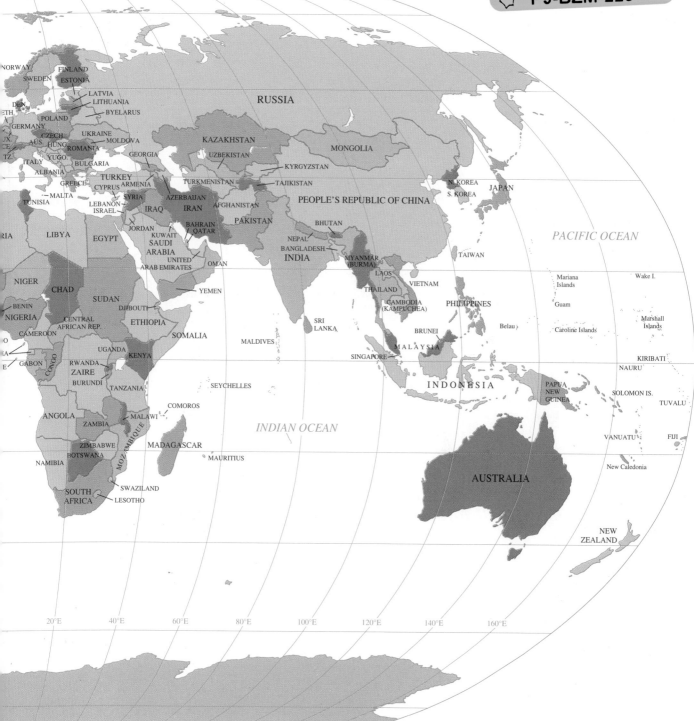

Marketing

Eighth Edition

HOUGHTON MIFFLIN COMPANY   BOSTON   TORONTO

DALLAS   GENEVA, ILLINOIS   PALO ALTO

PRINCETON, NEW JERSEY

Marketing

Concepts and Strategies

William M. Pride

TEXAS A&M UNIVERSITY

O. C. Ferrell

MEMPHIS STATE UNIVERSITY

To Nancy, Michael, and Allen Pride

To Linda Ferrell

Sponsoring Editor: *Diane McOscar*
Development Editor: *Susan Kahn*
Project Editor: *Mary Ann Carberry*
Electronic Production Specialist: *Victoria Levin*
Production/Design Coordinator: *Martha Drury*
Senior Manufacturing Coordinator: *Priscilla Bailey*

Part Opening Images: Part I, Tony Stone Worldwide; Part II, David Forbert/Shostal Associates; Part III, Jon Feingersh/Tom Stack and Associates; Part IV, COMSTOCK; Part V, Frank Wing/Image Bank; Part VI, COMSTOCK; Part VII, COMSTOCK/Hartman-DeWitt.

Credits: Page 526, adapted table from *Advertising: Its Role in Modern Marketing,* Seventh Edition by S. Watson Dunn and Arnold M. Barban, copyright © 1990 by the Dryden Press, reprinted by permission of the publisher. Page 781, excerpted figure from *International Marketing,* Fourth Edition by Vern Terpstra, copyright © 1987 by the Dryden Press, reprinted by permission of the publisher.

Cover photography by Geoffrey Gove. Cover design by Len Massiglia.

Printed in the U.S.A.

Library of Congress Catalog Card Number: 92-72396

Student Book ISBN: 0-395-62965-9

Examination Copy ISBN: 0-395-63885-2

123456789-VH-96 95 94 93 92

CONTENTS

21. Implementing Strategies and Measuring Performance

Part VII
Selected Applications

22. Business-to-Business Marketing

MARKETING HAS ALWAYS BEEN a dynamic area of study, but recent changes in our social and economic systems provide new challenges. Marketers must focus on global market opportunities while being sensitive to cultural differences, environmental concerns, ethical issues, and technological changes, both domestically and globally. To provide insight into the dynamic world of marketing, we have revised the eighth edition of *Marketing: Concepts and Strategies* to fully integrate these changes in a comprehensive framework that includes traditional marketing concepts and the challenging realities of today.

Sweeping changes in eastern Europe and the Commonwealth of Independent States demonstrate how fragile closed political and economic systems can be in today's highly interdependent world. The formation of the European Community signifies a new era demanding businesses to recognize the importance of cooperation. As trade barriers tumble throughout the world, it is increasingly difficult to determine the country of origin for many products. Decisions in Tokyo can have almost as much impact on American business as decisions in Washington. In addition, world environmental concerns related to many aspects of marketing create new challenges that must be considered in developing marketing strategies.

Marketing: Concepts and Strategies is a leading introductory marketing text in the United States, United Kingdom, Ireland, and other parts of the world because it provides comprehensive coverage and stimulates student interest with its readable style and extensive use of interesting, real-life examples. This text provides up-to-date coverage that integrates global, environmental, and ethical concepts to provide full understanding of the contemporary marketing world of the 1990s.

Changes in the Eighth Edition

Marketing: Concepts and Strategies has always focused on the concepts most relevant to the development and implementation of marketing strategies. To keep pace with new developments in the teaching and practice of marketing, the eighth edition provides the most comprehensive and current coverage of global marketing and of marketing ethics and social responsibility.

- In the international marketing chapter, the section on regional trade alliances and markets has been significantly revised. New and updated topics include the U.S. and Canada Free Trade Agreement, Mexico free trade agreement, *maquiladora* industries, European Community, Pacific Rim Nations, and changing relations with eastern Europe and the Commonwealth of Independent States.
- We have included a new chapter entitled "Branding and Packaging" in Part II, Product Decisions. We have expanded our coverage of these important topics because of their importance to marketing strategy. Based on reviews and focus group research, the management of branding and packaging is a critical product decision that deserves more in-depth coverage.

- In addition to comprehensive strategic cases, part-ending ethics and social responsibility cases (most with videos available) have been added to give students an opportunity to integrate these important concepts into real-world situations.

The basic features and overall design of the text were carefully reviewed and revised to make the material as accessible, fresh, and appealing as possible.

- New Global Perspective features have been added in each chapter to highlight a business or provide an example of how the chapter content can be applied in a global situation.
- We have included many new examples of challenges facing real organizations as they market products and attempt to take advantage of new opportunities in this changing world.
- The Inside Marketing features integrate fundamental marketing issues and concepts with real-world marketing activities. These features are generally about well-known companies and focus on issues that students will be able to relate to easily.
- Each chapter continues to include two cases: half of them are completely new and the other half have been updated.
- A strategic case is included at the end of each part. Four of these cases are completely new; three have been revised and updated.
- New to this edition are part-ending cases (most with video support) focusing on ethical and social responsibility issues.
- We have created a new attractive visual presentation of the content to stimulate readers' interest. All of the more than 120 advertisements and photos are new. In addition, the writing style continues to be lively, readable, and concise.

In addition, text coverage has been completely revised and updated to include major changes and additions such as the following:

- New coverage related to organizational implications of market orientation based on studies supported by the Marketing Science Institute (see Chapter 1).
- New coverage of cultural diversity as a demographic force that is creating a more diverse customer base (see Chapter 2).
- Inclusion of companies that have developed ethics programs or workshops (see Chapter 3).
- New coverage of population changes based on the 1990 census and projected demographic changes in the 1990s (see Chapter 4).
- New data on marketing researchers' views of respondents' reactions to major data collection techniques (see Chapter 7).
- Expanded coverage of product positioning and repositioning (see Chapter 8).
- New coverage of concept testing used in the new product development process (see Chapter 9).
- More in-depth discussion of brand selection and protection (see Chapter 10).
- Greater coverage of strategic uses of packaging (see Chapter 10).
- New coverage related to global dimensions of changing patterns of wholesaling (see Chapter 12).
- New categories and revision of major types of retail stores (see Chapter 13).

- New coverage focusing on managing a culturally diverse sales force (see Chapter 17).
- A new section on total quality management used in conjunction with strategy implementation (see Chapter 21).
- Updated coverage of regional trade alliances and markets including the U.S.–Canada Free Trade Agreement, Mexico free trade proposals, as well as changing relations with eastern Europe and the Commonwealth of Independent States (see Chapter 24).

Even though we have made numerous changes, we believe that users of earlier editions will find the eighth edition to have the same strengths that have made previous editions so popular. This edition, like its predecessors, explores the depth and breadth of the field, combining comprehensive coverage of marketing concepts and strategies with detailed real world examples. By focusing on the universal concerns of marketing decision makers, we demonstrate that marketing is a vital and challenging field of study—and a part of our world that influences almost everything we do.

Features of the Eighth Edition

As always, our goal is to provide a comprehensive and practical introduction to marketing, easy both to teach and to read. The entire book is structured to excite students about marketing and to make learning comprehensive and efficient.

- *Learning objectives* open each chapter, providing students with an overview of new concepts.
- A *vignette* introduces each chapter's marketing issues.
- Examples of familiar products and organizations make concrete and specific the generalizations of marketing theory.
- An *Inside Marketing* feature in each chapter, focusing on recognizable firms and products, extends the discussion of marketing topics and decisions.
- For each chapter, a *Global Perspective* examines global issues, organizations, or products.
- Numerous *figures, tables, and photographs* augment the text and increase comprehension.
- A complete *chapter summary* reviews the major topics discussed.
- A *list of important terms* (highlighted in the text) provides a study aid, helping students expand their marketing vocabulary.
- *Discussion and review questions* encourage further study and exploration of chapter material.
- Two concise, stimulating *cases* at the end of each chapter help students to understand the application of chapter concepts.
- A *diagram of the text's organization* at the beginning of each part shows students how material in the upcoming part relates to the rest of the book.
- A *strategic case* at the end of each part helps students integrate concepts from that part.
- An *ethics and social responsibility case* at the end of each part raises students' awareness of ethical and social responsibility issues and can lead to lively class discussions. Most of these cases are accompanied by video support.

- A *glossary* at the end of the text defines more than 625 important marketing terms.
- *Appendices* discuss career opportunities in marketing and provide additional insights into financial analysis in marketing.
- A *name index* and a *subject index* enable students to find topics of interest quickly.

Text Organization

We have organized the seven parts of *Marketing: Concepts and Strategies* to give students a theoretical and practical understanding of marketing decision making. Part I presents an overview of marketing, discusses general marketing concepts, and considers the marketing environment, ethics and social responsibility, types of markets, target market analysis, buyer behavior, and marketing research. Part II focuses on the conceptualization, development, management, and branding and packaging of products. Part III examines marketing channels, institutions, and physical distribution. Part IV covers promotion decisions and methods, including advertising, personal selling, sales promotion, and publicity. Part V is devoted to pricing decisions and Part VI to marketing management and discussion of strategic market planning, organization, implementation, and control. Part VII explores strategic decisions in business-to-business, service, nonbusiness, and international marketing.

A Complete Package of Teaching and Learning Supplements

The complete package available for *Marketing: Concepts and Strategies* includes numerous instructor support materials: Instructor's Resource Manual, Instructor's Presentation Software, Test Bank, Computerized Test Bank, Color Transparencies, MVT: Marketing Videotapes, Ethics and Social Responsibility Videotapes, and Video Guide. For a description of these items, see the front of the Instructor's Resource Manual.

The package for this text also includes several aids for student learning:

- The *Study Guide* helps students to review and integrate chapter content.
- *MicroStudy Plus,* a self-instructional program for microcomputers, reinforces learning of key concepts.
- *Micromarket: Computer Applications,* a Lotus-based disk, includes exercises that provide hands-on experience in making marketing decisions.
- *Marketer: A Simulation,* Second Edition, gives student teams working on microcomputers valuable experience in making marketing decisions.
- *Exploring Marketing Strategy,* a microcomputer-assisted program, helps students understand the marketing mix and marketing strategy by incorporating multiple-choice and fill-in-the-blank questions with an exciting graphic presentation.

Through the years, professors and students have sent us many helpful suggestions for improving the text and ancillary components. We invite your comments, questions, and criticisms. We want to do our best to provide materials that enhance the teaching and learning of marketing concepts and strategies. Your suggestions will be sincerely appreciated.

Acknowledgments

Like most textbooks, this one reflects the ideas of a multitude of academicians and practitioners who have contributed to the development of the marketing discipline. We appreciate the opportunity to present their ideas in this book.

A number of individuals have made many helpful comments and recommendations in their reviews of this or earlier editions. We appreciate the generous help of these reviewers.

Joe F. Alexander
University of Northern Colorado

Mark I. Alpert
University of Texas at Austin

Linda K. Anglin
Mankato State University

George Avellano
Central State University

Emin Babakus
Memphis State University

Julie Baker
University of Texas, Arlington

Siva Balasabramanian
University of Iowa

Joseph Ballinger
Stephen F. Austin State University

Guy Banville
Creighton University

Joseph Barr
Framingham State College

Thomas E. Barry
Southern Methodist University

Charles A Bearchell
California State University—Northridge

Richard C. Becherer
Wayne State University

Russell Belk
University of Utah

W. R. Berdine
California State Polytechnic Institute

Stewart W. Bither
Pennsylvania State University

Roger Blackwell
Ohio State University

Peter Bloch
Louisiana State University

Wanda Blockhus
San Jose State University

Paul N. Bloom
University of North Carolina

James P. Boespflug
Arapahoe Community College

Joseph G. Bonnice
Manhattan College

James Brock
Montana State University

John R. Brooks, Jr.
Houston Baptist University

Jackie Brown
University of San Diego

William Brown
University of Nebraska at Omaha

William G. Browne
Oregon State University

John Buckley
Orange County Community College

Karen Burger
Pace University

Pat J. Calabro
University of Texas at Arlington

Linda Calderone
*State University of New York
College of Technology at Farmingdale*

Joseph Cangelosi
East Tennessee State University

James C. Carroll
University of Southwestern Louisiana

Terry M. Chambers
Appalachian State University

Lawrence Chase
Tompkins Cortland Community College

Larry Chonko
Baylor University

Barbara Coe
North Texas State University

Ernest F. Cooke
Loyola College—Baltimore

Robert Copley
University of Louisville

John I. Coppett
University of Houston—Clear Lake

Deborah L. Cowles
Virginia Commonwealth University

Melvin R. Crask
University of Georgia

William L. Cron
Southern Methodist University

Benjamin J. Cutler
Bronx Community College

Bernice N. Dandridge
Diablo Valley College

Norman E. Daniel
Arizona State University

Lloyd M. DeBoer
George Mason University

Sally Dibb
University of Warwick

Ralph DiPietro
Montclair State College

Peter T. Doukas
Westchester Community College

Lee R. Duffus
University of Tennessee

Robert F. Dwyer
University of Cincinnati

Thomas Falcone
Indiana University of Pennsylvania

Gwen Fontenot
University of Northern Colorado

Charles W. Ford
Arkansas State University

John Fraedrich
Southern Illinois University, Carbondale

David J. Fritzsche
University of Washington

Donald A. Fuller
University of Central Florida

Geoffrey L. Gordon
University of Kentucky

Robert Grafton-Small
University of Strathclyde

Harrison Grathwohl
California State University—Chico

Alan A. Greco
*University of North Carolina—
Charlotte*

Blaine S. Greenfield
Bucks County Community College

Shanna Greenwalt
Southern Illinois University

Thomas V. Greer
University of Maryland

Sharon F. Gregg
Middle Tennessee University

Jim L. Grimm
Illinois State University

Charles Gross
University of New Hampshire

Roy R. Grundy
College of DuPage

Joseph Guiltinan
University of Notre Dame

Joseph Hair
Louisiana State University

Robert R. Harmon
Portland State University

Michael Hartline
University of Arkansas, Little Rock

Timothy Hartman
Ohio University

Salah S. Hassan
George Washington University

Del I. Hawkins
University of Oregon

Dean Headley
Wichita State University

Esther Headley
Wichita State University

Debbora Heflin-Bullock
*California State Polytechnic
University—Pomona*

Merlin Henry
Rancho Santiago College

Neil Herndon
Southwest Missouri State University

Charles L. Hilton
Eastern Kentucky University

Elizabeth C. Hirschman
Rutgers, State University of New Jersey

Robert D. Hisrich
University of Tulsa

George C. Hozier
University of New Mexico

John R. Huser
Illinois Central College

Donald L. James
Fort Lewis College

Ken Jensen
University of Tampa

Theodore F. Jula
Stonehill College

Peter F. Kaminski
Northern Illinois University

Yvonne Karsten
Mankato State University

Jerome Katrichis
Temple University

Alvin Kelly
Langston University

Philip Kemp
DePaul University

Sylvia Keyes
Bridgewater State College

William M. Kincaid, Jr.
Oklahoma State University

Roy Klages
State University of New York at Albany

Douglas Kornemann
Milwaukee Area Technical College

Priscilla LaBarbara
New York University

Patricia Laidler
Massasoit Community College

Bernard LaLonde
Ohio State University

Richard A. Lancioni
Temple University

David M. Landrum
Central State University

Irene Lange
California State University—Fullerton

Geoffrey P. Lantos
Stonehill College

Charles L. Lapp
University of Dallas

Virginia Larson
San Jose State University

John Lavin
Waukesha County Technical Institute

Hugh E. Law
East Tennessee University

Ron Lennon
Barry University

Richard C. Leventhal
Metropolitan State College

Jay D. Lindquist
Western Michigan University

David H. Lindsay
University of Maryland

Paul Londrigan
Mott Community College

Anthony Lucas
Community College of Allegheny County

William Lundstrom
Old Dominion University

Stan Madden
Baylor University

Patricia M. Manninen
North Shore Community College

Gerald L. Manning
Des Moines Area Community College

Allen S. Marber
University of Bridgeport

Gayle J. Marco
Robert Morris College

James McAlexander
Iowa State University

John McFall
San Diego State University

Jack McNiff
*State University of New York
College of Technology at Farmingdale*

Lee Meadow
Northern Illinois University

Jeffrey A. Meier
Fox Valley Technical College

James Meszaros
County College of Morris

Brian Meyer
Mankato State University

Stephen J. Miller
Oklahoma State University

William Moller
University of Michigan

Kent B. Monroe
University of Illinois

Carlos W. Moore
Baylor University

Carol Morris-Calder
Loyola Marymount University

Keith Murray
Northeastern University

Sue Ellen Neeley
University of Houston—Clear Lake

Terrence V. O'Brien
Northern Illinois University

Allan Palmer
University of North Carolina at Charlotte

Teresa Pavia
University of Utah

J. Paul Peter
University of Wisconsin—Madison

Michael Peters
Boston College

Thomas Ponzurick
West Virginia University

Arthur Prell
Lindenwood College

William Prescutti
Duquesne University

Kathy Pullins
Columbus State Community College

Victor Quinones
University of Puerto Rico

Daniel Rajaratnam
Baylor University

James D. Reed
Louisiana State University—Shreveport

William Rhey
University of Tampa

Glen Riecken
East Tennessee State University

Winston Ring
University of Wisconsin—Milwaukee

Ed Riordan
Wayne State University

Robert A. Robicheaux
University of Alabama

Robert H. Ross
Wichita State University

Michael L. Rothschild
University of Wisconsin—Madison

Bert Rosenbloom
Drexel University

Kenneth L. Rowe
Arizona State University

Ronald Schill
Brigham Young University

Bodo Schlegelmilch
University of Edinburgh

Stanley Scott
Boise State University

Harold S. Sekiguchi
University of Nevada—Reno

Richard J. Semenik
University of Utah

Beheruz N. Sethna
Clarkson College

Steven J. Shaw
University of South Carolina

Terence A. Shimp
University of South Carolina

Steven Shipley
Governor's State University

Carolyn F. Siegel
Eastern Kentucky University

Dean C. Siewers
Rochester Institute of Technology

Lyndon Simkin
University of Warwick

Paul J. Solomon
University of South Florida

Robert Solomon
Stephen F. Austin State University

Sheldon Somerstein
City University of New York

Rosann L. Spiro
Indiana University

William Staples
University of Houston—Clear Lake

Bruce Stern
Portland State University

Claire F. Sullivan
Metropolitan State University

Hal Teer
James Madison University

Ira Teich
Long Island University—C.W. Post

Debbie Thorne
Memphis State University

Dillard Tinsley
Stephen F. Austin State University

Hale Tongren
George Mason University

James Underwood
University of Southwest Louisiana

Barbara Unger
Western Washington University

Tinus Van Drunen
Universiteit Twente (Netherlands)

Poondi Varadarajan
Texas A & M University

Dale Varble
Indiana State University

Charles Vitaska
Metropolitan State College

Kirk Wakefield
University of Mississippi

James F. Wenthe
University of Georgia

Sumner M. White
Massachusetts Bay Community College

Alan R. Wiman
Rider College

Ken Wright
West Australia College of Advanced Education—Churchland Campus

George Wynn
James Madison University

We deeply appreciate the assistance of Barbara Gilmer, Pam Swartz, and Gwyneth M. Vaughn for providing editorial suggestions, technical assistance, and support. For assistance in completing numerous tasks associated with the text and ancillary items, we express appreciation to Michael Hartline, Victoria Bush, Bruce Keillor, Jennifer Maloney, Jose Mireles, Marissa Salinas, Zed Eric Stephens, Debbie Thorne, and Brent Wren.

Our special thanks go to Carolyn F. Siegel, Eastern Kentucky University, and Sundar and Anandhi Bharadwaj, both at Texas A & M University, for creating and developing the exercises in the *Micromarket: Computer Applications* program. For creating *Marketer: A Simulation*, Second Edition, we wish to thank Jerald R. Smith, University of Louisville. A great deal of thanks also go to Edwin C. Hackleman for developing the computerized test preparation program and for creating *Microstudy Plus*. We appreciate the efforts of Margaret Cunningham, Queen's University, in developing the *Marketing Strategy* computer disk. We also wish to thank Kirk Wakefield, University of Mississippi, for developing the new class exercises included in the Instructor's Resource Manual. We especially thank Jim L. Grimm, Illinois State University, for drafting the financial analysis appendix.

We express appreciation for the support and encouragement given us by our colleagues at Texas A & M University and Memphis State University. We also appreciate the efforts of the marketing educators who contributed guest lectures, which are included in the Instructor's Resource Manual, and whose names are included in the Preface of that ancillary.

WILLIAM M. PRIDE
O. C. FERRELL

I An Analysis of Marketing Opportunities

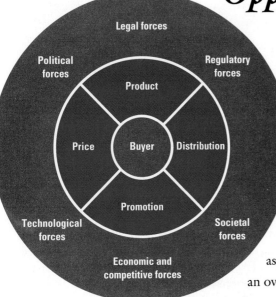

4 P's

In Part I we introduce the field of marketing and provide a broad perspective from which to explore and analyze various components of the marketing discipline. In the first chapter we define marketing and discuss why an understanding of it is useful in many aspects of everyday life, including one's career. We provide an overview of general strategic marketing issues, such as market opportunity analysis, target market selection, and marketing mix development. Marketers should understand how environmental forces can affect customers and their responses to marketing strategies. In Chapter 2 we discuss political, legal, regulatory, societal, economic and competitive, and technological forces in the environment. Chapter 3 deals with the role of ethics and social responsibility in marketing decisions and activities. Chapter 4 focuses on one of the major steps in the development of a marketing strategy: selecting and analyzing target markets. Understanding elements that affect buying decisions enables marketers to better analyze customers' needs and evaluate how specific marketing strategies can satisfy those needs. In Chapter 5 we examine consumer buying decision processes and factors that influence buying decisions. We stress organizational markets, organizational buyers, the buying center, and the organizational buying decision process in Chapter 6. Chapter 7 includes a discussion of the role of a marketing information system and the basic steps in the marketing research process.

1 An Overview of Strategic Marketing

OBJECTIVES

- To understand the definition of marketing

- To understand why a person should study marketing

- To gain insight into the basic elements of the marketing concept and its implementation

- To understand the major components of a marketing strategy

- To gain a sense of general strategic marketing issues, such as market opportunity analysis, target market selection, and marketing mix development

For forty years the Chevrolet Corvette—sometimes called America's only true sports car—has held the kind of mystique that creates dreams. Chevrolet has determined what customers want: excitement, image, and performance. The effectiveness of the company's marketing strategy can be seen in the ever-increasing value of classic Corvettes sold at the Bloomington Gold Corvettes USA show. Today, many 1970s models sell for 3 or 4 times their original price. Dubbed the world's largest classic Corvette event of the year, the show attracts Corvette owners and fans for four days every June to a 100-acre site in Bloomington, Illinois. By bringing together buyers and sellers of the classic sports cars and related parts and accessories, Bloomington Gold represents marketing in action.

At Bloomington Gold Corvettes USA, buyers, sellers, and lovers of Corvettes come together to exchange cars, products, services, and ideas and to have fun. One of the principal events is the show's Certification Meet, in which judges evaluate the restoration of contestants' cars. Cars restored to within 95 to 100 percent of the way they looked when they rolled off the assembly line are awarded the Bloomington Gold Certificate. Cars within 94 to 85 percent of their original condition receive a Silver or Bronze certificate. The Certification Meet has become so prestigious that the Gold, Silver, and Bronze certificates influence the market price for restored Corvettes, and owners are sure to advertise their certificates when selling a car.

Seminars and workshops show owners and Corvette lovers how to buy Corvettes and how to take care of and restore the classic automobiles. Buyers and sellers exchange Corvettes, parts, and accessories at the swap meet and auction. Entertainment events include the Silver Salute, a show of cars celebrating their twenty-fifth anniversary; the Road Tour, in which more than a thousand classic Corvettes parade in an uninterrupted line over a thirty-five-mile course; and music and many other family events. These products and services make Bloomington Gold Corvettes USA an exciting celebration of the Corvette automobile.[1]

Photo courtesy Bloomington Gold Corvettes USA.

THE CHEVROLET CORVETTE, introduced in 1953, is considered the only long-term U.S. success in the high-performance sports car market. Chevrolet has determined that the Corvette successfully provides the excitement, image, and performance that customers want in a sports car. The ever-increasing value of classic Corvettes sold at the Bloomington Gold Corvettes USA show is a reflection of this success. This annual event is also a part of Chevrolet's successful marketing strategy, helping to maintain the mystique of the Corvette.

This first chapter is an overview of the concepts and decisions covered in the text. In this chapter we first develop a definition of marketing and explain each element of the definition. Then we look at some of the reasons why people should study marketing. We introduce the marketing concept and consider several issues associated with implementing it. Next we define and discuss the major tasks associated with marketing strategy: market opportunity analysis, target market selection, marketing mix development, and management of marketing activities. We conclude by discussing the organization of this text.

Marketing Defined

If you ask several people what *marketing* is, they will respond with a variety of descriptions. Marketing encompasses many more activities than most people realize. Since it is practiced and studied for many different reasons, it has been, and continues to be, defined in many ways. According to one definition,

> Marketing is the process of planning and executing the conception, pricing, promotion, and distribution of ideas, goods, and services to create exchanges that satisfy individual and organizational goals.[2]

This definition, developed by the American Marketing Association (AMA), is widely accepted by academics and marketing managers.[3] It emphasizes that marketing focuses on planning and executing activities to satisfy customers' demands. Whereas earlier definitions restricted marketing as a business activity, this definition is broad enough to indicate that marketing can occur in nonbusiness organizations.

Although the AMA definition is certainly acceptable, we believe that marketing can be defined still more broadly. A definition of marketing should indicate that marketing consists of activities performed by individuals and organizations. In addition, it should acknowledge that marketing activities occur in a dynamic environment. Thus we define marketing as follows:

> **Marketing** consists of individual and organizational activities that facilitate and expedite satisfying exchange relationships in a dynamic environment through the creation, distribution, promotion, and pricing of goods, services, and ideas.

In this definition, an **exchange** is the provision or transfer of goods, services, and ideas in return for something of value. Any product may be involved in a marketing exchange. We assume only that individuals and organizations expect to gain a reward in excess of the costs incurred. So that our definition will be fully understood, we now examine each component more closely.

Marketing Mix Variables	Possible Decisions and Activities
Product	Develop and test-market new products; modify existing products; eliminate products that do not satisfy customers' desires; formulate brand names and branding policies; create product warranties and establish procedures for fulfilling warranties; plan packages, including materials, sizes, shapes, colors, and designs
Distribution	Analyze various types of distribution channels; design appropriate distribution channels; design an effective program for dealer relations; establish distribution centers; formulate and implement procedures for efficient product handling; set up inventory controls; analyze transportation methods; minimize total distribution costs; analyze possible locations for plants and wholesale or retail outlets
Promotion	Set promotional objectives; determine major types of promotion to be used; select and schedule advertising media; develop advertising messages; measure the effectiveness of advertisements; recruit and train salespersons; formulate compensation programs for sales personnel; establish sales territories; plan and implement sales promotion efforts; prepare and disseminate publicity releases
Price	Analyze competitors' prices; formulate pricing policies; determine method or methods used to set prices; set prices; determine discounts for various types of buyers; establish conditions and terms of sales

Table 1.1   Possible Decisions and Activities Associated with Marketing Mix Variables

Marketing Consists of Activities

Marketing products effectively requires many activities. Some are performed by producers; some are accomplished by intermediaries, who buy products from producers or from other intermediaries and resell them; and some are even performed by purchasers. Marketing does not include all human and organizational activities, but only those aimed at facilitating and expediting exchanges. Table 1.1 lists several major categories and examples of marketing activities. Note that this list is not all-inclusive. Each activity could be subdivided into more specific activities.

Marketing Is Performed by Individuals and Organizations

All organizations perform marketing activities to facilitate exchanges. Businesses as well as nonbusiness organizations—such as colleges and universities, charitable organizations, community theaters, and hospitals—perform marketing activities. For example, colleges and universities and their students engage in exchanges. To receive instruction, knowledge, entertainment, a degree, the use of facilities, and sometimes room and board, students give up time, money, and

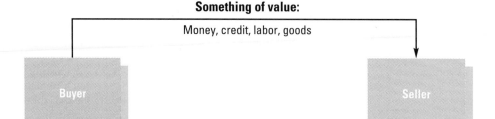

Figure 1.1

Exchange Between Buyer and Seller

Something of value:
Money, credit, labor, goods

Buyer

Seller

Something of value:
Goods, services, ideas

perhaps services in the form of labor; they may also give up opportunities to do other things. Likewise, many religious institutions engage in marketing activities to satisfy their "customers." For example, Willow Creek Community Church in South Barrington, Illinois, conducted a survey to determine why some of the residents did not attend any church in the community. The church used the survey results to develop programs to satisfy the religious needs of these residents.[4]

Marketing Facilitates Satisfying Exchange Relationships

For an exchange to take place, four conditions must exist. First, two or more individuals, groups, or organizations must participate. Second, each party must possess something of value that the other party desires. Third, each party must be willing to give up its "something of value" to receive the "something of value" held by the other party. The objective of a marketing exchange is to receive something that is desired more than what is given up to get it—that is, a reward in excess of costs. Fourth, the parties to the exchange must be able to communicate with each other to make their somethings of value available.[5]

Figure 1.1 illustrates the process of exchange. The arrows indicate that the parties communicate that each has something of value available to exchange. Note, though, that an exchange will not necessarily take place just because these four conditions exist. Nevertheless, even if there is no exchange, marketing activities still have occurred. The somethings of value held by the two parties are most often products and/or financial resources, such as money or credit. When an exchange occurs, products are traded for other products or for financial resources.

An exchange should be *satisfying* to both the buyer and the seller. In fact, in a study of marketing managers, 32 percent indicated that creating customer satisfaction was the most important concept in a definition of marketing.[6] Marketing activities, then, should be oriented toward creating and maintaining satisfying exchange relationships. To maintain an exchange relationship, the buyer must be satisfied with the good, service, or idea obtained in the exchange; the seller must be satisfied with the financial reward or something else of value received in the exchange. Inside Marketing focuses on the marketing efforts of

Binney & Smith to maintain satisfying relationships with customers purchasing its Crayola Crayons.

Maintaining a positive relationship with buyers is an important goal for a seller. Through buyer-seller interaction, the buyer develops expectations about the seller's future behavior. To fulfill these expectations, the seller must deliver on promises made. Over time, a healthy buyer-seller relationship results in interdependencies between the two parties. The buyer depends on the seller to furnish information, parts, and service; to be available; and to provide satisfying products in the future. For example, Figure 1.2 shows that Intel promises to satisfy its customers' current and future needs by providing an upgrade processor for their computer systems.

Marketing Occurs in a Dynamic Environment

The marketing environment consists of many changing forces: laws, regulations, political activities, societal pressures, changing economic conditions, and technological advances. Each of these dynamic forces has an impact on how effectively marketing activities can facilitate and expedite exchanges. For example, the development and acceptance of facsimile (fax) machines has given businesses another vehicle through which to promote their products. Some office supply sellers send advertisements about their products to businesses and individuals through their fax machines. However, some receivers of fax advertisements object to having their paper and fax machines used without their permission and want this type of advertising legally banned.

Figure 1.2

Customer Satisfaction

Intel hopes to build satisfying customer relationships through its new upgrade processor, which provides maximum flexibility for the customer.

Source: Reprinted with permission from Intel Corporation.

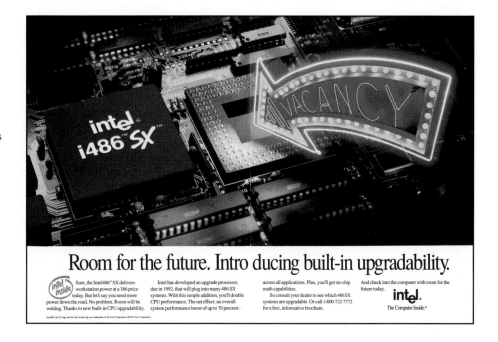

Room for the future. Introducing built-in upgradability.

Binney & Smith Brightens Marketing Strategy for Crayola Crayons

WHILE NINTENDO GAMES and MTV music videos have captured children's attention, Crayola Crayons have languished on store shelves. Now Binney & Smith, Inc., a division of Hallmark Cards, is fighting back with a new marketing strategy for the venerable crayon. The Easton, Pennsylvania–based company launched a $250 million, MTV-style campaign, which targets children rather than parents.

Traditionally Binney & Smith targeted Crayola Crayons at parents, using educational themes. But after recognizing that children's purchasing power and influence on family purchases have increased in recent years, the company decided to change the crayon's image as an old-fashioned toy to an exciting way for kids and teens to express themselves. To this end, the company developed new commercials featuring rock music, "hip" kids, and soaring colors that air on television shows seen by children.

After marketing research indicated that children prefer brighter colors, the company decided to retire blue gray, green blue, lemon yellow, maize, orange red, orange yellow, raw umber, and violet blue to the Crayola Hall of Fame, and replace them with the more vivid cerulean, dandelion, fuchsia, jungle green, royal purple, teal blue, vivid tangerine, and wild strawberry. This decision was controversial, however. The company was inundated with phone calls, letters, and petitions from people who missed the old colors. Protestors marched on the company, carrying placards with slogans like "We hate the new 8!" and "They call it a retirement, I call it a burial." RUMPS, the Raw Umber and Maize Preservation Society fi-

nally got their way. In late 1991 the company issued a commemorative tin containing the sixty-four-crayon box and a special pack of the eight colors dropped one year earlier. Even though kids liked the new colors, parents liked the old eight colors. The company issued a statement saying that the return of the old colors was done partly because the company is in the business of providing what the consumer wants.

Along with new advertisements and colors, the company introduced ColorWorks, a line of erasable crayon sticks and retractable colored pencils and pens. In 1991 the company brought out Silver Swirls, crayons that have twirls of silver mixed in with the wax color. Pictures colored with Silver Swirls can be buffed to a high sheen with tissue. The new line was not only tested by children, but also named by them.

Despite its new focus on children, Binney & Smith did not forget who actually holds the purse strings; the company continues to target parents with advertisements in women's and parents' magazines. The company hopes that its new strategy will lead more children to reach for Crayola Crayons instead of the Nintendo joystick.

Sources: Ellen Neuborne "Crayola Fans Have Old Colors Back," *USA Today,* Oct. 2, 1991, p. 2B; Ken Riddell, "Crayola Draws Brighter Lines in the Market," *Marketing (Maclean Hunter),* Jan. 21, 1991, p. 4; Virginia Daut, "Roses Were Reds, Violets Blues, Till They Redid Crayola's Hues," *Wall Street Journal,* Sept. 11, 1990, p. B1; and Cara Appelbaum, "Crayola Launches Hip, Bright Ads for Kids," *Adweek's Marketing Week,* Sept. 3, 1990, p. 8.

Marketing Involves Products, Distribution, Promotion, and Pricing

Marketing means more than simply advertising or selling a product; it involves developing and managing a product that will satisfy certain needs. It focuses on making the product available at the right place, at the right time, and at a price that is acceptable to customers. It also requires transmitting the kind of information that will help customers determine if the product will in fact be able to satisfy their needs.

Marketing Focuses on Goods, Services, and Ideas

We already have used the word *product* a number of times in this chapter. For purposes of discussion in this text, a *product* is viewed as being a good, a service, or an idea. A *good* is a physical entity one can touch. A Mazda Miata, a compact disc player, Kellogg's Frosted Flakes, a bar of soap, and a kitten in a pet store are examples of goods. A *service* is the application of human and mechanical efforts to people or objects to provide intangible benefits to customers. Airplane travel, dry cleaning, hair styling, banking, medical care, and day care are examples of services (Figure 1.3). *Ideas* include concepts, philosophies, images, and issues. For instance, a marriage counselor, for a fee, gives spouses ideas to help improve their relationships. Other marketers of ideas include political parties, churches, and schools.

Why Study Marketing?

After considering the definition of marketing, one can understand some of the obvious reasons why the study of marketing is relevant. In this section we discuss several perhaps less obvious reasons why one should study marketing.

Figure 1.3

Marketing Services

Services, such as the ski vacation packages Delta promotes, are just as real as goods, but an individual cannot actually touch them.

Source: Photo/Ad courtesy of Delta Air Lines, Inc.

Marketing Activities Are Used in Many Organizations

From 25 to 33 percent of all civilian workers in the United States perform marketing activities. The marketing field offers a variety of interesting and challenging career opportunities, such as personal selling, advertising, packaging, transportation, storage, marketing research, product development, wholesaling, and retailing. In addition, many individuals who work for nonbusiness organizations engage in marketing activities. Marketing skills are used to promote political, cultural, church, civic, and charitable activities. Whether a person earns a living through marketing activities or performs them without compensation in nonbusiness settings, marketing knowledge and skills are valuable assets.

Marketing Activities Are Important to Businesses and the Economy

A business organization must sell products to survive and to grow. Directly or indirectly, marketing activities help sell an organization's products. By doing so, they generate financial resources that can be used to develop innovative products. New products allow a firm to better satisfy customers' changing needs, which in turn enables the firm to generate more profits. For example, each year *Fortune* publishes a list of what its staff considers the top products. Recently, among these products of the year were the Minolta Maxxum 35mm camera, the Dodge Viper sports car, NCR's tablet-style computer, the Apple Macintosh PowerBook portable computer, products related to "step" aerobics, the drug Neupogen, low-fat beef products such as ConAgra's Healthy Choice Dinners and McDonald's McLean Deluxe and the Super Grip Velcro ball and paddle set.[7] All these products produce considerable profit for the firms that introduced them.

Our highly complex economy depends heavily on marketing activities. They help produce the profits that are essential not only to the survival of individual businesses, but also to the health and ultimate survival of the economy as a whole. Profits are essential to economic growth because without them businesses find it difficult, if not impossible, to buy more raw materials, hire more employees, attract more capital, and create the additional products that in turn make more profits.

Marketing Knowledge Enhances Consumer Awareness

Besides contributing to the well-being of our nation, marketing activities permeate our lives. In fact, they help us improve the quality of our lives. Studying marketing activities allows us to weigh costs, benefits, and flaws more effectively. We can see where they need to be improved and how to accomplish that goal. For example, if you have had an unsatisfactory experience with a warranty, you may have wished that laws were enforced more strictly to make sellers fulfill their promises. Similarly, you may have wished that you had more information about a product—or more accurate information—before you purchased it. Understanding marketing enables us to evaluate the corrective measures (such as laws, regulations, and industry guidelines) that may be required to stop unfair, damaging, or unethical marketing practices. Consumers today are demanding that the marketing claims of companies stating that they are environmentally responsible be an accurate portrayal of their products. Mobil discovered how serious those demands were when it had to pay $150,000 in fines and agree to stop making degradability claims about Hefty Degradable trash bags. Other companies, such as Colgate-Palmolive, have been able to answer environmentalists' criticisms by minimizing the amount of material in the product and packaging.[8]

Marketing Costs Consume a Sizable Portion of Buyers' Dollars

The study of marketing will make you aware that many marketing activities are necessary to provide people with satisfying goods and services. Obviously, these marketing activities cost money. In fact, about one-half of a buyer's dollar goes for marketing costs. A family with a monthly income of $2,000 that allocates $400 to taxes and savings spends about $1,600 for goods and services. Of this amount, $800 goes for marketing activities. Clearly, if marketing expenses consume that much of your dollar, you should know how this money is used.

The Marketing Concept

Some organizations have tried to be successful by buying land, building a factory, equipping it with people and machines, and then making a product that they believe consumers need. However, these organizations frequently fail to attract buyers with what they have to offer because they defined their business as "making a product" rather than as "helping potential customers satisfy their needs and wants." Such organizations have failed to implement the marketing concept.

According to the **marketing concept**, an organization should try to provide products that satisfy customers' needs through a coordinated set of activities that also allows the organization to achieve its goals. Customer satisfaction is the major aim of the marketing concept. First, an organization must find out what will satisfy customers. With this information, it then attempts to create satisfying products. But the process does not end there. The organization must continue to alter, adapt, and develop products to keep pace with customers' changing desires and preferences. The marketing concept stresses the importance of customers and emphasizes that marketing activities begin and end with them.

In attempting to satisfy customers, businesses must consider not only short-run, immediate needs, but also broad, long-term desires. Trying to satisfy customers' current needs by sacrificing their long-term desires will only create future dissatisfaction. For instance, people want efficient, low-cost energy to power their homes and automobiles, yet they react adversely to energy producers

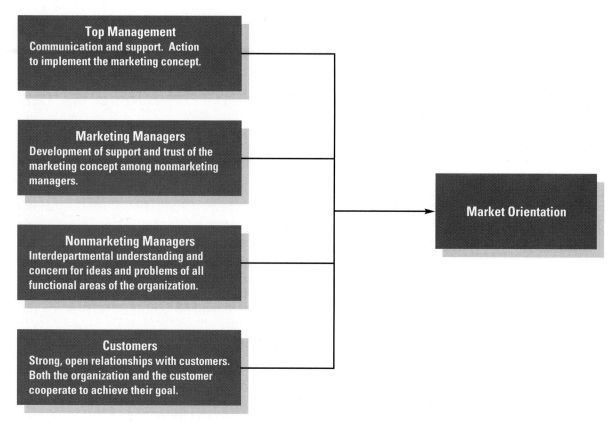

Figure 1.4 **Participants Needed to Develop Market Orientation**

who pollute the air and water, kill wildlife, or cause disease and birth defects. To meet these short- and long-run needs and desires, a firm must coordinate all its activities. Production, finance, accounting, personnel, and marketing departments must work together.

The marketing concept is not a second definition of marketing. It is a way of thinking—a management philosophy guiding an organization's overall activities. This philosophy affects all efforts of the organization, not just marketing activities. A firm's attempt to implement the marketing concept results in a market orientation. An organization whose overall activities are consistent with the marketing concept can be termed a marketing-oriented organization. A study of marketing managers supported by the Marketing Science Institute produced the following formal definition of market orientation:

> **Market orientation** is the organizationwide generation of market intelligence pertaining to current and future customer needs, dissemination of the intelligence across departments, and organizationwide responsiveness to it.[9]

As indicated in Figure 1.4, top management, marketing managers, nonmarketing managers, and customers are all important in developing and carrying out market orientation. The Marketing Science Institute study found that top management emerged as one of the most important factors in this process. Unless marketing managers provide continuous customer-focused leadership with minimal interdepartmental conflict, market orientation will be difficult. Nonmarketing managers need open communication with marketing managers to facilitate the sharing of information important to understanding the customer. Finally, market orientation involves being responsive to changing customer needs and wants. Developing a cooperative linkage with customers ensures that changes made in response to customer needs will result in customer satisfaction and at the same time allow the organization to achieve its goals.[10]

The marketing concept is not a philanthropic philosophy aimed at helping customers at the expense of the organization. A firm that adopts the marketing concept must not only satisfy its customers' objectives, but also achieve its own goals, or it will not stay in business long. The overall goals of a business might be directed toward increasing profits, share of the market, sales, or a combination of all three goals. The marketing concept stresses that an organization can best achieve its goals by providing customer satisfaction. Thus, implementing the marketing concept should benefit the organization as well as its customers.

Evolution of the Marketing Concept

The marketing concept may seem like an obvious and sensible approach to running a business. However, businesspeople have not always believed that the best way to make sales and profits is to satisfy customers. A famous example is Henry Ford's marketing philosophy for cars in the early 1900s: "The customers can have any color car they want as long as it is black." The philosophy of the marketing concept emerged in the third major era in the history of U.S. business, preceded by the production and the sales eras. Surprisingly, forty years after the marketing era began, many businesses still have not adopted the marketing concept.

The Production Era During the second half of the nineteenth century, the Industrial Revolution was in full force in the United States. Electricity, rail transportation, the division of labor, the assembly line, and mass production made it possible to manufacture products more efficiently. With new technology and new ways of using labor, products poured into the marketplace, where consumer demand for manufactured goods was strong. This production orientation continued into the early part of the twentieth century, encouraged by the scientific management movement that championed rigidly structured jobs and pay based on output.

The Sales Era In the 1920s, the strong consumer demand for products subsided. Businesses realized that products, which by this time could be made quite efficiently, would have to be "sold" to consumers. From the mid-1920s to the early 1950s, businesses viewed sales as the major means of increasing profits. As a result, this period came to have a sales orientation. Businesspeople believed that the most important marketing activities were personal selling and advertising.

The Marketing Era By the early 1950s, some businesspeople began to recognize that efficient production and extensive promotion of products did not guarantee that customers would buy them. These businesses, and many others since then, found that they must first determine what customers want and then produce it, rather than simply make products and try to change customers' needs to fit what is produced. As more organizations have realized the importance of knowing customers' needs, U.S. businesses have entered into the marketing era, one of customer orientation. Orientation toward customer satisfaction has resulted in an increased concern about ethics and social responsibility and an expansion into global markets. Many firms believe that we are in the "Total Quality Era," in which improved product quality, service emphasis, and customer orientation are a major focus on a global basis.

Implementing the Marketing Concept

A philosophy may sound reasonable and look good on paper, but that does not mean it can be put into practice easily. The marketing concept is a case in point. To implement it, an organization must focus on some general conditions and recognize several problems. Because of these conditions and problems, the marketing concept has yet to be fully accepted by American businesses.

Because the marketing concept affects all types of business activities, and not just marketing activities, the top management of an organization must adopt it wholeheartedly. High-level executives must incorporate the marketing concept into their philosophies of business management so completely that customers become the most important concern in the organization. Providing customers with high quality services is clearly important to Andersen Consulting, as shown in Figure 1.5.

As the first step, management must establish an information system that enables it to discover customers' real needs and to use the information to create satisfying products. Because such a system is usually expensive, management must be willing to commit money and time for development and maintenance. Without an adequate information system, an organization cannot be customer-oriented.

Management's second major task is to restructure the organization. We pointed out that if a company is to satisfy customers' objectives as well as its own, it must coordinate all activities. To achieve this, the internal operations and the overall objectives of one or more departments may need restructuring. If the head of the marketing unit is not a member of the organization's top-level management, he or she should be. Some departments may have to be abolished and new ones created. Implementing the marketing concept demands the support not only of top management, but also of managers and staff at all levels within the organization.

Even when the basic conditions of establishing an information system and reorganizing the company are met, the firm's new marketing approach may not work perfectly. First, there is a limit to a firm's ability to satisfy customers' needs for a particular product. In a mass production economy, most business organizations cannot tailor products to fit the exact needs of each customer. Second, although a company may try to learn what customers want, it may be unable to do so, and when it does correctly identify customers' needs, it often has a hard time developing a product that satisfies those needs. Many companies spend considerable time and money to research customers' needs and yet still create some products that do not sell well. Third, by striving to satisfy one segment of

Figure 1.5

Implementing the Marketing Concept

To successfully implement the marketing concept, organizations must place a high priority on satisfying customers. By emphasizing its business and technology skills, Andersen Consulting shows that it can help companies perform more effectively.

Source: Reprinted with permission of Andersen Consulting.

society, a firm sometimes dissatisfies other segments. Government and nonbusiness organizations also experience this problem. Fourth, a company may have trouble maintaining employee morale during any restructuring needed to coordinate the activities of various departments. Management must clearly explain the reasons for the changes and communicate its own enthusiasm for the marketing concept.

Marketing Strategy

To achieve the broad goal of expediting desirable exchanges, an organization's marketing managers are responsible for developing and managing marketing strategies. Specifically, a **marketing strategy** encompasses selecting and analyzing a target market (the group of people whom the organization wants to reach) and creating and maintaining an appropriate **marketing mix** (product, distribution, promotion, and price) that will satisfy those people. A marketing strategy articulates a plan for the best use of the organization's resources and tactics to meet its objectives.

Figure 1.6

**Components of the
Marketing Mix and
Marketing Environment**

Figure 1.6 — Components of the Marketing Mix and Marketing Environment. Concentric circle diagram with Buyer at center, surrounded by Product, Price, Distribution (Place), and Promotion. Outer ring shows Legal forces, Political forces, Regulatory forces, Technological forces, Societal forces, and Economic and competitive forces. Handwritten annotations: "demographics", "have control over", "Do not have control over", "have control over", "* Bases of the course".

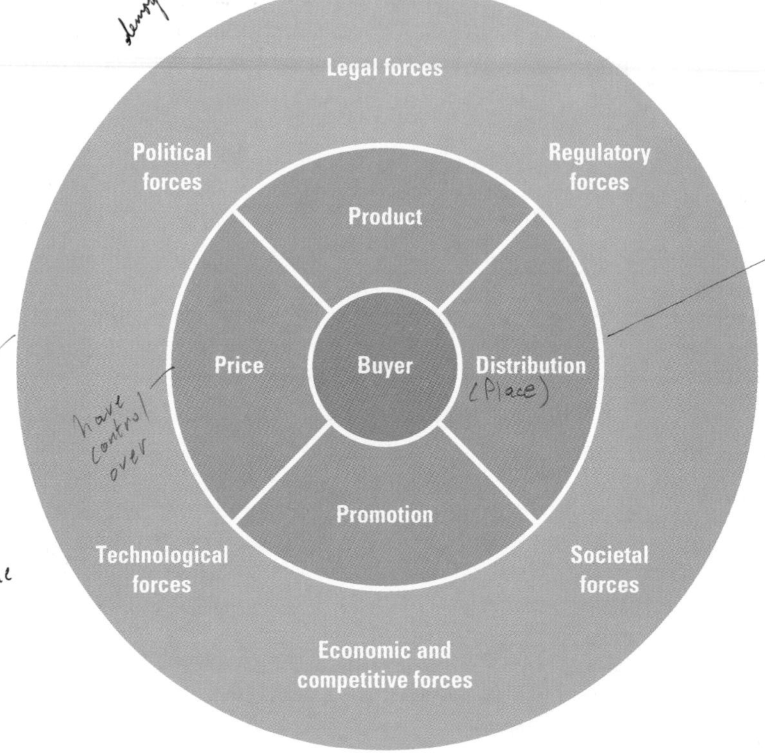

When marketing managers attempt to develop and manage marketing activities, they must deal with two broad sets of variables: those relating to the marketing mix and those that make up the marketing environment. The marketing mix decision variables—product, distribution, promotion, and price—are factors over which an organization has control. As Figure 1.6 shows, these variables are constructed around the buyer. The marketing environment variables are political, legal, regulatory, societal, economic and competitive, and technological forces. These factors are subject to less control by an organization but they affect buyers' needs as well as marketing managers' decisions regarding marketing mix variables.

To develop and manage marketing strategies, marketers must focus on several marketing tasks: marketing opportunity analysis, target market selection, marketing mix development, and effective marketing management. Figure 1.7 lists these tasks, along with the chapters of this book in which they are discussed.

Marketing Opportunity Analysis

A *marketing opportunity* exists when circumstances allow an organization to take action toward reaching a particular group of customers. An opportunity provides a favorable chance or opening for the firm to generate sales from identifiable markets. For example, after an early snowstorm, marketers of snow shovels have a marketing opportunity—an opportunity to reach customers who need snow shovels.

Marketers should be capable of recognizing and analyzing marketing opportunities. An organization's long-term survival depends on developing products that satisfy its customers. Few organizations can assume that products popular today will interest buyers ten years from now. A marketing organization can choose among several alternatives for continued product development through which it can achieve its objectives and satisfy buyers. It can modify existing products (for example, Citrus Hill and Minute Maid have added calcium to their orange juice products to address increasing health consciousness among customers), introduce new products (such as Microsoft's Windows software), and delete some that customers no longer want (such as Buick's Reatta).

A company may also try to market its products to a greater number of customers, convince current customers to use more of a product, or perhaps expand marketing activities into additional states or countries. Jeans companies such as Levi Strauss, Wrangler, and Lee are now targeting a much wider population. Their traditional target market, teenagers, is dwindling in size, so jeans marketers are now pursuing an older market. Industry leader Levi Strauss's new advertising campaigns target diverse audiences, including women, and Lee has developed campaigns to appeal to "thirty-something" women as well as to male jeans customers between ages 25 and 44.[11] Frito-Lay, in a recent television advertising campaign, encouraged current customers to increase their consumption of Doritos snack chips. The spots featured comedian Jay Leno telling viewers to "crunch all you want—we'll make more."

Figure 1.7

Marketing Strategy Tasks

Generic marketing management tasks

Marketing opportunity analysis and target market selection
- The marketing environment (Chapter 2)
- Marketing ethics and social responsibility (Chapter 3)
- Target market evaluation (Chapter 4)
- Consumer markets and buying behavior (Chapter 5)
- Organizational markets and buying behavior (Chapter 6)
- Marketing research and information systems (Chapter 7)

Marketing mix development
- Product decisions (Chapters 8, 9, and 10)
- Distribution decisions (Chapters 11, 12, 13, and 14)
- Promotion decisions (Chapters 15, 16, and 17)
- Price decisions (Chapters 18 and 19)

Marketing management
- Strategic market planning (Chapter 20)
- Implementing strategies and measuring performance (Chapter 21)

Diversification into new product offerings through internal efforts or through acquisitions of other organizations may also be viable options for a firm. For example, recent changes in Eastern Europe and the former Soviet Union have permitted jeans companies to sell more of their products to these markets. An organization's ability to pursue any of these alternatives successfully depends on its internal characteristics and the forces within the marketing environment.

Internal Organizational Factors   The primary factors inside an organization that should be considered when analyzing marketing opportunities are organizational objectives, financial resources, managerial skills, organizational strengths and weaknesses, and cost structures. Most organizations have overall organizational objectives. Some marketing opportunities may be consistent with these objectives; others are not, and to pursue them is hazardous. Frequently, the pursuit of such opportunities ends in failure or forces the company to alter its long-term objectives.

Obviously, a firm's financial resources constrain the type of marketing opportunities it can pursue. Typically, an organization does not develop projects that can bring economic catastrophe. In some situations, however, a firm must invest in a high-risk opportunity because the costs of not pursuing the project are so high. Thus a computer manufacturer, such as IBM, must do research and development and produce cutting-edge technology if it wants to remain competitive with other computer makers. Today IBM has less than 20 percent of the personal computer market and has joined with Apple Computer to develop a new class of personal computers and easy-to-use software.[12]

The skills and experience of an organization's management also limit the types of opportunities it can pursue. A company must be particularly cautious when exploring the possibility of entering unfamiliar markets with new products. If it lacks appropriate managerial skills and experience, the firm can sometimes acquire them by hiring additional managerial personnel.

Like people, most organizations have strengths and weaknesses. Because of the types of operations in which a firm is engaged, it normally has employees with specialized skills and technological information. Such characteristics are a strength when launching marketing strategies that require them. However, they may be a weakness if the company tries to compete in new, unrelated product areas.

An organization's cost structure may be an advantage if the company pursues certain marketing opportunities and a disadvantage if it pursues others. Such factors as geographic location, employee skills, access to raw materials, and type of equipment and facilities all can affect the cost structure.

Marketing Environment Forces   The *marketing environment,* which consists of political, legal, regulatory, societal, economic and competitive, and technological forces, surrounds the buyer and the marketing mix (see Figure 1.6). We explore each of these major environmental forces in considerable depth in Chapter 2. Although marketers know that they cannot predict changes in the marketing environment with certainty, they still must plan for them.

Marketing environment forces affect a marketer's ability to facilitate and expedite exchanges in three general ways. First, they influence customers by affecting their lifestyles, standards of living, and preferences and needs for products. Because a marketing manager tries to develop and adjust the marketing mix to satisfy consumers, the effects of environmental forces on customers also have an indirect impact on the marketing mix components. Second, marketing environment forces help determine whether and how a marketing manager can perform certain marketing activities. Third, the environmental forces may affect a marketing manager's decisions and actions by influencing buyers' reactions to the firm's marketing mix.

Although forces in the marketing environment sometimes are viewed as "uncontrollables," a marketing manager may be able to influence one or more of them. For example, when the recession of the early 1990s was having a major impact on new car sales, many dealers made discount financing available. New car rates were as low as 2.9% for 2 years. Dealers who lease cars promoted creative lease agreements which extended the number of years in the lease or otherwise minimized the monthly cost of the car. Car manufacturers responded to the competitive environment by promoting safety features such as antilock brakes and air bags.

Marketing environment forces fluctuate quickly and dramatically, which is one reason why marketing is so interesting and challenging. Because these forces are highly interrelated, a change in one may cause changes in others. For example, charging that cosmetic companies create "packaging and garbage" and sell "false hope and fantasy," Anita Roddick, founder of The Body Shop, responded to societal concerns about the natural environment by promoting refillable cosmetic packaging and developing campaigns for environmental causes.[13] The Body Shop has made millions of dollars in its 620 international franchise stores, which display window posters protesting rainforest destruction and the testing of cosmetics on animals. The Body Shop's social activism and success have changed competition in the cosmetics industry, and other companies are now moving away from animal testing as well.

Even though changes in the marketing environment produce uncertainty for marketers and, at times, hurt marketing efforts, they can also create opportunities. Marketers who are aware of changes in environmental forces can not only adjust to and influence them, but also capitalize on the opportunities such changes provide. For example, Procter & Gamble responded to consumers' concerns about wasteful packaging by developing and promoting concentrated refills for its Downy liquid fabric softener. Reebok has taken advantage of changes in consumer fitness habits by developing special shoes for step aerobics.

Marketing Strategy: Target Market Selection

A **target market** is a group of persons for whom a firm creates and maintains a marketing mix that specifically fits the needs and preferences of that group. When choosing a target market, marketing managers try to evaluate possible markets to see how entering them would affect the company's sales, costs, and profits. Marketers also attempt to determine if the organization has the resources to produce a marketing mix that meets the needs of a particular target market and if satisfying those needs is consistent with the firm's overall objectives. The size and number of competitors already marketing products in possible target markets is also of concern.

Marketing managers may define a target market as a vast number of people or as a relatively small group. Although a business may concentrate its efforts on one target market through a single marketing mix, businesses often focus on several target markets by developing and employing multiple marketing mixes. Reebok, for example, has different marketing mixes for several target markets. It markets different types of shoes to meet the specific needs of joggers, walkers, aerobics enthusiasts, and other groups.

Target market selection is crucial to generating productive marketing efforts. At times, products and organizations fail because marketers do not identify the appropriate customer groups at which to aim their efforts. For example, a study by *Self* magazine indicates that defining all women as a single target market may not be appropriate because of a growing polarization between homemakers and career-oriented women. Marketers must consider the many roles that women play in today's society. Women in this study expressed a wide range of characteristics when describing their self-image, with women under 50 placing more emphasis on attitude and less on beauty.[14]

Organizations that try to be all things to all people typically end up not satisfying the needs of any customer group very well. It is important for an organization's management to designate which customer groups the firm is trying to serve and to have adequate information about these customers. The identification and analysis of a target market provide a foundation on which a marketing mix can be developed.

Marketing Strategy: Marketing Mix Development

As mentioned earlier, the marketing mix consists of four major components: product, distribution, promotion, and price. These components are called marketing mix decision variables because a marketing manager decides what type of each component to use and in what amounts. A primary goal of a marketing manager is to create and maintain a marketing mix that satisfies consumers' needs for a general product type. Notice in Figure 1.6 that the marketing mix is built around the buyer (as is stressed by the marketing concept). Bear in mind, too, that the forces of the marketing environment affect the marketing mix variables in many ways.

Marketing mix variables often are viewed as controllable variables because they can be changed. However, there are limits to how much these variables can be altered. For example, because of economic conditions or government regulations, a manager may not be free to adjust prices daily. Changes in sizes, colors, shapes, and designs of most tangible goods are expensive; therefore, such product features cannot be altered very often. In addition, promotional campaigns and the methods used to distribute products ordinarily cannot be changed overnight.

Marketing managers must develop a marketing mix that precisely matches the needs of the people in the target market. Before they can do so, they must collect in-depth, up-to-date information about those needs. The information might include data about the age, income, race, sex, and educational level of people in the target market; their preferences for product features; their attitudes toward competitors' products; and the frequency and intensity with which they use the product. Armed with these kinds of data, marketing managers are better able to develop a product, distribution system, promotion program, and price that satisfy the people in the target market.

Figure 1.8

The Product Variable

Nestlé has addressed the product variable aspect of the marketing mix by designing a product—semi-sweet morsels—with desirable characteristics.

Source: Nestlé Food Company.

You can never be too rich or too creamy.

Rich. Creamy. Nestlé® Toll House® Morsels.
Make Your House A Toll House.

Let us look more closely at the decisions and activities related to each marketing mix variable (product, distribution, promotion, and price). Table 1.1 is a partial list of the decisions and activities associated with each marketing mix variable.

The Product Variable   As noted earlier, a product can be a good, a service, or an idea. The **product variable** is the aspect of the marketing mix that deals with researching consumers' product wants and designing a product with the desired characteristics. Figure 1.8 vividly communicates the desired characteristics—richness and creaminess—of Nestlé semi-sweet morsels. The product variable also involves the creation or alteration of packages and brand names and may include decisions regarding warranty and repair services. The actual production of products is not a marketing activity.

Product variable decisions and related activities are important because they are involved directly with creating products that satisfy consumers' needs and wants. The Global Perspective describes how Xerox Corporation Business Products and Systems regained global leadership by improving product quality. To maintain a satisfying set of products that will help an organization achieve its goals, a marketer must be able to develop new products, modify existing ones, and eliminate those that no longer satisfy buyers or yield acceptable profits.

The Distribution Variable   To satisfy consumers, products must be available at the right time and in a convenient location. In dealing with the **distribution**

Regaining Global Markets: Xerox Corporation Business Products and Systems

FOR ITS FIRST FIFTEEN YEARS, Xerox was without equal, best in an industry whose products were synonymous with its name. But in the mid-1970s challenges came from foreign competitors, such as Canon, and U.S. competitors, including IBM. Japanese and U.S. competition surpassed Xerox reprographic products in both cost and quality. Not even second best in some product categories, Xerox launched an ambitious quality improvement program in 1984 to arrest its decline in the world market it created. As a result, Xerox has not only halted loss of world market share, but also reversed it.

The phrase "Team Xerox" is not an empty slogan. It accurately reflects the firm's approach to tackling quality issues. Planning new products and services is based on detailed analyses of data specific to planning, managing, and evaluating quality improvement. Much of this wealth of data has been amassed through an extensive network of market surveillance and customer feedback, all designed to support systematic evaluation of customer requirements.

Customer analyses include exhaustive surveys of 55,000 Xerox equipment owners. The company uses this information to develop concrete business plans with measurable targets for achieving quality improvements necessary to meet customers' needs.

Xerox measures its performance in about 240 key areas of product, service, and business performance. The ultimate target for each attribute is the level of performance achieved by the world leader, regardless of industry. Gains in quality include a 78 percent decrease in the number of defects per one hundred machines; greatly increased product reliability, as measured by a 40 percent decrease in unscheduled maintenance; increased copy quality, which has strengthened the company's position as world leader; a 27 percent drop (nearly two hours) in service response time; and significant reductions in labor and material overhead. These improvements resulted in Xerox receiving the Malcolm Baldrige National Quality Award. Today the company has reestablished itself as a world leader in copier markets.

Source: Excerpted from U.S. Department of Commerce brochure, "Malcolm Baldrige National Quality Award, 1989 Award Winner."

variable, a marketing manager seeks to make products available in the quantities desired to as many customers as possible and to keep the total inventory, transportation, and storage costs as low as possible. A marketing manager may become involved in selecting and motivating intermediaries (wholesalers and retailers), establishing and maintaining inventory control procedures, and developing and managing transportation and storage systems.

The Promotion Variable The **promotion variable** relates to activities used to inform one or more groups of people about an organization and its products. Promotion can be aimed at increasing public awareness of an organization and of new or existing products. In addition, promotion can serve to educate consumers about product features or to urge people to take a particular stance on a political or social issue. It may also be used to keep interest strong in an established product that has been available for decades. The advertisement in Figure 1.9 is an example of creating sustained interest in Diet Coke.

The Price Variable The **price variable** relates to activities associated with establishing pricing policies and determining product prices. Price is a critical component of the marketing mix because consumers are concerned about the value obtained in an exchange. Price often is used as a competitive tool. Extremely intense price competition sometimes leads to price wars, but high price can also be used competitively to establish a product's image. For instance, if the makers of Calvin Klein's Obsession tried to sell that perfume in a one-gallon jug for $3.95, consumers probably would not buy it because the price would destroy the prestigious image of Obsession.

Developing and maintaining an effective marketing mix is a major requirement for a strong marketing strategy. Thus, as indicated in Figure 1.7, a large portion of this text (Chapters 8 through 19) focuses on the concepts, decisions, and activities associated with the components of the marketing mix.

Marketing Management

Marketing management is a process of planning, organizing, implementing, and controlling marketing activities to facilitate and expedite exchanges effectively and efficiently. Effectiveness and efficiency are important dimensions of this definition. *Effectiveness* is the degree to which an exchange helps achieve an organization's objectives. *Efficiency* is the minimization of resources an organization must spend to achieve a specific level of desired exchanges. Thus the

Figure 1.9

Promotion of an Established Brand

Coca-Cola promotes the taste of Diet Coke to differentiate it from other diet colas.

Source: © The Coca-Cola Company, reprinted by permission. All rights reserved.

overall goal of marketing management is to facilitate highly desirable exchanges and to minimize as much as possible the costs of doing so.

Planning is a systematic process of assessing opportunities and resources, determining marketing objectives, developing a marketing strategy, and developing plans for implementation and control. Planning determines when and how marketing activities will be performed and who is to perform them. It forces marketing managers to think ahead, to establish objectives, and to consider future marketing activities. Effective planning also reduces or eliminates daily crises.

Organizing marketing activities refers to developing the internal structure of the marketing unit. The structure is the key to directing marketing activities. The marketing unit can be organized by functions, products, regions, types of customers, or a combination of all four.

Proper implementation of marketing plans hinges on coordination of marketing activities, motivation of marketing personnel, and effective communication within the unit. Marketing managers must motivate marketing personnel, coordinate their activities, and integrate their activities both with those in other areas of the company and with the marketing efforts of personnel in external organizations, such as advertising agencies and research firms. An organization's communication system must allow the marketing manager to stay in contact with high-level management, with managers of other functional areas within the firm, and with personnel involved in marketing activities both inside and outside the organization.

The marketing control process consists of establishing performance standards, evaluating actual performance by comparing it with established standards, and reducing the difference between desired and actual performance. An effective control process has four requirements. It should ensure a rate of information flow that allows the marketing manager to quickly detect differences between actual and planned levels of performance. It must accurately monitor different kinds of activities and be flexible enough to accommodate changes. The control process must be economical so that its costs are low relative to the costs that would arise if there were no controls. Finally, the control process should be designed so that both managers and subordinates can understand it. To maintain effective marketing control, an organization needs to develop a comprehensive control process that evaluates marketing operations at regular intervals. In Chapters 20 and 21 we examine the planning, organizing, implementing, and controlling of marketing activities in greater detail.

The Organization of This Book

Figure 1.6 is a map of the overall organization of this book. Chapter 2 discusses the marketing environment variables listed in the outer portion of Figure 1.6, and Chapter 3 explores marketing ethics and social responsibility. Then we move to the center of the figure, analyzing markets, buyers, and marketing research in Chapters 4, 5, 6, and 7, respectively. Chapters 8 through 19 explore the marketing mix variables, starting with the product variable and moving clockwise around Figure 1.6. Chapters 20 and 21 discuss strategic market planning, organization, implementation, and control. Chapters 22, 23, and 24 scrutinize decisions and activities that are unique to business-to-business marketing, international marketing, and services marketing. If, as you study, you want to know where the text is leading, look again at Figure 1.6.

Summary

Marketing consists of individual and organizational activities that facilitate and expedite satisfying exchange relationships in a dynamic environment through the creation, distribution, promotion, and pricing of goods, services, and ideas. An exchange is the provision or transfer of goods, services, and ideas in return for something of value. Four conditions must exist for an exchange to occur: (1) two or more individuals, groups, or organizations must participate; (2) each party must have something of value desired by the other; (3) each party must be willing to give up what it has in order to receive the value held by the other; and (4) the parties to the exchange must be able to communicate with each other to make their somethings of value available. In an exchange, products are traded either for other products or for financial resources, such as cash or credit. Products can be goods, services, or ideas.

It is important to study marketing because it permeates our lives. Marketing activities are performed in both business and nonbusiness organizations. Moreover, marketing activities help business organizations generate profits, the lifeblood of a capitalist economy. The study of marketing enhances consumer awareness. Finally, marketing costs absorb about half of each consumer dollar.

The marketing concept is a management philosophy prompting a business organization to try to satisfy customers' needs through a coordinated set of activities that also allows the organization to achieve its goals. Customer satisfaction is the major objective of the marketing concept. The philosophy of the marketing concept emerged in the United States during the 1950s, after the production and the sales eras. To make the marketing concept work, top management must accept it as an overall management philosophy. Implementing the marketing concept requires an efficient information system and sometimes the restructuring of the organization.

Organizations that develop activities consistent with the marketing concept become market-oriented organizations. Market orientation is the generation of market information, and the coordination and communication of market information across departments. The participation of top management, marketing managers, and nonmarketing managers is important to the creation of a market-oriented organization. Open exchange of information and relationship-building activities with customers is also important in market orientation.

Marketing strategy involves selecting and analyzing a target market (the group of people whom the organization wants to reach) and creating and maintaining an appropriate marketing mix (product, distribution, promotion, and price) to satisfy this market. Marketing strategy requires that managers focus on four tasks to achieve set objectives: (1) marketing opportunity analysis, (2) target market selection, (3) marketing mix development, and (4) marketing management.

Marketers should be able to recognize and analyze marketing opportunities, which are circumstances that allow an organization to take action toward reaching a particular group of customers. Marketing opportunity analysis involves reviewing both internal factors (organizational objectives, financial resources, managerial skills, organizational strengths, organizational weaknesses, and cost structures) and external ones (the political, legal, regulatory, societal, economic and competitive, and technological forces of the marketing environment).

A target market is a group of persons for whom a firm creates and maintains a marketing mix that specifically fits the needs and preferences of that group. It is important for an organization's management to designate which customer groups the firm is trying to serve and to have some information about these customers. The identification and analysis of a target market provide a foundation on which a marketing mix can be developed.

The four variables that make up the marketing mix are product, price, promotion, and distribution. The product variable is the aspect of the marketing mix that deals with researching consumers' wants and designing a product with the desired characteristics. A marketing manager tries to make products available in the quantities desired to as many customers as possible and to keep the total inventory, transportation, and storage costs as low as possible—the distribution variable. The promotion variable relates to activities used to inform one or more groups of people about an organization and its products. The price variable refers to establishing pricing policies and determining product prices.

Marketing management is a process of planning, organizing, implementing, and controlling marketing activities to facilitate and expedite exchanges effectively and efficiently. Planning is a systematic process of assessing opportunities and resources, determining marketing objectives, developing a marketing strategy, and developing plans for implementation and control. Organizing marketing activities refers to developing the internal structure of the marketing unit. Properly implementing marketing plans depends on coordinating marketing activities, motivating marketing personnel, and effectively communicating within the unit. The marketing control process consists of establishing performance standards, evaluating actual performance by comparing it with established standards, and reducing the difference between desired and actual performance.

Important Terms

Marketing
Exchange
Marketing concept
Market orientation
Marketing strategy
Marketing mix

Target market
Product variable
Distribution variable
Promotion variable
Price variable
Marketing management

Discussion and Review Questions

1. What is marketing? How did you define marketing before you read this chapter?
2. Why should someone study marketing?
3. Discuss the basic elements of the marketing concept. Which businesses in your area use this concept? In your opinion, have these businesses adopted the marketing concept? Explain.
4. Identify several business organizations in your area that obviously have not adopted the marketing concept. What characteristics of these organizations indicate nonacceptance of the marketing concept?
5. Describe the major components of a marketing strategy. How are the components related?

6. Identify the tasks involved in developing a marketing strategy.
7. What are the primary issues that marketing managers consider when conducting a market opportunity analysis?
8. What are the variables in the marketing environment? How much control does a marketing manager have over environmental variables?
9. Why is the selection of a target market such an important issue?
10. Why are the elements of the marketing mix known as variables?
11. What types of management activities are involved in the marketing management process?

Cases

1.1   Two Grey Hills Trading Post

One of the last dozen or so trading posts remaining on the Navajo Indian Reservation, Two Grey Hills Trading Post has been in continuous operation since 1897. The post—which has been described as a general store as well as a place to buy, sell, and trade Native American–made products—is now owned and operated by Les Wilson. Although it faces a changing world and increasingly competitive environment, Two Grey Hills remains a valuable resource for Navajos living in and near the Chuska Mountains of northwestern New Mexico.

Trading posts have been vital to the economies of many Native American tribes for more than a century. In days past, the trading post served as a place to meet; to pick up mail, news, and gossip; and to exchange *naalyehe,* things of value. Navajo traders bartered groceries and dry goods for raw wool, rugs, piñon nuts, and native crafts, which were later sold or traded for more merchandise. Additionally, trading posts often served as pawn shops, holding silver and turquoise jewelry and other goods in exchange for cash, which would be used to purchase goods from the trader.

While Two Grey Hills's Les Wilson still serves as trader, grocer, banker, counselor, and occasional source of emergency support to native residents, today's trading posts have changed somewhat. Barter has been replaced by cash sales and purchases, and the trading posts have become more competitive with each other and with off-reservation businesses for the best crafts. Pawning is now discouraged at most trading posts. In competition with the large grocery and department stores off the reservation, they have become more like convenience stores, even renting videos. For many trading posts, tourist dollars have replaced the wool and piñon nuts of yesterday.

Although Two Grey Hills functions primarily as a general store for local residents, it is best known for its fine-quality Navajo rugs. Indeed, rugs woven in a particular geometric single- and double-diamond pattern have become so identified with the trading post that they are said to have the Two Grey Hills pattern. Except for the black border, the rugs are colored entirely by undyed shades of brown wool. They are woven by hand and take many months to complete. Most come from fifty weavers who live within ten miles of the trading post. Today, Two Grey Hills rugs fetch between $45 and $5,000 or higher.

Like small business owners everywhere, Les Wilson must take care to buy rugs and other Navajo crafts at good prices and to offer merchandise at competitive prices. When a weaver brings in a rug, Wilson must make a competitive offer; if the weaver does not like the offer, the rug is then sold elsewhere—to another trading post, to stores in Gallup or Farmington, New Mexico, or, if the weaving is of exceptional quality, to one of the galleries in Sante Fe. When tourists come in, Wilson must price the rug appropriately or the tourists will simply look elsewhere for a better price. And, because Two Grey Hills is off the beaten tourist path, good word-of-mouth advertising and good prices encourage the occasional tourist to brave the unpaved roads to the trading post.

Rug sales and tourist dollars are important to the post, but the sale of more mundane groceries, dry goods, hardware, and other supplies to nearby Navajo residents keeps the trading post alive. Among its wares are canned, dry, and fresh meat and produce; clothing and underwear; cloth, thread, and needles; hardware and auto parts; diesel and propane; lamp oil and laundry soap; and soft drinks and newspapers. Service station and mail services are also highly valued by customers.

When the Navajos traded horses and buckboard wagons for pickup trucks, it made it easier for them to drive off the reservation for supplies, leaving the trading post behind. Two Grey Hills faces strong competition from department and discount stores in Gallup and Farmington as well as Thriftway convenience stores scattered throughout the reservation. However, trading posts still offer credit, something more modern convenience stores don't allow. Les Wilson believes that credit and personal service will help Two Grey Hills and other trading posts survive on the reservation.

In 1989 Two Grey Hills was named to the New Mexico State Register of Cultural Properties and may soon achieve a listing as a historic property on the National Register of Historic Places. Wilson hopes this will bring more tourist attention for the post's famous rugs. While the future role of trading posts in Navajo society is unclear, Les Wilson says that they are not dying out and "will continue in the land of the Navajo as long as children herd sheep and weavers weave."[15]

Questions for Discussion

1. Discuss the various types of marketing exchanges that occur at Two Grey Hills Trading Post.
2. How does Two Grey Hills serve two target markets—tourists and Navajo residents?
3. How has Two Grey Hills developed a marketing strategy to deal with competition?

1.2   Saturn Reaches for the Stars with All-American Appeal

The fall of 1990 brought the introduction of a much-awaited new car company: Saturn Corporation. After seven long years of development, the General Motors Corporation-backed company debuted its first models in a crowded market of compact cars, which for years has been dominated by Japanese imports. Since 1985, GM's share of the U.S. passenger car market has fallen eleven points to 33 percent, while the Japanese car makers' share climbed seven points to 26 percent. For General Motors, Saturn represents not only the future of GM, but a last chance to challenge the Japanese.

GM established Saturn as a separate and independent subsidiary in Tennessee in 1985, claiming that it would be the key to GM's long-term competitiveness, survival, and success. Consequently, Saturn's management spent years developing the new company from scratch. New pace-setting labor relations, participatory management, and the latest technology and manufacturing methods were all supported financially by GM. With total support for their efforts, the leaders of Saturn embarked on a journey to build the car company of the future. Saturn's mission is to sell 80 percent of its cars to drivers who would not otherwise have bought a GM car. To achieve this goal, the company will have to pay careful attention to its product, price, promotion, and distribution, while closely monitoring and responding to changes in the marketing environment.

Most foreign-car buyers do not consider buying an American car, and a recent study by the research firm J. D. Power & Associates revealed that 42 percent of all new car shoppers won't even consider a GM car. Saturn's advertising agency, Hal Rhiney and Associates, was therefore faced with a challenge in promoting Saturn's cars. Should it stress the down-home feeling of buying American or stress the most ambitious, inspiring effort in manufacturing since World War II? The agency decided to put its $100 billion advertising effort into emphasizing the basic values and lifestyles of Americans. Consequently, Saturn advertisements have a down-home feeling and feature company employees talking about the cars and the Saturn concept.

Saturn's advertising is aimed at college-educated men and women ages 25 to 49. Commercials stress that by recapturing the United States' can-do spirit, Saturn knows how to make cars. The commercials feature the town of Spring Hill, Tennessee, where the plant is located, and the people who live and work there. This emphasizes the company's commitment to the community and its partnership with its residents. The company believes such values are key to the success of Saturn automobiles. Advertisements also tell the story of how employees took a risk in leaving Detroit for something new and exciting—to start from the drawing board and "build cars again . . . but in a brand new way." The employees symbolize the American pioneer spirit still at work in the 1990s.

Saturn is also employing a new pricing concept for its cars. Prices range from $9,000 to $12,000, competitive with import car prices, but are nonnegotiable. A price tag of, for example, $11,000 means $11,000—no dealer rebates, no promotions, no hidden added costs.

J. D. Power estimates that marketing, delivering, and selling cars through dealers account for 30 to 35 percent of a car's cost, so Saturn has paid close attention to the distribution of its cars. Saturn tries to limit outlets to one dealership in each metropolitan area. The first dealerships were set up primarily in areas where import car sales were high. The first seventy dealerships were located on the East and West coasts to avoid cannibalizing sales of other GM cars. In addition, Saturn chose dealers carefully to ensure that they know how to appeal to import car buyers.

First-day sales of the Saturn were tremendous. One dealership sold all nine of its Saturns on the first day with a backlog of orders. Saturn's sales continue to rise. In fact, its first 18 months' sales were stronger than some Japanese brands when they were introduced. The real test of Saturn is time—to test its product reliability and acceptance by the present foreign car–buying market. It will be several years before one of the most innovative companies in America will know whether it has truly set an example for auto companies to follow.

Questions for Discussion

1. What steps did General Motors take to implement customer orientation at Saturn?
2. What are Saturn's target market and marketing mix?
3. What aspects of the marketing environment will Saturn have to monitor to maintain success?

Chapter Notes

1. Based on information from Lowell C. Paddock, "Bloomington Gold," *Road & Track,* Feb. 1991, pp. 82–84; Sue Elliott, "Golden Opportunity," *Vette,* Nov. 1989, pp. 38–43; Dave Lundy, "A Celebration of the Sixties Survivors," *Vette,* Nov. 1989, pp. 46–47, 69; Tom Christmann and Paul Zazarine, "Field of Dreams," *Corvette Fever,* Nov. 1989, pp. 6–8; Rick Hanna, "The Man with the Midas Touch," *Corvette Fever,* Oct. 1989, pp. 22–25, 93–94; and "David Burroughs: The Man Behind Bloomington Gold," *CSA,* June 1989, pp. 69–87.
2. Reprinted from *Dictionary of Marketing Terms,* Peter D. Bennett, Ed., 1988, p. 54, published by the American Marketing Association. Used by permission.
3. O. C. Ferrell and George Lucas, "An Evaluation of Progress in the Development of a Definition of Marketing," *Journal of the Academy of Marketing Science,* Fall 1987, p. 17.
4. Thomas A. Stewart, "Turning Around the Lord's Business," *Fortune,* Sept. 25, 1989, pp. 116–128.
5. Philip Kotler, *Marketing Management: Analysis, Planning, Implementation, and Control,* 7th ed. (Englewood Cliffs, N.J.: Prentice-Hall, 1991), p. 7.
6. Ferrell and Lucas, p. 20.
7. Stephanie Losee, "Products of the Year," *Fortune,* Dec. 2, 1991, pp. 66–68, 72, 76.
8. "Selling Green," *Consumer Reports,* Oct. 1991, pp. 687–692.
9. Ajay K. Kohli and Bernard J. Jaworski, "Market Orientation: The Construct, Research Propositions and Managerial Implications," *Journal of Marketing,* Apr. 1990, pp. 1–18. Used by permission.
10. *Ibid.*
11. Cyndee Miller, "Jeans Marketers Look for a Good Fit with Older Men and Women," *Marketing News,* Sept. 16, 1991, pp. 1, 6.
12. "Gates' Vision: Putting Archives to Use," *USA Today,* Oct. 9, 1991, p. 8B.
13. Anita Roddick, *Body and Soul—Profits with Principles* (New York: Crown Publishers, 1991), pp. 1–10.
14. Cyndee Miller, "Study: Women Placing More Value on Attitude, Less on Beauty," *Marketing News,* Sept. 30, 1991, p. 5.
15. Kate McGraw, "Two Grey Hills Gets Listing," *Farmington Daily Times,* Dec. 16, 1989; Jean-Pierre Cativiela, "Two Grey Hills: Onions to Fine Weaving, Post Has It All," *The (Gallup, NM) Independent,* pp. 1–2; and Sharman Russell, "Trading on Tradition," *Westways,* Nov. 1989, pp. 62–64, 75.
16. Micheline Maynard, "18-Month-Old Saturn Walking Tall," *USA Today,* Feb. 24, 1992, p. 1B; James B. Treece, "Are the Planets Lining Up at Last for Saturn?" *Business Week,* April 8, 1991, pp. 32–33; James R. Healey, "Saturn Demand Delivers Excitement to Dealers," *USA Today,* Nov. 5, 1990, p. 1B; Raymond Serafin, "Saturn's Goal: To Be Worthy," *Advertising Age,* Nov. 5, 1990, p. 21; Stuart Elliott, "Campaign Takes Aim at Heartstrings," *USA Today,* Nov. 1, 1990, pp. 1B, 2B; Rich Ceppos, "Saturn—Finally, It's Here. But Is It Good Enough?" *Car and Driver,* Nov.

1990, pp. 132–138; Bob Garfield, "Down-to-Earth Ads Give Saturn an Underrated Liftoff," *Advertising Age,* Oct. 29, 1990, p. 68; Cindy Wolff, "First Saturn Here Runs Jag Off Road," *The (Memphis) Commercial Appeal,* Oct. 26, 1990, pp. A1, A12; Neal Templin and Joseph B. White, "GM's Saturn, In Early Orbit, Intrigues Buyers," *Wall Street Journal,* Oct. 25, 1990, pp. B1, B6; Barbara Lippert, "It's a Saturn Morning in America," *Adweek,* Oct. 15, 1990, p. 67; Raymond Serafin and Patricia Strand, "Saturn People Star in First Campaign," *Advertising Age,* Aug. 27, 1990, pp. 1, 38; Joseph B. White and Melinda Grenier Guiles, "Rough Launch," *Wall Street Journal,* July 9, 1990, pp. A1, A12; and James B. Treece, "Here Comes GM's Saturn," *Business Week,* April 9, 1990, pp. 56–62.

2 The Marketing Environment

OBJECTIVES

- To understand the concept of the marketing environment and the importance of environmental scanning and analysis

- To identify the types of political forces in the marketing environment

- To understand how laws and their interpretation influence marketing practices

- To determine how government regulations and self-regulatory agencies affect marketing activities

- To identify societal issues that marketers must deal with as they make decisions

- To understand how economic and competitive factors affect organizations' ability to compete and customers' willingness and ability to buy products

- To explore the effects of new technology on society and on marketing activities

Introducing *Healthy Sensation!*
At last, salad dressing as good as the salad.

Healthy Sensation! Now everything you ever wanted from a dressing comes in one bottle.

Marketers certainly want to promote the benefits of their products, but they must take care not to mislead consumers or violate federal regulations when making claims. One company that has had problems over such claims is Procter & Gamble.

In 1991 the Food and Drug Administration (FDA) complained that Procter & Gamble's use of the word *fresh* in its Citrus Hill Fresh Choice orange juice product was misleading and confusing because the beverage is actually made from concentrate. The federal agency repeatedly asked Procter & Gamble to remove the word from the product's label, but the company refused to back down, arguing that the "fresh" was part of the product's name. When negotiations broke down, the FDA seized 2,400 cases of Citrus Hill Fresh Choice from a Minneapolis warehouse. Within days, Procter & Gamble agreed to comply with the FDA's order and renamed the product Citrus Hill. The company also dropped "no cholesterol" claims from its Crisco corn oil and some other vegetable products in compliance with FDA requests. The products had never contained cholesterol. Only animal products contain cholesterol.

Procter & Gamble is not the only company to face off against the FDA, of course. However, because the company has recently become more aggressive in making broad health claims about a number of its products, it may be subject to more scrutiny by federal regulators. At the same time, the Food and Drug Administration has become more aggressive in enforcing federal regulations, after years of laxness. Indeed, some industry observers have charged that the FDA made an example out of Procter & Gamble to herald a new era of stricter enforcement of federal food and drug laws. Regardless, most food companies are examining their own policies and claims to ensure that no laws have been violated. To help deal with such problems in the future, Procter & Gamble has set up a new worldwide organization to handle regulatory issues. Whether the new organization will smooth the way for Procter & Gamble's products has yet to be tested.[1]

Photo courtesy of Thomas J. Lipton Company.

A s you can see from Procter & Gamble's experiences, various forces can have a tremendous impact on the decisions and activities of marketers. This chapter explores the political, legal, regulatory, societal, economic and competitive, and technological forces that make up the marketing environment. First we define the marketing environment and consider why it is critical to scan and analyze it. Then we discuss the political forces that generate government actions affecting marketing activities. We examine the effects of laws and regulatory agencies on these activities and describe the desires and expectations of society. Next we consider the effects of general economic conditions: prosperity, recession, depression, and recovery. We also examine several types of economic forces that influence companies' ability to compete and consumers' willingness and ability to buy. Finally, we analyze the major dimensions of the technological forces in the environment.

Examining and Responding to the Marketing Environment

The **marketing environment** consists of external forces that directly or indirectly influence an organization's acquisition of inputs and generation of outputs. Inputs might include personnel, financial resources, raw materials, and information. Outputs could be information, packages, goods, services, or ideas. As indicated in Chapter 1, we view the marketing environment as consisting of six categories of forces: political, legal, regulatory, societal, economic and competitive, and technological.

Whether they fluctuate rapidly or slowly, environmental forces are always dynamic. Changes in the marketing environment create uncertainty, threats, and opportunities for marketers. Although the future is not very predictable, marketers can estimate what will happen. We can say with certainty that marketers will continue to modify their marketing strategies in response to the dynamic environment. For example, in response to increased consumer interest in health foods, Kellogg Company of Battle Creek, one of the biggest proponents of health claims for its food products, developed Heartwise cereal. However, after settling a lawsuit with the state of Texas and receiving pressure from the Food and Drug Administration, Kellogg had to change the name from Heartwise to Fiberwise because there was no substantiation that the cereal benefitted the heart.[2] Marketing managers who fail to recognize changes in environmental forces leave their firms unprepared to capitalize on marketing opportunities or to cope with threats created by changes in the environment. Monitoring the environment is crucial to an organization's survival and to the long-term achievement of its goals.

Environmental Scanning and Analysis

To monitor changes in the marketing environment effectively, marketers must engage in environmental scanning and analysis. **Environmental scanning** is the process of collecting information about the forces in the marketing environ-

Figure 2.1

Products that Respond to Environmental Concerns

As this advertisement shows, marketing managers at Dakin have studied data about their industry's environment. To respond to environmental concerns about violent toys, Dakin markets its products as "toys you can feel good about."

Source: © 1990 Dakin, Inc. Available at fine gift and toy shops everywhere.

ment. Scanning involves observation; perusal of secondary sources, such as business, trade, government, and general-interest publications; and marketing research. However, managers must be careful not to gather so much information that sheer volume makes analysis impossible.

Environmental analysis is the process of assessing and interpreting the information gathered through environmental scanning. A manager evaluates the information for accuracy, tries to resolve inconsistencies in the data, and, if warranted assigns significance to the findings. Through analysis, a marketing manager seeks to describe current environmental changes and to predict future changes. By evaluating these changes, the manager should be able to determine possible threats and opportunities linked to environmental fluctuations. Understanding the current state of the marketing environment and recognizing the threats and opportunities arising from changes within it help marketing managers assess the performance of current marketing efforts and develop marketing strategies for the future. For example, Figure 2.1 illustrates how Dakin has used criticism about children's toys to promote its line of stuffed animals.

Responding to Environmental Forces

In responding to environmental forces, marketing managers can take two general approaches: to accept environmental forces as uncontrollable or to confront and mold them. If environmental forces are viewed as uncontrollable, the organization remains passive and reactive toward the environment. Instead of trying to influence forces in the environment, its marketing managers tend to adjust current marketing strategies to environmental changes. They approach market opportunities discovered through environmental scanning and analysis with caution. For example, ConAgra Inc. has introduced a 96 percent fat-free ground beef product that uses a new fat substitute made of oat flour to keep burgers juicy. ConAgra is hoping to lure Americans back to eating red meat and therefore, increase its market share relative to substitute products.[3] On the other hand, marketing managers who believe that environmental forces can be shaped adopt a proactive approach. For example, if a market is blocked by traditional environmental constraints, marketing managers may apply economic, psychological, political, and promotional skills to gain access to it or operate within it. Once they identify what blocks a market opportunity, marketers can assess the power of the various parties involved and develop strategies to try to overcome environmental forces.[4] For example, as part of the Clean Air Act compliance, the Environmental Protection Agency (EPA) issued sulfur emissions allowances to utilities, with the allowances decreasing over time. The utility industry, in cooperation with the Chicago Board of Trade, created a private market for the trading of rights to emit sulfur dioxide, thereby taking a proactive approach to coping with environmental constraints.[5]

In trying to influence environmental forces, marketing management may seek to create market opportunities or to extract greater benefits relative to costs from existing market opportunities. For instance, a firm losing sales to competitors with lower-priced products may strive to develop technology that would make its production processes more efficient; greater efficiency would allow it to lower the prices of its own products. Political action is another way of affecting environmental forces. A proactive approach, then, can be constructive and bring desired results. However, managers must recognize that there are limits on how much an environmental force can be shaped and that these limits vary across environmental forces. Although an organization may be able to influence the enactment of laws through lobbying, it is unlikely that a single organization can significantly increase the national birthrate or move the economy from recession to prosperity.

We cannot generalize and say that either of these approaches to environmental response is better than the other. For some organizations, the passive, reactive approach is most appropriate, but for other firms, the aggressive approach leads to better performance. The selection of a particular approach depends on an organization's managerial philosophies, objectives, financial resources, customers, and human skills and on the composition of the set of environmental forces within which the organization operates.

The rest of this chapter explores in detail each of the six environmental forces—political, legal, regulatory, societal, economic and competitive, and technological.

Political Forces

The political, legal, and regulatory forces of the marketing environment are closely interrelated. Legislation is enacted, legal decisions are interpreted by the courts, and regulatory agencies are created and operated, for the most part, by persons elected or appointed to political offices. Legislation and regulations (or their lack) reflect the current political outlook. Consequently, the political force of the marketing environment has the potential to influence marketing decisions and strategies.

Marketing organizations need to maintain good relations with elected political officials for several reasons. When political officials are well disposed toward particular firms or industries, they are less likely to create or enforce laws and regulations unfavorable to these companies. For example, political officials who believe that oil companies are making honest efforts to control pollution are unlikely to create and enforce highly restrictive pollution control laws. In addition, governments are big buyers, and political officials can influence how much a government agency purchases and from whom. Finally, political officials can play key roles in helping organizations secure foreign markets.

Many marketers view political forces as beyond their control; they simply try to adjust to conditions that arise from those forces. Some firms, however, seek to influence political events by helping to elect to political offices individuals who regard them positively. Much of this help is in the form of campaign contributions. Although laws restrict direct corporate contributions to campaign funds, corporate money may be channeled into campaign funds as personal contributions of corporate executives or stockholders. Such actions violate the spirit of the corporate campaign contribution laws. A sizable contribution to a campaign fund may carry with it an implicit understanding that the elected official will perform political favors for the contributing firm. A corporation may even contribute to the campaign funds of several candidates who seek the same office. Occasionally, some businesses find it so important to ensure favorable treatment that they make direct illegal corporate contributions to campaign funds.

Legal Forces

Know what each does ? how they are different

A number of laws influence marketing decisions and activities. Our discussion will focus on procompetitive and consumer protection laws and their interpretation.

Procompetitive Legislation

Procompetitive legislation is enacted to preserve competition. Table 2.1 briefly describes nine major procompetitive laws, most of which were enacted to end various practices deemed unacceptable by society. We describe the most important of these in greater detail below.

The Sherman Antitrust Act The **Sherman Antitrust Act** was passed in 1890 to prevent businesses from restraining trade and monopolizing markets. The act condemns "every contract, combination, or conspiracy in restraint of trade." It also prohibits monopolies or attempts by businesses to monopolize a particular market or industry. Enforced by the Antitrust Division of the Department of Justice, the Sherman Antitrust Act applies to firms operating in interstate commerce and to U.S. firms operating in foreign commerce.

Act	Purposes
Sherman Antitrust Act (1890)	Prohibits contracts, combinations, or conspiracies to restrain trade; establishes as a misdemeanor monopolizing or attempting to monopolize
Clayton Act (1914)	Prohibits specific practices such as price discrimination, exclusive dealer arrangements, and stock acquisitions in which the effect may notably lessen competition or tend to create a monopoly
Federal Trade Commission Act (1914)	Created the Federal Trade Commission; also gives the FTC investigatory powers to be used in preventing unfair methods of competition
Robinson-Patman Act (1936)	Prohibits price discrimination that lessens competition among wholesalers or retailers; prohibits producers from giving disproportionate services or facilities to large buyers
Wheeler-Lea Act (1938)	Prohibits unfair and deceptive acts and practices regardless of whether competition is injured; places advertising of foods and drugs under the jurisdiction of the FTC
Celler-Kefauver Act (1950)	Prohibits any corporation engaged in commerce from acquiring the whole or any part of the stock or other share of the capital or assets of another corporation when the effect substantially lessens competition or tends to create a monopoly
Consumer Goods Pricing Act (1975)	Prohibits the use of price maintenance agreements among manufacturers and resellers in interstate commerce
Trademark Counterfeiting Act (1980)	Provides civil and criminal penalties against those who deal in counterfeit consumer goods or any counterfeit goods that can threaten health or safety
Nutritional Labeling and Education Act (1990)	Prohibits exaggerated health claims and requires all processed foods to contain labels with nutritional information.

Table 2.1   Major Federal Laws Affecting Marketing Decisions

The Clayton Act   Because the Sherman Antitrust Act was written in rather vague terms, the courts have not always interpreted it as its creators intended. Consequently, the Clayton Act was passed in 1914 to limit specific activities that tend to reduce competition. The **Clayton Act** specifically prohibits price discrimination, tying and exclusive agreements, and the acquisition of stock in another corporation "where the effect may be to substantially lessen competition or tend to create a monopoly." In addition, the act prohibits members of one company's board of directors from holding seats on the boards of competing corporations. The Clayton Act also exempts farm cooperatives and labor organizations from antitrust laws.

The Federal Trade Commission Act and the Wheeler-Lea Act   Also passed in 1914, the **Federal Trade Commission Act** created the Federal Trade Commission (FTC), which today regulates the greatest number of marketing practices. Like the Clayton Act, the Federal Trade Commission Act was written to strengthen antimonopoly provisions of the Sherman Antitrust Act. Whereas the Clayton Act prohibits specific practices, the Federal Trade Commission Act more broadly prohibits unfair methods of competition. This act also empowers the FTC to work with the Department of Justice to enforce the provisions of the Clayton Act. Later sections of this chapter discuss the FTC's regulatory activities.

The creators of the Federal Trade Commission Act, like those of the Sherman Antitrust Act, found that the courts did not always interpret the act as they had intended. For instance, in the 1931 Raladam case, the Supreme Court ruled that a producer's misrepresentation of an obesity cure was not an unfair method of competition because the firm's action did not injure competition.[6] This ruling—among others—spurred Congress in 1938 to pass the **Wheeler-Lea Act**, which essentially makes unfair and deceptive acts or practices unlawful, regardless of whether they injure competition. It specifically prohibits false and misleading advertising of foods, drugs, therapeutic devices, and cosmetics. The Wheeler-Lea Act also provides penalties for violations and procedures for enforcement.

The Robinson-Patman Act   During the early 1930s, when the Depression was at its peak, the Federal Trade Commission found that many of the low prices that suppliers offered to chain stores could not be justified on the basis of cost savings arising from quantity purchases. Eventually, in 1936, after several years of economic hardship, pressure from the FTC and popular political support for further legislation led to the passage of the Robinson-Patman Act.

The **Robinson-Patman Act** is significant because it directly influences pricing policies. Its most important provision prohibits price discrimination among different purchasers of goods of similar grade and quality where the effect of such discrimination tends to reduce competition among the purchasers or gives one purchaser a competitive edge. The Robinson-Patman Act did *not* outlaw price differentials—price differentials are legal if they can be justified as cost savings or as meeting competition in good faith. The act also makes it unlawful to knowingly influence the setting of prices or to receive discriminatory prices when they are prohibited by the Robinson-Patman Act. Finally, it outlaws providing services or facilities to purchasers on terms not offered to all purchasers on more or less equal terms.

Thus the pricing provisions of the Robinson-Patman Act deal only with discriminatory price differentials. Price differentials become discriminatory when one purchaser (usually a retailer) can acquire similar quantities of goods of like grade and quality at lower prices than competing purchasers dealing with the same supplier. Such price differentials give that purchaser an unfair advantage in the market and ultimately reduce consumers' opportunities to choose from among a number of products, stores, and prices.

Consumer Protection Legislation

The second category of regulatory laws, **consumer protection legislation**, is not a recent development. During the mid-1800s, lawmakers in many states passed laws to prohibit the adulteration of food and drugs. However, consumer protection laws at the federal level mushroomed in the mid-1960s and early 1970s. A number of them deal with consumer safety—such as the food and drug acts, designed to protect people from actual and potential physical harm caused by adulteration or mislabeling of foods and drugs. Other laws prohibit the sale of various hazardous products, such as flammable fabrics and toys that may injure children.

To help consumers become better informed, Congress has passed several laws concerning the disclosure of information. Some laws require that information about specific products—such as textiles, furs, cigarettes, and automobiles—be provided on labels. Other laws focus on particular marketing activities—product development and testing, packaging, labeling, advertising, and consumer financing. For example, the 1990 Nutritional Labeling and Education Act attempts to prevent exaggerated health claims on food packages. Products affected by the new law include cereals claiming to reduce heart disease and peanut butter advertised to be cholesterol free (as a vegetable product, peanut butter by nature does not contain cholesterol to begin with).

Interpreting Laws

Laws certainly have the potential to influence marketing activities, but the actual effects of the laws are determined by how marketers and the courts interpret the laws. Laws seem to be quite specific because they contain many complex clauses and subclauses. In reality, however, many laws and regulations are stated in vague terms that force marketers to rely on legal advice rather than on their own understanding and common sense. Because of this vagueness, some organizations attempt to gauge the limits of certain laws by operating in a legally questionable way to see how far they can get with certain practices before being prosecuted. Other marketers, however, interpret regulations and statutes very conservatively and strictly to avoid violating a vague law.

Although court rulings directly affect businesses accused of specific violations, they also have a broader, less direct impact on other businesses. When marketers try to interpret laws in relation to specific marketing practices, they often analyze recent court decisions, both to understand better what the law is intended to do and to gain a clearer sense of how the courts are likely to interpret it in the future.

Regulatory Forces

Interpretation alone does not determine the effectiveness of laws and regulations; the level of enforcement by regulatory agencies is also significant. Some regulatory agencies are created and administered by government units; others are sponsored by nongovernmental sources. In our discussion, we first turn to federal, state, and local government regulatory units and then examine self-regulatory forces.

Federal Regulatory Agencies

Federal regulatory agencies influence many marketing activities, including product development, pricing, packaging, advertising, personal selling, and distribution. Usually, they have the power to enforce specific laws, such as the Federal Trade Commission Act, as well as some discretion in establishing operating rules and drawing up regulations to guide certain types of industry practices. Because of this discretion and overlapping areas of responsibility, confusion or conflict as to which agencies have jurisdiction over specific types of marketing activities is common.

The Federal Trade Commission Of all the federal regulatory units, the **Federal Trade Commission (FTC)** has the broadest powers to influence marketing activities. The agency consists of five commissioners, each appointed for a term of seven years by the president of the United States with Senate approval. Not more than three commissioners may be members of the same political party, and their terms of office are staggered to ensure continuity of experience in the judgment of cases. The FTC has many administrative duties under existing laws, but the policy underlying them all is to prevent monopolistic or anticompetitive practices and to provide the direct protection of consumers from unfair or deceptive trade practices.

One major function of the FTC is to enforce laws and regulatory guidelines falling under its jurisdiction. When it receives a complaint or otherwise has reason to believe that a firm is violating a law, the commission issues a complaint stating that the business is in violation. If the company continues the questionable practice, the FTC can issue a cease-and-desist order, which is simply an order for the business to stop doing whatever caused the complaint in the first place. The firm can appeal to the federal courts to have the order rescinded. However, the FTC can seek civil penalties in court, with a maximum penalty of $10,000 a day for each violation if a cease-and-desist order is violated.

The FTC also provides assistance and information to businesses so that they will know how to comply with laws. New marketing methods are evaluated every year. When general sets of guidelines are needed to improve business practices in a particular industry, the FTC sometimes encourages firms within that industry to establish a set of trade practices voluntarily. For example, the FTC has established guidelines proposed by marketers and trade groups for environmental claims about products. As a result of these guidelines, First Brands Corporation signed a consent agreement with the FTC to stop environmental claims concerning Glad trash bags.[7] The FTC may sponsor a conference to bring together industry leaders and consumers for this purpose. Although the FTC regulates a variety of business practices, it allocates a large portion of its resources to curbing false advertising, misleading pricing, and deceptive packaging and labeling.

The activities and policies of the Federal Trade Commission and other regulatory agencies are heavily influenced by the political environment, and specifically by the policies and agendas of the political administration in power at the time. During the administration of President Jimmy Carter, for example, the FTC actively regulated trade practices and strictly enforced FTC regulations. The administration of President Ronald Reagan, however, adopted a policy of laissez-faire (allowing business basically to regulate itself), and the FTC did not strictly enforce laws and regulations on advertising, pricing, and other business practices. In fact, the Reagan administration deregulated some industries, as we discuss later in this section. When George Bush succeeded Reagan as president in 1989, the FTC once again became more vigorous in enforcing business trade regulations. More recently, the FTC has targeted such areas as (1) promotional packages of the tobacco and alcohol industries; (2) health claims in food advertising; (3) children's advertising, including toy advertising such as "900" telephone services to "dial a Santa"; (4) advertising directed to the elderly on matters related to health, safety, and financial security; and (5) environmental "green" claims, such as those asserting a product is "biodegradable" or "environmentally safe."[8] It is therefore important for marketers to monitor the marketing environment to detect possible changes in policy resulting from changes in government administration.

Other Federal Regulatory Units Unlike the Federal Trade Commission, other regulatory units are limited to dealing with specific products, services, or business activities. For example, the Food and Drug Administration (FDA) enforces regulations that prohibit the sale and distribution of adulterated, misbranded, or hazardous food and drug products. Thus, the FDA outlawed the sale and distribution of most over-the-counter baldness remedies after research indicated that few of the products were effective in restoring hair growth, and as described in the opening example of this chapter, the FDA removed Citrus Hill Fresh Choice orange juice from the shelf until Procter & Gamble took the word *fresh* off the label of this juice actually made from concentrate. Table 2.2 outlines the major areas of responsibility of seven federal regulatory agencies.

As marketing activities become more complex, some of the responsibilities of federal units overlap. When authority over a specific product or marketing practice cannot be assigned to a single federal unit, marketers must try to comply with many different regulations and regulatory agencies.

State and Local Regulatory Agencies

All states—as well as many cities and towns—have regulatory agencies that enforce laws and regulations regarding marketing practices within their states or municipalities. State and local regulatory agencies try not to establish and enforce regulations that conflict with those of national regulatory agencies. Instead, they generally enforce laws dealing with the production and sale of particular goods and services. Utilities, insurance, financial, and liquor industries are among those commonly regulated by state agencies.

Nongovernmental Regulatory Forces

In the absence of governmental regulatory forces and in an attempt to prevent government intervention, some businesses try to regulate themselves. For example, Safeway requires all of the tuna sold in its stores (including cat food) to be certified "dolphin safe."[9] Trade associations in a number of industries have developed self-regulatory programs. Even though these programs are not a direct outgrowth of laws, many were established to stop or stall the development of laws and governmental regulatory groups that would regulate the associations' marketing practices. Sometimes trade associations establish codes of ethics by which their members must abide or risk censure by other members, or even exclusion from the program. For example, many cigarette manufacturers have agreed, through a code of ethics, not to advertise their products to children and teenagers.

Self-regulatory programs have several advantages over governmental laws and regulatory agencies. They are usually less expensive to establish and implement, and their guidelines are generally more realistic and operational. In addition, effective industry self-regulatory programs reduce the need to expand government bureaucracy. However, these programs also have several limitations. When a trade association creates a set of industry guidelines for its members, nonmember firms do not have to abide by them. In addition, many self-regulatory

Know these

Table 2.2 Major Federal Regulatory Agencies

Agency	Major Areas of Responsibility
Federal Trade Commission (FTC)	Enforces laws and guidelines regarding business practices; takes action to stop false and deceptive advertising and labeling
Food and Drug Administration (FDA)	Enforces laws and regulations to prevent distribution of adulterated or misbranded foods, drugs, medical devices, cosmetics, veterinary products, and particularly hazardous consumer products
Consumer Product Safety Commission (CPSC)	Ensures compliance with the Consumer Product Safety Act; protects the public from unreasonable risk of injury from any consumer product not covered by other regulatory agencies
Interstate Commerce Commission (ICC)	Regulates franchises, rates, and finances of interstate rail, bus, truck, and water carriers
Federal Communications Commission (FCC)	Regulates communication by wire, radio, and television in interstate and foreign commerce
Environmental Protection Agency (EPA)	Develops and enforces environmental protection standards and conducts research into the adverse effects of pollution
Federal Power Commission (FPC)	Regulates rates and sales of natural gas producers, thereby affecting the supply and price of gas available to consumers; also regulates wholesale rates for electricity and gas, pipeline construction, and U.S. imports and exports of natural gas and electricity

programs lack the tools or the authority to enforce guidelines. Finally, guidelines in self-regulatory programs are often less strict than those established by government agencies.

Better Business Bureaus   Perhaps the best-known nongovernmental regulatory group, the **Better Business Bureau** is a local regulatory agency supported by local businesses. Today more than 140 bureaus help settle problems between consumers and specific business firms. Each bureau also acts to preserve good business practices in a locality, although it usually does not have strong enforcement tools for dealing with firms that employ questionable practices. When a firm continues to violate what the Better Business Bureau believes to be good business practices, the bureau warns consumers through local newspapers or broadcast media.

The Council of Better Business Bureaus is a national organization comprising all the local Better Business Bureaus. The National Advertising Division (NAD) of the Council of Better Business Bureaus operates a self-regulatory program that investigates claims regarding alleged deceptive advertising. For example, after NAD reviewed a commercial for a Nintendo video game, it complained that the advertisement implied that Nintendo was the sole marketer of ice hockey video games, when in fact two other ice hockey games were on the market. Nintendo disagreed with the complaint, but agreed to consider NAD's concerns in future advertising campaigns.[10]

National Advertising Review Board   The Council of Better Business Bureaus and three advertising trade organizations have created a self-regulatory unit. Called the **National Advertising Review Board (NARB)**, it considers cases in which an advertiser challenges issues raised by the National Advertising Division about an advertisement. Cases are reviewed by panels drawn from NARB members, who represent advertisers, agencies, and the public. The following example describes a typical case handled by the panels:

> NAD claimed that Featherspring International's advertisements for flexible foot supports include therapeutic claims that could not be substantiated by "scientifically planned studies," and therefore were misleading. Featherspring countered that medical, professional, and consumer testimonials and endorsements, as well as pages copied from technical and scientific publications on foot and lower back problems, were adequate backing for its therapeutic claims and took the case to the NARB for a final decision.[11]

The NARB has no official enforcement powers. However, if a firm refuses to comply with its decision, the NARB may publicize the questionable practice and file a complaint with the FTC.

Deregulation

As mentioned earlier, the federal government attempted in the 1980s to deregulate some industries in an effort to reduce the costs and paperwork associated with enforcing regulations and maintaining regulatory agencies. Although deregulation of the airline, railroad, trucking, and banking industries has stirred controversy, most members of these industries continue to act responsibly without the enforcement of regulatory agencies and laws. Nevertheless, society's reaction to deregulation is still mixed. Although consumers enjoyed the low fares resulting from the airfare wars waged throughout the airline industry after deregulation, they are unhappy with the level of service quality provided by the airlines and are especially concerned about increasing accident rates. Similarly, in the banking industry, competition is more intense, and banks can offer new products because they are no longer restricted to traditional checking and savings accounts. On the negative side, the number of bank and savings and loan association failures has risen since deregulation, and some of those failures were attributed to unethical or illegal practices. Future administrations may seek to reregulate these industries.

Societal Forces

Societal forces comprise the structure and dynamics of individuals and groups and the issues that engage them. Society becomes concerned about marketers' activities when those activities have questionable or negative consequences. For example, in recent times publicized incidents of unethical behavior by marketers and others have perturbed and even angered consumers. Chapter 3 therefore takes a detailed look at marketing ethics and social responsibility. When marketers do a good job of satisfying society, praise or positive evaluation rarely follows. Society expects marketers to provide a high standard of living and to protect the general quality of life. In this section we examine some of society's expectations, the vehicles used to express those expectations, and the problems and opportunities that marketers experience as they try to deal with society's often contradictory wishes.

Living Standards and Quality of Life

In our society, we want more than just the bare necessities; we want to achieve the highest standard of living possible. For example, we want not only protection from the elements, but also comfort and a satisfactory lifestyle. We want food that is safe and readily available, in many varieties and in easily prepared forms. We use our clothing to protect our bodies, but most of us want a variety of clothing for adornment and to project an "image" to others. We want vehicles that provide rapid, safe, and efficient transportation. We desire communication systems that give us information from around the globe—a desire apparent in the popularity of products such as facsimile machines and the twenty-four-hour news coverage provided by the Cable News Network. In addition, we want sophisticated medical services that prolong our lives and improve our physical appearance. We also expect our education to equip us both to acquire and to enjoy a higher standard of living.

Our society's high material standard of living is not enough. We also desire a high degree of quality in our lives. Since we do not want to spend all our waking hours working, we seek leisure time for hobbies, recreation, and relaxation. The quality of life is enhanced by leisure time, clean air and water, an unlittered earth, conservation of wildlife and natural resources, and security from radiation and poisonous substances. A number of companies are expressing concerns about the quality of life. For example, Novell, a computer company, sends a clear message in Figure 2.2 that it is striving to be a responsible leader for the future.

Because of these desires, consumers have become increasingly concerned about environmental issues. Society's concerns have created both threats and opportunities for marketers. For example, one of society's biggest environmental problems is lack of space for garbage disposal, especially of plastic materials such as disposable diapers and polystyrene packaging, which are not biodegradable. Several cities have passed laws banning the use of all plastic packaging in stores and restaurants, and federal and local governments around the world are considering similar legislation. This trend has created problems for McDonald's and other fast food restaurants, which have now begun to develop packaging alternatives. Inside Marketing describes how McDonald's was forced to change its polystyrene packaging in response to consumer pressure. Some firms see environmental problems as opportunities. Procter & Gamble, for example, markets its Spic and Span cleaner in bottles made of recycled plastic.[12]

Environmentally responsible, or "green," marketing is even more extensive outside the United States. For example, German companies Audi, Volkswagen, and BMW are manufacturing "cleaner" automobiles, which do not pollute the atmosphere as much as traditional automobiles. Italian chemical companies are investing billions to reduce toxic wastes from their plants, and British industry is investing equally large sums to scrub acid emissions from power stations and to treat sewage more effectively.[13]

As these examples illustrate, changes in the forces of the marketing environment require careful monitoring and often demand a clear and effective response. Since marketing activities are a vital part of the total business structure, marketers have a responsibility to help provide what members of society want and to minimize what they do not want.

Figure 2.2

Corporate Responsibility

As a "responsible leader" in its industry, Novell believes that customers are better served if companies work together solving industry problems rather than fighting turf wars amongst themselves.

Source: Courtesy of Novell, Inc.

PART I   AN ANALYSIS OF MARKETING OPPORTUNITIES

McDonald's Changes Packaging to Satisfy Consumer Concerns

CONSUMERS TODAY are increasingly concerned about the environment, and they expect American businesses to be environmentally conscious as well. The McDonald's Corporation illustrates the pitfalls companies may experience as they attempt to balance consumer desires, environmental responsibility, and the need for profits. Although the Oak Brook, Illinois, restaurant company reduced its packaging size, phased out the use of ozone-damaging chlorofluorocarbons, and began using recycled materials in some packaging, the public continued to protest its use of the polystyrene clamshell hamburger container, which consumers viewed as environmentally irresponsible.

McDonald's has long advocated that polystyrene packaging is the better choice for the environment because it can be recycled and that the other alternative—polycoated paper, or paperboard—is more damaging. The company argued that paperboard requires more energy to produce and creates more pollution during production. After being contaminated by food, much of paperboard cannot be recycled, and it degrades slowly in landfills when covered up by other materials. The company also felt that the polystyrene packaging provides more benefit to customers by lengthening the time food stays fresh while stacked in bins and enabling the company to prepare hamburgers before rush hour, which speeds service and keeps costs and prices down.

To back its belief in polystyrene as the best environmental choice, McDonald's planned a long-term project to recycle waste polystyrene packaging. Together with its polystyrene suppliers, the company planned to invest $16 million to build seven polystyrene recycling plants across the United States. The plants would have turned the waste material into plastic resin pellets that could be used in the manufacture of videocassettes, food trays, and similar products.

Angry letters from consumers—particularly children—protests, and condemnations from environmental groups continued, however, and McDonald's retreated. It announced in late 1990 that it would stop using the polystyrene clamshell package. Although McDonald's continued to argue that polystyrene packaging is a better alternative for the environment, it made the change because it wanted its customers to be happy and the public to be comfortable with its attitude toward the environment.

Sources: Charles Campbell, "McDonald's Says Earth to Get Break," (*Memphis*) *Commercial Appeal*, Apr. 17, 1991, p. A1; Phyllis Berman, "McDonald's Caves In," *Forbes*, Feb. 4, 1991, pp. 73–74; Matthew Grimm, "McDonald's Flip-Flops Again and Ditches Its Clamshell," *Adweek's Marketing Week*, Nov. 5, 1990, pp. 4–5; Laura Medcalf, "Teaming Up for the Long Term," *Marketing*, Jan. 15, 1990, p. 10; and "Our Commitment to the Environment," *G+M*, Nov. 24, 1989, p. A18.

Cultural Diversity as a Societal Force

The number of immigrants into the United States has steadily risen during the last thirty years, with the result that America is becoming an increasingly multicultural society. In the 1960s, 3.2 million people immigrated to the United States; in the 1970s, 4.2 million came; and in the 1980s, America received over 6 million legal immigrants, very few of whom were of European origin. By the end of the 1990s, the population of the United States will have shifted from one dominated by whites to one consisting of three large racial and ethnic groups: whites, blacks, and Hispanics.

Another reason for the increasing cultural diversification of the United States is that most recent immigrants are relatively young, whereas citizens of European origin already in place are growing older. These younger immigrants also tend to have more children than their counterparts, further shifting the population balance. Table 2.3 illustrates this demographic mix.

Marketers must recognize these profound changes in the U.S. population for the unique problems and opportunities they bring. Changes in the population mean that U.S. companies must alter the way they look at their marketing practices. A diverse population means a more diverse customer base.

Consumer Movement Forces

The **consumer movement** is a diverse group of independent individuals, groups, and organizations that seeks to protect the rights of consumers. The main issues pursued by the consumer movement fall into three categories: environmental protection, product performance and safety, and information disclosure. The movement's major forces are individual consumer advocates, consumer organizations and other interest groups, consumer education, and consumer laws.

Table 2.3   **The United States Is Growing More Culturally Diverse**

| Age | Percentage of Total U.S. Population | | | | | |
	White	Black	Hispanic*	Asian/ Pacific Islander	Native American	Other Races
0 to 9	74.8%	15.0%	12.6%	3.3%	1.1%	5.9%
10 to 19	75.1	15.1	11.6	3.3	1.1	5.4
20 to 29	77.3	13.1	11.5	3.3	0.8	5.5
30 to 39	79.9	12.0	8.9	3.3	0.8	4.0
40 to 49	82.9	10.4	7.1	3.1	0.7	2.9
50 to 59	84.4	10.1	6.4	2.6	0.6	2.3
60 to 69	87.4	8.8	4.8	1.9	0.5	1.5
70 to 79	89.3	7.9	3.5	1.4	0.4	0.9
80 or older	90.4	7.5	3.2	1.0	0.3	0.8
All ages	80.3	12.1	9.0	2.9	0.8	3.9

*Hispanics may be of any race; therefore, the percentages do not total to 100.

Source: 1990 U.S. Census.

Figure 2.3

Children Learn to Fight Solid Waste Problems

A special school program teaches children to recycle their drink boxes and help reduce solid waste. This advertisment by the makers of drink boxes encourages communities to learn more about recycling.

Source: Tetra pak and Combibloc—Makers of the Drink Box. Photography by Kenneth Willardt '91.

Consumer advocates, such as Ralph Nader, take it upon themselves to protect the rights of consumers. They band together into consumer organizations, either independently or under government sponsorship. Some organizations, such as the National Consumers' League and the Consumer Federation of America, operate nationally, whereas others are active at state and local levels. They inform and organize other consumers, raise issues, help businesses develop consumer-oriented programs, and pressure lawmakers to enact consumer protection laws. Some consumer advocates and organizations encourage consumers to boycott products and businesses to which they have objections. The consumer movement has adopted corporate-style marketing and addresses a broad range of issues. Current campaigns include (1) the antifur campaign, (2) efforts to reduce liquor and cigarette billboard advertising in low-income, inner-city neighborhoods, and (3) efforts to encourage recycling.[14]

Educating consumers to make wiser purchasing decisions is perhaps one of the most far-reaching aspects of the consumer movement. Increasingly, consumer education is becoming a part of high school and college curricula and adult education programs. These programs cover many topics—for instance, what major factors should be considered when buying specific products, such as insurance, real estate, automobiles, appliances and furniture, clothes, and food; the provisions of certain consumer protection laws; and the sources of information that can help individuals become knowledgeable consumers. Figure 2.3 illustrates how 150 schools in ten states taught children to fight solid waste problems by recycling their lunch drink boxes.

Economic and Competitive Forces

The economic and competitive forces in the marketing environment influence both marketers' and customers' decisions and activities. In this section, we first examine the effects of general economic conditions. We also focus on buying power, willingness to spend, spending patterns, and competition. Then we look at competitive forces, including types of competitive structures, competitive tools, and methods for monitoring competitive behavior. In Chapter 24, we look at the United States' interdependence with the global economy.

General Economic Conditions

The overall state of the economy fluctuates in all countries. These changes in general economic conditions affect (and are affected by) the forces of supply and demand, buying power, willingness to spend, consumer expenditure levels, and the intensity of competitive behavior. Therefore, current economic conditions and changes in the economy have a broad impact on the success of organizations' marketing strategies. Fluctuations in the U.S. economy follow a general pattern often referred to as the business cycle. In the traditional view, the business cycle consists of four stages: prosperity, recession, depression, and recovery.

During **prosperity**, unemployment is low and total income is relatively high. Assuming a low inflation rate, this combination causes buying power to be high. To the extent that the economic outlook remains prosperous, consumers generally are willing to buy. In the prosperity stage, marketers often expand their product mixes (product, distribution, promotion, and price) to take advantage of the increased buying power. They sometimes capture a larger market share by intensifying distribution and promotion efforts.

Because unemployment rises during a **recession**, total buying power declines. The pessimism that accompanies a recession often stifles both consumer and business spending. As buying power decreases, many consumers become more price- and value-conscious; they look for products that are basic and functional. During a recession, some firms make the mistake of drastically reducing their marketing efforts and thus damage their ability to survive. Obviously, marketers should consider some revision of their marketing activities during a recessionary period. Because consumers are more concerned about the functional value of products, a company must focus its marketing research on determining precisely what product functions buyers want and then make sure that these functions become part of its products. Promotional efforts should emphasize value and utility. In Figure 2.4 the United States Postal Service promotes their low-cost, reliable, two-day mail service—Priority Mail.

A **depression** is a period in which unemployment is extremely high, wages are very low, total disposable income is at a minimum, and consumers lack confidence in the economy. The federal government has used both monetary and fiscal policies to offset the effects of recession and depression. Monetary policies are employed to control the money supply, which in turn affects spending, saving, and investment by both individuals and businesses. Through fiscal policies, the government can influence the amount of savings and expenditures by altering the tax structure and by changing the levels of government spending.

Some experts believe that effective use of monetary and fiscal policies can eliminate depressions from the business cycle.

Recovery is the stage of the business cycle in which the economy moves from depression or recession to prosperity. During this period, the high unemployment rate begins to decline, total disposable income increases, and the economic gloom that lessened consumers' willingness to buy subsides. Both the ability and the willingness to buy rise. Marketers face some problems during recovery— for example, the difficulty of ascertaining how quickly prosperity will return and forecasting the level of prosperity that will be attained. In this stage, marketers should maintain as much flexibility in their marketing strategies as possible to be able to make the needed adjustments as the economy moves from recession to prosperity.

Consumer Demand and Spending Behavior

Marketers must understand the factors that determine whether, what, where, and when people buy. In Chapters 5 and 6 we look at behavioral factors underlying these choices, but here we focus on the economic components: buying power, willingness to purchase, and spending patterns.

Buying Power The strength of a person's **buying power** depends on the size of the resources that enable the individual to purchase and on the state of the

Figure 2.4

Marketing During a Recessionary Period

Even the U.S. Postal Service is advertising and pricing its two-day service to compete directly with private companies such as Federal Express, United Parcel Service, and Airborne Express. The U.S. Postal Service hopes that promoting value and utility will help its express service thrive during difficult economic times.

Source: Courtesy of United States Postal Service.

Product	1980	1992	Percent Change
Fast Food Meal: McDonald's hamburger, regular fries and small soft drink	$1.21	$2.13	+76%
Grand Ole Opry: Nashville, adult admission	$8	$15.62	+95%
L.L. Bean Country Corduroy Pants	$30.50	$40	+31%
Round-Trip Flight: Full fare, NY–LA on American Airlines	$570	$1504	+164%
Oscar Mayer Hot Dogs: One pound, all-beef franks	$1.94	$2.99	+54%
People Weekly: Cover Price	$.75	$1.99	+165%
Pack of Camel Cigarettes	$.65	$1.75	+169%

Table 2.4   **A Comparison of 1980 and 1992 Prices for Selected Products**

economy. The resources that make up buying power are goods, services, and financial holdings. Fluctuations of the business cycle affect buying power because they influence price levels and interest rates. For example, during inflationary periods, when prices are rising, buying power decreases because more dollars are required to buy products. Table 2.4 compares 1980 and 1992 prices for selected products.

The major financial sources of buying power are income, credit, and wealth. From an individual's viewpoint, **income** is the amount of money received through wages, rents, investments, pensions, and subsidy payments for a given period, such as a month or a year. Normally, this money is allocated among taxes, spending for goods and services, and savings. The average annual family income in the United States is approximately $35,353.[15] However, because of the differences in people's educational levels, abilities, occupations, and wealth, income is not equally distributed in this country (or in other countries).

Marketers are most interested in the amount of money that is left after payment of taxes. After-tax income is called **disposable income** and is used for spending or saving. Because disposable income is a ready source of buying power, the total amount available in a nation is important to marketers. Several factors affect the size of total disposable income. One, of course, is the total amount of income. Total national income is affected by wage levels, rate of unemployment, interest rates, and dividend rates. These factors in turn affect the size of disposable income. Because disposable income is the income left after taxes are paid, the number of taxes and their amount directly affect the size of total disposable income. When taxes rise, disposable income declines; when taxes fall, disposable income increases.

Disposable income that is available for spending and saving after an individual has purchased the basic necessities of food, clothing, and shelter is called **discretionary income**. People use discretionary income to purchase entertainment, vacations, automobiles, education, pets and pet supplies, furniture, appliances, and so on. Changes in total discretionary income affect the sales of these products—especially automobiles, furniture, large appliances, and other costly durable goods.

Credit enables people to spend future income now or in the near future. However, credit increases current buying power at the expense of future buying power. Several factors determine whether consumers use or forego credit. First, credit must be available to consumers. Interest rates, too, affect consumers' decisions to use credit, especially for expensive purchases such as homes, appliances, and automobiles. When credit charges are high, consumers are more likely to delay buying expensive items. Use of credit is also affected by credit terms, such as the size of the down payment and the amount and number of monthly payments.

A person can have a high income and very little wealth. It is also possible, but not likely, for a person to have great wealth but not much income. **Wealth** is the accumulation of past income, natural resources, and financial resources. It may exist in many forms, including cash, securities, savings accounts, jewelry, antiques, and real estate. Like income, wealth is unevenly distributed. The significance of wealth to marketers is that as people become wealthier they gain buying power in three ways: they can use their wealth to make current purchases, to generate income, and to acquire large amounts of credit.

Buying power information is available from government sources, trade associations, and research agencies. One of the most current and comprehensive sources of buying power data is the *Sales & Marketing Management Survey of Buying Power*, published annually by *Sales & Marketing Management* magazine. As Table 2.5 shows, the *Survey of Buying Power* presents effective buying income data and the buying power index for specific geographic areas, including states, counties, and most cities with populations exceeding forty thousand. The *Survey of Buying Power* also contains population and retail sales data for the same geographic areas (not shown in Table 2.5).

The most direct indicators of buying power in the *Survey of Buying Power* are effective buying income and buying power index. **Effective buying income (EBI)** is similar to what we call disposable income; it includes salaries, wages, dividends, interest, profits, and rents, less federal, state, and local taxes. The **buying power index (BPI)** is a weighted index, consisting of population, effective buying income, and retail sales data.[16] The higher the index number, the greater the buying power. Like other indexes, the buying power index is most useful for comparative purposes. Marketers can use buying power indexes for a particular year to compare the buying power of one area with the buying power of another, or they can analyze trends for a particular area by comparing the area's buying power indexes for several years.

Income, wealth, and credit equip consumers to purchase goods and services. Marketing managers should be aware of current levels and expected changes in buying power in their own markets because buying power directly affects the types and quantities of goods and services that consumers purchase, as we see later in our discussion of spending patterns. Just because consumers have buying power, however, does not mean that they will buy. Consumers must also be willing to use their buying power.

Consumers' Willingness to Spend   People's **willingness to spend** is, to some degree, related to their ability to buy. That is, people are sometimes more willing to buy if they have the buying power. However, a number of other

Metro Area *County*	Total EBI ($000)	Median Household EBI	% of Households by EBI Group (A) $10,000–$19,999 (B) $20,000–$34,999 (C) $35,000–$49,000 (D) $50,000 & Over				Buying Power Index
			A	B	C	D	
San Francisco Area	110,377,269	35,963	11.1	21.7	18.4	33.0	3.0225
San Jose Area	26,770,972	42,126	12.1	20.1	19.1	40.8	.7270
Santa Clara County	26,770,972	42,126	12.1	20.1	19.1	40.8	.7270
Santa Barbara Area	5,377,477	29,502	20.2	24.3	17.3	24.7	.1539
Santa Barbara County	5,377,477	29,502	20.2	24.3	17.3	24.7	.1539
Santa Cruz Area	3,646,842	29,550	19.9	22.9	16.9	25.7	.1071
Santa Cruz County	3,646,842	29,550	19.9	22.9	16.9	25.7	.1071
Los Angeles–Riverside Area	216,697,063	31,456	18.2	23.3	17.3	27.6	6.2834
Los Angeles County	135,162,824	30,489	18.5	23.0	16.5	27.3	3.8702
Orange County	39,243,128	37,614	14.5	22.6	19.6	34.4	1.1500

Source: Reprinted by permission of *Sales & Marketing Management.* Copyright 1991, *Sales & Marketing Management, Survey of Buying Power,* August 19, 1991. (Data are from 1990.)

Table 2.5   Example of *Sales & Marketing Management*'s U.S. Metropolitan Area Projections

elements also influence willingness to spend. Some elements affect specific products; others influence spending in general. A product's absolute price and its price relative to the price of substitute products influence almost all of us. The amount of satisfaction currently received or expected in the future from a product already owned may also influence consumers' desire to buy other products. Satisfaction depends not only on the quality of the functional performance of the currently owned product, but also on numerous psychological and social forces.

Factors that affect consumers' general willingness to spend are expectations about future employment, income levels, prices, family size, and general economic conditions. If people are unsure whether or how long they will be employed, willingness to buy ordinarily declines. Willingness to spend may increase if people are reasonably certain of higher incomes in the future. Expectations of rising prices in the near future may also increase the willingness to spend in the present. For a given level of buying power, the larger the family, the greater the willingness to buy. One of the reasons for this relationship is that as the size of a family increases, a greater number of dollars must be spent to provide the basic necessities of life to sustain the family members. Finally, perceptions of future economic conditions influence willingness to buy.

Consumer Spending Patterns   Marketers must be aware of the factors that influence consumers' ability and willingness to spend, but they should also analyze how consumers actually spend their disposable incomes. Marketers obtain this information by studying consumer spending patterns. **Consumer spending patterns** indicate the relative proportions of annual family expenditures or the actual amount of money spent on certain kinds of goods and services. Families are usually categorized by one of several characteristics, including family income, age of the household head, geographic area, and family life cycle. There are two types of spending patterns: comprehensive and product-specific.

The percentages of family income allotted to annual expenditures for general classes of goods and services constitute **comprehensive spending patterns**. Comprehensive spending patterns or the data to develop them are available in government publications and in reports of the Conference Board—a national trade organization for businesses. Table 2.6 illustrates comprehensive spending patterns as classified by the life cycle of the family. Note the variation in expenditures between two-parent families and single-parent families.

Product-specific spending patterns indicate the annual dollar amounts families spend for specific products within a general product class. Information sources used to construct product-specific spending patterns include government publications, the Conference Board, trade publications, and consumer surveys. Table 2.7 illustrates a product-specific spending pattern. Notice the differences between this type of spending pattern and the comprehensive ones. The products listed fall into one general product category, and the figures are stated in dollar amounts.

A marketer uses spending patterns to analyze general trends in the ways that families spend their incomes for various kinds of products. For example, a person who is considering opening a bakery might use the data in Table 2.7 to estimate the demand for various categories of bakery products. Analyses of spending patterns yield information that a marketer can use to gain perspective and background for decision making. However, spending patterns reflect only general trends and thus should not be used as the sole basis for making specific decisions.

Assessment of Competitive Forces

Few firms, if any, operate free of competition. Broadly speaking, all firms compete with each other for consumers' dollars. From a more practical viewpoint, however, a business generally defines **competition** as those firms that market products that are similar to, or can be substituted for, its products in the same geographic area. For example, a local A & P supermarket manager views all grocery stores in town as competitors but almost never thinks of other types of local or out-of-town stores as competitors. In this section, we consider the types of competitive structures and the importance of monitoring competitors.

Types of Competitive Structures   The number of firms that control the supply of a product may affect the strength of competition. When only one or a few firms control supply, competitive factors will exert a different sort of influence on marketing activities than when there are many competitors. Four

Table 2.6 **Spending Based on Family Life Cycle**

Item	Husband and Wife Consumer Units					One Parent, at Least One Child Under 18	Single Person and Other Consumer Units
	Total Husband and Wife Consumer Units	Husband and Wife Only	Total Husband and Wife with Children	Other Husband and Wife Consumer Units			
Number of consumer units (thousands)	52,728	20,883	28,271	3,574	5,561	37,528	
Consumer unit characteristics:							
Income before taxes	$40,913	$37,183	$43,576	$42,171	$17,416	$20,260	
Average number of persons in consumer unit	3.2	2.0	3.9	4.9	2.9	1.6	
Average number of earners	1.8	1.2	2.1	2.4	1.0	.9	
Average annual expenditures	$34,826	$30,604	$37,580	$37,705	$19,186	$19,087	
Food	5,201	4,385	5,663	6,335	3,421	2,701	
Alcoholic beverages	294	300	285	323	128	292	
Housing	10,459	9,345	11,230	10,862	6,864	6,246	
Apparel and services	1,933	1,644	2,144	1,945	1,513	1,079	
Transportation	6,707	5,675	7,340	7,721	3,063	3,364	
Health care	1,780	2,003	1,582	2,051	663	991	
Entertainment	1,886	1,408	2,221	2,029	894	850	
Personal care products and services	442	406	466	463	299	265	
Reading	190	195	188	178	91	120	
Education	432	188	608	461	197	299	
Tobacco products and smoking supplies	293	245	317	385	184	228	
Miscellaneous	735	637	787	892	478	536	
Cash contributions	1,118	1,390	936	962	225	694	
Personal insurance and pensions	3,356	2,784	3,811	3,096	1,165	1,423	

Source: U.S. Department of Labor, Bureau of Labor Statistics, "Consumer Expenditure Survey," Nov. 30, 1990.

general types of competitive structures are presented in Table 2.8: monopoly, oligopoly, monopolistic competition, and perfect competition.

A **monopoly** exists when a firm turns out a product that has no close substitutes. Because the organization has no competitors, it completely controls the supply of the product and, as a single seller, can erect barriers to potential competitors. In actuality, most monopolies that survive today are local utilities, such as telephone, electricity, and cable companies, which are heavily regulated by local, state, or federal agencies. These monopolies are tolerated because of the tremendous financial resources needed to develop and operate them; few organizations can obtain the resources to mount any competition against a local electricity producer, for example.

An **oligopoly** exists when a few sellers control the supply of a large proportion of a product. In this case, each seller must consider the reactions of other sellers to changes in marketing activities. Products facing oligopolistic competition may be homogeneous, such as aluminum, or differentiated, such as cigarettes and automobiles. Usually, barriers of some sort make it difficult to enter the market and compete with oligopolies. For example, because of the enormous financial outlay required, few companies or individuals could afford to enter the oil-refining or steel-producing industries. Moreover, some industries demand special technical or marketing skills that block the entry of many potential competitors.

Monopolistic competition exists when a firm with many potential competitors attempts to develop a differential marketing strategy to establish its own market share. For example, Levi Strauss has established a differential advantage for its blue jeans through a well-known trademark, design, advertising, and a quality image. Although many competing brands of blue jeans are available, this firm has carved out its market share through use of a differential marketing strategy.

Perfect competition, if it existed at all, would entail a large number of sellers, not one of whom could significantly influence price or supply. Products would be homogeneous, and there would be full knowledge of the market and easy entry into it. The closest thing to an example of perfect competition would be an unregulated agricultural market.

Few, if any, marketers operate in a structure of perfect competition. Perfect competition is an ideal at one end of the continuum, with monopoly at the other end. Most marketers function in a competitive environment that falls somewhere between these two extremes.

Competitive Tools   Another set of factors that influences the level of competition is the number and types of competitive tools used by competitors. To survive, a firm uses one or several available competitive tools to deal with competitive economic forces. Once a company has analyzed its particular competitive environment and decided which factors in that environment it can or must adapt to or influence, it can choose among the variables that it can control to strengthen its competitive position in the overall marketplace.

Probably the first competitive tool that most organizations grasp is price. Bic Corp., for example, markets disposable pens and lighters that are similar to competing products but less expensive. However, there is one major problem with using price as a competitive tool: competitors will often match or beat the

Table 2.7 Annual Dollar Expenditures for Nonfrozen Bakery Products by Various Household Incomes

	Total		Household Income						
		Under $5,000	$5,000–$10,000	$10,000–$15,000	$15,000–$20,000	$20,000–$25,000	$25,000–$35,000	$35,000–$50,000	$50,000 and Above
Households (millions)	70.0	12.5	12.5	10.2	8.7	8.0	10.7	5.4	2.1
Distribution of households	100.0%	17.9	17.9	14.5	12.4	11.4	15.3	7.7	3.1
Average household size	2.6	1.9	2.1	2.4	2.8	3.0	3.1	3.4	3.3
Distribution of persons	100.0%	13.0	14.7	13.4	13.5	13.0	18.6	10.0	3.9
Distribution of income	100.0%	2.5	7.4	10.2	12.2	14.3	25.4	17.8	10.2
Expenditures of dollars	*Average*								
Nonfrozen bakery products	144.79	98.01	112.89	117.98	151.22	165.77	192.42	215.82	210.64
White bread	40.64	31.68	33.81	37.66	41.99	48.22	49.42	50.62	44.26
Bread other than white	16.98	11.91	14.52	15.45	17.27	17.67	21.14	23.00	28.60
Fresh biscuits, rolls, etc.	17.55	9.51	11.37	13.14	19.13	20.57	24.43	33.40	29.55
Cakes and cupcakes	16.29	9.57	14.10	11.50	18.23	17.44	22.44	25.38	25.21
Cookies	19.52	12.31	13.62	14.95	19.87	22.71	29.16	29.99	29.78
Crackers	11.23	7.79	8.59	9.66	10.70	13.03	14.50	16.65	19.74
Bread and cracker products	2.11	1.06	1.25	1.70	2.19	2.51	2.42	5.16	4.14
Doughnuts, sweetrolls, etc.	15.81	11.46	11.58	10.59	15.76	18.48	22.78	24.72	23.62
Fresh pies and tarts	4.67	2.72	4.05	3.32	6.09	5.16	6.12	6.90	5.73

Source: Consumer Research Center, *How Consumers Spend Their Money* (New York: Conference Board, 1984), pp. 20, 44. Used by permission.

price. This threat is one of the primary reasons for employing nonprice competitive tools that are based on the differentiation of market segments, product offering, promotion, distribution, or enterprise.[17]

By focusing on a specific market segment, a marketer sometimes gains a competitive advantage. For instance, Apple Computer, Inc., and International Business Machines Corp. (IBM) are working together in a joint venture to satisfy the user-friendly market segment with software and computers. But these firms will use different promotion, distribution, and products to compete.

Monitoring Competition   Marketers in an organization need to be aware of the actions of major competitors. They should monitor what competitors are currently doing and assess the changes occurring in the competitive environment. The Global Perspective describes how Benckiser, a small German consumer products firm, is successfully competing with Procter & Gamble, Unilever, and other consumer products giants. Monitoring allows firms to determine what specific strategies competitors are following and how those strategies affect their own. It can also guide marketers as they try to develop competitive advantages and aid them in adjusting current marketing strategies, as well as in planning new ones. Information may come from direct observation or from sources such as salespeople, customers, trade publications, syndicated marketing research services, distributors, and marketing studies.

An organization needs information about competitors that will allow its marketing managers to assess the performance of its own marketing efforts. Comparing their company's performance with that of competitors helps marketing managers recognize strengths and weaknesses in their own marketing strategies. Data about market shares, product movement, sales volume, and expenditure levels can be useful. However, accurate information on these matters is often difficult to obtain.

Technological Forces

The word *technology* brings to mind creations of progress such as computers, superconductors, lasers, and heart transplants. Even though such items are outgrowths of technology, none of them is technology. **Technology** has been defined as the knowledge of how to accomplish tasks and goals.[18] Often this knowledge comes from scientific research. The effects of technology are broad in scope and today exert a tremendous influence on our lives.

Technology grows out of research performed by businesses, universities, and nonprofit organizations. More than half of this research is paid for by the federal government, which supports investigations in a variety of areas, including health, defense, agriculture, energy, and pollution. Because much federally funded research requires the use of specialized machinery, personnel, and facilities, a sizable proportion of this research is conducted by large business organizations that already possess the necessary specialized equipment and people.

The rapid technological growth of the last several decades is expected to continue through the 1990s. Areas that hold great technological promise include digital electronics, artificial intelligence, superconductors, materials research, and biotechnology. Current research is investigating new forms of memory chips and computers that are a hundred times faster and smaller than current models. Because these and other technological developments will clearly have an impact on buyers' and marketers' decisions, we now turn, in our discussion, to the effects of technology on society and marketers. We then consider several factors that influence the adoption and use of technology.

The Impact of Technology

Marketers must be aware of new developments in technology and their possible effects because technology can and does affect marketing activities in many different ways. Consumers' technological knowledge influences their desires for goods and services. To provide marketing mixes that satisfy consumers, marketers must be aware of these influences.

The various ways in which technology affects marketing activities fall into two broad categories. It affects consumers and society in general, and it influences what, how, when, and where products are marketed.

Effects of Technology on Society   Technology determines how we, as members of society, satisfy our physiological needs. In various ways and to varying degrees, eating and drinking habits, sleeping patterns, sexual activities, and health care are all influenced by both existing technology and changes in

Table 2.8   **Selected Characteristics of Competitive Structures**

Type of Structure	Number of Competitors	Ease of Entry into Market	Product	Knowledge of Market	Example
Monopoly	One	Many barriers	Almost no substitutes	Perfect	Dayton (Ohio) Power and Light (gas and electricity service)
Oligopoly	Few	Some barriers	Homogeneous or differentiated (real or perceived differences) products	Imperfect	Philip Morris (cigarettes)
Monopolistic competition	Many	Few barriers	Product differentiation with many substitutes	More knowledge than oligopoly; less than monopoly	Levi Strauss (jeans)
Perfect competition	Unlimited	No barriers	Homogeneous products	Perfect	Vegetable farm (sweet corn)

German Consumer Products Firm Makes Impressive Gains over U.S. Competitors

FORMER HARVARD MARKETING PROFESSOR Thomas Bonoma made his mark in academic circles by writing scholarly articles and books on marketing implementation. Today, he heads the U.S. operations of Benckiser, a German consumer products firm that is making impressive gains against competitors such as Procter & Gamble. Benckiser, originally an industrial chemicals firm, moved into consumer goods in the late 1980s, buying small firms with products such as Electrasol dishwashing detergent, Cling Free fabric softener sheets, Jet-Dry dishwasher rinsing agent, Lime-A-Way, and Calgon afterbath lotion. Bonoma's Benckiser competes against market leaders by attempting to provide a quality product at a lower price without the packaging, advertising, and other expenses that many marketers believe is necessary.

Bonoma believes that providing high-quality products with minimum advertising and related marketing expenses is what consumers want. For example, he decided not to launch an advertising campaign to make dishwashing detergents fit a psychological profile—such as being sexy. Instead, he cut advertising and lowered the price on Electrasol to less than $2. He then insisted on printing the price on the box so shoppers understood that low price was the strategy. Before Benckiser purchased the Electrasol brand from Ecolab Inc. of St. Paul, Minnesota, the detergent had only a 3 percent market share. After Bonoma's strategy was launched, Electrasol gained more than a 10 percent share of a market previously dominated by Procter & Gamble's Cascade. Other well-known American brands purchased by Benckiser—Jet-Dry rinsing agent, Scrub Free and Lime-A-Way cleaners, and Clean & Smooth liquid hand soap—have done equally well in competition with U.S. consumer products.

Since divesting itself of all its industrial chemical holdings, formerly its core business, Benckiser has acquired eight consumer goods companies in ten countries and now owns leading household products in Italy, Spain, and the United States, to name a few. Benckiser's global marketing, headed by Thomas Bonoma, has pushed it into competition with such giants as Procter & Gamble, Unilever, and Japan's Kao Co. All corporate decisions are made by a five-member board, including Bonoma, but specific marketing plans are left to regional offices within individual countries. Benckiser, a German firm with the guidance of an American marketing professor, is changing the competitive environment for consumer packaged products in the United States.

Sources: "Lancaster Acquisitions Boosts Benckiser Sales," *Cosmetics Communications,* Vol. 15, Nov. 10, 1991, pp. 11–12; "Benckiser: From Calgon to Cosmetics in 18 Months," *European Cosmetic Markets,* Oct. 1991, p. 285; Peter Harf, "Dramatic Departure from the Status Quo," *Director & Boards,* Fall 1991, pp. 35–37; "Benckiser Breaks All Records," *European Cosmetic Markets,* May 1991, p. 129; Fara Warner, "Benckiser Who?" *Adweek's Marketing Week,* July 22, 1991, pp. 16–17; and Harold Seneker, "Reimann Family," *Forbes,* July 23, 1990, p. 224.

technology. For example, the $30-billion-a-year vending industry has developed new machines that allow the purchase of french fries, pizza, and even chicken that are prepared automatically for the customer. The first American Pizza Company machines hold up to 102 pizzas in six varieties. The six-inch pizzas cost $2.00–$2.50 and are cooked in two and one-half minutes by infrared heat.[19] Technological developments have improved our standard of living, thus giving us more leisure time, and have also enhanced information, entertainment,

Figure 2.5

The Impact of Technology

Technology can advance society's standard of living. Helping to improve the environment, Walther & Cie advertises products that promote clean air for future generations.

Source: Courtesy of Walther & Cie AG.

and education. As indicated in Figure 2.5, Walther & Cie AG, a German company, develops pollution control technology that is used on a worldwide basis.

Nevertheless, technology can detract from the quality of life through undesirable side effects, such as unemployment, polluted air and water, and other health hazards. Some people believe that further applications of technology can soften or eliminate these undesirable side effects; others argue that the best way to improve the quality of our lives is to decrease the use of technology.

Effects of Technology on Marketing   Technology also affects the types of products that marketers can offer. The introduction and general acceptance of cassette tapes and compact discs drove manufacturers of vinyl long-playing (LP) albums out of business or forced them to invest in new technology. Yet this technology provided new marketing opportunities for recording artists and producers, record companies, retailers, and those in related industries. The following items are only a few of the many thousands of existing products that were not available to consumers twenty years ago: home plaque-removal systems, disposable 35mm cameras, cellular telephones, ultralight laptop computers, and high-resolution television.

Computer technology helps make warehouse storage and keeping track of stored products more efficient, and therefore, less expensive. Often these savings can be passed on to consumers in the form of lower prices. Because of technological changes in communications, marketers now can reach large masses of people through a variety of media more efficiently.

Technological advances in transportation enable consumers to travel farther and more often to shop at a larger number of stores. Changes in transportation also have affected the producers' ability to get products to retailers and wholesalers. The ability of present-day manufacturers of relatively lightweight products to reach any of their dealers within twenty-four hours (via overnight express delivery services, such as Federal Express) would astound their counterparts of fifty years ago.

Adoption and Use of Technology

Through a procedure known as **technology assessment**, managers try to foresee the effects of new products and processes on their firm's operation, on other business organizations, and on society in general. With the information gained through a technology assessment, management tries to estimate whether the benefits of using a specific kind of technology outweigh the costs to the firm and to society at large. The degree to which a business is technologically based will also influence how its management responds to technology. Firms whose products and product changes grow out of recent technology strive to gather and use technological information.

Although available technology could radically improve their products (or other parts of the marketing mix), some companies may put off applying this technology as long as their competitors do not try to use it. K mart Corp., after being surpassed by Wal-Mart in the early 1990s, tried to improve its competitive position by implementing high-tech changes in its operations, such as a radarlike system that tracks customer traffic and high-tech signs and lighting to help customers shop more easily.[20]

The extent to which a firm can protect inventions stemming from research also influences its use of technology. How secure a product is from imitation depends on how easily it can be copied by others without violating its patent. If new products and processes cannot be protected through patents, a company is less likely to market them and make the benefits of its research available to competitors.

How a company uses (or does not use) technology is important for its long-run survival. A firm that makes the wrong decisions may well lose out to the competition. Poor decisions about technological forces may affect a company's profits by requiring expensive corrective actions and may even drive a firm out of business.

Summary

The marketing environment consists of external forces that directly or indirectly influence an organization's acquisition of inputs (personnel, financial resources, raw materials, information) and generation of outputs (information, packages, goods, services, ideas). The marketing environment includes political, legal, regulatory, societal, economic and competitive, and technological forces.

To monitor changes in these forces, marketers practice environmental scanning and analysis. Environmental scanning is the process of collecting information about the forces in the marketing environment; environmental analysis is the process of assessing and interpreting the information obtained in scanning. This information helps marketing managers predict opportunities and threats associated with environmental fluctuation. Marketing management may assume either a passive, reactive approach or a proactive, aggressive approach in responding to these environmental fluctuations. The choice depends on an organization's structure and needs and on the composition of the environmental forces that affect it.

The political, legal, and regulatory forces of the marketing environment are closely interrelated. The current political outlook is reflected in legislation and regulations or the lack of them. The political environment may determine what laws and regulations affecting specific marketers are enacted and how much the government purchases and from which suppliers; it can also be important in helping organizations secure foreign markets.

Federal legislation affecting marketing activities can be divided into procompetitive legislation—laws designed to preserve and encourage competition—and consumer protection laws. The Sherman Antitrust Act sought to prevent monopolies and activities that limit competition; subsequent legislation, such as the Clayton Act, the Federal Trade Commission Act, the Wheeler-Lea Act, and the Robinson-Patman Act, were directed toward more specific practices. Consumer protection laws generally relate to product safety and information disclosure. The actual effects of legislation are determined by how marketers and the courts interpret the laws.

Federal regulatory agencies influence most marketing activities. Federal, state, and local regulatory units usually have the power to enforce specific laws and some discretion in establishing operating rules and drawing up regulations to guide certain types of industry practices. Self-regulation by industry represents another regulatory force; marketers view this type of regulation more favorably than government action because they have more opportunity to take part in creating the guidelines. Self-regulation may be less expensive than government regulation, and its guidelines are generally more realistic. However, such regulation generally cannot assure compliance as effectively as government agencies.

Societal forces refer to the structure and dynamics of individuals and groups and the issues that concern them. Members of our society want a high standard of living and a high quality of life, and they expect business to help them achieve these goals. Another societal force is cultural diversity. With blacks and Hispanics representing a growing percentage of the population, the United States is becoming a multicultural society. For marketers, this increasingly diverse population means a more diverse consumer base. The consumer movement is a diverse group of independent individuals, groups, and organizations that attempts to protect the rights of consumers. The major issues taken up by the consumer movement fall into three categories: environmental protection, product performance and safety, and information disclosure. Consumer rights organizations inform and organize other consumers, raise issues, help businesses develop consumer-oriented programs, and pressure lawmakers to enact consumer protection laws.

The economic factors that can strongly influence marketing decisions and activities are general economic conditions, buying power, willingness to spend, spending patterns, and competitive forces. The overall state of the economy fluctuates in a general pattern known as a business cycle. The stages of the business cycle are prosperity, recession, depression, and recovery.

Consumers' goods, services, and financial holdings make up their buying power—that is, their ability to purchase. The financial sources of buying power are income, credit, and wealth. After-tax income used for spending or saving is called disposable income. Disposable income left after an individual has purchased the basic necessities of food, clothing, and shelter is called discretionary income. Two measures of buying power are effective buying income (which includes salaries, wages, dividends, interest, profits, and rents, less federal, state, and local taxes) and the buying power index (a weighted index consisting of population, effective buying income, and retail sales data). The factors that affect consumers' willingness to spend are product price, the level of satisfaction obtained from currently used products, family size, and expectations about future employment, income, prices, and general economic conditions. Consumer spending patterns indicate the relative proportions of annual family expenditures or the actual amount of money spent on certain kinds of goods and services. Comprehensive spending patterns specify the percentages of family income allotted to annual expenditures for general classes of goods and services. Product-specific spending patterns indicate the annual dollar amounts families spend for specific products within a general product class.

Although all businesses compete for consumers' dollars, a company's direct competitors are usually the businesses in its geographic area that market products that resemble its own or can be substituted for them. The number of firms that control the supply of a product may affect the strength of competition. There are four general types of competitive structures: monopoly, oligopoly, monopolistic competition, and perfect competition. Marketers should monitor what competitors are currently doing and assess the changes occurring in the competitive environment.

Technology is the knowledge of how to accomplish tasks and goals. Product development, packaging, promotion, prices, and distribution systems are all influenced directly by technology. Several factors determine how much and in what way a particular business will make use of technology; these factors include the firm's ability to use technology, consumers' ability and willingness to buy technologically improved products, the firm's perception of the long-run effects of applying technology, the extent to which the firm is technologically based, the degree to which technology is used as a competitive tool, and the extent to which the business can protect technological applications through patents.

Important Terms

Marketing environment
Environmental scanning
Environmental analysis
Procompetitive legislation
Sherman Antitrust Act
Clayton Act
Federal Trade Commission Act
Wheeler-Lea Act
Robinson-Patman Act
Consumer protection legislation
Federal Trade Commission (FTC)
Better Business Bureau
National Advertising Review Board (NARB)
Societal forces

Consumer movement
Prosperity
Recession
Depression
Recovery
Buying power
Income
Disposable income
Discretionary income
Wealth
Effective buying income (EBI)
Buying power index (BPI)
Willingness to spend
Consumer spending patterns
Comprehensive spending patterns

Product-specific spending patterns
Competition
Monopoly
Oligopoly

Monopolistic competition
Perfect competition
Technology
Technology assessment

Discussion and Review Questions

1. Why are environmental scanning and analysis so important?
2. How are political forces related to legal and governmental regulatory forces?
3. Describe marketers' attempts to influence political forces.
4. What types of procompetitive legislation directly affect marketing practices?
5. What was the major objective of most procompetitive laws? Do the laws generally accomplish this objective? Why or why not?
6. What are the major provisions of the Robinson-Patman Act? Which marketing mix decisions are influenced directly by this act?
7. What types of problems do marketers experience as they interpret legislation?
8. What are the goals of the Federal Trade Commission? List the ways in which the FTC affects marketing activities. Do you think a single regulatory agency should have such broad jurisdiction over so many marketing practices? Why or why not?
9. Name several nongovernmental regulatory forces. Do you believe that self-regulation is more or less effective than governmental regulatory agencies? Why?
10. Describe the consumer movement. Analyze some active consumer forces in your area.
11. In what ways can each of the business cycle stages affect consumers' reactions to marketing strategies?
12. What business cycle stage are we experiencing currently? How is this stage affecting business firms in your area?
13. Define income, disposable income, and discretionary income. How does each type of income affect consumer buying power?
14. How is consumer buying power affected by wealth and consumer credit?
15. How is buying power measured? Why should it be evaluated?
16. What factors influence a consumer's willingness to spend?
17. What does the term *technology* mean to you?
18. How does technology affect you as a member of society? Do the benefits of technology outweigh its costs and dangers?
19. Discuss the impact of technology on marketing activities.
20. What factors determine whether a business organization adopts and uses technology?

Cases

2.1 **BMG/Arista Makes Good for Milli Vanilli Lip-Synch Hijinx**

The recording industry was stunned by the disclosure that singers Rob Pilatus and Fabrice Morvan of the group Milli Vanilli did not perform the vocals for their Arista Records albums and lip-synched those recordings during their concert appearances. The group had only produced two albums—*Girl You Know It's*

True and *The Remix Album*—and one video recording when the announcement was made. The actions of the singers and Arista Records not only sent shock waves through the industry, but angered many fans and album purchasers as well.

On November 27, 1990, a state court judge in the Circuit Court of Cook County, Illinois, determined that the main lawsuit filed at the time—*Siegel* v. *Pilatus, et al.*—could proceed as a class-action suit on behalf of all recording/merchandise purchasers in the United States. In the class-action suit against Milli Vanilli, Arista, and the Bertelsmann Music Group (BMG), the plaintiffs claimed fraud, misrepresentation, negligence, breach of contract, and breach of warranty and sought monetary relief in the form of the return of amounts paid for Milli Vanilli's recordings, merchandise, and concert tickets. The plaintiffs also sought statutory and punitive damages, as well as attorney's fees. In addition to the main class-action suit, twenty-two other cases were also filed against the group and BMG/Arista, alleging violations of the federal Racketeer Influenced and Corrupt Organizations Act (RICO). Later that year, federal judges in Pennsylvania and California denied motions that would have allowed these twenty-two cases and others to become class-action suits as well.

On September 5, 1991, Judge Thomas J. O'Brien of the Circuit Court of Cook County, Illinois, preliminarily approved a proposed settlement agreed to by the plaintiffs in the *Siegel* case and BMG/Arista. Persons included in the settlement were divided into three classes: recordings, concert, and merchandise. Members of each class were allowed to obtain certain rebates provided that they met certain eligibility conditions. Those who had purchased a Milli Vanilli recording prior to November 27, 1990, were allowed to obtain a rebate of $1.00 for a single (cassette or record), $2.00 for an album (cassette or record), and $3.00 for a compact disc purchase. Class members who had purchased Milli Vanilli concert tickets prior to November 27, 1990, were allowed to obtain a rebate of 5 percent of the face value of a concert ticket (not to exceed $2.50). These members were allowed a rebate of $1.00 if their ticket stub did not reflect a purchase price. In the merchandise class, qualifying members were allowed to have their name included as a partial donor of $250,000 to one of three charities: the T. J. Martell Foundation for leukemia research, the American Foundation for AIDS Research, and the Rainforest Action Network and Cultural Survival. The maximum donation per class member was set at $5.00. Members of the recordings and concert classes were also allowed to donate their rebates to one of the three charities. In each case, class members were allowed to keep their recordings and merchandise. To be eligible for the rebates, class members had to send in proofs of purchase, such as liner notes from compact discs and cassettes and bar codes from records. Purchasers who did not want to accept these decisions were allowed to be excluded from the settlement.[21]

Questions for Discussion

1. How would you or one of your friends feel if you purchased a Milli Vanilli recording and found out the artists were not the real performers?
2. How might the settlement and its accompanying publicity affect Arista's marketing strategy?
3. What are the implications of this case for other industries and businesses?

2.2 The *Wall Street Journal* Faces a Challenging Environment

For more than a hundred years the *Wall Street Journal* has provided readers with important information on the business environment of the United States and the world. The paper started when Charles H. Dow, Edward D. Jones, and their silent partner, Charles M. Bergstresser, began printing a four-page afternoon business newspaper that sold for 2 cents a copy. In 1902, the publisher C. W. Barron purchased the paper and turned over its control to his wife. Today Barron's descendants still own a controlling interest in the paper.

Published by Dow Jones & Co., the *Wall Street Journal* is among the country's most prestigious papers. Its experienced staff and ultramodern printing facilities make the *Wall Street Journal* a lofty model for other newspapers. Businesspeople in many parts of the world read it almost religiously. Its reliability and relatively traditional format make the *Journal* a comfortable cornerstone of American business, and its nearly two million subscribers are clear evidence of the paper's success. However, recent developments have made many at the *Journal* uneasy about the future.

They worry that today's extremely busy businessperson simply does not have the time needed to peruse the paper every morning. Present-day businesspeople, especially high-ranking executives, must make decisions quickly and need immediate information. Electronic information systems, with their instantaneous data retrieval capabilities, might soon make the *Journal* obsolete.

Moreover, the *Journal's* subscription list is shrinking and advertising sales are down. Daily newspapers across the nation have extended their coverage of business, investments, and the economy; business programs on network and cable television now draw large audiences; and more people than ever are reading business magazines. As readers seek business information from these media, they are less likely to rely on the *Wall Street Journal*. Advertisers have diverted their funds as well, to cover the extended business press.

The *Journal's* staff attributes its problems to three major events: (1) the October 1987 stock market crash that reduced the number of investors; (2) the large number of layoffs that occurred because of mergers and streamlining efforts in corporate America; and (3) new competition, especially from electronic information transmittal. However, the paper's officials expect it to survive all challenges.

Ironically, another part of the Dow Jones & Co. family poses perhaps the greatest competitive threat to the *Wall Street Journal*. The Dow Jones Information Services Group is growing rapidly. Its new DowVision information system is on the cutting edge of electronic business information. By using Dow Jones News/Retrieval, subscribers can call up *Journal* stories on their personal computers early on publication day and also receive up-to-the-minute accounts of financial developments in London and Tokyo. One investment banker has indicated that the *Journal's* circulation problems during the last five years can be traced to Information Services.

Management at the *Journal* hopes that busy executives will continue to take time to read their newspaper. But as time becomes more valuable and crucial to businesspeople and investors, many may opt to get their business news directly from their personal computers. The staff at the *Wall Street Journal* believes that accurate, timely, important, and fair news coverage will be enough to hold their readers' attention and loyalty, whether it appears on a printed page or on a computer screen.[22]

Questions for Discussion

1. Which environmental forces are influencing the performance of the *Wall Street Journal* the most? Explain.
2. Could some of the environmental forces that are adversely affecting the *Journal* be treated as opportunities instead of threats?
3. Has the *Wall Street Journal*'s management employed an active or a passive approach in dealing with environmental forces? Explain.

Chapter Notes

1. Based on information from Alecia Swasy, "P&G Gets Mixed Marks as It Promotes Green Image," *Wall Street Journal*, Aug. 26, 1991, pp. B1, B2; Zachary Schiller and John Carey, "Procter & Gamble on a Short Leash," *Business Week*, July 22, 1991, pp. 76, 78; and Steven W. Colford, "FDA Getting Tougher," *Advertising Age*, Apr. 29, 1991, pp. 1, 53.
2. Fara Warner, "What Happened to the Truth?" *Adweek's Marketing Week*, Oct. 28, 1991, p. 4.
3. "Consumers Lured with Lean Meat," *Marketing News*, Oct. 28, 1991, p. 1.
4. Philip Kotler, "Megamarketing," *Harvard Business Review*, Mar.–Apr. 1986, pp. 117–124.
5. "Using Marketing Forces for Environmental Goals," *Business Ethics*, Sept./Oct. 1991, p. 12.
6. *Federal Trade Commission* v. *Raladam Company*, 283 U.S. 643, 1931.
7. Allan Hershkowitz, "Spurts and Starts Corporate Role in '90s Environmentalism, Hardly Consistent," *Advertising Age*, Oct. 28, 1991, pp. GR15–GR16.
8. Ray O. Werner, ed., "Legal Developments in Marketing," *Journal of Marketing*, Jan. 1991, p. 87.
9. Deborah Bihler, "Company Watch," *Business Ethics*, Sept./Oct. 1991, p. 11.
10. "NAD Polishes Off Cleaners' Dispute," *Advertising Age*, Jan. 16, 1989, p. 49.
11. "Two Marketers Challenge NAD on Ad Decisions," *Advertising Age*, June 19, 1989, p. 66.
12. Brian Bremner, "A New Sales Pitch: The Environment," *Business Week*, July 24, 1989, p. 50.
13. Robin Knight, with Eleni Dimmler, "The Greening of Europe's Industries," *U.S. News & World Report*, June 5, 1989, pp. 45–46.
14. Jenny C. McCune, "Consumer Activism Means Big Business," *Management Review*, Dec. 1990, pp. 16–19.
15. Current Population Reports, Money, Income of Households, Families, and Persons in the United States: 1990, Series P-60, No. 174, Aug. 1991, p. 3.
16. *Sales & Marketing Management 1989 Survey of Buying Power*, Aug. 7, 1989.
17. Wroe Alderson, *Dynamic Marketing Behavior* (Homewood, Ill.: Irwin, 1965), pp. 195–197.
18. Herbert Simon, "Technology and Environment," *Management Science*, June 1973, p. 1110.
19. Cyndee Miller, "Vending Industry Cooks Up New Meals in Machines," *Marketing News*, Oct. 28, 1991, p. 1.
20. "K-Mart Introduces High Tech Changes to Make Sales Come Back," *Marketing News*, Oct. 28, 1991, p. 7.
21. *Notice of Pendency of Class Action*, U.S. Circuit Court of Cook County, Illinois.
22. Alex Taylor III, "A Tale Dow Jones Won't Tell," *Fortune*, July 3, 1989, pp. 100–102, 106, 108–109; Dennis Farney, "One Newspaper's Century: The Inside Story," *Wall Street Journal*, June 23, 1989, pp. C1, C3–C4, C12; and Patrick Reilly, "Expanding Its Horizons," *Advertising Age*, June 19, 1989, pp. 43–44.

3 *Marketing Ethics and Social Responsibility*

O B J E C T I V E S

- To define and understand the importance of marketing ethics

- To recognize factors that influence ethical or unethical decisions

- To discuss some important ethical issues in marketing

- To identify ways to improve ethical decisions in marketing

- To understand the concept of social responsibility

- To explore several important issues of social responsibility

- To describe strategies for dealing with social dilemmas

Maybe you're the kind of basketball player who plays above the rim. Maybe you're on a plane. Maybe you open up the window shade. Maybe you see another player soaring high above the court in a pair of Air Flight™ Lite shoes, the lightest Nike basketball shoes on earth. Maybe you wish you were wearing a pair so you wouldn't have to listen to that screaming little brat in the seat behind you.

In the furious competition for market share in the maturing $5 billion athletic shoe industry, some companies are willing to take higher risks. One such company is Reebok International. For several years, Reebok and rival Nike, have engaged in an intense strategic marketing war. In early 1990 Reebok's ad agency struggled to come up with a brilliant ad campaign for the Reebok Pump shoe that would challenge the successful Nike Air campaign. The result was a television commercial featuring bungee jumpers—people who leap from high places tethered at the ankles by giant elastic ropes. The commercial opens with two men standing on a bridge, 180 feet above whitewater rapids and rocks. Both are wearing basketball shoes—one man in Nike Air hightops and the other in Reebok's Pump. Then the two men free–fall to the sound of their clothes flapping in the wind. At the end, the Reebok wearer is shown safely hanging upside down above the water; the other cord holds only a pair of empty Nike Airs. The announcer says, "The Pump from Reebok—it fits a little better than your ordinary athletic shoe."

The commercial certainly got attention and generated publicity, but it was the wrong kind. Many people viewed the sly joke about violent death as extraordinarily cruel, and consumers complained that children might try the dangerous stunt. Although the commercial was originally planned as an $8 million three-week campaign, Reebok pulled the advertisement off the air after six days. The company later attempted to rerun the commercial with disclaimers, but the major networks refused to air it.

Amongst the clutter of television advertising, how does a company get attention, make a statement? What is certain is that associating a competitor's product with death raises an ethical issue. This case highlights ethical and social responsibility concerns that advertisers have to the public. And the public *will* react when advertisers overlook these concerns. No matter how intense the competition is for market share, advertisers must consider the consequences of their actions. If ethical boundaries are crossed in an attempt to get attention, the consequences can be more negative than simply being number two in market share.[1]

Advertisement courtesy Nike Inc.

ISSUES SUCH AS THE REEBOK CONTROVERSY illustrate that all marketing activities can be judged as right or wrong by society, consumers, interest groups, competitors, and others. Although most marketers operate within the limits of the law, some marketers do engage in activities that are not considered acceptable by other marketers, consumers, and society in general. A number of recently publicized incidents in marketing, such as deceptive or objectionable advertising, misleading packaging, questionable selling practices, manipulation, corruption, and pollution, have raised questions as to whether specific marketing practices are acceptable and beneficial to society. The issues of what is acceptable in marketing practices and what obligations marketers have to society are issues of marketing ethics and social responsibility.

This chapter gives an overview of the role of ethics and social responsibility in marketing decision making. We first define marketing ethics and discuss the factors that influence ethical decision making in marketing. We also outline some specific ethical issues in marketing and discuss ways to improve ethics in marketing decisions. Then we address the issue of social responsibility and consider the impact of marketing decisions on society. Some strategies for dealing with social responsibility dilemmas are also developed. We close the chapter by comparing and contrasting the concepts of marketing ethics and social responsibility.

The Nature of Marketing Ethics

Though a very important concern in marketing decisions, ethics may be one of the most misunderstood and controversial concepts in marketing. No one has yet discovered a universally accepted approach to dealing with marketing ethics. However, this concept and its application need to be examined to foster marketing decisions that are acceptable and beneficial to society. In this section we consider the meaning of marketing ethics.

Marketing Ethics Defined

Ethics relate to moral evaluations of decisions and actions as right or wrong on the basis of commonly accepted principles of behavior. For our purposes, then, **marketing ethics** are moral principles that define right and wrong behavior in marketing. The most basic ethical issues have been formalized through laws and regulations to provide conformity to the standards of society. At a minimum, marketers are expected to conform to these laws and regulations. However, it is important to realize that marketing ethics go beyond legal issues; ethical marketing decisions foster mutual trust among individuals and in marketing relationships.

Although individual marketers often act in their own self-interest, there must be standards of acceptable behavior for marketing to be accepted as a socially approved behavior. Marketers need to operate in accordance with sound moral principles based on ideals such as fairness, justice, and trust.[2] Consumers generally regard unethical marketing activities—for instance, deceptive advertising, misleading selling tactics, misrepresentation of environmental impact, and the willful marketing of harmful products—as unacceptable and often refuse to do business with marketers that engage in such practices. Thus when marketers deviate from accepted moral principles to further their own interests at the expense of others, continued marketing exchanges become difficult, if not impossible.[3]

Marketing Ethics Are Controversial

Few topics in marketing are more controversial than ethics. Most marketing decisions can be judged as right or wrong, ethical or unethical. But everyone has different ideas as to what is ethical or unethical depending on personal values, the nature of the organization, and their experiences in life. Many marketers have such strong convictions about what is morally right or wrong that they deeply resent discussions of alternative ways to make ethical decisions.

In our society, we want to believe that individuals control their own destiny. Therefore, a very popular way of studying marketing ethics is to focus on the alternative philosophies individuals use to resolve personal moral decisions. However, many ethical decisions in marketing are resolved by groups, not individuals. These decisions are based on business, rather than personal, goals. Ethical decision making in marketing can include such issues as What is deceptive advertising? What constitutes a bribe in a personal selling situation? or What constitutes irrelevant or false claims about a product?

These and other ethics issues may seem straightforward and easy to resolve for some people, but in reality most marketers will need several years of experience within a specific industry to understand how to resolve close calls. For example, when does a salesperson's offer to take a customer on a fishing trip become a bribe rather than a good sales practice? While there are no easy answers to these questions, studying marketing ethics can help to prepare you to participate in many challenging decisions.

Regardless of how a person or an organization views the acceptability of a particular activity, if society judges that activity to be wrong or unethical, then this view directly affects the organization's ability to achieve its goals. Although not all activities deemed unethical by society may be illegal, consumer protests against a particular activity may result in legislation that restricts or bans it. When an organization engages in what society believes are unethical marketing activities, it may lose sales as dissatisfied consumers refuse to purchase its products. For example, when America's number-one kid's brand of home computer, Nintendo, announced it was entering the gambling business, there was a moral uproar. In a marketing test, the company sent ten thousand computers and modems to Minnesota families so that they could play the state lottery on their living room television. The Nintendo lottery plan was condemned in an editorial in the Twin Cities daily, the *Star Tribune,* and Minnesota state senate majority leader, Roger Moe, called the test "not only unethical, but insidiously destructive to society." Critics believe that Nintendo's decision to lend its technology and good name to a state lottery was a moral disaster—an idea that would be opposed by parents and educators alike.[4] Such examples illustrate the importance of understanding marketing ethics and recognizing ethical issues.

Because marketing ethics are so controversial, it is important to state that it is not the purpose of this chapter to question anyone's personal/ethical beliefs

Figure 3.1

**Factors That Influ-
ence the Ethical
Decision-Making
Process**

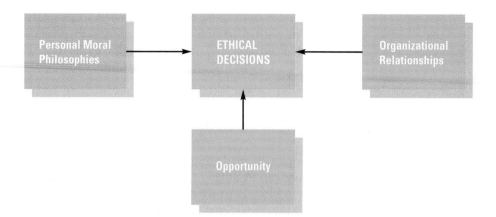

and convictions. Nor is it the purpose of this chapter to examine the behavior of consumers, although consumers, too, may be unethical (engaging, for instance, in coupon fraud, shoplifting, and other abuses). Instead, its goal is to underscore the importance of ethical issues and help you learn about ethical decision making in marketing. Understanding the impact of ethical decisions in marketing can help you recognize and resolve ethical issues within an organization.

Understanding the Ethical Decision-Making Process

To grasp the significance of ethics in marketing decision making, one must first examine the factors that influence the ethical decision-making process. Personal moral philosophies, organizational relationships, and opportunity are three factors that interact to determine ethical decisions in marketing (see Figure 3.1).

Moral Philosophies

Moral philosophies are principles or rules that individuals use to determine the right way to behave. They provide guidelines for resolving conflicts and ensuring mutual benefit for all members of society.[5] People learn these principles and rules through socialization by family members, social groups, religion, and formal education. It is widely believed that by identifying and improving one's moral philosophies, ethical decision making can be improved. Each moral philosophy has its own concept of rightness or ethicalness and rules for behavior. We discuss here two distinct moral philosophies: utilitarianism and ethical formalism.

Utilitarianism   Utilitarian moral philosophies are concerned with maximizing the greatest good for the greatest number of people. Utilitarians judge an action on the basis of the consequences for all the people affected by the action. In other words, in a situation with an ethical component, utilitarians compare all possible options and select the one that promises the best results. Under utilitarianism, then, it would be unethical to act in a way that leads to personal gain at the expense of society in general. Consider the following example of an organization adopting a utilitarian philosophy. In 1990, the offices of Delta Air Lines in Ireland received a telephone threat from terrorists that one of its transatlantic flights would be bombed. Delta decided to publicize the threat and announced that it would allow customers holding tickets on its transatlantic flights to transfer their tickets to other airlines without penalty.[6] When Pan Am received a bomb threat in 1988, it did not notify the public; the loss of more than two hundred lives in the terrorist bombing of Pan Am flight 103 and the negative publicity directed at Pan Am damaged the firm. Thus, after weighing the possible loss of life and the negative publicity surrounding a terrorist bombing or crash against the loss of revenues and profits, Delta executives probably concluded that publicizing the bomb threat and letting passengers decide whether to fly on Delta would be best.

Ethical Formalism Other moral philosophies focus on the intentions associated with a particular behavior and on the rights of the individual. Ethical formalism develops specific rules for behavior by determining whether an action can be taken consistently as a general rule without concern for alternative results.[7] Behavior is judged on the basis of whether it infringes on individual rights or universal rules. The Golden Rule—do unto others as you would have them do unto you—exemplifies ethical formalism. So does Immanuel Kant's categorical imperative: that every action should be based on reasons that everyone could act on, at least in principle, and that action must be based on reasons that the decision maker would be willing to have others use.[8] In marketing, ethical formalism is consistent with the idea of consumer choice. For example, consumers have a right to know about possible defects in an automobile or other products that relate to safety.[9] In Figure 3.2, Allstate offers consumers a free list of cars with air bags. Enabling consumers to make a choice is consistent with the idea of ethical formalism.

Applying Moral Philosophies to Marketing Decision Making Traditionally, it has been assumed that personal moral philosophies remain constant in both work and nonwork situations. However, research has shown that most business persons use one moral philosophy at work and a completely different one outside of work.[10]

Another study found that although personal moral philosophies and values enter into ethical decisions in business, they are not the central component guiding the decisions, actions, and policies of an organization.[11] This finding may explain why individuals switch moral philosophies between home and work and why personal values make up only one part of an organization's total value system.

Ethical behavior may be a function of two different dimensions of an organization's value structure: the organization's values and traditions, or corporate culture, and the personal moral philosophies of the organization's individual members. An employee assumes some measure of moral responsibility by agreeing to abide by an organization's rules and standard operating procedures. When a marketer decides to behave unethically or even illegally, it may be that competitive pressures and organizational rewards provided the incentive.

Living examples of people with air bags.

Each of these people is here today because of their air bag. There are hundreds like them. Since 1969, Allstate has been urging drivers and car manufacturers to install air bags. We're pleased this message is now catching on. But we won't stop until everyone who gets behind the wheel gets behind an air bag. (Remember: Air bags together with seat belts are the safest combination.)

See your Allstate agent or write for a free list of cars that come with driver and passenger air bags.

And get more out of life.

A member of the
Sears Financial Network

Allstate
You're in good hands.

For information on air bags, write: Allstate Insurance Company, Department 400, P.O. Box 7660, Mount Prospect, IL 60056-9961. © 1991 Allstate Insurance Company, Northbrook, Illinois.

Figure 3.2 **Ethical Formalism and Consumer Choice** Allstate illustrates the effectiveness of airbags and offers consumers a free list of cars with airbags. Enabling consumers to make an informed choice is consistent with the idea of ethical formalism. Source: Courtesy Allstate Insurance Company.

Organizational Relationships

People learn personal moral philosophies, and therefore ethical behavior, not only from society in general, but also from members of their social groups and their organizational environment. Relationships with one's employees, coworkers, or superiors create ethical problems, such as maintaining confidentiality in personal relations; meeting obligations, responsibilities and mutual agreements; and avoiding undue pressure that may force others to behave unethically. Employees may have to deal with assignments that they perceive as creating ethical dilemmas. For example, a salesperson may be asked to lie to a customer over the phone. Likewise, an employee who sees another employee cheating a customer must decide whether to report the incident.

Marketing managers must carefully balance their duties to the owners or stockholders who hired them to carry out the organization's objectives and to the employees who look to them for guidance and direction. In addition, managers must also comply with society's wishes and ethical evaluations. Striking an ethical balance among these areas, then, is a difficult task for today's marketing decision makers.

The role of top management is extremely important in developing the culture of an organization. Most experts agree that the chief executive officer or the vice president of marketing sets the ethical tone for the entire marketing organization. Lower-level managers obtain their cues from top management, yet they, too, impose some of their personal values on the company. This interaction between corporate culture and executive leadership helps determine the ethical value system of the firm.

Powerful superiors can affect employees' activities and directly influence behavior by putting into practice the company's standards of ethics. Young marketers in particular indicate that they often go along with their superiors to demonstrate loyalty in matters related to judgments of morality. The status and power of significant others is directly related to the amount of pressure they can exert on others to conform to their expectations. A manager in a position of authority can exert strong pressure to assure compliance on ethically related issues. In organizations where ethical standards are vague and supervision by superiors is limited, peers may provide guidance in an ethical decision.

The role of peers (co-workers) in the decision-making process depends on the person's ratio of exposure to unethical behavior to exposure to ethical behavior. The more a person is exposed to unethical activity in the organizational environment, the more likely it is that he or she will behave unethically.[12] Employees experience conflict between what is expected of them as workers and what they expect of themselves based on their own personal ethical standards.

Opportunity

Opportunity provides another pressure that may determine whether a person will behave ethically. Opportunity is a favorable set of conditions that limit barriers or provide rewards. Rewards may be internal or external. Internal rewards are the feelings of goodness and worth one experiences after an altruistic action. External rewards are what people expect to receive from others in terms of values generated and provided on an exchange basis. External rewards are often received from peers and top management in the form of praise, promotions, and raises.

If a marketer takes advantage of an opportunity to act unethically and is rewarded or suffers no penalty, he or she may repeat such acts as other opportunities arise. For example, a salesperson who receives a raise after using a deceptive sales presentation to increase sales is being rewarded and so will probably continue the behavior. Indeed, opportunity to engage in unethical conduct is often a better predictor of unethical activities than are personal values.[13]

Besides rewards and the absence of punishment, other elements in the business environment help to create opportunities. Professional codes of ethics and ethics-related corporate policy also influence opportunity by prescribing what behaviors are acceptable. The larger the rewards and the lesser the punishment for unethical behavior, the greater is the probability that unethical behavior will be practiced.

Ethical Issues in Marketing

A person will not make an ethical decision unless he or she recognizes that a particular issue or situation has an ethical or moral component. Thus developing awareness of ethical issues is important in understanding marketing ethics. An

ethical issue is an identifiable problem, situation, or opportunity requiring an individual or organization to choose from among several actions that must be evaluated as right or wrong, ethical or unethical. Anytime an activity causes consumers to feel deceived, manipulated, or cheated, a marketing ethical issue exists, regardless of the legality of that activity.

Ethical issues typically arise because of conflicts among individuals' personal moral philosophies and the marketing strategies, policies, and the organizational environment in which they work. Ethical issues may stem from conflicts between a marketer's attempts to achieve organizational objectives and customers' desires for safe and reliable products. Similarly, organizational objectives that call for increased profits or market share may pressure marketers to steal competitors' secrets, knowingly bring an unsafe product to market, or engage in some other questionable activity. What should a firm do when a disgruntled employee from a competitor mails top-secret new-product samples and offers to help the firm unravel a new technology for a small consulting fee? This actually happened to 3M Company and Johnson & Johnson. A 3M contract employee sent samples of a new casting tape for setting broken bones to Johnson & Johnson. 3M contends that Johnson & Johnson studied the tape and incorporated 3M's proprietary technology into its competing product. In 1991, a U.S. district court ordered Johnson & Johnson to pay 3M $116.3 million for infringing its patents and misappropriating trade secrets. Johnson & Johnson denies any wrongdoing and indicates that it has a strict policy against taking trade secrets.[14]

Regardless of the reasons behind specific ethical issues, once the issues are identified, marketers and organizations must decide how to deal with them. Thus it is essential to become familiar with many of the ethical issues that may arise in marketing so that they can be identified and resolved when they occur. We cannot, of course, discuss every possible issue that could develop in the different marketing mix elements. But our examination of a few issues can provide some direction and lead to an understanding of the ethical problems that marketers must confront.

Product Issues

In general, product-related ethical issues arise when marketers fail to disclose risks associated with the product or information regarding the function, value, or use of the product. Competitive pressures can also create product-related ethical issues. As competition intensifies and profit margins diminish, pressures can build to substitute inferior materials or product components to reduce costs. An ethical issue arises when marketers fail to inform customers about changes in product quality; this failure is a form of dishonesty about the nature of the product. Marketers may also seek to capitalize on public concerns, such as health, by using misleading terms in marketing their products. Under pressure from both federal and state regulatory groups, Kellogg had to change the name of its Heartwise cereal to Fiberwise because the company could not substantiate that the cereal was beneficial to the heart.[15] And Procter & Gamble had to stop calling Citrus Hill Fresh Choice orange juice by that name after a controversy over the word *fresh*. Since Citrus Hill is made from concentrate, the FDA considered the word *fresh* misleading and removed the juice from a warehouse until the company changed the name of the product.[16] When products do not possess the qualities implied in their promotion, ethical issues arise because consumers are being deceived.

It is important to recognize that most companies use an ethical approach to developing products and promoting them to customers. When ethical issues and problems related to the product emerge, the company usually gets back on course, and customers are usually quick to forgive a transgression. General Mills has rebounded from a health claim problem related to its now-defunct Benefit cereal and now leads the cereal industry with Cheerios, which it simply promotes as "made from whole grain oats" and having "the lowest sugar of the leading brands." The director of adult cereals at General Mills says, "You can't borrow from outside sources to build a brand's equity, because ultimately you're going to have to pay for it."[17]

Promotion Issues

The communication process provides a variety of situations that can create ethical issues: for instance, false and misleading advertising and manipulative or deceptive sales promotions, tactics, or publicity efforts. In this section we consider some ethical issues linked to advertising and personal selling. We also examine the use of bribery in personal selling situations.

Advertising   Unethical actions in advertising can destroy the trust customers have in an organization. Sometimes advertisements are questioned because they are unfair to a competitor. For example, after McDonald's introduced a chicken product in some regions, Kentucky Fried Chicken aired commercials featuring a clown named Mr. R. McDonald being questioned by a congressional committee. In one spot, when asked what McDonald's has that Kentucky Fried Chicken does not, Mr. McDonald replies, "Toys. . . . Lots of toys." CBS refused to air the spot, saying, "We felt the commercial was unfairly denigrating to the corporate image of McDonald's." Although both NBC and ABC aired the commercials, CBS considered the advertisements to be ethically questionable.[18]

Abuses in advertising can range from exaggerated claims and concealed facts to outright lying. Exaggerated claims cannot be substantiated; for example, commercial claims that a certain pain reliever or cough syrup is superior to any other on the market often cannot be verified by consumers or experts. Concealed facts are material facts deliberately omitted from a message. For example, there was much controversy over Mobil's advertising claim that its Hefty trash bags were biodegradable. Mobil agreed to stop making claims of biodegradability of its trash bags but made no admission of guilt for false advertising claims. The debate raged because environmentalists felt the trash bags would not deteriorate within a landfill environment.[19] When consumers learn that promotion messages are untrue, they may feel cheated and refuse to buy the product again; they may also complain to government or other regulatory agencies. Consequently, marketers should take care to provide all important facts and to avoid making claims that cannot be supported. Otherwise they risk alienating their customers.

Another form of advertising abuse involves ambiguous statements—statements using words so weak that the viewer, reader, or listener must infer advertisers' intended messages. These "weasel" words are inherently vague and enable the advertiser to deny any intent to deceive. For example, *help* is a common "weasel" word, as in, "helps prevent, helps fight, or helps make you feel."[20] Such advertising practices are questionable if they deceive the consumer outright. Although some marketers view such statements as acceptable, others do not. Thus vague messages remain an ethical issue in advertising.

Personal Selling A common problem in selling activities is judging what types of sales activities are acceptable. Consumers sometimes perceive salespeople as unethical because of the common belief that sales personnel often pressure customers to purchase products they neither need nor want. Nevertheless, the sales forces of most firms, such as IBM and Procter & Gamble, are well educated, well trained, and professional, and they know that they must act ethically or risk losing valuable customers and sales. Although most salespersons are ethical, some do engage in questionable actions. For example, some salespersons have used very aggressive and manipulative tactics to sell almost worthless securities, gemstones, vacations, or other products over the phone. Even though these salespeople may be fined and jailed for their activities, their unethical and often illegal actions contribute to consumers' mistrust of telephone selling and of personal selling in general.

At one time or another, most salespeople face an ethical conflict in their jobs. For example, a salesperson may have to decide whether to tell a customer the truth and risk losing the customer's business, or somehow mislead the customer to appease him or her and ensure a sale. Failure to adequately train salespeople in how to deal with such situations leaves them unprepared to cope with ethical issues when they arise. Furthermore, sales personnel who are untrained and confused about what action to take when facing an ethical dilemma often experience high levels of job frustration, anxiety, and stress.

Table 3.1

Which of These Gifts Could Be Considered a Bribe?

Pen and pencil set (with company logo)
Five-year supply of scratch pads (with company logo)
Dinner at a four-star French restaurant
Box of grapefruit shipped to your house each Christmas
Box of groceries delivered to your door each week
Season tickets to sport of your choice
Weekend cruise of the New England coast
Three-day, all-expenses-paid golfing vacation
Retreat to a Canadian fishing camp, via chartered jet
Lavish trip to an exotic foreign locale
$500 in cash

Source: Adapted from E. J. Muller, "Traffigraft; Is Accepting a Gift from a Vendor a Breach of Ethics? To Some People, It's Just a Perk. To Others, It's Poison." *Distribution*, January 1990, p. 38. © 1990 Distribution Magazine. Reprinted with permission.

Frequently, the problem of ethics has a snowball effect. Once a salesperson has deceived a customer, it becomes increasingly difficult to tell the truth later. If the customer learns of the deception, the sales representative will lose all credibility in the eyes of the customer, as well as that customer's associates and friends. Thus the manner in which a salesperson deals with an ethical issue can have far-reaching consequences for both the individual and the firm.

Bribery in Selling Situations When payments, gifts, or special favors are granted to obtain a sale or for some other reason, there is always some question of bribery. A bribe is anything given to improperly influence the outcome of a decision. Even when a bribe is offered to benefit the organization, it is usually considered unethical, and it hurts the organization in the long run for it jeopardizes trust and fairness. Imperial Oil has a corporate ethics code that "employees should neither give nor receive gifts of more than nominal value ($25) without the knowledge of managers who have authority to provide consent."[21] Table 3.1 lists some possible gifts that could be offered by a salesperson in an attempt to gain sales. As you can see, defining a bribe is often a matter of personal values and judgment. Bribes have led to the downfall of many marketers, legislators, and government officials. Such practices are harmful, for they stifle fair competition among businesses.

Pricing Issues

Price fixing, predatory pricing, and failure to disclose the full price associated with a purchase are typical ethical issues. The emotional and subjective nature of price creates many situations in which misunderstandings between the seller and buyer cause ethical problems. Marketers have the right to price their products so that they earn a reasonable profit, but ethical issues may crop up when a company seeks to earn high profits at the expense of its customers. For example, the Federal Communications Commission found that Nynex, which owns the New York and New England Telephone companies, had been inflating the prices it charged its subsidiaries for goods and services in order to boost its own profits.[22] Nynex ultimately settled the charges by paying $1.4 million to the U.S. Treasury and by offering a one-time $35.5 million reduction of its interstate charges to telephone companies. "It was clear we needed to get back into focus," said the Nynex vice president for ethics and business conduct.[23]

As discussed in Chapter 2, a number of laws address pricing issues. Both the Federal Trade Commission Act and the Wheeler-Lea Act prohibit deceptive pricing. For various reasons, marketers may wish to sell the same type of product at different prices. Provisions of the Robinson-Patman Act, as well as those of the Clayton Act, limit the use of such price differentials. Not all price differentials are illegal, but differentials can be questioned from an ethical perspective. For example, Nintendo, the videogame marketer, allegedly raised its prices by 20 to 30 percent during the Christmas buying season and manipulated the supply of games available at that time.[24] Note that this may be as much a legal issue as an ethical one if Nintendo takes advantage of consumers. If price differentials tend to lessen or injure competition, they are considered discriminatory and are prohibited.

Distribution Issues

Ethical issues in distribution involve relationships among producers and marketing middlemen. Marketing middlemen, or intermediaries (wholesalers and retailers), facilitate the flow of products from the producer to the ultimate consumer. Each intermediary performs a different role and agrees to certain rights, responsibilities, and rewards associated with that role. For example, producers can expect retailers to honor payment agreements and keep them informed of inventory needs. Failure to make payments in a timely manner may be considered an ethical issue.

The numerous relationships among marketing intermediaries present many opportunities for conflicts and disputes, including judgments about right or wrong, ethical or unethical behavior. Manipulating a product's availability for purposes of exploitation and using coercion to force intermediaries to behave in a specific manner are particularly serious ethical issues in the distribution sphere. For example, a powerful manufacturer can exert undue influence over an intermediary's choice whether to handle a product or how to handle it.

Other ethical issues in distribution relate to stores' attempting to bypass legitimate producers and wholesalers. For example, some record stores distribute bootleg recordings that were illegally made at artists' concerts or stolen from masters in studio recording files. And some computer software stores are "hacking," or making unauthorized copies of software, thus preventing producers from getting their due compensation. Anytime a retailer exploits or takes undue advantage of a wholesaler or producer, an ethical issue exists.

Much controversy also surrounds retailers such as Wal-Mart Stores, Inc., which does business with a producer rather than going through an intermediary. Wal-Mart has been accused of threatening to buy from other producers if firms refuse to sell directly to it. Similar buy-direct policies are in effect at Lowe's Companies, Inc., and at Builder's Square, a home improvement chain owned by K mart. These retailers, which emphasize low prices, maintain that the no-middleman approach cuts costs and does not involve any ethical issues.[25] However, some small companies cannot afford to maintain their own sales forces and must rely on intermediaries to sell their products to retailers. The refusal to deal with intermediaries effectively shuts these smaller companies out of the market because they cannot compete with companies that have their own sales forces.

Improving Ethical Decisions in Marketing

Conflicts between personal moral philosophies and corporate values, organizational pressures, and opportunity interact to create situations that may cause unethical behavior. It is possible to improve ethical behavior in an organization by eliminating unethical persons and improving the organization's ethical standards.

One way to approach improvement of an organization's ethical standards is by considering a "bad apple–bad barrel" analogy. Some people always do things in their own self-interest regardless of organizational goals or accepted moral standards; they are sometimes called "bad apples." To eliminate unethical be-

82

Figure 3.3

Improving Ethical Decisions

The Dreiford Group, a consulting organization, provides programs to help companies manage ethical issues and improve their ethical decision-making.

Source: © 1991, The Dreiford Group/DS and F

havior, an organization must rid itself of the bad apples, or unethical persons. It can attain this goal through screening techniques and through the enforcement of ethics codes.[26] However, organizations too sometimes become "bad barrels"—not because the individuals within them are bad, but because the pressures to survive and succeed create conditions that reward unethical behavior. A way of resolving the problem of the bad barrel is to redesign the organization's image and culture so that it conforms to industry and societal norms of ethical behavior.[27] Figure 3.3 illustrates the need for practical organizational solutions to ethical issues.

Table 3.2 provides an overview of five companies that are taking action to develop ethics programs to improve decision making within their organizations. A number of U.S. businesses are embracing in-house ethics programs; in fact, the Center for Business Ethics at Bentley College in Waltham, Massachusetts, found in 1991 that 45 percent of the one hundred largest U.S. companies had an ethics program or workshop, up from 35 percent in 1986.[28]

The perceived ethicalness of the organization has been shown to be a better predictor of an individual's ethical behavior in a work group than the individual's own moral philosophy or beliefs.[29] While this may sound surprising, keep in mind that most ethical issues in a business organization are not obviously illegal or easily identified as unethical by members of the organization or society in general. When we look at gray areas (and most daily ethical decision making involves borderline decisions), we look to our managers and coworkers for direction. We want to believe that it is the individual who makes the most

Niagara Mohawk Power	Held full-day ethics workshop for all senior managers, including the chairman
Pitney Bowes	Instituted ombudsman, ethics statement for employees, conduct-guide booklet, training seminars for top officers
Nynex	Instituted ethics officer, new code of conduct, training seminars for top- and middle-level executives, hotline
Pacific Bell	Established office of business conduct and standards, ethics advisory council, training seminars, whistle-blowers' hotline
Hershey Foods	Offered ethics-awareness training for senior- and middle-level managers

Source: Reprinted from September 23, 1991 issue of *Business Week* by special permission, copyright © 1991 by McGraw-Hill, Inc.

Table 3.2   **Companies That Have Developed Ethics Programs or Workshops**

difference in terms of ethical decision making, but many ethical training programs are now focusing on the importance of the work group in influencing and improving ethical decision making.

By sensitizing marketers to ethical issues and potential areas of conflict, it is possible to eliminate or defuse some of the ethical pressures that occur in daily marketing activities. Awareness and sensitivity toward ethical issues can eliminate the risk of making unethical decisions. Ethical values must be built into the organizational culture and marketing strategy.[30] This can be achieved by establishing codes of ethics and by controlling unethical behavior when it occurs.

Codes of Ethics

It is hard for employees to determine what is acceptable behavior within a company if the company does not have uniform policies and standards. Without standards of behavior, employees will generally make decisions based on their observations of how their peers and managers behave. **Codes of ethics** are formalized rules and standards that describe what the company expects of its employees. The Global Perspective highlights the code of ethics of Imperial Oil of Canada. Codes of ethics encourage ethical behavior by eliminating opportunities for unethical behavior because employees know both what is expected of them and the punishment for violating the rules. They also help marketers deal with ethical issues or dilemmas that develop in daily operations by prescribing or limiting certain activities. Codes of ethics do not have to be so detailed they take into account every situation, but they should provide general guidelines for achieving organizational goals and objectives in a morally acceptable manner. Top management should provide leadership in implementing the codes.

Table 3.3 is the American Marketing Association Code of Ethics. The code does not cover every ethical issue, but it is a useful overview of what marketers believe are sound moral principles for guiding marketing activities. This code could be used to help structure an organization's code of ethics.

The Code of Ethics of Imperial Oil

IMPERIAL OIL LIMITED, based in Toronto, Canada, has sought to define its corporate values and to encourage ethical behavior among its employees. The company therefore developed a twenty-three page booklet, "Our Corporate Ethics," which delineates its values and addresses specific ethical issues arising from its marketing and other business activities. Employees may use the booklet both as a guide to the values of Imperial Oil and its subsidiaries and as a tool to justify their actions to others.

Imperial's code first establishes the company's core values: integrity; employee well-being; quality, excellence, and continuous improvements in company practices and products; and a stimulating work environment. The code next offers general guidance for Imperial's relationships with employees, customers, sales associates, competitors, the community, suppliers and contractors, and shareholders. For example, because Imperial Oil benefits from the Canadian free-market system, its code of ethics discourages anticompetitive activities, mandating instead the offering of goods and services of superior value.

Imperial's code of ethics then addresses some specific issues related to the environment, transactions with stakeholders, conflicts of interest, gifts and entertainment, confidential information, dealings with the government, insider trading, outside directorships, outside business activity, and Canadian competi-tion. Regarding the environment, for example, the code specifies that the company and its subsidiaries incorporate environmental considerations into the design of products, facilities, and operations, and into all long-range planning, and that it support local environmental efforts. To help minimize conflicts of interest, employees are asked not to give or accept gifts and entertainment except where modest, infrequent, and appropriate.

Finally, the booklet provides an "Ethics Checklist" for employees to use when confronted with an ethical issue. When confronted with an ethical decision, employees should ask: Is it legal? Is it fair? Can I defend it? The code suggests throughout that employees who have questions about a particular activity should consult with their supervisor or a company ethics advisor.

Like most codes of ethics, Imperial Oil's code does not address every situation that may crop up in business. Rather, it attempts to provide guidelines for and values by which to judge actions taken in the name of the company. By delineating its corporate values and providing guidance in several general areas, Imperial Oil may foster more ethical behavior by its employees.

Source: Adapted from "Our Corporate Ethics" Imperial Oil Limited (111 St. Clair Ave. W., Toronto, Ont. M5W 1K3), March 1990.

Controlling Unethical Behavior

Ethical behavior in marketing must be based on a strong moral foundation, including personal moral development and an organizational structure that encourages and rewards desired ethical action. The pressures of competition must be understood and coped with to improve ethical behavior. The idea that marketing ethics is learned at home, at school, and in family relationships does not recognize the impact of opportunity and the organization on ethical decision makers.

If a company is to maintain ethical behavior, its policies, rules, and standards must be worked into its control system. If the number of employees making ethical decisions on a regular basis is not satisfactory, then the company needs to determine why and take corrective action through enforcement. Enforcement of standards is what makes codes of ethics effective. If codes are window dressing and do not relate to what is expected or what is rewarded in the corporate culture, then the codes serve no purpose except to give an illusion of concern about ethical behavior.

The Nature of Social Responsibility

The concepts of ethics and social responsibility are often used interchangeably, although each has a distinct meaning. **Social responsibility** in marketing refers to an organization's obligation to maximize its positive impact and minimize its negative impact on society. Whereas ethics relate to individual decisions, social responsibility concerns the impact of an organization's decisions on society.

Table 3.3 **Code of Ethics, American Marketing Association**

Members of the American Marketing Association (AMA) are committed to ethical professional conduct. They have joined together in subscribing to this Code of Ethics embracing the following topics:

Responsibilities of the Marketer
Marketers must accept responsibility for the consequences of their activities and make every effort to ensure that their decisions, recommendations, and actions function to identify, serve, and satisfy all relevant publics: consumers, organizations and society. Marketers' professional conduct must be guided by:

1. The basic rule of professional ethics: not knowingly to do harm;
2. The adherence to all applicable laws and regulations;
3. The accurate representation of their education, training and experience; and
4. The active support, practice and promotion of this Code of Ethics.

Honesty and Fairness
Marketers shall uphold and advance the integrity, honor, and dignity of the marketing profession by:

1. Being honest in serving consumers, clients, employees, suppliers, distributors and the public;
2. Not knowingly participating in conflict of interest without prior notice to all parties involved; and

3. Establishing equitable fee schedules including the payment or receipt of usual, customary and/or legal compensation for marketing exchanges

Rights and Duties of Parties
Participants in the marketing exchange process should be able to expect that:

1. Products and services offered are safe and fit for their intended uses;
2. Communications about offered products and services are not deceptive;
3. All parties intend to discharge their obligations, financial and otherwise, in good faith; and
4. Appropriate internal methods exist for equitable adjustment and/or redress of grievances concerning purchases.

It is understood that the above would include, *but is not limited to*, the following responsibilities of the marketer:

In the area of product development management:
Disclosure of all substantial risks associated with product or service usage

Identification of any product component substitution that might materially change the product or impact on the buyer's purchase decision

Identification of extra-cost added features

Figure 3.4 illustrates the concept of maximizing a positive impact on society through advertising. Here Russell Corporation provides a campaign to encourage student athletes to take their education seriously and to graduate.

For example, years ago Anheuser-Busch test-marketed a new adult beverage called Chelsea. Because the beverage contained less than one-half percent alcohol—about the same as apple cider—consumer groups labeled the beverage "kiddie beer" and protested that the company was being socially irresponsible by making an alcoholic drink available to minors. Anheuser-Busch's first reaction was defensive; it tried to claim that the beverage was not dangerous and would not lead children to stronger drink. However, the company later decided to withdraw the beverage from the marketplace and reformulate it so that it would be viewed as more acceptable by society.[31] Social responsibility, then, can be viewed as a contract with society, whereas ethics relate to carefully thought-out rules of moral values that guide individual and group decision making.

Table 3.3 (continued)

In the area of promotions:

Avoidance of false and misleading advertising

Rejection of high pressure manipulations, or misleading sales tactics

Avoidance of sales promotions that use deception or manipulation

In the area of distribution:

Not manipulating the availability of a product for purpose of exploitation

Not using coercion in the marketing channel

Not exerting undue influence over the resellers' choice to handle a product

In the area of pricing:

Not engaging in price fixing

Not practicing predatory pricing

Disclosing the full price associated with any purchase

In the area of marketing research:

Prohibiting selling or fund raising under the guise of conducting research

Maintaining research integrity by avoiding misrepresentation and omission of pertinent research data

Treating outside clients and suppliers fairly

Organizational Relationships

Marketers should be aware of how their behavior may influence or impact on the behavior of others in organizational relationships. They should not encourage or apply coercion to obtain unethical behavior in their relationships with others, such as employees, suppliers or customers.

1. Apply confidentiality and anonymity in professional relationships with regard to privileged information.
2. Meet their obligations and responsibilities in contracts and mutual agreements in a timely manner.
3. Avoid taking the work of others, in whole, or in part, and represent this work as their own or directly benefit from it without compensation or consent of the originator or owner.
4. Avoid manipulation to take advantage of situations to maximize personal welfare in a way that unfairly deprives or damages the organization or others.

Any AMA members found to be in violation of any provision of this Code of Ethics may have his or her Association membership suspended or revoked.

Source: Reprinted by permission of the American Marketing Association.

Impact of Social Responsibility on Marketing

Marketing managers try to determine what accepted relationships, obligations, and duties exist between the marketing organization and society. Recognition is growing that for a firm's survival and competitive advantage, the long-term value of conducting business in a socially responsible manner far outweighs short-terms costs.[32] To preserve socially responsible behavior while achieving organizational goals, organizations must monitor changes and trends in society's values. For example, companies around the world are developing and marketing more nutritional and healthier products in response to increasing public concerns about cancer and heart disease. Furthermore, marketers must develop control procedures to ensure that daily decisions do not damage their company's relations with the public. An organization's top management must assume some responsibility for the employees' conduct by establishing and enforcing policies.

Being socially responsible may be a noble and necessary endeavor, but it is not a simple one. For example, Anheuser-Busch says that, as part of a new direction for its Budweiser beer, it is abandoning the traditional portrayal in beer advertising of women as sex objects. The company says that in its future advertising, women will have equal roles and will be treated in an equal manner. The company claims to have heightened sensitivity to women's changing roles in society.[33] Stroh Brewery Co., on the other hand, decided to advertise its Old Milwaukee beer with the "Swedish Bikini Team." Although the campaign drew a lot of criticism and was even accused of promoting sexual harassment, Stroh's decision to use the campaign seems to indicate that it considers the risk of offending women to be worth taking in light of the fact that men make up the vast majority of the beer market.[34]

Marketers must determine what society wants and then predict the long-run effects of their decisions, often by turning to specialists such as lawyers, doctors, and scientists. However, specialists do not necessarily agree with each other, and the fields in which they work can yield findings that undermine previously acceptable marketing decisions. Forty years ago, for example, tobacco marketers promoted cigarettes as being good for one's health. Now, years after the discovery that cigarette smoking is linked to cancer and other medical problems, society's attitude toward smoking is changing, and marketers are confronted with new social responsibilities, such as providing a smoke-free atmosphere for customers. Most major hotel chains allocate at least some of their rooms for nonsmokers, and most other businesses within the food, travel, and entertainment industries provide smoke-free environments or sections.

Because society is made up of many diverse groups, finding out what society as a whole wants is difficult, if not impossible. In trying to satisfy the desires of one group, marketers may dissatisfy others. For example, in the smoking debate, marketers must balance smokers' desires to continue to smoke cigarettes against nonsmokers' desires for a smoke-free environment.

Moreover, there are costs associated with many of society's demands. For example, society wants a cleaner environment and the preservation of wildlife and habitats, but it also wants low-priced products. Figure 3.5 illustrates how ITT is attempting to renew forests as well as provide its cellulose-based products. Thus, companies must carefully balance the costs of providing low-priced

Figure 3.5

Supporting the Preservation of Natural Resources and Our Physical Environment

ITT seeks to ensure a never-ending supply of wood. Maintaining forests not only provides ITT with future manufacturing resources, it also creates an environment that is beneficial to people and wildlife.

Source: Courtesy ITT Corporation

By the time he's 21, we'll plant 20 million new trees.

We produce something called purified cellulose. A product that goes into making your eyeglass frames. And cosmetics. Your detergent and toothbrush. ITT Rayonier is a leading producer of cellulose from wood, with over 1.2 million acres of timberland. And each year, we renew our forests. Planting new trees to insure a never ending supply of wood. There are nine businesses in ITT. This is the one that helps you live better.

ITT RAYONIER   **ITT**

Table 3.4

Recycling Containers

	Percentage of cans and bottles recycled	
Containers	**1989**	**1990**
Aluminum cans	61%	64%
Aluminum-steel cans	22%	33%
Plastic bottles	28%	29%
Glass bottles	15%	20%

Source: National Soft Drink Association, reported in *USA Today,* Oct. 21, 1991, p. 1A. Copyright 1991, *USA Today.* Reprinted with permission.

products against the costs of manufacturing and packaging their products in an environmentally responsible manner. Recycling is another major issue today. Consumers are increasingly concerned with recycling containers, as shown by the figures in Table 3.4. Therefore, companies must go to the expense of using recycled materials as inputs to their production process and creating recyclable outputs. Balancing society's demands is difficult, if not impossible, to achieve the satisfaction of all members of society. Marketers must also evaluate the extent to which members of society are willing to pay for what they want. For instance, consumers may want more information about a product yet be unwilling to pay the costs the firm incurs in providing the data. Marketers who want to make socially responsible decisions may find the task difficult.

Social Responsibility Issues

Although social responsibility may seem to be an abstract ideal, managers make decisions related to social responsibility on a daily basis. To be successful, a business must determine what customers, government regulators, and competitors, as well as society in general, want or expect in terms of social responsibility. Table 3.5 summarizes three major categories of social responsibility issues: the consumer movement, community relations, and green marketing.

Consumer Movement   One of the most significant social responsibility issues in marketing is the consumer movement, which Chapter 2 defines as the efforts of independent individuals, groups, and organizations to protect the rights of consumers. A number of interest groups and individuals have taken actions such as lobbying government officials and agencies, letter-writing campaigns, public service announcements, and boycotts of companies they consider irresponsible.

Ralph Nader, one of the best-known consumer activists, continues to crusade for consumer rights. Consumer activism on the part of Nader and others has resulted in legislation requiring various safety features in cars: seat belts, padded dashboards, stronger door latches, head restraints, shatter-proof windshields, and collapsible steering columns. Activists' efforts have helped facilitate the passage of several consumer protection laws, such as the Wholesome Meat Act of 1967, the Radiation Control for Health and Safety Act of 1968, the Clean Water Act of 1972, and the Toxic Substance Act of 1976.

Also of great importance to the consumer movement are four basic rights spelled out in a consumer "bill of rights" drafted by President John F. Kennedy. These rights include the right to safety, the right to be informed, the right to choose, and the right to be heard.

Ensuring consumers' right to safety means that marketers have an obligation not to market knowingly a product that could harm consumers. This right can be extended to the idea that all products must be safe for their intended use, must include thorough and explicit instructions for proper and safe use, and must have been tested to ensure reliability and quality.

Consumers' right to be informed means that consumers should have access to and the opportunity to review all relevant information about a product before buying it. Many laws have been passed that require specific labeling on product packaging to satisfy this right. In addition, labels on alcoholic and tobacco products inform consumers that these products may cause illness and other problems.

The right to choose means that consumers must also have access to a variety of products and services at competitive prices. This means that they should be assured of satisfactory quality and service at a fair price. Activities that reduce competition among businesses in an industry jeopardize this right of consumers.

The right to be heard assures consumers that their interests will receive full and sympathetic consideration in the formulation of government policy. For

Table 3.5   **Social Responsibility Issues**

Issue	Description	Major Societal Concerns
Consumer Movement	Activities undertaken by independent individuals, groups, and organizations to protect their rights as consumers	The right to safety The right to be informed The right to choose The right to be heard
Community Relations	Society anxious to have marketers contribute to its well-being, wishing to know what businesses do to help solve social problems Communities demanding that firms listen to their grievances and ideas	Equality issues Disadvantaged members of society Safety and health Education and general welfare
Green Marketing	Consumers insisting not only on the quality of life but also on a healthful environment so that they can maintain a high standard of living during their lifetimes	Conservation Water pollution Air pollution Land pollution

example, when the Federal Communications Commission (FCC) was considering alternatives, including reregulation, to improve competition within the cable television industry, it invited comments from interest groups and the public.[35] The right to be heard also promises consumers fair treatment when they complain to marketers about their products. This right benefits marketers, too, because when consumers complain to manufacturers about a product, this information can help them modify the product to make it more satisfying.

Community Relations Social responsibility also extends to marketers' roles as community members. Individual communities expect marketers to contribute to the satisfaction and growth of their communities. Thus many marketers view social responsibility as including contributions of resources (money, products, time) to community causes such as education, the arts, recreation, disadvantaged members of the community, and others. Philip Morris, for example, sponsors several programs that focus on art and music. Shearson Lehman Hutton, a division of American Express, founded Project Access to Computer Training (PACT), a program that prepares qualified physically handicapped persons for computer-related jobs. Honeywell, Shell Oil, Ogilvy & Mather, Aetna Life and Casualty, and Hewlett-Packard all have programs that contribute funds, equipment, and personnel to educational reform. Similarly, IBM donates or reduces the price of computer equipment to educational institutions. All these efforts, of course, have a positive impact on local communities, but they also indirectly help the organizations in the form of good will, publicity, and exposure to potential future customers. Thus, although social responsibility is certainly a positive concept, most organizations do not embrace it without the expectation of some indirect long-term benefit.

Green Marketing **Green marketing** refers to the specific development, pricing, promotion, and distribution of products that do not harm the environment. For example, Figure 3.6 promotes Exxon Phase IV gasoline, which is designed to reduce air pollution. The Alliance for Social Responsibility, an independent coalition of environmentalists, scientists, ethicists, and marketers, is one group involved in evaluating products to determine their environmental impact and marketers' commitment to the environment. Several environmental groups have also joined together to create a seal of approval to distinguish products that are environmentally safe. Companies receiving the green seal will be able to use it in advertising and public information campaigns and on packaging.[36]

Developing a green marketing program is not easy, however. Procter & Gamble's experience in marketing its new Downy fabric softener refill product is a case in point. Although the Downy refill package does not carry a green label designation, it manifests the company's environmentally responsible approach: The product has 75 percent less packaging material (which does not waste resources and takes up less space in landfills). However, the Consumer Product Safety Commission has questioned the safety of the new Downy refill package because it is pint-sized and resembles a milk carton. The commission deems it inappropriate to package a household chemical in a container that children might confuse with a milk carton. Procter & Gamble claims that Downy is not hazardous and may cause only mild nausea if ingested.[37] Public approval of the refill product can be seen in the fact that, as of 1991, 40 percent of all Downy fabric softener sales were for the refill box.[38] This example illustrates the difficulty of being environmentally responsible in packaging and satisfying the concerns of all members of society at the same time. In addition, varying state legislation, especially regarding what can be said on labels about environmental impact, is making it difficult for businesses to implement green marketing. For example, New York City consumer affairs commissioner Mark Green challenged "environment friendly" claims about aerosol products marketed by Procter & Gamble, S.C. Johnson & Son, Gillette, and Revlon, charging that the claims were misleading and threatened the companies with civil lawsuits.[39]

As consumers have become more concerned about the effects of their buying actions on the natural environment, businesses have been attempting to exploit those concerns in their marketing strategies. Inside Marketing describes Wal-Mart's successful green marketing program in response to a marketing survey that showed customers were concerned about the environmental impact of the products they purchased and were willing to pay extra for environmentally safe ones. However, a recent study showed that U.S. consumers don't always buy the products that they claim to prefer. People who have positive attitudes toward green marketing and prefer environmentally conscious products are more likely to consume in line with those attitudes but in the end are still more likely to use the most convenient product when there is no efficient alternative. Attitude

Figure 3.6

Green Marketing

Exxon practices green marketing by researching and developing new petroleum products that are less harmful to the environment.

Source: Westlight Company/Courtesy of Exxon

Wal-Mart Focuses on "Green" Marketing

WITH A NEW ECOLOGICAL AWARENESS, consumers today want their environment protected from pollutants, toxins, and exploitation. Environmental, or "green," marketing is a way for marketers to appeal to this environmental concern. Green products are safer for the environment and include such items as packaging made from recycled paper and plastics and detergents that are free of phosphates. By effectively marketing such products, companies like Wal-Mart can improve their profits as well as the biosphere.

Wal-Mart Stores, Inc., was among the first businesses to embrace the notion of green marketing. The fastest-growing retailer in the United States and an influential leader in the retailing industry, Wal-Mart wants to offer shoppers the option of purchasing environmentally safe products instead of ones that contribute to pollution and landfill problems. The company makes a conscious effort to stock merchandise that is better for the environment in three respects—manufacturing, use, and disposal.

To promote environmentally safer products, Wal-Mart places green tags next to products that have undergone environmental improvements so that customers will be drawn to them. Wal-Mart knows that environmental issues affect everyday decisions: A survey of one thousand adults found that 77 percent were willing to pay extra for a product packaged with recyclable or biodegradable materials. More than 53 percent stated that they had not bought a particular product in the last year because they worried about that product's effect on the environment. Because Wal-Mart customers have become concerned about the quality of land, air, and water, the company wants to give them the opportunity to do something positive.

Additionally, Wal-Mart is setting up recycling centers in the parking lots of its 1,511 stores so that consumers have a place to dispose of their recyclable waste. Profits earned from the recycling centers are donated to United Way. Taking its own message to heart, company headquarters has reduced the amount of waste sent to landfills by 80 percent.

To help guide the company in the right direction, Wal-Mart has set up an environmental advisory board. One Wal-Mart executive says that environmental issues are bigger than retailing and consequently should not be made a competitive issue among retailers; instead, all retailers should do what they can to help the planet.

Sources: Christy Fisher, "Tending Wal-Mart's Green Policy," *Advertising Age,* Jan. 29, 1991, pp. 20, 22; Kevin Maney, "Companies Make Products Nicer to Nature," *USA Today,* Aug. 23, 1989, pp. 1B–2B; Christy Fisher and Judith Graham, "Wal-Mart Throws 'Green' Gauntlet," *Advetising Age,* Aug. 21, 1989, pp. 1, 66; and Jeremy Main, "Here Comes the Big New Cleanup," *Fortune,* Nov. 21, 1988, pp. 102–103, 106, 110, 112, 114, 118.

toward environmental consciousness seems to have a limited effect on consumer behavior.[40]

Strategies for Dealing with Social Responsibility Issues

There are four basic strategies for systematically dealing with social responsibility issues: reaction, defense, accommodation, and proaction.

Reaction Strategy   A business adopting a **reaction strategy** allows a condition or potential problem to go unresolved until the public learns about it. The situation may be known to management (as were one car maker's problems with gas tank combustibility) or it may be unknown (as was the sudden acceleration of the Audi 5000 without direct action from the driver). In either case, the business denies responsibility but tries to resolve the problem, deal with its consequences, and continue doing business as usual to minimize the negative impact.

Defense Strategy A business using a **defense strategy** tries to minimize or avoid additional obligations linked to a problem or problems. Commonly used defense tactics include legal maneuvering and seeking the support of trade unions that embrace the company's way of doing business and support the industry. Businesses often lobby to avoid government action or regulation. For example, Advo, a direct-mail firm, lobbied against an increase in bulk postal rates because it knew it would have to pass on these increases to its clients, advertisers, and advertising agencies. The company realized that sizable increases in postal rates could put it at a competitive disadvantage in relation to print media, such as newspaper inserts, which do not use the U.S. Postal Service. Thus Advo took a defensive position to protect its own and its clients' interests.

Accommodation Strategy A business using an **accommodation strategy** assumes responsibility for its actions. A business might adopt the accommodation strategy when special-interest groups are encouraging a particular action or when the business perceives that if it fails to react, Congress will pass a law to ensure compliance.

For example, McDonald's developed a nutrition-oriented advertising campaign to appease dietitians and nutritionists who had urged legal action in several states to require that accurate nutritional information be provided on all fast-food products. However, McDonald's campaign, instead of soothing the interest groups, riled them up. The groups claim that McDonald's portrayal of its food as healthful was inaccurate. A McDLT, fries, and shake contain 1,283 calories, approximately 60 percent of the entire recommended daily calorie intake for an adult woman. In addition, that meal contains 15 teaspoons of fat, 10 teaspoons of sugar, no fiber, and approximately 70 percent of the daily allowance of sodium. Dietitians and nutritionists petitioned the U.S. Food and Drug Administration in the hope that it would require product nutritional labeling to alert consumers to the high levels of fat, sodium, and sugar and low levels of starch and fiber.[41] McDonald's chose to take an accommodation strategy to curtail lobbying against nutritional information disclosure when it probably should have adopted a proactive strategy.

Proactive Strategy A business that uses a **proactive strategy** assumes responsibility for its actions and responds to accusations made against it without outside pressure or the threat of government intervention. A proactive strategy requires management, of its own free will, to support an action or cause. For example, in 1990, Coca-Cola and PepsiCo switched to bottles made from recycled plastic, making theirs the first food products to come in direct contact with recycled plastic packaging.[42] In another proactive move, the bottlers of Artesia water changed their label and logo—a picture of a mountain stream—out of concern that consumers would think the water came from a mountain stream. The bottled water actually comes from the same underground aquifer as the municipal drinking water of San Antonio, Texas.[43]

Social Responsibility and Marketing Ethics

Although the concepts of marketing ethics and social responsibility are often used interchangeably, it is important to remember that ethics relate to individual moral evaluations—judgments about what is right or wrong in a particular decision-making situation. Social responsibility is the obligation of an organization to maximize its positive impact and minimize its negative impact on society. Thus social responsibility deals with the total effect of marketing decisions on society. These two concepts work together because a company that supports both socially responsible decisions and individuals who act ethically is likely to have a positive impact on society.

One way to evaluate whether a specific behavior is ethical and socially responsible is to ask other persons in an organization if they approve of a specific behavior. For social responsibility issues, contact with concerned consumer groups and industry or government regulatory groups may be helpful. Also a check to see if there is a specific company policy about the activity may resolve the issue. If other persons in the organization approve of the activity and it is legal and customary within the industry, chances are the activity is acceptable from both an ethical and social responsibility perspective.

A rule of thumb for ethical and social responsibility issues is that if they can withstand open discussion and result in agreements or limited debate, then an acceptable solution may exist. Nevertheless, even after a final decision is reached, different viewpoints on the issue may remain. Openness is not the end-all solution to the ethics problem. However, it does create trust and facilitates learning relationships.[44]

Summary

Marketing ethics are moral principles that define right and wrong behavior in marketing. Most marketing decisions can be judged as ethical or unethical. Ethics are a very important concern in marketing decisions, yet ethics may be one of the most misunderstood and controversial concepts in marketing.

Personal moral philosophies, organizational factors, and opportunity are three important components of ethical decision making. Moral philosophies are principles or rules that individuals use to determine the right way to behave. They provide guidelines for resolving conflicts and ensuring mutual benefit for all members of society. Utilitarian moral philosophies are concerned with maximizing the greatest good for the greatest number of people. Ethical formalism philosophies, on the other hand, focus on general rules for guiding behavior and on the rights of the individual. Organizational relationships with one's employees or superiors create ethical problems, such as maintaining confidentiality in personal relations; meeting obligations, responsibilities, and mutual agreements; and avoiding undue pressure that may force others to behave unethically. Opportunity—a favorable set of conditions that limits barriers or provides internal or external rewards—to engage in unethical behavior provides another pressure that may determine whether a person behaves ethically. If an individual uses an opportunity afforded him or her to act unethically and escapes punishment or even gains a reward, that person is more likely to repeat such acts when circumstances favor them.

An ethical issue is an identifiable problem, situation, or opportunity requiring an individual or organization to choose from among alternatives that must be evaluated as right or wrong. Ethical issues typically arise because of conflicts among individuals' personal moral philosophies and the marketing strategies, policies, and the organizational environment in which they work. Product-related ethical issues may develop when marketers fail to disclose risks associated with the product or information that relates to understanding the function, value, or use of the product. Competitive pressures can also create product-related ethical issues. The promotion process provides situations that can result in ethical issues, such as false and misleading advertising and deceptive sales tactics. Sales promotions and publicity that use deception or manipulation also create significant ethical issues. Bribery may be an ethical issue in some selling situations. The emotional and subjective nature of price creates conditions in which misunderstandings between the seller and buyer lead to ethical problems. Ethical issues in distribution relate to conflicts among producers and marketing middlemen.

Codes of ethics, which formalize what an organization expects of its employees, eliminate the opportunity for unethical behavior because they provide rules to guide conduct and punishments for violating the rules. If the number of employees making ethical decisions on a regular basis is not satisfactory, the company needs to determine why and take corrective action through enforcement. Enforcement of an organization's standards is what makes codes of ethics effective.

Social responsibility in marketing refers to an organization's obligation to maximize its positive impact and minimize its negative impact on society. Marketing managers try to determine what accepted relationships, obligations, and duties exist between the business organization and society.

To be successful, a business must determine what customers, government regulators, and competitors, as well as society in general, want or expect in terms of social responsibility. Major categories of social responsibility issues include the consumer movement, community relations, and green marketing. The consumer movement refers to the activities of independent individuals, groups, and organizations in trying to protect the rights of consumers. Communities expect marketers to contribute to the satisfaction and growth of their communities. Green marketing refers to the specific development, pricing, promotion, and distribution of products that do not harm the environment.

Four basic strategies for dealing with social responsibility issues are reaction, defense, accommodation, and proaction. A business adopting a reaction strategy allows a condition or potential problem to go unresolved until the public learns about it. A business using the defense strategy tries to minimize or avoid additional obligations associated with a problem or problems. In the accommodation strategy, a business assumes responsibility for its actions. A business that uses the proactive strategy assumes responsibility for its actions and responds to accusations made against it without outside pressure or the threat of government intervention.

The concepts of marketing ethics and social responsibility work together because a company that has a corporate culture built on socially acceptable moral philosophies with individuals who have good personal values will generally make decisions that have a positive impact on society. If other persons in the organization approve of an activity and it is legal and customary within the industry, chances are the activity is acceptable from both an ethical and social responsibility perspective.

Important Terms

Marketing ethics	Green marketing
Moral philosophies	Reaction strategy
Ethical issue	Defense strategy
Codes of ethics	Accommodation strategy
Social responsibility	Proactive strategy

Discussion and Review Questions

1. Why is ethics an important consideration in marketing decisions?
2. How do the factors that influence ethical or unethical decisions interact?
3. What ethical conflicts could exist if business employees fly certain airlines just to receive benefits for their personal "frequent flier" program?
4. What are some of the areas that result in major ethical issues in marketing?
5. How can ethical decisions in marketing be improved?
6. How can people with different personal values join together to make ethical decisions in an organization?
7. What is the difference between ethics and social responsibility?
8. What are major social responsibility issues?
9. Describe strategies for dealing with social responsibility issues.
10. How do you determine when a gift or payment is a bribe in marketing?

Cases

3.1 Beech-Nut Sells Fake Apple Juice

Beech-Nut Nutrition Corporation is the second-largest manufacturer of baby food in the United States and has long enjoyed a reputation for quality and purity. The company's Beech-Nut apple juice was labeled and promoted as 100 percent fruit juice and touted as "good nutrition that tastes good." Unfortunately for Beech-Nut, its reputation was tarnished in the mid-1980s when the company was indicted for selling adulterated apple juice—that is, juice made from ingredients different from those specified, or from artificial ingredients.

Beech-Nut Nutrition Corp. began as a division of Squibb Corp. but was sold in 1973 to a group headed by entrepreneur Frank Nicholas. Nicholas and his partners bought the company in a leveraged buyout and were forced to operate Beech-Nut on a very limited budget. Under Nicholas's leadership, the company began to experience financial difficulties. Although Beech-Nut commanded 15 percent of the baby food market, its main competitor, Gerber Products Co., held 70 percent. Beech-Nut could not compete with Gerber's huge marketing budget and found it difficult to capture any more of the market.

In 1977 Interjuice Trading Corporation offered to sell apple juice concentrate at 20 percent below market price to Beech-Nut. Because apple juice products accounted for 30 percent of Beech-Nut's sales, its executives believed that buying the cheap concentrate could save the troubled company millions of dollars a year and improve its financial picture. So, Beech-Nut began buying the concentrate, but its financial problems persisted. In 1979, the company was sold to Nestlé S.A.

Suspicious of the low-cost concentrate, Beech-Nut chemists began testing the apple concentrate for purity. They soon determined that the concentrate contained beet sugar, apple flavor, caramel color, and corn syrup. When two Beech-

Nut employees were denied entry into Interjuice's concentrate-processing facility, their suspicions about the concentrate's purity increased. With this evidence, the director of research and development at Beech-Nut, Jerome LiCari, sent a memo to senior Beech-Nut executives, expressing his concerns about the purity of the apple concentrate. Senior executives at Beech-Nut, still under severe pressure to improve the company's financial position, failed to act on LiCari's information. When LiCari took his evidence of adulteration to the chief operating officer and president of the organization, the company threatened to fire him, and he eventually resigned in frustration.

In 1982, the Processed Apple Institute began investigating widespread rumors of apple juice adulteration in the industry. Investigators warned Beech-Nut that Interjuice's apple concentrate was adulterated and asked the company to join with other concentrate buyers in a lawsuit against Interjuice and other producers of adulterated concentrate. Beech-Nut refused, missing an opportunity to limit its liability.

Beech-Nut did cancel its contracts with Interjuice Trading Company, but it continued to sell apple juice made from the concentrate it had already purchased. Only after the Food and Drug Administration and the New York State Agriculture Department investigated and found that Beech-Nut's apple juice was indeed adulterated did the company recall the product.

At first, government investigators assumed that Beech-Nut had been a victim of unscrupulous dealers. But further investigation revealed evidence that Beech-Nut was aware of the adulteration, the most telling of which was Jerome LiCari's memo. In one instance, when the company learned that the Food and Drug Administration was about to seize a shipment of the adulterated apple juice, the company destroyed it to avoid the negative publicity that might have resulted from such a seizure.

In 1986, Beech-Nut and two top executives were indicted on 470 counts. The company pleaded guilty to 215 felony counts and willful violations of food and drug laws in 1987, and paid a $2.2 million fine. Charges against the top executives are still pending. In addition, five suppliers of adulterated apple juice concentrate were convicted and fined.

Beech-Nut tried to save money by using the low-cost concentrate, even after the company learned that the concentrate was not 100 percent apple juice. Ironically, the ensuing investigation and indictments cost the company more than $25 million in fines, legal fees, and lost sales. Beech-Nut's share of the juice market dropped 20 percent, and the company sustained near-record losses. Several years later, it still had not recovered from the damage caused by the scandal, and Nestlé sold Beech-Nut to Ralston Purina.[45]

Questions for Discussion

1. What are some of the important ethical issues in this case?
2. What are the key factors that influenced Beech-Nut's decision to continue the purchase of low-cost, artificial apple juice?
3. Discuss strategies for dealing with social responsibility issues and identify the strategy that Beech-Nut used. Which strategy would have been more effective?

3.2 Ben & Jerry's Homemade Balances Social Responsibility and Growth

Ben Greenfield and Jerry Cohen opened their first scoop shop in a converted gas station in Burlington, Vermont, in 1977, investing $12,000 in some second-hand equipment. Their rich, all-natural ice cream, full of sweet crunchy bits of cookies and candies, soon became popular. Before long they were packaging more and more ice cream to sell in local restaurants and grocery stores, gaining shelf space in 150 stores across the state. By 1990, Ben & Jerry's Homemade, Inc., topped $70 million in sales on six million gallons of ice cream; it projected sales of $91.5 million for 1991. Cohen and Greenfield have made it their business not just to taste sweet success but to give something back to their employees, their community, and the world at large.

With the company's rapid growth came questions and crises for the two "hippies" who never envisioned themselves in business suits. When Cohen and Greenfield first went into business together, they decided to write their own rules. Among these was a corporate mission statement focusing on the firm's social responsibilities: to initiate "innovative ways to improve the quality of life of a broad community—local, national, and international." But by the early 1980s, they feared their company's growth was out of control and veering away from their 1960s values; Jerry Greenfield even dropped out of the business for a time. When Cohen considered selling the company, a friend pointed out to him that he could make it into whatever he wanted. He soon developed the concept of "caring capitalism," which meant putting part of the company's profits into worthy causes, as well as finding creative ways to improve the quality of life of the firm's employees and the local community. Greenfield rejoined the company soon after.

When the company went public in 1984 as Ben & Jerry's Homemade, Inc., Cohen made it a statewide offering, with the idea that if local residents were part owners of the firm, the community would prosper as the business did. Then, in 1985, Cohen set up the Ben & Jerry's Foundation, which is dedicated to facilitating social change through the donation of 7.5 percent of Ben & Jerry's yearly pretax profits.

Ben & Jerry's social concern can be seen in many of the company's products. One of the firm's ventures is the Peace Pop, an ice cream bar on a stick, from which 1 percent of the profits are used to build awareness of and raise funds for peace. To help preserve endangered rainforests, the company purchases rainforest nuts for its Rainforest Crunch ice cream. It also buys brownies made by homeless people for its Chocolate Fudge Brownie and Brownie Bars.

Cohen and Greenfield extend their social awareness to their own employees as well. A seven-to-one salary ratio at the firm limits the salaries of top executives to seven times those earned by the lowest-paid workers. This helps give all employees a sense of working together as a team. And, when the company expanded nationally, perhaps too quickly (it went from 150 people to 300 almost overnight), executives made a conscious decision to slow growth to ensure that the plant's family atmosphere and the company's core values would not be lost. Employees also get three pints of ice cream a day, free health club memberships, and a partially subsidized company child care center.

Today, Ben & Jerry's continues to promote causes and events of value to the community rather than purchase advertising on television, radio, or in newspapers. The company sponsors peace, music, and art festivals around the country and tries to draw attention to the many social causes it undertakes. One such cause is opposition to bovine growth hormone (a substance injected into cows to increase milk production) because Greenfield and Cohen fear that its use will drive small dairy farmers out of business. A local venture is the Giraffe Project, which recognizes people willing to stick their own necks out and stand tall for what they believe; recipients of Giraffe Commendations are nominated by local customers at Ben & Jerry's ice cream shops.

Each year, Ben & Jerry's conducts a social audit to measure whether the company is fulfilling its self-stated obligations. Nonetheless, the company will continue to struggle in its efforts to balance growth and profits with social responsibility. And Ben & Jerry's customers—mostly twenty-five to forty-five-year-olds—will continue to buy its ice cream so that they may feel that they are doing something good for society.[46]

1. For some people, social responsibility is an abstract idea. How did Ben & Jerry's develop a company social responsibility philosophy?
2. How has Ben & Jerry's used its social responsibility philosophy to deal with issues like employee relations and consumer relations?
3. What type of social responsibility strategy does Ben & Jerry's use?

Chapter Notes

1. Based on information from Laura Jereski, "Can Paul Fireman Put the Bounce Back in Reebok?" *Business Week,* June 18, 1990, pp. 181–182; Bob Garfield, "Good Taste Takes Deep Dive in Bungee Ad for Reebok Pump," *Advertising Age,* Mar. 26, 1990, p. 52; Pat Sloan and Cleveland Horton, "Costly Controversies," *Advertising Age,* Mar. 26, 1990, pp. 1, 52; and Marcy Mageira, "Nike Edges Reebok, L.A. Gear Sprinting," *Advertising Age,* Sept. 25, 1989, p. 93.
2. Donald P. Robin and R. Eric Reidenbach, "Social Responsibility, Ethics in Marketing Strategy, Closing the Gap Between Concept and Application," *Journal of Marketing,* Jan. 1987, pp. 44–58.
3. Vernon R. Loucks, Jr., "A CEO Looks at Ethics," *Business Horizons,* Mar.–Apr. 1987, p. 4.
4. Rinler Buck, "Super Mario Fiasco," *Adweek's Marketing Week,* Sept. 30, 1991, p. 8.
5. James R. Rest, *Moral Development Advances in Research and Theory* (New York: Praeger, 1986), p. 1.
6. "CNN Worldday," Cable News Network (TV), Jan. 5, 1990.
7. F. Neil Brady, *Ethical Managing: Rules and Results* (New York: Macmillan, 1990), pp. 4–6.
8. O. C. Ferrell and Larry G. Gresham, "A Contingency Framework for Understanding Ethical Decision Making in Marketing," *Journal of Marketing,* Summer 1985, p. 90.
9. Ibid.
10. John Fraedrich, "Philosophy Type Interaction in the Ethical Decision Making Process of Retailers" (Ph.D. diss., Texas A&M University, 1988).
11. William C. Frederick and James Weber, "The Value of Corporate Managers and Their Critics: An Empirical Description and Normative Implications," in *Research in Corporate Social Performance and Social Responsibility,* ed. William C. Frederick and Lee E. Preston (Greenwich, Conn.: JAI Press, 1987), pp. 149–150.
12. O. C. Ferrell, Larry G. Gresham, and John Fraedrich, "A Synthesis of Ethical Decision Models for Marketing," *Journal of Macromarketing,* Fall 1989, pp. 58–59.

13. Ferrell and Gresham, p. 92.
14. Kevin Kelly, "When a Rival's Trade Secret Crosses Your Desk . . . ," *Business Week,* May 20, 1991, p. 48.
15. Fara Warner, "What Happened to the Truth?," *AdWeek's Marketing Week,* Oct. 28, 1991, p. 4.
16. Jennifer Lawrence, "P&G Gives In, Axes Its 'Fresh' Label," *Advertising Age,* Apr. 29, 1991, p. 1.
17. Warner, p. 5.
18. Scott Hume, "Squawk over KFC Ads—Company Challenges Y&R with New Strategy," *Advertising Age,* Jan. 15, 1990, p. 16.
19. Jennifer Lawrence, "Mobil," *Advertising Age,* Jan. 29, 1991, p. 12.
20. Archie B. Carroll, *Business and Society: Ethics and Stakeholder Management* (Cincinnati: South-Western Publishing, 1989), pp. 228–230.
21. Imperial Oil Limited, "Our Corporate Ethics," Toronto, Canada.
22. John R. Wilke and Mary Lu Carnevale, "Wrong Numbers: Nynex Overcharged Phone Units for Years, An FCC Audit Finds," *Wall Street Journal,* Jan. 9, 1990, pp. A1, A10.
23. Bruce Hager, "What's Behind Business's Sudden Fervor for Ethics?" *Business Week,* Sept. 23, 1991, p. 65.
24. Paul M. Barrett, "Nintendo-Atari Zapping Contest Goes to Washington," *Wall Street Journal,* Dec. 8, 1989, pp. B1, B4.
25. Karen Blumenthal, "A Few Big Retailers Rebuff Middlemen," *Wall Street Journal,* Oct. 21, 1986, p. 6.
26. Linda K. Trevino and Stuart Youngblood, "Bad Apples in Bad Barrels: A Causal Analysis of Ethical Decision Making Behavior," *Journal of Applied Psychology,* 1990.
27. Trevino and Youngblood, pp. 378–385.
28. Hager, p. 65.
29. Neil Herndon, "Commitment, Satisfaction and Turnover: The Impact of Individual Moral Structures When Exposed to a Conflicting or Matching Organizational Sales Culture" (Ph.D. diss., Texas A&M University, 1991), p. 201.
30. Robin and Reidenbach, pp. 44–58.
31. Carroll, p. 45.
32. Margaret A. Stroup, Ralph L. Newbert, and Jerry W. Anderson, Jr., "Doing Good, Doing Better: Two Views of Social Responsibility," *Business Horizons,* Mar.–Apr. 1987, p. 23.
33. Ira Teinowitz, "This Bud's for Her: Women to Get Equal Roles in New A-B Campaign," *Advertising Age,* Oct. 28, 1991, pp. 1, 49.
34. John P. Cortez and Ira Teinowitz, "More Trouble Brews for Stroh Bikini Team," *Advertising Age,* Dec. 9, 1991, p. 45.
35. Mary Lu Carnevale, "FCC Votes to Examine Cable-TV Rules, with an Eye on Beefing Up Competition," *Wall Street Journal,* Jan. 12, 1990, p. A3.
36. Christy Fisher, "Seal of Green Planned: Environmental Group to Give Product Approvals," *Advertising Age,* Nov. 20, 1989, p. 3.
37. Laurie Freeman, "Gov't Questions Downy Refill," *Advertising Age,* Nov. 20, 1989, p. 40.
38. Alice Z. Cuneo, "States Turn Marketers Sour on Green Pitches," *Advertising Age,* Nov. 4, 1991, p. 2.
39. "Spurts and Starts: Corporate Role in the 90's Environmentalism Hardly Consistent," *Advertising Age,* Oct. 28, 1991, p. GR16.
40. Joe Mandese, "New Study Finds Green Confusion," *Advertising Age,* Oct. 21, 1991, pp. 1, 56.
41. "McD Ads Draw Protests From Nutritional Experts," *Nation's Restaurant News,* June 22, 1987, p. 26.
42. "Spurts and Starts," *Advertising Age,* Oct. 28, 1991, p. GR15.

43. Alison Fahey, "H20 Marketers Mop Damage," *Advertising Age,* April 15, 1991, p. 49.
44. Sir Adrian Cadbury, "Ethical Managers Make Their Own Rules," *Harvard Business Review,* Sept.–Oct. 1987, p. 33.
45. Alix M. Freedman, "Nestlé Quietly Seeks to Sell Beech-Nut, Dogged by Scandal of Bogus Apple Juice," *Wall Street Journal,* July 6, 1989, p. B1; Betty Wong, "Conviction of Nestlé Unit's Ex-President Is Overturned on Appeal in Juice Case," *Wall Street Journal,* Mar. 31, 1989, p. B5; and Chris Welles, "What Led Beech-Nut Down the Road to Disgrace," *Business Week,* Feb. 22, 1988, pp. 124–128.
46. Maxine Lipner, "Ben & Jerry's: Sweet Ethics Evince Social Awareness," *COMPASS Readings,* July 1991, pp. 22–30; Eric J. Wieffering, "Trouble in Camelot," *Business Ethics,* Jan./Feb. 1991, pp. 16–19; and Erik Larson, "Forever Young," *INC.,* July 1988, pp. 50–62.

4 *Target Markets: Segmentation and Evaluation*

OBJECTIVES

- To understand the definition of a market

- To recognize the types of markets

- To learn how firms segment target markets

- To gain an understanding of sales potential

- To become familiar with sales forecasting methods

Two Texas women are taking advantage of the trend of both spouses working outside the home and smaller household size for a variety of family types. After developing a reputation in Brenham, Texas, for catering delicious nutritious meals, Virginia and Barbara Gaskamp incorporated into Market Place Casseroles to sell their homemade, family-sized frozen casseroles.

Barbara and Virginia Gaskamp (they're married to cousins) first analyzed market opportunities and targeted a specific group of consumers. They realized that today's busy families often do not have the time to prepare nutritious meals. Instead, they often purchase frozen dinners that go directly from freezer to microwave or oven in just minutes. The Gaskamps recognized that dual-income families would be willing to purchase family-sized, easy-to-prepare nutritious meals if they were a good value. Market Place Casseroles accordingly come in one- or two-pound family sizes, as well as single-serving microwavable packages, and are priced competitively with other frozen-dinner products. The casseroles have been successful thus far because of their convenient size and because they are home-cooked with high-quality ingredients and are promoted on that basis.

Market Place Casseroles grew out of the Gaskamps' Brenham catering business, which was particularly famous for its chicken spaghetti. The Gaskamps were soon making large batches of chicken spaghetti, freezing them, and selling them. They added more Texas-style recipes—King Ranch–styled chicken, tamale bake, and beef enchilada casserole, to name but a few—then added a freezer, and, finally moved to a larger building.

At first the Gaskamps sold Market Place Casseroles out of a small retail shop in Brenham, but they soon began distributing the casseroles to stores in central Texas. They do not want to expand their distribution area too quickly because they want to maintain the quality on which they have built their reputation. Although they are a small business, in 1991, Market Place Casseroles had sales of approximately $1 million.[1]

Photo: Market Place Casseroles

E VEN A SMALL-BUSINESS MARKETER such as Market Place Casseroles identifies or singles out groups of customers for its products and directs some or all of its marketing activities at those groups. It develops and maintains a marketing mix (a product, a distribution system, promotion, and price) that effectively satisfies the needs of customers in those groups.

In this chapter we explore markets and market segmentation. We first define the term *market* and describe the major types of markets. Then we examine the approaches and strategies typically used to select target markets, and the numerous variables commonly used to segment markets. Next we discuss market measurement and evaluation. Finally, we describe the primary sales forecasting techniques.

What Are Markets?

The word *market* has a number of meanings. People sometimes use it to refer to a specific location where products are bought and sold—for example, a flea market. A large geographic area may also be called a market. Sometimes the word refers to the relationship between the supply and demand of a specific product, as in the question "How is the market for low-fat food products?" At times, *market* is used as a verb to mean the act of selling something.

In this book, a **market** denotes an aggregate of people who, as individuals or as organizations, have needs for products in a product class and who have the ability, willingness, and authority to purchase such products. In general use, the term *market* sometimes refers to the total population—or mass market—that buys products. However, our definition is more specific; it refers to persons seeking products in a specific product category. For example, students are part of the market for textbooks, as well as the markets for calculators, pens and pencils, paper, food, music, and other products. Obviously, there are many different markets in our complex economy. In this section we discuss the requirements for a market and the general types of markets.

Requirements for a Market

For a group of people to be a market, it must meet the following four requirements:

1. The people must need or want a particular product. If they do not, then that group is not a market.
2. The people in the group must have the ability to purchase the product. Ability to purchase is a function of their buying power, which consists of resources, such as money, goods, and services, that can be traded in an exchange situation.
3. The people in the group must be willing to use their buying power.
4. The people in the group must have the authority to buy the specific products.

Individuals can have the desire, the buying power, and the willingness to purchase certain products but may not be authorized to do so. For example, high school students may have the desire, the money, and the willingness to buy alcoholic beverages, but a liquor producer does not consider them a market because until students are twenty-one years old, they are prohibited by law from buying alcoholic beverages. An aggregate of people that lacks any one of the four requirements thus does not constitute a market.

Types of Markets

Markets can be divided into two categories: consumer markets and organizational or business-to-business markets. These categories are based on the characteristics of the individuals and groups that make up a specific market and the purposes for which they buy products. A **consumer market** consists of purchasers and/or individuals in their households who intend to consume or benefit from the purchased products and who do not buy products for the main purpose of making a profit. Each of us belongs to numerous consumer markets for such products as housing, food, clothing, vehicles, personal services, appliances, furniture, and recreational equipment. Consumer markets are discussed in more detail in Chapter 5.

An **organizational**, or **business-to-business**, **market** consists of individuals or groups that purchase a specific kind of product for one of three purposes: resale, direct use in producing other products, or use in general daily operations. The four categories of organizational, or business-to-business, markets—producer, reseller, government, and institutional—are discussed in Chapter 6.

Selecting Target Markets

In Chapter 1 we say that a marketing strategy has two components: (1) the selection of the organization's target market and (2) the creation and maintenance of a marketing mix that satisfies that market's needs for a specific product. Regardless of the general types of markets on which a firm focuses, marketing management must select the firm's target markets. The next section examines two general approaches to identifying target markets: the total market approach and market segmentation.

Total Market, or Undifferentiated, Approach

An organization sometimes defines the entire market for a particular product as its target market. When a company designs a single marketing mix and directs it at the entire market for a particular product, it is using a **total market,** or **undifferentiated, approach,** shown in Figure 4.1. This approach assumes that all customers in the target market for a specific kind of product have similar needs and, therefore, that the organization can satisfy most customers with a single marketing mix. This single marketing mix consists of one type of product with little or no variation, one price, one promotional program aimed at everybody, and one distribution system to reach all customers in the total market. Products that can be marketed successfully through the total market approach

Figure 4.1

Total Market, or
Undifferentiated,
Approach

Organization   **Single marketing mix**   **Target market**

include staple food items, such as sugar and salt, and certain kinds of farm produce.

The total market approach can be effective under two conditions. First, a large proportion of customers in the total market must have similar needs for the product. A marketer using a single marketing mix for a total market of customers with a variety of needs will find that the marketing mix satisfies very few people. Anyone could predict that a "universal car," meant to satisfy everyone, would satisfy very few customers' needs for cars because it would not provide the specific attributes that a specific person wants. Second, the organization must be able to develop and maintain a single marketing mix that satisfies customers' needs. The company must be able to identify a set of product needs that are common to most customers in a total market, and it must have the resources and managerial skills to reach a sizable portion of that market. If customers' needs are dissimilar or if the organization is unable to develop and maintain a satisfying marketing mix, then a total market approach is likely to fail.

Although customers may have similar needs for a few products, in the case of most products these needs are decidedly different. In such instances, a company should use the market segmentation approach.

Market Segmentation Approach

Markets made up of individuals with diverse product needs are called **heterogeneous markets**. Not everyone wants the same type of car, furniture, or clothes. For example, some individuals want an economical car, others desire a status symbol, and still others seek an automobile that is roomy and comfortable for travel. The automobile market, then, is an example of a heterogeneous market. For such heterogeneous markets, the market segmentation approach is appropriate. Figure 4.2 illustrates the diverse market for women's shoes. The market for watches is also quite diverse. Timex provides a watch for $45 to $50 whereas Christian Dior's market seeks a more upscale, exclusive watch.

As Figure 4.3 shows, **market segmentation** is the process of dividing a total market into market groups consisting of people who have relatively similar product needs. The purpose is to design a marketing mix (or mixes) that more precisely matches the needs of individuals in a selected market segment (or segments). A **market segment** consists of individuals, groups, or organizations with one or more similar characteristics that cause them to have relatively similar product needs. For instance, the soft drink market can be divided into segments consisting of cola drinkers, noncola drinkers, and drinkers of diet drinks.

The principal rationale for segmenting markets is that in a diverse market, an organization is better able to develop a marketing mix that satisfies a relatively small portion of a total market than it is to develop a mix that meets the needs of all people. The segmentation approach differs from the total approach because it aims one marketing mix at one segment of a total market rather than directing a single marketing mix at a total market.

The market segmentation approach is widely used. In the next sections we analyze several of its main features, including the types of market segmentation strategies and the conditions required for effective segmentation.

Market Segmentation Strategies

There are two major segmentation strategies: the concentration strategy and the multisegment strategy.

Figure 4.2 **Heterogeneous Markets**   The women's shoe market is heterogeneous, as indicated by the need for expensive shoes, such as the F. Pinet fashion shoes, and the less expensive quality shoes, such as those made by Keds.   Source: F. Pinet ad: Courtesy of Russell and Bromley; Keds ad: Courtesy of the Keds Corporation © 1991.

Figure 4.3

Market Segmentation Approach

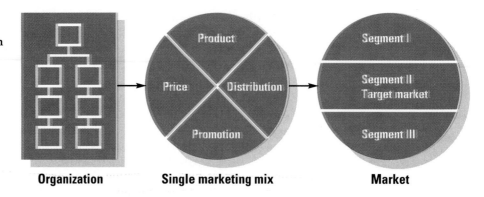

| Organization | Single marketing mix | Market |

Concentration Strategy When an organization directs its marketing efforts toward a single market segment by creating and maintaining one marketing mix, it is employing a **concentration strategy**. Lamborghini, for example, focuses on the luxury sports car segment and directs all its marketing efforts toward high-income individuals who want to own high-performance luxury cars. The chief advantage of the concentration strategy is that it allows a firm to specialize. The firm can analyze the characteristics and needs of a distinct customer group and then focus all its energies on satisfying that group's needs. A firm can generate a large sales volume by reaching a single segment. In addition, concentrating on a single segment permits a firm with limited resources to compete with much larger organizations, which may have overlooked some smaller segments.

Specialization, however, means that a company puts all its eggs in one basket—clearly a disadvantage. If a company's sales depend on a single segment and the segment's demand for the product declines, the company's financial strength also declines. Moreover, when a firm penetrates one segment and becomes well entrenched, its popularity may keep it from moving into other segments. For example, in the automobile market, Subaru, known for its small, low-price four-wheel-drive vehicles, may have trouble moving into the upscale, more affluent car segment, whereas Ferrari would find it difficult to enter the small, inexpensive automobile segment. The Global Perspective highlights the challenges faced by Subaru of America in expanding into new market segments in the United States.

Multisegment Strategy With a **multisegment strategy** (see Figure 4.4), an organization directs its marketing efforts at two or more segments by developing a marketing mix for each selected segment. After a firm uses a concentration strategy successfully in one market segment, it sometimes expands its efforts to additional segments. For example, Jockey underwear has traditionally been aimed at one segment: men. However, the company now markets underwear for women and children as well. The marketing mixes used for a multisegment strategy may vary as to product differences, distribution methods, promotion methods, and prices.

A business can usually increase its sales in the aggregate market through a multisegment strategy because the firm's mixes are being aimed at more people. Figure 4.5 illustrates how General Foods attempts to appeal to a new market segment for its Jell-O Brand Gelatin. Another example is the Gitano Group, which established its exclusive designer reputation by creating jeans targeted at teens. More recently, Gitano is attempting to attract the "older woman" segment of the jeans market with a product line called P.S. Gitano. While teenagers are still the core market, Gitano is now also targeting consumers anywhere from age thirty to over age sixty.[2] A company with excess production capacity may find a multisegment strategy advantageous because the sale of products to additional segments may absorb this excess capacity. On the other hand, multisegment strategy often demands a greater number of production processes, materials, and people; thus production costs may be higher than with concentration strategy. Keep in mind also that a firm using a multisegment strategy ordinarily experiences higher marketing costs. Because this strategy usually requires more research and several different promotion plans and distribution methods, the costs of planning, organizing, implementing, and controlling marketing activities increase.

Figure 4.4

Multisegment Strategy

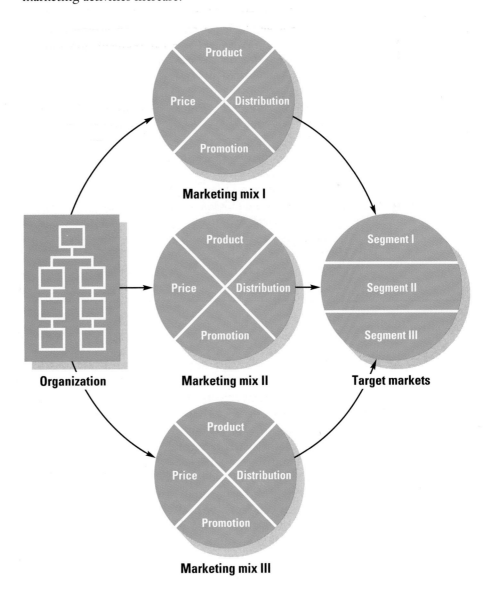

Subaru Targets New Markets in the United States

SUBARU OF AMERICA, a marketing subsidiary of the Japanese car maker, is defined in the United States by the small, inexpensive, durable four-wheel-drive import cars that it began selling here in 1968. While still popular among down-to-earth individuals who prefer utility, reliability, and ruggedness to fancy chrome and high tech (Subaru's top dealer is in Anchorage, Alaska), Subaru is struggling in the United States. In 1990 the company sold just 108,000 cars nationwide, down from 183,000 in 1986. Selling value cars that run well has endeared Subaru to one market segment, but this segment does not provide sufficient profits for the company to survive. To ensure its longevity, Subaru is altering its strategy to target more affluent, city-dwelling buyers. But in going upscale, the company risks losing the identity that made it a best seller in the United States for so many years.

To reach its new target segments, Subaru has introduced two new models. The Legacy, a luxury model selling from $12,000 to $19,000, offers most of the amenities expected in higher-priced luxury cars. The company also introduced the sleek new SVX sports car, which sells for $28,000. While the SVX has received good reviews in the automotive press, many critics wonder if consumers really want a Subaru that can go 140 miles per hour.

Additionally, Subaru no longer advertises the four-wheel-drive feature of the Legacy or many other models because research showed that upscale city dwellers associate four-wheel drive with trucks. When mentioned, the feature is now called all-wheel drive.

Although Subaru is trying to boost profits by targeting more segments of car buyers, its efforts to retain its rugged identity can be seen in a new advertising campaign, which attempts to position Subaru as practical, dignified, less ostentatious than other cars, and a great value. One print advertisement, for example, points out that "a car is a car. . . . It won't make you prettier. Or younger. And if it improves your standing with the neighbors, then you live among snobs with distorted values." Thus, although the company's new strategy is challenging, Subaru, with vehicles well-known for meeting difficult roads, seems ready to meet the challenge.

Sources: "Subaru Would Like to Introduce a Special New Feature for '92. The Truth," Subaru advertisement, Sept. 1991, Subaru of America; Bob Garfield, "Subaru Overhauls Image," *Advertising Age*, Aug. 19, 1991, pp. 1, 46; David Kiley, "Subaru Hits a Speed Bump," *Adweek's Marketing Week*, Aug. 19, 1991, p. 25; and David Kiley, "Can Subaru Survive in America?" *Adweek's Marketing Week*, Aug. 5, 1991, p. 27.

Conditions for Effective Segmentation

Whether a firm uses the concentration or the multisegment strategy, five conditions must exist for market segmentation to be effective. First, consumers' needs for the product must be heterogeneous. If they are not, there is little need to segment the market. Second, the segments must be identifiable and divisible. The company must find some basis for effectively separating individuals in a total market into groups, each of which has a relatively uniform need for the product. Third, the total market should be divided in such a way that the segments can be compared with respect to estimated sales potential, costs, and profits. Fourth, at least one segment must have enough profit potential to justify developing and maintaining a special marketing mix. Finally, the company must be able to reach the chosen segment with a particular marketing mix. Some market segments may be difficult or impossible to reach because of legal, social, or distribution constraints. For instance, marketers of Cuban rum and cigars are not permitted to sell to the U.S. market because of political and trade restrictions.

Choosing Segmentation Variables

Segmentation variables are the characteristics of individuals, groups, or organizations that are used for dividing a total market into segments. For example, location, age, sex, or rate of product usage can all be a means of segmenting.

Several factors are considered in selecting a segmentation variable. The segmentation variable should be related to customers' needs for, uses of, or behavior toward the product. Stereo marketers might segment the stereo market on the basis of income and age—but not on the basis of religion, because one person's music-listening needs do not differ much from those of persons of other religions. Furthermore, if individuals or organizations in a total market are to be classified accurately, the segmentation variable must be measurable. For example, age, location, and sex are measurable because such information can be obtained through observation or questioning. But segmenting a market on the basis of intelligence is extremely difficult because this attribute is harder to measure accurately.

A company's resources and capabilities affect the number and size of segment variables used. The type of product and the degree of variation in consumers'

Figure 4.5

Application of Multi-segment Strategy

General Foods attempts to reach a potentially new market segment for Jell-O Brand Gelatin by promoting its use in a recipe.

Source: Jell-O is a registered trademark of Kraft General Foods, Inc. Reproduced with permission.

Figure 4.6

Segmentation Variables for Consumer Markets

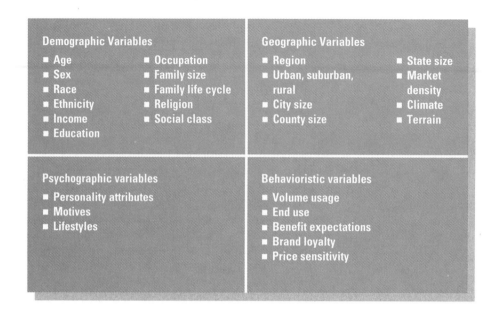

needs also dictate the number and size of segments targeted by a particular firm. In short, there is no best way to segment markets. For example, the number and size of the segments J.C. Penney's uses to divide the clothing market may not be appropriate for Borden to use in dividing the market for dairy products.

Choosing a segmentation variable or variables is a critical step in segmenting a market. Selecting an inappropriate variable limits the chances of developing a successful strategy. To help you understand better the possible segmentation variables, we now look closely at three aspects of the topic: the major types of variables used to segment consumer markets; the types used to segment organizational markets; and single-variable versus multivariable segmentation.

Variables for Segmenting Consumer Markets

A marketer shaping a segmentation strategy to reach a consumer market can choose one or several variables from a broad assortment of possible ones. As shown in Figure 4.6, segmentation variables can be grouped into four categories: (1) demographic, (2) geographic, (3) psychographic, and (4) behavioristic.

Demographic Variables   A demographer studies aggregate population characteristics, such as the distribution of age and sex, fertility rates, migration patterns, and mortality rates. The demographic characteristics that marketers commonly turn to in segmenting markets include age, sex, race, ethnicity, income, education, occupation, family size, family life cycle, religion, and social class. Marketers rely on these demographic characteristics both because they are often closely linked to customers' product needs and purchasing behavior and because they can be readily measured.

Because age is a commonly used variable for segmentation purposes, marketers need to be aware of the distribution of age and how that distribution is changing. All age groups (except the 5 to 13 group) that include persons now 34 years old or younger are expected to decrease, and all other age categories are expected to increase by the year 2000. In 1970, the average age of a U.S. citizen was 27.9; currently, it is about 32. According to projections, the average age in the year 2000 will be 35.5. Figure 4.7 shows how LEGO uses age as a segmentation variable.

Marketers are increasingly aiming their marketing efforts at children. Teenagers spend $33.5 billion on family grocery shopping, for in households with only one parent or where both parents work, children have to take on additional responsibilities such as cooking, cleaning, and grocery shopping. Moreover, the 42 million children under the age of 12 have about $6.2 billion to spend on their own. Marketers are beginning to recognize the buying power of today's children and are targeting more products at them. Polaroid, for example, designed its Cool Cam camera for the 9 to 14 age group, and Delta Air Lines created a frequent flier program for children aged 2 to 12. When H.J. Heinz learned that children eat one-third more ketchup than adults and often choose the family brand, the company created a youth-oriented advertising campaign to appeal to them.[3]

Gender is another demographic variable commonly used to segment a number of markets, including clothes, soft drinks, nonprescription medications, toiletries, magazines, and even cigarettes. The U.S. Census Bureau reports that girls and women account for 51.2 percent and boys and men 48.8 percent of the total U.S. population.[4] The deodorant market is a primary example of gender segmentation—Secret deodorant is marketed specifically to women, whereas Old Spice deodorant is directed toward men.

Figure 4.7

Age as a Segmentation Variable

LEGO targets its DUPLO Zoo Collection at children ages 2–5. Other LEGO products, such as the LEGOland Pirate System, are targeted at older children, ages 8–12.

Source: DUPLO advertisement courtesy of LEGO Systems, Inc.

Figure 4.8

Targeting the Upper-Income Market

The jewelry presented by Tabbah Jewelers is designed and marketed as "authentic and exclusive" for upper-income consumers.

Source: Tabbah International

Marketers have also turned to ethnicity as a means of segmenting markets for goods such as food, music, and clothing and for services such as banking and insurance. The U.S. Hispanic population illustrates the importance of ethnicity as a segmentation variable. Made up of people of Mexican, Cuban, Puerto Rican, and Central and South American heritage, this ethnic group is growing five times faster than the general population. Consequently, Campbell Soup Co., Procter & Gamble, and other companies are targeting U.S. Hispanic consumers. They view the Hispanic segment as attractive because of its size and growth potential. However, targeting Hispanic customers is not an easy task. For example, although marketers have long believed that Hispanic consumers are exceptionally brand loyal and prefer Spanish-language broadcast media, recent research has failed to support this notion. Not only do advertisers disagree about the merits of Spanish-language media, they also question whether it is suitable to advertise to Mexicans, Puerto Ricans, and Cubans using a common Spanish language.[5] Each culture has its own unique language—thus, to lump Hispanic groups together does not allow the message to effectively reach each segment. These findings suggest that marketers should carefully research the Hispanic market segment before developing marketing mixes for it.

Because it strongly influences people's product needs, income often provides a way of dividing markets. It affects the ability to buy (discussed in Chapter 2) and the aspirations for a certain style of living. Product markets segmented by income range from housing, furniture, clothing, and food to automobiles and certain kinds of sporting goods. Exclusive Tabbah watches are targeted to upper-income consumers in Figure 4.8.

Among the factors influencing household income and product needs are marital status and the presence and age of children. These characteristics can be combined into a single variable, sometimes called the *family life cycle*. Housing, appliances, food, automobiles, and boats are a few of the numerous product markets sometimes segmented by family life cycle.

Family life cycle can be broken down in various ways. Figure 4.9 shows a breakdown into nine categories according to age, marital status, and the presence or absence of children in the household. As can be seen in the figure, the composition of the American household in relation to family life cycle is changing. The "typical" American family of a single-earner married couple with children dropped from 21 percent of all households in 1970 to just 8 percent in 1990, and the number of nonfamily households—that is, households in which one person lives alone or with unrelated people—increased from 23 percent to 35 percent. Unmarried adults under age 45 headed just 3 percent of the households in 1970, but their share increased to 9 percent by 1990. Almost 60 percent of all adult women now work outside the home. Of these women, 40 percent have children below the age of 6. About 56 percent of all adults are married, but people are waiting longer to get married and are having fewer children. About half of all families do not have children younger than age 18.[6]

Figure 4.9 **The Nine Family Life Cycle Stages as a Percentage of All Households for 1970 and 1990** Source: Bureau of the Census, Current Population Survey, 1970 and 1990.

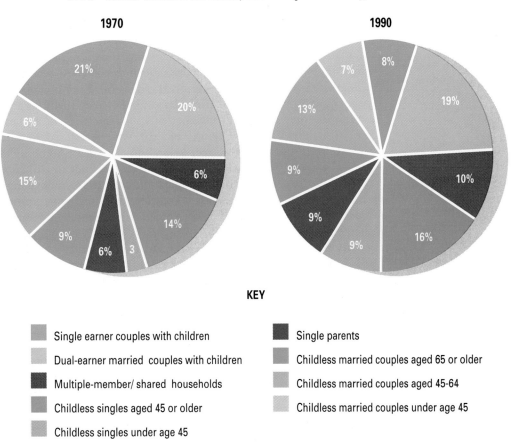

People of the same age may have diverse product needs because they are in different stages of the family life cycle. Persons in a particular life cycle stage may have very specific needs that can be satisfied by precisely designed marketing mixes. For example, family life cycle, age, income, and household size combine to explain differences in food spending. Middle-aged people spend more on food than do younger households, because older families have more members (households headed by someone under age 35 average 2.5 members, compared with 2.9 members for households headed by 45- to 54-year-olds). Householders who are under 35 years of age spend at least 40 percent of their annual food dollars in restaurants regardless of income, but there is a decline in restaurant spending among householders ages 55 to 64, especially those in lower-income groups.[7]

There are many more demographic variables. For instance, publishers of encyclopedias and dictionaries segment markets by education level; brewers sometimes aim their products at broad occupational categories; and producers of cosmetics and hair-care supplies may segment markets according to race. Certain types of foods and clothing are directed toward people of specific religious sects.

Geographic Variables   Geographic variables—climate, terrain, natural resources, population density, and subcultural values—also influence consumer product needs. Markets may be divided into regions because one or more geographic variables cause customers to differ from one region to another. A company that sells products to a national market might divide the United States into the following regions: Pacific, Southwest, Central, Midwest, Southeast, Middle Atlantic, and New England. A firm operating in one or several states might regionalize its market by counties, cities, zip code areas, or other units.

Marketers sometimes segment on the basis of state populations, and they use population figures in estimating demand. Between 1980 and 1990, the U.S. population grew by 10 percent, but the population in all regions did not grow proportionally. While the South and the West registered significant increases, the Midwest and East experienced only minor gains. Some areas—North Dakota, Wyoming, Iowa, West Virginia, and the District of Columbia—lost population.[8] Figure 4.10 shows the population change for each state between 1980 and 1990. To analyze the market accurately and segment it properly, marketers must be aware of both current population patterns and projected changes in these patterns.

City size can be an important segmentation variable. Some marketers want to focus their efforts on cities of a certain size. For example, one franchised restaurant organization will not locate in cities of less than 200,000 people. It has concluded that a smaller population base would not result in adequate profits. Other firms, however, seek opportunities in smaller towns.

Because cities often cut across political boundaries, the U.S. Census Bureau developed a system to classify metropolitan areas (any area with a city or an urbanized area of at least 50,000 population and a total metropolitan population of at least 100,000). Metropolitan areas are categorized as one of the following: a metropolitan statistical area (MSA), a primary metropolitan statistical area (PMSA), or a consolidated metropolitan statistical area (CMSA). An MSA is an urbanized area encircled by nonmetropolitan counties and is neither

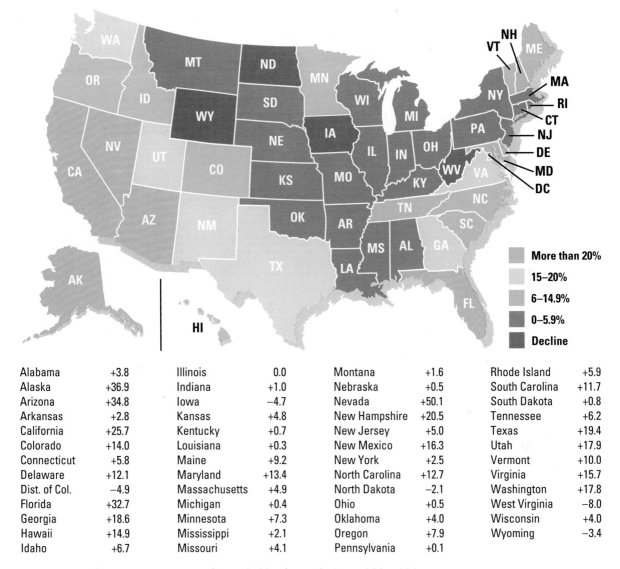

Alabama	+3.8	Illinois	0.0	Montana	+1.6	Rhode Island	+5.9
Alaska	+36.9	Indiana	+1.0	Nebraska	+0.5	South Carolina	+11.7
Arizona	+34.8	Iowa	−4.7	Nevada	+50.1	South Dakota	+0.8
Arkansas	+2.8	Kansas	+4.8	New Hampshire	+20.5	Tennessee	+6.2
California	+25.7	Kentucky	+0.7	New Jersey	+5.0	Texas	+19.4
Colorado	+14.0	Louisiana	+0.3	New Mexico	+16.3	Utah	+17.9
Connecticut	+5.8	Maine	+9.2	New York	+2.5	Vermont	+10.0
Delaware	+12.1	Maryland	+13.4	North Carolina	+12.7	Virginia	+15.7
Dist. of Col.	−4.9	Massachusetts	+4.9	North Dakota	−2.1	Washington	+17.8
Florida	+32.7	Michigan	+0.4	Ohio	+0.5	West Virginia	−8.0
Georgia	+18.6	Minnesota	+7.3	Oklahoma	+4.0	Wisconsin	+4.0
Hawaii	+14.9	Mississippi	+2.1	Oregon	+7.9	Wyoming	−3.4
Idaho	+6.7	Missouri	+4.1	Pennsylvania	+0.1		

Figure 4.10 **Percent Change in Total Population, 1980–1990** Source: 1990 U.S. Census.

socially nor economically dependent on any other metropolitan area. A metropolitan area within a complex of at least 1 million inhabitants can elect to be named a PMSA. A CMSA is a metropolitan area of at least 1 million consisting of two or more PMSAs. There are twenty CMSAs. The five largest CMSAs—New York, Los Angeles, Chicago, San Francisco, and Philadelphia—account for 20 percent of the population of the United States. The federal government provides a considerable amount of socioeconomic information about MSAs, PMSAs, and CMSAs that can aid market analysis and segmentation. Figure 4.11 provides an overview of the population changes expected in twenty CMSAs between 1990 and 1995. More than one-third of Americans live

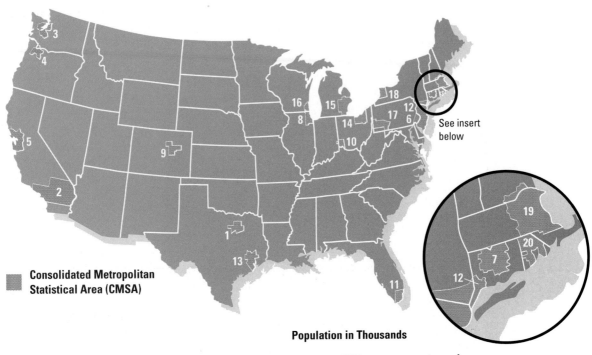

Population in Thousands

		1990 census	1995 projection	percentage change 1990–1995
1	Dallas–Fort Worth	3,885	4,334	+11.6
2	Los Angeles–Anaheim–Riverside	14,532	16,060	+10.5
3	Seattle–Tacoma	2,559	2,811	+9.8
4	Portland–Vancouver	1,478	1,586	+7.3
5	San Francisco–Oakland–San Jose	6,253	6,679	+6.8
6	Philadelphia–Wilmington–Trenton	5,899	6,254	+6.0
7	Hartford–New Britain–Middletown	1,086	1,151	+6.0
8	Chicago–Gary–Lake County	8,066	8,417	+4.4
9	Denver–Boulder	1,848	1,928	+4.3
10	Cincinnati–Hamilton	1,744	1,817	+4.2
11	Miami–Fort Lauderdale	3,193	3,301	+3.4
12	New York–Northern New Jersey–Long Island	18,087	18,272	+1.0
13	Houston–Galveston–Brazoria	3,711	3,715	+0.1
14	Cleveland–Akron–Lorain	2,760	2,747	−0.5
15	Detroit–Ann Arbor	4,665	4,626	−0.8
16	Milwaukee–Racine	1,607	1,586	−1.3
17	Pittsburgh–Beaver Valley	2,243	2,153	−4.0
18	Buffalo–Niagara Falls	1,189	1,139	−4.2
19	Boston–Lawerence–Salem	4,172	3,779	−9.4
20	Providence–Pawtucket–Fall River	1,142	944	−17.3

Figure 4.11   **Consolidated Metropolitan Statistical Areas and Projected Growth**
Sources: Thomas Exter, "America's Megamarkets," *American Demographics,* June 1991, p. 59; and
1990 U.S. Census. Reprinted with permission © *American Demographics,* June 1991.

in these twenty CMSAs. Between 1990 and 1995, total population in these
large market areas should increase by only 3.5 percent. As shown in Figure 4.11,
some areas will grow much faster than others.

Market density refers to the number of potential customers within a unit of land area, such as a square mile. Although market density is related generally to population density, the correlation is not exact. For example, in two different geographic markets of approximately equal size and population, the market density for office supplies might be much higher in one area than in another if one area contains a much greater proportion of business customers. Market density may be a useful segmentation variable because low-density markets often require different sales, advertising, and distribution activities than do high-density markets.

Climate is commonly used as a geographic segmentation variable because it has such a broad impact on people's behavior and product needs. The many product markets affected by climate include air-conditioning and heating equipment, clothing, gardening equipment, recreational products, and building materials.

Psychographic Variables Marketers sometimes use psychographic variables, such as personality characteristics, motives, and lifestyles, to segment markets. A psychographic dimension can be used by itself to segment a market, or it can be combined with other types of segmentation variables.

Personality characteristics are helpful when a product resembles many competing products and consumers' needs are not greatly affected by other segmentation variables. However, segmenting a market according to personality traits can be risky. Although marketing practitioners have long believed that consumer choice and product use vary with personality and lifestyle, until recently, marketing research had indicated only weak relationships. It is, of course, hard to gauge personality traits accurately—especially since most personality tests were developed for clinical use, and not for segmentation purposes. New, more reliable measurements devised for personality characteristics have indicated a stronger association between personality and consumer behavior.[9]

When appealing to a personality characteristic, a marketer almost always selects one that many people value positively. Individuals with this characteristic, as well as those who would like to have it, may be influenced to buy that marketer's brand. For example, the soft drink Dr Pepper has been promoted as "not for everyone," "the unusual," for those who are "independent," "strong-minded," or "outgoing." Marketers who take this approach do not worry about measuring how many people have the positively valued characteristic because they assume that a sizable proportion of people in the target market either have it or want to have it.

Motives are another means of segmenting markets. In such cases, a market is divided according to consumers' reasons for making a purchase. Product durability, economy, convenience, and status are motives that affect the types of product purchased and the choice of stores in which they are bought. For example, one motive for the purchase of soft drinks in two-liter bottles or six-packs is economy.

Lifestyle segmentation groups individuals according to how they spend their time, the importance of things in their surroundings (their homes or their jobs, for example), their beliefs about themselves and broad issues, and some socio-economic characteristics, such as income and education.[10] Figure 4.12 shows that Norwegian Cruise Line has segmented the cruise market based on people's interest in sports activities. Lifestyle analysis provides a broad view of buyers

because it encompasses numerous characteristics related to people's activities, interests, and opinions. Table 4.1 illustrates factors that are a part of the major dimensions of lifestyle.

One of the more popular studies of lifestyle is conducted by the Value and Lifestyle Program (VALS) of the Stanford Research Institute. This program surveys American consumers to select groups with identifiable values and lifestyles. The program has identified three broad consumer groups: Outer-Directed, Inner-Directed, and Need-Driven consumers. A VALS 2 classification was introduced that categorized consumers into five basic lifestyle groups: Strugglers, Action-Oriented, Status-Oriented, Principle-Oriented, and Actualizers. The VALS studies have been used to create products as well as to segment markets. VALS characteristics can also be used to select advertising media and determine advertising content. While the VALS studies are the most widely used basis for segmenting consumers by lifestyle, many other lifestyle classification systems do exist.

For example, one study divided supermarket shoppers into six segments based on their lifestyle activities. Avid Shoppers (about 25 percent of all shoppers) are the traditional supermarket shoppers who cook most of their meals, shop frequently, and look for bargains. Kitchen Strangers (20 percent) are usually childless men or women who seldom cook and eat take-out and restaurant food instead. Low-income families and individuals who usually buy only basic food products are classified as Constrained Shoppers. Hurried Shoppers are busy consumers who eat mostly at home but look for shopping and cooking short cuts. Older working people whose children have left home, leaving them more money to spend on groceries, are known as Unfettered Shoppers. Finally, Kitchen Birds, primarily the elderly, are very light eaters.[11] By segmenting markets in this way, supermarket chains can try to create marketing mixes that satisfy the needs of each segment. The Kroger and Safeway chains, for example, now offer full salad bars and take-out food to appeal to the Kitchen Stranger segment.

Even though psychographic variables can effectively divide a market, they are not used very much. For one thing, they are harder to measure accurately than other types of segmentation variables, and their links to consumers' needs are sometimes obscure and unproven. For another, segments based on psychographic variables may not be reachable. Thus a marketer may determine that highly compulsive individuals want a certain type of clothing, but no specific stores or specific media vehicles—such as television or radio programs, newspapers, or magazines—appeal precisely to this group and this group alone.

Behavioristic Variables Firms can divide a market on the basis of some feature of consumer behavior toward a product, commonly involving some aspect of product use. For example, a total market may be separated into users and nonusers. Users may then be classified as heavy, moderate, or light. To satisfy a specific group, such as heavy users, a marketer may have to create a distinctive product, set special prices, or initiate special promotion and distribution activities. Information on per capita expenditure patterns is helpful to companies such as Home Depot, Builder's Square, and Central Hardware. Economic census data show that per capita spending on building repair supplies at building material stores varies widely across the United States. For example, building supply stores in New Hampshire take an average of $537 for each resident, compared to $29 in Wyoming. This information will help companies in planning their expansion and allocating resources to stores.[12]

How customers use or apply the product may also determine segmentation. To satisfy customers who use a product in a certain way, some feature—say, packaging, size, texture, or color—may have to be designed precisely to make

Table 4.1

Lifestyle Dimensions

Activities	Interests	Opinions
Work	Family	Themselves
Hobbies	Home	Social issues
Social events	Job	Politics
Vacation	Community	Business
Entertainment	Recreation	Economics
Club membership	Fashion	Education
Community	Food	Products
Shopping	Media	Future
Sports	Achievements	Culture

Source: Reprinted, adapted, from Joseph Plummer, "The Concept and Application of Life Style Segmentation," *Journal of Marketing,* January 1974, p. 34, published by the American Marketing Association. Used by permission.

the product easier to use, safer, or more convenient. For instance, Crest, Colgate, and other brands of toothpaste are now packaged with pump dispensers because consumers wanted easier-to-use dispensers. In addition, special distribution, promotion, or pricing activities may have to be created.

Benefit segmentation is the division of a market according to the benefits that consumers want from the product. Although most types of market segmentation are based on the assumption that there is a relationship between the variable and customers' needs, benefit segmentation is different in that the benefits the customers seek *are* their product needs. Thus individuals are segmented directly according to their needs. By determining the benefits desired, marketers may be able to divide people into groups that are seeking certain sets of benefits.

The effectiveness of benefit segmentation depends on several conditions. First, the benefits sought must be identifiable. Second, using these benefits, marketers must be able to divide people into recognizable segments. Finally, one or more of the resulting segments must be accessible to the firm's marketing efforts. For example, Inside Marketing describes how Pier 1 reversed its slumping sales by identifying that the majority of its customers were looking for high-quality and unusual home furnishings. Kraft, as shown in Figure 4.13, determined a large segment of the market to be interested in low-fat foods.

As this brief discussion shows, consumer markets can be divided according to numerous characteristics. Some of these variables, however, are not particularly helpful for segmenting business-to-business or organizational markets.

Figure 4.13

Benefit Segmentation

Kraft recognized there was an accessible market for reduced-fat foods, meriting the development of light cheese slices.

Source: Kraft Light is a registered trademark of Kraft General Foods, Inc. Reproduced with permission.

Pier 1 Tries to Keep Pace with Their Target Market

WHEN PIER 1 FIRST OPENED in the 1960s, it understood how to meet the needs of its target market. True to the needs of the alternative-lifestyle members of the baby boom generation, Pier 1 sold mostly incense, baskets, and beads. The success Pier 1 enjoyed indicated that providing what customers want is the key to any good target marketing effort.

However, the problems this Fort Worth–based chain encountered in the late 1970s and early 1980s proved that target markets do not sit still for long. By the late 1970s, the aging baby boom generation had outgrown its younger days. The generation of the 1960s had become the generation of the 1980s, and buying houses was more important than buying beads and incense. Unfortunately, Pier 1 had not outgrown its early years. By the mid-1980s, the firm's sales had plummeted, and the number of stores had dropped by 18 percent.

In 1985, Pier 1 recruited new CEO Clark Johnson, who began to overhaul the company by questioning customers—mostly women aged 25 to 44 with household incomes of $40,000. Johnson asked these customers how Pier 1 could improve their shopping experiences. The answer: bigger stores in more accessible locations with more unusual, higher-quality products. Customers also indicated that they were willing to pay more for an up-to-date Pier 1.

Based on his research, Johnson began an immediate repositioning campaign for the chain. That was 1985. Today, Pier 1 is North America's leading specialty retailer of decorative home furnishings. The new merchandise ranges from home furnishings to brightly colored housewares, including some handmade items imported from over 44 countries. Since 1985 Pier 1 has opened 412 new stores—an average of 1 new store every four and one-half business days—to reach a 1991 total of 568 outlets. Existing stores were remodeled, and now the basic Pier 1 store is double its original size. Immediately after the changes, Pier 1 sales rose about 40 percent. In 1991, sales increased by 26 percent to approximately $700 million. In addition, stock prices have tripled as earnings per share rose about 26 percent.

Will Pier 1 make the same mistakes in the future? Probably not, says Johnson. The company is aggressively opening new stores near retirement communities, especially in Florida. As the baby boom generation turns gray, Pier 1 intends to keep up and not let them slip away again.

Sources: Pier 1, *1991 Annual Report*; Pier 1, *1990 Annual Report*; and Ret Autry, "Companies to Watch: Pier 1 Imports," *Fortune*, July 2, 1990, p. 93.

Variables for Segmenting Organizational Markets

Like consumer markets, business-to-business or organizational markets are sometimes segmented, but the marketers' aim is to satisfy the needs of organizations for products. Marketers may segment organizational markets according to geographic location, type of organization, customer size, and product use.

Geographic Location We noted that the demand for some consumer products can vary considerably among geographic areas because of differences in climate, terrain, customer preferences, or similar factors. Demand for organizational products also varies according to geographic location. For example, the producers of certain types of lumber divide their markets geographically because their customers' needs vary from region to region. Geographic segmentation may be especially appropriate for reaching industries that are concentrated in certain locations. Furniture producers, for example, are concentrated in the Southeast, whereas most iron and steel producers are located in the Great Lakes area.

Type of Organization   A company sometimes segments a market by the types of organizations within that market. Different types of organizations often require different product features, distribution systems, price structures, and selling strategies. Given these variations, a firm either may concentrate on a single segment with one marketing mix (concentration strategy) or focus on several groups with multiple mixes (multisegment strategy). A carpet producer could segment potential customers into several groups, such as automobile makers, commercial carpet contractors (firms that carpet large commercial buildings), apartment complex developers, carpet wholesalers, and large retail carpet outlets.

Customer Size   An organization's size may affect its purchasing procedures and the types and quantities of products it wants. Size can thus be an effective variable for segmenting an organizational market. To reach a segment of a particular size, marketers may have to adjust one or more marketing mix components. For example, customers who buy in extremely large quantities are sometimes offered discounts. In addition, marketers often have to expand personal selling efforts to serve larger organizational buyers properly. Because the needs of larger and smaller buyers tend to be quite distinct, marketers frequently use different marketing practices to reach various customer groups.

Product Use   Certain products, especially basic raw materials such as steel, petroleum, plastics, and lumber, are used in numerous ways. How a company uses products affects the types and amounts of the products purchased, as well as the method of making the purchase. For example, computers are used for engineering purposes, basic scientific research, and business operations, such as word processing, bookkeeping, and telephone service. A computer producer may segment the computer market by types of use because organizations' needs for computer hardware and software depend on the purpose for which the products are purchased.

Single-Variable Versus Multivariable Segmentation

Selecting the appropriate variable for market segmentation is an important marketing management decision because the variable is the primary factor in defining the target market. So far we have discussed segmentation by one variable. In fact, more than one variable can be used, and marketers must decide the number of variables to include.

Single-variable segmentation is achieved by using only one variable. The segmentation shown in Figure 4.14 is based on income alone. (Although the areas on the graph are the same size, this does not mean that the segments are the same size or equal in sales potential.) Single-variable segmentation, the simplest form of segmentation, is the easiest to perform. However, a single characteristic gives marketers only moderate precision in designing a marketing mix to satisfy individuals in a specific segment.

To achieve **multivariable segmentation**, more than one characteristic is used to divide a total market (see Figure 4.15). Notice in the figure that the market

Figure 4.14

Single-Variable Segmentation

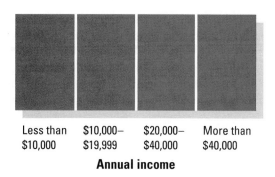

Less than $10,000 $10,000–$19,999 $20,000–$40,000   More than $40,000

Annual income

is segmented by three variables: income, population density, and volume usage. The people in the highlighted segment earn more than $40,000, are urban dwellers, and are heavy users. Multivariable segmentation provides more information about the individuals in each segment than does single-variable segmentation. More is known about the people in each segment of Figure 4.15 than about those in the segments of Figure 4.14. This additional information may allow a company to develop a marketing mix that will satisfy customers in a given segment more precisely. Knowing how to make customers comfortable in a retail environment requires detailed demographic and psychographic understanding. Knowing the median age group, educational background, income level, and buying habits of the target population is extremely important.[13]

The major disadvantage of multivariable segmentation is that the larger the number of variables used, the greater the number of resulting segments. This proliferation reduces the sales potential of many of the segments. Compare, for example, the number and size of the segments in Figure 4.14 with the number and size of those in Figure 4.15.

Figure 4.15

Multivariable Segmentation

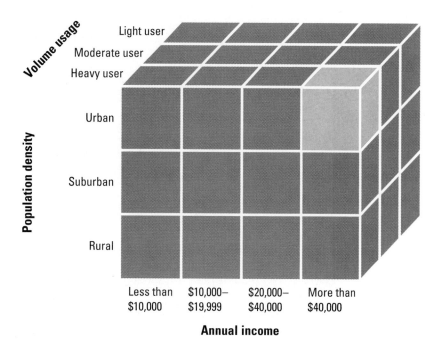

The use of additional variables can help create and maintain a more exact and satisfying marketing mix. However, when deciding on single-variable or multi-variable segmentation, a marketing manager must consider whether additional variables will actually help improve the firm's marketing mix. If using a second or third variable does not provide information that ensures greater precision, there is little reason to spend more money to gain information about the extra variables.

Evaluating Markets and Forecasting Sales

Whether taking a total market approach or opting for segmentation, a marketer must be able to measure the sales potential of the chosen target market or markets. Moreover, a marketing manager must determine the portion or share of the selected market that the firm can capture relative to its objectives, resources, and managerial skills, as well as to those of its competitors. Developing and maintaining a marketing mix consume a considerable amount of a company's resources. Thus the target market or markets selected must have enough sales potential to justify the cost of developing and maintaining one or more marketing mixes.

The potential for sales can be measured along several dimensions, including product, geographic area, time, and level of competition.[14] With respect to product, potential sales can be estimated for a specific product item (for example, Diet Coke) or an entire product line (for example, Coca-Cola, Coca-Cola Classic, Caffeine-Free Coke, Diet Coke, Diet Caffeine-Free Coke, Cherry Coca-Cola, and Diet Cherry Coca-Cola are one product line). A manager must also determine the geographic area to be included in the estimate. In relation to

Figure 4.16

The Relationship Between the Market Potential, Sales Potential, and Sales Forecast

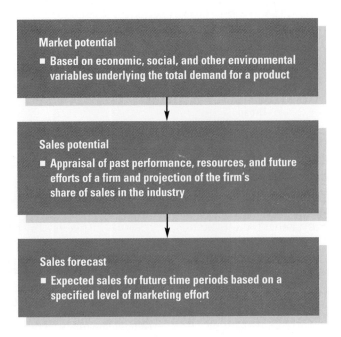

Market potential
- Based on economic, social, and other environmental variables underlying the total demand for a product

Sales potential
- Appraisal of past performance, resources, and future efforts of a firm and projection of the firm's share of sales in the industry

Sales forecast
- Expected sales for future time periods based on a specified level of marketing effort

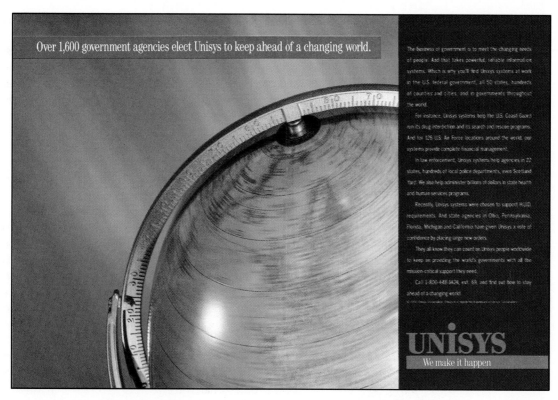

Figure 4.17 **Market Potential for Information Systems** Unisys assesses its market potential based on numbers of government agencies in need of reliable information systems.
Source: Unisys Corporation

time, sales potential estimates can be short range (one year or less), medium range (one to five years), or long range (longer than five years). The competitive level specifies whether sales are being estimated for a single firm or for an entire industry. Thus marketers measure sales potential for both the entire market and for their own firms and then develop a sales forecast (Figure 4.16).

Market and Sales Potentials

Market potential is the total amount of a product that customers will purchase within a specified period at a specific level of industrywide marketing activity. Market potential can be stated in terms of dollars or units and can refer to a total market or to a market segment. As shown in Figure 4.16, market potential is dependent on economic, social, and other marketing environment factors. When analyzing market potential, it is important to specify a time frame and to indicate the relevant level of industry marketing activities. In Figure 4.17, Unisys Corporation shows that it serves a market of over 1,600 government agencies.

Note that marketers have to assume a certain general level of marketing effort in the industry when they estimate market potential. The specific level of marketing effort certainly varies from one firm to another, but the sum of all firms' marketing activities equals industry marketing efforts. A marketing manager also must consider whether and to what extent industry marketing efforts will change. For instance, in estimating the market potential for the spreadsheet software industry, Microsoft Corp. must consider changes in marketing efforts by Lotus and other software producers. If marketing managers at Microsoft know that Lotus is planning to introduce a new version of the Lotus 1-2-3 Spreadsheet product with a new advertising campaign, this fact will contribute to Microsoft's estimate of the market potential for computer software.

Sales potential is the maximum percentage of market potential that an individual firm within an industry can expect to obtain for a specific product. Several general factors influence a company's sales potential. First, the market potential places absolute limits on the size of the company's sales potential. Second, the magnitude of industrywide marketing activities has an indirect but definite impact on the company's sales potential. Those activities have a direct bearing on the size of the market potential. When Domino's Pizza advertises home-delivered pizza, for example, it indirectly promotes pizza in general; its commercials may, in fact, help sell Pizza Hut's and other competitors' home-delivered pizza. Third, the intensity and effectiveness of a company's marketing activities relative to those of its competitors affect the size of the company's sales potential. If a company is spending twice as much as any of its competitors on marketing efforts and if each dollar spent is more effective in generating sales, the firm's sales potential will be quite high compared with that of its competitors.

There are two general approaches to measuring sales potential: breakdown and buildup. In the **breakdown approach**, the marketing manager first develops a general economic forecast for a specific time period. Next, market potential is estimated on the basis of this economic forecast. The company's sales potential is then derived from the general economic forecast and the estimate of market potential.

In the **buildup approach**, an analyst begins by estimating how much of a product a potential buyer in a specific geographic area, such as a sales territory, will purchase in a given period. Then the analyst multiplies that amount by the total number of potential buyers in that area. The analyst performs the same calculation for each geographic area in which the firm sells products and then adds the totals for each area to calculate the market potential. To determine the sales potential, the analyst must estimate, by specific levels of marketing activities, the proportion of the total market potential that the company can obtain.

For example, the marketing manager of a regional paper company with three competitors might estimate the company's sales potential for bulk gift-wrapping paper using the buildup approach. The manager might determine that each of the sixty-six paper buyers in a single sales territory purchases an average of 10 rolls annually. For that sales territory, then, the market potential is 660 rolls annually. The analyst follows the same procedure in each of the firm's other nine sales territories and then totals the sales potential for each sales territory (see Table 4.2). Assume that this total market potential is 18,255 rolls of paper (the quantity expected to be sold by all four paper companies). Then the marketing manager would estimate the company's sales potential by ascertaining that it could sell about 33 percent of the estimated 18,255 rolls at a certain

Table 4.2

The Sales Potential
Calculations for
Bulk Wrapping
Paper (Market
Potential: 18,255
Rolls)

Territory	Number of Potential Customers	Estimated Purchases	Total
1	66	10 rolls	660 rolls
2	62	10	620
3	55	5	275
4	28	25	700
5	119	5	595
6	50	20	1,000
7	46	10	460
8	34	15	510
9	63	10	630
10	55	10	550
		Total company sales potential	6,000 rolls

level of marketing effort. The marketing manager might develop several sales potentials, based on several levels of marketing effort.

Whether marketers use the breakdown or the buildup approach, they depend heavily on sales estimates. To get a clearer idea of how these estimates are derived, let us explore sales forecasting.

Developing Sales Forecasts

A **sales forecast** is the amount of a product that the company actually expects to sell during a specific period at a specified level of marketing activities. The sales forecast differs from the sales potential: It concentrates on what the actual sales will be at a certain level of marketing effort, whereas the sales potential assesses what sales are possible at various levels of marketing activities, assuming that certain environmental conditions will exist. Businesses use the sales forecast for planning, organizing, implementing, and controlling their activities. The success of numerous activities depends on the accuracy of this forecast. A study of retail business failures has shown that common problems in companies that fail are improper planning and lack of a realistic sales forecast. Overly ambitious sales forecasts lead to overbuying, overinvestment, and ultimately, a loss of financial flexibility.[15]

A sales forecast must be time-specific. Sales projections can be short (one year or less), medium (one to five years), or long (longer than five years). The length of time chosen for the sales forecast depends on the purpose and uses of the forecast, the stability of the market, and the firm's objectives and resources.

To forecast sales, a marketer can choose from a number of forecasting methods. Some of them are arbitrary; others are more scientific, complex, and time consuming. A firm's choice of method or methods depends on the costs involved, the type of product, the characteristics of the market, the time span of the forecast, the purposes of the forecast, the stability of the historical sales data, the availability of required information, and the forecasters' expertise and experience.[16] The common forecasting techniques fall into five categories: executive judgment, surveys, time series analysis, correlation methods, and market tests.

Executive Judgment   At times, a company forecasts sales chiefly on the basis of **executive judgment**, which is the intuition of one or more executives. This approach is highly unscientific but expedient and inexpensive. Executive judgment may work reasonably well when product demand is relatively stable and the forecaster has years of market-related experience. However, because intuition is swayed most heavily by recent experience, the forecast may be overly optimistic or overly pessimistic. Another drawback to intuition is that the forecaster has only past experience as a guide for deciding where to go in the future.

Surveys   A second way to forecast sales is to question customers, sales personnel, or experts regarding their expectations about future purchases.

Through a **customer forecasting survey**, marketers can ask customers what types and quantities of products they intend to buy during a specific period. This approach may be useful to a business that has relatively few customers. For example, a computer chip producer that markets to less than a hundred computer manufacturers could conduct a customer survey. PepsiCo, though, has millions of customers and cannot feasibly use a customer survey to forecast future sales.

Customer surveys have several drawbacks. Customers must be able and willing to make accurate estimates of future product requirements. Although industrial buyers can sometimes estimate their anticipated purchases accurately from historical buying data and their own sales forecasts, many cannot make such estimates. In addition, for a variety of reasons, customers may not want to take part in a survey. Occasionally, a few respondents give answers that they know are incorrect, making survey results inaccurate. Moreover, customer surveys reflect buying intentions, not actual purchases. Customers' intentions may not be well formulated, and even when potential purchasers have definite buying intentions, they do not necessarily follow through on them. Finally, customer surveys consume much time and money.

In a **sales-force forecasting survey**, members of the firm's sales force are asked to estimate the anticipated sales in their territories for a specified period of time. The forecaster combines these territorial estimates to arrive at a tentative forecast.

A marketer may survey the sales staff for several reasons. The most important one is that the sales staff is closer to customers on a daily basis than other company personnel; therefore it should know more about customers' future product needs. Moreover, when sales representatives assist in developing the forecast, they are more likely to work toward its achievement. Another advantage of this method is that forecasts can be prepared for single territories, for divisions consisting of several territories, for regions made up of multiple divisions, and then for the total geographic market. Thus the method readily provides sales forecasts from the smallest geographic sales unit to the largest.

Despite these benefits, a sales-force survey has certain limitations. Salespeople can be too optimistic or pessimistic because of recent experiences. In addition, salespeople tend to underestimate the sales potential in their territories when they believe that their sales goals will be determined by their forecasts. They also dislike paperwork because it takes up the time that could be spent selling. If the preparation of a territorial sales forecast is time consuming, the sales staff may not do the job adequately.

Nonetheless, sales-force surveys can be effective under certain conditions. If, for instance, the salespeople as a group are accurate—or at least consistent—estimators, the overestimates and underestimates should counterbalance each other. If the aggregate forecast is consistently over or under actual sales, then the marketer who develops the final forecast can make the necessary adjustments. Assuming that the survey is well administered, the sales force can have the satisfaction of helping to establish reasonable sales goals. It can also be assured that its forecasts are not being used to set sales quotas.

When a company wants an **expert forecasting survey**, it hires experts to help prepare the sales forecast. These experts are usually economists, management consultants, advertising executives, college professors, or other persons outside the firm who have solid experience in a specific market. Drawing on this experience and their analyses of available information about the company and the market, the experts prepare and present their forecasts or answer questions regarding a forecast. Using experts is expedient and relatively inexpensive. However, because they work outside the firm, experts may not be as motivated as company personnel to do an effective job.

Time Series Analysis   The technique by which the forecaster, using the firm's historical sales data, tries to discover a pattern or patterns in the firm's sales over time is called **time series analysis**. If a pattern is found, it can be used to forecast sales. This forecasting method assumes that the past sales pattern will continue in the future. The accuracy, and thus the usefulness, of time series analysis hinges on the validity of this assumption.

In a time series analysis, a forecaster usually performs four types of analysis: trend, cycle, seasonal, and random factor.[17] **Trend analysis** focuses on aggregate sales data, such as a company's annual sales figures, from a period of many years to determine whether annual sales are generally rising, falling, or staying about the same. Through **cycle analysis**, a forecaster analyzes sales figures (often monthly sales data) over a period of three to five years to ascertain whether sales fluctuate in a consistent, periodic manner. When performing **seasonal analysis**, the analyst studies daily, weekly, or monthly sales figures to evaluate the degree to which seasonal factors, such as climate and holiday activities, influence the firm's sales. **Random factor analysis** is an attempt to attribute erratic sales variations to random, nonrecurrent events, such as a regional power failure, a natural disaster, or political unrest in a foreign market. After performing each of these analyses, the forecaster combines the results to develop the sales forecast.

Time series analysis is an effective forecasting method for products with reasonably stable demand, but it is not useful for products with highly erratic demand. Joseph E. Seagram & Sons, Inc., an importer and producer of liquor and wines, uses several types of time series analyses for forecasting and has found them quite accurate. For example, Seagram's forecasts of industry sales volume have proved correct within ±1.5 percent, and the firm's sales forecasts have been accurate within ±2 percent.[18] Time series analysis is not always so dependable.

Correlation Methods   Like time series analysis, correlation methods are based on historical sales data. When using **correlation methods**, the forecaster attempts to find a relationship between past sales and one or more variables, such as population, per capita income, or gross national product. To determine whether a correlation exists, the forecaster analyzes the statistical relationships among changes in past sales and changes in one or more variables—a technique known as regression analysis. The objective of regression analysis is a mathematical formula that accurately describes a relationship between the firm's sales and one or more variables; however, the formula indicates only an association, not a causal relationship. Once an accurate formula has been established, the analyst plugs the necessary information into the formula to derive the sales forecast.

Correlation methods are useful when a precise relationship can be established. However, a forecaster seldom finds a perfect correlation. Furthermore, this method can be used only when the available historical sales data are extensive. Ordinarily, then, correlation techniques are futile for forecasting the sales of new products.

Market Tests   Conducting a **market test** involves making a product available to buyers in one or more test areas and measuring purchases and consumer responses to distribution, promotion, and price. Even though test areas are often cities with populations of 200,000 to 500,000, test sites can be larger metropolitan areas or towns with populations of 50,000 to 200,000. A market test provides information about consumers' actual purchases rather than about their intended purchases. In addition, purchase volume can be evaluated in relation to the intensity of other marketing activities—advertising, in-store promotions, pricing, packaging, distribution, and the like. On the basis of customer response in test areas, forecasters can estimate product sales for larger geographic units.

Because it does not require historical sales data, a market test is an effective tool for forecasting the sales of new products or the sales of existing products in new geographic areas. The test gives the forecaster information about customers' real actions rather than intended or estimated behavior. A market test also gives a marketer an opportunity to test various elements of the marketing mix. But these tests are often time consuming and expensive. In addition, a marketer cannot be certain that the consumer response during a market test represents the total market response or that such a response will continue in the future.

Using Multiple Forecasting Methods

Although some businesses depend on a single sales forecasting method, most firms use several techniques. A company is sometimes forced to use several methods when it markets diverse product lines, but even for a single product line several forecasts may be needed, especially when the product is sold in different market segments. Thus a producer of automobile tires may rely on one technique to forecast tire sales for new cars and on another to forecast the sales of replacement tires. Variation in the length of the needed forecasts may call for several forecast methods. A firm that employs one method for a short-range forecast may find it inappropriate for long-range forecasting. Sometimes a marketer verifies the results of one method by using one or several other methods and comparing results.

Summary

A market is an aggregate of people who, as individuals or as organizations, have needs for products in a product class and who have the ability, willingness, and authority to purchase such products. A consumer market consists of purchasers and/or individuals in their households who intend to consume or benefit from the purchased products and who do not buy products for the main purpose of making a profit. An organizational or business-to-business market consists of persons and groups who purchase a specific kind of product for resale, direct use in producing other products, or use in day-to-day operations. Because products are classified according to use, the same product may be classified as both a consumer product and an organizational product.

Marketers use two general approaches to identify their target markets: the total market and the market segmentation approaches. A firm using a total market approach designs a single marketing mix and directs it at an entire market for a particular product. The total market approach can be effective when a large proportion of individuals in the total market have similar needs for the product and the organization can develop and maintain a single marketing mix to satisfy those needs.

Markets made up of individuals with diverse product needs are called heterogeneous markets. The market segmentation approach divides the total market into groups consisting of people who have similar product needs. The purpose is to design a marketing mix (or mixes) that more precisely matches the needs of persons in a selected segment (or segments). A market segment is a group of individuals, groups, or organizations sharing one or more similar characteristics that cause them to have relatively similar product needs. There are two major types of market segmentation strategies. In the concentration strategy, the organization directs its marketing efforts toward a single market segment through one marketing mix. In the multisegment strategy, the organization develops different marketing mixes for two or more segments.

Certain conditions must exist for market segmentation to be effective. First, consumers' needs for the product should be heterogeneous. Second, the segments of the market should be identifiable and divisible. Third, the total market should be divided so that the segments can be compared with respect to estimated sales potential, costs, and profits. Fourth, at least one segment must have enough profit potential to justify developing and maintaining a special marketing mix for that segment. Fifth, the firm must be able to reach the chosen segment with a particular marketing mix.

Segmentation variables are the dimensions or characteristics of individuals, groups, or organizations that are used for dividing a total market into segments. The segmentation variable should be related to customers' needs for, uses of, or behavior toward the product. Segmentation variables for consumer markets can be grouped into four categories: demographic (age, gender, income, ethnicity, family life cycle), geographic (population, market density, climate), psychographic (personality traits, motives, and lifestyle), and behavioristic (use). Segmentation variables for organizational markets include geographic factors, type of organization, customer size, and product use. Besides selecting the appropriate segmentation variable, a marketer must also decide how many variables to use. Single-variable segmentation involves only one variable, but in multivariable segmentation, more than one characteristic is used to divide a total market.

Whether using a total market or a market segmentation approach, a marketer must be able to measure the sales potential of the target market or markets. Market potential is the total amount of a product that customers will purchase within a specified period at a specific level of industrywide marketing activity. Sales potential is the maximum percentage of market potential that an individual firm within an industry can expect to obtain for a specific product. There are two general approaches to measuring sales potential: breakdown and buildup. A sales forecast is the amount of a product that the company actually expects to sell during a specific period of time and at a specified level of marketing activities. Several methods are used to forecast sales: executive judgment, surveys (customer, sales force, and executive surveys), time series analysis (trend analysis, cycle analysis, seasonal analysis, random factor analysis), correlation methods, and market tests. Although some businesses may rely on a single sales forecasting method, most organizations employ several different techniques.

Important Terms

Market	Market potential
Consumer market	Sales potential
Organizational, or business-to-business, market	Breakdown approach
	Buildup approach
Total market, or undifferentiated, approach	Sales forecast
	Executive judgment
Heterogeneous markets	Customer forecasting survey
Market segmentation	Sales-force forecasting survey
Market segment	Expert forecasting survey
Concentration strategy	Time series analysis
Multisegment strategy	Trend analysis
Segmentation variables	Cycle analysis
Market density	Seasonal analysis
Benefit segmentation	Random factor analysis
Single-variable segmentation	Correlation methods
Multivariable segmentation	Market test

Discussion and Review Questions

1. What is a market? What are the requirements for a market?
2. In your local area, is there a group of people with unsatisfied product needs who represent a market? Could this market be reached by a business organization? Why or why not?
3. Identify and describe the two major types of markets. Give examples of each.
4. What is the total market approach? Under what conditions is it most useful? Describe a present market situation in which a company is using a total market approach. Is the business successful? Why or why not?

5. What is the market segmentation approach? Describe the basic conditions required for effective segmentation. Identify several firms that use the segmentation approach.
6. List the differences between the concentration and the multisegment strategies. Describe the advantages and disadvantages of each strategy.
7. Identify and describe four major categories of variables that can be used to segment consumer markets. Give examples of product markets that are segmented by variables in each category.
8. What dimensions are used to segment business-to-business or organizational markets?
9. How do marketers decide whether to use single-variable or multivariable segmentation? Give examples of product markets that are divided through multivariable segmentation.
10. Why is a marketer concerned about sales potential when trying to find a target market?
11. What is a sales forecast and why is it important?
12. Under what conditions are market tests useful for sales forecasting? Discuss the advantages and disadvantages of market tests.

Cases

4.1 How Do You Reach Teenagers? Tune to Channel One

For years, marketers have believed that the teen market is difficult, if not impossible, to reach with traditional advertising media. For the most part, teens do not watch a great deal of television or read magazines and newspapers to a great extent. Therefore marketers are left wondering how to reach the lucrative teenage market.

However, Chris Whittle may have the answer. Whittle, chairman of Knoxville, Tennessee–based Whittle Communications, has developed a concept known as Channel One. Channel One is a five-day-a-week news and information program delivered via satellite to thousands of middle and high school students around the country. Whittle loans television monitors, videocassette recorders, and satellite dishes to schools free of charge. In return, Channel One carries two minutes of commercial time in its twelve-minute-long daily news broadcast. Whittle refers to Channel One as the "Today" show for teenagers. As of 1991, over 9,000 U.S. high schools had signed on with Whittle, with the program reaching 45 percent of U.S. schools with more than 300 students.

The benefits of Channel One are obvious. First, schools receive the use of badly needed audiovisual equipment. In fact, in a time of budget cuts and decreased funding for education, Channel One represents an opportunity that few schools can afford to miss. Schools are allowed to use the equipment for other purposes besides Channel One, and Whittle is responsible for servicing the equipment. Second, students benefit from being exposed to current information and news from around the world. Some educators believe that the use of news broadcasts in class makes students more culturally literate. Finally, marketers have a means of reaching the elusive teenage market. The lure to marketers like Levi's, McDonald's, and M&Ms is very seductive; a captive audience of millions of teens giving their undivided attention to Channel One's advertisements.

Channel One is not without its critics. Many educators resent the idea of advertising to a captive teenage audience. Others resent the fact that the only means of obtaining badly needed equipment is the selling of the teenage audience to marketers. One of the biggest problems stems from Whittle's insistence that all students in participating schools watch Channel One every day. Channel One's approach is in stark contrast to that of Whittle's competitor, CNN "Newsroom." "Newsroom" contains no advertising and may be used by teachers whenever they choose. However, the CNN program is distributed by videotape and does not come with any equipment.

Whittle developed Channel One on the basis of extensive research. A Gallup poll commissioned by Whittle found that less than 1 percent of high school students watched cable television news in classrooms on any given day. Whittle also felt that traditional media were too "cluttered" and failed to deliver specific target audiences. Whereas media are usually developed and then distributed (as in the case of a news magazine), Whittle starts with a target audience in mind, and then develops a means of reaching it.

Whittle is somewhat of a pioneer in reaching untraditional target markets. In 1988, he launched *Special Reports*, a glossy, bimonthly magazine displayed in over 14,500 doctors' waiting rooms. In September 1990, Whittle debuted *American Style*, a bimonthly magazine distributed to 140,000 beauty parlors nationwide. Soon to be introduced is an expanded version of Channel One called WRTV (Waiting Room Television). Whittle's plan is to place 100,000 big-screen televisions in doctors' waiting rooms across the country. However, Whittle's next adventure is even bolder than the others. In 1991, Whittle announced a plan to put two million kids into a network of Whittle schools. Whittle Schools and Laboratories, his latest subsidiary, has started two years of research at a cost of $60 million. The goal: to reshape education in America.[19]

Questions for Discussion

1. How has Whittle defined his target market?
2. Does Channel One use a concentration strategy, or a multisegment strategy?
3. What segmentation variables could CNN use to compete with Channel One?

4.2 American Firms Increase Marketing Efforts to Hispanic Market

American marketers, from Anheuser-Busch to Coca-Cola and from Campbell Soup to Procter & Gamble, spend millions advertising products to Hispanics in the United States. Why has the Hispanic market segment suddenly become so attractive to marketers? The U.S. Hispanic population is growing at five times the rate of the total population and is the second-fastest-growing U.S. population group because of high birth rates and immigration from Latin America. The Hispanic market is also fairly concentrated, with approximately 90 percent of the Hispanic population found in eight states: California, Texas, New York, Florida, New Mexico, Arizona, New Jersey, and Colorado. Today, one out of every ten Americans is Hispanic.

The Hispanic market is appealing not only because of its rapid growth, but also for its significant buying power—more than $160 billion worth in 1991. The national average income for Hispanic households in 1991 was $31,300, and although this figure is one-third lower than the U.S. average, Hispanics tend to have larger families and to spend a larger percentage of their income on goods and services than do other segments of the U.S. market. In addition, 11 percent of all Hispanic families earn more than $50,000 a year. Marketers have long believed that Hispanic customers are also extremely brand loyal and often willing to pay extra for familiar name brands, though recent research has called this into question.

Marketers also have more advertising vehicles than ever to reach the American Hispanic population. The most widely used media is the nearly 200 Spanish-language radio stations in the United States. Three Spanish-language television networks—Univision, Telemundo, and Galavision—and 28 television stations across the nation also provide forums for marketers targeting U.S. Hispanics. In addition, there are more than 1,500 Hispanic magazines, journals, and newspapers.

In terms of Hispanic marketing, Miami is fast becoming the capital. Both Univision and Telemundo have moved their broadcast operations from Southern California to Miami. In addition, Miami-based advertising agencies are winning over national Spanish-language accounts—Pizza Hut, Coors, Carnival Cruise Lines, and Philip Morris, to name a few. In 1990, advertisers spent $92 million in Miami, second only to Los Angeles at $139.5 million.

One of the most popular advertising vehicles to reach Hispanics is the television program "Sabado Gigante," a popular game/talk/variety/advertisement show viewed by 4 million Hispanics on Saturday nights on the Univision network. The show, which reaches 37 percent of all U.S. Hispanic households, includes personal product endorsements from the host, promotional tie-ins, and audience sing-alongs of product jingles for common products such as Hamburger Helper, Mazola oil, and Coors beer. After being featured on "Sabado Gigante," sales to Hispanics of Reese's peanut butter cups tripled.

Despite the buying power and concentrated nature of the Hispanic market, Hispanics are not easy for marketers to reach. Educational achievement is lower for Hispanics than for non-Hispanics. Compared to an 11 percent high school drop-out rate for non-Hispanics, 40 percent of Hispanics fail to graduate from high school. Marketers also find it difficult to reach Hispanics effectively because the Hispanic market is actually three different market segments. Mexican-Americans comprise 60 percent of the U.S. Hispanic population; Central and South American Hispanics, 21 percent; and Caribbean Hispanics, the remaining 19 percent. Although there are many similarities among these three groups, there are subtle and important differences that complicate marketing activities directed at Hispanics. For example, when Borden advertised its ice cream under the Mexican slang term *nieve*, which literally means "snow," it successfully marketed ice cream to Hispanics from Texas to California. In the East, however, Cubans, Central Americans, and Puerto Ricans believed that the product actually *was* snow!

Because of these subtle but important differences among Hispanic market segments, the Campbell Soup Company decided to use different advertisements on Spanish-language television when it launched a major Hispanic marketing campaign for its soups. One commercial was targeted at Mexican-Americans, another at Hispanics of Caribbean origin. The Mexican-American advertisement showed a young woman preparing food in a southwestern-style kitchen while pop music played in the background. By contrast, the Caribbean ad had a grandmother cooking in a plant-filled kitchen with traditional Caribbean music in the background. By using these subtle differences in advertising, Campbell avoided targeting all Hispanics at once, a mistake frequently made by companies attempting to market to Hispanics for the first time.

In 1991, Coca-Cola Classic sponsored the "El Super Concurso De El Magnate" sweepstakes, which aired exclusively on the twenty-three Telemundo television affiliates around the country. The advertisements featured Andrés García, a popular star of Telemundo's "El Magnate" soap opera. The grand prize winner received a new Ferrari and got to appear on "El Magnate." The contest, one of the largest ever directed at the Hispanic market, generated over 500,000 responses for Coca-Cola.

Many other companies are pursuing sales from the Hispanic market. Coca-Cola has featured such Hispanic celebrities as Fernando Valenzuela in its commercials. Pepsi put the Miami Sound Machine on stage with the "Taste of a New Generation." American Express plans to feature well-known Hispanics in its award-winning "Portraits" campaign. Best Foods, the manufacturer of Mazola cooking oil, is particularly interested in the Hispanic segment because Hispanics use three to four times more cooking oil than the general public. Approximately 20 percent of Mazola's sales come from Hispanics. Thus, although targeting the U.S. Hispanic market is not easy, for marketers willing to make the extra effort, increased sales and brand loyalty from Hispanic customers are the reward.[20]

Questions for Discussion

1. Is there one U.S. Hispanic market, or can the market be divided into additional segments? Explain.
2. Could understanding the U.S. Hispanic market help a company in targeting a market in Latin America?
3. What segmentation variables are most useful in targeting the Hispanic market?

Chapter Notes

1. Based on information provided by Barbara Gaskamp and Virginia Gaskamp of Market Place Casseroles.
2. Cara Appelbaum, "Your Grandmother Wears Gitano Jeans," *Adweek's Marketing Week*, July 15, 1991, p. 6.
3. Patricia Sellers, "The ABC's of Marketing to Kids," *Fortune*, May 8, 1989, pp. 114–120.
4. *Statistical Abstract of the United States*, 111 Ed., U.S. Dept. of Commerce, 1991, p. 12.
5. Joseph G. Albonetti and Luis V. Dominguez, "Major Influences on Consumer-Goods Marketers' Decision to Target U.S. Hispanics," *Journal of Advertising Research*, Feb.-Mar. 1989, pp. 9–11.
6. Judith Waldorp, "Inside America's Households," *American Demographics*, Mar. 1989, p. 22.
7. "Marketing Tools Alert," *Special New Supplement to American Demographics*, Mar. 1991, p. 1.
8. *Statistical Abstract*, 1991, p. 6.
9. John L. Lastovicka and Erich A. Joachimsthaler, "Improving the Detection of Personality-Behavior Relationships in Consumer Research," *Journal of Consumer Research*, Mar. 1988, pp. 583–587.

10. Joseph T. Plummer, "The Concept and Application of Life Style Segmentation," *Journal of Marketing,* Jan. 1974, p. 33.

11. "Supermarket Shoppers Fall into Six Groups," *Wall Street Journal,* June 13, 1989, p. B1.

12. Joe Swartz and Thomas Exter, "Remodeling America," *American Demographics,* Nov. 1991, p. 48.

13. Jim Mitchell, "The Feel Good Convenience Store," *NPN: National Petroleum News,* Apr. 1991, p. 56.

14. Philip Kotler, *Marketing Management: Analysis, Planning, and Control,* 6th ed. (Englewood Cliffs, N.J.: Prentice-Hall, 1988), p. 257.

15. Gerald P. Buccino, "No More 'Business As Usual'—The Leadership Opportunity in Troubled Times," *Retail Control,* May–June 1991, pp. 14–20.

16. David Hurwood, Elliot S. Grossman, and Earl Bailey, *Sales Forecasting* (New York: Conference Board, 1978), p. 2.

17. Kenneth E. Marino, *Forecasting Sales and Planning Profits* (Chicago: Probus Publishing, 1986), p. 155.

18. Hurwood, Grossman, and Bailey, p. 61.

19. Dan Koeppel, "Why Channel One May Be Here to Stay," *Adweek's Marketing Week,* June 3, 1991, p. 22–23; Dan Koeppel, "Coming Next in Your Town: Christopher Whittle High," *Adweek's Marketing Week,* May 20, 1991, p. 6; John Birmingham, "Marketers—and Revisionists—Are Taking a Hard Look at Whittle," *Adweek's Marketing Week,* Apr. 9, 1990, pp. 20–21, 24, 28; Daniel M. Gold, "Education Officials Tune Out Channel One," *Adweek's Marketing Week,* Apr. 9, 1990, p. 24; and "Whittle Proposes Ad-Supported Twist to 'Educational' TV," *Broadcasting,* Jan. 23, 1989, pp. 149–150.

20. U.S. Population Reference Bureau, U.S. Department of Commerce, 1991; Carrie Goerne, "Targeting Hispanics: NutraSweet Educates While Coke Titillates," *Marketing News,* Nov. 11, 1991; Mike Clary, "The United States of Miami," *Adweek's Marketing Week,* July 15, 1991, pp. 19, 21–22; Fara Warner, "Goya Ice Cream, Coast to Coast," *Adweek's Marketing Week,* July 15, 1991, p. 6; Howard Schlossberg, "Hispanic Market Strong, But Often Ignored," *Marketing News,* Feb. 19, 1990, pp. 1, 12; Rick Marin, "3 1/2 Hours of 'Gigante' Advertising," *Insight,* July 17, 1989, pp. 60–61; Eva Pomice and Anne Moncreiff Arrarte, "It's a Whole *Nuevo Mundo* Out There," *U.S. News & World Report,* May 15, 1989, pp. 45–46; Shelly Garcia, "New Study Targets Changing Hispanic Markets," *Adweek,* Apr. 24, 1989, p. 59; Mary Westerman, "Death of the Frito Bandito," *American Demographics,* Mar. 1989, pp. 28–32; and José de Cordoba, "More Firms Court Hispanic Consumers—But Find Them a Tough Target Market," *Wall Street Journal,* Feb. 18, 1988, p. 25.

5 *Consumer Buying Behavior*

OBJECTIVES

- To understand the types of consumer buying behavior and stages in the consumer buying decision process

- To recognize the stages of the consumer buying decision process

- To explore how personal factors may affect the consumer buying decision process

- To learn about the psychological factors that may affect the consumer buying decision process

- To examine the social factors that influence the consumer buying decision process

- To understand why it is important that marketers attempt to understand consumer buying behavior

The nation's more than 100 million dogs and cats are eating better than ever. American dogs can dine on meat loaf made from lamb and brown rice and finish off the meal with ice cream. Cats can feast on Pacific mackerel in crab jelly or sardines and chicken. In fact, Americans spend more than $8 billion a year on dog and cat food, but only $1 billion on baby food.

Why are Americans lavishing such attention on their pets? Experts suggest that people are forming closer bonds with their pets, in part because there are more single people living alone and more couples without children. In addition, the trend toward better nutrition and fitness has been extended to pets, who are often considered family members.

Because of these trends, higher-priced, more nutritious "superpremium" pet foods are taking a larger percentage out of the pet food market. Whereas total pet food sales have been flat in recent years, sales of the superpremiums are growing. Canned gourmet cat food sales have been increasing, as are sales at specialty pet food stores that sell superpremium brands.

Marketers also understand buying behavior and are creating brand names for these new products that fit consumers' perceptions about premium pet food. For example, the nation's leading pet food marketer, Ralston Purina, offers O.N.E., a premium dry dog food made from corn, rice, and whole chicken; Fit & Trim, a low-calorie food for overweight dogs; and Unique, a line of gourmet cat foods. Many premium pet food products, such as Iams' dog and cat foods and Hill's Science Diets for dogs and cats, are distributed through veterinarians and pet stores rather than through traditional supermarkets. Premium pet snacks are also becoming more popular. Lick Your Chops, a Connecticut firm, markets a line of all-natural veterinarian-tested dog foods and snacks in consultation with a French baker. Finally, there is Frosty Paws, an ice cream specially formulated for dogs that contains less milk and sugar than ice cream made for humans.[1]

Photo: Quaker Oats Co. © 1991 The Quaker Oats Company.

A SYMBOLIC COMMUNICATION is expressed through the products that consumers buy and through the images that marketers present of their products. Brand names of premium pet foods are a good example of symbolic communication in marketing. Marketers need to be able to understand and take advantage of the symbolic communication expressed by consumers in their buying behavior. **Buying behavior** is the decision processes and acts of people involved in buying and using products.[2] **Consumer buying behavior** refers to the buying behavior of ultimate consumers, those persons who purchase products for personal or household use, not for business purposes. Marketers should analyze consumer buying behavior for several reasons. First, buyers' reactions to a firm's marketing strategy have a great impact on the firm's success. Second, as indicated in Chapter 1, the marketing concept stresses that a firm should create a marketing mix that satisfies customers. To find out what satisfies customers, marketers must examine the main influences on what, where, when, and how consumers buy. Third, by gaining a better understanding of the factors that affect buying behavior, marketers can better predict how consumers will respond to marketing strategies.

Although marketers may try to understand and influence consumer buying behavior, they cannot control it. Some critics credit them with the ability to manipulate buyers, but marketers have neither the power nor the knowledge to do so. Their knowledge of behavior comes from what psychologists, social psychologists, and sociologists know about human behavior in general. Even if marketers wanted to manipulate buyers, the lack of laws and principles in the behavioral sciences would prevent them from doing so.

Consumer behavior is pervasive in that everyone must acquire necessities to live. Even the homeless acquire possessions and products, but they do this quite differently from a typical consumer. Many of their necessities of life are found in the trash and the discarded possessions of others. Most interesting is that the homeless fulfill their needs in creative and innovative ways in order to survive.[3]

In this chapter we begin by examining the types of decision making that consumers engage in. We then analyze the major stages of the consumer buying decision process and consider the personal, psychological, and social factors that influence it. We conclude by assessing the importance of understanding consumer buying behavior.

Types of Consumer Buying Behavior

Consumers usually want to create and maintain a collection of products that satisfy their needs and wants in both the present and future. To achieve this objective, consumers make many purchasing decisions. For example, people must make several decisions daily regarding food, clothing, shelter, medical care, education, recreation, or transportation. As they make these decisions, they engage in different decision-making behaviors. The amount of effort, both mental and physical, that buyers expend in decision making varies considerably from situation to situation. Consumer decisions can thus be classified into one of three broad categories: routine response behavior, limited decision making, and extensive decision making.[4]

A consumer practices **routine response behavior** when buying frequently purchased, low-cost items that need very little search-and-decision effort. When buying such items, a consumer may prefer a particular brand, but he or she is familiar with several brands in the product class and views more than one as being acceptable. The products that are bought through routine response behavior are purchased almost automatically. Most buyers, for example, do not spend much time or mental effort selecting a soft drink or a snack food. If the nearest soft-drink machine does not offer Sprite, they will quite likely choose a 7-Up instead.

Buyers engage in **limited decision making** when they buy products occasionally and when they need to obtain information about an unfamiliar brand in a familiar product category. This type of decision making requires a moderate amount of time for information gathering and deliberation. For example, if Procter & Gamble introduces an improved Tide laundry detergent, buyers will seek additional information about the new product, perhaps by asking a friend who has used the product or watching a commercial, before they make a trial purchase.

The most complex decision-making behavior, **extensive decision making**, comes into play when a purchase involves unfamiliar, expensive, or infrequently bought products—for instance, cars, homes, or an education in a college or university. The buyer uses many criteria to evaluate alternative brands or choices and spends much time seeking information and deciding on the purchase.

By contrast, **impulse buying** involves no conscious planning but rather a powerful, persistent urge to buy something immediately. For some individuals, impulse buying may be the dominant buying behavior. Impulse buying, however, often provokes emotional conflicts. For example, a man may want to have the new golf bag he just saw right away and so purchases it on the spot, but he also feels guilty because he knows his budget is limited that month.

The purchase of a particular product does not always elicit the same type of decision-making behavior. In some instances, we engage in extensive decision making the first time we buy a certain kind of product but find that limited decision making suffices when we buy the product again. If a routinely purchased, formerly satisfying brand no longer pleases us, we may use limited or extensive decision processes to switch to a new brand. For example, if we notice that the gasoline brand we normally buy is making our automobile's engine knock, we may seek out a higher-octane brand through limited or extensive decision making.

The Consumer Buying Decision Process

As defined earlier, a major part of buying behavior is the decision process used in making purchases. The **consumer buying decision process**, shown in Figure 5.1, includes five stages: (1) problem recognition, (2) information search, (3) evaluation of alternatives, (4) purchase, and (5) postpurchase evaluation. Before we examine each stage, consider these important points. First, the actual act of purchasing is only one stage in the process; the process is begun several stages before the actual purchase. Second, even though, for discussion purposes, we indicate that a purchase occurs, not all decision processes lead to a purchase; the individual may end the process at any stage. Finally, all consumer decisions do not always include all five stages. Persons engaged in extensive decision making usually go through all stages of this decision process, whereas those engaged in limited decision making and routine response behavior may omit some stages.

Problem Recognition

Problem recognition occurs when a buyer becomes aware that there is a difference between a desired state and an actual condition. For example, consider a marketing student who wants a reliable, advanced calculator for use in a finance course. When her old calculator stops working, she recognizes that a difference exists between the desired state—a reliable calculator—and the actual condition—a nonworking calculator. She therefore decides to buy a new calculator.

Sometimes a person has a problem or need but is unaware of it. Marketers use sales personnel, advertising, and packaging to help trigger recognition of such needs or problems. For example, a university bookstore may advertise business and scientific calculators in the university newspaper at the beginning of the term. Students who see the advertisement may recognize that they need calculators for their course work. Figure 5.2 illustrates how Kellogg's reminds consumers of the need to monitor the healthfulness of their diet. The speed of consumer problem recognition can be rather slow or quite rapid.

Figure 5.1   **Consumer Buying Decision Process and Possible Influences on the Process**

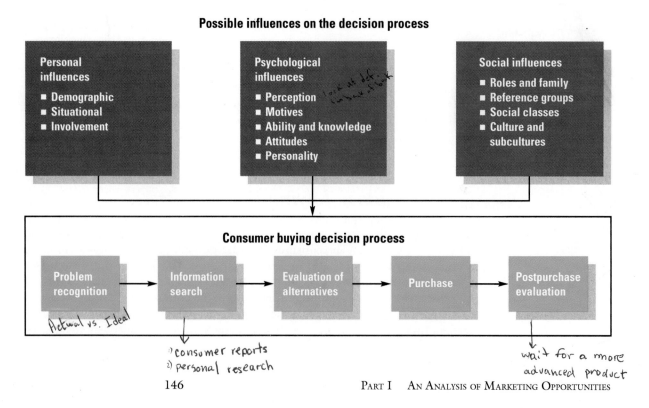

146   PART I   AN ANALYSIS OF MARKETING OPPORTUNITIES

Figure 5.2

Problem Recognition

When promoting their products, marketers draw attention to the specific consumer needs that the products will fulfill. Kellogg's promotes Common Sense Oat Bran cereal for those who have discovered the need for a low-fat, low-cholesterol diet.

Source: *Kellogg's*® and *Common Sense*™ are trademarks of Kellogg Company.

[handwritten margin notes:]

Secondary data collection

I. Internal
   A. Acct. Records
   B. Mkt. data bank

II. External Sources
   A. Census
   B. Periodicals
   C. Reports
   D. Private databanks

[handwritten note in left margin:] cognitive dissolence = is discomfort in your purchase

Information Search

After recognizing the problem or need, the buyer (if continuing the decision process) searches for information about products that will help resolve the problem or satisfy the need. For example, the above-mentioned student, after recognizing the need for a calculator, may search for information about different types and brands of calculators. Information is acquired over time from the consumer's surroundings. However, we must remember that the impact of the information depends on how the consumer interprets it.

There are two aspects to an information search. In the **internal search**, buyers first search their memory for information about products that might solve the problem. If they cannot retrieve enough information from their memory for a decision, they seek additional information in an **external search**. The external search may focus on communication with friends or relatives, comparison of available brands and prices, marketer-dominated sources, and/or public sources. An individual's personal contacts—friends, relatives, associates—often are credible sources of information because the consumer trusts and respects these sources. In fact, a consumer study has shown that word-of-mouth communication has a stronger impact on consumer judgments about products than printed communication does, unless the buyer has a well-defined prior impression of a product or unless the printed information about a product is extremely negative.[5] Utilizing marketer-dominated sources of information— such as salespersons, advertising, package labeling, and in-store demonstrations and displays—typically does not require much effort on the consumer's part.

Buyers can also obtain information from public sources—for instance, government reports, news presentations, publications such as *Consumer Reports,* and reports from product-testing organizations. Consumers frequently view information from public sources as highly credible because of its factual and unbiased nature.

Consumer groups are increasingly demanding access to all relevant product information. However, the greater the quantity of information available to buyers, the more the buyer may be overloaded with information. Research indicates that consumers make poorer choices when faced with large amounts of information.[6] Improving the quality of information and stressing features important to buyers in the decision process may help buyers make better purchase decisions.

How consumers use and process the information obtained in their search depends on a number of features of the information itself—namely, availability, quantity, quality, repetition, and format. If all the necessary information for a decision is available in the store, consumers may have no need to conduct an internal information search. Having all information externally available makes the consumer's decision process easier, increases utilization of the information, and may thus facilitate a purchase.[7]

Repetition, a technique well known to advertisers, increases consumer learning of information. When seeing or hearing an advertising message for the first time, the recipient may not grasp all its important details but learns more details as the message is repeated. Nevertheless, even when commercials are initially effective, repetition eventually causes the phenomenon of "wearout": consumers pay less attention to the commercial and respond to it less favorably than they did at first.[8]

The format in which information is transmitted to the buyer may also determine its use. Information can be presented verbally, numerically, or visually. For a wide variety of consumer tasks, pictures are remembered better than words, and the combination of pictures and words further enhances learning.[9] Consequently, marketers pay great attention to the creation of the visual components of their advertising materials.

A successful information search yields a group of brands that a buyer views as possible alternatives. This group of products is sometimes called the buyer's *evoked set.* For example, an evoked set of calculators might include those made by Texas Instruments, Hewlett-Packard, Tandy, Sharp, and Casio.

Evaluation of Alternatives

To evaluate the products in the evoked set, a buyer establishes criteria for comparing the products. These criteria are the characteristics or features that the buyer wants (or does not want). For example, one calculator buyer may want a solar-powered calculator with a large display and large buttons, whereas another may have no preference as to the size of features but happens to dislike solar-powered calculators. The buyer also assigns a certain level of importance to each criterion; some features and characteristics carry more weight than others. Using the criteria, a buyer rates and eventually ranks the brands in the evoked set. The evaluation stage may yield no brand that the buyer is willing to purchase; in that case, a further information search may be necessary.

Marketers can influence consumers' evaluation by *framing* the alternatives—that is, by the manner in which the marketer describes the alternative and its attributes. Framing can make a characteristic seem more important to a consumer and can facilitate its recall from memory. For example, by stressing a car's superior gasoline mileage over that of a competitor's, a car maker can direct consumers' attention toward this point of superiority. Framing affects the decision processes of inexperienced buyers more than those of experienced ones.[10] If the evaluation of alternatives yields one or more brands that the consumer is willing to buy, the consumer is ready to move on to the next stage of the decision process—the purchase.

Purchase

In the purchase stage, the consumer chooses the product or brand to be bought. The selection is based on the outcome of the previous evaluation stage and on other dimensions. Product availability may influence which brand is purchased. For example, if the brand ranked the highest in evaluation is not available, the buyer may purchase the brand that is ranked second.

During this stage, the buyer also picks the seller from whom he or she will buy the product. The choice of the seller may affect the final product selection—and so may the terms of sale, which, if negotiable, are determined during the purchase decision stage. Other issues such as price, delivery, warranties, maintenance agreements, installation, and credit arrangements are discussed and settled. Finally, the actual purchase takes place during this stage, unless, of course, the consumer terminates the buying decision process before reaching that point.

Postpurchase Evaluation

After the purchase, the buyer begins evaluating the product to ascertain if its actual performance meets expected levels. Many of the criteria used in evaluating alternatives are applied again during the postpurchase evaluation. The outcome of this stage is either satisfaction or dissatisfaction. These feelings strongly influence consumers' motivation and information processing. Consumers' satisfaction or dissatisfaction determines whether they make a complaint, communicate with other possible buyers, and purchase the product again.[11]

Shortly after a purchase of an expensive product, the postpurchase evaluation may result in **cognitive dissonance**—doubts that occur because the buyer questions whether the right decision was made in purchasing the product. For example, after buying an expensive calculator, the marketing student may feel guilty about the purchase or have doubts about whether she purchased the right brand and quality. A buyer who experiences cognitive dissonance may attempt to return the product or may seek positive information about it to justify that choice.

As shown in Figure 5.1, three major categories of influences are believed to affect the consumer buying decision process: personal, psychological, and social factors. The remainder of this chapter focuses on these factors. Although we discuss each major factor separately, keep in mind that their effects on the consumer decision process are interrelated.

Time-Pressured Parents Look for Quick Ways to Feed the Kids

THERE IS A SILENT TREND taking place in America today: the disappearance of the family dinner in dual-income and single-parent families. As more and more parents face the pressures of long work days and little free time, finding time to have a sit-down meal with the entire family has become an extremely difficult task. For parents who do not come home until six or seven o'clock, just feeding the kids has become almost impossible. That's why a few companies in the prepared foods industry are quickly moving to take advantage of changing consumer needs. As more and more Americans face time shortages, any product that can make food preparation more efficient and convenient has an advantage in the market.

Enter shelf-stable and frozen prepared foods targeted to kids. Products like Tyson's Looney Tunes Meals, ConAgra's Banquet Kid Cuisine, and Hormel's Kid's Kitchen entrees have made preparing lunch or dinner for kids as easy as pushing buttons on a microwave. In fact, preparing these foods is so easy, the hope is that kids will learn to cook for themselves. Children are assuming more responsibility for their own food preparation. They have a curiosity to know how things work, and they like information. Traditional kid food brands like Chef Boyardee and Franco American are also jumping on the bandwagon by adding new products to their lines.

Why target to kids? Kids are fickle and very finicky when it comes to eating. Parents often have a problem getting their kids to eat properly. Shelf-stable and frozen food marketers are trying to bridge the gap between parents and kids by making their products both fun and nutritious. Tyson signed a multiyear deal with Warner Bros. to use Looney Tunes characters like Bugs Bunny, Sylvester and Tweety, and Yosemite Sam to give their products a fun image. ConAgra includes a Fun Pak with puzzles and games inside every Kid Cuisine entree. Keeping food interesting and exciting gets kids' attention. While the kids get the fun, the parents get the convenience and information on the products' nutritional values as well. With the meals priced at about $2 per serving, many parents are finding the combination too good to pass up.

Many industry analysts say that kids' meals are only a flash in the pan. The entire prepared-foods industry is growing by leaps and bounds as consumers demand more convenience in food preparation. Many question whether it is really convenient to buy a special meal for the kids. Others ask if it is wise to teach kids to cook for themselves. Recent research shows that 81 percent of kids ages six to fourteen have a microwave and know how to use it. With numbers like that, targeting prepared foods to kids may be a wise move after all.

Sources: Christy Fisher, "Tyson Cooks Pasta for Kids," *Advertising Age,* Sept. 9, 1991, p. 10; Brian Bagot, "What's Up, Kids?," *Marketing and Media Decisions,* May 1990, pp. 49–50, 52; Mike Duff, "New Children's Meals: Not Just Kid Stuff," *Supermarket Business,* May 1990, pp. 89–95; and Judann Dagnoli and Julie L. Erickson, "The Looming Battle for Center of the Plate," *Advertising Age,* Nov. 13, 1989, pp. S10–S12.

Personal Factors Influencing the Buying Decision Process

Personal factors are ones that are unique to a particular person. Numerous personal factors can influence purchasing decisions. In this section we consider three categories of them: demographic factors, situational factors, and level of involvement.

Demographic Factors

Demographic factors are individual characteristics, such as age, sex, race, ethnicity, income, family life cycle, and occupation. (These and other characteristics were discussed in Chapter 4 as possible variables for segmentation purposes.) Demographic factors have a bearing on who is involved in family decision making. For example, children are assuming more responsibility and taking part in more purchase decisions from groceries to clothes and even family vacations.[12] Inside Marketing describes how companies in the prepared foods industry are taking advantage of changing family lifestyles by targeting prepared meals to children. Demographic factors may also partially govern behavior during a specific stage of the decision process. During the information stage, for example, a person's age and income may affect the number and types of information sources used and the amount of time devoted to seeking information.

Demographic factors also affect the extent to which a person uses products in a specific product category. Consumers in the fifteen- to twenty-four-year-old age group often purchase furniture, appliances, and other household basics as they establish their own households. On the other hand, those in the forty-five- to fifty-four-year-old age group spend more money on luxury and leisure products after their children have left home.[13] Ralph Lauren's Furniture Collection, as shown in Figure 5.3, is targeted to such a group. Brand preferences, store choice, timing of purchases, and inclination to shop at all are other areas on which demographic factors have some impact. For example, a study of working and nonworking wives showed that working wives dislike shopping more than

Figure 5.3

Demographic Factors

Factors such as age, income, and family life cycle influence consumers' decisions, and marketers target products accordingly. The Ralph Lauren furniture collection is targeted to an older age group that has more money to spend on luxury products.

Source: Courtesy of Polo Ralph Lauren Corporation.

nonworking wives, perhaps because of the perceived time, as opposed to the actual time, involved.[14]

Occupation clearly affects consumer buying behavior. Consider, for example, how differences in occupation result in variations in product needs. A college professor may earn almost as much annually as a plumber does. Yet the professor and the plumber spend their incomes differently because the product needs that arise from these two occupations vary considerably. Although both occupations require the purchase of work clothes, the professor purchases suits, and the plumber buys overalls and work shirts. The types of vehicles they drive also vary to some extent. The plumber is more likely to drive a truck or van, whereas the professor may drive a smaller car. What and where they eat for lunch are likely to be different. Finally, the "tools" that they purchase and use in their work are not the same.

Situational Factors

Situational factors are the external circumstances or conditions that exist when a consumer is making a purchase decision. Sometimes a consumer engages in buying decision making as a result of an unexpected situation. For example, a person may hurriedly buy an airline ticket to spend the last few days with a dying relative. Or a situation may arise that causes a person to lengthen or terminate the buying decision process. For instance, a consumer who is considering the purchase of a personal computer and is laid off from work during the stage of evaluating alternatives may decide to reject the purchase entirely.

Situational factors can influence a consumer's actions during any stage of the buying decision process, and in a variety of ways. Uncertainty about future marital status may sway a consumer against making a purchase. On the other hand, a conviction that the supply of necessary products is sharply limited may impel people to buy them. For example, consumers have purchased and hoarded gasoline and various food products when these products were believed to be in short supply. Even the weather may affect buying behavior. A hurricane warning usually sends coastal residents rushing to stock up on bottled water, batteries, and emergency food supplies and to fill up their cars' gas tanks. These and other situational factors can change rapidly; their influence on purchase decisions can be sudden and can also subside quickly.

The time available to make a decision is a situational factor that strongly influences consumer buying decisions. If there is little time for selecting and purchasing a product, a person may make a quick choice and purchase a readily available brand. The amount of available time also affects the way consumers process the information contained in advertisements and the length of the stages within the decision process.[15] For example, if a family is planning to buy a washing machine for a new home, its members may gather and consider a great deal of information. They may read *Consumer Reports,* talk to friends and salespersons, look at a number of advertisements, and spend a good deal of time on comparative shopping in a number of stores. However, if the family's twenty-year-old Kenmore washing machine suddenly breaks down and cannot be repaired, the extent of the information search, the number of alternatives considered, and the amount of comparative shopping may be much more re-stricted. Indeed, given the limited-time factor, if these family members were

Figure 5.4

High Involvement Product

Consumers spend much time and effort in making their purchase decision on a product such as this Honda motorcycle.

Source: Courtesy of Honda (UK).

reasonably satisfied with the performance of the old machine, they may buy another Kenmore because they know the brand.

Level of Involvement

Many aspects of consumer buying decisions are affected by the individual's **level of involvement**—the importance and intensity of interest in a product in a particular situation. A buyer's level of involvement determines why he or she is motivated to seek information about certain products and brands but virtually ignores others. The extensiveness of the buying decision process varies greatly with the consumer's level of involvement. The sequence of the steps in this process may also be altered. Low-involvement buyers may form an attitude about a product and evaluate its features after purchasing it rather than before.[16] Conversely, high-involvement buyers spend much time and effort researching their purchase beforehand. Figure 5.4 illustrates a high-involvement product—the Honda motorcycle. Computers are also products that undergo a great deal of investigation before they are chosen.

A consumer's level of involvement depends on a number of factors. Consumers tend to be more involved in the purchase of high-priced goods and of products that are visible to others, such as clothing, furniture, or automobiles. As levels of perceived risk increase, involvement levels are likely to rise. Furthermore, individuals may experience enduring involvement with a product class. *Enduring involvement* is an ongoing interest in a product class because of personal relevance. For example, people often have enduring involvement with products associated with their leisure activities. Their search and information-gathering processes for these products occur over extensive periods of time. Photography enthusiasts enjoy reading about and examining new types of cameras and films; snow skiers frequent sports stores even during the summer months.

Buyers may also experience *situational involvement* resulting from the particular circumstance or environment in which they find themselves. This type of involvement is temporary because the conditions that triggered the high degree of involvement may change.[17] If a person is searching for a silver serving tray to buy for a wedding gift, for example, he or she may experience a high level of involvement in the purchase decision. The person's information search and evaluation of alternatives may be extensive. However, once the selection has been made, he or she no longer sees a silver serving tray as being personally relevant.

Many purchase decisions do not generate great involvement on the consumer's part. When the involvement level is low, as with routine response purchases, the buying is almost automatic, and the information search and evaluation of alternatives are extremely limited. For example, grocery shopping represents low-involvement purchase decisions for many consumers; products are chosen out of habit and with minimal effort.

Psychological Factors Influencing the Buying Decision Process

Psychological factors operating within individuals partly determine people's general behavior and thus influence their behavior as consumers. The primary psychological influences on consumer behavior are (1) perception, (2) motives, (3) ability and knowledge, (4) attitudes, and (5) personality. Even though these psychological factors operate internally, later in this chapter we will see that they are very much affected by social forces outside the individual.

Perception

Are the horsemen in Figure 5.5 riding to the left or to the right? It could be either way depending on how you perceive the riders. Different people perceive the same thing at the same time in different ways. Similarly, the same individual at different times may perceive the same item in a number of ways. **Perception** is the process of selecting, organizing, and interpreting information inputs to produce meaning. **Information inputs** are the sensations received through sight, taste, hearing, smell, and touch. When we hear an advertisement, see a friend, smell polluted air or water, or touch a product, we receive information inputs. A study of music in advertising indicates that music is an important stimulus that works independently to create meaning or context. In fact, music as a functional component of advertising can be used in almost as many ways as language can be used.[18]

As the definition indicates, perception is a three-step process. Although we receive numerous pieces of information at once, only a few of them reach

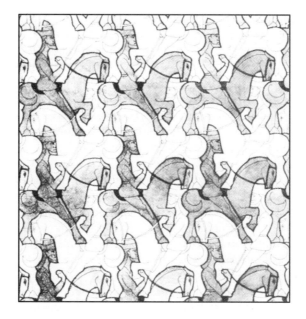

awareness. We select some inputs and ignore many others because we do not have the ability to be conscious of all inputs at one time. This phenomenon is sometimes called **selective exposure** because we select inputs that are to be exposed to our awareness. If you are concentrating on this paragraph, you probably are not aware that cars are outside making noise, that the light is on, or that you are touching this book. Even though you are receiving these inputs, you ignore them until they are mentioned.

There are several reasons why some types of information reach awareness while others do not. An input is more likely to reach awareness if it relates to an anticipated event. For example, a person hoping to attend an upcoming concert is likely to listen to a radio advertisement containing ticket information for the concert. An input is likely to reach consciousness if the information helps satisfy current needs. Thus you are more likely to notice a commercial for Burger King if you are hungry. Finally, if the intensity of an input changes significantly, the input is more likely to reach awareness. When a store manager reduces a price slightly, we may not notice because the change is not significant, but if the manager cuts the price in half, we are much more likely to recognize the reduction.

The selective nature of perception leads to two other conditions: selective distortion and selective retention. **Selective distortion** is changing or twisting currently received information. This condition can occur when a person receives information that is inconsistent with personal feelings or beliefs. For example, on seeing an advertisement promoting a brand that he or she dislikes, a person may distort the information to make it more consistent with prior views. This distortion substantially lessens the effect of the advertisement on the individual. In the **selective retention** phenomenon, a person remembers information inputs that support personal feelings and beliefs and forgets inputs that do not. After hearing a sales presentation and leaving the store, a customer may forget many of the selling points if they contradict prior beliefs.

The information inputs that do reach awareness are not received in an organized form. To produce meaning, an individual must enter the second step of the perceptual process—organize and integrate the new information with that already stored in memory. Ordinarily, this organizing is done rapidly.

Interpretation—the third step in the perceptual process—is the assignment of meaning to what has been organized. A person bases interpretation on what is familiar, on knowledge already stored in memory. For this reason, a manufacturer that changes a package design faces a major problem. Since people look for the product in the old, familiar package, they might not recognize it in the new one. Unless a package change is accompanied by a promotional program that makes people aware of the change, a firm may lose sales.

Although marketers cannot control people's perceptions, they often try to influence them. Several problems may arise from such attempts, however. First, a consumer's perceptual process may operate in such a way that a seller's information never reaches that person. For example, a buyer may block out a store clerk's sales presentation. Second, a buyer may receive a seller's information but perceive it differently than was intended. For example, when a toothpaste producer advertises that "35 percent of the people who use this toothpaste have fewer cavities," a customer could infer that 65 percent of the people who use the product have more cavities. Third, a buyer who perceives information inputs that are inconsistent with prior beliefs is likely to forget the information quickly. Thus if a salesperson tells a prospective car buyer that a particular model is highly reliable and requires few repairs, but the customer does not believe it, the customer probably will not retain the information very long.

In addition to perceptions of packages, products, brands, and organizations, individuals also have self-perceptions. That perception is called the person's **self-concept** or self-image. Research has shown that buyers purchase products that reflect and enhance their self-concept and that purchase decisions are important to the maintenance and development of a stable, harmonious self-concept.[19] For instance, a person might purchase Levi's jeans and rugby shirts to project a casual, relaxed self-concept.

Motives

A **motive** is an internal energizing force that orients a person's activities toward satisfying a need or achieving a goal. Motivation is the set of mechanisms for controlling movement toward goals.[20] A buyer's actions at any time are affected by a set of motives rather than by just one motive. At a single point in time, some motives in the set have priority, but the priorities of motives vary from one time to another. For example, a person's motives for having a cup of coffee are much stronger right after waking up than just before going to bed. Motivation also affects the direction and intensity of behavior. Individuals must choose which goals to pursue at a particular time.

Motives that influence where a person purchases products on a regular basis are called **patronage motives**. A buyer may shop at a specific store because of such patronage motives as price, service, location, honesty, product variety, or friendliness of salespeople. For example, Tianguis, a chain of southern California grocery stores, stocks a wide variety of Hispanic products, such as empanadas and tortilla mixes, with Spanish labels and has Spanish-speaking check-out clerks, as well as mariachi bands, to encourage the area's large Hispanic population to frequent its stores.[21] To capitalize on patronage motives, a marketer should try to determine why regular customers patronize a store and then emphasize these characteristics in the store's marketing mix.

Marketers conduct motivation research to analyze the major motives that influence consumers to buy or not buy their products. Motives, which often operate at a subconscious level, are difficult to measure. Because people ordinarily do not know what motivates them, marketers cannot simply ask them about their motives. Most motivation research relies on interviews or projective techniques.

When researchers study motives through interviews, they may use depth interviews, group interviews, or a combination of the two. In a **depth interview**, the researcher tries to get the subject to talk freely about anything to create an informal atmosphere. The researcher may ask general, nondirected questions and then probe the subject's answers by asking for clarification. A depth interview may last for several hours. In a **group interview**, the interviewer—through leadership that is not highly structured—tries to generate discussion about one or several topics among a group of six to twelve people. Through what is said in the discussion, the interviewer attempts to discover people's motives relating to some issue, such as the use of a product. The researcher usually cannot probe as far in a group interview as in a depth interview. To determine the subconscious motives reflected in the interviews, motivation researchers must be extremely well trained in clinical psychology. Their skill in uncovering subconscious motives from what is said in an interview determines the effectiveness of their research. Both depth and group interview techniques can yield a variety of information. For example, they might help marketers discover why customers continue to buy high-calorie fried foods even though most say they are trying to reduce their intake of cholesterol and calories.

Projective techniques are tests in which subjects are asked to perform specific tasks for particular purposes while in fact they are being evaluated for other purposes. Such tests are based on the assumption that subjects unconsciously will "project" their motives as they perform the required tasks. However, subjects should always be informed that the test is an unstructured evaluation. Researchers trained in projective techniques can analyze the materials a subject produces and can make predictions about the subject's subconscious motives. Some common types of projective techniques are word-association tests and sentence-completion tests. Such tests can be helpful in developing advertising campaigns. For example, Bell Telephone abandoned the proposed theme "The System is the Solution" when subjects in a word-association test responded with the negative "Big Brother is watching you."[22]

Motivation research techniques can be reasonably effective but are far from perfect. Marketers who want to research people's motives should obtain the services of psychologists skilled in the methods of motivation research.

Ability and Knowledge

Individuals vary in their **ability**—their competence and efficiency in performing tasks. One ability of interest to marketers is an individual's capacity to learn. **Learning** refers to changes in a person's behavior caused by information and experience. The consequences of behavior strongly influence the learning process. Behaviors that result in satisfying consequences tend to be repeated. For example, when a consumer buys a Snickers candy bar and likes it, he or she is more likely to buy a Snickers the next time. In fact, the individual will probably continue to purchase that brand until it no longer provides satisfaction. But when the effects of the behavior are no longer satisfying, the person will switch to a different brand, perhaps, or stop eating candy bars altogether.

When making purchasing decisions, buyers have to process information. Individuals have differing abilities in this regard. For example, when purchasing a home computer, a well-educated potential buyer who has experience with computer systems may be able to read, comprehend, and synthesize the considerable quantities of information found in the technical brochures for various competing brands. On the other hand, another buyer with more limited abilities may be incapable of performing this task and will have to rely on information obtained from advertisements or from a sales representative of a particular brand.

Another aspect of an individual's ability is knowledge. **Knowledge** is made up of two components: familiarity with the product and expertise, which is the individual's ability to apply the product.[23] The duration and intensity of the buying decision process depends on the buyer's familiarity with or prior experience in purchasing and using the product. For example, it has been found that many consumers are very aware and knowledgeable about the frequency of special sale events in stores and special deals in price reductions, especially when an often-purchased specific brand is involved.[24] The individual's knowledge influences his or her search for, recall of, and use of information.[25]

When making purchase decisions, inexperienced buyers may use different types of information than more experienced shoppers who are familiar with the product and purchase situation. Inexperienced buyers use price as an indicator of quality more frequently than buyers who have some knowledge of a particular product category.[26] Thus two potential purchasers of an antique desk may use quite different types of information in making their purchase decision. The inexperienced buyer is likely to judge the desk's value by the price, whereas the more experienced buyer may seek information about the craftsman, time period, and place of origin to judge the desk's quality and value.

Consumers who lack expertise may seek the advice of others when making a purchase or take along a "purchase pal." More experienced buyers have greater confidence; they also have more knowledge about the product or service and can tell which product features are reliable cues to product quality. For example, consider two young students who want reliable cars for travel back and forth to college. One has no expertise with regard to automobiles and is unsure about what features to use to judge a car. He finds the information given in the automobile brochures confusing and feels intimidated by the salesperson. Therefore he goes for advice to his father, who has purchased many cars, and takes him along to the car dealership when making the purchase. The other student has been interested in cars all her life and has worked in a large car dealership for several summers. Even though this is her first car purchase, she is an expert with regard to cars and knows what features are important. She is confident and knowledgeable and makes her purchase decision unassisted.

Marketers sometimes help customers to learn about their products and to gain experience with them. Free samples encourage trial and reduce purchase risk.

In-store demonstrations aid consumers in acquiring knowledge of product uses. Test drives give new car purchasers some experience with an automobile's features. Consumers also learn when they experience products indirectly, by way of information from salespersons, advertisements, friends, and relatives. Through sales personnel and advertisements, marketers offer information before (and sometimes after) purchases to influence what consumers learn and to create a more favorable attitude toward the products.

Although marketers seek to influence what a consumer learns, their attempts are seldom fully successful. Marketers encounter problems in attracting and holding consumers' attention, providing consumers with the kinds of information that are important for making purchase decisions, and convincing them to try the product.

Attitudes

Attitudes refer to knowledge and positive or negative feelings about an object or activity. The objects or acts toward which we have attitudes may be tangible or intangible, living or nonliving. For example, we have attitudes toward sex, religion, politics, and music, just as we do toward cars, football, and pizza. Attitudes toward products can have tremendous impact on sales. For example, Vuarnet sunglasses are preferred by trendsetters who have positive attitudes toward skiing.[27]

An individual learns attitudes through experience and interaction with other people. Just as attitudes are learned, they can also be changed. Nevertheless, an individual's attitudes remain generally stable and do not change from moment to moment. Likewise, at any one time, a person's attitudes do not all have equal impact; some are stronger than others.

Consumer attitudes toward a firm and its products greatly influence the success or failure of the firm's marketing strategy. When consumers have strong negative attitudes toward one or more aspects of a firm's marketing practices, they may not only stop using the firm's product but also urge their relatives and friends to do likewise. For example, when an oil spill from the supertanker *Exxon Valdez* fouled beaches and killed wildlife in Alaska's Prince William Sound, the public judged Exxon's response to cleaning up the spill as inadequate and cosmetic. As a result, many consumers boycotted Exxon products. Nearly twenty thousand Exxon credit card holders cut up their cards and sent them back to Exxon, exhorting their friends to do the same.

Since attitudes can play such an important part in determining consumer behavior, marketers should measure consumer attitudes toward prices, package designs, brand names, advertisements, salespeople, repair services, store locations, features of existing or proposed products, and social responsibility activities. Several methods can help marketers gauge these attitudes. One of the simplest ways is to question people directly. An attitude researcher for Keytronics, a computer keyboard manufacturer, for example, might ask respondents what they think about the style and design of Keytronics' newest keyboard. Projective techniques used in motivation research can also be employed to measure attitudes. Marketers also evaluate attitudes through attitude scales.

An **attitude scale** usually consists of a series of adjectives, phrases, or sentences about an object. Subjects are asked to indicate the intensity of their feelings toward the object by reacting to the adjectives, phrases, or sentences in a certain way. For example, if a marketer were measuring people's attitudes toward shopping, respondents might be asked to state the degree to which they agree or disagree with a number of statements, such as "Shopping is more fun than watching television." By using such an attitude scale, the consulting firm of Management Horizons was able to classify six major shopper types of clothing purchasers. The scale was based on attributes found to be predictive of shopping behavior, as profiled by demographics, media use, and purchase behavior.[28]

When marketers determine that a significant number of consumers have strong negative attitudes toward an aspect of a marketing mix, they may try to change consumer attitudes to make them more favorable. This task is generally long, expensive, and difficult and may require extensive promotional efforts. For example, the Beef Industry Council, an organization of beef producers, has attempted to use advertising to change consumers' attitudes toward beef by presenting it as a nutritious food. Some of the advertisements contain information about the caloric content, fat, cholesterol, sodium, and protein levels. In the same vein, both business and nonbusiness organizations try to change people's attitudes about many things, from health and safety to product prices and features.

Personality

Personality is all the internal traits and behaviors that make a person unique. Each person's unique personality arises from heredity and personal experiences. Personalities typically are described as having one or more characteristics, such as compulsiveness, ambitiousness, gregariousness, dogmatism, authoritarianism,

Figure 5.6

Appealing to Personalities

Recognizing the relationship between personality characteristics and buying behavior, Nike appeals to tennis enthusiasts who consider themselves to be bold and stylish.

Source: Reprinted with permission of Nike, Inc. © 1990 Bob Peterson, photographer.

introversion, extroversion, aggressiveness, and/or competitiveness. Marketing researchers attempt to find relationships among such characteristics and buying behavior. Even though a few links among several personality characteristics and buyer behavior have been determined, the results of many studies have been inconclusive. Some researchers see the apparently weak association between personality and buying behavior as due to unreliable measures rather than a lack of relationship.[29] A number of marketers are convinced that a consumer's personality does influence the types and brands of products purchased. For example, the type of clothing, jewelry, or automobile that a person buys may reflect one or more personality characteristics. Figure 5.6 provides an example of the personality type Nike wishes to attract to its Air Track Challenge II court shoe.

At times, marketers aim advertising campaigns at general types of personalities. In doing so, they use positively valued personality characteristics, such as security consciousness, gregariousness, independence, or competitiveness. For example, in analyzing the personality traits of its shoppers, K mart has found that they are looking for security and desire a shopping experience that represents their inner values and needs as they age.[30]

Social Factors Influencing the Buying Decision Process

The forces that other people exert on buying behavior are called **social factors**. As shown in Figure 5.1, they can be grouped into four major areas: (1) roles and family influences, (2) reference groups, (3) social classes, and (4) culture and subcultures.

Roles and Family Influences

All of us occupy positions within groups, organizations, and institutions. Associated with each position is a **role**—a set of actions and activities that a person in a particular position is supposed to perform, based on the expectations of both the individual and surrounding persons. Because people occupy numerous positions, they also have many roles. For example a man may perform the roles of son, husband, father, employee or employer, church member, civic organization member, and student in an evening college class. Thus there are several sets of expectations placed on each person's behavior.

An individual's roles influence both general behavior and buying behavior. The demands of a person's many roles may be inconsistent and confusing. To illustrate, assume that the man mentioned above is thinking about buying a boat. While he wants a boat for fishing, his children want one suitable for water skiing. His wife wants him to delay the boat purchase until next year. A co-worker insists that he should buy a particular brand, known for high performance. Thus an individual's buying behavior is partially affected by the input and opinions of family and friends.

Family roles relate directly to purchase decisions. The male head of household is likely to be involved heavily in the purchase of products such as tools and automobile tires. Although female roles have changed, women still make buying decisions related to many household items, including health-care products, laundry supplies, paper products, and foods. Husbands and wives participate jointly in the purchase of a variety of products, especially durable goods. A study indicates that when attitudinal, role relationships, and other explanations have been taken into account, it appears that women are still more involved than men in Christmas shopping. Women tend to give gifts to more recipients, shop earlier, shop more time per recipient, and report more success in their shopping than men. In general, men take Christmas shopping more lightly than do women.[31]

Some students aged sixteen to twenty-four may be rebellious; their brand loyalty can be quite changeable. Marketers frequently promote their products during spring break to catch this hard-to-reach group at a time when they are more receptive to a promotional message.[32] Children are making many purchase decisions and influencing numerous household purchase decisions that traditionally were made only by husbands and wives. When two or more family members participate in a purchase, their roles may dictate that each is responsible for performing certain tasks: initiating the idea, gathering information, deciding whether to buy the product, or selecting the specific brand. The particular tasks performed depend on the types of products being considered.

Marketers need to be aware of how roles affect buying behavior. To develop a marketing mix that precisely meets the needs of the target market, marketers must know not only who does the actual buying, but also what other roles influence the purchase. Because sex roles are changing so rapidly in our country, marketers must ensure that their information is current and accurate.

Reference Groups

A group becomes a **reference group** when an individual identifies with it so much that he or she takes on many of the values, attitudes, or behaviors of group members. The person who views a group as a reference group may or may not know the actual size of the group. Most people have several reference groups, such as families, friends, fraternities and sororities, and civic and professional organizations.

A group can be a negative reference group for an individual. Someone may have been a part of a specific group at one time but later rejected the group's values and members. One can also specifically take action to avoid a particular group.[33] However, in this discussion we refer to reference groups as those that the individual involved views positively.

A reference group may serve as a point of comparison and a source of information for an individual. A customer's behavior may change to be more in line with the actions and beliefs of group members. For example, a person might stop buying one brand of audiocassettes and switch to another on the advice of members of the reference group. Generally, the more conspicuous a product, the more likely it is that the brand decision will be influenced by reference groups. An individual may also seek information from the reference group about other factors regarding a prospective purchase, such as where to buy a certain product. The degree to which a reference group will affect a purchase decision depends on an individual's susceptibility to reference-group influence and the strength of his or her involvement with the group.

A marketer sometimes tries to use reference-group influence in advertisements by suggesting that people in a specific group buy a product and are highly satisfied with it. In this type of appeal, the advertiser hopes that many people will accept the suggested group as a reference group and buy (or react more favorably to) the product. Whether this kind of advertising succeeds depends on three factors: how effectively the advertisement communicates the message, the type of product, and the individual's susceptibility to reference-group influence.

Social Classes

Within all societies, people rank others into higher or lower positions of respect. This ranking results in social classes. A **social class** is an open group of individuals who have similar social rank. A class is referred to as "open" because people can move into and out of it. The criteria for grouping people into classes vary from one society to another. In the United States, we take into account many factors, including occupation, education, income, wealth, race, ethnic group, and possessions. In Russia, wealth and income are less important than education and occupation in determining social class: Although Russian doctors and scientists do not make a great deal of money, they are highly valued in Russian society. A person who is ranking someone does not necessarily apply all of a society's criteria. The number and the importance of the factors chosen depend on the characteristics of the individual being ranked and the values of the person who is doing the ranking.

To some degree, persons within social classes develop and assume common patterns of behavior. They may have similar attitudes, values, language patterns, and possessions. Social class influences many aspects of our lives. For example, it affects our chances of having children and their chances of surviving infancy. It influences our childhood training, choice of religion, selection of occupation, and how we spend our time. Because social class has a bearing on so many aspects of a person's life, it also affects buying decisions. For example, upper-class Americans seem to prefer luxury automobiles, such as the BMW and Mercedes-Benz, that symbolize their status, income, and financial comfort.

Analyses of social class commonly divide people in the United States into three to seven categories. Social scientists Richard Coleman and Lee Rainwater developed the Coleman-Rainwater classification, which comprises seven categories. They are as follows:

1. Upper Americans
   a. *Upper-upper class* (0.3 percent): high society; includes those of inherited wealth, aristocratic names
   b. *Lower-upper class* (1.2 percent): the newer social elite, drawn from current professional, corporate leadership
   c. *Upper-middle class* (12.5 percent): the rest of college graduate managers and professionals; lifestyle centers on private clubs, causes, and the arts
2. Middle Americans
   a. *Middle class* (32 percent): average-pay white-collar workers and their blue-collar friends; live on "the better side of town," try to "do the proper things"

b. *Working class* (38 percent): average-pay blue-collar workers; lead "working class" lifestyle whatever the income, school background, and job
3. Lower Americans
   a. *Lower class* (9 percent): working, not on welfare; living standard is just above poverty
   b. *Lower-lower class* (7 percent): on welfare, visibly poverty stricken; often have no steady employment.[34]

Coleman suggests that for purposes of consumer analysis and mass marketing the consuming public should be divided into the four major status groups shown in Table 5.1, but he cautions marketers to remember that there is considerable diversity in people's life situations within each status group.

Social class determines to some extent the type, quality, and quantity of products that a person buys and uses. Social class also affects an individual's shopping patterns and the types of stores patronized. Advertisements are sometimes based on an appeal to a specific social class.

Culture and Subculture

Culture is everything in our surroundings that is made by human beings. It consists of tangible items—such as foods, furniture, buildings, clothing, and tools—and intangible concepts, such as education, welfare, and laws. Culture also includes the values and wide range of behaviors that are acceptable within a specific society. The concepts, values, and behaviors that make up a culture are learned and passed on from one generation to the next.

Culture influences buying behavior because it permeates our daily lives. Our culture determines what we wear and eat, where we reside and travel. Certainly, society's interest in the healthfulness of food has affected companies' approaches to developing and promoting their products. It also influences how we buy and use products and our satisfaction from them. In American culture, time scarcity is a growing problem because of the rise in the number of women who work and the current emphasis we place on physical and mental self-development. Many people do time-saving shopping and buy time-saving products to cope with this scarcity.[35]

Because culture, to some degree, determines how products are purchased and used, it in turn affects the development, promotion, distribution, and pricing of products. Food marketers, for example, have had to make a multitude of changes in their marketing efforts. Thirty years ago most families in our culture ate at least two meals a day together, and the mother devoted four to six hours a day to preparing those meals. Now more than 60 percent of the women in the 25- to 54-year-old age group are employed outside the home, and average family incomes have risen considerably. These shifts, along with the problem of time scarcity, have resulted in dramatic changes in the national per capita consumption of certain foods: frozen dinners; shelf-stable foods, such as Lunch Bucket (see Figure 5.7) and Top Shelf; and take-out foods.[36]

When U.S. marketers sell products in other countries, they often see the tremendous impact that culture has on the purchase and use of products. International marketers find that people in other regions of the world have different attitudes, values, and needs, which in turn call for different methods of

doing business, as well as different types of marketing mixes. Some international marketers fail because they do not or cannot adjust to cultural differences. The effect of culture on international marketing programs is discussed in greater detail in Chapter 24.

A culture can be divided into **subcultures** according to geographic regions or human characteristics, such as age or ethnic background. In our country, we have a number of different subcultures: West Coast, teenage, and Asian-American, for example. Within subcultures, there are even greater similarities in people's attitudes, values, and actions than within the broader culture. Relative to other subcultures, individuals in a certain subculture may have stronger preferences for specific types of clothing, furniture, or foods. For example, there is a greater per capita consumption of rice among southerners than among New Englanders or midwesterners. American teenagers want to wear the latest fashions—for example, the surfwear and sports clothing made by Quiksilver, Inc.

Marketers must recognize that with growing international markets and increasing U.S. subcultures, there will be considerable variation in what products people buy. There will also be differences in how people make purchases—and variations in when they make them as well. To deal effectively with these differences, marketers may have to alter their products, promotion, distribution systems, or price to satisfy members of particular subcultures. The Global Perspective describes some of the differences between the buying patterns of Indians in urban India and those of the immigrant subculture in the United States.[37]

Class (% of Population)	Behavioral Traits	Buying Characteristics
Upper (14%); includes upper-upper, lower-upper, upper-middle	Income varies among the groups, but goals are the same Various lifestyles: preppy, conventional, intellectual, etc. Neighborhood and prestigious schooling important	Prize quality merchandise Favor prestigious brands Products purchased must reflect good taste Invest in art Spend money on travel, theater, books, and tennis, golf, and swimming clubs
Middle (32%)	Often in management Considered white collar Prize good schools Desire an attractive home in a nice, well-maintained neighborhood Often emulate the upper class Enjoy travel and physical activity Often very involved in children's school and sports activities	Like fashionable items Consult experts via books, articles, etc., before purchasing Will spend for experiences they consider worthwhile for their children (e.g., ski trips, college education) Tour packages; weekend trips Attractive home furnishings
Working (38%)	Emphasis on family, especially for economic and emotional supports (e.g., job opportunity tips, help in times of trouble) Blue collar Earn good incomes Enjoy mechanical items and recreational activities Enjoy leisure time after working hard	Buy vehicles and equipment related to recreation, camping, and selected sports Strong sense of value Shop for best bargains at off-price and discount stores Purchases automotive equipment for making repairs Enjoy local travel; recreational parks
Lower (16%)	Often down and out through no fault of their own (e.g., layoffs, company takeovers) Can include individuals on welfare; the homeless Often have strong religious beliefs May be forced to live in less desirable neighborhoods In spite of their problems, often good-hearted toward others Enjoyment of everyday activities when possible	Most products purchased are for survival Ability to convert good discards into usable items

Source: Adapted with permission from Richard P. Coleman, "The Continuing Significance of Social Class to Marketing," *Journal of Consumer Research*, pp. 265–280, 1983, 10 (December), with data from J. Paul Peter and Jerry C. Olson, *Consumer Behavior: Marketing Strategy Perspective* (Homewood, Ill.: Irwin, 1987), p. 433.

Table 5.1   **Social Class Behavioral and Purchasing Characteristics**

Buying Behaviors: Urban India and the U.S. Immigrant Indian Subculture

TODAY MARKETERS ARE CONCERNED with the behavior of consumers in different countries and as the American population becomes increasingly diverse, marketers are moving to better understand subcultures in the United States. Of particular importance are the social factors that influence the buying decision process—family, reference groups, social class, and culture. A study of Indians in India and Indian immigrants to the United States can be used to understand consumer behavior in India and how a change in culture affected Indians' buying behavior in the United States.

Indian immigrants are an interesting group in which to examine the effect of changing cultures on consumer behavior. U.S. immigration policy since 1965 has led to an influx of Indian immigrants quite unlike immigrants from other countries. Indians are typically better educated and more highly paid than most other immigrants and some natural-born citizens. This fact makes Indians better able to adapt to the U.S. culture and freer to maintain their Indian identities.

When coming to the United States, Indians face an immediate change in consumer values. U.S. consumers are highly individualistic and tend to buy products that are strongly associated with their self-identities. For example, many U.S. consumers buy automobiles to reflect status and prestige; often to the point where the person *is* what he or she drives. This sort of open materialism does not exist in India.

Using qualitative depth interviews and photographic methods, the researchers found several differences between Indian consumers and those who had immigrated to the United States. Domestic Indians tend to buy products more for religious and family

reasons. To these consumers, products for family recreation, such as televisions, videocassette recorders, and other electronic products represent status and prestige. In contrast, Indian immigrants to the United States also buy products for religious and family reasons, but to a much lesser extent. As compared with domestic Indian homes, immigrants' homes have many more possessions per room, often to the point of being cramped for space. Indian immigrants also tend to buy products associated with American holidays, such as Christmas and Thanksgiving. However, although Indian immigrants are more mobile than their domestic counterparts, they do not totally embrace U.S. materialism. To them, family and traditional values are still of utmost importance.

The pressures to conform when entering the U.S. culture are tremendous. Immigrants coming to the United States are faced with the pressure to fit in and the desire to hold on to traditional values. The results of this research show that Indian immigrants adapt by buying products associated with external images and public acceptance. However, they are still true to traditional Indian values such as religion and family in the privacy of their own homes.

Sources: Raj Mehta and Russell W. Belk, "Artifacts, Identity, and Transition: Favorite Possessions of Indians and Indian Immigrants to the United States," *Journal of Consumer Research*, Mar. 1991, pp. 398–411; T. G. Vaidyanathan, "Authority and Identity in India," *Daedalus*, Fall 1989, pp. 147–169; and Arthur W. Helweg, "Why Leave India For America? A Case Study Approach to Understanding Migrant Behaviour," *International Migration*, June 1987, pp. 165–177.

Understanding Consumer Buying Behavior

Marketers try to understand consumer buying behavior so that they can offer consumers greater satisfaction. Yet a certain amount of customer dissatisfaction remains. Some marketers have not adopted the marketing concept and so are not consumer-oriented and do not regard customer satisfaction as a primary objective. Moreover, because the tools for analyzing consumer behavior are imprecise, marketers may not be able to determine accurately what is highly satisfying to buyers. Finally, even if marketers know what increases consumer satisfaction, they may not be able to provide it.

Understanding consumer behavior is an important task for marketers. Even though research on consumer buying behavior has not supplied all the knowledge that marketers need, progress has been made during the last twenty years and is likely to continue in the next twenty. Not only will refinements in research methods yield more information about consumer behavior, but the pressures of an increasingly competitive business environment will make such information much more urgent for marketers.

Summary

Buying behavior is the decision processes and acts of people involved in buying and using products. Consumer buying behavior refers to the buying behavior of ultimate consumers, those who purchase products for personal or household use, not for business purposes. Analyzing consumer buying behavior is important to marketers; if they are able to determine what satisfies customers, they can implement the marketing concept and better predict how consumers will respond to different marketing strategies.

Consumer decisions can be classified into three categories: routine response behavior, limited decision making, and extensive decision making. A consumer uses routine response behavior when buying frequently purchased, low-cost items that require very little search-and-decision effort. Limited decision making is used for products that are purchased occasionally and when a buyer needs to acquire information about an unfamiliar brand in a familiar product category. Extensive decision making is used when purchasing an unfamiliar, expensive, or infrequently bought product. Impulse buying is not a consciously planned buying behavior but involves a powerful, persistent urge to buy something immediately. The purchase of a certain product does not always elicit the same type of decision-making behavior.

The consumer buying decision process includes five stages: problem recognition, information search, evaluation of alternatives, purchase, and postpurchase evaluation. All decision processes do not always culminate in a purchase, and all consumer decisions do not always include all five stages. Problem recognition occurs when a buyer becomes aware that there is a difference between a desired state and an actual condition. After recognizing the problem or need, the buyer searches for information about products that will help resolve the problem or satisfy the need. In the internal search, buyers search their memories for information about products that might solve the problem. If they are unable to retrieve from memory sufficient information to make a decision, they seek additional information through an external search. A successful search will yield a group of brands, called an evoked set, that a buyer views as possible alternatives. To evaluate the products in the evoked set, a buyer establishes certain criteria by which to compare, rate, and rank the different products. Marketers can influence consumers' evaluation by framing the alternatives.

In the purchase stage, the consumer selects the product or brand on the basis of results from the evaluation stage and on other dimensions. The buyer also chooses the seller from whom he or she will buy the product. After the purchase, the buyer evaluates the product to determine if its actual performance meets expected levels. Shortly after the purchase of an expensive product, for example, the postpurchase evaluation may provoke cognitive dissonance, which is dissatisfaction brought on by the consumer's doubts as to whether he or she should have bought the product in the first place or would have been better off buying another brand that had also ranked high in the evaluation.

Three major categories of influences are believed to affect the consumer buying decision process: personal, psychological, and social factors. A personal factor is one that is unique to a particular person. Personal factors include demographic factors, situational factors, and level of involvement. Demographic factors are individual characteristics such as age, sex, race, ethnicity, income, family life cycle, and occupation. Situational factors are the external circumstances or conditions that exist when a consumer is making a purchase decision. The time available to make a decision is a situational factor that strongly influences consumer buying decisions. An individual's level of involvement—the importance and intensity of interest in a product in a particular situation—also affects the buying decision process. Enduring involvement is an ongoing interest in a product class because of personal relevance. Situational involvement is a temporary interest resulting from the particular circumstance or environment in which buyers find themselves.

Psychological factors operating within individuals partly determine people's general behavior and thus influence their behavior as consumers. The primary psychological influences on consumer behavior are perception, motives, ability and knowledge, attitudes, and personality. Perception is the process of selecting, organizing, and interpreting information inputs (the sensations received through sight, taste, hearing, smell, and touch) to produce meaning. Selective exposure is the phenomenon of people selecting the inputs that are to be exposed to their awareness; selective distortion is changing or twisting currently received information. When a person remembers information inputs that support personal feelings and beliefs and forgets inputs that do not, the phenomenon is called selective retention. The second step of the perceptual process requires organizing and integrating the new information with that already stored in memory. Interpretation—the third step in the perceptual process—is the assignment of meaning to what has been organized. In addition to perceptions of packages, products, brands, and organizations, individuals also have a self-concept, or self-image.

A motive is an internal energizing force that orients a person's activities toward satisfying a need or achieving a goal. Patronage motives influence where a person purchases products on a regular basis. To analyze the major motives that influence consumers to buy or not buy their products, marketers conduct motivation research, using interviews or projective techniques.

Individuals vary in their ability—their competency and efficiency in performing tasks. Ability includes both learning and knowledge. Learning refers to changes in a person's behavior caused by information and experience. Knowledge is made up of two components: familiarity with the product and expertise—the individual's ability to apply the product.

Attitude refers to knowledge and positive or negative feelings about an object or activity. Consumer attitudes toward a firm and its products greatly influence the success or failure of the firm's marketing strategy. Marketers measure consumers' attitudes with projective techniques and attitude scales.

Personality comprises all the internal traits and behaviors that make a person unique. Some marketers believe that a person's personality does influence the types and brands of products purchased.

The forces that other people exert on buying behavior are called social factors. Social factors include the influence of roles and family, reference groups, social classes, and culture and subcultures. All of us occupy positions within groups, organizations, and institutions, and each position has a role—a set of actions and activities that a person in a particular position is supposed to perform, based on the expectations of both the individual and surrounding persons. A group is a reference group when an individual identifies with the group so much that he or she takes on many of the values, attitudes, or behaviors of group members. A social class is an open group of individuals who have similar social rank. Culture is everything in our surroundings that is made by human beings. Cultures vary widely from country to country around the world. A culture can be divided into subcultures on the basis of geographic regions or human characteristics, such as age or ethnic background.

Marketers try to understand consumer buying behavior so that they can offer consumers greater satisfaction. Refinements in research methods will yield more information about consumer behavior, and the pressure of an increasingly competitive business environment will spur marketers to seek fuller understanding of consumer decision processes.

Important Terms

Buying behavior
Consumer buying behavior
Routine response behavior
Limited decision making
Extensive decision making
Impulse buying
Consumer buying decision process
Internal search
External search
Cognitive dissonance
Personal factors
Demographic factors
Situational factors
Level of involvement
Psychological factors
Perception
Information inputs
Selective exposure
Selective distortion
Selective retention
Self-concept
Motive

Patronage motives
Depth interview
Group interview
Projective techniques
Ability
Learning
Knowledge
Attitude
Attitude scale
Personality
Social factors
Role
Reference group
Social class
Culture
Subcultures

Discussion and Review Questions

1. Name the types of buying behavior consumers use. List some products that you have bought using each type of behavior. Have you ever bought a product on impulse?
2. What are the major stages in the consumer buying decision process? Are all these stages used in all consumer purchase decisions?
3. What are the personal factors that affect the consumer buying decision process? How do they affect the process?
4. How does a consumer's level of involvement affect his or her purchase behavior?
5. What is the function of time in a consumer's purchasing decision process?
6. What is selective exposure? Why do humans engage in it?
7. How do marketers attempt to shape consumers' learning?
8. Why are marketers concerned about consumer attitudes?
9. How do roles affect a person's buying behavior?
10. Describe reference groups. How do they influence buying behavior? Name some of your own reference groups.
11. In what ways does social class affect a person's purchase decisions?
12. What is culture? How does it affect a person's buying behavior?
13. Describe the subcultures to which you belong. Identify buying behavior that is unique to your subculture.

Cases

5.1 Burger King Revamps Its Image

After years of declining market share, unsuccessful advertising campaigns, management upheaval, and finally, a takeover by British-owned Grand Metropolitan, PLC, Burger King Corp. wanted to change consumers' perceptions of the company and their attitudes toward it. Under new chief executive officer, Barry Gibbons, Burger King altered its marketing mix to stem its declining market share (17 percent of the $60 billion fast-food market) and to change its image by relating the Burger King experience to consumers' self-concepts. In a break from fast-food marketers' traditional focus on price and treatment of their products as "commodities," Burger King developed a new advertising campaign, designed to set it apart from competitors and its own troubled past.

A random survey showed that the consumers who already patronized Burger King restaurants were overwhelmingly positive about the chain. Such satisfied patrons help boost sales by positive word-of-mouth advertising. But to push up sales and lure competitors' customers, Burger King had to develop a new promotional campaign—a campaign that would enhance consumers' perceptions of the second-largest hamburger chain. Using "attitude advertising," Burger King tried to establish a positive relationship with consumers and create a different image with its daring "sometimes you've gotta break the rules" advertising campaign.

The 1989–1990 $150 million campaign focused on getting both consumers and Burger King management to think differently about the company. The resulting advertisements downplayed traditional product shots and jingles and focused instead on entertainment, humor, and a spirit of independence.

Although most fast-food advertisements usually have mouth-watering shots of food, the Burger King ads included only occasional glimpses of Burger King signs or products and avoided the traditional Burger King flame-broiling action shot. They attempted instead to provide an image of a Burger King experience that is fun and entertaining.

Over the first year of the new campaign, franchisees were disappointed and concerned that the "sometimes you've gotta break the rules" campaign was confusing to customers, and did not clearly convey Burger King's image. In 1990–1991, Burger King budgeted $200 million on image advertisements to improve the clarity of the "you've gotta break the rules" campaign. At the same time, Burger King started launching special promotions with Fox Broadcasting Company's hit series, *The Simpsons,* and movies such as *Teenage Mutant Ninja Turtles.* With these promotions, Burger King competed for the children's segment of the market on the same footing with McDonald's. Also in 1991, Burger King developed the value-priced menu as a strategy to compete head-on with McDonald's, Taco Bell, and other fast food chains that offer lower-priced food items. Burger King sales continued to increase and franchisees were happy about the tie-ins with popular television and movie characters. However, they continued to complain about the "sometimes you've gotta break the rules" commitment.

With increased emphasis on pricing and promotion strategies, the "sometimes you've gotta break the rules" campaign slid into obscurity toward the end of 1991. While executives still wanted to continue to appeal to customer's attitudes, they decided to use more traditional tactics to increase sales in three key groups: children, women, and teens (the traditional customer base).

To continue to appeal to children, Burger King signed a promotional deal with Walt Disney Company. Their children's meal promotions featured Disney character figurines such as Mickey Mouse, Donald Duck, Roger Rabbit, and Goofy, as well as a tie-in with the movie *Beauty and the Beast.* In addition to the Disney tie-ins, Burger King tried joint promotions with popular products such as Kool-Aid Kool Pop frozen treats and Snickers ice cream bars. To appeal to women and teens, Burger King expanded product lines and tested new products, such as Weight Watchers' low-calorie foods and Domino's pizza. In addition, value-pricing continues to stay competitive with other fast food franchises.

All these actions have been taken to support the theme of entertainment, humor, and a fun, economical experience. The changes in Burger King's marketing mix should help alter consumers' view of the company and make the Burger King image more consistent with consumers' interests, leading to a more positive attitude toward the firm.[38]

Questions for Discussion

1. Burger King claims to use "attitude advertising." Based on the text discussion on attitudes, what should this advertising accomplish?
2. How effective was attitude advertising at Burger King?
3. How does Burger King's value-pricing and joint promotions with Disney relate to consumer behavior concepts discussed in this chapter?

5.2 Don't Mess with Texas!

In the early 1980s, Texas taxpayers paid $24 million annually for litter pickup along Texas roads and highways. Previous antilitter programs and promotional campaigns had been unsuccessful in persuading Texans to stop throwing litter onto the roadside. A budget crunch in the mid-1980s forced the Texas Department of Highways and Public Transportation to take drastic steps to cut back the amount of money spent picking up litter.

Research conducted in 1985 by the Institute for Applied Research found that the primary Texas litterer was male, eighteen to thirty-four years old, and more blue collar than professional. Texas-based advertising agency Gurasich, Spence, Darilek and McClure (GSD&M), known for its innovative ideas, was asked to create a marketing campaign to encourage these men (whom that state labeled "Bubbas") to change their littering behavior and help the state reduce its spending on litter cleanup. The agency's tough goal: reduce litter 25 percent by August 31, 1986.

GSD&M recognized that antilitter slogans that might appeal to people from other states would not move Texans. They had to talk bold and tough to get Bubba's attention. To appeal to Texans' state pride and ego, the agency developed the theme "Don't Mess with Texas." Texans in general are quite proud of their state and their frontier heritage; Bubba in particular would probably sit up and listen to such an appeal.

In planning the campaign television and radio spots, the agency chose Bubba's favorite stars to voice the message. In one commercial, the late Stevie Ray Vaughan—a popular Texas guitarist—played the state's theme song, "The Eyes of Texas," seated before a giant Texas flag. Other commercials featured Texas musicians, such as the Fabulous Thunderbirds and Willie Nelson, playing or singing antilitter ditties. Johnny Rodriguez sang the message in Spanish to reach the state's large Hispanic population. Texas sports heroes, such as Ed "Too Tall" Jones, Randy White, and Mike Scott, set an example by picking up roadside litter in some spots. To increase the impact, advertisements ran more often during the spring and summer months, when littering seemed to hit its peak. Some of the spots were so popular that radio listeners and television viewers called the stations and requested that the advertisements be run more often!

Other forms of promotion carried the message too. Free bumper stickers, litter bags, and decals with the "Don't Mess with Texas" message were distributed; the message also appeared on highway road signs. Texas businesses, civic groups, and individuals sponsored the message on T-shirts, coffee cups, key chains, store windows, company trucks, billboards, and even grocery sacks. The state also held "The Great Texas Trash-Off" to encourage Texans to kick the littering habit for one day; sixteen thousand volunteers picked up trash along roadsides. The trash-off has since become an annual event.

When the Institute for Applied Research again surveyed the amount of litter on Texas roadsides in 1986, it found that roadside litter had been reduced by 29 percent in less than one year! Deliberate littering dropped 41 percent, and accidental littering (trash blowing out of the back of pickup trucks, car windows, and so on) dropped 18 percent. The Institute, which has conducted similar litter surveys across the nation, cited the 29 percent one-year drop in roadside litter as the largest one-year reduction in litter it had ever measured. A follow-up study conducted three years later found that overall littering on Texas highways had declined 60 percent since the campaign began. State highway cleanup crews have reported that they are collecting less trash and making their rounds faster, and, more importantly, are spending less state money to pick up trash.

The "Don't Mess with Texas" campaign was greatly expanded after achieving its initial goals. New commercials ask all Texans, not just Bubba, to think before they litter. Some advertisements address litter on Texas beaches, rivers, and lakes, as well as highways. Texas is the only state that relies entirely on a commercial advertising campaign to reduce roadside litter.

The "Don't Mess with Texas" campaign was quite effective in achieving its objective: to get young, blue-collar Texas men to stop throwing trash on the highway. The agency carefully defined its target and spoke directly to that target in words and gestures that group used every day. The slogan also made Texans feel better about their state and gave them a new rallying cry in addition to "Remember the Alamo!"[39]

Questions for Discussion

1. How did personal factors influence the consumer behavior of throwing litter along Texas roads and highways?
2. Discuss the psychological and sociological factors that could influence decisions to stop littering.
3. Evaluate the promotion used to control littering in Texas, based on consumer behavior factors discussed in this chapter.

Chapter Notes

1. Based on information from Vic Sussman, "No Sign of Recession at Fluffy's Mealtime," *U.S. News & World Report,* Oct. 14, 1991, p. 98; Marcia Staimer, "Food for Thought," *USA Today,* Oct. 12, 1989, p. 1A; Sam Gugino, "Haute Dog: Market for Canine, Kitty Cuisine Going Upscale," *Eagle,* June 14, 1989, p. 4C; Michelle Manges, "For Today's Pampered Pets, It's a Dog-Eat-Steak World," *Wall Street Journal,* May 18, 1989, p. B1.

2. James F. Engel, Roger D. Blackwell, and Paul W. Miniard, *Consumer Behavior,* 6th ed. (Hinsdale, Ill.: Dryden Press, 1990), p. 3.

3. Ronald Paul Hill and Mark Stamey, "The Homeless in America: An Examination of Possessions and Consumption Behaviors," *Journal of Consumer Research,* Dec. 1990, pp. 303–321.

4. John A. Howard and Jagdish N. Sheth, *The Theory of Buyer Behavior* (New York: Wiley, 1969), pp. 27–28.

5. Paul M. Herr, Frank R. Kardes, and John Kim, "Effects of Word-of-Mouth and Product-Attribute Information on Persuasion: An Accessibility-Diagnosticity Perspective," *Journal of Consumer Research,* Mar. 1991, pp. 454–462.

6. Kevin L. Keller and Richard Staelin, "Effects of Quality and Quantity of Information on Decision Effectiveness," *Journal of Consumer Research,* Sept. 1987, pp. 200–213.

7. Gabriel Biehal and Dipankar Chakravarti, "Consumers' Use of Memory and External Information in Choice: Macro and Micro Perspectives," *Journal of Consumer Research,* Mar. 1986, pp. 382–405.

8. Bobby J. Calder and Brian Sternthal, "Television Commercial Wearout: An Information Processing View," *Journal of Marketing Research,* May 1980, pp. 173–186.

9. Michael J. Houston, Terry L. Childers, and Susan E. Heckler, "Picture-Word Consistency and the Elaborative Processing of Advertisements," *Journal of Marketing Research,* Nov. 1987, pp. 359–369.

10. James R. Bettman and Mita Sujan, "Effects of Framing on Evaluation of Comparable and Noncomparable Alternatives by Expert and Novice Consumers," *Journal of Consumer Research,* Sept. 1987, pp. 141–154.

11. Robert A. Westbrook, "Product/Consumption–Based Affective Responses and Postpurchase Processes," *Journal of Marketing Research,* Aug. 1987, pp. 258–270.

12. Jon Berry, "The New Creation of Kids and Ads," *Adweek's Marketing Week,* Apr. 15, 1991, p. 26.

13. Judith Waldrop, "Inside America's Households," *American Demographics,* March 1989, pp. 20–27.

14. Thomas D. Jensen, C. P. Rao, and Randy Hilton, "Working Versus Nonworking Wives' Psychographic Profiles: A Longitudinal Analysis," *Journal of Business Research,* Dec. 1989, pp. 255–265.

15. Houston, Childers, and Heckler, pp. 359–369.

16. Thomas S. Robertson and Hubert Gatignon, "Competitive Effects on Technology Diffusion," *Journal of Marketing,* July 1986, pp. 1–12.

17. Ibid.

18. Linda M. Scott, "Understanding Jingles and Needledrop: A Rhetorical Approach to Music in Advertising," *Journal of Consumer Research,* Sept. 1990, pp. 223–236.

19. John W. Schouten, "Selves in Transition: Symbolic Consumption in Personal Rites of Passage and Identity Reconstruction," *Journal of Consumer Research,* Mar. 1991, pp. 412–425.

20. James R. Bettman, *An Information Processing Theory of Consumer Choice* (Reading, Mass.: Addison-Wesley, 1979), pp. 18–24.

21. Alfredo Corchado, "Hispanic Supermarkets Are Blossoming," *Wall Street Journal,* Jan. 23, 1989, p. B1.

22. David Aaker and George Day, *Marketing Research* (New York: John Wiley & Sons, 1990), p. 172.

23. Joseph W. Alba and J. Wesley Hutchinson, "Dimensions of Consumer Expertise," *Journal of Consumer Research*, Mar. 1987, pp. 411–454.

24. Arabhna Krishna, Imran S. Currim, and Robert W. Shoemaker, "Consumer Perceptions of Consumer Activity," *Journal of Marketing*, Apr. 1991, p. 4.

25. Akshay R. Rao and Kent B. Monroe, "The Moderating Effect of Prior Knowledge on Cue Utilization in Product Evaluations," *Journal of Consumer Research*, Sept. 1988, pp. 253–264.

26. Rao and Monroe, ibid.

27. "Rely on Vision: Secrets of Selling 'Life-Style' Products," *Success*, Dec. 1990, p. 12.

28. Rebecca Piirto, "Clothes with Attitude," *American Demographics*, Oct. 1990, pp. 10, 52, 54.

29. John L. Lastovika and Erich A. Joachimsthaler, "Improving the Detection of Personality-Behavior Relationships in Consumer Research," *Journal of Consumer Research*, Mar. 1988, pp. 583–587.

30. Howard Schlossberg, "K Mart's New Approach Aims Straight for the Heart," *Marketing News*, Apr. 1, 1991, pp. 8, 21.

31. Eileen Fischer and Stephen J. Arnold, "More Than a Labor of Love: Gender Roles and Christmas Gift Shopping," *Journal of Consumer Research*, Dec. 1990, pp. 333–345.

32. Martha T. Moore, "Spring Break: Brand Names Chase Sales," *USA Today*, Mar. 17, 1989, p. B1.

33. Henry Assael, *Consumer Behavior and Marketing Action* (Boston: Kent Publishing, 1987), p. 369.

34. Richard P. Coleman, "The Continuing Significance of Social Class in Marketing," *Journal of Consumer Research*, Dec. 1983, p. 267. Copyright © The Journal of Consumer Research, Inc., 1983. Reprinted by permission of the University of Chicago Press.

35. Leonard L. Berry, "The Time-Sharing Consumer," *Journal of Retailing*, Winter 1979, p. 69.

36. Mona Doyle, "The Metamorphosis of the Consumer," *Marketing Communications*, Apr. 1989, pp. 18–22.

37. Raj Mehta and Russell W. Belk, "Artifacts, Identity, and Transition: Favorite Possessions of Indians and Indian Immigrants to the United States," *Journal of Consumer Research*, Mar. 1991, pp. 393–411.

38. Scott Hume and Cleveland Horton, "BK Picks Mickey; Disney Promotion Leaves McDonald's Out, *Advertising Age*, Aug. 12, 1991, p. 1; Scott Hume, "Burger King, Langstaff Breaking up; Franchisees Blame 'Rules' Theme, No Follow-Through," *Advertising Age*, Mar. 4, 1991, p. 6; Scott Hume, "Burger King May Break Off 'Rules,'" *Advertising Age*, Nov. 5, 1990, p. 68; Scott Hume, "Burger King Tinkers with 'Break the Rules,'" *Advertising Age*, Sept. 10, 1990, p. 3; Scott Hume, "Burger King Nabs 'The Simpsons,'" *Advertising Age*, Apr. 30, 1990, p. 3; Jane Weaver, "Getting Attitude: Creatives Scrutinize Ads Without Products," *Adweek*, Oct. 23, 1989, p. 27; Bob Garfield, "Burger King Breaks from Indecisive Past," *Advertising Age*, Oct. 2, 1989, pp. 1, 68; Scott Hume, "A New 'Personality,'" *Advertising Age*, Oct. 2, 1989, pp. 1, 66; Scott Hume, "Burger King Ads Will Count," *Advertising Age*, Oct. 2, 1989, p. 66; and James Cox, "Bold Campaign Aims to Beef Up Market Share," *USA Today*, Sept. 28, 1989, pp. 1B, 2B.

39. "Campaign Gets 'Bubbas' to Quit Messin,'" *Marketing News,* June 19, 1987, p. 16; "Don't Mess with Texas: A Phenomenal Success," Gurasich, Spence, Darilek and McClure, Austin, Texas, 1987; "How to Talk Trash to Texans . . . Plus, the Antidote for Boring Advertising," Gurasich, Spence, Darilek and McClure, Austin, Texas, 1987; Seth Kantor, "Engineer's Survey Helped Shape State's Ad Campaign Against Highway Littering," *Eagle,* Aug. 4, 1989, p. 2D; Michael McCullar, "Trash on Roads Down 29% After Ads," *Austin American-Statesman,* Sept. 22, 1986, pp. A1, A8; press release issued by the Texas State Department of Highways and Public Transportation, Sept. 22, 1986; and a telephone conversation with Nick Turnham, public affairs officer, Brazos County, Texas Department of Highways and Public Transportation, Bryan, Texas, June 25, 1987.

6 *Organizational Markets and Buying Behavior*

OBJECTIVES

- To become familiar with the various types of organizational markets

- To identify the major characteristics of organizational buyers and transactions

- To understand several attributes of organizational demand

- To become familiar with the major components of a buying center

- To understand the stages of the organizational buying decision process and the factors that affect this process

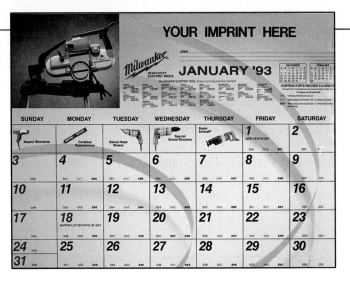

Sigma Marketing Concepts is a publisher of high-quality, creatively designed promotional calendars, which are sold directly to businesses for use as marketing tools. The product line includes wall calendars, wall planners, pocket planners, diaries, and other paper imprint items that can be used to promote a company and its products.

After carefully analyzing the characteristics of its organizational buyers and the organizational buying decision process, Sigma refined its target market. Sigma was focusing on large, customer contact companies that distributed their calendars through their sales forces. They usually supplied Sigma with an imprint or art design for the firm's customized calendar.

For years Sigma heard from customers that an effective calendar program would require too much of their staff's time to implement. Sigma seized this opportunity by marketing its "Total Service Package," a program where the entire calendar promotion is handled by Sigma, including conception, design, production, and delivery.

With its own computer order tracking and manifest system in place, Sigma was able to offer its customers and prospects an efficient and cost-saving order and distribution system. With a customer list provided, calendars could be shipped to as many as 20,000 locations for a single account. This was particularly helpful to those accounts that had dealers scattered across the country.

This achievement led Sigma to take its experience one step further. Using the customer-supplied list, they began marketing the calendars directly to the customers' distributors. Flyers and samples were mailed by and returned directly to Sigma. Now a single company's order may consist of over 1,000 different calendar imprints.

Sigma learned how its customers make decisions about specialty advertising purchases and developed a program to satisfy their needs.

The new strategy appears very successful. The company has added to its list of satisfied customers including Milwaukee Electric Tool Corp., International Paper Company, and Nabisco Brands, Inc.[1]

Photo courtesy of Sigma Marketing Concepts.

A N UNDERSTANDING OF ORGANIZATIONAL MARKETS and the buying decision process is required to effectively serve those markets. Sigma Marketing Concepts' understanding of their organizational buyers allows them to effectively sell their promotional calendars to large international companies, their divisions, and dealers. We define an organizational or business-to-business market in Chapter 4 as consisting of individuals or groups that purchase a specific type of product for resale, for use in making other products, or for use in daily operations.

In this chapter we look more closely at organizational markets and organizational buying decision processes. We first discuss the various kinds of organizational markets and the types of buyers that make up these markets. Next we explore several dimensions of organizational buying, such as the characteristics of the transactions, the attributes and concerns of the buyers, the methods of buying, and the distinctive features of the demand for products sold to organizational purchasers. Finally, we examine organizational buying decisions by considering how they are arrived at and who makes the purchases.

Types of Organizational Markets

In Chapter 4 we identify four kinds of organizational, or business-to-business, markets: producer, reseller, government, and institutional. The following section describes the characteristics of the customers that make up each of these markets.

Producer Markets

Individuals and business organizations that purchase products for the purpose of making a profit by using them to produce other products or by using them in their operations are classified as **producer markets**. Producer markets include buyers of raw materials, as well as purchasers of semifinished and finished items used to produce other products. For example, a manufacturer buys raw materials and component parts to use directly in the production of products. Grocery stores and supermarkets are part of the producer markets for numerous support products, such as paper and plastic bags, counters, scanners, and floor-care products. Farmers are part of the producer markets for farm machinery, fertilizer, seed, and livestock. A broad array of industries make up producer markets; the industries range from agriculture, forestry, fisheries, and mining to construction, transportation, communications, and utilities. As the data in Table 6.1 indicate, the number of business units in national producer markets is enormous.

Manufacturers are geographically concentrated. More than half are located in only seven states: New York, California, Pennsylvania, Illinois, Ohio, New Jersey, and Michigan. This concentration sometimes enables a business-to-business marketer to serve customers more efficiently. Within certain states, production in just a few industries may account for a sizable proportion of total industrial output.

Table 6.1

Number of Firms in Industry Groups

Industry	Number of Firms
Agriculture, forestry, fishing	357,000
Mining	121,100
Construction	1,651,000
Manufacturing	433,000
Transportation, public utilities	592,800
Finance, insurance, real estate	1,227,200
Services	5,937,700

Source: *Statistical Abstract of the United States,* 1991, p. 533.

Reseller Markets

Reseller markets consist of intermediaries, such as wholesalers and retailers, who buy finished goods and resell them to make a profit. (Wholesalers and retailers are discussed in Chapters 12 and 13.) Other than making minor alterations, resellers do not change the physical characteristics of the products they handle. With the exception of items that producers sell directly to consumers, all products sold to consumer markets are first sold to reseller markets.

Wholesalers purchase products for resale to retailers, to other wholesalers, and to producers, governments, and institutions. Of the 439,200 wholesalers in the United States, a large percentage are located in New York, California, Illinois, Texas, Ohio, Pennsylvania, and New Jersey.[2] Although some highly technical products are sold directly to end users, many products are sold through wholesalers who, in turn, sell products to other firms in the distribution system. Thus wholesalers are very important in helping to get a producer's product to customers. Wholesalers often carry many products, perhaps as many as 250,000 items. When inventories are vast, the reordering of products normally is automated and the wholesaler's initial purchase decisions are made by professional buyers and buying committees.

Retailers purchase products and resell them to final consumers. There are approximately 2.3 million retailers in the United States. They employ about 18 million people and generate close to $1.5 trillion in annual sales.[3] Some retailers carry a large number of items. Drugstores, for example, may stock up to 12,000 items, and some supermarkets may handle as many as 20,000 different products. In small, family-owned retail stores, the owner frequently makes purchasing decisions. Large department stores have one or more employees in each department who are responsible for buying products for that department. As for chain stores, a buyer or buying committee in the central office frequently decides whether a product will be made available for selection by store managers. For most products, however, local store management makes the actual buying decisions for a particular store.

When making purchase decisions, resellers consider several factors. They evaluate the level of demand for a product to determine in what quantity and at what prices the product can be resold. They assess the amount of space required

to handle a product relative to its potential profit. Retailers sometimes evaluate products on the basis of sales per square foot of selling area. In Figure 6.1, Rich Products Corporation's message to grocers deals with the product's appeal to customers and the minimal expense and effort involved in carrying the product. Since customers often depend on a reseller to have a product when they need it, a reseller typically evaluates a supplier's ability to provide adequate quantities when and where wanted. Resellers also take into account the ease of placing orders and the availability of technical assistance and training programs from the producer. More broadly, when resellers consider buying a product not previously carried, they try to determine whether the product competes with or complements products the firm is currently handling. These types of concerns distinguish reseller markets from other markets. Marketers dealing with reseller markets must recognize these needs and be able to serve them.

Government Markets

Federal, state, county, and local governments make up **government markets**. They spend billions of dollars annually for a variety of goods and services to support their internal operations and to provide citizens with such products as highways, education, water, energy, and national defense. For example, the U.S. federal government spends about $300 billion annually on defense.[4] Governmental expenditures annually account for about 20 percent of the U.S. gross national product.

Besides the federal government, there are 50 state governments, 3,042 county governments, and 83,186 other local governments.[5] The amount spent by federal, state, and local units during the last thirty years has increased rapidly because the total number of government units and the services they provide have both increased. In addition, the costs of providing these services have increased. In Table 6.2, notice that the federal government spends over half of the total amount spent by all governments.

The types and quantities of products bought by government markets reflect societal demands on various government agencies. As citizens' needs for government services change, so does the demand for products by government markets. Because government agencies spend public funds to buy the products needed to provide services, they are accountable to the public. This accountability explains their relatively complex set of buying procedures.

Some firms do not even try to sell to government buyers because they do not want to deal with so much red tape. However, many marketers have learned to deal efficiently with government procedures and do not find them to be a stumbling block. For certain products, such as defense-related items, the government may be the only customer. The U.S. Government Printing Office publishes and distributes several documents explaining buying procedures and describing the types of products various federal agencies purchase.

The government makes its purchases through bids or negotiated contracts. Although companies may be reluctant to approach government markets because of the complicated bidding process, once the rules of this process are understood, it becomes quite routine to penetrate this market.[6] To make a sale under the bid system, a firm must apply for and be approved in order to be placed on a list of qualified bidders. When a government unit wants to buy, it sends out a detailed description of the products to qualified bidders. Businesses that wish to sell such products submit bids. The government unit usually is required to accept the lowest bid.

Table 6.2

Annual Expenditures by Government Units for Selected Years (in billions of dollars)

Year	Total Government Expenditures	Federal Government Expenditures	State and Local Expenditures
1960	151	90	61
1970	333	185	148
1975	560	292	268
1980	959	526	432
1981	1,110	625	485
1983	1,351	786	565
1985	1,581	1,032	658
1987	1,810	1,149	775
1988	1,920	1,215	827

Source: *Statistical Abstract of the United States,* 1991, p. 279.

When buying nonstandard or highly complex products, a government unit often uses a negotiated contract. Under this procedure, the government unit selects only a few firms and then negotiates specifications and terms; it eventually awards the contract to one of the negotiating firms. Most large defense-related contracts held by such companies as McDonnell Douglas, General Dynamics, and Northrop are made through negotiated contracts.

Although government markets can have complicated requirements, they can also be very lucrative. When the Postal Service or other government agencies modernize obsolete computer systems, successful bidders can gain a billion dollars during the contract life, which is usually five years or more. Governments seem to be increasingly willing to spend money to update computer software. Many governmental agencies are trying to become more efficient by buying packaged software to reduce internal development costs.[7] Some firms have established separate departments to facilitate marketing to government units.

Institutional Markets

Organizations that seek to achieve charitable, educational, community, or other nonbusiness goals constitute **institutional markets**. Members of institutional markets include churches, some hospitals, civic clubs, fraternities and sororities, colleges, and charitable organizations. Institutions purchase millions of dollars' worth of products annually to provide goods, services, and ideas to congregations, students, patients, club members, and others. Because institutions often have different goals and fewer resources than other types of organizations, marketers may use special marketing activities to serve these markets. Sam's Club, a division of Wal-Mart Stores, Inc., has targeted institutional markets. Giant warehouse outlets permit institutional as well as other qualified members to purchase supplies on a self-service cash basis at prices lower than in stores oriented to the consumer market, and lower than those charged by high-service wholesalers. Sam's Club even publishes *Buy-Line,* a members-only newspaper with tips on effective management.[8]

Dimensions of Organizational Buying

Having gained an understanding of the different types of organizational customers, we now need to consider the dimensions of organizational buying. First we examine several characteristics of organizational transactions. Then we discuss the attributes of organizational buyers and some of their primary concerns when making purchase decisions. Next we consider methods of organizational buying and the major types of purchases. We conclude the section with a discussion of how the demand for industrial products differs from the demand for consumer products.

Characteristics of Organizational Transactions

Organizational (or business-to-business) transactions differ from consumer sales in several ways. Orders by organizational buyers tend to be much larger than individual consumer sales. Suppliers often must sell their products in large quantities to make profits; consequently, they prefer not to sell to customers who place small orders.

Generally, organizational purchases are negotiated less frequently than consumer sales. Some purchases involve expensive items, such as machinery, that are used for a number of years. Other products, such as raw materials and component items, are used continuously in production and may have to be supplied frequently. However, the contract regarding the terms of sale of these items is likely to be a long-term agreement, requiring negotiations, for example, every third year.

Negotiations in organizational sales are less frequent than in consumer sales and usually take longer. Surveys show, however, that the amount of time industrial sales representatives spend with customers is decreasing.[9] Purchasing decisions are often made by a committee; orders are frequently large and expensive; and products may be custom-built. There is a good chance that several people or departments in the purchasing organization will be involved. One department might express a need for a product; a second department might develop its specifications; a third might stipulate the maximum amount to be spent; and a fourth might actually place the order.

One practice unique to organizational sales is **reciprocity**, an arrangement in which two organizations agree to buy from each other. The risks associated with cooperation are great, but companies that develop long-term relationships based on reciprocity and trust can find that cooperation can be an effective competitive tool.[10] Reciprocal agreements that threaten competition are illegal. The Federal Trade Commission and the Justice Department take action to stop anticompetitive reciprocal practices. Nonetheless, it is reasonable to believe that a certain amount of reciprocal dealing occurs among small businesses and, to a lesser extent, among larger companies as well. Because reciprocity influences purchasing agents to deal only with certain suppliers, it can lower morale among agents and lead to less-than-optimal purchases. The Global Perspective focuses on the problems of Japanese auto factories in the United States in selecting suppliers.

Attributes of Organizational Buyers

We usually think of organizational buyers as being different from consumer buyers in their purchasing behavior because they are better informed than consumer buyers about the products they purchase. To make purchasing decisions that fulfill an organization's needs, organizational buyers demand detailed information about products' functional features and technical specifications.

Organizational buyers, however, also have personal goals that may influence their buying behavior. Most organizational purchasing agents seek the psychological satisfaction that comes with organizational advancement and financial rewards. Agents who consistently exhibit rational organizational buying behavior are likely to achieve these personal goals because they are performing their jobs in ways that help their firms achieve organizational objectives. Suppose, though, that an organizational buyer develops a close friendship with a certain supplier. If the buyer values friendship more than organizational promotion or financial rewards, he or she may behave irrationally from the firm's point of view. Dealing exclusively with that supplier regardless of better prices, product

Sourcing Decisions Determine
What Is an "American-Made" Car

IN THEIR ATTEMPTS at becoming more "American," Japanese car makers have transplanted automobile factories from Japan to the United States and Canada. The premise behind transplanted factories is that American-made parts, along with foreign-made parts, are assembled in foreign-owned factories based in North America. These transplants not only provide jobs and income for American citizens, but they allow the foreign car makers to claim that their cars are "American-made." Owners of these transplanted factories include Honda (Marysville, Ohio, and Alliston, Ontario), Nissan (Smyrna, Tennessee), Toyota (Georgetown, Kentucky), Mitsubishi (Normal, Illinois), Subaru-Isuzu (Lafayette, Indiana), and Mazda (Flat Rock, Michigan). In 1990, 39 percent of Japanese vehicles sold in the United States were built in North America, a figure up from 9 percent in 1986. Of those cars, Honda claims to have the highest percentage.

Defining "American-made" has, however, proved controversial and could have a real bottom-line influence on profits. Transplanted factories operate in producer markets, where raw materials and semifinished goods are assembled to create a total, finished automobile. These raw materials and semifinished goods come from Pacific Rim countries, such as Japan and Korea, as well as from North American countries to assembly plants in the United States, Canada, and Mexico. For an automobile to be classified as "American-made" and to obtain tariff-free import to the United States, at least 50 percent of the parts in the finished automobile must come from North American suppliers. By failing to purchase from U.S. suppliers, these companies could lose their tariff-free import status.

Initially, most of the Customs Department effort has been directed at Honda Motor Company. The investigators claim that Honda violated the rules of the U.S.–Canadian free trade agreement by overstating the North American content of its Civics. Customs found only $51.75 worth of U.S. parts and materials in Honda engines, and only 15 percent of the overall parts in the Honda Civic to be from North America. Honda executives claim that 75 percent of the parts in their automobiles come from North American suppliers. The disagreement stems from the definition of a North American supplier. Honda includes parts from U.S.–owned suppliers and U.S.–based suppliers that are owned by foreign companies. The costs for labor, depreciation, and overhead are also included in the Honda estimates. In contrast, the Customs Department only includes parts that are supplied by U.S.–owned companies. As a result, the Customs Department claims that most of the "American-made" parts that Honda buys are really supplied by a network of foreign-owned suppliers. The claims of the Customs Department were backed up by an independent study conducted by the University of Michigan. That study found that only 16 percent of the Honda Civic's content consisted of parts purchased from U.S.–owned suppliers.

The price for not being "American-made" could be very costly to Honda. In 1992, Honda lost the first round in the battle with U.S. Customs. The company was ordered to pay millions in back tariffs for a single year, and its reputation as "American-made" could be tarnished. The United States is not the only country investigating transplanted factories. Canada has recently begun its own investigation. Perhaps the true definition of an "American-made" car will result from these investigations. Then again, the answer to the question may ultimately depend upon whom you ask.

Sources: David E. Sanger, "U.S. Tariffs on Hondas Roil Japanese," *New York Times,* Mar. 4, 1992, p. 4; Paul Magnusson, "Big Flap Over the Customs Audit," *Business Week,* Nov. 18, 1991, p. 108; and Paul Magnusson, James B. Treece, and William C. Symonds, "Honda: Is It an American Car?," *Business Week,* Nov. 18, 1991, pp. 105–109, 112.

qualities, or services from competitors may indicate a questionable relationship between the buyer and seller.

Primary Concerns of Organizational Buyers

Today, organizational buyer behavior is being influenced more by longer-term strategic considerations than by short-term operational concerns. This is because companies are purchasing more of the products they use and sell, and rapidly changing technology and global competition are putting more pressures on decision makers.[11] When they make purchasing decisions, organizational customers take into account a variety of factors. Among their chief considerations are quality, service, and price.

Most organizational customers try to achieve and maintain a specific level of quality, or absence of variation, in the products they offer to their target markets.[12] To achieve this goal, most firms establish standards (usually stated as a percentage of defects allowed) for these products and buy them on the basis of a set of expressed characteristics, commonly called *specifications*. Thus an organizational buyer evaluates the quality of the products being considered to determine whether they meet specifications. Most firms have a continuous improvement process in which they search for high levels of quality by eliminating defects.[13]

Meeting specifications is extremely important to organizational customers. If a product fails to meet specifications and malfunctions for the ultimate consumer, the organizational customer may drop that product's supplier and switch to a different one. On the other hand, organizational customers are ordinarily cautious about buying products that exceed specifications because such products often cost more and thus increase an organization's production costs. As customer wants are evaluated, specifications that do not contribute to meeting these wants are considered wasteful. In Figure 6.2, International Paper promotes several types of copier paper to meet a variety of specifications.

Organizational buyers value service. The services offered by suppliers influence directly and indirectly organizational customers' costs, sales, and profits. When tangible goods are the same or quite similar—as is true in the case of most raw materials—the goods may be sold at the same price in the same kind of containers and may have the same specifications. Under such conditions, the mix of services provided to customers is likely to be the major way that the marketer gains a competitive advantage. Services are only as good as the customer's evaluation says they are good.

Specific services vary in importance. Among those commonly desired are market information, inventory maintenance, on-time delivery, repair services, and credit. Organizational buyers are likely to need technical product information, data regarding demand, information about general economic conditions, or supply and delivery information. Maintaining an adequate inventory is critical because it helps make products accessible when an organizational buyer needs them and reduces the buyer's inventory requirements and costs. Since organizational buyers are usually responsible for ensuring that the products are on hand and ready for use when needed, on-time delivery is crucial. Furthermore, reliable, on-time delivery saves organizational customers money, enabling them to carry less inventory. Purchasers of machinery are especially concerned

Figure 6.2

Product Specifications

International Paper recognizes that customers have differing paper needs. To meet those needs, it advertises the quality of its papers and the availability of different types of paper for specific applications.

Source: Reprinted with permission of Hammermill Papers. Division of International Paper.

about obtaining repair services and replacement parts quickly because inoperable equipment is costly. Caterpillar Inc., a manufacturer of earth-moving, construction, and materials-handling machinery, has built an international reputation, as well as high profits, by providing prompt service and replacement parts for its products around the world.

Suppliers can also give extra value to buyers by offering credit. Credit helps improve cash flow and reduces the peaks and valleys of capital requirements, thus lowering the firm's cost of capital. Although a single supplier cannot provide every possible service to its customers, a market-oriented supplier creates a service mix that satisfies the target market.

Providing service has become even more critical because customer expectations about service have broadened. In Figure 6.3, Ernst & Young shows that it helps companies respond to customer demands that something be done "right the first time." Approaching service quality based on traditional manufacturing and accounting systems is not enough. Now, for instance, communication channels that allow customers to ask questions, complain, submit orders, and trace shipments are indispensable aspects of service. Most overnight small-package delivery services can track a customer's package constantly. Marketers also need to strive for uniformity of service, simplicity, truthfulness, and accuracy; develop customer service objectives; and monitor or audit their customer service programs. Firms can monitor their service by formally surveying customers or informally calling on customers and asking questions about the service they received. Taking the time and effort to make sure customers are happy can be very beneficial for marketers. One study found that boosting customer retention 2 percent can have the same effect as cutting costs by 10 percent.[14]

Price matters greatly to an organizational customer because it influences operating costs and costs of goods sold, and these costs affect the customer's selling price and profit margin. When purchasing major equipment, an industrial buyer views the price as the amount of investment necessary to obtain a certain level of return or savings. Thus an organizational purchaser is likely to compare the price of a machine with the value of the benefits that the machine will yield. An organizational buyer does not compare alternative products strictly by price; as we discussed, other factors, such as product quality and supplier services, are also major elements in the purchase decision. A survey to determine the importance of various criteria that buyers place on suppliers resulted in the following considerations: (1) ease of placing order, (2) availability, (3) delivery when requested, and (4) length and consistency of the ordering cycle.[15] Customers want dependable suppliers and consistency in the purchasing relationship. Daewoo, a supplier for many industries, promotes its products and their ability to help customers grow (Figure 6.4).

Methods of Organizational Buying

Although no two organizational buyers go about their jobs in the same way, most use one or more of the following purchase methods: *description, inspection, sampling,* or *negotiation.* When the products being purchased are commonly standardized according to certain characteristics (such as size, shape, weight, and color) and are normally graded using such standards, an organizational

Figure 6.3

Maintaining the Quality of Services

Providing quality goods and services to business customers is critical in today's environment. The management consulting firm Ernst & Young promotes its services— helping companies use their innovative approach to develop total quality management.

Source: Ernst & Young.

Figure 6.4

Concerns of Organizational Buyers

Daewoo, one of South Korea's four largest conglomerates, is a supplier for many industries throughout the world including shipping, consumer electronics, and telecommunications. Here, Daewoo promotes the quality of its products and its spirit of innovation to potential buyers.

Source: Bernard S. Owett, Creative Director, J. Walter Thompson.

THE UNIVERSAL LANG UAGE OF INNOVATION.

At Daewoo, we bend over backwards to find new ways of looking at old problems. It's part of an innovative spirit that is shared by each of the almost 100,000 people that make up Daewoo. And that same spirit has helped make Daewoo, in little more than two decades, a universal name in fields as diverse as trading and shipbuilding, aeronautics and electronics, construction and telecommunications, finance and heavy industry. To find out how the innovative spirit behind Daewoo's growth can spur your own, call Daewoo.

Daewoo International (America) Corp. (212) 909-8200.

DAEWOO

buyer may be able to purchase simply by describing or specifying quantity, grade, and other attributes. Agricultural products often fall into this category. In some cases, a buyer may specify a particular brand or its equivalent when describing the desired product. Purchases on the basis of description are especially common between a buyer and seller who have established an ongoing relationship built on trust.

Certain products, such as large industrial equipment, used vehicles, and buildings, have unique characteristics and may vary regarding their condition. For example, a particular used truck might have a bad transmission. Consequently, organizational buyers of such products must base their purchase decisions on inspection.

In buying based on sampling, a sample of the product is taken from the lot and evaluated. It is assumed that the characteristics of this sample represent the entire lot. This method is appropriate when the product is homogeneous—for instance, grain—and examination of the entire lot is not physically or economically feasible.

Some industrial purchasing relies on negotiated contracts. In certain instances, an organizational buyer describes exactly what is needed and then asks sellers to submit bids. The buyer may take the most attractive bids and negotiate with those suppliers. In other cases, the buyer may not be able to identify specifically what is to be purchased but can provide only a general description—as might be the case for a special piece of custom-made equipment. A buyer and seller might negotiate a contract that specifies a base price and contains provisions for the payment of additional costs and fees. These contracts are most likely to be used for one-time projects, such as buildings and capital equipment.

Types of Organizational Purchases

Most organizational purchases are one of three types: new-task purchase, modified rebuy purchase, or straight rebuy purchase. In a **new-task purchase**, an organization makes an initial purchase of an item to be used to perform a new job or to solve a new problem. A new-task purchase may require the development of product specifications, vendor specifications, and procedures for future purchases of that product. To make the initial purchase, the organizational buyer usually needs much information. A new-task purchase is important to a supplier, for if the organizational buyer is satisfied with the product, the supplier may be able to sell the buyer large quantities of the product for a period of years.

In a **modified rebuy purchase**, a new-task purchase is changed the second or third time it is ordered or the requirements associated with a straight rebuy purchase are modified. For example, an organizational buyer might seek faster delivery, lower prices, or a different quality level of product specifications. A modified rebuy situation may cause regular suppliers to become more competitive to keep the account. Competing suppliers may have the opportunity to obtain the business.

A **straight rebuy purchase** occurs when a buyer purchases the same products routinely under approximately the same terms of sale. Buyers require little information for these routine purchase decisions. The buyer tends to use familiar suppliers that have provided satisfactory service and products in the past. These suppliers try to set up automatic reordering systems to make reordering easy and convenient for organizational buyers. A supplier may even monitor the organizational buyer's inventory and indicate to the buyer what needs to be ordered.

Demand for Industrial Products

Products sold to organizational customers are called industrial products, and consequently, the demand for these products is called industrial demand. Unlike consumer demand, industrial demand is (1) derived, (2) inelastic, (3) joint, and (4) more fluctuating. As we discuss each of these characteristics, remember that the demand for different types of industrial products varies.

Derived Demand   Because organizational customers, especially producers, buy products to be used directly or indirectly in the production of goods and services to satisfy consumers' needs, the demand for industrial products derives from the demand for consumer products; therefore it is called **derived demand**. For example, the demand for certain types of computer chips derives from consumers' demands for faster and smaller personal computers. In the long run, no industrial demand is totally unrelated to the demand for consumer goods.

The derived nature of industrial demand is usually multilevel. Industrial sellers at different levels are affected by a change in consumer demand for a particular product. For instance, consumers today are more concerned with health and good nutrition than ever before, and as a result are purchasing more products with less cholesterol and salt. When consumers stopped buying high-cholesterol shortenings and margarine, the demand for equipment used in manufacturing these products also dropped. Thus factors influencing consumer buying of various food products affected food processors, equipment manufacturers, suppliers of raw materials, and even fast-food restaurants, which have had to switch to vegetable oils for frying. Changes in derived demand result from a chain reaction. When consumer demand for a product changes, a wave is set in motion that affects demand for all firms involved in the production of that consumer product.

Inelastic Demand **Inelastic demand** for many industrial products simply means that a price increase or decrease will not significantly alter demand for the item. (The concept of price elasticity of demand is discussed further in Chapter 19.) Because many industrial products contain a number of parts, price increases that affect only one or two parts of the product may yield only a slightly higher per-unit production cost. Of course, when a sizable price increase for a component represents a large proportion of the product's cost, then demand may become more elastic because the price increase in the component causes the price at the consumer level to rise sharply. For example, if manufacturers of aircraft engines substantially increase the price of these engines, forcing Boeing to raise the prices of the aircraft it manufactures, the demand for airliners may become more elastic as airlines reconsider whether they can afford to buy new aircraft. An increase in the price of windshields, however, is unlikely to greatly affect the price of the airliners or the demand for them.

The characteristic of inelasticity applies only to industry demand for the industrial product, not to the demand curve faced by an individual firm. Suppose that a spark plug producer increases the price of spark plugs sold to manufacturers of small engines, but its competitors continue to maintain their lower prices. The spark plug company would probably experience reduced unit sales because most small-engine producers would switch to the lower-priced brands. A specific firm is vulnerable to elastic demand, even though industry demand for a particular product is inelastic.

Joint Demand The demand for certain industrial products, especially raw materials and components, is subject to joint demand. **Joint demand** occurs when two or more items are used in combination to produce a product. For example, a firm that manufactures axes needs the same number of ax handles as it does ax blades; these two products are demanded jointly. If there is a shortage of ax handles, then the producer will buy fewer ax blades.

Understanding the effects of joint demand is particularly important for a marketer selling multiple jointly demanded items. Such a marketer must realize that when a customer begins purchasing one of the jointly demanded items, a good opportunity exists for selling related products. Similarly, when customers purchase a number of jointly demanded products, the producer must exercise extreme caution to avoid shortages of any one of them because such shortages jeopardize the marketer's sales of all the jointly demanded products.

Demand Fluctuations As already mentioned, the demand for industrial products may fluctuate enormously because it is derived from consumer demand. In general, when particular consumer products are in high demand, their producers buy large quantities of raw materials and components to ensure that they can meet long-run production requirements. In addition, these producers may expand their production capacity, which entails the acquisition of new equipment and machinery, more workers, and more raw materials and component parts.

Conversely, a decline in the demand for certain consumer goods significantly reduces the demand for industrial products used to produce those goods. In fact, under such conditions, a marketer's sales of certain products may come to a temporary standstill. When consumer demand is low, industrial customers cut their purchases of raw materials and components and stop buying equipment and machinery, even for replacement purposes.

A marketer of industrial products may notice changes in demand when its customers change their inventory policies, perhaps because of expectations about future demand. For example, if several dishwasher manufacturers who buy timers from one producer increase their inventory of timers from a two-week to a one-month supply, the timer producer will have a significant immediate increase in demand.

Sometimes price changes can lead to surprising temporary changes in demand. A price increase for an industrial item may initially cause organizational customers to buy more of the item because they expect the price to rise further. Similarly, demand for a business-to-business product may be significantly lower following a price cut because buyers are waiting for further price reductions. Fluctuations in demand can be significant in industries in which price changes occur frequently.

Organizational Buying Decisions

Organizational (or **business-to-business**) **buying behavior** refers to the purchase behavior of producers, resellers, government units, and institutions. Although several of the same factors that affect consumer buying behavior (discussed in Chapter 5) also influence organizational buying behavior, a number of factors are unique to the latter. In this section we first analyze the buying center to learn who participates in making organizational purchase decisions. Then we focus on the stages of the buying decision process and the factors that affect it.

The Buying Center

Relatively few organizational purchase decisions are made by just one person; mostly, they are made through a buying center. The **buying center** refers to the group of people within an organization who are involved in making organizational purchase decisions. These individuals include users, influencers, buyers, deciders, and gatekeepers.[16] One person may perform several of these roles. These participants share some goals and risks associated with their decisions.

Users are the organization members who actually use the product being acquired. They frequently initiate the purchase process and/or generate the specifications for the purchase. After the purchase, they also evaluate the product's performance relative to the specifications. Influencers are often technical personnel, such as engineers, who help develop the specifications and evaluate alternative products. Technical personnel are especially important influencers when the products being considered involve new, advanced technology.

Buyers are responsible for selecting suppliers and actually negotiating the terms of purchase. They may also become involved in developing specifications. Buyers are sometimes called purchasing agents or purchasing managers. Their choices of vendors and products, especially for new-task purchases, are heavily influenced by persons occupying other roles in the buying center. For straight rebuy purchases, the buyer plays a major role in the selection of vendors and in negotiations with them. Deciders actually choose the products and vendors. Although buyers may be the deciders, it is not unusual for different people to occupy these roles. For routinely purchased items, buyers are commonly the deciders. However, a buyer may not be authorized to make purchases that exceed a certain dollar limit, in which case higher-level management personnel are the deciders. Gatekeepers, such as secretaries and technical personnel, control the flow of information to and among the persons who occupy the other roles in the buying center. Buyers who deal directly with vendors also may be gatekeepers because they can control the flow of information. The flow of information from supplier sales representatives to users and influencers often is controlled by personnel in the purchasing department.

The number and structure of an organization's buying centers are affected by the organization's size and market position, by the volume and types of products being purchased, and by the firm's overall managerial philosophy regarding exactly who should be involved in purchase decisions. Varying goals among the members of the buying center can have both positive and negative impacts on the purchasing process. Inside Marketing looks at the most common causes and the resultant outcomes of interdepartmental conflicts within the buying center.

A marketer attempting to sell to an organizational customer should determine who is in the buying center, the types of decisions each individual makes, and which individuals are the most influential in the decision process. Because in some instances many people make up the buying center, marketers cannot contact all participants; instead, they must be certain to contact a few of the most influential.

Stages of the Organizational Buying Decision Process

Like consumers, organizations follow a buying decision process, which is summarized in the right side of Figure 6.5. In the first stage, one or more individuals recognize that a problem or need exists. Problem recognition may arise under a variety of circumstances—for instance, when a machine malfunctions or a firm is modifying an existing product or introducing a new one. Individuals in the buying center—such as users, influencers, or buyers—may be involved in problem recognition, but it may be stimulated by external sources, such as sales representatives.

The second stage of the process—development of product specifications—requires organizational participants to assess the problem or need and determine what will be necessary to resolve or satisfy it. During this stage, users and influencers, such as technical personnel and engineers, often provide information and advice for developing product specifications. By assessing and describing needs, the organization should be able to establish product specifications.

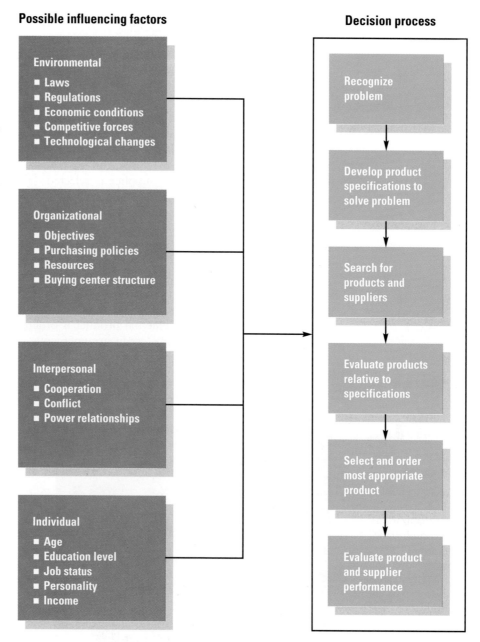

Figure 6.5

Organizational Buying Decision Process and Factors That May Influence It

Source: Adapted from Frederick E. Webster, Jr., and Yoram Wind, *Organizational Buying Behavior,* 1972, pp. 33–37. Adapted by permission of Prentice-Hall, Englewood Cliffs, N.J.

Possible influencing factors

Environmental

■ Laws
■ Regulations
■ Economic conditions
■ Competitive forces
■ Technological changes

Organizational

■ Objectives
■ Purchasing policies
■ Resources
■ Buying center structure

Interpersonal

■ Cooperation
■ Conflict
■ Power relationships

Individual

■ Age
■ Education level
■ Job status
■ Personality
■ Income

Decision process

Recognize problem

Develop product specifications to solve problem

Search for products and suppliers

Evaluate products relative to specifications

Select and order most appropriate product

Evaluate product and supplier performance

Searching for possible products to solve the problem and locating suppliers is the third stage in the decision process. Search activities may involve looking in company files and trade directories, contacting suppliers for information, soliciting proposals from known vendors, and examining catalogs and trade publications. The industrial advertisement in Figure 6.6 is an example of information available in trade publications. Some vendors may not be viewed as acceptable because they are not large enough to supply the needed quantities, and others may have poor records of delivery and service. In some instances the product is not available from any existing vendor and the buyer must find a company that can design and build the product. Innovative companies, like 3M, are sought.

If all goes well, the search stage will result in a list of several alternative products and suppliers. The fourth stage is evaluating the products on the list to determine which ones (if any) meet the product specifications developed in the second stage. At this point, too, various suppliers are evaluated according to multiple criteria, such as price, service, and ability to deliver.

The results of the deliberations and assessments in the fourth stage are used during the fifth stage to select the product to be purchased and the supplier from whom to buy it. In some cases, the buyer may decide to choose several suppliers. In others, only one supplier is selected—a situation known as **sole sourcing.** Sole sourcing has traditionally been discouraged except when a product is available from only one company; firms that have contracts with the federal government are still required to have several sources for an item. Sole sourcing is becoming more popular today, partly because such an arrangement means better communications between buyer and supplier, stability and higher profits for the supplier, and often lower prices for the buyer. However, most organizations still prefer to purchase goods and services from several suppliers because this approach lessens the possibility of disruption caused by strikes, shortages, or bankruptcy. The actual product is ordered in this fifth stage and specific details regarding terms, credit arrangements, delivery dates and methods, and technical assistance are worked out.

Figure 6.6

Trade Publication Information

When searching for products to solve problems, organizations often consult trade publications. BASF uses industrial advertising to inform potential customers about its chemical products.

Source: Agency: Warner Bicking, Morris and Partners. Client: BASF Specialty Chemicals. Photo: Pete Turner/Image Bank.

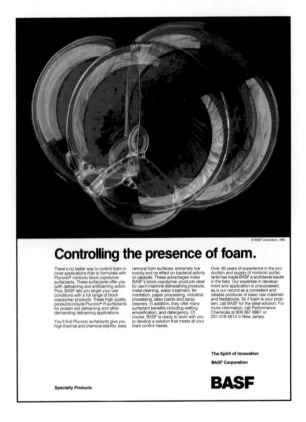

Controlling the presence of foam.

There's no better way to control foam in most applications than to formulate with Pluronic® nonionic block copolymer surfactants. These surfactants offer you both defoaming and antifoaming action. Plus, BASF lets you target your use conditions with a full range of block copolymer products. These high quality products include Pluronic® R surfactants for protein soil defoaming and other demanding defoaming applications.

You'll find Pluronic surfactants give you high thermal and chemical stability, easy

removal from surfaces, extremely low toxicity and no effect on bacterial activity or catalysts. These advantages make BASF's block copolymer products ideal for use in machine dishwashing products, metal cleaning, water treatment, fermentation, paper processing, industrial processing, latex paints and spray cleaners. In addition, they offer many surfactant benefits including wetting, emulsification, and detergency. Of course, BASF is ready to work with you to develop a solution that meets all your foam control needs.

Over 30 years of experience in the production and supply of nonionic surfactants has made BASF a worldwide leader in the field. Our expertise in development and application is unsurpassed, as is our record as a consistent and reliable producer of basic raw materials and feedstocks. So if foam is your problem, call BASF for the ideal solution. For more information, call Performance Chemicals at 800-367-9861 or 201-316-4610 in New Jersey.

The Spirit of Innovation

BASF Corporation

BASF

Specialty Products

Interdepartmental Conflict
Affects Buying Center Performance

PRACTICALLY ALL ORGANIZATIONAL BUYING DECISIONS are made through the buying center—a group of people from different departments given the responsibility of purchasing products and services for the organization. Many times, members of the buying center will have different goals and objectives, depending upon the particular department for which they work. As these members attempt to reach acceptable purchase choices, weighing such factors as product specifications, supplier capabilities, service, and price, the potential for conflict is always present.

Conflict within the buying center can have both good and bad outcomes on the purchase decision. Conflict in the purchasing process can ensure that the organization's best interests as a whole are preserved. Similarly, conflict can slow down the purchase decision, ensuring that careful consideration is given to product specifications and the choice of supplier *before* the actual purchase is made. However, conflict can also cause problems. Too much conflict can slow the purchasing process to the point of being inefficient. In addition, conflict can create negative feelings among members of the buying center—ultimately creating frustration and confusion in the purchasing process.

What causes conflict in the buying center? Recent research indicates that there are at least three major causes of buying conflict. First, organizations that reward employees for attaining departmental, rather than organizational, goals tend to have a greater amount of conflict in their purchasing process because different departments are working for different goals. For example, the engineering department may demand that an expensive piece of equipment be purchased because of its unique specifications. However, if the accounting department hesitates in spending the needed money, conflict is bound to occur. Overcoming this problem requires that management change the reward system to emphasize the achievement of overall organizational goals, rather than departmental ones.

The second and third reasons for conflict—unclear responsibilities and barriers to communication—are closely related. Different members of the buying center must take on clear responsibilities in the purchasing process. However, buying center members cannot hope to understand their responsibilities without clear, open communication between all members of the buying center, as well as communication between the buying center and top management. The key to eliminating conflict in the buying center is promoting full, open communication among departments. In this way, organizational members will understand their responsibilities and work toward fulfilling organizational goals.

Sources: Donald W. Barclay, "Interdepartmental Conflict in Organizational Buying: The Impact of the Organizational Context," *Journal of Marketing Research,* May 1991, pp. 145–159; Ajay Kohli, "Determinants of Influence in Organizational Buying: A Contingency Approach," *Journal of Marketing,* July 1989, pp. 50–65; and Robert J. Thomas, "Industrial Market Segmentation on Buying Center Purchase Responsibilities," *Journal of the Academy of Marketing Science,* Summer 1989, pp. 243–252.

During the sixth stage, the product's performance is evaluated by comparing it with specifications. Sometimes, even though the product meets the specifications, its performance does not adequately solve the problem or satisfy the need recognized in the first stage. In that case, the product specifications must be adjusted. The supplier's performance is also evaluated during this stage, and if it is found wanting, the organizational purchaser seeks corrective action from the supplier or searches for a new supplier. The results of the evaluation become feedback for the other stages and influence future organizational purchase decisions.

This organizational buying decision process is used in its entirety primarily for new-task purchases. Several of the stages, but not necessarily all, are used for modified rebuy and straight rebuy situations.

Influences on Organizational Buying

Figure 6.5 also lists the four major categories of factors that influence organizational buying decisions: environmental, organizational, interpersonal, and individual.

You may remember from Chapter 2 that environmental factors are uncontrollable forces, such as politics, laws, regulations and regulatory agencies, activities of interest groups, changes in the economy, competitors' actions, and technological changes. These forces generate a considerable amount of uncertainty for an organization, and the uncertainty can make individuals in the buying center apprehensive about certain types of purchases. Changes in one or more environmental force can create new purchasing opportunities and threats. For example, changes in competition and technology can make buying decisions difficult for products like computers, a field in which competition is increasingly being affected by new cooperative strategies between companies. Compaq Computer, for instance, grew into a billion-dollar company by competing only against IBM and developing cooperative relationships with all other potential competitors.[17]

Organizational factors influencing the organizational buying decision process include the buyer's objectives, purchasing policies, and resources, as well as the size and composition of its buying center. An organization may have certain buying policies to which buying center participants must conform. For instance, a firm's policies may mandate long-term contracts, perhaps longer than most sellers desire. The nature of an organization's financial resources may require special credit arrangements. Any of these conditions could affect purchase decision processes.

The interpersonal factors are the relationships among the people in the buying center. The use of power and the level of conflict among buying center participants influence organizational buying decisions. Certain persons in the buying center may be better communicators than others and may be more convincing. Often these interpersonal dynamics are hidden, making them difficult for marketers to assess.

Individual factors are the personal characteristics of individuals in the buying center, such as age, education, personality, income, and position in the organization. For example, a 55-year-old manager who has been in the organization for 25 years may affect the decisions made by the buying center differently than a 30-year-old person who has been employed only two years. How influential these factors are depends on the buying situation, the type of product being purchased, and whether the purchase is new-task, modified rebuy, or straight rebuy. The negotiating styles of people vary within an organization and from one organization to another. To be effective, a marketer must know customers well enough to be aware of these individual factors and the effects they may have on purchase decisions.

Summary

Organizational markets consist of individuals and groups that purchase a specific kind of product for resale, for direct use in producing other products, or for use in day-to-day operations. Producer markets include those individuals and business organizations that purchase products for the purpose of making a profit by using them to produce other products or by using them in their operations. Intermediaries who buy finished products and resell them for the purpose of making a profit are classified as reseller markets. Government markets consist of federal, state, and local governments, which spend billions of dollars annually for goods and services to support their internal operations and provide citizens with needed services. Organizations that seek to achieve charity, education, community, or other not-for-profit goals constitute institutional markets.

Organizational transactions differ from consumer transactions in several ways. Organizational transactions tend to be larger, and negotiations occur less frequently, though they are often lengthy. Organizational transactions sometimes involve more than one person or one department in the purchasing organization. They may also involve reciprocity, an arrangement in which two organizations agree to buy from each other. Organizational customers are usually viewed as more rational than ultimate consumers and as more likely to seek information about a product's features and technical specifications.

When purchasing products, organizational customers are particularly concerned about quality, service, and price. Quality is important because it directly affects the quality of products the buyer's firm produces. To achieve an exact level of quality, organizations often buy their products on the basis of a set of expressed characteristics, called specifications. Because services can have such a direct influence on a firm's costs, sales, and profits, such matters as market information, on-time delivery, and availability of parts can be crucial to an organizational buyer. Although an organizational customer does not depend solely on price to decide which products to buy, price is of prime concern because it directly influences a firm's profitability.

Organizational buyers use several purchasing methods, including description, inspection, sampling, and negotiation. Most organizational purchases are new-task, modified rebuy, or straight rebuy. In a new-task purchase, an organization makes an initial purchase of an item to be used to perform a new job or to solve a problem. In a modified rebuy purchase, a new-task purchase is changed the second or third time it is ordered or the requirements associated with a straight rebuy purchase are modified. A straight rebuy purchase occurs when a buyer purchases the same products routinely under approximately the same terms of sale.

Industrial demand differs from consumer demand along several dimensions. Industrial demand derives from the demand for consumer products. At the industry level, industrial demand is inelastic. If the price of an industrial item changes, demand for the product will not change as much proportionally. Some industrial products are subject to joint demand, which occurs when two or more items are used in combination to make a product. Finally, because business-to-business demand derives from consumer demand, the demand for business-to-business products can fluctuate widely.

Organizational, or business-to-business, buying behavior refers to the purchase behavior of producers, resellers, government units, and institutions. Organizational purchase decisions are made through a buying center—the group of people who are involved in making organizational purchase decisions. Users are those in the organization who actually use the product. Influencers help develop the specifications and evaluate alternative products for possible use. Buyers are responsible for selecting the suppliers and negotiating the terms of the purchases. Deciders choose the products and vendors. Gatekeepers control the flow of information to and among persons who occupy the other roles in the buying center.

The stages of the organizational buying decision process are problem recognition, the development of product specifications to solve the problem, the search for products and suppliers, evaluation of products relative to specifications, selection and ordering of the most appropriate product, and evaluation of the product's and the supplier's performance.

Four categories of factors influence organizational buying decisions: environmental, organizational, interpersonal, and individual. The environmental factors include laws and regulations, economic conditions, competitive forces, and technological changes. Organizational factors influencing the organizational buying decision process include the buyer's objectives, purchasing policies, and resources, as well as the size and composition of its buying center. The interpersonal factors are the relationships among the people in the buying center. Individual factors are the personal characteristics of individuals in the buying center, such as age, education, personality, position in the organization, and income.

Important Terms

Producer markets
Reseller markets
Government markets
Institutional markets
Reciprocity
New-task purchase
Modified rebuy purchase
Straight rebuy purchase
Derived demand
Inelastic demand
Joint demand

Organizational (or business-to-business) buying behavior
Buying center
Sole sourcing

Discussion and Review Questions

1. Identify, describe, and give examples of four major types of organizational markets.
2. Regarding purchasing behavior, why are organizational buyers generally considered more rational than ultimate consumers?
3. What are the primary concerns of organizational buyers?
4. List several characteristics that differentiate organizational transactions from consumer ones.
5. What are the commonly used methods of organizational buying?
6. Why do buyers involved in a straight rebuy purchase require less information than those making a new-task purchase?

7. How does industrial demand differ from consumer demand?
8. What are the major components of a buying center?
9. Identify the stages of the organizational buying decision process. How is this decision process used when making straight rebuys?
10. How do environmental, organizational, interpersonal, and individual factors affect organizational purchases?

Cases

6.1 **Faber-Castell Markets Low-Tech Products to Organizational Markets**

When Faber-Castell Corporation finalized its acquisition of Eberhard Faber Inc., the rejoining of two major writing instrument companies was complete. Both firms trace their ancestry to Kaspar Faber, the inventor of pencil lead as we know it. In the late nineteenth century, the Faber pencil business split into three separate companies: German-based A.W. Faber-Castell Corp., Faber-Castell Corp., and Eberhard Faber.

Eberhard Faber, the originator of the familiar yellow pencil, had been producing wood-cased pencils since 1849, maintaining a 10 percent share of the $100 million pencil market. The company's sales of pencils, pens, erasers, and rubber bands had been increasing in Third World countries, but recent U.S. sales had been essentially static. As a result, Eberhard Faber's U.S. pencil sales accounted for less than 20 percent of its worldwide sales, and earnings had declined during recent years.

When the pencil market became particularly competitive in the early 1980s, Eberhard Faber's top management concluded that the key to greater domestic profitability was marketing. At first the firm made some mistakes. For example, after producing yellow pencils for nearly a century, the company decided to introduce a natural-looking pencil: bare cedar wood covered with a coat of clear lacquer. Eberhard Faber projected a 15 percent market share for the new product, thinking that the current trend toward naturalness would carry over into the pencil market. But pencil dealers avoided the new product, preferring to stick with a proven seller.

Another strategic miscalculation involved the company's redoubled efforts in art supplies, a market that yields greater profit margins than the highly competitive office products market. Because Eberhard Faber's Design markers were already successful, the company acquired several art supply firms, such as NSM, maker of leather portfolios. At the same time, however, the company began to neglect the commercial office products field that accounted for two-thirds of its total sales. In this market, which includes sales to corporations under private labels as well as the Eberhard Faber name, the firm found itself gaining a reputation for noncompetitive pricing and sluggish new-product development, despite the consistently good quality and service it offered.

New executives tried to revamp every aspect of the company's ineffective marketing operation. To build sales among office product wholesalers, they increased the advertising budget, created new promotional programs, and redesigned the company's catalogs and order sheets. They developed new products, such as five-sided erasers in stylish colors. With commodity products such as rubber bands, they marketed quality and price. Nearly every product package was updated. Office products distributors say such moves definitely improved the company's image.

Continuing to struggle despite its efforts, Eberhard Faber began seeking a buyer. Faber-Castell, seeing an opportunity to increase market share and protect the Faber trade name, bought Eberhard Faber. Faber-Castell is best known for its Uni-ball roller pen which holds a commanding 40 percent of the roller pen market. Still, Faber-Castell is a clear pencil giant. The company owns a major share of the $127.6 million pencil market. In addition, the pencil market is expected to grow at a rate of 5.4 percent per year through 1997. With Faber-Castell's control over the writing instrument market, there will probably always be a place for the familiar yellow pencil.[18]

Questions for Discussion

1. What types of organizational markets (as classified in this chapter) purchase the products Faber-Castell makes?
2. Most purchases of Faber-Castell's office products would be of what type: new-task, modified rebuy, or straight rebuy? Why?
3. Why were the "natural-looking" pencils less than successful?
4. Evaluate changes made in this firm's marketing efforts.

6.2   Intel Serves Organizational Markets

A company in Santa Clara, California, has a kind of monopoly that the old-time capitalists of the early 1900s would be proud to control. More than 70 percent of all personal computers (PCs) rely on Intel technology. Intel supplied the "brain" to IBM's first personal computer and to every IBM personal computer assembled since then. Many IBM compatibles also rely on Intel's chips, particularly its 80386 microprocessor, which has contributed $2 billion to the company's profits. Even Japanese computer companies consume massive numbers of Intel's chips. Now, however, the firm is facing its toughest competition yet to supply the "brains" of the computer industry.

Although Intel has maintained a virtual monopoly as supplier of 80386 and other chips for personal computers, the field is heating up with chips from Advanced Micro Devices Inc. (AMD), Chips & Technologies Inc., and other newcomers. Already AMD has captured 15 percent of the PC market with its clone of Intel's 386DX chip. Other companies are beginning to market clones of Intel's most advanced microprocessor, the 80486 chip. Moreover, Intel is under investigation by the Federal Trade Commission for anticompetitive behavior.

Compounding the problem of competition, faster and more sophisticated computer work stations are giving PCs a strong challenge as *the* technological tool for scientists, engineers, and businesspeople. Work stations are becoming more powerful and less expensive—and more popular. Intel's current and very challenging goal is to maintain its PC "monopoly" while dominating the market for the new RISC (reduced instruction set computing) chip, which will likely revolutionize the computer work stations of the future.

Some computer analysts think that Intel may eventually control the RISC market, though smaller companies like Sun and MIPS are eager to give Intel a strong fight. Because Intel is so devoted to its PC market and the development of the RISC, it has in the past missed opportunities to enter some other lucrative markets. It seems that the market for "handmaiden" chips (chips that enhance performance and provide additional functions, such as graphics) could have easily been controlled by Intel. But Intel executives did not aggressively pursue this product area, and now other computer technology companies are reaping large financial gains.

Because of these and similar events, Intel executives have modified their company strategy somewhat. To battle the competition, they have begun a marketing campaign to convince computer manufacturers and consumers that the best PCs have "Intel inside," even paying computer manufacturers to advertise Intel chips in their own advertisements. The company is now committed to strengthening its other products, such as semiconductors, memory chips, and personal computers. Intel has devoted more funds to research and development ($700 million in 1992), investing huge amounts in leading-edge CAD (computer-aided design) equipment to reduce product development time. Intel management is particularly excited by a new technology it recently purchased for an estimated, and surprisingly low, price of $20 million. Digital Video Interactive, DVI, will bring a full-motion color picture and stereo sound to PCs. Computer users having access to DVI capabilities will be able to extensively manipulate the images on their computer screens.

Believing that the company was becoming bloated and outdated, Intel management has closed eight obsolete plants since 1984. It has also reduced the work force by six thousand employees and made a new commitment to customer service, trying to remedy its reputation as an unresponsive and sometimes arrogant supplier.

Andrew S. Grove, Intel's chief executive officer, has said that his primary hope for the future is to position Intel as the heart, spine, and framework of the entire computer industry. Because so much of today's software has been written for IBM personal computers, this software is designed to work with Intel's chips and will likely guarantee the continued success of Intel, at least for the forseeable future.

Employee turnover, especially among management, is extremely low at Intel, which is unusual for a computer company. This and Intel's reputation as a leading innovator make it an attractive firm for young and talented engineers, designers, programmers, and managers. Armed with ingenuity and an improved marketing strategy, Intel is not afraid of the microchip wars. However, it is not overconfident either. A group of 128 Japanese companies has been trying to perfect a technology called TRON that could compete head to head with Intel's PC microprocessors. Chief executive officer Grove takes this still-hypothetical confrontation seriously. He has remarked that he never laughs at anything Japanese because the Japanese never give up. It does not appear that Intel will give up either.[19]

Questions for Discussion

1. What types of organizational markets does Intel serve?
2. When purchasing Intel computer chips, what type of organizational buying method or methods would a personal computer manufacturer use?
3. What are the characteristics of the demand for Intel computer chips?

Chapter Notes

1. Based on interviews with Donald Sapit, Michael Sapit, Deborah Yates and Linda Johnson, Sigma Marketing Concepts, Orange Park, Florida, March 10, 1992.
2. *Statistical Abstract of the United States,* 1991, p. 781.
3. Ibid., p. 773.
4. *Statistical Abstract of the United States,* 1990, p. 330.
5. Ibid., p. 330.
6. Richard J. Maturi, "States: A Mother Lode Ripe for Mining," *Industry Week,* June 17, 1991, pp. 79–83.
7. Mike Bucken, "Aging Software Base in Need of Updating," *Software Magazine,* Jan. 1989, pp. 96–97.
8. *Sam's Buy-Line,* Winter 1991, pp. 1–36.
9. Arthur Bragg, "Getting Face-to-Face with Customers," *Sales & Marketing Management,* Feb. 1991, pp. 44–48.
10. J. Carlos Jarillo and Howard H. Stevenson, "Cooperative Strategies: The Payoffs and the Pitfalls," *Long Range Planning,* Feb. 1991, pp. 64–70.
11. Louis J. DeRose, "Meet Today's Buying Influences with Value Selling," *Industrial Marketing Management,* May 1991, pp. 87–90.

12. Otis Port and John Carey, "Questing for the Best," *Business Week,* Oct. 25, 1991, p. 8.
13. Ibid.
14. Larry Armstrong, "Beyond May I Help You," *Business Week,* Oct. 25, 1991, p. 102.
15. M. Bixby, J. Cooper, Cornelia Droge, and Patricia J. Daugherty, "How Buyers and Operations Personnel Evaluate Service," *Industrial Marketing Management,* Feb. 1991, pp. 81–85.
16. Frederick E. Webster, Jr., and Yoram Wind, *Organizational Buying Behavior* (Englewood Cliffs, N.J.: Prentice-Hall, 1972), pp. 78–80.
17. J. Carlos Jarillo and Howard H. Stephenson, "Cooperative Strategies—The Payoffs and the Pitfalls," *Long Range Planning,* Feb. 1991, pp. 64–70.
18. Walter A. Kleinschrod, "Writing in Style," *Today's Office,* Oct. 1990, pp. 6, 11; Gloria M. Curry, "Versatile Is the Word for Today's Writing Instruments," *Office,* Nov. 1989, pp. 82, 90–92; "Faber-Castell Acquires Eberhard Faber," *Office Systems,* Feb. 1988, p. 12; and Sylvia H. Wright, "Writing Instruments: The Business at Hand," *Office,* Nov. 1987, pp. 98, 113–114.
19. Russell Mitchell, "Intel Isn't Taking This Lying Down," *Business Week,* Sept. 30, 1991, pp. 32–33; Carrie Gottlieb, "Intel's Plan for Staying on Top," *Fortune,* Mar. 27, 1989, pp. 98–100; Stuart Gannes, "IBM and DEC Take on the Little Guys," *Fortune,* Oct. 10, 1988, pp. 108–109, 112, 114; and Richard Brandt and Otis Port, "Intel: The Next Revolution," *Business Week,* Sept. 26, 1988, pp. 74–78, 80.

7 Marketing Research and Information Systems

OBJECTIVES

- To understand the importance of and relationship between research and information systems in marketing decision making

- To distinguish between research and intuition in solving marketing problems

- To learn the five basic steps for conducting a marketing research project

- To understand the fundamental methods of gathering data for marketing research

- To communicate the importance of ethics in marketing research

3 ways of Collecting Data

1) Observation
2) Survey
3) Experience

You should always start w/ secondary research
SR is not up to date

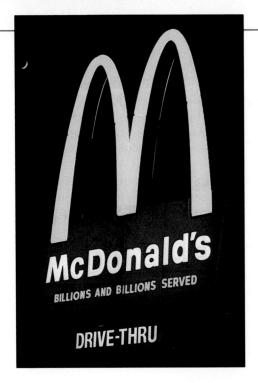

Five years ago, if you asked someone what types of food McDonald's served, the answer would probably have been hamburgers and french fries. Today, however, the answer to that question is not so clear. The nation's number-one restaurant chain has opened itself to previously unimaginable changes in recent years in an effort to stay number one and fight off some very stiff competition.

McDonald's conducts research by creating new test products and then seeing if consumers like them. Products like grilled chicken and steak sandwiches, pizza, and beef and chicken fajitas have been introduced in test markets in recent years. The goal of this type of research is to find out if consumers like the products before they are offered worldwide. This approach can be used because it is relatively inexpensive to create and test new food products compared to creating and testing highly complex products like computers.

Some of these experimental products do not last long. The Chicken McSwiss sandwich, Hula Burgers, fried chicken, and a hamburger-shaped hot dog are examples of products that missed the mark. However, some of McDonald's best-known products were once experimental. Chicken fajitas and breakfast burritos were invented by franchises in El Paso, Texas and are very successful. Other successful franchise-invented items include the McLean Deluxe, Egg McMuffin, Filet-O-Fish, and the Big Mac. McDonald's latest introductions include baked apple pie, McHoagie sandwiches, skinless oven-roasted chicken, and McSticks—fresh fruit and vegetable sticks.

McDonald's uses a systematic and well-thought-out approach to conducting research. In fact, all aspects of its retail operations are subject to investigation. McDonald's recently opened the Golden Arch Cafe—a 1950s-style diner without the McDonald's name—in Hartsville, Tennessee. McDonald's is experimenting with the cafe concept to find out what consumers want in a restaurant other than fast food. By not using the McDonald's name, the company is free to experiment with new menu items and concepts without risking confusion with the fast-food image.[1]

Photo: Stock Boston, © William Johnson.

THE MARKETING RESEARCH conducted by McDonald's demonstrates that in order to implement the marketing concept, marketers require information about the characteristics, needs, and wants of their target markets. Given the intense competition in today's marketplace, especially in the fast-food industry, it is unwise in most cases to develop a product and then look for a market where it can be profitably sold without information or research. Marketing research and information systems that provide practical, unbiased information help firms avoid the assumptions and misunderstandings that could result in poor marketing performance.

In this chapter we focus on the ways of gathering information needed to make marketing decisions. We first distinguish between managing information within an organization (a marketing information system) and conducting marketing research. Then we discuss the role of marketing research in decision making and problem solving, compare it with intuition, and examine the individual steps of the marketing research process. We also take a close look at experimentation and various methods of collecting data. In the final section, we consider the importance of marketing research and marketing information systems.

Defining Marketing Research and Marketing Information Systems

Marketing research is the systematic design, collection, interpretation, and reporting of information to help marketers solve specific marketing problems or take advantage of marketing opportunities. It is a process for gathering information not currently available to decision makers. Marketing research is conducted on a special-project basis, with the research methods adapted to the problems being studied and to changes in the environment. The American Marketing Association defines marketing research as follows:

> Marketing research is the function which links the consumer, customer, and public to the marketer through information—information used to identify and define marketing opportunities and problems; generate, refine, and evaluate marketing actions; monitor marketing performance; and improve understanding of marketing as a process. Marketing research specifies the information required to address these issues; designs the method for collecting information; manages and implements the data collection process; analyzes the results; and communicates the findings and their implications.[2]

A **marketing information system (MIS)** is the framework for the day-to-day management and structuring of information gathered regularly from sources both inside and outside an organization. As such, an MIS provides a continuous flow of information about prices, advertising expenditures, sales, competition, and distribution expenses. When information systems are strategically created and then institutionalized throughout an organization, their value is enhanced.[3] Figure 7.1 illustrates the chief components of an MIS.

The inputs into a marketing information system include the information sources inside and outside the firm assumed to be useful for future decision making. Processing information involves classifying it and developing categories for meaningful storage and retrieval. Marketing decision makers then determine

Figure 7.1

An Organization's
Marketing Information System

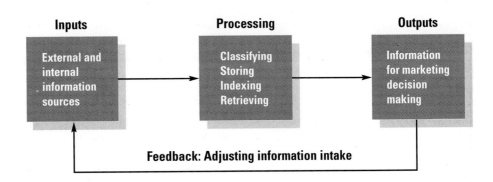

Inputs	Processing	Outputs
External and internal information sources	Classifying Storing Indexing Retrieving	Information for marketing decision making

Feedback: Adjusting information intake

which information—the output—is useful for making decisions. Finally, feedback enables those who are responsible for gathering internal and external data to adjust the information inputs systematically.

Regular reports of sales by product or market categories, data on inventory levels, and records of salespersons' activities are all examples of information that is useful in making decisions. In the MIS, the means of gathering data receive less attention than do the procedures for expediting the flow of information. The main focus of the marketing information system is on data storage and retrieval, as well as on computer capabilities and management's information requirements. RJR Nabisco, for example, handles hundreds of thousands of consumer contacts each year, usually inquiries about product usage, nutrition, and ingredients. This consumer feedback is computerized and made available on demand throughout the company's operating divisions. Inside Marketing describes how new technology has been used to develop VideOcarts that gather important data from shoppers for marketing information systems and marketing research.

The main difference between marketing research and marketing information systems is that marketing research is an information-gathering process for specific situations, whereas an MIS provides continuous data input for an organization. Nonrecurring decisions that deal with the dynamics of the marketing environment often call for a data search structured according to the problem and decision. Marketing research is usually characterized by in-depth analyses of major problems or issues. Often the information needed is available only from sources outside an organization's formal channels of information. For instance, an organization may want to know something about its competitors or to gain an unbiased understanding of its own customers. Such information needs may require an independent investigation by a marketing research firm. The packaged goods industry is still among the heaviest users of market research, but service firms are also adopting marketing research.[4]

Data brought into the organization through marketing research become part of its **marketing databank,** a file of data collected through both the MIS and marketing research projects. The marketing databank allows researchers to retrieve information that is useful for addressing problems quite different from those that prompted the original data collection. Often a research study developed for one purpose proves valuable for developing a research method or indicating problems in researching a particular topic. For instance, data obtained from a study by Ford Motor Co. on the buying behavior of purchasers of its Mustang model may be used in planning a new two-seat sports car to be

VideOcart Rolls On

TO CUT THROUGH PROMOTIONAL CLUTTER in supermarkets and retail stores and to better understand consumers' shopping behavior, marketers are testing a new electronic innovation. Developed by Information Resources, Inc. (IRI), a marketing research company, the VideOcart is a shopping cart with a liquid crystal video display screen mounted on its handles. Each VideOcart carries advertisements, directory information, and entertainment.

Here's how VideOcart works. As a shopper pushes a VideOcart down the aisles, sensors in the screen pick up signals from control units throughout the store. When the cart passes a control unit on a store shelf—in the coffee section, for example—it triggers an advertisement for specific related brands, such as Folger's. Shoppers may also use the unit to help locate specific items in the store or to obtain an overall map of the store. While the shopper is waiting in line, recipes, movie information, or local news may flash on the screen.

By tracking shoppers' paths through the store, VideOcart collects valuable information on traffic flow and the amount of time shoppers spend in each section. Data obtained from the carts will allow marketers to analyze shopping patterns and to determine whether some areas are more congested than others and plan for the optimal placement of products. The information can also be used to gauge the success of displays and special promotions. In addition, VideO-

cart has been designed to collect shoppers' opinions about various products, and it stores this data at the checkout for future collection and analysis.

VideOcart charges participating advertisers $4 per thousand consumers, much less costly than newspaper inserts or television advertising. In return, the advertisers receive tracking information that helps them determine advertising, promotion, or point-of-purchase effectiveness.

The company has plans to manufacture 120,000 VideOcarts with IBM. Toys R Us is testing a version of VideOcart that provides suggestions for children's gifts by age level. Industry observers are now predicting that the VideOCart will be the electronic point-of-purchase medium of the 1990s. If true, VideOcart could be rolling soon to a store near you.

Sources: William H. Bolen, "Shopper Takes VideOcart for Test Drive, Finds it a Pleasant Experience," *Marketing News*, March 16, 1992, p. 18; Bradley Johnson, "Retailers Check Out In-Store," *Advertising Age*, Dec. 16, 1991, p. 23; "VideOcart, IBM Ink Deal," *Adweek's Marketing Week*, Aug. 5, 1991, p. 8; David Kiley, "After a Successful Test, VideOcart Rolls East," *Adweek's Marketing Week*, Nov. 12, 1990, p. 46; Julie Liesse Erickson, "Shoptalk," *Advertising Age*, Nov. 21, 1988, p. 12; Catherine Hedgecock, "Soon You Can Watch As You Shop for Groceries," *USA Today*, Sept. 14, 1988, p. 7B; Susan Dillingham, "Grocery Cart Extra: Data via Video Screen," *Insight*, May 30, 1988, p. 43.

introduced in the future. Consequently, marketers should classify and store in the databank all data from marketing research and the MIS to facilitate use of the information in future marketing decisions.

Databanks vary widely from one organization to another. In a small organization, the databank may simply be a large notebook, but many organizations employ a computer storage and retrieval system to handle the large volume of data. Figure 7.2 illustrates how marketing decision makers combine research findings with data from an MIS to develop a databank. Although many organizations do not use the term *databank*, they still have some system for storing information. Smaller organizations may not use the terms *MIS* and *marketing research,* but they normally do perform these marketing activities.

After a marketing information system—of whatever size and complexity—has been established, information should be related to marketing planning. The

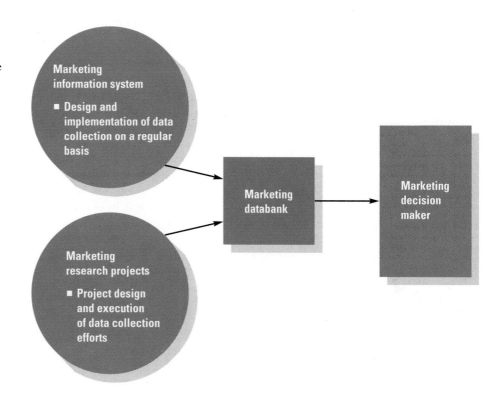

following section discusses how marketers use marketing information, intuition, and judgment in making decisions.

Information Needs and Decision Making

The real value of marketing research and marketing information systems is measured by improvements in a marketer's ability to make decisions. Marketers should treat information in the same manner as other resources utilized by the firm, and they must weigh the costs of obtaining information against the benefits derived. Information is worthwhile if it results in marketing activities that better satisfy the needs of the firm's target markets, leads to increased sales and profits, or helps the firm achieve some other goal. Nielsen Marketing Research promotes its Procision Integrated Information Service as one that delivers bottom-line success (Figure 7.3).

There is concern that marketing research has been used incorrectly by some firms. The major problem comes from bias and distortion because the researcher wants to obtain favorable results. Consider the following examples: (1) Levi Strauss purportedly asked students which clothes would be most popular this year. Ninety percent said Levi's 501 jeans. Apparently, Levi's were the only jeans on the list for students to select. (2) A Gallup poll sponsored by the disposable diaper industry asked: "It is estimated that disposable diapers account for less than 2 percent of the trash in today's landfills. In contrast, beverage containers, third-class mail, and yard waste are estimated to account for about 21 percent of the trash in landfills. Given this, in your opinion, would it be fair to ban disposable diapers?" Eighty-four percent of those interviewed said no.[5]

These examples illustrate research conducted for public consumption and to further the interests of the parties involved in conducting the research. Most research is conducted objectively for internal decision making. Marketing researchers want to know about behavior and opinions, and they want accurate data to help in making decisions. Careful wording of questions is very important because a biased or emotional word can change the results tremendously. Marketing research and marketing information systems provide the organization with customer feedback, without which a marketer cannot understand the dynamics of the marketplace. As managers recognize its benefits, they assign marketing research a much larger role in decision making.

The increase in marketing research activities represents a transition from intuitive to scientific problem solving. In relying on *intuition,* marketing managers base decisions on personal knowledge and past experience. One study found that experienced marketers rated more information as useful for new-product decisions and used general information more effectively than did less experienced managers.[6] However, in *scientific decision making,* managers take an orderly and logical approach to gathering information. They seek facts on a systematic basis, and they apply methods other than trial and error or generalization from experience.

Despite the obvious value of formal research, marketing decisions are often made without it. Certainly, minor problems that must be dealt with at once can

Figure 7.3

Marketing Information

Nielsen is the largest marketing research company in the world. It provides accurate information to assist marketers in making decisions that will maximize promotion effectiveness.

Source: Nielsen Marketing Research.

PART I   AN ANALYSIS OF MARKETING OPPORTUNITIES

	Research	Intuition
Nature	Formal planning, predicting based on scientific approach	Preference based on personal feelings
Methods	Logic, systematic methods, statistical inference	Experience and demonstration
Contributions	General hypotheses for making predictions, classifying relevant variables, carrying out systematic description and classification	Minor problems solved quickly through consideration of experience, practical consequences

and should be handled on the basis of personal judgment and common sense. If good decisions can be made with the help of currently available information, then costly formal research may be superfluous. However, as the financial, social, or ethical risks increase or the number of courses of action multiplies, full-scale research as a prerequisite for marketing decision making becomes both desirable and rewarding.

We are not suggesting here that intuition has no value in marketing decision making. Successful decisions blend both research and intuition. Statistics, mathematics, and logic are powerful tools in problem solving, and the information they provide can reduce the uncertainty of predictions based on limited experience. But these tools do not necessarily bring out the right answers. Consider an extreme example. A marketing research study conducted for Xerox Corporation in the late 1950s indicated a very limited market for an automatic photocopier. Xerox management judged that the researchers had drawn the wrong conclusions from the study and decided to launch the product anyway. That product, the Xerox 914 copier, was an instant success. An immediate backlog of orders developed, and the rest is history. Though the Xerox example is an extreme one, by and large a proper blend of research and intuition offers the best formula for a correct decision. Table 7.1 distinguishes between the roles of research and intuition in decision making.

The Marketing Research Process

To maintain the control needed for obtaining accurate information, marketers approach marketing research in logical steps. The difference between good and bad research depends on the quality of the input, which includes effective control over the entire marketing research process. Figure 7.4 illustrates the five steps of the marketing research process: (1) defining and locating problems, (2) developing hypotheses, (3) collecting data, (4) interpreting research findings, and (5) reporting research findings. These five steps should be viewed as an

Figure 7.4 The Five Steps of the Marketing Research Process

overall approach to conducting research rather than as a rigid set of rules to be followed in each project. In planning research projects, marketers must think about each of the steps and how they can best be adjusted for each particular problem.

Defining and Locating Problems

Problem definition, the first step toward finding a solution or launching a research study, focuses on uncovering the nature and boundaries of a negative, or positive, situation or question. The first sign of a problem is usually a departure from some normal function, such as conflicts between or failures in attaining objectives. If a corporation's objective is a 12 percent return on investment and the current return is 6 percent, this discrepancy should be a warning flag. It is a symptom that something inside or outside the organization has blocked the attainment of the desired goal or that the goal is unrealistic. Decreasing sales, increasing expenses, or decreasing profits also signal problems. Conversely, when an organization experiences a dramatic rise in sales, or some other positive event, it may conduct marketing research to discover the reasons and maximize the opportunities stemming from them.

To pin down the specific causes of the problem through research, marketers must define the problem and its scope in a way that requires probing beneath the superficial symptoms. The interaction between the marketing manager and the marketing researcher should yield a clear definition of the problem. Researchers and decision makers should remain in the problem definition stage until they have determined precisely what they want from the research and how they will use it.

The research objective specifies what information is needed to solve the problem. Deciding how to refine a broad, indefinite problem into a clearly defined and researchable statement is a prerequisite for the next step in planning the research: developing the type of hypothesis that best fits the problem.

Developing Hypotheses

The objective statement of a marketing research project should include hypotheses drawn from both previous research and expected research findings. A **hypothesis** is an informed guess or assumption about a certain problem or set of circumstances. It is based on all the insight and knowledge available about the problem from previous research studies and other sources. As information is gathered, a researcher can test the hypothesis. For example, a consumer food products manufacturer such as H. J. Heinz might propose the hypothesis that children today have more influence on their families' buying decisions for ketchup and other grocery products. A marketing researcher would then gather data, perhaps through surveys of children and their parents, and draw conclusions as to whether the hypothesis is correct. Sometimes several hypotheses are developed during the actual study; the hypotheses that are accepted or rejected become the study's chief conclusions.

Collecting Data

The kind of hypothesis being tested determines which approach will be used for gathering general data: exploratory, descriptive, or causal. When marketers need more information about a problem or want to make a tentative hypothesis more specific, they may conduct **exploratory studies**. For instance, they may review the information in the firm's databank or examine publicly available data. Questioning knowledgeable people inside and outside the organization may also yield new insights into the problem. An advantage of the exploratory approach is that it permits marketers to conduct ministudies with a very restricted database.

If marketers need to understand the characteristics of certain phenomena to solve a particular problem, **descriptive studies** can aid them. Such studies may range from general surveys of consumers' education, occupation, or age to specifics on how many consumers purchased Ford Escorts last month or how many adults between the ages of 18 and 30 eat some form of oat bran at least three times a week. Some descriptive studies require statistical analysis and predictive tools. For example, a researcher trying to find out how many people will vote for a certain political candidate may have to survey registered voters to predict the results. Descriptive studies generally demand much prior knowledge and assume that the problem is clearly defined. The marketers' major task is to choose adequate methods for collecting and measuring data.

Hypotheses about causal relationships call for a more complex approach than a descriptive study. In **causal studies**, it is assumed that a particular variable X causes a variable Y. Marketers must plan the research so that the data collected prove or disprove that X causes Y. To do so, marketers must try to hold constant all variables except X and Y. For example, to find out whether new carpeting, miniblinds, and ceiling fans increase the number of rentals in an apartment complex, marketers need to keep all variables constant except the new furnishings. Table 7.2 compares the features of these three types of research studies.

Marketing researchers have two types of data at their disposal. **Primary data** are observed and recorded or collected directly from respondents. This type of data must be gathered by observing phenomena or surveying respondents. **Secondary data** are compiled inside or outside the organization for some purpose other than the current investigation. Secondary data include general reports supplied to an enterprise by various data services. Such reports might concern

Table 7.2

Comparison of
Data-Gathering
Approaches

Project Component	Exploratory Studies	Descriptive or Causal Studies
Purpose	Provide general insights	Confirm insights Verify hypotheses
Data Sources	Ill-defined	Well-defined
Collection Form	Open-end	Structured
Sample	Small	Large
Collection Procedure	Flexible	Rigid
Data Analysis	Informal	Formal
Recommendations	Tentative	Conclusive

Source: Adapted from A. Parasuraman, *Marketing Research,* © 1986 by Addison-Wesley Publishing Company, Inc. Reprinted with permission of the publisher.

market share, retail inventory levels, and consumers' buying behavior. Figure 7.5 illustrates how primary and secondary sources differ. Commonly, secondary data are already available in private or public reports or have been collected and stored by the organization itself. Figure 7.6 shows that *Hispanic Media and Markets* provides secondary data about the Spanish-language market. In the next section, we discuss the methods of gathering both secondary and primary data.

Secondary Data Collection

Marketers often begin the marketing research process by gathering secondary data. They may use available reports and other information from both internal and external sources to study a marketing problem. The Global Perspective presents the results of an international quality study developed by the American Society for Quality Control and is an example of the wide range of secondary data available to marketers.

Internal sources of secondary data can contribute tremendously to research. An organization's marketing databank may contain information about past marketing activities, such as sales records and research reports, which can be used to test hypotheses and pinpoint problems. An organization's accounting records are also an excellent source of data but, strangely enough, are often overlooked. The large volume of data an accounting department collects does not automatically flow to the marketing area. As a result, detailed information about costs, sales, customer accounts, or profits by product category may not be part of the MIS. This condition develops particularly in organizations that do not store marketing information on a systematic basis.

Secondary data can also be gleaned from periodicals, government publications, and unpublished sources. Periodicals such as *Business Week,* the *Wall Street*

Journal, Sales & Marketing Management, American Demographics, Marketing Research, and *Industrial Marketing* print general information that is helpful for defining problems and developing hypotheses. *Survey of Buying Power,* an annual supplement to *Sales & Marketing Management,* contains sales data for major industries on a county-by-county basis. Many marketers consult federal government publications such as the *Statistical Abstract of the United States,* the *Census of Business,* the *Census of Agriculture,* and the *Census of Population,* available from the Superintendent of Documents in Washington, D.C. Table 7.3 summarizes the major external sources of secondary data, excluding syndicated services.

Syndicated data services periodically collect general information, which they sell to clients. Arbitron, for example, supplies television stations and media buyers with estimates of the number of viewers at specific times. Selling Areas Marketing, Inc. (SAMI) furnishes monthly information that describes market shares for specific types of manufacturers. The A. C. Nielsen Company Retail Index provides data about products primarily sold through food stores and drugstores. This information includes total sales in a product category, sales of clients' own brands, and sales of important competing brands. Most of this data is obtained from scanners used in retail checkout operations. The availability of

Figure 7.5

Approaches to Collecting Data

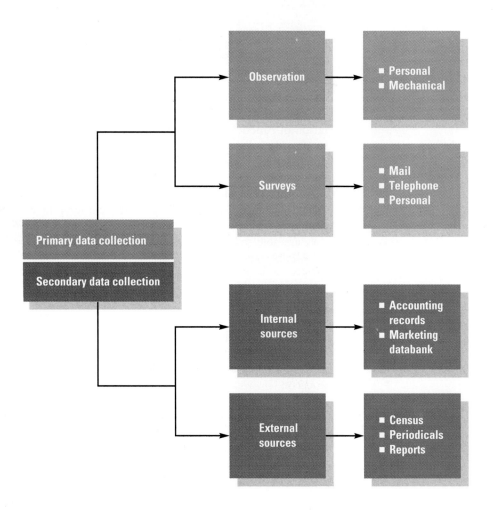

Figure 7.6

Secondary Data

Hispanic Media and Markets is a publication that provides extensive Spanish-language market data summaries and information about media vehicles that reach that market. Such secondary data enable marketers to develop detailed advertising plans.

Source: Reprinted with permission from Standard Rate and Data Service.

an increasing amount of scanner data is enabling marketers to assess the market's sensitivity to a range of marketing strategies.[7] The Market Research Corporation of America (MRCA) collects data through a national panel of consumers to provide information about purchases. MRCA maintains data on consumer purchases of brands classified by age, race, sex, education, occupation, and family size.

Another type of secondary data, which is available for a fee, is demographic analysis. Companies that specialize in demographic databanks use sophisticated computer systems to work with the U.S. Census Bureau databank. As a result, they are able to respond to specialized requests that the Census Bureau cannot or will not handle.

Primary Data Collection

The collection of primary data is a more lengthy and complex process than the collection of secondary data. The acquisition of primary data often requires an experimental approach to determine which variable or variables caused an event to occur.

Experimentation **Experimentation** involves maintaining certain variables constant so that the effects of the experimental variables may be measured. For instance, when the WordPerfect Corp. tests a change in its WordPerfect word processing computer program, all variables should be held constant except the change in the program. **Marketing experimentation** is a set of rules and

Quality Perceptions in the United States, Germany, and Japan

AN INTERNATIONAL QUALITY SURVEY conducted for the American Society for Quality Control by the Gallup Organization illustrates the value of data available to all businesses. Researchers conducted personal interviews with 1,008 consumers in the United States, 1,446 in Japan, and 1,000 in Germany. The survey was designed to compare opinions of consumers in the world's three most powerful economies on a number of issues related to product and service quality. Similar studies were conducted in the United States in 1988 and 1985, thus allowing trends in U.S. consumer opinion to be studied.

The results showed that American consumers' opinions of the quality of American products and services in 1991 had increased since 1988. Back in 1985, 51 percent of those surveyed gave American products high marks on quality. By 1988, this percentage had slipped to only 48 percent. But the 1991 study indicated that a full 55 percent felt that American products were of high quality. Unfortunately, Japanese and German consumers do not agree. Only 17 percent of Japanese consumers and 26 percent of German consumers rate American products as being high quality.

A surprising part of the study was the rankings given to the products of each country by the different consumer groups. American consumers ranked American products first, German products second, and Japanese products third. Japanese consumers ranked their own products first, German products second, and American products third. Consumers in Germany also ranked their own products first but ranked American products higher than those from Japan. In every case, consumers ranked their own country's products first, with the exception of televisions and videocassette recorders, for which all consumers favor Japanese products.

Consumers were also asked open-ended questions about what was important in determining the quality of a product. American and Japanese consumers ranked a well-known brand name as most important, whereas German consumers chose price. Having a well-known brand name was the second choice for Germans. After their first choices, American consumers look at word-of-mouth, past experience, and performance in determining product quality. In contrast, German consumers emphasize appearance and durability; while Japanese consumers consider performance and ease of use to be important.

Results from the 1991 study also indicate the effects of a recessionary climate on quality perceptions. When the 1991 study was conducted, the United States was in the midst of a recession, including a very sluggish economy and higher unemployment. As a result, many American consumers were hesitant to spend their hard-earned dollars. Not surprisingly, when the results were compared with those from 1988, American consumers were found to place more emphasis on price and warranty as important factors in determining quality.

The results of the international quality study are important because they show that the United States has a long way to go to improve the international perception of the quality of its products. As quality becomes an even more important aspect of success in the global marketplace, the United States must move to increase the quality of its products or risk becoming known as second-rate. This information can be of value in assessing country-of-origin brand names in the development of the marketing strategy of selected products.

Source: From "Looking for Quality in a World Marketplace," summary of a 1991 ASQC/Gallup Survey.

procedures by which data gathering is organized to expedite analysis and interpretation.

In experimentation, an **independent variable** (a variable not influenced by or dependent on other variables) is manipulated and the resulting changes are

Trade Journals	Virtually every industry or type of business has a trade journal. These journals give a feel for the industry—its size, degree of competition, range of companies involved, and problems. To find trade journals in the field of interest, check *Ulrich's,* a reference book that lists American and foreign periodicals by subject.
Trade Associations	Almost every industry, product category, and profession has its own association. Depending on the strength of each group, they often conduct research, publish journals, conduct training sessions, and hold conventions. A call or a letter to the association may yield information not available in published sources. To find out which associations serve which industries check the *Encyclopedia of Associations.*
International Sources	Periodical indexes, such as the *F&S Index International,* are particularly useful for overseas product or company information. More general sources include the *United Nations Statistical Yearbook* and the *International Labour Organization's Yearbook of Labour Statistics.*
Government	The federal government, through its various departments and agencies, collects, analyzes, and publishes statistics on practically everything. Government documents also have their own set of indexes: the *Monthly Catalog.* Other useful indexes for government-generated information are the *American Statistical Index* and the *Congressional Information Service.*
Books in Print (BIP)	BIP is a two-volume reference book found in most libraries. All books issued by U.S. publishers and currently in print are listed by subject, title, and author.
Periodical Indexes	The library's reference section contains indexes on virtually every discipline. The *Business Periodicals Index,* for example, indexes each article in all major business periodicals.
Computerized Literature-Retrieval Databases	Literature-retrieval databases are periodical indexes stored in a computer. Books and dissertations are also included. Key words (such as the name of a subject) are used to search a database and generate references.

Table 7.3   Guide to External Sources of Secondary Data

measured in a **dependent variable** (a variable contingent on, or restricted to, one value or a set of values assumed by the independent variable). Figure 7.7 illustrates the relationship between these variables. For example, when Houghton Mifflin Company introduces a new edition of its *American Heritage Dictionary,* it may want to estimate the number of dictionaries that could be sold at various levels of advertising expenditure and prices. The dependent variable would be sales, and the independent variables would be advertising expenditures and price. Researchers would design the experiment so that other independent variables that might influence sales—such as distribution and variations of the product—would be controlled.

In designing experiments, marketing researchers must ensure that research techniques are both reliable and valid. A research technique has **reliability** if it produces almost identical results in successive repeated trials. But a reliable technique is not necessarily valid. To have **validity**, the method must measure what it is supposed to measure, not something else. A valid research method provides data that can be used to test the hypothesis being investigated. A study to measure the effectiveness of advertising would be valid if advertising could be isolated from other factors or variables that affect sales. It would be reliable if the study or experiment on the effectiveness of advertising could be repeated in successive trials.

Experiments may be conducted in the laboratory or in the field; each research setting has advantages and disadvantages. In *laboratory settings,* participants or respondents are invited to a central location to react or respond to experimental stimuli. In such an isolated setting it is possible to control independent variables that might influence the outcome of an experiment. The features of laboratory settings might include a taste kitchen, video equipment, slide projectors, tape recorders, one-way mirrors, central telephone banks, and interview rooms. In an experiment to determine the influence of price (independent variable) on sales of a new canned soup (dependent variable), respondents would be invited to a laboratory—a room with table, chairs, and sample soups—before the soup was available in stores. The soup would be placed on a table with competitors' soups. Analysts would then question respondents about their reactions to the soup at various prices.

One problem with a laboratory setting is its isolation from the real world. It is simply not possible to duplicate all the conditions that affect choices in the marketplace. On the other hand, by controlling variables that cannot be controlled in the real world, laboratory experiments can focus on variables that marketers think may be significant for the success of a marketing strategy.

The experimental approach can also be used in *field settings.* A taste test of a new Slice soft-drink flavor conducted in a grocery store is one example of an experiment in a field setting. Field settings give the marketer an opportunity to obtain a more direct test of marketing decisions than laboratory settings do.

There are several limitations to field experiments. Field experiments can be influenced or biased by inadvertent events, such as weather or major economic news. Carry-over effects of field experiments are impossible to avoid. What respondents have been asked to do in one time period will influence what they do in the next. For example, evaluating competing advertisements may influence attempts to obtain objective evaluations of new proposals for a firm's future advertising. The fact that previous advertising has been viewed influences respondents' evaluation of future advertising. Respondent cooperation may be difficult because respondents do not understand their role in the experiment.

Figure 7.7

Relationship Between Independent and Dependent Variables

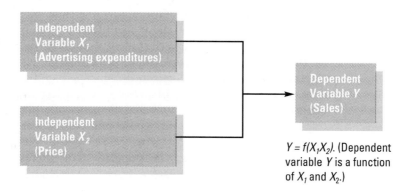

Independent Variable X_1 (Advertising expenditures)

Independent Variable X_2 (Price)

Dependent Variable Y (Sales)

$Y = f(X_1, X_2)$. (Dependent variable Y is a function of X_1 and X_2.)

Finally, only a small number of variables can be controlled in field experiments. It is impossible, for example, to control competitors' advertising or their attempts to influence the outcome of the experiment. Tactics that competitors can use to thwart field efforts include couponing, reducing prices temporarily, and increasing advertising frequency.

Experimentation is used in marketing research to improve hypothesis testing. However, whether experiments are conducted in the laboratory or in the field, many assumptions must be made to limit the number of factors and isolate causes. Marketing decision makers must recognize that assumptions may diminish the reliability of the research findings. For example, viewing proposed advertisements on a videocassette recorder in a laboratory is different from watching the advertisements on television at home.

The gathering of primary data through experimentation may involve the use of sampling, survey methods, observation, or a combination of techniques.

Sampling By systematically choosing a limited number of units, or a **sample**, to represent the characteristics of a total population, marketers can project the reactions of a total market or market segment. The objective of **sampling** in marketing research, therefore, is to select representative units from a total population. Sampling procedures are used in studying the likelihood of events based on assumptions about the future. In Figure 7.8, Survey Sampling, Inc. promotes their responsiveness to marketers' needs for accurate, efficient samples for marketing surveys.

Since the time and the resources available for research are limited, it would be almost impossible to investigate all members of a population. A **population**, or "universe," comprises all elements, units, or individuals that are of interest to researchers for a specific study. For example, if a Gallup poll is designed to predict the results of a presidential election, all registered voters in the United States would constitute the population. A representative national sample of several thousand registered voters would be selected in the Gallup poll to project the probable voting outcome. The projection would be based on the assumption that no major political events would occur before the election.

Sampling techniques allow marketers to predict buying behavior fairly accurately on the basis of the responses from a representative portion of the population of interest.

When marketers employ **random sampling**, all the units in a population have an equal chance of appearing in the sample. Random sampling is basic probability sampling. The various events that can occur have an equal or known chance of taking place. For example, a specific card in a regulation deck should have a 1/52 probability of being drawn at any one time. Similarly, if each student at a university or college has a unique identification number and these numbers are mixed up in a large basket, each student's number would have a known probability of being selected. Sample units are ordinarily chosen by selecting from a table of random numbers statistically generated so that each digit, zero through nine, will have an equal probability of occurring in each position in the sequence. The sequentially numbered elements of a population are sampled randomly by selecting the units whose numbers appear in the table of random numbers.

In **stratified sampling**, the population of interest is divided into groups according to a common characteristic or attribute, and then a probability sample

is conducted within each group. The stratified sample may reduce some of the error that could occur in a simple random sample. By ensuring that each major group or segment of the population receives its proportionate share of sample units, investigators avoid including too many or too few sample units from each stratum. Usually, samples are stratified when researchers believe that there may be variations among different types of respondents. For example, many political opinion surveys are stratified by sex, race, and age.

Area sampling involves two stages: (1) selecting a probability sample of geographic areas, such as blocks, census tracts, or census enumeration districts, and (2) selecting units or individuals within the selected geographic areas for the sample. This approach is a variation of stratified sampling, with the geographic areas serving as the segments, or primary units, used in sampling. To select the units or individuals within the geographic areas, researchers may choose every nth house or unit, or random selection procedures may be used to pick out a given number of units or individuals from a total listing within the selected geographic areas. Area sampling may be used when a complete list of the population is not available.

Quota sampling differs from other forms of sampling in that it is judgmental—that is, the final choice of respondents is left to the interviewers. A study of consumers who wear eyeglasses, for example, may be conducted by interviewing any person who wears eyeglasses. In quota sampling, there are some controls—usually limited to two or three variables, such as age, sex, and education—over the selection of respondents. The controls attempt to ensure that representative categories of respondents are interviewed.

	Mail Surveys	Telephone Surveys	Personal Interview Surveys
Economy	Potentially the lowest cost per interview if there is an adequate return rate; increased postage rates are raising costs	Avoids interviewers' travel expenses; less expensive than in-home interviews; most common survey method	In-home interviewing is the most expensive interviewing method; shopping mall, focus-group interviewing may lower costs
Flexibility	Inflexible; questionnaire must be short, easy for respondents to complete; no probing questions; may take more time to implement than other survey methods	Flexible because interviewers can ask probing questions, encourage respondents to answer questions; rapport may be gained, but observations are impossible	Most flexible method; respondents can react to visual materials, help fill out questionnaire; because observation is possible, demographic data are more accurate; in-depth probes are possible
Interviewer Bias	Interviewer bias eliminated; questionnaires can be returned anonymously	Some anonymity; may be hard to develop trust in respondents	Refusals may be decreased by interviewers' rapport-building efforts; interviewers' personal attributes may bias respondents
Sampling and Respondents' Cooperation	Obtaining a complete mailing list is difficult; nonresponse is a major disadvantage	Sample must be limited to respondents with telephones. Telephone answering machines used to screen calls, busy signals, and refusals are problems	Not-at-homes are more difficult to deal with; focus-groups, shopping mall interviewing may overcome these problems

Table 7.4   **Comparison of the Three Basic Survey Methods**

Quota samples are unique because they are not probability samples; not everyone has an equal chance of being selected. Therefore, sampling error cannot be measured statistically. Quota samples are used most often in exploratory studies, when hypotheses are being developed. Often a small quota sample will not be projected to the total population, although the findings may provide valuable insights into a problem. Quota samples are useful when people with some unusual characteristic are found and questioned about the topic of interest. A probability sample used to study people allergic to cats would be highly inefficient.

Survey Methods   **Survey methods** include interviews by mail or telephone and personal interviews. Selection of a survey method depends on the nature of the problem, the data needed to test the hypothesis, and the resources, such as funding and personnel, that are available to the researcher. Table 7.4 summarizes and compares the advantages of the various methods. Researchers must know exactly what type of information is needed to test the hypothesis and what type of information can be obtained through interviewing. Table 7.5 lists the most frequently used consumer survey techniques and perceived respondent reaction to these techniques. The data are based on a survey of managers and marketing research firms that use these survey methods to collect data. Table 7.6 indicates that marketing researchers expect that it will be more difficult to gather data from the public in the future, particularly through telephone interviewing and in-person at-home interviewing.

Gathering information through surveys is becoming more difficult because response rates are declining. Many researchers believe that nonresponse is the single biggest problem facing the research industry.[8] Some of the concerns of respondents that cause them not to respond include fear of their privacy being invaded, overly long questionnaires, dull topics, time pressures, and general skepticism regarding the personal benefits of participating in a research study.[9] Moreover, fear of crime makes respondents unwilling to trust personal interviewers. The use of "sugging"—sales techniques disguised as market surveys—has also contributed to decreased respondent cooperation.

In *mail surveys,* questionnaires are sent to respondents, who are encouraged to complete and return them. Mail surveys are used most often when the individuals chosen for questioning are spread over a wide area and funds for the survey are limited. A mail survey is the least expensive survey method as long as the response rate is high enough to produce reliable results. The main disadvantages of this method are the possibility of a low response rate or of misleading results if respondents are significantly different from the population being sampled.

Researchers can boost mail survey response rates by offering respondents some incentive to return the questionnaire. When using mail survey techniques, incentives and follow-ups have been found to consistently increase response rates. But promises of anonymity, special appeals for cooperation, and questionnaire length have no apparent impact on the response rate. Other techniques for increasing the response rate, such as advance notification, personalization of survey materials, type of postage, corporate or university sponsorship, or

Table 7.5 **Marketing Researchers' Views of Respondent Reactions Toward Major Data Collection Techniques**

	Very Negative	Somewhat Negative	Neither Neg. nor Positive	Somewhat Positive	Very Positive
Telephone	20.8%	59.8%	12.9%	6.0%	0.4%
In-person at home	5.8%	17.9%	36.7%	32.4%	7.2%
Mall Intercept	2.3%	27.6%	38.3%	31.0%	0.8%
Focus Groups	0.2%	0.8%	7.3%	52.5%	39.2%
Mail Surveys	1.5%	15.8%	49.0%	31.3%	2.5%

Source: 1990 Industry Image Study, Walker Research, Inc., Indianapolis, IN.

	Harder	Easier	No Difference
In the future, will it be harder or easier to collect data from the public via the use of:			
Telephone	89.2%	2.7%	8.1%
In-person at home	74.0%	3.8%	22.3%
Mall Intercept	41.9%	10.4%	47.7%
Focus Groups	22.4%	21.2%	56.4%
Mail	47.2%	10.6%	42.2%

Source: 1990 Industry Image Study, Walker Research, Inc., Indianapolis, IN.

foot-in-the-door techniques have had mixed results, varying according to the population surveyed.[10] Although such techniques may help increase the response rates, they can introduce sample-composition bias, or nonresponse bias, which results when those responding to a survey differ in some important respect from those not responding to the survey. In other words, response-enhancing techniques may alienate some people in the sample and appeal to others, making the results nonrepresentative of the population of interest. Perhaps because of these problems and the others discussed earlier, firms surveyed in Table 7.6 feel that it will be increasingly more difficult to collect mail marketing research data.[11]

Premiums or incentives encouraging respondents to return questionnaires have been effective in developing panels of respondents who are regularly interviewed by mail. Mail panels, which are selected to represent a market or market segment, are especially useful for evaluating new products, providing general information about consumers, and providing records of consumers' purchases. As Table 7.5 indicates most negative attitudes are toward telephone, at-home, and mall intercept interviewing.[12] Consumer mail panels and consumer purchase diaries are much more widely used than custom mail surveys, but they do have shortcomings. Research indicates that the people who take the time to fill out a consumer diary have higher income and are more educated than the general population. If researchers include less educated consumers in the panel, they must risk poorer response rates.[13]

In *telephone surveys,* respondents' answers to a questionnaire are recorded by interviewers on the phone. A telephone survey has some advantages over a mail survey. The rate of response is higher because it takes less effort to answer the telephone and talk than to fill out a questionnaire and return it. If there are enough interviewers, telephone surveys can be conducted very quickly. Thus they can be used by political candidates or organizations seeking an immediate reaction to an event. In addition, this survey technique permits interviewers to gain rapport with respondents and ask probing questions. Moreover, the use of WATS (Wide Area Telecommunications Service) lines reduces the expense of long-distance telephone interviewing. According to a survey by the Council of American Survey Research Organizations (CASRO), telephone interviewing is the preferred survey method in more than 40 percent of the projects conducted by commercial survey research firms.[14] The data in Table 7.5 show that telephone surveying has a somewhat negative image. Table 7.6 indicates that 89 percent of the researchers surveyed believe it is going to be harder to collect data through telephone interviews in the future.

Telephone interviews do have drawbacks. They are limited to oral communication; visual aids or observation cannot be included. Interpreters of results must make adjustments for subjects who are not at home or who do not have telephones. Many households are excluded from telephone directories by choice (unlisted numbers) or because the residents moved after the directory was published. Telephone answering machines are often used to screen calls and prevent access to potential respondents.

These findings have serious implications for the use of telephone samples in conducting surveys. Some adjustment must be made for groups of respondents that may be undersampled because of a smaller-than-average incidence of telephone listings. Nondirectory telephone samples can overcome such bias. Various methods are available, including random-digit dialing (adding random numbers to the telephone prefix) and plus-one telephone sampling (adding one to the last digit of a number in the directory). These methods make it feasible to dial any working number, whether it is or is not listed in a directory.

Telephone surveys, like mail and personal interview surveys, are sometimes used to develop panels of respondents who can be interviewed repeatedly to measure changes in attitudes or behavior. Reliance on such panels is increasing.

Computer-assisted telephone interviewing permits an integration of questionnaire, data collection, and tabulations and provides data to aid decision makers in the shortest time possible. In computer-assisted telephone interviewing, the paper questionnaire is replaced by a computer monitor or video screen. Responses are entered on a terminal keyboard, or the interviewer can use a light pen (a pen-shaped flashlight) to record a response on a light-sensitive screen. On the most advanced devices, the interviewer merely points at the appropriate response on a touch-sensitive screen with his or her finger. Open-ended responses can be typed on the keyboard or recorded with paper and pencil.

Computer-assisted telephone interviewing saves time and facilitates monitoring the progress of interviews. Entry functions are largely eliminated; the computer determines which question to display on the screen, skipping irrelevant questions. Because data are available as soon as they are entered into the system, cumbersome hand computations are avoided and interim results can be quickly retrieved.

Marketing researchers have traditionally favored the *personal interview survey*, chiefly because of its flexibility. Various audiovisual aids—pictures, products, diagrams, or prerecorded advertising copy—can be incorporated into a personal interview. Rapport gained through direct interaction usually permits more in-depth interviewing, including probes, follow-up questions, or psychological tests. In addition, because personal interviews can be longer, they can yield more information. Finally, respondents can be selected more carefully, and reasons for nonresponse can be explored. In one study, it was found that respondents questioned by personal contact methods had the most favorable attitudes toward survey research in general. The respondent liked seeing the person who was asking the questions and having the personal contact that is part of the interview.[15]

The nature of personal interviews has changed. In the past, most personal interviews, which were based on random sampling or prearranged appointments, were conducted in the respondent's home. Today, most personal interviews are conducted in shopping malls. *Shopping mall intercept interviews* involve interviewing a percentage of persons passing by certain "intercept" points in a mall. Although there are many variations of this technique, Table 7.5 indicates that the reaction toward mall intercept research is mixed, nearly equally split among positive, negative, and neutral. Almost half of major consumer goods and services companies use this technique, and report that shopping mall intercept interviewing was their major expenditure on survey research.[16]

Like any face-to-face interviewing method, mall intercept interviewing has many advantages. The interviewer is in a position to recognize and react to respondents' nonverbal indications of confusion. Respondents can be shown product prototypes, videotapes of commercials, and the like, and reactions can be sought. The mall environment lets the researcher deal with complex situations. For example, in taste tests, researchers know that all the respondents are reacting to the same product, which can be prepared and monitored from the mall test kitchen or some other facility. In addition, lower cost, greater control, and the ability to conduct tests requiring bulky equipment make shopping mall intercept interviews popular.

Research indicates that given a comparable sample of respondents, shopping mall intercept interviewing is a suitable substitute for telephone interviewing.[17] In addition, there seem to be no significant differences in the completeness of consumer responses between telephone interviewing and shopping mall intercept interviewing. In fact, for questions dealing with socially desirable behavior, shopping mall intercept respondents appear to be more honest about their past behavior.[18] On the other hand, when shopping mall intercept studies are done at central locations within a mall, data gathered are likely to be from individuals who spend more time at the location. It is possible to adjust sample results based on length of stay as well as frequency of visits in a mall.[19]

On-site computer interviewing, a variation of the mall intercept interview, consists of respondents completing a self-administered questionnaire displayed on a computer monitor. A microcomputer-based software package can be used to conduct such interviews in shopping malls. After a brief lesson on how to operate the software, respondents can proceed through the survey at their own pace. Adaptive design questionnaires may be developed so that the respondent sees only those questionnaire items (usually a subset of an entire scale) that provide useful information about the respondent's attitude.[20]

The object of a *focus-group interview* is to observe group interaction when members are exposed to an idea or concept. Often these interviews are conducted informally, without a structured questionnaire. Consumer attitudes, behavior, lifestyles, needs, and desires can be explored in a flexible and creative manner through focus-group interviews. Table 7.5 indicates that the focus group interviews have a generally positive image and Table 7.6 indicates little change in the ease of gathering data using this technique. Questions are open-ended and stimulate consumers to answer in their own words. Researchers can ask probing questions to clarify something they do not fully understand or something unexpected and interesting that may help explain consumer behavior. Cadillac used information obtained from focus groups to change its advertising so that the safety features of Cadillacs might be emphasized. The new advertisements increased Cadillac sales by 36 percent in test markets.[21]

Another research technique is the *in-home (door-to-door) interview*. As Table 7.6 indicates, 74 percent of researchers believe that it will become more difficult to gather data through this type of interview. However, the in-home interview offers a clear advantage when thoroughness of self-disclosure and the elimination of group influence are important. In an in-depth interview of forty-five to ninety minutes, respondents can be probed to reveal their real motivations, feelings, behaviors, and aspirations.

Questionnaire Construction   A carefully constructed questionnaire is essential to the success of any survey. Questions must be designed to elicit information that meets the study's data requirements. These questions must be clear, easy to understand, and directed toward a specific objective. Researchers need to define the objective before trying to develop a questionnaire because the objective determines the substance of the questions and the amount of detail. A common mistake in constructing questionnaires is to ask questions that interest the researchers but do not yield information useful in deciding whether to accept or reject a hypothesis. Finally, the most important rule in composing questions is to maintain impartiality.

The questions are usually of three kinds: open-ended, dichotomous, and multiple choice.

OPEN-ENDED QUESTION
What is your general opinion of the American Express Optima Card?

_____

_____

_____

DICHOTOMOUS QUESTION
Do you presently have an American Express Optima Card?

Yes _____   No _____

MULTIPLE-CHOICE QUESTION
What age group are you in?

Under 20	_____	40–49	_____
20–29	_____	50–59	_____
30–39	_____	60 and over	_____

Researchers must be very careful about questions that a respondent might consider too personal or that might require him or her to admit activities that other people are likely to condemn. Questions of this type should be worded in such a way as to make them less offensive.

For testing special markets where individuals (for instance, executives, scientists, and engineers) are likely to own or have access to a personal computer, questionnaires may be programmed on a computer disk and the disks delivered through the mail. This technique may cost less than a telephone interview and eliminate bias by simplifying flow patterns in answering questions. Respondents see less clutter on the screen than on a printed questionnaire; the novelty of the approach may also spark their interest and compel their attention.

Observation Methods In using **observation methods**, researchers record respondents' overt behavior, taking note of physical conditions and events. Direct contact with respondents is avoided; instead, their actions are examined and noted systematically. For example, researchers might use observation methods to answer the question "How long does the average McDonald's restaurant customer have to wait in line before being served?"

Observation may also be combined with interviews. For example, during personal interviews, the condition of a respondent's home or other possessions may be observed and recorded, and demographic information such as race, approximate age, and sex can be confirmed by direct observation.

Data gathered through observation can sometimes be biased if the respondent is aware of the observation process. An observer can be placed in a natural market environment, such as a grocery store, without biasing or influencing shoppers' actions. However, if the presence of a human observer is likely to bias the outcome or if human sensory abilities are inadequate, mechanical means may be used to record behavior. **Mechanical observation devices** include cameras, recorders, counting machines, and equipment to record physiological changes in individuals. For instance, a special camera can be used to record eye movements of respondents looking at an advertisement; the sequence of reading and the parts of the advertisement that receive greatest attention can be detected. The electronic scanners in supermarkets mentioned earlier in the chapter are mechanical observation devices that offer an exciting opportunity for marketing research. Scanner technology can provide accurate data on sales and consumers' purchase patterns, and marketing researchers may buy such data from the supermarket.

Observation is straightforward and avoids a central problem of survey methods: motivating respondents to state their true feelings or opinions. However, observation tends to be descriptive. When it is the only method of data collection, it may not provide insights into causal relationships. Another drawback is that analyses based on observation are subject to the biases of the observer or the limitations of the mechanical device.

Interpreting Research Findings

After collecting data to test their hypotheses, marketers interpret the research findings. Interpretation of the data is easier if marketers carefully plan their data analysis methods early in the research process. They should also allow for continual evaluation of the data during the entire collection period. They can then gain valuable insight into areas that ought to be probed during the formal interpretation.

The first step in drawing conclusions from most research is displaying the data in table format. If marketers intend to apply the results to individual categories of the things or people being studied, cross tabulation may be quite useful, especially in tabulating joint occurrences. For example, using the two variables, gender and purchase rates of automobile tires, a cross tabulation could show how men and women differ in purchasing automobile tires.

After the data are tabulated, they must be analyzed. **Statistical interpretation** focuses on what is typical or what deviates from the average. It indicates how widely responses vary and how they are distributed in relation to the variable being measured. This interpretation is another facet of marketing research that relies on marketers' judgment or intuition. Moreover, when they interpret statistics, marketers must take into account estimates of expected error or deviation from the true values of the population. The analysis of data may lead researchers to accept or reject the hypothesis being studied. As shown in Figure 7.9, SPSS, a noted statistical analysis package producer for marketing research, provides data analysis and presentation graphics.

Data require careful interpretation by the marketer. If the results of a study are valid, the decision maker should take action; however, if it is discovered that a question has been incorrectly worded, the results should be ignored. For example, if a study by an electric utility company reveals that 50 percent of its customers believe that meter readers are "friendly," is that finding good, bad, or indifferent? Two important benchmarks help interpret the result: how the 50 percent figure compares with that for competitors and how it compares with a previous time period. Managers must understand the research results and relate the results to a context that permits effective decision making.[22]

Figure 7.9

Data Analysis

SPSS provides software for the statistical analysis of market research data. This kind of analysis helps researchers interpret data resulting from the testing of their hypotheses.

Source: Courtesy of SPSS Inc.

Reporting Research Findings

The final step in the marketing research process is reporting the research findings. Before preparing the report, the marketer must take a clear, objective look at the findings to see how well the gathered facts answer the research question or support or negate the hypotheses posed in the beginning. In most cases, it is extremely doubtful that the study can provide everything needed to answer the research question. Thus in the report the researcher must point out the deficiencies and the reasons for them.

The report presenting the results is usually a formal, written report. Researchers must allow time for the writing task when they plan and schedule the project. Since the report is a means of communicating with the decision makers who will use the research findings, researchers need to determine beforehand how much detail and supporting data to include. They should keep in mind that corporate executives prefer reports that are short, clear, and simply expressed. Often researchers will give their summary and recommendations first, especially if decision makers do not have time to study how the results were obtained. A technical report allows its users to analyze data and interpret recommendations because it describes the research methods and procedures and the most important data gathered. Thus, researchers must recognize the needs and expectations of the report user and adapt to them.

When marketing decision makers have a firm grasp of research methods and procedures, they are better able to integrate reported findings and personal experience. If marketers can spot limitations in research from reading the report, then personal experience assumes additional importance in the decision-making process. For example, it is important for marketing decision makers who are studying potential markets in Russia to know that marketing research in Russia is extremely difficult due to the magnitude of product shortages. In Russia the last brand purchased is more of an indication of availability than of brand preference. In fact, brand names have little meaning to the average Russian consumer, although country of origin does have meaning.[23]

Marketers who cannot understand basic statistical assumptions and data gathering procedures may misuse research findings. Consequently, report writers should be aware of the backgrounds and research abilities of those who will rely on the report in making decisions. Clear explanations presented in plain language make it easier for decision makers to apply the findings and diminish the chances of a report being misused or ignored. Talking with potential research users before writing a report can help researchers supply information that will indeed improve decision making.

The Importance of Ethical Marketing Research

Marketing research and systematic information gathering make successful marketing more likely. In fact, many companies, and even entire industries, have failed because of a lack of marketing research. Marketing managers and other professionals are relying more and more on marketing research to make better decisions. Clearly, marketing research and information systems are vital to marketing decision making. It is therefore essential that professional standards be established by which such research may be judged reliable.

To improve the quality of marketing research data, it has been suggested that research firms should be audited to evaluate their procedures and that professional certification of marketing researchers would be beneficial.[24] In the Walker Image study cited in Table 7.5, 64 percent of the researchers surveyed believe that there is a need for professional certification. One part of professional certification is a measure of competence to recognize and abide by marketing research industry ethical codes. In this same study, only 38 percent of the researchers indicated that their firms had a written code of ethical conduct.

In recent years, the courts have also addressed the question of what survey research may be considered reliable. Table 7.7 summarizes the guidelines judicial decisions have determined for survey research to be admissible as evidence in court cases. Although these requirements may be slightly narrow for private users of research, they do provide guidelines for what are considered professional marketing research procedures.[25]

In any field, ethics are a vital part of professional standards. Ethical issues in marketing research include researcher honesty, manipulation of research techniques, data manipulation, invasion of privacy, and failure to disclose the purpose or sponsorship of a study in some situations. Too often respondents are unfairly manipulated and research clients are not told about flaws in data.

One common practice that hurts the image of marketing research is "sugging" ("selling under the guise of marketing research"). A leading marketing research association (ESOMAR) is attempting to get research companies and marketing research firms worldwide to adopt codes and policies prohibiting this practice.[26]

Because so many parties are involved in the marketing research process, developing shared ethical concern is difficult. The relationships among respondents who cooperate and share information, interviewing companies, marketing research agencies that manage projects, and organizations that use the data are interdependent and complex. Ethical conflict typically occurs because the parties involved in the marketing research process often have different objectives. For example, the organization that uses data tends to be result-oriented, and success is often based on performance rather than a set of standards. On the other hand, a data-gathering subcontractor is evaluated based on the ability to follow a specific set of standards or rules. The relationships among all participants in marketing research must be understood so that decision making becomes ethical. Without clear understanding and agreement, including mutual adoption of standards, ethical conflict will lead to mistrust and questionable research results.[27]

Summary

To implement the marketing concept, marketers need information about the characteristics, needs, and wants of their target markets. Marketing research and information systems that furnish practical, unbiased information help firms avoid the assumptions and misunderstandings that could lead to poor marketing performance.

Marketing research is the systematic design, collection, interpretation, and reporting of information to help marketers solve specific marketing problems or

1. **Universe Definition and Sample Selection**
   a. The universe should include all relevant respondents and exclude inappropriate, unknowledgeable, or unconcerned respondents.
   b. The universe must be defined in the context of the research question being investigated.
   c. Convenience and nonprobability sampling must be justifiable.
   d. Sample size must be intuitively justifiable.
   e. Sampling should not appear to be biased toward any viewpoint or opinion group.

2. **Design of Survey Instrument**
   a. Questionnaires should be pretested.
   b. Questions that appear to predispose respondents must be avoided.
   c. Question wording must be direct, clear, and unambiguous.
   d. Respondents must appear to be capable of understanding the topics that questions are raising.
   e. Survey questions must relate directly to the research questions being investigated.
   f. Objective questions must include properly stated, complete sets of response scales.
   g. Respondents should be explicitly instructed not to guess.

3. **Administration of Survey Instrument**
   a. Results must not appear to be an artifact of the research design.
   b. Respondent tasks must appear possible to perform.
   c. Surveys should not omit necessary respondent tasks.

   d. Research designs must be devised in the context of normal marketplace conditions, subject to the research questions being investigated.
   e. Contrived or deceptive research designs will not only be unconvincing, but may be held against the researcher.

4. **Interviewers' Qualifications and Techniques**
   a. Interviewers should not know the name of the organization sponsoring the survey.
   b. Interviewers should not know the purpose of the research project.
   c. Interviewer decision making, through probing questions or intervention during questioning, should be minimized.

5. **Data Analysis and Presentation**
   a. Assumptions underlying data interpretations must be obvious and justifiable.
   b. Multiple responses to an open-ended question should not be combined unless the groupings are obvious and justifiable.
   c. The frequencies and order of mention of multiple responses to a question should be reported.

6. **Administration of Overall Project**
   a. The survey administrator must be a recognized expert, based on peer review, in survey research.
   b. The survey administrator must continuously and closely supervise all steps in the research project.

Source: Adapted from Fred W. Morgan, "Judicial Standards for Survey Research: An Update and Guidelines," *Journal of Marketing*, 1990, p. 63. Used by permission.

Table 7.7   **Methodological Guidelines for Conducting Survey Research Admissible in Court**

take advantage of marketing opportunities. Marketing research is conducted on a special-project basis, with the research methods adapted to the problems being studied and to changes in the environment.

The marketing information system (MIS) is a framework for the day-to-day managing and structuring of information regularly gathered from sources both inside and outside an organization. The inputs into a marketing information system include the information sources inside and outside the firm considered useful for future decision making. Processing information involves classifying information and developing categories for meaningful storage and retrieval.

Marketing decision makers then determine which information—the output—is useful for making decisions. Feedback enables those who are responsible for gathering internal and external data to adjust the information inputs systematically. Data brought into the organization through marketing research become part of its marketing databank, a file of data collected through both the MIS and marketing research projects.

The increase in marketing research activities represents a transition from intuitive to scientific problem solving. Intuitive decisions are made on the basis of personal knowledge and past experience. Scientific decision making is an orderly, logical, and systematic approach. Minor, nonrecurring problems can be handled successfully by intuition. As the number of risks and alternative solutions increases, the use of research becomes more desirable and rewarding.

The five basic steps of planning marketing research are (1) defining and locating problems, (2) developing hypotheses, (3) collecting data, (4) interpreting research findings, and (5) reporting the findings.

Defining and locating the problem—the first step toward finding a solution or launching a research study—means uncovering the nature and boundaries of a negative, or positive, situation or question. A problem must be clearly defined for marketers to develop a hypothesis—an informed assumption about that problem or set of circumstances—which is the second step in the research process.

To test the accuracy of hypotheses, researchers collect data—the third step in the research process. Researchers may use exploratory, descriptive, or causal studies. Secondary data are compiled inside or outside the organization for some purpose other than the current investigation. Secondary data may be collected from an organization's databank and other internal sources; from periodicals, government publications, and unpublished sources; and from syndicated data services, which collect general information and sell it to clients.

Primary data are observed and recorded or collected directly from respondents. Experimentation involves maintaining as constants those factors that are related to or may affect the variables under investigation so that the effects of the experimental variables may be measured. Marketing experimentation is a set of rules and procedures under which the task of data gathering is organized to expedite analysis and interpretation. In experimentation, an independent variable is manipulated and the resulting changes are measured in a dependent variable. Research techniques are reliable if they produce almost identical results in successive repeated trials; they are valid if they measure what they are supposed to measure and not something else. Experiments may take place in laboratory settings, which provide maximum control over influential factors, or in field settings, which are preferred when marketers want experimentation to take place in natural surroundings.

Other methods for collecting primary data include sampling, surveys, and observation. Sampling involves selecting representative units from a total population. In random sampling, all the units in a population have an equal chance of appearing in the sample. In stratified sampling, the population of interest is divided into groups according to a common characteristic or attribute, and then a probability sample is conducted within each group. Area sampling involves selecting a probability sample of geographic areas such as blocks, census tracts, or census enumeration districts and selecting units or individuals within the selected geographic areas for the sample. Quota sampling differs from other forms of sampling in that it is judgmental.

There are numerous survey methods, ranging from mail surveys, telephone surveys, computer-assisted telephone interviews, personal interview surveys, and shopping mall intercept interviews to on-site computer interviews, focus-group interviews, and in-home interviews. Questionnaires are instruments used to obtain information from respondents and to record observations; they should be unbiased and objective. Observation methods involve researchers recording respondents' overt behavior and taking note of physical conditions and events. Observation may be facilitated by mechanical observation devices.

To apply research findings to decision making, marketers must interpret and report their findings properly. Statistical interpretation is analysis that focuses on what is typical or what deviates from the average. After interpreting the research findings, the researchers must prepare a report of the findings that the decision makers can use and understand.

Marketing research and systematic information gathering increase the probability of successful marketing. In fact, marketing research is essential in planning and developing marketing strategies. Because of this, attempts to eliminate unethical marketing research practices and establish generally acceptable procedures for conducting research are important goals. However, because so many parties are involved in the marketing research process, shared ethical concern is difficult.

Important Terms

Marketing research	Dependent variable
Marketing information system (MIS)	Reliability
Marketing databank	Validity
Problem definition	Sample
Hypothesis	Sampling
Exploratory studies	Population
Descriptive studies	Random sampling
Causal studies	Stratified sampling
Primary data	Area sampling
Secondary data	Quota sampling
Syndicated data services	Survey methods
Experimentation	Observation methods
Marketing experimentation	Mechanical observation devices
Independent variable	Statistical interpretation

Discussion and Review Questions

1. What is the MIS likely to include in a small organization? Do all organizations have a marketing databank?
2. What is the difference between marketing research and marketing information systems? In what ways do marketing research and the MIS overlap?
3. How do the benefits of decisions guided by marketing research compare with those of intuitive decision making? How do marketing decision makers know when it will be worthwhile to conduct research?
4. Give specific examples of situations in which intuitive decision making would probably be more appropriate than marketing research.
5. What is the difference between defining a research problem and developing a hypothesis?

6. What are the major limitations of using secondary data to solve marketing problems?

7. List some problems of conducting a laboratory experiment on respondents' reactions to the taste of different brands of beer. How would these problems differ from those of a field study of beer taste preferences?

8. In what situation would it be best to use random sampling? Quota sampling? Stratified or area sampling?

9. *Nonresponse* is the inability or refusal of some respondents to cooperate in a survey. What are some ways to decrease nonresponse in personal door-to-door surveys?

10. Make some suggestions for ways to encourage respondents to cooperate in mail surveys.

11. If a survey of all homes with listed telephone numbers is conducted, what sampling design should be used?

12. Give some examples of marketing problems that could be solved through information gained from observation.

Cases

7.1 How Marketing Research Helped Create a New "Cadillac Style"

When the 1980s began, Americans could choose from among 408 different automobile models; by 1990 that figure had grown to 572. Every car maker wants to sell in the United States—the world's richest market—and many new brands—Isuzu, Daihatsu, Mitsubishi, Hyundai, Geo, Saturn, and others—have been introduced in the last ten years. But with so many different models available, consumers have become simultaneously liberated, confused, and less brand-loyal. Consequently, car makers are having a harder time keeping customers, as well as getting customers to buy their brands in the first place. In this environment, marketing research is crucial in helping automobile manufacturers determine what car buyers need and want in a new car.

One company using marketing research to stay ahead of the pack is General Motor's Cadillac division. Cadillac, the best-selling domestic luxury car since 1948, has long been associated with high quality, luxury, and value. Competition from new models, however, has made reaching affluent car buyers more difficult. Along with other well-established luxury brands—Lincoln, Mercedes-Benz, Volvo, and BMW—Cadillac has found itself competing with Japanese luxury sedans, such as Honda's Acura, Nissan's Infiniti, and Toyota's Lexus.

Marketing research showed Cadillac that luxury car makers were not effectively targeting affluent consumers because traditional advertising efforts missed the activities where affluent consumers spend most of their leisure time (art, theater, golf, for example). With this information, Cadillac decided to alter its promotional activities. It recently signed on to sponsor a series of PGA Seniors golf tournaments in the 1990s. It is also getting involved with other upscale lifestyle promotions, such as sponsoring yachting regattas, horse shows, and polo matches.

Lifestyle activities such as these have been a part of Cadillac advertising for many years. Going into the 1990s, however, Cadillac felt that the time had come to move toward a new concept of "Cadillac Style." The problem was in deciding how to approach this new concept. Marketing research had already shown that consumers are less brand-loyal than they have been in the past. And the recent introductions of Lexus and Infiniti meant that Cadillac *had* to choose the correct strategy for the 1990s.

Again, Cadillac found the answer through marketing research. A national survey by the *Wall Street Journal* of potential car buyers indicated that 60 percent of the respondents wanted anti-lock brakes in their next car, and 50 percent said they wanted to buy a car with air bags. The same survey respondents, however, showed little interest in features such as turbo engines and electronic dashboards. When Cadillac conducted focus-group interviews with potential buyers who already owned luxury imports, it found that 50 percent would consider buying a redesigned Cadillac Eldorado or Seville; previous research of this type had found only 10 percent of potential buyers were willing to consider a Cadillac.

The fact that car buyers wanted more safety features posed a problem for Cadillac, in part because the Big Three car makers had long held the belief that safety does not sell cars. However, Cadillac decided to ignore this theory and designed safer Eldorados and Sevilles for the 1992 model year. Cadillac immediately changed its advertising to emphasize the cars' safety features, rather than their upscale image. Company officials felt that the well-established Cadillac image would promote styling, luxury, and prestige in and of itself. A new advertising campaign, which used the theme "Building a Safer Automobile, Cadillac Style," showed more of Cadillac's antilock brakes and air-bag features and fewer upscale images.

Additionally, Cadillac has returned to designing automobiles to satisfy its traditional Cadillac buyers: the age-fifty-and-over market. Although the company had made smaller Eldorado, Seville, DeVille, and Fleetwood models in the mid-1980s, research suggested that luxury car buyers preferred the old "boulevard barges" with lavish interiors and massive size. The company therefore enlarged and restyled these cars beginning with the 1988 and 1989 model years. The Fleetwood and DeVille sedans gained nine inches in length, and all Cadillacs got a more powerful V-8 engine in 1988. The company also reduced its cars' defect rates by 40 percent over three years. To gain sales from younger import buyers, the company is attempting to use more distinctive styling in Cadillacs, particularly in the Seville.

In 1990, Cadillac won the Malcolm Baldrige National Quality Award. The 1992 Seville won many automobile-magazine awards and quickly became a top-selling model. Cadillac will continue to conduct marketing research to determine the needs and wants of Cadillac buyers and to develop products and promotions accordingly.[28]

Questions for Discussion

1. How has marketing research helped Cadillac improve its promotional activities?
2. What kinds of risks were involved for Cadillac in redesigning the 1992 Eldorado and Seville and emphasizing safety features as suggested by focus-group research?
3. Why do you think the 1992 Eldorado and Seville were so successful?

7.2 Why Products Fail: A Marketing Research Gap

The importance of marketing research and information systems is best understood by looking at product failures. Eight out of ten new products eventually fail. To highlight the importance of strong marketing research, this case reviews several product failures.

Fab 1 Shot was introduced in 1987 as a single-packet detergent and fabric softener. To beat competitors to the market, Colgate-Palmolive introduced the product nationally without first test marketing it. The company targeted promotion for the product at large families, when, in fact, the actual consumers were singles, college students, and apartment dwellers. These consumers want convenience at any price, whereas large families are more concerned with cost and controlling the amount of detergent in each load. Without marketing efforts targeting the appropriate segment, Fab 1 Shot was a failure. Thus accurate market test data are invaluable in positioning a product to the appropriate demographic segment.

When the film *Crocodile Dundee* was popular, so too was anything Australian. In jumped Australia's Foster's Lager beer in the late 1980s. Foster's promotion revolved around its Australian heritage. But when the Australian fever ended, Foster's lost more than 40 percent of its sales. In a highly competitive market, Foster's failed to convey a clear image to consumers beyond its Australian origins, and the product never found a market niche of its own. Targeting a saturated market requires marketing research to determine niches that may have an interest in the product.

In the late 1980s, four new colognes for men and women were introduced. There was nothing too unusual about the colognes except their brand name: Bic. Upon introducing the product, Bic put $18 million into its marketing campaign, but disappointing sales contributed to a 22 percent drop in company profits. Advertising for the colognes focused more on the novel shape of the package—similar to a lighter—and less on the fragrance. Consumers were confused by the packaging and reluctant to purchase a cologne that they could not test before purchasing. More extensive marketing research could have revealed that the Bic brand name had been overextended. What makes for a great pen, lighter, or razor doesn't necessarily create a great cologne.

When PepsiCo introduced Slice soda, its advertising proclaimed the drink was made with 10 percent real fruit juice. Will all the concern toward health issues, Slice's appeal seemed to fit with changing attitudes and behavior. When consumers are offered products with health benefits, conceptual tests indicate they rank the product high. But actual soda consumption revealed that consumers are more concerned with taste than health benefits. Therefore, Slice offered consumers an unnecessary benefit. PepsiCo has since trimmed its Slice product line, reduced the amount of juice in the products, and repositioned them for the orange and lemon-lime soda categories.

When R.J. Reynolds test marketed Uptown menthol cigarettes, the product was targeted to the black segment of the population. But test marketing backfired when the public learned that the product was specifically targeted at blacks. Many felt that the whole project represented insensitivity to a market's concerns and that it was exploitative. A great deal of hostility toward R.J. Reynolds was generated through the media by local communities and the federal government. Further attitude research could have revealed consumer sensitivity to racial segmentation in controversial product categories such as cigarettes.

When the Campbell Soup Company introduced Souper Combos, a microwavable soup and a side entree, test results showed the product had great appeal for office lunches and for dinners where families dined at various times. When Campbell's took the product national, however, the test results were no longer indicative. The company's support of the product, competitive activity, and consumer expectations all had changed. Even though test marketing had been conducted to support the ultimate product launch, the company did not conduct follow-up research to evaluate external and internal changes that could directly affect the product. Marketing research is necessary throughout a product's launch and life span to monitor changes in the marketing environment.

These cases highlight the importance of marketing research, test marketing, and establishing marketing information systems both within and outside of the company. Without critical research, products may fail, resulting in substantial losses.[29]

Questions for Discussion

1. What mistakes were common to all these product failures?
2. Which product failure could have been prevented with only an inexpensive research project?
3. What were the ethical issues in marketing research for Uptown cigarettes?

Chapter Notes

1. Based on information from Kevin Maney, "A Taste of Fast Food's Future," *USA Today,* Aug. 16–18, 1991, pp. 1A–2A; Laurie Petersen, "Pretesting Brand Strategies," *Adweek's Marketing Week,* Dec. 3, 1990, pp. 32–33; and Scott Hume, "McD's Sizzles with New Ideas," *Advertising Age,* Sept. 3, 1990, pp. 1, 53.
2. Reprinted from *Dictionary of Marketing Terms,* Peter D. Bennett, Ed., 1988, pp. 117–118, published by the American Marketing Association. Used by permission.
3. Andrea Dunham, "Information Systems Are the Key to Managing Future Business Needs," *Marketing News,* May 23, 1986, p. 11.
4. Melanie Payne, "Execs Tell What They Need from Research in the 90s," *Marketing News,* Jan. 7, 1991, p. 18.
5. Cynthia Crossen, "Margin of Error," *Wall Street Journal,* Nov. 14, 1991, p. A7.
6. W. Steven Perkins and Ram C. Rao, "The Role of Experience in Information Use and Decision Making by Marketing Managers," *Journal of Marketing Research,* Feb. 1990, pp. 1–10.
7. Greg M. Allenby, "Hypothesis Testing with Scanner Data: The Advantage of Bayesian Methods," *Journal of Marketing Research,* Nov. 1990, pp. 379–389.
8. Lynn G. Coleman, "Researchers Say Non-Response Is the Single Biggest Problem," *Marketing News,* Jan. 7, 1991, p. 32.
9. Ibid.
10. Jeffrey S. Conant, Denise T. Smart, and Bruce J. Walker, "Mail-Survey Facilitation Techniques: An Assessment and Proposal Regarding Reporting Practices" (working paper, Texas A&M University, 1990).
11. 1990 Industry Image Study, Walker Research, Inc., Indianapolis, IN.
12. Ibid.
13. Martha Farnsworth Riche, "Who Says Yes?" *American Demographics,* Feb. 1987, p. 8.
14. Diane K. Bowers, "Telephone Legislation," *Marketing Research,* Mar. 1989, p. 47.

15. Cynthia Webster, "Consumers' Attitudes Toward Data Collection Methods," Robert L. King, Ed., *Marketing: Toward the 21st Century,* Proceedings of the Southern Marketing Association, Atlanta, GA, Nov. 1991, p. 221.

16. *Practices, Trends and Expectations for the Market Research Industry 1987,* Market Facts, Inc., Apr. 29, 1987.

17. Alan J. Bush and A. Parasuraman, "Mall Intercept Versus Telephone-Interviewing Environment," *Journal of Advertising Research,* Apr.-May 1985, p. 42.

18. Alan J. Bush and Joseph F. Hair, Jr., "An Assessment of the Mall Intercept as a Data Collecting Method," *Journal of Marketing Research,* May 1985, p. 162.

19. Clifford Nowell and Linda S. Stanley, "Length-Bias Sampling in Mall Intercept Surveys," *Journal of Marketing Research,* Nov. 1991, pp. 478–479.

20. Jagdip Singh, Roy D. Howell, and Gary K. Rhoads, "Adaptive Designs for Likert-Type Data: An Approach for Implementing Marketing Surveys," *Journal of Marketing Research,* Aug. 1990, pp. 304–321.

21. James B. Treece and Wendy Zellner with Walecia Konrad, "Detroit Tries to Rev Up," *Business Week,* June 12, 1989, p. 82.

22. Michael J. Olivette, "Marketing Research in the Electric Utility Industry," *Marketing News,* Jan. 2, 1987, p. 13.

23. Jerry Stafford and Neil Ubmeyer, "Product Shortages Hamper Research in the Soviet Union," *Marketing News,* Sept. 3, 1990, p. 6.

24. Bruce L. Stern and Edward L. Grubb, "Alternative Solutions to The Marketing Research Industry's 'Quality Control Program,'" Robert L. King, Ed., *Marketing: Toward the 21st Century,* Proceedings of the Southern Marketing Association, Atlanta, GA, Nov. 1991, pp. 225–229.

25. Fred W. Morgan, "Judicial Standards for Survey Research: An Update and Guidelines," *Journal of Marketing,* Jan. 1990, pp. 59–70.

26. Lynn Colemar, "It's Selling Disguised as Research," *Marketing News,* Jan. 4, 1988, p. 1.

27. O. C. Ferrell and Steven J. Skinner, "Ethical Behavior and Bureaucratic Structure in Marketing Research Organizations," *Journal of Marketing Research,* Feb. 1988, pp. 103–104.

28. Jacqueline Mitchell, "Cadillac Seville Ads Aim for Younger Laps of Luxury," *Wall Street Journal,* Aug. 26, 1991, p. B4; Wendy Zellner, "The Boulevard Barge Is Cruising Again," *Business Week,* Feb. 5, 1990, pp. 52–53; Lesa Doll, "Prospecting Goes Further Upscale," *Advertising Age,* Jan. 22, 1990, pp. S10–S11; Paul Ingrassia and Gregory A. Patterson, "Is Buying a Car a Choice or a Chore?" *Wall Street Journal,* Oct. 24, 1989, p. B1; Raymond Serafin and Patricia Strand, "Ads, Cadillac-Style," *Advertising Age,* Sept. 18, 1989, p. 84; and Raymond Serafin, "Caddy Goes for Golf," *Advertising Age,* Aug. 21, 1989, p. 16.

29. Cara Appelbaum, "Overextending a Brand," *Adweek's Marketing Week,* Nov. 5, 1990, p. 21; Cara Appelbaum, "Targeting the Wrong Demographic," *Adweek's Marketing Week,* Nov. 5, 1990, p. 20; Laura Bird, "Unnecessary 'Innovations,'" *Adweek's Marketing Week,* Nov. 5, 1990, p. 24; Matthew Grimm, "Targeting a Saturated Market," *Adweek's Marketing Week,* Nov. 5, 1990, p. 21; David Kiley, "Conditions That Change," *Adweek's Marketing Week,* Nov. 5, 1990, p. 25; and Dan Koeppel, "Insensitivity to a Market's Concern," *Adweek's Marketing Week,* Nov. 5, 1990, p. 25.

Stew Leonard's: The World's Largest Dairy Store

Stew Leonard's is the top-grossing, highest-volume food store in the world. Built on the philosophy that the customer is always right, Stew Leonard's offers food shoppers low prices, high product quality, excellent customer service, and a festive, Disney-like atmosphere. The Norwalk, Connecticut store draws 100,000 shoppers a week, some from as far away as Massachusetts, Rhode Island, Pennsylvania, and New York. Annual sales total $100 million.

Milkman and entrepreneur Stewart Leonard opened his store in 1969 after the state of Connecticut decided to route a highway through the small dairy he had inherited from his father. The original Stew Leonard's offered only eight products, but customers were attracted to the dairy store by the prices and Leonard's showmanship and marketing flair. In fact, the original store made the decision to standardize their milk containers by offering only half-gallon cartons. Strategies such as these helped Stew Leonard's control costs by minimizing overhead and inventory. Today, after twenty-six expansions, family-owned Stew Leonard's is a 106,000-square-foot complex built around a highly automated milk-processing operation. The store continues to present a narrow product mix—about 750 items, as compared to the 15,000 items conventional supermarkets stock. Nevertheless, Stew Leonard's sells in such volume that the store's per square foot sales of $2,974 earned the business a place in the Guinness Book of World Records. While many large grocery stores have reported slumping sales, Stew Leonard's sales continue to grow by 25 percent annually.

Each year Stew Leonard's customers buy 10 million quarts of milk, 1 million pints of cream, 100 tons of cottage cheese, 2.9 million quarts of orange juice, and more than 500,000 pounds of butter. They also buy 1,040 tons of ground beef, 1,820 tons of Perdue poultry products, and 800 tons of fixings from the store's salad bar. According to the Food Marketing Institute, the in-store bake shop sells twenty times more baked goods than any other in-store bakery in the country—almost 3 million muffins, 500,000 pies, and 348 tons of chocolate chip cookies annually. In addition, the store sells 2,000 pounds of pistachio nuts a week, which is 1 percent of the country's entire pistachio crop. These figures are even more amazing when you consider that Stew Leonard's has no wholesale customers; it sells only to the public.

Customer Orientation

Stew Leonard's low prices—about 10 to 20 percent lower than prices at stores nearby—are partly responsible for the store's popularity, but even more important is the store's responsiveness to customers. Indeed, the store opened in response to requests from Leonard's former milk route customers. Today, customer demand continues to dictate what products the store carries. Although Stew Leonard's may testmarket as many as 10,000 different products in a year, an item must sell 1,000 units weekly to remain in inventory. Thus the store carries only the best-selling brands of such items as cereal, yogurt, and peanut butter. Stew Leonard's also emphasizes product quality. Because of its enormous sales volume, the store can buy directly from producers, passing along the savings to customers. Stew Leonard's also has the leverage to order house brands made to its own specifications. For example, Stew Leonard's sells its own brand of potato chips and sliced bread.

Stew Leonard's strong customer orientation is reflected in the two rules carved in a huge, three-ton granite boulder just outside the door. Rule 1 states that "the customer is always right." Rule 2 says, "If the customer is ever wrong, reread Rule 1." Customer service is the top priority at Stew Leonard's. To eliminate long lines, the Leonards have equipped the store with 25 cash registers. Should any line back up to more than three customers, an employee immediately passes out free ice cream or snacks to waiting customers. The Leonards also actively solicit ideas from their customers, both to keep up with trends and to improve service. About once a month, focus groups of customers are invited to critique the store's products and policies—and management listens. For example, at the focus groups' suggestion, Stew Leonard's began to sell strawberries loose, instead of packaged. Originally the store's profit margin on strawberries decreased, but sales increased tenfold; the store was able to get a better deal from the supplier, and ultimately profits on strawberries were higher.

Stew Leonard's also acts promptly on the hundred-odd messages dropped into the store's suggestion box each day. When the Leonards followed one customer's suggestion that English muffins be displayed near bacon and eggs, muffin sales increased 50 percent. Another customer reported that he would have bought deli roast beef on special if the hard rolls had not been located clear across the store at the bakery. Leonard moved some rolls near the deli counter; sales of both rolls and deli roast beef doubled.

At Stew Leonard's nothing is too good for a customer. When a woman complained to Leonard the day after Thanksgiving that her turkey had been too dry, he immediately handed her a $20 turkey free of charge, knowing that her weekly business meant more to the store than the price of a single turkey. Leonard also had high praise for the courtesy booth employee who surprised a distraught customer with $50 in gift certificates after the customer was unable to find her missing sterling silver pen. Leonard's oft-repeated slogan gets the point across to all employees: "*S*atisfy the Customer; *T*eamwork gets it done; *E*xcellence makes it better; *W*ow makes it fun!"

The "Wow!" is a reminder of Leonard's deeply held conviction that a food retailer must give customers a pleasant and memorable shopping experience if the store is to remain competitive. Hence Stew Leonard's is full of surprises reminiscent of Leonard's hero, Walt Disney. In the parking lot, for example, is "The Little Farm," a collection of one hundred live cows, goats, chickens, sheep, and geese. Inside the store, employees dressed as farm animals and cartoon characters pass out balloons to children and tell shoppers about store specials. Installed above display cases are larger-than-life musical robots, such as a big banjo-playing dog and a cow singing nursery rhymes with a farmer. Purchases totaling more than $100 set off electronic mooing at the cash registers and gets the customer a free ice-cream cone.

Employee Motivation

The Leonards recognize that only happy employees can produce satisfied customers. A nonunion operation, Stew Leonard's offers employee benefits on the scale of a large corporation. The Leonards also encourage initiative by giving employees public recognition for their ideas. The Leonards look for "a good attitude" in potential employees and tell their team members, "If you're training the person under you to do a better job than you do, you're valuable to the company and will be promoted." About one hundred of the employees currently working at the store have graduated from Dale Carnegie courses conducted inhouse. Outstanding employees also are rewarded with plaques, dinners, gift certificates, recognition in the company newsletter, and (for managers) profit sharing. On the store's walls are framed pictures of employees of the month and team members whose suggestions have saved the organization money. Leonard's own efforts earned him a Presidential Award for Entrepreneurial Achievement. He was also named Connecticut's Small Business Advocate

of the Year by the U.S. Small Business Administration, and the store is featured in the book *A Passion for Excellence* as one of the best-run companies in America.

Until recently, Stew Leonard's was a single-store operation. However, after having developed all available space on the original site, the Leonards opened a second store in Danbury, Connecticut. The new store—a two-story, 272,000-square foot facility on a 44-acre site—employs about 400 persons and includes all the features of the Norwalk store, plus a garden center and parking space for 800 cars. It is a state-of-the-art facility which is on target to gross over $75 million dollars in its first year. Apparently, the new store has the same drawing power as the original Stew Leonard's.

In response to the demand for his management techniques, Stew Leonard has branched out into training and consulting services. The list of services includes lectures at various organizations, a training video entitled, "Creating the Customer's Dream," and even a university (Stew U.). Stew U. is actually a one-day seminar which is held periodically at the Norwalk store. Participants tour the store and hear lectures on the Stew Leonard way of doing business. The training and consulting services are just another way that Stew Leonard's is able to spread the word about the benefits of customer service. Perhaps more companies will adopt Stew Leonard's devotion to developing loyalty and trust among customers and employees.

Questions for Discussion

1. Has Stew Leonard's adopted the philosophy of the marketing concept? Explain your answer.
2. In what ways does Stew Leonard's demonstrate a strong customer orientation?
3. What types of marketing research does Stew Leonard's use?
4. How does Stew Leonard's understanding of customer needs contribute to the firm's success?

Sources: Richard M. Petreycik, "Crucial Steps to More Effective Management," *Progressive Grocer,* June 1991, pp. 24–27; Everett T. Suters, "Stew Leonard: Soul of a Leader," *Executive Excellence,* June 1991, pp. 13–14; Diane Feldman, "Quality Chitchat, Chickens, and Customer Service", *Management Review,* May 1989, pp. 8–9; "Supermarket Whiz Tells Bankers: Create Some Fun," *Marketing,* April 1989, p. 16; "Stew Leonard's In-Store Disneyland," *Incentive,* Jan. 1989, pp. 26, 30; Joanne Kaufman, "In the Moo: Shopping at Stew Leonard's," *Wall Street Journal,* Sept. 17, 1987, p. 26; Stew Leonard's Fact Sheet, B.L. Ochman Public Relations, New York; "Stew Leonard's Launches a New Invasion," *Progressive Grocer*, May 1986, p. 18; and Margaret Mahar, "Supermarketer," *Success!,* March 1986, pp. 50–53.

Hershey Foods' Ethics and Social Responsibility

The Hershey Foods Corporation is the number-one confectionery in North America. The Hershey Chocolate U.S.A. division, the nation's largest chocolate producer, makes up approximately 44 percent of the U.S. chocolate industry. Hershey's sales were $2.9 billion with $219.5 million in profits for fiscal 1991. Hershey manufactures more than 55 brands of confectionery products including such familiar brands as Hershey's milk chocolate bar, Hershey's syrup, Hershey's cocoa, Almond Joy, Mr. Goodbar, Hershey's Kisses, Kit Kat, and Reese's peanut butter cups. In its Confectionery Division, Hershey sells ready-to-eat puddings in four candy bar flavors. Hershey Pasta group is the second-largest pasta producer in the United States and manufactures regionally distributed brands of pasta including San Giorgio, Skinner, and Ronzoni pasta. The confectionery companies Mars and Nestlé are Hershey's major competitors.

Milton Hershey was born in 1857 of Pennsylvania Dutch descent. He became an apprentice to a candy maker in 1872 at age 15. By age 30, Hershey had begun the Lancaster Caramel Company. He visited the Chicago Exhibition in 1893 and became interested in a new chocolate-making machine. He sold the caramel factory and built a large chocolate factory in Derry Church, Pennsylvania, in 1905, and the city was renamed Hershey in 1906. Hershey pioneered modern confectionery mass production techniques by developing much of the machinery for making and packaging his milk chocolate products.

From the beginning, Milton Hershey was concerned about doing what was right. His firm was built with high standards of fairness, integrity, honesty, and respect. Mr. Hershey also believed in fairness to consumers, and provided the highest-quality mass market product. Everything that he did was based on what he believed to be the highest ethical standards. These high ethical standards influenced his relationship with the community, customers, and employees.

Community Focus

An example of his concern for the community was the founding of the Hershey Industrial School, now called the Milton Hershey School, an orphanage, in 1909. Many of the children who attended the school became Hershey employees, and former Hershey chairman William Dearden (1976–1984) was a graduate of the Hershey School. Today, the 10,000-acre school houses and provides education for nearly 1,200 socially-disadvantaged children. Although Hershey is now a public company, the school is supported by a trust that owns 42 percent of Hershey Foods. This stock ownership provides substantial dividends to offset the costs of operating the school. In addition, the Hershey trust owns 77 percent of the Hershey Foods' voting shares and 100 percent of the Hershey Entertainment and Resort Company, a theme park developed by Milton Hershey.

Another example of Hershey's commitment to youth is the sponsorship of the Hershey's National Track and Field Youth Program. In 1990, more than 350,000 U.S. children, aged 9 to 14, participated in this physical fitness program. Hershey Foods also supports the Children's Miracle Network, a national program benefiting children's hospitals across the United States.

It is often said that Hershey was more concerned with benevolence than with profits. He put people to work when they were unemployed, and did everything possible to treat his employees fairly. During the Great Depression of the 1930s, Hershey hired people to construct a hotel, golf courses, a library, theaters, a museum, a stadium and other facilities in Hershey, Pennsylvania.

Hershey employees have responded to this socially-concerned corporate culture by contributing $570,000 to the United Way in 1990. Employees may also have their gifts to institutions of higher learning matched via an employee gifts matching program. Hershey contributed more than $6 million in cash, products, and services to a variety of charities in 1990.

Hershey's Ethics and Value System

The strong value system that was put in place by Milton Hershey is still the guiding philosophy of Hershey Foods today. His system dictates that all employees conduct their business in an ethical manner. While some companies may have codes of ethics on the wall or other outward appearances of ethics standards, Hershey's ethical values are an integral part of the corporate culture. Employees know that their company will support them as long as they focus on quality, integrity, and honesty. All Hershey employees have specific policies that provide guidance for handling ethical issues. Specific policies also exist for relationships with stockholders, suppliers, employees, and customers. The following statements are from the Hershey Foods' Corporate Philosophy:

- Honesty, integrity, fairness and respect must be key elements in all dealings with our employees, shareholders, customers, consumers, suppliers and society in general.
- Our operations will be conducted within regulatory guidelines and in a manner that does not adversely affect our environment.
- Employees will be treated with respect, dignity and fairness.
- Our ongoing objective is to provide quality products and services of real value at competitive prices that will also insure an adequate return on investment.

Concern for Customers and Employees

Hershey has always emphasized quality products and good relationships with consumers. Today, Hershey's Quality Assurance division makes certain that customers get full value for their money. By using the highest quality ingredients and numerous quality control checks, the firm even assures that the right number of almonds go into each Almond Joy.

The company values employee cultural diversity and is able to attract and retain the most qualified employees. Hershey is a corporate sponsor of the National Minority Supplier Development Council which seeks to expand business opportunities for minority-owned businesses.

Ethics and social responsibility are not just words at Hershey; they are an important part of the corporate culture and the way business is conducted on a daily basis. All managers go through ethical training programs to make sure they understand how to handle the many complex issues they deal with in operating the company. Employees have a clear idea of the company's ethical values and know that they will be supported in following them. The company continues to be the most profitable company in the confectionery market and has outperformed the stock market over the last ten years.

Questions for Discussion

1. What impact did Milton Hershey's personal moral philosophies have on the Hershey corporate philosophy of ethics today?
2. How has social responsibility at Hershey helped the company attain success?
3. Identify what you believe as the most significant ethics or social responsibility program at Hershey today? Why do you believe it is so significant to the company?
4. What can other firms learn from Hershey's ethical and social responsibility actions?

Sources: "The Business Week 1,000," *Business Week*, 1992 Special Bonus Issue, p. 128; Gary Hoover, Alta Campbell, and Patrick J. Spain, *Hoover's Handbook*, 1991 (California Publishers Group West), p. 287; "Hershey Foods Philosophy and Values," Hershey Foods Corporation videotape, 1990; "A Tradition of Excellence," Hershey Foods Corporation, August 1990; Hershey Foods Corporation 1990 Annual Report; and Steven S. Ross, "Green Groceries," *Mother Jones*, February/March 1989 (vol. 14 #2), pp. 48–49.

PREVIEW:

MICROMARKET COMPUTER APPLICATION I

Fun Times, Inc.: Developing Sales Forecasts

This exercise produces information that upper management will use in making a decision to either build a new production facility or eliminate a current product. Specifically, sales trends are analyzed and sales forecasts are made using three tools: 1) a graph of recent sales figures, 2) an ordinary least squares (OLS) projection of future sales, and 3) a weighted moving average (WMA) projection of future sales. The OLS and WMA calculations are done manually and with Lotus 1-2-3. Additionally, the differences between OLS and WMA are contrasted. The exercise concludes with a written memo reporting the findings of the analysis and case questions.

II *Product Decisions*

We are now prepared to analyze the decisions and activities associated with developing and maintaining effective marketing mixes. In Parts II through V we focus on the major components of the marketing mix: product, distribution, promotion, and price. Specifically, in Part II we explore the product ingredient of the marketing mix. Chapter 8 introduces basic concepts and relationships that must be understood if one is to make effective product decisions. In Chapter 9 we analyze a variety of dimensions regarding product management, including product modification, new product development, and product elimination. Branding, packaging, and labeling are discussed in Chapter 10.

8 *Product Concepts*

OBJECTIVES

- To understand the concept of a product

- To understand how to classify products

- To become familiar with the concepts of product item, product line, and product mix and understand how they are connected

- To understand the concept of product life cycle

- To become aware of how products are positioned and repositioned

- To gain insight into the types of organizational structures used for managing products

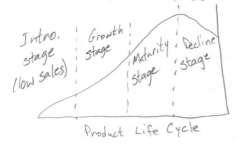

Product Life Cycle

Intro. Stage - low Sales, High cost per customer

Growth Stage - High Sales, profits

Mature Stage - Sales peak, low cost per customer, high profits,

Decline Stage - Low profits, low Sales.

In the future, what is it going to be like to watch television? Televisions have already evolved from sealed-off boxes that transform broadcast signals into black-and-white images, to versatile pieces of technology that can offer viewers hundreds of channels on cable and recent Hollywood movies using videocassette recorders. The next rung on the evolutionary ladder appears to be high-definition television (HDTV), a system conveying more information and sharper images to the screen. Whoever wins the global race to develop the newest generation of televisions and related equipment stands to carve a sizable niche in what promises to be a multibillion-dollar market. Although consumer electronics has languished in the United States, Zenith Electronics Corporation hopes to reverse that trend with HDTV.

In partnership with AT&T, Zenith has developed an all-digital system for HDTV transmission. Receiving digital information instead of electrical waves allows HDTV to produce theater-quality pictures and compact-disc-quality sound with negligible interference. Current technology transmits a signal that is reassembled as a picture on a few hundred television screen lines. HDTV transmits more information and reassembles the signal on over 1,000 television screen lines. To accommodate both those with standard televisions and those with HDTVs, the Zenith–AT&T system will send traditional signals on existing channels and digital signals on those channels not currently being used.

Over the last several years, Zenith's share of the color television market has dropped from 17.5 percent to 11.6 percent. Zenith is hoping to make a comeback with HDTV. Before sets become available, the Federal Communications Commission (FCC) must approve a signal transmission system. If Zenith's system is the first to be approved by the FCC, Zenith will receive royalties on every HDTV sold, as well as a manufacturing head start. The FCC's rejection of a proposed Japanese HDTV transmitting system for the United States makes Zenith the front runner, but competitors like General Instruments, Toshiba, and Hitachi are also positioning to enter the market.[1]

Photo courtesy of Zenith Electronics Corporation.

T HE PRODUCT IS an important variable in the marketing mix. Products such as the high-definition television being developed by Zenith are among a firm's most crucial and visible contacts with buyers. If a company's products do not meet its customers' desires and needs, the company will fail unless it makes adjustments. Developing a successful product, as Zenith is attempting to do, requires knowledge of fundamental marketing and product concepts.

In this chapter we first introduce and define the concepts that help clarify what a product is and how buyers view products. Next we examine the concepts of product line and product mix to help us understand product planning. We then explore the stages of the product life cycle. Each life cycle stage generally requires a specific marketing strategy, operates within a certain competitive environment, and has its own sales and profit pattern. We next discuss product positioning and repositioning. We conclude this chapter with a look at several organizational approaches used to manage products.

What Is a Product?

A **product** is everything, both tangible and intangible, that one receives in an exchange, including functional, social, and psychological utilities or benefits. A product can be an idea, a service, a good, or any combination of these three. This definition also covers supporting services that go with goods, such as installation, guarantees, product information, and promises of repair or maintenance. A **good** is a tangible physical entity, such as a box of Kellogg's Frosted Flakes or a Bic pen. A **service**, by contrast, is intangible; it is the result of the application of human and mechanical efforts to people or objects. Examples of services include Federal Express overnight delivery, medical examinations, and child day care. (Chapter 23 provides a detailed discussion of services marketing.) **Ideas** are concepts, philosophies, images, or issues. They provide the psychological stimulation that aids in solving problems or adjusting to the environment. For example, the World Wildlife Fund promotes endangered-wildlife conservation issues.

When buyers purchase a product, they are really buying the benefits and satisfaction they think the product will provide. A Mazda Miata sports car, for example, is purchased for excitement and fun, not just for transportation. Services, in particular, are purchased on the basis of promises of satisfaction. Promises, with the images and appearances of symbols, help consumers make judgments about tangible and intangible products.[2] Often, symbols and cues are used to make intangible products more tangible or real to the consumer. Merrill Lynch, for example, uses a bull to symbolize the firm's financial power and strength.

Classifying Products

Products fall into one of two general categories. Products purchased to satisfy personal and family needs are **consumer products**. Those bought to use in a firm's operations, to resell, or to make other products are **business-to-business**

products. Consumers buy products to satisfy their personal wants, whereas business buyers seek to satisfy the goals of their organizations.

The same item can be both a consumer product and a business product. For example, when consumers purchase light bulbs for their homes, light bulbs are classified as consumer products. However, when a large corporation purchases light bulbs to provide lighting in a factory or office, the light bulbs are considered business products because they are used in the daily operations of the firm. Thus the buyer's intent—or the ultimate use of the product—determines whether an item is classified as a consumer or a business product.

Why do we need to know about product classifications? The main reason is that classes of products are aimed at particular target markets, and this affects distribution, promotion, and pricing decisions. Furthermore, the types of marketing activities and efforts needed differ among the classes of consumer or business products. In short, the entire marketing mix can be affected by how a product is classified. In this section we examine the characteristics of consumer and business products and explore the marketing activities associated with some of them.

Consumer Products

The most widely accepted approach to classifying consumer products relies on the common characteristics of consumer buying behavior. It divides products into four categories: convenience, shopping, specialty, and unsought products. However, not all buyers behave in the same way when purchasing a specific type of product. Thus a single product can fit into all four categories. To minimize this problem, marketers think in terms of how buyers *generally* behave when purchasing a specific item. In addition, they recognize that the "correct" classification can be determined only by considering a particular firm's intended target market. With these thoughts in mind, let us examine the four traditional categories of consumer products.

Convenience Products **Convenience products** are relatively inexpensive, frequently purchased items for which buyers exert only minimal purchasing effort. They range from bread, soft drinks, and chewing gum to gasoline and newspapers. The buyer spends little time planning the purchase or comparing available brands or sellers. Even a buyer who prefers a specific brand will readily choose a substitute if the preferred brand is not conveniently available.

Classifying a product as a convenience product has several implications for a firm's marketing strategy. A convenience product is normally marketed through many retail outlets. Because sellers experience high inventory turnover, per-unit gross margins can be relatively low. Producers of convenience products, such as Lay's potato chips and Crest toothpaste, expect little promotional effort at the retail level and thus must provide it themselves with advertising and sales promotion. Packaging is also an important element of the marketing mix for convenience products. The package may have to sell the product because many convenience items are available only on a self-service basis at the retail level.

Shopping Products **Shopping products** are items for which buyers are willing to expend considerable effort in planning and making the purchase. Buyers

Figure 8.1

Shopping Product

Raleigh Bicycles as well as most other brands of bicycles are shopping products. That is, buyers spend considerable effort in planning their purchase.

Source: Permission by Derby Cycle Corporation, Kent, WA.

allocate much time for comparing stores and brands with respect to prices, product features, qualities, services, and perhaps warranties. Appliances, furniture, stereos, cameras, and bicycles (as shown in Figure 8.1) are examples of shopping products. These products are expected to last a fairly long time and thus are purchased less frequently than convenience items. Even though shopping products are more expensive than convenience products, few buyers of shopping products are particularly brand loyal. If they were, they would be unwilling to shop and compare among brands.

To market a shopping product effectively, a marketer considers several key issues. Shopping products require fewer retail outlets than convenience products. Because shopping products are purchased less frequently, inventory turnover is lower, and middlemen expect to receive higher gross margins. Although large sums of money may be required to advertise shopping products, an even larger percentage of resources is likely to be used for personal selling. Usually, the producer and the middlemen expect some cooperation from one another with respect to providing parts and repair services and performing promotional activities.

Specialty Products **Specialty products** possess one or more unique characteristics, and a significant group of buyers is willing to expend considerable effort to obtain them. Buyers actually plan the purchase of a specialty product; they know exactly what they want and will not accept a substitute. Examples of specialty products include a Jaguar automobile or a painting by Andy Warhol. When searching for specialty products, buyers do not compare alternatives; they are concerned primarily with finding an outlet that has a preselected product available.

The fact that an item is a specialty product can affect a firm's marketing efforts in several ways. Specialty products are often distributed through a limited number of retail outlets. Like shopping products, they are purchased infrequently, causing lower inventory turnover and thus requiring relatively high gross margins.

Unsought Products **Unsought products** are products purchased when a sudden problem must be solved, products of which customers are unaware, and products that people do not necessarily think of purchasing. Emergency automobile repairs and some types of auto accessories, such as snow chains, are examples of products needed quickly to solve a problem. Life insurance and cemetery plots are products that individuals do not necessarily think about buying.

Business-to-Business Products

Business-to-business products are usually purchased on the basis of an organization's goals and objectives. Generally, the functional aspects of the product are more important than the psychological rewards sometimes associated with consumer products. Business-to-business products can be classified into seven categories according to their characteristics and intended uses: raw materials, major equipment, accessory equipment, component parts, process materials, consumable supplies, and business-to-business services.[3]

Raw Materials **Raw materials** are the basic natural materials that actually become part of a physical product. They include minerals, chemicals, agricultural products, and materials from forests and oceans. They are usually bought and sold according to grades and specifications, and in relatively large quantities.

Major Equipment **Major equipment** includes large tools and machines used for production purposes, such as cranes and stamping machines. Normally, major equipment is expensive and intended to be used in a production process for a considerable length of time. Some major equipment is custom-made to perform specific functions for a particular organization, but other items are standardized and perform similar tasks for many types of firms. Because major equipment is so expensive, purchase decisions are often made by high-level management. Marketers of major equipment frequently must provide a variety of services, including installation, training, repair and maintenance assistance, and even aid in financing the purchase.

Accessory Equipment **Accessory equipment** does not become a part of the final physical product but is used in production or office activities. Examples include typewriters, fractional-horsepower motors, calculators, and tools. Compared with major equipment, accessory items are usually much cheaper; purchased routinely, with less negotiation; and treated as expense items rather than capital items because they are not expected to last as long. Accessory products are standardized items that can be used in several aspects of a firm's operations.

More outlets are required for distributing accessory equipment than for major equipment, but sellers do not have to provide the multitude of services expected of major equipment marketers.

Component Parts **Component parts** become a part of the physical product and are either finished items ready for assembly or products that need little processing before assembly. Although they become part of a larger product, component parts can often be easily identified and distinguished. Spark plugs, tires, clocks, and switches are all component parts of the automobile. Buyers purchase such items according to their own specifications or industry standards. They expect the parts to be of specified quality and delivered on time so that production is not slowed or stopped. Producers that are primarily assemblers, such as most lawn mower or computer manufacturers, depend heavily on the suppliers of component parts.

Process Materials **Process materials** are used directly in the production of other products. Unlike component parts, however, process materials are not readily identifiable. For example, Reichhold Chemicals, Inc., markets a treated fiber product—a phenolic-resin sheet-molding compound—that is used in the production of aircraft flight deck instrument panels and cabin interiors. Although the material is not identifiable in the finished aircraft, it retards burning, smoke, and formation of toxic gas if molded components are subjected to

Figure 8.2 **Industrial Service** AT&T 800 services usually are classified as industrial services. As this advertisement illustrates, florists rely on this intangible product for success in their operations. Source: Courtesy of AT&T.

fire or high temperatures. As with component parts, process materials are purchased according to industry standards or the purchaser's specifications.

Consumable Supplies   **Consumable supplies** facilitate production and operations but do not become part of the finished product. Paper, pencils, oils, cleaning agents, and paints are in this category. Because such supplies are standardized items used in a variety of situations, they are purchased by many different types of organizations. Consumable supplies are commonly sold through numerous outlets and are purchased routinely. To ensure that supplies are available when needed, buyers often deal with more than one seller. Because these supplies can be divided into three subcategories—maintenance, repair, and operating (or overhaul) supplies—they are sometimes called **MRO items**.

Business-to-Business Services   **Business-to-business services** (also called industrial services) are the intangible products that many organizations use in their operations. They include financial, legal, marketing research, computer programming and operation, and janitorial services. Telecommunication services, like those discussed in Figure 8.2, fall into the business-to-business services category. Firms must decide whether to provide their own services internally or obtain them outside the organization. This decision depends on the costs associated with each alternative and how frequently the services are needed.

Product Line and Product Mix

Marketers must understand the relationships among all the products of their organization if they are to coordinate the marketing of the total group of products. The following concepts help describe the relationships among an organization's products. A **product item** is a specific version of a product that can be designated as a distinct offering among an organization's products, for example, Mead's Five Star two-subject spiral notebook. A **product line** includes a group of closely related product items that are considered to be a unit because of marketing, technical, or end-use considerations. All the spiral notebooks manufactured by Mead constitute one of its product lines. To come up with the optimum product line, marketers must understand buyers' goals. Figure 8.3 depicts part of Sony's Walkman personal stereo line. Specific product items in a product line usually reflect the desires of different target markets or the different needs of consumers.

A **product mix** is the composite, or total, group of products that an organization makes available to customers. For example, all the health care, beauty care, laundry and cleaning, food and beverage, paper, cometic, and fragrance products that Procter & Gamble manufactures constitute its product mix. The **depth** of a product mix is measured by the number of different products offered in each product line. The Global Perspective points out how Procter & Gamble is adding depth to several product lines to be more competitive in international markets. The **width** of the product mix is measured by the number of product lines a company offers. Figure 8.4 illustrates these concepts by showing the width of the product mix and the depth of each product line for selected Procter & Gamble products. Procter & Gamble is known for using distinctive branding,

packaging, and consumer advertising to promote individual items in its detergent product line. Tide, Bold, Gain, Dash, Cheer, and Oxydol—all Procter & Gamble detergents—share the same distribution channels and similar manufacturing facilities. Yet each is promoted as distinctive, and this claimed uniqueness adds depth to the product line. Branding and packaging are discussed further in Chapter 10.

Product Life Cycles

Just as biological cycles progress through growth and decline, so do product life cycles. As Figure 8.5 shows, a **product life cycle** has four major stages: (1) introduction, (2) growth, (3) maturity, and (4) decline. As a product moves through its cycle, the strategies relating to competition, promotion, distribution, pricing, and market information must be periodically evaluated and possibly changed. Astute marketing managers use the life cycle concept to make sure that the introduction, alteration, and termination of a product are timed and executed properly. By understanding the typical life cycle pattern, marketers are better able to maintain profitable products and drop unprofitable ones. (Marketing strategies for different life cycle stages are discussed in Chapter 9.)

Introduction

The **introduction stage** of the life cycle begins at a product's first appearance in the marketplace, when sales are zero and profits are negative. Profits are below zero because initial revenues are low and at the same time the company generally must cover large expenses for promotion and distribution. Notice in Figure 8.5 how sales should move upward from zero, and profits also should move upward from a position in which profits are negative because of high expenses.

Because of cost, very few product introductions represent major inventions. Developing and introducing a new product can mean an outlay of $20 million or more. The failure rate for new products is quite high, ranging from 60 to 90 percent, depending on the industry and how product failure is defined. For example, in the food and beverage industry, 80 percent of all new products fail.[4] More typically, product introductions involve a new packaged convenience food, a new automobile model, or a new fashion in clothing rather than a major product innovation.

Potential buyers must be made aware of the new product's features, uses, and advantages. Two difficulties may arise at this point. Only a few sellers may have

Figure 8.4 **The Concepts of Product Mix Width and Depth Applied to Selected Procter & Gamble Products** Source: "Facts About Procter & Gamble" (Procter & Gamble, January 1992), pp. 5–9. Reprinted by permission of Procter & Gamble.

Laundry Detergents	Toothpastes	Bar Soaps	Deodorants	Shampoos	Coffees
Oxydol 1914	Gleem 1952	Ivory 1879	Secret 1956	Prell 1946	Folgers (vacuum packed) 1850
Ivory Snow 1930	Crest 1955	Kirk's 1885	Sure 1972	Head & Shoulders 1961	
Dreft 1933	Denquel 1980	Lava 1893		Pert Plus 1979	Instant Folgers (coffee crystals) 1963
Tide 1946		Camay 1926		Ivory 1983	
Cheer 1950		Zest 1952			Instant High Point 1975
Dash 1954		Safeguard 1963			
Bold 1965		Coast 1974			Folgers (decaffeinated) 1984
Gain 1966					
Era 1972					Instant Folgers (decaffeinated) 1984
Solo 1979					
Liquid Tide 1984					Folgers (Special Roast Flaked) 1986
Liquid Bold-3 1985					
Liquid Cheer 1986					Folgers (Gourmet Supreme) 1989
Liquid Lemon Dash 1987					
Tide with bleach 1988					
Liquid Dreft 1989					
Liquid Ivory Snow 1989					

Product line depth

Product mix width

Revlon Acquisition Energizes
Procter & Gamble's Global Push

EVERY YEAR the venerable Cincinnati-based firm of Procter & Gamble sells about $24 billion worth of brand name detergents and other household products. However, as increasingly price-conscious American consumers save money by selecting less expensive store brands, Procter & Gamble's domestic sales are slowing down. Recognizing that cosmetics offer the company not only significant profit potential, but plenty of room for international growth, Procter & Gamble is pushing aggressively into the global personal care and beauty market.

Owning brands like top-selling Pert-Plus shampoo, Cover Girl and Clarion makeups, Oil of Olay facial treatment, and Navy and Old Spice fragrances, Procter & Gamble is hardly a novice at marketing beauty products. Since its purchase of Oil of Olay in 1985, the firm has boosted sales of the beauty fluid 60 percent by increasing advertising, broadening its target market, and extending the product line. Mass market Navy perfume is now a $25 million brand, and Cover Girl makeup commands 23 percent of a $4 billion market. Encouraged by its successes, Procter & Gamble recently paid $1.1 billion for Revlon's Max Factor and Betrix cosmetic brands.

In keeping with its intent to expand outside of mature domestic markets, the firm picked two of Revlon's best international brands. Max Factor's popularity in Great Britain, especially its SK-II skin care line, and Betrix cosmetics' rank as the top seller in Germany make Procter & Gamble an instant European powerhouse. Company executives believe that the acquisition will raise Procter & Gamble's cosmetic sales to $1.3 billion worldwide. Previously the firm's Japanese sales of fragrances and cosmetics were zero but immediately catapulted to $237 million after the sale.

Revitalizing Procter & Gamble's international business is foremost among the goals of CEO Edwin Artzt. When he assumed his position, overseas sales accounted for 26 percent of the company's total, but this figure is already up to 40 percent. Artzt, along with other industry experts, believes that the Revlon acquisition will speed up Procter & Gamble's global expansion by at least five years. For example, transforming the Cover Girl brand into an international competitor will be simplified because a distribution and marketing network is already in place in Europe and Japan. Company executives realize, of course, that securing a foothold doesn't assure success; mass-marketing cosmetics across Europe presents cultural obstacles, and Japanese Kao Corporation and Anglo-Dutch Unilever Group are powerful, well-established rivals.

The joke goes that if Procter & Gamble, master of household products, sold nail polish, the company would market only one color, but it would come in "large," "family," and "economy" sizes. However, the company is proving as adept at mass-marketing cosmetics as it is at selling diapers and soap, and no one is laughing. As doors to formerly Communist countries open, and the European Community takes charge, Procter & Gamble is there in force.

Sources: Barbara Buell, "P&G Recession-Proof? No Soap," *Business Week*, Apr. 29, 1991, pp. 30–31; Zachary Schiller and Larry Light, "Procter & Gamble Is Following Its Nose," *Business Week*, Apr. 22, 1991, p. 28; Cara Appelbaum, "A New World of Beauty for P&G," *Adweek's Marketing Week*, Apr. 15, 1991, pp. 4–5; Anthony Ramirez, "P. & G. Gets Revlon's Max Factor," *New York Times*, Apr. 11, 1991, pp. D1, D5; Randall Smith, Kathleen Deveny, and Alecia Swasy, "Perelman Launches Sale of Revlon Units to Procter & Gamble for $1.14 Billion," *Wall Street Journal*, Apr. 11, 1991, p. A4; Alecia Swasy, "Procter & Gamble Is to Buy Some of Revlon Inc.'s Lines," *Wall Street Journal*, Apr. 10, 1991 p. A3; Larry Light and Monica Roman, "Why Perelman Faces Life Without Makeup," *Business Week*, Apr. 1, 1991, pp. 71–72; Cara Appelbaum, "P&G Cuts Back on Ads, but Forges Ahead with Its Beauty Blitz," *Adweek's Marketing Week*, Mar. 4, 1991, p. 5; and Laura Bird, "The Great Cosmetics Consolidation," *Superbrands 1990* (supplement to *Adweek's Marketing Week*), pp. 124, 128.

Figure 8.5

The Four Stages of the Product Life Cycle

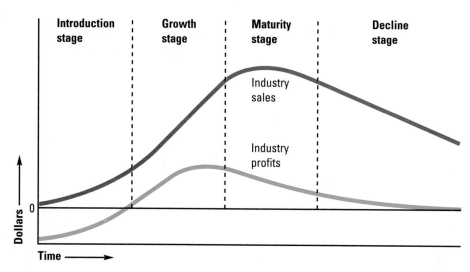

the resources, technological knowledge, and marketing know-how to launch the product successfully; and the initial product price may have to be high, to recoup expensive marketing research or development costs. Given these difficulties, it is not surprising that many products never get beyond the introduction stage.

Growth

During the **growth stage**, sales rise rapidly and profits reach a peak and then start to decline (see Figure 8.5). The growth stage is critical to a product's survival because competitive reactions to the product's success during this period will affect the product's life expectancy. For example, the maker of California Cooler successfully marketed the first "wine cooler" but today competes against numerous other brands. Profits decline late in the growth stage as more competitors enter the market, driving prices down and creating the need for heavy promotional expenses. At this point a typical marketing strategy encourages strong brand loyalty and competes with aggressive emulators of the product. During the growth stage, an organization tries to strengthen its market share and develop a competitive niche by emphasizing the product's benefits. Also, aggressive pricing, including price cuts, is typical during the growth stage. Inside Marketing describes the marketing steps taken by the makers of Nutra-Sweet as this product enters the growth stage of the aspartame market.

Maturity

During the **maturity stage**, the sales curve peaks and starts to decline and profits continue to decline (see Figure 8.5). This stage is characterized by severe competition, as many brands are in the market. Competitors emphasize improvements and differences in their versions of the product. As a result, during the maturity stage weaker competitors are squeezed out or lose interest in the product. For example, some brands of videocassette recorders will perish as the VCR moves through the maturity stage.

During the maturity phase, the producers who remain in the market must make fresh promotional and distribution efforts; advertising and dealer-oriented promotions are typical during this stage of the product life cycle. The promoters must also take into account the fact that, as the product reaches maturity, buyers' knowledge of it attains a high level. Consumers of the product are no longer inexperienced generalists but instead are experienced specialists.

Decline

During the **decline stage**, sales fall rapidly (see Figure 8.5). New technology or a new social trend may cause product sales to take a sharp turn downward. When this happens, the marketer considers pruning items from the product line to eliminate those not earning a profit. At this time, too, the marketer may cut promotion efforts, eliminate marginal distributors, and, finally, plan to phase out the product.

Because most businesses have a product mix consisting of multiple products, a firm's destiny is rarely tied to one product. A composite of life cycle patterns is formed when various products in the mix are at different cycle stages. As one product is declining, other products are in the introduction, growth, or maturity stage. Marketers must deal with the dual problem of prolonging the life of existing products and introducing new products to meet organizational sales goals. For example, Kodak has prolonged the product life cycle of its 110mm cameras by adding built-in flashes, waterproof bodies, and other features. But Kodak has also continued to introduce new products, including the disposable 35mm Kodak Fling; Breeze, a new line of 35mm cameras; and Ektar, a new line of color films specifically for 35mm single-lens reflex cameras. In the next chapter you will learn more about how products can be managed in their various life cycle stages.

Product Positioning and Repositioning

The term **product positioning** refers to the decisions and activities intended to create and maintain a certain concept of the firm's product (relative to competitive brands) in customers' minds. When marketers introduce a product, they attempt to position it so that it seems to possess the characteristics the target market most desires. This projected image is crucial. Crest is positioned as a fluoride toothpaste that fights cavities, and Close-Up is positioned as a whitening toothpaste that enhances the user's sex appeal. As shown in Figure 8.6, Puma is positioned carefully for the target markets.

Product position is customers' perceptions of a product's attributes relative to those of competitive brands. Buyers make a large number of purchase decisions on a regular basis. To avoid a continuous reevaluation of numerous products, buyers tend to group or "position" products in their minds to simplify buying decisions. Rather than allowing customers to position products independently, marketers often try to influence and shape consumers' concepts or perceptions of products through advertising. Marketers sometimes analyze product positions by developing perceptual maps, as shown in Figure 8.7. Perceptual maps are created by questioning a sample of consumers regarding their perceptions of products, brands, and organizations with respect to two or more dimensions. To develop a perceptual map like the one in Figure 8.7, respondents would be asked how they perceive selected pain relievers in regard to price and type of pain for which they are used.

Product positioning is a part of a natural progression when market segmentation is used. Segmentation lets the firm aim a given brand at a portion of the total market. Effective product positioning helps serve a specific market segment by creating an appropriate concept in the minds of customers in that market segment. Gillette Co.'s Dippity-Do hair gel product had been on the decline since its heydey in the 1960s, in part because women who used it then associated it with that era's popular bouffant hair styles. Gillette therefore repositioned Dippity-Do for today's hair styles by appealing to teenagers who have no memories of the product's former use.[5]

A firm can position a product to compete head-on with another brand, as Pepsi has done against Coca-Cola, or to avoid competition, as 7-Up has done relative to other soft-drink producers. Head-to-head competition may be a marketer's positioning objective if the product's performance characteristics are at least equal to competitive brands and if the product is priced lower. Head-to-head positioning may be appropriate even when the price is higher if the product's performance characteristics are superior. Conversely, positioning to avoid competition may be best when the product's performance characteristics are not significantly different from competing brands. Moreover, positioning a brand to avoid competition may be appropriate when that brand has unique characteristics that are important to some buyers. Volvo, for example, has for years positioned itself away from competitors by focusing on the safety characteristics of

Figure 8.6

Product Positioning

Puma is positioned as a middle of the road, medium-priced shoe rather than an expensive, high-tech shoe. Its marketers hope the shoe will be clearly distinguished and will appeal to members of the target market.

Source: PUMA USA.

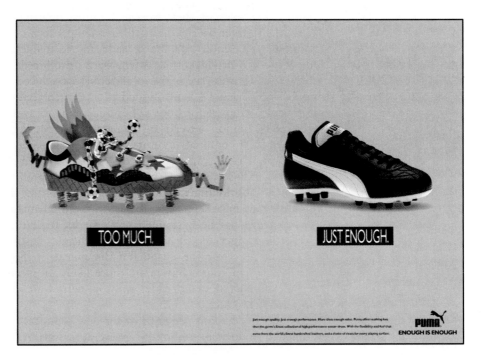

Figure 8.7

Hypothetical Perceptual Map for Pain Relievers

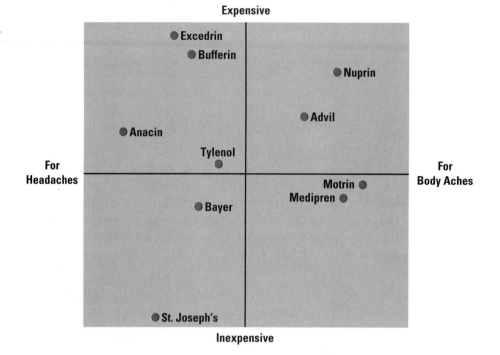

its cars. Competitors sometimes mention safety issues in their advertisements but are more likely to focus on style, fuel efficiency, or performance.

Avoiding competition is critical when a firm introduces a brand into a market in which it already has one or more brands. Marketers usually want to avoid cannibalizing sales of their existing brands, unless the new brand generates substantially larger profits. Sometimes attempts to avoid cannibalization can be troublesome. Tylenol was a brand leader in the analgesic market for many years until ibuprofen products, like Advil, were introduced. To remain competitive, Johnson & Johnson (the maker of Tylenol) introduced Medipren, an ibuprofen brand. Since Tylenol was positioned as a headache remedy, Johnson & Johnson positioned Medipren for body aches and pains to avoid cannibalization. Even with a $40 million advertising campaign for Medipren's introductory year, consumers were confused about its uses. Many consumers believed the Medipren was for menstrual pain. Thus, Advil took considerable share from Tylenol. Johnson & Johnson should have positioned Medipren for headache pain. Even though this positioning would have cannibalized some Tylenol sales, Johnson & Johnson would have kept a larger share of the total analgesic market.[6]

If a product has been planned properly, its attributes and brand image will give it the distinct appeal needed. Style, shape, construction, quality of work, and color help create the image and the appeal. If they can easily identify the benefits, then of course buyers are more likely to purchase the product. When the new product does not offer some preferred attributes, there is room for another new product.

Positioning decisions are not just for new products. Evaluating the positions of existing products is important for several reasons. A brand's market share and

NutraSweet Enters a New Life Cycle Stage

DURING THE 1980s, NutraSweet sugar substitute made its way into low-calorie soft drinks and three thousand other "guilt-free" products. Sales soared to over $900 million. Capturing 75 percent of the artificial sweetener market, NutraSweet's red-swirl trademark became synonymous with its chemical name, aspartame. With its patent due to expire soon and competitors ready to grab market share, the company is modifying the NutraSweet strategy so that the product can successfully compete in the growth stage of its life cycle.

NutraSweet's plans follow the strategy prescribed by marketing experts: lower production costs and pass on the savings to customers, encourage brand loyalty, provide better customer service, and expand the product's uses while developing product variations. By laying off 12 percent of its work force, the firm has already taken the first steps toward its goal of lowering production costs 60 percent. NutraSweet has always encouraged its customers to promote the NutraSweet name by displaying the logo on their own packages and in their own advertising, a strategy that earned its brand a 96 percent awareness level. To maintain loyalty when competition hits the market, consumers will soon be bombarded with "brand identification" advertisements on network and cable television. Although NutraSweet's relations with customers like Coca-Cola and Kraft have been cool at best, the firm is hoping to warm things up by offering better service. In addition to relaxing control over decisions like how to display the logo on packages, which the firm has traditionally dictated, NutraSweet is earmarking $20 million worth of advertising for direct support of customers' NutraSweet-containing products. Hoping to expand its market beyond soft drinks and cold food, Monsanto, makers of NutraSweet, is petitioning the Federal Drug Administration for permission to put aspartame in heated products. Company scientists are also developing

Sweetener 2000, a sugar substitute that has no calories, an indefinite shelf life, can be used in baking, and is ten thousand times sweeter than sugar. Although NutraSweet won't seek FDA approval before 1994, company executives are already heralding it as the "sugar replacement of the twenty-first century."

NutraSweet is counting on an aggressive strategy to protect its market share from a growing number of hungry competitors. Acesulfame-K, known as ACK, received limited FDA approval and is already sweetening Trident sugarless gum. Johnson & Johnson expects the FDA's authorization soon to market Sucralose, a sweetener that can be used in baked goods. In development is Pfizer's Alitame, and Coca-Cola recently patented its own class of artificial sweeteners. Some analysts predict that in the first year NutraSweet's patent expires, annual NutraSweet sales will fall by $750 million. That the company will have to lower prices to remain competitive is clear; in Europe, NutraSweet's prices fell quickly after its patent ran out there several years ago. However, the company's CEO remains optimistic that brand strength and new customer sensitivity will land his firm enough contracts to offset price reductions and keep NutraSweet a growing global powerhouse.

Sources: "As NutraSweet Patent Runs Out, Critics Rekindle Debate on Safety," *Bryan–College Station (TX) Eagle,* July 7, 1991, p. 3A; "Competitors Drool as Patent Clock Ticks Away Future of NutraSweet," *Bryan–College Station (TX) Eagle,* July 1, 1991, p. 5A; Fara Warner, "NutraSweet Launches New Ads," *Adweek's Marketing Week,* May 20, 1991, p. 6; Lois Therrien, "NutraSweet Tries Being More of a Sweetie," *Business Week,* Apr. 18, 1991, p. 88; "Monsanto Touts New Sugar Substitute as Sweetest Yet," *Wall Street Journal,* Mar. 3, 1991, p. B1; Bruce Oman, "Bittersweet Success," *Beverage World,* Jan. 1991, pp. 58–59; and Gregory D. L. Morris, "Canada's Competition Board Scolds NutraSweet," *Chemicalweek,* Oct. 17, 1990, p. 10.

profitability may be strengthened considerably by product repositioning. For example, several years ago Kraft was on the verge of discontinuing Cheez Whiz because its sales had declined considerably. Kraft marketers repositioned Cheese Whiz as a fast, convenient microwavable cheese sauce, causing its sales to rebound to new heights. When introducing a new product into a product line, one or more existing brands may have to be repositioned to minimize cannibalization of established brands and to assure a favorable position for the new brand.

Organizing to Manage Products

After reviewing the concepts of product line and mix, life cycles, positioning, and repositioning, it should be obvious that managing products is a complex task. Often the traditional functional form of organization—in which managers specialize in business functions such as advertising, sales, and distribution—does not fit a company's needs. Consequently, management must find an organizational approach that accomplishes the tasks necessary to develop and manage products. Alternatives to functional organization include the product manager approach, the market manager approach, and the venture team approach.

A **product manager** is responsible for a product, a product line, or several distinct products that make up an interrelated group within a multiproduct organization. A **brand manager**, on the other hand, is responsible for a single brand. General Foods Corp., for example, has one brand manager for Maxim coffee and one for Maxwell House coffee. A product or brand manager operates cross-functionally to coordinate the activities, information, and strategies involved in marketing an assigned product. Product managers and brand managers plan marketing activities to achieve objectives by coordinating a mix of distribution, promotion (especially sales promotion and advertising), and price. They must consider packaging and branding decisions and work closely with personnel in research and development, engineering, and production. Marketing research helps product managers to understand consumers and find target markets. The product or brand manager approach to organization is used by many large, multiple-product companies in the consumer package goods business.

A **market manager** is responsible for managing the marketing activities that serve a particular group or class of customers. This organizational approach is particularly effective when a firm engages in different types of marketing activities to provide products to diverse customer groups. A company might have one market manager for industrial markets and another for consumer markets. These broad market categories might be broken down into more limited market responsibilities.

A **venture team** is designed to create entirely new products that may be aimed at new markets. Unlike a product or market manager, a venture team is responsible for all aspects of a product's development: research and development, production and engineering, finance and accounting, and marketing. Venture teams work outside established divisions to create inventive approaches to new products and markets. As a result of this flexibility, new products can be developed to take advantage of opportunities in highly segmented markets.

The members of a venture team come from different functional areas of an organization. When the commercial potential of a new product has been demonstrated, the members may return to their functional areas, or they may join a new or existing division to manage the product. The new product may be turned over to an existing division, a market manager, or a product manager. Innovative organizational forms such as venture teams are necessary for many companies, especially well-established firms operating primarily in mature markets. These companies must take a dual approach to marketing organization. They must accommodate the management of mature products and also encourage the development of new ones.[7]

Summary

A product is everything, both favorable and unfavorable, that one receives in an exchange. It is a complex set of tangible and intangible attributes, including functional, social, and psychological utilities or benefits. A product can be an idea, a service, a good, or any combination of these three. When consumers purchase a product, they are buying the benefits and satisfaction that they think the product will provide.

Products can be classified on the basis of the buyer's intentions. Thus consumer products are those purchased to satisfy personal and family needs. Business-to-business products, on the other hand, are purchased for use in a firm's operations, to resell, or to make other products. Consumer products can be subdivided into convenience, shopping, specialty, and unsought products. Business-to-business products can be divided into raw materials, major equipment, accessory equipment, component parts, process materials, consumable supplies, and business-to-business services.

A product item is a specific version of a product that can be designated as a distinct offering among an organization's products. A product line is a group of closely related product items that are considered a unit because of marketing, technical, or end-use considerations. The composite, or total, group of products that an organization makes available to customers is called the product mix. The depth of a product line is measured by the number of different products offered in each product line. The width of the product mix is measured by the number of product lines a company offers.

The product life cycle describes how product items in an industry move through (1) introduction, (2) growth, (3) maturity, and (4) decline. The life cycle concept is used to make sure that the introduction, alteration, and termination of a product are timed and executed properly. The sales curve is at zero at introduction, rises at an increasing rate during growth, peaks at maturity, and then declines. Profits peak toward the end of the growth stage of the product life cycle. The life expectancy of a product is based on buyers' wants, the availability of competing products, and other environmental conditions. Most businesses have a composite of life cycle patterns for various products. It is important to manage existing products and develop new ones to keep the overall sales performance at a desired level.

Product positioning comprises the decisions and activities intended to create and maintain a certain concept of the firm's product (relative to competitive brands) in customers' minds. Product positioning is part of a natural progression when market segmentation is used. A firm can position a product to compete head-on with another brand or to avoid competition. Existing products are sometimes repositioned to make them more competitive.

Developing and managing products is critical to an organization's survival and growth. The various approaches available for organizing product management share common activities, functions, and decisions necessary to guide a product through its life cycle. A product manager is responsible for a product, a product line, or several distinct products that make up an interrelated group within a multiproduct organization. A brand manager is a product manager who is responsible for a single brand. Market managers are responsible for managing the marketing activities that serve a particular group or class of customers. A venture team is sometimes used to create entirely new products that may be aimed at new markets.

Important Terms

Products
Goods
Services
Ideas
Consumer products
Business-to-business products
Convenience products
Shopping products
Specialty products
Unsought products
Raw materials
Major equipment
Accessory equipment
Component parts
Process materials
Consumable supplies
MRO items

Business-to-business services
Product item
Product line
Depth of product mix
Product mix
Width of product mix
Product life cycle
Introduction stage
Growth stage
Maturity stage
Decline stage
Product positioning
Product manager
Brand manager
Market manager
Venture team

Discussion and Review Questions

1. List the tangible and intangible attributes of a spiral notebook. Compare the benefits of the spiral notebook with those of an intangible product, such as life insurance.
2. A product has been referred to as a "psychological bundle of satisfaction." Is this a good definition of a product? Why or why not?
3. Is a roll of carpeting in a store a consumer product or a business-to-business product? Defend your answer.
4. How do convenience products and shopping products differ? What are the distinguishing characteristics of each type of product?
5. Would a stereo system that sells for $869 be a convenience, shopping, or specialty product?
6. In the category of business-to-business products, how do component parts differ from process materials?
7. How does an organization's product mix relate to its development of a product line? When should an enterprise add depth to its product lines rather than width to its product mix?

8. How do industry profits change as a product moves through the four stages of its life cycle?

9. What is the relationship between the concepts of product mix and product life cycle?

10. What organizational alternatives are available to a firm with two product lines having four product items in each line?

11. When is it more appropriate to use a product manager than a market manager? When might an alternative or combined approach be used?

12. What type of organization might use a venture team to develop new products? What are the advantages and disadvantages of such a team?

Cases

8.1 Kodak's Disposable Cameras

Eastman Kodak Co. is one of the world's leading photographic companies, controlling about 75 percent of the market for color film, black-and-white film, and photographic paper. Following a tradition for making innovation a part of its everyday company strategy, Kodak recently introduced a line of single-use, or disposable, cameras. These cameras are very simple to operate; all one needs to do is aim and push a button. There are no adjustments for light level, exposure time, or focusing. After shooting all the exposures, the customer turns in the entire camera to the film processor. Depending on the model, these cameras retail from $8.35 for the Fling to around $16.00 for the more specialized versions. One model is a modified wide-angle camera; another can take pictures up to twelve feet underwater. They all use 35mm color film.

Very inexpensive to produce, these cameras are basically just a roll of film in an encasement of plastic with an elementary lens on the front and a minimum of internal parts. Industry experts predict that sales of disposable cameras (Kodak prefers the name "single-use" cameras) will grow 20 to 25 percent yearly worldwide, encouraging Kodak executives' expectations that these cameras will become highly profitable despite stiff competition from Fuji's disposable Quick Snap and new disposable telephoto camera, the Quick Snap Tele.

The idea for Kodak's waterproof disposable camera, the Weekend 35, emerged from a Kodak engineer's rafting trip that exposed his camera equipment to water damage. In the Weekend 35, the ultrasonically sealed plastic outer body protects the camera's internal parts and film from sand and dirt, as well as from water, snow, and rain. Since Kodak engineers originally designed the disposable prototype on a three-dimensional computer-aided system, they found it fairly easy to devise a waterproof disposable and perfect their new design on a computer terminal. They even contrived a special viewfinder suitable for use with a scuba mask.

Kodak set up a task force to seek ways of expanding an emerging market for disposable cameras. After members of this force talked with a consumer who was frustrated in attempting to photograph the Grand Canyon with a disposable model, the Stretch 35 came into existence. Already having a lens that was capable of producing extra-wide photos, Kodak engineers built a camera around it, bringing this model from the drawing board to the retail shelves in less than one year. One potential drawback to the Stretch is that its prints come, not in the standard size, but in a longer format. To keep this model viable, Kodak must convince photofinishers to print unusually shaped photos.

Newest in Kodak's single-use line-up is the recyclable Fun Saver 35. Designed for indoor or outdoor use, this model possesses a built-in electronic flash. Users return the entire camera to a photofinisher, who processes the film and returns the camera to Kodak for recycling. After a New York public affairs organization recently named disposable cameras among the worst examples of nonrecyclable consumer goods, Kodak announced that the Fling, Stretch, and Weekend will soon be recyclable as well.

Kodak management targets the cameras at several different groups. The first segment consists of children who are just learning about photography. The company views the disposables as ideal starter cameras. They are easy to use, and the photographer is almost guaranteed an acceptable print. Youngsters might not be able to afford more expensive cameras, and their parents are spared the agony of thinking what a $300 model will look like after an enthusiastic child gets through with it.

Another target is the impulse buyer, who might spot the camera on the way out of a grocery store and purchase it because it could be ready for special occasions, such as a spontaneous picnic or sporting event. According to Kodak marketers, serious or professional photographers might also be interested in owning a low-cost camera when a particular assignment might put the expensive equipment in jeopardy. Smaller disposable cameras are also easy to tote around. Still others who might opt for one of the disposable models are tourists who don't want to risk expensive equipment while traveling or who simply forget their cameras. However, forgetful individuals should beware; a disposable camera can cost twice as much as a roll of film.[8]

Questions for Discussion

1. Does the addition of disposable cameras to Kodak's product mix add depth, width, or both of these dimensions to this product mix?
2. If Kodak is the only seller of disposable cameras, then is positioning needed? If yes, explain why and indicate how the product should be positioned. If no, explain why.
3. To what degree, if any, does the sale of disposable cameras reduce or cut into the sales of Kodak's other cameras?

8.2 WD-40 Has One Formula for Success

Don't wander up and down the aisles of the local supermarket or hardware store searching for WD-39 or WD-41; it won't be there because it doesn't exist. There is just one WD-40, a spray lubricant in a blue, yellow, and red can. Comprised of about 20 cents worth of chemical distillates and some mineral spirits, WD-40 is sprayed by millions of people all over the world on bicycle chains that get rusty, bolts that won't turn, scissors that are too stubborn to cut, or just about anything that misbehaves. Consumers are amazingly loyal to WD-40 and have turned up their noses at perfectly good competitors like 3M's Q4 and Valvoline's 1-2-99. Enjoying profits of $15.5 million and resisting the current trend to bring out several new products or brand extensions every year, WD-40 keeps all its eggs in one basket and concentrates all its energies on its target market.

When company president John Barry began marketing WD-40 in 1969, retailers predicted that, with only one product to sell, he would have trouble maintaining shelf space. After 21 years, and still only one product to sell, retailers no longer complain. A recent survey by Family Media reveals that WD-40's 70 percent household penetration is the largest for any U.S. brand. Another poll identifies the lubricant as one of the top 40 brands, based on consumer esteem. WD-40's current yearly sales of almost $84 million are a far cry above sales of $2 million in 1969, and the company achieves this phenomenal success with a total of 135 employees running the show. *Business Month* recently named WD-40 one of the five best-run corporations in the United States, evidence that one-brand companies can succeed.

The concentrate is manufactured in the company's headquarters in San Diego and then shipped to contract packagers in the United States and Canada. When the lubricant is ready in its colorful can, WD-40 sells it solely to distributors and retailers with enough outlets to ensure that it gets the most overall shelf space. Believing that an in-house sales force would market its product more aggressively and effectively, the organization recently replaced manufacturers' sales representatives with its own sales force.

Selling a single product helps keep the company's advertising and promotion budget manageable without cramping creative style. Although WD-40 markets to a diverse group of commercial users—including farms, factories, garages, and offices—the company directs the bulk of its promotions toward household consumers. Because the firm's president believes that free samples are an excellent marketing tool, several times a year the company runs giveaways of its six-ounce cans. Various promotions are designed to appeal to a range of consumers. For example, the organization sponsored magazine ads with the U.S. Park Service, touting WD-40 as a lubricant for fishing gear. And when WD-40 buyers switched long-distance phone companies to sign up with U.S. Sprint, they got sixty free minutes of long-distance calls.

The down side of WD-40's remarkable household penetration is a nearly saturated market in the United States. Company executives perceive that long-term growth depends on the European market. International sales currently account for about 27 percent of the product's sales; in one year alone, the firm's export business grew 42 percent, with Korean sales up by 70 percent and Mexican sales up by 300 percent. Company president Barry predicts that by the mid 1990s, 50 percent of WD-40's sales will be international. To increase the likelihood of that happening, WD-40 is moving forward with its overseas strategy. A recently built manufacturing plant in Great Britain will facilitate European distribution, and soon the firm will have representatives in Germany, France, Spain, and Italy. With the economic unification of European Community members, WD-40 is already on the inside looking out at any U.S. competitors. Executives are hopeful that 800 million prospective customers in recently opened Eastern bloc countries will compensate for a current sales dip resulting from recession in Canada and Europe. Although the firm denies having specific plans for doing business in the Commonwealth of Independent States, it has already put in an application there to register the WD-40 brand. To offset slowing U.S. sales, the company recently instituted its first price increase in nine years. There are, however, no plans to introduce any new products to the WD-40 line of one. Over the years, shareholders and other interested parties have suggested over two hundred brand extensions, such as crankcase additives and corrosion inhibitors. They have also suggested packaging changes, such as individualized labels on cans destined for drugstores, supermarkets, auto parts shops, or sporting goods stores. Barry, however, believes in the old adage "If it isn't broken, don't fix it" and is convinced that different labels and different products only confuse customers. Made confident by past and continuing success, the company is not afraid to remain a "one-act play." Unlike the movies, where sequel after sequel is the consumer's daily fare, a WD-40 sequel will not be appearing soon.[9]

Questions for Discussion

1. WD-40 could be viewed as a consumer product or as a business-to-business product. When viewed as a consumer product, how would it be classified? If viewed as a business-to-business product, how would it be classified?
2. Describe the dimensions of the WD-40 Company's product mix.
3. In what product life cycle stage is WD-40?
4. What are the major advantages and disadvantages of having only one product in a product mix?
5. Does the WD-40 Company use product positioning? Explain.

Chapter Notes

1. Based on information from Lois Therrien, "HDTV Isn't Clearing Up Zenith's Picture," *Business Week*, Feb. 25, 1991, pp. 56–57; Robert L. Rose and Michael W. Miller, "Zenith, AT&T to Offer Digital HDTV Version," *Wall Street Journal*, Dec. 18, 1990, pp. B1, B4; Jonathan Weber, "Zenith, AT&T Offer Plan for Digital HDTV," *Los Angeles Times*, Dec. 18, 1990, pp. D2, D16; James Flanigan, "New Era Dawning in Home Entertainment," *Los Angeles Times*, Nov. 14, 1990, pp. D1, D4; and Michael Schrage, "These People Want to Adjust Your TV Set," *Los Angeles Times*, June 28, 1990, pp. D1, D14.
2. Theodore Levitt, "Marketing Intangible Products and Product Intangibles," *Harvard Business Review*, May–June 1981, pp. 94–102.
3. Robert W. Haas, *Industrial Marketing Management*, 3rd ed. (Boston: Kent Publishing, 1986), pp. 15–25.
4. "Why Products Fail," *Adweek's Marketing Week*, Nov. 5, 1990, pp. 20, 24.
5. Ronald Alsop, "Giving Fading Brands a Second Chance," *Wall Street Journal*, Jan. 24, 1989, p. B1.
6. Calvin L. Hodock, "Strategies Behind the Winners and Losers," *Journal of Business Strategy*, September–October 1990, pp. 4–7.
7. Roger C. Bennet and Robert G. Cooper, "The Product Life Cycle Trap," *Business Horizons*, September–October 1984, pp. 7–16.
8. "Recyclable 35mm Camera to Be Offered by October," *Wall Street Journal*, July 5, 1990, p. A3; Jay Palmer, "The Picture Brightens: At Eastman Kodak, Things Are Looking Up at All Divisions," *Barron's*, June 25, 1990, pp. 8–9, 57–59; "Kodak Recycling," *New York Times*, Feb. 10, 1990, p. 35; John Birmingham, "Can Kodak Hold on to Its Share in a Rapidly Changing Market?" *Adweek's Marketing Week*, Jan. 1, 1990, pp. 18–19; Francesca Lunzer Kritz, "Cameras for Forgetful Snapshooters," *U.S. News & World Report*, July 10, 1989, pp. 58–59; Dan Richards, "Kodak's Wild Disposables Are Wide and Wet; Fuji's Is a Tele," *Popular Photography*, July 1989, pp. 26, 85, 95; Leslie Helm, "Playing Leapfrog in Disposable Cameras," *Business Week*, May 1, 1989, p. 34; Clare Ansberry, "Kodak, Fuji Unveil Models to Expand Disposable Lines," *Wall Street Journal*, Apr. 19, 1989, p. B6; "New Products from Kodak,"

New York Times, Apr. 19, 1989, p. D4; and "Kodak Develops Cameras for the Young and Forgetful," *Machine Design,* Apr. 7, 1988, p. 18.

9. "WD-40 Company," *San Diego (CA) Business Journal,* Dec. 17, 1990; Herbert Lockwood, "Barry Predicts WD-40 Income Will Be Down, Sales Flat in 1991," *San Diego (CA) Daily Transcript,* Dec. 4, 1990; David Kiley, "Going It Alone: One-Brand Companies," *Adweek's Marketing Week,* Nov. 26, 1990, pp. 20–22; David S. Leibowitz, "A Basket Full of Golden Eggs," *FW,* Feb. 20, 1990, p. 90; and "WD-40 Sticking By One Product but Moves Overseas for Its Growth," *San Diego (CA) Daily Transcript,* Jan. 4, 1990.

9 *Developing and Managing Products*

OBJECTIVES

- To understand the importance and role of product development in the marketing mix

- To become aware of how existing products can be modified

- To gain insight into how businesses develop a product idea into a commercial product

- To acquire knowledge about the management of products during various life cycle stages

- To learn how product elimination can be used to improve product mixes

In the early 1980s, the minivan, family transportation with the benefits of a pickup truck and the ride and handling of a sedan, hastened the demise of the big station wagon and achieved tremendous success. This popularity explosion was largely due to Chrysler's introduction of the Dodge Caravan and the Plymouth Voyager.

Although Chrysler's minivans are still the most popular choice among consumers, a growing number of car manufacturers are entering the market with new designs or improving upon their old ones. Among recent challengers are the Chevrolet Lumina APV, the Ford Aerostar, the Mazda MPV, the Nissan Axxess, and newest to the competition, the Toyota Previa. What makes some of these versions of the minivan striking—and appealing—is their sleek and aerodynamic exteriors, especially in comparison to the more boxlike shape of the Caravan and Voyager.

Although Chrysler spent $650 million redesigning its 1991 minivans, the exterior doesn't look too different. To keep them competitive, however, Chrysler made numerous changes to the interior. Rather than the typical practice of relying exclusively on "motorist focus groups" and the opinions of expert consultants, Chrysler based most of its changes on suggestions from customers, who have written thousands of letters expressing their ideas. Some of the interior changes requested most often include a more legible dashboard, addition of a traditional glove compartment—without removing the existing storage bin on the passenger side—a high-mounted rear brake light, foldback outside mirrors, optional second-row bucket seats, rear shoulder belts, child safety option, driver's side airbag, and a handle on the back of the front passenger seat to assist passengers climbing into the rear. Chrysler added every one of these features to their new minivans, and will emphasize this fact in several advertisements.

Since the introduction of its Voyager and Caravan over six years ago, Chrysler minivans have maintained their popularity. Sales more than quadrupled between 1983 and 1990, giving Chrysler a 55 percent share of the minivan market.[1]

Photo courtesy of Chrysler Corporation.

To compete effectively and achieve its goals, an organization such as Chrysler must be able to adjust its product mix in response to changes in buyers' preferences. A firm often has to modify existing products, introduce new products, or eliminate products that were successful perhaps only a few years ago. To provide products that satisfy target markets and achieve the organization's objectives, a marketer must develop, alter, and maintain an effective product mix. An organization's product mix may need several types of adjustments. Because customers' attitudes and product preferences change over time, their desire for certain products may wane.

In some cases a company needs to alter its product mix for competitive reasons. A marketer may have to delete a product from the mix because a competitor dominates the market for that product. Similarly, a firm may have to introduce a new product or modify an existing one, as Chrysler has done with its minivans, to compete more effectively. A marketer may expand a firm's product mix to take advantage of excess marketing and production capacity.

Regardless of the reasons for altering a product mix, the product mix must be managed. In strategic market planning, many marketers rely on the portfolio approach for managing the product mix. The product portfolio approach tries to create specific marketing strategies to achieve a balanced mix of products that will bring maximum profits in the long run. (We examine product portfolio models in Chapter 20 in the discussion of strategic market planning.) This chapter examines several ways to improve an organization's product mix, including modifying the quality, function, or aesthetic attributes of existing products and developing new products from idea generation to commercialization. We also consider issues and decisions associated with managing products during life cycle stages. Finally, we focus on eliminating weak products from the product mix.

Modifying Existing Products

Product modification means changing one or more characteristics of a firm's product. It is most likely to be used in the maturity stage of the product life cycle to give a firm's existing brand a competitive advantage. Altering a product mix this way entails less risk than developing a new product.

Under certain conditions, product modification can indeed improve a firm's product mix. First, the product must be modifiable. Second, existing customers must be able to perceive that a modification has been made (assuming that the modified item is still aimed at them). Third, the modification should make the product more consistent with customers' desires so that it provides greater satisfaction. There are three major ways to modify products: quality modifications, functional modifications, and aesthetic modifications.

Quality Modifications

Quality modifications are changes that relate to a product's dependability and durability. Usually they are executed by altering the materials or the production process. Reducing a product's quality may allow an organization to lower its price and direct the item at a larger target market.

By contrast, increasing the quality of a product may give a firm an advantage over competing brands. In fact, over the last twenty years, increased global competition, rapid technological changes, and more demanding customers have forced marketers to improve product integrity to remain competitive.[2] Higher quality may enable a company to charge a higher price by creating customer loyalty and by lowering customer sensitivity to price. However, higher quality may require the use of more expensive components and processes, thus necessitating an organization to cut costs in other areas. Some firms, such as Caterpillar, are finding ways to both increase quality and reduce costs.

Functional Modifications

Changes that affect a product's versatility, effectiveness, convenience, or safety are called **functional modifications;** they usually require that the product be redesigned. Typical product categories that have undergone considerable functional modifications include office and farm equipment, appliances and cleaning products. Procter & Gamble, for example, modified Tide by adding bleach, which improved the detergent's effectiveness. Panasonic, as shown in Figure 9.1, modified one of its camcorders by adding a stabilization feature. Functional modifications can make a product useful to more people, which enlarges its market. This type of change can place a product in a favorable competitive position by providing benefits competing items do not offer. Functional modifications can also help an organization achieve and maintain a progressive image. At times, too, functional modifications are made to reduce the possibility of

Figure 9.1

Functional Modification

Panasonic has modified one of its camcorders to add a stabilization feature. With this new feature that improves the product's versatility and effectiveness, Panasonic hopes to enlarge the market for the product and enhance the company's image as being innovative.

Source: Matsushita Electric Corporation of America.

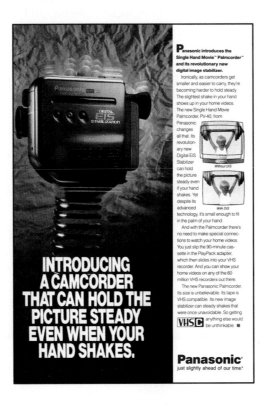

product liability claims. Recently, marketers have been modifying products (especially electronics) to make them easier to use. Inside Marketing explores this trend toward simplicity in more detail.

Aesthetic Modifications

Aesthetic modifications change the sensory appeal of a product by altering its taste, texture, sound, smell, or visual characteristics. In making a purchase decision a buyer is swayed by how a product looks, smells, tastes, feels, or sounds. Thus an aesthetic modification may strongly affect purchases. For years automobile makers have relied on aesthetic modifications.

Through aesthetic modifications, a firm can differentiate its product from competing brands and thus gain a sizable market share. The major drawback in using aesthetic modifications is that their value is determined subjectively. Although a firm may strive to improve the product's sensory appeal, customers may actually find the modified product less attractive.

Developing New Products

In addition to modifying existing products, a firm may develop new products as a means of enhancing its product mix. Developing and introducing new products is frequently expensive and risky. The development of Gillette's Sensor razor took over eight years and resulted in a $200 million investment.[3] Thousands of new consumer products are introduced annually, and, as indicated in Chapter 8, anywhere from 60 to 90 percent of them fail. Lack of research is a leading cause of new-product failure. Other often-cited causes are technical problems in design or production and errors in timing the product's introduction. Although new-product development is risky, so is failure to introduce new products. For example, the makers of Timex watches gained a large share of the U.S. watch market through effective marketing strategies during the 1960s and early 1970s. By 1983, Timex's market share had slipped considerably, in part because Timex had failed to introduce new products. In recent times, however, Timex has introduced a number of new products and regained market share.

The term *new product* can have more than one meaning. A genuinely new product—like the VCR once was—offers innovative benefits. But products that are different and distinctly better are often viewed as new. The following items (listed in no particular order) are product innovations of the last thirty years: Post-It note pads, fax machines, birth-control pills, personal computers, felt-tip pens, disposable razors, compact-disc players, quartz watches, and camcorders. Thus, a new product can be an innovative product that has never been sold by any organization, such as Kodak's disposable camera. It can also be a product that a given firm has not marketed previously, although similar products may have been available from other companies. The first company to introduce a VCR, for example, clearly was launching a new product. However, if Boeing introduced a VCR brand, this would also be viewed as a new product for Boeing because that organization has not previously marketed VCRs. Finally, a product can be viewed as new when it is brought to one or more markets from another,

Figure 9.2

Phases of New-
Product Development

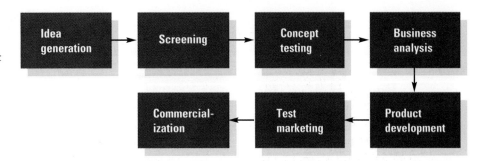

such as American football being brought to European markets by the World League of American Football (see the Global Perspective).

Before a product is introduced, it goes through the seven phases of **new-product development** shown in Figure 9.2: (1) idea generation, (2) idea screening, (3) concept testing, (4) business analysis, (5) product development, (6) test marketing, and (7) commercialization. A product may be dropped, and many are, at any stage of development. In this section, we will look at the process through which products are developed, from the inception of an idea to fully commercialized product.

Idea Generation

Businesses and other organizations seek product ideas that will help them achieve their objectives. This activity is **idea generation**. The fact that only a few ideas are good enough to be commercially successful underscores the difficulty of the task. Although some organizations get their ideas almost by chance, firms that are trying to effectively manage their product mixes usually develop systematic approaches for generating new product ideas. At the heart of innovation is a purposeful, focused effort to identify new ways to serve a market. Unexpected occurrences, incongruities, new needs, industry and market changes, and demographic changes all may indicate new opportunities.[4]

New product ideas can come from several sources. They may come from internal sources—marketing managers, researchers, sales personnel, engineers, or other organizational personnel. Brainstorming and incentives or rewards for good ideas are typical intrafirm devices for stimulating the development of ideas. For example, the idea for 3M Post-It adhesive-backed yellow notes came from an employee. As a church choir member, he used slips of paper for marking songs in his hymnal. Because the pieces of paper fell out, he suggested developing an adhesive-backed note. Hewlett-Packard Co. keeps its labs open to engineers twenty-four hours a day to help generate ideas; it also encourages its researchers to devote 10 percent of company time to exploring their own ideas for new products.[5]

New product ideas may also arise from sources outside the firm—customers, competitors, advertising agencies, management consultants, and private research organizations. Johnson & Johnson, for example, acquired the technology for its new clear orthodontic braces through a joint venture with Saphikon, the developer of the technology behind the braces.[6] Sometimes potential buyers of a product are questioned in depth to discover what attributes would appeal to

Product Modification: Simplify, Simplify, Simplify

AT THE MCCANN ELECTRONICS SERVICE CENTER, telephones ring all day. Most of the calls are from people who don't understand how to operate their videocassette recorders. Driven to frustration by complicated programming instructions for his new VCR, one customer called the service center and said, "I tried to follow the instructions, and I'm not an ignorant man. But I absolutely could not figure out what to do!" He is not alone. In one year's time, Sony Corporation's fifty-five product information specialists received about 500,000 calls for help. Increasingly, consumers are complaining about what is being dubbed "hypergadgetry"—intricate, button-laden, high-tech, difficult-to-use products.

How did electronic products become overloaded with complex features and operations that consumers can't figure out? Industry analysts point to the microchip as the culprit, because that tiny invention makes it possible to squeeze many functions into very small devices at negligible costs. Technology that began with push-button phones expanded to include photocopiers and VCRs too complicated for the average person to work. Surveys indicate that 75 percent of VCR owners never learn how to record a television program. Ricoh Company of Japan interviewed its fax customers and learned that 95 percent of them never used the three key features deliberately built into the machines to increase their appeal. Xerox Corporation's state-of-the-art 8200 Office Copier so perplexed office workers with its buttons and visual display that customers abandoned it, costing Xerox a significant share of the U.S. copier market.

In conjunction with ideas from anthropologists, sociologists, and cognitive psychologists, product designers are scrapping features people don't like or use

and working to create "user-friendly" products instead. Citibank's automated teller machines have visual menus that list all possible transactions and clearly tell users how to get them. The newest generation of VCRs have on-screen programming that provides step-by-step instructions for taping future shows, and several firms are developing VCR prototypes that understand and use spoken words. Philips Consumer Electronics is coming out with its new Easy Line of simple-to-use clock radios, VCRs, and tape players. To convince consumers that it understands their frustration and is doing something about it, GoldStar Electronics recently began a $15 million advertising campaign promoting its "designed with real people in mind" VCRs and microwaves.

Human factors experts insist that the true mark of a well-designed product is simplicity; average people should be able to look at it, understand it, and use it right away. Americans aren't against technology. They just want to be able to operate their VCRs, compact disk players, message machines, electronic thermostats, keypad burglar alarms, digital clocks, microwaves, programmable phones, and home computers.

Sources: Joel Achenbach, "'Hypergadgetry' Curse of Our Time," *Bryan–College Station (TX) Eagle,* June 30, 1991, p. 8B; Bruce Nussbaum and Robert Neff, "'I Can't Work This Thing,'" *Business Week,* Apr. 29, 1991, pp. 58–62, 66; Kim Foltz, "GoldStar Promoting 'User-Friendlier' Image," *New York Times,* Nov. 6, 1990, p. D17; "VCR Still a Mystery? Try Talking to It," *New York Times,* Oct. 10, 1990, p. D9; Carla Lazzareschi, "Enough with the Gadgets," *Los Angeles Times,* Aug. 22, 1990, pp. A1, A18; and Keith Bradsher, "Coping with Home Electronics," *New York Times,* Jan. 13, 1990, p. 52.

them. Asking weekend fishermen what they wanted in a sonar fish finder led Techsonic Industries Inc. to develop its LCR (liquid crystal recorder) fish finder. Annual sales of the LCR reached $31 million within one year. The practice of asking customers what they want from its products has helped Techsonic maintain its leadership in the industry.[7]

Screening

In the process of **screening,** those ideas with the greatest potential are selected for further review. During screening, product ideas are analyzed to determine whether they match the organization's objectives and resources. The company's overall ability to produce and market the product is also analyzed. Other aspects of an idea that should be weighed are the nature and wants of buyers and possible environmental changes. Compared with other phases, the largest number of new-product ideas are rejected during the idea-screening phase.

At times a checklist of new-product requirements is used when making screening decisions. It encourages evaluators to be systematic and so reduces the chances of their overlooking some fact. If a critical factor on the checklist remains unclear, the type of formal research described in Chapter 7 may be needed. To screen ideas properly, it may be necessary to test product concepts: a product concept and its benefits can be described or shown to consumers. Several product concepts may be tested to discover which might appeal most to a particular target market.

Concept Testing

Concept testing is a phase in which a small sample of potential buyers is presented with a product idea through a written or oral description (and perhaps a few drawings) to determine their attitudes and initial buying intentions regarding the product. For a single product idea, an organization can test one or several concepts of the same product. Concept testing is a low-cost procedure for an organization to determine customers' initial reactions to a product idea prior to investing considerable resources in product research and development. The results of concept testing can be used by product development personnel to better understand the product attributes and product benefits that are most important to potential customers.

Figure 9.3 shows a concept test for a proposed tick and flea control product. Notice that the concept is briefly described; a series of questions is then presented. The types of questions that are asked vary considerably depending on the type of product being tested. Typical questions are: In general, do you find this proposed product attractive? Which benefits are especially attractive to you? Which features are of little or no interest to you? Do you feel that this proposed product would work better for you than the product that you are currently using? Compared with your current product, what are the primary advantages of the proposed product? If this product were available at an appropriate price, would you buy it? How often would you buy this product? How could this proposed product be improved?

Business Analysis

During the **business analysis** stage, the product idea is evaluated to determine its potential contribution to the firm's sales, costs, and profits. In the course of a business analysis, evaluators ask a variety of questions: Does the product fit in

Figure 9.3

Concept Test for a
Tick and Flea Control
Product

Product description: An insecticide company is considering the development and introduction of a new tick and flea control product for pets. This product would consist of insecticide and a liquid dispensing brush for applying the insecticide to dogs and cats. The insecticide is in a cartridge that is installed in the handle of the brush. The insecticide is dispensed through the tips of the bristles when they touch the pet's skin (which is where most ticks and fleas are found). The actual dispensing works very much like a felt-tip pen. Only a small amount of insecticide actually is dispensed on the pet because of this unique dispensing feature. Thus, the amount of insecticide that is placed on your pet is minimal compared to conventional methods of applying a tick and flea control product. One application of insecticide will keep your pet free from ticks and fleas for fourteen days.

Questions: Please answer the following questions:

1. In general, how do you feel about using this type of product on your pet?

2. What are the major advantages of this product compared to the existing product that you are currently using to control ticks and fleas on your pet?

3. What characteristics of this product do you especially like?

4. What suggestions do you have for improving this product?

5. If available at an appropriate price, how likely are you to buy this product?

   Very likely   Semi-likely   Not likely

6. Assuming that a single purchase would provide 30 applications for an average size dog or 48 applications for an average size cat, approximately how much would you pay for this product?

with the organization's existing product mix? Is demand strong enough to justify entering the market and will the demand endure? What types of environmental and competitive changes can be expected, and how will these changes affect the product's future sales, costs, and profits? Are the organization's research, development, engineering, and production capabilities adequate? If new facilities must be constructed, how quickly can they be built and how much will they cost? Is the necessary financing for development and commercialization on hand or obtainable at terms consistent with a favorable return on investment?

In the business analysis stage, firms seek market information. The results of consumer polls, along with secondary data, supply the specifics needed for estimating potential sales, costs, and profits. At this point, a research budget should explore the financial objectives and related considerations for the new product.

Exporting American Football

WHEN THE LONDON MONARCHS faced off against the Frankfurt Galaxy in the opening game of the World League of American Football, a crowd of more than 23,000 cheered them on. Flag-waving, song-singing fans sat in the rain and cold in Barcelona to watch the New York–New Jersey Knights battle the hometown Dragons, even though many didn't seem to know the difference between a first down and a touchdown. From the enthusiasm the ten-team WLAF is generating overseas, it looks like Europeans will embrace football the way they have cheeseburgers and MTV.

Over 750 million fans in more than fifty countries watched the last Superbowl on television, and National Football League exhibition games in Europe, Canada, and Japan have drawn huge crowds. Pointing to that popularity as an indicator of football's universal appeal, promoters created a new spring league made up of seven American and Canadian teams and two European ones. Cynics say that the WLAF is professional ball without agents, talk shows, and a coach for every kicking tee. Players are mostly unknowns who are too light or too slow for the NFL, salaries average a modest $20,000 a year, accommodations are far from glamorous, and playing fields often don't meet regulations. What all of this adds up to is a game that lacks the machinelike quality American fans have come to expect from the NFL but

exudes a spontaneity and vitality that European fans are enjoying. European franchises consistently beat U.S. WLAF franchises in game attendance, and British newspapers regularly feature more items on the WLAF than do newspapers in the United States. While ABC draws dismal ratings for its Sunday telecasts of WLAF games, the World Bowl at London's Wembly Stadium attracted a near-sellout crowd.

To survive, the WLAF needs to increase its number of fans. Experts agree that the league can boost television ratings in the United States by adding franchises in high-television-viewing states like California, changing broadcast networks from USA network (which most devoted football fans do not watch), and reducing the number of games per weekend from the present four. The league's best chance for success, however, seems to rest with European fans, who aren't inundated with the National Football League, basketball, hockey, and baseball. Potential locations for expansion include Paris, Helsinki, and Tokyo, where promoters hope the sport won't be just another "Spring League," but "American Football."

Sources: Rick Reilly, "One to Remember," *Sports Illustrated*, June 17, 1991, p. 46; Charles Leerhsen, Daniel Pedersen, and Howard Manly, "Hold That Helmet Cam!" *Newsweek*, May 20, 1991, p. 60; and Rick Reilly, "World Premiere," *Sports Illustrated*, Apr. 1, 1991, pp. 40–43.

Product Development

Product development is the phase in which the organization finds out if it is technically feasible to produce the product and if it can be produced at costs low enough to make the final price reasonable. To test its acceptability, the idea or concept is converted into a prototype, or working model. The prototype should reveal tangible and intangible attributes associated with the product in consumers' minds. The product's design, mechanical features, and intangible aspects must be linked to wants in the marketplace. Through marketing research and concept testing, product attributes that are important to buyers are identified. These characteristics must be communicated to customers through the design of the product. Failure to determine how consumers feel about the product and how they would use it may lead to the product's failure. For example, Coca-Cola

Company's Minute Maid division developed Minute Maid Squeeze-Fresh orange juice concentrate so that consumers could make one glass of juice at a time rather than mix and store a half gallon. In tests, however, the company discovered that consumers did not like Squeeze-Fresh because it was messy and they did not know how much concentrate to use to make one glass of juice. Testing to determine how consumers view the product idea is therefore very important in the product development stage.

After a company has developed a prototype, its functionality must be tested. This means that its performance, safety, convenience, and other functional qualities are tested in a laboratory as well as in the field. Functional testing should be rigorous and long enough to thoroughly test the product.

A crucial question that arises during product development is how much quality to build into the product. A major dimension of quality is durability. Higher quality often calls for better materials and more expensive processing, which increase production costs and, ultimately, the product's price. In determining the specific level of quality, a marketer must ascertain approximately what price the target market views as acceptable. In addition, a marketer usually tries to set a level for a specific product that is consistent with the firm's other products that carry a similar brand. Obviously, the quality of competing brands is a consideration.

The development phase of a new product is frequently lengthy and expensive; thus a relatively small number of product ideas are put into development. If the product appears sufficiently successful during this stage to merit test marketing, then during the latter part of the development stage marketers begin to make decisions regarding branding, packaging, labeling, pricing, and promotion for use in the test marketing stage.

Table 9.1   **Popular Test Markets for New Products**

Akron, OH	Detroit, MI	Marion, IN	St. Louis, MO
Ann Arbor, MI	Durham, NC	Melbourne, FL	Salem, NC
Asheville, NC	Elkhart, IN	Midland, TX	Salt Lake City, UT
Austin, TX	Evansville, IN	Mobile, AL	San Francisco, CA
Bangor, ME	Fort Collins, CO	Montgomery, AL	Scranton, PA
Beaumont, TX	Fort Wayne, IN	New Orleans, LA	Sioux Falls, SD
Boise, ID	Grand Junction, CO	Oklahoma City, OK	Spokane, WA
Buffalo, NY	Greensboro, NC	Orlando, FL	Springfield, IL
Cedar Rapids, IA	Hartford, CT	Philadelphia, PA	Syracuse, NY
Charleston, WV	Huntsville, AL	Pittsfield, MA	Tampa, FL
Chicago, IL	Jacksonville, FL	Portland, OR	Troy, NY
Colorado Springs, CO	Kansas City, MO	Providence, RI	Washington, DC
Columbus, OH	Las Vegas, NV	Raleigh, NC	Wichita, KS
Dallas, TX	Little Rock, AK	Richmond, VA	Yakima, WA
Decatur, IL	Lubbock, TX	Rockford, IL	

Source: "The Nation's Most Popular Test Markets," *Sales & Marketing Management,* March 1989, pp. 65–66. Reprinted by permission of Sales & Marketing Management. Copyright 1989.

Test Marketing

A limited introduction of a product in geographic areas chosen to represent the intended market is called **test marketing**. Its aim is to determine the reactions of probable buyers. For example, Pepsi test-marketed a caffeine-charged soft drink called Pepsi A.M. aimed at buyers who wanted a caffeine drink in the morning but do not like coffee or tea. Due to mediocre sales volume during test marketing, Pepsi marketers decided not to launch this product. Test marketing is not an extension of the development stage; it is a sample launching of the entire marketing mix. Test marketing should be conducted only after the product has gone through development and after initial plans regarding the other marketing mix variables have been made.

Companies of all sizes use test marketing to lessen the risk of product failure. The dangers of introducing an untested product include undercutting already-profitable products and, should the new product fail, loss of credibility with distributors and customers. Frito-Lay, for example, believed that it understood consumers' snack preferences well enough to introduce a new snack cracker called MaxSnax without first test marketing it. Even with strong advertising support, the product did not sell, and Frito-Lay was forced to eliminate the product from its snack line.[8]

Test marketing provides several benefits. It lets marketers expose a product in a natural marketing environment to gauge its sales performance. While the product is being marketed in a limited area, the company can strive to identify weaknesses in the product or in other parts of the marketing mix. A product weakness discovered after a nationwide introduction can be expensive to correct. Moreover, if consumers' early reactions are negative, marketers may not be able to convince consumers to try the product again. Thus making adjustments after test marketing can be crucial to the success of a new product. Test marketing also allows marketers to experiment with variations in advertising, price, and packaging in different test areas and to measure the extent of brand awareness, brand switching, and repeat purchases that result from alterations in the marketing mix.

The accuracy of test marketing results often hinges on where the tests are conducted. Selection of appropriate test areas is very important. The validity of test market results depends heavily on selecting test sites that provide accurate representation of the intended target market. Table 9.1 lists some of the most popular test market cities. The criteria used for choosing test cities depend on the product's characteristics, the target market's characteristics, and the firm's objectives and resources. Even though the selection criteria will vary from one company to another, the kind of questions that Table 9.2 presents can be helpful in assessing a potential test market.

Test marketing is not without risks, however. Not only is it expensive, but a firm's competitors may try to interfere. A competitor may attempt to "jam" the test program by increasing advertising or promotions, lowering prices, and offering special incentives—all to combat the recognition and purchase of a new brand. Any such devices can invalidate test results. Sometimes, too, competitors copy the product in the testing stage and rush to introduce a similar product. It is therefore desirable to move quickly and commercialize as soon as possible after testing. Clorox spent over four years and several million dollars test marketing a detergent with bleach. During this period Procter & Gamble launched

Table 9.2

Questions to Consider When Choosing Test Markets

1. Is the area typical of planned distribution outlets?
2. Is the city relatively isolated from other cities?
3. What local media are available, and are they cooperative?
4. Does the area have a dominant television station? Does it have multiple newspapers, magazines, and radio stations?
5. Does the city contain a diversified cross section of ages, religions, and cultural/societal preferences?
6. Are the purchasing habits atypical?
7. Is the city's per capita income typical?
8. Does the city have a good record as a test city?
9. Would testing efforts be easily "jammed" by competitors?
10. Does the city have stable year-round sales?
11. Are retailers who will cooperate available?
12. Are research and audit services available?
13. Is the area free from unusual influences, such as one industry's dominance or heavy tourist traffic?

Source: Adapted from "A Checklist for Selecting Test Markets," copyright 1982 *Sales & Marketing Management*. Reprinted by permission of Sales & Marketing Management. Copyright 1982.

and went national with Tide with Bleach. Several other brands were also introduced during this period, and Clorox withdrew from the detergent market.[9]

Because of these risks, many companies are using alternative methods to gauge consumer preferences. One such method is simulated test marketing. Typically, consumers at shopping centers are asked to view an advertisement for a new product and are given a free sample to take home. These consumers are subsequently interviewed over the phone and asked to rate the product. The major advantages of simulated test marketing are speed, lower costs, and tighter security, which reduces the flow of information to competitors and reduces jamming. For example, Gillette's Personal Care Division spends less than $200,000 for a simulated test that takes three to five months. A live test market costs Gillette $2 million, counting promotion and distribution, and takes one to two years to complete.[10] Several marketing research firms, such as A. C. Nielsen Company, offer test marketing services to help provide independent assessment of products.

Commercialization

During the **commercialization** phase, plans for full-scale manufacturing and marketing must be refined and settled, and budgets for the project must be prepared. Early in the commercialization phase, marketing management analyzes the results of test marketing to find out what changes in the marketing mix are needed before the product is introduced. For example, the results of test marketing may tell the marketers to change one or more of the product's physical attributes, modify the distribution plans to include more retail outlets, alter promotional efforts, or change the product's price. However, as more and more changes are made based on test marketing findings, the test marketing projections may become less valid.

During the early part of this stage, marketers not only must gear up for larger-scale production, but they also must make decisions about warranties, repairs, and replacement parts. A *warranty* specifies what the producer will do if the product malfunctions. The type of warranty a firm provides can be a critical issue for buyers, especially when expensive, technically complex goods such as appliances are involved. Maytag, for example, provides a money-back guarantee on its refrigerators. Because warranties must be more precise today due to stricter government regulations, marketers such as car makers are using them more vigorously as tools to give their brands a competitive advantage. Establishing an effective system for providing repair services and replacement parts is necessary to maintain favorable customer relationships. Although the producer may furnish these services directly to buyers, it is more common for the producer to provide such services through regional service centers. Regardless of how services are provided, it is important to customers that they be performed quickly and correctly.

The product enters the market during the commercialization phase. When introducing a product, marketers often spend enormous sums of money for advertising, personal selling, and other types of promotion. These expenses, together with capital outlays for plant and equipment, can make commercialization extremely costly; such expenditures may not be recovered for several years. For example, when Giorgio introduced the fragrance Red for Men, the company spent $3 million on advertising to communicate the new product's attributes.[11]

Commercialization is easier when customers accept the product rapidly. There is a better chance of this occurring if marketers can make them aware of a product's benefits. The following stages of the **product adoption process** are generally recognized as those that buyers go through in accepting a product:

1. *Awareness.* The buyer becomes aware of the product.
2. *Interest.* The buyer seeks information and is receptive to learning about the product.
3. *Evaluation.* The buyer considers the product's benefits and determines whether to try it.
4. *Trial.* The buyer examines, tests, or tries the product to determine its usefulness relative to his or her needs.
5. *Adoption.* The buyer purchases the product and can be expected to use it when the need for this general type of product arises again.[12]

This adoption model has several implications for the commercialization phase. First, the company must promote the product to create widespread awareness of its existence and its benefits. Samples or simulated trials should be arranged to help buyers make initial purchase decisions. At the same time, marketers should emphasize quality control and provide solid guarantees to reinforce buyer opinion during the evaluation stage. Finally, production and physical distribution must be linked to patterns of adoption and repeat purchases. (The product adoption process is also discussed in Chapter 15.)

Products are not usually launched nationwide overnight but are introduced through a process called a roll-out. Through a roll-out, a product is introduced in stages, starting in a set of geographic areas and gradually expanding into

Figure 9.4

Product Rollout

Glade Plug-Ins air freshener was rolled out over a period of time. That is, it was introduced in stages which eventually resulted in nationwide distribution.

Source: SC Johnson Wax.

adjacent areas. Glade Plug-Ins air freshener (see Figure 9.4) is an example of a product that was rolled out. It may take several years to market the product nationally. Sometimes the test cities are used as initial marketing areas, and the introduction becomes a natural extension of test marketing. A product test-marketed in Sacramento, Fort Collins, Dallas, St. Louis, and Jacksonville, as the map in Figure 9.5 shows, could be introduced first in those cities. After the stage 1 introduction is complete, stage 2 could include market coverage of the states in which the test cities are located. In stage 3, marketing efforts could be extended into adjacent states. All remaining states would then be covered in stage 4. Gradual product introductions do not always occur state by state, however; other geographic combinations are used as well, such as groups of counties that overlap across state borders.

Gradual product introduction is popular for several reasons. It reduces the risks of introducing a new product. If the product fails, the firm will experience smaller losses if the item has been introduced in only a few geographic areas than if it has been marketed nationally. Furthermore, a company cannot introduce a product nationwide overnight because the system of wholesalers and retailers, necessary to distribute a product, cannot be established that quickly. The development of a distribution network may take considerable time. Keep in mind also that the number of units needed to satisfy the national demand for a successful product can be enormous, and a firm usually cannot produce the required quantities in a short time.

Despite the good reasons for introducing a product gradually, marketers realize that this approach creates some competitive problems. A gradual introduction allows competitors to observe what a firm is doing and to monitor results, just as the firm's own marketers are doing. If competitors see that the newly introduced product is successful, they may enter the same target market quickly with similar products. In addition, as a product is introduced region by region, competitors may expand their marketing efforts to offset promotion of the new product.

Managing Products After Commercialization

Most new products start off slowly and seldom generate enough sales to produce profits immediately. As buyers learn about the new product, marketers should be alert for product weaknesses and make corrections quickly to prevent its early demise. Marketing strategy should be designed to attract the segment that is most interested and has the fewest objections. If any of these factors need adjustment, this action, too, must be taken quickly to sustain demand. As the sales curve moves upward and the break-even point is reached, the growth stage begins.

Figure 9.5 **Stages of Expansion into a National Market During Commercialization**
Source: Adapted from *Business: An Involvement Approach,* by Herbert G. Hicks, William M. Pride, and James D. Powell. Copyright © 1975 by McGraw-Hill. Used with permission of McGraw-Hill Book Company.

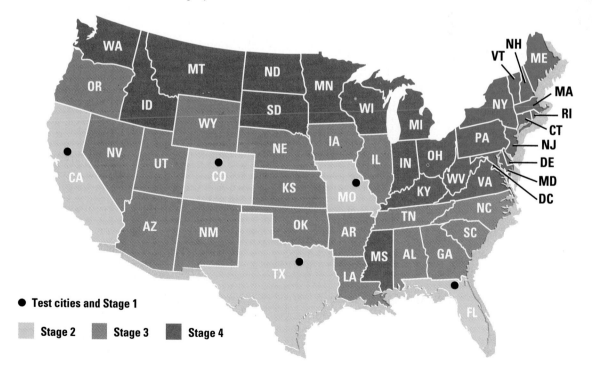

Marketing Strategy in the Growth Stage

As sales increase, management must support the momentum by adjusting the marketing strategy. The goal is to establish the product's position and to fortify it by encouraging brand loyalty. As profits increase, the organization must brace itself for the entrance of aggressive competitors, who may make specialized appeals to selected market segments.

During the growth stage, product offerings may have to be expanded. To achieve greater penetration of an overall market, segmentation may have to be used more intensely. That would require developing product variations to satisfy the needs of people in several different market segments. Marketers should analyze the product position regarding competing products and correct weak or omitted attributes. Quality, functional, or aesthetic modifications may be required.

Gaps in the marketing channels should be filled during the growth period. Once a product has won acceptance, new distribution outlets may be easier to obtain. Sometimes marketers tend to move from an exclusive or selective exposure to a more intensive network of dealers to achieve greater market penetration. Marketers must also make sure that the physical distribution system is running efficiently and delivering supplies to distributors before their inventories are exhausted. Because competition increases during the growth period, service adjustments and prompt credit for defective products are important marketing tools.

Advertising expenditures may be lowered slightly from the high level of the introductory stage but are still quite substantial. As sales increase, promotion costs should drop as a percentage of total sales. A falling ratio between promotion expenditures and sales should contribute significantly to increased profits. The advertising messages should stress brand benefits. Coupons and samples may be used to increase market share.

After recovering development costs, a business may be able to lower prices. As sales volume increases, efficiencies in production can result in lower costs. These savings may be passed on to buyers. If demand remains strong and there are few competitive threats, prices tend to remain stable. If price cuts are feasible, they can improve price competition and discourage new competitors from entering the market. For example, when compact disc players were introduced in the early 1980s, they sported a $1,000 price tag. Primarily because of the price, the product was positioned as a "toy for audiophiles"—a very small market segment. To generate mass market demand, compact disc player manufacturers dropped their prices to around $200, and the cost of discs dropped from $22 to about $15. The price is now at a point where the margin is low, but unit sales are rising.

Marketing Strategy for Mature Products

Because many products are in the maturity stage of their life cycles, marketers must deal with these products and be prepared to improve the marketing mix constantly. During maturity, the competitive situation stabilizes, and some of the weaker competitors drop out. It has been suggested that as a product matures, its customers become more experienced and specialized (especially for industrial products). As these customers gain knowledge, the benefits they seek may change as well. Thus new marketing strategies may be called for.[13]

Marketers may need to alter the product's quality or otherwise modify the product offering. Mattel marketers, for example, have effectively managed the Barbie doll (see Figure 9.6) by modifying the product and continuing to provide Barbie-related accessories. A product may be rejuvenated through different packaging, new models, or aesthetic changes. For example, Pillsbury introduced a line of refrigerated prepared dough products in 1960, and sales grew steadily until 1970. Then sales declined slowly until 1980. In 1980 Pillsbury improved product quality, changed its distribution system, refocused its advertising toward consumers instead of the trade, and reduced the price to revitalize these mature products.[14] Sales and market share may be maintained or strengthened by developing new uses for the product. Kraft, for instance, revived Cheez Whiz by repositioning it as a microwavable cheese sauce and promoting numerous uses as a sauce (see Figure 9.7).

During the maturity stage of the life cycle, marketers actively encourage dealers to support the product. Dealers may be offered promotional assistance in lowering their inventory costs. In general, marketers go to great lengths to serve dealers and provide incentives for selling the manufacturer's brand.

To maintain market share during the maturity stage requires moderate and sometimes large advertising expenditures. Advertising messages focus on differentiating a brand from numerous competitors, and sales promotion efforts are aimed at both consumers and resellers.

A greater mixture of pricing strategies is used during the maturity stage. Strong price competition may occur, and price wars may break out. Firms may also compete in other ways, such as product quality or service, rather than

Figure 9.6

Effective Management of a Mature Product

Mattel's Barbie Doll remains a highly successful product due to effective management during its mature stage.

Source: Used with permission of Mattel, Inc.

Figure 9.7

Promoting New Uses of a Product

Kraft attempts to strengthen the market share for Cheez Whiz by suggesting new uses for the product.

Source: Cheez Whiz is a registered trademark of Kraft General Foods, Inc. Reproduced with permission.

through price. Marketers develop price flexibility to differentiate offerings in product lines. Markdowns and price incentives are more common, but prices may rise if distribution and production costs increase.

Marketing Strategy for Declining Products

As a product's sales curve turns downward, industry profits continue to fall. A business can justify maintaining a product as long as it contributes to profits or enhances the overall effectiveness of a product mix. In this stage, marketers must determine whether to eliminate the product or seek to reposition it in an attempt to extend its life. Usually, a declining product has lost its distinctiveness because similar competing products have been introduced. Competition engenders increased substitution and brand switching as buyers become insensitive to minor product differences. For these reasons, marketers do little to change a product's style, design, or other attributes during its decline. New technology, product substitutes, or environmental considerations may also indicate that the time has come to delete a product.

During a product's decline, outlets with strong sales volumes are maintained, and unprofitable outlets are weeded out. An entire marketing channel may be eliminated if it does not contribute adequately to profits. Sometimes a new marketing channel, such as a factory outlet, will be used to liquidate remaining inventory of an obsolete product. As sales decline, the product becomes more obscure, but loyal buyers seek out dealers who carry it.

Advertising expenditures are at a minimum. Advertising of special offers may slow the rate of decline. Sales promotions, such as coupons and premiums, may temporarily regain buyers' attention. As the product continues to decline, the sales staff shifts its emphasis to more profitable products.

To have a product return a profit may be more important to a firm than to maintain a certain market share through repricing. To squeeze out all possible remaining profits, marketers may maintain the price despite declining sales and competitive pressures. Prices may even be increased as costs rise if a loyal core market still wants the product. In other situations, the price may be cut to reduce existing inventory so that the product can be deleted. Severe price reductions may be required if a new product is making an existing product obsolete.

Product Elimination

Generally, a product cannot satisfy target market customers and contribute to the achievement of an organization's overall goals indefinitely. **Product elimination** is the process of deleting a product from the product mix when it no longer satisfies a sufficient number of customers. A declining product reduces an organization's profitability and drains resources that could be used instead to modify other products or develop new ones. A marginal product may require shorter production runs, which can increase per-unit production costs. Finally, when a dying product completely loses favor with customers, the negative feelings may transfer to some of the company's other products.

Most organizations find it difficult to eliminate a product. A decision to drop a product may be opposed by management and other employees who feel the product is necessary in the product mix. Salespeople who still have some loyal customers are especially upset when a product is dropped. Considerable resources and effort are sometimes spent trying to change the product's marketing mix to improve its sales and thus avoid having to eliminate it.

Some organizations delete products only after they have become heavy financial burdens. A better approach is some form of systematic review in which each product is evaluated periodically to determine its impact on the overall effectiveness of the firm's product mix. Such a review should analyze a product's contribution to the firm's sales for a given period and include estimates of future sales, costs, and profits associated with the product. It should also gauge the value of making changes in the marketing strategy to improve the product's performance. A systematic review allows an organization to improve product performance and to ascertain when to eliminate products. Although many companies do systematically review their product mixes, a research study found that few companies have formal, written policies on the process of deleting products. The study also found that most companies based their decisions to eliminate weak products on poor sales and profit potential, low compatibility with the firm's business strategies, unfavorable market outlook, and historical declines in profitability.[15]

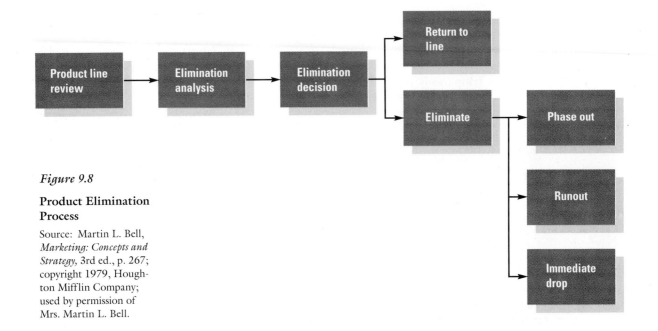

Figure 9.8

Product Elimination Process

Source: Martin L. Bell, *Marketing: Concepts and Strategy*, 3rd ed., p. 267; copyright 1979, Houghton Mifflin Company; used by permission of Mrs. Martin L. Bell.

Basically, there are three ways to eliminate a product: phase it out, run it out, or drop it immediately (see Figure 9.8). A *phaseout* approach lets the product decline without a change in the marketing strategy. No attempt is made to give the product new life. A *runout* policy exploits any strengths left in the product. Intensifying marketing efforts in core markets or eliminating some marketing expenditures, such as advertising, may cause a sudden spurt of profits. This approach is commonly taken for technologically obsolete products, such as older models of computers and calculators. Often the price is reduced to get a sales spurt. The third alternative, *dropping* an unprofitable product immediately, is the best strategy when losses are too great to prolong the product's life.

Summary

The product portfolio approach attempts to create specific marketing strategies to achieve a balanced product mix that will produce maximum long-run profits. To maximize the effectiveness of a product mix, an organization usually has to alter its mix through modification of existing products, new-product development, or elimination of a product. Product modification is changing one or more characteristics of a firm's product. This approach to altering a product mix can be effective when the product is modifiable, when customers can perceive the change, and when customers want the modification. Quality modifications are changes that relate to a product's dependability and durability. Changes that affect a product's versatility, effectiveness, convenience, or safety are called functional modifications. Aesthetic modifications change the sensory appeal of a product.

A new product may be an innovation that has never been sold by any organization; it can be a product that a given firm has not marketed previously, although similar products may have been available from other organizations; or it can be a product brought from one market to a new market. Before a product is introduced, it goes through the seven phases of new-product development. In the idea generation phase, new product ideas may come from internal or external sources. In the process of idea screening, those ideas with the greatest potential are selected for further review. Concept testing, the third phase, involves having a small sample of potential customers review a brief description of the product idea to determine their initial perceptions of the proposed product and their early buying intentions. During the business analysis stage, the product idea is evaluated to determine its potential contribution to the firm's sales, costs, and profits. Product development is the stage in which the organization finds out if it is technically feasible to produce the product and if it can be produced at costs low enough so that the final price is reasonable. Test marketing is a limited introduction of a product in areas chosen to represent the intended market. The decision to enter the commercialization phase means that full-scale production of the product begins and a complete marketing strategy is developed. The process that buyers go through in accepting a product includes awareness, interest, evaluation, trial, and adoption.

As a product moves through its life cycle, marketing strategies may require continual adaptation. In the growth stage, it is important to develop brand loyalty and a market position. In the maturity stage, a product may be modified, or new market segments may be developed to rejuvenate its sales. A product that is declining may be maintained as long as it makes a contribution to profits or enhances the product mix. Marketers must determine whether to eliminate the declining product or try to reposition it to extend its life.

Product elimination is the process of deleting a product that no longer satisfies a sufficient number of customers. Although a firm's personnel may oppose product elimination, weak products are unprofitable, consume too much time and effort, may require shorter production runs, and can create an unfavorable impression of the firm's other products. A product mix should be systematically reviewed to determine when to delete products. Products to be eliminated can be phased out, run out, or dropped immediately.

Important Terms

Product modification
Quality modifications
Functional modifications
Aesthetic modifications
New-product development
Idea generation
Idea screening
Concept testing

Business analysis
Product development
Test marketing
Commercialization
Warranty
Product adoption process
Product elimination

Discussion and Review Questions

1. Compare and contrast the three major ways of modifying a product.
2. Identify and briefly explain the seven major phases of the new-product development process.
3. Do small companies that manufacture one or two products need to be concerned about developing new products? Why or why not?
4. Why is product development a cross-functional activity within an organization? That is, why must finance, engineering, manufacturing, and other functional areas be involved?

5. Managers in some firms believe that they can omit the test-marketing stage. What are some of the advantages and disadvantages of test marketing?
6. What is the major purpose of concept testing and how is it accomplished?
7. What are the major tasks to be performed during the commercialization stage?
8. Why does commercialization sometimes take a considerable amount of time?
9. In what ways does the marketing strategy for a mature product differ from the marketing strategy for a growth product?
10. What types of problems are caused by a weak product in a product mix?
11. Why are marketers hesitant to drop weak products?
12. What is the most effective approach for eliminating weak products from the product mix?

Cases

9.1 Nabisco Enjoys Sweet Success with Teddy Grahams

Graham crackers: a cookie almost everyone loves but stops eating by the age of five. They've been around since the late 1800s, but until recently most cookie manufacturers considered graham crackers stodgy and antiquated, not fit for a "yuppie" society. However, the senior director of marketing at Nabisco Brands, Inc. believes that graham, with its "good-for-you" aura, is the right product for the times. When Nabisco came out with its first new line of cookies in years, what was it? Graham crackers. They don't look like graham crackers, but despite their tiny size and cute teddy bear shape, Teddy Grahams are still graham crackers.

Long the undisputed "cookie king" in the United States, Nabisco controls 34 percent of a market that ships over 1.5 billion pounds of product a year. Its Oreos and Chips Ahoy! are the two top-selling cookie brands. Success taught Nabisco that knowledge of current trends in the world of snack food greatly increases the chances that a new cookie will be a top seller. Before settling on the type of cookie they were going to introduce, Nabisco experts researched trade publications extensively. What did the research reveal? Miniaturizing foods, producing snacks that can be eaten right out of the box, is the number-one snack food trend. A society that eats on the move needs portable food. Parents driving their children all over town to gymnastics, baseball practice, and the mall need "hand-to-mouth" food to serve. The success of Sunshine's Grahamy Bears, Keebler's Townhouse Cheddar Jrs, and even Nabisco's own Ritz Bits is testimony to the popularity of "down-sizing" snack foods. In addition to the trend toward smaller size, Nabisco researchers discovered that clever snack shapes, especially animal shapes, attract shoppers. Finally, although statistics reveal that snacking in general is on the rise, consumers are increasingly health conscious, looking for foods with less fat, less cholesterol, and more fiber. Taking into account the results of its research, Nabisco came up with tiny, low-fat, high-fiber, chocolate, cinnamon, and honey-flavored, bear-shaped Teddy Grahams, hoping that these cookies would be small enough, cute enough, and healthy enough to be a winner.

Before introducing its tiny teddies, Nabisco did pre–market testing, selecting families to do in-home evaluations of the product. But because of its strength in the market and the scope of its sales and distribution—3,500 of its sales people call on stores several times a week—Nabisco felt no necessity to test-market Teddy Grahams before introducing them nationwide. Smaller or unestablished companies have to pay supermarket chains $60,000 to $80,000 in slotting fees to obtain initial shelf space and can display products only as long as they sell well. Nabisco was able to distribute Teddy Grahams and achieve immediate visibility without paying slotting fees.

To present Teddy Grahams to the public, Nabisco held a press conference at F.A.O. Schwartz, a prestigious New York toy store, featuring actress and child advocate Sally Struthers. Following this high-profile debut, Teddy Grahams burst onto the television screen with three oversized bears—"Teddy," "Freddy," and "Eddy"—singing, "Won't you let us be your Teddy Grahams," a takeoff on an Elvis Presley song. In keeping with its traditional advertising strategy, Nabisco restricted advertising to television, believing that television is more efficient than print. Thirty-second spots programmed on Saturday morning cartoons like "Ghostbusters" targeted the children's market with costuming, dance moves, and reference to "scrumptious taste." Airing during soap operas, game shows, and nighttime fare like "Lifestyles of the Rich and Famous," adult-oriented advertisements emphasized wholesomeness and fewer calories. In a scene designed to evoke a nostalgic response, the Beatles-like Rock'n Bears stepped down from a plane into a throng of screaming fans. Nabisco executives refused to disclose how much they spent on advertising their product, but according to trade journals, spots on network, syndicated, and cable channels cost Nabisco approximately $7.4 million during Teddy Graham's first nine months on the market. In addition to its television campaign, Nabisco promoted its product by giving away 200 million Teddy Graham coupons and offering a poster of the singing bears with proof of purchase.

Results of Nabisco's promotion and advertising are phenomenal. In a $3.5-billion-dollar industry, Nabisco could have made big profits even if it only captured a small portion of the market. But it sold $100 million worth of Teddy Grahams in the first six months, and by the end of the first year, captured 5 percent of the market and the number-three-selling cookie spot in the United States. Nabisco added a production line at its Philadelphia bakery just to produce Teddy Grahams, partly because store managers complained that Nabisco wasn't delivering the cookies fast enough to meet demand. Nabisco attributes the new cookie's success to its appealing taste, fun shape, and eye-catching packaging. But it also credits the company's strength and emphasis on product promotion for making consumers more receptive to something new from Nabisco.

Maintaining Teddy Grahams' momentum requires continued promotion and product development. Additions to the Teddy Grahams product line include vanilla-flavored cookies, snack packs featuring three individually wrapped packages in three different flavors, and T. G. Bearwich, a sweeter, cream-filled sandwich version of the original. There is a fan club, giving members a Teddy on Tour Fun Kit including a board game, music cassette, poster, and membership certificate when they enroll. The company hired a West Coast licensing firm to represent Teddy Grahams in licensing deals, paving the way for Teddy Graham T-shirts and toys. Nabisco is also taking its best-selling product from the cookie jar into the cereal bowl, introducing its first-ever children's cereal, Teddy Grahams Breakfast Bears. Nabisco is spending about $10 million to launch the new cereal, believing it is guaranteed a trial simply because of the cookie's popularity. The television advertisement features the now-famous bears singing an old rock-and-roll hit, "Wake Up Little Susie."

When Teddy Grahams came on to the market, the American Marketing Association named them one of that year's best new products. If sales are indicative of excellence, these little bears must be outstanding. The only recent snack product whose success approaches that of Teddy Grahams is Nabisco's Ritz Bits, but that tiny cracker is really a line extension of the already-popular larger Ritz Crackers. Teddy Grahams is not a Newton Bear or a Chips Ahoy! Bear. An old cracker formula with an innovative size and shape, Teddy Grahams are selling beyond expectations and rapidly becoming a new classic in what experts often label a "no-growth market."[16]

Questions for Discussion

1. Is Teddy Grahams a product modification or a new product for Nabisco? Discuss.
2. Evaluate Nabisco's decision not to test-market Teddy Grahams.
3. Why have Teddy Grahams become so successful?

9.2 Harley-Davidson's Product Management

Harley-Davidson Motor Co., headquartered in Milwaukee, has come roaring back to profitability after a decade of troubles. Strong competition from Japanese motorcycle manufacturers—Honda, Suzuki, Yamaha, and Kawasaki—caused Harley's market share for superheavyweight motorcycles (motorcycles with engine displacements greater than 850 cubic centimeters) to drop from 99.7 percent in 1972 to 23 percent in 1983. Harley's hard-core image—black leather jackets, chains, and tattooed riders—turned consumers off. More importantly, Harley simply could not compete with Japan's high-tech machines, low prices, and attractive designs. Company executives were forced to re-evaluate their entire organization. Largely because of its commitment to new-product development and improved product quality, Harley's net income has risen 38 percent to $32.9 million, and today Harley is once again the U.S. market share leader (almost 60 percent) for superheavyweight motorcycles.

Because of huge growth in the early 1970s, Harley was more interested in increasing production than in developing new products or improving product quality. The resulting motorcycles, infamous for being leaky and unreliable, were inferior and outdated when compared with Japanese vehicles. When Harley sales figures plummeted, its executives knew that they had to undertake drastic modifications to ensure the company's survival. They increased the annual research and development budget from $2 million to $14 million.

Realizing the importance of product quality, Harley product managers decided to turn to their customers for help. Instead of conducting extensive (and expensive) market research to determine what was wanted in or on a motorcycle, Harley executives communicated directly with customers, even attending meetings of the H.O.G. (Harley Owners Group). While mingling and listening, company representatives learned that bikers are very vocal about their likes and dislikes; enthusiasts are eager to share their views on Harley products and how they can be improved. Harley is equally eager to give its customers what they want.

Willie G. Davidson, Harley's vice president for styling and the grandson of one of the founders, began attending biker rallies to gather ideas for potential product innovations. Noticing that many bikers liked to customize their motorcycles after purchase, he suggested that Harley mimic this variety in the factory. The company would produce various models and options that would roll off the factory line and into the dealerships. In 1980, Harley engineers created a completely redesigned chassis and the new Nova line of engines, ranging from 883 to 1340 cubic centimeters displacement. These new engines made Harley products directly competitive with Japanese high-performance bikes. Davidson invented a new model, the Super Glide; then he introduced other successful models, such as the Low Rider and the Wide Glide. Currently enjoying great success is the Softail, called by many "Harley's ultimate custom bike." Bikers can now choose among twenty-eight Harley custom models, each with its own individual touch.

One senior vice president at Harley-Davidson views Davidson as an artistic genius. According to this executive, Davidson performed virtual miracles by simply manipulating decals and paint in the years before the company was able to bring new engines on-stream. Harley's survival may be due to the new models Davidson was able to create by cosmetically changing existing models. Japanese motorcycle makers have started copying Harley designs.

However, only about 5 percent of Japanese motorcycles fail to pass inspection when coming off the assembly line, compared with about 50–60 percent of new Harleys. This disappointing statistic, coupled with customer complaints, prompted the company to introduce its Quality Audit Program. A few days before a new model, the Cafe Racer, was scheduled to come off the production line, an employee shocked a Harley executive with news of severe defects in the model. Deciding to make the Cafe Racer the new symbol of Harley-Davidson product quality, the chief executive officer dispatched a team of engineers, service supervisors, and manufacturing managers to correct the problems. It cost the company about $100,000 to mend only a hundred Cafe Racers, but management believed that the investment in quality was worth it. Thereafter, the Quality Audit Program was applied to all models.

Harley improved the quality of its products by implementing three integrated programs: just-in-time manufacturing (called "materials-as-needed," or "MAN," at Harley), statistical operator control (SOC), and heavy reliance on employee involvement. The MAN system frees Harley from a bulky inventory and increases plant productivity. SOC gives assembly-line operators responsibility for the quality of individual parts and allows them to know before completing a faulty part that the system isn't working properly. By consulting with line operators, Harley managers and engineers have been able to improve manufacturing processes and consequently improve motorcycles. None of these successful programs required large capital investments; Harley improved product quality by enhancing procedures.

As Harley's foreign sales grow to about fifteen thousand bikes a year, demand for the company's motorcycles is currently outrunning supply. Never again complacent, Harley's product development strategies continue to evolve as the company grows stronger. The company has even called its new power train the Evolution Engine. Harley executives are determined to keep their customers happy and the product innovations rolling while keeping the bikes looking big, mean, and American.[17]

Questions for Discussion

1. Why did Harley's share of the superheavyweight motorcycle market drop so drastically between 1972 and 1983?
2. What sources did Harley use to generate new product ideas?
3. What steps has Harley taken to regain its competitiveness?

Chapter Notes

1. Based on information from James B. Treece, "The Streetwise Makeover of Chrysler's Minivans," *Business Week*, Sept. 24, 1990, pp. 110–113; Amy Duncan, "You Don't Have to Pay the Maximum for a Minivan," *Personal Business*, Apr. 30, 1990, pp. 120–121; Dan McCosh, "Automotive Newsfront," *Popular Science*, Apr. 1990, pp. 29–39; Raymond Serafin and Patricia Strnad, "Chrysler Readies for Van Fight," *Advertising Age*, Feb. 6, 1990, p. 50; Rich Taylor, "The Light Vantastics," *Popular Mechanics*, Feb. 1990, pp. 62–67; "Testing the New Vans," *Consumer Reports*, Feb. 1990, pp. 110–120; and Greg Gardner, "Mini-Van Wars Are a Show of Industry's Maximum Competition," *Detroit Free Press*, July 17, 1989.
2. Kim B. Clark and Takahiro Fujimoto, "The Power of Product Integrity," *Harvard Business Review*, November–December 1990, pp. 108–118.
3. "Product Development: Where Planning and Marketing Meet," *Journal of Business Strategy*, September–October 1990, pp. 13–16.
4. Peter F. Drucker, "The Discipline of Innovation," *Harvard Business Review*, May–June 1985, pp. 67–68.
5. Jonathan B. Levine, "Keeping New Ideas Kicking Around," *Business Week*, Innovation 1989 issue, p. 128.
6. Joseph Weber, "Going Over the Lab Wall in Search of New Ideas," *Business Week*, Innovation 1989 issue, p. 132.
7. Joshua Hyatt, "Ask and You Shall Receive," *Inc.*, September 1989, pp. 90–101.
8. "Oops! Marketers Blunder Their Way Through the 'Herb Decade,'" *Advertising Age*, Feb. 13, 1989, p. 66.
9. Fara Warner, "Clorox Dumps Its Detergents and Sticks to Core Brands," *Adweek's Marketing Week*, May 27, 1991, p. 6.
10. Leslie Brennan, "Meeting the Test," *Sales & Marketing Management*, Mar. 1990, pp. 57–60.
11. Marcy Magiera, "Red Turns to Men," *Advertising Age*, Apr. 29, 1991, p. 4.
12. Adapted from Everett M. Rogers, *Diffusion of Innovations* (New York: Macmillan, 1962), pp. 81–86.
13. F. Stewart DeBruicker and Gregory L. Summe, "Make Sure Your Customers Keep Coming Back," *Harvard Business Review*, January–February 1985, pp. 92–98.
14. Michael Paxton, "Company Study: Managing Mature Markets," *Journal of Consumer Marketing*, Summer 1991, pp. 63–67.
15. Douglas M. Lambert and Jay U. Sterling, "Identifying and Eliminating Weak Products," *Business*, July–September 1988, pp. 3–10.
16. Jon Berry, "Nabisco Unleashes a New Batch of Teddies," *Adweek's Marketing Week*, Sept. 24, 1990, p. 2; Brian Bagot, "Bear Essentials," *Marketing and Media Decisions*, Mar. 1990, pp. 71–73; Judann Dagnoli, "Making Breakfast Bear-able," *Advertising Age*, Oct. 16, 1989, pp. 3, 77; "Nabisco Subsidiary to Unveil Today New Line of Cookies," *Wall Street Journal*, Sept. 7, 1989, p. 32; Mark Meltzer, "Teddy Graham

Cookie Uses Recipe for Success," *(Lawrenceville, GA) Gwinnett Daily News,* Apr. 16, 1989; and Judith A. Osborne, "Nabisco, Sunshine Add Flavor to Market," *(Newark, NJ) Star-Ledger,* Feb. 6, 1989.

17. Robert L. Rose, "After Nearly Stalling, Harley-Davidson Finds New Crowd of Riders," *Wall Street Journal,* Aug. 31, 1990, pp. A1, A6; Kate Fitzgerald, "Kathleen Demitros Helps Spark Comeback at Harley-Davidson," *Advertising Age,* Jan. 8, 1990, p. 32; Peter C. Reid, *Well Made in America: Lessons From Harley-Davidson on Being the Best* (New York: McGraw-Hill, 1990); "How Harley Beat Back the Japanese," *Fortune,* Sept. 25, 1989, pp. 155, 157, 162, 164; Doron P. Levin, "Motorcycle Makers Shift Tactics," *New York Times,* Sept. 16, 1989, pp. 33, 46; Gary Miller, "Harley's Teerlink Thrives as Rank-and-File Kind of Guy," (Milwaukee, WI) *Business Journal,* July 17, 1989, TRN 39:E9; Vaughn Beals, "Operation Recovery," *Success,* Feb. 1989, p. 16; Tani Mayer, "Harley-Davidson Rides High," *Financial World,* Oct. 18, 1988, pp. 16, 18; and Vaughn Beals, "Harley-Davidson: An American Success Story," *Journal for Quality and Participation,* June 1988, pp. A19–A23.

10 Branding and Packaging

OBJECTIVES

- To understand the types and benefits of brands and how to select, protect, and license them

- To become aware of the major packaging functions and design considerations and how packaging is used in marketing strategies

- To examine the functions of labeling and the legal issues associated with labeling

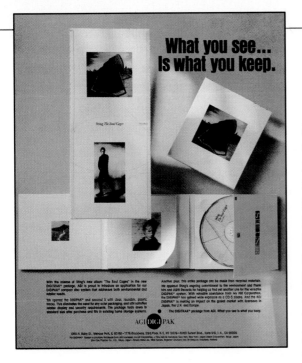

Music retailers in Europe and Japan rejected it. Canada banned it altogether. The Grateful Dead, Peter Gabriel, Sting, U2, and R.E.M., are among famous musical artists protesting against it. "It" is the bulky cardboard compact disc package, known as the longbox. The 6-inch by 12-inch longbox houses the 5-inch by 5 ½-inch "jewel box" containing the actual CD, and the packaging uses about twice as much paper as is needed. Every year, Americans purchase 250 million CDs whose packaging later becomes about 20 million pounds of trash. As more artists demanded environmentally responsible packaging, a "Ban the Box" movement gained momentum throughout the music industry.

Opposing the movement were many record manufacturers, dealers, and merchants. Retailers, especially those with smaller stores that can't afford expensive electronic antitheft devices, wanted to keep the longbox because its size discourages shoplifting. Because two CD longboxes fit precisely into a bin where one record album fit before, music retailers saved extensive remodeling costs by preserving that style of packaging.

In response to a record merchandiser's challenge to develop environmentally accountable prototypes, designers came up with a wide range of possibilities. The CD Browser Pack, thinner than the longbox, contains only the booklet and an inventory card that customers present at the counter to get the disc. Great Tapes displays the jewel box on a spinning rack that must be unlocked by a clerk. The Quadratag system eliminates the longbox and attaches a combination security-price tag directly to the jewel box. For one Sting release, A&M Records used Digi-Track packages comprised of materials stiff enough to stand without hard plastic boxes. The Eco-Pack, made mostly of recycled paper, folds down to become the disc's cover.

After continued pressure from environmentally-concerned performers and groups such as Ban the Box, the American recording industry opted for change. The president of the Recording Industry Association of America announced that six major U.S. record labels agreed to replace the longbox with a smaller, more ecological container.[1]

Photo: AGI Digi Pak

BRANDS AND PACKAGES are part of a product's tangible features, the verbal and physical cues that help customers identify the products they want and influence their choices when they are unsure. As such, branding and packaging play an important role in marketing strategy. A good brand is distinct and memorable; without one, firms could not differentiate their products, and shoppers' choices would essentially be arbitrary. A good package design is cost-effective, safe, environmentally responsible (such as the new compact disc packages), and valuable as a promotional tool.

In this chapter we define branding, including its benefits to customers and sellers, and the various types of brands. We then discuss how companies choose brands, how they protect them, the various branding policies that companies employ, and brand licensing. Next, we examine packaging's critical role as part of the product and how it is marketed. We explore the functions of packaging, issues to consider in packaging design, how the package can be a major element in marketing strategy, and packaging criticisms. We conclude with a discussion of labeling and other product-related features, including the product's physical characteristics and supportive product-related services.

Branding

In addition to making decisions about actual products, marketers must make many decisions associated with branding, such as brands, brand names, brand marks, trademarks, and trade names. A **brand** is a name, term, design, symbol, or any other feature that identifies one seller's good or service as distinct from those of other sellers. A brand may identify one item, a family of items, or all items of that seller.[2] A **brand name** is that part of a brand that can be spoken—including letters, words, and numbers—such as 7 Up. A brand name is often a product's only distinguishing characteristic. Without the brand name, a firm could not identify its products. To consumers, brand names are as fundamental as the product itself. Brand names simplify shopping, guarantee a specific level of quality, and allow self-expression.[3] Table 10.1 lists the twenty most powerful brands in the United States and the twenty most powerful brands in the world based on surveys of over ten thousand respondents in the United States, Japan, and Europe. These ratings reflect both brand recognition (awareness) and esteem scores.

The element of a brand that is not made up of words, but is often a symbol or design, is called a **brand mark**. One example is the red-and-white checkerboard square on Ralston Purina pet foods and Chex cereals. A **trademark** is a legal designation indicating that the owner has exclusive use of a brand or a part of a brand and that others are prohibited by law from using it. To protect a brand name or brand mark in the United States, an organization must register it as a trademark with the U.S. Patent and Trademark Office. As of 1990, the Patent and Trademark Office had 680,000 trademark registrations—100,000 more than in 1984.[4] Finally, a **trade name** is the full and legal name of an organization, such as Ford Motor Company, rather than the name of a specific product.

World	United States	World	United States
1. Coca-Cola	1. Coca-Cola	11. Rolls-Royce	11. Levi's
2. Sony	2. Campbell's	12. Honda	12. GE
3. Mercedes-Benz	3. Disney	13. Panasonic	13. Sears
4. Kodak	4. Pepsi-Cola	14. Levi's	14. Hallmark
5. Disney	5. Kodak	15. Kleenex	15. Johnson & Johnson
6. Nestlé	6. NBC	16. Ford	16. Betty Crocker
7. Toyota	7. Black & Decker	17. Volkswagen	17. Kraft
8. McDonald's	8. Kellogg's	18. Kellogg's	18. Kleenex
9. IBM	9. McDonald's	19. Porsche	19. Jell-O
10. Pepsi-Cola	10. Hershey's	20. Polaroid	20. Tylenol

Source: Landor Associates' ImagePower Survey, 1990 (New York). Used by permission.

Table 10.1   **The Twenty Most Powerful Brands in the World and the Twenty Most Powerful Brands in the United States**

Benefits of Branding

Branding provides benefits for both buyers and sellers. Brands help buyers identify specific products that they do and do not like, which in turn facilitates the purchase of items that satisfy their needs and reduces the time required to purchase the product. Without brands, product selection would be quite random because buyers could have no assurance that they were purchasing what they preferred. A brand also helps buyers evaluate the quality of products, especially when they are unable to judge a product's characteristics. That is, a brand may symbolize a certain quality level to a purchaser, and in turn the person lets that perception of quality represent the quality of the item. A brand helps to reduce a buyer's perceived risk of purchase. In addition, a brand may offer a psychological reward that comes from owning a brand that symbolizes status. Certain brands of watches (Rolex) and automobiles (Mercedes-Benz), for example, fall into this category.

Sellers benefit from branding because each company's brands identify its products, which makes repeat purchasing easier for consumers. Branding helps a firm introduce a new product that carries the name of one or more of its existing products because buyers are already familiar with the firm's existing brands. Branding also facilitates promotional efforts because the promotion of each branded product indirectly promotes all other products that are similarly branded.

Branding also helps sellers by fostering brand loyalty. To the extent that buyers become loyal to a specific brand, the company's market share for that product achieves a certain level of stability, allowing the firm to use its resources more efficiently. When a firm develops some degree of customer loyalty to a brand, it can charge a premium price for the product. For example, brand loyal buyers of Bayer aspirin are willing to pay two or three times more for Bayer than

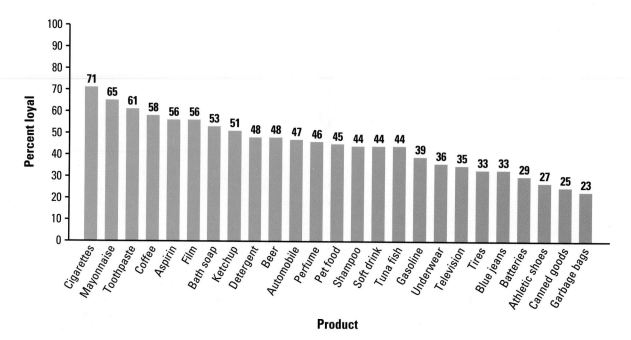

Figure 10.1 **Percentage of Users of Selected Products Who Are Loyal to One Brand**
Source: *Wall Street Journal*, Oct. 19, 1989, p. B1. Reprinted by permission of the *Wall Street Journal,* © 1989 Dow Jones & Company, Inc. All Rights Reserved Worldwide.

for a store brand of aspirin even though both have the same amount of pain-relieving agent. However, brand loyalty is declining, partly because of marketers' increased reliance on sales, coupons, and other short-term promotions, and partly because of the sometimes overwhelming array of similar new products from which consumers can choose. A *Wall Street Journal* survey found that 12 percent of consumers are not loyal to any brand, whereas 47 percent are brand loyal for one to five product types. Only 2 percent of the respondents were brand loyal for more than sixteen product types (see Figure 10.1). To stimulate loyalty to their brands, some marketers are stressing image advertising, mailing personalized catalogs and magazines to regular users, and creating membership clubs for brand users.[5]

Types of Brands

There are three categories of brands: manufacturer brands, private distributor brands, and generic brands. **Manufacturer brands** are initiated by producers and ensure that producers are identified with their products at the point of purchase—for example, Green Giant, Apple Computer, and Levi's jeans (see Figure 10.2). A manufacturer brand usually requires a producer to become involved in distribution, promotion, and, to some extent, pricing decisions. Brand loyalty is encouraged by promotion, quality control, and guarantees; it is a valuable asset to a manufacturer. The producer tries to stimulate demand for the product, which tends to encourage middlemen to make the product available.

Private distributor brands (also called **private brands**, **store brands**, or **dealer brands**), are initiated and owned by resellers—wholesalers or retailers.

The major characteristic of private brands is that the manufacturers are not identified on the products. Retailers and wholesalers use private distributor brands to develop more efficient promotion, to generate higher gross margins, and to improve store images. Private distributor brands give retailers or wholesalers freedom to purchase products of a specified quality at the lowest cost without disclosing the identity of the manufacturer. Wholesaler brands include IGA (Independent Grocers' Alliance) and Topmost (General Grocer). Familiar retailer brand names include Sears' Kenmore and J.C. Penney's Stafford Executive (see Figure 10.2). Many successful private brands are distributed nationally. Sears' Kenmore washers are as well known as most manufacturer brands. Sometimes retailers with successful distributor brands start manufacturing their own products to gain more control over product costs, quality, and design with the hope of increasing profits. While one might think that store brands have their strongest appeal among either lower-income shoppers or upscale shoppers who compare labels, studies indicate that private brand buyers have characteristics that match those of the overall population.[6]

Some marketers of products that have traditionally been branded have embarked on a policy of not branding, often called generic branding. A **generic brand** indicates only the product category (such as aluminum foil) and does not include the company name or other identifying terms. Usually generic brands are sold at lower prices than are comparable branded items. Although at one time generic brands may have represented as much as 10 percent of all retail grocery sales, today they account for less than 1 percent.[7]

Figure 10.2   **Type of Brands**   Levi's is a manufacturer brand. Stafford, owned and sold by J.C. Penney, is a private brand.   Sources: Levi Strauss and Company; Courtesy of J.C. Penney.

Competition between manufacturer brands and private distributor brands (sometimes called "the battle of the brands") is intensifying in several major product categories, particularly cheese, orange juice, sugar, and soft drinks. Private distributor brands now account for slightly over 18 percent of all retail grocery sales.[8] As shown in Figure 10.3, both men and women are quite favorable toward private brands of food products, with women (still the major grocery purchasers) even more favorable than men. For manufacturers, developing multiple manufacturer brands and distribution systems has been an effective means of combating the increased competition from private brands. By developing a new brand name, a producer can adjust various elements of a marketing mix to appeal to a different target market. For example, Scott Paper has developed lower-priced brands of paper towels; it has tailored its new products to a target market that tends to purchase private brands.

Manufacturers find it hard to ignore the marketing opportunities that come from producing private distributor brands for resellers. If a manufacturer refuses to produce a private brand for a reseller, a competing manufacturer will. Moreover, the production of private distributor brands allows the manufacturer to use excess capacity during periods when its own brands are at nonpeak production. The ultimate decision whether to produce a private or a manufacturer brand depends on a company's resources, production capabilities, and goals.

Selecting a Brand Name

Marketers should consider a number of factors when they select a brand name. The name should be easy for customers (including foreign buyers, if the firm intends to market its products in other countries) to say, spell, and recall. Short, one-syllable names such as Cheer often satisfy this requirement. The brand name should indicate the product's major benefits and, if possible, should suggest in a positive way the product's uses and special characteristics; negative or offensive references should be avoided. For example, a deodorant should be branded with a name that connotes freshness, dryness, or long-lasting protection, as do Ban, Dry Idea, and Ice Blue Secret. The brand should be distinctive, to set it apart from competing brands. If a marketer intends to use a brand for a product line,

Figure 10.3

Preference for Private Brands of Food Products by Age and Sex

Source: *Yankelovich Monitor,* © 1991. Used by permission.

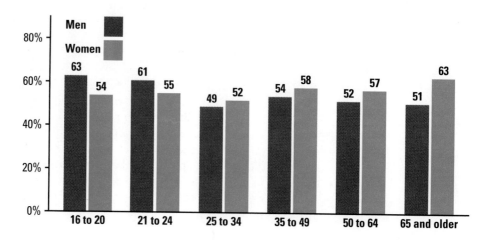

it must be compatible with all products in the line. Finally, a brand should be designed so that it can be used and recognized in all of the various types of media. Finding the right brand name has become a challenging task because many obvious product names have already been used. In 1990, the U.S. Patent and Trademark Office registered 56,515 new trademarks, over three times the number registered in 1980.[9]

How are brand names derived? Brand names can be created from single or multiple words—for example, Bic or Dodge Grand Caravan. Initials, numbers, or sometimes combinations are used to create brands such as IBM PC or PS 2. At times, words, numbers, and initials are combined to yield brand names such as Mazda RX7 or Mitsubishi 3000GT. To avoid terms that have negative connotations, marketers sometimes use fabricated words that have absolutely no meaning at the point that they are created—for example, Kodak and Exxon. Occasionally, a brand is simply brought out of storage and used as is or is modified. Firms often maintain banks of registered brands, some of which may have been used in the past. Cadillac, for example, has a bank of approximately 360 registered trademarks. The LaSalle brand, used in the 1920s and 1930s, may be called up for a new Cadillac model soon to be introduced.[10] Possible brand names sometimes are tested in focus groups or in other settings to assess customers' reactions.

Who actually creates brand names? Brand names can be created internally by the organization. Sometimes a name is suggested by individuals who are close to the development of the product. Some organizations have committees that participate in brand name creation and approval. Large companies that introduce numerous new products annually are likely to have a department that develops brand names. At times, outside consultants are used in the process of developing brand names. An organization may also hire a company that specializes in brand name development.

Even though most of the important branding considerations apply to both goods and services, services branding has some additional dimensions. The brand of the service is usually the same as the company name. For example, American Express, Paine Webber, Lube King, Kwik-Kopy, and Sheraton are names of companies and the services that they provide. Whereas companies that produce tangible goods (such as Procter & Gamble) can use separate brand names for separate products (such as Prell, Head & Shoulders, Pert Plus, and Ivory), service providers (such as United Air Lines) are perceived by customers as having one brand name, even though they offer multiple products (first class, business class, and coach). Because the service brand name and company name are so closely interrelated, a service brand name must be flexible enough to encompass a variety of current services as well as new ones that the company might offer in the future. Geographical references like "western" and descriptive terms like "trucking" limit the scope of associations that can be made with the brand name. "Northwest Airlines" is not a good name if the company begins flying south and east. But "Humana," with its connotations of kindness and compassion, is flexible enough to encompass all services that the company offers—hospitals, insurance plans, and health care memberships.[11] Frequently, a service marketer will employ a symbol along with its brand name to make the brand distinctive and to communicate a certain image. For example, Merrill Lynch uses a bull, AT&T uses a globe, and Travelers' Insurance uses an umbrella, as shown in Figure 10.4.

Figure 10.4

Using a Symbol with a Brand Name

Traveler's Insurance uses an umbrella to make its brand distinctive. Marketers hope this symbol will conjure images of safety and protection for consumers.

Source: The Traveler's Insurance Company.

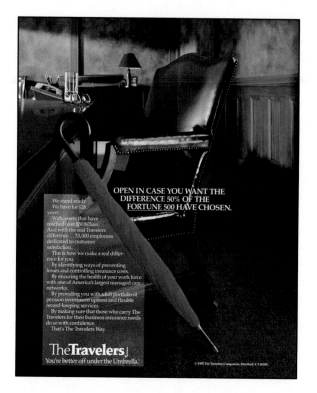

Protecting a Brand

A marketer should also design a brand that can be protected easily through registration. A series of court decisions has created a broad hierarchy of protection based on brand type. From most protectable to least protectable, these brand types are fanciful (Exxon), arbitrary (Dr Pepper), suggestive (Spray 'n Wash), descriptive (Minute Rice), and generic (aluminum foil). Generic words are not protectable. Surnames and descriptive geographic or functional names are difficult to protect.[12] Because of their designs, some brands can be legally infringed upon more easily than others. Although registration protects trademarks domestically for ten years and can be renewed indefinitely, a firm should develop a system for ensuring that its trademarks will be renewed as needed. To protect its exclusive rights to a brand, the company must make certain that the selected brand is not likely to be considered an infringement on any existing brand already registered with the U.S. Patent and Trademark Office. This task may be complex because infringement is determined by the courts, which base their decisions on whether a brand causes consumers to be confused, mistaken, or deceived about the source of the product. McDonald's is one company that aggressively protects its trademarks against infringement; it has brought charges against a number of companies with "Mc" names because it fears that the use of the "Mc" will give consumers the impression that these companies are associated with or owned by McDonald's.

If possible, a marketer must guard against allowing a brand name to become a generic term used to refer to a general product category. Generic terms cannot be protected as exclusive brand names. For example, names such as aspirin, escalator, and shredded wheat—all brand names at one time—eventually were declared generic terms that refer to product classes; thus they no longer could be protected. To keep a brand name from becoming a generic term, the firm should spell the name with a capital letter and use it as an adjective to modify the name of the general product class, as in Kool-Aid Brand Soft Drink Mix.[13] Including the word *brand* just after the brand name is also helpful. An organization can deal with this problem directly by advertising that its brand is a trademark and should not be used generically. The firm can also indicate that the brand is a registered trademark by using the symbol ®.

To strengthen trademark protection, Congress enacted the 1988 Trademark Law Revision Act, which is the only major federal trademark legislation since the Lanham Act passed in 1946. The purpose of this recent legislation is to increase the value of the federal registration system for U.S. firms relative to foreign competitors and to better protect the public from counterfeiting, confusion, and deception.[14]

A U.S. firm that tries to protect a brand in a foreign country frequently encounters problems. In many countries, brand registration is not possible; the first firm to use a brand in such a country has the rights to it. In some instances, a U.S. company actually has had to buy its own brand rights from a firm in a foreign country because the foreign firm was the first user in that country.

Marketers trying to protect their brands must also contend with brand counterfeiting. In the United States, for instance, one can purchase fake General Motors parts, fake Cartier watches, fake Jordache jeans, fake Vuitton handbags, fake Walt Disney character dolls, and a host of other products that are illegally marketed by manufacturers that do not own the brands. Many counterfeit products are manufactured overseas—in South Korea, Italy, or Taiwan, for example—but some are counterfeited in the United States. The International Anti-Counterfeiting Coalition estimates that roughly $60 billion in annual world trade involves counterfeit merchandise. The sale of this merchandise, obviously, reduces the brand owners' revenues from marketing their own legitimate products.

Brand counterfeiting is particularly harmful because the usually inferior counterfeit product undermines consumers' confidence in the brand and their loyalty to it. After unknowingly purchasing a counterfeit product, the buyer may blame the legitimate manufacturer if the product is of low quality or—even worse—if its use results in damage or injury. Since the counterfeiting problem has grown so serious, many firms are taking legal action against counterfeiters. Others have adopted such measures as modifying the product or the packaging to make counterfeit items easier to detect, conducting public awareness campaigns, and monitoring distributors to ensure that they stock only legitimate brands.[15]

Branding Policies

Before it establishes branding policies, a firm must first decide whether to brand its products at all. If a company's product is homogeneous and similar to competitors' products, it may be difficult to brand. Raw materials—such as coal, sand, and farm produce—are hard to brand because of the homogeneity of such products and their physical characteristics.

If a firm chooses to brand its products, it may opt for one or more of the following branding policies: individual, overall family, line family, and brand-extension branding. **Individual branding** is a policy of naming each product differently. Procter & Gamble relies on an individual branding policy for its line of detergents, which includes Tide, Bold, Dash, Cheer, and Oxydol. A major advantage of individual branding is that if an organization introduces a poor product, the negative images associated with it do not contaminate the company's other products. An individual branding policy may also facilitate market segmentation when a firm wishes to enter many segments of the same market. Separate, unrelated names can be used, and each brand can be aimed at a specific segment.

In **overall family branding**, all of a firm's products are branded with the same name or at least part of the name, such as Kraft. In some cases, a company's name is combined with other words to brand items. Arm & Hammer uses its name on all its products along with a generic description of the item, such as Arm & Hammer Heavy Duty Detergent, Arm & Hammer Pure Baking Soda, and Arm & Hammer Carpet Deodorizer. Unlike individual branding, overall family branding means that the promotion of one item with the family brand promotes the firm's other products.

Sometimes an organization uses family branding only for products within a single line. This policy is called **line family branding**. Procter & Gamble, for example, produces a line of soaps in several forms and for different uses, all

Figure 10.5

Line Family Branding

Heinz USA uses line family branding in that it uses the Heinz name for condiments and baby food, but uses other names for different lines. These other lines include Weight Watchers dietetic foods, Chico San rice cakes, Alba dry milk products, and Near East boxed rice products.

Source: Heinz USA

under the name Ivory. Procter & Gamble also produces several brands of tooth-paste, none of which carry the Ivory brand. As depicted in Figure 10.5, Heinz USA uses line family branding.

Brand-extension branding occurs when a firm uses one of its existing brand names as part of a brand for an improved or new product that is usually in the same product category as the existing brand. The makers of Arrid deodorant eventually extended the name Arrid to Arrid Extra-Dry and Arrid XX. There is one major difference between line family branding and brand-extension brand-ing. With line family branding, all products in the line carry the same name, but with brand-extension branding, this is not the case. The producer of Arrid deodorant, for example, also makes other brands of deodorants. Line family branding and brand-extension branding are popular. Of the 6,125 new products introduced in the first five months of 1991, 95 percent were brand or line extensions.[16] Inside Marketing focuses on some of the advantages and disadvantages of brand extensions.

An organization is not limited to a single branding policy. Instead, branding policy is influenced by the number of products and product lines the company produces, the characteristics of its target markets, the number and types of competing products available, and the size of its resources. Anheuser-Busch, Inc., for example, uses both individual and brand-extension branding. Most of the brands are individual brands; however, the Michelob Light brand is an extension of the Michelob brand.

Brand Licensing

A recent trend in branding strategies involves the licensing of trademarks. By means of a licensing agreement, a company may permit approved manufacturers to use its trademark on other products for a licensing fee. Royalties may be as low as 2 percent of wholesale revenues or better than 10 percent. The licensee is responsible for all manufacturing, selling, and advertising functions and bears the costs if the licensed product fails. Not long ago, only a few firms licensed their corporate trademarks but today licensing is a multibillion dollar business, and it is growing. Harley-Davidson, for example, has authorized the use of its name on nonmotorcycle products such as cologne, wine coolers, gold rings, and shirts. McDonald's has licensed a line of children's sportswear, called McKids, to Sears.

The advantages of licensing range from extra revenues and low cost to free publicity, new images, and trademark protection. For example, Coca-Cola has licensed its trademark for use on glassware, radios, trucks, and clothing in the hope of protecting its trademark. Similarly, Winnebago Industries licensed a line of tents, air mattresses, and other camping gear to keep its name from becoming a generic term for "recreational vehicle." However, brand licensing is not with-out drawbacks. The major ones are a lack of manufacturing control, which could hurt the company's name, and bombarding consumers with too many unrelated products bearing the same name. Licensing arrangements can also fail because of poor timing, inappropriate distribution channels, or mismatching of product and name.

Brand Extensions: Lucrative or Dangerous?

ARM & HAMMER INTRODUCES a carpet deodorizer and an oven cleaner bearing the same name. Arrid Deodorant is followed by Arrid Extra-Dry, which is followed by Arrid XX. These products are examples of brand extension, the practice of using an existing brand name as part of a brand for an improved or new product. Similar to movie sequels, such as "Back to the Future III" and "Rocky V," these products are designed to capitalize on their parents' successes. Marketers hope that an older brand's familiarity to consumers and the positive associations they have with it will induce them to buy the new one. But some experts warn that brand extension is not a panacea and advise companies to proceed with caution when considering this alternative.

Two advantages of brand extension are lower product introduction costs and better chances for success in the marketplace. Rather than risk the expense involved in introducing a new product—between $50 million and $100 million—companies gravitate toward less expensive brand extension. The cost of test marketing may be reduced by using brand extensions, and the cost for advertising and promotion is about one-third less per customer for extensions than for completely new products. Evidence indicates that success is more likely for a product with an old name. In a recent study of ninety-three supermarket products, two-thirds of those grossing over $15 million were brand extensions. Consumers, reassured by a proven brand name, are more likely to try a related newcomer. Examples of highly successful brand extensions include Sunkist Juice Bars, Jell-O Pudding Pops, Tartar Control Crest, and diet Coke.

Some potential disadvantages in marketing brand extensions warrant consideration. When consumers associate too many products with one brand name, marketers are risking "putting all the company eggs in one basket." If one product is harmful, or defective, or merely unpopular, sales of all products with that name can suffer. Overextension occurs by introducing too many products with the parent brand's name. Consumers may become confused and a brand's identity undermined. Can Betty Crocker, for example, introduce dry packaged salads without diluting its image as a producer of quality cake mixes? Cannibalization, when brand extensions compete too directly with their own parent brands, can reduce sales of previously well received products. Unsuccessful attempts at brand extension are well documented. Levi Strauss, long-time leader among jeans and casual clothing manufacturers, attempted to sell slacks and blazers marketed as "classically tailored clothes from Levi's." Associating Levi's strongly with blue jeans and a casual lifestyle, men who buy classically tailored clothes rejected the line, and it failed.

Some debunkers of brand extension warn that the current trend toward extending existing brands rather than introducing innovative new ones will stifle product innovation. Procter & Gamble has not introduced a new brand in two years, and Kraft General Foods has no new products on the drawing board.

Will consumers continue to be satisfied with familiar products and their sequels? Probably yes, says a Nielsen Marketing Research study that revealed that nineteen out of twenty-two best-selling brands from 1925 or before still led their product categories sixty years later.

Sources: Karen Springen and Annetta Miller, "Sequels for the Shelf," *Newsweek*, July 9, 1990, pp. 42–43; David Aaker, "Brand Extensions: The Good, the Bad, and the Ugly," *Sloan Management Review*, Summer 1990, pp. 47–56; "Brand-Stretching Can Be Fun—and Dangerous," *The Economist*, May 5, 1990, pp. 77–78, 80; Peter Doyle, "Building Successful Brands: The Strategic Options," *Journal of Consumer Marketing*, Spring 1990, pp. 5–20; Patricia Winters, "Diet Coke's Formula: Stress Taste, Not Calories," *Advertising Age*, Jan. 1, 1990, p. 16; David A. Aaker and Kevin Lane Keller, "Consumer Evaluations of Brand Extensions," *Journal of Marketing*, Jan. 1990, pp. 27–41; and Tom Buday, "Capitalizing on Brand Extensions," *Journal of Consumer Marketing*, Fall 1989, pp. 27–30.

Packaging

Packaging involves the development of a container and a graphic design for a product. A package can be a vital part of a product, making it more versatile, safer, or easier to use. Like a brand name, a package can influence customers' attitudes toward a product and so affect their purchase decisions. For example, several producers of jellies, sauces, and ketchups have packaged their products in squeezable containers to make use and storage more convenient. Package characteristics help shape buyers' impressions of a product at the time of purchase or during use. In this section we examine the main functions of packaging and consider several major packaging decisions. We also analyze the role of the package in a marketing strategy.

Packaging Functions

Effective packaging means more than simply putting products in containers and covering them with wrappers. First of all, packaging materials serve the basic purpose of protecting the product and maintaining its functional form. Fluids such as milk, orange juice, and hair spray need packages that preserve and protect them; the packaging should prevent damage that could affect the product's usefulness and increase costs. Since product tampering has become a problem for marketers of many types of goods, several packaging techniques have been developed to counter this danger. Some packages are also designed to foil shoplifting.

Another function of packaging is to offer convenience for consumers. For example, small aseptic packages—individual-sized boxes or plastic bags that contain liquids and do not require refrigeration—strongly appeal to children and young adults with active lifestyles. The size or shape of a package may relate to the product's storage, convenience of use, or replacement rate. Small, single-serving cans of vegetables, for instance, may prevent waste and make storage easier. A third function of packaging is to promote a product by communicating its features, uses, benefits, and image. At times, a reusable package is developed to make the product more desirable. For example, the Cool Whip package doubles as a food-storage container.

Major Packaging Considerations

As they develop packages, marketers must take many factors into account. Obviously, one major consideration is cost. Although a variety of packaging materials, processes, and designs is available, some are rather expensive. In recent years, buyers have shown a willingness to pay more for improved packaging, but there are limits. Marketers should try to determine, through research, just how much customers are willing to pay for packages.

As already mentioned, developing tamper-resistant packaging is very important. Although no package is tamper-proof, marketers can develop packages that are difficult to tamper with. At a minimum, all packaging must comply with the Food and Drug Administration's packaging regulations. However, packaging should also make any product tampering evident to resellers and consumers.

Because new, safer packaging technologies are being explored, marketers should be aware of changes in packaging technology and legislation and be prepared to make modifications that will ensure consumer safety. One packaging innovation includes an inner pouch that displays the word *open* when air has entered the pouch after opening. Marketers also have an obligation to inform the public of the possibilities and risks of product tampering by educating consumers on how to recognize possible tampering and by placing warnings on packaging.[17] For example, nonprescription medications such as Advil are typically packaged in plastic containers with protective foil seals under child-proof caps; the container is then packaged in a cardboard box. Both the box and the container carry warnings stating, "If imprinted foil seal under cap is broken or missing when purchased, do not use." Although effective tamper-resistant packaging may be expensive to develop, when balanced against the costs of lost sales, loss of consumer confidence and company reputation, and potentially expensive product liability lawsuits, the costs of ensuring consumer safety are minimal.[18]

Marketers should consider how much consistency is desirable among an organization's package designs. No consistency may be the best policy, especially if a firm's products are unrelated or aimed at vastly different target markets. To promote an overall company image, a firm may decide that all packages are to be similar or include one major element of the design. This approach is called **family packaging**. Sometimes it is used only for lines of products, as with Campbell soups, Weight Watchers foods, and Planters nuts.

A package's promotional role is an important consideration. Through verbal and nonverbal symbols, the package can inform potential buyers about the product's content, features, uses, advantages, and hazards. A firm can create desirable images and associations by its choice of color, design, shape, and texture. Many cosmetics manufacturers, for example, design their packages to create impressions of richness, luxury, and exclusiveness. A package performs a promotional function when it is designed to be safer or more convenient to use, if such characteristics help stimulate demand.

To develop a package that has a definite promotional value, a designer must consider size, shape, texture, color, and graphics. Beyond the obvious limitation that the package must be large enough to hold the product, a package can be designed to appear taller or shorter. For instance, thin vertical lines make a package look taller; wide horizontal stripes make it look shorter. A marketer may want a package to appear taller because many people perceive something that is taller as being larger.

Colors on packages are often chosen to attract attention. People associate specific colors with certain feelings and experiences. Red, for example, is linked with fire, blood, danger, and anger; yellow suggests sunlight, caution, warmth, and vitality; blue can imply coldness, sky, water, and sadness.[19] When selecting packaging colors, marketers must decide whether a particular color will evoke positive or negative feelings when it is linked to a specific product. Rarely, for example, do processors package meat or bread in green materials because customers may associate green with mold. Marketers must also decide whether a specific target market will respond favorably or unfavorably to a particular color. Cosmetics for women are more likely to be sold in pastel packaging than are personal-care products for men. Packages designed to appeal to children often use primary colors and bold designs.

Packaging must also meet the needs of resellers. Wholesalers and retailers consider whether a package facilitates transportation, storage, and handling. Resellers may refuse to carry certain products if their packages are cumbersome.

A final consideration is whether to develop packages that are environmentally responsible. A Cable News Network report on the growing garbage disposal problem in the United States stated that nearly 50 percent of all garbage consists of discarded plastic packaging, such as polystyrene containers, plastic soft-drink bottles, carryout bags, and other packaging.[20] Plastic packaging material does not biodegrade, and paper requires the destruction of valuable forest lands. Consequently, a number of companies are exploring packaging alternatives; they are also recycling more materials. Lever Brothers uses recycled plastic as mentioned in Figure 10.6. Procter & Gamble markets Downy fabric softener in concentrated form, which requires less packaging than the ready-to-use version; H. J. Heinz is looking for alternatives to its plastic ketchup squeeze bottles. Customers' responses to Wendy's new paper plates and coffee cups have been mixed; some customers prefer the old nondegradable foam packages. Other companies searching for alternatives to environmentally harmful packaging have experienced similar problems.[21] Thus marketers must carefully balance society's desires to preserve the environment against consumers' desires for convenience. Environmental packaging issues in global markets are discussed in the Global Perspective.

Packaging and Marketing Strategy

Packaging can be a major component of a marketing strategy. A new cap or closure, a better box or wrapper, or a more convenient container may give a

Figure 10.6

Environmentally Responsible Packages

Lever Brothers has determined that in addition to having convenient, quality products, helping protect the environment is a major concern for consumers. To address this, they have taken the responsibility of using recyclable plastic in their packages.

Source: Courtesy of Lever Brothers.

product a competitive advantage. The right type of package for a new product can help it gain market recognition very quickly. In the case of existing brands, marketers should reevaluate packages periodically. Especially for consumer convenience products, marketers should view packaging as a major strategic tool. In this section we examine several ways in which packaging can be used strategically.

Altering the Package At times, a marketer changes a package because the existing design is no longer in style, especially when compared with competitive products. Quaker Oats had a package design company redesign its Rice-A-Roni package to give the product the appearance of having evolved with the times but still having its traditional taste appeal. Rice-A-Roni sales jumped 44 percent in one year, with no other marketing mix changes.[22] A package also may be redesigned because new product features need to be highlighted on the package, or because new packaging materials have become available. An organization may decide to change a product's packaging to make the product more convenient or safer to use, or to reposition the product. A major redesign of a simple package costs about $20,000, and the redesign for a line of products may cost up to $250,000.[23]

Secondary-Use Packaging   A secondary-use package is one that can be reused for purposes other than its initial use. For example, a margarine container can be reused to store leftovers, a jelly container can be used as a drinking glass, and a L'eggs egg can be used for making crafts, such as Christmas tree ornaments. Secondary-use packages can be viewed by customers as adding value to products. If customers value this type of packaging, then its use should stimulate unit sales.

Category-Consistent Packaging Category-consistent packaging means that the product is packaged in line with the packaging practices associated with a particular product category. Some product categories—for example, mayonnaise, mustard, ketchup, and peanut butter—have traditional package shapes. Other product categories are characterized by recognizable color combinations—red and white for soup; red and yellow for tea; red, white, and blue for Ritz-like crackers. When an organization introduces a brand in one of these product categories, marketers will often use traditional package shapes and color combinations to ensure that customers will recognize the new product as being in that specific product category.

Innovative Packaging   Sometimes, a marketer will employ a unique cap, design, applicator, or other feature to make the product competitively distinctive. Using such packaging can be effective when the innovation makes the product safer or easier to use, or when the unique package provides better protection for the product (as shown in Figure 10.7). In some instances, marketers use innovative or unique packages that are inconsistent with traditional packaging practices to make the brand stand out relative to its competitors. Procter & Gamble, for example, used an innovative crush-proof cylinder to package its Pringles potato chips. Innovative packaging generally requires a considerable amount of resources, not only in package design but also in making customers aware of the unique package and its benefit.

Figure 10.7

Innovative Packaging

Sanka brand coffee is packaged in innovative vacuum packs to protect and seal in its fresh taste.

Source: Sanka is a registered trademark of Kraft General Foods, Inc. Reproduced with permission.

Multiple Packaging Rather than packaging a single unit of the product, marketers sometimes use twin packs, tri-packs, six-packs, or other forms of multiple packaging. For certain types of products, multiple packaging is used to increase demand because it increases the amount of the product available at the point of consumption (in one's house, for example). However, multiple packaging does not work for all types of products. One would not use additional table salt simply because an extra box is in the pantry. Multiple packaging can make products easier to handle and store, as in the case of six-packs for soft drinks; it can also facilitate special price offers, such as two-for-one sales. In addition, multiple packaging may increase consumer acceptance of the product by encouraging the buyer to try the product several times.

Handling-Improved Packaging Packaging of a product may be changed to make it easier to handle in the distribution channel—for example, changing the outer carton, special bundling, shrink-wrapping, or palletizing. In some cases the shape of the package may need to be changed. For example, an ice-cream producer may change from a cylindrical package to a rectangular one to facilitate handling. In addition, at the retail level, the ice-cream producer may be able to get more shelf-facings with a rectangular package as opposed to a round one. Outer containers for products are sometimes changed so that they will proceed more easily through automated warehousing systems.

As package designs improve, it becomes harder for any one product to dominate because of packaging. However, marketers still attempt to gain a competitive edge through packaging. Skilled artists and package designers who have

Packaging for Global Markets

THROUGHOUT EASTERN EUROPE and the former Soviet Union, capitalism is taking the place of communism. Economies are growing in Japan, Korea, and other Pacific Rim countries. Formerly isolationist China is making tentative gestures toward international commerce. To remain competitive, American firms are turning to global markets. The world may be a smaller place, but as the globe shrinks, the marketplace expands. To successfully market products on a global scale, attention to packaging is essential. Experts agree that firms need to package products to meet specific governmental regulations and appeal to people in specific cultures.

To market products in Europe, firms must meet increasingly strict environmental regulations regarding packaging. The European Community is considering a directive requiring that 60 percent of packaging waste be recoverable for recycling or other uses, and international marketers are already repackaging environmentally friendly brand extensions. As part of a program called Duales System Deutschland, manufacturers, including U.S. firms Procter & Gamble and Unilever United States, are marking products with a green spot that indicates their packaging is part of a recycling system. Analysts predict that products carrying the green spot will be big sellers with environmentally concerned shoppers. In many of its European markets, Procter & Gamble sells Ariel liquid detergent in plastic bottles and refill pouches made from 25 percent recycled materials. Lever Bros. reduced the amount of packaging for its U.K. detergent brand, Radion.

For those foreign companies marketing products in the United States, packaging issues focus more on meeting American expectations than on meeting environmental regulations. To upgrade its packaging and please American consumers, China enlisted help from U.S. marketing consultants, who toured the country's packaging facilities, held seminars, and arranged exhibits of the best Western packaging. The tour turned up many packaging problems, including poorly attached labels, blurry and dull colors, and inconsistent labeling that robbed companies of a chance for brand recognition. Some boxes were designed so poorly that they couldn't entirely contain their products. In addition, some companies did not make sure their products' names would appeal to Americans; marketing consultants assured one Chinese baker that Americans would not buy Void Pit Shortbread Bisquits no matter how delicious they might be.

With package designs costing anywhere from $20,000 for one product to $250,000 for multiproduct brands, firms may hesitate before developing culturally specific packages for all of their markets. Sometimes a universal package might work. When winemaker Freixenet wanted to market its Cordon Negro in a black bottle to Americans, the company's U.S. distributor warned that to Americans, black symbolizes death. Freixenet went ahead, and not only did Americans buy the wine, but black became a trendy U.S. packaging color. Despite success stories like this, experts strongly recommend culturally specific packaging. After all, packages speak for the product, so they had better speak in a language shoppers can understand.

Sources: Dagmar Mussey and Juliana Koranteng, "Packaging Strict Green Rules," *Advertising* Age, Dec. 2, 1991, p. S-10; Laura Bird, "Romancing the Package," *Adweek's Marketing Week*, Jan. 21, 1991, pp. 10–14; Laura Bird, "Packaging Paints It Black," *Adweek's Marketing Week*, Sept. 11, 1990, p. 17; George White, "U.S. Consultants Teaching China to Wrap," *Los Angeles Times*, Aug. 13, 1990; and John S. Blyth, "Packaging for Competitive Advantage," *Management Review*, May 1990, p. 64.

experience in marketing research test packaging to see what sells well, not just what is aesthetically appealing. Since the typical large store stocks fifteen thousand items or more, products that stand out are more likely to be bought.

Criticisms of Packaging

During the last several decades, we have seen a number of improvements in packaging. However, some packaging problems still need to be resolved.

Some packages suffer from functional problems in that they simply do not work well. The packaging for flour and sugar is, at best, nothing other than poor. Both grocers and consumers are very much aware that these packages leak and are easily torn. Can anyone open and close a bag of flour without spilling at least a little bit? Certain packages such as canned biscuits, milk cartons with foldout spouts, and potato chip bags are frequently difficult to open. The traditional shapes of packages for products such as ketchup and salad dressing make the product inconvenient to use. Have you ever questioned when tapping on a ketchup bottle why the producer didn't put ketchup in a mayonnaise jar?

As discussed earlier, certain types of packaging are being questioned in regard to recyclability and biodegradability. For example, throw-away bottles take considerably more resources to produce than do reusable glass bottles.

Although many steps have been taken to make packaging safer, critics still focus on the safety issues. Containers with sharp edges and easily broken glass bottles are sometimes viewed as a threat to safety. Certain types of plastic packaging and aerosol containers represent possible health hazards.

At times, packaging is viewed as being deceptive. Package shape, graphic design, and certain colors may be used to make a product appear larger than it actually is. The inconsistent use of certain size designations—such as giant, economy, family, king, and super—can certainly lead to customer confusion. Although customers in this country traditionally have liked attractive, effective, convenient packaging, the cost of such packaging is high. For some products, such as cosmetics, the cost of the package is higher than the cost of the product itself.

Labeling

Labeling is very closely interrelated with packaging and can be used in a variety of promotional, informational, and legal ways. The label can be used to facilitate the identification of a product by presenting the brand and a unique graphic design. For example, Heinz's ketchup is easy to identify on a supermarket shelf because the brand name is easy to read and is coupled with a distinctive crownlike graphic design. Labels have a descriptive function. For certain types of products, the label indicates the grade of the product, especially for canned fruit. Labels can describe the source of the product, its contents and major features, how to use the product, how to care for the product, nutritional information, type and style of the product, and size and number of servings. The label can play a promotional function through the use of graphics that attract attention.

Several federal laws deal directly or indirectly with packaging and labeling. For instance, federal laws require disclosure of such information as textile identification, potential hazards, and nutritional information. Although consumers have responded favorably to this type of information on labels, evidence as to whether they actually use it has been mixed. Several studies indicate that consumers do not use nutritional information, whereas other studies indicate that they do. In 1966, Congress passed the Fair Packaging and Labeling Act, one of the most comprehensive pieces of labeling and packaging legislation. This law focuses on mandatory labeling requirements, voluntary adoption of packaging standards by firms within industries, and the provision of power to the Federal Trade Commission and the Food and Drug Administration to establish and enforce packaging regulations. For example, the Food and Drug Administration has established labeling requirements by which food processors must indicate the amount of calories, protein, fat, carbohydrates, and vitamins that are in a product.

The label for many products includes a **universal product code (UPC)**, which is a series of thick and thin lines that identifies the product and provides inventory and pricing information that is read by an electronic scanner. The UPC is electronically machine-read at the retail check-out counter. This information is used by retailers and producers for price and inventory control purposes.

Color and eye-catching graphics on labels overcome the jumble of words—known to designers as "mouse print"—that have been added to satisfy government regulations. Because so many similar products are available, an attention-getting device or silent salesperson is needed to attract interest. As one of the most visible parts of a product, the label is an important element in a marketing mix.

Summary

A brand is a name, term, design, symbol, or any other feature that identifies one seller's good or service and distinguishes it from those of other sellers. A brand name is that part of a brand that can be spoken; the element that cannot be spoken is called a brand mark. A trademark is a legal designation indicating that the owner has exclusive use of a brand or part of a brand and that others are prohibited by law from using it. A trade name is the legal name of an organization. Branding helps buyers identify and evaluate products, helps sellers facilitate repeat purchasing and product introduction, and fosters brand loyalty. A manufacturer brand, initiated by the producer, makes it possible to more easily associate the firm with its products at the point of purchase. A private distributor brand is initiated and owned by a reseller. A generic brand indicates only the product category and does not include the company name or other identifying terms. Manufacturers combat the growing competition from distributor brands by developing multiple brands. When selecting a brand, a marketer should choose one that is easy to say, spell, and recall, and that alludes to the product's uses, benefits, or special characteristics. Brand names are created inside an organization by individuals, committees, or branding departments, or by outside consultants. Brand names can be devised from words, initials, numbers, nonsense words, or a combination of these. Services as well as products are branded, often with the company name and an accompanying symbol that makes the brand distinctive or conveys a desired image.

Producers protect ownership of their brands through registration with the U.S. Patent and Trademark Office. Marketers at a company must make certain that their selected brand name does not infringe on an already-registered brand by confusing or deceiving consumers about the source of the product. In most foreign countries, brand registration is on a first-come, first-serve basis, making protection more difficult. Brand counterfeiting, increasingly common, has potential for undermining consumer confidence in and loyalty to a brand. Companies brand their products in several ways: Individual branding designates a unique name for each of a company's products; overall family branding identifies all of a firm's products with the single name; line family branding assigns all products within a single line the same name; and brand-extension branding applies an existing name to a new or improved product. Trademark licensing enables producers to earn extra revenue, receive low-cost or free publicity, and protect their trademarks. Through a licensing agreement, and for a licensing fee, a firm may permit approved manufacturers to use its trademark on other products.

Packaging involves development of a container and graphic design for a product. Effective packaging offers protection, economy, safety, and convenience. It can influence the customer's purchase decision by promoting features, uses, benefits, and image. When developing a package, marketers must consider cost relative to how much the target market is willing to pay. Other considerations include how to make the package tamper-resistant, whether to use multiple packaging and family packaging, how to design the package as an effective promotional tool, how best to accommodate resellers, and whether to develop environmentally responsible packaging. Packaging can be an important part of an overall marketing strategy. Firms choose particular colors, designs, shapes, and textures to create desirable images and associations. Producers alter packages to convey new features or to make them safer or more convenient. If a package has a secondary use, the product's value to the consumer may be increased. Category-consistent packaging makes products more easily recognized by consumers, and innovative packaging enhances a product's distinctiveness. Consumers may criticize packaging that doesn't work well, poses health or safety problems, is deceptive in some way, or is not biodegradable or recyclable.

Labeling is an important aspect of packaging for promotional, informational, and legal reasons. Because labels are attention-getting devices, they are significant features in the marketing mix. Various regulatory agencies can require that products be labeled or marked with warnings, instructions, certifications, nutritional information, and manufacturer's identification.

Important Terms

Brand
Brand name
Brand mark
Trademark
Trade name
Manufacturer brands
Private distributor brands (private, store, or dealer brands)
Generic brand
Individual branding
Overall family branding

Line family branding
Brand-extension branding
Family packaging
Labeling
Universal product code (UPC)

1. What is the difference between a brand and a brand name? Compare and contrast the terms *brand mark* and *trademark*.
2. How does branding benefit customers and organizations?
3. What are the distinguishing characteristics of private distributor brands?
4. Given the competition between private distributor brands and manufacturer brands, should manufacturers be concerned about the popularity of private distributor brands? How should manufacturers fight back in the brand battle? At what point should a manufacturer make private brands?
5. Identify and explain the major considerations when selecting a brand.
6. The brand name Xerox is sometimes used generically to refer to photocopying machines. How can Xerox Corporation protect this brand name?
7. Identify and explain the four major branding policies and give examples of each. Can a firm use more than one policy at a time? Explain your answer.
8. What are the major advantages and disadvantages of licensing?
9. Describe the functions that a package can perform. Which function is most important? Why?
10. When developing a package, what are the major issues that a marketer should consider?
11. In what ways can packaging be used as a strategic tool?
12. What are the major criticisms of packaging?
13. What are the major functions of labeling?

Cases

10.1 Chiquita Banana Revitalizes Its Brand Name

When it comes to making purchase decisions, well-known brand names can be powerful inducements for choosing one product over another. If consumers cannot judge a product's quality by simply examining it, they may trust a brand name alone to ensure that quality. Commodities such as fruits and vegetables present a more complicated picture. In the produce aisle, shoppers are able to judge apples based on how red and shiny they look or on how many soft spots they have. They don't need a label to guide them. Executives at Chiquita Banana, however, believe that there is a strong consumer preference for well-known banana brands. Keeping in mind that banana consumption is about 25 pounds per person annually, Chiquita hopes that the famous name on those little blue stickers will provide the company with the lion's share of a growing market.

Over the last few years, consumer preference for Chiquita bananas has eroded. In the past, the company advertised aggressively, but it has not done so in recent years. Company executives believe this advertising lapse is the culprit to blame for declining brand awareness. Years before the current focus on healthy eating, Chiquita positioned its fruit as a healthful alternative to other snacks. In the 1960s, campaign themes included "Eat Bananas for Goodness' Sake" and "Wear It in Good Health." In the 1980s, advertisements emphasized bananas' low sodium and high fiber, advising consumers to "Take One a Day" like a vitamin. But complacency set in at Chiquita, and advertising slacked off. Then worrisome competitors like Dole and Delmonte began nibbling away at Chiquita's market share. Hoping to rejuvenate equity in its brand name (and simultaneously increase sales), Chiquita launched a new advertising campaign with a familiar theme and a familiar theme song.

Ever since 1945, when a singing and dancing banana named Miss Chiquita first tuned the words, "I'm a Chiquita banana, and I'm here to say . . . ," the company's theme song has been intrinsic to the brand. Although Chiquita has launched many campaigns to reinforce the banana's image since then, the song has been used sparingly. Several years ago, it played on radio in a promotional campaign, but other than this very limited exposure, it has not been heard lately. That is changing. In a major new multimedia campaign for radio, network, spot, and cable television, consumers now hear a modernized version of the old familiar Chiquita Banana song. The campaign theme, "Quite possibly, the world's perfect food," continues to position bananas as a healthy food. Television spots, including a biker refreshing himself with a banana and a grandfather doing the same after romping with his twin grandsons, focus on the fruit's ability to replenish active bodies depleted of particular vitamins and minerals. In the background of these advertisements are heard the strains of the updated Chiquita Banana song. Chiquita's advertisers are counting on the tune to strike a nostalgic note with older consumers and to become linked with the brand in the minds of new generations of banana eaters. Renewed popularity of the song, say company executives, will infuse new life into the Chiquita Banana brand.

With its new advertising campaign, Chiquita is outspending all of its rival banana advertisers. The question remains, however, is it worth investing so much to brand a banana? The company proudly asserts that when asked about banana brands, 70 percent of responding consumers name Chiquita first. With respect to produce, however, high brand recognition doesn't necessarily translate into good sales. When shoppers want bananas, but no Chiquitas are available, they will probably buy whatever brand is in the bin as long as the bananas are firm and yellow. Noteworthy examples of Chiquita's failure to cash in on its well-known brand name include the company's inability to make headway into the packaged food market and its unsuccessful attempt to introduce frozen juice bars, which cost the company about $30 million. Ironically, in these cases the brand name may have worked against the products, because in the minds of most consumers, Chiquita is just a banana company.

As concerns over food quality and safety grow, Chiquita's executives expect brands to become increasingly important in the fresh-produce market. That confidence is reflected in Chiquita's continued investment in revitalizing the Chiquita brand. The company is even trying out branded kiwis in one midwestern test market.[24]

Questions for Discussion

1. What are the major problems associated with trying to brand produce?
2. Evaluate the success of other producers or processors that have been involved in branding fruit.
3. Given the difficulties of branding fruit, why do producers and processors continue to brand fruit? What benefits can accrue to these branders?
4. Should Chiquita get involved with brand-extension branding again? Would brand licensing be advisable?

When some people died several years ago after taking cyanide-containing Tylenol capsules, consumer confidence in over-the-counter medications plummeted. As a direct result of that tragedy, the drug industry voluntarily redesigned packages to make them more tamper-resistant. Years without incident renewed consumer faith. Recently, however, the specter of fear and doubt surfaced again when two people in Washington State died, and one became critically ill, from cyanide-laced Sudafed 12 Hour decongestant capsules.

Burroughs Wellcome Company, manufacturers of Sudafed, responded promptly with a nationwide recall of all packages of 12 Hour capsules, which make up about 15 percent of the product's $109 million in annual sales. Among the recalled stock, the FBI found one cyanide-containing capsule out of 124,000 they examined, and two boxes that displayed evidence of tampering. Replicating the steps Johnson & Johnson took after the Tylenol poisoning, Burroughs immediately suspended regular advertising, established a toll-free telephone line for concerned consumers, and offered a $100,000 reward for information leading to the capture of the perpetrator. In addition, the company provided refunds or replacements for any boxes consumers returned. A week-long $2.5 million national television campaign featured company president and CEO, Philip Tracy, in a sixty-second spot. He announced that Burroughs was working closely with the Food and Drug Administration and the FBI to catch the guilty party, furnished the toll-free number, and reassured consumers that Sudafed was safe to take. Ads with a similar message ran in Washington State newspapers. Despite these measures, Pay N Save Drug Stores and Western Drug Distributors Drug Emporiums, the two chains that carried the tainted Sudafed, stopped selling all brands of over-the-counter capsules.

In the past decade, episodes of over-the-counter drug poisoning in the United States have resulted in ten deaths, indicating that the likelihood of consumer poisoning is slim. Yet whether or not any widespread danger exists, consumers react intensely to an event like this one, compelling both manufacturers and federal agencies to act. In the case of Burroughs, that action involved recall and reassurance. For the Food and Drug Administration, that action takes the form of a task force investigation that could result in a ban of all thirty-seven over-the-counter capsule brands. If such a ban is initiated, the drug industry will fight back, protesting the burden of tremendous costs required to reformulate medications and the profit losses from some inevitable consumer dissatisfaction with alternate forms. In addition, experts maintain that no matter what they do, no packaging is tamper-proof. They insist that consumers must assume some responsibility for checking the packages they buy, because a motivated person can get to any product in any package. Sudafed packages have three tamper-resistant features—tamper-evident tape on the box ends, a blister pack, and a blue gelatin band around the middle of each capsule—yet someone was able to slit the outer seal, remove a capsule, and substitute a poisoned one.

Rumors are circulating that Burroughs has about $60 million worth of malicious-product-tamper insurance, which has been available only a short time. Industry experts are skeptical, because the nature of capsules makes them very susceptible to tampering and therefore difficult to insure. If Burroughs has such a policy, coverage would include losses from products contaminated by someone not demanding a ransom, costs of recall and scientific examination, and fees for any security or public relations consultants brought in during the crisis. Johnson & Johnson, not covered by such a plan, continues to face lawsuits from survivors claiming the firm's liability. Because Sudafed is sold in tamper-resistant packages that go beyond the FDA's recommendations, insurance experts do not expect Burroughs to be found negligent in marketing its capsules.

Some experts insist that Tylenol never completely recovered from its tampering tragedy. Johnson & Johnson was forced to spend tremendous amounts of money on promotion and advertising to regain market share, and Tylenol has not been able to command the price it did before the tampering. In addition, the firm lost many loyal customers when it eliminated capsules altogether from its product line. Although Sudafed holds the number-two spot after Nyquil in the $1 billion cold medication category, noncapsule competitors such as Drixoral, Comtrex, and Benadryl are likely to gain market share in the aftermath of the tragedy. What will happen to Sudafed's market share is not clear, but analysts predict that the product's solid brand name affords it strong potential for bouncing back from temporary losses. A question more critical to the drug industry as a whole is whether it will be allowed to continue marketing capsules at all, and if so, what form the packaging will take.[25]

Questions for Discussion

1. To what extent can packages be designed to prevent tampering?
2. Through package design, is it possible to overprotect products from tampering? Explain.
3. Evaluate Burroughs' handling of this incident. Then assess the impact of this incident on Sudafed's brand share.

Chapter Notes

1. Based on information from Renee Graham, "In Bow to Ecology, Record Makers Agree on Small CD Package," *Boston Globe*, Feb. 28, 1992, p. 1; Peter Newcomb, "Ban the Box!" *Forbes*, May 13, 1991, p. 70; Amy Duncan, "The CD Packaging Debate," *Christian Science Monitor*, Apr. 15, 1991, p. 14; Stephen Holden, "CD Packaging Attacked as Wasteful," *New York Times*, Dec. 25, 1990, p. 28; "New CD Packages Cut Down on Trash," *Wall Street Journal*, Oct. 10, 1990, p. B1; James R. Oestreich, "CD's Cut Down to Size," *New York Times*, Sept. 23, 1990, p. H28; and "Are CDs Recyclable?" *Wall Street Journal*, Apr. 18, 1990, p. A22.
2. Peter D. Bennett, ed., *Dictionary of Marketing Terms* (Chicago: American Marketing Association, 1988), p. 18.
3. James U. McNeal and Linda Zeren, "Brand Name Selection for Consumer Products," *MSU Business Topics,* Spring 1981, p. 35.
4. "No Brand Like an Old Brand," *Forbes*, June 11, 1990, p. 180.
5. Ronald Alsop, "Brand Loyalty Is Rarely Blind Loyalty; Rise in Coupons, Choices Blamed for '80s Erosion," *Wall Street Journal*, Oct. 19, 1989, pp. B1, B6.
6. Chip Walker, "What's in a Name?" *American Demographics*, Feb. 1991, pp. 54–57.
7. Alan Miller, "Gains Share in Dollars and Units During 1990 Third Quarter," *Private Label*, January–February 1991, pp. 85-89.

8. Phil Fitzell, "Private Label's 7th Annual U.S. Supermarket Report," *Private Label*, January–February 1991, p. 12.

9. Telephone conversation with U.S. Patent and Trademark Office personnel, Sept. 11, 1991.

10. "No Brand Like an Old Brand."

11. Leonard L. Berry, Edwin E. Lefkowith, and Terry Clark, "In Services, What's in a Name?" *Harvard Business Review*, September–October, 1988, pp. 2–4.

12. Dorothy Cohen, "Trademark Strategy," *Journal of Marketing*, January 1986, p. 63.

13. "Trademark Stylesheet," U.S. Trademark Association, no. 1A.

14. Dorothy Cohen, "Trademark Strategy Revisited," *Journal of Marketing*, July 1991, pp. 46–59.

15. Ronald F. Bush, Peter H. Bloch, and Scott Dawson, "Remedies for Product Counterfeiting," *Business Horizons*, January–February 1989, pp. 59–65; Pete Engardio, with Todd Vogel and Dinah Lee, "Companies Are Knocking Off the Knockoff Outfits," *Business Week*, Sept. 26, 1988, pp. 86–88; and Michael Harvey, "A New Way to Combat Product Counterfeiting," *Business Horizons*, July–August 1988, pp. 19–28.

16. Mark Landler, "What's in a Name? Less and Less," *Business Week*, July 8, 1991, pp. 66–67.

17. Fred W. Morgan, "Tampered Goods: Legal Developments and Marketing Guidelines," *Journal of Marketing*, Apr. 1988, pp. 86–96.

18. Ibid.

19. James U. McNeal, *Consumer Behavior: An Integrative Approach* (Boston: Little, Brown, 1982), pp. 221–222.

20. "Not in My Backyard," CNN Special Report, Cable News Network, Dec. 19, 1988.

21. Alecia Swasy, "Ecology and Buyer Wants Don't Jibe," *Wall Street Journal*, Aug. 23, 1989, p. B1.

22. Howard Schlossberg, "Effective Packaging Talks to Consumers," *Marketing News*, Aug. 6, 1990, p. 6.

23. Laura Bird, "Romancing the Package," *Adweek's Marketing Week*, Jan. 21, 1991, p. 11.

24. Laura Bird, "Chiquita's Ad Archive: The Picture of Health," *Adweek's Marketing Week*, Jan. 7, 1991, pp. 32–33; Stephen Phillips, "Chiquita May Be a Little Too Ripe," *Business Week*, Apr. 30, 1990, p. 100; and Patricia Strnad, "Modern Chiquita: Banana Song Updated for New Campaign," *Advertising Age*, Feb. 26, 1990, p. 4.

25. Judann Dagnoll, "Brief Slump Expected for Sudafed," *Advertising Age*, Mar. 18, 1991, p. 53; "Cyanide in Decongestant Capsules Kills Two in US," *Packaging Week*, Mar. 13, 1991, pp. 1, 3; Paul H. Rubin, "Sudafed's the Last Thing to Be Afraid Of," *Wall Street Journal*, Mar. 13, 1991, p. A14; David Kiley, "Sudafed Deaths Spark a Backlash Against Capsules," *Adweek's Marketing Week*, Mar. 11, 1991, p. 6; Stacy Shapiro, "Sudafed-Type Capsules Hard to Insure," *Business Insurance*, Mar. 11, 1991, pp. 2, 4; and Philip J. Hilts, "Cyanide in a Drug Kills 2 and Forces a National Recall," *New York Times*, Mar. 4, 1991, pp. A1, B6.

Rogaine: Prescription Treatment for Thinning Hair

Estimates indicate that there are 33 million balding men in the United States, and they spend approximately $300 million annually on over-the-counter hair growth aids. In 1986, hoping to tap this market, Upjohn introduced "Rogaine," a revolutionary hair loss treatment requiring a physician's prescription. Rogaine has faced hurdles to get its message to the public. It is hailed by some as a "miracle cure" and derided by others who label it the "ultimate yuppie drug" and express the concern that development of Rogaine is the result of misplaced research priorities. Although Upjohn is disappointed by lower-than-expected sales, they have no plans to remove the product from the market. With recent FDA approval to allow brand-name advertising of prescription drugs and with projects under development to broaden its usage, Upjohn is confident about the future of Rogaine.

Research and Development

Upjohn discovered Rogaine by accident. While testing a blood pressure medication called "minoxidil" in the 1960s, researchers discovered a side-effect; the drug produced hair growth on patients' foreheads and cheeks. In 1979, Upjohn began testing the effectiveness of a liquified version as a hair restorer, using 2,300 male patients at 27 medical centers throughout the United States as subjects. Some were given Rogaine to use, while others were given a placebo and told it was the actual drug. Based on patient self-evaluation at the end of four months, 26 percent of the subjects using the medication reported moderate to dense hair growth, while 11 percent of those using a placebo reported the same. At the end of 12 months, 48 percent of those using the Rogaine rated their hair growth as moderate or better. From their studies, Upjohn concluded that Rogaine, while not a "miracle hair restorer," can provide effective long-term treatment for male pattern baldness. Although Upjohn's researchers did not discover how Rogaine works to stimulate hair growth, the Federal Drug Administration approved the drug for sale to the public.

With the public's anticipation of a baldness remedy that actually worked, Upjohn stock went up. A $450 investment in 1984 was worth $3,045 by July of 1987.

When Rogaine finally came on the market, drug industry analysts predicted sales of $1 billion. Although Upjohn spent $15 million more on advertising than originally budgeted, sales were well below expectations. From November of 1988 through January of 1989, the number of Rogaine prescriptions filled grew slightly. Despite these rising sales—$32 million in the first quarter of 1990, up from the same period in 1989—the $175 million in sales predicted for the year was nowhere near the enthusiastic figure of $1 billion originally forecasted.

Product Introduction Obstacles

Difficulties in launching the product fall primarily into two categories. The first is the problem with advertising Rogaine, and the second is problems with the product itself. Because Rogaine is not an over-the-counter product, the Federal Drug Administration placed tight advertising restrictions on it. To use its brand name on television or in print, Upjohn would have had to include a long explanation of testing procedures, information on effectiveness, and a list of all possible side effects. Deeming this type of advertisement too negative and cumbersome, Upjohn decided to produce ads which, without mentioning the name Rogaine, informed men that if hair loss is a problem, seeing a physician could provide a solution. The original advertisements merely showed a young barefoot man walking along a beach and a voice-over stating, "If you're concerned about hair loss, see your doctor." Upjohn was unwilling to reveal how much it spent on this first campaign, but considering production and media costs, the expenditure was not minimal. Many experts and consumers judged the commercial to be too vague; resulting sales were not overwhelming.

Difficulties with the product itself have been more troublesome for Upjohn to overcome than a problematic advertising campaign. Rogaine's effectiveness is limited. Even when it works, sometimes the hair that grows in is different in texture and color from the rest. In the best of circumstances, Rogaine remains a treatment and not a cure. To maintain hair growth and prevent a reversal of the effects, Rogaine must be applied twice daily in the proper dosage for the rest of the user's life, a long-term commitment that is discouraging to many consumers. The high cost of Rogaine may be prohibitive. A year's supply costs between $550 and $900, and most health insurance companies regard hair growth as cosmetic and do not reimburse for Rogaine prescriptions.

Changing to Improve Sales

With FDA approval to use the Rogaine name in print and on television advertisements, Upjohn is beginning more aggressive advertising, hoping to improve acceptance and increase use of its product. In conjunction with the new campaign, the firm is targeting new markets and improving its product.

In August 1989, the name Rogaine first appeared in advertisements. Commercials now name the product, emphasizing that Rogaine is the only hair regrowth product approved by the FDA. A toll-free number for consumer questions is also provided. Upjohn says that print ads now appearing in magazines like *Time, Newsweek, GQ,* and *Sports Illustrated* have doubled consumer awareness of Rogaine. To reach a wider market, Upjohn has also distributed 150,000 copies of informational videos to hairdressers around the United States, offered a rebate for a six-month supply, and held a sweepstakes through beauty and barber shops in Atlanta, Los Angeles, and New York.

As a means to increase sales, Upjohn is considering changes in Rogaine itself as well as addition of new related products to the market. Possible Rogaine formulations include one with a stronger concentration of minoxidil requiring only one application per day and a milder over-the-counter version. An easier-to-use gel is being introduced in Europe. Already developed is a shampoo called "Progaine," packaged with the Rogaine trademark and marketed to be used in conjunction with the prescription drug. Upjohn has recently entered into an agreement with Procter & Gamble to develop other hair-related consumer products.

Targeting Another Market

For several years, Upjohn has been investigating the possibility of marketing Rogaine to women. Because the FDA had only approved its use for men, the organization could not aim the product at women. Recently, however, the FDA approved Rogaine's use for women too, and Upjohn is going ahead with plans to target women in television and magazine advertisements. This strategy seems promising in light of a recent Gallup poll indicating that 38.6 percent of women questioned say they would seek treatment if they were losing their hair compared to 30.4 percent of the men asked.

Industry analysts are skeptical concerning the future success of Rogaine. They suggest that the only way to increase sales is to lower the cost of the product and make it more effective. Upjohn remains optimistic and is forging ahead with new advertising strategies and continuing product development. The drug is currently being sold in more than 50 countries under the name, "Regaine." But Rogaine has to do well quickly. In 1996, Upjohn's patent runs out and it faces competition from other minoxidil-based hair growth products.

Questions for Discussion

1. What are some of the major barriers Upjohn had to overcome when introducing Rogaine?
2. Which part of Upjohn's business analysis phase appeared to be least accurate? Explain.
3. Evaluate the statement that the development of Rogaine is the result of misplaced research priorities.
4. In what stage of the product life cycle is Rogaine? Explain.

Sources: "Upjohn To Market Rogaine Hair Treatment to Women," *Bryan-College Station Eagle,* Aug. 28, 1991; David Woodruff, "For Rogaine, No Miracle Cure—Yet," *Business Week,* June 4, 1990, p. 100; Patricia Winters and Laurie Freeman, "Nicorette, Rogaine Seek TV OK," *Advertising Age,* Nov. 27, 1989, p. 31; Laurie Freeman, "Can Rogaine Make Gains Via Ads?" *Advertising Age,* Sept. 11, 1989, pp. 12–13; Rick Ratliff, "Rogaine Ad Tells All," *Detroit Free Press,* Aug. 17, 1989; Susan Tompor, "Rogaine Gets Brand-Name Treatment in New Upjohn Ads," *Detroit News,* Aug. 15, 1989; Michael Chandler, "Upjohn's Drug May Produce Hair But Sales Hopes Have Been Trimmed," *Detroit Free Press,* May 21, 1989; Laurie Freeman, "Upjohn Takes a Shine to Balding Women," *Advertising Age,* Feb. 27, 1989, p. S-1; Matt Roush, "Rogaine Sales Thin At First," *Kalamazoo Gazette,* Feb. 26, 1989; Paul Keep, "Upjohn Hopes Its TV Message Will Take Root," *Kalamazoo Gazette,* Nov. 23, 1988; and Nancy Brachey, "Baldness Drug Arrives in Region," *Charlotte Observer,* Sept. 10, 1988.

Procter & Gamble: Environmental Quality Leader

In the 1960s, consumer-product giant Procter & Gamble introduced disposable diapers, and many welcomed it as the product of the decade. For years afterwards, thousands of parents enjoyed the freedom and convenience of diapers that they could simply use and throw away. Then in the late 1980s, public concerns about protecting the environment led to worries about using disposable diapers. People began to feel guilty that the millions of diapers they were throwing away contributed to the enormous amount of garbage piling up in landfills. After consumer action groups began publicizing the environmental impact of disposable diapers, calls from concerned customers began pouring in to Procter & Gamble's corporate headquarters.

Founded over 150 years ago, Procter & Gamble markets the top three brands in over 30 categories of consumer products and records sales of over $20 billion a year. Some of its well-known brands include Crest toothpaste, Tide laundry detergent, Ivory soap, and one of the targets of environmental concern, Pampers disposable diapers. When consumers began urging marketers to do more to protect the environment, Procter & Gamble responded, investigating ways to minimize the environmental impact of each of its products. Company executives realized that their commitment to protect the environment will help sustain Procter & Gamble's position as a market leader, but they also recognized that the company has a duty to serve society and act as a responsible global citizen.

Products

Procter & Gamble's manager of environmental marketing recently stated that his company is committed to incorporating an environmentally correct element into every product it introduces. Procter & Gamble's Fry-Max is a restaurant shortening formulated to require smaller amounts for frying and to last longer. When the Cracker Barrel Restaurant chain switched to Fry-Max, it was able to reduce dramatically the amount of cooking oil used in one year. That reduction represents 200,000 gallons of used oil and 45,000 pounds of packaging material that did not end up in landfills all over the United States. To decrease the air pollution

resulting from the manufacturing process of one of its laundry detergents, Procter & Gamble changed the product's formula. Now, when a plant in Venezuela manufactures Bold III, there are fewer and less harmful by-products in stack emissions.

When it comes to disposable diapers, Procter & Gamble's efforts are ongoing to make them a more environmentally responsible product. First introduced in 1986, Superabsorbent Pampers are only half the size of earlier Pampers, and they contribute about half as much trash as they did with the bigger, bulkier variety. Procter & Gamble is also striving to increase the percentage of its disposable diapers that can be turned into compost. The company is developing materials to replace plastic liners, waistbands, and tape tabs, and hopes to begin testing a new 100 percent compostable diaper soon.

Packaging

In countries around the world, concerned customers can purchase Procter & Gamble products in packaging that is more environmentally responsible. From cleaning products to personal care items, Procter & Gamble is reducing the amount of packaging and making it increasingly recyclable and biodegradable. Liquid Tide and Cheer laundry detergents come in recycled plastic bottles, and concentrated powder versions in relatively small boxes. The Worldwide Fund for Nature recently endorsed Procter & Gamble's "Dash Ultra" for using less packaging. Downy fabric softener is available in refill boxes, making it possible for customers to reuse one plastic bottle indefinitely and throw away only a very small container. In Germany, Procter & Gamble markets refill packs for almost all of its liquid laundry aid, household cleaner, and personal care brands. In Japan, the company changed the way it wraps three bars of soap. Instead of putting each bar in its own box, shrink wrapping them individually, and then shrink wrapping them a second time as a unit, the company now puts all three bars in one box that requires about 18 percent less packaging material.

Concern for air quality led Procter & Gamble to change the way it packages hair spray. Instead of using propellants that cause permanent damage to the global ozone layer, the company packages its German brand of hair spray, Shamtu, in compressed air cylinders. To use it, people pump it a few times to build up air pressure, and push; the hair spray comes out using only air.

Labeling

At Procter & Gamble, marketers believe it is their responsibility to make it easier for customers to locate and understand environmental information by creating standard definitions for green products and using a uniform labeling policy. To facilitate customer understanding and ensure communication that is not misleading, Procter & Gamble is working with an industry-wide coalition to propose such labeling guidelines to the Federal Trade Commission. Procter & Gamble has already initiated its own companywide guidelines for environmental labeling. These mandate that all Procter & Gamble packages include relevant information concerning the product's recycled content, recyclability, and disposability, as well as a statement on the product's biodegradability, and that each brand establish a consistent location for this information on the product or package.

Consumer Perceptions

From the results of a recent *Advertising Age/Gallup* "green marketing" study, it is clear that consumers recognize Procter & Gamble's ongoing environmental efforts. When asked to name one company that is most environmentally conscious, the largest percentage of respondents named Procter & Gamble. When asked to rate products that they considered least harmful to the environment, Procter & Gamble brands topped the list

in many categories. Tide was the winner in the laundry soap category, Downy refill cartons in the fabric softener category, and Pampers in the disposable diaper category.

More general questions in the survey reveal that consumers want marketers to do more for the environment and are willing to change their purchasing behavior to favor companies they perceive as environmentally sensitive. Procter & Gamble is committed to continuing its research for new ideas that meet consumer needs while protecting the environment.

Questions for Discussion

1. What types of risks is Procter & Gamble taking when it modifies its products to make them more environmentally responsible?
2. Which major issues has Procter & Gamble focused on when attempting to make its packaging more environmentally sensitive?
3. What major problem has Procter & Gamble tried to overcome through its labeling program?
4. Does Procter & Gamble have an ethical responsibility to be environmentally sensitive?

Sources: Thomas A. Hemphill, "Marketer's New Motto: It's Keen To Be Green," *Business & Society Review*, Summer 1991, pp. 39–44; Judann Dagnoli, "Whose Job Is It To Define 'Green'?" *Advertising Age*, Feb. 4, 1991, p. 13; Laurie Freeman and Dagmar Mussey, "Germans Set P&G's Green Test Agenda," *Advertising Age*, Feb. 4, 1991, pp. 25–26; Dennis Chase, "The Green Revolution: P&G Gets Top Marks in AA Survey," *Advertising Age*, Jan. 29, 1991, pp. 8–10; Laurie Freeman, "The Green Revolution: Procter & Gamble," *Advertising Age*, Jan. 29, 1991, pp. 16, 34; and "Environmental Quality Leaders," Procter & Gamble videotape.

PREVIEW:
MICROMARKET COMPUTER APPLICATION II

Howe, Inc.: Selecting Test Markets

The goal of this exercise is the selection of the most appropriate test market(s) for a new microwave oven Howe wishes to introduce. These selections are made from among twelve potential test market cities. The cities are ranked using a cumulative market index value which is calculated on Lotus 1-2-3. The selection decision is complicated by a limited test market budget and the threat of jamming by one of Howe's competitors. The exercise concludes with a written memo to a marketing executive making recommendations for test market cities.

III *Distribution Decisions*

Providing customers with satisfying products is important but not enough for successful marketing strategies. These products must also be available in adequate quantities in accessible locations at the times when customers desire them. The chapters in Part III deal with the distribution of products and the marketing channels and institutions that provide the structure for making products available. In Chapter 11 we discuss the structure and functions of marketing channels and present an overview of institutions that make up these channels. In Chapter 12 we analyze the types of wholesalers and their functions. In Chapter 13 we focus on retailing and retailers. Specifically, we examine the types of retailers and their roles and functions in marketing channels. Finally, in Chapter 14 we analyze the decisions and activities associated with the physical distribution of products, such as order processing, materials handling, warehousing, inventory management, and transportation.

11 *Marketing Channels*

OBJECTIVES

- To understand the marketing channel concept and the types of marketing intermediaries in the channel

- To discuss the justification of channel members

- To examine the structure and function of the channel system

- To explore the power dimensions of channels, especially the concepts of cooperation, conflict, and leadership

AutoZone is a chain of 700 retail auto parts stores in twenty states—mostly in the Sunbelt. It competes in an industry supplying auto parts through other distribution outlets, such as automotive dealers, independent repair shops, national repair chains, discount stores, and mail-order suppliers. The company prides itself on clean stores, low prices, and an abundance of friendly service. In fact, AutoZone's combination of low prices and service is setting a new standard in the auto parts industry.

Why the great success at AutoZone? Industry analysts cite two reasons: AutoZone chairman J. R. Hyde and the dramatic increase in the do-it-yourself (DIY) auto parts market. Hyde was a member of Wal-Mart's board of directors for seven years. During that time, he learned a great deal about the importance of people. At AutoZone, Hyde strives for a company culture similar to Wal-Mart's by encouraging team spirit and good service among his "AutoZoners." Hyde spends a great deal of time in the stores, where he waits on customers with other AutoZoners.

Another reason for AutoZone's success is the rapid growth of the DIY market. By 1990, over 62 percent of all light vehicles on the road were over five years old, with the average car being 7.8 years old. This, along with an average mechanic's labor charge of $39 per hour, has led to an increase in the number of do-it-yourselfers in the United States. Even with the increased sophistication of today's cars, the DIY market continues to expand. As long as DIYers can remove old parts and put on new ones, the DIY market should continue to grow. AutoZone is helping this market grow by making it easy to find replacement parts and by providing advice on servicing and repairing automobiles.

AutoZone only accounts for 3 percent of the industry's sales. It is competing against other auto supply stores such as NAPA, Chief Auto Parts, Parts Plus, as well as Wal-Mart, K mart, and other discount stores. As the company puts it, if AutoZone's sales grow at 20 percent a year, and the DIY market stays the same, the company's market share would be 20 percent by the year 2000.[1]

Photo courtesy of AutoZone.

AutoZone has excelled at making auto parts available to the do-it-yourself auto repair market. **Distribution** refers to activities that make products available to customers when and where they want to purchase them. Choosing which channels of distribution to use is a major decision in the development of marketing strategies.

This chapter focuses on the description and analysis of channels of distribution, or marketing channels. (Chapter 14 discusses the physical distribution of products.) We first discuss the main types of channels and their structures and then explain the need for intermediaries as well as analyze the functions they perform. Next we outline several forms of channel integration. We explore how marketers determine the appropriate intensity of market coverage for a product and how they consider a number of factors when selecting suitable channels of distribution. Finally, after examining behavioral patterns within marketing channels, we look at several legal issues that affect channel management.

The Structures and Types of Marketing Channels

A **channel of distribution** (sometimes called a **marketing channel**) is a group of individuals and organizations that directs the flow of products from producers to customers. Providing customer benefits should be the driving force behind all marketing channel activities. Buyers' needs and behavior are therefore important concerns of channel members.

Table 11.1

Marketing Channel Activities Performed by Intermediaries

Category of Marketing Activities	Possible Activities Required
Marketing information	Analyze information such as sales data; perform or commission marketing research studies
Marketing management	Establish objectives; plan activities; manage and coordinate financing, personnel, and risk taking; evaluate and control channel activities
Facilitating exchange	Choose product assortments that match the needs of buyers
Promotion	Set promotional objectives, coordinate advertising, personal selling, sales promotion, publicity, and packaging
Price	Establish pricing policies and terms of sales
Physical distribution	Manage transportation, warehousing, materials handling, inventory control, and communication

Figure 11.1

Retailers Make Products Available to Ultimate Consumers

The Pop Swatch watch in this ad is being promoted as available at Filene's, an upscale department store.

Source: Courtesy of SWATCH WATCH.

Making products available benefits customers. Channels of distribution make products available at the right time, in the right place, and in the right quantity by providing such product-enhancing functions as service, transportation, and storage. Although consumers do not see the distribution of a product, they value the product availability that channels of distribution make possible.

Most, but not all, channels of distribution have marketing intermediaries. A **marketing intermediary**, or middleman, links producers to other middlemen or to ultimate users of the products. Marketing intermediaries perform the activities described in Table 11.1. There are two major types of intermediaries: merchants and functional middlemen (agents and brokers). **Merchants** buy products and resell them, whereas **functional middlemen** do not take title.

Both retailers and wholesalers are intermediaries. Retailers purchase products for the purpose of reselling them to ultimate consumers. For example, in Figure 11.1, Swatch is promoted as being available to consumers at Filene's department stores. Merchant wholesalers resell products to other wholesalers and to retailers. Functional wholesalers, such as agents and brokers, expedite exchanges among producers and resellers and are compensated by fees or commissions. For purposes of discussion in this chapter, all wholesalers are considered merchant middlemen unless otherwise specified.

Channel members share certain significant characteristics. Each member has different responsibilities within the overall structure of the distribution system, but mutual profit and success can be attained only if channel members cooperate in delivering products to the market.

Although distribution decisions need not precede other marketing decisions, they do exercise a powerful influence on the rest of the marketing mix. Channel decisions are critical because they determine a product's market presence and buyers' accessibility to the product. The strategic significance of these decisions is further heightened by the fact that they entail long-term commitments. For example, it is much easier to change prices or packaging than distribution systems.

Because the marketing channel most appropriate for one product may be less suitable for another, many different distribution paths have been developed in most countries. The links in any channel, however, are the merchants (including producers) and agents who oversee the movement of products through that channel. Although there are many various marketing channels, they can be classified generally as channels for consumer products or channels for business-to-business products.

Channels for Consumer Products

Figure 11.2 illustrates several channels used in the distribution of consumer products. Besides the channels listed, a manufacturer may use sales branches or sales offices (discussed in Chapter 12).

Channel A describes the direct movement of goods from producer to consumers. Customers who harvest their own fruit from commercial orchards or buy cookware from door-to-door salespeople are acquiring products through a direct channel. A producer that sells its goods directly from its factory to end users and ultimate consumers is using a direct-marketing channel. Inside Marketing describes a unique direct-marketing channel for computer software. Although this channel is the simplest, it is not necessarily the most effective method of distribution.

Figure 11.2

Typical Marketing Channels for Consumer Products

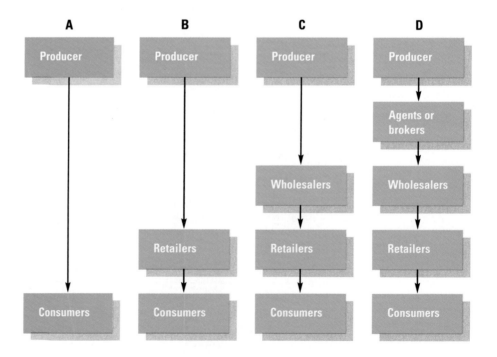

PART III   DISTRIBUTION DECISIONS

Shareware Distribution: Try Before You Buy

ALTHOUGH MOST PEOPLE buy computer programs from stores or mail-order outlets, a new method of distribution has developed in recent years. Computer users can now obtain some software from friends, work, electronic bulletin boards, and other unusual sources, and they pay for such software only if they like it and plan to use it. Unlike most commercial computer software, these programs, known as *shareware*, can be copied and distributed at little or no cost.

Suppose a coworker tells you about a great new shareware spreadsheet and offers to make you a copy. After you try it out, if you decide you do not like the program, you do nothing. If you do like it and plan to use it, you send the developer of the program a registration fee, generally less than $100. In return for registering the program, you get technical support, free upgrades, manuals, and other materials, just as you do with commercial software. You can also freely distribute copies of the program to others without fear of violating the author's copyright. Indeed, shareware programmers *want* others to make copies of these programs and to give those copies to others—that's how they get new customers.

One of the first shareware programs was PC-Write, a word-processing program created by Bob Wallace of Quicksoft, Inc. At the time, Wallace knew little about conventional marketing techniques for software, so when he introduced PC-Write at a San Francisco

computer fair in 1983, he handed out copies and told users to send him $75 only if they liked the program. By 1990 there were more than 47,000 registered users of PC-Write. Other software developers who lack resources or access to conventional software marketing channels have found similar success by making their programs shareware.

Because developers of shareware spend little on packaging, advertising, and distribution, shareware programs usually cost far less than comparable commercial programs. There are shareware programs available to fill most personal and business needs. Some deal with specialized uses, such as stargazing, genealogy, and golf-score tracking. Programs for word processing, spreadsheets, telecommunications, and other more widespread uses are also available. In many cases shareware programs have been judged better than commercial programs that do the same tasks. Although individuals are the biggest users of shareware, corporations as diverse as Caterpillar, MCI Communications, Du Pont, and Ford Motor Co. have registered shareware programs.

Sources: Teresa Reeder, "Software for Sharing," *Nation's Business,* Aug. 1990, pp. 33–37; Janet Ruhl, "Shareware: An Alternative Tool," *Computerworld,* May 1, 1989, p. 136; and Mike Hogan, "Try It, You'll Like It," *Forbes,* Nov. 28, 1988, pp. 227–228.

Channel B, which moves goods from producer to retailers and then to consumers, is the frequent choice of large retailers, for they can buy in quantity from a manufacturer. Such retailers as J.C. Penney, K mart, and Sears, for example, sell clothing, stereos, and many other items that they have purchased directly from the producers. Automobiles are also commonly sold through this type of marketing channel.

A long-standing distribution channel, especially for consumer products, channel C takes goods from producer to wholesalers, then to retailers, and finally to consumers. It is a very practical option for a producer that sells to hundreds of thousands of consumers through thousands of retailers. A single producer finds it hard to do business directly with thousands of retailers. For example, consider the number of retailers that market Wrigley's chewing gum. It would be extremely difficult, if not impossible, for Wrigley's to deal directly with all the retailers that sell its brand of gum. Manufacturers of tobacco products, some home appliances, hardware, and many convenience goods sell their products to wholesalers, who then sell to retailers, who in turn do business with individual consumers. Chapters 12 and 13 discuss in greater detail the functions of wholesalers and retailers in the marketing channel.

Channel D—through which goods pass from producer to agents to wholesalers to retailers and only then to consumers—is frequently used for products intended for mass distribution, such as processed food. For example, to place its cracker line in specific retail outlets, a food processor may hire an agent (or a food broker) to sell the crackers to wholesalers. The wholesalers then sell the crackers to supermarkets, vending machine operators, and other retail outlets.

Contrary to popular opinion, a long channel may be the most efficient distribution channel for consumer goods. When several channel intermediaries are available to perform specialized functions, costs may be lower than if one channel member is responsible for all the functions.

Channels for Business-to-Business Products

Figure 11.3 shows four of the most common channels for business-to-business products. As with consumer products, manufacturers of business-to-business products sometimes work with more than one level of wholesalers.

Channel E illustrates the direct channel for business-to-business products. In contrast to consumer goods, many business-to-business products—especially expensive equipment, such as steam generators, aircraft, and computers—are sold directly to the buyers. For example, Mitsubishi Aircraft International Corporation, a subsidiary of Mitsubishi Heavy Industries, Ltd., sells its jets directly to corporate buyers. The direct channel is most feasible for many manufacturers of business-to-business goods because they have fewer customers, and those

Figure 11.3

Typical Marketing Channels for Business-to-Business Products

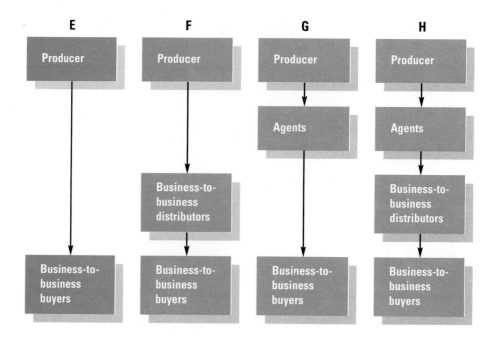

PART III   DISTRIBUTION DECISIONS

customers are often clustered geographically. Buyers of complex business-to-business products also can receive technical assistance from the manufacturer more easily in a direct channel.

If a particular line of business-to-business products is aimed at a large number of customers, the manufacturer may use a marketing channel that includes business-to-business distributors, merchants who take title to products (channel F). Mitsubishi fork lifts and other construction products, for example, are sold through business-to-business distributors. Building materials, operating supplies, and air-conditioning equipment are frequently channeled through business-to-business distributors.

Channel G—producer to agents to business-to-business buyers—is often the choice when a manufacturer without a marketing department needs market information, when a company is too small to field its own sales force, or when a firm wants to introduce a new product or enter a new market without using its own salespeople. Thus a large soybean producer might sell its product to animal-food processors through an agent.

Channel H is a variation of channel G: goods move from producer to agents to business-to-business distributors and then to business-to-business buyers. A manufacturer without a sales force may rely on this channel if its business-to-business customers purchase products in small quantities or if they must be resupplied frequently and therefore need access to decentralized inventories. Japanese manufacturers of electronic components, for example, work through export agents that sell to business-to-business distributors serving small producers or dealers in the United States. Chapter 22 presents more information about marketing channels for business-to-business products.

Multiple Marketing Channels

To reach diverse target markets, a manufacturer may use several marketing channels simultaneously, with each channel involving a different group of intermediaries. For example, a manufacturer turns to multiple channels when the same product is directed to both consumers and business-to-business customers. When Del Monte Corp. markets ketchup for household use, the ketchup is sold to supermarkets through grocery wholesalers or, in some cases, directly to the retailers, whereas ketchup going to restaurants or institutions follows a different distribution channel. In some instances, a producer may prefer **dual distribution**: the use of two or more marketing channels for distributing the same products to the same target market. Kellogg Co. sells its cereals directly to large retail grocery chains and to food wholesalers that, in turn, sell them to retailers. Dual distribution can cause dissatisfaction among wholesalers and smaller retailers that must compete with large retail grocery chains that make direct purchases from manufacturers like Kellogg.

Justifications for Intermediaries

Even if producers and buyers are located in the same city, there are costs associated with exchanges. As Figure 11.4 shows, if four buyers purchase the products of four producers, sixteen transactions are required. If one intermedi-

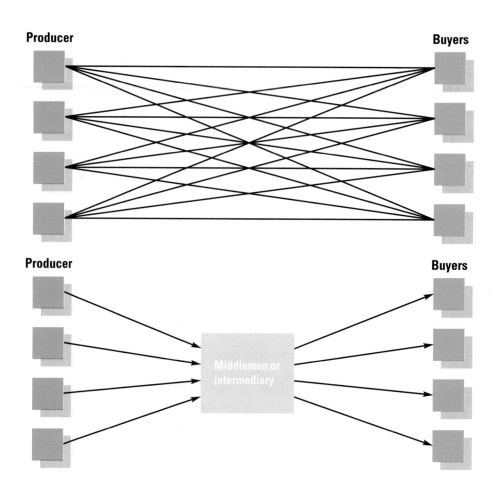

Figure 11.4

Efficiency in Exchanges Provided by an Intermediary

ary serves both producers and buyers, the number of transactions can be reduced to eight. Intermediaries become specialists in facilitating exchanges. They provide valuable assistance because of their access to, and control over, important resources for the proper functioning of the marketing channel.

Nevertheless, the press, consumers, public officials, and other marketers freely criticize intermediaries, especially wholesalers. Table 11.2 indicates that in a national survey of the general public 74 percent believed that "wholesalers frequently make high profits, which significantly increase prices that consumers pay." The critics accuse wholesalers of being inefficient and parasitic. Consumers often wish to make the distribution channel as short as possible, assuming that the fewer the intermediaries, the lower the price. Because suggestions to eliminate wholesalers come from both ends of the marketing channel, they must be careful to perform only those marketing activities that are truly desired. To survive, they must be more efficient and more service-oriented than alternative marketing institutions.

Critics who suggest that eliminating wholesalers would lower prices for consumers do not recognize that this would not eliminate the need for the services wholesalers provide. Other institutions would have to perform those services, and consumers would still have to fund them. In addition, all producers would have to deal directly with retailers or consumers, meaning that every producer

Table 11.2

Consumer Misunderstanding about Wholesalers

Statement: Wholesalers frequently make high profits, which significantly increase prices that consumers pay.

	Total %	Male %	Female %
Strongly agree	35.5	33	38
Somewhat agree	38	40	36
Neither agree nor disagree	16	14	18
Somewhat disagree	8	9	7
Strongly disagree	2.5	4	1
	100	100	100

Source: O. C. Ferrell and William M. Pride, National sample of 2,045 households.

would have to keep voluminous records and hire enough personnel to deal with every customer. Even in a direct channel, consumers might end up paying a great deal more for products because prices would reflect the costs of inefficient producers' operations.

To illustrate the efficient service that wholesalers provide, assume that all wholesalers were eliminated. Because there are more than 1.5 million retail stores, a widely purchased consumer product—say candy—would require an extraordinary number of sales contacts, possibly more than a million, to maintain the current level of product exposure. For example, Mars, Inc. would have to deliver its candy, purchase and service thousands of vending machines, establish warehouses all over the country, and maintain fleets of trucks. Selling and distribution costs for candy would skyrocket. Instead of a few contacts with food brokers, large retail organizations, and various merchant wholesalers, candy manufacturers would face thousands of expensive contacts with and shipments to smaller retailers. Such an operation would be highly inefficient, and its costs would be passed on to consumers. Candy bars would cost more, and they would be harder to find. Wholesalers are more efficient and less expensive, not only for manufacturers, but for consumers as well.

Functions of Intermediaries

Before we examine the functions of intermediaries in some detail, we should note that a distribution network helps overcome two major distribution problems: discrepancies in quantity and discrepancies in assortment. Consider a firm that manufactures jeans. The company specializes in the goods it can produce most efficiently, denim clothing. To make jeans the most economical way possible, the producer turns out a hundred thousand pairs of jeans each day. Few persons, however, want to buy a hundred thousand pairs of jeans. Thus the quantity of jeans that the company can produce efficiently is more than the average customer wants. We call this a *discrepancy in quantity*.

An **assortment** is a combination of products put together to provide benefits. A consumer creates and holds an assortment. The set of products made available to customers is an organization's assortment. Most consumers want a broad assortment of products. In addition to jeans, a consumer wants to buy shoes, food, a car, a stereo, soft drinks, and many other products. Yet our jeans manufacturer has a narrow assortment because it makes only jeans (and perhaps a few other denim clothes). There is a *discrepancy in assortment* because a consumer wants a broad assortment, but an individual manufacturer produces a narrow assortment.

Quantity and assortment discrepancies are resolved through the sorting activities of intermediaries in a marketing channel. **Sorting activities** are functions that allow channel members to divide roles and separate tasks. Sorting activities, as Figure 11.5 shows, may be grouped into four main tasks: sorting out, accumulation, allocation, and assorting of products.[2]

Sorting Out

Sorting out, the first step in developing an assortment, is separating conglomerates of heterogeneous products into relatively uniform, homogeneous groups based on product characteristics such as size, shape, weight, or color. Sorting out is especially common in the marketing of agricultural products and other raw materials, which vary widely in size, grade, and quality and would be largely unusable in an undifferentiated mass. A tomato crop, for example, must be sorted into tomatoes suitable for canning, those for making tomato juice, and those for sale in retail food stores.

Sorting out for specific products follows a set of predetermined standards. The sorter must know how many classifications to use and the criteria for each classification and must usually provide for a group of miscellaneous leftovers as well. Certain product characteristics can be categorized more easily than others; appearance and size of agricultural products are more readily apparent than flavor or nutritional content, for instance. Because the overall quality of a crop or supply of raw material most likely will vary from year to year or from region to region, classifications must be somewhat flexible.

Changing consumer needs and new manufacturing techniques influence the sorting-out process. If sorting out results in manufactured goods with minor defects, these damaged or irregular products are often marketed at lower prices through factory outlet stores, which are growing in consumer popularity. Im-

Figure 11.5

Sorting Activities Conducted by Intermediaries

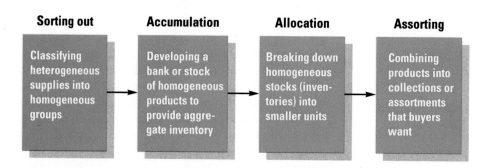

Sorting out	Accumulation	Allocation	Assorting
Classifying heterogeneous supplies into homogeneous groups	Developing a bank or stock of homogeneous products to provide aggregate inventory	Breaking down homogeneous stocks (inventories) into smaller units	Combining products into collections or assortments that buyers want

proved processing also permits the use of materials that might have been culled previously, such as the paper and aluminum now being recycled. In some industries, producers have stopped using natural materials because the manufacturing process demands uniformity that is possible only with synthetic materials. Sorting out thus helps alleviate discrepancies in assortment by making relatively homogeneous products available for the next step, accumulation.

Accumulation

Accumulation is the development of a bank or inventory of homogeneous products that have similar production or demand requirements. Farmers who grow relatively small quantities of tomatoes, for example, transport their sorted tomatoes to central collection points, where tomatoes are accumulated in large lots for movement into the next level of the channel.

Combining many small groups of similar products into larger groups serves several purposes. Products move through subsequent marketing channels more economically in large quantities because transportation rates are lower for bulk loads. In addition, accumulation gives buyers a steady supply of products in large volumes. If Del Monte had to frequently purchase small amounts of tomatoes from individual farmers, the company's tomato products would be produced much less efficiently. Instead, Del Monte buys bulk loads of tomatoes through brokers, thus maintaining a continuous supply of uniform-quality materials for processing. Accumulation lets producers continually use up stocks and replenish them, thus minimizing losses from interruptions in the supply of materials.

For both buyer and seller, accumulation also alleviates some of the problems associated with price fluctuations and highly seasonal materials. Buyers may obtain large-volume purchases at lower prices because sellers are anxious to dispose of perishable goods; purchasing agents may accumulate stocks of materials in anticipation of price hikes. In other cases, sellers may receive higher prices because they enter into long-term supply contracts with producers or they agree to store accumulated materials until the producer is ready for them. Accumulation thus relieves discrepancies in quantity. It enables intermediaries to build up specialized inventories and allocate products according to customers' needs.

Allocation

Allocation is the breaking down of large homogeneous inventories into smaller lots. This process, which addresses discrepancies in quantity, enables wholesalers to buy efficiently in truckloads or carloads and then apportion products by cases to other channel members. A food wholesaler, for instance, serves as a depot, allocating products according to market demand. The wholesaler may divide a single truckload of Del Monte canned tomatoes among several retail food stores.

Because supply and demand are seldom in perfect balance, allocation is influenced by several factors (and can sometimes resemble rationing). At times price is the overriding consideration. The highest bidder, or perhaps the buyer placing the largest order, is allocated most of the stock. At other times an intermediary gives preference to customers whose loyalty has been established or to those whose businesses show the most growth potential. In still other cases, products are allocated through compromise and negotiation.

Depending on the product, allocation may begin with the manufacturer and continue through several levels of intermediaries, including retailers. Allocation ends when the ultimate user selects the desired quantity of a particular product from the assortment of products available.

Assorting

Assorting is the process of combining products into collections or assortments that buyers want to have available in one place. Assorting eliminates discrepancies in assortment by grouping products in ways that satisfy buyers. The same food wholesaler supplying supermarkets with Del Monte tomato products may also buy canned goods from competing food processors so that grocery stores can choose from a wide assortment of canned fruits and vegetables.

Buyers want an assortment of products at one location because of some task they want to perform or some problem they want solved. A buyer looking for a variety of products, all serving different purposes, requires a broad assortment from which to choose; a buyer with more precise needs or interests will seek out a narrower, and deeper, product assortment.

Assorting is especially important to retailers, and they strive to create assortments that match the demands of consumers who patronize their stores. Although no single customer is likely to buy one of everything in the store, a retailer must anticipate the probability of purchase and provide a satisfactory range of product choices. The risk involved is greater for some retailers than for others. For example, supermarkets purchase staple foods repeatedly, and these items can be stocked with little risk. But clothing retailers who misjudge consumer demand for "hot" fashion items can lose money if their assortments contain too few (or too many) of these products. Discrepancies in assortment reappear, in fact, when retailers fail to keep pace with shifts in consumer attitudes. New specialists—such as retail outlets for computer products—may even enter the market to provide assortments existing retailers do not offer.

Channel Integration

Channel functions may be transferred between intermediaries and to producers and even customers. This section examines how channel members can either combine and control most activities or pass them on to another channel member. Remember, though, that the channel member cannot eliminate functions; unless buyers themselves perform the functions, they must pay for the labor and resources needed for the functions to be performed. The statement that "you can eliminate middlemen but you can't eliminate their functions" is an accepted principle of marketing.

Many marketing channels are determined by consensus. Producers and intermediaries coordinate their efforts for mutual benefit. Some marketing channels, however, are organized and controlled by a single leader, which can be a producer, a wholesaler, or a retailer, depending on the industry. The channel leader may establish channel policies and coordinate the development of the marketing mix. Sears, for example, is a channel leader for several of the many products it sells.

The various links or stages of the channel may be combined under the management of a channel leader either horizontally or vertically. Integration may stabilize supply, reduce costs, and increase coordination of channel members.

Vertical Channel Integration

Combining two or more stages of the channel under one management is **vertical channel integration**. One member of a marketing channel may purchase the operations of another member or simply perform the functions of the other member, eliminating the need for that intermediary as a separate entity. Total vertical integration encompasses all functions from production to ultimate buyer; it is exemplified by oil companies that own oil wells, pipelines, refineries, terminals, and service stations.

Whereas members of conventional channel systems work independently and seldom cooperate, participants in vertical channel integration coordinate their efforts to reach a desired target market. This more progressive approach to distribution enables channel members to regard other members as extensions of their own operations. A vertically integrated channel is often more effective against competition because of increased bargaining power, the ability to inhibit competitors, and the sharing of information and responsibilities.[3] At one end of an integrated channel, for example, a manufacturer might provide advertising and training assistance, and the retailer at the other end would buy the manufacturer's products in quantity and actively promote them.

In the past, integration has been successfully institutionalized in marketing channels called vertical marketing systems. A **vertical marketing system (VMS)** is a marketing channel in which a single channel member coordinates or manages channel activities to achieve efficient, low-cost distribution aimed at satisfying target market customers. Crate and Barrel (Figure 11.6) operates a vertical marketing system, managing wholesale and retail activities. Because efforts of individual channel members are combined in a VMS, marketing activities can be coordinated for maximum effectiveness and economy, without duplication of services. Vertical marketing systems are also competitive, accounting for a growing share of retail sales in consumer goods. Marketers of services, such as health care, can also benefit from vertical marketing systems. Hospitals often have the structure and resources available to successfully operate and control a vertically integrated channel.[4] Outreach facilities and hospitals in remote locations can be under the control of a central marketing unit.

Most vertical marketing systems today take one of three forms: corporate, administered, or contractual. The *corporate* VMS combines all stages of the marketing channel, from producers to consumers, under a single ownership. For example, The Limited established a corporate VMS operating corporate-owned production facilities and retail stores. Supermarket chains that own food-processing plants and large retailers that purchase wholesaling and production

Figure 11.6

Vertical Channel Integration

Crate and Barrel has integrated wholesaling and retailing functions to provide efficient distribution of housewares.

Source: Crate and Barrel.

facilities are other examples of corporate VMSs. Figure 11.7 contrasts a conventional marketing channel with a VMS, which consolidates marketing functions and institutions.

In an *administered* VMS, channel members are independent, but a high level of interorganizational management is achieved by informal coordination. Members of an administered VMS may agree, for example, to adopt uniform accounting and ordering procedures and to cooperate in promotional activities. Although individual channel members maintain their autonomy, as in conventional marketing channels, one channel member (such as the producer or a large retailer) dominates the administered VMS, so that distribution decisions take into account the system as a whole. Because of its size and power as a retailer, Wal-Mart exercises a strong influence over the independent manufacturers in its marketing channels, as do Kellogg Co. (cereal) and Magnavox (television and other electronic products).

Under a *contractual* VMS, the most popular type of vertical marketing system, interorganizational relationships are formalized through contracts. Channel members are linked by legal agreements that spell out each member's rights and obligations. For instance, franchise organizations such as McDonald's and KFC are contractual VMSs. Other contractual VMSs include wholesaler-sponsored groups, such as IGA (Independent Grocers' Alliance) stores, in which independent retailers band together under the contractual leadership of a wholesaler. Retailer-sponsored cooperatives, which own and operate their own wholesalers, are a third type of contractual VMS.

Horizontal Channel Integration

Combining institutions at the same level of operation under one management constitutes **horizontal channel integration**. An organization may integrate horizontally by merging with other organizations at the same level in a marketing channel level. For example, the owner of a dry cleaning firm might buy and combine several other existing dry cleaning establishments. Horizontal integration may enable a firm to generate sufficient sales revenue to integrate vertically as well.

Although horizontal integration permits efficiencies and economies of scale in purchasing, market research, advertising, and specialized personnel, it is not always the most effective method of improving distribution. Problems of "bigness" often follow, resulting in decreased flexibility, difficulties in coordination, and the need for additional marketing research and large-scale planning. Unless distribution functions for the various units can be performed more efficiently under unified management than under the previously separate managements, horizontal integration will not reduce costs or improve the competitive position of the integrating firm.

Figure 11.7

Comparison of a Conventional Marketing Channel and a Vertical Marketing System

Source: *Strategic Marketing*, by David J. Kollat, Roger D. Blackwell, and James F. Robeson (Holt, Rinehart and Winston, 1972). Reprinted by permission of the authors.

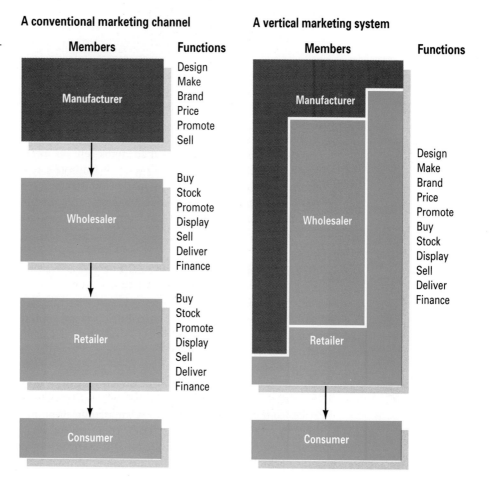

Intensity of Market Coverage

Characteristics of the product and the target market determine the kind of coverage a product should get—that is, the number and kinds of outlets in which it is sold. To achieve the desired intensity of market coverage, distribution must correspond to the behavior patterns of buyers. Chapter 8 divides consumer products into three categories—convenience products, shopping products, and specialty products—according to how consumers make purchases. In considering products for purchase, consumers take into account the replacement rate, product adjustment (services), duration of consumption, time required to find the product, and similar factors.[5] These variables directly affect the intensity of market coverage. Three major levels of market coverage are intensive, selective, and exclusive distribution.

Intensive Distribution

In **intensive distribution**, all available outlets are used for distributing a product. Intensive distribution is appropriate for convenience products such as bread, chewing gum, beer, and newspapers. To consumers, availability means a store located nearby and minimum time necessary to search for the product at the store. Sales may have a direct relationship to availability. The successful sale of products such as bread and milk at service stations or of gasoline at convenience grocery stores has shown that the availability of these products is more important than the nature of the outlet. Convenience products have a high replacement rate and require almost no service. To meet these demands, intensive distribution is necessary, and multiple channels may be used to sell through all possible outlets.

Producers of consumer packaged items rely on intensive distribution. In fact, intensive distribution is one of Procter & Gamble's key strengths. It is fairly easy for this company to formulate marketing strategies for many of its products (soaps, detergents, food and juice products, and personal-care products) because consumers want availability provided quickly and intensively.

Selective Distribution

In **selective distribution**, only some available outlets in an area are chosen to distribute a product. Selective distribution is appropriate for shopping products. Durable goods such as typewriters and stereos usually fall into this category. Such products are more expensive than convenience goods. Consumers are willing to spend greater searching time visiting several retail outlets to compare prices, designs, styles, and other features.

Selective distribution is desirable when a special effort—such as customer service from a channel member—is important. Shopping products require differentiation at the point of purchase. To motivate retailers to provide adequate presale service, selective distribution and company-owned stores are often used. Many business-to-business products are sold on a selective basis to maintain a certain degree of control over the distribution process. For example, agricultural herbicides are distributed on a selective basis because dealers must offer services to buyers, such as instructions about how to apply the herbicides safely or the option of having the dealer apply the herbicide. Evinrude outboard motors are sold by dealers on a selective basis.

Exclusive Distribution

In **exclusive distribution**, only one outlet is used in a relatively large geographic area. Exclusive distribution is suitable for products that are purchased rather infrequently, consumed over a long period of time, or require service or information to fit them to buyers' needs. Exclusive distribution is not appropriate for convenience products and many shopping products. It is used often as an incentive to sellers when only a limited market is available for products. For example, automobiles such as the Bentley, made by Rolls-Royce, are sold on an exclusive basis. Exclusive distribution affords a company tighter image control because the types of distributors and retailers that distribute the product are closely monitored.[6] A producer that uses exclusive distribution generally expects a dealer to be very cooperative with respect to carrying a complete inventory, sending personnel for sales and service training, participating in promotional programs, and providing excellent customer service. Some products may be appropriate for exclusive distribution when they are first introduced, but as competitors enter the market and the product moves through its life cycle, other types of market coverage and distribution channels often become necessary. For example, NEXT, Inc., a computer manufacturer, established an exclusive distribution agreement with Businessland Inc., a computer retailer, that was expected to generate sales of $100 million in less than two years. However, NEXT's computer workstation was soon met with intense competition, and many of the functions and features that once distinguished the workstation could be attained at a lower cost from other retailers.[7]

Selection of Distribution Channels

The process of selecting appropriate distribution channels for a product is often complex for a variety of reasons. Producers must choose specific intermediaries carefully, evaluating their sales and profit levels, performance records, other products carried, clientele, availability, and so forth. But producers must also examine other factors that influence distribution channel selection, including organizational objectives and resources, market characteristics, buyer behavior, product attributes, and environmental forces. At times these factors may cause producers to utilize multiple channels of distribution. Some products, such as insurance services, can be distributed through sales account representatives, telemarketers, or electronic systems. The decision to distribute insurance services through multiple channels is largely based on customer requirements, buying power, and costs associated with contacting customers.[8]

Organizational Objectives and Resources

A producer must consider what it is trying to accomplish in the marketplace and what resources can be brought to bear on the task. A company's objectives may be broad, such as higher profits, increased market share, and greater responsiveness to customers, or narrow, such as replacing an intermediary that has left the channel. The organization may possess sufficient financial and marketing clout to control its distribution channels—for example, by engaging in direct marketing or by operating its own trucking fleet. On the other hand, an organization may have no interest in performing distribution services or may be forced by lack of resources and experience to depend on middlemen.

The company must also evaluate the effectiveness of past distribution relationships and methods in light of its current goals. One firm might decide to maintain its basic channel structure but add members for increased coverage in new territories. Another company might alter its distribution channel so as to provide same-day delivery on all orders. When selecting distribution channels, organizational factors and objectives are important considerations.

Market Characteristics

Beyond the basic division between consumer markets and industrial markets, several market variables influence the design of distribution channels. Geography is one factor; in most cases, the greater the distance between the producer and its markets, the less expensive is distribution through intermediaries rather than through direct sales. A related consideration is market density. If customers tend to be clustered in several locations, the producer may be able to eliminate middlemen. Transportation, storage, communication, and negotiation are specific functions performed more efficiently in high-density markets. Market size—measured by the number of potential customers in a consumer or business-to-business market—is yet another variable. Direct sales may be effective if a producer has relatively few buyers for a product, but for larger markets the services of middlemen may be required.[9]

Buyer Behavior

Buyer behavior is a crucial consideration in selecting distribution channels. To be able to match intermediaries with customers, the producer must have specific, current information about customers who are buying the product and when and where they are buying it.[10] How customers buy is important as well. A manufacturer might find direct selling economically feasible for large-volume sales but inappropriate for small orders.

The producer must also understand how buyer specifications vary according to whether buyers perceive products as convenience, shopping, or specialty items (see Chapter 8). Customers for chewing gum, for example, are likely to buy the product frequently (even impulsively) from a variety of outlets. Buyers of home computers, however, carefully evaluate product features, dealers, prices, and postsale services. Buying patterns influence the selection of channels.

Buyers may be reached most effectively when producers are creative in opening up new distribution channels. Hanes, manufacturer of L'eggs pantyhose, concluded that hosiery customers would be attracted to a product they could buy conveniently while grocery shopping. As a result of L'eggs' innovative strategy, supermarkets are now included in the distribution channels for several brands of women's hosiery.

Product Attributes

Another variable in the selection of distribution channels is the product itself. Because producers of complex business-to-business products must often provide technical services to buyers both before and after the sale, these products are usually shipped directly to buyers. Perishable or highly fashionable consumer products with short shelf lives are also marketed through short channels. In other cases, distribution patterns are influenced by the product's value; the lower the price per unit, the longer the distribution chain. Additional factors to consider are the weight, bulkiness, and relative ease of handling the products. Producers may find wholesalers and retailers reluctant to carry items that create storage or display problems.[11]

Environmental Forces

Finally, producers making decisions about distribution channels must consider forces in the total marketing environment—that is, such issues as competition, ecology, economic conditions, technology, society, law, and the global economy. Technology, for example, has made possible electronic scanners, computerized inventory systems, telemarketing, and teleshopping devices, all of which are altering present distribution systems and making it harder for technologically unsophisticated firms to remain competitive. Changing family patterns and the emergence of important minority consumer groups are driving producers to seek new distribution methods for reaching market segments, and sometimes this search results in nontraditional approaches that increase competitive pressures. Interest rates, inflation, and other economic variables affect members of distribution channels at every level. Environmental forces are numerous and complex and must be taken into account if distribution efforts are to be appropriate, efficient, and effective.

Behavior of Channel Members

The marketing channel is a social system with its own conventions and behavior patterns. Each channel member performs a different role in the system and agrees (implicitly or explicitly) to accept certain rights, responsibilities, rewards, and sanctions for nonconformity. Moreover, each channel member expects certain things of every other channel member. Retailers, for instance, expect wholesalers to maintain adequate inventories and deliver goods on time. For their part, wholesalers expect retailers to honor payment agreements and keep them informed of inventory needs. In this section we discuss several issues related to channel member behavior, including cooperation, conflict, and leadership. Marketers need to understand these behavioral issues to make effective channel decisions.

Channel Cooperation

Channel cooperation is vital if each member is to gain something from other members.[12] Without cooperation, neither overall channel goals nor member goals can be realized. Policies must be developed that support all essential channel members; otherwise, failure of one link in the chain could destroy the channel. All channel members must recognize and understand that the success of one firm in the channel depends, in part, on the other firms in the channel. Thus, marketing channel members should take actions that provide a coordinated effort at satisfying market requirements. Channel cooperation leads to greater trust among channel members and improves the overall functioning of the channel.[13]

There are several ways to improve channel cooperation. A marketing channel should consider itself a unified system, competing with other systems. This way, individual members will be less likely to take actions that would create disadvantages for other members. Similarly, channel members should agree to direct their efforts toward a common target market so that channel roles can be structured for maximum marketing effectiveness, which in turn can help members achieve their individual objectives. It is crucial to define precisely the tasks that each member of the channel is to perform. This provides a basis for reviewing the intermediaries' performance and helps reduce conflicts because each channel member knows exactly what is expected of it.

Channel Conflict

Although all channel members work toward the same general goal—distributing products profitably and efficiently—members may sometimes disagree about the best methods for attaining this goal. Each channel member wants to maximize its own profits while maintaining as much autonomy as possible. However, if this self-interest creates misunderstanding about role expectations, the end result is frustration and conflict for the whole channel. For individual organizations to function together in a single social system, each channel member must clearly communicate and understand role expectations. Communication difficulties are a potential form of channel conflict because ineffective communication leads to frustration, misunderstandings, and ill-coordinated strategies.[14]

Because channel integration and coordination are achieved through role behavior, channel conflict often stems from perceived or real unmet role expectations. That is, members of the channel expect a given channel member to conduct itself in a certain way and to make a particular contribution to the total system. Wholesalers expect producers to monitor quality control and production scheduling, and they expect retailers to market products effectively. Producers and retailers expect wholesalers to provide coordination, functional services, and communication. But if members do not fulfill their roles—for example, if whole-

Favoritism in International Marketing Channels

U.S. MANUFACTURERS ARE COMPLAINING about favoritism in the international channels of distribution to Japan and Malaysia. Many U.S. manufacturers feel that Japanese channel members provide more support to Japanese products, while giving little or no support to U.S. products. In effect, U.S. businesses see this intentional favoritism as a nontariff barrier to conducting business in Japan. Similarly, U.S. exporters to Malaysia complain that local distributors pay more attention to best-selling U.S. goods and provide little support to slow-selling products that need help the most. As a type of trade barrier, this favoritism greatly reduces the size of the market for U.S. goods in Malaysia. These policies by local agents have caused a great deal of conflict between U.S. businesses and Japanese and Malaysian distributors.

Are these problems associated with international trade real or imagined? A recent study of 131 retail stores in Japan found that U.S. products receive fair treatment in Japanese markets. However, reports from U.S. analysts in Kuala Lumpur suggest that attitudes within the Malaysian culture are partly to blame for their favoritism. All analysts are quick to point out that favoritism by foreign channel members is difficult to prove. In most cases, the best way for U.S. distributors to limit negative favoritism is to visit a foreign country first-hand to learn its culture and hand-pick an agent to support their products.

Sources: Norm Borin, Cynthia Van Vranken, and Paul W. Farris, "A Pilot Test of Discrimination in the Japanese Distribution System," *Journal of Retailing,* Spring 1991, pp. 93–106; "Boosting Sales to Malaysia by 'Selling the Market,'" *East Asian Executive Reports,* Feb. 15, 1991, pp. 15–17; and Isaac Shapiro and Constance C. Hamilton, "How to Succeed in Japan: Time for U.S. Firms to Focus on Post-Entry Survival—Part II," *East Asian Executive Reports,* May 15, 1990, pp. 8, 13–18.

salers or producers fail to deliver products on time or the producers' pricing policies cut into the margins of downstream channel members—conflict may ensue. The Global Perspective deals with potential conflict in international marketing channels.

Channel conflicts also arise when dealers overemphasize competing products or diversify into product lines traditionally handled by other, more specialized, intermediaries. In some cases, conflict develops because producers strive to increase efficiency by circumventing intermediaries, as is happening in marketing channels for microcomputer software. Many software-only stores are establishing direct relationships with software producers, bypassing wholesale distributors altogether. Some dishonest retailers are also pirating software or making unauthorized copies, thus cheating other channel members out of their due compensation.

A manufacturer embroiled in channel conflict may ship late (or not at all), withdraw financing, use promotion to build consumer brand loyalty, and operate or franchise its own retail outlet. To retaliate, a retailer may develop store brands, refuse to stock certain items, focus its buying power on one supplier or group of suppliers, and seek to strengthen its position in the marketing channel. Although there is no single method for resolving conflict, an atmosphere of cooperation can be reestablished if two conditions are met. First, the role of each channel member must be specified. To minimize misunderstanding, all

Figure 11.8

Determinants of Channel Leadership

Source: Reprinted by permission of Publishing Horizons, Inc., from *Marketing Channels and Strategies*, 2nd ed., by R. D. Michman and S. D. Sibley, 1980, p. 413.

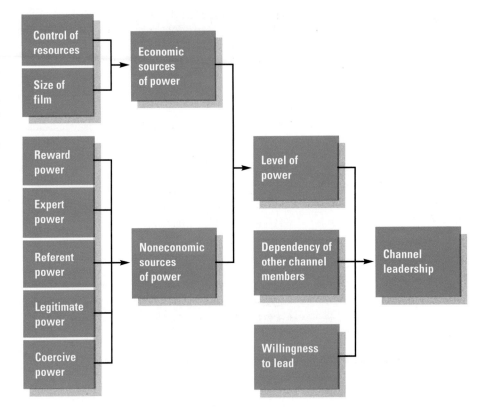

members must be able to expect unambiguous, agreed-on levels of performance from each other. Second, channel members must institute certain measures of channel coordination, which requires leadership and the benevolent exercise of control.[15] To prevent channel conflict, producers, or other channel members, may provide competing resellers with different brands, allocate markets among resellers, define direct-sales policies to clarify potential conflict over large accounts, negotiate territorial issues between regional distributors, and provide recognition to certain resellers for the importance of their role in distributing to others. Hallmark, for example, distributes its Ambassador greeting-card line in discount stores and its name brand Hallmark line in upscale department stores and Hallmark stores, thus limiting the amount of competition between retailers carrying its products.[16]

Channel Leadership

The effectiveness of marketing channels hinges on channel leadership. Producers, retailers, or wholesalers may assume this leadership. To become a leader, a channel member must want to influence and direct overall channel performance. Furthermore, to attain desired objectives, the leader must possess **channel power**, which is the ability to influence another channel member's goal achievement. As Figure 11.8 shows, the channel leader derives power from seven sources, two of them economic and five noneconomic.

The five noneconomic powers—reward, expert, referent, legitimate, and coercive—are crucial for establishing leadership. A channel leader gains reward power by providing financial benefits. Sears (Figure 11.9) is a channel leader in carpet sales. Expert power exists when other channel members believe that the leader provides special expertise required for the channel to function properly. Referent power emerges when other members strongly identify with and emulate the leader. Legitimate power is based on a superior-subordinate relationship. Coercive power is a function of the leader's ability to punish other channel members.[17] The power structure of a marketing channel, including sources of power, affects the relationships between channel members. The member who becomes the channel leader will accept the responsibilities and exercise the power associated with this role.[18]

In the United States, producers assume the leadership role in many marketing channels. A manufacturer—whose large-scale production efficiency demands increasing sales volume—may exercise power by giving channel members financing, business advice, ordering assistance, advertising, and support materials. For example, after Rubbermaid increased distribution for its products from sixty thousand to a hundred thousand outlets, it improved cooperative advertising plans and increased channel members' margins, both to motivate new channel members and to appease older channel members, which now had to compete with more outlets carrying Rubbermaid products.[19] This is an example of reward power. Coercion causes dealer dissatisfaction that is stronger than any impact from rewards, so the use of coercive power can be a major cause of channel conflict.[20] Because of its buying power, Wal-Mart has refused to buy from some middlemen, preferring to deal directly with the supplier.

Figure 11.9

Channel Leadership

Sears is a channel leader for the distribution of carpeting. Sears has considerable power in the marketing channel because of its share of the carpeting market.

Source: Courtesy of Sears, Roebuck and Company.

Retailers can also function as channel leaders, and with the rise of national chain stores and private-label merchandise, they are increasingly doing so. Small retailers, too, may share in the leadership role when they command particular consumer respect and patronage in local or regional markets. Among large retailers, K mart, J.C. Penney, and Kroger base their channel leadership on wide public exposure to their products. These retailers control many brands and sometimes replace uncooperative producers. As the channel leader in the marketing of its private-label power tools, paints, tires, motor oil, batteries, and appliances, Sears exercises two types of power. First, its high-volume sales enable the company to offer profit reward to producers that supply the private-label goods; second, its marketing expertise means that many of the producers depend on Sears to perform all marketing activities.

Wholesalers assume channel leadership roles as well, although they were more powerful decades ago, when most manufacturers and retailers were small, under-financed, and widely scattered. Today wholesaler leaders may form voluntary chains with several retailers, which they supply with bulk buying or management services or which market their own brands. In return, the retailers shift most of their purchasing to the wholesaler leader. The Independent Grocers' Alliance (IGA) is one of the best-known wholesaler leaders in the United States. IGA's power is based on the expert advertising, pricing, and purchasing knowledge it makes available to independent business owners. Other wholesaler leaders might also help retailers with store layouts, accounting, and inventory control.

Legal Issues in Channel Management

The multitude of federal, state, and local laws governing channel management are based on the general principle that the public is best served when competition and free trade are protected. Under the authority of such federal legislation as the Sherman Antitrust Act, the Clayton Act, the Federal Trade Commission Act, the Robinson-Patman Act, and the Celler-Kefauver Act, the courts and regulatory agencies determine under what circumstances channel management practices violate this underlying principle and must be restricted and when these practices may be permitted. Although channel managers are not expected to be legal experts, they should be aware that attempts to control distribution functions may have legal repercussions. The following practices are among those frequently subject to legal restraint.

Dual Distribution

A producer that distributes the same product through two or more different channel structures or sells the same or similar products through different channels under different brand names is engaging in dual distribution.[21] Liz Claiborne (Figure 11.10) makes clothing available through both department stores and their own retail outlets. The courts do not consider this practice illegal when it promotes competition. For example, a manufacturer can legally open its own retail outlets where no other retailers are available to carry the manufacturer's products. But the courts view as a threat to competition a manufacturer who

Figure 11.10

Dual Distribution

Liz Claiborne makes their products available through various department stores, as well as Liz Claiborne retail stores.

Source: Agency: Altschiller Reitzfeld/Tracy-Locke; Client: Liz Claiborne Hosiery; Writer: Rosalind Greene; Art Director: Steve Mitsch; Creative Directors: David Altschiller, Robert Reitzfeld; Photographer: Dennis Stock.

uses company-owned outlets to dominate or drive out of business independent retailers or distributors who handle its products. In such cases, dual distribution is a violation of the law. To avoid this interpretation, a producer should use a retail price that does not severely undercut the independent retailer's price.

Restricted Sales Territories

To tighten its control over the distribution of its products, a manufacturer may try to prohibit intermediaries from selling its products outside designated sales territories. The intermediaries themselves often favor this practice because it gives them exclusive territories, letting them avoid competition for the producer's brands within these territories. Many companies have long followed the policy of restricting sales in this fashion. In recent years, the courts have adopted conflicting positions in regard to restricted sales territories. Although the courts have deemed restricted sales territories a restraint of trade among intermediaries handling the same brands (except for small or newly established companies), the courts have also held that exclusive territories can actually promote competition between dealers handling different brands. At present, the producer's intent in establishing restricted territories and the overall effect of doing so on the market must be evaluated for each case individually.

Tying Contracts

When a supplier (usually a manufacturer or franchiser) furnishes a product to a channel member stipulating that the channel member must purchase other products as well, a **tying contract** exists.[22] Suppliers, for instance, may institute tying arrangements to move weaker products along with more popular items. To use another example, a franchiser may tie the purchase of equipment and supplies to the sale of franchises, justifying the policy as necessary for quality control and protection of the franchiser's reputation.

A related practice is *full-line forcing*. In this situation, a supplier requires that channel members purchase the supplier's entire line to obtain any of the supplier's products. Manufacturers sometimes use full-line forcing to ensure that intermediaries accept new products and that a suitable range of products is available to customers.

The courts accept tying contracts when the supplier alone can provide products of a certain quality, when the intermediary is free to carry competing products as well, and when a company has just entered the market. Most other tying contracts are considered illegal.

Exclusive Dealing

When a manufacturer forbids an intermediary to carry products of competing manufacturers, the arrangement is called **exclusive dealing**. A manufacturer receives considerable market protection in an exclusive dealing arrangement and may cut off shipments to an intermediary who violates such an agreement.

The legality of an exclusive dealing contract is generally determined by applying three tests. If the exclusive dealing blocks competitors from as much as 10 percent of the market, if the sales revenue involved is sizable, and if the manufacturer is much larger (and thus more intimidating) than the dealer, the arrangement is considered anticompetitive.[23] If, on the other hand, dealers and customers in a given market have access to similar products or if the exclusive dealing contract strengthens an otherwise-weak competitor, the arrangement is allowed.

Refusal to Deal

For nearly seventy years, the courts have held that producers have the right to choose the channel members with whom they will do business (and the right not to choose others). Within existing distribution channels, however, suppliers may not refuse to deal with wholesalers or dealers just because these wholesalers or dealers had resisted policies that are anticompetitive or in restraint of trade. Suppliers are further prohibited from organizing some channel members in refusal-to-deal actions against other members who choose not to comply with illegal policies.[24]

Summary

Distribution refers to activities that make products available to customers when and where they want to purchase them. A channel of distribution, or marketing channel, is a group of individuals and organizations that directs the flow of products from producers to customers. In most channels of distribution, producers and customers are linked by marketing intermediaries or middlemen, called merchants if they take title to products and functional middlemen if they do not take title. Channel structure reflects the division of responsibilities among members.

Channels of distribution are broadly classified as channels for consumer products or channels for business-to-business products. Within these two broad categories, different marketing channels are used for different products. Although some consumer goods move directly from producer to consumers, consumer product channels that include wholesalers and retailers are usually more economical and efficient. Business-to-business goods move directly from producer to end users more frequently than do consumer goods. Channels for business-to-business products may also include agents, business-to-business distributors, or both. Most producers have dual or multiple channels so that the distribution system can be adjusted for various target markets.

Although intermediaries can be eliminated, their functions are vital and cannot be dropped; these activities must be performed by someone in the marketing channel or passed on to customers. Because intermediaries serve both producers and buyers, they reduce the total number of transactions that would otherwise be needed to move products from producer to ultimate users. Intermediaries' specialized functions also help keep down costs.

An assortment is a combination of products assembled to provide benefits. Intermediaries perform sorting activities essential to the development of product assortments. Sorting activities allow channel members to divide roles and separate tasks. Through the basic tasks of sorting out, accumulating, allocating, and assorting products for buyers, intermediaries resolve discrepancies in quantity and assortment. The number and characteristics of intermediaries are determined by the assortments and by the expertise needed to perform distribution activities.

Integration of marketing channels brings various activities under the management of one channel member. Vertical integration combines two or more stages of the channel under one management. The vertical marketing system is managed centrally for the mutual benefit of all channel members. Vertical marketing systems may be corporate, administered, or contractual. Horizontal integration combines institutions at the same level of channel operation under a single management.

A marketing channel is managed so that products receive appropriate market coverage. In choosing intensive distribution, producers strive to make a product available to all possible dealers. In selective distribution, dealers are screened to choose those most qualified for exposing a product properly. Exclusive distribution usually gives one dealer exclusive rights to sell a product in a large geographic area.

When selecting distribution channels for products, manufacturers evaluate potential channel members carefully. Producers also consider the organization's objectives and available resources; the location, density, and size of a market; buyers' behavior in the target market; characteristics of the product; and outside forces in the marketing environment.

A marketing channel is a social system in which individuals and organizations are linked by a common goal: the profitable and efficient distribution of goods and services. The positions or roles of channel members are associated with rights, responsibilities, and rewards, as well as sanctions for nonconformity. Channels function most efficiently when members cooperate, but when they deviate from their roles, channel conflict can arise. Effective marketing channels are usually a result of channel leadership.

Channel leaders can facilitate or hinder the attainment of other members' goals, and they derive this power from authority, coercion, rewards, referents, or expertise. Producers are in an excellent position to structure channel policy and to use technical expertise and consumer acceptance to influence other channel members. Retailers gain channel control through consumer confidence, wide product mixes, and intimate knowledge of consumers. Wholesalers become channel leaders when they have expertise that other channel members value and when they can coordinate functions to match supply with demand.

Federal, state, and local laws regulate channel management to protect competition and free trade. The courts may prohibit or permit a given practice depending on whether it violates this underlying principle. Various procompetitive legislation applies to distribution practices. The channel management practices frequently subject to legal restraint include dual distribution, restricted sales territories, tying contracts, exclusive dealing, and refusal to deal. When these practices strengthen weak competitors or increase competition among dealers, they may be permitted; in most other cases they are deemed illegal.

Important Terms

Distribution
Channel of distribution (marketing channel)
Marketing intermediary
Merchants
Functional middlemen
Dual distribution
Assortment
Sorting activities
Sorting out
Accumulation

Allocation
Assorting
Vertical channel integration
Vertical marketing system (VMS)
Horizontal channel integration
Intensive distribution
Selective distribution
Exclusive distribution
Channel power
Tying contract
Exclusive dealing

Discussion and Review Questions

1. Compare and contrast the four major types of marketing channels for consumer products. Through which type of channel is each of the following products most likely to be distributed: (a) new automobiles, (b) saltine crackers, (c) cut-your-own Christmas trees, (d) new textbooks, (e) sofas, (f) soft drinks?
2. "Shorter channels are usually a more direct means of distribution and therefore are more efficient." Comment on this statement.
3. Describe a business-to-business distributor. What types of products are marketed through business-to-business distributors?
4. Under what conditions is a producer most likely to use more than one marketing channel?
5. Why do consumers often blame intermediaries for distribution inefficiencies? List several of the reasons.
6. How do the major functions that intermediaries perform help resolve the discrepancies in assortment and quantity?
7. How does the number of intermediaries in the channel relate to the assortments retailers need?
8. Can one channel member perform all channel functions?
9. Identify and explain the major factors that influence decision makers' selection of marketing channels.

10. Name and describe firms that use (a) vertical integration and (b) horizontal integration in their marketing channels.

11. Explain the major characteristics of each of the three types of vertical marketing systems (VMSs).

12. Explain the differences between intensive, selective, and exclusive methods of distribution.

13. "Channel cooperation requires that members support the overall channel goals to achieve individual goals." Comment on this statement.

14. How do power bases within the channel influence the selection of the channel leader?

15. Under what conditions are tying contracts, exclusive dealing, and dual distribution judged illegal?

Cases

11.1 Tyson Foods Develops Global Marketing Channels

Most people don't realize that the chicken capital of the world is Springdale, Arkansas. But the residents of this small northwest Arkansas town know it very well. Springdale is the headquarters of Tyson Foods, Inc., the nation's leading poultry producer and an international leader in the distribution of chicken products.

The story of Tyson Foods is a textbook case of a business success story. In the 1980s, Tyson Foods led all *Fortune* 500 companies in total return to investors, almost 50 percent annually. The secret behind Tyson's success is the leadership of Don Tyson, the company's chief executive officer. Since he took control of the company in 1967, Tyson has emphasized aggressive growth through acquisitions of new companies and opening up new marketing channels to reach diverse markets.

For example, at a time when more and more Americans were getting out of the kitchen and eating out, Tyson had the vision to focus his company's efforts on the "food service" segment (restaurants, hospitals, hotels, schools, and other nonsupermarket sales). The effort paid off in 1980 when Tyson became McDonald's sole supplier of Chicken McNuggets (a Don Tyson creation). In 1982, against the advice of company officials, Tyson acquired a company called Mexican Original. Today the company is posting record sales as a major supplier to Taco Bell. As a result of this company focus, Tyson Foods became the largest producer of food service poultry.

When Tyson experienced diminishing returns, it acquired former rival, the Holly Farms Corporation of Memphis, Tennessee. Holly Farms was one of the largest poultry suppliers at the retail level, and its acquisition supplied Tyson with another marketing channel to reach the U.S. poultry market. The combined companies gave Tyson a 20 percent share of the total poultry market—more than twice that of Tyson's nearest rival, ConAgra.

Tyson's marketing principle—"Segmentate, Concentrate, Dominate"—highlights the importance Tyson Foods places on finding new ways to distribute the company's products to diverse markets. Moving into the 1990s, Tyson's latest goal is to double the size of his $4 billion company by 1995. Part of the strategic plan includes extending the Tyson label to poultry products overseas and pork products in the United States. By exporting domestic production overseas to Great Britain, the firm is attempting to expand market share. Tyson's expertise domestically has been with conducting marketing research to create new chicken products, creating consumer demand, and it plans to continue this strategy on a global basis. The company is expanding its international channels to ensure that it remains on the leading edge of global competition. Tyson's international presence is evident in its exports to Pacific Rim countries, Russia and the former Soviet Republics, the Middle East, and Saudi Arabia, as well as its number-one status in Tokyo.

Tyson is also one of a few U.S. companies that operates border assembly plants in Mexico. These *maquiladoras* import component items and then export the finished product to the United States. They are an excellent way for companies involved in agricultural production to reduce the cost of labor. Further, Mexicans are able to find well-paying jobs at home, and U.S. consumers can purchase good products at more reasonable prices. Despite these advantages, few agricultural producers have ventured into Mexico. Tyson can be considered an innovator in utilizing and serving foreign markets.

Not only is Tyson well informed and innovative in foreign markets, but the company still utilizes the same expertise at home. For instance, Tyson Foods, ConAgra, and Perdue Farms have worked together to dispel the myth that poultry products are commodities. Each company has differentiated its products from those of competitors by offering specialty poultry items. Tyson's strategy involves segmenting the total market into more definable target markets. Products are then developed to be marketed to the appropriate consumers based on target market characteristics, such as demographics and values. Each target market may require a different marketing channel or distribution outlet. To meet these needs Tyson experiments with its own channels of distribution.

Tyson is an innovative company that has capitalized on Holly Farms's beef and pork products, has introduced new chicken products, and has expanded into international markets. The company now outsells its major competitor, ConAgra, by nearly a two-to-one margin in chicken products. Tyson supplies top fast-food restaurant chains and is increasing its presence in supermarkets. Over the next five years, it expects its beef and pork products to generate more than $1 billion in sales. Because Tyson must reach a large number of customers with a diverse group of products, distribution plays a major role in its strategic plan and company focus. Clearly, how Tyson chooses to distribute its products will be a factor in its future success.[25]

Questions for Discussion

1. What types of marketing channels does Tyson use to distribute its products?
2. How does Tyson maintain leadership in managing its marketing channels?
3. How can Tyson maintain its channel leadership as it moves into international markets?

11.2 Channel Selection for Cincinnati Microwave's Escort Radar Detector

For years motorists with a penchant for exceeding posted speed limits have been beating a mail-order path to the door of Cincinnati Microwave, maker of the Escort radar detector, a device that alerts speeding drivers to police radar signals. Though in recent years the radar detector's sales have declined when compared with the exponential sales figures of its early years, the executives at Cincinnati Microwave think they can regain the product's old momentum.

The Escort came into being in 1981 when electrical engineers James Jaeger and Michael Valentine analyzed the workings of a radar detector Jaeger had just purchased and saw how the model could be improved. The two first offered their idea to Electrolert Inc., maker of the Fuzzbuster, the best-selling detector at that time. When Electrolert showed no interest, Valentine and Jaeger formed a partnership to build their own detectors. Working out of Jaeger's basement on money Valentine's father had lent them, the two entrepreneurs used sophisticated heterodyne technology to produce a detector with a microwave system to amplify and filter incoming signals, thereby increasing the detector's range and reducing false alarms.

To attract an upscale clientele, Jaeger and Valentine introduced the Escort at $245, a price almost twice that of competing models. They also decided to sell the product exclusively by mail. The fledgling company could not afford retail distribution, and direct marketing would minimize risk because the detectors could be manufactured as orders arrived and would not need to be shipped until customers' checks or credit card payments had cleared. In addition, mail-order distribution would enable Jaeger and Valentine to expand the company without tying up borrowed capital in extensive inventory.

Jaeger and Valentine published a toll-free telephone number in *Road & Track* and *Motor Trend* and took turns answering the phone. At first orders trickled in at a rate of 250 or so per month. By the end of the first year, Cincinnati Microwave had sold about 1,800 units. Then *Car & Driver* published results of comparison tests on radar detectors, calling the Escort the most reliable and sensitive model on the market. The magazine also exposed the fraudulent claims of a competing firm, whose entry was merely an Escort with a different exterior. Escort sales took off. Within six months Cincinnati Microwave was swamped with more than 1,400 orders every month; at one point the company was thirty-three weeks behind in filling orders.

After a year of rapid growth, Cincinnati Microwave regained control of operations by expanding production, computerizing many functions, and hiring more personnel. (During one period the company was adding ten to twenty new employees per week.) Four years after its founding, Cincinnati Microwave's revenues had risen from $2.1 million to $57.1 million. During the start-up period, Jaeger was in charge of production and Valentine handled marketing. After disagreements over strategy, however, Jaeger bought out Valentine and his father, took the company public, and began to delegate management functions to other executives.

The demand for radar detectors leveled off after a few years, and increased competition from low-priced radar detectors, including some Japanese models, hurt the company's sales immensely. More than 85 percent of all radar detectors sold cost less than $200, and Cincinnati Microwave had nothing in that price range. Industry analysts think that Cincinnati Microwave made a huge mistake in not meeting competitors' prices on comparable radar detectors. The firm's sales have also been hampered by the actions taken by some states to restrict the use of detectors.

Cincinnati Microwave's efforts to diversify into other product areas have not been successful, and the company has discontinued ventures into satellite television receivers, luggage, and cellular telephones. Cincinnati Microwave executives had great expectations from a product they named the Guardian Interlock, but this device—an auto ignition interlock system designed to keep intoxicated drivers from starting their cars—never met anticipated sales predictions. The company lost a total of $10 million in two years on these investments.

Recently, Cincinnati Microwave won a $3.6 million contract to supply home incarceration equipment to the government of Singapore. Sold under the Guardian Technologies name, this equipment allows officials to monitor non-violent criminals in their homes, thereby reducing the problems associated with overflowing prison populations. The contract represents the company's first venture into export marketing.

Cincinnati Microwave's major strengths are its reputation for excellent customer service and a mailing list of two million names. By expanding its product mix, the company hopes to regain the success it once had. However, Cincinnati Microwave does not intend to abandon the radar detector industry. It has increased its investment in electronics research and development and plans to continue offering premium-performance items while becoming more competitive as to price.[26]

Questions for Discussion

1. Why did Cincinnati Microwave initially select a direct-distribution channel for its radar detectors?
2. What are the advantages and disadvantages of using a direct channel of distribution for products such as radar detectors?
3. If Cincinnati Microwave were to use a second marketing channel in addition to the direct channel, what channel would you recommend? Explain.

Chapter Notes

1. Based on information from AutoZone Inc., 1992 Second Quarter Report and 1991 Annual Report; and Shelley Neumeier, "Companies to Watch: AutoZone," *Fortune,* Dec. 2, 1991.
2. Wroe Alderson, *Marketing Behavior and Executive Action* (Homewood, Ill.: Irwin, 1957), pp. 201–211.
3. Jordan D. Lewis, "Using Alliances to Build Market Power," *Planning Review*, September–October 1990, pp. 4–9, 48.
4. Douglas L. Fugate and Phillip J. Decker, "Channel Leadership in Health Care Marketing: A Natural Role for Hospitals," *Health Marketing Quarterly*, nos. 3–4, 1990, pp. 189–199.
5. Leo Aspinwall, "The Marketing Characteristics of Goods," in *Four Marketing Theories* (Boulder: University of Colorado Press, 1961), pp. 27–32.
6. Allan J. Magrath, "Differentiating Yourself via Distribution," *Sales & Marketing Management*, Mar. 1991, pp. 50–57.
7. Amiel Kornel and James Daly, "NEXT Finds Revolution a Long March," *Computerworld*, June 18, 1990, pp. 1, 130–131.
8. David W. Cravens, Thomas N. Ingram, and Raymond W. LaForge, "Evaluating Multiple Sales Channel Strategies," *Journal of Business and Industrial Marketing*, Summer–Fall 1991, pp. 3–4.
9. Bert Rosenbloom, *Marketing Channels: A Management View* (Hinsdale, Ill.: Dryden, 1987), p. 160.
10. Ibid., p. 161.
11. Ibid., pp. 254–255.

12. Wroe Alderson, *Dynamic Marketing Behavior* (Homewood, Ill.: Irwin, 1965), p. 239.

13. James C. Anderson and James A. Narus, "A Model of Distributor Firm and Manufacturer Firm Working Partnerships," *Journal of Marketing*, Jan. 1990, pp. 42–58.

14. Jakki Mohr and John R. Nevin, "Communication Strategies in Marketing Channels: A Theoretical Perspective," *Journal of Marketing*, Oct. 1990, pp. 36–51.

15. Adel I. El-Ansary, "Perspectives on Channel System Performance," in *Contemporary Issues in Marketing Channels*, ed. Robert F. Lusch and Paul H. Zinszer (Norman: University of Oklahoma Press, 1979), p. 50.

16. Kenneth G. Hardy and Allan J. Magrath, "Ten Ways for Manufacturers to Improve Distribution Management," *Business Horizons*, November–December 1988, p. 68.

17. Ronald D. Michman and Stanley D. Sibley, *Marketing Channels and Strategies* (Columbus, Ohio: Grid Publishing, 1980), pp. 412–417.

18. Janet E. Keith, Donald W. Jackson, and Lawrence A. Crosby, "Effect of Alternative Types of Influence Strategies Under Different Channel Dependence Structures," *Journal of Marketing*, July 1990, pp. 30–41.

19. Hardy and Magrath, p. 68.

20. John F. Gaski and John R. Nevin, "The Differential Effects of Exercised and Unexercised Power Sources in a Marketing Channel," *Journal of Marketing Research*, July 1985, p. 139.

21. Rosenbloom, p. 91.

22. Ibid, p. 98.

23. Ibid., pp. 92–93.

24. Ibid., pp. 96–97.

25. Stephanie Anderson Forest, "Tyson Is Winging Its Way to the Top," *Fortune*, Feb. 25, 1991, pp. 57, 60; Joel Millman, "There's Your Solution," *Forbes*, Jan. 7, 1991, pp. 72, 76; Charles Conner, "Tyson CEO Will Relocate to England to Build Sales," *(Memphis) Commercial Appeal*, Oct. 28, 1990, pp. C1, C5; and Joe G. Thomas and J. M. Koonce, "Differentiating a Commodity: Lessons from Tyson Foods," *Planning Review*, September–October 1989, pp. 24–29.

26. Mike Boehmer, "Cincinnati Microwave Adding Sales, Production Workers," *Greater Cincinnati Business Record*, Sept. 30, 1991, p. 3; Mike Boyer, "Not Off Critical List Yet," *Cincinnati Enquirer*, July 24, 1991, p. E5; Mike Boyer, "Diversity Zapped Cincinnati Microwave," *Cincinnati Enquirer*, June 5, 1991, p. B8; "New Market Detected," *Cincinnati Enquirer*, July 6, 1989; "Is Microwave's Future Calling with GTE Deal?" *(Cincinnati) Business Record*, Mar. 6, 1989; "Microwave Learning from Its Mistakes," *Cincinnati Enquirer*, Aug. 10, 1987, p. D6; "Sales Drop Signals Problems for Cincinnati Microwave," *Cincinnati Enquirer*, Aug. 10, 1987, p. D1; "Microwave to Transfer Subsidiary's Product," *Cincinnati Business Courier*, Mar. 8, 1987, p. 9; Warren Brown, "Radar Detector Maker Thrives Despite Attacks," *Washington Post*, June 1, 1986, p. F1; and Michael Rogers, "Speed Bumps Ahead for Cincinnati Microwave," *Fortune*, Apr. 28, 1986, p. 84.

12 *Wholesaling*

OBJECTIVES

- To understand the nature of wholesaling in the marketing channel

- To learn about wholesalers' activities

- To understand how wholesalers are classified

- To examine organizations that facilitate wholesaling

- To explore changing patterns in wholesaling

Super Valu is one of the leading food distributors in the United States, with sales of over $12 billion. It provides food and nonfood items to 2,700 independent retailers in 33 states. Its customers range from convenience stores to giant superstores. Super Valu supplies its retailers from 17 nationwide distribution centers and provides them with more than one hundred retail support services. It monitors stores' performances and makes suggestions on how the stores might improve.

Super Valu understands its retail customers and also engages in retail activities itself. It operates the Cub chain of superwarehouse-style stores and the ShopKo chain of discount general-merchandise stores. Super Valu is not an isolated case of a wholesaler engaging in retailing activities. Many wholesalers are vertically integrating into retailing because many large retailers are taking over wholesale activities. In 1991, Super Valu spent over half its budget on wholesale operations, a key factor in the company's commitment to serving retailers.

A computer innovation—Super Valu's electronic data interchange (EDI) system—has allowed the company to monitor store orders and inventories more effectively. EDI is a communications operation that uses electronic versions of such common business documents as purchase orders and invoices. By electronically communicating with retailers, Super Valu has cut down on ordering errors and provides much quicker service. In addition, the inventories of Super Valu's retailers have been reduced because they no longer have to overbuy to preserve sufficient stock levels. Super Valu executives are trying to convince their own suppliers to adopt EDI systems. They are pleased with the system's results and are eager to extend its applications.

In 1991, Super Valu intended to sell all but 48 percent of ShopKo in order to finance the expansion of the Cub Foods line. With its commitment to expansion and continued profitability, many Wall Street analysts consider Super Valu to be the best-managed company in its industry.[1]

Photo courtesy of Super Valu Stores, Inc.

I N THIS CHAPTER we focus on wholesaling activities (such as those provided by Super Valu) within a marketing channel. We view wholesaling as all exchanges among organizations and individuals in marketing channels, except transactions with ultimate consumers. First we examine the importance of wholesalers and their functions, noting the services they render to producers and retailers alike. We then classify various types of wholesalers and facilitating organizations. Finally, we explore changing patterns in wholesaling.

The Nature and Importance of Wholesaling

Wholesaling comprises all transactions in which the purchaser intends to use the product for resale, for making other products, or for general business operations. It does not include exchanges with ultimate consumers. Wholesaling establishments are engaged primarily in selling products directly to business-to-business, reseller, government, and institutional users. The United States has a $2.5 trillion wholesaling industry.[2]

A **wholesaler** is an individual or organization engaged in facilitating and expediting exchanges that are primarily wholesale transactions. Only occasionally does a wholesaler engage in retail transactions, which are sales to ultimate consumers. There are more than 470,000 wholesaling establishments in the United States. Wholesale sales rose from $1,258 billion in 1977 to $2,525 billion in 1987.[3]

The Activities of Wholesalers

Approximately 60 percent of all products sold in the United States pass through wholesalers.[4] It is important to remember, however, that the distribution of all goods requires wholesaling activities, whether or not a wholesaling institution is involved. Wholesaling activities are not limited just to goods. Service companies, such as financial institutions, also have active wholesale networks. For example, a number of banks are buying loans in bulk from other financial institutions rather than originating loans with their customers. Sometimes intermediaries package singe-family mortgages and make them available to banks that want to own and manage the mortgages.[5] Table 12.1 lists the major activities wholesalers perform. The activities are not mutually exclusive; individual wholesalers may perform more or fewer activities than Table 12.1 shows. Wholesalers provide marketing activities for organizations above and below them in the marketing channel. In Figure 12.1, Sweetheart Cup Company promotes their product and encourages retailers to contact a Sweetheart wholesale distributor or company sales representative.

Services for Producers

Producers, above wholesalers in the marketing channel, have a distinct advantage when they use wholesalers. Wholesalers perform specialized accumulation and allocation functions for a number of products, thus allowing producers to

Figure 12.1

Wholesale Activities

Sweetheart Cup Company, Inc. ships its products directly to customers and, at the same time, encourages customers to contact wholesale distributors who make the product available to retailers.

Source: Courtesy of Sweetheart Cup Co., Inc.

concentrate on developing and manufacturing products that match consumers' wants.

Wholesalers provide other services to producers as well. By selling a manufacturer's products to retailers and other customers and by initiating sales contacts with the manufacturer, wholesalers serve as an extension of the producer's sales force. Wholesalers also provide four forms of financial assistance. They often pay the costs of transporting goods; they reduce a producer's warehousing expenses and inventory investment by holding goods in inventory; they extend credit and assume the losses from buyers who turn out to be poor credit risks; and when they buy a producer's entire output and pay promptly or in cash, they are a source of working capital. In addition, wholesalers are conduits for information within the marketing channel, keeping manufacturers up-to-date on market developments and passing along the manufacturers' promotional plans to other middlemen in the channel.

Ideally, many producers would like more direct interaction with retailers. Wholesalers, however, usually have closer contact with retailers because of their strategic position in the marketing channel. Besides, even though a producer's own sales force is probably more effective in its selling efforts, the costs of maintaining a sales force and performing the activities normally done by wholesalers are usually higher than the benefits received from better selling. Wholesalers can also spread their costs over many more products than most producers, resulting in lower costs per product unit. For these reasons, many producers have chosen to control promotion and influence the pricing of products and shifted transportation, warehousing, and financing functions to wholesalers.

Services for Retailers

Independent wholesalers are helpful to retailers trying to target specific markets. The wholesaler supports the retailer by playing a key role in assisting with marketing strategy development and implementation of marketing activities.[6] Wholesalers also help their retailer customers select inventory. In industries where obtaining supplies is important, skilled buying is essential. A wholesaler who buys is a specialist in understanding market conditions and an expert at negotiating final purchases. For example, based on its understanding of local customer needs and market conditions, Lawrence R. McCoy & Co., a Massachusetts building supply wholesaler, purchases inventory ahead of season so that it can provide its retail customers with the building supplies they want when they want them.[7] A retailer's buyer can thus avoid the responsibility of looking for and coordinating supply sources. Moreover, if the wholesaler makes purchases for several different buyers, expenses can be shared by all customers. Another advantage is that a manufacturer's salespersons can offer retailers only a few products at a time, but independent wholesalers have a wide range of products available.

Table 12.1

Major Wholesaling Activities

Activity	Description
Wholesale management	Planning, organizing, staffing, and controlling wholesaling operations
Negotiating with suppliers	Serving as the purchasing agent for customers by negotiating supplies
Promotion	Providing a sales force, advertising, sales promotion, and publicity
Warehousing and product handling	Receiving, storing and stockkeeping, order processing, packaging, shipping outgoing orders, and materials handling
Transportation	Arranging and making local and long-distance shipments
Inventory control and data processing	Controlling physical inventory, bookkeeping, recording transactions, keeping records for financial analysis
Security	Safeguarding merchandise
Pricing	Developing prices and providing price quotations
Financing and budgeting	Extending credit, borrowing, making capital investments, and forecasting cash flow
Management and marketing assistance to clients	Supplying information about markets and products and providing advisory services to assist customers in their sales efforts

By buying in large quantities and delivering to customers in smaller lots, a wholesaler can perform physical distribution activities (covered in Chapter 14)—such as transportation, materials handling, inventory planning, communication, and warehousing—more efficiently and can provide more service than a producer or retailer would be able to do with its own physical distribution system. Furthermore, wholesalers can provide quick and frequent delivery even when demand fluctuates. They are experienced in providing fast delivery at low cost, which lets the producer and the wholesalers' customers avoid risks associated with holding large product inventories.

Because they carry products for many customers, wholesalers can maintain a broad product line at a relatively low cost. For example, a small Chrysler-Plymouth dealer in the Midwest discovered that it was cheaper to let wholesale suppliers provide automobile parts than to maintain a parts inventory at the dealership. Often wholesalers can perform storage and warehousing activities more efficiently, permitting retailers to concentrate on other marketing activities. When wholesalers provide storage and warehousing, they generally take on the ownership function as well, an arrangement that frees retailers' and producers' capital for other purposes. Inside Marketing deals with the variety of services that McKesson provides to retailers.

Wholesalers are very important in reaching global markets. Approximately 85 percent of all prescription drugs sold in Europe go through wholesalers that are within the national borders of the country in which the products are sold.[8] In the future it is anticipated that more wholesalers will operate without considering national borders between countries and will penetrate global markets.[9]

Classifying Wholesalers

Many types of wholesalers meet the different needs of producers and retailers. In addition, new institutions and establishments develop in response to producers and retail organizations that want to take over wholesaling functions. Wholesalers adjust their activities as the contours of the marketing environment change.

Wholesalers are classified along several dimensions. Whether a wholesaler is owned by the producer influences how it is classified. Wholesalers are also grouped as to whether they take title to (actually own) the products they handle. The range of services provided is another criterion used for classification. Finally, wholesalers are classified according to the breadth and depth of their product lines. Using these dimensions, we discuss three general categories, or types, of wholesaling establishments: (1) merchant wholesalers, (2) agents and brokers, and (3) manufacturers' sales branches and offices.

Merchant Wholesalers

Merchant wholesalers are wholesalers that take title to goods and assume the risks associated with ownership. These independently owned businesses, which make up about 83 percent of all wholesale establishments, generally buy and resell products to business-to-business or retail customers.[10] A producer is likely

McKesson Uses Technology to Become the Leading Health Care Wholesaler

MCKESSON CORPORATION is the leading wholesale distributor of health care products in the United States. Throughout its existence, McKesson has revolutionized the health care industry by providing health care retailers with distribution innovations, new avenues of customer support, and electronic information systems.

McKesson set out to assist in particular smaller retail drugstores that were competing with the larger health care chains. It organized these stores into purchasing cooperatives that could then receive volume discounts comparable to the ones given to giant chain operations. Using research gathered by its sales force, McKesson learned that the smaller stores wanted help with marketing research, shelf-management planning, centralized warehousing and storage, and cooperative advertising and joint marketing. McKesson assisted them in all these areas, thus establishing a loyal base of customers. Because of McKesson's efforts, the smaller drugstores were able to offer consumers reduced prices and better services—making them more profitable and stable enterprises.

McKesson has reduced retailers' labor costs, product costs, and inventory holding costs by developing the most advanced computer system in the industry,

which allows orders to be handled electronically. Hand-held order entry devices allow retailers to automatically order products. McKesson has developed a communications system so complex that it has satellites, small dish antennas, and expert systems that help resolve any problems in inventory control quickly. In fact, McKesson has been a pioneer working with IBM's national service division to determine how to use technology best to achieve customer satisfaction. The use of advanced inventory technology has allowed McKesson to differentiate itself from other drug wholesalers.

Sources: Paul Desmond, "McKesson Expert Net Tool Just Keeps Getting Smarter," *Network World,* May 20, 1991, pp. 1, 59; "Satellite Keeps Watchful Eye on McKesson," *Chain Store Age Executive,* October 1990, pp. 81–82; William L. Trombetta, "Channel Systems: An Idea Whose Time Has Come in Health Care Marketing," *Journal of Health Care Marketing,* September 1989, pp. 26–35; "IBM Means Service, but What Does Service Mean Today?," *IBM Directions,* Fall 1989, pp. 2–7; and Meghan O'Leary, "Getting the Most Out of Buying at Cost," *CIO,* August 1989, pp. 86–88.

to use merchant wholesalers when selling directly to customers would be economically unfeasible. From the producer's point of view, merchant wholesalers are also valuable for providing market coverage, making sales contacts, storing inventory, handling orders, collecting market information, and furnishing customer support.[11] Some merchant wholesalers are even involved in packaging and developing private brands to help their retailer customers be competitive.

During the past thirty years, merchant wholesalers have expanded their share of the wholesale market, despite competition from other types of intermediaries. They currently employ approximately 4.5 million people and have an annual payroll of approximately $100 billion in the United States.[12] In 1987 merchant wholesalers accounted for more than half (58 percent) of all wholesale revenues.[13] However, between 1987 and 1992, merchant wholesalers' profits as a percentage of sales shrank under pressure from retailers demanding lower prices.[14] As a rule, merchant wholesalers for business-to-business products are better established and earn higher profits than consumer goods merchant wholesalers; the latter normally deal in products of lower unit value and face more competition from other middlemen. Business-to-business products wholesalers are also more likely to have selective distribution arrangements with manufacturers because of the technical nature of many business-to-business products.

Merchant wholesalers go by various names, including wholesaler, jobber, distributor, assembler, exporter, and importer.[15] They fall into one of two broad categories: full-service and limited-service. Figure 12.2 illustrates the different types of merchant wholesalers.

Full-Service Merchant Wholesalers **Full-service wholesalers** are middlemen who offer the widest possible range of wholesaling functions. Their customers rely on them for product availability, suitable assortments, bulk breaking (breaking large quantities into smaller ones), financial assistance, and technical advice and service.[16] Full-service wholesalers provide numerous marketing services to interested customers. Many large grocery wholesalers, for example, help retailers with store design, site selection, personnel training, financing, merchandising, advertising, coupon redemption, and scanning. Although full-service wholesalers often earn higher gross margins than other wholesalers, their operating expenses are also higher because they perform a wider range of functions. Full-service merchant wholesalers may handle either consumer products or business-to-business products and are categorized as general-merchandise, limited-line, or specialty-line wholesalers.

General-Merchandise Wholesalers **General-merchandise wholesalers** are middlemen who carry a wide product mix but offer limited depth within the product lines. They deal in such products as drugs, hardware, nonperishable

Figure 12.2

Types of Merchant Wholesalers

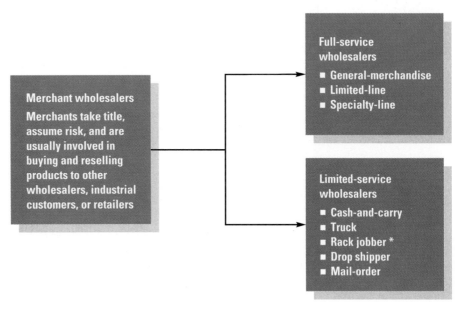

* Rack jobbers, in many cases, provide such a large number of services that they can be classified as full-service, specialty-line wholesalers.

Figure 12.3

Wholesalers

Cereal Foods is a wholesaler and manufacturer of flour, cereal, and bakery products.

Source: Courtesy of Charles Haines Ltd.

foods, cosmetics, detergents, and tobacco. General-merchandise wholesalers develop strong, mutually beneficial relationships with neighborhood grocery stores, hardware and appliance shops, and local department stores, which are their typical customers. The small retailers often obtain everything they need from these wholesalers. General-merchandise wholesalers for business-to-business customers provide supplies and accessories and are sometimes called *business-to-business distributors* or *mill supply houses.*

Limited-Line Wholesalers **Limited-line wholesalers** are wholesalers that carry only a few product lines—such as groceries, lighting fixtures, or oil-well drilling equipment—but offer an extensive assortment of products within those lines. In Figure 12.3, Cereal Foods, a New Zealand manufacturer, promotes the lines of flour they carry. They provide a range of services similar to those of full-service merchandise wholesalers. Limited-line wholesalers for industrial goods serve relatively large geographic areas and provide technical expertise; in consumer goods, they supply single- or limited-line retailers. Leading Edge Products, Inc., for example, is a limited-line wholesaler of computer equipment and supplies. The company markets printers, modems, screens, and its own private-label computer disks to the retailers that serve users of home and office computers.

Specialty-Line Wholesalers Of all the wholesalers, **specialty-line wholesalers** are the middlemen who carry the narrowest range of products, usually a single product line or a few items within a product line. For example, wholesalers that carry shellfish, fruit, or other food delicacies are specialty-line wholesalers. Specialty-line wholesalers understand the particular requirements of the ultimate buyers and offer customers detailed product knowledge and depth of choice. To provide sales assistance to retailers, specialty wholesalers may set up displays and arrange merchandise. In industrial markets, specialty wholesalers often are better able than manufacturers to give customers technical advice and service.

Rack jobbers are specialty-line wholesalers that own and maintain their own display racks in supermarkets and drugstores. They specialize in nonfood items—particularly branded, widely advertised products sold on a self-serve basis —that the retailers themselves prefer not to order and stock because of risk or inconvenience. Health and beauty aids, toys, books, magazines, hardware, housewares, and stationery are typical products rack jobbers handle. The rack jobbers send out delivery persons to set up displays, mark merchandise, stock shelves, and keep billing and inventory records; retailers need only furnish the space. Most rack jobbers operate on consignment and take back unsold products.

Limited-Service Merchant Wholesalers **Limited-service wholesalers** provide only some marketing services and specialize in a few functions. Producers perform the remaining functions, or the functions are passed on to customers or other middlemen. Limited-service wholesalers take title to merchandise, but in many cases they do not deliver merchandise, grant credit, provide marketing information, store inventory, or plan ahead for customers' future needs. Because they offer only restricted services, limited-service wholesalers are compensated with lower rates and thus earn smaller profit margins than full-service wholesalers.

Although certain types of limited-service wholesalers are few in number (and are not even categorized separately by the Census Bureau), they are important in the distribution of such products as specialty foods, perishable items, construction materials, and coal. In this section we discuss the specific functions of four typical limited-service wholesalers: cash-and-carry wholesalers, truck wholesalers, drop shippers, and mail-order wholesalers. (Table 12.2 summarizes the services these wholesalers provide.)

Cash-and-Carry Wholesalers **Cash-and-carry wholesalers** are middlemen whose customers—usually small retailers and small industrial firms—will pay cash and furnish transportation. In some cases, full-service wholesalers set up cash-and-carry departments because they cannot otherwise supply small retailers profitably. Cash-and-carry middlemen usually handle a limited line of products with a high turnover rate—for instance, groceries, building materials, electrical supplies, or office supplies.

Cash-and-carry wholesaling developed after 1920, when independent retailers began experiencing competitive pressure from large chain stores. Today cash-and-carry wholesaling offers advantages to wholesaler and customers alike. The wholesaler has no expenditures for outside salespersons, marketing, research, promotion, credit, or delivery, and the customer benefits from lower prices and immediate access to products. Many small retailers whose accounts were refused by other wholesalers have survived because of cash-and-carry wholesalers. The Global Perspective describes how Sam's Club is serving a growing number of small cash-and-carry organizations and is exporting the wholesale-club idea abroad.

Truck Wholesalers **Truck wholesalers**, sometimes called truck jobbers or wagon jobbers, are middlemen who transport a limited line of products directly to customers for on-the-spot inspection and selection. These wholesalers are often small operators who own and drive their own trucks. Usually, truck wholesalers have regular routes and call on retailers and institutions to determine their needs.

Truck wholesalers play an important part in supplying small grocery stores with perishables, such as fruits and vegetables, which other wholesalers often choose not to carry. They may also sell meat, potato chips, supplies for service stations, and tobacco products. Although truck wholesalers perform selling, promotional, and transportation functions, they are generally classified as limited-service wholesalers because they do not extend credit. As a result of their low-volume sales and wide range of customer services, their operating costs are high.

Drop Shippers **Drop shippers**, also known as desk jobbers, are intermediaries who take title to goods and negotiate sales but never take actual possession of products. They forward orders from retailers, business-to-business buyers, or other wholesalers to manufacturers and then arrange for carload shipments of items to be delivered directly from producers to customers. The drop shipper assumes responsibility for the products during the entire transaction, including the costs of any unsold goods.

Drop shippers are most commonly used in large-volume purchases of bulky goods, such as coal, oil, chemicals, lumber, and building materials. Normally sold in carload quantities, these products are expensive to handle and ship relative to their unit value; extra loading and unloading is an added (and unnecessary) expense. One trend in this form of wholesaling is the use of more drop shipping from manufacturers to supermarkets. A drop shipment eliminates

Table 12.2 **Various Services That Limited-Service Merchant Wholesalers Provide**

	Cash-and-Carry	Truck	Drop Shipper[a]	Mail Order
Physical possession of merchandise	Yes	Yes	No	Yes
Personal sales calls on customers	No	Yes	No	No
Information about market conditions	No	Some	Yes	Yes
Advice to customers	No	Some	Yes	No
Stocking and maintenance of merchandise in customers' stores	No	No	No	No
Credit to customers	No	Some	Yes	Some
Delivery of merchandise to customers	No	Yes	No	No

[a]Also called *desk jobber.*

Sam's Club Brings Small-Business Wholesale Club to Mexico

SAM'S CLUB is a highly successful warehouse/wholesale club operated by Wal-Mart Stores, Inc., that combines cash-and-carry wholesaling features with discount retailing. With approximately 150 outlets, Sam's Club's sales reached $6.6 billion in 1991, an average of $44 million per unit.

Sam's Club focuses on small-business owners and institutional customers, such as schools and churches, who for a nominal annual fee (about $25) may purchase products at wholesale prices for business use or resale. It also offers small-business members special hours for their exclusive patronage of stores and *Sam's Buy-line,* a news publication that provides helpful tips and information on how to run a small business more effectively. The goal of Sam's Club is to concentrate on group members who are organizational buyers and shop at Sam's Clubs on a regular basis. This gives Sam's the high-volume members that make up the majority of their business.

In July 1991, Wal-Mart/Sam's Club announced a joint venture with CIFRA, Mexico's largest distributor. Together they plan to introduce the wholesale club concept in Mexico. The first two clubs, called Club Aurrera, opened at the beginning of 1992. Mexico's economy has been improving, and the current policy is to view its proximity to the United States as a business opportunity. Foreign investment is being encouraged, and a free trade agreement with the United States is being negotiated. With all aspects of the Mexican economy improving, the Sam's Club–CIFRA venture has the potential to expand the small-business wholesale club concept to Mexico.

Sources: Matt Moffett, "A 1980's Style Boom Is Just Now Reaching an Awakening Mexico," *Wall Street Journal,* Dec. 18, 1991, pp. A1, A12; *Sam's Buy-line,* Winter 1991, p. 3; and Wal-Mart 1991 Annual Report, p. 2.

---

warehousing and deferred deliveries to the stores, and large supermarkets can sell entire truckloads of products rapidly enough to make drop shipping profitable.[17]

Because drop shippers incur no inventory costs and provide only minimal promotional assistance, they have low operating costs and can pass along some of the savings to their customers. In some cases, drop shippers do offer planning services, credit, and personal selling.

Mail-Order Wholesalers **Mail-order wholesalers** use catalogs instead of sales forces to sell products to retail, industrial, and institutional buyers. This is a convenient and effective method of selling small items to customers in remote areas. Mail order enables buyers to choose particular catalog items and then send in their orders and receive shipments through United Parcel Service, the U.S. Postal Service, or other carriers. Wholesalers can thus generate sales in locations that otherwise would be unprofitable to service.

Wholesale mail-order houses generally feature cosmetics, specialty foods, hardware, sporting goods, business and office supplies, and automotive parts. They usually require payment in cash or by credit card, and they give discounts for large orders. Mail-order wholesalers hold goods in inventory and offer some planning services but seldom provide assistance with promotional efforts.

Agents and Brokers

Agents and brokers (see Figure 12.4) negotiate purchases and expedite sales but do not take title to products. They are **functional middlemen**, intermediaries who perform a limited number of marketing activities in exchange for a commission, which is generally based on the product's selling price. **Agents** are middlemen who represent buyers or sellers on a permanent basis. **Brokers** are usually middlemen that either buyers or sellers employ temporarily. Together, agents and brokers account for 10.4 percent of the total sales volume of all wholesalers.[18]

Although agents and brokers perform even fewer functions than limited-service wholesalers, they are usually specialists in particular products or types of customers and can provide valuable sales expertise. They know their markets well and often form long-lasting associations with customers. Agents and brokers enable manufacturers to expand sales when resources are limited, to benefit from the services of a trained sales force, and to hold personal selling costs down. However, despite the advantages they offer, agents and brokers face increased competition from merchant wholesalers, manufacturers' sales branches and offices, and direct-sales efforts.

Here we look at three types of agents: manufacturers' agents, selling agents, and commission merchants. We also examine the brokers' role in bringing about exchanges between buyers and sellers. Table 12.3 summarizes these services.

Manufacturers' Agents **Manufacturers' agents**—which account for over half of all agent wholesalers—are independent middlemen who represent two or more sellers and usually offer customers complete product lines. They sell and take orders year round, much like a manufacturer's sales office does. Restricted

Figure 12.4

Types of Agents and Brokers

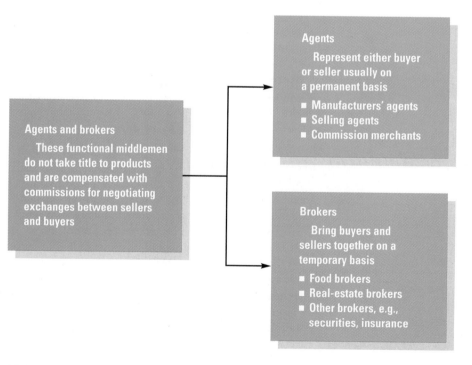

	Manufacturers' Agents	Selling Agents	Commission Merchants	Brokers
Physical possession of merchandise	Some	No	Yes	No
Long-term relationship with buyers or sellers	Yes	Yes	Yes	No
Representation of competing product lines	No	No	Yes	Yes
Limited geographic territory	Yes	No	No	No
Credit to customers	No	Yes	Some	No
Delivery of merchandise to customers	Some	Yes	Yes	No

Table 12.3   **Various Services Agents and Brokers Provide**

to a particular territory, a manufacturers' agent handles noncompeting and complementary products. The relationship between the agent and each manufacturer is governed by written agreements explicitly outlining territories, selling price, order handling, and terms of sale relating to delivery, service, and warranties. Manufacturers' agents are commonly used in the sale of apparel and accessories, machinery and equipment, iron, steel, furniture, automotive products, electrical goods, and certain food items.

Although most manufacturers' agents run small enterprises, their employees are professional, highly skilled salespersons. The agents' major advantages, in fact, are their wide range of contacts and strong customer relationships. These intermediaries help large producers minimize the costs of developing new sales territories and adjust sales strategies for different products in different locations. Agents are also useful to small producers that cannot afford outside sales forces of their own because the producers incur no costs until the agents have actually sold something. By concentrating on a limited number of products, agents can mount an aggressive sales effort that would be impossible with any other distribution method except producer-owned sales branches and offices. In addition, agents are able to spread operating expenses among noncompeting products and thus can offer each manufacturer lower prices for services rendered.

The chief disadvantage of using agents is the higher commission rate (usually 10 to 15 percent) they charge for new-product sales. When sales of a new product begin to build, total selling costs go up, and producers sometimes transfer the selling function to in-house sales representatives. For this reason, agents try to avoid depending on a single product line; most work for more than one manufacturer.

Manufacturers' agents have little or no control over producers' pricing and marketing policies. They do not extend credit, and they may not be able to provide technical advice. They do occasionally store and transport products, assist with planning, and provide promotional support. Some agents help retailers advertise and maintain a service organization. The more services offered, the higher the agent's commission.

Selling Agents **Selling agents** market either all of a specified product line or a manufacturer's entire output. They perform every wholesaling activity except taking title to products. Selling agents usually assume the sales function for several producers at a time and are often used in place of a marketing department. In contrast to other agent wholesalers, selling agents generally have no territorial limits and have complete authority over prices, promotion, and distribution. They play a key role in the advertising, marketing research, and credit policies of the sellers they represent, at times even advising on product development and packaging.

Selling agents, who account for about 1 percent of the wholesale trade, are used most often by small producers or by manufacturers who find it difficult to maintain a marketing department because of seasonal production or other factors. A producer having financial problems may also engage a selling agent. By so doing, the producer relinquishes some control of the business but may gain working capital by avoiding immediate marketing costs.

To avoid conflicts of interest, selling agents represent noncompeting product lines. The agents play an important part in the distribution of coal and textiles, and they also sometimes handle canned foods, household furnishings, clothing, lumber, and metal products. In these businesses, competitive pressures increase the importance of marketing relative to production, and the selling agent is a source of essential marketing and financial expertise.

Commission Merchants **Commission merchants** are agents that receive goods on consignment from local sellers and negotiate sales in large central markets. Most often found in agricultural marketing, commission merchants take possession of truckload quantities of commodities, arrange for any necessary grading or storage, and transport the commodities to auction or markets where they are sold. When sales have been completed, an agent deducts a commission, plus the expense of making the sale, and then turns over the profits to the producer.

Sometimes called factor merchants, these agents may have broad powers regarding prices and terms of sale, and they specialize in obtaining the best price possible under market conditions. Commission merchants offer planning assistance and sometimes extend credit, but they do not usually provide promotional support. Because commission merchants deal in large volumes, their per-unit costs are usually low. Their services are most useful to small producers that must get products to buyers but choose not to field a sales force or accompany the goods to market themselves. In addition to farm products, commission merchants may handle textiles, art, furniture, or seafood products.

Businesses—including farms—that use commission merchants have little control over pricing, although the seller can specify a minimum price. Generally, too, the seller is able to supervise the agent's actions through a check of the commodity prices published regularly in newspapers. Large producers, however, need to maintain closer contact with the market and therefore have limited need for commission merchants.

Brokers Brokers seek out buyers or sellers and help negotiate exchanges. In other words, a broker's primary purpose is to bring buyers and sellers together. Thus brokers perform fewer functions than other intermediaries. They are not involved in financing or physical possession, have no authority to set prices, and assume almost no risks. Instead, they offer their customers specialized knowledge of a particular commodity and a network of established contacts.

Brokers are especially useful to sellers of certain types of products that market those products only occasionally. Sellers of used machines, seasonal food products, financial securities, and real estate may not know of potential buyers. A broker can furnish this information. The party who engages the broker's services—usually the seller—pays the broker's commission when the transaction is completed.

In the food industry—where brokers are most commonly found—**food brokers** are intermediaries that sell food and general merchandise items to retailer-owned and merchant wholesalers, grocery chains, business-to-business buyers, and food processors. Food brokers enable buyers and sellers to adjust to fluctuating market conditions; they also provide assistance in grading, negotiating, and inspecting foods (in some cases they store and deliver products). Because of the seasonal nature of food production, the association between food broker and producer is temporary. Many mutually beneficial broker-producer relationships, however, are resumed year after year. Because food brokers provide a range of services on a somewhat permanent basis and operate in specific geographic territories, they can more accurately be described as manufacturers' agents.

Manufacturers' Sales Branches and Offices

Sometimes called manufacturers' wholesalers, manufacturers' sales branches and offices resemble merchant wholesalers' operations. According to the *Census of Wholesale Trade,* these producer-owned middlemen account for about 9 percent of wholesale establishments and generate approximately one-third (31 percent) of all wholesale sales.[19]

Sales branches are manufacturer-owned middlemen selling products and providing support services to the manufacturer's sales force, especially in locations where large customers are concentrated and demand is high. They offer credit, deliver goods, give promotional assistance, and furnish other services. In many cases, they carry inventory (although this practice often duplicates the functions of other channel members and is now declining). Customers include retailers, business-to-business buyers, and other wholesalers. Branch operations are common in the electrical supplies (Westinghouse Electric Corp.), plumbing (Crane Co. and American Standard), lumber, and automotive parts industries.

Sales offices are manufacturer-owned operations that provide services normally associated with agents. Like sales branches, they are located away from manufacturing plants, but unlike branches, they carry no inventory. A manufacturer's sales offices or branches may sell products that enhance the manufacturer's own product line. For example, Hiram Walker, a liquor producer, imports wine from Spain to increase the number of products that its sales offices can offer wholesalers. United States Tobacco Company imports Borkum Riff smoking tobacco from Sweden to add variety to its chewing tobacco and snuff lines.

Manufacturers may set up sales branches or sales offices so they can reach customers more effectively by performing wholesaling functions themselves. A manufacturer may also set up these branches or offices when needed specialized wholesaling services are not available through existing middlemen. In some situations, however, a manufacturer may bypass its wholesaling organization entirely—for example, if the producer decides to serve large retailer customers directly. One major distiller bottles private-label bourbon for California supermarkets and separates this operation completely from the company's sales office, which serves other retailers.

Facilitating Agencies

The total marketing channel is more than a chain linking the producer, intermediary, and buyer. **Facilitating agencies**—transportation companies, insurance companies, advertising agencies, marketing research agencies, and financial institutions—may perform activities that enhance channel functions. Note, however, that any of the functions these facilitating agencies perform may be taken over by the regular marketing intermediaries in the marketing channel.

The basic difference between channel members and facilitating agencies is that channel members perform the negotiating functions (buying, selling, and transferring title), whereas facilitating agencies do not.[20] In other words, facilitating agencies assist in the operation of the channel but do not sell products. The channel manager may view the facilitating agency as a subcontractor to which various distribution tasks can be farmed out according to the principle of specialization and division of labor.[21] Channel members (producers, wholesalers, or retailers) may rely on facilitating agencies because they believe that these independent businesses will perform various activities more efficiently and more effectively than they themselves could. Facilitating agencies are functional specialists performing special tasks for channel members without getting involved in directing or controlling channel decisions. The following sections describe the ways in which facilitating agencies provide assistance in expediting the flow of products through marketing channels.

Public Warehouses

Public warehouses are storage facilities available for a fee. Producers, wholesalers, and retailers may rent space in a warehouse instead of constructing their own facilities or using a merchant wholesaler's storage services. Many warehouses also order, deliver, collect accounts, and maintain display rooms where potential buyers can inspect products.

To use goods as collateral for a loan, a channel member may place products in a bonded warehouse. If it is too impractical or expensive to physically transfer goods, the channel member may arrange for a public warehouser to verify that goods are in the member's own facilities and then issue receipts for lenders.[22] Under this arrangement, the channel member retains possession of the products, but the warehouser has control. Many public warehousers know where their clients can borrow working capital and are sometimes able to arrange low-cost loans.

Finance Companies

Wholesalers and retailers may be able to obtain financing by transferring ownership of products to a sales finance company, bank, or savings and loan association while retaining physical possession of the goods. Often called "floor planning," this form of financing enables wholesalers and retailers—especially automobile and appliance dealers—to offer a greater selection of products for customers and thus increase sales. When a product is sold, the dealer may have to pay off the loan immediately. The products financed through floor plans are usually well known, sell relatively easily, and present little risk.

Other financing functions are performed by factors—organizations that provide clients with working capital by buying their accounts receivable or by loaning money, using the accounts receivable as collateral. Most factors minimize their own risks by specializing in particular industries, the better to evaluate individual channel members within those industries. Factors usually lend money for a longer time than banks. They may help clients improve their credit and collection policies and may also provide management expertise.

Transportation Companies

Rail, truck, air, and other carriers are facilitating organizations that help manufacturers and retailers transport products. Each form of transportation has its own advantages. Railroads ship large volumes of bulky goods at low cost; in fact, a "unit train" is the cheapest form of overland transportation for ore, grain, or other commodities. Air transport is relatively expensive but often preferred for shipping high-value or perishable goods. Trucks, which usually carry short-haul, high-value goods, now carry more and more products because factories are moving closer to their markets. As a result of technological advances, pipelines now transport powdered solids and fluidized solid materials, as well as petroleum and natural gas.

Transportation companies sometimes take over the functions of other middlemen. Because of the ease and speed of using air transportation for certain types of products, air freight companies, such as the one shown in Figure 12.5, can eliminate the need of maintaining large inventories and branch warehouses. In other cases, freight forwarders perform accumulation functions by combining less-than-full shipments into full loads and passing on the savings to customers—perhaps charging a carload rate rather than a less-than-carload rate.

Trade Shows and Trade Marts

Trade shows and trade marts enable manufacturers or wholesalers to exhibit products to potential buyers and thus help the selling and buying functions. **Trade shows** are industry exhibitions that offer both selling and nonselling benefits.[23] On the selling side, trade shows let vendors identify prospects; gain access to key decision makers; disseminate facts about their products, services, and personnel; and actually sell products and service current accounts through

Figure 12.5

Facilitating Agencies

Air express companies, such as Federal Express, facilitate and sometimes perform functions of marketing channel members.

Source: Courtesy of Federal Express.

**WE DELIVER TO EVERY CORNER OF THE EARTH.
(INCLUDING THE CORNER OF 東 AND 西.)**

Federal Express now serves more than 100 countries worldwide.

contacts at the show.[24] The London International Fashion Show in Figure 12.6 makes many manfacturers' fashions available to retailers. Trade shows also allow a firm tc reach potential buyers who have not been approached through regular selling efforts. In fact, research indicates that most trade show visitors have not been contacted by a sales representative of any company within the past year, and many are therefore willing to travel several hundred miles to attend trade shows to learn about new goods and services.[25] The nonselling benefits include opportunities to maintain the company image with competitors, customers, and the industry; gather information about competitors' products and prices; and identify potential channel members.[26] Trade shows have a positive influence on other important marketing variables, including maintaining or enhancing company morale, product testing, and product evaluation.

Trade shows can permit direct buyer-seller interaction and may eliminate the need for agents. Companies exhibit at trade shows because of the high concentration of prospective buyers for their products. Studies show that it takes, on the average, 5.1 sales calls to close a business-to-business sale but less than 1 sales call (0.8) to close a trade show lead. The explanation for the latter figure is that more than half of the customers who purchase a product based on information gained at a trade show order the product by mail or by phone after the show. When customers use these more impersonal methods to gather information, the need for major sales calls to provide such information is eliminated.

Trade marts are relatively permanent facilities that firms can rent to exhibit products year round. At these marts, such products as furniture, home decorating supplies, toys, clothing, and gift items are sold to wholesalers and retailers. In the United States, trade marts are located in several major cities, including

New York, Chicago, Dallas, High Point (North Carolina), Atlanta, and Los Angeles. The Dallas Market Center—which includes the Dallas Trade Mart, the Home-furnishing Mart, the World Trade Center, the Decorative Center, Market Hall, InfoMart, and the Apparel Mart—is housed in six buildings designed specifically for the convenience of professional buyers.

Changing Patterns in Wholesaling

The wholesaling industry is becoming much more competitive in the 1990s. The distinction between wholesaling activities that any business can perform and the traditional wholesaling establishment is blurring. Changes in the nature of the marketing environment itself have transformed various aspects of the industry. For instance, they have brought about increasing reliance on computer technology to expedite the ordering, delivery, and handling of goods. This efficient technology is allowing retailers to take over many of wholesalers' functions. Fleming, the largest U.S. food wholesaler, lost $400 million worth of business when Albertson's, a major supermarket chain, decided to handle its own distribution. Other Fleming customers are poised to do the same thing as they grow larger and as inventory controls and computerized systems on the check-out lines become more sophisticated and effective.[27] The trend toward globalization of world markets has resulted in other changes, and astute wholesalers are responding to them. The two predominant shifts in wholesaling today are the consolidation of the wholesaling industry and the development of new types of wholesalers.

Figure 12.6

Trade Show

The London International Fashion Show is an example of an industry exhibition that lets vendors identify prospects and disseminate facts about their products.

Source: Courtesy of Philbeach Events Limited.

Wholesalers Consolidate Power

Like most major industries, the wholesale industry is experiencing a great number of mergers. In fact, some experts believe that the current wave of mergers will leave only 285,000 independent wholesalers, down from the 340,000 in existence now. Wholesalers that grow through geographic expansion, merger or acquisition, or improved productivity will control most of the wholesale business by the year 2000.[28] Wholesaling firms are acquiring or merging with other firms primarily to achieve more efficiency in the face of declining profit margins. Consolidation also gives larger wholesalers more pricing power over producers. Some analysts have expressed concern that wholesalers' increased price clout will increase the number of single-source supply deals.

On the other hand, consolidation is being demanded by wholesalers' larger customers, such as Du Pont and Union Carbide. These firms want to deal with a few suppliers who provide specialized services and deliver reliable products on time.[29] In some cases companies are buying everything from one wholesaler.

One of the results of the current wave of consolidation in the wholesale industry is that more wholesalers are specializing. For example, McKesson Corp. once distributed chemicals, wines, and spirits but now focuses only on drugs. The new larger wholesalers can also afford to purchase and make use of more modern technology to physically manage inventories, provide computerized ordering services, and even help manage their retail customers' operations.

New Types of Wholesalers

The trend toward larger retailers—superstores and the like (discussed in Chapter 13)—will offer opportunities to, as well as threaten, wholesaling establishments. Opportunities will develop from the expanded product lines of these mass merchandisers. A merchant wholesaler of groceries, for instance, may want to add other low-cost, high-volume products that are sold in superstores. Some limited-function merchant wholesalers, however, may no longer have a role to play. For example, the volume of sales may eliminate the need for rack jobbers, who usually handle slow-moving products that are purchased in limited quantities. The future of independent wholesalers, agents, and brokers depends on their ability to delineate markets and furnish desired services. Merchant wholesalers that assume more marketing functions in order to respond to the increased competitive pressures may be able to expand their share of the wholesale market.[30]

Summary

Wholesaling includes all transactions in which the purchaser intends to use the product for resale, for making other products, or for general business operations. It does *not* include exchanges with the ultimate consumers. Wholesalers are individuals or organizations that facilitate and expedite primarily wholesale transactions.

More than half of all goods are exchanged through wholesalers, although the distribution of any product requires that someone must perform wholesaling activities, whether or not a wholesaling institution is involved. For producers, wholesalers perform specialized accumulation and allocation functions for a number of products, letting the producers concentrate on manufacturing the products. For retailers, wholesalers provide buying expertise, wide product lines, efficient distribution, and warehousing and storage services.

Various types of wholesalers serve different market segments. How a wholesaler is classified depends on whether the wholesaler is owned by a producer, whether it takes title to products, the range of services it provides, and the breadth and depth of its product lines. The three general categories of wholesalers are merchant wholesalers, agents and brokers, and manufacturers' sales branches and offices.

Merchant wholesalers are independently owned businesses that take title to goods and assume risk; they make up about two-thirds of all wholesale firms. They are either full-service wholesalers, offering the widest possible range of wholesaling functions, or limited-service wholesalers, providing only some marketing services and specializing in a few functions. Full-service merchant wholesalers include general-merchandise wholesalers, which offer a wide but relatively shallow product mix; limited-line wholesalers, which offer extensive assortments in a few product lines; and specialty-line wholesalers, which offer great depth in a single product line or in a few items within a line. Rack jobbers are specialty-line wholesalers that own and service display racks in supermarkets and drugstores. There are four types of limited-service merchant wholesalers. Cash-and-carry wholesalers sell to small businesses, require payment in cash, and do not deliver. Truck wholesalers sell a limited line of products from their own trucks directly to customers. Drop shippers own goods and negotiate sales but never take possession of products. Mail-order wholesalers sell to retail, business-to-business, and institutional buyers through direct-mail catalogs.

Agents and brokers, sometimes called functional middlemen, negotiate purchases and expedite sales but do not take title to products. They are usually specialists and provide valuable sales expertise. Agents represent buyers or sellers on a permanent basis. Manufacturers' agents offer customers the complete product lines of two or more sellers; selling agents market a complete product line or a producer's entire output and perform every wholesaling function except taking title to products; commission merchants receive goods on consignment from local sellers and negotiate sales in large central markets. Brokers, such as food brokers, negotiate exchanges between buyers and sellers on a temporary basis.

Manufacturers' sales branches and offices are vertically integrated units owned by manufacturers. Branches sell products and provide support services for the manufacturer's sales force in a given location. Sales offices carry no inventory and function much as agents do.

Facilitating agencies do not buy, sell, or take title but perform certain wholesaling functions. They include public warehouses, finance companies, transportation companies, and trade shows and trade marts. In some instances, these organizations eliminate the need for a wholesaling establishment.

The nature of the wholesaling industry is changing in response to changes in the marketing environment. The predominant changes are the increasing consolidation of the wholesaling industry and the growth of new types of wholesalers.

Important Terms

Wholesaling
Wholesaler
Merchant wholesalers
Full-service wholesalers
General-merchandise wholesalers
Limited-line wholesalers
Specialty-line wholesalers
Rack jobbers
Limited-service wholesalers
Cash-and-carry wholesalers
Truck wholesalers
Drop shippers
Mail-order wholesalers

Functional middlemen
Agents
Brokers
Manufacturers' agents
Selling agents
Commission merchants
Food brokers
Sales branches
Sales offices
Facilitating agencies
Public warehouses
Trade shows
Trade marts

Discussion and Review Questions

1. Is there a distinction between wholesalers and wholesaling? If so, what is it?
2. Would it be appropriate for a wholesaler to stock both interior wall paint and office supplies? Under what circumstances would this product mix be logical?
3. What services do wholesalers provide to producers and retailers?
4. Drop shippers take title to products but do not accept physical possession. Commission merchants take physical possession of products but do not accept title. Defend the logic of classifying drop shippers as wholesale merchants and commission merchants as agents.
5. What are the advantages of using agents to replace merchant wholesalers? What are the disadvantages?
6. What, if any, are the differences in the marketing functions that manufacturers' agents and selling agents perform?
7. Why are manufacturers' sales offices and branches classified as wholesalers? Which independent wholesalers are replaced by manufacturers' sales branches? Which independent wholesalers are replaced by manufacturers' sales offices?
8. "Public warehouses are really wholesale establishments." Please comment.
9. Discuss the role of facilitating organizations. Identify three facilitating organizations and explain how each type performs this role.

Cases

12.1 Anheuser-Busch Grows with Its Wholesalers

St. Louis–based Anheuser-Busch, Inc., is the world's largest brewing company, with a market share that is increasing steadily. It currently produces 44 percent of all beer sold in the United States. Anheuser-Busch's brewery sales have recently neared $8.16 billion. Its products include Budweiser, Bud Light, Bud Dry Draft, Michelob, Michelob Light, Michelob Classic Dark, and O'Doul's, a non-alcoholic brew.

In the United States and in Caribbean countries, Anheuser-Busch distributes beer through a network of about 900 independently owned wholesalers and 12 company-owned wholesale operations—a distribution system considered the strongest in the brewing industry. Anheuser-Busch's independent wholesalers employ about 30,000 people, more than 18,000 of whom work in direct beer marketing positions. (One Anheuser-Busch distributor is Frank Sinatra, who owns Somerset Distributing in California.) Company-owned distributorships employ about 1,600 people. Wholesalers handle volumes ranging from 870 barrels to over 1 million barrels annually.

Anheuser-Busch's effective distribution system is bolstered by a variety of cooperative arrangements with wholesalers. For example, the company tries to ensure that its beers are sold to wholesalers FOB (free on board) from the "least cost" brewery. That is, the wholesaler must supply or pay for transportation from the brewery that can provide the product at the lowest shipping cost. But if a product must be shipped at a higher cost—perhaps because the nearest brewery does not produce a specific package—Anheuser-Busch compensates the wholesaler for the difference in cost. The company's traffic department also helps wholesalers arrange transportation. A wholesaler advisory panel, a cross section of wholesalers and top company managers, meets regularly to discuss and act on industry issues.

In addition, the ten distributorships in the company's wholesale operations division serve as a testing ground for programs that are made available to independent wholesalers. In one case, the company developed computer software to help wholesalers maximize retail shelf space. Anheuser-Busch wholesalers receive group discounts on computers, trucks, and insurance and can take company courses ranging from draught beer basics to dynamics of business readings. To build morale among wholesalers, Anheuser-Busch puts top executives in charge of its biggest-volume states (the company's president, August Busch III, handles California himself). Furthermore, every three years, the company throws a Las Vegas–style wholesalers' convention, with appearances by such celebrities as Bob Hope and Paul Newman.

Anheuser-Busch's most evident support for its distributors is its backing of special promotions: sporting events, rodeos, and festivals. The company may pay as much as half the cost of these events, in cooperation with local wholesalers. To improve sales of Michelob Light, for example, a local New York distributor decided to hold a Michelob Light Concentration Day. On that day the distributor delivered only Michelob Light to retailers. Tuxedo-clad representatives from the St. Louis headquarters rode on delivery trucks, accompanied by two Playboy Playmates. The distributorship sold 21,000 cases of Michelob Light in one day (it normally takes twenty days to sell that amount), and Anheuser-Busch is now staging Concentration Days in other cities.

The company has helped support everything from Chicago's Lithuanian festival to the Iron Man Triathlon in Hawaii. Just before Coors moved into the New York–New Jersey market, Anheuser-Busch supplied its wholesalers with a three-hundred-page "Coors Defense Plan," along with funding for promotional events that might have attracted Coors sponsorship. Coors was unable to reach an agreement with any major beer wholesalers and had to distribute through a soft-drink bottler instead.

For distributors, however, the price of such generous corporate support is unquestioned loyalty. Anheuser-Busch asks more of its wholesalers than any other brewer. Each year all distributors are requested to contribute ideas for local promotions—one for every brand. Furthermore, although the distributors are independent business owners, technically free to sell whatever they choose, Anheuser-Busch takes a dim view of wholesalers who decide to carry a competing product. When a Florida distributorship added Heineken and Amstel Light to its line, twenty-two Anheuser-Busch field managers swarmed in and rode the company's trucks for a week, and the distributor and his general manager were summoned to St. Louis for a meeting with top management.

Anheuser-Busch defends its policies, maintaining that the company will not allow "greedy" wholesalers to jeopardize market share. Although Anheuser-Busch has a lead over all other brewers, the company is taking no chances. It has enthusiastically entered and is actively pursuing its foreign markets, especially in Britain, where it is trying to establish an equally effective distribution system. Anheuser-Busch has launched several nonbeer beverages in recent years, including L.A. (a low-alcohol beer), Dewey Stevens (a low-calorie wine cooler aimed at women), and Zeltzer Seltzer (a flavored sparkling water). So far these products have not been marketed aggressively, and they may never be highly profitable. But with rival brewers entering these new markets, Anheuser-Busch wants to be able to supply its distributors with competing products. Along with its share of the market, say Anheuser-Busch executives, the company intends to maintain its share of wholesalers.[31]

Questions for Discussion

1. Are Anheuser-Busch's wholesalers merchant wholesalers? Explain your answer. Are they full-service or limited-service wholesalers? Why?
2. Why does Anheuser-Busch give its wholesale distributors so much support?
3. Why has Anheuser-Busch introduced nonbeer products? Evaluate this practice.

12.2 Fleming Companies, Inc. Strives to Be Competitive

Fleming Companies, Inc., a food wholesaler based in Oklahoma City, services more than 4,800 food retailers in 36 states. It is now the industry leader in sales and is eager to retain this position. Fleming's annual $12 billion in sales makes it the largest food wholesaler in the United States, ahead of such tough competitors as Minneapolis-based Super Valu Stores and Wetterau, located in Hazelwood, Missouri. As the wholesaling industry continues to consolidate and retailers demand more services from wholesalers, food wholesalers such as Fleming are forced to keep pace with these shifts.

Fleming gets approximately 29 percent of its sales volume from chain retailers. However, it considers the independent food retailers to be very important, and its executives see helping the independents to remain viable and competitive as a major task. One way the company tries to meet this task is by providing independent retailers with the same services and techniques used by the chain retailers. Although Fleming considers itself mostly a supplier of rural stores, its urban customers include Philadelphia's Carrefour hypermarket as well as Super Center stores and Wal-Mart's Hypermart USA stores.

Much of Fleming's growth in the past several years stems from its acquisition of other wholesale firms, a policy that has boosted its buying power, provided economies of scale, and allowed the company to spread fixed costs. With fewer than three hundred food wholesalers now remaining, Fleming is pursuing additional growth strategies to prepare for the inevitable day when there are no more companies to acquire. Recently, Fleming acquired Malone & Hyde, a Memphis-based food wholesaler known for its innovative food-distribution system. Fleming's CEO says that the firm will continue to acquire companies when there are mutual benefits for both Fleming and the company being bought.

Another of Fleming's growth strategies is to increase market share by offering a high degree of customer service. Fleming has long assisted its retail buyers with store planning and development, financial and insurance services, consumer services, printing, advertising, and other services—over one hundred services in all. Such information ultimately helps retailers determine which products can be handled most economically. For years, too, Fleming has provided an extensive line of private labels—including IGA, Thriftway, and Piggly Wiggly—to give retailers a competitive tool against national brands. Such private-label brands contribute 8 percent of the company's sales. In addition, Fleming has established a Sales Training Institute to equip its sales and service representatives to meet retailers' needs more effectively. The institute covers such topics as electronic retail systems and retail counseling.

Fleming has always been a technological leader in the food wholesale industry. The company is experimenting with computerized shelf tags in grocery stores and plans to launch this service to all customers. These tags provide the consumer with the price, size, and other information about a product and can be controlled by the retailer from a single control point, resulting in instantaneous price changes rather than the time-consuming manual method. Fleming is also experimenting with automatic ordering techniques that transfer inventory information directly from the check-out stand to a distribution center.

Through mechanization and computerization, Fleming plans to continue to improve its transportation, distribution, and warehouse systems. According to its top management, the company and the retailers already have unique market share positions in many of the leading cities throughout the United States. Fleming is striving to improve those market shares even more.[32]

Questions for Discussion

1. How would you classify Fleming as to type of wholesaler?
2. In what ways is Fleming trying to gain an edge over its competitors?
3. What services is Fleming likely to provide to producers?

Chapter Notes

1. Based on information from Super Valu 1991 Annual Report; Ann Merrill, "ShopKo Likely to Fuel Cub Foods Growth," *Minneapolis-St. Paul City Business,* Aug. 29, 1991, p. 3; Harlan S. Byrne, "Super Valu Stores: Food Wholesaler Gives Thanks for Its Retail Operations," *Barron's,* Nov. 19, 1990, pp. 51–52; Jay L. Johnson, "Twin Valu Opens Second 'Supercenter,'" *Discount Merchandiser,* June 1990, pp. 21–23; Harlan S. Byrne, "Super Value Stores Inc.," *Barron's,* Apr. 24, 1989, pp. 49–50; and

Torrey Byles, "Grocery Chain Says Invoices Key to Managing Inventory," *Journal of Commerce,* Jan. 26, 1989, p. F9.

2. *Statistical Abstract of the United States,* 1991, p. 779.
3. Ibid., p. 779.
4. David E. Gumpert, "They Can Get It for You Wholesale," *Working Woman*, Aug. 1990, pp. 33–36, 94.
5. "Mortgage Wholesaling: Wave of the Future," *United States Banker,* Apr. 1991, pp. 40–43.
6. Robert F. Dwyer and Sejo Oh, "A Transaction Cost Perspective on Vertical Contractual Structure and Interchannel Competitive Strategies," *Journal of Marketing,* Apr. 1988, pp. 21–34.
7. Clarence Casson, "1988 Wholesaler Giants; Making All the Right Moves," *Building Supply Home Centers,* September 1988, p. 56.
8. Rebecca Rolfes, "Wholesaling Without Borders," *Medical Marketing & Media,* Feb. 1991, pp. 74–76.
9. Ibid.
10. *Statistical Abstract of the United States,* 1991, p. 779.
11. Bert Rosenbloom, *Marketing Channels: A Management View* (Hinsdale, Ill.: Dryden Press, 1987), p. 63.
12. John G. F. Bonnanzio, "NAW: Distribution's Watchdog," *Industrial Distribution,* May 1990, pp. 43–46, and *Statistical Abstract of the United States,* 1991, p. 779.
13. *Census of Wholesale Trade,* May 1987, p. US9.
14. Joseph Weber, "Wholesaling," *Business Week,* Jan. 13, 1992, p. 82.
15. Rosenbloom, p. 34.
16. Ibid., p. 63.
17. "Drop-Shipping Grows to Save Depot Costs," *Supermarket News,* Apr. 1, 1985, pp. 1, 17.
18. *Census of Wholesale Trade,* May 1987, p. US9.
19. Ibid.
20. Rosenbloom, p. 61.
21. Ibid.
22. Ibid., p. 62.
23. Thomas V. Bonoma, "Get More Out of Your Trade Shows," *Harvard Business Review,* January–February 1983, pp. 75–83.
24. Rosenbloom, p. 185.
25. "Trade Shows—Part 1; A Major Sales and Marketing Tool," *Small Business Report,* June 1988, pp. 34–39.
26. Rosenbloom, p. 185.
27. Anthony Baldo, "Fleming: Food Fight," *Financial World,* Jan. 8, 1991, pp. 40–41.
28. Ronald D. Michman, "Managing Structural Changes in Marketing Channels," *Journal of Consumer Marketing,* Fall 1990, pp. 33–42.
29. Weber, p. 82.
30. Michman, pp. 33–42.
31. *Anheuser-Busch Companies Fact Book 91/92,* 1991; Anheuser-Busch, Inc., *Marketing Fact Sheet,* 1991; Anheuser-Busch Companies, Inc., 1990 Annual Report; Paul Hemp, "'King of Beers' in a Bitter Battle in Britain," *Wall Street Journal,* June 9, 1988, p. 26; Patricia Sellers, "How Busch Wins in a Doggy Market," *Fortune,* June 22, 1987, pp. 99–100; and Michael Oneal, "Anheuser-Busch: The Scandal May Be Small Beer After All," *Business Week,* May 11, 1987, pp. 72–73.

32. Fleming Companies 1991 Annual Report; Richard Turcsik, "Fleming's Future," *Supermarket News,* Mar. 4, 1991, p. 1; Steve Weinstein, "Fleming's Goal: Be the Best," *Progressive Grocer,* June 1990, pp. 38–44; "Fleming Companies, Inc.," *Wall Street Transcript,* Apr. 17, 1989, pp. 352–393; "Wholesaling," *Supermarket News,* Mar. 13, 1989, pp. 13–14, 16, 18, 20, 22–23; "Current Corporate Reports," *Barron's,* Feb. 13, 1989, p. 108; and "Fleming Profit Declines 32%," *Supermarket News,* Feb. 13, 1989, p. 48.

13 Retailing

OBJECTIVES

- To understand the purpose and function of retailers in the marketing channel

- To describe and distinguish major types of retailers

- To understand nonstore retailing and franchising

- To learn about strategic issues in retailing

After a period of almost exponential growth, The Limited Inc. is fighting a fashion slump. The past few years have not been good to the retail clothing industry in general. Yet although its own sales figures have declined, The Limited, based in Columbus, Ohio, is still out-guessing and outselling its competitors.

While other clothing store executives have adopted a "wait-and-see" strategy, The Limited is aggressively trying to attract more new customers and dazzle its regular shoppers. Although The Limited once targeted its fashion goods primarily toward teenagers, it now caters to older, more affluent consumers. The company is building larger stores that carry children's clothing and menswear in addition to women's sportswear. The atmosphere of these new stores is sleek and stylish.

The Limited already has more than 4,000 stores in operation, and more are scheduled to open. The company owns retailing chains which include Victoria's Secret (a lingerie chain), Lane Bryant, Limited Too (a children's fashion store), Lerner New York (women's fashions), and Abercrombie & Fitch. The Limited's strategies seem to be paying off. The per-square-foot sales in its stores are about $60 higher than the industry average.

Aggressive retailing and marketing tactics have made The Limited one of the top clothing retailers in the world. A company executive once predicted that one company would dominate the industry—and that company would be The Limited. The Limited has grown quickly from 1,000 stores with $1 billion in sales to 4,000 stores with $5 billion in sales. It responds quickly to fashion trends and even more quickly to marketing errors. As other retailers wait quietly for the fashion slump to end, The Limited is trying to activate a recovery.[1]

Photo courtesy of The Limited.

B Y USING EFFECTIVE MARKETING EFFORTS, The Limited is becoming successful again—repositioning itself as a major specialty retailer. Marketing methods that satisfy consumers serve well as the guiding philosophy of retailing. Retailers are an important link in the marketing channel because they are both marketers and customers for producers and wholesalers. They perform many marketing activities, such as buying, selling, grading, risk taking, and developing information about consumers' wants. Of all marketers, retailers are the most visible and accessible to ultimate consumers. They are in a strategic position to gain feedback from consumers and to relay ideas to producers and intermediaries in the marketing channel. Retailing is an extraordinarily dynamic area of marketing.

In this chapter we examine the nature of retailing and its importance in supplying consumers with goods and services. We discuss the major types of retail stores—department stores, traditional general-merchandise retail stores, emerging general-merchandise retailers, and specialty retailers—and describe several forms of nonstore retailing, such as in-home retailing, telemarketing, automatic vending, and mail-order retailing. We also look at franchising, a retailing form that continues to grow in popularity. Finally, we present several strategic issues in retailing: location, product assortment, retail positioning, atmospherics, store image, scrambled merchandising, and the wheel of retailing.

The Nature of Retailing

Retailing includes all transactions in which the buyer intends to consume the product through personal, family, or household use. The buyers in retail transactions are ultimate consumers. A **retailer**, then, is an organization that purchases products for the purpose of reselling them to ultimate consumers. Although most retailers' sales are to consumers, nonretail transactions occasionally occur when retailers sell products to other businesses. Retailing activities usually take place in a store or in a service establishment, but exchanges through telephone selling, vending machines, and mail-order retailing occur outside stores.

It is fairly common knowledge that retailing is important to the national economy. There are approximately 1.51 million retailers operating in the United States.[2] This number has remained relatively constant for the past twenty years, but sales volume has increased more than fourfold, suggesting that the average size of stores has increased. Most personal income is spent in retail stores, and nearly one out of every seven persons employed in the United States works in a retail store.

The face of retailing in the United States is changing. Wal-Mart has passed Sears and K mart as the number one retailer in the country in terms of sales volume. In one year Wal-Mart can increase its sales by $10 billion by building more stores. K mart's and Sears's penetration of the market does not allow similar store growth opportunities.[3] No longer is it enough to simply offer consumers a building with merchandise, checkers, and credit. Consumers must have a defined reason to seek out retailers in this intensely competitive marketplace. Many of the keys to success in the future will relate to a strong customer focus, focused product development, database marketing, innovative advertisements to break through the clutter, and fashionable value.[4]

By providing assortments of products that match consumers' wants, retailers create place, time, and possession utilities. *Place utility* is moving products from wholesalers or producers to a location where consumers want to buy them. *Time utility* is the maintaining of specific business hours so that products are available when consumers want them. *Possession utility* involves facilitating the transfer of ownership or use of a product to consumers.

In the case of services such as hair styling, dry cleaning, restaurants, and automotive repair, retailers themselves develop most of the product utilities. The services of such retailers provide aspects of form utility associated with the production process. Retailers of services usually have more direct contact with consumers and more opportunity to alter the product component of the marketing mix.

The American retail markets are splintered, causing many retailers to create broad product offerings and target their products to many market segments. Consumers with different tastes, and with the ability and willingness to purchase, support a variety of retail establishments. In the following section we take a closer look at the major types of these establishments.

Major Types of Retail Stores

Retail stores seek to provide product mixes to match consumers' shopping preferences. These factors are important in classifying the stores according to four main types: department stores, mass merchandisers, emerging general-merchandise retailers, and specialty retailers. However, there is generally much variation among stores of a particular type.

Department Stores

Department stores are large retail organizations employing at least twenty-five people and characterized by wide product mixes. To facilitate marketing efforts and internal management in these stores, related product lines are organized into separate departments, such as cosmetics, housewares, apparel, home furnishings, and appliances. Each department functions much as a self-contained business, and the buyers for individual departments are fairly autonomous.

Department stores are distinctly service-oriented. Their total product includes credit, delivery, personal assistance, merchandise returns, and a pleasant atmosphere. Although some so-called department stores are actually large, departmentalized specialty stores, most department stores are shopping stores. That is, consumers compare price, quality, and service at one store with those at competing stores. Along with large discount stores, department stores are often considered the retailing leaders in a community and are found in most communities with populations of more than 25,000 people.

Typical department stores—Macy's, Marshall Field's, and Neiman Marcus—obtain a large proportion of their sales from apparel, accessories, and cosmetics. (Table 13.1 lists the top fifteen department store chains, ranked by sales volume.) Other products these stores carry include gift items and luggage.

Table 13.1

The Top U.S.
Department Stores
(ranked by sales
volume)

Rank	Department Store	Annual Sales (in millions)	Number of Stores
1	J.C. Penney	$14,616	1,312
2	Mervyn's	4,055	227
3	Dillard's	3,606	186
4	Macy's Northeast	3,090	46
5	Nordstrom	2,894	63
6	Dayton-Hudson	1,880	37
7	Macy's South/Bullock's	1,750	48
8	Macy's-California	1,520	25
9	Saks Fifth Avenue	1,280	48
10	Bloomingdale's	1,295	17
11	Neiman Marcus	1,245	24
12	Foleys	1,150	36
13	Lord & Taylor	1,047	47
14	The Broadway	1,105	44
15	Marshall Fields	1,025	24

Source: "The Top 100 Department Stores," *Stores Magazine*, July 1991, pp. 31–42. Used by permission.

General-merchandise department stores carry a larger number of product lines. To attract additional customers, many general-merchandise department stores have recently added automotive, recreational, and sports equipment departments, as well as services such as insurance, hair care, travel advice, optical services, and income tax preparation. In some cases, space for these specialized services is leased out, with the proprietors managing their own operations and paying rent to the department stores.

Corporate chain department stores generate tremendous sales volume, which gives them considerable control over a wide range of the products they sell. J.C. Penney, Sears, and Montgomery Ward, for example, have many more store units and far greater sales volume than certain conventional department store units that usually operate regionally. Sears has been very successful both in integrating marketing activities and in owning or controlling production. Consumers' loyalty and trusted private store brands make Sears extremely powerful in channel leadership and competitive status. Sears has recently opened specialty stores trading on their strong name recognition. These stores specialize in paints and hardware, automotive supplies, and appliances. Inside Marketing describes how J.C. Penney is changing its image to respond to competition in the 1990s. Chain stores have high name recognition and advertise through many forms of media.

Corporate chain department stores have encountered problems in recent years. Their overhead and operating expenses (about 35 percent of sales) are higher than those of most other retailers, partly because of the variety of services they offer. Many have been forced into bankruptcy or near bankruptcy and have streamlined their product offerings, modified their appeal, or undergone major remodeling to sustain and generate profitability, and some are

J.C. Penney Goes Upscale

THE FOURTH-LARGEST RETAILER and the largest fashion-oriented department store in the United States, J.C. Penney Co. experienced a long sales slump in the mid-1970s that lasted until the early 1980s. J.C. Penney's management is turning the company around with a new strategy that emphasizes niche marketing, remodeling drab, older stores, and upgrading the retailer's image. The company wants consumers to associate J.C. Penney with stores such as Bloomingdale's and Macy's rather than K mart or Sears.

To begin the transformation, Penney's management eliminated the sporting goods, photography, and home electronics lines, as well as paint, hardware, and automotive supplies from all stores. By the early 1990s, it had spent more than $2 billion on store renovation and expected to spend $1 billion more by 1995. Because J.C. Penney's catalog sales have been steadily growing, the company is enlarging its catalogs and expanding catalog services, such as twenty-four-hour order handling. By the mid-1990s, J.C. Penney is expected to be the largest catalog marketer in the United States. The company also discontinued its Telaction subsidiary—an experimental home shopping service. Finally, J.C. Penney moved its headquarters from Manhattan to Dallas and trimmed its headquarters staff.

J.C. Penney is trying to prove to consumers that its lower prices do not mean poor quality. The "new" J.C. Penney is designed to attract suburban, middle-to upper-middle-class shoppers (80 percent of J.C. Penney's stores are in malls) who appreciate a mixture of fashion and comfort in their apparel. Rather than pursue exclusive designer clothes, Penney executives have chosen to improve the company's more profitable private-label fashions while attracting popular national brands like Levi's and Bugle Boy jeans, Van Heusen, Joneswear, Maidenform, Henry Grethel, and others. Indeed, the company is now Levi's largest account. J.C. Penney is clearly a company that is trying new methods to make it more competitive and improve sales.

Sources: Harlan S. Byrne, "J.C. Penney Co.," *Barron's*, Oct. 14, 1991, pp. 37–38; J.C. Penney 1990 Annual Report; Thomas C. Hayes, "New Shine on a Tarnished Penney," *New York Times*, Apr. 23, 1989, p. F4; Amy Dunkin and Brian Bremner, "The Newly Minted Penney: Where Fashion Rules," *Business Week*, Apr. 17, 1989, pp. 88–90; and Caroline E. Mayer, "Specialty Stores Get Special Push," *Washington Post*, Feb. 4, 1988, pp. E1, E3.

expanding their budget-priced lines to ease the competitive pressure from discount and specialty stores. Population growth is now centered in the suburbs; to stay close to their customers, many department stores have opened branch stores in outlying shopping centers and malls. To attract and hold customers, some department stores are adding, rather than reducing, services. Macy's and Neiman Marcus, for example, offer personal shopping services to interested customers.[5]

Mass Merchandisers

Mass merchandisers are retailers that generally offer fewer customer services than department stores and emphasize lower prices, high turnover, and large sales volumes. They usually have a wider—and sometimes shallower—product mix than department stores. They are less likely than department stores to reorder sold-out sizes and styles. These general merchandisers are characterized by single-story, low-cost facilities, centralized check-out, and higher-volume, multiple purchases. They appeal to large, heterogeneous target markets, especially price-conscious consumers. With their relatively low operating costs, general merchandisers project an image of efficiency and economy. These operations include discount stores, supermarkets, superstores, home improvement centers, hypermarkets, warehouse/wholesale clubs, and warehouse and catalog showrooms.

Discount Stores **Discount stores** are self-service, general-merchandise outlets that regularly offer brand-name merchandise at low prices. Discounters accept lower margins than conventional retailers in exchange for high sales volume. To keep turnover high, they carry a wide but carefully selected assortment of products, from appliances to housewares and clothing. Major discount establishments also offer toys, automotive services, garden supplies, and sports equipment. Often a food supermarket is operated as a department within a discount store. Table 13.2 lists the top ten discount stores in the United States. Many of the discounters are regional organizations. Most operate in large (50,000 to 80,000 square feet) no-frills facilities, often in low-rent areas. Discount stores that offer everyday low prices, such as Wal-Mart, K mart, and Target—as well as low-cost retailers and warehouse-type stores like CostCo, Price Club, Sam's, Waban, and Home Depot—are outperforming retailers that rely on one-day sales events.[6]

Discount retailing developed on a large scale in the early 1950s, when postwar production began to catch up with consumer demand for appliances, home furnishings, and other hard goods. Discount stores in those days were often cash-only operations in warehouse districts, offering goods at savings of 20 to 30 percent over conventional retailers. Through the years, facing increased competition from department stores and other discount stores, discounters generally have improved store services, atmosphere, and location, raising prices and sometimes blurring the distinction between discount houses and depart-

Table 13.2

The Top Ten U.S. Discount Stores (ranked by retail sales)

Rank	Chain	Estimated Annual Sales (in millions)
1	Wal-Mart Stores, Inc.	$26,023
2	K mart Corporation	25,000
3	Target Stores	8,200
4	Ames Department Stores	3,000
5	Meijer Thrifty Acres	2,650
6	Marshall's, Inc.	2,183
7	Hills Department Stores	2,141
8	Bradlees	1,920
9	Caldor	1,574
10	ShopKo	1,714

Source: "The Top 51 Companies in Sales," *Discount Merchandiser,* June 1991, p. 52. Reprinted by permission.

Table 13.3

The Top Ten U.S.
Supermarket Chains
(ranked by sales
volume)

Rank	Company	Annual Sales (in millions)
1	American Stores	$21,156
2	Kroger	20,261
3	Safeway	14,874
4	Great Atlantic & Pacific Tea	11,164
5	Winn-Dixie Stores, Inc.	9,745
6	Albertson's	8,219
7	Supermarkets General	6,126
8	Publix	5,821
9	Food Lion	5,584
10	Vons	5,334

Source: "The 50 Largest Retailing Companies," *FORTUNE*, June 3, 1991, p. 274. Reprinted by permission from the FORTUNE Service 500, 1991.

ment stores. Other discounters continue to focus on price alone. For example, Toys "R" Us, the nation's leading toy retailer, has long relied on a policy of using supermarket-style stores selling huge selections of toys at cut-rate prices. The success of their concept has spurred large-scale plans for international growth, including the first Toys "R" Us in Japan, whose opening in 1992 was attended by President George Bush. Generally, however, many better-known discount houses have assumed the characteristics of department stores. As discounters upgrade their merchandise and facilities and provide more customer services, their risks and operating expenses increase.

Supermarkets **Supermarkets** are large, self-service stores that carry a complete line of food products, as well as some nonfood products, such as cosmetics and nonprescription drugs. The average supermarket has minimum annual sales of $2 million, according to the Food Marketing Institute. Supermarkets are arranged in departments for maximum efficiency in stocking and handling products but have central check-out facilities. They offer lower prices than smaller neighborhood grocery stores, and they usually provide free parking and may also cash checks. Supermarkets may be independently owned but more often are part of a chain operation. Table 13.3 lists the top ten supermarket chains in the United States.

Supermarkets, the first general merchandisers, originated more than fifty years ago, when most food retailers were still small, limited-line organizations. Responding to competitive pressures from chain food stores, certain independent food retailers began combining broad assortments of food products with low-price, self-service operations. Three factors made the high-volume experiment a success: the price consciousness of Depression-era consumers; improved packaging and refrigeration technologies; and the widespread use of automobiles, which enabled the stores to attract many customers who formerly had patronized neighborhood stores. Within a few years, the supermarket became the dominant form of food retailing.

Today consumers make more than three-quarters of all their grocery purchases in the 30,750 supermarkets currently in operation. Even so, the supermarkets' total share of the food market is declining because consumers now have widely varying food preferences and buying habits, and in most communities they can choose from among a number of convenience stores, discount stores, and specialty food stores, as well as a wide variety of restaurants.

To remain competitive, some supermarkets are cutting back services, emphasizing low prices, and using promotion methods such as games or coupons. Other supermarkets have converted to discount or warehouse retailing or both. Still other supermarkets have taken the opposite approach, dramatically expanding both services and product mixes. For example, at Gromer's Super Market in Elgin, Illinois, customers can use the post office, pay utility bills, buy lottery tickets, get documents notarized or photocopied, have film processed, pick up license plates and transfer auto titles, cash checks or use an automatic teller machine, rent rug-cleaning machines, and even get fingerprinted. The Superquinn supermarket chain in Ireland conducts regular focus group sessions with customers to find out what goods and services they want (and do not want).[7] About 60 percent of all supermarkets have service delis; many also offer floral departments, pharmacies, and photo-finishing services.[8] Still, other supermarkets try to differentiate their product lines with unique meats, high-quality in-store restaurants, and an upscale, well-merchandized environment in which to shop.

Supermarkets are also trying to increase their efficiency and competitiveness with technological changes. Most supermarkets have replaced the cash registers at their check-out counters with electronic scanners, which identify and record purchases via bar codes on each product. Such detailed sales data allow management to maintain inventories, track unit sales and consumer preferences, and improve store and shelf layouts. Regardless of the technology used, supermarkets must be operated efficiently because net profits after taxes are usually less than 1 percent of sales.

Superstores **Superstores**—which originated in Europe but are fairly new to U.S. markets—are giant retail outlets that carry not only all food and nonfood products ordinarily found in supermarkets, but also many consumer products that are purchased routinely. In addition to a complete food line, superstores sell housewares, hardware, small appliances, clothing, personal-care products, garden products, and tires—in all, about four times as many items as supermarkets sell. Services available at superstores include laundry and dry cleaning, automotive repair, check cashing, bill paying, and snack bars.

Superstores combine features of discount houses and supermarkets. Examples include Meijer-Thrifty Acres in Michigan and some Kroger stores. To cut handling and inventory costs, they use sophisticated operating techniques and often tall, visible shelving to display entire assortments of products. Most superstores have an area of about 40,000 square feet (compared with 20,000 square feet in supermarkets), although some are as large as 100,000 square feet. Their sales volume is two to three times that of supermarkets, partly because they locate near good transportation networks that help generate the in-store traffic needed for profitability.

Consumers are most attracted to superstores by the lower prices and the one-stop shopping feature. Consequently, other food retailers, too, have started handling general merchandise because gross margin and net profit are higher on those items than on food items. Several supermarket chains, including Winn-Dixie, have added supersized units or enlarged existing stores and product mixes. But superstores require large investments, stringent cost controls, appropriate facilities, and managers who can coordinate broad product assortments. Conventional supermarkets, hampered by economic uncertainty and lack of space for physical expansion, find it difficult to compete effectively with superstores.

Fastest Growing

Home Improvement Centers **Home improvement centers** represent a combination of the traditional hardware store and lumberyard. These centers provide the services and resources to assist do-it-yourselfers in remodeling and redecorating their homes. Products available include lumber, paint, hardware, lighting, electrical supplies, wallpaper, plumbing and fixtures, tools, lawn and garden supplies, and a wide array of building materials.

The merchandise in many home improvement centers is presented in a warehouse arrangement. Home Depot, the largest of the home improvement centers, focuses on providing home improvement with service at a discount price. Its goal is to educate the amateur on how to do simple tasks, hoping they will return later when they undertake bigger projects, such as decks and room remodeling. The do-it-yourself market represents $104 billion in sales.[9] As consumers are faced with a greater challenge in selling their homes, many turn to remodeling instead, spurring the growth in this industry. In recent years, approximately 75 percent of all homeowners undertook some kind of home improvement project.[10] The typical home center generates sales of approximately $3.5 million, with larger stores generating $10–$12 million. Home Depot, classified by many as a category killer (dominating the home improvement business when it enters the market), has average store sales of $23.4 million.[11] Home improvement expenditures vary greatly by the area of the country, with New Hampshire showing the greatest, $537 per capita, and Wyoming showing the lowest, $29 per capita.[12]

The home improvement market is expected to grow at a rate that outperforms overall retail sales growth. Many of the fourteen million homes built in the 1950s are in need of repair and remodeling, and many consumers enjoy the satisfaction of completing home projects themselves.

Hypermarkets **Hypermarkets** combine supermarket and discount store shopping in one location. Larger even than superstores, they measure an average of 225,000 square feet and offer 45,000 to 60,000 different types of products at low prices. They commonly allocate 40 to 50 percent of their selling space to grocery products and the remainder to general merchandise, including athletic shoes, designer jeans, and other apparel; refrigerators, televisions, and other appliances; housewares; cameras; toys; jewelry; hardware; and automotive supplies.[13] Many lease space to noncompeting businesses, such as banks, optical shops, and fast-food restaurants. Because they offer so many diverse products in one location, hypermarkets have been referred to as "malls without walls."[14] Wal-Mart and Cullum Cos. jointly operate several Hypermart U.S.A.s; other hypermarkets in the United States include Carrefour and Bigg's (a partnership between Euromarché and wholesaler Super Valu). All focus on low prices and vast selections of goods.

Although they are now becoming a popular retailing trend in the United States, hypermarkets are not new. The concept began in France after World War II. French-owned Carrefour successfully operates more than a hundred hypermarkets in France, Spain, and South America. The hypermarket concept was first introduced in the United States in the 1970s by the Oshawa Group and Fed Mart but was abandoned largely because sales of general merchandise were slow, resulting in low overall margins for the stores, even though grocery products sold well. Analysts believe that today's hypermarkets face possible failure for the same reasons.[15] Although many consumers enjoy shopping in such a comprehensive environment, some are overwhelmed by the size of the stores and the time required both to shop and to wait in line to check out. Nonetheless, Hypermart U.S.A., Carrefour, and Bigg's all have plans to add new hypermarkets; Super Valu, K mart, Auchan (a French retailer), and other retailers also plan to develop their own hypermarkets.[16]

Warehouse/Wholesale Clubs   **Warehouse/wholesale clubs** are the newest form of mass merchandising—large-scale, members-only selling operations that combine cash-and-carry wholesaling features with discount retailing. Small-business owners account for about 60 percent of a typical warehouse club's sales. (Thus a warehouse/wholesale club could be viewed as a wholesaler.) For a nominal annual fee (usually about $25), small retailers may purchase products at wholesale prices for business use or for resale. Warehouse clubs also sell to ultimate consumers who are affiliated with government agencies, credit unions, schools, hospitals, and banks, but instead of paying a membership fee, individual consumers pay about 5 percent more on each item than do retailers.

Sometimes called buying clubs, warehouse clubs offer the same types of products as discount stores do, but in a limited range of sizes and styles. Whereas most discount stores carry 40,000 items, a warehouse club handles only 4,000 to 5,000 different products, usually acknowledged brand leaders.[17] But because their product lines are shallow and sales volumes high, warehouse clubs can offer a broad range of merchandise, including nonperishable foods, beverages, books, appliances, housewares, automotive parts, hardware, furniture, and sundries.

To keep their prices 20 to 40 percent lower than those of supermarkets and discount stores, warehouse clubs provide few services. They generally do not advertise, except through direct mail. Their facilities are often located in industrial parks and have concrete floors and aisles wide enough for fork lifts. Merchandise is stacked on pallets or displayed on pipe racks. All payments must be in cash, and customers must transport purchases themselves.

Still, warehouse clubs appeal to many price-conscious consumers and small retailers who may be unable to obtain wholesaling services from larger distributors. The sales volume of most warehouse clubs is four to five times that of a typical department store. With stock turning over at the average rate of eighteen times a year, warehouse clubs sell their goods before manufacturers' payment periods are up, virtually eliminating the need for capital.[18]

The warehouse club concept, which has spread widely in the last few years, was pioneered in the United States in the late 1970s by Price Company, which has annual sales of $110 million per warehouse club.[19] The largest warehouse club chains are Sam's Club, a division of Wal-Mart (annual sales $6.6 billion), Price Club ($5.3 billion), and CostCo ($4.1 billion).[20] As competition increases, the clubs may begin to offer more services. Sam's Club now has an optical department as well as automotive services.

Warehouse and Catalog Showrooms **Warehouse showrooms** are retail facilities with five basic characteristics: (1) a large, low-cost building, (2) use of warehouse materials-handling technology, (3) use of vertical merchandise display space, (4) a large on-premises inventory, and (5) minimum services.

Although some superstores, hypermarkets, and discount supermarkets have used warehouse retailing, most of the best-known showrooms are operated by large furniture retailers. Wickes Furniture and Levitz Furniture Corporation brought sophisticated mass merchandising to the highly fragmented furniture industry. These high-volume, low-overhead operations stress fewer personnel and services. Lower costs are possible because some marketing functions have been shifted to consumers, who must transport, finance, and perhaps store merchandise. Most consumers carry away their purchases in the manufacturer's carton, although the stores will deliver for a fee.

In **catalog showrooms**, one item of each product is on display, often in a locked case, and remaining inventory is stored out of the buyer's reach. Using catalogs that have been mailed to their homes or are on counters in the store, customers order products by phone or in person. Clerks fill the orders from the warehouse area, and products are presented in the manufacturer's carton. In contrast to traditional catalog retailers, which offer no discounts and require that customers wait for delivery, catalog showrooms regularly sell below list price and often provide goods immediately.

Catalog showrooms usually sell jewelry, luggage, photographic equipment, toys, small appliances and housewares, sporting goods, and power tools. They advertise extensively and carry established brands and models that are not likely to be discontinued. Because catalog showrooms have higher product turnover, fewer losses through shoplifting, and lower labor costs than department stores, they are able to feature lower prices. They offer minimal services, however. Customers may have to stand in line to examine items or place orders. Pressure is being applied to catalog showrooms with the rapid growth from discounters and warehouse clubs. Service Merchandise, Best Products, and Consumer Distributing are three of the largest catalog showroom retailers.

Specialty Retailers

In contrast to department stores and mass merchandisers, which offer broad product mixes, specialty retailers emphasize the narrowness and depth of their product lines. Despite their name, specialty retailers do not sell specialty items (except when the specialty goods complement the overall product mix). Instead, these retailers offer substantial assortments in a few product lines. In this section we examine two types of specialty stores: traditional specialty retailers and off-price retailers.

Traditional Specialty Retailers **Traditional specialty retailers** are stores carrying a narrow product mix with deep product lines. They are sometimes called *limited-line retailers;* if they carry unusual depth in one main product category, they may be referred to as *single-line retailers.*

Shopping goods such as apparel, jewelry, sporting goods, art supplies, fabrics, computers, and pet supplies are commonly sold through specialty retailers. For example, The Foot Locker, owned by Kinney Shoe Corp., specializes in a product mix of various types of athletic footwear. The Limited, Radio Shack, Hickory Farms, and The Gap are other retailers that offer limited product lines but great depth within those lines. Specialty apparel retailing accounted for $45 billion in sales in 1990. The fastest growth in the past decade has come in the women's and children's markets. In 1990 the women's segment represented 73 percent of the apparel industry, men's 21 percent, and children's 6 percent.[21]

Although the number of chain specialty stores is increasing, most specialty stores are independently owned. Specialty stores occupy about two-thirds of the space in most shopping centers and malls and account for 40 to 50 percent of all general-merchandise sales.[22] Florists, bakery shops, and bookstores are among the small independent specialty retailers that appeal to local target markets, although these stores can, of course, be owned and managed by large corporations. Even if this kind of retailer adds a few supporting product lines, the store may still be classified as a specialty store.

Because they are usually small, specialty stores may have high costs in proportion to sales, and to satisfy customers they may have to carry some products with low turnover rates. On the other hand, these stores sometimes obtain lower prices from suppliers because they buy limited lines of merchandise in large quantities. Successful specialty stores understand their customer types and know what products to carry, thus reducing the risk of unsold merchandise. Specialty stores usually offer better selections and more sales expertise than department stores, their main competitors. By capitalizing on fashion, service, personnel, atmosphere, and location, specialty retailers can position themselves strategically to attract customers in specific market segments. They may even become exclusive dealers in their markets for certain products. Through specialty stores, small-business owners can provide unique services to match consumers' varied desires. For consumers dissatisfied with the impersonal nature of large retailers, the close, personal contact offered by a small specialty store can be a welcome change.

Off-Price Retailers **Off-price retailers** are stores that buy manufacturers' seconds, overruns, returns, and off-season production runs at below-wholesale prices for resale to consumers at deep discounts. Unlike true discount stores, which pay regular wholesale prices for their goods and usually carry second-line brand names, off-price retailers offer limited lines of national-brand and designer merchandise, usually clothing, shoes, or housewares. The number of off-price retailers has grown rapidly since the mid-1980s and now includes such major chains as T.J. Maxx (see Figure 13.1), Stein Mart, Burlington Coat Factory, and Marshall's. Marshall's, the largest off-price retailer in the United States in terms of sales, has 317 stores and plans to open 200 more by 1994; T. J. Maxx has 328 stores and plans to open 45 more per year.[23]

Off-price stores charge 20 to 50 percent less than do department stores for comparable merchandise but offer few customer services. They often feature community dressing rooms, central check-out counters, and no credit, returns, or exchanges. Off-price stores may or may not sell goods with original labels intact (Filene's Basement Stores do, Loehmann's outlets do not). They turn over

SATURDAY TO THE MAXX.

T·J·maxx

The maxx for the minimum.

their inventory nine to twelve times a year, three times as often as traditional specialty stores. They compete with department stores for the same customers: price-conscious members of suburban households who are knowledgeable about brand names. Another form of off-price retailer is the manufacturer's outlet mall, which makes available manufacturer overstocks and unsold merchandise from other retail outlets. The prices are low, and a diversity of manufacturers are represented in these malls. As of 1991 there were 270 manufacturers' outlet malls in the United States, with 160 more in the development phase.[24]

To ensure a regular flow of merchandise into their stores, off-price retailers must establish long-term relationships with suppliers that can provide large quantities of goods at reduced prices. Manufacturers may approach the retailers with samples, discontinued products, or items that have not sold well; or the retailers may seek out producers, offering to pay cash for goods produced during the manufacturers' off-season. Although manufacturers benefit from such arrangements, they also risk alienating their specialty and department store customers. Department stores tolerate off-price stores as long as they do not advertise brand names, limit their merchandise to lower-quality items, and are located away from the department stores. But when off-price retailers are able to obtain large stocks of in-season, top-quality merchandise—as many do—tension builds between department stores and manufacturers. In fact, some department stores, including Neiman Marcus and Woodward & Lothrop, are opening separate stores for selling their marked-down goods, in direct competition with the off-price retailers.[25]

Nonstore Retailing and Direct Marketing

Nonstore retailing is the selling of goods or services outside the confines of a retail facility. This form of retailing accounts for an increasing percentage of sales and includes personal sales methods, such as in-home retailing and telemarketing, and nonpersonal sales methods, such as automatic vending and mail-order retailing (which includes catalog retailing).

Certain nonstore retailing methods are in the category of **direct marketing**: the use of nonpersonal media to introduce products to consumers, who then purchase the products by mail or telephone. In the case of telephone orders, salespersons may be required to complete the sales. Telemarketing and mail-order and catalog retailing are all examples of direct marketing, as are sales generated by coupons, direct mail, and toll-free 800 numbers.

In-Home Retailing

In-home retailing is selling via personal contacts with consumers in their own homes. Organizations such as Avon (see Figure 13.2), Electrolux, and Fuller Brush Company send representatives to the homes of preselected prospects. Merchandise such as *World Book Encyclopedia*s, Kirby vacuum cleaners, Amway products, and Mary Kay cosmetics are also sold to consumers in their homes.

Traditionally, in-home retailing relied on a random door-to-door approach. Some companies (such as World Book and Kirby, both divisions of Scott & Fetzer Co.) now use a more efficient approach. They first identify prospects by reaching them by phone or mail or intercepting them in shopping malls or at consumer trade fairs. These initial contacts are limited to a brief introduction and the setting of appointments. Several large retailers, such as J.C. Penney,

Figure 13.2

In-Home Retailing

Avon is an in-home retailer that advertises department store quality at discount store prices. Customers can pick and choose at home on their own schedule.

Source: Avon Products, Inc.

offer in-home decorating services. Consumers find in-home selling of rugs, draperies, and home improvements helpful because these products must be coordinated with existing home interiors.

Some in-home selling, however, is still undertaken without information about sales prospects. Door-to-door selling without a prearranged appointment is a tiny proportion of total retail sales, probably less than 1 percent. Because it has so often been associated with unscrupulous and fraudulent techniques, door-to-door selling is illegal in some communities. Generally, this technique is regarded unfavorably because so many door-to-door salespersons are under-trained and poorly supervised. A big disadvantage of door-to-door selling is the large expenditure, effort, and time it demands. Sales commissions are usually 25 to 50 percent (or more) of the retail price; as a result, consumers often pay more than a product is worth. Door-to-door selling is used most often when a product is unsought—for instance, encyclopedias, which most consumers would not be likely to purchase in a store.

A variation of in-home retailing is the home demonstration or party plan, which such companies as Tupperware, Stanley Home Products, and Mary Kay Cosmetics use successfully. One consumer acts as host and invites a number of friends to view merchandise at his or her home, where a salesperson is on hand to demonstrate the products. The home demonstration is more efficient for the sales representative than contacting each prospect door-to-door, and the conge-nial atmosphere partly overcomes consumers' suspicions and encourages them to buy. Home demonstrations also meet the buyers' needs for convenience and personal service. Commissions and selling costs make this form of retailing expensive, however. Additionally, successful party-plan selling requires both a network of friends and neighbors who have the time to attend such social gatherings and a large number of effective salespersons. With so many house-hold members now holding full-time jobs, both prospects and sales representa-tives are harder to recruit. The growth of interactive telephone-computer home shopping may also cut into party-plan sales.

Telemarketing

More and more organizations—IBM, Merrill Lynch, Allstate, Avis, Ford, Time, and American Express, to name a few—are using the telephone to strengthen the effectiveness of traditional marketing methods. **Telemarketing** is direct selling of goods and services by telephone, based on either a cold canvass of the telephone directory or a prescreened list of prospective clients. (In some areas, certain telephone numbers are listed with an asterisk to indicate the people who do not want to receive telephone sales calls.) Telemarketing can generate sales leads, improve customer service, speed up collection of past-due accounts, raise funds for nonprofit groups, and gather market data.

In some cases, telemarketing uses advertising that encourages consumers to initiate a call or to request information about placing an order. This type of retailing is only a small part of total retail sales, but its use is growing. Accord-ing to AT&T, U.S. companies spent $13.6 billion in one year on telemarketing phone calls and equipment (phones, lines, and computers). Research indicates that telemarketing is most successful when combined with other marketing strategies, such as direct mail or advertising in newspapers, radio, and television.

Automatic Vending

Automatic vending makes use of machines and accounts for less than 2 percent of all retail sales. Approximately six million vending units generate about $25 billion in retail sales annually.[26] Vending machine locations and the percentage of sales each generates are as follows:[27]

Plants and factories	38%
Public locations (e.g., stores)	26%
Offices	16%
Colleges and universities	6%
Government facilities	3%
Hospitals and nursing homes	3%
Primary and secondary schools	2%
Others	6%

Video game machines provide an entertainment service, and many banks now offer machines that dispense cash or offer other services, but these uses of vending machines are not reported in total vending sales volume.

Automatic vending is one of the most impersonal forms of retailing. Small, standardized, routinely purchased products (chewing gum, candy, newspapers, cigarettes, soft drinks, coffee) can be sold in machines because consumers usually buy them at the nearest available location. Machines in areas of heavy traffic provide efficient and continuous services to consumers. Such high-volume areas may have more diverse product availability—for example, hot and cold sandwiches as well as soups. The elimination of sales personnel and the small amount of space necessary for vending machines give this retailing method some advantages over stores. The advantages are partly offset by the expense of the frequent servicing and repair needed.

Mail-Order Retailing

Mail-order retailing involves selling by description because buyers usually do not see the actual product until it arrives in the mail. Sellers contact buyers through direct mail, catalogs, television, radio, magazines, and newspapers. A wide assortment of products, such as compact discs, books, and clothing, is sold to consumers through the mail. Placing mail orders by telephone is increasingly common. The advantages of mail-order selling include efficiency and convenience. Mail-order houses, such as Williams-Sonoma, Crate & Barrel, and L.L. Bean, can be located in remote, low-cost areas and forgo the expenses of store fixtures. Eliminating personal selling efforts and store operations may result in tremendous savings that can be passed along to consumers in the form of lower prices. On the other hand, mail-order retailing is inflexible, provides limited service, and is more appropriate for specialty products than for convenience products. Some mail-order retailers, such as Williams-Sonoma and Crate & Barrel, have opened stores in major cities.

When **catalog retailing** (a specific type of mail-order retailing) is used, customers receive their orders by mail (see Figure 13.3), or they may pick them up if the catalog retailer has stores, as do Montgomery Ward and Sears. Sears is

testing the elimination of in-store pickup of merchandise after marketing research showed 90 percent of Sears's customers favored home delivery. The shift in service would save the company more than $50 million annually.[28] Although in-store visits result in some catalog orders, most are placed by mail or telephone. Catalog retailers, such as Lands' End, J. Crew, and L.L. Bean, have experienced significant growth and success through offering casual fashions at an affordable price with a high level of service. These retailers are also able to reach many two-income families who have more money and less time for special shopping. Catalog sales increased 12 percent in 1991.[29]

Franchising

Franchising is an arrangement whereby a supplier, or franchiser, grants a dealer, or franchisee, the right to sell products in exchange for some type of consideration. For example, the franchiser may receive some percentage of total sales in exchange for furnishing equipment, buildings, management know-how, and marketing assistance to the franchisee. The franchisee supplies labor and capital, operates the franchised business, and agrees to abide by the provisions of the franchise agreement. In the next section we look at the major types of retail franchises, the advantages and disadvantages of franchising, and trends in franchising.

Major Types of Retail Franchises

Retail franchise arrangements can generally be classified as one of three general types. In the first arrangement, a manufacturer authorizes a number of retail stores to sell a certain brand-name item. This franchise arrangement, one of the oldest, is common in the sales of passenger cars and trucks, farm equipment, shoes, paint, earth-moving equipment, and petroleum. About 90 percent of all gasoline is sold through franchised independent retail service stations, and franchised dealers handle virtually all sales of new cars and trucks. The second type of retail franchise occurs when a producer licenses distributors to sell a given product to retailers. This franchising arrangement is common in the soft-drink industry. Most national manufacturers of soft-drink syrups—Coca-Cola, Dr Pepper, Pepsi-Cola—franchise independent bottlers, which then serve retailers. In the third type of retail franchise, a franchiser supplies brand names, techniques, or other services, instead of a complete product. The franchiser may provide certain production and distribution services, but its primary role in the arrangement is the careful development and control of marketing strategies. This approach to franchising, which is the most typical today, is used by many organizations, including Holiday Inn, AAMCO, McDonald's, Dairy Queen, Avis, Hertz, KFC, and H&R Block. Hardee's (Figure 13.4) is another example of a fast-food franchiser.

Advantages and Disadvantages of Franchising

Franchising offers several advantages to both the franchisee and the franchiser. It enables a franchisee to start a business with limited capital and to make use of the business experience of others. Moreover, an outlet with a nationally advertised name, such as Midas or Burger King, is often assured of customers as soon as it opens. If business problems arise, the franchisee can obtain guidance and advice from the franchiser at little or no cost. Franchised outlets are generally more successful than independently owned businesses: Only 5 to 8 percent of franchised retail businesses fail during the first two years of operation, whereas approximately 54 percent of independent retail businesses fail during that period.[30] The franchisee also receives materials to use in local advertising and can take part in national promotional campaigns sponsored by the franchiser.

The franchiser gains fast and selective distribution of its products through franchise arrangements without incurring the high cost of constructing and operating its own outlets. The franchiser therefore has more capital available to expand production and to use for advertising. At the same time, it can ensure, through the franchise agreement, that outlets are maintained and operated by its own standards. The franchiser also benefits from the fact that the franchisee, being a sole proprietor in most cases, is likely to be very highly motivated to succeed. The success of the franchise means more sales, which translate into higher royalties for the franchiser.

Despite their numerous advantages, franchise arrangements also have several drawbacks. The franchiser can dictate many aspects of the business: decor, the design of employees' uniforms, types of signs, and numerous details of business operations. In addition, franchisees must pay to use the franchiser's name, products, and assistance. Usually, there is a one-time franchise fee and continu-

Figure 13.4

Fast-food Retail Franchise

Hardee's is a familiar fast-food franchiser.

Source: Courtesy of Hardee's.

ing royalty and advertising fees, often collected as a percentage of sales. Table 13.4 shows the one-time fees for the ten most expensive and the ten least expensive franchises. In addition, franchisees often must work very hard, putting in ten- and twelve-hour days, six days a week. In some cases, franchise agreements are not uniform: one franchisee may pay more than another for the same services. The franchiser also gives up a certain amount of control when entering into a franchise agreement. Consequently, individual establishments may not be operated exactly the way that the franchiser would wish to operate them.

Trends in Franchising

Franchising has been used since the early 1900s, primarily for service stations and car dealerships. However, it has grown enormously since the mid-1960s. This growth has generally paralleled the expansion of the fast-food industry—the industry in which franchising is most widely used. Of course, franchising is not limited to fast foods. Franchise arrangements for health clubs, exterminators, hair salons, tax preparers, and travel agencies are widespread. The real estate industry has also experienced a rapid increase in franchising. Even professionals, such as dentists and lawyers, participate in franchise arrangements. The total number of franchised units in the United States grew from 396,000 in 1970 to 533,000 in 1990, a 35 percent increase. But the average sales per unit skyrocketed from $302,000 in 1970 to $1,344,000 in 1990, a 345 percent increase in sales volume.[31] The largest franchising sectors, ranked by sales, are automobile and truck dealers (50.6 percent), gasoline service stations (16.1 percent), restaurants (10.7 percent), and nonfood retailing (4.0 percent).[32]

10 Most Expensive Franchises		10 Least Expensive Franchises	
Company	Start-Up Cost and Franchise Fee	Company	Start-Up Cost and Franchise Fee
1. Hampton Inn	$2.3 million	1. Packy the Shipper	$995
2. Quality Inns Intl.	$1.9 million	2. Novus Windshield Repair	$2,000
3. Econo Lodge	$1.8 million	3. Sunshine Polishing Systems	$2,675
4. Hardee's	$433,000	4. Coverall	$4,200
5. Roy Rogers	$396,000	5. Stork News	$5,000
6. McDonald's	$363,000	6. Chem-Dry	$9,000
7. Ponderosa Steakhouse	$342,000	7. Coustic Glo	$11,250
8. Jack-in-the-Box	$331,000	8. Jani-King	$13,500
9. Round Table Pizza	$322,000	9. Duraclean	$16,800
10. Super 8 Motels	$320,000	10. Video Data Services	$16,950

Source: *USA Today*, Feb. 11, 1988, p. 8B. Copyright 1988 USA TODAY. Reprinted with permission.

Table 13.4   **The Ten Most Expensive and the Ten Least Expensive Franchises**

Strategic Issues in Retailing

Consumers often have vague reasons for making a retail purchase. Whereas most business-to-business purchases are based on economic planning and necessity, consumer purchases often result from social influences and psychological factors. Because consumers shop for a variety of reasons—to search for specific items, to escape boredom, or to learn about something new—retailers must do more than simply fill space with merchandise; they must make desired products available, create stimulating environments for shopping, and develop marketing strategies that increase store patronage. In this section we discuss how store location, product assortment, retail positioning, atmospherics, store image, scrambled merchandising, and the wheel of retailing affect these retailing objectives.

Location

Location, the least flexible of the strategic retailing issues, is one of the most important because location dictates the limited geographic trading area from which a store must draw its customers. Retailers consider a variety of factors when evaluating potential locations, including the location of the firm's target market within the trading area, the kinds of products being sold, the availability of public transportation, customer characteristics, and competitors' locations. Southern Florida, thought by many to be an older community, is a dynamic, thriving area comprised of ethnically diverse younger individuals. Stores seeking to expand and penetrate this market include Wal-Mart, CostCo, Ross, Home Depot, Sports Authority, and Winn-Dixie. New retailers entering this competitive, established area are focusing on value, service, and the renovation needs of the market.[33]

In choosing a location, retailers evaluate the relative ease of movement to and from the site, including pedestrian and vehicular traffic, parking, and transportation. Most retailers prefer sites with high pedestrian traffic, although preliminary site investigations often include a pedestrian count to determine how many of the passers-by are truly prospective customers. Similarly, the nature of the area's vehicular traffic is analyzed. Certain retailers, such as service stations and convenience stores, depend on large numbers of driving customers but try to avoid overly congested locations. In addition, parking space must be adequate for projected demand, and transportation networks (major thoroughfares and public transit) must be able to accommodate customers and delivery vehicles.

Retailers also evaluate the characteristics of the site itself: the types of stores in the area; the size, shape, and visibility of the lot or building under consideration; and the rental, leasing, or ownership terms under which the building may be occupied. Retailers also look for compatibility with nearby retailers because stores that complement each other draw more customers for everyone. When making site location decisions, retailers must select from among several general types of locations: free-standing structures, traditional business districts, neighborhood shopping centers, community shopping centers, regional shopping centers, or nontraditional shopping centers.

Free-Standing Structures Free-standing structures are buildings that are not connected to other buildings. An organization may build a structure or lease or buy one. A retailer, for example, may find that it is most successful when its stores are in free-standing structures close to a shopping mall but not in the mall. The use of free-standing structures allows retailers to physically position themselves away from or close to their competitors. It is not unusual for quick-service oil change dealers and fast-food restaurants to use free-standing structures and locate close to each other.

Traditional Business Districts Traditional business districts consist of structures usually attached to one another and located in a central part of a town or city—for example, downtown. Often these structures are older. In some cities the traditional business districts are decaying and are not seen as viable locations for retailers. However, a number of towns and cities have taken steps to preserve or reinvigorate their traditional business districts, thus making them very attractive locations for certain types of retailers. Some cities have enclosed walkways, shut off streets from traffic, and provided free parking and trolley systems to help their traditional business districts compete with shopping malls more effectively.

Neighborhood Shopping Centers **Neighborhood shopping centers** usually consist of several small convenience and specialty stores, such as small grocery stores, gas stations, and fast-food restaurants. They serve consumers who live less than ten minutes' driving time from the center. Many of these retailers consider their target markets to be consumers who live within a two- to three-mile radius of their stores. Because most purchases are based on convenience or personal contact, there is usually little coordination of selling efforts within a neighborhood shopping center. Generally, product mixes consist of essential products, and the depth of the product lines is limited. Convenience stores are most successful when they are closer to the consumer than, for example, supermarkets. A good strategy for neighborhood centers is to locate near hotels or interstate highways, or to be along the way for potential consumers headed to a regional shopping center.

Community Shopping Centers **Community shopping centers** include one or two department stores and some specialty stores, as well as convenience stores. They serve a larger geographic area and draw consumers who are looking for shopping and specialty products that are not available in neighborhood shopping centers. Consumers drive longer distances to community shopping centers than to neighborhood shopping centers. The community shopping center is planned and coordinated to attract shoppers. Special events, such as art exhibits, automobile shows, and sidewalk sales, are used to stimulate traffic. The overall management of a community shopping center looks for tenants that complement the center's total assortment of products. Such centers have wide product mixes and deep product lines.

Regional Shopping Centers **Regional shopping centers** usually have the largest department stores, the widest product mixes, and the deepest product lines of all shopping centers. Many shopping malls are regional shopping centers, although some malls are community shopping centers. Regional shopping centers carry most products found in a downtown shopping district. With 150,000 or more consumers in their target market, regional shopping centers must have well-coordinated management and marketing activities. The Galleria in Houston (Figure 13.5) is an example of a major regional shopping center.

Figure 13.5

Regional Shopping Centers

Houston's Galleria is a well-known major regional shopping center in Texas.

Source: The Galleria, Houston, Texas.

Target markets may include consumers traveling from extended distances to find products and prices not available in their hometown.

Because of the expense of leasing space in regional shopping centers, tenants are more likely to be national chains than small independent stores. These large centers usually advertise, have special events, furnish transportation to some consumer groups, and carefully select the mix of stores. When it is completed in 1992, Mall of America, near Minneapolis, will be one of the largest shopping malls in the world. It will contain eight hundred stores, including Nordstrom's and Bloomingdale's, and one hundred restaurants and nightclubs. The shopping center will feature Camp Snoopy, a theme park based on Charlie Brown's famous dog, as well as hotels, miniature golf courses, and water slides.[34]

Nontraditional Shopping Centers Three new types of discount malls or shopping centers are emerging that differ significantly from traditional shopping centers. The factory outlet mall features discount and factory outlet stores carrying traditional manufacturer brands, such as Van Heusen, Levi Strauss, Munsingwear, HealthTex, and Wrangler. Manufacturers own these stores and must make a special effort to avoid conflict with traditional retailers of their products. Manufacturers claim that their stores are in noncompetitive locations, and indeed most factory outlet malls are located outside metropolitan areas. Not all factory outlets stock close-outs and irregulars, but most strive to avoid comparison with discount houses. The factory outlet mall attracts customers because of lower prices for quality and major brand names. The factory outlet mall operates in much the same way as the regional shopping center but probably draws traffic from a larger shopping radius. Promotional activity is at the heart of these new shopping centers. Craft and antique shows, contests, and special events attract a great deal of traffic.

Another nontraditional shopping center is the miniwarehouse mall. These loosely planned centers sell space to retailers, who operate what are essentially retail stores out of warehouse bays. The developers of the miniwarehouse mall may also sell space to wholesalers or even to light manufacturers that maintain a retail facility in their warehouse bay. Some of these miniwarehouses are located in high-traffic areas and provide ample customer parking, as well as display windows that can be seen from the street. Home improvement materials, specialty foods, pet supplies, and garden and yard supplies are often sold in these malls. Unlike the traditional shopping center, the miniwarehouse mall usually does not have a coordinated promotional program and store mix. These nontraditional shopping centers come closest to a neighborhood or community shopping center.

A third type of shopping center is emerging, one that does not include a traditional anchor department store. Most malls have one to three main anchor department stores to ensure a continuous stream of traffic for the mall. With traditional mall sales declining, this new type of shopping mall may be anchored by a store like The Gap. One such mall in Wheaton, Illinois, has a 17,000-square-foot Gap and is surrounded by other specialty stores, such as Banana Republic and Gap Kids. Other likely stores for the new malls include Toys "R" Us, Circuit City, and Home Depot.

The retailing industry is in a transition period, and new developments are inevitable. Price Waterhouse predicts that one-half of all major retailers will be out of business by the end of the century![35]

Figure 13.6

Relationships Between Merchandise Breadth and Depth for a Typical Discount Store, Department Store, and Specialty Store

Source: Robert F. Hartley, *Retailing: Challenge and Opportunity*, 3rd ed., p. 118. Copyright © 1984 by Houghton Mifflin Company. Used by permission.

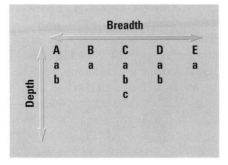

Discount store

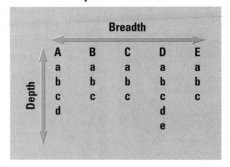

Department store

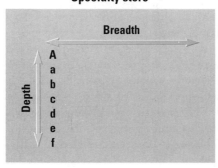

Specialty store

The capital letters represent the number of product lines, and the small letters depict the choices in any one product line. Thus it can be seen that discount stores are wide and shallow in merchandise assortment. Specialty stores, at the other extreme, have few product lines, but much more depth in the few they carry. The typical department store falls in between, having a broad assortment with many merchandise lines and medium depth in each line.

Product Assortment

The product assortments that retailers develop vary considerably in breadth and depth. As discussed earlier, retail stores are often classified according to their product assortments. Conversely, a store's type affects the breadth and depth of the store's product offerings, as shown in Figure 13.6. Thus a specialty store has a single product line, but considerable depth in that line. Godiva chocolate stores and Fannie May Candy Shops, for example, carry only one line of products but many items within that line. In contrast, discount stores may have a wide product mix (such as housewares, automotive services, apparel, and food), but few products within each line. Department stores may have a wide product mix with different product line depths. Nevertheless, it is usually difficult to maintain a wide and deep product mix because of the inventories required. In addition, some producers prefer to distribute through retailers that offer less variety so that their products get more exposure and are less affected by the presence of competing brands.

Issues of product assortment are often a matter of what and how much to carry. Retailers decide what should be included in their product assortments, considering the assortment's purpose, status, and completeness. *Purpose* relates to how well an assortment satisfies consumers and at the same time furthers the retailer's goals. *Status* identifies by rank the relative importance of each product in an assortment: for example, motor oil might have low status in a store that sells convenience foods. *Completeness* means that an assortment includes the products necessary to satisfy a store's customers; the assortment is incomplete when some products are missing. An assortment of convenience foods must include milk to be complete because most consumers expect to be able to buy milk when purchasing other food products. New products are added to (and declining products are deleted from) an assortment when they meet (or fail to meet) the retailer's standards of purpose, status, and completeness.

The retailer also considers the quality of the products to be offered. The store may limit its assortments to expensive, high-quality goods for upper-income market segments; it may stock cheap, low-quality products for low-income buyers; or it may try to attract several market segments by offering a range of quality within its total product assortment.

How much to include in an assortment depends on the needs of the retailer's target market. A discount store's customers expect a wide and shallow product mix, whereas specialty-store shoppers prefer narrow and deep assortments. If a retailer can increase sales by increasing product variety, the assortment may be enlarged. For example, The Gap stores have been successful in enlarging their assortment to include clothing for the entire family, not just teenagers. Since The Gap implemented this strategy, company sales have tripled, and profits have grown to six times the previous level.[36] If a broader product mix ties up too much floor space or creates storage problems, the retailer may stock only the products that generate the greatest sales. Other factors that affect product assortment decisions are the personnel, store image, inventory control methods, and the financial risks involved.

Retail Positioning

Because of the emergence of new types of stores (warehouse clubs, hypermarkets, and deep discounters) and the expansion of product offerings by traditional stores, competition among retailers is intense. Thus it is important for management to consider the retail organization's market positioning. **Retail positioning** involves identifying an unserved or underserved market niche, or segment, and serving the segment through a strategy that distinguishes the retailer from others in the minds of persons in that segment.[37] In international marketing, understanding the target market is critical. Several Canadian firms have found marketing their products in the United States quite difficult. In Canada, competition is more limited, and prices are higher than in the United States. To be successful in exporting their products to the United States, Canadian retailers must position themselves differently than at home.[38] The Global Perspective describes how The Body Shop has positioned itself as a unique global retailer.

There are several ways in which retailers position themselves. A retailer may position itself as a seller of high-quality, premium-priced products and provide many services. A store such as Neiman Marcus, which specializes in expensive high-fashion clothing and jewelry, sophisticated electronics, and exclusive home furnishings, might be expected to provide wrapping and delivery, valet parking, personal shopping consultants, and fine-dining facilities. Von Maur, a high-quality midwestern department store, emphasizes topnotch service. It wraps and mails packages at no charge all over the country during the holidays and even hires pianists to play in the main lobbies of its stores. Another type of retail organization, such as Wal-Mart, may be positioned as a marketer of reasonable-quality products at everyday low prices.

Atmospherics

Atmospherics is often used to help position a retailer. **Atmospherics** describes the physical elements in a store's design that appeal to consumers' emotions and encourage consumers to buy. Exterior and interior characteristics, layout, and displays all contribute to a store's atmosphere. Department stores, restaurants, hotels, service stations, and shops combine these elements in different ways to create specific atmospheres that may be perceived as warm, fresh, functional, or exciting.

Exterior atmospheric elements include the appearance of the storefront, display windows, store entrances, and degree of traffic congestion. Exterior atmospherics is particularly important to new customers, who tend to judge an unfamiliar store by its outside appearance and may not enter the store if they feel intimidated by the building or inconvenienced by the parking lot. Because consumers form general impressions of shopping centers and business districts, the businesses and neighborhoods surrounding a store will affect how buyers perceive the atmosphere of a store.

Interior atmospheric elements include aesthetic considerations, such as lighting, wall and floor coverings, dressing facilities, and store fixtures. Interior sensory elements also contribute significantly to atmosphere. Color, for example, can attract shoppers to a retail display. Many fast-food restaurants use bright colors, such as red and yellow, because these have been shown to make customers feel hungrier and eat faster, which increases turnover. Sound is another important sensory component of atmosphere and may consist of silence, soft music, or even noisiness. Scent may be relevant as well; within a store, the odor of perfume suggests an image different from that suggested by the smell of prepared food. A store's layout—arrangement of departments, width of aisles, grouping of products, and location of check-out areas—is yet another determinant of atmosphere. Closely related to store layout is the element of crowding. A crowded store may restrict exploratory shopping, impede mobility, and decrease shopping efficiency.

Once the exterior and interior characteristics and store layout have been determined, displays are added. Displays enhance the store's atmosphere and give customers information about products. When displays carry out a storewide theme—during the Christmas season, for instance—they attract customers' attention and generate sales. So do displays that present several related products in a group, or ensemble. Interior displays of products stacked or hanging neatly on racks create one kind of atmosphere; marked-down items grouped together on a sale table produce a different kind.

Retailers must determine the atmosphere the target market seeks and then adjust atmospheric variables to encourage the desired awareness and action in consumers. High-fashion boutiques generally strive for an atmosphere of luxury and novelty. Ralph Lauren's Polo Shops offer limited amounts of merchandise with large open areas and props such as saddles or leather chairs adding to the exclusive look and image. Discount department stores must not seem too exclusive and expensive. To appeal to multiple market segments, a retailer may create different atmospheres for different operations within the store; for example, the discount basement, the sports department, and the women's shoe department may each have a unique atmosphere.

The Body Shop Practices Global Social Responsibility

IN 1976, ANITA RODDICK, then a 33-year-old housewife, opened a store in Brighton, England, to sell natural body lotions. Since then, sales and profits of The Body Shop's retail chain have grown an average of 50 percent a year. By January 1992, the company had 709 Body Shop stores (94 percent franchised) in thirty-seven countries, with pretax profits of $26 million on sales of $238 million. Annual return to investors has averaged 97 percent over the past five years. Much of The Body Shop's success can be attributed to smart retailing practices combined with a strong sense of social responsibility.

The Body Shop stores sell all-natural cosmetics made from high-quality biodegradable ingredients packaged in recyclable containers. Its products are not developed in laboratories or tested on animals like those of many other cosmetic companies. Each store is designed to be self-service, and the salespersons, while very knowledgeable about Body Shop products, provide information and do not force sales. To educate consumers about how its products are made and where their ingredients come from, the company uses bright graphics, videos, and a sense of style and humor.

Anita Roddick has tried to bring a global focus and unusual values to The Body Shop. She believes that companies must be concerned with more than profits, that they must be accountable for their actions and how they affect the environment, just as people are responsible for themselves and their neighbors. This is further emphasized by The Body Shop's support of such causes as saving endangered whales and vanishing rainforests. All of these issues surround customers in the form of banners, pamphlets, T-shirts, and posters emphasizing the importance of social issues.

The Body Shop's unusual philosophy has helped create a passion in its employees and customers. The company maintains a school in London to teach employees about its products and the value of being socially conscious. Additionally, employees are required to put in one hour of paid company time each week toward a community project. By instigating a philosophy of social responsibility, Roddick believes that her employees will be motivated by feeling good about what they are doing.

The lesson to be learned by The Body Shop's operation is that business does not have to focus solely on the science of making money. By focusing on its responsibilities to customers and employees, as well as society as a whole, business can be truly successful.

Sources: Rahul Jacob, "Body Shop International: What Selling Will Be Like in the '90's," *Fortune*, Jan. 13, 1992, pp. 63–64; Bo Burlingham, "This Woman Has Changed Business Forever," *Inc.*, June 1990, pp. 34–48; The Body Shop 1990 Annual Report; 1989 Annual Report; Bernice Huxtable, "Body-Care Firm Joins Rainforest Campaign," *Calgary Herald*, July 11, 1989, p. E5; and Dan Parle, "Back to Nature," *Business Journal*, January–February 1989, pp. 24–29.

Store Image

To attract customers, a retail store must project an image—a functional and psychological picture in the consumer's mind—that is acceptable to its target market. Although heavily dependent on atmospherics, a store's image is also shaped by its reputation for integrity, the number of services offered, location, merchandise assortments, pricing policies, promotional activities, and community involvement.

Characteristics of the target market—social class, lifestyle, income level, and past buying behavior—help form store image as well. How consumers perceive the store can be a major determinant of store patronage. Pier 1 Imports promotes a casual, affordable image, as shown in Figure 13.7. Consumers from lower socio-economic groups tend to patronize small, high-margin, high-service food stores and prefer small, friendly loan companies over large, impersonal banks, even though these companies charge high interest. Affluent consumers look for exclusive, high-quality establishments that offer prestige products and labels.

Retailers should be aware of the multiple factors that contribute to store image and recognize that perceptions of image vary. For example, one study found that consumers perceive Wal-Mart and K mart differently, although the two sell almost the same products in stores that look quite similar, offer the same prices, and even have similar names. Researchers discovered that Wal-Mart shoppers spend more money at Wal-Mart and are more satisfied with the store than K mart shoppers are with K mart, in part because of differences in the retailers' images. For example, Wal-Mart employees wear vests; K mart employees do not. Wal-Mart purchases are bagged in paper sacks, whereas K mart uses plastic bags. Wal-Mart has wider aisles, recessed lighting, and carpeting in some departments. Even the retailers' logos affect consumers' perceptions: Wal-Mart's simple white-and-brown logo appears friendly and "less blatantly commercial" than K mart's flashier red-and-white logo. These atmospheric elements give consumers the impression that Wal-Mart is warmer, friendlier, and more "upscale," than K mart.[39]

Figure 13.7

Image

Pier 1 Imports maintains an image as an importer of decorative household items, furniture, and clothing.

Source: Courtesy of Pier 1 Imports.

Scrambled Merchandising

When retailers add unrelated products and product lines—particularly fast-moving items that can be sold in volume—to an existing product mix, they are practicing **scrambled merchandising**. For example, a convenience store might start selling lawn fertilizer. Retailers adopting this strategy hope to accomplish one or more of the following: (1) convert their stores into one-stop shopping centers, (2) generate more traffic, (3) realize higher profit margins, (4) increase impulse purchases.

However, in scrambling merchandise, retailers must deal with diverse marketing channels and thus may reduce their own buying, selling, and servicing expertise. The practice can also blur a store's image in consumers' minds, making it more difficult for a retailer to succeed in today's highly competitive, saturated markets. Finally, scrambled merchandising intensifies competition among traditionally distinct types of stores and forces suppliers to adjust distribution systems so that new channel members can be accommodated.

The Wheel of Retailing

As new types of retail businesses come into being, they strive to fill niches in the dynamic environment of retailing. One hypothesis regarding the evolution and development of new types of retail stores is the **wheel of retailing**. According to this theory, new retailers often enter the marketplace with low prices, margins, and status. The new competitors' low prices are usually the result of innovative cost-cutting procedures, and they soon attract imitators. Gradually, as these businesses attempt to broaden their customer base and increase sales, their operations and facilities become more elaborate and more expensive. They may move to more desirable locations, begin to carry higher-quality merchandise, or add customer services. Eventually, they emerge at the high end of the price/cost/service scales, competing with newer discount retailers following the same evolutionary process.[40]

For example, supermarkets have undergone many changes since their introduction in 1921. Initially, they provided limited services in exchange for lower food prices. However, over time they developed a variety of new services, including free coffee, gourmet food sections, and children's play areas. Now supermarkets are being challenged by superstores and hypermarkets, which offer more product choices than the original supermarkets and have undercut supermarket prices.

Figure 13.8 illustrates the wheel of retailing for department stores and discount houses. Department stores such as Sears started out as high-volume, low-cost merchants competing with general stores and other small retailers; discount houses developed later, in response to the rising expenses of services in department stores. Many discount houses now appear to be following the wheel of retailing by offering more services, better locations, quality inventories, and, therefore, higher prices. Some discount houses are almost indistinguishable from department stores.

Like most hypotheses, the wheel of retailing may not fit every case. For example, it does not adequately explain the development of convenience stores,

Figure 13.8

The Wheel of Retailing, Which Explains the Origin and Evolution of New Types of Retail Stores

Source: Adapted from Robert F. Hartley, *Retailing: Challenge and Opportunity*, 3rd ed., p. 42. Copyright © 1984 by Houghton Mifflin Company. Used by permission.

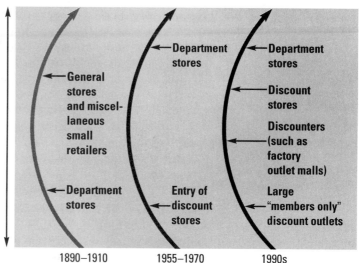

If the "wheel" is considered to be turning slowly in the direction of the arrows, then the department stores around 1900 and the discounters later can be viewed as coming on the scene at the low end of the wheel. As it turns slowly, they move with it, becoming higher-price operations, and at the same time leaving room for lower-price firms to gain entry at the low end of the wheel.

specialty stores, department store branches, and vending machine operations. Another major weakness of the theory is that it does not predict what retailing innovations will develop, or when. Still, the hypothesis works reasonably well in industrialized, expanding economies.

Summary

Retailing includes all transactions in which the buyer intends to consume the product through personal, family, or household use. Retailers, which are organizations that sell products primarily to ultimate consumers, are important links in the marketing channel because they are customers for wholesalers and producers. Most retailing takes place inside stores or service establishments, but retail exchanges may also occur outside stores through in-home retailing, telemarketing, vending machines, and mail-order catalogs. Retail institutions provide place, time, and possession utilities. In the case of services, retailers develop most of the product's form utility as well.

Retail stores are usually classified according to width of product mix and depth of product lines. The major types of retail stores are department stores, general merchandisers, and specialty stores. Department stores are large retail organizations employing at least twenty-five people and characterized by wide product mixes in considerable depth for most product lines. Their product lines are organized into separate departments that function much as self-contained businesses do.

Mass merchandisers generally offer fewer customer services than do department stores and emphasize lower prices, high turnover, and large sales volumes. Mass merchandisers include discount stores (self-service, low-price general-merchandise outlets) and supermarkets (large, self-service food stores that also carry some nonfood products). Emerging general-merchandise retailers include superstores (giant retail outlets that carry all products found in supermarkets and most consumer products purchased on a routine basis), home improvement centers (retailers that provide services and resources to assist do-it-yourselfers in remodeling or redecorating their homes), hypermarkets (one-stop combination supermarket and discount stores), warehouse/wholesale clubs (large-scale, members-only discount operations), and warehouse and catalog showrooms (low-cost operations characterized by warehouse methods of materials handling and display, large inventories, and minimum services).

Specialty retailers offer substantial assortments in a few product lines. They include traditional specialty retailers, which carry narrow product mixes with deep product lines, and off-price retailers, which sell brand-name manufacturers' seconds and production overruns to consumers at deep discounts.

Nonstore retailing is the selling of goods or services outside the confines of a retail facility. Direct marketing is the use of nonpersonal media to introduce products to consumers, who then purchase the products by mail or telephone. Forms of nonstore retailing include in-home retailing (selling via personal contacts with consumers in their own homes), telemarketing (direct selling of goods and services by telephone, based either on a cold canvass of the telephone directory or on a prescreened list of prospective clients), automatic vending (selling through machines), and mail-order retailing (selling by description because buyers usually do not see the actual product until it arrives in the mail).

Franchising is an arrangement whereby a supplier grants a dealer the right to sell products in exchange for some type of consideration. Retail franchises are of three general types: a manufacturer may authorize a number of retail stores to sell a certain brand-name item; a producer may license distributors to sell a given product to retailers; or a franchiser may supply brand names, techniques, or other services instead of a complete product. Franchise arrangements have a number of advantages and disadvantages over traditional business forms, and their use is increasing.

To increase sales and store patronage, retailers must consider several strategic issues. Location determines the trading area from which a store must draw its customers and should be evaluated carefully. When evaluating potential sites, retailers take into account a variety of factors, including the location of the firm's target market within the trading area, the kinds of products being sold, the availability of public transportation, customer characteristics, and competitors' locations. Retailers can choose among several types of locations: freestanding structures, traditional business districts, neighborhood shopping centers, community shopping centers, regional shopping centers, or nontraditional shopping centers. The width, depth, and quality of the product assortment should be of the kind that can satisfy the retailer's target market customers.

Retail positioning involves identifying an unserved or underserved market niche, or segment, and serving the segment through a strategy that distinguishes the retailer from others in the minds of persons. Atmospherics comprises the physical elements of a store's design that can be adjusted to appeal to consumers' emotions and thus induce consumers to buy. Store image, which various consumers perceive differently, derives not only from atmosphere, but also from location, products offered, customer services, prices, promotion, and the store's overall reputation. Scrambled merchandising adds unrelated product lines to an existing product mix and is being used by a growing number of stores to generate sales.

The wheel-of-retailing hypothesis holds that new retail institutions start as low-status, low-margin, and low-price operators. As they develop, they increase service and prices and eventually become vulnerable to newer institutions, which enter the market and repeat the cycle. However, the wheel-of-retailing hypothesis may not apply in every case.

Important Terms

Retailing
Retailer
Department stores
Mass merchandisers
Discount stores
Supermarkets
Superstores
Hypermarkets
Warehouse/wholesale clubs
Warehouse showrooms
Catalog showrooms
Traditional specialty retailers
Off-price retailers
Nonstore retailing
Direct marketing
In-home retailing

Telemarketing
Automatic vending
Mail-order retailing
Catalog retailing
Franchising
Neighborhood shopping centers
Community shopping centers
Regional shopping centers
Retail positioning
Atmospherics
Scrambled merchandising
Wheel of retailing

Discussion and Review Questions

1. What are the major differences between discount houses and department stores?
2. How does a superstore differ from a supermarket?
3. Should a warehouse/wholesale club be classified as a wholesaler or as a retailer?
4. In what ways are traditional specialty stores and off-price retailers similar? How do they differ?
5. Evaluate the following statement: "Direct marketing and nonstore retailing are about the same thing."
6. Why is door-to-door selling a form of retailing? Some consumers feel that direct mail-orders skip the retailer. Is this true?
7. If you were to open a retail business, would you prefer to open an independent store or to own a store under a franchise arrangement? Explain your preference.
8. What major issues should be considered when determining a retail site location?
9. Describe the three major types of shopping centers. Give examples of each type in your area.
10. How does atmosphere add value to products sold in a store? How important is atmospherics for convenience stores?
11. How should one determine the best retail store atmosphere?
12. Discuss the major factors that help determine a retail store's image.

13. Is it possible for a single retail store to have an overall image that appeals to sophisticated shoppers, extravagant ones, and bargain hunters? Why or why not?

14. In what ways does the use of scrambled merchandising affect a store's image?

Cases

13.1 Mrs. Fields Cookies Uses High Tech to Control Retail Outlets

In 1977, 20-year-old Debbi Fields was studying English and history at a community college and wondering what to do with her life. The former Oakland A's ball girl did not want a traditional nine-to-five job and was willing to take some risks to avoid it. She occasionally baked cookies for her husband Randy to take to work. His clients loved the cookies, and the Fields got the idea to go into business selling the cookies.

Debbi borrowed $50,000, bought used ovens and mixers and opened her first shop in an international food arcade near Stanford University in Palo Alto, California. To drum up customers for the fledgling shop, Debbi spent her first day in business giving away cookies to pedestrians. At the end of the day, Debbi had made $75. Today, Mrs. Fields Cookies operates over 600 retail outlets in the United States that generated over $130 million in revenue in 1991.

The secret to Mrs. Fields' success had always been the tight control that Debbi held over the company. In the beginning, Debbi would visit stores and mop floors, make cookie batter, and even change light bulbs. However, this control eventually spurred the company's decline. In the late 1980s, Debbi began to realize that her micromanagement techniques left her with little time to focus on larger decisions. Along with this problem, the company also faced rising rents and costs and stiff competition from other cookie companies like Famous Amos Chocolate Chip Cookie Co., Blue Chip Cookies, and the Great American Chocolate Chip Cookie Co. As a result of these difficulties, the company had to close some stores and pull out of overseas expansion efforts.

Faced with a declining organization, Debbi Fields was forced to give up some of her control and bring others into the organization. The company hired a new layer of management, including area sales managers, district managers, and regional directors of operations. In addition, Randy Fields designed an innovative and sophisticated management information system called Retail Operations Intelligence (ROI) to provide a constant flow of information between every store manager and corporate headquarters.

The ROI system allows every store manager, district manager, and regional director to have daily contact via computer with Debbi and the rest of the company's top management. Information within the system is exchanged two ways. The first is FormMail, the company's version of an electronic mail system. FormMail allows employees to send information to and ask questions of anyone within the company, including Debbi, with a promised response time of 24 to 48 hours.

The second way of exchanging information is through an automated computer system that connects each store to the company's headquarters. This part of the ROI system contains twenty applications ranging from production planning and inventory to sales reporting and analysis. The system allows Mrs.

Fields to achieve two objectives that are unusual for most cookie retailers. First, by automating (and thus speeding up) routine tasks, the system frees store managers from time-consuming paperwork and administrative chores. Second, because the system allows Debbi to be involved in daily operations, her enthusiastic, people-first management style is present in each store. This system enables managers to duplicate the high quality standards and effective selling that first made Debbi a success.

For example, at the start of every business day, using the Day Planner software, a store manager examines his or her store's performance for the three previous weeks and calculates how many customers will be needed and how many cookies must be sold that day to meet sales projections. The computer also helps the manager schedule that day's cookie baking to meet sales demand and yet have minimum leftovers. Although, if necessary, the manager could make these calculations personally, the computer saves valuable time. Then, throughout the day, the manager enters sales figures into the computer (the company is beginning to equip its stores with cash registers that transmit this information automatically to the computer). The computer, in turn, adjusts hourly projections and offers selling advice if customer count or total sales drop below predicted levels.

The computer assists with other managerial activities as well. It helps the manager determine how many employees to schedule for the upcoming two-week period, based on sales projections and mixing and baking times. With a special series of interview questions, it evaluates prospective employees and initiates the paperwork with the Park City office when the manager makes the final hiring decision. By asking the manager questions, the system also troubleshoots when equipment malfunctions, and it generates repair requests and alerts headquarters to pay the bill when repair services are required. In short, because the computer reorganizes and makes accessible the information that managers provide about their own operations, every store manager is equipped to make better day-to-day decisions.

Although the company does have area, district, and regional managers, the responsibility for monitoring the stores' daily reports and weekly inventory reports rests with just a few store controllers in Park City, who make sure that the reports tally with sales figures. In case of discrepancies, the controllers go, whenever possible, to the source of the problem. With store controllers tracking the routine figures, the company's executives are free to deal with the exceptions—the differences between expected outcome and actual outcome. They can concentrate on people, not numbers, just as Debbi Fields wants them to.

By using the ROI system, Mrs. Fields has increased productivity, increased sales, and lowered employee turnover. In fact, the system has been so successful that the company formed the Fields Software Group in 1988 to develop and market the ROI system. Since then, eight companies have agreed to purchase the system—the most notable buyer being the Miami-based Burger King Corporation.

Since Debbi Fields delegated much of her control over the company to other managers and the ROI system, she is more accessible to her employees and has more opportunity to visit stores and brainstorm on new promotional ideas. She has even started a new franchise-type program whereby the most productive store managers can purchase their stores from Mrs. Fields. The company expected 25 managers to take advantage of this option in 1992.

With time to concentrate on more important issues, Debbi is overseeing the company's second attempt at expansion. The company recently signed a licensing arrangement with Ambrosia Chocolate to market Mrs. Fields Semi-Sweet Chocolate Chips in supermarkets. Mrs. Fields chocolate chips sell for about 10 cents more than competing chips and are available in 23 midsize American cities. In addition, Mrs. Fields signed a licensing agreement with Marriott to open new outlets in locations such as airports and highway travel plazas where Marriott controls the food franchise. As of early 1992, ten stores had opened with fifty more planned by 1995.

Likewise, the company is experimenting with combination bakery-cafes that offer soups, sandwiches, bagels, brownies, and cookies. The company also markets Mrs. Fields coffee and macadamia nuts, and is experimenting with frozen cookie dough. Debbi Fields' latest experiment involves opening bakeries in national supermarket chains like Cub Foods. Offering cookies and brownies, these Mrs. Fields stores are run by Cub employees trained by Mrs. Fields, Inc.

In spite of its difficulties, Mrs. Fields is still the largest cookie retailer in the country for several reasons. Debbi Fields constantly sets goals to motivate herself and her employees and to keep tabs on the company's progress. She pays unyielding attention to detail, particularly to maintaining product quality. When she opened her first store, Debbi established a policy that all cookies would have a maximum shelf life of two hours. Cookies not sold after two hours were given to charity. That policy is now in effect at all Mrs. Fields locations. Debbi also treats her employees as well as she treats her customers. She believes it is unrealistic to expect a poorly treated employee to provide a potential cookie buyer with a pleasant experience.[41]

Questions for Discussion

1. With all of the benefits associated with franchising, why did it take Debbi Fields so long to give up control of day-to-day operations and finally implement a franchise system?
2. How has Mrs. Fields' ROI system enabled managers to manage hundreds of retail outlets effectively?
3. By definition, Mrs. Fields is a specialty retailer. With this in mind, evaluate Mrs. Fields' expansion into other retail and product areas. How do each of these areas relate to Mrs. Fields' basic business of selling cookies?

13.2 Dell Computers Wins with Direct Marketing

Dell Computers was born when then 19-year-old Michael Dell started building personal computers (PCs) in his dorm room at the University of Texas. He eventually dropped out of the university to concentrate on building a computer company. By age 26 Dell saw his company's sales reach $546 million, with his own 35 percent stake in the company worth nearly $200 million. Dell Computers now ranks sixth in the U.S. personal computer market. The company has achieved its success in a highly competitive personal computer market by building a reliable brand-name reputation and selling through direct marketing.

At first, Dell targeted his computers at a small group of technically oriented users and avoided competition with IBM, Apple, and other big computer makers in the general-purpose market. Today Dell focuses on manufacturing and selling high-end IBM-compatibles, with half its sales coming from PCs with Intel's 80386 chip; it offers machines based on the 80486 chip as well. Dell also markets multiuser systems based on the UNIX operating system.

Most computer marketers use a lengthy distribution channel: manufacturer to dealer to customer. Dell Computers, however, bypasses the high-cost dealer system and sells directly to the customer. Not only does this help the company keep its computer prices low, it keeps Dell in close touch with the needs and wants of its market.

Customers order Dell's PCs through a toll-free 800 telephone number, which they may find in *Computer Shopper*, computer magazines, or trade journals. When a customer calls, a sales representative asks about the customer's computing needs and uses, and then helps the customer determine an appropriate model and options to satisfy those needs. The sales representative then checks the customer's creditworthiness and releases the customer's order to manufacturing. Unlike most companies, Dell manufactures computers after receiving an order, not before, with each computer built to the customer's specifications. It strives for a delivery time of five days because customers who do not want to wait can get comparable PCs from other dealers. Most orders go out in one to two days.

Dell has only a few basic models of PCs, but these can be manufactured using up to one hundred different configurations of hard drives, monitors, add-in boards, and other hardware. Dell handles only the assembly and testing of its products. Components are manufactured by suppliers such as Intel. Dell can therefore focus on the computers and leave keeping up with rapidly changing technology to its suppliers.

Service is a crucial component of Dell's product. A staff of 150 technicians stands by to help solve customers' problems; Michael Dell says that 95 percent of customer problems are solved over the phone. Additionally, the company provides next-day, on-site service on its products through a unit of Xerox Corp. The company's strong service allows it to pay attention to its customers and maintain good relationships with them. That it has succeeded is evident by the firm's number-one rank in a personal computer customer-satisfaction survey by J.D. Power & Associates (a marketing research firm).

However, the company has not always had such a good reputation for service. Before the company went public in June 1988, it had difficulty meeting orders—with delivery times stretching from three days to a dismal thirty-five. The company raised $31 million from the stock sale, which funded additional inventory and the capacity to reduce its delivery time. In September 1989, the company moved into a larger, 126,000-square-foot facility to enhance its manufacturing capacity.

Although most sales come through direct marketing, Dell has a sales team that targets the largest 1,000 U.S. companies, as well as companies in Canada, Great Britain, Germany, and Australia. Its reputation in the corporate world is increasing: Dell was ranked the top vendor of 80386-chip PCs and ranked number one in customer support by top corporate personal computer purchasers.

Dell's success with direct mail marketing may well be indicative of the future of computer marketing in general. According to WorkGroup Technologies, Inc., a marketing research firm, direct marketing will account for 29 percent of all PC sales in 1995, up from 22 percent in 1991. Consumers have discovered that mail-order PCs are generally as good as store brands (and sometimes better) and may cost as much as 30 percent less. Dell Computers is therefore well positioned to continue growth and innovation through direct marketing.[42]

Questions for Discussion

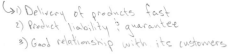
— Deals with customers directly w/o the middleman

1. Explain why Dell is a nonstore retailer and how Dell competes with computer stores. *lower prices & better service*
2. How would you describe the retailing strategy of Dell?
3. What are some of the issues that Dell must consider to ensure future success?
↳1) Delivery of products fast
2) Product liability & guarantee
3) Good relationship with its customers

Chapter Notes

1. Based on information from Rita Koselka, "Fading Into History," *Forbes*, Aug. 19, 1991, p. 70; John Dorfman, "Heard on the Street: Limited's Stock Remains Hot But More Missteps May Alter That," *Wall Street Journal–Europe*, Aug. 12, 1991; The Limited 1990 Annual Report; Carol Hymowitz, "Limited Inc., on New Tack, Pulls Ahead of Retail Gang," *Wall Street Journal*, Feb. 24, 1989, pp. B1, B4; "The Limited's Approach," *Chain Store Age Executive*, December 1988, pp. 28, 30, 36; and Annette Tapert, "Happy Landings," *Working Woman*, September 1988, pp. 114–118.
2. *Statistical Abstract of the United States, 1991*, p. 769.
3. Laura Zinn, "Shoppers Sightings Reported" *Business Week*, Jan. 13, 1992, p. 81.
4. Laura Zinn, "The New Stars of Retailing," *Business Week*, Dec. 16, 1991, pp. 120–122.
5. Leonard L. Berry and Larry G. Gresham, "Relationship Retailing: Transforming Customers into Clients," *Business Horizons*, November–December 1986, pp. 44–45.
6. Maggie Mahar, "Last of the Big Spenders? A New-Style Consumer Will Scale Down, Save More," *Barron's*, Mar. 11, 1991, pp. 10–11, 34–40.
7. "Service Equals Success in Supermarkets," *Marketing Communications*, April 1989, pp. 24–25, 31.
8. Ruth Hamel, "Food Fight," *American Demographics*, March 1989, pp. 36–39, 60.
9. Patrick McDonnell, "A Chain's Weak Links," *Forbes*, Jan. 21, 1991, pp. 76–80.
10. Home Depot 1990 Annual Report, p. 10.
11. Kimberly D. Hendrix, "The 1990's: It's a Rough Time for Home Improvement Retailing," *Chain Store Age Executive*, Aug. 1991, pp. 34A–36A.
12. Joe Schwartz and Thomas Exter, "Remodeling America," *American Demographics*, Nov. 1991, pp. 46–49.
13. David Rodgers, "Hypermarkets Need 'Something Special' to Succeed," *Supermarket Business*, May 1988, pp. 25–26, 158.
14. Priscilla Donegan, "Hypermarkets: Is America Ready?" *Progressive Grocer*, July 1988, pp. 21–34.
15. Ibid., pp. 23–24.

16. Bill Saporito, "Retailers Fly into Hyperspace," *Fortune,* Oct. 24, 1988, pp. 148–152.

17. J. Barry Mason and Morris L. Mayer, *Modern Retailing Theory and Practice* (Plano, Texas: Business Publications, 1987), pp. 65–66.

18. Mason and Mayer, p. 66.

19. Andrew Kupfer, "The Final Word in No-Frills Shopping?" *Fortune,* Mar. 13, 1989, p. 30.

20. "The Discount Industry's Top 150 Chains," *Discount Store News,* July 22, 1991, p. 35.

21. Amanda Putnam, "Demographic Tail Wind Spurs Growth of Specialty Apparel Retailing," *Chain Store Age Executive,* Aug. 1991, pp. 28A–30A.

22. Barry Berman and Joel Evans, *Retail Management: A Strategic Approach* (New York: Macmillan, 1986), p. 99.

23. Judith Graham, "Marshall's, T. J. Maxx Duel over Off-Price Leadership," *Advertising Age,* June 26, 1989, p. 3.

24. Zinn, p. 81.

25. Teri Agins, "Upscale Retailers Head to Enemy Turf," *Wall Street Journal,* Aug. 25, 1989, p. B1.

26. *Vending Times,* Census of Industry, 1990.

27. "V/T Census of the Industry Issue—1988," *Vending Times,* 1988, p. 49. Reprinted by permission.

28. Francine Schwadel, "Sears to Roebuck to Streamline Catalog Business," *Wall Street Journal,* Jan. 8, 1992, p. B2.

29. Zinn, p. 81.

30. Al Urbanski, "The Franchise Option," *Sales & Marketing Management,* February 1988, pp. 28–33.

31. *Statistical Abstract of the United States, 1991,* p. 778.

32. Ibid. 1991, p. 778.

33. "Renovating Under the Palms," *Chain Store Age Executive,* Aug. 1991, pp. 37–42.

34. "The Minnesota Mallers," *U.S. News & World Report,* June 26, 1989, p. 12.

35. Adrienne Ward, "The Gap Opens Door to New Mall Concept," *Advertising Age,* Jan. 21, 1991, p. 39.

36. Susan Caminiti, "How the Gap Keeps Ahead of the Pack," *Fortune,* Feb. 12, 1990, pp. 129–131.

37. George H. Lucas, Jr., and Larry G. Gresham, "How to Position for Retail Success," *Business,* April–June 1988, pp. 3–13.

38. Nicholas Hirst, "How to Succeed in U.S. Retailing," *Canadian Business,* October 1991, pp. 77–84.

39. Francine Schwadel, "Little Touches Spur Wal-Mart's Rise; Shoppers React to Logo, Decor, Employee Vests," *Wall Street Journal,* Sept. 22, 1989, p. B1.

40. Stephen Brown, "The Wheel of Retailing: Past and Future," *Journal of Retailing,* Summer 1990, pp. 143–149.

41. Alan Prendergast, "Learning to Let Go," *Working Woman,* Jan. 1992, pp. 42, 44–45; Michael Garry, "Cub Embraces Non-Foods," *Progressive Grocer,* Dec. 1991, pp. 45–48; Jack Schember, "Mrs. Fields' Secret Weapon," *Personnel Journal,* Sept. 1991, pp. 56–58; Brian Quinton, "Mrs. Fields Bakery Cafes Seek New Fortune Beyond Cookies," *Restaurants and Institutions,* Feb. 20, 1991, p. 21; Bradley Johnson, "Mrs. Fields Sells Name for Dough," *Advertising Age,* Apr. 23, 1990, p. 75; and Buck Brown, "How the Cookie Crumbled at Mrs. Fields," *Wall Street Journal,* Jan. 26, 1989, p. B1.

42. Stephanie Anderson Forest, "PC Slump? What PC Slump?" *Business Week*, July 1, 1991, pp. 66–67; Lois Therrien, "So You Wanna Be a Mail-Order Star . . . ," *Business Week*, July 1, 1991, pp. 66–67; Robert Cohen, "Precise Targeting Key to Direct Mail," *Marketing (Maclean Hunter)*, Feb. 4, 1991, p. 26; Neal E. Boudette, "Simple, Flexible, Manual," *Industry Week*, Nov. 6, 1989, pp. 48, 50; and Kevin Kelly, "Dell Computer Hits the Drawing Board," *Business Week*, Apr. 24, 1989, p. 138.

14 *Physical Distribution*

OBJECTIVES

- To understand how physical distribution activities are integrated into marketing channels and overall marketing strategies

- To examine three important physical distribution objectives: customer service, total distribution costs, and cost trade-offs

- To learn how efficient order processing facilitates product flow

- To illustrate how materials handling is a part of physical distribution activities

- To learn how warehousing facilitates the storage and movement functions in physical distribution

- To understand how inventory management is conducted to develop and maintain adequate assortments of products for target markets

- To gain insight into how transportation modes, which bridge the producer-customer gap, are selected and coordinated

M. S. Carriers is a fairly young truckload carrier with a low-key approach to managing quality physical distribution service to marketing channel members. Whereas many companies spend a great deal to promote their quality improvement efforts to potential customers and the general public, M. S. Carriers chooses not to flaunt its customer orientation. In a short time M. S. Carriers has become a leader in its industry and was recently rated in the top five in its division by *Distribution* magazine. Instead of promoting their efforts externally, the company focuses internally to constantly improve the way they serve their customers—marketing channel members.

One of M. S. Carriers' divisions provides service to private companies. In some cases they take over a manufacturer's private trucking operations. Manufacturers, retailers, or wholesalers often run their trucks empty on a return trip after delivering cargo, but M. S. Carriers uses its service and marketing network to contract cargo to haul back on the return. The channel member benefits by reducing costs and distribution problems, while M. S. Carriers makes a profit.

In an effort to place even more emphasis on continuous process improvement through quality management, M. S. Carriers hired Darryl Jackson, their external quality consultant, as executive vice president and chief operating officer to oversee the day-to-day operations of the company. This move allows the company's CEO, Mike Starnes, to focus on developing and expanding "niche" markets while providing missing links in customer service. M. S. Carriers' basic quality service principles are customer focus, total employee involvement, proper performance measurement, and improving the systems and processes within the company. Over 75 percent of the company's 1,800 employees are truck drivers, and a great deal of effort has been directed at helping them do a better job. In an industry in which turnover is rampant, M. S. Carriers improved its driver turnover rate 35 percent from 1990 to 1991 by allocating more money for training and boosting driver wages 24 percent. M. S. Carriers is succeeding in an industry in which many transportation firms have failed in recent years.[1]

Photo courtesy of M. S. Carriers.

THE TRANSPORTATION FIRM M. S. Carriers provides quality customer service to marketing channel members. The company's service orientation facilitates manufacturers, wholesalers, and retailers in physical distribution of their products. Physical distribution deals with the movement and handling of goods and the processing of orders, activities necessary to provide a level of service that will satisfy customers. Even though physical distribution is costly, it creates time and place utility, which maximizes the value of products by delivering them when and where they are wanted.

This chapter describes how marketing decisions are related to physical distribution. After considering basic physical distribution concepts, we outline the major objectives of physical distribution. We then examine each major distribution function: order processing, materials handling, warehousing, inventory management, and transportation. We close the chapter with a discussion of marketing strategy considerations in physical distribution. When reading this chapter, keep in mind how important customer service is to physical distribution and how physical distribution is related to marketing channels.

The Importance of Physical Distribution

Physical distribution (or logistics) is a set of activities—consisting of order processing, materials handling, warehousing, inventory management, and transportation—used in the movement of products from producers to consumers and end users. Planning an effective physical distribution system can be a significant decision in developing a marketing strategy. A company that has the right goods in the right place, at the right time, in the right quantity, and with the right support services is able to sell more than competitors who fail to accomplish these goals. Physical distribution is an important variable in a marketing strategy because it can decrease costs and increase customer satisfaction. In fact, speed of delivery, along with services and dependability, is often as important to buyers as cost.

Physical distribution deals with physical movement and inventory holding (storing and tracking inventory until it is needed) both within and among marketing channel members. Often one channel member will arrange the movement of goods for all channel members involved in exchanges. For example, a packing company ships fresh California fruit to remote markets on a routine basis. Frequently, buyers are found while the fruit is in transit.

The physical distribution system is often adjusted to meet the needs of a channel member. For example, a construction equipment dealer who keeps a low inventory of replacement parts requires the fastest and most dependable service when parts not in stock are needed. In this case, the distribution cost may be a minor consideration when compared with service, dependability, and timeliness.

Physical Distribution Objectives

For most companies, the main objective of physical distribution is to decrease costs while increasing service. In the real world, however, few distribution systems manage to achieve these goals in equal measure. The large inventories

Figure 14.1

Customer Service

Ryder Transportation emphasizes that they keep customers happy with total transportation management of complex distribution needs.

Source: Courtesy of Ryder Truck Rental Inc.

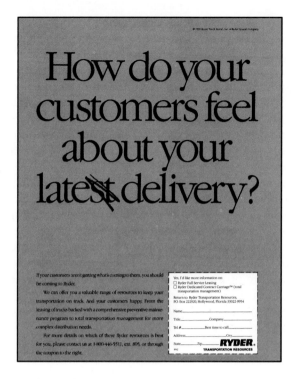

and rapid transportation essential to high levels of customer service drive up costs. On the other hand, reduced inventories and slower, cheaper transportation methods cause customer dissatisfaction. Physical distribution managers strive for a reasonable balance between service, costs, and resources. They determine what level of customer service is acceptable, yet realistic, develop a "system" outlook of figuring total distribution costs, and trade higher costs at one stage of distribution for savings in another. In this section we examine these three performance objectives more closely.

Customer Service

In varying degrees, all organizations attempt to satisfy customer needs and wants through a set of activities known collectively as customer service. Many companies claim that service to the customer is their top priority. Clearly, without customers, there would be no profit. Service may be as important in attracting customers and building sales as the cost or quality of the organization's products. In Figure 14.1, Ryder Transportation Resources focuses on their reliability in service.

Customers require a variety of services. At the most basic level, they need fair prices, acceptable product quality, and dependable deliveries. In the physical distribution area, availability, timeliness, and quality are the most important dimensions of customer service. These are the main factors that determine how satisfied customers are likely to be with a supplier's physical distribution activities.[2] Customers seeking a higher level of customer service may also want sizable inventories, efficient order processing, availability of emergency shipments, progress reports, postsale services, prompt replacement of defective items, and warranties. Customers' inventory requirements influence the level of physical distribution service they expect. For example, customers that want to minimize inventory storage and shipping costs may require that suppliers assume the cost of maintaining inventory in the marketing channel, or the cost of premium transportation.[3] Because service needs vary from customer to customer, companies must analyze—and adapt to—customer preferences. Attention to customer needs and preferences is crucial to increasing sales and obtaining repeat sales. A company's failure to provide the desired level of service may mean the loss of customers.

Companies must also examine the service levels competitors offer and match those standards, at least when the costs of providing the services can be balanced by the sales generated. Many companies are guaranteeing service performance to win customers over. For example, through their Premium 500 service, CF Truckload Services of Palo Alto, California, guarantees on-time delivery of single-bill, full-truckload shipments or the customer receives a $500 refund.[4]

Services are provided most effectively when service standards are developed and stated in terms that are specific, measurable, and appropriate for the product: for example, "98 percent of all orders filled within forty-eight hours." Standards should be communicated clearly to both customers and employees and rigorously enforced. In many cases, it is necessary to maintain a policy of minimum order sizes to ensure that transactions are profitable; that is, special service charges are added to orders smaller than a specified quantity. Many service policies also spell out delivery times and provisions for backordering, returning goods, and obtaining emergency shipments. The overall objective of any service policy should be to improve customer service just to the point beyond which increased sales would be negated by increased distribution costs.

Total Distribution Costs

Although physical distribution managers try to minimize the costs of each element in the system—order processing, materials handling, inventory, warehousing, and transportation—decreasing costs in one area often raises them in another. By using a total cost approach to physical distribution, managers can view the distribution system as a whole, not as a collection of unrelated activities. The emphasis shifts from lowering the separate costs of individual functions to minimizing the total cost of the entire distribution system.

The total cost approach calls for analyzing the costs of all possible distribution alternatives, even those considered too impractical or expensive. Total cost analyses weigh inventory levels against warehousing expenses, materials handling costs against various modes of transportation, and all distribution costs against customer service standards. The costs of potential sales losses from lower performance levels are also considered. In many cases, accounting procedures and statistical methods can be used to figure total costs. Where hundreds of combinations of distribution variables are possible, computer simulations may be helpful. In no case is a distribution system's lowest total cost the result of using a combination of the cheapest functions; instead, it is the lowest overall cost compatible with the company's stated service objectives.

It is expected that through the mid-1990s, transportation, warehousing, inventory handling, and other physical distribution costs will rise faster than the inflation rate. These cost increases will be caused mainly by fuel price increases, labor shortages, and the aging of the transportation infrastructure.[5]

Cost Trade-offs

A distribution system that attempts to provide a specific level of customer service for the lowest possible total cost must use cost trade-offs to resolve conflicts about resource allocations. That is, higher costs in one area of the distribution system must be offset by lower costs in another area if the total system is to remain cost effective.

Trade-offs are strategic decisions to combine (and recombine) resources for greatest cost effectiveness. When distribution managers regard the system as a network of interlocking functions, trade-offs become useful tools in a unified distribution strategy. Trade-offs are apparent in the American distribution strategy of Swedish furniture retailer IKEA, which sells large selections of stylish, ready-to-assemble furniture in several U.S. stores (see Case 14.1). To ensure that each store carries enough inventory to satisfy customers in the area, IKEA groups its American retail outlets into regions, each served by a separate distribution center. In addition, each IKEA store carries a five-week back stock of inventory. Thus IKEA has chosen to trade higher inventory warehousing costs for improved customer service.[6]

Order Processing

Order processing—the first stage in a physical distribution system—is the receipt and transmission of sales order information. Although management sometimes overlooks the importance of these activities, efficient order processing facilitates product flow. Computerized order processing, used by many firms, speeds the flow of information from customer to seller.[7] When carried out quickly and accurately, order processing contributes to customer satisfaction, repeat orders, and increased profits.

Generally, there are three main tasks in order processing: order entry, order handling, and order delivery.[8] Order entry begins when customers or salespersons place purchase orders by mail, telephone, or computer. In some companies, sales service representatives receive and enter orders personally and also handle complaints, prepare progress reports, and forward sales order information.

The next task, order handling, involves several activities. Once an order has been entered, it is transmitted to the warehouse, where the availability of the product is verified, and to the credit department, where prices, terms, and the customer's credit rating are checked. If the credit department approves the purchase, the warehouse begins to fill the order. If the requested product is not in stock, a production order is sent to the factory or the customer is offered a substitute item.

When the order has been filled and packed for shipment, the warehouse schedules pickup with an appropriate carrier. If the customer is willing to pay for rush service, priority transportation is used. The customer is sent an invoice, inventory records are adjusted, and the order is delivered.

Order processing can be manual or electronic, depending on which method provides the greatest speed and accuracy within cost limits. Manual processing suffices for a small volume of orders and is more flexible in special situations. **Electronic data interchange (EDI)** is a process that lets a company integrate order processing, production planning, inventory, accounting, and transportation planning into a total information system.[9] Wal-Mart and several hundred of its suppliers use EDI networks. Instead of sending paper purchase orders—which take five to ten days to reach their destination and then must be keyed into a supplier's system—Wal-Mart transmits purchase orders directly from its main data processing center to a participating vendor's computer. Consolidated Freightways recently installed a nationwide EDI system to file shipping documents the day after a shipment is delivered. This system has reduced their order processing time from ten days to one day and has greatly increased their ability to serve customers.[10] The Global Perspective describes how Benetton uses an EDI system to improve order processing in its international distribution system.

Materials Handling

Materials handling, or physical handling of products, is important in efficient warehouse operations, as well as in transportation from points of production to points of consumption. The characteristics of the product itself often determine how it will be handled. For example, bulk liquids and gases have unique characteristics that determine how they can be moved and stored.

Materials handling procedures and techniques should increase the usable capacity of a warehouse, reduce the number of times a good is handled, improve service to customers, and increase their satisfaction with the product. Packaging, loading, movement, and labeling systems must be coordinated to maximize cost reduction and customer satisfaction.

Internal packaging is also an important consideration in materials handling. Goods must be packaged correctly to prevent damage or breakage during handling and transportation procedures. An ongoing debate in physical distribution concerns the use of polystyrene peanuts as a cushioning material, which environmentalists reject.[11] As discussed in Case 14.2, there are several alternatives to polystyrene; however, many of these alternatives have problems of their own, and most are more expensive.

In Chapter 8 we note that the protective functions of packaging are important considerations in product development. Appropriate decisions about packaging materials and methods allow for the most efficient physical handling; most companies employ packaging consultants or specialists to accomplish this important task. Materials handling equipment is used in the design of handling systems. **Unit loading** is grouping one or more boxes on a pallet or skid; it permits movement of efficient loads by mechanical means, such as fork lifts, trucks, or conveyor systems. **Containerization** is the practice of consolidating many items into a single large container that is sealed at its point of origin and opened at its destination. The containers are usually eight feet wide, eight feet high, and ten, twenty, twenty-five, or forty feet long. They can be conveniently stacked and shipped via rail or waterway. Once the containers reach their destinations, wheel assemblies can be added to make them suitable for ground transportation.[12] Because individual items are not handled in transit, containerization greatly increases efficiency and security in shipping. Figure 14.2 is an advertisement for Cast, a container shipping company.

Warehousing

Warehousing, the design and operation of facilities for storing and moving goods, is an important physical distribution function. Warehousing provides time utility by enabling firms to compensate for dissimilar production and consumption rates. That is, when mass production creates a greater stock of goods than can be sold immediately, companies may warehouse the surplus goods until customers are ready to buy. Warehousing also helps stabilize the prices and availability of seasonal items. Here we describe the basic functions of warehouses and the different types of warehouses available. We also examine the distribution center concept, a special warehouse operation designed so that goods can be moved rapidly.

Figure 14.2

Containerization

Cast is a container shipping firm that ships products world-wide.

Source: Courtesy of Cast North America (1983) Inc.

Benetton's International Electronic Data Interchange System

How IMPORTANT can eight people be to a multinational clothing manufacturer and retailer? To Benetton, the Italian sportswear company, the eight people who run the warehouse that handles the distribution of 50 million pieces of clothing a year are extremely important. These eight people are responsible for processing 230,000 articles of clothing a day to serve 4,500 stores, of which 700 are located in the United States. Though sales in the garment industry have sagged recently, Benetton is still moving tremendous amounts of knit and cotton clothing. After their small clothing business expanded into an international fashion sensation, executives at Benetton realized that highly efficient physical distribution methods were a must.

Benetton has linked its sales agents, factory, and warehouse together using an international electronic data interchange (EDI) system. Suppose a student in San Francisco wants to buy a Benetton sweater identical to his older brother's. He goes to a Benetton store and searches for it, only to be disappointed when he finds that the sweater is not there. The salesperson assures him that the sweater will arrive in a month. The salesperson then calls a Benetton sales agent, who places the sweater order on a personal computer. Three times a day, this information is collected and sent to the company's mainframe system in Italy, where the computer searches inventory data to find out if the requested item is in stock. If not, an order automatically travels to a machine that cuts the material and immediately starts to knit the sweater. Workers put the finished sweater in a box with a bar-coded label and send it to the warehouse. In the warehouse, a computer commands a robot to retrieve the sweater and any other merchandise that needs to be transported to the same store.

Through efficient management of physical distribution activities and the use of the latest technologically advanced equipment, Benetton ensures that its products are available to consumers when and where they want them. Close attention to physical distribution activities has helped the company achieve its objectives and become a major competitor in the fashion industry.

Sources: Barbara DePompa, "More Power at Your Fingertips," *Information Week,* Dec. 23, 1991, p. 22; Lory Zottola, "The United Systems of Benetton," *Computerworld,* Apr. 2, 1990, p. 70; Brian Dumaine, "How Managers Can Succeed Through Speed," *Fortune,* Feb. 13, 1989, p. 59; and Martha Groves, "Retailer Benetton Hopes to Crack Soviet Market," *Los Angeles Times,* Jan. 7, 1989, sec. IV, pp. 2, 4.

Warehousing Functions

Warehousing is not limited simply to storage of goods. When warehouses receive goods by carloads or truckloads, they break down the shipments into smaller quantities for individual customers; when goods arrive in small lots, the warehouses assemble the lots into bulk loads that can be shipped out more economically.[13] Warehouses perform the following basic distribution functions:

1. *Receiving goods.* The merchandise is accepted, and the warehouse assumes responsibility for it.
2. *Identifying goods.* The appropriate stockkeeping units are recorded, along with the quantity of each item received. The item may be marked with a physical code, tag, or other label, or it may be identified by an item code (a code on the carrier or container) or by physical properties.

3. *Sorting goods.* The merchandise is sorted for storage in appropriate areas.
4. *Dispatching goods to storage.* The merchandise is put away for later retrieval when necessary.
5. *Holding goods.* The merchandise is kept in storage and properly protected until needed.
6. *Recalling and picking goods.* Items customers have ordered are efficiently retrieved from storage and readied for the next step.
7. *Marshaling the shipment.* The items making up a single shipment are brought together and checked for completeness or explainable omissions. Order records are prepared or modified as necessary.
8. *Dispatching the shipment.* The consolidated order is packaged suitably and directed to the right transport vehicle. Necessary shipping and accounting documents are prepared.[14]

Types of Warehouses

A company's choice of warehouse facilities is an important strategic consideration. By using the right warehouse, a company may be able to reduce transportation and inventory costs or improve its service to customers; the wrong warehouse may drain company resources. Besides deciding how many facilities to operate and where to locate them, a company must determine which type of warehouse will be most appropriate. Warehouses fall into two general categories, private and public. In many cases, a combination of private and public facilities provides the most flexible approach to warehousing.

Private Warehouses **Private warehouses** are operated by companies for shipping and storing their own products. Private warehouses are usually leased or purchased when a firm believes that its warehouse needs in given geographic markets are so substantial and so stable that it can make a long-term commitment to fixed facilities. They are also appropriate for firms that require special handling and storage features and want to control the design and operation of the warehouse.

Some of the largest users of private warehouses are retail chain stores.[15] Retailers such as Sears, Radio Shack, and even Burger King find it economical to integrate the warehousing function with purchasing for and distribution to their retail outlets. When sales volumes are fairly stable, ownership and control of a private warehouse may provide benefits, such as property appreciation. Private warehouses, however, face fixed costs, such as insurance, taxes, maintenance, and debt expense. They also allow little flexibility when firms wish to move inventories to more strategic locations. Before tying up capital in a private warehouse or entering into a long-term lease, a company should consider its resources, the level of its expertise in warehouse management, and the role of the warehouse in its overall marketing strategy.

Public Warehouses **Public warehouses** rent storage space and related physical distribution facilities to other companies and sometimes provide distribution services, such as receiving and unloading products, inspecting, reshipping, filling orders, financing, displaying products, and coordinating shipments. They are especially useful to firms with seasonal production or low-volume storage needs, companies with inventories that must be maintained in many locations, firms that are testing or entering new markets, and business operations that own private warehouses but occasionally require additional storage space. Public warehouses can also serve as collection points during product-recall programs. Whereas private warehouses have fixed costs, public warehouses have variable (and often lower) costs because users rent space and purchase warehousing services only as needed.

In addition, many public warehouses furnish security for products that are being used as collateral for loans, a service that can be provided at either the warehouse or the site of the owner's inventory. **Field public warehouses** are warehouses established by public warehouses at the owner's inventory location. The warehouser becomes the custodian of the products and issues a receipt that can be used as collateral for a loan. Public warehouses can also provide **bonded storage**, a warehousing arrangement under which imported or taxable products are not released until the owners of the products have paid U.S. customs duties, taxes, or other fees. Bonded warehouses enable firms to defer tax payments on such items until the products are delivered to customers.

Distribution Centers   **Distribution centers** are large, centralized warehouses that receive goods from factories and suppliers, regroup them into orders, and ship them to customers quickly, with the focus being on active movement of goods rather than passive storage.[16] Distribution centers are specially designed for the rapid flow of products. They are usually one-story buildings (to eliminate elevators) and have access to transportation networks, such as major highways or railway lines. Many distribution centers are highly automated, with computer-directed robots, fork lifts, and hoists collecting and moving products to loading docks. Although some public warehouses offer such specialized services, most distribution centers are privately owned. They serve customers in regional markets and in some cases function as consolidation points for a company's branch warehouses.

Distribution centers offer several benefits. Foremost among them is improved customer service. Distribution centers ensure product availability by maintaining full product lines. The speed of their operations cuts delivery time to a minimum. In addition, distribution centers reduce costs. Instead of having to make many smaller shipments to scattered warehouses and customers, factories can ship large quantities of goods directly to distribution centers at bulk-load rates, which lowers transportation costs; furthermore, rapid turnover of inventory lessens the need for warehouses and cuts storage costs. Some distribution centers also facilitate production by receiving and consolidating raw materials and providing final assembly for some products.

Inventory Management

Inventory management involves developing and maintaining adequate assortments of products to meet customers' needs. Because a firm's investment in inventory usually represents 30 to 50 percent of its total assets, inventory decisions have a significant impact on physical distribution costs and the level of customer service provided. When too few products are carried in inventory, the

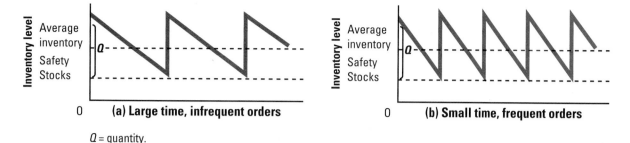

Q = quantity.

Figure 14.3 Effects of Order Size on an Inventory System

result is **stockouts**, or shortages of products, which cause brand switching, lower sales, and loss of customers. But when too many products (or too many slow-moving products) are carried, costs increase, as do the risks of product obsolescence, pilferage, and damage. The objective of inventory management, therefore, is to minimize inventory costs while maintaining an adequate supply of goods.

There are three types of inventory costs. *Carrying costs* are holding costs; they include expenditures for storage space and materials handling, financing, insurance, taxes, and losses from spoilage of goods. *Replenishment costs* are related to the purchase of merchandise. The price of goods, handling charges, and expenses for order processing contribute to replenishment costs. *Stockout costs* include sales lost when demand for goods exceeds supply on hand and the clerical and processing expenses of backordering. All costs of obtaining and maintaining inventory must be controlled if profit goals are to be achieved.

Inventory managers deal with two issues of particular importance. They must know when to reorder and how much merchandise to order. The **reorder point** is the inventory level that signals that more inventory should be ordered. Three factors determine the reorder point: the anticipated time between the date an order is placed and the date the goods are received and made ready for resale to customers; the rate at which a product is sold or used up; and the quantity of **safety stock** on hand, or inventory needed to prevent stockouts. The optimum level of safety stock depends on the general demand and the standard of customer service to be provided. If a firm is to avoid shortages without tying up too much capital in inventory, some systematic method for determining reorder points is essential.

The inventory manager faces several trade-offs when reordering merchandise. Large safety stocks ensure product availability and thus improve the level of customer service; they also lower order-processing costs because orders are placed less frequently. Small safety stocks, on the other hand, cause frequent reorders and higher order-processing costs but reduce the overall cost of carrying inventory. (Figure 14.3 illustrates two order systems involving different order quantities but the same level of safety stocks. Figure 14.3(a) shows inventory levels for a given demand of infrequent orders; Figure 14.3(b) illustrates levels needed to fill frequent orders at the same demand.)

To quantify this trade-off between carrying costs and order-processing costs, a model for an **economic order quantity (EOQ)** has been developed (see Figure 14.4); it specifies the order size that minimizes the total cost of ordering and

Figure 14.4

**Economic Order
Quantity (EOQ)
Model**

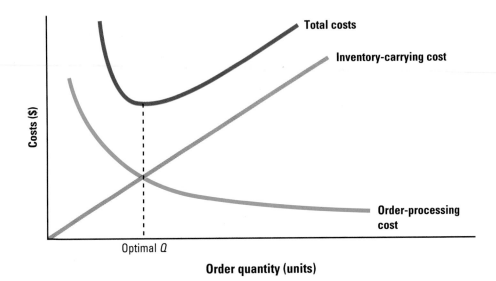

carrying inventory.[17] The fundamental relationships underlying the widely accepted EOQ model are the basis of many inventory control systems. Keep in mind, however, that the objective of minimum total inventory cost must be balanced against the customer service level necessary for maximum profits. Therefore, because increased costs of carrying inventory are usually associated with a higher level of customer service, the order quantity will often lie to the right of the optimal point in the figure, leading to a higher total cost for ordering and larger carrying inventory.

When management miscalculates reorder points or order quantities, inventory problems develop. Warning signs include an inventory that grows at a faster rate than sales, surplus or obsolete inventory, customer deliveries that are consistently late or lead times that are too long, inventory that represents a growing percentage of assets, and large inventory adjustments or write-offs.[18] However, there are several tools for improving inventory control. From a technical standpoint, an inventory system can be planned so that the number of products sold and the number of products in stock are determined at certain checkpoints. The control may be as simple as tearing off a code number from each product sold so that the correct sizes, colors, and models can be tabulated and reordered. A sizable amount of technologically advanced electronic equipment is available to aid in inventory management. Figure 14.5 indicates that fax machines have made billing and ordering much more efficient for companies. In many larger stores, such as Wal-Mart and Toys "R" Us, check-out terminals connected to central computer systems instantaneously update inventory and sales records. For continuous, automatic updating of inventory records, some firms use pressure-sensitive circuits installed under ordinary industrial shelving to weigh inventory, convert the weight to units, and display any inventory changes on a video screen or computer printout.

Various techniques have also been used successfully to improve inventory management. The **just-in-time (JIT)** concept, widely used in Japanese as well as in American companies, has replaced the EOQ concept for the most part.[19] JIT calls for companies to maintain low inventory levels and purchase products and materials in small quantities, just at the time they are needed for production.

Ford Motor Company, for example, sometimes receives supply deliveries as often as every two hours.[20] Just-in-time inventory management depends on a high level of coordination between producers and suppliers, but the technique enables companies to eliminate waste and reduce inventory costs significantly. When Harley-Davidson implemented JIT techniques in an effort to reduce its investment in inventories, the company lowered its inventory holdings by 75 percent. The end result was a 50 percent boost in productivity, greater cash reserves, and a profit margin that more than doubled.[21]

Another inventory management technique, the 80/20 rule, holds that fast-moving products should generate a higher level of customer service than slow-moving products, on the theory that 20 percent of the items account for 80 percent of the sales. Thus an inventory manager attempts to keep an adequate supply of fast-selling items and a minimal supply of the slower-moving products.

Transportation

Transportation adds time and place utility to a product by moving it from where it is made to where it is purchased and used.[22] Because product availability and timely deliveries are so dependent on transportation functions, a firm's choice of transportation directly affects customer service. A firm may even build its distribution and marketing strategy around a unique transportation system if

Figure 14.5

Inventory Management

Fax machines have become an efficient technological method to aid in inventory management.

Source: Pitney Bowes.

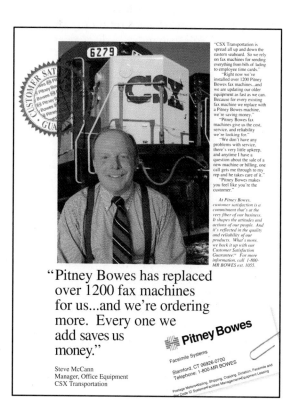

the on-time deliveries, which that system ensures, will give the firm a competitive edge. In this section we consider the principal modes of transportation, the criteria companies use to select one transportation mode over another, and several methods of coordinating transportation services.

Transportation Modes

As Figure 14.6 indicates, there are five major **transportation modes**, or methods of moving goods: railways, motor vehicles, inland waterways, airways, and pipelines. Each mode offers unique advantages; many companies have adopted physical handling procedures that facilitate the use of two or more modes in combination. Table 14.1 illustrates typical transportation modes for various products.

Railways Railways carry heavy, bulky freight that must be shipped overland for long distances. Railways commonly haul minerals, sand, lumber, pulp, chemicals, and farm products, as well as low-value manufactured goods and an increasing number of automobiles. They are especially efficient for transporting full carloads, which require less handling—and can therefore be shipped at lower rates—than less-than-carload quantities. Many companies locate their factories or warehouses near major rail lines or on spur lines for convenient loading and unloading.

Although railways haul more intercity freight than any other mode of transportation, accounting for more than one-third of all cargo ton-miles carried, their share of the transportation market declined from a high of 75 percent in the 1920s to 35 percent in 1990.[23] High fixed costs, shortages of rail cars during peak periods, poor maintenance of tracks and equipment, and increased

Figure 14.6 **Ton-Miles of Domestic Intercity Freight Traffic—Percent Distribution by Type of Transportation, 1970 to 1989** Source: *Statistical Abstract of the United States*, 1991, p. 603.

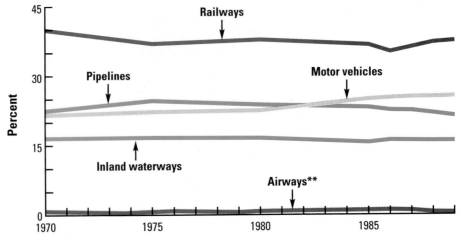

* A ton-mile is the movement of 1 ton (2,000 pounds) of freight for the distance of 1 mile.
** Airways represent less than 1% intercity traffic.

Railways	Motor Vehicles	Waterways	Pipelines	Airways
Coal	Clothing	Petroleum	Oil	Flowers
Grain	Paper goods	Chemicals	Processed coal	Perishable food
Chemicals	Computers	Iron ore	Natural gas	Instruments
Lumber	Books	Bauxite	Water	Emergency parts
Automobiles	Fresh fruit	Grain		Overnight mail
Iron	Livestock			

Table 14.1   **Typical Transportation Modes for Various Products**

competition from other carriers, mainly trucks, have plagued railroad companies and diminished profits.

To improve customer service, railroads have turned to a variety of innovations. Several years ago, Railbox, a nationwide pool of 25,000 general-service boxcars, was formed; the boxcars belong to no single rail company and can be dispatched around the country wherever boxcars are in short supply. Rail yards are also speeding up the formation of outbound trains by using optical scanners to read coded labels on the sides of cars, which helps sort cars by destination. Other special services include unit trains, which carry a single commodity from point of origin to destination and bypass classification yards; run-through trains, which also run nonstop but carry more than one product; and minitrains, which run often and are therefore useful in just-in-time inventory systems. These innovations and others enabled the nation's 170 rail carriers to haul a record 1.031 trillion ton-miles of freight in 1990.[24]

Motor Vehicles   Motor vehicles provide the most flexible schedules and routes of all major transportation modes because they can go almost anywhere. As indicated in Table 14.2, Yellow Freight is the nation's top trucking company in terms of revenue. Trucks usually haul small shipments of high-value goods over short distances. Because trucks have a unique ability to move goods directly from factory or warehouse to customer, they are often used in conjunction with other forms of transport that cannot provide door-to-door deliveries. In Figure 14.7, New Jersey is promoted as an attractive location for many companies because of its proximity to major markets and extensive transportation network.

The Interstate Commerce Commission (ICC) classifies motor vehicles (along with other transportation firms) as common, contract, private, or exempt carriers. Common carriers are legally obligated to serve all customers requesting their services, assuming that the carriers have the necessary equipment. Contract carriers function much the same as private transportation systems and only haul freight for customers that have written agreements with them. Private carriers are company-owned transport systems; although they are not economically regulated by the ICC, they are subject to safety regulations and prohibited from carrying other companies' products. Exempt carriers are freight haulers in any category who are carrying products exempted from regulation, such as unprocessed agricultural goods. As in many other industries, brokers bring together those wanting transport services and those providing them.

Although motor vehicles usually travel much faster than trains, they are somewhat more vulnerable to bad weather, and their services are more expensive. Trucks are also subject to the size and weight restrictions of the products they carry. In addition, motor carriers, especially common carriers, are sometimes criticized for high levels of loss and damage to freight and for delays from rehandling small shipments. In response, the trucking industry is turning to computerized tracking of shipments and developing new equipment to speed up loading and unloading.[25]

There is a great deal of competition between rail and motor carriers. Their latest dispute is whether longer combination vehicles (LCVs) should be authorized by Congress for use on the nation's highways. LCVs are trucks that haul either three 28-foot trailers (triples) or two 48-foot trailers (doubles).[26] Motor carriers want to use LCVs to help cut costs and improve efficiency. However, rail carriers argue that LCVs will give the trucking industry a competitive advantage that could hurt the already-troubled rail industry.[27]

Inland Waterways Water transportation is the cheapest method of shipping heavy, low-value, nonperishable goods, such as ore, coal, grain, sand, and petroleum products. Water carriers offer considerable capacity. Tugboat-powered barges that travel along inland rivers, canals, and navigation systems can haul at least ten times the weight of one rail car, and deep-draft vessels operating within the Great Lakes–St. Lawrence Seaway system can carry up to 65,000 tons.[28]

However, many markets are accessible to water only with supplementary rail or truck transport. Furthermore, water transport is extremely slow and sometimes comes to a standstill during freezing weather. Companies that depend on water may ship their entire inventory during the summer and then store it for

Table 14.2

The Top Ten U.S. Trucking Companies

Company	Revenue (in millions)
1. Yellow Freight	$2,189.6
2. Consolidated Freightways	1,894.9
3. Roadway Express	1,835.5
4. Overnite	697.8
5. ABF Freight	630.1
6. Carolina Freight	538.9
7. ANR Freight	416.3
8. Preston Trucking	366.9
9. St. Johnsbury Trucking	313.6
10. Central Transport	276.9

Source: "RCCC Lists Top 10 Truckers," *Inbound Logistics,* July 1990, p. 12. Reprinted with permission from *Inbound Logistics,* July 1990, Thomas Publishing Company, Five Penn Plaza, 8th floor, New York, NY 10001, (212) 629–1560.

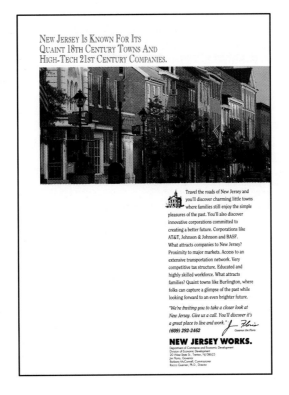

winter use. Droughts and floods also create difficulties for users of inland waterway transportation. Nevertheless, because water transportation is extremely fuel efficient, its use will continue to increase in the future.

Airways   Air transportation is the fastest and most expensive form of shipping. It is used most often for perishable goods; for high-value, low-bulk items; and for products that must be delivered quickly over long distances, such as emergency shipments. The capacity of air transport is limited only by the capacity of individual aircraft. Medium-range jets can haul about 60,000 pounds of freight, and some new jet cargo planes equipped to carry containers can accommodate more than 220,000 pounds.[29] Most air carriers transport a combination of passengers, freight, and mail.[30]

Although air transport accounts for only 2 percent of total ton-miles carried, its importance as a mode of transportation is growing. Despite its expense, air transit can reduce warehousing and packaging costs and also losses from theft and damage, thus helping lower total costs (however, the truck transportation needed for pickup and final delivery adds to cost and transit time). The benefits provided by air transportation are especially important for companies using JIT techniques.[31]

Pipelines   Pipelines, the most automated transportation mode, usually belong to the shipper and carry the shipper's products. Most pipelines carry petroleum products or chemicals. For example, the Trans-Alaska Pipeline, owned and operated by a consortium of oil companies that includes Exxon, Mobil, and British Petroleum, transports crude oil from remote oil-drilling sites in central

	Cost	Transit Time	Reliability	Capability	Accessibility	Security	Traceability
Most	Air	Water	Pipeline	Water	Truck	Pipeline	Air
	Truck	Rail	Truck	Rail	Rail	Water	Truck
	Rail	Pipeline	Rail	Truck	Air	Rail	Rail
	Pipeline	Truck	Air	Air	Water	Air	Water
Least	Water	Air	Water	Pipeline	Pipeline	Truck	Pipeline

Source: Some of this information has been adapted from J. L. Heskett, Robert Ivie, and J. Nicholas Glaskowsky, *Business Logistics* (New York: Ronald Press, 1973). Used by permission.

Table 14.3   **Ranking of Transportation Modes by Selection Criteria, Highest to Lowest**

Alaska to shipping terminals on the coast for its owners. Slurry pipelines have been developed to carry pulverized coal, grain, or wood chips suspended in water. Even though pipelines have limited accessibility because of their fixed routes, pipeline use accounts for about 21 percent of all intercity ton-miles.

Pipelines move products slowly but continuously and at relatively low cost. They are a reliable mode of transportation and ensure low product damage and theft. However, their contents are subject to as much as 1 percent shrinkage, usually from evaporation, and products must be shipped in minimum quantities of 25,000 barrels for efficient pipeline operation.[32] They have also been a source of concern to environmentalists, who fear that installation and leaks could harm plants and animals.

Criteria for Selecting Transportation

Marketers select a transportation mode on the basis of costs, transit time (speed), reliability, capability, accessibility, security, and traceability.[33] Table 14.3 summarizes various cost and performance considerations that help determine the selection of transportation modes. It is important to remember that these relationships are approximations and that the choice of a transportation mode involves many trade-offs.

Costs   Marketers compare alternative modes of transportation to determine whether the benefits from a more expensive mode are worth the higher costs. Air freight carriers—for instance, United Parcel Service (Figure 14.8)—provide many benefits, such as high speed, reliability, security, and traceability, but at higher costs relative to other transportation modes. When speed is less important, marketers prefer lower costs. For example, bicycles are often shipped by rail because an unassembled bicycle can be shipped more than a thousand miles on a train for as little as $3.60. Bicycle wholesalers plan their purchases far enough in advance to be able to capitalize on this cost advantage.

Generally, marketers have been able to cut expenses and increase efficiency since transportation was deregulated in the late 1970s and early 1980s. Railroads, airlines, trucks, barges, and pipeline companies all have become more competitive and more responsive to customers' needs. In recent years transportation costs per hundredweight and as a percentage of sales have declined, now averaging $33.45 per hundredweight, or 7.5 percent of sales.

Transit Time   Transit time is the total time a carrier has possession of goods, including the time required for pickup and delivery, handling, and movement between the points of origin and destination. Closely related to transit time is frequency, or number of shipments per day. Transit time obviously affects a marketer's ability to provide service, but there are some less obvious implications as well. A shipper can take advantage of transit time to process orders for goods en route, a capability especially important to agricultural and raw materials shippers. Some railroads also let carloads already in transit be redirected, for maximum flexibility in selecting markets. For example, a carload of peaches may be shipped to a closer destination if the fruit is in danger of ripening too quickly.

Reliability   The total reliability of a transportation mode is determined by the consistency of service provided. Marketers must be able to count on their carriers to deliver goods on time and in an acceptable condition. Along with transit time, reliability affects a marketer's inventory costs, including sales lost when merchandise is not available. Unreliable transportation necessitates higher inventory levels so that stockouts will be avoided. Reliable delivery service, on the other hand, enables customers to carry smaller inventories, at lower cost. To maintain desired levels of inventory, Wal-Mart ships more than 75 percent of its stock through its own distribution network, which includes nineteen distribution centers and a private fleet of trucks.[34]

Figure 14.8

Air Express Services

UPS promotes guaranteed delivery in over 180 countries. They provide computerized tracking services and prices that are significantly less than what other air express companies charge.

Source: Courtesy of United Postal Service.

Capability Capability is the ability of a transportation mode to provide the appropriate equipment and conditions for moving specific kinds of goods. For example, many products must be shipped under controlled temperature and humidity. Other products, such as liquids or gases, require special equipment or facilities for shipment. In the railroad industry, a shipper with unusual transport needs can consult the *Official Railway Equipment Register*, which lists the various types of cars and equipment each railroad owns.

Accessibility A carrier's ability to move goods over a specific route or network (rail lines, waterways, or truck routes) is its accessibility. For example, marketers evaluating transportation modes for reaching Great Falls, Montana, would realistically consider rail lines, truck routes, and scheduled airline service but would eliminate water-borne carriers because Great Falls is inaccessible by water.

Some carriers differentiate themselves by serving areas their competitors do not. After deregulation, for instance, many large railroad companies sold off or abandoned unprofitable routes, making rail service inaccessible to shippers located on spur lines. Some shippers were forced to buy their own truck fleets just to get their products to market. In recent years, however, small, short-line railroad companies have started buying up track and creating networks of low-cost feeder lines to reach those underserved markets. Small shippers are regaining access to rail service, and the short-line companies are profiting.[35]

Security A transportation mode's security is measured by the physical condition of goods upon delivery. A firm does not incur costs directly when goods are lost or damaged because the common carrier is usually held liable. Nevertheless, poor service and lack of security indirectly lead to increased costs and lower profits for the firm because damaged or lost goods are not available for immediate sale or use.

Security problems vary considerably among transportation companies and geographic regions. In the Northeast, for example, truck hijacking is a rapidly growing crime. According to the Federal Bureau of Investigation (FBI), approximately 19,000 truck tractors and 47,000 trailers are listed as stolen each year. In the United States, over $8 billion a year is lost to cargo theft.[36] To combat the hijacking problem, The Federated Group, which operates a chain of electronics stores, implemented a two-way radio security system for all its trucks. This allows Federated to track the location of each truck, its status, and its estimated time of arrival at the next location. In the event of a hijacking, the radio in each truck includes a hidden "panic button" that drivers can push to alert an operator at the company's communication headquarters, who then calls the police to give the location of the truck.[37] However, all transportation modes have security problems, and marketers must evaluate the relative risk of each mode.

Traceability Traceability is the relative ease with which a shipment can be located and transferred (or found if it is lost). Quick traceability is a convenience that some firms value highly. Shippers have learned that the tracing of shipments, along with prompt invoicing and processing of claims, increases customer loyalty and improves a firm's image in the marketplace. Federal Express, for example, relies on special computer systems to process and track the more than one million packages it receives each day for overnight delivery. At each stage of processing, from pickup to delivery, the location of every package is logged into the company's central computer in Memphis, Tennessee. If Federal Express is unable to track down a package within thirty minutes of a customer's query, the customer is charged nothing for the shipment.[38]

Coordinating Transportation Services

To take advantage of the benefits various types of carriers offer, and to compensate for their deficiencies, marketers often must combine and coordinate two or more modes of transportation. In recent years, **intermodal transportation**, as this integrated approach is sometimes called, has become easier because of new developments within the transportation industry. Inside Marketing describes how the Norfolk-Southern Railroad expanded its business by using new technology to establish its intermodal transportation system.

Several kinds of intermodal shipping are available, all combining the flexibility of trucking with the low cost or speed of other forms of transport. Containerization, discussed earlier, facilitates intermodal transportation by consolidating shipments into sealed containers for transport by piggyback (shipping that combines truck trailers and railway flatcars), fishyback (truck trailers and water carriers), and birdyback (truck trailers and air carriers). As transportation costs increase, intermodal services gain popularity. Intermodal services have been estimated to cost 25 to 40 percent less than all-highway transport and account for about 12 to 16 percent of total freight transportation business.[39]

Specialized agencies, **freight forwarders**, provide other forms of transport coordination. These firms combine shipments from several organizations into efficient lot sizes. Small loads (less than five hundred pounds) are much more expensive to ship than full carloads or truckloads and frequently must be consolidated. The freight forwarder takes small loads from various shippers, buys transport space from carriers, and arranges for the goods to be delivered to their respective buyers. The freight forwarder's profits come from the margin between the higher, less-than-carload rates charged to each shipper and the lower carload rates the agency pays. Because large shipments require less handling, the use of a freight forwarder can speed transit time. Freight forwarders can also determine the most efficient carriers and routes and are useful for shipping goods to foreign markets.

One other transportation innovation is the development of **megacarriers**, which are freight transportation companies that provide several methods of shipment, such as rail, truck, and air service. CSX, for example, has trains, barges, container ships, trucks, and pipelines, which allows it to provide a multitude of transportation services. Air carriers have increased their ground transportation services. As they have expanded the range of transportation alternatives, carriers have also put greater stress on customer service.

Strategic Issues in Physical Distribution

The physical distribution functions discussed in this chapter—order processing, materials handling, warehousing, inventory management, and transportation—account for about half of all marketing costs. Moreover, these functions have a significant impact on customer service and satisfaction, which are of prime

Norfolk-Southern Goes Intermodal with RoadRailer Service

NORFOLK-SOUTHERN, the nation's most profitable railroad company, operates on the forefront of intermodal technology. In 1985, the Norfolk, Virginia company purchased North American Van Lines in an effort to move into trucking and offset some of the railroad's lost business. That same year, the company introduced its RoadRailer, a 48-foot trailer that can be used on both railroad tracks and highways, and began offering its Triple Crown service. For one price, Norfolk-Southern can pick up and deliver freight door-to-door in a manner that outperforms or equals the on-time performance of trucks.

Freight is picked up from a customer by a truck that hauls a RoadRailer unit. At the railroad terminal, the units are lined up on tracks and turned into railcars by retracting the rubber tires and extending steel wheels. Several of these units on a track form a train that can be hauled anywhere on Norfolk-Southern's line. Once the train reaches its destination, the process is reversed, and trucks once again haul each RoadRailer unit to its delivery point. Today, Norfolk-Southern has over 1,800 RoadRailers in operation, with an average of 82 RoadRailer trains per week and over 100,000 loads per year. This intermodal service accounts for 20 percent of the company's rail shipments, up from 16.8 percent in 1988.

Intermodal transportation represents a golden opportunity for Norfolk-Southern. Many shippers are hesitant to use railroads because they traditionally provide much less service and slower delivery times than trucks. A recent survey of shippers indicated that door-to-door service was a major factor in choosing a freight carrier. Intermodal services are the best means for a company to deliver door-to-door and better satisfy customers.

According to Norfolk-Southern's CEO Arnold B. McKinnon, the secret of the company's success has been to think like a truck line in serving customer needs. This means working with the shipper's schedule rather than following a traditional rail schedule. The use of the RoadRailer units and Triple Crown service has enabled the company to compete effectively against truckers in door-to-door ability. Even with their success, Norfolk-Southern continues to look toward the future. The next major step for the company is to make greater use of electronic data interchange technologies (EDI); a move that will increase the company's ability to offer just-in-time (JIT) services.

Sources: Peter Bradley, "Bundle Up or Pack It In," *Purchasing,* Feb. 21, 1991, pp. 44–48; Ronit Addis, "Southern Comfort," *Forbes,* Jan. 8, 1990, p. 202; Norfolk-Southern Corporation, 1990 Annual Report; Luther S. Miller, "A Strategy For the '90s," *Railway Age,* August 1989, pp. 33, 36, 38, 40, 77; Daniel F. Kelly, "Intermodal Industry Faces Glut in Doublestack Cars; NS Stresses North-South Run," *Traffic World,* July 3, 1989, pp. 15–16; Peter Bradley, "Workin' On the Railroads," *Purchasing,* May 4, 1989, pp. 98–103; and James Cook, "Tending the Base Business," *Forbes,* Dec. 26, 1988, pp. 108, 110.

importance to marketers. Effective marketers accept considerable responsibility for the design and control of the physical distribution system. They work to ensure that the organization's overall marketing strategy is enhanced by physical distribution, with its dual objectives of decreasing costs while increasing customer service.

The strategic importance of physical distribution is evident in all elements of the marketing mix. Product design and packaging must allow for efficient stacking, storage, and transport; decisions to differentiate products by size, color, and style must take into account the additional demands that will be placed on warehousing and shipping facilities. Competitive pricing may depend on a firm's ability to provide reliable delivery or emergency shipments of replacement parts; a firm trying to lower its inventory costs may offer quantity discounts to encourage large purchases. Promotional campaigns must be coordinated with distribution functions so advertised products will be available to buyers; order-processing departments must be able to handle additional sales order information efficiently. Distribution planners must consider warehousing and transportation costs, which may influence—for example—the firm's policy on stockouts or its choice to centralize (or decentralize) its inventory.

No single distribution system is ideal for all situations, and any system must be evaluated continually and adapted as necessary. For instance, pressures to adjust service levels or reduce costs may lead to totally restructuring the marketing channel relationships; changes in transportation, warehousing, materials handling, and inventory may affect speed of delivery, reliability, and economy of service. Marketing strategists must consider customers' changing needs and preferences and recognize that changes in any one of the major distribution functions will affect all other functions. Consumer-oriented marketers analyze the characteristics of their target markets and then design distribution systems to provide products at acceptable costs.

Summary

Physical distribution is a set of activities that moves products from producers to consumers, or end users. These activities include order processing, materials handling, warehousing, inventory management, and transportation. An effective physical distribution system can be an important component of an overall marketing strategy because it can decrease costs and increase customer satisfaction. Physical distribution activities should be integrated with marketing channel decisions and should be adjusted to meet the unique needs of a channel member. For most firms, physical distribution accounts for about one-fifth of a product's retail price.

The main objective of physical distribution is to decrease costs while increasing customer service. To this end, physical distribution managers strive to balance service, distribution costs, and resources. Companies must adapt to customers' needs and preferences, offer service comparable to or better than their competitors, and develop and communicate desirable customer service policies. Costs of providing service are minimized most effectively through the total-cost approach, which evaluates the costs of the system as a whole rather than as a collection of separate activities. Cost trade-offs must often be used to offset higher costs in one area of distribution with lower costs in another area.

Order processing, the first stage in a physical distribution system, is the receipt and transmission of sales order information. Order processing consists of three main tasks. Order entry is placing purchase orders from customers or salespersons by mail, telephone, or computer. Order handling involves checking customer credit, verifying product availability, and preparing products for shipping. Order delivery is provided by the carrier most suitable for a desired level of customer service. Order processing may be done manually or electronically through an EDI network, depending on which method gives the greatest speed and accuracy within cost limits.

Materials handling, or the physical handling of products, is an important element of physical distribution. Packaging, loading, and movement systems must be coordinated to take into account both cost reduction and customer requirements. Basic handling systems include unit loading on pallets or skids, movement by mechanical devices, and containerization.

Warehousing involves the design and operation of facilities for storing and moving goods. Private warehouses are owned and operated by a company for the purpose of distributing its own products. Public warehouses are business organizations that rent storage space and related physical distribution facilities to other firms. Public warehouses may furnish security for products that are being used as collateral for loans by establishing field warehouses. They may also provide bonded storage for companies wishing to defer tax payments on imported or taxable products. Distribution centers are large, centralized warehouses specially designed for the rapid movement of goods to customers. In many cases, a combination of private and public facilities is the most flexible approach to warehousing.

The objective of inventory management is to minimize inventory costs while maintaining a supply of goods adequate for customers' needs. All inventory costs—carrying, replenishment, and stockout costs—must be controlled if profit goals are to be met. To avoid stockouts without tying up too much capital in inventory, a firm must have a systematic method for determining a reorder point, the inventory level at which more inventory is ordered. The trade-offs between the costs of carrying larger average safety stocks and the costs of frequent orders can be quantified in the economic order quantity (EOQ) model. Inventory problems may take the form of surplus inventory, late deliveries, write-offs, and inventory that is too large in proportion to sales or assets. Methods for improving inventory management include systems for determining the number of products sold and in stock and management techniques such as just-in-time (JIT) and the 80/20 rule.

Transportation adds time and place utility to a product by moving it from where it is made to where it is purchased and used. The five major modes of transporting goods in the United States are railways, motor vehicles, inland waterways, airways, and pipelines. Marketers evaluate transportation modes with respect to costs, transit time (speed), reliability, capability, accessibility, security, and traceability; final selection of a transportation mode involves many trade-offs. Intermodal transportation allows marketers to combine the advantages of two or more modes of transport; it is facilitated by containerization; freight forwarders, who coordinate transport by combining small shipments from several organizations into efficient lot sizes; and megacarriers, freight transportation companies that offer several methods of shipment.

Physical distribution affects every element of the marketing mix: product, price, promotion, and distribution. To give customers products at acceptable prices, marketers consider consumers' changing needs and any shifts within the major distribution functions. Then they adapt existing physical distribution systems for greater effectiveness. Physical distribution functions account for about half of all marketing costs and have a significant impact on customer satisfaction. Therefore, effective marketers are actively involved in the design and control of physical distribution systems.

Important Terms

Physical distribution
Order processing
Electronic data interchange (EDI)
Materials handling
Unit loading
Containerization
Warehousing
Private warehouses
Public warehouses
Field public warehouses
Bonded storage
Distribution centers
Stockouts

Reorder point
Safety stock
Economic order quantity (EOQ)
Just-in-time (JIT)
Transportation
Transportation modes
Intermodal transportation
Freight forwarders
Megacarriers

Discussion and Review Questions

1. Discuss the cost and service trade-offs in developing a physical distribution system.
2. What factors must physical distribution managers consider when developing a customer service mix?
3. Why should physical distribution managers develop service standards?
4. What is the advantage of using a total distribution cost approach?
5. What are the main tasks involved in order processing?
6. Discuss the advantages of using an electronic order-processing system. Which types of organizations are most likely to utilize electronic order processing?
7. How does a product's package affect materials handling procedures and techniques?
8. What is containerization? Discuss the major benefits of containerization.
9. Explain the major differences between private and public warehouses. What is a field public warehouse?
10. Under what circumstances should a firm use a private warehouse instead of a public one?
11. The focus of distribution centers is on active movement of goods. Discuss how distribution centers are designed for the rapid flow of products.
12. Describe the costs associated with inventory management.
13. Explain the trade-offs inventory managers face when reordering merchandise.
14. How can managers improve inventory control? Give specific examples of techniques.
15. Compare the five major transportation modes as to costs, transit time, reliability, capability, accessibility, security, and traceability.
16. What is transit time, and how does it affect physical distribution decisions?
17. Discuss the ways marketers can combine or coordinate two or more modes of transportation. What is the advantage of doing this?
18. Identify the types of containerized shipping available to physical distribution managers.
19. Discuss how the four elements of the marketing mix affect physical distribution strategy.

IKEA, one of Europe's largest furniture retailers, has invaded the U.S. market. The Swedish firm made its debut in this country with a two-story, six-acre store just outside Philadelphia. As of 1991, IKEA had seven U.S. stores in the Baltimore, Pittsburgh, New York City, Washington, D.C., and Los Angeles metropolitan areas. Worldwide, IKEA's 95 stores in 23 countries generated over $3.7 billion in revenue for 1991.

The attractive Scandinavian styling and bright colors of IKEA's ready-to-assemble furniture and decorating accessories were an immediate success with American shoppers. Do-it-yourself furniture, however, is nothing new. British-based Conran's introduced European design to American mass markets several years before IKEA arrived, and other firms that sell Scandinavian furniture, both assembled and knocked down, have been located within the United States since the 1960s. What sets IKEA apart, besides its low prices, is its transnational distribution system. Both benefits are possible partly because of IKEA's innovative flat-pack technology.

About 95 percent of IKEA's fourteen thousand product offerings are sold knocked down in flat boxes, which lowers prices by saving storage space and cutting shipping costs. IKEA's central warehouse in Amhult, Sweden, is staffed by just three people using computerized fork lifts and thirteen robots. Through a command from the keyboard operator, a fork lift glides down the aisles of the 200-yard-long building to locate the designated pallets and bring them to the robots. The robots then follow magnetic strips on the floor to deliver the pallets to the shipping dock. Once the products reach an IKEA store, they are held (still boxed) in a self-service warehouse adjoining the store's showrooms. After shoppers browse through the showrooms and examine IKEA's glossy catalog, they push supermarket-style carts into the self-service area, pull their boxed selections from bins and shelves, and proceed to the check-out line. The customers themselves transport most purchases home, although delivery service for heavy items such as sofas and cabinets is available from outside companies for a fee.

IKEA is continually experimenting with ways to flat-pack more product per box. Whereas fully assembled bentwood chairs, for example, are usually shipped six to a pallet, IKEA engineers have figured out how to pack in twenty-eight chairs unassembled. By farming out its in-house designs to the most efficient manufacturers and suppliers it can find, IKEA cuts costs even further. IKEA's "creative sourcing" might mean that a carpenter supplies wooden parts for tables; a shirt manufacturer, seat covers; and a third supplier, screws and bolts. In total, the company employs 1,500 suppliers in more than 45 countries. As a result, IKEA's retail prices are up to 50 percent lower than those of its competitors.

American shoppers took to the IKEA system quickly—so quickly in fact that at first the Philadelphia store was almost overwhelmed. During the four-day grand opening, 130,000 shoppers made their way through the store's stylish room settings. Sales for the first three months totaled $8 million, up $2 million from initial projections. There was a similar response to the opening of the Elizabeth, New Jersey, store. The New Jersey Turnpike was backed up for nine miles as over 26,000 shoppers jammed into the store. The Elizabeth IKEA racked up over $1 million in sales that day alone, doubling the company's opening-day record.

But success has not been without problems. First, the U.S. stores are too small. Inadequate warehouse space and loading platforms have necessitated a night shift just to replenish the stock. Second, demand has routinely exceeded supply in some product categories. At one point, the Philadelphia store had a backlog of 15,000 requests for out-of-stock items, and the Elizabeth store was taking reservations to place back orders on a particular bookcase. IKEA maintains two distribution centers in Canada to service its stores there, but most of the stock for the U.S. stores comes from the main warehouse in Sweden, spending six to eight weeks in transit before arriving at one of the company's huge distribution centers. The stockouts are troublesome, because many of IKEA's product designs are modular: If one piece is unavailable, sales of the other pieces are delayed. IKEA is also concerned about first-time shoppers who find an item out of stock and never return for a second visit. IKEA has responded by increasing its warehouse stock.

IKEA managers have alleviated many supply problems by building a multi-million-dollar distribution center in the Philadelphia area, and a new terminal is planned for California. The company also intends to use a greater number of domestic suppliers. At present Canadian manufacturers provide some of the products for the U.S. stores (as well as about 20 percent of the items in Canadian stores), and some of IKEA's sofas are now made in Knoxville, Tennessee. Another possibility for avoiding distribution delays is the purchase of a private shipping line. Although IKEA offers mail-order service in Europe (and, in fact, started out as a mail-order furniture company), the company has no current plans to establish a mail-order business in the United States, despite a deluge of requests from customers.

Instead, IKEA's long-range U.S. strategy calls for several new stores over the next few years, supported by five regional distribution and marketing systems. For now, IKEA is concentrating on setting up new stores on both coasts. By 1993, the company plans to have eight of its huge stores in the Los Angeles and New York markets alone.[40]

Questions for Discussion

1. What actions has IKEA taken to reduce its physical distribution problems?
2. Explain how IKEA's physical distribution system influences other parts of this organization's marketing strategies.
3. In the future, what types of physical distribution problems must IKEA resolve with respect to its U.S. stores?

14.2 Transportation Industry Faces a Packaging Dilemma

Many companies are facing a dilemma in their choice of cushioning materials to protect their products during distribution. The use of polystyrene peanuts, the most common cushioning material, is facing increasing criticism from both consumers and environmentalists for several reasons. First, polystyrene peanuts are made from petroleum, a nonrenewable resource. Second, the peanuts are not biodegradable; they stay in the environment from four hundred to a thousand years. Third, some peanuts contain chlorofluorocarbons (CFCs) that are released during incineration. CFCs are widely known for their damaging effects to the earth's ozone layer. Finally, the peanuts produce static electricity, making them useless for cushioning sensitive electronic equipment.

The purpose of any cushioning material is to protect a package's contents from harm during the distribution process. Internal packaging is important because if it fails to do its job, the quality of the package's contents becomes a secondary concern. However, in the face of increased environmental awareness, many companies are discovering that their choice of packaging materials is fast becoming an important issue with their customers.

There are several alternatives to polystyrene peanuts, each having advantages and disadvantages. One of the most clever alternatives is popcorn, which many industry experts say could be the answer to the dilemma. Popcorn is an attractive alternative because it is biodegradable and costs one-fourth as much as polystyrene peanuts. Likewise, unpopped popcorn is less expensive to ship and store before it is needed. However, popcorn is not a viable option at present because the Food and Drug Administration (FDA) recognizes it as a food, not a packaging material. The FDA currently forbids the use of popcorn as a cushioning material until a method can be found to prevent people from eating it after it has been used for shipping purposes.

Billed as a direct alternative to polystyrene peanuts, Eco-Foam is made from a special hybrid corn and is composed of 95 percent cornstarch, making it fully biodegradable and less prone to static electricity. Eco-Foam, which looks a lot like polystyrene peanuts, is an attractive alternative because it can be used with the same dispensing equipment as peanuts. Since different dispensing equipment is not needed, a company that currently uses peanuts can switch to Eco-Foam with very little inconvenience. However, Eco-Foam is more expensive and has one major drawback: It fully disintegrates when it gets wet. This makes Eco-Foam impractical for use in shipping liquid-filled containers or in situations in which the threat of water damage is high. In addition, Eco-Foam has a tendency to shrink when exposed to high heat and humidity, which is always a possibility in a truck trailer or railcar.

Quadra-Pak, a third alternative, is fully biodegradable and recyclable, contains no CFCs, and is produced totally from refuse materials. Quadra-Pak is made by stacking heavyweight paper in layers that are then cut into four-inch lengths an eighth of an inch wide. The cut lengths are then compacted into an accordion shape that makes them act as if spring-loaded. The finished product measures about one inch long but expands when it is jostled. The result is a packing material that protects from all sides while preventing a carton's contents from moving about. Although Quadra-Pak possesses superior cushioning properties over peanuts, it is more expensive to manufacture and cannot be used with current dispensing equipment.

Other alternatives include Bio-Puffs—a loose-fill foam packaging peanut that biodegrades within weeks or months—and vermiculite, a naturally occurring mineral used by the military to ship munitions in Operation Desert Storm. With so many alternatives and the relentless pressure of environmentalists to use more environmentally friendly packing materials, the Polystyrene Packaging Council (PPC) is crying foul. PPC admits that CFCs were once a problem, but even then, it argues, only 2 percent of all polystyrene contained CFCs, and their use was phased out of polystyrene production in 1989. To curb negative publicity, the PPC—along with four producers of polystyrene peanuts—is creating a peanut recycling program in about 1,400 locations nationwide. Already the Free-Flow Packaging Corp. of Redwood City, California, manufactures peanuts from 100 percent recycled polystyrene. In addition, Dow Chemical Company recently introduced a polystyrene resin that is photodegradable—it breaks down when exposed to ultraviolet light from the sun.

While many packaging options exist, there is no perfect answer to the current dilemma. All of the options have good and bad characteristics. For the most part, companies currently choose a packing material on the basis of cost and performance. Ultimately, however, which material to use will depend more and more upon the needs of the customer and the material's impact on the environment.[41]

Questions for Discussion

1. What are the advantages and disadvantages to each of the packaging alternatives discussed above?
2. How does the choice of packaging materials affect a company's ability to serve customer needs?
3. Overall, which packing material would you choose? Why? Would your decision change if you were shipping electronic equipment? Glass? Liquid-filled containers?

Chapter Notes

1. Based on information from David Yawn, "M. S. Carriers Looks into Satellite-Tracking System," *Memphis Business Journal,* Nov. 18–22, 1991, p. 8; David Flaum, "Adviser Gets Role at M. S. Carriers," *(Memphis) Commercial Appeal,* Nov. 11, 1991, p. B3; and Mike Eigo, "Partnership Pays for TL Carrier," *Fleet Owner,* November 1988, pp. 103–108.
2. John T. Mentzer, Roger Gomes, and Robert E. Krapfel, Jr., "Physical Distribution Service: A Fundamental Marketing Concept?" *Journal of the Academy of Marketing Science,* Winter 1989, p. 59.
3. Lloyd M. Rinehart, M. Bixby Cooper, and George D. Wagenheim, "Furthering the Integration of Marketing and Logistics Through Customer Service in the Channel," *Journal of the Academy of Marketing Science,* Winter 1989, p. 67.
4. Thomas F. Dillon, "Carriers Offering Service Guarantees," *Inbound Logistics,* July 1990, p. 6.
5. "Logistics Costs to Rise," *Inbound Logistics,* November 1990, p. 6.
6. Bill Saporito, "IKEA's Got 'Em Lining Up," *Fortune,* Mar. 14, 1991, p. 72; and Judith Graham, "IKEA Furnishing Its U.S. Identity," *Advertising Age,* Sept. 14, 1989, p. 79.
7. Rinehart, Cooper, and Wagenheim, p. 67.
8. Carl M. Guelzo, *Introduction to Logistics Management* (Englewood Cliffs, N.J.: Prentice-Hall, 1986), pp. 35–36.
9. Michael Oskrobz, "EDI or Die?" *Inbound Logistics,* May 1990, pp. 18–21.
10. Thomas F. Dillon, "Competition Improves Service," *Inbound Logistics,* July 1991, p. 10.
11. Bob Freiday, "Popcorn, Peanuts, and Quadra-Paks," *Inbound Logistics,* February 1991, pp. 25–28.
12. Thomas F. Dillon, "Containerization: An Idea That Made Sense," *Inbound Logistics,* April 1991, pp. 25–28.

13. Guelzo, p. 102.

14. Adapted from *Physical Distribution Systems* by John F. Magee. Copyright 1967 McGraw-Hill, Inc.

15. James C. Johnson and Donald F. Wood, *Contemporary Physical Distribution & Logistics,* 3rd ed. (New York: Macmillan, 1986), p. 344.

16. Guelzo, p. 102.

17. The EOQ formula for the optimal order quantity is EOQ = 2DR/I, where EOQ = optimum average order size, D = total demand, R = cost of processing an order, and I = cost of maintaining one unit of inventory per year. For a more complete description of EOQ methods and terminology, see Frank S. McLaughlin and Robert C. Pickardt, *Quantitative Techniques for Management Decisions* (Boston: Houghton Mifflin, 1978), pp. 104–119.

18. "Watch for These Red Flags," *Traffic Management,* January 1983, p. 8.

19. Martin J. Schneider, "JIT's Missing Link," *Inbound Logistics,* November 1991, p. 16.

20. David N. Burt, "Managing Suppliers Up to Speed," *Harvard Business Review,* July–August 1989, p. 128.

21. Sharon Moshavi, "J-I-T Ignites Harley-Davidson," *Inbound Logistics,* May 1990, pp. 24–27.

22. Peter D. Bennett, ed., *Dictionary of Marketing Terms* (Chicago: American Marketing Association, 1988), p. 204.

23. Walter L. Weart, "Railroads Get Back on Track," *Inbound Logistics,* November 1990, pp. 22–25.

24. Alan J. Montgomery, "Railroads Flex Their Muscles," *Inbound Logistics,* November 1991, pp. 20–22; and "Rails Set Ton-Mile, Intermodal Records," *Inbound Logistics,* February 1991, p. 4.

25. Guelzo, pp. 50–52.

26. "In This Corner, Weighing In At . . . ," *Inbound Logistics,* December 1990, p. 4.

27. Felecia Stratton, "I Want My LCVs," *Inbound Logistics,* September 1991, pp. 24–26; and Walter L. Weart, "Just Another Vehicle on the Road?," *Inbound Logistics,* July 1991, pp. 21–25, 37.

28. Donald F. Wood and James C. Johnson, *Contemporary Transportation* (Tulsa, Okla.: Petroleum Publishing, 1980), pp. 290, 303.

29. *Jane's All the World's Aircraft 1991–92,* 82nd ed. (Alexandria, VA: Jane's Information Group, 1991).

30. Charles A. Taff, *Management of Physical Distribution and Transportation* (Homewood, Ill.: Irwin, 1984), p. 126.

31. Mark W. Lyon, "Inventory Busters," *Inbound Logistics,* November 1991, pp. 28, 30–31.

32. Guelzo, p. 53.

33. John J. Coyle, Edward Bardi, and C. John Langley, Jr., *The Management of Business Logistics* (St. Paul, Minn.: West, 1988), pp. 327–329.

34. Wal-Mart Stores, Inc., 1991 Annual Report, p. 2–4.

35. Gary Slutsker, "Working on the Railroads," *Forbes,* Mar. 24, 1986, p. 126.

36. Felecia Stratton, "Cargo Cops: To Catch a Thief," *Inbound Logistics,* March 1991, p. 22.

37. "Federated Group Stymies Hijackers with Two-Way Radio," *Chain Store Age Executive,* November 1985, pp. 172, 175.

38. Federal Express Corporation, 1990 Annual Report.

39. Dillon, "Containerization," pp. 25–28; and Allen R. Wastler, "Intermodal Leaders Ponder Riddle of Winning More Freight," *Traffic World,* June 19, 1989, pp. 14–15.

40. Jeffrey A. Trachtenberg, "IKEA Furniture Chain Pleases with Its Prices, Not with Its Service," *Wall Street Journal,* Sept. 17, 1991, pp. A1, A5; Barbara Solomon, "A Swedish Company Corners the Business: Worldwide," *Management Review,* April 1991, pp. 10–13; Bill Saporito, "IKEA's Got 'Em Lining Up," *Fortune,* Mar. 14, 1991, p. 72; Diane Harris, "Money's Store of the Year," *Money,* December 1990, pp. 144–153; Jim Moses, "IKEA Cashes In," *Global Trade,* October 1990, pp. 44, 46; Ela Schwartz, "The Swedish Invasion," *Discount Merchandiser,* July 1990, pp. 52, 56; Janet Bamford, "Why Competitors Shop for Ideas at IKEA," *Business Week,* Oct. 9, 1989, p. 88; Judith Graham, "IKEA Furnishing Its U.S. Identity," *Advertising Age,* Sept. 18, 1989, p. 79; and Peter Fuhrman, "The Workers' Friend," *Forbes,* Mar. 21, 1988, pp. 124, 128.

41. Jerry Drisaldi, "Protective Packaging: It's Your Responsibility," *Inbound Logistics,* November 1991, p. 39; Walter L. Weart, "Packaging Dilemmas: The Sequel," *Inbound Logistics,* June 1991, pp. 27–29; Bob Freiday, "Popcorn, Peanuts, and Quadra-Paks," *Inbound Logistics,* February 1991, pp. 25–28; and "Environmental Concerns Influence Packaging," *Inbound Logistics,* June 1990, p. 4.

Channel Decisions for TI's microLaser Printer*

Texas Instruments (TI), founded in the 1930s, employs 75,000 people worldwide, with major manufacturing sites in North America, South America, Europe, Asia, and Australia. TI serves a wide range of electronics markets and is divided into six major groups of specific applications. The Information Technology Group is comprised of Computer Systems, Industrial Automation, and Peripheral Products. The Peripheral Products Division (PPD), located in Temple, Texas, produces printers and portable computers and terminals. Because all phases of a new product introduction—including engineering, manufacturing, and marketing—are located together, the communication and coordination needed for a successful product launch exists.

The Laser Printer Market

The popularity of personal computers has prompted the growth of printers as a complementary product. Today, laser printers are the fastest-growing segment of the entire printer industry. Laser technology has become popular because it offers excellent print quality, fast printing, quiet operation, and flexibility with graphics and styles of letters on a page. Laser printers are designed for environments where data/word processing, specialty publishing, and business communications are integral to daily operations. Laser printers require minimal user training and are considered a commodity in some markets. For this reason, the price of laser printers has decreased dramatically over the past several years.

The Introduction of the microLaser Printer

In late 1989, TI introduced the microLaser laser printer. TI hoped that the microLaser would become the laser printer of choice in the world. When compared to leading competitors, the microLaser offered greater functionality in a smaller package. It was designed to fit easily on a desktop and perform numerous applications.

*This case researched and written by Debbie M. Thorne, Memphis State University

By virtue of its size, ease of use, and affordability, the microLaser has been positioned as a personal laser printer. It is small and relatively inexpensive. TI marketers hoped these attributes would encourage companies to purchase a microLaser for use with every personal computer they owned.

TI Explores New Distribution Channels

As with any new product introduction, careful attention was given to a distribution strategy. In the past, TI had relied on distributors, original equipment manufacturers (OEMs), and value added resellers (VARs) to market its laser printers. OEMs would specify a high level of customization and remarket the printer under their own brand name, usually as a part of a system. The OEM might even request functional modifications to meet its customer needs. The printer was usually integrated with a computer and software to form a system that the OEM would sell as its own. A VAR was more likely to purchase the printer with the TI name on it and then integrate it with other brands of computers and software to form a system. Texas Instruments' authorized distributors, VARs, and OEMs usually sold into large volume accounts, such as governmental agencies, financial institutions and Fortune 1000 companies.

Thus far, little attention had been given to retailers and less sophisticated end-users. Although the Texas Instruments name was recognized by many consumers, market research showed that little was known about TI laser printers. Most people either associated TI with its educational products, semiconductors, or for being forced out of the personal computer market. Perhaps these associations are reasons why retail distribution had not been pursued by the Peripheral Products Division. Additionally, from 1986 to 1989, Peripheral Products had no products suitable for the retail market.

The development of the microLaser prompted PPD Marketing to explore new channels of distribution. Research revealed that 48 percent of laser printer purchases were made through retailers. Distributors and wholesalers accounted for an additional 20 percent of laser printer sales. Texas Instruments had mainly sold through the reseller market. However, data such as these proved that the market demanded new distribution channels. Retailers did sell to individual users and small business owners, but now larger corporations with decentralized buying were going to retail outlets for their purchases.

After much thought and analysis, TI executives decided to re-enter the retail market. The nature of the printer market and the increased popularity of laser printers demanded new distribution channels. However, the move into retail was to be gradual. Support for retailers, including promotional campaigns, had to be designed, tested, and implemented. This channel demanded more support than the others and required that TI "pull" customers into the stores. PPD Marketing had to find ways to reach end-users and purchasers to build name recognition and establish TI as a producer of high quality printers.

TI Enters the Retail Market

Although nearly half of all laser printer purchases were made through retailers, the microLaser printer presented several challenges to TI. There are many laser printers to choose from and there is not a great deal of differentiation among them. First, the printer was essentially a "me-too" product. Most laser printers have similar warranties and software compatibilities. Generally, the size, weight, and output quality of the printers are only slightly different. In many ways, the products can be considered homogeneous, so buyers will often use price as a means of differentiation among competitors. This elastic price situation means that new entrants into the laser printer market should have a very low price to encourage sales. The TI microLaser had a price lower than two-thirds of its competitors in the laser printer industry.

Although the printer had a reasonable price, TI did not provide the promotional support necessary to "pull" end-users into retail stores. TI advertised in trade journals but did little else to establish itself as viable competitor in the laser printer market. Co-op advertising and sales force incentives might have been excellent strategies for building recognition among retailers.

The microLaser was similar to other products and there were few end-users specifically requesting the printer. Further, entrenched competitors, such as Hewlett-Packard and IBM, made it difficult for TI to persuade retailers to add another laser printer to their product mix. Finally, TI had much more experience in dealing with large accounts and industrial merchandis-ing which may have put them at a disadvantage in dealing with the competitive retail market.

The Future of TI Laser Printers

Although TI has enjoyed only moderate success with its microLaser printer, the company has expanded on the microLaser product line. By late 1991, the microLaser PS17 and PS35, the microLaser XL, microLaser Turbo printers, and microLaser Plus printers had been introduced by TI. Each of the new printers offers either improved print engine speed or greater font capability at an affordable price. Despite these improvements, TI's presence and movement in retail markets remains relatively slow. In fact, the company has signed agreements to distribute the microLaser product line through an original equipment manufacturer (OEM) and a national computer distributor. There has been no announcement of a contract to distribute the microLasers through large national retailers.

Questions for Discussion

1. The microLaser was introduced in a highly competitive and price-sensitive market. Explain how these factors affected the marketing strategy for the microLaser.
2. Evaluate TI's decision to enter retail markets. What could they have done differently?
3. Now that TI has a product line of laser printers, explain how the company might position itself to end users, to retailers, and to distributors.

Sources: Daniel M. Kehoe, "Fonts Unlimited: Seven Smart Lasers for Under $3,000," *PC World*, Sept. 1990; Alfred Poor, "Small-Footprint 6-ppm TI microLaser," *PC Magazine*, Apr. 24, 1990; a marketing study on Texas Instruments prepared by John Barnes, Jamie Holmes, Danny Lester, Truman Murray, and Mike Shelton, Memphis State University, 1991; Peter H. Lewis, "Texas Instruments Gets Personal," *New York Times*, Nov. 5, 1989, p. A2; Whitney Lynn, "Selling Computer Products in Changing Channels," *Computer Reseller News*, Aug. 28, 1989, pp. 83–84; Personal interview with Bruce Foster (Channel Marketing Manager for Texas Instruments' Peripheral Products Division), Aug. 16, 1989; Rowland T. Moriarty and Thomas J. Kosnick, "High Tech Marketing: Concepts, Continuity, and Change," *Sloan Management Review*, Summer 1989, pp. 7–17; *Texas Instruments*, (promotional booklet), 1988; *Marketrends/1988: The State of the Printer Industry*, pp. 3–4; and "Desktop Publishing Drives a High-Tech Company," *Modern Office Technology*, May 1988, pp. 80, 85, 88.

The History of Dayton Hudson's Social Responsibility

The Department Store division, consisting of Dayton's, Hudson's, and Marshall Field's, is one of three operating divisions of Dayton Hudson Corporation. The stores in this division dominate the markets in Minneapolis, Detroit, and Chicago, respectively. Dayton Hudson, one of America's largest retailers, has been known for its community involvement and social responsibility activities for over a century.

The Stores

Dayton's has been the upper Midwest's leading department store since its beginning in Minneapolis in 1902. Founder George Draper Dayton emphasized dependable merchandise at a low price. His basic philosophy was integrity and innovation. An example of his high standards of integrity included an offer of $1 paid for any inaccuracy found in the store's advertising. Therefore, consumers read and believed his ads. Dayton showed concern for his employees by providing many benefits and showing personal concern for each salesperson. Since 1946, the company has donated 5 percent of its taxable income (the maximum allowable) to charitable programs in the communities in which it does business. These contributions have totaled more than $200 million over the past half century. George Dayton also established the Dayton Foundation that today contributes more than $33 million to a variety of community projects and organizations.

Hudson's, another part of the Dayton Hudson Department Store Division with historical roots in social responsibility, has epitomized integrity in retailing ever since it opened its doors in Detroit in 1881. At the start of his career, Joseph L. Hudson established an unmatched reputation for honesty by exceeding the terms of an earlier bankruptcy, paying his creditors more than required and adding compound interest. When Joseph Hudson died in 1912, his four nephews took over and expanded the business. In 1928, the Hudson's in downtown Detroit became the second largest retail store building in the United States, and Hudson's eventually grew to 25 stores. The Hudson stores were always community-oriented and contributed to many charities, especially in the Detroit metropolitan area.

Marshall Field's, purchased in 1990, was founded by Marshall Field in 1892. Marshall Field also gained legendary status as a generous philanthropist. When this chain was purchased, it added 24 high-end department stores making Dayton Hudson the dominant Midwest department store operator. Some of Marshall Field's innovative community activities include family events such as Mother Nature Day and Dad's Day at the Zoo. Marshall Field's emphasizes superior customer service and makes significant contributions to local charities. In 1990, Marshall Field's contributed $1.6 million to social action and arts programs in the store's communities.

Social Responsibility at Dayton Hudson

The now-combined Dayton's, Hudson's and Marshall Field's have won recognition for continued efforts to serve their store communities. Dayton Hudson has won recognition for a high rate of participation in United Way campaigns. Several company programs are designed to make it easier for employees to donate their time to community organizations and programs of their choice. The company recently won recognition from the Public Management Institute as America's most generous retailer from the best-selling book, *The 100 Best Companies to Work for in America*, and from the Business Committee for the Arts in *Forbes* magazine for distinguished achievement in arts support. In 1989, the Dayton Hudson Corporation was awarded the America's Corporate Conscience Award by the Council on Economic Priorities.

The mission of Dayton's, Hudson's and Marshall Field's is to meet the needs of its quality-conscious customers through:

- customer service that exceeds all expectations
- fashion leadership
- high integrity and social responsibility, as demonstrated by prominent community involvement
- maintaining the traditions and individual distinctiveness of Dayton's, Hudson's, and Marshall Field's stores
- attracting and retaining the finest employees by seeking people of diverse backgrounds, recognizing

and rewarding excellence, communicating company goals honestly and clearly, and fostering personal growth.

Dayton Hudson believes in partnering with their communities. The corporation manages a unified corporatewide giving program which concentrates on two areas: social action and the arts. Forty percent of the funds from this giving program support projects that address social concerns. Another 40 percent of the funds support community arts programs.

Dayton Hudson's Environmental Concerns

Dayton Hudson Corporation has not only been involved in external activities to help their community, but there have been efforts directed toward getting their own house in order to make a positive environmental impact. The department stores are making major advances to meet environmental challenges that face all retailers. Solid waste reduction is a major concern. The environmental guidelines encourage:

- reduction in consumption of materials and energy,
- decreasing output of waste by recycling materials whenever possible, and
- using recycled or recyclable materials wherever practical and encourages its suppliers to do the same.

The department stores now print all of their credit statements on recycled paper. The company has reduced or eliminated the use of styrofoam packaging peanuts and styrofoam coffee cups, and minimum standards have been set for recycling all cardboard, fine paper, glass, cans, plastic, and hangers where possible. Advertising materials, computer-generated reports, and all copy machine paper use 100 percent preconsumer recycled paper. If possible, 100 percent recycled paper and recycled plastic bags are used for customer checkout containers.

Dayton Hudson Earns Respect and Success

The company carries on a tradition of integrity and innovation established by its founders. In a period of time when many department stores are struggling to survive, Dayton Hudson continues to be highly profitable. The Department Store Division had sales of over $3 billion in 1991 with 62 stores and a workforce of approximately 40,000. Although it is difficult to measure the impact of social responsibility on profits, Dayton Hudson seems well poised for the twenty-first century.

Questions for Discussion

1. What impact did the personal moral philosophies of George Draper Dayton, Joseph L. Hudson and Marshall Field have on the development of current ethics and social responsibility concerns at Dayton Hudson?
2. What is the role of high integrity and social responsibility, as demonstrated by high prominent community involvement, in building a department store marketing strategy?
3. How is the stores' internal concern for the environment contributing to social responsibility and community involvement.

Sources: Dayton Hudson Corporation 1990 Annual Report; Gary Hoover, Alta Campbell, and Patrick J. Spain, *Hoover's Handbook*, 1991 (California Publishers Group West), p. 202; "History of Dayton's," Dayton Hudson videotape, 1991; and "Seven Companies Given Awards," *New York Times*, March 3, 1989, p. 18D.

PREVIEW:

MICROMARKET COMPUTER APPLICATION III

Lonestar Auto Parts: Inventory Control

The warehouse manager for Lonestar Auto Parts must compare the benefits and costs of carrying large or small inventories to determine the optimum inventory level for each product. This exercise requires the use of the Economic Order Quantity (EOQ) technique to determine the inventory level for one product, Never Fail Wiper Blades. EOQ calculations are made using Lotus 1-2-3. The sensitivity of the EOQ is also analyzed by varying the level of demand, holding costs, order cost, and real EOQ over a four-year period. The application concludes with a written memo and case questions.

IV Promotion Decisions

Part IV focuses on communication with target market members. A specific marketing mix cannot satisfy people in a particular target market unless they are aware of the product and where to find it. Some promotion decisions and activities relate to a specific marketing mix, whereas others, broader in scope, are geared to promoting the whole organization. Chapter 15 presents an overview of promotion. We describe the communication process and the major promotion methods that can be included in promotion mixes. In Chapter 16, we analyze the major steps required to develop an advertising campaign, and we explain what publicity is and how it can be used. Chapter 17 deals with the management of personal selling and the role it can play in a firm's promotion mix. This chapter also explores the general characteristics of sales promotion and sales promotion techniques.

15 *Promotion: An Overview*

OBJECTIVES

■ To understand the role of promotion in the marketing mix

■ To examine the process of communication

■ To understand the product adoption process and its implications for promotional efforts

■ To explore the elements of the promotion mix

■ To acquire an overview of the major methods of promotion

■ To explore factors that affect the choice of promotional methods

Does electronic networking signal the demise of a paper-oriented society? Not if sales of IBM and Sears, Roebuck's Prodigy are any indication. According to its advertisers, personal computers were invented for services like Prodigy that provide on-line shopping, banking, education, news, and entertainment for a monthly fee. But so far, the number of subscriptions to the $600 million joint venture into the world of electronic networking has been less than expected. Prodigy marketing strategists are staging a multifaceted promotional effort designed to attract more families and casual home computer users.

Although the purchase price for Prodigy is $49.95, a special introductory promotion waives that charge and the fees for the first three months. Direct-mail promotions include coupons for free software and one month's free service. When prospective subscribers try Prodigy, they receive a free gift, either a *Sports Illustrated* video or software developed by *Money Magazine*.

When Prodigy began airing 30-second commercials with the theme "You Gotta Get This Thing," it became the first and only on-line service to advertise on television. Each of four advertisements focused on a different piece of available software—the 21-volume encyclopedia, the airline flight information, the financial data, or the at-home shopper. Prodigy ads appear in print as well.

Prodigy is staging a number of different events in association with Time Warner Corporation, its partner in a new cross-media contract. Inserts in *Time*, *Sports Illustrated*, *People*, and *Money* welcome subscribers by name and give them the address of the nearest Prodigy dealers. Cable television networks air commercials that promote the magazine issues containing the "personalized advertising message from Prodigy," and newspaper stands display placards to publicize them.

So far, are these promotional efforts working? Analysts insist that despite a 20 to 30 percent growth in the industry in general, an increase in Prodigy subscribers from 50,000 its first year to 400,000 to date, and a greater than 50 percent subscriber renewal rate, the companies are losing money on Prodigy. Undaunted, IBM and Sears continue promotional efforts.[1]

Photo courtesy of Prodigy Services Company.

O RGANIZATIONS SUCH AS PRODIGY use various promotional approaches to communicate with target markets, as the Prodigy example illustrates. This chapter looks at the general dimensions of promotion. First we define and examine the role of promotion. Next, to understand how promotion works, we analyze the meaning and process of communication, as well as the product adoption process. The remainder of the chapter discusses the major types of promotional methods and the factors that influence an organization's decision to use specific methods of promotion.

The Role of Promotion

People's attitudes toward promotion vary. Some hold that promotional activities, particularly advertising and personal selling, paint a distorted picture of reality because they provide only selected information to the customer. According to this view, the repetition of similar themes in promotion has brought about changes in social values, such as increased materialism.[2] Promotional activities are seen as unnecessary and wasteful, and promotion costs (especially advertising) as high—sometimes excessively so—resulting in higher prices. Still others take a positive view: that advertising messages often project wholesome values, such as affection, generosity, or patriotism,[3] or that advertising, as a powerful economic force, can free countries from poverty by communicating information.[4] Some observe that advertising of consumer products was a factor in the decline of communism and the move toward a free enterprise system in eastern Europe. However, none of these impressions is completely accurate.

The role of **promotion** is to communicate with individuals, groups, or organizations to directly or indirectly facilitate exchanges by informing and persuading one or more audiences to accept an organization's products. A variety of organizations spend considerable resources on promotion efforts. For example, Rock Against Drugs (RAD), a nonprofit organization, employs popular rock musicians to communicate its antidrug messages to teenagers and young adults. Marketers indirectly facilitate exchanges by focusing information about company activities and products on interest groups (such as environmental and consumer groups), current and potential investors, regulatory agencies, and society in general. Some marketers use *cause-related marketing*, which links the purchase of their products to philanthropic efforts for a particular cause favored by their target market. Cause-related marketing often helps a marketer boost sales and generate good will through contributions to causes that members of its target markets want to support. Marketers also sponsor special events, which often leads to news coverage and positive promotion of an organization and its brands. Inside Marketing discusses event sponsorship as part of the total marketing strategy.

Viewed from this wider perspective, promotion can play a comprehensive communication role. Some promotional activities, such as publicity and public relations, can be directed toward helping a company justify its existence and maintain positive, healthy relationships between itself and various groups in the marketing environment. For example, Russell Corporation, a large athletic uniform manufacturer, sponsors a Stay in School program to encourage students to remain in school and get an education (see Figure 15.1).

Figure 15.1

Promotion of Socially Responsible Activities

Russell Corporation promotes a program that encourages students to stay in school.

Source: Russell Corporation.

Although a company can direct a single type of communication—such as an advertisement—toward numerous audiences, marketers often design a communication precisely for a specific target market. A firm frequently communicates several different messages concurrently, each to a different group. For example, McDonald's may direct one communication toward customers for its Big Mac, a second message toward investors about the firm's stable growth, and a third communication toward society in general regarding the company's social awareness in supporting Ronald McDonald Houses, which provide support to families of children suffering from cancer.

To gain maximum benefit from promotional efforts, marketers must make every effort to properly plan, implement, coordinate, and control communications. Effective promotional activities are based on information from the marketing environment, often obtained from an organization's marketing information system (see Figure 15.2). How effectively marketers can use promotion to maintain positive relationships depends largely on the quantity and quality of information an organization takes in. For example, consumer research on zip-top plastic storage bags revealed that many customers were unsure whether the bags were properly sealed. Glad therefore developed a two-color seal for its bags—one side yellow, one side blue—which when the bag is effectively sealed appears as a green color. Because the basic role of promotion is to communicate, we should analyze what communication is and how the communication process works.

Promotion and the Communication Process

Communication can be viewed as the transmission of information. For communication to take place, however, both the sender and the receiver of the information must share some common ground. They must share a common understanding of the symbols used to transmit information, usually pictures or words. For instance, an individual transmitting the following message may believe he or she is communicating with you:

在工廠吾人製造化粧品,在商店吾人銷售希望。

However, communication has not taken place because few of you understand the intended message.[5] Thus we define **communication** as a sharing of meaning.[6] Implicit in this definition is the notion of transmission of information because sharing necessitates transmission.

As Figure 15.3 shows, communication begins with a source. A **source** is a person, group, or organization that has a meaning it intends and attempts to share with an audience. For example, a source could be a salesperson who wishes to communicate a sales message or an organization that wants to send a message to thousands of consumers through an advertisement. A **receiver** or audience is the individual, group, or organization that decodes a coded message. An audience is two or more receivers who decode a message. The intended receivers or audience of an advertisement for Motorola cellular telephones, for example, might be business persons who must frequently travel by car.

To transmit meaning, a source must convert the meaning into a series of signs that represent ideas or concepts. This is called the **coding process**, or *encoding*. When coding meaning into a message, a source must take into account certain characteristics of the receiver or audience. First, to share meaning, the source should use signs that are familiar to the receiver or audience. Marketers who understand this fact realize how important it is to know their target market and to make sure that an advertisement, for example, is written in language that the target market can understand. Thus when Du Pont advertises its Stainmaster carpeting, it does not mention the name of the chemical used to make the carpet resistant to spotting because it would have little meaning to consumers seeing the advertisement. There have been some notable problems in translating English advertisements into Spanish for the U.S. Hispanic market segment. A beer advertisement with the tag line "Sueltate" was supposed to mean "Let go!" but actually invited Hispanics to "Get diarrhea!" And an airline advertisement intended to entice Hispanics to fly first class on leather seats invited them instead to fly naked.[7] Thus it is important that people understand the language used in promotion.

Figure 15.2

Information Flows Into and Out of an Organization

Promoting Organizations and Brands Through Event Sponsorship

WHEN THE AMERICAN BOWL football game took place in London, its sponsor, Inter-Continental Hotels, received publicity from the media when its name, emblazoned across the stadium scoreboard, appeared on television screens in thousands of homes during the game. When Hiram Walker sponsored a free skiing party in Providence, Rhode Island, to introduce its new Fris Vodka, the $8,000 in charitable donations it collected generated goodwill in the community. What is the common denominator in these two scenarios? They are both examples of event sponsorship, which, except for the initial cost of underwriting the event, can provide companies with considerable amounts of free media coverage.

Sponsoring special events is an effective means of increasing brand recognition with relatively minimal investment. Even before the final round of the Nintendo World Championships, the promotional competition helped to boost sales of the company's entertainment system and hand-held Game Boy by 30 percent. In Cleveland, where one of the semifinal rounds was held, major press organizations treated the championship like an Olympic event. Television spots about the competition aired 27 times in three days. Even the *New Yorker*, which usually reviews highbrow events like ballet and art exhibits, ran an article on the Nintendo phenomenon in its "Talk of the Town" column. Company executives were thrilled that the publicity resulted in exposing about 378 million consumers worldwide to Nintendo.

Sometimes a company sponsors a special event to enhance its reputation as a philanthropic and caring organization. Minute Maid's sponsorship of the 1992 Olympic Games was the core of its "consumer cause" campaign; advertisements focused heavily on Minute Maid's program to donate a portion of its sales revenue to the Olympic Training Fund. By associating the Minute Maid brand with the Olympics' positive image, the company hopes to make consumers think less of rivals like Tropicana, which said, "Buy our juice because it's delicious," and more of Minute Maid, which said, "Buy our juice because every time you do, you give a young Olympic hopeful a chance."

Marketing experts know that event sponsorship must be a part of the total product marketing strategy. They try to make sure that their product and an event target a consistent audience. Associating a 10-kilometer run with Nike shoes makes better business sense than associating it with Pampers disposable diapers. Companies also make sure that sponsorship is profitable, using tools specifically created to evaluate the exposure provided for the cost, and compare the value of sponsorship with other promotional opportunities. Organizations are always on the lookout for less expensive means to achieve brand name recognition and consumer goodwill, and whether employed primarily as a product mover or an image enhancer, the $2.1 billion special-event marketing industry is likely to grow considerably over the next decade.

Sources: "Promotion News and Trends," *Adweek's Marketing Week*, Aug. 13, 1990, pp. 33D–40D; Jennifer Lawrence, "Minute Maid Teams with '92 Games," *Advertising Age*, July 23, 1990, pp. 3, 45; Erika Penzer, "And Now, A Word from Our Sponsor," *Incentive*, May 1990, pp. 49–56; Scott Hume, "GM Scrutinizes Sponsorships," *Advertising Age*, Apr. 2, 1990, p. 32; Erika Penzer, "American Football, British Style," *Incentive*, January 1990, pp. 34–35; Jon Lafayette, "Y & R Steps Up Event Marketing," *Advertising Age*, Oct. 9, 1989, p. 53; and Judith Graham, "Warner Canto: AmEx Exec on Prowl for Special Events," *Advertising Age*, July 31, 1989, p. 26.

Figure 15.3

The Communication
Process

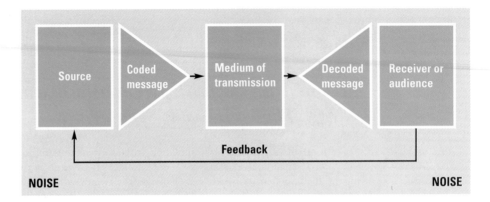

Second, when coding a meaning, a source should try to use signs that the receiver or audience uses for referring to the concepts the source intends. Marketers should generally avoid signs that can have several meanings for an audience. For example, a national advertiser of soft drinks should avoid using the word *soda* as a general term for soft drinks. Although in some parts of the United States soda means "soft drink," in other regions it may connote bicarbonate of soda, an ice cream drink, or something that one mixes with Scotch whisky.

To share a coded meaning with the receiver or audience, a source must select and use a medium of transmission. A **medium of transmission** carries the coded message from the source to the receiver or audience. Transmission media include ink on paper, vibrations of air waves produced by vocal cords, chalk marks on a chalkboard, and electronically produced vibrations of air waves—in radio and television signals, for example.

When a source chooses an inappropriate medium of transmission, several problems may arise. A coded message may reach some receivers, but not the right ones. For example, suppose a community theater spends most of its advertising dollars on radio advertisements. If theatergoers depend mainly on newspapers for information about local drama, then the theater will not reach its intended target audience. Coded messages may also reach intended receivers in an incomplete form because the intensity of the transmission is weak. For example, radio signals can be received effectively only over a limited range that may vary depending on climatic conditions. Members of the target audience who live on the fringe of the broadcast area may receive a weak signal; others well within the broadcast area may also receive an incomplete message if they listen to their radios while driving or studying.

In the **decoding process**, signs are converted into concepts and ideas. Seldom does a receiver decode exactly the same meaning that a source coded. When the result of decoding is different from what was coded, **noise** exists. Noise has many sources and may affect any or all parts of the communication process. Noise sometimes arises within the medium of transmission itself. Radio static, faulty printing processes, and laryngitis are sources of noise. Noise also occurs when a source uses a sign that is unfamiliar to the receiver or that has a different meaning from the one the source intended. Noise also may originate in the receiver. As Chapter 4 discusses, a receiver may be unaware of a coded message because his or her perceptual processes block it out.

The receiver's response to a message is **feedback** to the source. The source usually expects and normally receives feedback, although it may not be immediate. During feedback, the receiver or audience is the source of a message that is directed toward the original source, which then becomes a receiver. Feedback is coded, sent through a medium of transmission, and is decoded by the receiver, the source of the original communication. It is logical, then, to think about communication as a circular process.

During face-to-face communication, such as a personal selling situation or product sampling, both verbal and nonverbal feedback can be immediate. Instant feedback lets communicators adjust their messages quickly to improve the effectiveness of their communication. For example, when a salesperson realizes through feedback that a customer does not understand a sales presentation, the salesperson adapts the presentation to make it more meaningful to the customer. In interpersonal communication, feedback occurs through talking, touching, smiling, nodding, eye movements, and other body movements and postures.

When mass communication such as advertising is used, feedback is often slow and difficult to recognize. If Disney World increased advertising to increase the number of visitors, it might be six to eighteen months before the firm could recognize the effects of the expanded advertising. Although it is harder to recognize, feedback does exist for mass communication. The advertisement by the Colorado Tourism Board (Figure 15.4) is designed to aid in getting feedback by including a toll-free number and an information blank. Advertisers, for example, obtain feedback in the form of changes in sales volume or in consumers' attitudes and awareness levels. Thus after the state of Texas created its "Don't Mess with Texas" antilitter advertising campaign, the state found that roadside littering declined by 60 percent over the course of the campaign.[8] This

Figure 15.4

Obtaining Feedback

The Colorado Tourism Board will be able to measure feedback from this advertisement by the number of calls received on the 800 number, and by the number of information blanks returned.

Source: Jeff Andrews Photography.

feedback—the decline in littering—made it clear that the advertising campaign was effective in communicating its antilitter message.

Each communication channel has a limit on the volume of information it can handle effectively. This limit, called **channel capacity**, is determined by the least efficient component of the communication process. To illustrate, think about communications that depend on vocal speech. An individual source can talk only so fast, and there is a limit to how much an individual receiver can take in aurally. Beyond that point, additional messages cannot be decoded; thus meaning cannot be shared. Although a radio announcer can read several hundred words a minute, a one-minute advertising message should not exceed 150 words because most announcers cannot articulate the words into understandable messages at a rate beyond 150 words per minute. This figure is the limit for both source and receiver, and marketers should keep this in mind when developing radio commercials. At times, a firm creates a television advertisement that contains several types of visual materials and several forms of audio messages, all transmitted to viewers at the same time. Such communication may not be totally effective because receivers cannot decode all the messages simultaneously.

Now that we have explored the basic communication process, we consider more specifically how promotion is used to influence individuals, groups, or organizations to accept or adopt a firm's products. Although we briefly touch on the product adoption process in Chapter 9, we discuss it more fully in the following section to gain a better understanding of the conditions under which promotion occurs.

Promotion and the Product Adoption Process

Marketers do not promote simply to inform, educate, and entertain; they communicate to facilitate satisfying exchanges. One long-run purpose of promotion is to influence and encourage buyers to accept or adopt goods, services, and ideas. At times, an advertisement may be informative or entertaining, yet it may fail to get the audience to purchase the product. The ultimate effectiveness of promotion is determined by the degree to which it affects product adoption among potential buyers or increases the frequency of current buyers' purchases.

To establish realistic expectations about what promotion can do, one should not view product adoption as a one-step process. Rarely can a single promotional activity cause an individual to buy a previously unfamiliar product. The acceptance of a product involves many steps. Although there are several ways to look at the **product adoption process**, one common approach is to view it as consisting of five stages: awareness, interest, evaluation, trial, and adoption.[9]

In the *awareness stage*, individuals become aware that the product exists, but they have little information about it and are not concerned about getting more. When Nissan introduced its Infiniti automobile, for example, it used provocative teaser advertisements, which showed fields and oceans but not the car. Consumers enter the *interest stage* when they are motivated to get information about the product's features, uses, advantages, disadvantages, price, or location. During the *evaluation stage*, individuals consider whether the product will satisfy certain criteria that are crucial for meeting their specific needs. In the *trial stage*, they use or experience the product for the first time, possibly by purchas-

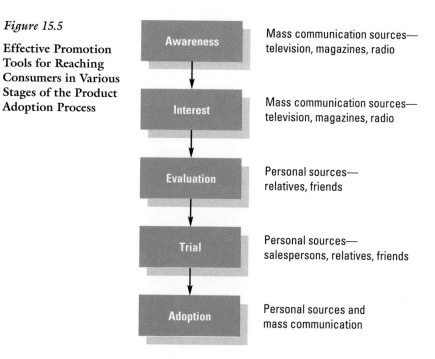

Figure 15.5

Effective Promotion Tools for Reaching Consumers in Various Stages of the Product Adoption Process

Awareness — Mass communication sources—television, magazines, radio

Interest — Mass communication sources—television, magazines, radio

Evaluation — Personal sources—relatives, friends

Trial — Personal sources—salespersons, relatives, friends

Adoption — Personal sources and mass communication

ing a small quantity, by taking advantage of a free sample or demonstration, or by borrowing the product from someone. Supermarkets, for example, frequently offer special promotions to encourage consumers to taste products. During this stage, potential adopters determine the usefulness of the product under the specific conditions for which they need it.

Individuals move into the *adoption stage* by choosing the specific product when they need a product of that general type. Do not assume, however, that because a person enters the adoption process she or he will eventually adopt the new product. Rejection may occur at any stage, including adoption. Both product adoption and product rejection can be temporary or permanent.

For the most part, people respond to different information sources at different stages of the adoption process. Figure 15.5 illustrates the most effective sources for each stage. Mass communication sources, such as television advertising, are often effective for moving large numbers of people into the awareness stage. Producers of consumer goods commonly use massive advertising campaigns when introducing new products. They do so to create product awareness as quickly as possible within a large portion of the target market.

Mass communications may also be effective for people in the interest stage who want to learn more about a product. During the evaluation stage, individuals often seek information, opinions, and reinforcement from personal sources—relatives, friends, and associates. In the trial stage, individuals depend on salespersons for information about how to use the product properly to get the most out of it. Marketers must use advertising carefully when consumers are in the trial stage. If advertisements greatly exaggerate the benefits of a product, the consumer may be disappointed when the product does not meet expectations.[10] It is best to avoid creating expectations that cannot be satisfied because rejection at this stage will prevent adoption. Friends and peers may also be

Figure 15.6

Distribution of Product Adopter Categories

Source: Reprinted with permission of The Free Press, a Division of Macmillan Inc., from *Diffusion of Innovations*, 3rd ed., by Everett H. Rogers. Copyright © 1962, 1983 by The Free Press.

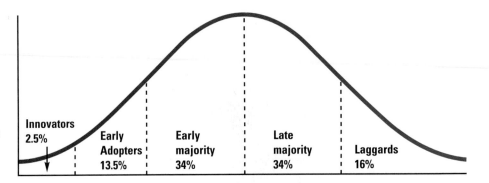

important sources during the trial stage. By the time the adoption stage has been reached, both personal communication from sales personnel and mass communication through advertisements may be required. Even though the particular stage of the adoption process may influence the types of information sources consumers use, marketers must remember that other factors, such as the product's characteristics, price, uses, and the characteristics of customers, also affect the types of information sources that buyers desire.

Because people in different stages of the adoption process often require different types of information, marketers designing a promotional campaign must determine what stage of the adoption process a particular target audience is in before they can develop the message. Potential adopters in the interest stage will need different information than people who have already reached the trial stage.

When an organization introduces a new product, people do not all begin the adoption process at the same time, and they do not move through the process at the same speed. Of those people who eventually adopt the product, some enter the adoption process rather quickly, whereas others start considerably later. For most products, too, there is a group of nonadopters who never begin the process.

Depending on the length of time it takes them to adopt a new product, people can be divided into five major adopter categories: innovators, early adopters, early majority, late majority, and laggards.[11] Figure 15.6 illustrates each adopter category and the percentage of total adopters that it typically represents. **Innovators** are the first to adopt a new product. They enjoy trying new products and tend to be venturesome. **Early adopters** choose new products carefully and are viewed as "the people to check with" by persons in the remaining adopter categories. Persons in the **early majority** adopt just prior to the average person; they are deliberate and cautious in trying new products. **Late majority** people, who are quite skeptical of new products, eventually adopt new products because of economic necessity or social pressure. **Laggards**, the last to adopt a new product, are oriented toward the past. They are suspicious of new products, and when they finally adopt the innovation, it may already have been replaced by a newer product. When developing promotional efforts, a marketer should bear in mind that persons in different adopter categories often need different forms of communication and different types of information.

To gain a better understanding of how promotion can move people closer to the acceptance of goods, services, and ideas, we turn to the major promotional methods available to an organization.

The Promotion Mix

Several types of promotional methods can be used to communicate with individuals, groups, and organizations. When an organization combines specific ingredients to promote a particular product, that combination constitutes the promotion mix for that product. The four possible ingredients of a **promotion mix** are advertising, personal selling, publicity, and sales promotion (see Figure 15.7). For some products, firms use all four ingredients; for other products, only two or three suffice. In this section we analyze the major ingredients of a promotion mix and the chief factors that influence an organization to include specific ingredients in the promotion mix for a specific product. In Chapters 16 and 17 we analyze the promotion mix in greater detail.

Promotion Mix Ingredients

At this point we consider some general characteristics of advertising, personal selling, publicity, and sales promotion.

Advertising   Advertising is a paid form of nonpersonal communication about an organization and its products that is transmitted to a target audience through a mass medium such as television, radio, newspapers, magazines, direct mail, mass transit vehicles, outdoor displays, or catalogs. Individuals and organizations use advertising to promote goods, services, ideas, issues, and people. Because it is highly flexible, advertising offers the options of reaching an extremely large target audience or focusing on a small, precisely defined segment of the population. For instance, McDonald's advertising focuses on a large audience of potential fast-food consumers, ranging from children to adults, whereas advertising for DeBeers's diamonds focuses on a much smaller and more specialized target market.

Advertising offers several benefits. It can be an extremely cost-efficient promotional method because it can reach a vast number of people at a low cost per

Figure 15.7

Possible Ingredients for a Promotion Mix

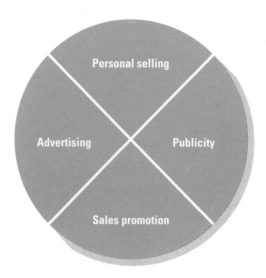

person. For example, the cost of a four-color, one-page advertisement in *Time* magazine is $128,000. Because the magazine reaches four million subscribers, the cost of reaching 1,000 subscribers is only $32. Advertising also lets the user repeat the message a number of times. Calvin Klein advertises many of its products (lingerie, cologne, clothes) on television, in magazines, and through outdoor advertising. In addition, advertising a product a certain way can add to its value. For example, Geo, which is sold and serviced by Chevrolet, is advertised as having more dealers than Honda, Toyota, and other Japanese companies combined. The visibility that an organization gains from advertising enhances the firm's public image.

Advertising also has several disadvantages. Even though the cost per person reached may be low, its absolute dollar outlay can be extremely high, especially for commercials during popular television shows. These high costs can limit, and sometimes prevent, the use of advertising in a promotion mix. Moreover, advertising rarely provides rapid feedback. Measuring its effect on sales is difficult, and it ordinarily has less persuasive impact on customers than personal selling.

Personal Selling Personal selling involves informing customers and persuading them to purchase products through personal communication in an exchange situation. The phrase *purchase products* should be interpreted broadly to encompass the acceptance of ideas and issues. Telemarketing, which Chapter 13 describes as direct selling over the telephone, relies heavily on personal selling.

Personal selling has both advantages and limitations when compared with advertising. Advertising is general communication aimed at a relatively large target audience, whereas personal selling involves more specific communication aimed at one or several persons. Reaching one person through personal selling costs considerably more than it does through advertising, but personal selling efforts often have greater impact on customers. Personal selling also provides immediate feedback, which allows marketers to adjust their message to improve communication. It helps them determine and respond to customers' needs for information.

When a salesperson and customer meet face to face, they use several types of interpersonal communication. Obviously, the predominating communication form is language—both speech and writing. In addition, a salesperson and customer frequently use **kinesic communication**, which is communication through the movement of heads, eyes, arms, hands, legs, or torsos. Winking, head nodding, hand gestures, and arm motions are forms of kinesic communication. A good salesperson can often evaluate a prospect's interest in a product or presentation by watching for eye contact and head nodding. **Proxemic communication**, a less obvious form of communication used in personal selling situations, occurs when either person varies the physical distance that separates the two people. When a customer backs away from a salesperson, for example, that individual may be saying that he or she is not interested in the product or may be expressing dislike for the salesperson. Touching, or **tactile communication**, can also be a form of communication, although it is not as popular in the United States as it is in many other countries. Handshaking is a common form of tactile communication in many countries.

Publicity Publicity refers to nonpersonal communication in news story form about an organization or its products, or both, that is transmitted through a mass medium at no charge. Examples of publicity include magazine, newspaper, radio, and television news stories about new retail stores, new products, or personnel changes in an organization. Although both advertising and publicity are transmitted through mass communication, the sponsor does not pay the media costs for publicity and is not identified. Nevertheless, publicity should never be viewed as free communication. Clearly there are costs associated with preparing news releases and encouraging media personnel to broadcast or print them. A firm that uses publicity regularly must have employees to perform these activities or must obtain the services of a public relations firm. Either way, the firm bears the costs of the activities.

Publicity must be planned and implemented so that it is compatible with, and supportive of, other elements in the promotion mix. However, publicity cannot always be controlled to the extent that other elements of the promotion mix can be. For example, Domino's, the largest pizza-delivery company in the world, has received much negative publicity about the driving record of its delivery people. The company has experienced criticism about pressures from the company that all pizzas be delivered within thirty minutes, regardless of weather and driving conditions. Because of the heightened awareness of this issue, Domino's is minimizing its emphasis on the thirty-minute guarantee and focusing instead on product quality.

Sales Promotion Sales promotion is an activity or material that acts as a direct inducement, offering added value, or incentive for the product, to resellers, salespersons, or consumers.[12] Examples of sales promotion include coupons (see Figure 15.8), bonuses, and contests used to enhance the sales of a product. The term *sales promotion* should not be confused with *promotion;* sales promotion is

Figure 15.8

Example of Sales Promotion Method

Minute Maid uses coupons to increase the market share of its frozen concentrate orange juice.

Source: © The Coca-Cola Company, reprinted by permission. All rights reserved.

but a part of the more comprehensive area of promotion. Currently, marketers spend about one and a half times as much on sales promotion as they do on advertising. Sales promotion appears to be growing in use more than advertising.

Marketers frequently rely on sales promotion to improve the effectiveness of other promotion mix ingredients, especially advertising and personal selling. For example, some firms allocate 25 percent of their annual promotion budget to trade shows in order to introduce new products, meet key industrial personnel, and identify likely prospects.[13]

Marketers design sales promotion to produce immediate sales increases. For example, Denny's used sales promotion to introduce its Flintstones Fun Meals, in which children received a free Flintstones toy with each meal ordered from the children's menu. During the first week of the launch, Denny's sales rose 20 percent.[14]

Generally, if a company employs advertising or personal selling, it either depends on them continuously or turns to them cyclically. However, a marketer's use of sales promotion tends to be irregular. Many products are seasonal. A company such as Toro may offer more sales promotions in July and August than in the peak selling season of April or May, when more people buy tractors, lawn mowers, and other gardening equipment.

Now that we have discussed the basic components of an organization's promotion mix, we need to consider how that mix is created. We must examine what factors and conditions affect the selection of the promotional methods that a specific organization uses in its promotion mix for a particular product.

Selecting Promotion Mix Ingredients

Marketers vary the composition of promotion mixes for many reasons. Although all four ingredients can be included in a promotion mix, frequently a marketer selects fewer than four. In addition, many firms that market multiple product lines use several promotion mixes simultaneously.

An organization's promotion mix (or mixes) is not an unchanging part of the marketing mix. Marketers attempt to measure the effectiveness of their promotion mixes and change them when necessary. The specific promotion-mix ingredients employed and the intensity at which they are used depend on a variety of factors, including the organization's promotional resources, objectives, and policies; characteristics of the target market; characteristics of the product; and cost and availability of promotional methods.

Promotional Resources, Objectives, and Policies   The quality of an organization's promotional resources affects the number and relative intensity of promotional methods that can be included in a promotion mix. If a company's promotional budget is extremely limited, the firm is likely to rely on personal selling because it is easier to measure a salesperson's contribution to sales than to measure the effect of advertising. A business must have a sizable promotional budget if it is to use regional or national advertising and sales promotion activities. Organizations with extensive promotional resources usually can include more ingredients in their promotion mixes. However, having more promotional dollars does not imply that they necessarily will use a greater number of promotional methods.

An organization's promotional objectives and policies also influence the types of promotion used. If a company's objective is to create mass awareness of a new convenience good, its promotion mix is likely to lean heavily toward advertising, sales promotion, and possibly publicity. If a company hopes to educate consumers about the features of durable goods, such as home appliances, its promotion mix may combine a moderate amount of advertising, possibly some sales promotion efforts designed to attract customers to retail stores, and a great deal of personal selling because this method is an excellent way to inform customers about these types of products. If a firm's objective is to produce immediate sales of consumer nondurables, the promotion mix will probably stress advertising and sales promotion efforts. The Global Perspective describes how Häagen-Dazs relies heavily on advertising and sales promotion in marketing its ice cream in Europe.

Characteristics of the Target Market The size, geographic distribution, and socioeconomic characteristics of an organization's target market also help dictate the ingredients to be included in a product's promotion mix. To some degree, market size determines the composition of the mix. If the size is quite limited, the promotion mix will probably emphasize personal selling, which can be quite effective for reaching small numbers of people. Organizations that sell to industrial markets and firms that market their products through only a few wholesalers frequently make personal selling the major component of their promotion mixes. When markets for a product consist of millions of customers, organizations use advertising and sales promotion because these methods can reach masses of people at a low cost per person.

The geographic distribution of a firm's customers can affect the combination of promotional methods used. Personal selling is more feasible if a company's customers are concentrated in a small area than if they are dispersed across a vast region. When the company's customers are numerous and dispersed, advertising may be more practical. In Figure 15.9, a combination of advertising and sales promotion can benefit both Alaska Airlines and Pepto-Bismol.

The distribution of a target market's socioeconomic characteristics, such as age, income, or education, may dictate the types of promotional techniques that a marketer selects. For example, personal selling may be much more successful than print advertisements for communicating with less-educated people.

Characteristics of the Product Generally, promotion mixes for business-to-business products concentrate on personal selling. In promoting consumer goods, on the other hand, advertising plays a major role. Treat this generalization cautiously, however. Business-to-business marketers do use some advertising to promote goods. Advertisements for computers, road building equipment, and aircraft are not altogether uncommon, and some sales promotion occasionally is used to promote business-to-business products. Personal selling is used extensively for consumer durables, such as home appliances, automobiles, and houses, and consumer convenience items are promoted mainly through advertising and sales promotion. Publicity appears in promotion mixes for both business-to-business and consumer products.

Figure 15.9

Combination Promotion

Alaska Airlines and Pepto-Bismol benefit from this advertisement that promotes both of their products.

Source: Alaska Airlines Inc.

Marketers of highly seasonal products are often forced to emphasize advertising, and possibly sales promotion, because off-season sales will not support an extensive year-round sales force. Although many toy producers have sales forces to sell to resellers, a number of these companies depend to a large extent on advertising to promote their products.

The price of a product also influences the composition of the promotion mix. High-priced products call for more personal selling because consumers associate greater risk with the purchase of such products and usually want the advice of a salesperson. Few of us, for example, would be willing to purchase a refrigerator from a self-service establishment. For low-priced convenience items, marketers use advertising rather than personal selling at the retail level.

A further consideration in creating an effective promotion mix is the stage of the product life cycle. During the introduction stage, a good deal of advertising may be necessary for both business-to-business and consumer products to make potential users aware of a new product. For many products, personal selling and sales promotion are helpful as well in this stage. In the case of consumer nondurables, the growth and maturity stages call for a heavy emphasis on advertising. Business-to-business products, on the other hand, often require a concentration of personal selling and some sales promotion efforts during these stages. In the decline stage, marketers usually decrease their promotional activities, especially advertising. Promotional efforts in the decline stage often center on personal selling and sales promotion efforts.

The intensity of market coverage is still another factor affecting the composition of the promotion mix. When a product is marketed through intensive distribution, the firm depends strongly on advertising and sales promotion.

Häagen-Dazs in Europe: The Cream Rises to the Top

THE CHOCOLATE COMES from the Netherlands and the vanilla from Madagascar. The coffee is from Brazil, and the strawberries are picked in Oregon. From Switzerland, Hawaii, and Georgia come almonds, macadamias, and pecans. All of these luscious ingredients combine to make Häagen-Dazs ice cream the number one U.S. brand in the superpremium ice cream category. Over 300 shops in the United States, Canada, Japan, and Europe dish up the frozen treat. In only two years, sales in Britain, France, and Germany skyrocketed from $2 million to $30 million. Encouraged by these figures, Häagen-Dazs has embarked on a $50 million promotional campaign to expand its European sales.

Although its name sounds exotic, Häagen-Dazs was born in the Bronx, New York, over thirty years ago. Pillsbury's buyout of the company in 1983 did not change the domestic focus. However, when British firm Grand Metropolitan PLC took over in 1989, Häagen-Dazs ventured overseas and soon had Europe eating eighteen different flavors out of its hands. In Britain, where they pronounce the ice cream "Hargen-Darz," customers are willing to pay two to three times the price of homegrown varieties. London's Leicester Square shop served almost one million ice-cream lovers its first year, adding up to $2.5 million in sales. In France, where sweet tooths run to napoleons and éclairs, Häagen-Dazs recently opened four cafes in fashionable Paris districts, as well as its first European factory. The company's second-busiest store in the world at Victor Hugo Plaza caters to French taste with its gold and ivory decor, rather than the traditional red-and-white stripes. Häagen-Dazs has plans for shops in Italy, Spain, and Scandinavia, expecting that by mid-decade, over half of its total sales will come from international markets.

Company marketers believe that once customers try Häagen-Dazs, they will buy it. The firm has therefore relied on free taste testing to sell its product, giving away over five million little cupfuls in Europe alone. To ensure that potential customers tasted the ice cream at its best, the company supplied thousands of retailers with freezers. Marketers didn't want the notoriously poor quality of most European freezers to damage their product. Recently, Häagen-Dazs targeted $20 million toward more aggressive European promotion, especially advertising. Although marketers are underscoring Häagen-Dazs's imaginative flavors, fine ingredients like fresh cream and cane sugar, and lack of additives, some European advertisements are raising eyebrows. In one spot, a seminude man and woman feed Häagen-Dazs ice cream to each other.

One Häagen-Dazs executive says that in Europe, the company is trying to do in three years what took thirty to do in the United States: bring annual sales of Häagen-Dazs to $300 million. Every year, companies all over the world produce more than three billion gallons of ice cream, and Europeans eat about 22 percent of it. Häagen-Dazs hopes to increase that figure by tempting more of them to consume treats like vanilla ice-cream bars hand-dipped in Belgian chocolate and rolled in roasted almonds.

Sources: "European Push by Häagen-Dazs," *New York Times*, Nov. 12, 1991; Mark Maremont, "They're All Screaming for Häagen-Dazs," *Business Week*, Oct. 14, 1991, p. 121; Nigella Lawson, "It's Really Cool," *The Spectator*, June 9, 1990, pp. 30–31, 33; and "A Better Class of Chill," *New Statesman & Society*, May 4, 1990, pp. 43–44.

A number of convenience products, such as lotions, cereals, and coffee, are promoted through samples, coupons, and cash refunds. Where marketers have opted for selective distribution, marketing mixes vary considerably as to type and amount of promotional methods. Items handled through exclusive distribution frequently demand more personal selling and less advertising. Expensive watches, furs, and high-quality furniture are typical products promoted heavily through personal selling.

Figure 15.10

Personal Product

The maker of Clearplan Easy relies heavily on advertising to promote its product.

Source: Whitehall Laboratories.

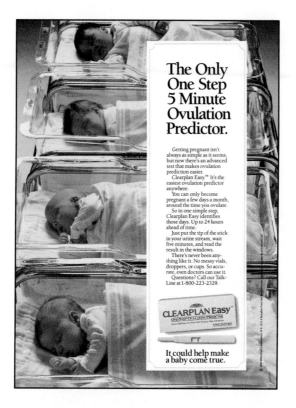

The Only One Step 5 Minute Ovulation Predictor.

Getting pregnant isn't always as simple as it seems, but now there's an advanced test that makes ovulation prediction easier.

Clearplan Easy.™ It's the easiest ovulation predictor anywhere.

You can only become pregnant a few days a month, around the time you ovulate.

So in one simple step, Clearplan Easy identifies those days. Up to 24 hours ahead of time.

Just put the tip of the stick in your urine stream, wait five minutes, and read the result in the windows.

There's never been anything like it. No messy vials, droppers, or cups. So accurate, even doctors can use it. Questions? Call our Talk-Line at 1-800-223-2329.

CLEARPLAN Easy™

It could help make a baby come true.

A product's use also affects the combination of promotional methods. Manufacturers of highly personal products, such as nonprescription contraceptives, feminine hygiene products, and hemorrhoid medications, count on advertising for promotion because many users do not like to talk with salespersons about such products (see Figure 15.10).

Cost and Availability of Promotional Methods   The costs of promotional methods are major factors to analyze when developing a promotion mix. National advertising and sales promotion efforts require large expenditures. For example, the average cost of producing a national television commercial is approximately $150,000. However, if the efforts are effective in reaching extremely large numbers of people, the cost per individual reached may be quite small, possibly a few pennies per person. Not all forms of advertising are expensive, however. Many small, local businesses advertise their products through local newspapers, magazines, radio and television stations, and outdoor and transit signs.

Another consideration that marketers must explore when formulating a promotion mix is the availability of promotional techniques. Despite the tremendous number of media vehicles in the United States, a firm may find that no available advertising medium effectively reaches a certain market. For example, a stockbroker may discover that no advertising medium precisely targets investors and potential investors in the Boston Celtics basketball team. The problem of media availability becomes even more pronounced when marketers try to advertise in foreign countries. Some media, such as television, simply may not be available. The media that are available may not be open to certain types of advertisements. For example, in Germany, advertisers are forbidden to make brand comparisons on television. Other promotional methods have limitations as well. A firm may wish to increase the size of its sales force but be unable to find qualified personnel. In addition, some state laws prohibit the use of certain types of sales promotion activities, such as contests. Those techniques are thus "unavailable" in those locales.

Push Policy Versus Pull Policy

Another element that marketers should consider when they plan a promotion mix is whether to use a push policy or a pull policy. With a **push policy**, the producer promotes the product only to the next institution down the marketing channel. For instance, in a marketing channel with wholesalers and retailers, the producer promotes to the wholesaler because in this case the wholesaler is the channel member just below the producer (see Figure 15.11). Each channel member in turn promotes to the next channel member. A push policy normally stresses personal selling. Sometimes sales promotion and advertising are used in conjunction with personal selling to push the products down through the channel.

As Figure 15.11 shows, a firm using a **pull policy** promotes directly to consumers with the intention of developing a strong consumer demand for the products. It does so primarily through advertising and sales promotion. Because consumers are persuaded to seek the products in retail stores, retailers will in turn go to wholesalers or the producer to buy the products. The policy is thus intended to "pull" the goods down through the channel by creating demand at the consumer level.

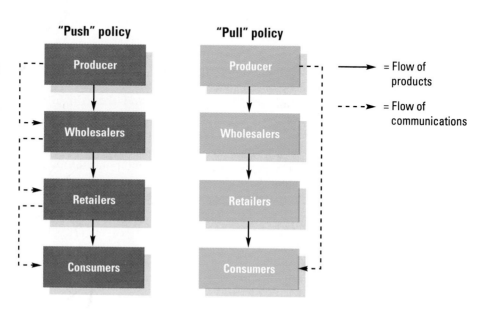

Figure 15.11

Comparison of Push and Pull Promotional Strategies

Summary

The primary role of promotion is to communicate with individuals, groups, or organizations in the environment to directly or indirectly facilitate exchanges.

Communication is a sharing of meaning. The communication process involves several steps. First, the source translates the meaning into code, a process known as coding or encoding. The source should employ signs familiar to the receiver or audience and choose signs that the receiver or audience uses for referring to the concepts or ideas being promoted. The coded message is sent through a medium of transmission to the receiver or audience. The receiver or audience then decodes the message and usually supplies feedback to the source. When the decoded message differs from the encoded one, a condition called noise exists.

The long-run purpose of promotion is to influence and encourage customers to accept or adopt goods, services, and ideas. The product adoption process consists of five stages. In the awareness stage, individuals become aware of the product. People move into the interest stage when they seek more information about the product. In the evaluation stage, individuals decide whether the product will meet certain criteria that are crucial for satisfying their needs. During the trial stage, the consumer actually tries the product. In the adoption stage, the consumer decides to use the product on a regular basis. Rejection of the product may occur at any stage. The adopters can be divided into five major categories—innovators, early adopters, early majority, late majority, and laggards—according to the length of time it takes them to start using a new product.

The promotion mix for a product may include four major promotional methods: advertising, personal selling, publicity, and sales promotion. Advertising is a paid form of nonpersonal communication about an organization and its products that is transmitted to a target audience through a mass medium. Personal selling is a process of informing customers and persuading them to purchase products through personal communication in an exchange situation. Publicity is nonpersonal communication in news story form, regarding an organization, its products, or both, that is transmitted through a mass medium at no charge. Sales promotion is an activity or material that acts as a direct inducement, offering added value to or incentive for the product, to resellers, salespersons, or consumers.

There are several major determinants of what promotional methods to include in a promotion mix for a product: the organization's promotional resources, objectives, and policies; the characteristics of the target market; the characteristics of the product; and the cost and availability of promotional methods. Marketers must also consider whether to use a push policy or a pull policy. With a push policy, the producer promotes the product only to the next institution down the marketing channel. Normally, a push policy stresses personal selling. A firm that uses a pull policy promotes directly to consumers with the intention of developing a strong consumer demand for the products. Once consumers are persuaded to seek the products in retail stores, retailers in turn go to wholesalers or the producer to buy the products.

Important Terms

Promotion
Communication
Source
Receiver

Coding process
Medium of transmission
Decoding process
Noise

Feedback
Channel capacity
Product adoption process
Innovators
Early adopters
Early majority
Late majority
Laggards
Promotion mix
Kinesic communication
Proxemic communication

Tactile communication
Push policy
Pull policy

Discussion and Review Questions

1. What is the major task of promotion? Do firms ever use promotion to accomplish this task and fail? If so, give several examples.
2. What is communication? Describe the communication process. Is it possible to communicate without using all the elements in the communication process? If so, which ones can be omitted?
3. Identify several causes of noise. How can a source reduce noise?
4. Describe the product adoption process. Under certain circumstances, is it possible for a person to omit one or more of the stages in adopting a new product? Explain your answer.
5. Describe a product that many persons are in the process of adopting. Have you begun the adoption process for this product? If so, what stage have you reached?
6. Identify and briefly describe the four major promotional methods that can be included in an organization's promotion mix. How does publicity differ from advertising?
7. What forms of interpersonal communication besides language can be used in personal selling?
8. How do market characteristics determine which promotional methods to include in a promotion mix? Assume that a company is planning to promote a cereal to both adults and children. Along what major dimensions would these two promotional efforts have to be different?
9. How can a product's characteristics affect the composition of its promotion mix?
10. Evaluate the following statement: "Appropriate advertising media are always available if a company can afford them."
11. Explain the difference between a pull policy and a push policy. Under what conditions should each policy be used?

Cases

15.1 Southwest Airlines: Are We Having Fun Yet?

Southwest Airlines, the ninth-largest airline in the United States, has been one of the most innovative promoters in the competitive airline industry. Chairman Herbert Kelleher has proven that a company can be run for both fun and profit. The keys to Southwest's success are the lowest operating costs in the industry, (about 6 cents a seat per mile), loyal employees, no-frills on-board service, low prices, and playful but effective promotion.

The focus of much of Southwest's promotion is Kelleher's zaniness and personal involvement with employees, passengers, and the general public. New employees watch "Southwest Shuffle," a rap-music video in which a number of employees, including Kelleher, rap out descriptions of their jobs and praise for the company. Kelleher often appears in television advertisements serving peanuts on his planes to illustrate Southwest's low-fare, no-frill service. He has also been known to board his planes dressed as the Easter Bunny or a leprechaun. He knows many of his seven thousand employees by name, and they call him Uncle Herb or Herbie. In a way, Kelleher is personally selling Southwest as a fun airline to both customers and Southwest employees. It is fitting that the company's theme song is a take-off on the Beach Boys hit "Fun, Fun, Fun."

In the airline's early days, female flight attendants broke with tradition by wearing miniskirts, and on one recent Christmas flight they dressed as reindeer (with musical accompaniment by the carol-singing pilot). There are Halloween costume contests among flight attendants and in-flight contests among passengers. The pilot might announce that anyone possessing a 1929 nickel wins a free trip. Attendants often sing their cabin announcements. To bring the same whimsical spirit from the airplane to the board room, a recent annual report had a paper cutout of a Southwest 737 on its back cover.

One sales promotion event paired Southwest with the Chili's restaurant chain in a two-for-one "Partner Pass" airline ticket giveaway with the purchase of one meal. Southwest viewed the promotion as a way to increase passenger traffic during the early months of the year, a traditionally slow period for all airlines. In another promotion, to herald the opening of Sea World in San Antonio, Kelleher had one of his 737 jets painted to look like a killer whale, one of Sea World's most popular attractions. Obviously, much publicity resulted.

Doing things differently is a source of pride at Southwest Airlines. It advertises service without meals or first-class seating; its tickets resemble grocery store receipts; it employs nonrestrictive work rules that allow, for example, a mechanic to help load baggage or a pilot to help board passengers; it flies straight-line routes, avoiding hubs and major city airports; and travel agents cannot use computers to book travelers on its flights, saving the airline $25 million annually in booking fees.

Despite its no-frills philosophy, the company's playful attitude and promotions have made it popular with travelers. The number of Southwest passengers a day continues to rise. Southwest has had eighteen straight years of profitability, a record that none of the larger airlines can match. In a feat made more impressive when viewed against a backdrop of the current economic slowdown and the struggle for survival by other airlines, Southwest's profits rose from $58 million to $71.6 million during a recent year. When the company recently achieved revenues of $1 billion, the Transportation Department elevated it to the status of "major airline." Even with rock-bottom fares, Southwest has been profitable because its costs average 30 percent below those of its competitors. Moreover, the Department of Transportation's monthly consumer report routinely ranks Southwest among the airlines lowest in complaints and highest in on-time flights. Southwest's on-time flight record can be attributed partly to a fifteen-minute turnaround time for planes versus an industry average of forty-five minutes.

Southwest's style makes it an easy target for competitors' put-downs, but they are taken in stride. In one advertisement, Kelleher wears a paper bag on his head and offers such a bag to anyone embarrassed to fly on Southwest. If travelers are willing to give up meals and legroom and choose Southwest Airlines, they can still have the bag to hold all the money they will save by flying Southwest.

Some analysts suggest that Southwest will eventually be squashed by the competition, but competition does not scare Kelleher. To keep Southwest growing in revenue and profits, he has plans to double his fleet of airplanes to 170 by the late 1990s and to increase the frequency of flights on existing routes, as well as to open new ones. Expanding to California is his number-one priority, but although Southwest recently began daily flights from Burbank to Oakland, the airline has been denied gates at many California airports. Until this situation changes, Southwest's competitors in California can breathe easier. Meanwhile, Kelleher continues to put pressure on his advertising firm, GSD&M of Austin, to devote more creative resources to the $20 million account, and to make promotions a key consideration in working toward his objectives.[15]

Questions for Discussion

1. What is the promotion mix at Southwest Airlines?
2. What role does Herbert Kelleher play in the promotion of Southwest Airlines?
3. What is the importance of publicity in Southwest Airline's promotion mix?

15.2   Nissan Uses Promotion to Change Its Image

Nissan Motor Co., the American marketing subsidiary of the Japanese Nissan, has experienced declining sales and market share in recent years, due in large part to consumer confusion about Nissan's image. In 1958, Nissan began selling a compact car called the Bluebird in the United States. In Japan, the Bluebirds were called Datsuns, and the name stuck in the United States, too. Thus, without much planning, the nameplate on the whole line of cars sold in the United States became Datsun over the next two decades. Many Americans associated the name Datsun with efficiency, reliability, and performance, and the sporty Datsun models 240Z and 280ZX sold well.

However, the Japan-based Nissan wanted to convey a uniform image around the world, and so in 1981 the company started marketing all its cars under the name Nissan. Out went "Datsun—We Are Driven," and in came "The Name is Nissan." With the introduction of the 1985 Maxima model, the Datsun nameplate disappeared. But many Americans continued to refer to the company's cars and trucks as Datsuns, and the name Nissan meant little to consumers; some even believed Nissan was a division of Toyota. The confusion over the name may explain why Nissan experienced a decline in sales and market share of its automobiles and trucks in the United States during the late 1980s.

Another factor in Nissan's image problem was the company's change from mostly numbered models (210s, 510s, 280s) to mostly named ones (Stanzas, Maximas). Many consumers confused the Pulsar with a watch brand and the Maxima with interest-bearing checking accounts. Automobile analysts say that the confusion caused by this inconsistency led to fewer Nissan sales. In the same time period that Honda sold 362,000 Accords and Toyota sold 257,000 Camrys, Nissan sold just 42,736 Stanzas. At one point, Nissan had a one-hundred-day supply of unsold cars in showrooms and on loading docks, forty days above the industry average. By comparison, Toyota had only a twenty-day supply. As others in the automobile industry began promoting new models, Nissan was still flooded with older cars. New cars also piled up because Nissan had no "all-new" cars to sell. Every model was a carry-over from the previous model year with only slight modifications.

When Nissan's "Built for the Human Race" advertisements failed to bring prospective buyers into the showroom, sales fell by 40 percent, and the company kept the slogan, but dropped the advertisements that went with it. Soon after, Nissan initiated a sales promotion offering rebates of up to $1,000 on selected cars. Many industry experts predicted that such sales promotions would bring only short-run sales results and could not build the long-term brand image Nissan wanted.

To solve its image and declining sales problems, Nissan fired its advertising agency, retired many employees, and reorganized its U.S. operations under eleven regional managers. A dealer operations manager coordinates all regional operations, and customer service and owner loyalty managers create and supervise local programs. It also introduced an aggressive owner-satisfaction program, called Owner 1, to make sure that owners were satisfied with their purchases of new cars, as well as repairs of older cars. In addition, Nissan sought to add flash to a complete line of new cars with distinctive and innovative designs.

Commercials for five of the new cars stress sex, speed, and dreams, but to promote its restyled Maxima four-door sedan, Nissan opted for a more straightforward approach. Television spots targeted the "aging babyboomer" by emphasizing reliability coupled with youthful styling. Print advertisements gave potential customers a toll-free phone number to call in order to receive a free Maxima preview kit and test-drive offer. Those who made a test drive and filled out an evaluation form afterward received a free flashlight. Nissan's direct-mail campaign that advertised a free set of luggage for anyone purchasing a Maxima received an Echo award from the Direct Marketing Association.

Early advertisements for Nissan's new Infiniti line of luxury cars (which compete with Mercedes-Benz, BMW, Jaguar, and Audi) were offbeat, showing images of waves, fields, or clouds, but never a car. Market research firm Video Storyboard Tests recently named these Zen-inspired spots third in the top ten most-remembered television advertisements, the best showing ever for a new-car campaign. Other surveys show rising scores in unaided brand awareness and recognition. However, although Infiniti dealers have been overwhelmed with "tire-kickers," sales are lagging about 30 percent behind Nissan's goals. Largely in response to dealer insistence, the most recent Infiniti ads are more tangible, emphasizing steering and comfort instead of rocks and trees. Two-page ads in newspapers across the country not only display the car at last, but do it from fifteen different angles. For Infiniti, however, the goal remains to establish an identity that will make it stand out from its toughest competitor, the Toyota Lexus.

To date, Nissan's most successful promotion has been its "Test-Drive Challenge." Shoppers were invited to test-drive a Nissan Stanza, Honda Accord, and Toyota Camry. Anyone purchasing either of the competitors' products after the test drive received $100 from Nissan. Nissan gave away about $424,000, but Stanza sales increased rapidly, dealers were very pleased, and the company extended the promotion. Nissan's president of sales says it was the "best half million dollars" he ever spent.

Although Nissan continues to wrestle with its image problem in the United States, it is fighting back with offbeat promotions and a revamped line-up. The future will see a sleek replacement for the aging Sentra, a minivan, and an innovative new Stanza. Designed, engineered, and produced in the United States, the new Stanza will have an aerodynamic forward-sloping hood like the new minivans from Toyota and GM. Promotion will continue to play a key role in informing and persuading buyers to form a new image of Nissan cars. After years of decline, sales in 1990 and 1991 were up. Company executives believe Nissan is finally re-establishing itself and its reputation for making bold, exciting cars with distinctive and innovative designs.[16]

Questions for Discussion

1. What went wrong with Nissan's promotion in the 1980s?
2. What can Nissan do to improve its promotion in the 1990s?
3. Is "sex and speed" a socially responsible message to use in automobile advertising?

Chapter Notes

1. Based on information from Alison Fahey, "Prodigy Loads Up," *Advertising Age*, Sept. 10, 1990, p. 24; Thomas R. King, "Time Signs Prodigy to Cross-Media Deal," *Wall Street Journal*, Sept. 10, 1990, p. 38; Margie G. Quimpo, "Prodigy Venture Plans More Computer Services," *Washington Post*, Sept. 6, 1990, pp. E1, E6; Eben Shapiro, "New Features Are Planned by Prodigy," *New York Times*, Sept. 6, 1990, p. D19; Michael Alexander, "Videotex: Struggling for Acceptance," *Computerworld*, July 16, 1990, p. 22; Judy Getts, "Prodigy Plows Ahead," *PC World*, July 1990, p. 72; Tom Sherman, "The Prodigy Service: A Glimpse of the Future?" *Link-Up*, May–June 1990, pp. 24, 26–27; Mick O'Leary, "Prodigy, IPS, and OLTV," *Information Today*, May 1990, pp. 9–10, 12; and Fred Kapner, "Prodigy Begins Regional Blitz," *Baltimore Daily Record*, Mar. 1, 1989.
2. Richard W. Pollay, "On the Value of Reflections on the Values in 'The Distorted Mirror,'" *Journal of Marketing*, July 1987, pp. 104–109.
3. Morris B. Holbrook, "Mirror, Mirror, on the Wall, What's Unfair in the Reflections on Advertising," *Journal of Marketing*, July 1987, pp. 95–103.
4. Richard N. Farmer, "Would You Want Your Granddaughter to Marry a Taiwanese Marketing Man?" *Journal of Marketing*, October 1987, pp. 111–116.
5. In case you do not read Chinese, this says, "In the factory we make cosmetics, and in the store we sell hope." Prepared by Chih Kang Wang.

6. Terence A. Shimp, *Promotion Management and Marketing Communication* (Hinsdale, Ill.: Dryden Press, 1990), p. 38.

7. Carlos E. Garcia, "Hispanic Market Is Accessible if Research Is Designed Correctly," *Marketing News,* Jan. 4, 1988, p. 46.

8. Seth Kantor, "Engineer's Survey Helped Shape State's Ad Campaign Against Highway Littering," *Bryan–College Station(TX) Eagle,* Aug. 4, 1989, p. 2D.

9. Adapted from Everett M. Rogers, *Diffusion of Innovations* (New York: Free Press, 1962), pp. 81–86, 98–102.

10. Lawrence J. Marks and Michael A. Kamins, "Product Sampling and Advertising Sequence, Belief Strength, Confidence and Attitudes," *Journal of Marketing Research,* August 1988, pp. 266–281.

11. Rogers, pp. 247–250.

12. Don E. Schultz and William A. Robinson, *Sales Promotion Management* (Chicago: Crain, 1982), p. 8.

13. Roger A. Kerin and William L. Cron, "Assessing Trade Show Functions and Performance: An Exploratory Study," *Journal of Marketing,* July 1987, pp. 87–94.

14. Laurie Petersen, "CPSA Honors Repeat Campaigns," *Adweek's Marketing Week,* Apr. 29, 1991, p. 33.

15. "Chili's, Southwest Airlines Proceed with Promotion," *Adweek,* Jan. 21, 1991, p. 3; "GSD&M Keeps Account of Southwest Airlines," *New York Times,* July 26, 1990, p. D17; Jennifer Lawrence and Ira Teinowitz, "Airline Agencies Face Rough Summer," *Advertising Age,* June 11, 1990, p. 27; James Ott, "Analysts Call Consolidation a Threat to Weak Carriers," *Aviation Week and Space Technology,* Feb. 26, 1990, pp. 64–65; Robert E. Dallos, "Locked Out at the Gate," *Los Angeles Times,* Feb. 12, 1990, pp. D1, D4; Denise Gellene, "Airline Battle Is Shaping Up in California," *Los Angeles Times,* Feb. 1, 1990, pp. D1, D7; Doug Carroll, "No-Frills Firm Flies Against the Ordinary," *USA Today,* Aug. 24, 1989, pp. 1B, 2B; Michael Hiestand, "Flying the Wacky Skies with Southwest's CEO," *Adweek's Marketing Week,* July 10, 1989, p. 31; Kevin Kelly, "Southwest Airlines: Flying High with 'Uncle Herb,'" *Business Week,* July 3, 1989, pp. 53–54; Oliver Sutton, "Southwest Airlines Offers Something Special in Texas," *Interavia,* May 1989, pp. 416, 418, 420; Stuart Manning, "Burger King, Southwest Airlines Offer 'Buddy Pass' Promo," *Dallas/Fort Worth Business Journal,* Dec. 5, 1988; and Dean Lampman, "Herb Kelleher, Chief of America West's Arch Rival, Keeps Lighter Side of Business in Mind," *Phoenix Business Journal,* May 2, 1988.

16. David Kiley, "Looking for Solutions, Nissan Goes Local," *Adweek's Marketing Week*, Jan. 28, 1991, p. 9; Larry Armstrong, "So Far, Nissan's Catch-Up Plan Hasn't Caught On," *Business Week*, Sept. 17, 1990, pp. 59, 62, 66; "Nissan's U.S. Exec Drives Ahead," *Advertising Age*, Aug. 20, 1990, p. 20; Kristine Stiven Breese, "Cash Deal Jump-Starts Stanza Sales," *Automotive News*, June 18, 1990, p. 4; Francis J. Gawronski, "Infiniti," *Automotive News*, Mar. 26, 1990, p. 101; Larry Armstrong, "The American Drivers Steering Japan Through the States," *Business Week*, Mar. 12, 1990, pp. 98–99; Michael Garry, "To the Max," *Marketing and Media Decisions*, March 1990, pp. 39–40, 42; Mark Landler and Wendy Zellner, "No Joyride for Japan," *Business Week*, Jan. 15, 1990, pp. 20–21; Joseph B. White, "Nissan Motors Back to Basics: Sex, Speed," *Wall Street Journal*, Nov. 9, 1989, p. B6; James R. Healey, "Enthusiasm, Lines Welcome Nissan's Infiniti," *USA Today*, Nov. 8, 1989, p. 1B; David Landis, "Hot Models Re-charge Sales Image," *USA Today*, Sept. 13, 1989, pp. 1B, 2B; and Michael Lev, "Nissan Tries to Build an Image Where There Was None," *Torrance (CA) Daily Breeze*, June 5, 1988.

16 Advertising and Publicity

OBJECTIVES

- To explore the uses of advertising

- To become aware of the major steps involved in developing an advertising campaign

- To find out who is responsible for developing advertising campaigns

- To gain an understanding of publicity

- To analyze how publicity can be used

In the days before compact disc players, car phones, and the power lunch, people associated sneakers with sweat, and children wore $10 gym shoes in school during physical education. Renamed "athletic shoes" and repositioned to symbolize fitness and style, sneakers now command an upscale price to go along with an up-scale image. Despite the high prices, sales of athletic shoes rose 14.8 percent in one year. Intensely competitive for the lion's share of the market, the top three sneaker companies, L.A. Gear, Nike, and Reebok, spend about $300 million a year on celebrity endorsements and television commercials to convince consumers that they need these high-tech expensive shoes.

While Nike edged ahead with consistently well received advertising, Reebok floundered. First came its "U.B.U." campaign, which many retailers and consumers hated, followed by the equally unsuccessful "The Physics Behind the Physique" campaign. Reebok's most controversial and short-lived commercial was the infamous Bungee jumping spot in which two people, one wearing Reebok's Pump and one wearing Nike shoes, jump off of a bridge. The Reebok jumper bounces back on the bungee cord, but the Nike wearer's cord bounces back empty.

Reebok's agency recently introduced its newest theme, "It's Time to Play," believing that the concept of play covers a whole range of activities from parents playing one-on-one basketball with their children in the driveway to professionals playing in the National Basketball Association. Viewers see Americans in Reebok footwear running, dancing, and just enjoying life to the tune of a country-western song, "Come from the Heart." Reebok negotiated with controversial pop star Madonna to endorse its Side One casual shoes, going as far as producing two test commercials featuring "the material girl." Recently announcing there would be no deal with Madonna, executives expressed concern that the controversy surrounding her lyrics and videos made her an inappropriate Reebok spokesperson.[1]

Photo courtesy of LA Gear.

A THLETIC-SHOE PRODUCERS such as Reebok and Nike rely heavily on advertising and on publicity generated from event sponsorship. This chapter explores the many dimensions of advertising and publicity. Initially, we focus on the nature and uses of advertising. We then examine the major steps in developing an advertising campaign and describe who is responsible for developing such campaigns. As we analyze publicity, we compare its characteristics with those of advertising and explore the different forms it may take. We then consider how publicity is used and what is required for an effective publicity program. Finally, we discuss negative publicity and some problems associated with the use of publicity.

The Nature of Advertising

Advertising permeates our daily lives. At times people view it positively; at other times they avoid it by taping television programs and then zapping over the commercials with the fast-forward button of their videocassette recorders. Some advertising informs, persuades, or entertains us; some of it bores, even offends us. Benetton, the clothing manufacturer and retailer, received over 800 complaints in the first week after launching an advertising campaign with billboards showing a placenta-covered newborn with umbilical cord still attached. The company decided to remove the posters.[2]

As mentioned in Chapter 15, **advertising** is a paid form of nonpersonal communication that is transmitted through mass media such as television, radio, newspapers, magazines, direct mail, mass transit vehicles, and outdoor displays. An organization can use advertising to reach a variety of audiences, ranging from small, precise groups, such as the stamp collectors of Idaho, to extremely large groups, such as all athletic shoe purchasers in the United States.

When people are asked to name major advertisers, most immediately mention business organizations. However, many types of organizations—including governments, churches, universities, civic groups, and charitable organizations—take advantage of advertising. In 1990, for example, the U.S. government was the thirty-ninth largest advertiser in the country, spending $304 million.[3] So even though we analyze advertising in the context of business organizations here, remember that much of what we say applies to all types of organizations.

Under certain conditions, advertising can work effectively for an organization. The questions in Table 16.1 raise some points that a marketer should consider when assessing the potential value of advertising as an ingredient in a product's promotion mix. The list is not all-inclusive. Many factors have a bearing on whether advertising should be used at all, and if so, to what extent.

The Uses of Advertising

Advertising can serve a variety of purposes. Individuals and organizations use it to promote products and organizations, to stimulate demand, to offset competitors' advertising, to make salespersons more effective, to increase the uses of a product, to remind and reinforce customers, and to reduce sales fluctuations.

Promoting Products and Organizations

Advertising is used to promote goods, services, ideas, images, issues, people, and indeed anything that the advertiser wants to publicize or foster. Depending on what is being promoted, advertising can be classified as institutional or product advertising. **Institutional advertising** promotes organizational images, ideas,

Table 16.1 Some Issues to Consider When Deciding Whether to Use Advertising

1. **Does the product possess unique, important features?**
Although homogeneous products, such as cigarettes, gasoline, and beer, have been advertised successfully, they usually require considerably more effort and expense than other products. On the other hand, products that are differentiated on physical rather than psychological dimensions are much easier to advertise. Even so, "being different" is rarely enough. The advertisability of product features is enhanced when buyers believe that those unique features are important and useful.

2. **Are "hidden qualities" important to buyers?**
If by viewing, feeling, tasting, or smelling the product buyers can learn all there is to know about the product, advertising will have less chance of increasing demand. Conversely, if not all product benefits are apparent to consumers, advertising has more of a story to tell, and the probability that it can be profitably used increases. The "hidden quality" of vitamin C in oranges once helped explain why Sunkist oranges could be advertised effectively, whereas the advertising of lettuce has been a failure.

3. **Is the general demand trend for the product favorable?**
If the generic product category is experiencing a long-term decline, it is less likely that advertising can be used successfully for a particular brand within the category.

4. **Is the market potential for the product adequate?**
Advertising can be effective only when there are sufficient actual or prospective users of the brand in the target market.

5. **Is the competitive environment favorable?**
The size and marketing strength of competitors and their brand shares and loyalty will greatly affect the possible success of an advertising campaign. For example, a marketing effort to compete successfully against Kodak film, Morton salt, or Campbell soups would demand much more than simply advertising.

6. **Are general economic conditions favorable for marketing the product?**
The effects of an advertising program and the sale of all products are influenced by the overall state of the economy and by specific business conditions. For example, it is much easier to advertise and sell luxury leisure products (stereos, sailboats, recreation vehicles) when disposable income is high.

7. **Is the organization able and willing to spend the money required to launch an advertising campaign?**
As a general rule, if the organization is unable or unwilling to undertake an advertising expenditure that as a percentage of the total amount spent in the product category is at least equal to the market share it desires, advertising is less likely to be effective.

8. **Does the firm possess sufficient marketing expertise to market the product?**
The successful marketing of any product involves a complex mixture of product and buyer research, product development, packaging, pricing, financial management, promotion, and distribution. Weakness in any area of marketing is an obstacle to the successful use of advertising.

Source: Adapted from Charles H. Patti, "Evaluating the Role of Advertising," *Journal of Advertising,* Fall 1977, pp. 32–33. Used by permission.

Figure 16.1

Product Advertisement

This product advertisement for Purina Dog Chow focuses on specific product characteristics, such as taste and nutrition.

Source: © 1990, Ralston Purina Company. Ad produced by Check Mark Communications. Tim Cenova, art; Susan McMichael, copy. Reproduced with permission of Ralston Purina Company.

or political issues. For example, both Anheuser-Busch and Miller Brewing Co. employ advertising to promote responsible drinking and reduce teenage consumption.[4] These advertisements help to build a socially responsive image for these companies.

Product advertising promotes goods and services. Business, government, and private nonbusiness organizations turn to it to promote the uses, features, images, and benefits of their products. For example, in Figure 16.1, Ralston Purina promotes the good taste and nutritional value of Purina Dog Chow.

Stimulating Primary and Selective Demand

When a specific firm is the first to introduce an innovation, it tries to stimulate *primary demand*—demand for a product category rather than a specific brand of the product—through pioneer advertising. **Pioneer advertising** informs people about a product: what it is, what it does, how it can be used, and where it can be purchased. Because pioneer advertising is used in the introductory stage of the product life cycle when there are no competitive brands, it neither emphasizes the brand name nor compares brands. The first company to introduce the compact disc player, for instance, initially tried to stimulate primary demand by emphasizing the benefits of compact disc players in general rather than the benefits of its brand. Product advertising is also used sometimes to stimulate primary demand for an established product. Occasionally, an industry trade group, rather than a single firm, sponsors advertisements to stimulate primary demand. For example, to stimulate demand for flowers, the American Floral Marketing Council sponsors advertisements that promote flowers as gifts (see Figure 16.2).

To build *selective demand,* or demand for a specific brand, an advertiser turns to competitive advertising. **Competitive advertising** points out a brand's uses, features, and advantages that benefit consumers but may not be available in competing brands.

An increasingly popular form of competitive advertising is **comparative advertising**, in which two or more specified brands are compared on the basis of one or more product attributes. Figure 16.3 is a comparative advertisement for Fresh Start detergent. In 1988, Colgate Palmolive produced this comparative advertisement for Fresh Start Laundry Detergent. It revealed the findings of one particular test under very specific conditions. Comparative advertising is prevalent among manufacturers of hamburgers, soft drinks, toothpastes, aspirin, tires, automobiles, and a multitude of other products. However, under the 1988 Trademark Law Revision Act, marketers using comparative advertising must not misrepresent the qualities or characteristics of the competitive product. The Global Perspective describes Pepsi's problems with using comparative advertising in Japan.

Offsetting Competitors' Advertising

When marketers advertise to offset or lessen the effects of a competitor's promotional program, they are using **defensive advertising**. Although defensive advertising does not necessarily increase a company's sales or market share, it may prevent a loss in sales or market share. For example, to combat the advertising efforts for AT&T's Universal credit card, Sears advertised its Discover card, heavily, with emphasis on its "no annual fee" feature, a feature that was also heavily promoted in the Universal card advertisement.[5] Defensive advertising is used most often by firms in extremely competitive consumer product markets, such as the fast-food industry.

Figure 16.2

Stimulating Primary Demand

American Floral Marketing Council attempts to stimulate primary demand for flowers.

Source: Poster courtesy of the American Floral Marketing Council © 1989 AFMC.

Figure 16.3

Using Comparative Advertising

This comparative advertisement for Fresh Start Laundry Detergent is based on the findings of one particular test.

Source: Courtesy of Colgate-Palmolive Company.

Making Salespersons More Effective

Business organizations that stress personal selling often use advertising to improve the effectiveness of sales personnel. Advertising created specifically to support personal selling activities tries to presell a product to buyers by informing them about its uses, features, and benefits and by encouraging them to contact local dealers or sales representatives. This form of advertising helps salespeople find good sales prospects. Advertising is often designed to support personal selling efforts for business-to-business products, insurance, and consumer durables, such as automobiles and major household appliances. For example, advertising may bring a prospective buyer to a showroom, but usually a salesperson plays a key role in closing the sale.

Increasing the Uses of a Product

The absolute demand for any product is limited because people in a market will consume only so much of it. Given both this limit on demand and competitive conditions, marketers can increase sales of a specific product in a defined geographic market only to a certain point. To improve sales beyond this point, they must either enlarge the geographic market and sell to more people or develop and promote a larger number of uses for the product. If a firm's advertising convinces buyers to use its products in more ways, then the sales of the products go up. When promoting new uses, an advertiser attempts to increase the demand for its own brand without driving up the demand for competing brands.

Japanese Pepsi Ad Dares to Compare

"VISION 2000" IS THE NAME of PepsiCo International's plan to double sales outside of the United States. Several years ago, the company spent $128 million on international advertising, most of it on its snack food division. Now its energy and dollars will go behind the Pepsi soft-drink brand.

Of all the locations targeted for international growth, PepsiCo executives consider Japan the top priority. With an aggressive new advertising campaign, the firm hopes to double its share of the $18.5 billion Japanese soft-drink market. Until now, Pepsi's efforts have been less than exciting. Its uninspiring advertising slogan has been "Pepsi Loves You." In a television commercial showing Japanese consumers taking the "Pepsi Challenge"—comparing the taste of Coke and Pepsi—Japanese networks made Pepsi cover up Coke's name, diminishing the advertisement's impact. Recently, however, Japan's Fair Trade Commission eased restrictions against comparative advertising.

Taking advantage of regulatory changes, Pepsi aired a spot flaunting the comparison between Coke and Pepsi. The commercial features popular rap singer M.C. Hammer drinking Pepsi between numbers on stage. After switching to Coke, he suddenly starts singing a subdued sentimental song, but when a fan hands him a Pepsi, he resumes his high-energy style. The advertisement was certain to capture attention and stir controversy because it ignored Japanese television's continuing reluctance to air comparative ads. Most Japanese consumers consider it arrogant to compare one product to another in an advertisement, and most Japanese business people believe that openly challenging a competitor is unethical. Pepsi officials, however, maintained that Japanese youth, who make up the majority of Japanese soft-drink consumers, would appreciate the advertisement, especially in light of M.C. Hammer's tremendous popularity in Japan.

PepsiCo executives were gratified by the results of an independent consumer survey showing that Pepsi's sales were up 50 percent during the two months the spot ran on Japan's five major commercial television stations. Celebrations, however, were short-lived. When Pepsi requested to continue the advertisements, Japanese television stations said no. The firm filed a complaint with Japan's Fair Trade Commission, charging that rival Coca-Cola pressured major television stations into dropping the controversial advertisements. Coca-Cola concedes that it notified key television stations that Pepsi's use of the Coca-Cola trademark in commercials was unauthorized and that the advertisements tarnished Coke's image.

The future of Pepsi's comparative advertisement is still undecided, but analysts believe that if Pepsi succeeds, other companies will follow suit. Japanese firms have been airing more advertisements that specify their products' advantages, and print advertisements more frequently name competitors and compare prices. However, the Japanese taboo regarding television commercials that put down the competition remains in place; for now, competing brands of laundry detergent, soap, or even soft drinks will probably be labeled Brand X.

Sources: "Pepsi, Coke Spar in Japan over Comparative TV Ad," *Wall Street Journal*, Mar. 8, 1991, p. B6; Yumiko Ono, "Pepsi Challenges Japanese Taboo as It Ribs Coke," *Wall Street Journal*, Mar. 6, 1991, pp. B1, B3; and David Kilburn, "Pepsi's Challenge: Double Japan Share," *Advertising Age*, Dec. 10, 1990, p. 36.

Reminding and Reinforcing Customers

Marketers sometimes employ **reminder advertising** to let consumers know that an established brand is still around and that it has certain uses, characteristics, and benefits. Procter & Gamble, for example, reminds consumers that its Crest toothpaste is still the best one for preventing cavities. **Reinforcement advertising**, on the other hand, tries to assure current users that they have made the right choice and tells them how to get the most satisfaction from the product. AT&T's advertising tells customers that its services are "the right choice." The aim of both reminder and reinforcement advertising is to prevent a loss in sales or market share.

Reducing Sales Fluctuations

The demand for many products varies from month to month because of such factors as climate, holidays, seasons, and customs. A business, however, cannot operate at peak efficiency when sales fluctuate rapidly. Changes in sales volume translate into changes in the production or inventory, personnel, and financial resources required. To the extent that marketers can generate sales during slow periods, they can smooth out the fluctuations. When advertising reduces fluctuations, a manager can use the firm's resources more efficiently.

Advertising is often designed to stimulate sales during sales slumps. For example, advertisements promoting price reductions of lawn-care equipment or air conditioners can increase sales during fall and winter months. On occasion, a business advertises that customers will get better service by coming in on certain days rather than others. During peak sales periods, a marketer may refrain from advertising to prevent overstimulating sales to the point where the firm cannot handle all the demand. For example, coupons for the delivery of pizza are often valid only Monday through Thursday, not Friday through Sunday, which are the peak delivery times.

A firm's use of advertising depends on the firm's objectives, resources, and environmental forces. The degree to which advertising accomplishes the marketer's goals depends in large part on the advertising campaign.

Developing an Advertising Campaign

An **advertising campaign** involves designing a series of advertisements and placing them in various advertising media to reach a particular target market. As Figure 16.4 indicates, the major steps in creating an advertising campaign are (1) identifying and analyzing the advertising target, (2) defining the advertising objectives, (3) creating the advertising platform, (4) determining the advertising appropriation, (5) developing the media plan, (6) creating the advertising message, (7) executing the campaign, and (8) evaluating the effectiveness of the advertising. The number of steps and the exact order in which they are carried out may vary according to an organization's resources, the nature of its product, and the types of target markets or audiences to be reached. These general guidelines for developing an advertising campaign are appropriate for all types of organizations.

Identifying and Analyzing the Advertising Target

The **advertising target** is the group of people at which advertisements are aimed. For example, advertisements for Barbie cereal are targeted toward young girls who play with Barbie dolls, whereas the advertising target for Special K cereal is health-conscious adults. Identifying and analyzing the advertising target are critical processes; the information they yield helps determine the other steps in developing the campaign. The advertising target often includes everyone in a firm's target market. Marketers may, however, direct a campaign at only a portion of the target market.

Advertisers research and analyze advertising targets to establish an information base for a campaign. Information commonly needed includes the location and geographic distribution of the target group; the distribution of age, income, race, sex, and education; and consumer attitudes regarding the purchase and use of both the advertiser's products and competing products. The exact kinds of information that an organization will find useful depend on the type of product being advertised, the characteristics of the advertising target, and the type and amount of competition. Generally, the more advertisers know about the advertising target, the more likely they are to develop an effective advertising campaign. When the advertising target is not precisely identified and properly analyzed, the campaign may not succeed.

Defining the Advertising Objectives

The advertiser's next step is to consider what the firm hopes to accomplish with the campaign. Because advertising objectives guide campaign development, advertisers should define their objectives carefully. Advertising campaigns based on poorly defined objectives seldom succeed.

Advertising objectives should be stated clearly, precisely, and in measurable terms. Precision and measurability allow advertisers to evaluate advertising success at the end of the campaign, assessing whether or not the objectives have been met. To provide precision and measurability, advertising objectives should contain benchmarks—the current condition or position—and indicate how far

Figure 16.4

General Steps for Developing and Implementing an Advertising Campaign

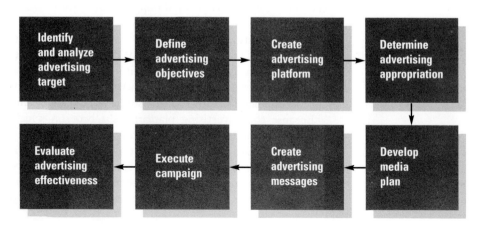

the advertiser wishes to move from these benchmarks. For example, the advertiser should state the current sales level (the benchmark) and the amount of sales increase that is sought through advertising. An advertising objective also should specify a time frame, so that advertisers know exactly how long they have to accomplish the objective. Thus an advertiser with average monthly sales of $450,000 (the benchmark) might set the following objective: "Our primary advertising objective is to increase average monthly sales from $450,000 to $540,000 within twelve months." This also tells the advertiser when evaluation of the campaign should begin.

If an advertiser defines objectives based on sales, the objectives focus on raising absolute dollar sales, increasing sales by a certain percentage, or increasing the firm's market share. Even though an advertiser's long-run goal is to increase sales, not all campaigns are designed to produce immediate sales. Some campaigns are designed to increase product or brand awareness, make consumers' attitudes more favorable, or increase consumers' knowledge of a product's features. These objectives are stated in terms of communication. For example, when Apple Computer introduced home computers, its initial campaign did not focus on sales but on creating brand awareness and educating consumers about the features and uses of home computers. A specific communication objective might be to increase product feature awareness from 0 to 40 percent in the target market by the end of six months.

Creating the Advertising Platform

Before launching a political campaign, party leaders develop a political platform, which states the major issues that will be the basis of the campaign. Like a political platform, an **advertising platform** consists of the basic issues or selling points that an advertiser wishes to include in the advertising campaign. A single advertisement in an advertising campaign may contain one or several issues in the platform. Although the platform sets forth the basic issues, it does not indicate how they should be presented.

A marketer's advertising platform should consist of issues that are important to consumers. One of the best ways to determine what those issues are is to survey consumers about what they consider most important in the selection and use of the product involved. The selling features must not only be important to consumers; if possible, they should also be features that competitive products do not have.

Although research is the most effective method for determining the issues of an advertising platform, it is expensive. As a result, the advertising platform is most commonly based on the opinions of personnel within the firm and of individuals in the advertising agency, if an agency is used. This trial-and-error approach generally leads to some successes and some failures.

Because the advertising platform is a base on which to build the message, marketers should analyze this stage carefully. A campaign can be perfect as to the selection and analysis of its advertising target, the statement of its objectives, its media strategy, and the form of its message. But the campaign will still fail if the advertisements communicate information that consumers do not consider important when they select and use the product.

Rank	Company	Advertising Expenditures	Sales	Advertising Expenditures as Percent of Sales
1	Procter & Gamble	$2284.5	$15,276	15.0
2	Phillip Morris	2210.2	36,014	6.1
3	Sears, Roebuck	1507.1	55,972	2.7
4	General Motors	1502.8	86,967	1.7
5	Grand Metropolitan	882.6	8,025	11.0
6	PepsiCo	849.1	14,047	6.0
7	AT&T	796.5	37,285	2.1
8	McDonald's	764.1	3,871	19.7
9	K mart	693.2	32,070	2.2
10	Time Warner	676.9	8,550	7.9
11	Eastman Kodak	664.8	20,229	3.3
12	Johnson & Johnson	653.7	5,427	12.0
13	RJR Nabisco	636.1	12,125	5.2
14	Nestlé	635.9	36,511	1.7
15	Warner-Lambert	630.8	2,445	25.8
16	Ford	616.0	56,902	1.1
17	Toyota	580.7	71,400	0.8
18	Kellogg	577.7	3,044	19.0
19	Unilever	568.9	8,680	6.6
20	General Mills	539.0	6,377	8.5
21	Chrysler	528.4	26,887	2.0
22	Anheuser-Busch	459.2	11,612	4.0
23	Walt Disney	435.7	5,844	7.5
24	Bristol-Myers Squibb	428.7	7,017	6.1
25	American Home Products	415.4	4,608	9.0

Source: Adapted with permission from "100 Leading National Advertisers with U.S. Sales," *Advertising Age*, Sept. 25, 1991, pp. 2–71. Reprinted with permission from *Advertising Age*, Sept. 25, 1991. Copyright Crain Communications Inc. All rights reserved.

Table 16.2   **Sales Volume and Advertising Expenditures for the Top Twenty-five U.S. Advertisers (in millions of dollars)**

Determining the Advertising Appropriation

The **advertising appropriation** is the total amount of money that a marketer allocates for advertising for a specific time period. It is difficult to decide how much to spend on advertising for a specific period of time because there is no way to measure what the precise effects will be.

Many factors affect a firm's decision about how much to appropriate for advertising. The geographic size of the market and the distribution of buyers within the market have a great bearing on this decision. As Table 16.2 shows, both the type of product advertised and a firm's sales volume relative to competitors' sales volumes also play a part in determining what proportion of a firm's revenue is spent on advertising. Advertising appropriations for business-to-business products are usually quite small relative to the sales of the products, whereas consumer convenience items, such as soft drinks, soaps, and cosmetics, generally have large appropriations.

Of the many techniques used to determine the advertising appropriation, one of the most logical is the **objective-and-task approach**. Using this approach, marketers initially determine the objectives that a campaign is to achieve and then attempt to list the tasks required to accomplish them. The costs of the tasks are then calculated and added to arrive at the amount of the total appropriation. This approach has one main problem: marketers sometimes find it hard to accurately estimate the level of effort needed to achieve certain objectives. A coffee marketer, for example, might find it extremely difficult to determine how much to increase national television advertising to raise a brand's market share from 8 to 12 percent.

In the more widely used **percent-of-sales approach**, marketers simply multiply a firm's past sales, plus a factor for planned sales growth or declines, by a standard percentage that is based on both what the firm traditionally spends on advertising and what the industry averages. This approach has one major flaw: it is based on the incorrect assumption that sales create advertising, rather than the reverse. Consequently, a marketer using the approach at a time of declining sales will reduce the amount spent on advertising. But such a reduction may further diminish sales. Though illogical, this technique has gained wide acceptance because it is easy to use and less disruptive competitively; it stabilizes a firm's market share within an industry. However, in times of declining sales, the fact remains that many firms do increase the percentage of their contribution to advertising in the hope of reversing the decline.

Table 16.3

Total Advertising Expenditures (in millions of dollars)

	1970	1975	1980	1985	1990
Newspapers	$ 5,704	$ 8,234	$14,794	$25,170	$ 32,281
Magazines	1,292	1,539	3,279	5,341	6,803
Television	3,596	5,263	11,366	20,738	28,405
Radio	1,308	1,980	3,777	6,490	8,726
Outdoor	234	335	600	945	1,084
Direct mail	2,766	4,124	7,596	15,500	23,370
Business press	740	919	1,674	2,375	2,875
Miscellaneous	3,910	5,558	10,767	18,159	25,096
Total	$19,550	$27,952	$53,853	$94,718	$128,640

Source: DDB Needham, *Worldwide Media Trends*, 1987 Edition and Robert J. Coen, "Coen: Little Ad Growth," *Advertising Age*, May 6, 1991, pp. 1, 16.

Another way to determine the advertising appropriation is the **competition-matching approach**. Marketers who follow this approach try to match their major competitors' appropriations in terms of absolute dollars or to allocate the same percentage of sales for advertising as their competitors do. Although a wise marketer should be aware of what competitors spend on advertising, this technique should not be used by itself because a firm's competitors probably have different advertising objectives and different resources available for advertising. Many companies and advertising agencies engage in quarterly competitive spending reviews, comparing competitors' dollar expenditures in print, radio, and television with their own spending levels. Competitive tracking of this nature occurs at both the national and regional levels.

At times, marketers use the **arbitrary approach**: a high-level executive in the firm states how much can be spent on advertising for a certain time period. The arbitrary approach often leads to underspending or overspending. Although hardly a scientific budgeting technique, it is expedient.

Establishing the advertising appropriation is critically important. If it is set too low, the campaign cannot achieve its full potential for stimulating demand. When too much money is appropriated for advertising, overspending results, and financial resources are wasted.

Developing the Media Plan

As Table 16.3 shows, advertisers spend tremendous amounts of money on advertising media. These amounts have grown rapidly during the past two decades. To derive the maximum results from media expenditures, a marketer must develop an effective media plan. A **media plan** sets forth the exact media vehicles to be used (specific magazines, television stations, newspapers, and so forth) and the dates and times that the advertisements will appear. The effectiveness of the plan determines how many people in the advertising target will be exposed to the message. It also determines, to some degree, the effects of the message on those individuals. Media planning is a complex task that requires thorough analysis of the advertising target.

To formulate a media plan, the planner selects the media for a campaign and prepares a time schedule for each medium. The media planner's primary goal is to reach the largest number of persons in the advertising target per dollar spent on media. In addition, a secondary goal is to achieve the appropriate message reach and frequency for the target audience while staying within the budget. *Reach* refers to the percentage of consumers in the advertising target actually exposed to a particular advertisement in a stated time period. *Frequency* is the number of times these targeted consumers were exposed to the advertisement.

Media planners begin with rather broad decisions; eventually, however, they must make very specific choices. A planner must first decide which major kinds of media to use: radio, television, newspapers, magazines, direct mail, outdoor displays, mass transit vehicles, or a combination of two or more of these. After making the general media decision, the planner selects specific subclasses within each medium.

Media planners take many factors into account as they devise a media plan. They analyze the location and demographic characteristics of people in the advertising target because the various media appeal to particular demographic

Figure 16.5

Black and White Advertisement Compared to Color Advertisement

This example highlights the importance of using color in advertisements for certain types of products, such as food.

Source: Courtesy of the Dial Corporation.

groups in particular locations. For example, there are radio stations especially for teenagers, magazines for men in the 18 to 34 age group, and television programs aimed at adults of both sexes. Media planners also should consider the sizes and types of audiences specific media reach. Several data services collect and periodically publish information about the circulations and audiences of various media.

The content of the message sometimes affects the choice of media. Print media can be used more effectively than broadcast media to present many issues or numerous details in single advertisements. If an advertiser wants to promote beautiful colors, patterns, or textures, media that offer high-quality color reproduction—magazines or television—should be used instead of newspapers. For example, food can be effectively promoted in a full-color magazine advertisement, but the ad would be far less effective in black and white. Compare the black and white and color versions of the advertisement in Figure 16.5.

The cost of media is an important but troublesome consideration. Planners try to obtain the best coverage possible for each dollar spent, yet there is no accurate way of comparing the cost and impact of a television commercial with the cost and impact of a newspaper advertisement. A **cost comparison indicator** lets an advertiser compare the costs of several vehicles within a specific medium (such as two magazines) in relation to the number of persons reached by each vehicle. For example, the "cost per thousand" (CPM) is the cost comparison indicator for magazines; it shows the cost of exposing a thousand persons to a one-page advertisement.

Table 16.3 shows that the extent to which each medium is used varies quite a bit and that the pattern of use has changed over the years. For example, the proportion of total media dollars spent on magazines has declined since 1970, whereas that spent on television advertising has increased. The media selected are determined by weighing the various characteristics, advantages, and disadvantages of each (see Table 16.4).

Table 16.4 Characteristics, Advantages, and Disadvantages of Major Advertising Media

Medium	Types	Unit of Sale	Factors Affecting Rates	Cost Comparison Indicator	Advantages	Disadvantages
Newspaper	Morning Evening Sunday Sunday supplement Weekly Special	Agate lines Column inches Counted words Printed lines	Volume and frequency discounts Number of colors Position charges for preferred and guaranteed positions Circulation level	Milline rate = cost per agate line × 1,000,000 divided by circulation	Reaches large audience; purchased to be read; national geographic flexibility; short lead time; frequent publication; favorable for co-operative advertising; merchandising services	Not selective for socioeconomic groups; short life; limited reproduction capabilities; large advertising volume limits exposure to any one advertisement
Magazine	Consumer Farm Business	Pages Partial pages Column inches	Circulation level Cost of publishing Type of audience Volume discounts Frequency discounts Size of advertisement Position of advertisement (covers) Number of colors Regional issues	Cost per thousand (CPM) = cost per page × 1,000 divided by circulation	Socioeconomic selectivity; good reproduction; long life; prestige; geographic selectivity when regional issues are available; read in leisurely manner	High absolute dollar cost; long lead time

Table 16.4 (Continued)

Direct mail	Letters Catalogs Price lists Calendars Brochures Coupons Circulars Newsletters Postcards Booklets Broadsides Samplers	Not applicable	Cost of mailing lists Postage Production costs	Cost per contact	Little wasted circulation; highly selective; circulation controlled by advertiser; few distractions; personal; stimulates actions; use of novelty; relatively easy to measure performance; hidden from competitors	Expensive; no editorial matter to attract readers; considered junk mail by many; criticized as invasion of privacy
Radio	AM FM	Programs: sole sponsor, cosponsor, participative sponsor Spots: 5, 10, 20, 30, 60 seconds	Time of day Audience size Length of spot or program Volume and frequency discounts	Cost per thousand (CPM) = cost per minute × 1,000 divided by audience size	Highly mobile; low-cost broadcast medium; message can be quickly changed; reaches large audience; geographic selectivity; socioeconomic selectivity	Provides only audio message; has lost prestige; short life of message; listeners' attention limited because of other activities while listening
Television	Network Local CATV	Programs: sole sponsor, cosponsor, participative sponsor Spots: 5, 10, 15, 30, 60 seconds	Time of day Length of program Length of spot Volume and frequency discounts Audience size	Cost per thousand (CPM) = cost per minute × 1,000 divided by audience size	Reaches large audience; low cost per exposure; uses audio and video; highly visible; high prestige; geographic and socioeconomic selectivity	High dollar costs; highly perishable message; size of audience not guaranteed; amount of prime time limited

Table 16.4 (Continued)

Medium	Types	Unit of Sale	Factors Affecting Rates	Cost Comparison Indicator	Advantages	Disadvantages
Inside transit	Buses Subways	Full, half, and quarter showings are sold on a monthly basis	Number of riders Multiple-month discounts Production costs Position	Cost per thousand riders	Low cost; "captive" audience; geographic selectivity	Does not reach many professional persons; does not secure quick results
Outside transit	Buses Taxicabs	Full, half, and quarter showings; space also rented on per-unit basis	Number of advertisements Position Size	Cost per thousand exposures	Low cost; geographic selectivity; reaches broad, diverse audience	Lacks socioeconomic selectivity; does not have high impact on readers
Outdoor	Papered posters Painted displays Spectaculars	Papered posters: sold on monthly basis in multiples called "showings" Painted displays and spectaculars: sold on per-unit basis	Length of time purchased Land rental Cost of production Intensity of traffic Frequency and continuity discounts Location	No standard indicator	Allows for repetition; low cost; message can be placed close to point of sale; geographic selectivity; operable 24 hours a day	Message must be short and simple; no socioeconomic selectivity; seldom attracts readers' full attention; criticized as traffic hazard and blight on countryside

Sources: Adapted table from *Advertising: Its Role in Modern Marketing*, Seventh Edition by S. Watson Dunn and Arnold M. Barban, copyright © 1990 by the Dryden Press, reprinted by permission of the publisher; and Anthony F. McGann and J. Thomas Russell, *Advertising Media* (Homewood, Ill.: Irwin, 1981).

Creating the Advertising Message

The basic content and form of an advertising message are a function of several factors. The product's features, uses, and benefits affect the content of the message. Characteristics of the people in the advertising target—their sex, age, education, race, income, occupation, and other attributes—influence both the content and form. When Procter & Gamble promotes its Crest toothpaste to children, the company emphasizes the importance of daily brushing and cavity control. When Crest is marketed to adults, tartar and plaque are discussed. To communicate effectively, an advertiser must use words, symbols, and illustrations that are meaningful, familiar, and attractive to the people who constitute the advertising target.

The objectives and platform of an advertising campaign also affect the content and form of its messages. For example, if a firm's advertising objectives involve large sales increases, the message demands hard-hitting, high-impact language and symbols. When campaign objectives aim at increasing brand awareness, the message may use much repetition of the brand name and words and illustrations associated with it. Thus, the advertising platform is the foundation on which campaign messages are built.

The choice of media obviously influences the content and form of the message. Effective outdoor displays and short broadcast spot announcements require concise, simple messages. Magazine and newspaper advertisements can include much detail and long explanations. Because several different kinds of media offer geographic selectivity, a precise message content can be tailored to a particular

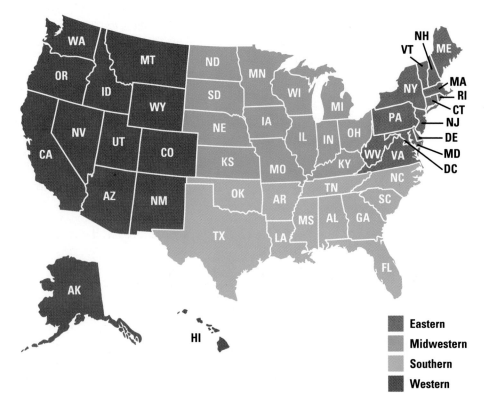

Figure 16.6

Geographic Divisions for *Sports Illustrated* Regional Issues

Source: *Sports Illustrated*.

Figure 16.7

Components of a Print Advertisement

This advertisement, for 3M's Thinsulate Insulation, clearly differentiates the basic components of print advertising.

Source: Photo from 3M Insulation and Specialty Fabrics.

geographic section of the advertising target. Some magazine publishers produce **regional issues,** in which, for a particular issue, the advertisements and editorial content of copies appearing in one geographic area differ from those appearing in other areas. As Figure 16.6 shows, *Sports Illustrated* publishes four regional issues. A clothing manufacturer that advertises in *Sports Illustrated* might decide to use one message in the western region and another in the rest of the nation. A company may also choose to advertise in only one region. Such geographic selectivity lets a firm use the same message in different regions at different times.

The basic components of a print advertising message are shown in Figure 16.7. The messages for most advertisements depend on the use of copy and artwork. Let us examine these two elements in more detail.

Copy **Copy** is the verbal portion of an advertisement. It includes headlines, subheadlines, body copy, and the signature (see Figure 16.7). When preparing advertising copy, marketers attempt to move readers through a persuasive sequence called AIDA: attention, interest, desire, and action. Not all copy need be this extensive, however.

The headline is critical because often it is the only part of the copy that people read. It should attract readers' attention and create enough interest to make them want to read the body copy. The subheadline, if there is one, links the headline to the body copy. Sometimes it helps explain the headline.

Body copy for most advertisements consists of an introductory statement or paragraph, several explanatory paragraphs, and a closing paragraph. Some copywriters have adopted a pattern or set of guidelines to develop body copy systematically: (1) identify a specific desire or problem, (2) recommend the product as

Volvo's Controversial Advertising

TWENTY YEARS AGO, the U.S. Supreme Court ruled that demonstration advertisements could not contain "any form of mock-ups or deception." Leading to the ruling were two Federal Trade Commission investigations of national advertisers whose product demonstrations were judged to be misrepresentative. One case was against Campbell Soup Company for putting marbles in soup bowls to make the vegetables rise to the top. The other was against the Colgate-Palmolive Company for a commercial presumably demonstrating how quickly Rapid Shave could deliver a smooth shave to a piece of sandpaper; what television viewers didn't know was that the "sandpaper" was really plexiglas. The Texas attorney general's recent discovery that Volvo produced and released a deceptive advertisement brings to mind these past debacles.

The controversial Volvo advertisement depicts a giant "monster" truck named Bear Foot rolling over the tops of several different cars, crushing all but the Volvo. It aired primarily on cable networks like ESPN and CNN, and a photo of the unscathed Volvo with the caption, "Can you spot the Volvo?" appeared as an advertisement in *Time, Newsweek, Sports Illustrated, Forbes,* and *Fortune.* Claiming to be footage of an actual event, the advertisement was really staged. The production company, Perretti Productions, hired four hundred spectators and altered the cars to weaken the competition and strengthen the Volvo 240 station wagon. The first attempt to film the scene resulted in a crushed Volvo. Hoping for success the next time, workers cut the roof supports on competing cars and put a steel reinforcement inside the Volvo station wagon. To the company's dismay, angry spectators recognized the trickery and reported it to the attorney general's office, prompting a state probe.

Investigators concluded that Volvo deceived consumers and ordered the company to remove the advertisement, issue a corrective one, and reimburse the state of Texas for over $300,000 it spent on the investigation. Volvo's president published a letter in nineteen Texas newspapers, *USA Today,* and the *Wall Street Journal* acknowledging that his company "inaccurately characterized the event as a car-crushing exhibition when in fact it was a dramatization of the actual event." But fallout from the affair continued. The Federal Trade Commission launched a probe (including an examination of four older Volvo "stacking" advertisements); Volvo conducted its own internal investigation; Scali, McCabe, Slover, Volvo's advertising agency since 1967, resigned its $40 million account; and network executives are expressing concern that consumer trust has been jeopardized.

Since 1956, when Volvo entered the U.S. automobile market, all of its advertisements have emphasized safety, reliability, and longevity. Trust is the cornerstone of Volvo's popularity, captured in its slogan, "A car you can believe in." But in light of recent events, is Volvo still a company consumers will believe in? Doubts may arise about the authenticity of previous commercials, such as the one in which several cars and a truck stacked on top of a Volvo do not crush it. Nationwide, Volvo's sales dropped 11.3 percent in the first ten months after the story broke but the company has no current plans to change its emphasis on safety. Accelerating production of new advertisements with a safety theme, Volvo will let consumers be the judge.

Sources: "As Volvo Sales Slide, Do Ads Share Blame?" *Wall Street Journal,* Dec. 3, 1990, p. B1; Raymond Serafin and Jennifer Lawrence, "Four More Volvo Ads Scrutinized," *Advertising Age,* Nov. 26, 1990, p. 3; "Taking 'Em for a Ride," *Time,* Nov. 19, 1990, p. 85; Stuart Elliot, "Ad Agency Quits over Volvo Ad," *USA Today,* Nov. 14, 1990, p. 1; Joann A. Lublin, "WPP's Scali Gives Up the Volvo Account," *Wall Street Journal,* Nov. 14, 1990, p. B6; David Kiley, "Candid Camera: Volvo and the Art of Deception," *Adweek's Marketing Week,* Nov. 12, 1990, pp. 4–5; Raymond Serafin and Gary Levin, "Ad Industry Suffers Crushing Blow," *Advertising Age,* Nov. 12, 1990, pp. 1, 76–77; Krystal Miller, "Such an Ad Was Almost Certain to Make Somebody Hit the Roof," *Wall Street Journal,* Nov. 8, 1990, p. B1; and "Volvo Settles with Texas," *Wall Street Journal,* Nov. 6, 1990, p. B10.

the best way to satisfy that desire or solve that problem, (3) state the advantages and benefits of the product and indicate why the product is the best for the buyer's particular situation, (4) substantiate the advertising claims, and (5) ask the buyer for action. When substantiating claims, it is important to present the substantiation in a credible manner. Clearly, the proof of claims should strengthen product and company integrity. Inside Marketing presents an example in which both product and organizational integrity were damaged.

The signature identifies the sponsor of the advertisement. It may contain several elements, including the firm's trademark, logo, name, and address. The signature should be designed to be attractive, legible, distinctive, and easy to identify in a variety of sizes.

Because radio listeners often are not fully "tuned in" mentally, radio copy should be informal and conversational to attract listeners' attention, resulting in greater impact. The radio message is highly perishable. Thus radio copy should consist of short, familiar terms. Its length should not require a rate of speech exceeding approximately two and one-half words per second.

In television copy, the audio material must not overpower the visual material and vice versa. However, a television message should make optimal use of its visual portion. As Figure 16.8 illustrates, copy for a television commercial is initially written in parallel script form. The video is described in the left column and the audio in the right column. When the parallel script is approved, the copywriter and artist combine the copy with the visual material through use of a **storyboard** (see Figure 16.9), which depicts a series of miniature television screens to show the sequence of major scenes in the commercial. Beneath each screen is a description of the audio portion that is to be used with the video message shown. Technical personnel use the storyboard as a blueprint when they produce the commercial.

Artwork   **Artwork** consists of the illustration and layout of the advertisement (see Figure 16.7). Although **illustrations** are often photographs, they can also be drawings, graphs, charts, and tables. Illustrations are used to attract attention, to encourage the audience to read or listen to the copy, to communicate an idea quickly, or to communicate an idea that is difficult to put into words.[6] They are especially important because consumers tend to recall the visual portion of advertisements better than the verbal portions. Advertisers use a variety of illustration techniques, which are identified and described in Table 16.5.

The **layout** of an advertisement is the physical arrangement of the illustration, headline, subheadline, body copy, and signature. The arrangement of these parts in Figure 16.7 is only one possible layout. These same elements could be arranged in many ways. The final layout is the result of several stages of layout preparation. As it moves through these stages, the layout helps people involved in developing the advertising campaign exchange ideas. It also provides instructions for production personnel.

Executing the Campaign

The execution of an advertising campaign requires an extensive amount of planning and coordination. Regardless of whether an organization uses an advertising agency, many people and firms are involved in the execution of a

Figure 16.8

Example of a Parallel Script

In a parallel script, the audio and video components of a television commercial are depicted.

```
Philips Lighting Company
200 Franklin Square Drive
P.O. Box 6800
Somerset, NJ  08875-6800

TITLE:  "SO ATTRACTIVE" -- PASTELS :15


        VISUAL                          AUDIO

Man on couch.  Woman walks     |  OLD MAN:  My wife put
behind him with Pastel bulbs.  |
Room is lit but lamp behind    |  Philips Softone Pastel
couch is not.                  |
                               |  light bulbs all over the
                               |
                               |  house.
                               |
                               |
She walks over to lamp,        |  MAN:  She says they make
changes bulb.                  |
                               |  things look more
                               |
                               |  attractive.
She turns on light, turns and  |
looks at him.  Room is now     |
bathed in soft warm glow.      |
                               |
Cut to her point of view of    |  MAN:  I don't know about
guy (same wardrobe, same       |
voice) but he has been         |  that.
transformed into movie star    |
stud.                          |
                               |
                               |
Cut back to her looking at     |  WIFE:  I do.
him.                           |
                               |
All the colors are             |  ANNCR:  New Softone
represented.  Each bulb        |
lights up in sequence from     |  Pastels.  It's time to
left to right.  "Philips"      |
clicks on.                     |  change your bulb to
                               |
                               |  Philips.
                               |
```

campaign. Production companies, research organizations, media firms, printers, photoengravers, and commercial artists are just a few of the people and firms that contribute to a campaign.

Implementation requires detailed schedules to ensure that various phases of the work are done on time. Advertising management personnel must evaluate the quality of the work and take corrective action when necessary. In some instances, changes have to be made during the campaign so that it meets campaign objectives more effectively.

Evaluating the Effectiveness of the Advertising

There are a variety of ways to test the effectiveness of advertising. They include measuring achievement of advertising objectives; assessing the effectiveness of copy, illustrations, or layouts; and evaluating certain media.

Advertising can be evaluated before, during, and after the campaign. Evaluations performed before the campaign begins are called **pretests** and usually attempt to evaluate the effectiveness of one or more elements of the message. To pretest advertisements, marketers sometimes use a **consumer jury**, a number of persons who are actual or potential buyers of the advertised product. Jurors are asked to judge one or several dimensions of two or more advertisements. Such tests are based on the belief that consumers are more likely than advertising experts to know what will influence them.

To measure advertising effectiveness during a campaign, marketers usually take advantage of "inquiries." In the initial stages of a campaign, an advertiser

Figure 16.9

Storyboard

This is a storyboard for a Philips Softone Pastels advertisement.

Source: Courtesy of Philips Lighting.

may use several advertisements simultaneously, each containing a coupon or a form requesting information. The advertiser records the number of coupons that are returned from each type of advertisement. If an advertiser receives 78,528 coupons from advertisement A, 37,072 coupons from advertisement B, and 47,932 coupons from advertisement C, advertisement A is judged superior to advertisements B and C.

Evaluation of advertising effectiveness after the campaign is called a **posttest**. Advertising objectives often indicate what kind of posttest will be appropriate. If an advertiser sets objectives in terms of communication—product awareness, brand awareness, or attitude change—then the posttest should measure changes in one or more of these dimensions. Advertisers sometimes use consumer surveys or experiments to evaluate a campaign based on communication objectives. These methods are costly, however.

For campaign objectives that are stated in terms of sales, advertisers should determine the change in sales or market share that can be attributed to the campaign. Unfortunately, changes in sales or market share brought about by advertising cannot be measured precisely; many factors independent of advertisements affect a firm's sales and market share. Competitive actions, government actions, and changes in economic conditions, consumer preferences, and weather are only a few factors that might enhance or diminish a company's sales or market share. However, by using data about past and current sales and advertising expenditures, an advertiser can make gross estimates of the effects of a campaign on sales or market share.

Because consumer surveys and experiments are so expensive, and because it is difficult to determine the direct effects of advertising on sales, many advertisers

Illustration Technique	Description
Product alone	Simplest method; advantageous when appearance is important, when identification is important, when trying to keep a brand name or package in the public eye, or when selling through mail order
Emphasis on special features	Shows and emphasizes special details or features as well as advantages; used when product is unique because of special features
Product in setting	Shows what can be done with product; people, surroundings, or environment hint at what product can do; often used in food advertisements
Product in use	Puts action into the advertisement; can remind readers of benefits gained from using product; must be careful not to make visual cliché; should not include anything in illustration that will divert attention from product; used to direct readers' eyes toward product
Product being tested	Uses test to dramatize product's uses and benefits versus competing products
Results of product's use	Emphasizes satisfaction from using product; can liven up dull product; useful when nothing new can be said
Dramatizing headline	Appeal of illustration dramatizes headline; can emphasize appeal but dangerous to use illustrations that do not correlate with headlines
Dramatizing situation	Presents problem situation or situation in which problem has been resolved
Comparison	Compares product with "something" established; the something must be positive and familiar to audience
Contrast	Shows difference between two products or two ideas or differences in effects between use and nonuse; before-and-after format is a common technique
Diagrams, charts, and graphs	Used to communicate complex information quickly; may make presentations more interesting
Phantom effects	X-ray or internal view; can see inside products; helpful to explain concealed or internal mechanism
Symbolic	Symbols used to represent abstract ideas that are difficult to illustrate; effective if readers understand symbol; must be positive correlation between symbol and idea
Testimonials	Actually shows the testifier; should use famous person or someone to whom audience can relate

Sources: Dorothy Cohen, *Advertising* (Glenview Ill.: Scott Foresman, 1988), pp. 284–288; and S. Watson Dunn and Arnold M. Barban, *Advertising: Its Role in Modern Marketing*, 7th ed. (Hinsdale, Ill.: Dryden Press, 1990), pp. 307–308.

Table 16.5 **Illustration Techniques for Advertisements**

evaluate print advertisements according to the degree to which consumers can remember them. The posttest methods based on memory include recognition and recall tests. Such tests are usually performed by research organizations through consumer surveys. If a **recognition test** is used, individual respondents are shown the actual advertisement and asked whether they recognize it. If they do, the interviewer asks additional questions to determine how much of the advertisement each respondent read. When recall is evaluated, the respondents are not shown the actual advertisement but instead are asked about what they have seen or heard recently.

Recall can be measured through either unaided or aided recall methods. In an **unaided recall test**, subjects are asked to identify advertisements that they have seen recently but are not shown any clues to help them remember. A similar procedure is used with an **aided recall test**, except that subjects are shown a list of products, brands, company names, or trademarks to jog their memories. Several research organizations, including Daniel Starch and Gallup & Robinson, provide research services that test recognition and recall of advertisements.

The major justification for using recognition and recall methods is that people are more likely to buy a product if they can remember an advertisement about it than if they cannot. However, recalling an advertisement does not necessarily lead to buying the product or brand advertised. Research shows that the more "likable" an advertisement is, the more persuasive it will be with consumers. Compared to those who are neutral toward an advertisement, people who enjoy an advertisement are twice as likely to be convinced that the advertised brand is best.[7] The type of program in which the product is advertised can also affect consumers' feelings about the commercial and the product it promotes. Viewers judge commercials placed in happy programs as more effective and recall them somewhat better.[8]

Researchers are also using a sophisticated technique called single-source data to help evaluate advertisements. With this technique, individuals' behaviors are tracked from television sets to the check-out counter. Monitors are placed in preselected homes, and microcomputers record when the television set is on and which station is being viewed. At the supermarket check-out, the individual in the sample household presents an identification card. The checker records the purchases by scanner, and the data are sent to the research facility. This technique is bringing more insight into people's buying patterns than ever before. Several researchers have found that for selected products in specific markets, increases in advertising expenditures do not generate enough additional sales to warrant the extra advertising expense.[9]

Who Develops the Advertising Campaign?

An advertising campaign may be handled by an individual or a few persons within the firm, an advertising department within the organization, or an advertising agency.

In very small firms, one or two individuals are responsible for advertising (and many other activities as well). Usually these individuals depend heavily on personnel at local newspapers and broadcast stations for copywriting, artwork, and advice about scheduling media.

In certain types of large businesses—especially in larger retail organizations—advertising departments create and implement advertising campaigns. Depending on the size of the advertising program, an advertising department may consist of a few multiskilled persons or a sizable number of specialists, such as copywriters, artists, media buyers, and technical production coordinators. An advertising department sometimes obtains the services of independent research organizations and also hires free-lance specialists when they are needed for a particular project.

When an organization uses an advertising agency, such as Ogilvy & Mather or BBD&O, the firm and the agency usually develop the advertising campaign jointly. How much each party participates in the campaign's total development depends on the working relationship between the firm and the agency. Ordinarily, a firm relies on the agency for copywriting, artwork, technical production, and formulation of the media plan.

An advertising agency can assist a business in several ways. An agency, especially a larger one, supplies the firm with the services of highly skilled specialists—not only copywriters, artists, and production coordinators, but also media experts, researchers, and legal advisers. Agency personnel often have had broad experience in advertising and are usually more objective than a firm's employees about the organization's products.

Because an agency traditionally receives most of its compensation from a 15 percent media commission on media purchases, a firm can obtain some agency services at a low or moderate cost. For example, if an agency contracts for $400,000 of television time for a firm, it receives a commission of $60,000 from the television station. Although the traditional compensation method for agen-

Figure 16.10

Example of a News Release

Mattel Toys issued this information release to publicize a new African-American doll, Jamal, for its Shani line.

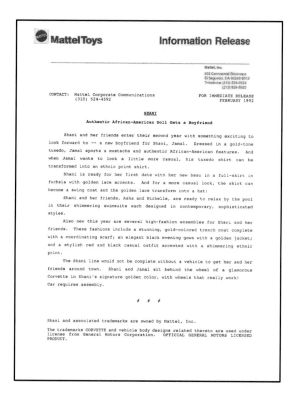

cies is changing and now includes other factors, the media commission still offsets some costs of using an agency.

Now that we have explored advertising as a potential promotion-mix ingredient, let us consider a related ingredient, publicity.

Publicity

As indicated in Chapter 15, **publicity** is communication in news story form, about an organization, its products, or both, that is transmitted through a mass medium at no charge. Publicity can be presented through a variety of vehicles, several of which we examine in this section.

Within an organization, publicity is sometimes viewed as part of public relations—a larger, more comprehensive communication function. **Public relations** is a broad set of communication activities used to create and maintain favorable relations between the organization and its publics: customers, employees, stockholders, government officials, and society in general. Publicity is the result of various public relations efforts. For example, when Wal-Mart decided to make a special effort to stock environmentally safe products and packaging, its public relations department sent out press releases to various newspapers, magazines, and television contacts, as well as to its suppliers. The result was publicity in the form of magazine articles, newspaper acknowledgments, and television coverage.

Publicity and Advertising Compared

Although publicity and advertising both depend on mass media, they differ in several respects. Advertising messages tend to be informative or persuasive, whereas publicity is primarily informative. Advertisements are sometimes designed to have an immediate impact on sales; publicity messages are more subdued. Publicity releases do not identify sponsors; advertisements do. The sponsor pays for media time or space for advertising, but not for publicity. Communications through publicity are usually included as part of a program or a print story, but advertisements are normally separated from the broadcast programs or editorial portions of print media so that the audience or readers can easily recognize (or ignore) them. Publicity may have greater credibility than advertising among consumers because as a news story it may appear more objective. Finally, a firm can use advertising to repeat the same messages as many times as desired; publicity is generally not subject to repetition.

Kinds of Publicity

There are several types of publicity mechanisms. The most common is the **news release**, which is usually a single page of typewritten copy containing fewer than three hundred words. A news release, sometimes called a press release, also gives the firm's or agency's name, its address and phone number, and the contact person. Automobile companies often use news releases to introduce new products. Figure 16.10 is an example of a news release introducing a new product. A

feature article is a longer manuscript (up to three thousand words) that is usually prepared for a specific publication. A **captioned photograph** is a photograph with a brief description explaining the picture's content. Captioned photographs are especially effective for illustrating a new or improved product with highly visible features.

There are several other kinds of publicity. A **press conference** is a meeting called to announce major news events. Media personnel are invited to a press conference and are usually supplied with written materials and photographs. In addition, letters to the editor and editorials are sometimes prepared and sent to newspapers and magazines. However, newspaper editors frequently allocate space on their editorial pages to local writers and national columnists. Finally, films and tapes may be distributed to broadcast stations in the hope that they will be aired.

A marketer's choice of specific types of publicity depends on considerations that include the type of information being transmitted, the characteristics of the target audience, the receptivity of media personnel, the importance of the item to the public, and the amount of information that needs to be presented. Sometimes a marketer uses a single type of publicity in a promotion mix. In other cases, a marketer may use a variety of publicity mechanisms, with publicity being the primary ingredient in the promotion mix.

Uses of Publicity

Publicity has a number of uses. It can make people aware of a firm's products, brands, or activities; help a company maintain a certain level of positive public visibility; and enhance a particular image, such as innovativeness or progressiveness. Companies also try to overcome negative images through publicity. Some firms seek publicity for a single purpose and others for several purposes. As Table 16.6 shows, publicity releases can tackle a multitude of specific issues.

Requirements of a Publicity Program

For maximum benefit, a firm should create and maintain a systematic, continuous publicity program. A single individual or department—within the organization or from its advertising agency or public relations firm—should be responsible for managing the program.

It is important to establish and maintain good working relationships with media personnel. Often personal contact with editors, reporters, and other news personnel is essential, for without their input a company may find it hard to design its publicity program so as to facilitate the work of media newspeople.

Media personnel reject a great deal of publicity material because it is poorly written or not newsworthy. To maintain an effective publicity program, a firm must strive to avoid these flaws. Guidelines and checklists can aid it in this task.

Finally, a firm has to evaluate its publicity efforts. Usually, the effectiveness of publicity is measured by the number of releases actually published or broadcast. To monitor print media and determine which releases are published and how often, an organization can hire a clipping service—a firm that clips and sends published news releases to client companies. To measure the effectiveness of television publicity, a firm can enclose a card with its publicity releases and

Table 16.6

Possible Issues for Publicity Releases

Changes in marketing personnel	New products
Support of a social cause	Creation of a new slogan
Improved warranties	Research developments
Reports on industry conditions	Company's history and development
New uses for established products	Employment, production, and
Product endorsements	sales records
Winning of quality awards	Award of contracts
Company name changes	Opening of new markets
Interviews with company officials	Improvements in financial position
Improved distribution policies	Opening of an exhibit
International business efforts	History of a brand
Athletic event sponsorship	Winners of company contests
Visits by celebrities	Logo changes
Reports on new discoveries	Speeches of top management
Innovative marketing activities	Merit awards to the organization
Economic forecasts	Anniversary of inventions
Packaging changes	

request that the station record its name and the dates when the news item is broadcast, but station personnel do not always comply. Though some television and radio tracking services do exist, they are extremely costly.

Dealing with Unfavorable Publicity

Up to this point we have discussed publicity as a planned promotion-mix ingredient. However, companies may have to deal with unfavorable publicity regarding an unsafe product, an accident, the actions of a dishonest employee, or some other negative event. For example, when an airline experiences a plane crash, it is faced with a negative situation. Unfavorable publicity from such events can be quick and dramatic. A single negative event that produces unfavorable publicity can wipe out a company's favorable image and destroy positive consumer attitudes that took years to build through promotional efforts. Moreover, the mass media today can disseminate information faster and to larger audiences than ever before, and bad news generally receives much attention in the media. Thus the negative publicity surrounding an unfavorable event now reaches more people.[10] By dealing effectively with a negative situation, an organization can minimize the damage from unfavorable publicity.

To protect an organization's image, it is important to avoid unfavorable publicity or at least to lessen its effects. First and foremost, the organization can directly reduce negative incidents and events through safety programs, inspections, and effective quality control procedures. But because firms obviously cannot eliminate all negative occurrences, they need to establish policies and procedures for the news coverage of such events. These policies should aim at reducing negative impact.

In most cases, organizations should expedite news coverage of negative events rather than try to discourage or block it. Facts are likely to be reported accurately, but if news coverage is discouraged, rumors and misinformation may be passed along. An unfavorable event can easily balloon into a scandal or a tragedy. It can even cause public panic. Openness with the media not only tends to diminish the fallout from negative events, but also fosters a positive relationship with media personnel. Such a relationship is essential if news personnel are to cooperate with a company and broadcast favorable news stories about it.

Limitations in Using Publicity

The use of publicity has several drawbacks. If company messages are to be published or broadcast, media personnel must judge them newsworthy. Consequently, messages must be timely, interesting, and accurate. Many communications simply do not qualify. It may take time and effort to convince media personnel of the news value of publicity releases.

Although marketers usually encourage media personnel to air a publicity release at a certain time, they control neither the content nor the timing of the communication. Media personnel alter the length and content of publicity releases to fit publishers' or broadcasters' requirements and may even delete the parts of the message that the firm deems most important. Furthermore, media personnel use publicity releases in time slots or positions that are most convenient for them; thus the messages often appear at times or in locations that may not reach the firm's target audiences. These limitations can be frustrating. Nevertheless, as you have seen in the earlier portions of this section, properly managed publicity offers an organization substantial benefits.

Summary

Advertising is a paid form of nonpersonal communication that is transmitted to consumers through mass media, such as television, radio, newspapers, magazines, direct mail, mass transit vehicles, and outdoor displays. Both nonbusiness and business organizations use advertising.

Marketers use advertising in many ways. Institutional advertising promotes organizations' images and ideas, as well as political issues and candidates. Product advertising focuses on uses, features, images, and benefits of goods and services. To make people aware of a new or innovative product's existence, uses, and benefits, marketers rely on pioneer advertising in the introductory stage to stimulate primary demand for a general product category. They switch to competitive advertising to boost selective demand by promoting a particular brand's uses, features, and advantages.

Through advertising, a company can sometimes lessen the impact of a competitor's promotional program or make its own sales force more effective. To increase market penetration, an advertiser sometimes focuses a campaign on promoting a greater number of uses for the product. Some advertisements for an established product remind consumers that the product is still around and that it has certain characteristics and uses. Marketers may try to assure users of a particular brand that they are selecting the best brand. Marketers also use advertising to smooth out fluctuations in sales.

Although marketers may vary in how they develop advertising campaigns, they should follow a general pattern. First, they must identify and analyze the advertising target. Second, they should establish what they want the campaign to accomplish by defining the advertising objectives. The third step is creating the advertising platform, which contains the basic issues to be presented in the campaign. Fourth, advertisers must decide how much money to spend on the campaign; they arrive at this decision through the objective-and-task approach, the percent-of-sales approach, the competition-matching approach, or the arbitrary approach. Fifth, they must develop the media plan by selecting and scheduling the media to be used in the campaign. In the sixth stage, advertisers use copy and artwork to create the message. In the seventh stage, the execution of an advertising campaign requires extensive planning and coordination. Finally, advertisers must devise one or more methods for evaluating the effectiveness of the advertisements.

Advertising campaigns can be developed by personnel within the firm or in conjunction with advertising agencies. When a campaign is created by the firm's personnel, it may be developed by only a few people, or it may be the product of an advertising department within the firm. The use of an advertising agency may be advantageous to a firm because an agency can provide highly skilled, objective specialists with broad experience in the advertising field at low to moderate costs to the firm.

Publicity is communication in news story form, regarding an organization, its products, or both, that is transmitted through a mass medium at no charge. Generally, publicity is part of the larger, more comprehensive communication function of public relations. Publicity is mainly informative and usually more subdued than advertising. There are many types of publicity, including news releases, feature articles, captioned photographs, press conferences, editorials, films, and tapes. Marketers can use one or more of these forms to achieve a variety of objectives. To have an effective publicity program, someone—either in the organization or in the firm's agency—must be responsible for creating and maintaining systematic and continuous publicity efforts.

An organization should avoid negative publicity by reducing the number of negative events that result in unfavorable publicity. To diminish the impact of unfavorable publicity, an organization should institute policies and procedures for dealing with news personnel when negative events do occur. Problems that organizations confront when seeking publicity include the reluctance of media personnel to print or air releases and a lack of control over the timing and content of messages.

Important Terms

Advertising
Institutional advertising
Product advertising
Pioneer advertising
Competitive advertising
Comparative advertising
Defensive advertising
Reminder advertising
Reinforcement advertising

Advertising campaign
Advertising target
Advertising platform
Advertising appropriation
Objective-and-task approach
Percent-of-sales approach
Competition-matching approach
Arbitrary approach
Media plan

Cost comparison indicator
Regional issues
Copy
Storyboard
Artwork
Illustrations
Layout
Pretests
Consumer jury
Posttest
Recognition test

Unaided recall test
Aided recall test
Publicity
Public relations
News release
Feature article
Captioned photograph
Press conference

Discussion and Review Questions

1. What is the difference between institutional and product advertising?
2. When should advertising be used to stimulate primary demand? When should advertising be used to stimulate selective demand?
3. What are the major steps in creating an advertising campaign?
4. What is an advertising target? How does a marketer analyze the target audience after it has been identified?
5. Why is it necessary to define advertising objectives?
6. What is an advertising platform, and how is it used?
7. What factors affect the size of an advertising budget? What techniques are used to determine this budget?
8. Describe the steps required in developing a media plan.
9. What is the role of copy in an advertising message?
10. What role does an advertising agency play in developing an advertising campaign?
11. Discuss several ways to posttest the effectiveness of advertising.
12. What is publicity? How does it differ from advertising?
13. How do organizations use publicity? Give several examples of publicity releases that you observed recently in local media.
14. How should an organization handle negative publicity? Identify a recent example of a firm that received negative publicity. Did the firm deal with it effectively?
15. Explain the problems and limitations associated with using publicity. How can some of these limitations be minimized?

Cases

16.1 Nintendo Advertising Targets an Older Market

An anecdote circulating at Nintendo of America relates the story of two advertising executives playing the company's hand-held Game Boy during an airline flight. So the story goes, a businessman on the flight approached and asked what they were doing. The men invited him to join, but he declined, saying that his position as a corporate vice president forbade such frivolous pursuits. The players, however, convinced the businessman to join by revealing that it was all right; they too were vice presidents. Perhaps it was this enlightening real-life event that sparked Nintendo's new $15 million advertising campaign directed at men between the ages of 18 and 40. But it might be an industry report that Nintendo sales are down or experts' belief that the videogame market is nearing saturation that convinced Nintendo's new advertising agency, Foote, Cone, & Belding, to promote the idea that Nintendo isn't just for kids.

Nintendo surpasses all of its competition, owning the largest share of the $3.5 billion videogame business. Part of this astonishing success results from the popularity of its hand-held Game Boy, a videogame with the capability to play many different games on one machine. Action occurs on a two-and-one-half-inch screen possessing digital sound, and there are even headphones for privacy. Citing recent research revealing that 40 percent of Game Boy buyers are over the age of 18, Nintendo's advertising manager insists that this product is completely appropriate for adults.

Previous advertising exclusively targeted young boys, and despite the presence of adults in the commercials, children were always portrayed as the potential consumers—even though Mom and Dad might foot the bill. The new campaign does not entirely abandon children, but one of the new 30-second spots, called "Never Get Old," positions Game Boy as an adult way to have fun. Relying on statistics showing that 60 percent of adult Game Boy consumers are male, the ad portrays three professional men in suits playing with Game Boy at work. An announcer says, "You don't stop playing because you get old, but you could get old if you stop playing." By slowly transforming the background music from classical to electric-guitar rock, advertisers reinforce their theme that playing Game Boy keeps men young. Commercials will air during sports and late-night programming and during prime time on the Fox network. Nintendo executives expect the new ads to increase Game Boy sales to 20 million units, making retail sales about $1 billion. They are also hoping to increase sales of the older Nintendo Entertainment System by targeting this same 18- to 40-year-old male market. The new adult-oriented commercials, scheduled to air soon, will cost the company between $10 million and $15 million for media time.

Realizing that the children's market can be fickle, and that Game Boy's popularity may fade like Cabbage Patch Dolls and Transformers, Nintendo hopes to convince a more stable adult market that its product is not just a "plaything." Toward this end, the company is introducing a new software series called InfoGenius, to be marketed by its licensee, Gametek. Initially, it will consist of five adult-interest cartridges for Game Boy, including French and Spanish translators, a personal organizer, a travel guide, and a spelling checker. Under development as well is a Nintendo Entertainment System network that will allow Nintendo players across the United States to compete via a modem. If the company follows through with tentative plans to expand this system to include banking, shopping, and the stock market, Nintendo may enhance its adult appeal, becoming a serious competitor against on-line information systems such as Prodigy.

Nintendo continues to fight competition in a steadily maturing videogame industry. Advertising executives insist that targeting an older consumer group is not a frightened reaction to a saturated market. They admit, however, that their most important job right now is to preserve their product's edge in the battle for dominance. The current plan of attack is to broaden the scope of its appeal. Nintendo is confident that men with money to spend on trendy upscale technology like car phones and designer electric razors will also be willing to spend money on trendy upscale fun like videogames.[11]

Questions for Discussion

1. What is the purpose of Nintendo's advertising campaign aimed at men?
2. Are the objectives for this campaign based on sales or communication?
3. Is going after the 18- to 40-year-old male segment of the market a sound approach? Evaluate.

16.2   The Energizer Bunny Marches On

"Nothing outlasts the Energizer. They keep going and going . . . ." To effectively communicate the message that its Energizer batteries last a long, long time, the Eveready Battery Co. introduced what has been called one of the most clever advertising campaigns in television history.

In a series of television commercials, the Energizer Bunny's batteries last so long that he escapes from a real advertisement for the batteries and marches through parodied commercials for fictional products such as instant coffee, air freshener, late-night albums by obscure artists, soft drinks, and Chateau Marmoset wine. After several seconds of a seemingly real advertisement for "Chug-a-Cherry Cola," for example, E.B. encounters a young man dancing upside down on the ceiling. In an advertisement for a fictitious phone company, the bunny knocks down the partition dividing two callers, poking fun at long-distance phone advertising. After following the real sixty-second battery commercial for several weeks, the fifteen-second parody spots now air alone, enhancing the surprise effect.

Chiat/Day/Mojo Inc., the campaign's creators, pay attention to the tiniest details in the parodied commercials, even down to a "use only as directed" disclaimer for the fake nasal spray. The ads emphasize that "nothing outlasts the Energizer. They keep going and going and going . . . ," just like E.B. keeps going and going, even into other commercials. The campaign works because of the elements of surprise and humor. The long-lasting message is clearly evident, and the phony spots amuse consumers while standing out from the barrage of television advertising. Company executives say they have received hundreds of positive letters about the campaign, and one Energizer Bunny ad recently won a Clio award for the year's best video spot.

Emboldened by the success of the campaign, E.B. is turning up in surprisingly new places. He marches through advertisements for real products like Purina Cat Chow. (Ralston Purina Co. is the corporate parent for both Eveready and Cat Chow.) In this commercial, E.B. dances along with a woman and her cat to the well-known "chow-chow-chow" step of the Purina Cat Chow campaign. He breaks through a page of full type in print ads running in issues of *Newsweek*,

People, Sports Illustrated, Time, and *U.S. News and World Report.* In his movie debut, appearing in over one thousand theaters across the country, he interrupts a preview parody for a fictitious French film, *Dance with Your Feet.* Right in the middle of a dancer's romantic interlude, in barges E.B. He is even appearing soon on packages of Eveready batteries and in in-store promotions.

One nagging concern for both Eveready and its advertising agency is continuing customer confusion over which brand of battery the bunny commercials promote. In a recent survey by Video Storyboard Tests, Inc., 40 percent of the respondents who remember the bunny think he advertises Duracell batteries, Eveready's number-one competitor. Although some experts are advising the company to spend more time advertising the Energizer name and less on the bunny, Eveready is confident that this is a normal "lag time" before people consistently link the bunny to the battery.

Despite its overwhelming popularity, the campaign's effect on sales is ambiguous. Recent Nielsen figures place Duracell in the number-one spot with 42.1 percent of all alkaline battery sales, and Eveready in second place with 36.7 percent, down slightly from the previous year. Eveready's own internally calculated figures, however, indicate that it is the undisputed market-share leader. In addition, Eveready consumer research shows unaided brand awareness up 33 percent, television commercial awareness up 43 percent, and recall of the product's "long-lasting" message up 49 percent.

Increasing consumer demand from the campaign has forced retailers to respond by moving Energizer battery displays to more prominent spaces in their stores. In fact, E.B. is so popular that an offer for a stuffed E.B. doll (for $14.95 and three proofs of purchase) drew twenty thousand requests in two weeks—a response twenty times larger than a typical mail offer generates. The bunny gained some extra publicity when an imposter E.B. appeared on the "Late Night with David Letterman" show. In a recent Coors Brewing Company commercial, actor Leslie Nielsen dressed in bunny ears, cottontail, and pink bunny feet, marches through an advertisement for light beer while a voice-over announces that Coors Light sales keep on "growing and growing." Although Eveready initiated talks with Coors to try and stop the advertisement from airing, some analysts assert that battery sales will actually benefit from the humor and extra exposure. So far, Ralston Purina has turned down hundreds of offers to license E.B. for sale in retail stores, but the success of California Raisins toys and the Domino's Pizza Noid doll may encourage company executives to do so. Building on E.B.'s popularity with consumers, Eveready's $25 million to $30 million advertising campaign should help to "energize" its battle against competitors in the battery market and increase its percent share of this $3 billion business.[12]

Questions for Discussion

1. Why are the Energizer battery advertisements so successful?
2. What is the advertising platform for the Energizer Bunny campaign?
3. What is the nature of publicity that Eveready gained with the Energizer Bunny campaign? Distinguish between the publicity and the advertising in this campaign.

Chapter Notes

1. Based on information from Brian Dumaine, "Design That Sells and Sells and . . . ," *Fortune*, Mar. 11, 1991, pp. 86–94; "A Blowout in Sneakers," *Time*, Feb. 4, 1991, p. 60; Gary Levin, "New Exec Works to Put Reebok Back on Top," *Advertising Age*, Sept. 10, 1990, p. 72; Barbara Lippert, "Reebok Takes a Breather," *Adweek's Marketing Week*, Aug. 13, 1990, p. 53; Laura Raposa, "Reebok Ads Try to Catch a Nation at Play," *Boston Herald*, July 26, 1990; Frederic M. Biddle, "Reebok, Madonna out of 'Vogue,'" *Boston Globe*, July 16, 1990; Tom Nutile, "Proposed Reebok Ads Play Up Madonna as Quite the Fun-Loving Gal," *Boston Herald*, May 9, 1990; Tom Nutile, "Can Madonna–Reebok Ad Material-ize into Sales?" *Boston Herald*, May 8, 1990; Pat Sloan and Marcy Magiera, "Madonna Nears Reebok Deal," *Advertising Age*, May 7, 1990, pp. 1, 8; Denise Smith, "Shoe Wars," *St. Petersburg (FL) Times*, May 7, 1990; Pat Sloan, "Reebok's Fresh Start," *Advertising Age*, Apr. 23, 1990, p. B1; Anthony E. Heffernan, "Shoe Sales Soar on 'Cool' Looks," *(Lawrenceville, GA) Gwinnett Daily News*, Feb. 11, 1990; and Pat Sloan, "Reebok Chief Looks Beyond Nike," *Advertising Age*, Jan. 29, 1990, pp. 16, 57.

2. Elena Bowes, "Benetton Forges Ahead," *Advertising Age*, Sept. 9, 1991, p. 14.

3. "100 Leading National Advertisers by Rank," *Advertising Age*, Sept. 25, 1991, p. 1.

4. Julia Flynn Siler, "It Isn't Miller Time Yet, and This Bud's Not for You," *Business Week*, June 24, 1991, p. 52.

5. Kate Fitzgerald, "Discover Goes on the Offensive," *Advertising Age*, Apr. 18, 1991, p. 4.

6. S. Watson Dunn and Arnold M. Barban, *Advertising: Its Role in Modern Marketing*, 7th ed. (Hinsdale, Ill.: Dryden Press, 1990), p. 307.

7. Ronald Alsop, "TV Ads That Are Likeable Get Plus Ratings for Persuasiveness," *Wall Street Journal*, Feb. 20, 1986, p. 21.

8. Marvin E. Goldberg and Gerald J. Gorn, "Happy and Sad TV Programs: How They Affect Reactions to Commercials," *Journal of Consumer Research*, December 1987, pp. 387–403.

9. Magid A. Abraham and Leonard M. Lodish, "Getting the Most Out of Advertising and Promotion," *Harvard Business Review*, May–June 1990, pp. 50–60.

10. Marc G. Weinberger and Jean B. Romeo, "The Impact of Negative Product News," *Business Horizons*, January–February 1989, p. 44.

11. Matthew Grimm, "Nintendo's Game Boy Heads into Adulthood," *Adweek's Marketing Week,* Oct. 19, 1990, p. 10; Cleveland Horton, "Nintendo Adopts Dual Strategy," *Advertising Age,* Sept. 10, 1990, p. 40; Thomas R. King, "Nintendo's New Sales Campaign Separates the Men from the Boys," *Wall Street Journal,* Aug. 31, 1990, p. B4; David W. Tice, "More Fund and Games?" *Barron's,* June 18, 1990, pp. 18, 20, 22; "Nintendo Picks Foote, Cone," *Wall Street Journal,* June 18, 1990, p. B5; Cleveland Horton and Kate Fitzgerald, "Nintendo Zaps McCann," *Advertising Age,* June 4, 1990, pp. 1, 53; and Frank Vizard, "Game Boy Versus Lynx," *Popular Mechanics,* June 1990, pp. 32, 103, 105.

12. Ira Teinowitz, "Coors in a (Rabbit) Stew over Parody," *Advertising Age,* Apr. 29, 1991, pp. 1, 50; Julie Liesse, "Bunny Back to Battle Duracell," *Advertising Age,* Sept. 17, 1990, pp. 4, 78; "Eveready's Bunny to Be in the Movies," *Los Angeles Times,* Sept. 11, 1990, p. D6; Joann S. Lublin, "Bunny at the Movies," *Wall Street Journal,* Sept. 11, 1990, p. B6; Joanne Lipman, "Too Many Think the Bunny is Duracell's, Not Eveready's," *Wall Street Journal,* July 31, 1990, pp. B1, B7; Dan Cook, "The Rabbit's Feat," *California Business,* June 1, 1990; Stuart Elliott and Sal Ruibal, "E.B. and Bo Led '89 Dream Team," *USA Today,* Dec. 28, 1989, p. 6B; Stuart Elliott, "He's Back: Energizer Bunny's Beat Goes On," *USA Today,* Dec. 6, 1989, p. 2B; Julie Liesse Erickson, "Energizer Bunny Will Plug Purina," *Advertising Age,* Dec. 4, 1989, pp. 1, 54; Stuart Elliott, "Energizer Ads March to Different Drummer," *USA Today,* Oct. 24, 1989, p. 1B; Julie Liesse Erickson, "Energizer Bunny Gets the Jump," *Advertising Age,* Oct. 23, 1989, p. 4; and Bob Garfield, "Energizer's Parody Campaign Is One Bunny of a Concept," *Advertising Age,* Oct. 23, 1989, p. 120.

17 *Personal Selling and Sales Promotion*

OBJECTIVES

- To understand the major purposes of personal selling

- To learn the basic steps in the personal selling process

- To identify the types of sales force personnel

- To gain insight into sales management decisions and activities

- To become aware of what sales promotion activities are and how they can be used

- To become familiar with specific sales promotion methods used

Anyone walking down the cookie and cracker aisle in almost any U.S. grocery store can't help but notice Nabisco's Oreos, Fig Newtons, Chips Ahoy!, Ritz Crackers, Wheat Thins, and Triscuits. Nabisco Biscuit Company, a subsidiary of RJR Nabisco, definitely has a successful product; it produces eight of the ten top-selling brands in the cookie/cracker category and sells one billion pounds of its products a year. Is this achievement proof that a really good product "sells itself"? Nabisco's 4,000-person sales force says no. They believe their success is the result of extensive training, dedicated service to the customer, and personal commitment to the products and the company—not just a reputation for making delicious cookies. Recently winning *Sales & Marketing Management's* Best Sales Force award confirms that Nabisco's belief in and reliance on its salespeople is well-founded.

Good training prepares Nabisco's people to go into the field and do an excellent job. Nabisco spends about $1 million a year holding thirteen strategy meetings for sales personnel. At these sessions, salespeople learn current sales figures, set new goals together, devise sales and marketing strategies, find out about new products, upcoming promotions and advertising campaigns, and work together to improve their selling skills.

Equipped with exceptional training, sales personnel go out into the field and provide exceptional service. Salespeople set up the cookie/cracker department, picking the best location and putting the products on the shelves themselves. Using the data they carry with them in their laptop computers, sales personnel often share with outlet managers information to help boost store sales.

Nabisco's sales force is able to maintain its high level of enthusiasm in part because of an intense commitment to the company, commitment enhanced by personal input and involvement. Sales representatives communicate with decision makers in the corporate marketing department. Through this communication, sales representatives get the satisfaction of knowing that their suggestions and ideas matter.[1]

Photo courtesy of Nabisco Foods Group.

N ABISCO'S WELL-TRAINED, HIGHLY MOTIVATED, and strongly committed sales force plays a major role in the organization's success. As indicated in Chapter 15, personal selling and sales promotion are two possible ingredients in a promotion mix. Sometimes personal selling is a company's sole promotional tool, although it is generally used in conjunction with other promotion mix ingredients. Personal selling is becoming more professional and sophisticated, with sales personnel acting more as consultants and advisors. Sales promotion, too, plays an increasingly important role in marketing strategies.

This chapter focuses on personal selling and sales promotion. We consider the purposes of personal selling, its basic steps, the types of salespersons, and how they are selected. We also discuss the major sales-force management decisions and activities, including setting objectives for the sales force and determining its size; recruiting, selecting, training, compensating, and motivating salespeople; managing sales territories; and controlling and evaluating sales personnel. We then examine several characteristics of sales promotion, the reasons for using sales promotion, and the sales promotion methods available for use in a promotion mix.

The Nature of Personal Selling

Personal selling is a process of informing customers and persuading them to purchase products through personal communication in an exchange situation. For example, a salesperson describing the benefits of a Kenmore dryer to a customer in a Sears store is using personal selling. Personal selling gives marketers the greatest freedom to adjust a message to satisfy customers' information needs. In comparison with other promotion methods, personal selling is the most precise, enabling marketers to focus on the most promising sales prospects. Other promotion mix ingredients are aimed at groups of people, some of whom may not be prospective customers. A major disadvantage of personal selling is its cost. Generally, it is the most expensive ingredient in the promotion mix. Personal selling costs are increasing faster than advertising costs.

Businesses spend more money on personal selling than on any other promotion mix ingredient. Millions of people, including increasing numbers of women, earn their living through personal selling. A sales career can offer high income, a great deal of freedom, a high level of training, and a high level of job satisfaction. Unfortunately, customers sometimes view personal selling negatively. However, major corporations, professional sales associations, and academic institutions are attempting to change the negative stereotypes of salespeople.

Personal selling goals vary from one firm to another. However, they usually involve finding prospects, convincing prospects to buy, and keeping customers satisfied. Identifying potential buyers who are interested in an organization's products is critical. Because most potential buyers seek information before they make a purchase, salespersons must ascertain prospects' informational needs and then provide the relevant information. To do so, sales personnel must be well trained, both in regard to their products and in regard to the selling process in general.

Salespeople need to be aware of their competitors. They need to monitor new products being developed, and they should be aware of competitors' sales activities in their sales territories. Salespeople must emphasize the advantages their products provide when their competitors' products do not offer that specific advantage. Later in this chapter we discuss this issue in greater detail.

Few businesses survive solely on profits from one-sale customers. For long-run survival, most marketers depend on repeat sales. A company has to keep its customers satisfied to obtain repeat purchases. Besides, satisfied customers help attract new ones by telling potential customers about the organization and its products. Even though the whole organization is responsible for providing customer satisfaction, much of the burden falls on salespeople. The salesperson is almost always closer to customers than anyone else in the company and often provides buyers with information and service after the sale. Such contact not only gives salespeople an opportunity to generate additional sales, but also offers them a good vantage point for evaluating the strengths and weaknesses of the company's products and other marketing mix ingredients. Their observations are helpful in developing and maintaining a marketing mix that better satisfies both customers and the firm.

A salesperson may be involved with achieving one or more of the three general goals. In some organizations, there are persons whose sole job is to find prospects. This information is relayed to salespeople, who contact the prospects. After the sale, these same salespeople may do the follow-up work, or a third group of employees may have the job of maintaining customer satisfaction. In some organizations, such as Amway (see the Global Perspective), salespeople handle all these functions. No matter how many groups are involved, several major sales tasks must be performed to achieve these general goals.

Elements of the Personal Selling Process

The exact activities involved in the selling process vary among salespersons and differ for particular selling situations. No two salespersons use exactly the same selling methods. Nonetheless, many salespersons—either consciously or unconsciously—move through a general selling process as they sell products. This process consists of seven elements, or steps, as outlined in Figure 17.1: prospecting and evaluating, preparing, approaching the customer, making the presentation, overcoming objections, closing, and following up.

Figure 17.1

General Steps in the Personal Selling Process

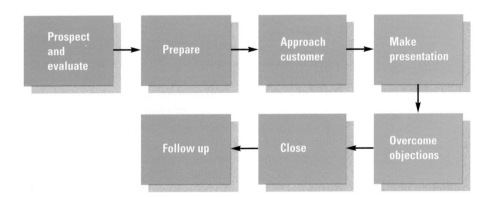

Figure 17.2

Prospecting Assistance

MapInfo aids marketers in the prospecting stage of the personal selling process.

Source: MapInfo Corporation.

Prospecting and Evaluating

Developing a list of potential customers is called **prospecting**. A salesperson seeks the names of prospects from the company's sales records, referrals, trade shows, computer data banks (see Figure 17.2), newspaper announcements (of marriages, births, deaths, and so on), public records, telephone directories, trade association directories, and many other sources. Sales personnel also use responses from advertisements that encourage interested persons to send in an information request form. Seminars and meetings targeted at particular types of clients, such as attorneys or accountants, may also produce good leads.

After developing the prospect list, a salesperson evaluates whether each prospect is able, willing, and authorized to buy the product. On the basis of this evaluation, the prospects are ranked according to their desirability or potential.

Preparing

Before contacting acceptable prospects, a salesperson should find and analyze information about each prospect's specific product needs, current use of brands, feelings about available brands, and personal characteristics. The most successful salespeople are thorough in their preparation. They prepare by identifying key decision makers, reviewing account histories and reports, contacting other clients for information, assessing credit histories and problems, preparing sales presentations, identifying product needs, and obtaining all relevant literature.[2] A salesperson with a lot of information about a prospect is better equipped to develop a presentation that precisely communicates with the prospect.

Amway in Japan: Successful Blend of East and West

ALTHOUGH AMWAY CORPORATION, marketer of home and personal care products, derives its name from "American Way," the firm's success is translating well into Japanese. According to a study conducted by Japan's Ministry of International Trade and Industry, Amway is the seventh-fastest growing company, foreign or domestic, currently operating in Japan. Enjoying unprecedented sales, Amway Japan Ltd. is outperforming giants like IBM, Coca-Cola, and Du Pont. Although the company has been in business in Japan for a relatively short time, sales nearly equal those in the United States, where the firm has been operating for over thirty-one years.

In Japan, working for Amway provides an attractive alternative for more and more young people striving to succeed outside the rigid hierarchy of Japanese big business. Amway is luring those 20- and 30-year-olds who are tired of salary based on seniority rather than on performance and who want to work for themselves. Personal effort reaps personal reward in the form of 30 percent commissions on all product sales plus excellent bonuses for bringing new members to the Amway family. For those reluctant to risk leaving a secure and well-established career, selling Amway part time is an alternative; for women, who have not yet achieved acceptance in much of corporate Japan, selling Amway is another option for earning income.

Where many other American companies have failed, Amway is flourishing, in part because its own corporate style blends well with Japanese traditions. Amway's techniques, which include frequent intense group meetings and pep rallies and urging those who buy Amway products to sell to others, fit well with the Japanese belief that group participation and close personal relationships are intrinsic to good business. In Japanese society, building one's *jinmyaku* (network of human contacts) is very important, making Amway's system of selling products through acquaintances work well. The firm's independent distributors handle customers personally, distributing catalogs, making phone contacts, even conducting sales pitches at the neighborhood coffee shop.

When Amway began operations in Japan, 13 employees offered consumers 9 different products. Today, 450 full-time staff and more than 500,000 distributors (out of 1 million worldwide) market over 150 products. To the surprise of company executives and industry analysts alike, Japanese consumers like to see the "Made in America" prominently displayed on Amway products. What ambitious Japanese salespeople like about Amway is the almost-limitless possibility for success through independent effort.

Sources: Robert Trost, "Japanese Subsidiary of Amway Is Readied for Public Stock Sale," *Grand Rapids (MI) Press,* Apr. 16, 1991; Yumiko Ono, "Amway Translates with Ease into Japanese," *Wall Street Journal,* Sept. 21, 1990, pp. B1, B3; Isao Shinorhara, "Amway (Japan) Achieves a Smashing Success," *Tokyo Business Today,* September 1990, pp. 24–25; Jim Harger, "Amway Aims at $2 Billion by Offering More Products," *Kalamazoo (MI) Gazette,* June 7, 1990; and Ronald E. Yates, "Patience Pays Off for U.S. Firm's Business in Japan," *Washington Post,* Jan. 28, 1990, pp. H1, H9.

Approaching the Customer

The **approach**—the manner in which a salesperson contacts a potential customer—is a critical step in the sales process. In more than 80 percent of initial sales calls, the purpose is to gather information about the buyer's needs and objectives. Creating a favorable impression and building rapport with the prospective client are also important tasks in the approach because the prospect's first impression of the salesperson is usually a lasting one, with long-run consequences. During the initial visit, the salesperson strives to develop a relationship rather than just push a product. The salesperson may have to call on a prospect several times before the product is considered.[3]

One type of approach is based on referrals. The salesperson approaches the prospect and explains that an acquaintance, an associate, or a relative had suggested the call. The salesperson who uses the cold canvass method calls on potential customers without their prior consent. Repeat contact is another common approach; when making the contact, the salesperson mentions a prior meeting. The exact type of approach depends on the salesperson's preferences, the product being sold, the firm's resources, and the characteristics of the prospect.

Making the Presentation

During the sales presentation, the salesperson must attract and hold the prospect's attention to stimulate interest and stir up a desire for the product. The salesperson should have the prospect touch, hold, or actually use the product. If possible, the salesperson should demonstrate the product and get the prospect more involved with it to stimulate greater interest. Audiovisual materials may be used to enhance the presentation, as shown in Figure 17.3.

During the presentation, the salesperson must not only talk but listen. The sales presentation gives the salesperson the greatest opportunity to determine the prospect's specific needs by listening to questions and comments and observing responses. Even though the salesperson has planned the presentation in advance, she or he must be able to adjust the message to meet the prospect's information needs.

Figure 17.3

Enhancing the Sales Presentation

Video equipment helps salespeople show a product's applications, uses, and benefits.

Source: Matsushita Electric Corporation of America.

Overcoming Objections

An effective salesperson usually seeks out a prospect's objections in order to address them. If they are not apparent, the salesperson cannot deal with them, and they may keep the prospect from buying. One of the best ways to overcome a prospect's objections is to anticipate and counter them before the prospect has an opportunity to raise them. However, this approach can be risky because the salesperson may mention some objections that the prospect would not have raised. If possible, the salesperson should handle objections when they arise. They also can be dealt with at the end of the presentation.

Closing

Closing is the element in the selling process whereby the salesperson asks the prospect to buy the product or products. During the presentation, the salesperson may use a "trial close" by asking questions that assume the prospect will buy the product. For example, the salesperson might ask the potential customer about financial terms, desired colors or sizes, delivery arrangements, or the quantity to be purchased. The reactions to such questions usually indicate how close the prospect is to buying. A trial close allows prospects to indicate indirectly that they will buy the product without having to say those sometimes difficult words, "I'll take it."

A salesperson should try to close at several points during the presentation because the prospect may be ready to buy. One closing strategy involves asking the potential customer to place a low-risk tryout order. Often an attempt to close the sale will result in objections. Thus closing can be an important stimulus that uncovers hidden objections, which can then be addressed.

Following Up

After a successful closing, the salesperson must follow up the sale. In the follow-up stage, the salesperson should determine whether the order was delivered on time and installed properly, if installation was required. He or she should contact the customer to learn what problems or questions have arisen regarding the product. The follow-up stage can also be used to determine customers' future product needs.

Types of Salespersons

To develop a sales force, a marketing manager must decide what kind of salesperson will sell the firm's products most effectively. Most business organizations use several different kinds of sales personnel. Based on the functions they perform, salespersons can be classified into three groups: order getters, order takers, and support personnel. One salesperson can, and often does, perform all three functions.

Order Getters

To obtain orders, a salesperson must inform prospects and persuade them to buy the product. The **order getter**'s job is to increase the firm's sales by selling to new customers and by increasing sales to present customers. This task sometimes is called creative selling. It requires that salespeople recognize potential buyers' needs and then give them the necessary information. Order-getting activities sometimes are divided into two categories: current-customer sales and new-business sales.

Current-Customer Sales Sales personnel who concentrate on current customers call on people and organizations that have purchased products from the firm at least once. These salespeople seek more sales from existing customers by following up previous sales. Current customers can also be sources of leads for new prospects.

New-Business Sales Business organizations depend on sales to new customers, at least to some degree. New-business sales personnel locate prospects and convert them to buyers. Salespersons in many industries help to generate new business, but industries that depend in large part on new-customer sales are real estate, insurance, appliances, heavy industrial machinery, and automobiles.

Order Takers

Taking orders is a repetitive task that salespersons perform to perpetuate long-lasting, satisfying relationships with customers. **Order takers** seek repeat sales. One of their major objectives is to be absolutely certain that customers have sufficient product quantities where and when they are needed. Most order takers handle orders for standardized products that are purchased routinely and therefore do not require extensive sales efforts.[4] There are two groups of order takers: inside order takers and field order takers.

Inside Order Takers In many businesses, inside order takers, who work in sales offices, receive orders by mail and telephone. Certain producers, wholesalers, and even retailers have sales personnel who sell from within the firm rather than in the field. That does not mean that inside order takers never communicate with customers face to face. For example, salespersons in retail stores are classified as inside order takers.

Field Order Takers Salespersons who travel to customers are referred to as outside, or field, order takers. Often a customer and a field order taker develop an interdependent relationship. The buyer relies on the salesperson to take orders periodically (and sometimes to deliver them), and the salesperson counts on the buyer to purchase a certain quantity of products periodically. Use of laptop computers can improve the field order taker's tracking of inventory and orders.

Field and inside order takers should not be thought of as passive functionaries who simply record orders in a machinelike manner. Order takers generate the bulk of many organizations' total sales.

Support Personnel

Support personnel facilitate the selling function but usually are not involved solely with making sales. They are engaged primarily in marketing business-to-business products. They locate prospects, educate customers, build goodwill, and provide service after the sale. Although there are many kinds of sales support personnel, the three most common are missionary, trade, and technical.

Missionary Salespersons **Missionary salespersons**, who are usually employed by manufacturers, assist the producer's customers in selling to their own customers. A missionary salesperson may call on retailers to inform and persuade them to buy the manufacturer's products. If the call is successful, the retailers purchase the products from wholesalers, who are the producer's customers. Manufacturers of medical supplies and pharmaceutical products often use missionary salespersons to promote their products to physicians, hospitals, and retail druggists.

Trade Salespersons **Trade salespersons** are not strictly support personnel because they usually perform the order-taking function as well. However, they direct much of their efforts toward helping customers, especially retail stores, promote the product. They are likely to restock shelves, obtain more shelf space, set up displays, provide in-store demonstrations, and distribute samples to store customers. Food producers and processors commonly employ trade salespersons.

Technical Salespersons **Technical salespersons** give technical assistance to the organization's current customers. They advise customers on product characteristics and applications, system designs, and installation procedures. Because this job is often highly technical, the salesperson usually needs to have formal training in one of the physical sciences or in engineering. Technical sales personnel often sell technical business-to-business products, such as computers, heavy equipment, and steel.

When hiring sales personnel, marketers seldom restrict themselves to a single category because most firms require different types. Several factors dictate how many of each type of salesperson a particular company should have. A product's uses, characteristics, complexity, and price influence the kind of sales personnel used, as do the number of customers and their characteristics. The kinds of marketing channels and the intensity and type of advertising also have an impact on the selection of sales personnel.

Management of the Sales Force

The sales force is directly responsible for generating an organization's primary input: sales revenue. Without adequate sales revenue, a business cannot survive long. A firm's reputation is often determined by the ethical conduct of the sales force. On the other hand, the morale, and ultimately the success, of a firm's sales force is determined in large part by adequate compensation, room for advancement, adequate training, and management support, all key areas of sales management. When these elements are not satisfying to salespersons, they may leave for more satisfying jobs. It is important to evaluate the input of salespeople because effective sales-force management determines a firm's success.

In this section we explore eight general areas of sales management: (1) establishing sales-force objectives, (2) determining sales-force size, (3) recruiting and selecting salespeople, (4) training sales personnel, (5) compensating salespeople, (6) motivating salespeople, (7) managing sales territories, and (8) controlling and evaluating sales-force performance.

Establishing Sales-Force Objectives

To manage a sales force effectively, a sales manager must develop sales objectives. Sales objectives tell salespersons what they are expected to accomplish during a specified time period. They give the sales force direction and purpose and serve as performance standards for the evaluation and control of sales personnel. As with all types of objectives, sales objectives should be stated in precise, measurable terms and should specify the time period and the geographic areas involved.

Sales objectives are usually developed for both the total sales force and each salesperson. Objectives for the entire force are normally stated in terms of sales volume, market share, or profit. Volume objectives refer to a quantity of dollars or sales units. For example, the objective for an electric drill producer's sales force might be to sell $10 million worth of drills annually or 600,000 drills annually. When sales goals are stated in terms of market share, they usually call for an increase in the proportion of the firm's sales relative to the total number of products sold by all businesses in that particular industry. When sales objectives are based on profit, they are generally stated in terms of dollar amounts or return on investment.

Sales objectives, or quotas, for individual salespersons are commonly stated in terms of dollar or unit sales volume. Other bases used for individual sales objectives include average order size, average number of calls per time period, and the ratio of orders to calls.

Determining Sales-Force Size

Deciding how many salespersons to use is important because it influences the company's ability to generate sales and profits. Moreover, the size of the sales force affects the compensation methods used, salespersons' morale, and overall sales-force management. Sales-force size must be adjusted from time to time because a firm's marketing plans change, as do markets and forces in the marketing environment. One danger is to cut back the size of the sales force to increase profits. The sales organization could lose its strength and resiliency, preventing it from rebounding when growth rebounds or better market conditions prevail. The organization that loses capacity from cutbacks may not have the energy to accelerate.[5]

There are several analytical methods for determining the optimal size of the sales force. One method involves determining how many sales calls per year are necessary for an organization to effectively serve its customers and then dividing this total by the average number of sales calls that a salesperson makes annually. A second method is based on marginal analysis, whereby additional salespeople are added to the sales force until the costs of an additional salesperson equals the additional sales generated by that person. Although marketing managers may use one or several analytical methods, they normally temper their decisions with a good deal of subjective judgment.

Recruiting and Selecting Salespeople

To create and maintain an effective sales force, a sales manager must recruit the right type of salespeople. **Recruiting** is a process by which the sales manager develops a list of applicants for sales positions. The cost of hiring, training, and retaining a salesperson is soaring; currently, costs can reach $80,000 or more.[6]

To ensure that the recruiting process results in a pool of qualified salespersons from which to hire, a sales manager should establish a set of required qualifications before beginning to recruit. Although for years marketers have attempted to enumerate a set of traits that characterize effective salespeople, there is currently no such set of generally accepted characteristics. Therefore a sales manager must develop a set tailored to the sales tasks in a particular company. Two activities can help establish this set of requirements. The sales manager should prepare a job description that lists the specific tasks salespersons are to perform. The manager also should analyze the characteristics of the firm's successful salespersons, as well as those of ineffective sales personnel. From the job description and the analysis of traits, the sales manager should be able to develop a set of specific requirements and be aware of potential weaknesses that could lead to failure.

A sales manager generally recruits applicants from several sources: departments within the firm, other firms, employment agencies, educational institutions, respondents to advertisements, and individuals recommended by current employees. The specific sources a sales manager uses depend on the type of salesperson required and the manager's experiences with particular sources.

The process of hiring a sales force varies tremendously from one company to another. One technique used to determine whether potential candidates will be good salespeople is an assessment center. Assessment centers are intense training environments that place candidates in realistic problem settings in which they must give priorities to their activities, make decisions, and act on their decisions. Candidates are judged by experienced managers or trained observers. Assessment centers have proven valuable in selecting good salespeople.[7]

Sales management should design a selection procedure that satisfies the company's specific needs. The process should include enough steps to yield the information needed for making accurate selection decisions. However, because each step incurs a certain expense, there should be no more steps than necessary. The stages of the selection process should be sequenced so that the more expensive steps, such as physical examination, are near the end. Fewer people will then move through the higher-cost stages.

Recruitment should not be sporadic; it should be a continuous activity aimed at reaching the best applicants. The selection process should systematically and effectively match applicants' characteristics and needs with the requirements of specific selling tasks. Finally, the selection process should ensure that new sales personnel are available where and when they are needed.

Recruitment and selection of salespeople are not one-time decisions. The market and marketing environment change, as do an organization's objectives, resources, and marketing strategies. Maintaining the proper mix of salespeople thus requires the firm's sales management's continued decision making.

Training Sales Personnel

Many organizations have formal training programs; others depend on informal on-the-job training. Some systematic training programs are quite extensive; others are rather short and rudimentary. Regardless of whether the training program is complex or simple, its developers must consider what to teach, who to train, and how to train them.

A sales training program can concentrate on the company, on products, or on selling methods. Training programs often cover all three areas. Training for experienced company salespersons usually emphasizes product information, although salespeople also must be informed about new selling techniques and any changes in company plans, policies, and procedures.

Training programs can be aimed at newly hired salespeople, at experienced salespersons, or both. Ordinarily, new sales personnel require comprehensive training, whereas experienced personnel need both refresher courses about established products and training that gives them new-product information. Training programs can be directed at the entire sales force or at a segment of it.

Sales training may be done in the field, at educational institutions, in company facilities, or in several of these locations. Some firms train new employees before assigning them to a specific sales position. Other businesses, however, put them into the field immediately and provide formal training only after the new salespersons have gained a little experience. Training programs for new personnel can be as short as several days or as long as three years; some are even longer. Sales training for experienced personnel is often scheduled during a period when sales activities are not too demanding. Because training of experienced salespeople is usually a recurring effort, a firm's sales management must determine the frequency, sequencing, and duration of these activities.

Sales managers, as well as other salespeople, often engage in sales training—whether daily on the job or periodically in sales meetings. Salespeople sometimes receive training from technical specialists within their own organizations. In addition, a number of individuals and organizations sell special sales training programs. Appropriate materials for sales training programs range from films, texts, manuals, and cases to programmed learning devices and audio- and videocassettes. As for teaching methods, lectures, demonstrations, simulation exercises, and on-the-job training can all be effective. The choice of methods and materials for a particular sales training program depends on the type and number of trainees, the program's content and complexity, its length and location, the size of the training budget, the number of teachers, and the teachers' preferences.

Compensating Salespeople

To develop and maintain a highly productive sales force, a business must formulate and administer a compensation plan that attracts, motivates, and retains the most effective individuals. The plan should give sales management the desired level of control and provide sales personnel with an acceptable level of freedom, income, and incentive. It should also be flexible, equitable, easy to administer, and easy to understand. Good compensation programs facilitate and encourage proper treatment of customers.

Even though these requirements appear to be logical and easily satisfied, it is actually quite difficult to incorporate them all into a simple program. Some of them will be satisfied, and others will not. Studies evaluating the impact of financial incentives on sales performance indicate five general responses. For money-sensitive individuals, an increase in incentives will usually increase their sales efforts, and a decrease in financial rewards will diminish their efforts. Unresponsive salespeople will sell at the same level regardless of the incentive. Leisure-sensitive salespeople tend to work less when the incentive system is implemented. Income satisfiers normally adjust their performance to match their income goal. Understanding potential reactions and analyzing the personalities of the sales force can help management evaluate whether an incentive program might work.[8] In formulating a compensation plan, sales management must strive for a proper balance of freedom, income, and incentives.

The developer of a compensation program must determine the general level of compensation required and the most desirable method of calculating it. In analyzing the required compensation level, sales management must ascertain a salesperson's value to the company on the basis of the tasks and responsibilities associated with the sales position. The sales manager may consider a number of factors, including salaries of other types of personnel in the firm, competitors' compensation plans, costs of sales-force turnover, and the size of nonsalary selling expenses.

Sales compensation programs usually reimburse salespersons for their selling expenses, provide a certain number of fringe benefits, and deliver the required compensation level. To do that, a firm may use one or more of three basic compensation methods: straight salary, straight commission, or a combination of salary and commission. In a **straight salary compensation plan**, salespeople are paid a specified amount per time period. This sum remains the same until they receive a pay increase or decrease. In a **straight commission compensation plan**, salespeople's compensation is determined solely by the amount of their sales for a given time period. A commission may be based on a single percentage of sales or on a sliding scale involving several sales levels and percentage rates. In a **combination compensation plan**, salespeople are paid a fixed salary and a commission based on sales volume. Some combination programs require a salesperson to exceed a certain sales level before earning a commission; others offer commissions for any level of sales.

Table 17.1 lists the major characteristics of each sales-force compensation method. Notice that the combination method is most popular. When selecting a compensation method, sales management weighs the advantages and disadvantages shown in Table 17.1.

Proper administration of the sales-force compensation program is crucial for developing high morale and productivity among sales personnel. A good salesperson is very marketable in today's work place, and successful sales managers switch industries on a regular basis. Basic knowledge and skills related to sales management are in demand, and sometimes new insights can be gained from different work experiences. To maintain an effective compensation program and retain productive employees, sales management should periodically review and evaluate the plan and make necessary adjustments.

Motivating Salespeople

A sales manager should develop a systematic approach for motivating salespersons to be productive. Motivating should not be viewed as a sporadic activity reserved for periods of sales decline. Effective sales-force motivation is achieved through an organized set of activities performed continuously by the company's sales management.

Although financial compensation is important, a motivational program must also satisfy nonfinancial needs. Sales personnel, like other people, join organizations to satisfy personal needs and achieve personal goals. Sales managers must become aware of their personnel's motives and goals and then attempt to create an organizational climate that lets sales personnel satisfy their personal needs. Recognition of individual goals is becoming more challenging as cultural diversity increases (see Inside Marketing).

A sales manager can use a variety of positive motivational incentives other than financial compensation. For example, enjoyable working conditions, power

Figure 17.4

Incentive Program

Travel can be an effective sales force incentive to provide motivation.

Source: Royal Caribbean Cruise Line.

Compensation Method	Frequency of Use (%)[*]	When Especially Useful	Advantages	Disadvantages
Straight salary	17.4	Compensating new salespersons; firm moves into new sales territories that require developmental work; salespersons need to perform many non-selling activities	Gives salesperson security; gives sales manager control over salespersons; easy to administer; yields more predictable selling expenses	Provides no incentive; necessitates closer supervision of salespersons; during sales declines, selling expenses remain constant
Straight commission	6.5	Highly aggressive selling is required; non-selling tasks are minimized; company cannot closely control sales-force activities	Provides maximum amount of incentive; by increasing commission rate, sales managers can encourage salespersons to sell certain items; selling expenses relate directly to sales resources	Salespersons have little financial security; sales manager has minimum control over sales force; may cause salespeople to give inadequate service to smaller accounts; selling costs less predictable
Combination	76.1	Sales territories have relatively similar sales potentials; firm wishes to provide incentive but still control sales-force activities	Provides certain level of financial security; provides some incentive; selling expenses fluctuate with sales revenue	Selling expenses less predictable; may be difficult to administer

*The figures are computed from "Alternative Sales Compensation and Incentive Plans," *Sales & Marketing Management,* Feb. 17, 1986, p. 57. *Note:* The percentage for Combination includes compensation methods that involved any combination of salary, commission, or bonus.

Source: Based on the *Harvard Business Review* article "How to Pay Your Sales Force" by John P. Steinbrink (July/August 1978).

Table 17.1 **Characteristics of Sales-Force Compensation Methods**

and authority, job security, and an opportunity to excel are effective motivators. Salespeople can be motivated by their company's efforts to make their job more productive and efficient.

Sales contests and other incentive programs can also be effective motivators. Sales contests can motivate salespersons to focus on increasing sales or new accounts, promote special items, achieve greater volume per sales call, cover territories better, and increase activity in new geographic areas.[9] Some companies have found such incentive programs to be powerful motivating tools that marketing managers can use to achieve corporate goals. In Figure 17.4 Royal Caribbean promotes its cruises as potential salesperson incentives. Properly designed, an incentive program can pay for itself many times over. Recognition programs that acknowledge outstanding performance with symbolic awards, such as plaques or rings, can be quite effective. Although some experts believe that the best recognition programs reward less than 30 percent of the sales force at one time, some research efforts indicate that the most successful recognition programs reward 30 to 50 percent of the sales force.[10] Some organizations also use negative motivational measures: financial penalties, demotions, even terminations.

Managing Sales Territories

The effectiveness of a sales force that must travel to its customers is influenced, to some degree, by management's decisions regarding sales territories. Sales managers deciding on territories must consider size, shape, routing, and scheduling.

Creating Sales Territories   Several factors enter into the design of the size and shape of sales territories. First, sales managers must construct the territories so that sales potentials can be measured. Thus sales territories often consist of several geographic units for which market data are obtainable, such as census tracts, cities, counties, or states. Sales managers usually try to create territories that have similar sales potentials or that require about the same amount of work. If territories have equal sales potentials, they will almost always be unequal in geographic size. The salespersons who get the larger territories will have to work longer and harder to generate a certain sales volume. Conversely, if sales territories that require equal amounts of work are created, sales potentials for those territories will often vary. If sales personnel are partially or fully compensated through commissions, they will have unequal income potentials. Many sales managers try to balance territorial workloads and earning potentials by using differential commission rates. Although a sales manager seeks equity when developing and maintaining sales territories, some inequities will always prevail.

A territory's size and shape should also be designed to help the sales force provide the best possible customer coverage and to minimize selling costs. Territory size and shape should take into account the density and distribution of customers.

Routing and Scheduling Salespeople   The geographic size and shape of a sales territory are the most important factors affecting routing and scheduling of sales calls. Next are the number and distribution of customers within the territory, followed by the frequency and duration of sales calls. The person in charge of routing and scheduling must consider the sequence in which customers are called on, the specific roads or transportation schedules to be used, the number of calls to be made in a given period, and what time of day the calls will occur. In some firms, salespeople plan their own routes and schedules with little or no assistance from the sales manager; in other organizations, the sales manager draws up the routes and schedules. No matter who plans the routing and scheduling, the major goals should be to minimize salespersons' nonselling time (the time spent traveling and waiting) and maximize their selling time. The planners should try to achieve these goals in a way that holds a salesperson's travel and lodging costs to a minimum.

Managing a Culturally Diverse Sales Force

IN THE UNITED STATES TODAY, demographic studies reveal dramatic growth among Hispanic, Asian, and black populations. Although estimates vary, experts predict that by the year 2000, one of every four U.S. workers will come from a minority group. No longer can American companies operate under the assumption that every employee or every customer has the same values, beliefs, and expectations. Managing a sales force in a diverse society requires understanding and insight into cultural differences.

To succeed in sales, good communication is a necessity. If the majority of a sales representative's customers speak Spanish, for example, it makes sense for that representative to understand and speak Spanish as well. Ethnocentric hiring, says the president of Avon, would eliminate potential markets for their personal-care products. To make sure that its salespeople can understand and respond to clients, Avon strives to hire staff who match the demographics of their specific customer base. Operating in six Florida counties with residents from more than twelve countries gives Equitable Insurance Company's Suquet Agency first-hand experience in the importance of recruiting people who reflect the market. For example, agents have learned that older clients especially react positively to someone familiar with their culture, language, and traditions. Suquet's manager values his multicultural sales force's ability to open doors to new markets. When Monsanto Agricultural Company realized that most of those using its Round-up weedkiller were Hispanic farm workers

who spoke little English, it began sending interpreters along with sales representatives and hired a Spanish-speaking Round-up spokesperson.

To recruit and keep a skilled culturally diverse sales staff, these companies cultivate an environment that accepts and values employee differences. Avon encourages a cultural network that helps new minority employees adjust, organizes cultural events, and provides feedback to a top-level cultural diversity council. The Suquet Agency incorporates religious observances into the company calendar. At Monsanto, the Value Diversity task force raises awareness through sensitivity training, discussions at staff meetings, publications that highlight task force activities, and films.

In a recent poll of 645 national companies, three-fourths expressed concern for the problems connected with a multicultural work force and client base. Increasingly, American firms are awakening to the reality that, both in the workplace and out, good relations with people of diverse backgrounds translate into good business.

Sources: Renee Loth, "The Big New Mix," *Boston Globe Magazine*, Oct. 13, 1991, pp. 18–19; "A Sampling of Diversity Programs," *Training & Development Journal*, March 1991, pp. 40–44; Sherri K. Lindenburg, "Managing a Multi-Ethnic Field Force," *National Underwriter*, Jan. 7, 1991, pp. 16, 18, 24; Abby Livingston, "12 Companies That Do the Right Thing," *Working Woman*, January 1991, pp. 57, 59–60; and Shari Caudron, "Monsanto Responds to Diversity," *Personnel Journal*, November 1990, pp. 72–80.

Controlling and Evaluating Sales-Force Performance

To control and evaluate sales-force activities properly, sales management needs information. A sales manager cannot observe the field sales force daily and so relies on call reports, customer feedback, and invoices. Call reports identify the customers called on and present detailed information about interaction with those clients. Traveling sales personnel often must file work schedules indicating where they plan to be during specific future time periods.

The dimensions used to measure a salesperson's performance are determined largely by sales objectives. These objectives are normally set by the sales manager. If an individual's sales objective is stated in terms of sales volume, then that person should be evaluated on the basis of sales volume generated. Even though a salesperson may be assigned a major objective, he or she is ordinarily expected to achieve several related objectives as well. Thus salespeople are often judged along several dimensions. Sales managers evaluate many performance indicators, including average number of calls per day, average sales per customer, actual sales relative to sales potential, number of new-customer orders, average cost per call, and average gross profit per customer.

To evaluate a salesperson, a sales manager may compare one or more of these dimensions with a predetermined performance standard. However, sales management commonly compares one salesperson's performance with the performance of other employees operating under similar selling conditions or compares current performance with past performance. Sometimes management judges factors that have less direct bearing on sales performance, such as personal appearance, knowledge of the product, and competitors.

After evaluating salespeople, sales managers must take any needed corrective action to improve the performance of the sales force. They may have to adjust performance standards, provide additional training, or try other motivational methods. Corrective action may demand comprehensive changes in the sales force.

Many industries, especially technical ones, are monitoring their sales forces and increasing productivity through the use of laptop (portable) computers. In part, the increasing use of computers in technical sales is a response to customers' greater technical sophistication. Product information—especially information on price, specifications, and availability of products—helps salespeople to be more valuable.

The Nature of Sales Promotion

As defined earlier, **sales promotion** is an activity or material (or both) that acts as a direct inducement, offering added value or incentive for the product, to resellers, salespersons, or consumers.[11] It encompasses all promotional activities and materials other than personal selling, advertising, and publicity. In competitive markets, where products are very similar, sales promotion provides additional inducements that encourage purchases. For example, Evian Waters of France launched its Evian Hydration Patrol, consisting of information vans and sampling crews who gave free samples to over 175,000 people at beaches, parks, fairs, and colleges. Sales in that geographic market jumped by 14 percent.[12] Sales promotions such as this one are designed to generate sales and good will toward the promoter.

Sales promotion has grown dramatically in the last ten years, largely because of the focus of American business on short-term profits and value and the perceived need for promotional strategies that produce short-term sales boosts.[13] The most significant change in promotion expenditures in recent years has been the transfer of funds usually earmarked for advertising to sales promotion. Fundamental changes in marketing, which have led to a greater emphasis on sales promotion, mean that advertising agencies have had to increase their participation in sales promotion to maintain revenues.[14]

An organization often uses sales promotion activities in concert with other promotional efforts to facilitate personal selling, advertising, or both. Sales promotion efforts are not always secondary to other promotion mix ingredients. Companies sometimes use advertising and personal selling to support sales promotion activities. For example, marketers frequently use advertising to promote contests, free samples, and premiums. Manufacturers' sales personnel occasionally administer sales contests for wholesale or retail salespersons. The most effective sales promotion efforts are highly interrelated with other promotional activities. Decisions regarding sales promotion therefore often affect advertising and personal selling decisions, and vice versa.

Sales Promotion Opportunities and Limitations

Sales promotion can increase sales by providing an extra incentive to purchase. There are many opportunities to motivate consumers, resellers, and salespeople to take a desired action. Some kinds of sales promotion are designed specifically to stimulate resellers' demand and effectiveness; some are directed at increasing consumer demand; and others focus on both resellers and consumers. Regardless of the purpose, marketers need to ensure that the sales promotion objectives are consistent with the organization's overall objectives, as well as its marketing and promotion objectives.

Although sales promotion can support a brand image, excessive price-reduction sales promotion, such as coupons, can affect brand image. Firms therefore must decide between short-term sales increases and the long-run need for a desired reputation and brand image.[15] While there has been increased emphasis on sales promotion, in the future, brand advertising may become more important relative to sales promotion. Some firms that shifted from brand advertising to sales promotion have lost market share.

For example, Minute Maid orange juice (owned by Coca-Cola Foods) experienced its most dramatic sales declines after shifting the majority of advertising spending to sales promotion while one of its major competitors, Tropicana, continued to focus on brand advertising. Minute Maid's advertising budget was reduced by approximately 40 percent from 1984 to 1988. Consequently, Minute Maid's share of the fruit beverage category dropped from 12.4 percent to 9.5 percent. To counter Minute Maid's decline in market share, Coca-Cola introduced a $30 million advertising campaign for Minute Maid in 1989 to provide a sustained brand image for Minute Maid orange juice. Similarly, when General Foods boosted the advertising budget for its Maxwell House coffee by 50 percent, Maxwell House gained a 30 percent share of the coffee market.[16] These examples do not mean that advertising always works better than sales promotion. There are trade-offs between these two forms of promotion, and the marketing manager must determine the right balance to achieve maximum promotional effectiveness.

Sales Promotion Methods

Most sales promotion methods can be grouped into the categories of consumer sales promotion and trade sales promotion. **Consumer sales promotion techniques** encourage or stimulate consumers to patronize a specific retail store or to try a particular product. **Trade sales promotion methods** stimulate wholesalers and retailers to carry a producer's products and to market these products aggressively.

Marketers consider a number of factors before deciding which sales promotion methods to use. They must take into account both product characteristics (size, weight, costs, durability, uses, features, and hazards) and target market characteristics (age, sex, income, location, density, usage rate, and shopping patterns). How the product is distributed and the number and types of resellers may determine the type of method used. The competitive and legal environment may also influence the choice.

In this section we look closely at several consumer and trade sales promotion methods to learn what they entail and what goals they can help marketers achieve.

Consumer Sales Promotion Methods

Consumer sales promotion by manufacturers and resellers amounts to approximately the same level of expenditure as for advertising.[17] In this section we discuss coupons, demonstrations, frequent-user incentives, point-of-purchase displays, free samples, money refunds, premiums, cents-off offers, and consumer contests and sweepstakes.

Coupons **Coupons** are used to stimulate consumers to try a new or established product, to increase sales volume quickly, to attract repeat purchasers, or to introduce new package sizes or features. Coupons usually reduce the purchase price of an item. The makers of Alpo Lite dog food offered a coupon to promote its product (see Figure 17.5). The savings may be deducted from the purchase price or offered as cash. For best results, coupons should be easy to recognize and state the offer clearly. The nature of the product (seasonality, maturity, frequency of purchase, and the like) is the prime consideration in setting up a coupon promotion.

Many consumer-products manufacturers distribute coupons, which are used by approximately 80 percent of all households. In 1990, over 300 billion coupons were distributed, with an average value of 49 cents.[18] One study found that price consciousness and pride and satisfaction from obtaining savings through the use of coupons were the most important determinants of coupon use.[19] Another study showed that the major determinants are size of the coupon offer, how easily the consumer can redeem the offer, how brand-loyal the consumer is, and the extent to which the consumer is generally favorable toward using coupons.[20]

Coupons are distributed on and in packages, through free-standing inserts (FSIs), print advertising, direct mail, and in stores. When deciding on the proper vehicle for their coupons, marketers should consider strategies and objec-

Figure 17.5

Manufacturer's Coupon

Alpo employs coupons to gain market share for Alpo Lite.

Source: Copyright Alpo Pet Foods, Inc.

tives, redemption rates, availability, circulation, and exclusivity. The whole coupon distribution and redemption area has become very competitive. To draw customers to their stores, grocers may double and sometimes even triple the value of the coupons they bring in. But because the practice of doubling and tripling coupons is expensive, many of these retailers have asked manufacturers to reduce the face value of the coupons they offer.[21]

There are several advantages to using coupons. Print advertisements with coupons are often more effective than nonpromotional advertising for generating brand awareness. Generally, the larger the coupon's cash offer, the better the recognition generated. Another advantage is that coupons are a way to reward present users of the product, win back former users, and encourage purchases in larger quantities. Coupons also let manufacturers determine whether the coupons reached the intended target market because they get the coupons back.

Coupons also have drawbacks. Fraud and misredemption are possible, and the redemption period can be quite lengthy. The approximate redemption rate is 3.6 percent, with 10 to 15 percent of the coupons accepted being misredemptions. In addition, some experts believe that coupons are losing their value because so many manufacturers are offering them, and consumers have therefore learned not to buy without some incentive, whether it be a coupon, a rebate, or a refund. There has been a general decline in brand loyalty among heavy coupon users. On the other hand, many consumers only redeem coupons for products they normally buy. Studies have shown that about 75 percent of coupons are redeemed by people who already use the brand on the coupon. So, as an incentive to try and to continue to use a new brand or product, coupons have questionable success. Another problem with coupons is that stores often do not have enough of the coupon item in stock. This situation can generate ill will toward both the store and the product.[22]

Although the use of coupons as a sales promotion technique is expected to grow in the next few years, a concern among marketers about their effectiveness could well diminish their appeal. However, coupons will probably remain a major sales promotion component for stimulating trial of new products. Coupons will also be used to increase the frequency of purchase for established products that show sluggish sales. On the other hand, successful established products may be reducing their profits if 75 percent of the coupons are redeemed by brand-loyal customers.[23]

Demonstrations   **Demonstrations** are excellent attention getters. Manufacturers often use them temporarily either to encourage trial use and purchase of the product or to actually show how the product works. Because labor costs can be extremely high, demonstrations are not used widely. They can, however, be highly effective for promoting certain types of products, such as appliances, cosmetics, and cleaning supplies. Cosmetics marketers such as Clinique (owned by Estee Lauder), for example, sometimes offer potential customers "make-overs" to demonstrate their products' benefits and proper application.

Frequent-User Incentives   Many firms develop incentive programs to reward individual consumers who engage in repeat (frequent) purchases. For example, most major airlines offer a frequent-flyer program through which customers who have flown a specified number of miles are rewarded with free tickets for additional travel. Thus frequent-user incentives help foster customer loyalty to a specific company or group of cooperating companies that provide extra incentives for patronage. Frequent-user incentives have also been used by service businesses, such as auto rental agencies, hotels, and credit card companies, as well as by marketers of consumer goods. Procter & Gamble, for example, launched the GiftLink Shoppers Reward program, in conjunction with Ralston Purina, Kraft, Campbell Soup, and Ocean Spray, to reward brand-loyal customers for their regular support. Consumers enrolled in the program earn "points" each time they purchase a brand listed in the program. They can redeem these points for merchandise—for instance, Samsonite luggage or Black & Decker small appliances.[24]

An older frequent-user incentive is trading stamps. **Trading stamps** are dispensed in proportion to the amount of a consumer's purchase and can be accumulated and redeemed for goods. Retailers use trading stamps to attract consumers to specific stores. Stamps can be attractive to consumers as long as they do not drive up prices. Trading stamps were very popular, but their use as a sales promotion method has declined.

Point-of-Purchase Displays   **Point-of-purchase (P-O-P) materials** include such items as outside signs, window displays, counter pieces, display racks, and self-service cartons. Innovations in P-O-P displays include sniff-teasers, which give off a product's aroma in the store as consumers walk within a radius of four feet, and computerized interactive displays. These items, which are often supplied by producers, attract attention, inform customers, and encourage retailers to carry particular products. A retailer is likely to use point-of-purchase materials if they are attractive, informative, well-constructed, and in harmony with the store. A survey of retail store managers indicated that almost 90 percent believed that P-O-P materials sell products. The retailers surveyed also said that P-O-P is essential for product introductions. Different forms of display material are carried by different types of retailers. Convenience stores, for example, favor window banners and "shelf talkers" (on-the-shelf displays or signs), whereas chain drugstores prefer floor stands and devices that provide samples.[25]

Free Samples   Marketers use **free samples** for several reasons: to stimulate trial of a product, to increase sales volume in the early stages of a product's life cycle, or to obtain desirable distribution. Sampling is the most expensive of all sales promotion methods because production and distribution through such channels as mail delivery, door-to-door delivery, in-store distribution, and on-package distribution entail very high costs. In designing a free sample, marketers should consider certain factors, such as the seasonality of the product, the characteristics of the market, and prior advertising. Free samples are not appropriate for mature products and slow-turnover products.

Money Refunds   With **money refunds**, consumers submit proof of purchase and are mailed a specific amount of money. Usually, manufacturers demand multiple purchases of the product before a consumer can qualify for a refund. This method, used primarily to promote trial use of a product, is relatively low in cost. Nevertheless, because money refunds sometimes generate a low response rate, they have limited impact on sales.

One of the problems with money refunds or rebates is that many people perceive the redemption process as too complicated. Consumers also have negative perceptions of manufacturers' reasons for offering rebates. They may believe that these are new, untested products or products that haven't sold well. If these perceptions are not changed, rebate offers may degrade the image and desirability of the product being promoted. If the promotion objective in the rebate offer is to increase sales, then an effort should be made to simplify the redemption process and proof-of-purchase requirements.[26]

Premiums   **Premiums** are items offered free or at minimum cost as a bonus for purchasing a product. They are used to attract competitors' customers, introduce different sizes of established products, add variety to other promotional efforts, and stimulate loyalty. Inventiveness is necessary, however; if an offer is to stand out and achieve a significant number of redemptions, the premium must be matched to both the target audience and the brand's image. To be effective, premiums must be easily recognizable and desirable. Premiums are placed on or in packages and can also be distributed by retailers or through the mail. Examples include a service station giving free glasses with a fill-up, a free toothbrush available with a tube of toothpaste, or a free plastic box given with the purchase of Kraft Cheese Singles.

Cents-off Offers   When a **cents-off offer** is used, buyers receive a certain amount off the regular price shown on the label or package. Similar to coupons, this method can be a strong incentive for trying the product; it can stimulate product sales, yield short-lived sales increases, and promote products in off-seasons. It is an easy method to control and is used frequently for specific purposes. However, if used on an ongoing basis, it reduces the price to customers who would buy at the regular price, and frequent use of cents-off offers may cheapen a product's image. In addition, the method often requires special handling by retailers.

Consumer Contests and Sweepstakes In **consumer contests**, individuals compete for prizes based on their analytical or creative skill. This method generates traffic at the retail level. As shown in Figure 17.6, Pulsar sponsored a mystery map contest through which winning contestants were awarded all-expenses-paid vacations. However, marketers should exercise care in setting up a contest. Problems or errors may anger consumers or result in lawsuits. Contestants are usually more involved in consumer contests than they are in sweepstakes, which we discuss next, even though the total participation may be lower. Contests may be used in conjunction with other sales promotion methods, such as coupons.

The entrants in a **consumer sweepstakes** submit their names for inclusion in a drawing for prizes. Sweepstakes are used to stimulate sales and, as with contests, are sometimes teamed with other sales promotion methods. Sweepstakes are used more often than consumer contests, and they tend to attract a greater number of participants. The cost of a sweepstakes is considerably less than the cost of a contest. Successful sweepstakes can generate widespread interest and short-term increases in sales or market share. However, sweepstakes are prohibited in some states.

Trade Sales Promotion Methods

Producers use sales promotion methods to encourage resellers, especially retailers, to carry their products and promote them effectively. The methods include buy-back allowances, buying allowances, counts and recounts, free merchandise, merchandise allowances, cooperative advertising, dealer listings, premium or push money, sales contests, and dealer loaders.

Buy-Back Allowances A **buy-back allowance** is a certain sum of money given to a purchaser for each unit bought after an initial deal is over. This method is a secondary incentive in which the total amount of money that resellers can receive is proportional to their purchases during an initial trade deal, such as a coupon offer. Buy-back allowances foster cooperation during an initial sales promotion effort and stimulate repurchase afterward. The main drawback of this method is its expense.

Buying Allowances A **buying allowance** is a temporary price reduction to resellers for purchasing specified quantities of a product. A soap producer, for example, might give retailers $1 for each case of soap purchased. Such offers may be an incentive to handle a new product, achieve a temporary price reduction, or stimulate the purchase of an item in larger than normal quantities. The buying allowance, which takes the form of money, yields profits to resellers and is simple and straightforward to use. There are no restrictions on how resellers use the money, which increases the method's effectiveness. One hazard of buying allowances is that customers will buy forward, meaning that they buy large amounts that keep them supplied for many months. Another problem is that

Figure 17.6

Consumer Contest

Pulsar promotes its watches, sponsoring a contest for a vacation.

Source: David Zimmerman ©.

competitors can match (or beat) the reduced price, which can mean lower profits for all sellers.[27]

Counts and Recounts   The **count-and-recount** promotion method is based on the payment of a specific amount of money for each product unit moved from a reseller's warehouse in a given time period. Units of a product are counted at the start of the promotion and again at the end to determine how many have moved from the warehouse. This method can reduce retail stockouts by moving inventory out of warehouses and can also clear distribution channels of obsolete products or packages and reduce warehouse inventories. The count-and-recount method might benefit a producer by decreasing resellers' inventories, making resellers more likely to place new orders. However, this method is often difficult to administer and may not appeal to resellers who have small warehouses.

Free Merchandise   **Free merchandise** is sometimes offered to resellers who purchase a stated quantity of the same or different products. Occasionally, free merchandise is used as payment for allowances provided through other sales promotion methods. To avoid handling and bookkeeping problems, the giving of free merchandise usually is accomplished by reducing the invoice.

Merchandise Allowances   A **merchandise allowance** is a manufacturer's agreement to pay resellers certain amounts of money for providing special promotional efforts, such as advertising or displays. This method is best suited to high-volume, high-profit, easily handled products. One major problem with using merchandise allowances is that some retailers perform their activities at a minimally acceptable level simply to obtain the allowances. Before paying retailers, manufacturers usually verify their performance. Manufacturers hope that the retailers' additional promotional efforts will yield substantial sales increases.

Cooperative Advertising   **Cooperative advertising** is an arrangement whereby a manufacturer agrees to pay a certain amount of a retailer's media costs for advertising the manufacturer's products. The amount allowed is usually based on the quantities purchased. Before payment is made, a retailer must show proof that advertisements did appear. These payments give retailers additional funds for advertising. Some retailers exploit cooperative advertising programs by crowding too many products into one advertisement. Surprisingly, though, not all available cooperative advertising dollars are used. Some retailers cannot afford to advertise; others can afford it but do not want to advertise. Approximately 80 to 90 percent of all cooperative advertising dollars are spent on newspaper advertisements.[28]

Dealer Listings   A **dealer listing** is an advertisement that promotes a product and identifies the names of participating retailers who sell the product. Dealer listings can influence retailers to carry the product, build traffic at the retail level, and encourage consumers to buy the product at participating dealers.

Premium or Push Money   **Premium** or **push money** is used to push a line of goods by providing additional compensation to salespeople. This promotion method is appropriate when personal selling is an important part of the marketing effort; it is not effective for promoting products that are sold through self-service. Although this method often helps a manufacturer obtain commitment from the sales force, often it can be very expensive.

Sales Contests   A **sales contest** is designed to motivate distributors, retailers, and sales personnel by recognizing outstanding achievements. To be effective, this method must be equitable for all salespersons involved. One advantage to the method is that it can achieve participation at all levels of distribution. However, the positive effects may be temporary, and prizes are usually expensive.

Dealer Loaders   A **dealer loader** is a gift to a retailer who purchases a specified quantity of merchandise. Often dealer loaders are used to obtain special display efforts from retailers by offering essential display parts as premiums. For example, a manufacturer might design a display that includes a sterling silver tray as a major component and give the tray to the retailer. Marketers use dealer loaders to obtain new distributors and push larger quantities of goods.

Summary

Personal selling is the process of informing customers and persuading them to purchase products through personal communication in an exchange situation. The three general purposes of personal selling are finding prospects, convincing them to buy, and keeping customers satisfied.

Many salespersons—either consciously or unconsciously—move through a general selling process as they sell products. In prospecting, the salesperson develops a list of potential customers. Before contacting acceptable prospects, the salesperson prepares by finding and analyzing information about the prospects and their needs. The approach is the manner in which a salesperson contacts a potential customer. During the sales presentation, the salesperson must attract and hold the prospect's attention to stimulate interest and desire for the product. If possible, the salesperson should handle objections when they arise. Closing is the stage in the selling process when the salesperson asks the prospect to buy the product or products. After a successful closing, the salesperson must follow up the sale.

In developing a sales force, marketing managers must consider which types of salespersons will sell the firm's products most effectively. The three classifications of salespersons are order getters, order takers, and support personnel. Order getters inform both current customers and new prospects and persuade them to buy. Order takers seek repeat sales and fall into two categories: inside order takers and field order takers. Sales support personnel facilitate the selling function, but their duties usually extend beyond making sales. The three types of support personnel are missionary, trade, and technical salespersons.

The effectiveness of sales-force management is an important determinant of a firm's success because the sales force is directly responsible for generating an organization's sales revenue. The major decision areas and activities on which sales managers must focus are establishing sales-force objectives, determining sales-force size, recruiting and selecting salespeople, training sales personnel, compensating salespeople, motivating salespeople, managing sales territories, and controlling and evaluating the sales force.

Sales objectives should be stated in precise, measurable terms and specify the time period and the geographic areas involved. The size of the sales force must be adjusted from time to time because a firm's marketing plans change, as do markets and forces in the marketing environment.

Recruiting and selecting salespeople involves attracting and choosing the right type of salesperson to maintain an effective sales force. When developing a training program, managers must consider a variety of dimensions, such as who should be trained, what should be taught, and how the training should occur. Compensation of salespeople involves formulating and administrating a compensation plan that attracts, motivates, and holds the right types of salespeople for the firm. Motivation of salespeople should allow the firm to attain high productivity. Managing sales territories, another aspect of sales-force management, focuses on such factors as size, shape, routing, and scheduling. To control and evaluate sales-force performance, the sales manager must use information obtained through salespersons' call reports, customer feedback, and invoices.

Sales promotion is an activity or material (or both) that acts as a direct inducement, offering added value or incentive for the product, to resellers, salespersons, or consumers. Marketers use sales promotion to identify and attract new customers, to introduce a new product, and to increase reseller inventories. Sales promotion techniques fall into two general categories: consumer and trade. Consumer sales promotion methods encourage consumers to trade at specific stores or to try a specific product. These methods include coupons, demonstrations, frequent-user incentives, free samples, money refunds, premiums, cents-off offers, and consumer sweepstakes and contests. Trade sales promotion techniques stimulate resellers to handle a manufacturer's products and market these products aggressively. These techniques include buy-back allowances, buying allowances, counts and recounts, free merchandise, merchandise allowances, cooperative advertising, dealer listings, premium or push money, sales contests, and dealer loaders.

Important Terms

Personal selling
Prospecting
Approach
Closing
Order getter
Order taker
Support personnel
Missionary salespersons
Trade salespersons
Technical salespersons
Recruiting
Straight salary compensation plan
Straight commission compensation
  plan
Combination compensation plan
Sales promotion
Consumer sales promotion techniques
Trade sales promotion methods
Coupons

Demonstrations
Trading stamps
Point-of-purchase (P-O-P) materials
Free samples
Money refunds
Premiums
Cents-off offer
Consumer contests
Consumer sweepstakes
Buy-back allowance
Buying allowance
Count-and-recount
Free merchandise
Merchandise allowance
Cooperative advertising
Dealer listing
Premium or push money
Sales contest
Dealer loader

Discussion and Review Questions

1. What is personal selling? How does personal selling differ from other types of promotional activities?
2. What are the primary purposes of personal selling?
3. Identify the elements of the personal selling process. Must a salesperson include all these elements when selling a product to a customer? Why or why not?
4. How does a salesperson find and evaluate prospects? Do you consider any of these methods questionable ethically?
5. Are order getters more aggressive or creative than order takers? Why or why not?
6. Identify several characteristics of effective sales objectives.
7. How should a sales manager establish criteria for selecting sales personnel? What are the general characteristics of a good salesperson?
8. What major issues or questions should be considered when developing a training program for the sales force?
9. Explain the major advantages and disadvantages of the three basic methods of compensating salespersons. In general, which method do you most prefer? Why?
10. What major factors should be taken into account when designing the size and shape of a sales territory?
11. How does a sales manager—who cannot be with each salesperson in the field on a daily basis—control the performance of sales personnel?
12. What is sales promotion? Why is it used?

13. For each of the following, identify and describe three techniques and give several examples: (a) consumer sales promotion methods and (b) trade sales promotion methods.
14. What types of sales promotion methods have you observed recently?

Cases

17.1 DEC's Sales Force Goes On-Line

Since 1957, when Digital Equipment Company was established, it has risen to the spot of number-two computer maker in the world, just below its chief competitor, IBM. Faced with more hardware and software challengers in the market as well as an industrywide slowdown, DEC is now struggling to remain at the top. Only a few years ago company profits rose 38 percent, but more recently DEC has experienced a drop in its market share and cut its work force by 10,000 people. Declining sales have served as a catalyst for change. By linking personal computers to information networking technology, DEC is automating its sales force—presumably a more efficient sales force capable of maintaining a competitive edge.

With buzzwords like "Microserver," "Microvax II," and "ethernet" in its vocabulary, networking conjures images of science fiction full of robots and other futuristic technology usurping humanity's place in the world. But it is really only a tool designed to serve, and in large corporations and small firms alike, it is doing just that. Hewlett-Packard and Fina Oil and Chemical equip all salespeople with laptop computers, and several small businesses have saved themselves from going under by automating their sales forces. All that is needed is a computer, a modem, and the communications software, which is becoming increasingly available. The most recent *Directory of Marketing Software,* a comprehensive list of sales marketing and sales software, catalogs almost 700 packages available for microcomputers, minicomputers, and mainframes, compared with only 250 entries just a few years earlier. Turn on the switch and there is an electronic sales assistant, a desktop library with 24-hour access to current information, and a worldwide communication system.

DEC's software, called Easynet Network, links sales, marketing, and service personnel in five hundred offices and thirty-three countries, allowing communication anytime and anyplace. Every DEC salesperson has an Easynet account accessible at the office, the customer site, or at home via a personal computer. Sales personnel can use three different electronic ordering systems. Electronic Store provides customers with descriptions and pricing for every DEC product and service; over 100,000 customers have used this option to place orders. DECdirect, with a "mailing list" of 500,000 customers, is an electronic catalog for smaller-priced items, with salespeople available for on-line customer assistance. One of DEC's goals over the next few years is to use DECdirect to place at least 80 percent of its orders. EDI (electronic data interchange) provides computer-to-computer exchange of documents, such as purchase orders, enabling the sales force to respond to orders and ship products sooner. Sales representatives receive credit toward bonuses and membership in "top sales" clubs for all orders they place electronically.

Asked what they like most about being "on-line," DEC salespeople place access to information, as well as to others in the company, at the top of the list. Seventeen informational data bases satisfy the sales representative's "need to know," offering information on topics such as account management, customer service, and telemarketing. One DEC sales manager reports that Easynet saves sales representatives more than one hour of research time for every sale, as well as about sixty phone calls per month, translating into a savings of $12.5 million. Easynet provides communication between sales, marketing, finance, and engineering personnel through electronic mail (person-to-person messages), conferencing (group discussions), and electronic bulletin boards (companywide information). As communication becomes easier, geography becomes less relevant to the sales process. On a large project, the sales manager in San Francisco can communicate with the project manager in Washington, who can talk to the support personnel in Maryland, without playing telephone tag or waiting for conventional mail. Thanks to Easynet, DEC is now restructuring its sales organization from territory-based to industry-based. A person formerly responsible for a geographic area, such as New England, for example, may become the sales manager for a specific industry, such as insurance or banking.

Why automate a sales force? Critics warn that computer technology may be difficult for new people to learn, and the amount of available information may overwhelm the sales force. DEC believes computerized selling frees people from paperwork and streamlines the ordering process, giving salespeople more time to create demands for their products and propose solutions to meet those demands. DEC saves money and gets a better prepared, more knowledgeable sales force. After more than twenty years in business, the president of DEC remains committed to his vision of a technology-driven operation. His goal is to use electronics in a continuous effort to satisfy any customer's needs for any of DEC's 100,000 products or services in less and less time at lower and lower cost.[29]

Questions for Discussion

1. In what ways does the automation of DEC's sales force help the company's sales managers do their jobs more effectively?
2. What competitive advantages are provided by DEC's sales force being equipped with advanced information technology?

17.2 Dr Pepper's Sales Promotion Efforts

Dr Pepper was once an also-ran in the race to be the top-selling American soft drink. While Coke and Pepsi battled for the number-one spot, Dr Pepper remained what its commercials told everyone—"so misunderstood." Today, many soft-drink consumers are looking for cola alternatives. Although the cola giants continue waging market-share wars, Dr Pepper has become "just what the Doctor ordered"—the number-one-selling noncola soft drink in America. Dr Pepper executives credit the company's strong promotional program with the soft drink's growing popularity and market share.

Underlying Dr Pepper's promotional strategy is one fundamental objective, to increase sales. To accomplish that goal, company executives formulated specific guidelines for creating effective sales promotions. Because the soft drink's unusual taste is a key selling point, sales promotions must reinforce that characteristic. Dr Pepper's marketers always plan sales promotion efforts that target specific channels or packages. If the objective is to increase sales of two-liter bottles, for example, a promotional game will involve that size only. Because the organization's bottling companies and retailers (such as supermarkets and discount stores) offer many sales promotions of their own, Dr Pepper always times sales promotions to complement those of the retailer. Sales promotion techniques must be easy for shoppers to understand, as well as be fun and rewarding for participants. In addition to providing an overall strategy for specific promotional campaigns, Dr Pepper's executives believe strongly in couponing. In one recent year, the company distributed over 74 million coupons.

Dr Pepper's most recent sales promotion gives away trips, vehicles, thousands of dollars in cash prizes, and, of course, free Dr Pepper products. To drive sales of two-liter bottles of Dr Pepper and Diet Dr Pepper, the company came up with its "Hover over Hawaii" promotion, which gives customers a chance to win vacations to Hawaii, pairs of airlines tickets, cash prizes, or coupons for free two-liter bottles of Dr Pepper simply by checking the back of the label. "Peel-a-Pepper," also created for the two-liter market, rewards one out of twelve customers with a free two-liter bottle. In the single-drink channel, the "Pepper Payday" promotion gives away a free Payday candy bar to those who find a specially marked bottle cap on their sixteen- or twenty-ounce bottle of Dr Pepper. One of the company's biggest promotions is called "Explore America." Soft-drink customers who buy specially marked twelve-pack cases of Dr Pepper can win Ford Explorers, trips for two anywhere in the United States, a year's supply of Dr Pepper or Diet Dr Pepper, or coupons for 55 cents off their next purchase. In keeping with Dr Pepper's promotional strategy, all of its games are designed for one specific package or channel and are easy to play. Even though winning the big prize is a long shot, Dr Pepper drinkers still win lots of the soft drinks.

In addition to nationally sponsored promotions, Dr Pepper lovers can usually find local sales promotions. One bottling company promoted the opening of the Stephen King thriller *Graveyard Shift* by giving away forty-four-ounce Dr Peppers with a paid admission. In Hannibal, Missouri, and Quincy, Illinois, McDonald's offered a free Dr Pepper with every salad. Baseball fans in Little Falls, Minnesota, could win in a drawing for free 12-packs of Dr Pepper by sending cards with favorite Minnesota Twins players to a local radio station.

Between 1987 and 1991, Dr Pepper's share of the soft-drink market grew 67 percent. Diet Dr Pepper, the oldest diet noncola, is now America's fastest-growing soft drink brand. In an industry with a yearly increase in sales of about 3 percent, total Dr Pepper sales were up 14 percent. Dr Pepper's sales promotion efforts continue to build brand awareness, increase total sales volume, and persuade more soft-drink consumers to try Dr Pepper. Diet Dr Pepper's slogan, "There's no stopping the taste," can easily be amended to predict the company's future—"There's no stopping Dr Pepper."[30]

Questions for Discussion

1. Identify the major sales promotion methods used by Dr Pepper.
2. Why are Dr Pepper's sales promotion methods focused on either package sizes or channels?
3. Evaluate the overall effectiveness of Dr Pepper's sales promotion efforts.

Chapter Notes

1. Based on information from "When the Chips Were Down, Nabisco Didn't Crumble," *Sales & Marketing Management,* June 1990, pp. 74–76; Judann Dagnoli and Judith Graham, "Aggressive Marketer to Head RJR," *Advertising Age,* Mar. 20, 1989, p. 4; and Robert H. Klein, "Nabisco Packages a Meeting for Field Managers," *Sales & Marketing Management,* Nov. 11, 1985, pp. 88–90.
2. Thomas W. Leigh and Patrick F. McGraw, "Mapping the Procedural Knowledge of Industrial Sales Personnel: A Script-Theoretic Investigation," *Journal of Marketing,* January 1989, pp. 16–34.
3. Leigh and McGraw, pp. 16–34.
4. William C. Moncrief, "Five Types of Industrial Sales Jobs," *Industrial Marketing Management,* 17 (1988), p. 164.
5. A. J. Magrath, "Are You Overdoing 'Lean and Mean'?" *Sales & Marketing Management,* January 1988, pp. 46–53.
6. "1991 Sales Manager's Budget Planner," *Sales & Marketing Management,* June 17, 1991, pp. 72–98.
7. Patrick C. Fleenor, "Selling and Sales Management in Action: Assessment Center Selection of Sales Representatives," *Journal of Personal Selling & Sales Management,* May 1987, pp. 57–59.
8. Rene Y. Darmon, "The Impact of Incentive Compensation on the Salesperson's Work Habits: An Economic Model," *Journal of Personal Selling & Sales Management,* May 1987, pp. 21–32.
9. Sandra Hile Hart, William C. Moncrief, and A. Parasuraman, "An Empirical Investigation of Salespeople's Performance, Effort and Selling Method During a Sales Contest," *Journal of the Academy of Marketing Science,* Winter 1989, pp. 29–39.
10. Thomas A. Wotruba, John S. Macfie, and Jerome A. Colletti, "Effective Sales Force Recognition Programs," *Industrial Marketing Management,* 20, (1991), pp. 9–15.
11. Don E. Schultz and William A. Robinson, *Sales Promotion Management* (Chicago: Crain Books, 1982), p. 8.
12. Laurie Peterson, "CPSA Honors Repeat Campaigns," *Adweek's Marketing Week,* Apr. 29, 1991, p. 33.
13. Thomas McCann, "Promotions Will Gain More Clout in the '90s," *Marketing News,* Nov. 6, 1989, pp. 4, 24.
14. Laurie Petersen, "Agencies See Gold in Promo Field," *Adweek,* Oct. 23, 1989, pp. 1, 76.
15. W. E. Phillips and Bill Robinson, "Continued Sales (Price) Promotion Destroys Brands: Yes; No," *Marketing News,* Jan. 16, 1989, pp. 4, 8.
16. Laurie Freeman and Jennifer Lawrence, "Brand Building Gets New Life," *Advertising Age,* Sept. 4, 1989, pp. 3, 34.
17. Daniel M. Gold, "A Shift in Direction?" *Adweek's Marketing Week,* Apr. 13, 1992, pp. 26–27.
18. Laurie Petersen, "Clutter Anyone?" *Adweek's Marketing Week,* Apr. 8, 1991, pp. 22–23.
19. Emin Babakus, Peter Tat, and William Cunningham, "Coupon Redemption: A Motivational Perspective," *Journal of Consumer Marketing,* Spring 1988, p. 40.
20. Goutam Chakraborty and Catherine Cole, "Coupon Characteristics and Brand Choice," *Psychology and Marketing,* Fall 1991, pp. 145–159.
21. Alison Fahey, "Coupon War Fallout," *Advertising Age,* Sept. 4, 1989, p. 2.
22. Donna Campanella, "Sales Promotion: Couponmania," *Marketing and Media Decisions,* June 1987, pp. 118–122.
23. Ibid.
24. Michael J. McCarthy, "Rewarding 'Frequent Buyer' for Loyalty," *Wall Street Journal,* June 21, 1989, p. B1.
25. Alison Fahey, "Study Shows Retailers Rely on P-O-P," *Advertising Age,* Nov. 27, 1989, p. 83.

26. Peter Tat, William A. Cunningham, and Emin Babakus, "Consumer Perceptions of Rebates," *Journal of Advertising Research*, August–September 1988, p. 48.

27. Magid M. Abraham and Leonard Lodish, "Getting the Most out of Advertising and Promotion," *Harvard Business Review*, May–June 1990, pp. 50–60.

28. Robert D. Wilcox, "Getting Your Money's Worth," *Sales & Marketing Management*, May 1991, pp. 64–68.

29. Thayer C. Taylor, "DEC Gets Its House in Order," *Sales & Marketing Management*, July 1990, pp. 59–66; "Our 1990 Marketing Software Directory," *Business Marketing*, June 1990, pp. 54, 56–58, 60–61, 70, 72; "DEC Fires Up an Enterprise-Wide Networking Strategy," *Electronics*, September 1988; Leslie Helm, "What Next for Digital?" *Business Week*, May 16, 1988, pp. 88–92, 96; Russ Lockwood, "What's New in On-Line Services," *Personal Computing*, June 1987, pp. 151–161; "Digital's High-Tech Coup," *Dun's Business Month*, December 1986, pp. 28–29; and Nick Sullivan, "Making On-Line Information Work for You," *Working Woman*, April 1986, pp. 111–113.

30. *Clockdial*, Dr Pepper Company, no. 3, 1991; *Clockdial*, Dr Pepper Company, no. 1, 1991; Barbara Lippert, "The Doctor's Imitation Blues," *Adweek's Marketing Week*, Oct. 8, 1990; and *Clockdial*, Dr Pepper Company, no. 3, 1990.

MasterCard's Promotional Mix

Including funds from customer fees, interest on outstanding balances, and charges assessed to merchants, banks receive more profit from charge cards than from all other sources combined. If asked, most bankers would probably point to credit cards as the only bright spot in the suffering banking industry. In one year alone, Citibank collected $3.6 billion in credit card interest. But with more than 260 million cards in circulation and the average American owning three cards, credit cards are no longer considered an easy growth market. Hoping to induce potential customers to switch to a new card or to own just one more, credit card companies are lowering prices, increasing services, targeting new markets, initiating new promotions, and adding incentives such as purchase protection, cash dividends, and frequent flier miles. The Discover card has no yearly fee and offers its users rebates for purchases they make. AT&T's card offers purchase protection and extended warranties on items purchased with the card, a 10 percent discount on long distance calls, and no interest charges on balances paid in full. American Express, long acknowledged as a card for "upscale" customers, is attempting to broaden its appeal by targeting less affluent customers, such as college students, and encouraging discount retailers, such as Wal-Mart, to accept the card.

In recent years, MasterCard has had some internal troubles. U.S. banks issuing the card recently suffered $1.2 billion in bad debt losses on it, and MasterCard's market share fell from 37.3 percent to 36 percent. Analysts blame declining credit card use on inflation and increased competition, but agree that some unsuccessful ad campaigns and sales promotions have not improved MasterCard's standing. After stumbling several times, however, MasterCard is back on the road to market share with a more successful promotional mix.

Advertising

Traditional credit card advertising appeals to customers' fantasies. In typical Visa spots, for example, beautiful couples spontaneously jet off to exotic places such as Australia or Paris. American Express advertisements have featured superstars, such as Paul Newman. After MasterCard canceled an unsuccessful and short-lived advertising campaign centered around the slogan,

"Master the Possibilities," the credit card's marketers re-evaluated the message they wanted to convey.

Hoping to differentiate itself from the pack, MasterCard began targeting mainstream cardholders. In its ongoing campaign with the theme "Master the Moment," MasterCard's spots portray the way people really live. Magazine advertisements and spots airing on network television shows focus on real-life, everyday uses for the card, such as the cash advances available through MasterCard's network of automated teller machines. Even advertisements for the premium Gold Card, that is targeted at a more upscale audience, do not focus on glamorous uses for the card. One new spot promotes the Gold Card's "Road Assist" program that serves customers whose cars break down, dispatching a towing service, usually at lower-than-market rates in about 30 minutes. Gold Card advertisements will appear on network news programs. Altogether, MasterCard will spend over $12.5 million for network television advertising alone.

Sales Promotions

Similar to its attempts in the realm of advertising, MasterCard tried a series of sales promotions that were unsuccessful. Hoping to appeal to consumer goodwill, one holiday promotion centered around donating money to charitable causes every time members used their cards. Cardholders were uninspired when MasterCard asked them to "Choose to Make a Difference." Appealing to cardholders' self-interest met with no more success than appealing to their altruism. Supported by print, radio, and direct mail advertising, a "Win Cash" promotion gave shoppers a chance to win a $198,000 grand prize every time they used their cards. After spending approximately $9 million on this promotion, MasterCard deemed it a failure.

After these attempts fell short of expectations, MasterCard came up with a promotion that is succeeding in increasing card use among current holders and attracting new ones. Entitled "MasterValues," this promotion began by offering cardholders discounts at major retail stores such as Toys "R" Us, K mart, Casual Corner, and B. Dalton Booksellers. When customers use the card in conjunction with coupons available at the store or provided in their monthly statements, they receive discounts at the checkout counters of retail outlets nationwide.

Hoping to be more successful this time, MasterCard hired Minneapolis-based U.S. Communications to handle the MasterValues promotion, spending approximately $10 million for advertising. Forty million monthly statements included inserts outlining the program. Keeping with the "Master the Moment" theme, television commercials detailed the promotion and mentioned all of the retail partners. Radio and print advertising, in-store signage, and a national public relations program were all included in the campaign.

MasterValues has been so successful that MasterCard is continuing it indefinitely, recently adding six new retailers, and supporting the sales promotion extension with about $10 million in radio spots, magazine advertisements, and a network and cable television advertising campaign. The promotion's ongoing strength, say MasterCard's executives, is attributable to its point-of-purchase nature. Just as customers at 5,000 retailers nationwide are deciding how to pay for their purchases, they spot the MasterValues in-store signs and pull out their MasterCards.

Event Sponsorship

As part of its new global strategy, MasterCard is sponsoring the 1994 World Cup of Soccer, the card's largest event sponsorship ever. Designed to build brand awareness, stimulate card acquisition, and enhance MasterCard's image as a global payment system, the 3-year sponsorship will cost between $30 and $60 million and give the card media exposure at over 200 soccer events around the world. As an official World Cup sponsor, MasterCard can advertise on stadium boards hosting international soccer matches leading up to the World Cup Championship, as well as at the final 52 matches to be held in twelve U.S. cities. In addition, MasterCard has the first option to buy advertising time on all World Cup English-language telecasts.

This is not the first time the company has sponsored World Cup Soccer. In 1990, MasterCard sponsored the World Cup Championship in Italy. Unfortunately, the company did not buy stadium advertising, and got very little exposure or benefit from the sponsorship. This time, in an effort to avoid its previous mistake, MasterCard will begin advertising well in advance of the championship match. The name MasterCard will appear in ads on stadium boards, on television commercials that emphasize MasterCard's worldwide acceptance, even on hot air balloons drifting above the crowd at soccer matches. Because the United States is hosting the 1994 World Cup Championship, MasterCard executives believe it will be easier to reach American consumers than it was the last time around.

MasterCard's Future

As Americans become less optimistic about the economy, many are cutting down on their use of credit cards. To remain competitive, MasterCard continues to look for new ways to promote the card. One of its newest attempts is a program called "co-branding," in which MasterCard issues jointly-sponsored credit cards. For example, the Air Travel Card, used by corporations to charge tickets on about 30 airlines, is introducing the MasterCard Business Card that companies can offer to their employees for air travel.

In recent years, MasterCard's share in the $343-billion charge card market has decreased dramatically, and most of its lost business has gone to its number-one competitor, Visa International. MasterCard's promotional efforts, however, are not aimed at tumbling Visa from its number-one spot. The company hopes that it can convince those who might choose the Discover Card, American Express "Optima" Card, or even cash to use MasterCard instead.

Questions for Discussion

1. In general, what types of problems do credit card companies face when trying to promote their products?
2. How has MasterCard attempted to differentiate its advertising from competitors' advertising?
3. Why is MasterCard's "MasterValues" program successful?
4. What benefits are provided to MasterCard through event sponsorship?

Sources: Gary Levin, "Co-Branding Trend Takes Credit Cards," *Advertising Age*, Nov. 11, 1991, p. 69; Gary Levin, "MasterCard Multiplies," *Advertising Age*, August 19, 1991, pp. 2, 45; "American Credit Cards: The Non-Banks Muscle In," *The Economist*, May 25, 1991, pp. 84, 89; Alison Fahey, "MasterCard Scores," *Advertising Age*, March 25, 1991, pp. 3, 45; John McManus and Kate Fitzgerald, "MasterCard Turns Up Heat," *Advertising Age*, July 16, 1990, pp. 1, 42; Mark D. Fefer, "Who's Winning the Credit Card War," *Fortune*, July 2, 1990, pp. 66–71; Brian Bagot, "Charged Up," *Marketing & Media Decisions*, April, 1990, pp. 73–78; Russell Mitchell, "The Failed Vision: Jim Robinsons's Big Plans for American Express Aren't Working," *Business Week*, March 19, 1990, pp. 108–113; Judith Graham, "MasterCard Sets 'Win Cash' Promotion," *Advertising Age*, August 21, 1989, p. 60; Judith Graham, "MasterCard, Visa Plan Holiday Push," *Advertising Age*, June 5, 1989, p. 2; Judith Graham, "MasterCard Readies $20M Ad Campaign," *Advertising Age*, March 13, 1989, p. 3; and "Is MasterCard Mastering the Possibilities?" *Business Week*, October 10, 1988, p. 123.

R. J. Reynolds Tobacco Company:
Joe Camel Under Fire

The Surgeon General of the United States reports that every year about 390,000 Americans lose their lives because of smoking cigarettes and that average male smokers are fifteen times more likely to die of lung cancer than non-smokers. Despite these grim statistics, Americans continue to spend about $42 billion a year on cigarettes. Ever since citizens of Jamestown, Virginia planted the first commercial tobacco crop in 1612, cigarettes have been part of American life and the tobacco industry a powerful force in the American economy.

Although Americans continue lighting up in large numbers, sales of older cigarette brands, such as R. J. Reynolds's Camel Filters, have slowed down significantly. However, in 1987, Reynolds introduced a new advertising campaign featuring the cartoon camel known as Old Joe. In three years, the brand's market share grew from 2.7 percent to 3.1 percent, a notable rise for a 75-year-old brand in a declining market. Industry analysts attribute Camel cigarettes' sales increase to the popularity of advertisements and sales promotions featuring Old Joe. The news for RJR Tobacco, however, is not all good. Anti-smoking activists repeatedly criticize the manufacturer for creating a campaign that they say targets underage smokers and demand the demise of Old Joe Camel.

Historical Perspective

Ever since the American Tobacco Company introduced Lucky Strike cigarettes in 1916, tobacco ads have been the subject of controversy. Companies have employed famous people to make claims about the benefits of specific cigarette brands. Magazines featured cigarette ads making health claims (relief from fatigue, aid to digestion, protection from the common cold), and celebrities such as Bing Crosby, Bob Hope, and Ronald Reagan regularly promoted various brands of cigarettes.

In the late 1950s came the first studies linking smoking and cancer, and the Federal Trade Commission prohibited cigarette ads from making health claims. In 1966, five years after studies proved that cigarette smoking causes lung cancer, cigarette manufac-

turers were required to put cautionary health warnings on their packages. In 1971, with growing evidence about the dangers of cigarette smoking and mounting public pressure, cigarette advertising was banned entirely from radio and television, and the mandatory warning on cigarette packages was changed from "may be hazardous" to "is dangerous."

Camel's Old Joe Campaign

When R. J. Reynolds could no longer rely on radio and television to sell its cigarettes, the company, along with other tobacco manufacturers, turned to print and direct mail for the bulk of its promotion. Despite more than a decade of these efforts, sales of the venerable Camel brand continued declining, until ads featuring Old Joe rejuvenated it. Whether dressed for adventure or a night on the town, Old Joe, is depicted as a "smooth character," who has style and class. Recently, Video Storyboard Tests, a market research firm, rated ads featuring the sophisticated camel as second in popularity only to ads by Calvin Klein. Video Storyboard points out that Old Joe's message appeals strongly to younger people—and that is precisely what has given rise to controversy.

Ethical Considerations

RJR executives openly admit picking a "spokescartoon" with a contemporary image to attract younger consumers, but the question many critics are raising is just how young? Three studies recently published in the *Journal of American Medical Association* suggest that Old Joe's audience is far too young, that recognition of the character is lower among adults than children, and that cartoon camel ads and promotions encourage children to smoke. The first study asserts that the campaign's popularity boosted RJR's share of the illegal children's cigarette market from .5 percent prior to the campaign to over 30 percent today. The second study shows that among all age groups, children aged 12 and 13 are the most familiar with the "Smooth

Character" campaign. The third study concludes that a majority of 6-year-olds associate Old Joe with cigarettes as clearly as they do Mickey Mouse with the Disney Channel. Thirty percent of 3-year-olds questioned correctly matched Old Joe with a picture of a cigarette.

R. J. Reynolds disputes all three of the studies. Company officials contend that the statistics are inaccurate, deny that the Old Joe campaign is targeted toward children, and assert that just because children can identify the logo doesn't mean they will buy the product. One company spokesperson argues that it is contrary to the industry's best interests for those under age to smoke, because it increases the likelihood that the government, trying to protect children, will ban cigarette advertising altogether. As evidence of the company's goodwill, RJR points to its ongoing billboard and print campaign to discourage children from smoking.

Even before the Joe Camel studies were published, the U.S. Congress was looking into RJR's direct-marketing practices involving a Joe Camel t-shirt offer. Calling a toll-free number advertised in *Sports Illustrated*, a 14-year-old boy received not only the desired t-shirt, but three packs of Camel cigarettes. The results of the JAMA studies only fanned the fire of controversy surrounding the Joe Camel campaign. Several health-related groups are insisting that R. J. Reynolds get rid of the Old Joe character, and the Coalition on Smoking and Health petitioned the FTC to take action against the company's cartoon camel. The American Medical Association and the U.S. Surgeon General are demanding that RJR voluntarily remove Joe from all advertising and promotion for Camel cigarettes. Some activists are even hoping that the study's information will lead to a complete ban on cigarette advertising.

For now, RJR has no plans to drop the popular Joe. The American Association of Advertisers supports the company, decrying what it terms unconstitutional restrictions on advertising. From the results of a recent *Advertising Age* poll, it seems that many Americans agree. Over half of the respondents who believe that Old Joe strongly influences children to smoke also believe that RJR should not bow to outside pressures to get rid of him.

Questions for Discussion

1. Does the banning of cigarette advertising violate a tobacco company's first amendment constitutional rights?
2. As long as the sale of tobacco products is legal, is it ethical for a company to promote a product that kills almost 400,000 people in the United States annually? Discuss.
3. Is it ethical for RJR to use a promotional campaign that is highly effective in reaching children?
4. Evaluate RJR's response to the criticisms of its Old Joe Camel campaign.

Sources: William Ecenbarger, "The Strange History of Tobacco," *Reader's Digest*, April, 1992, pp. 139–142; Adrienne Ward, "Old Joe Lights Up AA Faxes," *Advertising Age*, March 23, 1992, pp. 3, 46; "Should Old Joe Stay or Go?" *Advertising Age*, March 16, 1992, p. 52; Walecia Konrad, "I'd Toddle a Mile for a Camel," *Business Week*, Dec. 2, 1991, p. 34; Judann Dagnoli, "'JAMA' Lights New Fire Under Camel's Ads," *Advertising Age*, Dec. 16, 1991, pp. 3, 32; Kim Foltz, "Old Joe is Paying Off for Camel," *New York Times*, Aug. 7, 1990; Steven W. Colford and Judann Dagnoli, "RJR Now Hit for Camel Mail Mix-up," *Advertising Age*, March 5, 1990, pp. 3, 41; and "American Heart Video Journal, Volume II, Tobacco Advertising," American Heart Association, 1987.

PREVIEW:

MICROMARKET COMPUTER APPLICATION IV

Eatin' Treats, Inc.: Managing the Sales Force

This exercise allocates Eatin' Treats' sales force to four geographic regions and three customer types as constrained by a limited sales force budget. The equalized workload method is employed and calculated on Lotus 1-2-3. The number of outlets, frequency of calls for each customer type, and number of calls a salesperson makes each day are varied, one at a time, to investigate different "what if" scenarios. A written memo discussing recommendations and case questions conclude this exercise.

V *Pricing Decisions*

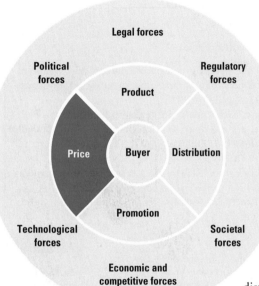

If an organization is to provide a satisfying market-ing mix, the price must be acceptable to target market members. Pricing decisions can have numer-ous effects on other parts of the marketing mix. For example, a product's price can influence how customers perceive it, what types of marketing institutions are used in distributing the product, and how the product is promoted. In Chapter 18, we discuss the importance of price and look at some of the characteristics of price and nonprice competition. We then examine the ma-jor factors that affect marketers' pricing decisions. Eight major stages used by marketers in establishing prices are discussed in Chapter 19.

579

18 *Pricing Concepts*

OBJECTIVES

- To understand the nature and importance of price

- To become aware of the characteristics of price and nonprice competition

- To examine various pricing objectives

- To explore key factors that may influence marketers' pricing decisions

- To consider issues affecting the pricing of products for industrial markets

Before the days of home video, the only way to see a hit movie was in a theater. Now studios release films on video soon after they play in theaters and rent them at a cost most movie-lovers can afford. Because renting is such a bargain, few industry experts believe there is a viable market for home video sales. Sales account for only about 10 percent of the business at Blockbuster Video, one of America's biggest video chains. Contending that about 50 percent of U.S. households have already purchased videos, some firms maintain that sales will soar into the millions if the price is right.

LIVE Home Video believes that $14.95 is the right price and plans to release 40 recent titles at that price. Although LIVE is one of the earliest supporters of the $14.95 movie, other suppliers are joining the fold. FoxVideo and MCA/Universal Pictures Home Video recently announced promotions in this price category, and after conducting a survey on various pricing options, Orion Home Video is going even lower by selling six titles for $7.98 each. Special offers can reduce prices even further. Orion's supermarket promotion offers six titles for $5.99 each with a minimum grocery purchase, and Disney Home Video is giving a limited-time $5 rebate on the purchase of two Disney full-length films. Industry analysts credit an intensifying battle for shelf space and competition from grocery and drugstore chains for the rising popularity of budget pricing. They also assert that customers are more likely to indulge in impulse buying when the price for a video suddenly drops from $20 to $14.95.

Shoppers cannot, however, count on finding all the movies they want for $14.95. In fact, prices vary enough to boggle the mind. At the same time that Family Home Entertainment, LIVE's children's line, releases a new series of animated Mutant Ninja Turtle videos for a retail price of $12.95, it continues selling other animated children's films for anywhere between $10 to $15, while Disney Home Video promotes a "low" $24.99 price for its animated "Year-Round Classics" like *Bambi* and *Robin Hood*. Action films usually retail for about $25, and, without apparent consistency, many titles continue to sell for $60 to $100.[1]

Photo courtesy of Blockbuster Video.

M OVIE VIDEO COMPANIES are using price, along with other elements, to distinguish their products from those of competitors. As in the case of these firms, pricing is a crucial element in most organizations' marketing mixes. In this chapter we focus first on the nature of price and its importance to marketers. We then consider some of the characteristics of price and nonprice competition. Next we explore the various types of pricing objectives that marketers may establish, and we examine in some detail the numerous factors that can influence pricing decisions. Finally, we discuss selected issues related to the pricing of products for business-to-business markets.

The Nature of Price

To a buyer, **price** is the value placed on what is exchanged. Something of value —usually buying power—is exchanged for satisfaction or utility. As described in Chapter 2, buying power depends on a buyer's income, credit, and wealth. It is a mistake to believe that price is always money paid or some other financial consideration. In fact, trading of products—**barter**—is the oldest form of exchange. Money may or may not be involved.

Buyers' interest in price stems from their expectations about the usefulness of a product or the satisfaction they may derive from it. Because buyers have limited resources, they must allocate their buying power so that they can obtain the most desired products. Buyers must decide whether the utility gained in an exchange is worth the buying power sacrificed. Almost anything of value— ideas, services, rights, and goods—can be assessed by a price because in our society the financial price is the measurement of value commonly used in exchanges. For example, a painting by Picasso may be valued, or priced, at $2 million. Financial price, then, quantifies value. It is the basis of most market exchanges.

Terms Used to Describe Price

Price is expressed in different terms for different exchanges. For instance, automobile insurance companies charge a *premium* for protection from the cost of injuries or repairs stemming from an automobile accident. An officer who stops you for speeding writes a ticket that requires you to pay a *fine*. If a lawyer defends you, a *fee* is charged, and if you use a railway or taxi, a *fare* is charged. A *toll* is charged for the use of bridges or turnpikes. *Rent* is paid for the use of equipment or an apartment. A *commission* is remitted to a broker for the sale of real estate. *Dues* are paid for membership in a club or group. A *deposit* is made to hold or lay away merchandise. A *tip* helps pay waitresses or waiters for their services. *Interest* is charged for the loan that you obtain, and *taxes* are paid for government services. The value of many products is called *price*. Although price may be expressed in a variety of ways, it is important to remember that the purpose of this concept is to quantify and express the value of the items in a market exchange.

The Importance of Price to Marketers

As pointed out in Chapter 9, developing a product may be a lengthy process. It takes time to plan promotion and to communicate benefits. Distribution usually requires a long-term commitment to dealers who will handle the product. Often price is the only thing a marketer can change quickly to respond to changes in demand or to the actions of competitors. Bear in mind, however, that under certain circumstances the price variable may be relatively inflexible.

Price is also a key element in the marketing mix because it relates directly to the generation of total revenue. The following equation is an important one for the entire organization:

$$\text{Profits} = \text{Total Revenues} - \text{Total Costs}$$

or

$$\text{Profits} = (\text{Prices} \times \text{Quantities Sold}) - \text{Total Costs}$$

Prices affect an organization's profits, which are its lifeblood for long-term survival. Price affects the profit equation in several ways. It directly influences the equation because it is a major component. It has an indirect impact because it can be a major determinant of the quantities sold. Even more indirectly, price influences total costs through its impact on quantities sold.

Because price has a psychological impact on customers, marketers can use it symbolically. By raising a price, they can emphasize the quality of a product and try to increase the status associated with its ownership. By lowering a price, they can emphasize a bargain and attract customers who go out of their way—spending extra time and effort—to save a small amount. Price can have a strong effect on sales.

Price and Nonprice Competition

A product offering can compete on a price or nonprice basis. The choice will affect not only pricing decisions and activities, but also those associated with other marketing mix decision variables.

Price Competition

When **price competition** is used, a marketer emphasizes price as an issue and matches or beats the prices of competitors. As discussed in Inside Marketing, Toys "R" Us engages in price competition by pricing its products below competitors' prices and by emphasizing low prices in its advertisements. To compete effectively on a price basis, a firm should be the low-cost producer of the product. If all firms producing goods in an industry charge the same price, the firm with the lowest costs is the most profitable. Firms that stress low price as a key element in the marketing mix tend to produce standardized products. A seller using price competition may change prices frequently or at least must be willing and able to do so. Whenever competitors change their prices, the seller

Lower Prices Make Toys "R" Us Number One

WITH 457 STORES WORLDWIDE, profits of $321.1 million, and a 25 percent share of the $13 billion U.S. retail toy market, Toys "R" Us has transformed a seasonal business into a year-round moneymaker. At a recent Financial Executives Conference, a corporate officer from Toys "R" Us asserted that no one makes a profit in the toy business except KayBee and Toys "R" Us. The company's formula for becoming the world's largest toyseller is to combine self-service, huge inventories, and most notably, discount prices.

Toys "R" Us is one of the first retail stores to put the concept of "everyday low prices" to work, believing strongly that consumers prefer knowing they can come to the store on any day to buy what they want instead of waiting for a sale. Toys "R" Us is determined not to permit any of its competitors to offer lower prices. Not every one of the store's 18,000 items costs less, but comparative shopping allows the company, overall, not to be undersold.

Being the undisputed champion of toy stores has not made Toys "R" Us complacent. The company was dissatisfied on the rare occasions when a competitor had a sale that undercut its prices. To prevent that from happening too often, Toys "R" Us initiated a new pricing scheme called "Check It Out," designed to further underprice its competitors. One company executive predicted that once the new prices went into effect, Toys "R" Us would "get market share from everybody." The tactics are to offer selected merchandise below the sale price of other stores. From Barbie dolls to baby strollers, the prices will tell customers there is no reason to wait for a sale. Board games like Monopoly and Clue sell for $1–$2 less than at competitors' stores. Hawaiian Fun Barbie sells for $5.99, $2 below the regular retail price and $1 lower than even the sale price.

To introduce "Check It Out," advertisements ran in 650 newspapers, reaching about 65 million readers. The advertisements explained the new pricing policy, accenting certain items and prices and urging consumers to "Check It Out." In-store displays support the newspaper campaign. For the first time in the company's history, Toys "R" Us is advertising on television outside of the Christmas season. The new commercial uses the familiar "I'm a Toys 'R' Us Kid" theme in a 30-second spot promoting various brand-name bicycles.

Retailing all over the United States is currently suffering, and many well-known stores are closing their doors permanently. Child World, at one time the number-two toy retailer, recently went up for sale. But Toys "R" Us is thriving, branching out into a children's clothing chain called Kids "R" Us. The organization recently opened a $40 million distribution center that holds 45 percent more merchandise than its existing warehouse but takes up only two-thirds of the space. This innovative warehouse will lower handling costs, which in turn will help Toys "R" Us to continue to beat everyone's prices.

Sources: Alison Fahey, "Toys 'R' Us Sets Lower Pricing," *Advertising Age*, Mar. 4, 1991, p. 4; "Top Executive Symposium—New Realities for Retailing in the Next Decade: Question and Answer Session," *Retail Control*, October 1990, pp. 3–8; Susan Caminiti, "The New Champs of Retailing," *Fortune*, Sept. 24, 1990, pp. 85–100; and Faye Rice, "Superelf Plans for Xma$," *Fortune*, Sept. 11, 1989, p. 151.

must respond quickly and aggressively. As shown in Figure 18.1, Airborne Express engages in price competition with Federal Express.

Price competition gives a marketer flexibility. Prices can be altered to account for changes in the firm's costs or in demand for the product. If competitors try to gain market share by cutting prices, an organization competing on a price basis can react quickly to such efforts. However, a major drawback of price competition is that competitors, too, have the flexibility to adjust their prices. Thus they can quickly match or beat an organization's price cuts. A price war

may result, as has occurred in the fast-food industry. When the Taco Bell and Wendy's chains reduced the price of many of their menu items to less than $1, other fast-food chains were forced to lower prices or offer specials to remain competitive. Furthermore, if a user of price competition is forced to raise prices, competing firms that are not under the same pressures may decide not to raise their prices.

Nonprice Competition

Nonprice competition occurs when a seller elects not to focus on price and instead emphasizes distinctive product features, service, product quality, promotion, packaging, or other factors to distinguish its product from competing brands. Thus nonprice competition is based on factors other than price. Nonprice competition gives an organization the opportunity to increase its brand's unit sales through means other than changing the brand's price. As shown in Figure 18.2, Frigidaire engages in nonprice competition by emphasizing quality and value in advertising its washing machines. One major advantage of nonprice competition is that a firm can build customer loyalty toward its brand. If customers prefer a brand because of nonprice issues, they may not be easily lured away by competing firms and brands. But when price is the primary reason that customers buy a particular brand, the competition can attract such customers through price cuts.

Nonprice competition is workable under the right conditions. A company must be able to distinguish its brand through unique product features, higher quality, customer service, promotion, packaging, and the like. Buyers not only must be able to perceive these distinguishing characteristics but must also view them as desirable. The distinguishing features that set a particular brand apart from its competitors should be difficult, if not impossible, for competitors to imitate. Finally, the organization must extensively promote the distinguishing characteristics of the brand to establish its superiority and to set it apart from competitors in the minds of buyers.

Foreign firms put less emphasis on price than do their U.S. counterparts. They look for a competitive edge by concentrating on promotion, research and development, marketing research, and marketing channel considerations.

A marketer attempting to compete on a nonprice basis is still not able to simply ignore competitors' prices, however. The organization must be aware of competitors' prices and will probably price its brand near or slightly above competing brands. As an example, Sony sells television sets in a highly competitive market and charges higher prices for them. It is successful nonetheless. Sony's emphasis on high product quality both distinguishes it from its competitors and allows it to set higher prices. Therefore, price still remains a crucial marketing mix component in situations that call for nonprice competition.

Pricing Objectives

Pricing objectives are overall goals that describe what the firm wants to achieve through its pricing efforts. Because pricing objectives influence decisions in most functional areas—including finance, accounting, and production—the

Figure 18.2

Nonprice Competition

Companies that compete on a nonprice basis generally promote quality features and value.

Source: Courtesy Frigidaire Company.

objectives must be consistent with the organization's overall mission and purpose. Since deregulation, banks have become more interested in pricing. As competition intensified, bank executives realized that their products had to be priced to meet not only short-term profit goals, but also long-term strategic objectives.[2] Because of the many areas involved, a marketer often uses multiple pricing objectives. In this section we look at a few of the typical pricing objectives that companies might set for themselves.

Survival

A fundamental pricing objective is survival. Most organizations will tolerate difficulties, such as short-run losses and internal upheaval, if they are necessary for survival. Because price is a flexible variable, it is sometimes used to increase sales volume to levels that match the organization's expenses.

Profit

Although businesses may claim that their objective is to maximize profits for their owners, the objective of profit maximization is rarely operational because its achievement is difficult to measure. Because of this difficulty, profit objectives tend to be set at levels that the owners and top-level decision makers view as satisfactory. Specific profit objectives may be stated in terms of actual dollar amounts or in terms of percentage change relative to the profits of a previous period.

Return on Investment

Pricing to attain a specified rate of return on the company's investment is a profit-related pricing objective. Most pricing objectives based on return on investment (ROI) are achieved by trial and error because not all cost and revenue data needed to project the return on investment are available when prices are set. General Motors, for example, uses ROI pricing objectives.

The objective of return on investment may be used less as managers and marketers in diversified companies stress the creation of shareholder value. When shareholder value is used as a performance objective, strategies—including those involving price—are evaluated on the basis of the impact they will have on the value investors perceive in the firm.[3]

Market Share

Market share, which is a product's sales in relation to total industry sales, can be an appropriate pricing objective. Many firms establish pricing objectives to maintain or increase market share. For years both Coke and Pepsi have set pricing objectives aimed at gaining market share. Recently, ConAgra, Inc. introduced Budget Gourmet Light and Healthy Dinners, priced at about $1 below

Figure 18.3

Market Share Pricing Objective

ConAgra, Inc., maker of Healthy Choice, launched Budget Gourmet Light and Healthy Dinners to gain additional market share.

Source: The All American Gourmet Company.

Healthy Choice (also made by ConAgra), to gain additional market share (see Figure 18.3).

Maintaining or increasing market share need not depend on growth in industry sales. Remember that an organization can increase its market share even though sales for the total industry are decreasing. On the other hand, an organization's sales volume may, in fact, increase while its market share within the industry decreases, assuming that the overall market is growing.

Cash Flow

Some organizations set prices to recover cash as fast as possible. Financial managers are understandably interested in quickly recovering capital spent to develop products. This objective may have the support of the marketing manager who anticipates a short product life cycle.

Although it may be acceptable in some situations, the use of cash flow and recovery as an objective oversimplifies the value of price in contributing to profits. A disadvantage of this pricing objective could be high prices, which might allow competitors with lower prices to gain a large share of the market.

Status Quo

In some cases, an organization may be in a favorable position and, desiring nothing more, may set an objective of status quo. Status quo objectives can focus on several dimensions—maintaining a certain market share, meeting (but not beating) competitors' prices, achieving price stability, or maintaining a favorable public image. A status quo pricing objective can reduce a firm's risks by helping stabilize demand for its products. The use of status quo pricing objectives sometimes minimizes pricing as a competitive tool, leading to a climate of nonprice competition in an industry.

Product Quality

A company might have the objective of product quality leadership in the industry. This goal normally dictates a high price to cover the high product quality and, in some instances, the high cost of research and development. Although the company has had to reduce prices recently, Compaq Computers, for example, has charged high prices and has been viewed as a quality leader in the business computer industry. Jenn-Air products, shown in Figure 18.4, are premium-priced to cover higher production costs and to facilitate a high-quality image.

Factors Affecting Pricing Decisions

Pricing decisions can be complex because of the number of details that must be considered. Frequently there is considerable uncertainty about the reactions to price on the part of buyers, channel members, competitors, and others. Price is also an important consideration in marketing planning, market analysis, and

Figure 18.4

Product Quality Pricing Objective

Jenn-Air promotes higher quality at a slightly higher price.

Source: Jenn-Air Company.

sales forecasting. It is a major issue when assessing a brand's position relative to competing brands. Most factors that affect pricing decisions can be grouped into one of the eight categories shown in Figure 18.5. In this section we explore how each of these eight groups of factors enters into price decision making.

Organizational and Marketing Objectives

Marketers should set prices that are consistent with the organization's goals and mission. For example, a retailer trying to position itself as value-oriented may wish to set prices that are quite reasonable relative to product quality. In this case, a marketer would not want to set premium prices on products but would strive to price products in line with this overall organizational goal.

The firm's marketing objectives must also be considered. Decision makers should make pricing decisions that are compatible with the organization's marketing objectives. Say, for instance, that one of a producer's marketing objectives is a 12 percent increase in unit sales by the end of the next year. Assuming that buyers are price-sensitive, increasing the price or setting a price above the average market price would not be in line with the firm's sales objective.

Types of Pricing Objectives

The type of pricing objectives a marketer uses obviously will have considerable bearing on the determination of prices. An objective of a certain target return on investment requires that prices be set at a level that will generate a sales volume high enough to yield the specified target. A market share pricing objective usually causes a firm to price a product below competing brands of similar

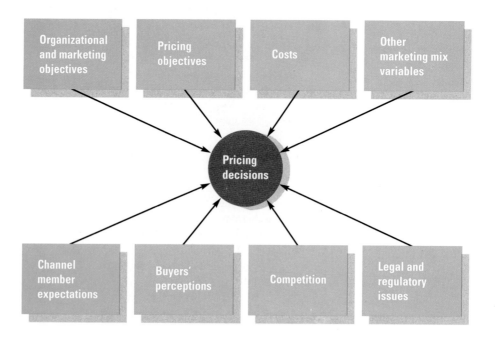

Figure 18.5

Factors That Affect Pricing Decisions

quality to attract competitors' customers to the company's brand. This type of pricing can lead to lower profits. A marketer sometimes uses temporary price reductions in the hope of gaining market share. A cash flow pricing objective may cause an organization to set a relatively high price, which can place the product at a competitive disadvantage. On the other hand, a cash flow pricing objective sometimes results in a long, sustained low price. However, this type of objective is more likely to be addressed by using temporary price reductions, such as sales, rebates, and special discounts.

Costs

Obviously, costs must be an issue when establishing price. A firm may temporarily sell products below cost to match competition, to generate cash flow, or even to increase market share, but in the long run it cannot survive by selling its products below cost. Even when a firm has a high-volume business, it cannot survive if each item is sold slightly below what it costs. A marketer should be careful to analyze all costs so that they can be included in the total cost associated with a product.

Besides considering the costs associated with a particular product, marketers must also take into account the costs that the product shares with others in the product line. Products often share some costs, particularly the costs of research and development, production, and distribution. Most marketers view a product's cost as a minimum, or floor, below which the product cannot be priced. We discuss cost analysis in more detail in the next chapter and in Chapter 21.

Other Marketing Mix Variables

All marketing mix variables are highly interrelated. Pricing decisions can influence decisions and activities associated with product, distribution, and promotion variables. A product's price frequently affects the demand for the item. A high price, for instance, may result in low unit sales, which in turn may lead to higher production costs per unit. Conversely, lower per-unit production costs may result from a low price. For many products, buyers associate better product quality with a high price and poorer product quality with a low price. This perceived price/quality relationship influences customers' overall image of products or brands. Sony, for example, prices its television sets higher than average to help communicate that Sony television sets are high-quality electronic products. The price sometimes determines the degree of status associated with ownership of the product.

Pricing decisions influence the number of competing brands in a product category. When a firm introduces a product, sets a relatively high price, and achieves high unit sales, competitors may be attracted to this product category. If a firm uses a low price, the low profit margin may be unattractive to potential competition.

The price of a product is linked to several dimensions of its distribution. Premium-priced products often are marketed through selective or exclusive distribution; lower-priced products in the same product category may be sold through intensive distribution. For example, Cross pens are distributed through selective distribution and Bic pens through intensive distribution. The manner in which a product is stored and transported may also be associated with its price. When a producer is developing the price of a product, the profit margins of marketing channel members, such as wholesalers and retailers, must be considered. Channel members must be adequately compensated for the functions they perform. Inadequately compensated channel members will withdraw from a marketing channel.

The way a product is promoted can be affected by its price. Bargain prices are often included in advertisements, whereas premium prices are less likely to appear in advertising messages. The issue of a premium price is sometimes included in advertisements for upscale items, such as luxury cars or fine jewelry. Higher-priced products are more likely to require personal selling efforts than lower-priced ones. A customer may purchase an inexpensive watch in a self-service environment but hesitate to buy an expensive watch in the same store, if it is available there.

The price structure can affect a salesperson's relationship with customers. A complex pricing structure takes longer to explain to customers, is more likely to confuse the buyer, and may cause misunderstandings that result in long-term customer dissatisfaction. For example, the pricing structures of many airlines are complex and frequently confuse ticket sales agents and travelers alike.

Channel Member Expectations

When making price decisions, a producer must consider what distribution channel members (such as wholesalers and retailers) expect. A channel member certainly expects to receive a profit for the functions it performs. The amount of profit expected depends on what the intermediary could make if it were handling a competing product instead. Also, the amount of time and the resources required to carry the product influence intermediaries' expectations.

Channel members often expect producers to provide discounts for large orders and quick payment. (Discounts are discussed later in this chapter.) At times, resellers expect producers to provide several support activities, such as sales training, service training, repair advisory service, cooperative advertising, sales promotions, and perhaps a program for returning unsold merchandise to the producer. These support activities clearly have costs associated with them, and a producer must consider these costs when determining prices. Failure to price the product so that the producer can provide some of these support activities may cause resellers to view the product less favorably.

Buyers' Perceptions

One important question that marketers should assess when making price decisions is "How important is the price to people in the target market?" The importance of price is not absolute; it can vary from market segment to market segment and from person to person. Members of one market segment may be more sensitive to price than members in a different target market. Moreover, the importance of price will vary across different product categories. Price may be a more important factor in the purchase of gasoline than in the purchase of a pair of jeans because buyers may be more sensitive to the price of gasoline than to the price of jeans.

For numerous products, buyers have a range of acceptable prices. This range can be fairly narrow in some product categories but wider in others. A marketer should become aware of the acceptable range of prices in the relevant product category. (This and related issues are discussed in more detail in Chapter 19.)

Consumers' perceptions of price may also be influenced by all products in a firm's product line. The perception of price depends on a product's actual price, plus the consumer's reference price—that is, the consumer's expectation of price. Exposure to a range of prices in a product line affects the consumer's expectations and perceptions of acceptable prices.[4] Customers' ranges of price acceptability can change for certain products over time, as discussed in the Global Perspective.

Buyers' perceptions of a product relative to competing products may allow or encourage a firm to set a price that differs significantly from the prices of competing products. If the product is deemed superior to most of the competition, a premium price may be feasible. Strong brand loyalty sometimes provides the opportunity to charge a premium price. Schwinn, for instance, has developed strong customer loyalty for its high-quality bicycles. Thus it is able to charge premium prices for its products. On the other hand, if buyers view the product unfavorably (assuming that they are not extremely negative), a lower price may be required to generate sales. There is a considerable body of research on the relationship between price and consumers' perceptions of quality. Consumers use price as an indicator of quality when brands are unfamiliar, and the perceived risk of making unsatisfactory choices is high. They also rely on price if there is little information available and judging a product's attributes is difficult.[5]

Competition

A marketer needs to know competitors' prices so that the firm can adjust its own prices accordingly. This does not mean that a company will necessarily match competitors' prices; it may set its price above or below theirs. However, matching competitors' fares is an important strategy for survival in the airline industry.[6]

When adjusting prices, a marketer must assess how competitors will respond. Will competitors change their prices (some, in fact, may not), and if so, will they raise or lower them? In Chapter 2 we describe several types of competitive market structures. The structure that characterizes the industry to which a firm belongs affects the flexibility of price setting.

When an organization operates as a monopoly and is unregulated, it can set whatever prices the market will bear. However, the company may avoid pricing the product at the highest possible level for fear of inviting government regulation or because it wants to penetrate a market by using a lower price. If the monopoly is regulated, it normally has less pricing flexibility; the regulatory body lets it set prices that generate a reasonable, but not excessive, return. A government-owned monopoly may price products below cost to make them

Haute Couture Moves Downscale

NAMES LIKE Yves Saint Laurent, Givenchy, Christian Dior, and Giorgio Armani are synonymous with haute couture, one-of-a-kind, hand-crafted fashions priced beyond the means of all but an elite few. In the best French fashion houses, women like Princess Caroline of Monaco and Jackie Kennedy Onassis pay $30,000 for one dress, flying to Paris for fittings and waiting three months for delivery. Even "luxury ready-to-wear" commands extravagant prices. Most women can only admire an $1,800 dress, let alone spend $10,000 for a Saint Laurent Rive Gauche suit. To attract a larger market, many European couturiers are offering more moderately priced collections, known in the fashion industry as bridge lines.

Certainly, global recession has had an impact on the world of high fashion. The chairman of the Fédération Française reports that orders for French haute couture and upscale ready-to-wear are declining steadily, and the president of Yves Saint Laurent says orders for his custom-made line are down by 50 percent. In style-conscious Italy, sales of chic apparel dropped 12 percent in one year. As the glamorous 1980s crashed headlong into the price-conscious 1990s, consumers became less willing to spend their dollars on clothes just to make a fashion statement.

Many European couturiers, however, are counting on consumer willingness to spend $100 to $900 for bridge-collection labels. Among the down-to-earth lines are Givenchy's Life, Ungaro's Emanuel, Yves Saint Laurent's Variation, and Christian Dior's Coordonnes. In France, a Variation sports jacket sells for about $200 American dollars. Although an Ungaro white sequin dress costs about $2,500, European shoppers can pick up a similar dress from the less-expensive Emanuel line for $698. In the United States, almost everything in Ungaro's Emanuel collection is priced under $500. Instead of luxurious fabrics and delicate craftsmanship, Armani Jeans offers casual apparel like cotton T-shirts and denim jackets. For about $110, shoppers can walk out of a shop wearing a pair of Armani Jeans white stretch pants and an Armani Jeans T-shirt. While these figures still look pricey, fashion marketers are confident that the prosperous middle class can afford them.

Since European haute couture houses were born in the days of Napoleon III, some women have always spent a fortune on fashion. Industry experts believe that, for the most part, those days are over. They predict that less-expensive bridge lines will flourish into a $1 billion worldwide market, with the United States as the most enthusiastic customer. Boutiques featuring second collections are already flourishing on Rodeo Drive in Beverly Hills and in New York and Washington, D.C. Some designers, however, refuse to jump on the bandwagon for fear that cheaper collections will pollute the glamorous image of haute couture.

Sources: Barbara Rudolph, "Why Chic Is Now Cheaper," *Time*, Nov. 11, 1991, pp. 68–70; Zina Sawaya, "Alter Egos," *Forbes*, June 24, 1991, pp. 58, 61; and Blanca Riemer, Laura Zinn, and Fred Kapner, "Haute Couture That's Not So Haute," *Business Week*, Apr. 22, 1991, p. 108.

accessible to people who otherwise could not afford them. Transit systems, for example, are sometimes operated this way. However, government-owned monopolies sometimes charge higher prices to control demand. In states with state-owned liquor stores, the price of liquor tends to be higher than in states where liquor stores are not owned by a government body.

In an oligopoly there are only a few sellers and there are high barriers to competitive entry. The automotive, mainframe-computer, and steel industries exemplify oligopolies. A firm in such industries can raise its price, hoping that its competitors will do the same. When an organization cuts its price to gain a competitive edge, other firms are likely to follow suit. Thus very little is gained through price cuts in an oligopolistic market structure.

A market structure characterized by monopolistic competition means numerous sellers with differentiated product offerings. The products are differentiated by physical characteristics, features, quality, and brand images. The distinguishing characteristics of its product may allow a company to set a different price than its competitors. However, firms engaged in a monopolistic competitive market structure are likely to practice nonprice competition, discussed earlier in this chapter.

Under conditions of perfect competition, there are many sellers. Buyers view all sellers' products as the same. All firms sell their products at the going market price, and buyers will not pay more than that. This type of market structure, then, gives a marketer no flexibility in setting prices.

Legal and Regulatory Issues

At times government action sways marketers' pricing decisions. To curb inflation, the federal government may invoke price controls, "freeze" prices at certain levels, or determine the rates at which prices can be increased. In some states, regulatory agencies set prices on such products as insurance, dairy goods, and electricity.

Many regulations and laws affect pricing decisions and activities. The Sherman Antitrust Act prohibits conspiracies to control prices, and in interpreting the act, courts have ruled that price fixing among firms in an industry is illegal. Not only must marketers refrain from fixing prices; they must also develop independent pricing policies and set prices in ways that do not even suggest collusion. Both the Federal Trade Commission Act and the Wheeler-Lea Act prohibit deceptive pricing. In establishing prices, marketers must not deceive customers.

The Robinson-Patman Act has had a strong impact on pricing decisions. For various reasons, marketers may wish to sell the same type of product at different prices. Provisions in the Robinson-Patman Act, as well as those in the Clayton Act, limit the use of such price differentials. If price differentials tend to lessen or injure competition, they are considered discriminatory and are forbidden. However, not all price differentials are discriminatory. Marketers can use them for a product if any one of the following conditions is satisfied:

1. The price differentials do not injure or lessen competition.
2. The price differentials result from differences in the costs of selling to various customers.
3. The customers are not competitors.
4. The price differentials arise because the firm has had to cut its price to a particular buyer to meet competitors' prices.

Until 1975, manufacturers of consumer goods could set and enforce minimum retail prices for their products in some states. Now the Consumer Goods Pricing Act prohibits the use of price maintenance agreements between producers and resellers involved in interstate commerce.

Retailers and wholesalers in states that have effective unfair trade practices acts are limited in their use of pricing as a competitive tool. Because such acts place a "floor" under prices that retailers and wholesalers can regularly charge, marketers who compete on the basis of price must be aware of legal constraints on their competitors' pricing policies.

Pricing for Business-to-Business Markets

As previously mentioned, business-to-business markets consist of individuals and organizations that purchase products for resale, for use in their own operations, or for producing other products. Establishing prices for this category of buyers is sometimes different from setting prices for consumers. Business-to-business markets have experienced much change because of economic uncertainty, sporadic supply shortages, and an increasing interest in service. Differences in the size of purchases, geographic factors, and transportation considerations require sellers to adjust prices. In this section, we discuss several issues unique to the pricing of business-to-business products, including discounts, geographic pricing, transfer pricing, and price discrimination.

Price Discounting

Producers commonly provide intermediaries with discounts off list prices. Although there are many types of discounts, they usually fall into one of five categories: trade, quantity, cash, seasonal, and allowances.

Trade Discounts A reduction off the list price given by a producer to an intermediary for performing certain functions is called a **trade**, or **functional**, **discount**. A trade discount is usually stated in terms of a percentage or series of percentages off the list price. Intermediaries are given trade discounts as compensation for performing various functions, such as selling, transporting, storing, final processing, and perhaps providing credit services. Although certain trade discounts are often a standard practice within an industry, discounts do vary considerably among industries. It is important that a manufacturer provide a large-enough trade discount to offset the intermediary's costs, plus a reasonable profit, to entice the reseller to carry the product. For example, QMS, Inc., a producer of high-quality, moderately-priced laser jet printers, offered retailers a trade discount that was too low to retailers' costs of ordering, displaying, and selling QMS printers. Thus retailers simply didn't order the printer, leaving $71 million in printers in QMS warehouses. QMS had to borrow money to help cover the carrying costs of this excess inventory.[7]

Quantity Discounts Deductions from list price that reflect the economies of purchasing in large quantities are called **quantity discounts**. Price quantity discounts are used to pass cost savings, gained through economies of scale, to the buyer. Cost savings usually occur in four areas. First, fewer but larger orders reduce per-unit selling costs. Second, fixed costs, such as billing and sales contracts, remain the same—or even go down. Third, there are lower costs for raw materials because quantity discounts are often available to the seller. Fourth, longer production runs mean no increases in holding costs.[8] Finally, a large purchase may shift some of the storage, finance, and risk-taking functions to the buyer. Thus quantity discounts usually reflect legitimate reductions in costs.

Quantity discounts can be either cumulative or noncumulative. **Cumulative discounts** are quantity discounts aggregated over a stated period of time. Purchases of $10,000 in a three-month period, for example, might entitle the buyer to a 5 percent, or $500, rebate. Such discounts are supposed to reflect economies in selling and encourage the buyer to purchase from one seller. **Noncumulative discounts** are one-time reductions in prices based on the number of units purchased, the dollar value of the order, or the product mix purchased. Like cumulative discounts, these discounts should reflect some economies in selling or trade functions.

Cash Discounts   A **cash discount**, or price reduction, is given to a buyer for prompt payment or cash payment. Accounts receivable are an expense and a collection problem for many organizations. A policy to encourage prompt payment is a popular practice and sometimes a major concern in setting prices.

Discounts are based on cash payments or cash paid within a stated time. For example, "2/10 net 30" means that a 2 percent discount will be allowed if the account is paid within 10 days. However, if the buyer does not make payment within the 10-day period, the entire balance is due within 30 days without a discount. If the account is not paid within 30 days, interest may be charged.

Seasonal Discounts   A price reduction to buyers who purchase goods or services out of season is a **seasonal discount**. These discounts let the seller maintain steadier production during the year. For example, automobile rental agencies offer seasonal discounts in winter and early spring to encourage firms to use automobiles during the slow months of the automobile rental business.

Allowances   Another type of reduction from the list price is an **allowance**—a concession in price to achieve a desired goal. Trade-in allowances, for example, are price reductions granted for turning in a used item when purchasing a new one. Allowances help give the buyer the ability to make the new purchase. This type of discount is popular in the aircraft industry. Another example is promotional allowances, which are price reductions granted to dealers for participating in advertising and sales support programs intended to increase sales of a particular item.

Geographic Pricing

Geographic pricing involves reductions for transportation costs or other costs associated with the physical distance between the buyer and the seller. Prices may be quoted as being F.O.B. (free-on-board) factory or destination. An **F.O.B. factory** price indicates the price of the merchandise at the factory, before it is loaded onto the carrier vehicle, and thus excludes transportation costs. The buyer must pay for shipping. An **F.O.B. destination** price means that the producer absorbs the costs of shipping the merchandise to the customer. This policy may be used to attract distant customers. Although F.O.B. pricing is an easy way to price products, it is sometimes difficult for marketers to administer, especially when a firm has a wide product mix or when customers are dispersed widely. Because customers will want to know about the most economical method of shipping, the seller must keep abreast of shipping rates.

To avoid the problems involved in charging different prices to each customer, **uniform geographic pricing**, sometimes called postage-stamp pricing, may be used. The same price is charged to all customers regardless of geographic location, and the price is based on average shipping costs for all customers. Gasoline, paper products, and office equipment are often priced on a uniform basis.

Zone prices are regional prices that take advantage of a uniform pricing system; prices are adjusted for major geographic zones as the transportation costs increase. For example, a Florida manufacturer's prices may be higher for buyers on the Pacific Coast and in Canada than for buyers in Georgia.

Base-point pricing is a geographic pricing policy that includes the price at the factory, plus freight charges from the base point nearest the buyer. This approach to pricing has virtually been abandoned because its legal status has been questioned. The policy resulted in all buyers paying freight charges from one location—say, Detroit or Pittsburgh—regardless of where the product was manufactured.

When the seller absorbs all or part of the actual freight costs, **freight absorption pricing** is being used. The seller might choose this method because it wishes to do business with a particular customer or to get more business; more business will cause the average cost to fall and counterbalance the extra freight cost. This strategy is used to improve market penetration and to retain a hold in an increasingly competitive market.

Transfer Pricing

When one unit in a company sells a product to another unit, **transfer pricing** occurs. The price is determined by one of the following methods:

Actual full cost: calculated by dividing all fixed and variable expenses for a period into the number of units produced

Standard full cost: calculated on what it would cost to produce the goods at full plant capacity

Cost plus investment: calculated as full cost, plus the cost of a portion of the selling unit's assets used for internal needs

Market-based cost: calculated at the market price less a small discount to reflect the lack of sales effort and other expenses

The choice of a method of transfer pricing depends on the company's management strategy and the nature of the units' interaction. The company might initially choose to determine price by the actual-full-cost method. But later price changes could result in a market-based method or another method that the management of the company decides is best for its changed business situation.[9]

An organization must also ensure that transfer pricing is fair to all units that must purchase its goods or services. For example, Bellcore, the centralized research organization that supports the seven regional telephone companies formed from the breakup of AT&T, found that the prices charged by its secretarial, word processing, graphics, and technical publications divisions for the services they provided were too high. As a result, engineers and researchers had to take time away from their duties to type documents and prepare presentation materials to reduce their own costs. Upon investigation, Bellcore discovered that the four service divisions were themselves paying more than their share for overhead and rent expenses. Bellcore revised its methods of allocating overhead and rent. Lower overhead and rental charges coupled with improved efficiency in the four service divisions allowed them to reduce their costs by 31 percent and to charge more reasonable prices for services provided to other divisions.[10]

Price Discrimination

A policy of **price discrimination** results in different prices being charged to give a group of buyers a competitive advantage. Price differentiation becomes discriminatory, and illegal, when a seller gives one reseller or business-to-business buyer an advantage over competitors by providing products at a price lower than other similar customers can obtain. As mentioned earlier, price differentials are legal when they can be justified on the basis of cost savings, when they are used to meet competition in good faith, or when they do not damage competition. Thus if customers are not in competition with each other, different prices may be charged legally.

Price differentiation is a form of market segmentation that companies use to provide a marketing mix that satisfies different segments. Because different market segments perceive the value of a particular product differently, depending on the product's importance and value to the business-to-business buyer, marketers may charge different prices to different market segments. Price discrimination can also be used to modify demand patterns, support sales of other products, help move obsolete goods or excessive inventories, fill excess production capacity, and respond to competitors' activities in particular markets.[11] Table 18.1 shows the principal forms of price discrimination. For price discrimination to work, several conditions are necessary: (1) the market must be segmentable; (2) the cost of segmenting should not exceed the extra revenue from price discrimination; (3) the practice should not breed customer ill will; (4) competition should not be able to steal the segment that is charged the higher price; and (5) the practice should not violate any applicable laws.

Summary

Price is the value placed on what is exchanged. The buyer exchanges buying power—which depends on the buyer's income, credit, and wealth—for satisfaction or utility. Price is not always money paid; barter, the trading of products, is the oldest form of exchange. Price is a key element in the marketing mix because it relates directly to the generation of total revenue. The profit factor can be determined mathematically by multiplying price by quantity sold to get total revenues, and then subtracting total costs. Price is the only variable in the marketing mix that can be adjusted quickly and easily to respond to changes in the external environment.

A product offering can compete on either a price or a nonprice basis. Price competition emphasizes price as the product differential. Prices fluctuate frequently, and price competition among sellers is aggressive. Nonprice competition emphasizes product differentiation through distinctive features, services, product quality, or other factors. Establishing brand loyalty by using nonprice

Table 18.1

Principal Forms of Price Discrimination

Bases of Discrimination	Examples
Buyers' incomes	Income-based sliding scale for doctors' fees
Buyers' earning power	Royalties paid for use of patented machines and processes
Buyers' age and sex	Children's haircuts, lower admission charges for individuals in uniform, senior citizen rates
Buyers' location	Zone prices, in-state versus out-of-state tuition, lower export prices (dumping)
Buyers' status	Lower prices to new customers, quantity discounts to big buyers
Use of product	Railroad rates, public utility rates
Qualities of products	Relatively higher prices for deluxe models
Labels on products	Lower prices of unbranded products
Sizes of products	Relatively lower prices for larger sizes (the "giant economy" size)
Peak and off-peak services	Lower prices for off-peak services, excursion rates in transportation, off-season rates at resorts, holiday and evening telephone rates

competition works best when the product can be physically differentiated and the customer can recognize these distinguishing characteristics.

Pricing objectives are overall goals that describe the role of price in a firm's long-range plans. The most fundamental pricing objective is the organization's survival. Price can be easily adjusted to increase sales volume or to combat competition so that the organization can stay alive. Profit objectives, which are usually stated in terms of sales dollar volume or percentage change, are normally set at a satisfactory level rather than at a level designed for profit maximization. A sales growth objective focuses on increasing the profit base by increasing sales volume. Pricing for return on investment (ROI) has a specified profit as its objective. A pricing objective to maintain or increase market share implies that market position is linked to success. Other types of pricing objectives include cash flow and recovery, status quo, and product quality.

Eight factors enter into price decision making: organizational and marketing objectives, pricing objectives, costs, other marketing mix variables, channel member expectations, buyers' perceptions, competition, and legal and regulatory issues. When setting prices, marketers should make decisions consistent with the organization's goals and mission. Pricing objectives heavily influence price-setting decisions. Most marketers view a product's cost as the floor below which a product cannot be priced. Due to the interrelation of the marketing mix variables, price can affect product, promotion, and distribution decisions. The revenue that channel members expect for the functions they perform must also be considered when making price decisions.

Buyers' perceptions of price vary. Some consumer segments are sensitive to price, but others may not be; thus before determining price, a marketer needs to be aware of its importance to the target market. Knowledge of the prices charged for competing brands is essential for the firm so that it can adjust its prices relative to those of competitors. Government regulations and legislation influence pricing decisions. Congress has enacted several laws to enhance perfect competition in the marketplace. Moreover, the government has the power to invoke price controls to curb inflation.

Unlike consumers, business-to-business buyers purchase products to use them in their own operations or for producing other products. When adjusting prices, business-to-business sellers take into consideration the size of the purchase, geographic factors, and transportation requirements. Producers commonly provide discounts off list prices to intermediaries. The categories of discounts include trade, quantity, cash, and seasonal discounts, and allowances. A trade discount is a price reduction for performing such functions as storing, transporting, final processing, or providing credit services. If an intermediary purchases in large-enough quantities, the producer gives a quantity discount, which can be either cumulative or noncumulative. A cash discount is a price reduction for prompt payment or payment in cash. Buyers who purchase goods or services out of season may be granted a seasonal discount. A final type of reduction from the list price is an allowance, such as a trade-in allowance.

Geographic pricing involves reductions for transportation costs or other costs associated with the physical distance between the buyer and the seller. A price quoted as F.O.B. factory means that the buyer pays for shipping from the factory; an F.O.B. destination price means that the producer pays for shipping. This is the easiest way to price products, but it can be difficult for marketers to administer. When the seller charges a fixed average cost for transportation, the practice is known as uniform geographic pricing. Zone prices take advantage of a uniform pricing system adjusted for major geographic zones as the transportation costs increase. Base-point pricing resembles zone pricing; prices are adjusted for shipping expenses incurred by the seller from the base point nearest the buyer. A seller who absorbs all or part of the freight costs is using freight absorption pricing.

When a price discrimination policy is adopted, different prices are charged to give a group of buyers a competitive advantage. Price differentials are legal only when they can be justified on the basis of cost savings, when they meet competition in good faith, or when they do not attempt to damage competition.

Important Terms

— Price
— Barter
— Price competition
Nonprice competition
— Pricing objectives
Trade, or functional, discount
— Quantity discount
Cumulative discount

Noncumulative discount
— Cash discount
— Seasonal discount
Allowance
Geographic pricing
— F.O.B. factory
— F.O.B. destination
Uniform geographic pricing

Zone prices
Base-point pricing
Freight absorption pricing

Transfer pricing
Price discrimination

Discussion and Review Questions

1. Why are pricing decisions so important to an organization?
2. Compare and contrast price and nonprice competition. Describe the conditions under which each form works best.
3. How does a pricing objective of sales growth and expansion differ from an objective to increase market share?
4. Why is it crucial that marketing objectives and pricing objectives be considered when making pricing decisions?
5. In what ways do other marketing mix variables affect pricing decisions?
6. What types of expectations may channel members have about producers' prices, and how do these expectations affect pricing decisions?
7. How do legal and regulatory forces influence pricing decisions?
8. Compare and contrast a trade discount and a quantity discount.
9. What is the reason for using the term F.O.B.?
10. What is the difference between a price discount and price discrimination?

Cases

18.1   MCI Uses Price Competition

Since the break up of AT&T in 1984, U.S. spending on long-distance calls has increased about 10 percent a year, while long-distance rates have plummeted almost 40 percent. What this means is good news for customers, and intense competition among long-distance carriers for the biggest share of the $55 billion industry. MCI, along with its two major rivals, AT&T and U.S. Sprint, tout their own special services and quality, enticing customers with an array of promotions and discounts.

When MCI first initiated long-distance phone service at cut-rate costs, it was known to some customers as a company where consumers got what they paid for: static, echoes, and lots of extra digits to dial. Today, MCI is the number-two long-distance marketer, with earnings of $558 million a year and quality equaling that of AT&T. However, the road has not always been smooth for MCI.

Although the 1984 breakup of AT&T heralded the end of a powerful dynasty, it also caused trouble for MCI. At that time, the Federal Communications Commission phased out a discounting policy that had allowed MCI to virtually own the low-cost long-distance-calling niche. Profits fell, and the organization laid off 15 percent of its 16,000-person work force. MCI then began changing its focus to developing a reputation not only for low prices, but also for excellent quality and service. By 1987, the company had returned to profitability.

Persuading customers that one type of service is significantly better than another or that the quality of one call is noticeably better is difficult; most can't appreciate the differences. What consumers can appreciate is the money they save by paying cheaper phone rates; that makes pricing the key to acquiring market share. MCI, along with other leading long-distance marketers, offers a variety of service plans that compute rates differently. All include some type of standard plan with prices based on distance, time of day, and length of the call, as well as various discount plans. MCI's most popular discount plan, Prime-Time, charges an hour's worth of calls at a flat rate, with the price of all calls after that based on time of day and length of call. AT&T has a similar and directly competing plan called Reach Out America. Regardless of the plan, MCI is often less expensive than AT&T. For example, a weekday evening 12-minute phone call from Chicago to Washington, D.C., costs $1.77 at MCI's base rate versus $1.89 on AT&T's basic plan. With MCI's Prime-Time, that same call costs $1.29, significantly less than the $1.61 it costs at AT&T's comparable Reach Out America evening rate.

Despite possible confusion over the diverse pricing plans, MCI believes that offering lots of choices continues to be the best strategy for attracting consumers and meeting the widest variety of needs. The company's recent attempt to step ahead of its competition is its Friends and Family plan. Long-standing and new MCI customers alike can take advantage of a 20 percent discount on calls to 12 households of their choice (the consumer gives the list to a MCI representative), as long as all parties use MCI as their long-distance carrier. Because the company will gain new customers, and customers will get a substantial price break, MCI views Friends and Family as a winner. Several months before the discounts went into effect, MCI began airing 30-second teaser spots on network television. Featuring such celebrities as Zsa Zsa Gabor, George Burns, Regis Philbin, and New York Giants coach Bill Parcells, the advertisements did not reveal specifics but merely promised something new from MCI. Advertisers hoped to tantalize viewers with the teasing tactic, maximizing interest in the plan when it was revealed at long last.

Because the new discount program can be used by consumers who are already MCI customers, analysts warn that the company could lose revenue. MCI insists that a temporary loss of profit is worth the gains in market share that it is certain will result from the lower prices.

Ever since the number of long-distance carriers began to proliferate, competition among companies challenging AT&T has been based mostly on price, not quality. Number-three long-distance carrier U.S. Sprint takes a different approach. Although the company offers a variety of pricing schemes, its advertising focuses on its state-of-the-art technology and the quality and reliability of its service. Sprint executives say they will not enter a price war to compete with MCI's Friends and Family. AT&T's official response has been similarly subdued, but it is surely no coincidence that the company recently began advertising its Select Saver program for the first time. The 30-second television spots promote AT&T's discount prices on calls made to one area code, a concept conspicuously similar to that of MCI's newest pricing scheme. While its competitors debunk or ignore the Friends and Family plan, MCI keeps forging ahead with new products like personal 800 service and Call USA, a cheaper overseas calling plan.[12]

Questions for Discussion

1. MCI and most of its competitors are engaged in price competition. What are the major strengths and weaknesses of price competition for MCI?
2. What type of pricing objective is associated with MCI's Friends and Family plan?

3. Do most residential telephone customers perceive big differences among major long-distance telephone companies relative to the quality of service provided? How do these buyer perceptions affect the pricing of long-distance telephone services?

18.2 The Coke and Pepsi Price War

Coca-Cola Company and PepsiCo, Inc., have long fought for soft-drink supremacy on supermarket shelves, in vending machines, at soda fountains, and in the media. In the $46 billion retail soft-drink market, both firms want to be the clear market leader. A one-percentage-point shift in the $16 billion food store soft-drink market amounts to $160 million in sales. In the scramble for consumer dollars and market-share bragging rights, a price war broke out between the two companies as each slashed prices to attract customers.

At a store in Tempe, Arizona, traffic jams developed in the parking lot, and checkout lines stretched to the meat department as shoppers hauled away cases of Coke priced at 59 cents per six-pack. The store was selling Coca-Cola at the rate of 2,900 cases a day. At another Tempe store, six-packs of Pepsi priced at 79 cents were selling almost as quickly.

While overall grocery prices were increasing, soft-drink prices were declining sharply. Traditionally, price wars intensified around holidays and in the summer, but now battles are fought daily. In food stores, where the price war is primarily centered, 90 percent of the soft drinks sold are on sale. Customers have become accustomed to looking for soft drinks on sale at the end-of-aisle displays. Sometimes, by featuring their own price specials to draw consumers, retailers play the two companies against each other, pressuring them to continue to either lower prices more, offer lower prices for longer periods of time, or both.

Both companies are eager to become the choice of the average American—who drinks over 42 gallons of soft drinks a year. Despite the continuing warfare, however, the gap between Coke and Pepsi never changes much. Current figures indicate Coca-Cola leads the overall industry with 41 percent of the market. Although the disastrous introduction of New Coke temporarily helped Pepsi to take over the lead in the supermarket category, Coke has recently edged ahead with 34.1 percent of the food store share as compared to Pepsi with 32.1 percent.

When the soft-drink giants wage price wars, the producers of brands such as Dr Pepper, Royal Crown Cola, and 7-Up suffer the most. Because 75 percent of the soft-drink market belongs to Coca-Cola and Pepsi, smaller competitors must continuously try to underprice them. When Coca-Cola and Pepsi lower prices, earnings at the smaller firms decrease rapidly.

Pepsi's own internal bottling division accounts for 40 percent of the Pepsi sold in the United States. Coca-Cola owns 49 percent of its primary bottler. Both companies sell soft-drink concentrate to their bottlers, and it is the bottlers who actually combine the syrup with carbonated water and sell it to grocers. The cola war is especially heated in Los Angeles, Phoenix, and several Texas cities where respective company-owned bottlers compete directly with each other. In the midst of the cola price war, Pepsi and Coca-Cola bottlers are on the front line.

Some marketers think that the price war may last indefinitely, believing it unlikely that one company will raise prices if the other does not. There are increasing indications, however, that prices are beginning to turn around, and a truce in the cola wars may be on the horizon, at least on the pricing front. In a recent 9-month period, soft-drink prices rose 3.3 percent, and the average supermarket price for 2-liter bottles of Coke and Pepsi went up about 10 cents. Industry experts are not entirely surprised that the war is slacking off, citing as unexpected casualties both cola brand loyalty and profits for smaller-brand bottlers. Reasons for the subsiding price war include increased competition from alternatives like bottled water and fruit juice, increased pressure for bottlers to raise prices due to rising costs of packaging and corn sweeteners, a change of focus from pricing to promotions (like Superbowl ticket give-aways and Olympic sponsorship), high-profile celebrity advertising, franchise business (like Wendy's and Burger King), and burgeoning European markets. If consumers, accustomed to paying low prices, reject these higher prices altogether, they might look to other brands to satisfy their thirsts.[13]

Questions for Discussion

1. What type of pricing objectives are Coca-Cola and Pepsi most likely to have? Explain.
2. Does a price war help to build brand loyalty? Why or why not? If brand loyalty were stronger among cola drinkers, would a price war be advisable? Explain.
3. What major factors are most likely to influence which company will win an extended price war?

Chapter Notes

1. Based on information from Jim McCullaugh, "A LIVE One: 40-Title Surge on $14.95 Vid Sell-Thru," *Billboard*, July 6, 1991, pp. 45–46; Paul Sweeting, "Orion Hopes for Fast Track on Slow-Speed Budget Vids," *Billboard*, June 29, 1991, pp. 9, 79; and Jim McCullaugh, " 'Robin' to Perk Up Midsummer Nights," *Billboard*, May 18, 1991, p. 64.
2. Robert P. Ford, "Pricing Operating Services," *Bankers Magazine*, May–June 1987.
3. George S. Day and Liam Fahey, "Valuing Market Strategies," *Journal of Marketing*, July 1988, pp. 45–57.
4. Susan M. Petroshius and Kent B. Monroe, "Effect of Product-Line Pricing Characteristics on Product Evaluations," *Journal of Consumer Research*, March 1988, pp. 511–519.
5. Valerie A. Zeithaml, "Consumer Perceptions of Price, Quality and Value: A Means-End Model and Synthesis of Evidence," *Journal of Marketing*, July 1988, pp. 2–22.
6. Andrew T. Chalk and John A. Steiber, "Managing the Airlines in the 1990's," *Journal of Business Strategy*, Winter 1987, pp. 87–91.

7. Allan J. MaGrath, "Ten Timeless Truths About Pricing," *Journal of Consumer Marketing,* Winter 1991, pp. 5–13.

8. James B. Wilcox, Roy D. Howell, Paul Kuzdrall, and Robert Britney, "Price Quantity Discounts: Some Implications for Buyers and Sellers," *Journal of Marketing,* July 1987, pp. 60–61.

9. Robert G. Eccles, "Control with Fairness in Transfer Pricing," *Harvard Business Review,* November–December 1983, pp. 149–161.

10. Edward J. Kovac and Henry P. Troy, "Getting Transfer Prices Right: What Bellcore Did," *Harvard Business Review,* September–October 1989, pp. 148–154.

11. Michael H. Morris, "Separate Prices as a Marketing Tool," *Industrial Marketing Management,* 16, 1987, pp. 79–86.

12. Kate Fitzgerald, "MCI: We Have AT&T's Number," *Advertising Age,* Mar. 25, 1991, p. 51; Jon Berry, "MCI Reaches Out for Leads," *Adweek's Marketing Week,* Mar. 20, 1991, p. 2; Kate Fitzgerald, "MCI Spots Tease New Discount Plan," *Advertising Age,* Feb. 25, 1991, p. 2; "MCI and Sprint Pitch 800 Services to Households," *Wall Street Journal,* Oct. 16, 1990; "Beating High Phone Rates Abroad," *New York Times,* July 17, 1990; "The Book Can Wait," *Forbes,* May 28, 1990, p. 252; Judith D. Schwartz, "Sprint Dials T for Technology in Its Battle with AT&T, MCI," *Adweek's Marketing Week,* May 14, 1990, pp. 42–43; Troy Segal, "Getting a Line on Long-Distance Phone Deals," *Business Week,* Mar. 26, 1990, pp. 106–107; and "The K-Mart Contract: How MCI Beat AT&T and Learned Lessons on Keeping Competitive," *Washington Post,* Feb. 19, 1990.

13. Alison Fahey, "Pepsi Bridges Generation Gap in Ads," *Advertising Age,* Jan. 20, 1992; Mark Landler and Walecia Konrad, "Pepsi: Memorable Ads, Forgettable Sales," *Business Week,* Oct. 21, 1991, p. 36; Walecia Konrad, "The Real Thing Is Getting Real Aggressive," *Business Week,* Nov. 26, 1990, pp. 94, 96, 100, 104; John Marcom, Jr., "Cola Attack," *Forbes,* Nov. 26, 1990, pp. 48–49; Thomas R. King, "For Colas, the Fault Is in Too Many Stars," *Wall Street Journal,* Jan. 24, 1990, pp. B1, B4; Joshua Levine, "We Can't Let Pepsi Outflesh Us," *Forbes,* Nov. 27, 1989, pp. 270, 272; Patricia Winters, "Jackson, Houston Hard Acts to Follow," *Advertising Age,* Sept. 11, 1989, pp. S13, S14; Mike Duff, "Soft Drinks," *Supermarket Business,* September 1989, pp. 217–222; Michael J. McCarthy, "Guns Falling Silent in Cola Price Wars," *Wall Street Journal,* Aug. 4. 1989, pp. B1, B3; Karen Hoggan, "Head to Head," *Marketing,* June 22, 1989, pp. 20–21; and Stephen W. Quickel, "Coke vs. Pepsi: A 100 Years War," *Business Month,* January 1989, pp. 10–11.

19 *Setting Prices*

OBJECTIVES

- To understand eight major stages of the process used to establish prices

- To explore issues connected with selecting pricing objectives

- To grasp the importance of identifying the target market's evaluation of price

- To gain insight into demand curves and the price elasticity of demand

- To examine the relationships among demand, costs, and profits

- To learn about analyzing competitive prices

- To understand the different types of pricing policies

- To scrutinize the major kinds of pricing methods

Nancy Reagan styles at Barbara Bush prices.

Now you can easily design a stylish new home at a very practical price. Just select the furniture you want from our range of 12,000 coordinated items displayed in over 100 room settings. From entire living rooms and kitchens to lamps, textiles, cookware, plants and flooring. You'll find quality furniture that's been designed in Sweden, not only to look good, but also to be flat-packed in easy-to-carry boxes. So you can take it home immediately and do the simple, final assembly yourself. That way you save time and money. At IKEA, you don't need to spend 8 years and a lot of money to design a beautiful new home.

It's a big country. Someone's got to furnish it.

On the day that IKEA opened up a new outlet in Elizabeth, New Jersey, the section of turnpike leading to the store was backed up for nine miles, and 26,000 shoppers spent $1 million. Shoppers entered planning to purchase a sofa, and they went home with a sofa, a chair, some lamps, and excitement about a new place to buy home furnishings at unbelievable bargains.

Founder Ingvar Kamprad's philosophy, to market a wide range of well-designed and functional home furnishings at prices so low that the majority of people can afford to buy them, has worked well from Stockholm to Newark. There are almost 90 stores in 22 countries worldwide, and in the last four years alone, IKEA's sales have added up to $3.2 billion. In 1990, 100 million people shopped at the 100,000-square-foot stores, spending about $400 per square foot. That same year, IKEA leaped from 24th to 15th in *Furniture Today*'s ranking of home-furnishing stores and was named *Money Magazine*'s "Store of the Year."

Amazingly low prices are the key to IKEA's success. Prices on everything every day are 25 to 50 percent lower than at other stores. Five-foot-high bookcases sell for $39.00, sofa beds for $149.00, and table lamps for $7.50. Prices are kept low to encourage multiple purchases. By operating a self-service system offering unassembled flat-packaged furniture, the company saves money on shipping, storage, and assembly, the three most expensive aspects of furniture retailing. These savings are passed on to customers. IKEA also keeps prices down by designing its furniture for low-cost manufacture and distribution and producing all of its 27 different catalogs in-house.

From its catalogs that direct attention to special bargains with the tag "Impossible Price," to its tongue-in-cheek advertisements promoting "Nancy Reagan style at Barbara Bush prices," IKEA maximizes its reputation for rock-bottom prices. Industry analysts predict that the rate of household formation will decrease in the 1990s, forcing furniture retailers to work harder to attract customers. Because IKEA seems to have the right approach, it will probably be one of the survivors.[1]

Photo courtesy of IKEA.

ONE OF THE REASONS that IKEA is successful is its prices. At IKEA, pricing is used as a major competitive tool. Setting prices of products such as furniture requires careful analysis of numerous issues. In this chapter we examine eight stages of a process that marketers can use when setting prices.

Figure 19.1 illustrates these eight stages. Stage 1 is the development of a pricing objective that is congruent with the organization's overall objectives and its marketing objectives. In stage 2, both the target market's evaluation of price and its ability to buy must be assessed. Then, in stage 3, marketers should examine the nature and price elasticity of demand. Stage 4, which consists of analyzing demand, cost, and profit relationships, is necessary for estimating the economic feasibility of alternative prices. Evaluation of competitors' prices, which constitutes stage 5, helps determine the role of price in the marketing strategy. Stage 6 is the selection of a pricing policy, or the guidelines for using price in the marketing mix. Stage 7 involves choosing a method for calculating the price charged to customers. Stage 8, the determining of the final price, depends on environmental forces and marketers' understanding and use of a systematic approach to establishing prices. These stages are not rigid steps that all marketers must follow but rather guidelines that provide a logical sequence for establishing prices. In some situations, additional stages may need to be included in the price-setting process; in others, certain stages may not be necessary.

Selection of Pricing Objectives

In Chapter 18 we discussed the various types of pricing objectives. Selecting pricing objectives is an important task because pricing objectives form the basis for decisions about other stages of pricing. Thus pricing objectives must be explicitly stated. The statement of pricing objectives should include the time period during which the objectives are to be accomplished.

Figure 19.1

Stages for Establishing Prices

Marketers must be certain that the pricing objectives they set are consistent with the organization's overall objectives and marketing objectives. Inconsistent objectives cause internal conflicts and confusion and can prevent the organization from achieving its overall goals. Furthermore, pricing objectives inconsistent with organizational and marketing objectives may cause marketers to make poor decisions during the other stages in the price-setting process.

Organizations normally have multiple pricing objectives, some short-term and others long-term. For example, the pricing objective of gaining market share is normally short-term because it often requires the firm to price its product quite low relative to competitors' prices. An organization should have one or more pricing objectives for each product. For the same product aimed at different market segments, marketers sometimes choose different pricing objectives. A marketer typically alters pricing objectives over time.

Assessing the Target Market's Evaluation of Price and Its Ability to Buy

Although we generally assume that price is a significant issue for buyers, the importance of price depends on the type of product, the type of target market, and the purchase situation. For example, in general, buyers are probably more sensitive to gasoline prices than to luggage prices. With respect to the type of target market, the price of an airline ticket is much more important to a tourist than to a business traveler. The purchase situation also affects the buyer's view of price. Most movie goers would never pay, in other situations, the prices paid for soft drinks, popcorn, and candy at movie concession stands. By assessing the target market's evaluation of price, a marketer is in a better position to know how much emphasis to place on price. Information about the target market's price evaluation may also help a marketer determine how far above the competition a firm can set its prices.

As we point out in Chapter 4, the people who make up a market must have the ability to buy a product. Buyers must need a product, be willing to use their buying power, and have the authority (by law or social custom) to buy. Their ability to buy and their evaluation of price, have direct consequences for marketers. The ability to purchase involves such resources as money, credit, wealth, and other products that could be traded in an exchange. Understanding customers' buying power and knowing how important a product is to them in comparison with other products helps marketers correctly assess the target market's evaluation of price. The Global Perspective discusses the problems in pricing products for international markets.

Determining Demand

Determining the demand for a product is the responsibility of marketing managers, who are aided in this task by marketing researchers and forecasters. Marketing research and forecasting techniques yield estimates of sales potential

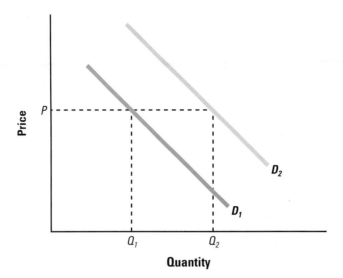

or the quantity of a product that could be sold during a specific period. (Chapter 4 describes such techniques as surveys, time series analyses, correlation methods, and market tests.) These estimates are helpful in establishing the relationship between a product's price and the quantity demanded.

The Demand Curve

For most products, the quantity demanded goes up as the price goes down, and as the price goes up, the quantity demanded goes down. Thus there is an inverse relationship between price and quantity demanded. As long as the marketing environment and buyers' needs, ability (purchasing power), willingness, and authority to buy remain stable, this fundamental inverse relationship will continue.

Figure 19.2 illustrates the effect of one variable—price—on the quantity demanded. The classic **demand curve** (D1) is a graph of the quantity of products expected to be sold at various prices, if other factors remain constant.[2] It illustrates that as price falls the quantity demanded usually rises. Demand depends on other factors in the marketing mix, including product quality, promotion, and distribution. An improvement in any of these factors may cause a shift to, say, demand curve D2. In such a case, an increased quantity (Q2) will be sold at the same price (P).

There are many types of demand and not all conform to the classic demand curve shown in Figure 19.2. Prestige products, such as selected perfumes and jewelry, seem to sell better at high prices than at low ones. For example, the Rolex Watch in Figure 19.3 is known to be expensive and thus has a prestigious image. These products are desirable partly because their expense makes buyers feel elite. If the price fell drastically and many people owned them, they would lose some of their appeal.

The demand curve in Figure 19.4 shows the relationship between price and quantity for prestige products. Demand is greater, not less, at higher prices. For a certain price range—from P1 to P2—the quantity demanded (Q1) goes up to

Figure 19.3

Prestige Product

The high price of prestige products such as Rolex watches adds to their attractiveness.

Source: Courtesy of The Richards Group.

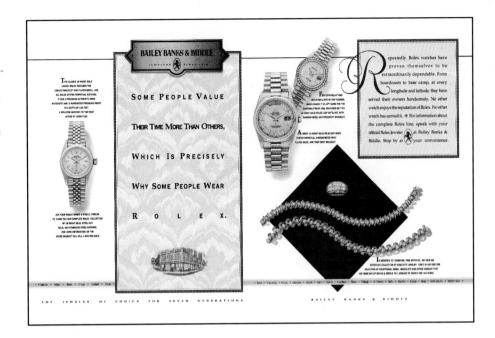

Q2. After a certain point, however, raising the price backfires. If the price of a product goes too high, the quantity demanded goes down. The figure shows that if the price is raised from P2 to P3, quantity demanded goes back down from Q2 to Q1.

Demand Fluctuations

Changes in buyers' needs, variations in the effectiveness of other marketing mix variables, the presence of substitutes, and dynamic environmental factors can influence demand. Restaurants and utility companies experience large fluctuations in demand daily. Toy manufacturers, fireworks suppliers, and air-conditioning and heating contractors also face demand fluctuations because of the seasonal nature of these items. The demand for fax machines, single-serving low-calorie meals, and fur coats has changed significantly over the last few years. In some cases, demand fluctuations are predictable. It is no surprise to restaurants and utility company managers that demand fluctuates. However, changes in demand for other products may be less predictable, and this leads to problems for some companies. Although demand can fluctuate unpredictably, some firms have been able to anticipate changes in demand by correlating demand for a specific product to demand for the total industry or to some other economic variable. If a brand maintains a fairly constant market share, its sales can be estimated as a percentage of industry sales.

Gauging Price Elasticity of Demand

Up to this point, we have been discussing how marketers identify the target market's evaluation of price and its ability to purchase and how they examine demand to learn whether price is related inversely or directly to quantity. The

Pricing for International Markets

AS THE WORLD SHRINKS and global business expands, companies often vary advertising, promotions, logos, or prices to attract customers in diverse markets around the world. Pricing for specific international markets is complicated by the need to understand relevant local laws, as well as local attitudes and economies.

Differences in price from one country to another often relate directly to indigenous governmental regulations, such as taxes or subsidies, or even to the prevailing political climate. An example of government's influence on pricing is the cost of gasoline at pumps worldwide. While Americans complain about paying $1.30 per gallon, Germans pay $3.04, and Japanese, $4.18; yet drivers in Mexico pay only 90 cents per gallon and those in the former Soviet Union pay 25 cents. What accounts in part for the disparity is whether a government saves consumers money by subsidizing the price, or taxes them, which adds to the price. Japanese pay $1.60 in tax on every gallon of gas they buy, whereas Russian drivers have benefited from government subsidies that keep prices low. Prices often fall prey to politics, as is the case in Korea. Government officials there decided that Korea is importing too many cars and dramatically raised the number of mandatory subway bonds consumers must buy when purchasing a foreign car. Someone choosing a Mercedes-Benz, for example, must include in the purchase price $20,000 worth of bonds.

A product's image in various world markets often affects its price. International wine pricing, for example, is particularly sensitive to image. To Europeans, California wines typically suggest lower jug-type quality, especially in comparison with the best French and Italian wines. After adding importers' fees, du-ties, and shipping, Gallo charges £4.75 (about $10) in Great Britain for a bottle of wine that retails for about $5 in the United States. At that price, Gallo's low-quality image can't compete with choice European wines. Industry experts believe that California can perform better overseas by exporting higher-priced, high-quality wines.

Adding to the complexity of pricing for the global community is the wide diversity in income and standard of living. An affluent Japanese driver may find it easy to pay $4 a gallon for gas, whereas a Russian citizen may be unable to pay $1. To buy the least expensive GM car available in Poland, a Polish customer has to spend 125 times the average monthly salary. In Moscow, an average Russian worker will pay at least two days' wages to buy a McDonald's meal for the family. Clearly, sensitivity to the ability of customers around the world to pay the price is essential.

Sources: Damon Darlin, "U.S. Auto Firms Push Their Efforts to Sell Cars in Asian Market," *Wall Street Journal*, Mar. 21, 1991, p. A1; Allen R. Myerson, "Setting Up an Island in the Soviet Storm," *New Yorks Times*, Dec. 30, 1990, pp. F1, F6; Lawrence M. Fisher, "California Wineries Look Overseas," *New York Times*, Dec. 26, 1990, pp. D1, D5; "G.M. Is Selling Cars in Poland," *New York Times*, Aug. 28, 1990, p. D4; Linda Feldmann, "Muscovites Have Fallen in Love with a Pair of Golden Arches," *Christian Science Monitor*, Aug. 20, 1990, p. 11; Damon Darlin, "South Korea Regresses on Opening Markets, Trade Partners Say," *Wall Street Journal*, June 12, 1990, pp. A1, A15; Masha Hamilton, "1st 'Beeg Mak' Attack Leaves Moscow Agog," *Los Angeles Times*, Feb. 1, 1990, pp. A1, A12; and Richard Homan, "Gas Peddled at Wide Range of Prices," *Washington Post*, Jan. 12, 1991.

next stage in the process is to gauge price elasticity of demand. **Price elasticity of demand** provides a measure of the sensitivity of demand to changes in price. It is formally defined as the percentage change in quantity demanded relative to a given percentage change in price (see Figure 19.5).[3] The percentage change in quantity demanded caused by a percentage change in price is much greater for elastic demand than for inelastic demand. For a product such as electricity, demand is relatively inelastic. When its price is increased, say, from P1 to P2, quantity demanded goes down only a little, from Q1 to Q2. For products such as recreational vehicles, demand is relatively elastic. When price rises sharply, from P1 to P2, quantity demanded goes down a great deal, from Q1 to Q2.

If marketers can determine price elasticity of demand, then setting a price is much easier. By analyzing total revenues as prices change, marketers can determine whether a product is price-elastic. Total revenue is price times quantity; thus 10,000 rolls of wallpaper sold in one year at a price of $10 per roll equals $100,000 of total revenue. If demand is *elastic,* a change in price causes an opposite change in total revenue—an increase in price will decrease total revenue, and a decrease in price will increase total revenue. An *inelastic* demand results in a change in the same direction in total revenue—an increase in price will increase total revenue, and a decrease in price will decrease total revenue. The following formula determines the price elasticity of demand:

$$\text{Price Elasticity of Demand} = \frac{\text{\% Change in Quantity Demanded}}{\text{\% Change in Price}}$$

For example, if demand falls by 8 percent when a seller raises the price by 2 percent, the price elasticity of demand is −4 (the negative sign indicating the inverse relationship between price and demand). If demand falls by 2 percent when price is increased by 4 percent, then elasticity is −½. The less elastic the demand, the more beneficial it is for the seller to raise the price. Products without readily available substitutes and for which consumers have strong needs (for example, electricity, appendectomies) usually have inelastic demand.

Marketers cannot base prices solely on elasticity considerations. They must also examine the costs associated with different volumes and see what happens to profits.

Figure 19.4

Demand Curve Illustrating the Relationship Between Price and Quantity for Prestige Products

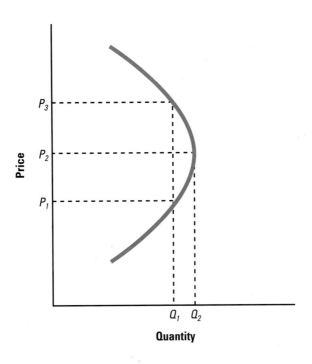

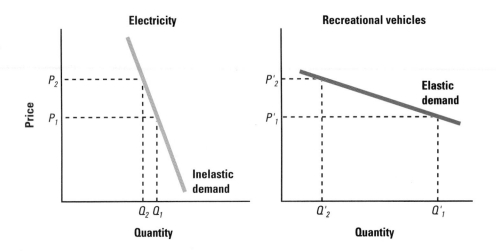

Figure 19.5

Elasticity of Demand

Analysis of Demand, Cost, and Profit Relationships

Having examined the role of demand in setting prices and the various costs and their relationships, we can now explore the relationships among demand, cost, and profit. To stay in business, a company has to set prices that cover all its costs. There are two approaches to understanding demand, cost, and profit relationships: marginal analysis and breakeven analysis.

Marginal Analysis

Marginal analysis is the examination of what happens to a firm's costs and revenues when production (or sales volume) is changed by one unit. Both production costs and revenues must be evaluated. To determine the costs of production, it is necessary to distinguish among several types of costs. **Fixed costs** do not vary with changes in the number of units produced or sold. The cost of renting a factory does not change because production increases from one shift to two shifts a day or because twice as much wallpaper is sold. Rent may go up, but not because the factory has doubled production or revenue. **Average fixed cost** is the fixed cost per unit produced and is calculated by dividing fixed costs by the number of units produced.

Variable costs vary directly with changes in the number of units produced or sold. The wages for a second shift and the cost of twice as much paper are extra costs that occur when production is doubled. Variable costs are usually constant per unit; that is, twice as many workers and twice as much material produces twice as many rolls of wallpaper. **Average variable cost**, the variable cost per unit produced, is calculated by dividing the variable costs by the number of units produced.

Total cost is the sum of average fixed costs and average variable costs times the quantity produced. The **average total cost** is the sum of the average fixed cost and the average variable cost. **Marginal cost (MC)** is the extra cost a firm

1	2	3	4	5	6	7
Quantity	Fixed Cost	Average Fixed Cost (2) ÷ (1)	Average Variable Cost	Average Total Cost (3) + (4)	Total Cost (5) × (1)	Marginal Cost
1	$40	$40.00	$20.00	$60.00	$ 60	$10
2	40	20.00	15.00	35.00	70	5
3	40	13.33	11.67	25.00	75	15
4	40	10.00	12.50	22.50	90	20
5	40	8.00	14.00	22.00	110	30
6	40	6.67	16.67	23.33	140	40
7	40	5.71	20.00	25.71	180	

Table 19.1 Costs and Their Relationships

incurs when it produces one more unit of a product. Table 19.1 illustrates various costs and their relationships. Notice that the average fixed cost declines as the output increases. The average variable cost follows a U shape, as does the average total cost. Because the average total cost continues to fall after the average variable cost begins to rise, its lowest point is at a higher level of output than that of the average variable cost. The average total cost is lowest at 5 units at a cost of $22.00, whereas the average variable cost is lowest at 3 units at a cost of $11.67. As shown in Figure 19.6, marginal cost equals average total cost at the latter's lowest level. In Table 19.1 this occurs between 5 and 6 units of production. Average total cost decreases as long as the marginal cost is less than the average total cost, and it increases when marginal cost rises above average total cost.

Marginal revenue (MR) is the change in total revenue that occurs when a firm sells an additional unit of a product. Figure 19.7 depicts marginal revenue and a demand curve. Most firms in the United States face downward-sloping demand curves for their products. In other words, they must lower their prices to sell additional units. This situation means that each additional product sold provides the firm with less revenue than the previous unit sold. MR then

Figure 19.6

Typical Marginal Cost and Average Total Cost Relationship

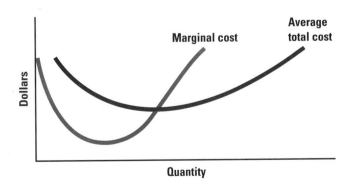

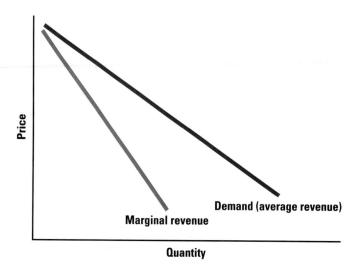

Figure 19.7

Typical Marginal Revenue and Average Revenue Relationship

Price

Demand (average revenue)

Marginal revenue

Quantity

becomes less than average revenue, as Figure 19.7 shows. Eventually, MR reaches zero, and the sale of additional units merely hurts the firm.

However, before the firm can determine whether a unit makes a profit, it must know its cost, as well as its revenue, because profit equals revenue minus cost. If MR is a unit's addition to revenue and MC is a unit's addition to cost, then MR minus MC tells us whether the unit is profitable or not. Table 19.2 illustrates the relationships among price, quantity sold, total revenue, marginal revenue, marginal cost, and total cost. It indicates where maximum profits are possible at various combinations of price and cost.

Profit is maximized where MC = MR (see Table 19.2). In this table MC = MR at four units. The best price is $33.75 and the profit is $45.00. Up to this

Table 19.2   **Marginal Analysis: Method of Obtaining Maximum Profit-Producing Price**

1	2	3	4	5	6	7
Price	Quantity Sold	Total Revenue $(1) \times (2)$	Marginal Revenue	Marginal Cost	Total Cost	Profit $(3) - (6)$
$57.00	1	$ 57	$57	$—	$ 60	–$ 3
55.00	2	110	53	10	70	40
40.00	3	120	10	5	75	45
33.75*	**4**	**135**	**15**	**15**	**90**	**45**
30.00	5	150	15	20	110	40
27.00	6	162	12	30	140	22
25.00	7	175	13	40	180	–5

* Boldface indicates best price-profit combination.

point, the additional revenue generated from an extra unit sold exceeds the additional total cost. Beyond this point, the additional cost of another unit sold exceeds the additional revenue generated, and profits decrease. If the price was based on minimum average total cost—$22.00 (Table 19.1)—it would result in less profit: only $40.00 (Table 19.2) for five units at a price of $30.00 versus $45.00 for four units at a price of $33.75.

Graphically combining Figures 19.6 and 19.7 into Figure 19.8 shows that any unit for which MR exceeds MC adds to a firm's profits, and any unit for which MC exceeds MR subtracts from a firm's profits. The firm should produce at the point where MR equals MC because this is the most profitable level of production.

This discussion of marginal analysis may give the false impression that pricing can be highly precise. If revenue (demand) and cost (supply) remained constant, then prices could be set for maximum profits. In practice, however, cost and revenue change frequently. The competitive tactics of other firms or government action can quickly undermine a company's expectations of revenue. Thus marginal analysis is only a model from which to work. It offers little help in pricing new products before costs and revenues are established. On the other hand, in setting prices of existing products, especially in competitive situations, most marketers can benefit by understanding the relationship between marginal cost and marginal revenue.

Breakeven Analysis

The point at which the costs of producing a product equal the revenue made from selling the product is the **breakeven point**. If a wallpaper manufacturer has total annual costs of $100,000 and the same year it sells $100,000 worth of wallpaper, then the company has broken even.

Figure 19.9 illustrates the relationships of costs, revenue, profits, and losses involved in determining the breakeven point. Knowing the number of units

Figure 19.8

Combining the Marginal Cost and Marginal Revenue Concepts for Optimal Profit

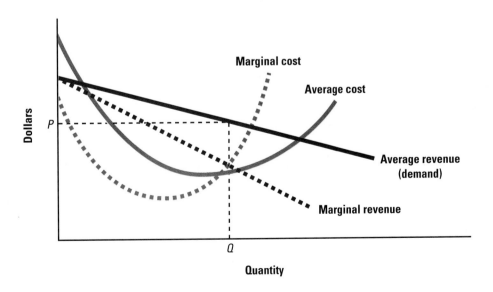

Figure 19.9

Determining the
Breakeven Point

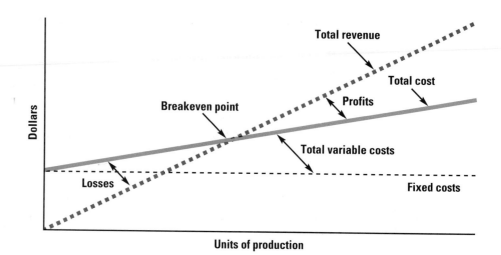

necessary to break even is important in setting the price. If a product priced at $100 per unit has an average variable cost of $60 per unit, then the contribution to fixed costs is $40. If total fixed costs are $120,000, here is the way to determine the breakeven point in units:

$$\text{Breakeven Point} = \frac{\text{Fixed Costs}}{\text{Per Unit Contribution to Fixed Costs}}$$

$$= \frac{\text{Fixed Costs}}{\text{Price} - \text{Variable Costs}}$$

$$= \frac{\$120,000}{\$40}$$

$$= 3,000 \text{ Units}$$

To calculate the breakeven point in terms of dollar sales volume, multiply the breakeven point in units by the price per unit. In the preceding example, the breakeven point in terms of dollar sales volume is 3,000 (units) times $100, or $300,000.

To use breakeven analysis effectively, a marketer should determine the breakeven point for each of several alternative prices. This determination allows the marketer to compare the effects on total revenue, total costs, and the breakeven point for each price under consideration. Although this comparative analysis may not tell the marketer exactly what price to charge, it will identify highly undesirable price alternatives that should definitely be avoided.

Breakeven analysis is simple and straightforward. It does assume, however, that the quantity demanded is basically fixed (inelastic) and that the major task in setting prices is to recover costs. It focuses more on how to break even than on how to achieve a pricing objective, such as percentage of market share or return on investment. Nonetheless, marketing managers can use this concept to determine whether a product will achieve at least a breakeven volume. In other words, it is easier to answer the question "Will we sell at least the minimum volume necessary to break even?" than the question "What volume of sales will we expect to sell?"

Evaluation of Competitors' Prices

In most cases, marketers are in a better position to establish prices when they know the prices charged for competing brands. Learning competitors' prices may be a regular function of marketing research. Some grocery and department stores, for example, have full-time comparative shoppers who systematically collect data on prices. Companies may also purchase price lists, sometimes weekly, from syndicated marketing research services.

Finding out what prices competitors are charging is not always easy, especially in producer and reseller markets. Competitors' price lists are often closely guarded. Even if a marketer has access to price lists, they may not reflect the actual prices at which competitive products are sold because those prices may be established through negotiation.

Knowing the prices of competing brands can be very important for a marketer. Competitors' prices and the marketing mix variables that they emphasize partly determine how important price will be to customers. Marketers in an industry in which nonprice competition prevails need competitive price information to ensure that their organization's prices are the same as its competitors' prices. In some instances, an organization's prices are designed to be slightly above competitors' prices to give its products an exclusive image. Alternatively, another company may use price as a competitive tool and attempt to price its product below those of competitors. Toys "R" Us, for example, has acquired a large market share through aggressive competitive pricing.

Selection of a Pricing Policy

A **pricing policy** is a guiding philosophy or course of action designed to influence and determine pricing decisions. Pricing policies set guidelines for achieving pricing objectives. They are an important component of an overall marketing strategy. Generally, pricing policies should answer this recurring question: How will price be used as a variable in the marketing mix? This question may relate to (1) introduction of new products, (2) competitive situations, (3) government pricing regulations, (4) economic conditions, or (5) implementation of pricing objectives. Pricing policies help marketers solve the practical problems of establishing prices. Let us examine the most common pricing policies.

Pioneer Pricing Policies

Pioneer pricing—setting the base price for a new product—is a necessary part of formulating a marketing strategy. The base price is easily adjusted (in the absence of government price controls), and its establishment is one of the most fundamental decisions in the marketing mix. The base price can be set high to recover development costs quickly or to provide a reference point for developing discount prices to different market segments.

When marketers set base prices, they also consider how quickly competitors will enter the market, whether they will mount a strong campaign on entry, and what effect their entry will have on the development of primary demand. If competitors will enter quickly, with considerable marketing force, and with limited effect on the primary demand, then a firm may adopt a base price that will discourage their entry.

Price Skimming   **Price skimming** is charging the highest possible price that buyers who most desire the product will pay. This pioneer approach provides the most flexible introductory base price. Demand tends to be inelastic in the introductory stage of the product life cycle.

Price skimming can provide several benefits, especially when a product is in the introductory stage of its life cycle. A skimming policy can generate much-needed initial cash flows to help offset sizable developmental costs. When introducing a new model of camera, Polaroid initially uses a skimming price to defray large research and development costs. Price skimming protects the marketer from problems that arise when the price is set too low to cover costs. When a firm introduces a product, its production capacity may be limited. A skimming price can help keep demand consistent with a firm's production capabilities. The use of a skimming price may attract competition into an industry because the high price makes that type of business appear to be quite lucrative.

Penetration Price   A **penetration price** is a price below the prices of competing brands and is designed to penetrate a market and produce a larger unit sales volume. When introducing a product, a marketer sometimes uses a penetration price to gain a large market share quickly. As shown in Figure 19.10, Brother is using penetration pricing for its color copiers. This approach places the marketer

Figure 19.10

Penetration Pricing

To gain market share, Brother Industries employs a penetration pricing policy for its color copier.

Source: Brother International Corporation.

in a less flexible position than price skimming because it is more difficult to raise a penetration price than to lower or discount a skimming price. It is not unusual for a firm to use a penetration price after having skimmed the market with a higher price.

Penetration pricing can be especially beneficial when marketers suspect that competitors could enter the market easily. First, if the penetration price lets one marketer gain a large market share quickly, competitors might be discouraged from entering the market. Second, entering the market may be less attractive to competitors when a penetration price is used because the lower per-unit price results in lower per-unit profit; this may cause competitors to view the market as not being especially lucrative. Mazda, for instance, used penetration pricing when it introduced the MX-5 Miata to gain market share quickly and to discourage competitors from entering that market segment.

A penetration price is particularly appropriate when demand is highly elastic. Highly elastic demand means that target market members would purchase the product if it was priced at the penetration level, but few would buy the item if it was priced higher. A marketer should consider using a penetration price when a lower price would result in longer production runs, increasing production significantly and reducing the firm's per-unit production costs.

Psychological Pricing

Psychological pricing encourages purchases based on emotional rather than rational responses. It is used most often at the retail level. Psychological pricing has limited use for business-to-business products.

Odd-Even Pricing   Through **odd-even pricing**—that is, ending the price with certain numbers—marketers try to influence buyers' perceptions of the price or the product. Odd pricing assumes that more of a product will be sold at $99.95 than at $100. Supposedly, customers will think, or at least tell friends, that the product is a bargain—not $100, mind you, but $99, plus a few insignificant pennies. Also, customers are supposed to think that the store could have charged $100 but instead cut the price to the last cent, to $99.95. Some claim, too, that certain types of customers are more attracted by odd prices than by even ones. However, there are no substantial research findings that support the notion that odd prices produce greater sales. Nonetheless, even prices are far more unusual today than odd prices.

Even prices are used to give a product an exclusive or upscale image. An even price supposedly will influence a customer to view the product as being a high-quality, premium brand. A shirt maker, for example, may print on a premium shirt package a suggested retail price of $32.00 instead of $31.95; the even price of the shirt is used to enhance its upscale image.

Customary Pricing   In **customary pricing**, certain goods are priced primarily on the basis of tradition. The customary price of a standard package of chewing gum is 25¢, as shown in Figure 19.11. Recent economic uncertainties have made most prices fluctuate fairly widely, but the classic example of the customary, or traditional, price is the candy bar. For scores of years, the price of a candy bar was 5 cents. A new candy bar would have had to be something very special

Figure 19.11

Customary Pricing

The prices of products such as chewing gum are usually determined by customary pricing.

Source: Courtesy of Wm. Wrigley Jr. Company.

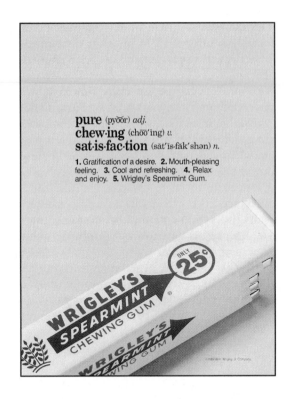

pure (pyŏor) *adj.*
chew·ing (chōō'ing) *v.*
sat·is·fac·tion (săt'is-făk'shən) *n.*

1. Gratification of a desire. **2.** Mouth-pleasing feeling. **3.** Cool and refreshing. **4.** Relax and enjoy. **5.** Wrigley's Spearmint Gum.

to sell for more than a nickel. This price was so sacred that rather than change it, manufacturers increased or decreased the size of the candy bar itself as chocolate prices fluctuated. Now, of course, the nickel candy bar has disappeared, probably forever. Yet most candy bars still sell at a consistent but obviously higher price. Thus customary pricing remains the standard for this market.

Prestige Pricing   In **prestige pricing**, prices are set at an artificially high level to provide prestige or a quality image. Prestige pricing is used especially when buyers associate a higher price with higher quality. Pharmacists report that some consumers complain when a prescription does not cost enough. Apparently, some consumers associate a drug's price with its potency. Typical product categories in which selected products are prestige-priced include perfumes, automobiles, liquor, and jewelry. If producers that use prestige pricing lowered their prices dramatically, it would be inconsistent with the perceived high-quality images of such products.

Price Lining   When an organization sets a limited number of prices for selected groups or lines of merchandise, it is using **price lining**. A retailer may have various styles and brands of similar quality men's shirts that sell for $15. Another line of higher-quality shirts may sell for $22. Price lining simplifies consumers' decision making by holding constant one key variable in the final selection of style and brand within a line. In product line pricing, the company should look at the prices of the overall product line to ensure that the price of the new model lies within the range of existing prices for that line. Failure to consider the impact of the new model's price relative to the existing product line may change buyers' perceptions of all the models in the line.[4]

The basic assumption in price lining is that the demand is inelastic for various groups or sets of products. If the prices are attractive, customers will concentrate their purchases without responding to slight changes in price. Thus a women's dress shop that carries dresses priced at $85, $55, and $35 might not attract many more sales with a drop to, say, $83, $53, and $33. The "space" between the prices of $55 and $35, however, can stir changes in consumer response. With price lining, the demand curve looks like a series of steps, as shown in Figure 19.12.

Professional Pricing

Professional pricing is used by persons who have great skill or experience in a particular field or activity. Some professionals who provide such products as medical services feel that their fees (prices) should not relate directly to the time and involvement in specific cases; rather, a standard fee is charged regardless of the problems involved in performing the job. Some doctors' and lawyers' fees are prime examples: $35 for a checkup, $400 for an appendectomy, and $199 for a divorce. Other professionals set prices in other ways.

The concept of professional pricing carries with it the idea that professionals have an "ethical" responsibility not to overcharge unknowing customers. In some situations, a seller can charge customers a high price and continue to sell many units of the product. Medicine offers several examples. If a diabetic requires one insulin treatment per day to survive, the individual will buy that treatment whether its price is $1 or $10. In fact, the patient surely would purchase the treatment even if the price went higher. In these situations sellers could charge exorbitant fees. Drug companies claim that despite their positions of strength in this regard, they charge "ethical" prices rather than what the market will bear. Burroughs-Wellcome Co. reduced the price of its AIDS-treatment drug AZT by 20 percent partly in response to pressure from AIDS patients and activists. However, some feel that the $6,400 annual price tag of AZT treatments is still far too high.[5]

Figure 19.12

Price Lining

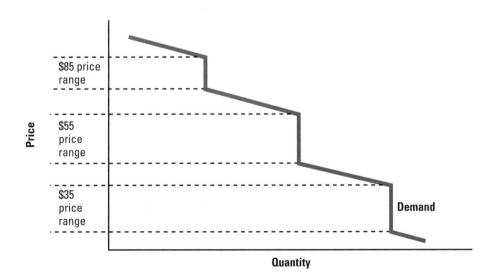

Promotional Pricing

Price is an ingredient in the marketing mix, and it often is coordinated with promotion. The two variables sometimes are so interrelated that the pricing policy is promotion-oriented. Some examples of promotional pricing include price leaders, special-event pricing, superficial discounting, and experience curve pricing.

Price Leaders Sometimes a firm prices a few products below the usual markup, near cost, or below cost, which results in prices known as **price leaders**. This type of pricing is used most often in supermarkets and department stores to attract consumers by giving them special low prices on a few items. Management hopes that sales of regularly priced merchandise will more than offset the reduced revenues from the price leaders.

Special-Event Pricing To increase sales volume, many organizations coordinate price with advertising or sales promotions for seasonal or special situations. **Special-event pricing** involves advertised sales or price cutting that is linked to a holiday, season, or event. As shown in Figure 19.13, Jordan Marsh uses St. Patrick's Day as a basis for special-event pricing. If the pricing objective is survival, then special sales events may be designed to generate the necessary operating capital. Special-event pricing also entails coordination of production, scheduling, storage, and physical distribution. Whenever there is a sales lag, special-event pricing is an alternative that marketers should consider.

Figure 19.13

Special-Event Pricing

Special days, such as St. Patrick's Day, provide opportunities for special-event pricing.

Source: Courtesy of Jordan Marsh.

Superficial Discounting **Superficial discounting**, sometimes called "was-is pricing" is fictitious comparative pricing—for example, "Was $259, is $199." The Federal Trade Commission and the Better Business Bureau discourage these deceptive markdowns. Legitimate discounts are not questioned, but when a pricing policy gives only the illusion of a discount, it is unethical and in some states illegal.

As an example of superficial discounting, consider one retailer that sells 93 percent of its power tools on sale with discounts ranging from 10 to 40 percent. The retailer's frequent special events or sales mean that the tools are sold at sale prices most of the year. To combat such superficial discounting, Canada requires retailers to post a base price for at least six months before discounting a product.

Experience Curve Pricing

In **experience curve pricing**, a company fixes a low price that high-cost competitors cannot match and thus expands its market share. This practice is possible when a firm gains cumulative production experience and is able to reduce its manufacturing costs at a predictable rate through improved methods, materials, skills, and machinery. Texas Instruments used this strategy in marketing its calculators. The experience curve depicts the inverse relationship between production costs per unit and cumulative production quantity. To take advantage of the experience curve, a company must gain a dominant market share early in a product's life cycle. An early market share lead, with the greater cumulative production experience that it implies, will place a company further down the experience curve than its competitors. To avoid antitrust problems, companies must objectively examine the competitive structure of the market before and after implementing the experience curve strategy. The strategy should not be anticompetitive, and the company must have specific and accurate data that will be unshakable in a court of law.

Development of a Pricing Method

After selecting a pricing policy, a marketer must choose a **pricing method**, a mechanical procedure for setting prices on a regular basis. The pricing method structures the calculation of the actual price. The nature of a product, its sales volume, or the amount of product the organization carries will determine how prices are calculated. For example, a procedure for pricing the thousands of products in a supermarket must be simpler and more direct than that for calculating the price of a new earth-moving machine manufactured by Caterpillar. In this section we examine three types of market-oriented pricing methods: cost-oriented, demand-oriented, and competition-oriented pricing.

Cost-Oriented Pricing

In **cost-oriented pricing**, a dollar amount or percentage is added to the cost of a product. The method thus involves calculations of desired margins or profit margins. Cost-oriented pricing methods do not necessarily take into account the economic aspects of supply and demand, nor do they necessarily relate to a specific pricing policy or ensure the attainment of pricing objectives. They are, however, simple and easy to implement. Two common cost-oriented pricing methods are cost-plus and markup pricing.

Cost-Plus Pricing   In **cost-plus pricing**, the seller's costs are determined (usually during a project or after a project is completed), and then a specified dollar amount or percentage of the cost is added to the seller's cost to set the price. When production costs are difficult to predict cost-plus pricing is appropriate. Custom-made equipment and commercial construction projects are often priced by this method. The government frequently uses such cost-oriented pricing in granting defense contracts. One pitfall for the buyer is that the seller may increase costs to establish a larger profit base. Furthermore, some costs, such as overhead, may be difficult to determine.

In periods of rapid inflation, cost-plus pricing is popular, especially when the producer must use raw materials that are fluctuating in price. For industries in which cost-plus pricing is common and sellers have similar costs, price competition may not be especially intense.

Markup Pricing   A common pricing method among retailers is **markup pricing**. In markup pricing, a product's price is derived by adding a predetermined percentage of the cost, called *markup*, to the cost of the product. Although the percentage markup in a retail store varies from one category of goods to another (35 percent of cost for hardware items and 100 percent of cost for greeting cards, for example), the same percentage often is used to determine the price on items within a single product category, and the same or similar percentage markup may be standardized across an industry at the retail level. Using a rigid percentage markup for a specific product category reduces pricing to a routine task that can be performed quickly.

Markup can be stated as a percentage of the cost or as a percentage of the selling price. The following example illustrates how percentage markups are determined and points out the differences in the two methods. Assume that a retailer purchases a can of tuna at 45 cents, adds 15 cents to the cost, and then prices the tuna at 60 cents. Here are the figures:

$$\text{Markup as a Percentage of Cost} = \frac{\text{Markup}}{\text{Cost}}$$

$$= \frac{15}{45}$$

$$= 33.3\%$$

$$\text{Markup as a Percentage of Selling Price} = \frac{\text{Markup}}{\text{Selling Price}}$$

$$= \frac{15}{60}$$

$$= 25.0\%$$

Obviously, when discussing a percentage markup, it is important to know whether the markup is based on cost or selling price.

Markups normally reflect expectations about operating costs, risks, and stock turnovers. Wholesalers and manufacturers often suggest standard retail markups that are considered profitable. An average percentage markup on cost may be as high as 100 percent or more for jewelry or as low as 20 percent for the textbook you are reading. To the extent that retailers use similar markups for the same product category, price competition is reduced. In addition, using rigid markups is convenient—the major reason that retailers, who face numerous pricing decisions, favor this method.

Demand-Oriented Pricing

Rather than basing the price of a product on its cost, marketers sometimes use a pricing method based on the level of demand for the product: **demand-oriented pricing**. This method results in a high price when demand for the product is strong and a low price when demand is weak. Most long-distance telephone companies, such as MCI, Sprint, and AT&T, use demand-oriented pricing. To use this method, a marketer must be able to estimate the amounts of a product that consumers will demand at different prices. The marketer then chooses the price that generates the highest total revenue. Obviously, the effectiveness of this method depends on the marketer's ability to estimate demand accurately.

A marketer may favor a demand-oriented pricing method called **price differentiation** when the firm wants to use more than one price in the marketing of a specific product. Price differentiation can be based on such considerations as type of customer, type of distribution channel used, or the time of the purchase. For example: A twelve-ounce canned soft drink costs less from a supermarket than from a vending machine. Florida hotel accommodations are more expensive in the winter than in the summer. A home owner pays more for air conditioner filters than does an apartment complex owner, who purchases the same-size filters in greater quantity. Christmas tree ornaments are usually cheaper on December 26 than on December 16. Holiday Inn, as shown in Figure 19.14, offers special weekend prices in their hotels.

For price differentiation to work properly, the marketer must be able to segment a market on the basis of different strengths of demand and then keep the segments separate enough so that segment members who buy at lower prices cannot then sell to buyers in segments that are charged a higher price. This isolation could be accomplished, for example, by selling to geographically separated segments.

Price differentiation is often facilitated in international marketing by the geographic distance between markets. For example, Matsushita Electric Co. sells cordless Panasonic telephones in Japan at eight times what cordless telephones of slightly lower quality sell for in the United States. When a Japanese trading company reimported the U.S. cordless phones and sold them for $80 instead of the Japanese model, which cost $657, consumers lined up to buy the cheaper telephone. To combat the reimportation, Matsushita bought up all the unsold made-for-export Panasonic telephones it could find to eliminate the wide price differential. (The major difference between the telephones was that the U.S. telephone had a range of forty meters and the Japanese telephone had a range of fifty meters, which is surprising, because the average Japanese home is much

smaller than the average U.S. home.) For years, U.S. manufacturers have accused the Japanese of subsidizing foreign trade wars with high profits from their relatively closed home market.[6]

Price differentiation can also be based on employment in a public service position. For example, most airlines permit 50 percent off each regular one-way or round-trip fare for all U.S. military personnel on active duty, leave, furlough, or a pass.

Compared with cost-oriented pricing, demand-oriented pricing places a firm in a better position to reach higher profit levels, assuming that buyers value the product at levels sufficiently above the product's cost. To use demand-oriented pricing, however, a marketer must be able to estimate demand at different price levels, which is often difficult to do accurately.

Competition-Oriented Pricing

In using **competition-oriented pricing**, an organization considers costs and revenue secondary to competitors' prices. The importance of this method increases if competing products are almost homogeneous and the organization is serving markets in which price is the key variable of the marketing strategy. A firm that uses competition-oriented pricing may choose to be below competitors' prices, above competitors' prices, or at the same level. The price that the bookstore paid to the publishing company for this textbook was determined using competition-oriented pricing. Competition-oriented pricing should help attain a pricing objective to increase sales or market share. Competition-oriented pricing methods may be combined with cost approaches to arrive at

Carnival Cruise Lines Discounts Luxury

CRUISING THE CARIBBEAN on a luxury liner named *Carnivale, Fantasy,* or *Ecstasy* is no longer a diversion for the wealthy alone. Since 1980, the number of Americans walking up the gangplank every year has increased 600 percent, and more than 30 percent of those are under forty years old earning under $50,000 a year. Thanks in large part to Carnival Cruise Lines, pleasure cruising has become a $5-billion-a-year mass market industry that attracts a younger, less affluent clientele. From its precarious beginnings in 1972, Carnival now boasts a net income of $54.6 million and a fleet of nine liners and is the market leader in the pleasure cruise industry.

Carnival rules the waves because it creates attractive all-inclusive vacations and offers them at affordable prices, usually at least 20 percent below the cost of the competition. Although cruises range in price from $2,395 per person for a seven-day cruise with premium accommodations to $395 per person for a three-day cruise with less luxurious cabins, the average passenger pays about $1,200 for a package that includes air fare to Miami, food, and entertainment. Carnival permits bargain hunters to lower the rates in numerous ways. They can plan to travel at a time of the year when the "value" rates are in effect, rather than the higher "base" or "season" rates; they can deduct $100 to $200 from the package cost if they opt for "cruise-only," which includes no air fare; they can pay a cheaper per-person rate for the third and fourth occupant staying in one stateroom; they can book six months in advance and save about 10 percent; or they can book as close as three weeks in advance and save almost 50 percent. When budgeting their expenses, however, cruisers must be sure to include the cost of gratuities; for a seven-day two-party cruise, passengers should expect to pay a minimum of $100.

Considering the quality of service Carnival extends to passengers—including gourmet meals, Las Vegas–style entertainment and gambling casinos, and even an on-board children's day camp—it seems surprising that the company realizes such tremendous profits. It does so by filling the ships to capacity. By booking three and four people in two-passenger cabins, Carnival averages 110 percent occupancy on most cruises. By offering a variety of promotions and advertising heavily on television, the company attracts a tremendous number of customers with the message that a holiday at sea is within reach of almost everyone.

Carnival recently received two awards that demonstrate the wide appeal of its cruise vacations. The American Society of Travel Agents voted the company as the best overall cruise line over thirty-five others serving the North American market. Carnival also claimed *Family Circle* magazine's "1991 Family Resorts of the Year" award in the cruise line category.

Sources: Carnival Cruise Lines Press Kit, 1991; Willima G. Glanagan and Evan McGlinn, "Man the Pumps?" *Forbes,* Dec. 10, 1990, pp. 116, 120–122, 124, 128; "Added Capacity Boosts Carnival's Profit 31%," *Journal of Commerce* (New York), July 3, 1990, pp. 14–15; and Faye Rice, "How Carnival Stacks the Decks," *Fortune,* Jan. 16, 1989, pp. 9–11.

price levels necessary for a profit. Carnival Cruise Lines, for example, has become the market leader partially through its use of both competition-oriented and cost-oriented pricing (see Inside Marketing).

Determining a Specific Price

A pricing method (or combination of them) will yield a certain price. However, this price is likely to need refinement. The price may need alteration to make it consistent with pricing practices in a particular market or industry. For example, a manager may set the final retail price of a hand-blown glass vase at $180.00 if the pricing method resulted in an initial price of $177.61.

Pricing policies and methods should help in setting a final price. If they are to do so, it is important for marketers to establish pricing objectives, to know something about the target market, and to determine demand, price elasticity, costs, and competitive factors. Also, the manner in which pricing is used in the marketing mix will affect the final price.

Although we suggest a systematic approach to pricing, in practice prices often are finalized after only limited planning, or they may be set without planning, just by trial and error. Then marketers determine whether revenue, minus costs, yields a satisfactory profit. This approach to pricing is not recommended because it makes it difficult to discover pricing errors.

In the absence of government price control, pricing remains a flexible and convenient way to adjust the marketing mix. In most situations, prices can be adjusted quickly—in a matter of minutes or over a few days. This flexibility and freedom do not characterize the other components of the marketing mix.

Summary

The eight stages in the process of establishing prices are (1) selecting pricing objectives; (2) assessing the target market's evaluation of price and its ability to purchase; (3) determining demand; (4) analyzing demand, cost, and profit relationships; (5) analyzing competitors' prices; (6) selecting a pricing policy; (7) developing a pricing method; and (8) determining a specific price.

The first stage, setting pricing objectives, is critical because pricing objectives form a foundation on which the decisions of subsequent stages are based. Organizations may use numerous pricing objectives: short-term and long-term ones, and different ones for different products and market segments.

The second stage in establishing prices is an assessment of the target market's evaluation of price and its ability to purchase. This stage tells a marketer how much emphasis to place on price and may help the marketer determine how far above the competition the firm can set its prices. Understanding customers' buying power and knowing how important a product is to the customers in comparison with other products helps marketers correctly assess the target market's evaluation of price.

In the third stage, the organization must determine the demand for its product. The classic demand curve is a graph of the quantity of products expected to be sold at various prices, if other factors are held constant. It illustrates that, as price falls, the quantity demanded usually increases. However, for prestige products, there is a direct positive relationship between price and quantity demanded: demand increases as price increases. Next, price elasticity of demand—the percentage change in quantity demanded relative to a given percentage change in price—must be determined. If demand is elastic, a change in price causes an opposite change in total revenue. Inelastic demand results in parallel change in total revenue when a product's price is changed.

Analysis of demand, cost, and profit relationships—the fourth stage of the process—can be accomplished through marginal analysis or breakeven analysis. Marginal analysis is the examination of what happens to a firm's costs and revenues when production (or sales volume) is changed by one unit. Marginal analysis combines the demand curve with a firm's costs to develop an optimum price for maximum profit. Fixed costs do not vary with changes in the number of units produced or sold; average fixed cost is the fixed cost per unit produced. Variable costs vary directly with changes in the number of units produced or sold. Average variable cost is the variable cost per unit produced. Average total cost is the sum of average fixed cost and average variable cost times the quantity produced. The optimum price is the point at which marginal cost (the cost associated with producing one more unit of the product) equals marginal revenue (the change in total revenue that occurs when one additional unit of the product is sold). Marginal analysis is only a model; it offers little help in pricing new products before costs and revenues are established.

Breakeven analysis (determining the number of units necessary to break even) is important in setting the price. The point at which the costs of production equal the revenue from selling the product is the breakeven point. To use breakeven analysis effectively, a marketer should determine the breakeven point for each of several alternative prices. This determination makes it possible to compare the effects on total revenue, total costs, and the breakeven point for each price under consideration. However, this approach assumes that the quantity demanded is basically fixed and that the major task is to set prices to recover costs.

A marketer needs to be aware of the prices charged for competing brands. This allows a firm to keep its prices the same as competitors' prices when nonprice competition is used. If a company uses price as a competitive tool, it can price its brand below competing brands.

A pricing policy is a guiding philosophy or course of action designed to influence and determine pricing decisions. Pricing policies help marketers solve the practical problems of establishing prices. Two types of pioneer pricing policies are price skimming and penetration pricing. With price skimming, an organization charges the highest price that buyers who most desire the product will pay. A penetration price is a lower price designed to penetrate the market and produce a larger unit sales volume. Psychological pricing, another pricing policy, encourages purchases that are based on emotional rather than rational responses. It includes odd-even pricing, customary pricing, prestige pricing, and price lining. A third pricing policy, professional pricing, is used by people who have great skill or experience in a particular field. Promotional pricing, in which price is coordinated with promotion, is another type of pricing policy. Price leaders, special-event pricing, and superficial discounting are examples of promotional pricing. Experience curve pricing fixes a low price that high-cost competitors cannot match. Experience curve pricing is possible when experience reduces manufacturing costs at a predictable rate.

A pricing method is a mechanical procedure for assigning prices to specific products on a regular basis. Three types of pricing methods are cost-oriented, demand-oriented, and competition-oriented pricing. In using cost-oriented pricing, a firm determines price by adding a dollar amount or percentage to the cost of the product. Two common cost-oriented pricing methods are cost-plus and markup pricing. Demand-oriented pricing is based on the level of demand for the product. To use this method, a marketer must be able to estimate the amounts of a product that buyers will demand at different prices. Demand-oriented pricing results in a high price when demand for a product is strong and a low price when demand is weak. In the case of competition-oriented pricing, costs and revenues are secondary to competitors' prices. Competition-oriented pricing and cost approaches may be combined to arrive at price levels necessary for a profit.

Demand curve
+ Price elasticity of demand
+ Fixed costs
− Average fixed cost
+ Variable costs
− Average variable cost
+ Total cost
− Average total cost
Marginal cost (MC)
Marginal revenue (MR)
+ Breakeven point
Pricing policy
+ Price skimming
+ Penetration price
+ Psychological pricing
+ Odd-even pricing
Customary pricing
− Prestige pricing
Price lining
Professional pricing
Price leaders
Special-event pricing
Superficial discounting
Experience curve pricing

Pricing method
Cost-oriented pricing
− Cost-plus pricing
+ Markup pricing
− Demand-oriented pricing
Price differentiation
+ Competition-oriented pricing

Discussion and Review Questions

1. Identify the eight stages that make up the process of establishing prices.
2. Why do most demand curves demonstrate an inverse relationship between price and quantity?
3. List the characteristics of products that have inelastic demand. Give several examples of such products.
4. Explain why optimum profits should occur when marginal cost equals marginal revenue.
5. The Chambers Company has just gathered estimates for doing a breakeven analysis for a new product. Variable costs are $7 a unit. The additional plant will cost $48,000. The new product will be charged $18,000 a year for its share of general overhead. Advertising expenditures will be $80,000, and $55,000 will be spent on distribution. If the product sells for $12, what is the breakeven point in units? What is the breakeven point in dollar sales volume?
6. Why should a marketer be aware of competitors' prices?
7. For what type of products would a pioneer price-skimming policy be most appropriate? For what type of products would penetration pricing be more effective?
8. Why do consumers associate price with quality? When should prestige pricing be used?
9. Are price leaders a realistic approach to pricing?
10. What are the benefits of cost-oriented pricing?

11. Under what conditions is cost-plus pricing most appropriate?
12. If a retailer purchases a can of soup for 24 cents and sells it for 36 cents, what is the percentage markup on selling price?

Cases

19.1 Dr. Denton Cooley's Cut-Rate Heart Surgery

Dr. Denton A. Cooley, the renowned heart specialist who pioneered American heart transplants and implanted the first human artificial heart, has brought "everyday low prices" to heart bypass surgery. Surgeons perform coronary artery bypass surgery to treat angina, a severe chest pain that occurs when the heart muscle is deprived of oxygenated blood, and bypass surgery is Cooley's specialty. He is an expert at replacing older, clogged arteries with new ones. As the population of the United States ages overall, bypass surgery is likely to become more common. In one recent year, 270,000 bypass surgeries were performed in the United States alone. Dr. Cooley's pricing strategy makes this sophisticated surgery more affordable and may also prove to be an effective marketing tool in an area that is relatively new to marketing.

Dr. Cooley's marketing approach is to create a high-volume, low-cost business. Cooley charges a flat rate for a standard bypass—about $25,000. This rate is 40 percent less than the national average for similar surgery. If Dr. Cooley is successful with his flat-fee surgery, surgeons using other surgical procedures may adopt this approach. The medical field may adopt its own version of a price war.

It usually takes a surgeon three to four hours to perform the triple-bypass operation that Dr. Cooley performs in one and a half to two hours, thanks to his expert team of five surgeons. Working through the Texas Heart Institute at St. Luke's Episcopal Hospital in Houston, Cooley performs six to eight surgeries a day and has no plan to slow down in the future. He works five days a week, often twelve hours at a time with only small breaks. Some physicians have criticized Cooley's business, calling it "assembly-line surgery." Dr. Cooley responded by remarking, "If it's assembly line, it's a Rolls-Royce line."

Because 30 percent of Dr. Cooley's income comes from the work his team performs, he is looking for ways to increase volume. Cooley offers a "bundled" service that allows patients or their insurance companies to pay for everything—services, supplies, and specialists—with one fee. This more practical billing procedure makes Dr. Cooley's operations even more attractive to patients and insurance companies. A study by the Inspector General's office, the overseer of U.S. health agencies, has concluded that Medicare could reduce its $1.5-billion-a-year bill for heart surgery by 13 percent if Medicare patients were operated on by Dr. Cooley and his team. The 13 percent savings includes the costs of transporting the patients to Houston and housing them there.

Dr. Cooley is marketing his reputation as well as low prices. In thirty years of practice, he and his team have performed over 80,000 heart operations, more than any other physician in the world. Almost 90 percent of his bypass patients live at least five years, while 74 percent live ten years or longer. Dr. Cooley is constantly seeking and experimenting with new technology in his battle with heart disease, the number-one killer in the United States today. The battle is strenuous, but the rewards—patient lives, intrinsic rewards, and the $9.7 million a year he receives—are exceptional.[7]

Questions for Discussion

1. Is the flat-fee approach effective for pricing major medical services such as open-heart surgery? Explain.
2. Is Dr. Cooley using demand-oriented, cost-oriented, or competition-oriented pricing methods? Explain.
3. Evaluate the price elasticity of demand for open-heart surgery.

19.2   Keds Stomps Competitors' Prices

During the 1980s climate of rampant consumption, the humble sneaker evolved into a high-tech status symbol with a high-end price tag. By the end of the decade, these bio-engineered fashion statements could cost up to $200 a pair and were generating about $10 billion in annual sales in the United States. As the appeal of the yuppie lifestyle wanes in the 1990s and recession hits consumers' wallets, back-to-basics seems to be the current trend in the athletic shoe market. Most people can't afford to spend $60 per foot anymore, even if the shoes fill with air for a springier step, or all the cool kids are wearing them. Keds, the company that practically invented sneakers, is taking advantage of changing consumer preferences to market the simple design and affordable price synonymous with the name Keds for seventy-five years.

At the beginning of the twentieth century, shoemakers glued vulcanized rubber onto canvas tops and came up with sneakers. In 1917, the U.S. Rubber Company introduced Keds, the first widely marketed sneaker. Originally, Keds were all light brown canvas with black soles, and over the years, the company expanded its line to include several different styles and colors. Although the U.S. sneaker industry grew consistently, with more brands appearing on the market, the shoes themselves looked pretty much the same until the late 1970s. When exercising changed from shooting baskets on the driveway and walking the dog to serious efforts such as jogging and aerobics, sneakers changed too. Along came Adidas, Nike, and Reebok shoes that were lighter and provided better traction than plain old sneakers like Keds. In the wake of intense competition from state-of-the-art athletic shoes and those that make a fashion statement, Keds fell out of favor. Even sales of Pro-Keds, the company's offering in the high-tech category, were not inspiring.

As the economic climate changes and America's spending habits with it, Keds is still here with the same basic design it has been marketing for decades. Annual sales have climbed to $270 million. At $20 a pair, about a third the price of the average leather Nike or Reebok, people are buying more than one pair at a time. What was once primarily a children's brand is now popular with adults, too. In fact, Keds is increasingly aiming advertising at women, emphasizing simplicity and affordability. Owning over 5 percent of the market, Keds is now America's fourth-largest sneaker brand, recently passing Converse, Inc. Stride Rite Corporation, owner of Keds, reports that 30 percent of its revenues now come from sneaker sales.

Encouraged by the resurgence of Keds, other sneaker manufacturers are offering more down-to-earth and affordable brands. One of the fastest-growing shoes in the United States is the Adidas Phantom, which, at $55 a pair, recorded sales of $22 million in 1991. Other low-tech newcomers include Converse's $30 canvas hightop, Chuck Taylor All Stars, PF Flyers, and, of course, Pro-Keds.

Increasingly, customers recognize that, except for those that meet the needs of professional athletes, all shoes are pretty much the same. Customers may still want Nikes, but they are more likely to buy the $65 Keds Quantum Force than the $85 Nike Air. Companies may promote their $150 shoes, but most shoppers trade down when it comes time to write the check. As retailers turn to less expensive sneakers, footwear manufacturers are watching sales of their top-of-the-line styles fall. Although sales are slumping, analysts predict that even in the current recession, Keds will flourish because of their low price.[8]

Questions for Discussion

1. What are the primary pricing objectives for Keds?
2. Which type of pricing method is Keds using?
3. In what ways are environmental forces influencing the demand for Keds shoes?

Chapter Notes

1. Based on information from Thomas Exter, "Nice Niches for Furniture," *American Demographics*, March 1991, p. 6; Dianne Harris, "Money's Store of the Year," *Money*, December 1990, pp. 144–146, 148–150; Ela Schwartz, "The Swedish Invasion," *Discount Merchandiser*, July 1990, pp. 52, 56; Cara Appelbaum, "How IKEA Blitzes a Market," *Adweek's Marketing Week*, June 11, 1990, pp. 18–19; Seth Chandler, "Swedish Marketers Going Global," *Advertising Age*, Apr. 16, 1990, p. 38; and Bill Saporito, "IKEA's Got 'Em Lining Up," *Fortune*, Mar. 11, 1991, p. 72.
2. Reprinted from *Dictionary of Marketing Terms*, Peter D. Bennett, Ed., 1988, p. 54, published by the American Marketing Association. Used by permission.
3. Bennett, p. 150.
4. Kent B. Monroe, "Effect of Product Line Pricing Characteristics on Product Evaluation," *Journal of Consumer Research*, March 1987, p. 518.
5. Marylin Chase, "Burroughs-Wellcome Cuts Price of AZT Under Pressure from AIDS Activists," *Wall Street Journal*, Sept. 19, 1989, p. A3.
6. "Frantic Cheap Phone Buy-Up Reveals a Lot About Japanese Marketing," *Ann Arbor News* (Ann Arbor, Mich.), Feb. 14, 1988, p. C9.
7. Updated information from the Texas Heart Institute, February 1991; Terri Cotten, "Cost of Bypass Surgery Sparks Debate over Its Use," *Colorado Springs Gazette Telegraph*, Aug. 19, 1990; Mark Ivey, "Will Denton Cooley Make Medical History Again?" *Business Week*, Mar. 27, 1989, pp. 56, 58; Carol Stevens, "Is This the Beginning of DRG's for Doctors?" *Medical Economics*, Jan. 16, 1989, pp. 27–28, 33–34, 36; and Kathy A. Fackelmann, "Shopping for Bypass Discounts," *Perspectives*, Sept. 21, 1987, pp. 1–4.
8. Matthew Grimm, "Dump the Pump," *Adweek's Marketing Week*, Dec. 16, 1991, p. 15; Anthony Ramirez, "The Pedestrian Sneaker Makes a Comeback," *New York Times*, Oct. 14, 1990; Jay Palmer, "Hooray for the Inefficient Market!" *Barron's*, Apr. 30, 1990, pp. 22, 34; and Gerald Eskenazi, "Once a Canvas Shoe, Now a Big-Time Player," *New York Times*, Mar. 11, 1990.

Taco Bell Prospers With Value Pricing

General Motors marketed a two-door Grand Prix for $9,000 less than the model's price the previous year. Sears created a marketing strategy around the concept of "everyday low prices." From cars to clothing, companies are delivering high quality at lower costs on a regular basis, not just during sales and specials. In the restaurant business, Taco Bell, a subsidiary of PepsiCo, is employing "value pricing" with phenomenal success. By grouping most of its menu offerings into three price categories all under $1, Taco Bell is fast becoming known as the chain with the best deals on meals, and its profits reflect its reputation. While many fast-food chains languish due to competition and recession, Taco Bell's net sales are increasing, revenues are up 14 percent, and the company currently owns almost 75 percent of the $3.5 billion U.S. Mexican-style restaurant category.

Taco Bell Searches for a Pricing Strategy

When Glen Bell opened his first Taco Bell in California, he hoped consumers would welcome Mexican food such as tacos and burritos as attractive alternatives to hamburgers and french fries. Customers came, but they did not come often enough. With specialty items costing $2.99 and most others priced around $1.65, prices were too high to attract heavy users who eat at fast-food restaurants almost every weekday. To offer the kind of values that keep customers coming back, Taco Bell searched for a scheme; an "all-you-can-eat" promotion failed, and a 39-cent taco sold well but ate up the profits. Raising the price of a taco to 49 cents, however, made Taco Bell a profit and kept the cost low enough so that customers didn't mind ordering three or four tacos for lunch. The company expanded discount offerings to include 59-cent items. When customer transactions shot up 35 percent, the firm knew it was on to something. It wasn't long before Taco Bell divided most of its food items into three price groups, 59 cents, 79 cents, or 99 cents, called it the "Value Menu," and became the fast food discount leader.

Taco Bell's Value Pricing

Industry analysts hail Taco Bell's pricing strategy as a return to common sense in the fast-food business. To attract customers, many chains have been adding items that cost more and take longer to prepare, but Taco Bell's menu gets back to basic speed and economy. An intense television advertising campaign promotes the new menu's simplicity as well as its low prices. In addition to providing the value menu, the chain reduced prices on other items so that customers will feel comfortable "trading up." To expand the value menu, Taco Bell recently introduced several low-priced chicken items, including a 79-cent taco and 99-cent burrito, and lowered the price on the previously-available chicken soft taco. A spokesperson for the company said that although Taco Bell is trying to keep in step with the industry's trend toward better nutrition, the ad campaign for the new chicken selections will continue to focus on value.

Taco Bell executives, resolving that food could still be a little cheaper and that they could still go a little lower, introduced the "Fiesta Menu," featuring smaller tacos and burritos starting at 39 cents each. The snack-sized items, about 60 percent the size of regular offerings, are designed to attract afternoon customers as well as calorie counters. Taco Bell also hopes the low prices will encourage customers to order more food.

The newest Taco Bell attack on high fast-food prices is its introduction of a breakfast menu, including among other items, four varieties of breakfast burritos, all priced from 39 cents to 79 cents. After thousands of Taco Bell's customers said yes to eating Mexican food first thing in the morning at 200 outlets in the Los Angeles area, the restaurant began offering its breakfast menu in cities all over the United States. Although fast-food chains, doughnut and coffee shops, and family-style restaurants all compete in the $10-billion breakfast market, Taco Bell hopes its low prices will attract enough customers to give it the largest share. The Fiesta Breakfast burrito with sausage, potato, cheese, and salsa costs only 39 cents. Other items include a sausage and bacon burrito for 59 cents, a muffin sandwich for 99 cents, hash browns for 39 cents, and caramel rolls for 59 cents. The cost of these items is not arbitrary. Taco Bell's prices deliberately go head-to-head with specific items at McDonald's. For example, all of Taco Bell's burritos cost less than the 99 cents customers pay for a burrito at McDonald's, and at 99 cents, Taco Bell's muffin sandwich is way below the price of an Egg McMuffin, which costs around $1.40.

Industry experts predict that the low prices on Taco Bell's menu will force other chains to lower their breakfast prices. Taco Bell's president predicts that in a few years, 25 percent of the company's sales will come from the breakfast menu.

Taco Bell's success is proof that offering real value for less can attract customers and increase sales. The difficult part is maintaining profits at the same time, and Taco Bell is finding ways to do that. Company researchers came up with a taco shell that doesn't crumble easily during preparation, reducing waste. They also developed a way to cook and quick freeze seasoned ground beef outside the restaurant, reducing the needed kitchen space, and making the space available for seating instead. Redesigned restaurants now devote 70 percent of the floor space to seating, compared with 30 percent in the past. By increasing traffic and cutting costs, Taco Bell was able to increase operating profits by over 90 percent in three months.

Future Outlook For Value Pricing

At a recent fast-food operator's convention in Chicago, many companies called for an end to price wars, but it is difficult to find a chain that is sticking to that agreement. Del Taco/Naugles, Taco Bell's head-to-head rival in Southern California, has implemented a value-pricing strategy. Its 300 outlets sell several 49-cent items, promoting them with a radio ad campaign. Wendy's offers a wide variety of full-priced items, but includes a 99-cent value menu as well. Although fast-food leader McDonald's insists that it doesn't imitate its rivals' actions, the chain recently reduced prices on some of its items. Traditionally rejecting long-term discounting, McDonald's chooses short-term specials instead, like selling Big Macs for 99 cents. Competition is forcing McDonald's to change its strategy a little.

The chain now offers "Value Meals" like a Big Mac, fries, and a soft drink for $2.99. However, customers still won't find anything at McDonald's for 39 cents except a small cup of coffee.

Riding high on his continuing wave of success, Taco Bell president John E. Martin is not humble with his predictions for the future. He expects sales to reach $4 billion by the end of the year, and the current 3,200 outlets to swell to 10,000 by the turn of the century. Martin and Taco Bell plan to keep busy convincing consumers that tacos and burritos are as American as Big Macs, and a lot cheaper.

Questions for Discussion

1. What type of general pricing method is Taco Bell using with respect to its value pricing approach?
2. Are Wendy's and McDonald's employing the same general pricing method as is Taco Bell? Explain.
3. What type of pricing objectives is most likely to be associated with value pricing?

Sources: Michael J. McCarthy, "Taco Bell Plans Bargain Menu for Breakfast," *Wall Street Journal*, Oct. 22, 1991, p. B1; Dan Koeppel, "Taco Bell Drops Prices to 39 Cents," *Adweek's Marketing Week*, June 17, 1991, p. 5; Martha T. Moore, "Taco Bell Rings In A 39-cent Menu," *USA Today*, June 12, 1991; Bradley Johnson and Scott Hume, "Dueling Chicken," *Advertising Age*, Apr. 15, 1991, p. 4; Bruce Horovitz, "McDonald's: McLeader or McFollower?" *Los Angeles Times*, Mar. 14, 1991, p. D2; Joseph B. White, "'Value Pricing' Is Hot As Shrewd Consumers Seek Low-Cost Quality," *Wall Street Journal*, Mar. 12, 1991, pp. A1, A9; Michael Lev, "Taco Bell Finds Price of Success (59 Cents)," *New York Times*, Dec. 17, 1990, pp. D1, D9; Chris Woodyard, "Price Cuts Part of New Taco Bell Strategy," *Los Angeles Times*, Oct. 30, 1990, p. D1; and PepsiCo, Inc., 1990 Annual Report.

Yield Management Pricing at American Airlines

Those who frequently fly on commercial airlines sometimes use legitimate means to avoid paying for higher-priced tickets. Although the airline industry acknowledges the existence of rule breakers, it usually looks the other way when no laws are broken. Recently, however, American Airlines had a frequent business customer arrested for allegedly perpetrating a ticket fraud scheme that cost American Airlines over $200,000 in less than two years. What motivated a successful businessman and responsible citizen to allegedly cheat the airlines and break the law? Many experts believe that his behavior is indicative of growing customer resentment regarding what they consider unfair pricing. Almost everyone who flies knows that there are a mind-boggling number of ticket prices, and that factors such as class of service, date of booking, and flexibility to change or cancel usually determine how much a ticket costs. What customers are becoming indignant about is the vast and seemingly unfair disparity among those prices. For example, business customers, who use the airlines regularly but typically cannot book flights far in advance, often pay three times more for their tickets than the vacationers sitting next to them on the plane.

Yield Management Pricing

After airline price deregulation in 1978, low-cost discount airlines inundated the market. To remain competitive, American Airlines entered price wars that resulted in dramatically lower fares and filled-to-capacity airplanes, but lower profits. Although American ranks number two in the industry, controlling about 19 percent of the market, the organization has lost $279 million in the last two years. To reverse the downward trend and meet its objective—flying the most passengers possible at the highest possible fares—American Airlines has turned to an approach called yield management pricing. By carefully controlling its inventory of airline seats so that it can fill planes with a profitable mix of discount and full-fare passengers, American's yield management division is substantially raising company revenues.

Simply stated, yield management is a pricing method that helps firms increase sales revenue by selling the right product to the right type of customer at the right time for the right price. Using computer technology, yield management experts correlate past customer-use patterns with current demands, forecast future demands, and come up with a set of prices that generate the highest level of sales revenue. In the airline industry, there are several classes of service (first-class, full-fare, coach, and super-saver) with different prices for each. Although airlines would prefer to fill their planes with first-class and full-fare customers, to do so is unlikely. To carry fuller, more economical loads when they fly, airlines offer reduced fares to customers who are willing to meet required restrictions. What results is differentiated pricing that airlines say is the only way to make a profit and many customers say is unfair.

Putting Yield Management to Work at American Airlines

As soon as an American Airlines plane leaves the gate, the value of the unsold seats on that plane is lost. Those seats can't be sold at the end of the flight. By employing two techniques, overbooking and discount allocations, yield management allows American to control its inventory before departure in order to sell as many seats as possible.

Overbooking is the strategy of selling more reservations than there are physical seats on the plane. Statistics show that about 13 percent of those holding tickets do not show up for flights or cancel at the last minute. American would lose a considerable amount of money if it consistently allowed flights to leave with those seats empty. Holding them would also mean turning away customers who want to purchase a seat at the last minute. By overbooking, American not only accommodates millions of last-minute fliers, but generates over $250 million in revenue a year.

American could probably fill its planes if all seats went to discount passengers. Many people will only fly if they get reduced fares, even if means purchasing their tickets weeks in advance, flying only on Tuesdays through Thursdays between 10:00 p.m. and 4:00 a.m., and staying over Saturday night. Business travelers, however, are often willing to pay full fare to get a seat at the last minute. To accommodate the varying needs of its customers and realize a profit, American limits the number of discount seats. To calculate the best mix among its many types of fares, American employs discount allocations. From highest value to lowest, American ranks seats in eight categories and determines the number of seats available in each, always trying to have available the number of higher-priced seats forecasted to be sold.

Ethical Concerns

Is the use of ticketing requirements and travel restrictions by American Airlines an example of unfair price differentiation? Experts do not agree. Some argue that it is inequitable, for example, for business fliers to pay higher prices than pleasure fliers for seats in the same class of service on the same plane. Others counter that airlines are providing quality services, such as the last-minute ticket sales and affordable family fares, and service is costly. Using yield management pricing allows American Airlines to balance the number and types of fares in order to provide service while continuing to generate sufficient revenue.

In a recent effort to attract more air passengers, American Airlines reduced fares up to 50 percent on many of its domestic flights. However, the airline is not abandoning yield management pricing. American's executives assert that the organization's overall pricing structure will stay in place and customers will continue to pay different prices for different classes of service.

Questions for Discussion

1. Does the use of price differentiation by the airlines help to build positive customer relationships with air passengers? Explain.
2. Is it ethical for an airline to charge different prices to air travelers flying on the same plane in the same class of service?
3. Rule breakers cost the airlines millions of revenue dollars annually. Although not illegal, is it unethical for air travelers to break airline rules and restrictions in order to save money?

Sources: John Greenwald, "Fasten Your Seat Belts for the Fare War," *Time*, Apr. 27, 1992, p. 41; Del Jones, "Airline Claims Flier Broke Law To Cut Costs," *USA Today*, Apr. 21, 1992, pp. 1B–2B; Bridget O'Brian, "American Air Launches New Price Sortie," *Wall Street Journal*, Apr. 21, 1992, p. B1; Christopher P. Fotos, "Summer Traffic Reinforces Domination by 'Big 3' Airlines," *Aviation Week & Space Technology*, Sept. 23, 1991, pp. 28–29; Joseph P. Schwieterman, "Fare Is Fair in Airline Deregulation: Restrictions and the Pursuit of Allocative Efficiency," *Cato Review of Business & Government*, Summer 1991, pp. 29–34; John R. Lott, Jr. and Russell D. Roberts, "A Guide to the Pitfalls of Identifying Price Discrimination," *Economic Inquiry*, January 1991, pp. 14–23; Sheryl E. Kimes, "Yield Management: A Tool for Capacity-Constrained Service Firms," *Journal of Operations Management*, October 1989, pp. 348–363; and "Maximizing Revenue: A Look at AMR's Yield Management," American Airlines Corporate Communications videotape.

PREVIEW:

MICROMARKET COMPUTER APPLICATION V

KidGames Corp.: Using Breakeven Analysis for Pricing Decisions

This exercise produces input for the final "go or no-go" decision about the new game, kidVID. Specifically, breakeven analysis is conducted using Lotus 1-2-3. A number of "what if" scenarios are explored by varying sales price, production cost, and promotional cost in calculating the breakeven point. The sales quantity for target profit levels are also calculated. A written memo, including recommendations and case questions conclude the exercise.

VI Marketing Management

We have divided marketing into several sets of variables and have discussed the decisions and activities associated with each variable. By now, you should understand (1) how to analyze marketing opportunities and (2) the components of the marketing mix. It is time to put all these components together in a discussion of marketing management issues. In Chapter 20 we discuss strategic market planning, focusing on the planning process, the setting of marketing objectives, the assessment of opportunities and resources, and specific product/market matching approaches to strategic market planning. Chapter 21 deals with other marketing management issues, including organization, implementation, and control. It explores approaches to organizing a marketing unit, issues regarding strategy implementation, and techniques for controlling marketing strategies.

643

20 *Strategic Market Planning*

OBJECTIVES

- To understand the strategic market planning process

- To explore and examine three major tools to assist in strategic market planning: product-portfolio analysis, the market attractiveness–business position model, and Profit Impact on Marketing Strategy (PIMS)

- To evaluate strategic market planning and relate it to the development of functional marketing strategies and activities

- To gain an overview of the marketing plan

Who else but the color-crazy pioneers would run an ad that looks like this?

Where can consumers go to buy Sizzlers, Twisters, Hot Spots, and Jammerz? The names might suggest trendy restaurants or clothing boutiques, but to get them, shoppers can simply walk down the office supply aisle at the local Wal-Mart. Despite the whimsical names, the items are pens and pencils, part of an innovative line from Pentech International. Chairman Norman Melnick has taken a standard product, invigorated it with innovation and creativity, and in six years, built a $30 million company that goes head-to-head with giant competitors like Paper Mate and Bic.

In the $2 billion pen-and-pencil industry, most firms introduce one new item per year and rely on high-volume sales for profitability. Pentech's strategy, however, is to develop up to 30 new writing tools every year, patent them, test-market them for six months, and introduce them into the market quickly. The company has found its niche by attracting customers with its snazzy pens and pencils sporting offbeat shapes and unconventional inks. Newest in the Pentech lineup are the Grip Stick, a notched easy-to-hold pencil for children's hands, and Transformers, a set of seven pens that can create fourteen different colors. Essential to the company's strategy is acquiring shelf space. Most of its retail customers now carry between ten and fifty Pentech products.

Since its creation, Pentech has relied on low-cost overseas manufacturing in Asia, Israel, and Italy to keep production costs down. Recently, two of its largest customers, Wal-Mart and K mart, informed Pentech that they would buy more of its pens and pencils if they were made in the United States. In response, Pentech is opening a 500,000-square-foot state-of-the-art automated factory in New Jersey. When the wholly owned subsidiary, Sawdust Pencil Company, comes on-line, it will produce about 300,000 pencils a day.

In only six years, Pentech has made it onto *Business Week*'s annual list of the top 100 small corporations in the United States. Industry analysts acknowledge that credit for much of the organization's success goes to Melnick, who is skilled at predicting consumer buying habits. He is aware that Pentech would be unable to compete by selling mundane pens and pencils.[1]

Photo courtesy of Pentech.

ONE REASON THAT Pentech International is successful is due to strategic planning. Strategic planning requires a general management orientation rather than a narrow functional orientation. Nevertheless, with market analysis becoming more important, in many companies the lead responsibility for formulating corporate strategy is increasingly being entrusted to the marketing department. The corporate strategy determines the means for utilizing resources in functional areas of the organization in order to reach the organization's goals. Corporate strategy addresses the composition of the firm's distinct business operations and how the firm should divide business activities into manageable units.[2] Corporate strategic planning focuses on the decision-making process that governs the overall direction of the company, including many marketing considerations.

To understand the tools for strategic market planning, it is important to recognize that strategic market planning takes into account all aspects of a firm's strategy in the marketplace. Most of this book deals with marketing decisions and strategies. This chapter focuses on the recognition that all functional activities including marketing, research and development, production, finance, and personnel must be coordinated to reach organizational goals.

We begin this chapter with an overview of the strategic market planning process, including the development of organizational goals and corporate strategy. We also examine organizational opportunities and resources as they relate to planning. We then look at some tools used in strategic market planning: the product-portfolio analysis, the market attractiveness–business position model, and Profit Impact on Marketing Strategy (PIMS). Next we examine competitive strategies for marketing and close with a look at marketing planning and the development of a marketing plan. Other aspects of the marketing management process—organizing, implementing, and controlling—are covered in Chapter 21.

Strategic Market Planning Defined

A **strategic market plan** is an outline of the methods and resources required to achieve an organization's goals within a specific target market. It takes into account not only marketing, but also all functional aspects of a business unit that must be coordinated. These functional aspects include production, finance, and personnel. Environmental issues are an important consideration as well. The concept of the strategic business unit is used to define areas for consideration in a specific strategic market plan. Each **strategic business unit (SBU)** is a division, product line, or other profit center within the parent company. Borden's strategic business units, for example, consist of dairy products, snacks, pasta, niche grocery products such as RealLemon juice and Cremora coffee creamer, and other units such as glue and paints. Each sells a distinct set of products to an identifiable group of customers, and each competes with a well-defined set of competitors. Each SBU's revenues, costs, investments, and strategic plans can be separated and evaluated from those of the parent company. SBUs operate in a variety of markets, which have differing growth rates, opportunities, degrees of competition, and profit-making potential. Strategic planners therefore must recognize the different performance capabilities of each SBU and carefully allocate scarce resources among these divisions.

The process of **strategic market planning** yields a marketing strategy that is the framework for a marketing plan. A **marketing plan** includes the framework and entire set of activities to be performed; it is the written document or blueprint for implementing and controlling an organization's marketing activities. Thus a strategic market plan is *not* the same as a marketing plan; it is a plan of *all* aspects of an organization's strategy in the marketplace. A marketing plan, in contrast, deals primarily with implementing the market strategy as it relates to target markets and the marketing mix.[3]

Figure 20.1 shows the components of strategic market planning. The process is based on the establishment of an organization's overall goals, and it must stay within the bounds of the organization's opportunities and resources. When the firm has determined its overall goals and identified its resources, it can then assess its opportunities and develop a corporate strategy. Marketing objectives must be designed so that their achievement will contribute to the corporate strategy and so that they can be accomplished through efficient use of the firm's resources.

To achieve its marketing objectives, an organization must develop a marketing strategy, or a set of marketing strategies, as shown in Figure 20.1. The set of

Figure 20.1

Components of Strategic Market Planning

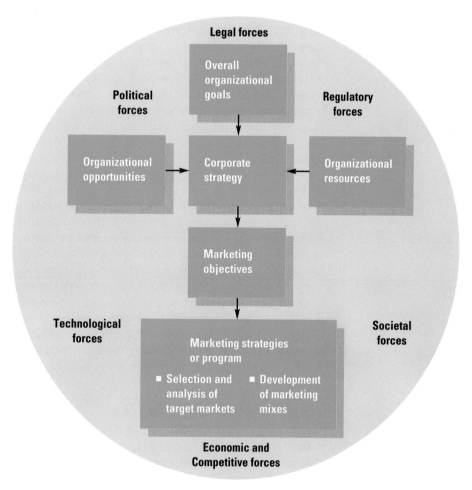

marketing strategies that are implemented and used at the same time is referred to as the organization's **marketing program**. Through the process of strategic market planning, an organization can develop marketing strategies that, when properly implemented and controlled, will contribute to the achievement of its marketing objectives and its overall goals. As we have mentioned before, to formulate a marketing strategy, the marketer identifies and analyzes the target market and develops a marketing mix to satisfy individuals in that market. Marketing strategy is best formulated when it reflects the overall direction of the organization and is coordinated with all the firm's functional areas.

As indicated in Figure 20.1, the strategic market planning process is based on an analysis of the environment, by which it is very much affected. Environmental forces can place constraints on an organization and possibly influence its overall goals; they also affect the amount and type of resources that a firm can acquire. However, these forces can create favorable opportunities as well—opportunities that can be translated into overall organizational goals and marketing objectives.

Marketers differ in their viewpoints concerning the effect of environmental variables on marketing planning and strategy. Some take a deterministic perspective, believing that firms must react to external conditions and tailor their strategies and organizational structures to deal with these conditions. According to others, however, companies can influence their environments by choosing what markets to compete in. Furthermore, they can change the structures of their industries, engaging in activities such as mergers and acquisitions, demand creation, or technological innovation.[4]

Regardless of which viewpoint is adopted, environmental variables play a part in the creation of a marketing strategy. When environmental variables affect an organization's overall goals, resources, opportunities, or marketing objectives, they also affect its marketing strategies, which are based on these factors. Environmental forces more directly influence the development of a marketing strategy through their impact on consumers' needs and desires. In addition, these forces have a bearing on marketing mix decisions. For instance, competition strongly influences marketing mix decisions. The organization must diagnose the marketing mix activities it performs, taking into account competitors' marketing mix decisions, and develop some competitive advantage to support a strategy. Thus as Honda and Toyota entered the luxury automobile market with the Acura and Lexus models, European car makers BMW, Mercedes-Benz, and Jaguar had to change their marketing strategies to maintain their market shares. They did so by lowering prices to compete with the new Japanese models.

In the next sections we discuss the major components of the strategic market planning process: organizational goals, organizational opportunities and resources, and corporate strategy, as well as the tools that aid in strategic market planning and some competitive marketing strategies.

Organizational Goals

A firm's organizational goals should be derived from its *mission,* the broad tasks that the organization wants to accomplish. IBM, for example, has stated that its mission is helping businesspeople make decisions. A company's mission and overall organizational goals should guide all its planning efforts. Its goals should specify the ends or results that are sought. For example, a firm in serious financial trouble may be concerned solely with short-run results needed for staying in business. There usually is an airline or major retailer being forced by cash shortages to take drastic action to stay in business. On the other hand, some companies have more optimistic goals. Often manufacturers such as General Motors have goals that relate to return on investment. A successful company, however, may want to sacrifice the current year's profits for the long run and at the same time pursue other goals, such as increasing market share.

Organizational Opportunities and Resources

There are three major considerations in assessing opportunities and resources: evaluating market opportunities, environmental scanning (discussed in Chapter 2), and understanding the firm's capabilities.

Market Opportunities

A **market opportunity** arises when the right combination of circumstances occurs at the right time to allow an organization to take action toward reaching a target market. An opportunity provides a favorable chance or opening for the firm to generate sales from identifiable markets. For example, because of concern over the hazards of dietary fat and cholesterol, consumers reduced consumption of baked goods, especially desserts. Entenmann's, a 93-year-old baking company (currently owned by Kraft General Foods), responded by introducing a line of thirty fat-free, cholesterol-free items aimed at diet-conscious customers.[5] In fact, many firms, such as the makers of Promise margarine (Figure 20.2) have capitalized on the market opportunities created by increased health concerns. The term *strategic window* has been used to describe what are often temporary periods of optimum fit between the key requirements of a market and the particular capabilities of a firm competing in that market.[6]

The attractiveness of market opportunities is determined by market factors, such as size and growth rate, as well as political, legal, regulatory, societal, economic, competitive, and technological forces. Because each industry and product are somewhat different, the factors that determine attractiveness tend to vary.

Market requirements relate to customers' needs or desired benefits. Market requirements are satisfied by components of the marketing mix that provide buyers with these benefits. Of course, buyers' perceptions of what requirements fulfill their needs and provide the desired benefits determine the success of any marketing effort. Marketers must devise strategies to outperform competitors by finding out what product attributes buyers use to select products. An attribute must be important and differentiating if it is to be useful in strategy development. When marketers fail to understand buyers' perceptions and market requirements, the result may be failure. First Nationwide Financial Corp., for

Figure 20.2

Responding to Marketing Opportunities

Consumers' desires to reduce cholesterol levels have produced numerous marketing opportunities, such as the promotion of Promise margarine.

Source: Van ben Bergh Foods Company, Lisle, IL 60532.

example, assumed that working-class consumers would want to take care of their banking needs while shopping for discount products. It opened 170 minibank branches in K mart stores in twelve states. But K mart shoppers were not interested or were reluctant to handle their banking needs outside of traditional banking channels, and First Nationwide was forced to close all the K mart branches.[7] The Global Perspective describes how the Walt Disney Company has attempted to identify Europeans' needs for a theme park. Two other theme park companies have apparently failed at meeting these needs.

Environmental Scanning

In Chapter 2 we define environmental scanning as the process of collecting information about the marketing environment because such knowledge helps marketers identify opportunities and assists in planning. Some companies have derived substantial benefits from establishing an "environmental scanning (or monitoring) unit" within the strategic planning group or including line management in teams or committees to conduct environmental analysis. Results of forecasting research show that even simple quantitative forecasting techniques outperform the unstructured intuitive assessments of experts.[8]

Environmental scanning to detect changes in the environment is extremely important if a firm is to avoid crisis management. An environmental change can suddenly alter a firm's opportunities or resources. Reformulated, more effective strategies may then be needed to guide marketing efforts. For example, after Congress passed legislation requiring that 10 percent of all cars sold in the United States in the late 1990s run on "clean" fuels, such as methanol and

Disney's Magic Debuts in France

THE FIRST EUROPEAN DISNEY THEME PARK recently opened on a 4,800-acre site fifteen miles from Paris, France. Newest home to Mickey Mouse, Donald Duck, and all the magic Disney has come to represent since its first park opened in California in 1955, the French Disneyland is expected to attract 11 million visitors its first year. Of three $150 million amusement parks that opened in France within the last few years, two have already been forced into bankruptcy. Master-marketer Disney, however, was not afraid to plunge in, confident that a new French edition couldn't miss.

Home to about 120 million more people than the United States, the European market presents enormous potential. Europeans' love of Disney is documented by the nearly 3 million of them who visit Disney's American parks every year, spending about $1.6 million on merchandise like Mickey Mouse T-shirts and *Little Mermaid* tapes. After considering 200 other European locations, Disney decided that the site near Paris provided the greatest likelihood of reaching its target market. Seventeen million people live within a two-hour drive from Paris and 100 million within six hours. Paris has two international airports, and once the tunnel under the English Channel is complete, the trip from London to Paris will only take about three hours.

Disney's successful history paved the way for timely, favorable financial arrangements. International sponsors include well-known firms like Renault and Nestlé. Disney controls 49 percent of Euro Disneyland, the maximum allowed by French law, with the balance selling publicly on European exchanges. In addition to securing 49 percent of the profits, the firm receives 10 percent of admission fees and 5 percent of food revenues, as well as management and incentive fees.

Not everyone in France is thrilled with Mickey's arrival. Fears that Disney characters will contaminate French culture prompted demonstrators to greet Disney's CEO by throwing eggs and waving signs demanding, "Mickey Go Home." Responding to the desires of its market, the French Magic Kingdom incorporates European flavor and themes. Both French and English are official park languages, and all guides are multilingual. In many attractions, Disney planners reveal their awareness that Pinocchio is an Italian boy, and Cinderella a French girl, and that Lewis Carroll, Hans Christian Andersen, and the Brothers Grimm are all European. Discoveryland is inspired by French science fiction writer Jules Verne, and a 360-degree-screen theater features a film on the history of Europe. Preserving ice-cream parlors on Main Street, U.S.A., and cowboys in Frontierland, Disney marketers believe that the French can love the Louvre, ballet, and Mickey, too.

Adding one more Disneyland to the list keeps the organization's most lucrative division growing, and Walt Disney Company thrives on the strategy of continual growth. Plans are already underway for a $3 billion French Disney-MGM, and Disney watchers can probably expect a European Epcot Center as well.

Sources: "An American in Paris," *Sight and Sound*, May 1991, p. 4; Steven Greenhouse, "Playing Disney in the Parisian Fields," *New York Times*, Feb. 17, 1991; Tatiana Pouschine and Thomas Bancroft, "Why Not Buy the Real Thing?" *Forbes*, Oct. 1, 1990, p. 208; and David Lawday, "Empire of the Sun," *U.S. News & World Report*, May 28, 1990, pp. 44–52.

ethanol, American car makers had to reformulate their strategies to provide for the development and marketing of automobiles that will cost more and will run on higher-priced fuels.[9] Because automobile manufacturers had engaged in environmental scanning and were aware that such legislation might indeed be enacted because of social and political concerns, most had already begun developing plans for cars powered by clean fuel. Ford Motor Company, for example, is already testing a car that can run on methanol, ethanol, gasoline, or any combination of those fuels.[10] Environmental scanning should identify new developments and determine the nature and rate of change.

Capabilities and Resources

A firm's capabilities relate to distinctive competencies that it has developed to do something well and efficiently. A company is likely to enjoy a differential advantage in an area where its competencies outmatch those of its potential competition.[11] Often a company may possess manufacturing or technical skills that are valuable in areas outside of its traditional industry. For example, BASF, known for its manufacture and development of audio- and videotapes, produced a new type of lightweight plastic that has uses in other industries.

Today marketing planners are especially concerned with resource constraints. Shortages in energy and other scarce economic resources often limit strategic planning options. On the other hand, planning to avoid shortages can backfire. Many electric utilities decided to build nuclear power plants in the 1970s, to compensate for an expected shortfall of fossil fuels, only to find the political, social, and technological problems of nuclear power almost impossible to overcome. Moreover, an adequate supply of fossil fuels still exists to power traditional plants that generate electricity. But as the public grows more concerned about pollution and the so-called greenhouse effect, nuclear power plants may once again become a plausible alternative.

Corporate Strategy

Corporate strategy determines the means for utilizing resources in the areas of production, finance, research and development, personnel, and marketing to reach the organization's goals. A corporate strategy determines not only the scope of the business but also its resource deployment, competitive advantages, and overall coordination of production, finance, marketing, and other functional areas. The term *corporate* in this context does not apply only to corporations; corporate strategy is used by all organizations, from the smallest sole proprietorship to the largest multinational corporation.

Corporate strategy planners are concerned with issues such as diversification, competition, differentiation, interrelationships between business units, and environmental issues. They attempt to match the resources of the organization with the opportunities and risks in the environment. Corporate strategy planners are also concerned with defining the scope and role of the strategic business units of the firm so that they are coordinated to reach the ends desired.

Tools for Strategic Market Planning

A number of tools have been proposed to aid marketing managers in their planning efforts. Based on ideas used in the management of financial portfolios, several models that classify an organization's product portfolio have been proposed. These models allow strategic business units or products to be classified and visually displayed according to the attractiveness of various markets and the business's relative market share within those markets. Three of these tools—the Boston Consulting Group (BCG) product-portfolio analysis, the market attractiveness–business position model, and the Profit Impact on Marketing Strategy (PIMS)—are discussed next.

The Boston Consulting Group (BCG) Product-Portfolio Analysis

Just as financial investors have different investments with varying risks and rates of return, firms have a portfolio of products characterized by different market growth rates and relative market shares. **Product-portfolio analysis**, the Boston Consulting Group approach, is based on the philosophy that a product's market growth rate and its relative market share are important considerations in determining its marketing strategy. All the firm's products should be integrated into a single, overall matrix and evaluated to determine appropriate strategies for individual SBUs and the overall portfolio strategies. However, a balanced product-portfolio matrix is the end result of a number of actions—not just the result of the analysis alone. Portfolio models can be created on the basis of present and projected market growth rate and proposed market share strategies (build share, maintain share, harvest share, or divest business). Managers can use these models to determine and classify each product's expected future cash contributions and future cash requirements.

Generally, managers who use a portfolio model must examine the competitive position of a product (or product line) and the opportunities for improving that product's contribution to profitability and cash flow.[12] The BCG analytical approach is more of a diagnostic tool than a guide for making strategy prescriptions.

Figure 20.3, which is based on work by the BCG, enables the marketing manager to classify a firm's products into four basic types: stars, cash cows, dogs, and problem children.[13] Stars are products with a dominant share of the market and good prospects for growth. However, they use more cash than they generate to finance growth, add capacity, and increase market share. Cash cows have a dominant share of the market but low prospects for growth; typically, they generate more cash than is required to maintain market share. Dogs have a subordinate share of the market and low prospects for growth; these products are often found in mature markets. Problem children, sometimes called "question marks," have a small share of a growing market and generally require a large amount of cash to build share.

The growth-share matrix in Figure 20.3 can be expanded to show a firm's whole portfolio by providing for each product (1) its dollar sales volume, illustrated by the size of a circle on the matrix; (2) its market share relative to competition, represented by the horizontal position of the product on the matrix, and (3) the growth rate of the market, indicated by the position of the product in the vertical direction. Figure 20.4 suggests marketing strategies appropriate for cash cows, stars, dogs, and problem children.

The long-term health of an organization depends on having some products that generate cash (and provide acceptable profits) and others that use cash to

Figure 20.3

Illustrative Growth-Share Matrix Developed by the Boston Consulting Group

Source: *Perspectives,* No. 66, "The Product Portfolio." Reprinted by permission from The Boston Consulting Group, Inc., Boston, MA. © Copyright 1970.

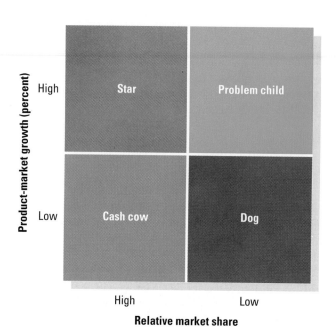

support growth. Among the indicators of overall health are the size and vulnerability of the cash cows, the prospects for the stars, if any, and the number of problem children and dogs. Particular attention must be paid to those products with large cash appetites. Unless the company has an abundant cash flow, it cannot afford to sponsor many such products at one time. If resources, including debt capacity, are spread too thin, the company will end up with too many marginal products and will be unable to finance promising new product entries or acquisitions in the future.

Market Attractiveness–Business Position Model

The **market attractiveness–business position model**, illustrated in Figure 20.5, is another two-dimensional matrix. However, rather than using single measures to define the vertical and horizontal dimensions of the matrix, the model employs multiple measurements and observations. The vertical dimension, *market attractiveness,* includes all strengths and resources that relate to the market, such as seasonality, economies of scale, competitive intensity, industry sales, and the overall cost and feasibility of entering the market. The horizontal axis, *business position,* is a composite of factors such as sales, relative market share, research and development, price competitiveness, product quality, and market knowledge as they relate to the product in building market share. The size of each circle represents the relative dollar sales. A slight variation of this matrix is called General Electric's Strategic Business Planning Grid because General Electric is credited with extending the product-portfolio planning tool to examine market attractiveness and business strength.

The best situation is for a firm to have a strong business position in an attractive market. The upper left area in Figure 20.5 represents the opportunity for an invest/grow strategy, but the matrix does not indicate how to implement

Stars

Characteristics

- Market leaders
- Fast growing
- Substantial profits
- Require large investment to finance growth

Strategies

- Protect existing share
- Reinvest earnings in the form of price reductions, product improvements, providing better market coverage, production efficiency, etc.
- Obtain a large share of the new users

Problem children

Characteristics

- Rapid growth
- Poor profit margins
- Enormous demand for cash

Strategies

- Invest heavily to get a disproportionate share of new sales
- Buy existing market shares by acquiring competitors
- Divestment (see Dogs)
- Harvesting (see Dogs)
- Abandonment (see Dogs)
- Focus on a definable niche where dominance can be achieved

Cash cows

Characteristics

- Profitable products
- Generate more cash than needed to maintain market share

Strategies

- Maintain market dominance
- Invest in process improvements and technological leadership
- Maintain price leadership
- Use excess cash to suppport research and growth elsewhere in the company

Dogs

Characteristics

- Greatest number of products fall in this category
- Operate at a cost disadvantage
- Few opportunities for growth at a reasonable cost
- Markets are not growing; therefore, little new business

Strategies

- Focus on a specialized segment of the market that can be dominated and protected from competitive inroads
- Harvesting—cut back all support costs to a minimum level; supports cash flow over the product's remaining life
- Divestment—sale of a growing concern
- Abandonment—elimination from the product line

Product-market growth — High / Low

Relative market share — High / Low

Figure 20.4 **Characteristics and Strategies for the Four Basic Product Types in the Growth-Share Matrix** Source: Concepts in this figure adapted from George S. Day, "Diagnosing the Product Portfolio," *Journal of Marketing*, April 1977, pp. 30–31.

this strategy. The purpose of the model is to serve as a diagnostic tool to highlight SBUs that have an opportunity to grow or that should be divested or approached selectively. SBUs that occupy the invest/grow position can lose their position through faulty marketing strategies.

Decisions on allocating resources to SBUs of medium overall attractiveness should be arrived at on a basis relative to other SBUs that are either more or less

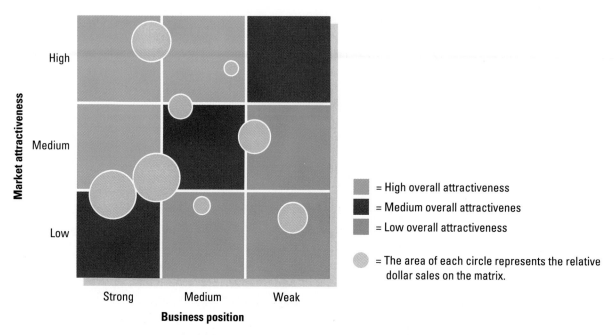

Figure 20.5 **Market Attractiveness–Business Position Matrix**   Source: Adapted from Derek F. Abell and John S. Hammond, *Strategic Market Planning: Problems and Analytical Approaches,* © 1979, p. 213. Reprinted by permission of Prentice-Hall, Inc., Englewood Cliffs, N.J.

attractive. The lower right area of the matrix is a low-growth harvest/divest area. Harvesting is a gradual withdrawal of marketing resources on the assumption that sales will decline at a slow rate but profits will still be significant at a lower sales volume. Harvesting and divesting may be appropriate strategies for SBUs characterized by low overall attractiveness.

Profit Impact on Marketing Strategy (PIMS)

The Strategic Planning Institute (SPI) developed a databank of information on three thousand strategic business units of two hundred different firms during the period 1970–1983 for the **Profit Impact on Marketing Strategy (PIMS)** research program.[14] The sample is somewhat biased because it is composed primarily of large, profitable manufacturing firms marketing mature products, and service firms and distribution companies are underrepresented. However, 19 percent of the sample is composed of international businesses.[15] The member organizations of the institute provide confidential information on successes, failures, and marginal products. Figure 20.6 shows a PIMS data form. The data are analyzed to provide members with information about how similar organizations have performed under a given set of circumstances and about the factors that contribute to success or failure in given market conditions.

The unit of observation in PIMS is the SBU. Table 20.1 shows the types of information provided on each business in the PIMS database. The PIMS database includes both diagnostic and prescriptive information to assist in analyzing marketing performance and formulating marketing strategies. The analysis focuses on options, problems, resources, and opportunities.

The PIMS project has identified more than thirty factors that affect the performance of firms. These factors can be grouped into three sets of variables: (1) those relating to the structure of the marketplace in which the firm competes; (2) those that describe the firm's competitive position within that market; and (3) those that relate to the strategy chosen by the firm.[16] These factors may interact, as well as directly affect performance and profitability. Some of the main findings of the PIMS project are discussed briefly below.

Strong Market Position Market position refers to the relative market share that a firm holds in relation to its competition. Firms that have a large share of a market tend to be the most profitable. However, it should be noted that market share does not necessarily create profitability. It is the result of business strategies such as the marketing of high-quality products, or the provision of good service.

Figure 20.6

Sample Page from PIMS Data Forms

Source: PIMS Data Form reproduced by permission of the Strategic Planning Institute (PIMS program), Cambridge, Mass., 1979.

103: **"LIFE CYCLE" STAGE OF PRODUCT CATEGORY**

How would you describe the stage of development of the types of products or services sold by this business during the last three years? *(Check one)*

... Introductory Stage: Primary demand for product just starting to grow; products or services still unfamiliar to many potential users ☐ 1

... Growth Stage: Demand growing at 10% or more annually in real terms; technology or competitive structure still changing ☐ 2

... Maturity Stage: Products or services familiar to vast majority of prospective users; technology and competitive structure reasonably stable ☐ 3

... Decline Stage: Products viewed as commodities; weaker competitors beginning to exit ☐ 4

104: What was this business's first year of commercial sales? *(Check one)*

Prior to 1930	1930-1949	1950-1954	1955-1959	1960-1964	1965-1969	1970-1974	1975-
☐ 0	☐ 1	☐ 2	☐ 3	☐ 4	☐ 5	☐ 6	☐ 7

105: At the time this business first entered the market, was it ... *(Check one)*

... One of the pioneers in first developing such products or services? ☐ 1

... An early follower of the pioneer(s) in a still growing, dynamic market? ☐ 2

... A later entrant into a more established market situation? ☐ 3

106-107: **PATENTS AND TRADE SECRETS**

Does this business benefit *to a significant degree* from patents, trade secrets, or other proprietary methods of production or operation ...

106: Pertaining to products or services?   NO ☐ 0   YES ☐ 1   107: Pertaining to processes?   NO ☐ 0   YES ☐ 1

108: **STANDARDIZATION OF PRODUCTS OR SERVICES**

Are the products or services of this business ... *(Check one)*

... More or less standardized for all customers? ☐ 0

... Designed or produced to order for individual customers? ☐ 1

109: **FREQUENCY OF PRODUCT CHANGES**

Is it typical practice for the business and its major competitors to change all or part of the line of products or services offered ... *(Check one)*

... Annually (for example, annual model changes)? ☐ 1

... Seasonally? ☐ 2

... Periodically, but at intervals longer than one year? ☐ 3

... No regular, periodic pattern of change? ☐ 4

110: **TECHNOLOGICAL CHANGE**

Have there been *major* technological changes in the products offered by the business or its major competitors, or in methods of production, during the last 8 years? *(If in doubt about whether a change was "major," answer NO.)*   NO ☐ 0   YES ☐ 1

Characteristics of the business environment
Long-run growth rate of the market
Short-run growth rate of the market
Rate of inflation of selling price levels
Number and size of customers
Purchase frequency and magnitude

Competitive position of the business
Share of the served market
Share relative to largest competitors
Product quality relative to competitors
Prices relative to competitors
Pay scales relative to competitors
Marketing efforts relative to competitors
Pattern of market segmentation
Rate of new-product introductions

Structure of the production process
Capital intensity (degree of automation, etc.)
Degree of vertical integration
Capacity utilization
Productivity of capital equipment
Productivity of people
Inventory levels

Discretionary budget allocations
Research and development budgets
Advertising and promotion budgets
Sales force expenditures

Strategic moves
Patterns of change in the controllable
    elements above

Operating results
Profitability results
Cash flow results
Growth results

Source: Reproduced by permission of the Strategic Planning Institute (PIMS program), Cambridge, Mass.

Table 20.1 **Types of Information Provided on Each Business in the PIMS Database**

High-Quality Products Organizations that offer higher-quality products tend to be more profitable than their competitors. They are able to demand higher prices for those products. Moreover, high-quality offerings instill customer loyalty, foster repeat purchases, insulate firms from price wars, and help build market share. In Figure 20.7, Lennox promotes its ongoing commitment to quality. It appears impossible for firms to overcome inferior offerings with high levels of marketing expenditures. Advertising is no substitute for product quality.

Lower Costs Firms achieve lower costs through economies of scale, ability to bargain with suppliers, or backward integration. Low costs heighten profitability levels.

Investment and Capital Intensity The higher the required investment to compete in an industry, the more pressure there is on a firm to fully use its production capacity. Moreover, these factors tend to have a negative impact on profitability.

Significance of Strategic Market Planning Approaches

The approaches presented here provide an overview of the most popular analytical methods used in strategic market planning. However, the Boston Consulting Group's portfolio analysis, the market attractiveness–business position model, and the Profit Impact on Marketing Strategy research program are used not only to diagnose problem areas or to recognize opportunities, but also to facilitate the allocation of resources among business units. They are not intended to serve as formulas for success or prescriptive guides that lay out cut-and-dried strategic action plans.[17] These approaches are supplements to, not substitutes for, the marketing manager's own judgment. The real test of each approach, or any integrated approach, is how well it helps management diagnose the firm's strengths and weaknesses and prescribe strategic actions for maintaining or improving performance. The emphasis should be on making sound decisions with the aid of these analytical tools.[18]

Another word of caution regarding the use of portfolio approaches is necessary. The classification of SBUs into a specific portfolio position hinges on four factors: (1) the operational definition of the matrix dimensions; (2) the rules used to divide a dimension into high and low categories; (3) the weighting of the variables used in composite dimensions, if composite dimensions are used; and (4) the specific model used.[19] In other words, changes in any of these four factors may well result in a different classification for a single SBU.

Results of a survey sponsored by the *Harvard Business Review* of top industrial firms indicate that portfolio planning and other depersonalized planning techniques help managers strengthen their planning process and solve the problems of managing diversified business-to-business companies. However, the results also indicate that analytical techniques alone do not result in success. Management must blend these analyses with managerial judgment to deal with the reality of the existing situation.

There are other tools that aid strategic market planning besides those examined here. For example, for many years marketing planners have used the

Figure 20.7

A Commitment to Quality

Lennox offers a high-quality product and remains a major competitor in the heating and air-conditioning equipment market.

Source: Lennox Industries, Inc.

product life cycle concept, discussed in Chapters 8 and 9. Many firms have their own approaches to planning that incorporate, to varying degrees, some of the approaches discussed here. All strategic planning approaches have some similarity in that several of the components of strategic market planning outlined in Figure 20.1 (especially market/product relationships) are related to a plan of action for reaching objectives.

Developing Competitive Strategies for Marketing

After analyzing business operations and business performance, the next step in strategic market planning is to determine future business directions and develop marketing strategies. A business may choose one or more competitive strategies, including intense growth, diversified growth, and integrated growth. Figure 20.8 shows these competitive strategies on a product-market matrix. This matrix can help in determining growth that can be implemented through marketing strategies.

Intense Growth

Intense growth can take place when current products and current markets have the potential for increasing sales. There are three main strategies for intense growth: market penetration, market development, and product development.

Market penetration is a strategy of increasing sales in current markets with current products. Wendy's, for example, cut prices on many of its menu items to 99 cents in an effort to enlarge its market share in the increasingly competitive fast-food industry.

Market development is a strategy of increasing sales of current products in new markets. For example, a European aircraft manufacturer was able to enter the U.S. market by offering airline companies financing that Boeing could not match.

Product development is a strategy of increasing sales by improving present products or developing new products for current markets. Tandem Computers Inc., for example, has marketed specialty computers for commercial use for

Figure 20.8

Competitive Strategies

Source: H.I. Ansoff, *Corporate Strategy*, McGraw-Hill, 1965, p. 109. Used by permission of the author.

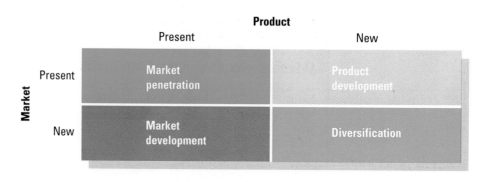

Figure 20.9

Product Development Intense Growth Strategy

Robitussin developed additional products to serve current customers.

Source: Courtesy of A.H. Robins Company.

When it comes to relieving coughs, Robitussin always comes through. Which may explain why more doctors and pharmacists recommend it than any other cough medicine. And why more mothers have made Robitussin the medicine they call on to doctor their family's coughs—any hour of the day or night.

Which Robitussin is right for you? Ask your doctor or pharmacist.

No One Has Made More House Calls.

Recommended by "Dr. Mom"

several years but only recently developed its first mainframe computer—the NonStop Cyclone—to compete head-on with IBM in Tandem's market.[20] Robitussin expanded its product offering to serve its current market (see Figure 20.9).

Inside Marketing discusses how Frito-Lay uses both market development and product development competitive strategies.

Diversified Growth

Diversified growth occurs when new products are developed to be sold in new markets. Firms have become increasingly diversified since the 1960s. Diversification offers some advantages over single-business firms because it allows firms to spread their risk across a number of markets. More importantly, it allows firms to make better and wider use of their management, technical, and financial resources. For example, marketing expertise can be used across businesses, and they may also share advertising themes, distribution channels, warehouse facilities, or even sales forces.[21] The three forms of diversification are horizontal, concentric, and conglomerate.

Horizontal diversification results when new products that are not technologically related to current products are introduced to current markets. Sony Corp., for example, has diversified from an electronics giant to a filmmaker through its purchase of Columbia Pictures. The purchase gave Sony a library of 2,700 movies, including *Ghostbusters 2* and *When Harry Met Sally*, as well as 23,000 television episodes, which it may use to help establish its new line of 8mm VCRs.[22]

In *concentric diversification*, the marketing and technology of new products are related to current products, but the new ones are introduced into new markets. For instance, Dow Chemical is diversifying into agricultural chemicals

New Strategies at Frito-Lay

FROM ALL INDICATIONS, Frito-Lay reigns supreme and secure in the salty-snack industry, owning nearly one-half of the $9.2 billion market. Its Doritos tortilla chips are the number-one-selling brand in the United States, and its Ruffles and Lay's potato chips are close behind. Why, then, should the company risk new marketing strategies when old ones have worked so well? Because Frito-Lay, long-time pioneer in fresh marketing techniques, has been quick to perceive that many historically loyal consumers are changing their eating habits at the same time that new target markets are becoming important. Frito-Lay wants to stay on top by changing right along with its customers. Promoting specific brands to precise niches and using innovative computer-assisted marketing techniques, along with unconventional strategies, are helping Frito-Lay succeed.

As babyboomers graduate to health-conscious middle age, their snacking habits are changing, a trend Frito-Lay hopes to exploit with its new Light line of snacks. Marketed not as a brand extension, but as a distinct line of products, Doritos Light, Ruffles Light, and Cheetos Light target those 35- to 54-year-old consumers who enjoy snacking but won't feel as guilty doing it if their old favorites contain less fat and cholesterol. In addition to promoting the Light line on network television, in print advertisements, with in-store and direct-mail sampling, and with special regional events, Frito will test the products in canister packaging, hoping that the resealability feature will attract the light and occasional snackers comprising this niche.

While focusing attention on the health-conscious segment, Frito-Lay is not ignoring those consumers who don't worry about reading the nutritional information on the back of the package. Repositioning its 60-year-old Fritos Corn Chips is an example of the company's eagerness to attract the biggest snacking segment, 9- to 18-year-olds. Over the last five years, sales of legendary Fritos dropped, even though the $635 million corn chip segment as a whole was flourishing. Recognizing that its traditional customer is aging, Frito redesigned its package and began a

youth-oriented campaign. Package colors are bolder, the logo is updated, and added to the old slogan, "Muncha buncha Fritos," are the words "right now," designed to appeal to the target group's desire for instant gratification. Company executives are willing to gamble that increasing the numbers of younger consumers can boost market share without sacrificing brand equity.

To attract the largest share of its diverse markets, Frito employs several innovative marketing techniques. When the company bought Smartfood, New England's top-selling brand of prepopped popcorn, executives elected to stick with what the company calls "guerilla marketing." Flying in the face of Frito tradition, this strategy uses no glamorous national advertising, just offbeat public relations that take the message and the product directly to consumers. People dressed up in Smartfood bags show up in surprising places doing surprising things—waving to drivers from highway overpasses and skiing down mountain slopes, for example.

With the help of two computer databases, the company applies "micromarketing," a technique enabling its sales force to analyze demographic profiles and physical store characteristics and then match the right product with the right neighborhood. Store-specific marketing allows Frito to spend its promotional dollars more efficiently.

Sources: Jennifer Lawrence, "Fritos, at Age 60, Thinks Young in New Ad Effort," *Advertising Age,* Feb. 25, 1991, pp. 3, 54; Barbara Holsomback, "F-L Takes Risk in Repositioning of Fritos Brand," *Adweek,* Feb. 25, 1991, pp. 1, 4; Jon Berry, "Hey, Dudes, Check Out Those Fritos!" *Adweek's Marketing Week,* Feb. 25, 1991, pp. 4–5; Jennifer Lawrence, "Frito's Micro-Move," *Advertising Age,* Feb. 12, 1990, p. 44; Jennifer Lawrence, "Frito Goes National with New Snack Line," *Advertising Age,* Feb. 5, 1990, pp. 3, 45; Jennifer Lawrence, "Frito's Kernels Plot 'Guerilla Marketing,'" *Advertising Age,* Apr. 9, 1990, pp. 3, 61; Jennifer Lawrence and Laurie Freeman, "Can-Do: Frito-Lay Snacks Take on Pringle's with New Package," *Advertising Age,* Jan. 9, 1989, pp. 3, 42.

and pharmaceuticals through joint ventures with corporations in those industries.[23]

Conglomerate diversification occurs when new products are unrelated to current technology, products, or markets and are introduced to markets new to the firm. For example, Bass P.L.C., a British brewer, acquired the American Holiday Inn hotel chain.

Integrated Growth

Integrated growth can occur in the same industry that the firm is in and in three possible directions: forward, backward, and horizontally. A company growing through forward integration takes ownership or increased control of its distribution system. For example, a shoe manufacturer might start selling its products through wholly owned retail outlets. In backward integration, a firm takes ownership or increased control of its supply systems. A newspaper company that buys a paper mill is integrating backward. Horizontal integration occurs when a firm takes ownership or control of some of its competitors. For example, Polly Peck International P.L.C., a British fruit grower and distributor, purchased Del Monte's fresh-fruit division.[24]

Marketing Planning

As we noted at the start, this chapter deals with the planning aspect of marketing management. In this section we describe how the strategic plan is implemented. **Marketing planning** is a systematic process that involves assessing marketing opportunities and resources, determining marketing objectives, and developing a plan for implementation and control. The objective of marketing planning is the creation of a marketing plan.

Figure 20.10 illustrates the **marketing planning cycle**. Note that marketing planning is a circular process. As the dotted feedback lines in the figure indicate, planning is not unidirectional. Feedback is used to coordinate and synchronize all stages of the planning cycle.

The duration of marketing plans varies. Plans that cover a period of one year or less are called **short-range plans**. **Medium-range plans** usually encompass two to five years. Marketing plans that extend beyond five years are generally viewed as **long-range plans**. These plans can sometimes cover a period as long as twenty years. Marketing managers may have short-, medium-, and long-range plans all at the same time. Long-range plans are relatively rare. However, as the marketing environment continues to change and business decisions become more complex, profitability and survival will depend more and more on the development of long-range plans.[25]

The extent to which marketing managers develop and use plans also varies. Although planning provides numerous benefits, some managers do not use formal marketing plans because they spend almost all their time dealing with daily problems, many of which would be eliminated by adequate planning. However, planning is becoming more important to marketing managers, who realize that planning is necessary to develop, coordinate, and control marketing

Figure 20.10

**The Marketing Plan-
ning Cycle**

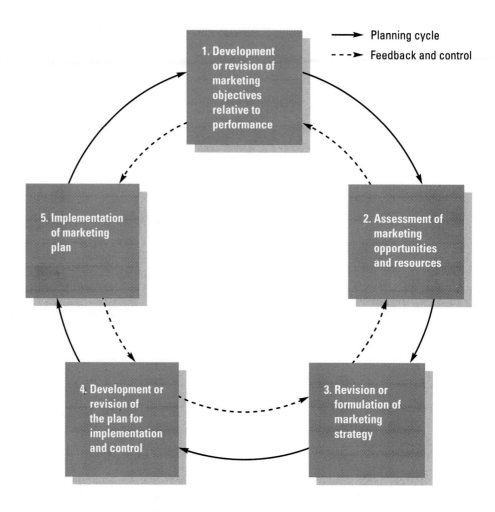

activities effectively and efficiently. When formulating a marketing plan, a new enterprise or a firm with a new product does not have current performance to evaluate or an existing plan to revise. Therefore, its marketing planning centers on analyzing available resources and options to assess opportunities. Managers can then develop marketing objectives and a strategy. In addition, many firms recognize the need to include information systems in their plans so that they can have continuous feedback and keep their marketing activities oriented toward objectives. (Information systems are discussed in Chapter 7.) One research study, which examined 207 different companies, found that those that had maintained or increased their planning departments during the preceding five years, and had increased their allocation of resources to planning activities, outperformed those whose planning departments had become smaller.[26]

The Marketing Plan

As mentioned earlier, the marketing plan is the written document or blueprint governing all of a firm's marketing activities, including the implementation and control of those activities. A marketing plan serves a number of purposes:

1. It offers a "road map" for implementing the firm's strategies and achieving its objectives.
2. It assists in management control and monitoring of implementation of strategy.
3. It informs new participants in the plan of their role and function.
4. It specifies how resources are to be allocated.
5. It stimulates thinking and makes better use of resources.
6. It assigns responsibilities, tasks, and timing.
7. It makes participants aware of problems, opportunities, and threats.[27]

A firm should have a plan for each marketing strategy it develops. Because such plans must be changed as forces in the firm and in the environment change, marketing planning is a continuous process.

Organizations use many different formats when devising marketing plans. Plans may be written for strategic business units, product lines, individual products or brands, or specific markets. Most plans share some common ground, however, by including an executive summary, opportunity and threat analysis, a description of environmental forces, an inventory of company resources, a description of marketing objectives, an outline of the marketing strategy, financial projections and budgets, and benchmarks or controls for monitoring and evaluating the action taken (see Table 20.2). In the following sections we consider the major parts of a typical marketing plan, as well as the purpose that each part serves.

Executive Summary

The executive summary is a synopsis (often only one or two pages long) outlining the main thrust of the entire report. It includes an introduction, the major aspects of the marketing plan, and a statement about the costs of implementing the plan. Such a summary helps executives who need to know what information the plan contains but are not involved in approving or making decisions related to the plan and can pass up the details.

Situation Analysis

The situation analysis provides an appraisal of the difference between the firm's current performance and past stated objectives. It includes a summary of data that relate to the creation of the current marketing situation. This information is obtained from both the firm's external and internal environment, usually through its marketing information system. Depending on the situation, details on the composition of target market segments, marketing objectives, current marketing strategies, market trends, sales history, and profitability may be included.

Opportunity and Threat Analysis

In the analysis of opportunities and threats, a detailed examination of opportunities or threats present in the firm's operating environment is provided. It examines opportunities and threats with regard to specific target markets along

Table 20.2

Components of a
Marketing Plan

I. **Executive Summary**

II. **Situation Analysis**
   A. Description of markets, current marketing strategies
   B. Description of measures of performance

III. **Opportunities and Threats**
   A. Greatest challenges or threats to future marketing activities
   B. Opportunity analysis

IV. **Environment**
   A. Legal, political, and regulatory factors
   B. Social and cultural factors
   C. Economic factors
   D. Competitive factors
   E. Technological factors

V. **Company Resources**
   A. Financial resources
   B. Human resources
   C. Experience and expertise

VI. **Marketing Objectives**

VII. **Marketing Strategies**
   A. Target market
   B. Marketing mix

VIII. **Financial Projections and Budgets**
   A. Delineation of costs
   B. Estimates of sales and revenues
   C. Expected return on investment for implementing the marketing plan

IX. **Controls and Evaluation**
   A. Measures of performance
   B. Monitoring and evaluating performance

with their size and growth potential. Possible market opportunities may be described in this section. It develops an ordering of priorities for action in light of the unit's internal capabilities for dealing with the circumstances.

Environmental Analysis

The environmental section of the marketing plan describes the current state of the marketing environment, including the legal, political, regulatory, technological, competitive, social, and economic forces, as well as ethical considerations. It also makes predictions about future directions of those forces.

As mentioned earlier, environmental forces can hamper an organization in achieving its objectives. The section also describes the possible impact of these forces on the implementation of the marketing plan. Most marketing plans include extensive analyses of competitive, legal, and regulatory forces, perhaps even creating separate sections for these influential forces of the marketing environment. It is important to note here that, because the forces of the marketing environment are dynamic, marketing plans should be reviewed and possibly modified periodically to adjust to change.

Company Resources

A firm's human and financial resources, as well as its experiences and expertise, are major considerations in developing a marketing plan. Thus the marketing plan should delineate the human, financial, and physical resources available for implementing the plan, as well as describe resource constraints that may affect implementation. It should also describe any distinctive competencies that may give the firm an edge in the marketplace. The plan should take into account strengths and weaknesses that may influence the firm's ability to implement a selected marketing strategy.

Marketing Objectives

This section describes the objectives underlying the plan. A **marketing objective** is a statement of what is to be accomplished through marketing activities. It specifies the results expected from marketing efforts. A marketing objective should be expressed in clear, simple terms so that all marketing personnel understand exactly what they are trying to achieve. It should be written in such a way that its accomplishment can be measured accurately. If a company has an objective of increasing its market share by 12 percent, the firm should be able to measure changes in its market share accurately. A marketing objective should also indicate the time frame for accomplishing the objective. For example, a firm that sets an objective of introducing three new products should state the time period in which this is to be done.

Objectives may be stated in terms of degree of product introduction or innovation, sales volume, profitability per unit, or gains in market share. They must also be consistent with the firm's overall organizational goals.

Marketing Strategies

This section provides a broad overview of the plan for achieving the marketing objectives, and ultimately, the organizational goals. Marketing strategy focuses on defining a target market and developing a marketing mix to gain long-run competitive and consumer advantages. There is a degree of overlap between corporate strategy and marketing strategy. Marketing strategy is unique in that it has the responsibility to assess buyer needs and the firm's potential for gaining competitive advantage, both of which ultimately must guide the corporate mission.[28] In other words, marketing strategy guides the firm's direction in relationships between customers and competitors. The bottom line is that a

Figure 20.11

Marketing Strategy That Meets Customers' Needs

Crayola Washable Markers fit the needs of both children and parents.

Source: Courtesy of Binney and Smith.

marketing strategy must be consistent with consumer needs, perceptions, and beliefs. As shown in Figure 20.11, Crayola provides a marketing strategy that is consistent with kids' and parents' needs. Thus this section should describe the firm's intended target market and how product, promotion, distribution, and price will be used to satisfy the needs of the members of the target market.

Financial Projections and Budgets

The financial projections and budgets section outlines the returns expected through implementation of the plan. The costs incurred will be weighed against expected revenues. A budget must be prepared to allocate resources to accomplish marketing objectives. It should contain estimates of the costs of implementing the plan, including the costs of advertising, sales force training and compensation, development of distribution channels, and marketing research.

Controls and Evaluation

This section details how the results of the plan will be measured. For example, results of an advertising campaign designed to increase market share may be measured in terms of increases in sales volume or improved brand recognition and acceptance by consumers. Next, a schedule for comparing the results achieved with the objectives set forth in the marketing plan is developed. Finally, guidelines may be offered outlining who is responsible for monitoring the program and taking remedial action.

Summary

A strategic market plan is an outline of the methods and resources required to achieve the organization's goals within a specific target market; it takes into account all functional areas of a business unit that must be coordinated. A strategic business unit (SBU) is a division, product line, or other profit center within the parent company and is used to define areas for consideration in a specific strategic market plan. The process of strategic market planning yields a marketing strategy that is the framework for a marketing plan. A marketing plan includes the framework and entire set of activities to be performed; it is the written document or blueprint for implementing and controlling an organization's marketing activities.

Through the process of strategic market planning, an organization can develop marketing strategies that, when properly implemented and controlled, will contribute to achieving the organization's overall goals. The set of marketing strategies that are implemented and used at the same time is referred to as the organization's marketing program. Environmental forces are important in the strategic market planning process and very much affect it. These forces imply opportunities and threats that influence an organization's overall goals.

A firm's organizational goals should be derived from its mission, the broad tasks the organization wants to achieve. These goals should guide planning efforts.

There are three major considerations in assessing opportunities and resources: evaluation of market opportunities, monitoring of environmental forces, and understanding the firm's capabilities. A market opportunity, or strategic window, opens when the right combination of circumstances occurs at the right time, and an organization can take action toward a target market. An opportunity offers a favorable chance for the company to generate sales from markets. Market requirements relate to the customers' needs or desired benefits. The market requirements are satisfied by components of the marketing mix that provide buyers with these benefits. Environmental scanning is a search for information about events and relationships in a company's outside environment; such information aids marketers in planning. A firm's capabilities relate to distinctive competencies that it has developed to do something well and efficiently. A company is likely to enjoy a differential advantage in an area where its competencies outmatch those of its potential competition.

Corporate strategy determines the means for utilizing resources in the areas of production, finance, research and development, personnel, and marketing to reach the organization's goals.

A number of tools have been developed to aid marketing managers in their planning efforts, including the Boston Consulting Group (BCG) product-portfolio analysis, the market attractiveness–business position model, and Profit Impact on Marketing Strategy (PIMS). The BCG approach is based on the philosophy that a product's market growth rate and its market share are key factors influencing marketing strategy. All the firm's products are integrated into a single, overall matrix and evaluated to determine appropriate strategies for individual SBUs and the overall portfolio strategies.

The market attractiveness–business position model is a two-dimensional matrix. The market attractiveness dimension includes all the sources of strength and resources that relate to the market; competition, industry sales, and the cost of competing are among the sources. The business position axis measures sales, relative market share, research and development, and other factors that relate to building a market share for a product.

The Profit Impact on Marketing Strategy (PIMS) research program has developed a databank of confidential information on the successes, failures, and marginal products of more than three thousand strategic business units of the two hundred members of the Strategic Planning Institute. The unit of observation in PIMS is an SBU. The results of PIMS include diagnostic and prescriptive information to assist in analyzing marketing performance and formulating marketing strategies. The analysis focuses on options, problems, resources, and opportunities.

These tools for strategic market planning are used only to diagnose problem areas or recognize opportunities. They are supplements to, not substitutes for, the marketing manager's own judgment. The real test of each approach, or any integrated approach, is how well it helps management diagnose the firm's strengths and weaknesses and prescribe strategic actions for maintaining or improving performance.

Competitive strategies that can be implemented through marketing include intense growth, diversified growth, and integrated growth. Intense growth includes market penetration, market development, or product development. Diversified growth includes horizontal, concentric, and conglomerate diversification. Integrated growth includes forward, backward, and horizontal integration.

Marketing planning is a systematic process that involves assessing opportunities and resources, determining marketing objectives, developing a marketing strategy, and developing plans for implementation and control. Short-range marketing plans cover one year or less; medium-range plans usually encompass two to five years; plans that last for more than five years are long-range.

A marketing plan is the written document or blueprint for implementing and controlling an organization's marketing activities. A well-written plan clearly specifies when, how, and who is to perform marketing activities. Typical marketing plans include an executive summary, situation analysis, opportunity and threat analysis, a description of the impact of the marketing environment forces, a summary of company resources, marketing objectives, marketing strategies, financial projections and budgets, and prescriptions for controlling and evaluating the results of the marketing plan.

Important Terms

Strategic market plan
Strategic business unit (SBU)
Strategic market planning
Marketing plan
Marketing program
Market opportunity
Market requirements
Corporate strategy
Product-portfolio analysis
Market attractiveness–business position model

Profit Impact on Marketing Strategy (PIMS)
Intense growth
Diversified growth
Integrated growth
Marketing planning
Marketing planning cycle
Short-range plans
Medium-range plans
Long-range plans
Marketing objective

1. Why should an organization develop a marketing strategy? What is the difference between strategic market planning and the strategy itself?
2. Identify the major components of strategic market planning, and explain how they are interrelated.
3. In what ways do environmental forces affect strategic market planning? Give specific examples.
4. What are some of the issues that must be considered in analyzing a firm's opportunities and resources? How do these issues affect marketing objectives and market strategy?
5. Why is market opportunity analysis necessary? What are the determinants of market opportunity?
6. In relation to resource constraints, how can environmental scanning affect a firm's long-term strategic market planning? Consider product costs and benefits affected by the environment.
7. What are the major considerations in developing the product-portfolio grid? Define and explain the four basic types of products suggested by the Boston Consulting Group.
8. When should marketers consider using PIMS for strategic market planning?
9. What benefits do marketing managers gain from planning? Is planning necessary for long-run survival? Why or why not?
10. How should an organization establish marketing objectives?

Cases

20.1 Timex Stands the Test of Time

During the 1970s, watches took a technological leap forward from wind-up spring mechanisms to quartz crystals, batteries, and digital displays. The Timex Corporation, however, lagged behind other manufacturers in making the changes. When the Swiss-made Swatch invaded U.S. department stores and convinced customers that their watches weren't just time-telling devices, but fashion statements, Timex wasn't ready to offer any competition. At Timex, reliability had always been the number-one priority, but certainly not style and fashion. For years, Timex's sales suffered because of a drab image, especially in comparison with the colorful Swatch.

Then came the 1990s, the decade of downscaling. As value takes precedence over status, more price-conscious consumers are attracted by quality at moderate prices than by designer labels. Timex is taking advantage of this trend to revive its 41-year-old brand, the old reliable Timex watch. By blending its "value pricing" message with some trendy new designs and diversifying its product for specific niche markets, Timex is making a comeback.

Consumers can still get an unadorned Timex watch for about $9.95, and analysts say that these simple styles with easy-to-read faces are the company's best sellers. To compete in a crowded market, however, Timex is developing stylish special collections for two separate adult divisions, dress watches and sports watches, as well as expanding its children's unit. The company even set up studios in France and the United States to design Timex renditions of colorful creative watches. In the adult fashion arena, Timex offers women its Images line with neon-accented hands, floral-patterned watch bands, and oversized faces, and men the Carriage III collection. For those with poor vision, Timex created the Easy Reader with large clear numbers. Sports watch buyers can choose among models with names like Surf, Brave Wave, and Magnum that are shock-resistant, water-resistant, and offer features like compasses, pedometers, chronographs, and thermometers. After soliciting educators' advice, the company came up with its Gizmoz watches that help children five to nine years old tell time. Colorful designs are on the band instead of the face, which displays all of the numbers and color-codes hour and minute hands. For example, black-faced watches have white hours and hour hands, but green minutes and green minute hands. There is even a Lefty Gizmo available. To appeal to parents, whose money really buys the Gizmos, Timex offers a Kids' Loss Protection Plan that replaces a watch for one-half the purchase price.

Timex's advertising strategy is to appeal to niche markets by reviving its traditional "durable yet inexpensive" positioning and revitalizing its powerful brand identity. The famous Timex theme, "It Takes a Licking and Keeps On Ticking," takes a humorous bent in television spots where Sumo wrestlers wear Timex watches strapped to their middles as they grapple on the mat, and rock musicians use Timex watches to strum their guitars. In a recent print advertising campaign, the firm features real people who, like the Timex watches they wear, have been through rough experiences but survived to tell the tale. On talk shows all over the United States, company executives introduced the Timex *Why Pay More* magazine, featuring Timex watches as part of fashion outfits selling for under $75. After each television appearance, about 1,000 people called Timex toll-free to order the magazine.

With watch sales in the United States down about 10 percent, most watch-makers are concerned. At Timex Corporation, however, executives are celebrating sales and market share increases. The company now controls a larger segment of the market than its four biggest competitors combined. Its newest cause-related promotional campaign not only won the firm a national award, but garnered about $300,000 for the American Heart Association. Timex is happy to be shedding its dowdy and boring image. Rising young professional people don't have to put their wrists behind their backs to hide a Timex anymore, or announce loudly to coworkers that they are only wearing a Timex while their Rolex is being repaired.[29]

Questions for Discussion

1. Which environmental forces are likely to be of greatest interest to marketing managers at Timex?
2. Identify the target markets toward which Timex is aiming its products.
3. What types of target markets should Timex marketers consider?

20.2 Paramount Pictures' Strategic Struggle

Although the products marketed by Hollywood studios differ from those of other companies, like any other business, they too are vulnerable to threats and open to opportunities. They must develop marketing strategies and implement them if they are to produce the blockbuster movies and hit television shows that consumers want to see. Paramount Pictures Corporation is one studio that has developed successful marketing strategies.

Business is good for Paramount today, with movie blockbusters and hit television shows such as "Cheers," "The Arsenio Hall Show," and "Star Trek: The Next Generation." But things were not always so glamorous for the studio division of Paramount Communications Inc. (formerly Gulf & Western). In early 1986, Paramount had a dismal 1.5 percent share of the market, down from a 1984 high of 19.1 percent. In addition, the management team that had led the studio to glory with the films *Flashdance, An Officer and a Gentleman,* and *Raiders of the Lost Ark* left for positions with 20th Century Fox and the Walt Disney Company. Paramount became owner of a large collection of movie flops, with the exception of one huge hit, *Beverly Hills Cop.*

Then, Frank Mancuso, a 27-year Paramount veteran, assumed the post of chairman of the company. Mancuso hired the industry's best production and marketing executives and began a strategy of establishing long-term relationships between the studio and major film producers and stars. This strategy proved to be the answer to Paramount's film production woes.

Shortly after Mancuso assumed the chairmanship of Paramount, the company began turning out one hit after another—often from ideas turned down by other film studios. One such idea was a script about young naval air cadets, which Paramount produced at a cost of more than $17.5 million under the name *Top Gun*. *Top Gun* went on to become the top-grossing hit of 1986 with revenues of $270 million. *Crocodile Dundee* in 1986 and *Beverly Hills Cop II, Fatal Attraction,* and *The Untouchables* in 1987 were other Paramount success stories. By the end of 1987, Paramount had captured the number-one position in the market two years in a row and a 20 percent share of the U.S. market. Despite the 1990 box office success of *The Hunt for Red October* and *Ghost,* a 7 percent decline in motion picture attendance and several disappointing films lowered the studio's market share to 16.4 percent.

The secret to Paramount's success lies partly in the whimsical entertainment tastes of American consumers. However, a great deal of its success can be attributed to its strategy of nurturing successful long-term relationships and projects. Paramount has carefully milked one of its oldest television cash cows, "Star Trek," with video releases of the original episodes, six feature films, and the number-two hit syndicated program "Star Trek: The Next Generation." Long-term relationships with other cash cows and stars, such as actor/comedians Eddie Murphy and Arsenio Hall and major directors Steven Spielberg and George Lucas, have also contributed to the studio's string of successes.

Nurturing such long-term relationships are the only means of securing successful sequel and television spinoff development. The enormous popularity of movie groups such as the *Indiana Jones* trilogy, the series of *Star Trek* movies, and more than half a dozen Eddie Murphy pictures bear out the importance of securing these long-term contracts. Within the industry, Paramount's exclusive contract with Eddie Murphy has been considered to be the best of them all. Murphy's movies with Paramount have a combined income of more than $1 billion, not counting the additional revenue generated through television, videocassettes, and cable television.

The success of these long-term relationships has allowed Paramount to be aggressive in marketing and media usage. A prime example is the deal struck by Paramount and Time Warner to promote the opening day of *Godfather III*. Paramount agreed to advertise heavily in Time Warner publications, especially in *People, Life,* and *Entertainment Weekly.* In return, Time Warner supported the movie's opening by showing *The Godfather* and *The Godfather II* on HBO shortly before the premier. It also aired a 30-minute special, "Making of the Godfather" and a television behind-the-scenes look at *Godfather* stars that gave out a 900 number offering viewers a gift package. Paramount's advertisements promoted the HBO showings as well as the movie. As the result of this and other promotions, Paramount is known as the master of publicity and word-of-mouth promotions.

A product-line style of movie-making strategy can be a gamble. Paramount risks staking its future on past successes and even on a single superstar. Some of the company's products, such as the *Star Trek* movies, are already mature because of the aging of the principal actors. Others have finished: *Indiana Jones and the Last Crusade* was the last of the highly successful trilogy featuring Harrison Ford. The danger of relying on a single star is becoming more evident to Paramount studios. There was some doubt as to whether or not Eddie Murphy would make *Beverly Hills Cop III,* considered to be an automatic $100 million movie.

Thus, despite its successful long-term relationships and successful products, Paramount must constantly look for new product ideas and hot new stars. To shore up a 4 percent drop in entertainment operating revenues, Paramount sold a 24-film package of premium movies to the USA network for about $2 million per title. The studio also trimmed its staff and halved the number of films in development to 125. Paramount is currently exploring the possibility of doing a string of movies based on its "Star Trek: The Next Generation" television series. It recently signed Arsenio Hall to an exclusive, long-term contract and announced its own talk show, "The Maury Povich Show," already sold to stations in 40 percent of the United States. The firm's European operation will produce 2 to 4 films annually.

Paramount has had to endure occasional setbacks. One example is a recent court ruling against the studio in favor of Art Buchwald's claim that Paramount "stole" his script, "King for a Day," and turned it into the very lucrative *Coming to America.* The studio continues to believe in its strategy of milking its cash cows, however. With a box-office share just below leader Disney Studios, a $420 million production budget, and more plans for big-budget, big-star films, its faith seems justified. But the studio is constantly looking for and developing new stars. One company executive insists that Paramount won't just sit back, make *Star Trek VII, VIII, IX* and call it a day.[30]

Questions for Discussion

1. What is the role of strategic market planning at Paramount Pictures?
2. Relate the product-portfolio matrix scheme to the analysis of products (movies) at Paramount Pictures.
3. Which environmental forces are most likely to affect the planning and the outcomes of Paramount's marketing strategies?

Chapter Notes

1. Based on information from Bob Weinstein, "Pointed Matters," *Continental Profiles,* June 1991, pp. 22, 53–59; "Keeping Score for Two Retailers," *Business Journal of New Jersey,* Oct. 1, 1990; Richard Sherwin, "N.J. Firm Is Write on Money," *New York Daily News,* Sept. 18, 1990; and Judith A. Osborne, "Pencil Maker Finds 'Style' Has Appeal," *Newark Star Ledger,* June 25, 1990.
2. Michael E. Porter, *Competitive Advantage* (New York: Free Press, 1985), p. 317.
3. Derek F. Abell and John S. Hammond, *Strategic Market Planning* (Englewood Cliffs, N.J.: Prentice-Hall, 1979), p. 10.
4. P. Rajan Varadarajan, Terry Clark, and William Pride, "Controlling the Uncontrollable: Managing the Market Environment," *Sloan Management Review,* Winter 1992.
5. "1991 Marketing Achievement Awards," *Sales & Marketing Management,* August 1991, pp. 33–39.
6. Derek F. Abell, "Strategic Windows," *Journal of Marketing,* July 1978, p. 21.
7. Ken Wells, "Bank Checks Out of K mart, Realizing That Interest at Stores Was Too Low," *Wall Street Journal,* Feb. 13, 1989, p. B3.
8. David M. Georgaff and Robert G. Mundick, "Managers' Guide to Forecasting," *Harvard Business Review,* January–February 1986, p. 120.
9. "The Bumpy Road to 'Clean Fuels,'" *U.S. News & World Report,* June 26, 1989, pp. 10–11.
10. Ibid.
11. Philip Kotler, *Marketing Management,* 7th ed. (Englewood Cliffs, N.J.: Prentice Hall, 1991), pp. 50–52.
12. Joseph P. Guiltinan and Gordon W. Paul, *Marketing Management: Strategies and Programs* (New York: McGraw-Hill, 1991), p. 43.
13. George S. Day, "Diagnosing the Product Portfolio," *Journal of Marketing,* April 1977, pp. 30–31.
14. Robert Jacobson, "Distinguishing Among Competing Theories of the Market Share Effect," *Journal of Marketing,* October 1988, pp. 68–80.
15. George S. Day, *Analysis for Strategic Market Decisions* (St. Paul, Minn.: West, 1986), pp. 117–118.
16. Robert D. Buzzell and Bradley T. Gale, *The PIMS Principles: Linking Strategy to Performance* (New York: Free Press, 1987).
17. Day, *Analysis for Strategic Market Decisions,* p. 10.

18. David W. Cravens, "Strategic Marketing's New Challenge," *Business Horizons,* March–April 1983, p. 19.

19. Yoram Wind, Vijay Majahan, and Donald J. Swire, "An Empirical Comparison of Standardized Portfolio Models," *Journal of Marketing,* Spring 1983, pp. 89–99.

20. Jonathan B. Levine, "This Cyclone Is Out to Rain on IBM's Parade," *Business Week,* Oct. 23, 1989, p. 114.

21. Roger A. Kerin, Vijay Majahan, and P. Rajan Varadarajan, *Contemporary Perspectives on Strategic Marketing Planning* (Boston: Allyn & Bacon, 1990).

22. Ronald Grover, "When Columbia Met Sony . . . A Love Story," *Business Week,* Oct. 9, 1989, pp. 44–45.

23. David Woodruff, "Has Dow Chemical Found the Right Formula?" *Business Week,* Aug. 7, 1989, pp. 62, 64.

24. Mark Maremont, with Judith H. Dobrzynski, "Meet Asil Nadir, the Billion-Dollar Fruit King," *Business Week,* Sept. 18, 1989, p. 32.

25. Ronald D. Michman, "Linking Futuristics with Marketing Planning, Forecasting, and Strategy," *Journal of Consumer Marketing,* Summer 1984, pp. 17, 23.

26. Vasudevan Ramanujam and N. Venkatraman, "Planning and Performance: A New Look at an Old Question," *Business Horizons,* May–June 1987, pp. 19–25.

27. William A. Cohen, *The Practice of Marketing Management: Analysis, Planning, and Implementation* (New York: Macmillan, 1991), pp. 45–46.

28. Yoram Wind and Thomas S. Robertson, "Marketing Strategy: New Directions for Theory and Research," *Journal of Marketing,* Spring 1983, p. 12.

29. Cara Appelbaum, "High Time for Timex," *Adweek's Marketing Week,* July 29, 1991, p. 24; Melissa Campanelli, "Motivating, MOTI Style," *Sales & Marketing Management,* June 1991, pp. 125–126; and Jennifer Pellet, "Watching Watch Trends," *DM,* November 1990, pp. 56–57.

30. Richard Behar, "Small Wonders," *Time*, Feb. 11, 1991, pp. 63–64; Charles Fleming, "Time Warner, Par in 'God Swap,'" *Film*, Oct. 8, 1990, p. 5, 85; "Paramount Hoping Povich 'Current Affair' Success Translates to New Talk Show," *Broadcasting*, Oct. 8, 1990, pp. 50–51; "Paramount, MCA Opt for USA over Syndication," *Broadcasting*, Oct. 1, 1990, p. 32; "Tribune, Paramount Part Company," *Broadcasting*, Oct. 1, 1990, p. 36; Michael Fleming, "Majors' Heavyweight Films to Slug It Out for Holiday Biz," *Film*, October 1990, pp. 5, 8; Paul Noglows and Judy Brennan, "Par's Net Hike by the Book," *Finance*, September 1990, pp. 73–74; Charles Fleming, "Sequel Sinks as Murphy Trawls for New Megadeals," *Variety*, Mar. 28, 1990, pp. 1, 4; Dennis McDougal, "Paramount's Net Profit Central to Buchwald Suit," *Los Angeles Times*, Mar. 23, 1990; Elizabeth Guider, "Writers Flex Their Muscles Thanks to Buchwald Win," *Variety*, Jan. 17, 1990, pp. 1, 4; Marcy Magiera, "Paramount Axes DMB&B As Studios Watch Costs," *Advertising Age*, Jan. 15, 1990, p. 4; Laura Landro, "Paramount Plans Movie Unit in London to Tap Growing International Market," *Wall Street Journal*, Jan. 12, 1990, p. B4; Laura Landro, "It's a Record Race for Movie Makers," *Wall Street Journal*, Nov. 3, 1989, p. B2; Ronald Grover, "Fat Times for Studios, Fatter Times for Stars," *Business Week*, July 24, 1989, p. 48; and Laura Landro, "Sequels and Stars Help Top Movie Studios Avoid Major Risks," *Wall Street Journal*, June 6, 1989, pp. A1, A18.

21 *Implementing Strategies and Measuring Performance*

OBJECTIVES

- To understand how the marketing unit fits into a firm's organizational structure

- To become familiar with the ways of organizing a marketing unit

- To examine several issues relating to the implementation of marketing strategies

- To understand the control processes used in managing marketing strategies

- To learn how cost and sales analyses can be used to evaluate the performance of marketing strategies

- To become aware of the major components of a marketing audit

For years, Pepsi-Cola and Coca-Cola have been slugging it out for market share in a soft-drink war, and Pepsi keeps coming in second. However, PepsiCo is more than just soft drinks. Since its 1965 merger with Frito-Lay, Inc., the company has continued to expand and now flourishes in soft drinks, snack foods, and restaurants. Since 1980, sales have quadrupled to $17.8 billion. According to industry analysts, PepsiCo's ability to implement and change its marketing strategies accounts for the firm's enormous profitability.

To satisfy changing tastes in the marketplace, Pepsi-Cola (the soft-drink arm of PepsiCo) strives to please its target markets. Because Pepsi is popular with teens, the company cultivates the product's youthful and exciting image. It constantly updates television advertising, using music and stars with youth appeal. The company introduced Diet Pepsi to attract diet-conscious American consumers. In the 1990s Pepsi will concentrate on international markets in the former Soviet Republics, Europe, and India.

PepsiCo's snack food division, Frito-Lay, is the number-one snack food company in the world. Identifying two distinct target markets, high-volume youthful snackers and older nutrition-conscious snackers, Frito-Lay developed separate product mixes, different packaging, and different styles of advertising and promotion for each. Adding spicier new flavors, modernizing packaging, and updating music in commercials are all ways Frito-Lay targets younger snackers. For consumers worried about fat and calories, the company introduced reduced-fat versions of popular snacks.

PepsiCo's three restaurant chains, Pizza Hut, Taco Bell, and KFC are closing in on their number-one competitor, McDonald's. Pizza Hut attracts fast-food customers with the guaranteed five-minute lunch. Taco Bell attracts frugal customers with value pricing. KFC attracts health-conscious customers with skinless fried chicken.

Pepsi-Cola tried to make the 1960s "the Pepsi Generation," but the 1990s may turn out to be the company's decade after all. In a recent *Fortune* survey of corporate reputations, PepsiCo ranked number five, one step ahead of archrival Coca-Cola.[1]

Photo courtesy of PepsiCo.

EFFECTIVE MANAGEMENT OF MARKETING STRATEGIES is a major source of Pepsi-Co's success. In the last chapter we examined planning, which is one dimension of managing marketing strategies. This chapter is devoted to other dimensions of managing marketing strategies, including organization, implementation, and control. First, we focus on the marketing unit's position in the organization and the ways the unit itself can be organized. We then examine several issues regarding the implementation of marketing strategies. Next we consider the basic components of the process of control and discuss the use of cost and sales analyses to evaluate the effectiveness of marketing strategies and measure the firm's performance. Finally, we describe a marketing audit.

Organizing Marketing Activities

The structure and relationships of a marketing unit, including lines of authority and responsibility that connect and coordinate individuals, strongly affect marketing activities. This section first looks at the place of marketing within an organization and examines the major alternatives available for organizing a marketing unit. Then it shows how marketing activities can be structured to fit into an organization so as to contribute to the accomplishment of overall objectives.

Centralization Versus Decentralization

The organizational structure that a company uses to connect and coordinate various activities affects its success. Basic decisions relate to how various participants in the company will work together to make important decisions, as well as to coordinate, implement, and control activities. Top managers create corporate strategies and coordinate lower levels. A **centralized organization** is one in which the top-level managers delegate very little authority to lower levels of the organization. In a **decentralized organization**, decision-making authority is delegated as far down the chain of command as possible. The decision to centralize or decentralize the organization directly affects marketing in the organization.

In a centralized organization, major marketing decisions originate with top management and are transmitted to lower levels of management. A decentralized structure gives marketing managers more opportunity for making key strategic decisions. IBM has adopted a decentralized management structure so that its marketing managers have a chance to customize strategies for customers. On the other hand, Hewlett-Packard Co. and 3M have become more centralized by consolidating functions or eliminating divisional managers.[2] Although decentralizing may foster innovation and a greater responsiveness to customers, a decentralized company may be inefficient or appear to have a blurred marketing strategy when dealing with larger customers. A centralized organization avoids confusion among the marketing staff, vagueness in marketing strategy, and autonomous decision makers who are out of control. Of course, overly centralized companies often become dependent on top management and re-

Figure 21.1

Organizational Structure

The insurance company AIG changed its organization so that it is more sensitive to changes in the marketplace.

Source: Tony Stone Worldwide/Leonard Nadel.

Our approach to structuring an organization is a little bit different.

In business, the pyramid principle can lead to a type of management in which those at the top keep those at the lower levels from exercising initiative. At AIG, we've built a new kind of insurance group. One that gives people at every level decision-making responsibility. This makes AIG far more sensitive to changes in the marketplace anywhere in the world. And far more responsive to your insurance needs. This approach explains why AIG companies are the largest underwriters of commercial and industrial risks in the U.S., and a leading global provider of life, accident and health insurance. To learn more, contact AIG, Dept. A, 70 Pine Street, New York, NY 10270. Then watch us turn things around for you.

Insurance Companies That Don't Think Like Insurance Companies **AIG**

spond too slowly to be able to solve problems or seize new opportunities. Obviously, finding the right degree of centralization for a particular company is a difficult balancing act.

The Place of Marketing in an Organization

Because the marketing environment is so dynamic, the position of the marketing unit within the organization has risen during the past twenty-five years. Firms that truly adopt the marketing concept develop a distinct organizational culture—a culture based on a shared set of beliefs that make the customer's needs the pivotal point of a firm's decisions about strategy and operations.[3] As mentioned in Figure 21.1, AIG Insurance is organized in a way so that it is sensitive to the needs of the marketplace. Instead of developing products in a vacuum and then trying to convince consumers to make purchases, companies using the marketing concept begin with an orientation toward their customers' needs and desires. As shown in Figure 21.2, Casual Corner strives to meet customers' needs. If the marketing concept serves as a guiding philosophy, the marketing unit will be closely coordinated with other functional areas, such as production, finance, and personnel.

Marketing must interact with other functional departments in a number of key areas. It needs to work with manufacturing in determining the volume and variety of the company's products. Those in charge of production rely on marketers for accurate sales forecasts. Research and development departments depend heavily on information gathered by marketers about product features and benefits desired by consumers. Decisions made by the physical distribution department hinge on information about the urgency of delivery schedules and cost/service trade-offs.[4]

A **marketing-oriented organization** concentrates on discovering what buyers want and providing it in a way that lets it achieve its objectives. Such a company

Figure 21.2

Meeting Customer Needs

Casual Corner promotes how it tries to satisfy customer needs.

Source: Casual Corner.

has an organizational culture that effectively and efficiently produces a sustainable competitive advantage. It focuses on customer analysis, competitor analysis, and the integration of the firm's resources to provide customer value and satisfaction, as well as long-term profits.[5] As Figure 21.3 shows, the marketing manager's position is at the same level as those of the financial, production, and personnel managers. Thus the marketing manager takes part in top-level decision making. Note, too, that the marketing manager is responsible for a variety of activities. Some of them—sales forecasting and supervision and product planning—would be under the jurisdiction of other functional managers in production- or sales-oriented firms.

Both the links between marketing and other functional areas (such as production, finance, and personnel) and the importance of marketing to management evolve from the firm's basic orientation. Marketing encompasses the greatest number of business functions and occupies an important position when a firm is marketing-oriented; it has a limited role when the firm views the role of marketing as simply selling products that the company makes. However, a marketing orientation is not achieved simply by redrawing the organizational chart; management must also adopt and use the marketing orientation as a management philosophy.

Major Alternatives for Organizing the Marketing Unit

How effectively a firm's marketing management can plan and implement marketing strategies depends on how the marketing unit is organized. Effective organizational planning can give the firm a competitive advantage. The organizational structure of a marketing department establishes the authority relationships among marketing personnel and specifies who is responsible for making certain decisions and performing particular activities. This internal structure provides the vehicle for directing marketing activities.

In organizing a marketing unit, managers divide the work into specific activities and delegate responsibility and authority for those activities to persons in various positions within the unit. These positions include, for example, the sales manager, the research manager, and the advertising manager.

To develop organizational plans that give a firm a competitive advantage, four issues should be considered:

1. Which jobs or levels of jobs need to be added, deleted, or modified? For example, if new products are important to the success of the firm, marketers with strong product development skills should be added to the organization.
2. How should reporting relationships be structured to create a competitive advantage? This question is discussed further in the following descriptions of organizational structure.
3. Who should be assigned the primary responsibility for accomplishing work? Identifying primary responsibility explicitly is critical for effective performance appraisal and reward systems.
4. Should any committees or task forces be organized?[6]

No single approach to organizing a marketing unit works equally well in all businesses. A marketing unit can be organized according to (1) functions, (2) products, (3) regions, or (4) types of customers. The best approach or approaches depend on the number and diversity of the firm's products, the characteristics and needs of the people in the target market, and many other factors.

Firms often use some combination of organization by functions, products, regions, or customer types. Product features may dictate that the marketing unit be structured by products, whereas customers' characteristics require that it be organized by geographic region or by types of customers. IBM has organized by product types (mainframe and midsize computers, personal computers, and so on), but many financial institutions organize by customers because personal

Figure 21.3 Organizational Chart of a Marketing-Oriented Firm

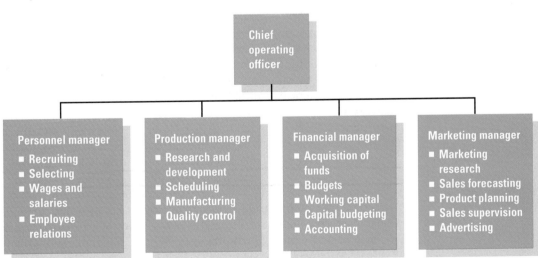

banking needs differ from commercial ones. By using more than one type of organization, a flexible marketing unit can develop and implement marketing plans to match customers' needs precisely.

Organizing by Functions Some marketing departments are organized by general marketing functions, such as marketing research, product development, distribution, sales, advertising, and customer relations. The personnel who direct these functions report directly to the top-level marketing executive. This structure is fairly common because it works well for some businesses with centralized marketing operations, such as Ford and General Motors. In more decentralized firms, such as grocery store chains, functional organization can raise severe coordination problems. The functional approach may, however, suit a large centralized company whose products and customers are neither numerous nor diverse.

Organizing by Products An organization that produces and markets diverse products may find the functional approach inadequate. The decisions and problems related to a single marketing function for one product may be quite different from those related to the same marketing function for another product. As a result, businesses that produce diverse products sometimes organize their marketing units according to product groups. Organizing by product groups gives a firm the flexibility to develop special marketing mixes for different products.

The product management system, which was introduced by Procter & Gamble, operates in about 85 percent of firms in the consumer packaged goods industry. In this structure, the product manager oversees all activities related to his or her assigned product. He or she develops product plans, sees that they are implemented, monitors the results, and takes corrective action as necessary. The product manager is also responsible for acting as a liaison between the firm and its marketing environment, transmitting essential information about the environment to the firm.[7] The product manager may also draw on the resources of specialized staff in the company.

Organizing by Regions A large company that markets products nationally (or internationally) may organize its marketing activities by geographic regions. Managers of marketing functions for each region report to their regional marketing manager; all the regional marketing managers report directly to the executive marketing manager. At Frito-Lay, for example, four regional marketing vice presidents who have responsibility for marketing efforts in their regions report to the senior vice president for marketing at the company's Dallas headquarters. Frito-Lay adopted this regional structure to put more senior management personnel into the field, to get closer to customers, and to enable the company to respond more quickly and efficiently to regional competitors.[8] This form of organization is especially effective for a firm whose customers' characteristics and needs vary greatly from one region to another.

A firm with marketing managers for each separate region has a complete marketing staff at its headquarters to provide assistance and guidance to regional marketing managers. Pizza Hut maintains a full marketing department in Wichita, Kansas, with regional offices having a regional marketing manager and regional marketing supervisors. However, not all firms organized by regions maintain a full marketing staff at their home offices. Firms that try to penetrate the national market intensively sometimes divide regions into subregions.

Organizing by Types of Customers   Sometimes the marketing unit is organized according to types of customers. This form of internal organization works well for a firm that has several groups of customers whose needs and problems differ significantly. For example, Bic Corp. may sell pens to large retail stores, wholesalers, and institutions. Retailers may want more rapid delivery of small shipments and more personal selling by the producer than do either wholesalers or institutional buyers. Because the marketing decisions and activities required for these two groups of customers differ considerably, the company may find it efficient to organize its marketing unit by types of customers.

In an organization with a marketing department broken down by customer group, the marketing manager for each group reports to the top-level marketing executive and directs most marketing activities for that group. A marketing manager directs all activities needed to market products to a specific customer group.

Implementing Marketing Activities

The planning and organizing functions provide purpose, direction, and structure for marketing activities. However, until marketing managers implement the marketing plan, exchanges cannot occur. In fact, organizers of marketing activities can become overly concerned with planning strategy while neglecting implementation. Proper implementation of a marketing plan depends on internal marketing to employees, the motivation of personnel who perform marketing activities, effective communication within the marketing organization, the coordination of marketing activities, and a focus on quality. The Global Perspective discusses MTV's implementation of marketing efforts in global markets.

Internal Marketing

Marketing activities cannot be effectively implemented without the cooperation of employees. Employees are the essential ingredient in increasing productivity, providing customer service, and beating the competition. Thus, in addition to marketing activities targeted at external customers, firms use internal marketing to attract, motivate, and retain qualified internal customers (employees) by designing internal products (jobs) that satisfy employees' wants and needs.[9] **Internal marketing** refers to the managerial actions necessary to make all members of the marketing organization understand and accept their respective roles in implementing the marketing strategy. This means that everyone, from the president of the company down to the hourly workers on the shop floor, must understand the role they play in carrying out their jobs and implementing the marketing strategy. Everyone must do his or her part to ensure that customers are satisfied. All personnel within the firm, both marketers and those who perform other functions, must recognize the tenet of customer orientation and service that underlies the marketing concept. Customer orientation is fostered

MTV's Strategies in Global Markets

IN 53 MILLION AMERICAN HOMES, pop music fans, mostly ages 16 to 34, tune in to enjoy superstars like Paula Abdul, Michael Jackson, and Madonna. Working like a Top 40 radio station, MTV rotates through about 60 different music videos, selling and airing advertising to make its money. Viacom International, owner of MTV, reports that about 20 percent of its $1.4 billion in revenue comes from its video network. In the last few years, the number of American MTV viewers has leveled off, and MTV's U.S. market seems to be reaching saturation. Hoping to attract new audiences and still retain its established market, MTV is concentrating on international expansion. MTV's goal, says the network's CEO, is to be in every home in the world.

When MTV made its first foreign licensing deal in Japan, company executives were just beginning to think about overseas expansion. They gave their Japanese affiliate little supervision regarding style and content. However, after one MTV executive reviewed some of the Japanese videos, she decided that they didn't convey the trendy and sophisticated image MTV tries to impart. Renegotiating the deal, the network took tighter control over quality. Subsequent expansion into Europe, South America, and Australia means that today, about 200 million fans in about 38 countries can enjoy the latest pop videos from around the world.

Other cable enterprises, including Cable News Network, broadcast internationally. Unlike executives at MTV, CNN's owner, cable giant Ted Turner, elects to broadcast solely in English, primarily targeting Americans traveling in all parts of the world. MTV attempts to be sensitive to other countries' cultures by responding to their musical styles and tastes. Although every broadcast must fit into MTV guidelines, foreign networks employ native video jockeys who highlight locally popular stars. In Japan, MTV VJs speak almost entirely in Japanese and focus on Japanese and other international artists. English is the language of choice on 24-hour European MTV, but European and other international musicians are the stars of the videos. MTV depends on music instead of language to link its 25-country European market.

Recognized as the leading pop music expert in the United States, MTV is rapidly becoming the authority on youth culture worldwide. The network is increasingly successful at convincing record companies that it can launch artists on a worldwide scale. Adding to its list of international advertisers like Nike, Levi's, and Fruit of the Loom is going a long way toward keeping MTV one step ahead of its fast-growing competitor, Video Jukebox Network.

Sources: Andy Fry, "The Year of European Media Revolution," *Marketing*, Mar. 28, 1991, pp. 25–26; Peter Newcomb, "Music Video Wars," *Forbes*, Mar. 4, 1991, pp. 68, 70; and Sara Nelson, "What's the Big Idea," *Working Woman*, July 1990, pp. 96, 98, 108.

by training and education and by keeping the lines of communication open throughout the firm.

Like external marketing activities, internal marketing may involve market segmentation, product development, research, distribution, and even public relations and sales promotion.[10] For example, an organization may sponsor sales contests to encourage sales personnel to boost their selling efforts. Some companies, including Chaparral Steel of Midlothian, Texas, and United Technologies, encourage employees to work for their companies' customers for a period of time, often while continuing to receive their regular salaries. This helps the employees (and ultimately the company) to understand better the customer's needs and problems, allows them to learn valuable new skills, and heightens their enthusiasm for their regular jobs. The ultimate result is more satisfied employees and improved customer relations.

Motivating Marketing Personnel

An important element in implementing the marketing plan, and in internal marketing, is motivating marketing personnel to perform effectively. People work to satisfy physical, psychological, and social needs. To motivate marketing personnel, managers must discover their employees' needs and then develop motivational methods that help employees satisfy those needs. It is crucial that the plan to motivate employees be fair, ethical, and well understood by employees. Additionally, rewards to employees must be tied to organizational goals. In general, to improve employee motivation, companies need to find out what workers think, how they feel, and what they want. Some of this information can be attained from an employee attitude survey. A firm can motivate its workers by directly linking pay with performance, informing workers how their performance affects department and corporate results, following through with appropriate compensation, promoting or implementing a flexible benefits program, and adopting a participative management approach.[11]

Consider the following example. Suppose a salesperson can sell product A or B to a particular customer, but not both products. Product A sells for $200,000 and contributes $20,000 to the company's profit margin. Product B sells for $60,000 and has a contribution margin of $40,000. If the salesperson receives a commission of 3 percent of sales, he or she would obviously prefer to sell product A, even though the sale of product B contributes more to the company's profits. If the salesperson's commission was based on contribution margin instead of sales and the firm's goal was to maximize profits, both the firm and the salesperson would benefit more from the sale of product B.[12] By tying rewards to organizational goals, the company encourages behavior that meets organizational goals.

Besides tying rewards to organizational goals, managers must use different motivational tools to motivate individuals. Selecting effective motivational tools has become more difficult because this country's work force is becoming more culturally diverse, meaning that there are greater differences between workers due to race, ethnicity, and gender. These differences lead to a broader range of individual value systems, which in turn call for a more diverse set of motivational tools. For example, an employee might value autonomy or recognition more than a slight pay increase. Managers can reward employees with money, plus additional fringe benefits, prestige or recognition, or even nonfinancial rewards such as job autonomy, skill variety, task significance, and increased feedback.

Communicating Within the Marketing Unit

With good communication, marketing managers can motivate personnel and coordinate their efforts. Marketing managers must be able to communicate with the firm's high-level management to ensure that marketing activities are consistent with the company's overall goals. Communication with top-level executives keeps marketing managers aware of the company's overall plans and achievements. It also guides what the marketing unit is to do and how its activities are to be integrated with those of other departments—such as finance, production, or personnel—with whose management the marketing manager must also communicate to coordinate marketing efforts. For example, marketing personnel must work with the production staff to help design products that customers want. To direct marketing activities, marketing managers must communicate with marketing personnel at the operations level, such as sales and advertising personnel, researchers, wholesalers, retailers, and package designers.

To facilitate communication, marketing managers should establish an information system within the marketing unit. The marketing information system (discussed in Chapter 7) should allow for easy communication among marketing managers, sales managers, and sales personnel. Marketers need an information system to support a variety of activities, such as planning, budgeting, sales analyses, performance evaluations, and the preparation of reports. An information system should also expedite communications with other departments in the organization and minimize destructive competition among departments for organizational resources.

Coordinating Marketing Activities

Because of job specialization and differences related to marketing activities, marketing managers must synchronize individuals' actions to achieve marketing objectives. In addition, they must work closely with managers in research and development, production, finance, accounting, and personnel to see that marketing activities mesh with other functions of the firm. Marketing managers must coordinate the activities of marketing staff within the firm and integrate those activities with the marketing efforts of external organizations—advertising agencies, resellers (wholesalers and retailers), researchers, and shippers, among others. In Figure 21.4, Ford promotes its quality commitment in a magazine advertisement. Coordinated efforts make this message evident to customers in television commercials and other media. Marketing managers can improve coordination by using internal marketing activities to make each employee aware of how his or her job relates to others and how his or her actions contribute to the achievement of marketing plans.

Total Quality Management

A primary concern today in some organizations is total quality management. Major reasons for this concern about quality are foreign competition, more demanding customers, and poorer profit performance due to reduced market shares and higher costs. Over the last few years several U.S. firms have lost the dominant, competitive positions that they held for decades.

Total quality management is the coordination of efforts directed at improving customer satisfaction, increasing employee participation and empowerment, forming and strengthening supplier partnerships, and facilitating an organizational culture of continuous quality improvement. Improving customer satisfaction can occur through higher-quality products and through better customer service, such as reduced delivery times, faster responses to customer inquiries, and simply treating customers better by showing them that the company really cares. Increasing employee involvement can mean allowing them to participate in decisions to a greater extent, developing self-managed work teams, and placing responsibility and accountability on employees for improving the quality of their work. Front-line customer-contact personnel should be empowered by management to deviate from company policies and procedures to meet customers' needs. Improved supplier partnerships translate into obtaining the right supplies and materials on time at lower costs. Quality improvement should not be viewed as achievable through one single program that has a target objective. Instead, a culture based on continuous improvement has proved to be the most effective approach in the long run.

Total quality management can provide several benefits. Overall financial benefits include lower operating costs, higher return on sales and investment, and an improved ability to use premium pricing rather than competitive pricing. Additional benefits include faster development of innovations, improved access to global markets, higher levels of customer retention, and an enhanced reputation.[13]

Although many factors influence the effectiveness of a total quality management program, two issues are crucial. First, top management must make a strong commitment to a total quality management program by treating quality improvement as a top priority and one that needs frequent attention. Establishing a total quality management program and then focusing on other priorities by top management generally leads to failure of quality improvement initiatives. Second, management must coordinate the specific elements of a total management program so that they work in harmony with each other. At times, an overemphasis on one aspect of a total quality management program can be detrimental to the efficacy of other parts of the program.

Figure 21.4

Coordinating Marketing

Ford's commitment to quality requires coordination of its marketing efforts.

Source: Courtesy of Ford Motor Company.

Figure 21.5

The Marketing Control Process

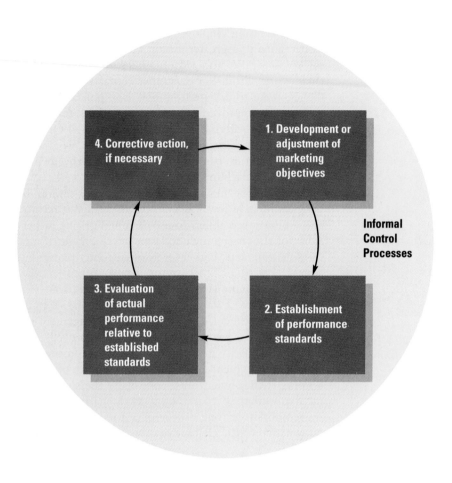

1. Development or adjustment of marketing objectives

2. Establishment of performance standards

3. Evaluation of actual performance relative to established standards

4. Corrective action, if necessary

Informal Control Processes

Controlling Marketing Activities

To achieve marketing objectives as well as general organizational objectives, marketing managers must effectively control marketing efforts. The **marketing control process** consists of establishing performance standards, evaluating actual performance by comparing it with established standards, and reducing the differences between desired and actual performance.

Although the control function is a fundamental management activity, it has received little attention in marketing. There are both formal and informal control systems in organizations. The formal marketing control process, as mentioned before, involves performance standards, evaluation of actual performance, and corrective action to remedy shortfalls (see Figure 21.5). The informal control process, however, involves self-control, social or group control, and cultural control through acceptance of a firm's value system. Which type of control system dominates depends on the environmental context of the firm.[14] We discuss these steps in the control process and consider the major problems they involve.

Establishing Performance Standards

Planning and controlling are closely linked because plans include statements about what is to be accomplished. For purposes of control, these statements function as performance standards. A **performance standard** is an expected level of performance against which actual performance can be compared. Examples of performance standards might be the reduction of customers' complaints by 20 percent, a monthly sales quota of $150,000, or a 10 percent increase per month in new customer accounts. Performance standards are also given in the form of budget accounts; that is, marketers are expected to achieve a certain objective without spending more than a given amount of resources. As stated earlier, performance standards should be tied to organizational goals. Performance standards can relate to product quality.

Evaluating Actual Performance

To compare actual performance with performance standards, marketing managers must know what marketers within the company are doing and have information about the activities of external organizations that provide the firm with marketing assistance. (We discuss specific methods for assessing actual performance later in this chapter.) Information is required about the activities of marketing personnel at the operations level and at various marketing management levels. Most businesses obtain marketing assistance from one or more external individuals or organizations, such as advertising agencies, intermediaries, marketing research firms, and consultants. To maximize benefits from external sources, a firm's marketing control process must monitor their activities. Although it may be difficult to obtain the necessary information, it is impossible to measure actual performance without it.

Records of actual performance are compared with performance standards to determine whether and how much of a discrepancy exists. For example, a salesperson's actual sales are compared with her or his sales quota. If there is a significant negative discrepancy, the marketing manager takes corrective action.

Taking Corrective Action

Marketing managers have several options for reducing a discrepancy between established performance standards and actual performance. They can take steps to improve actual performance, can reduce or totally change the performance standard, or do both. Changes in actual performance may require the marketing manager to use better methods of motivating marketing personnel or find more effective techniques for coordinating marketing efforts.

Sometimes performance standards are unrealistic when they are written. In other cases, changes in the marketing environment make them unrealistic. For example, a company's annual sales goal may become unrealistic if several aggressive competitors enter the firm's market. In fact, changes in the marketing environment may force managers to change their marketing strategy completely.

Requirements for an Effective Control Process

A marketing manager should consider several requirements in creating and maintaining effective control processes.[15] Effective control hinges on the quantity and quality of information available to the marketing manager and the speed at which it is received. The control process should be designed so that the flow of information is rapid enough to allow the marketing manager to quickly detect differences between actual and planned levels of performance. A single control procedure is not suitable for all types of marketing activities, and internal and environmental changes affect an organization's activities. Therefore, control procedures should be flexible enough to adjust to both varied activities and changes in the organization's situation. For the control process to be usable, its costs must be low relative to the costs that would arise if controls were lacking. Finally, the control process should be designed so that both managers and subordinates can understand it.

Problems in Controlling Marketing Activities

When marketing managers attempt to control marketing activities, they frequently run into several problems. Often the information required to control marketing activities is unavailable or is only available at a high cost. Even though marketing controls should be flexible enough to allow for environmental changes, the frequency, intensity, and unpredictability of such changes may hamper effective control. In addition, the time lag between marketing activities and their effects limits a marketing manager's ability to measure the effectiveness of marketing activities.

Because marketing and other business activities overlap, marketing managers cannot determine the precise cost of marketing activities. Without an accurate measure of marketing costs, it is difficult to know if the effects of marketing activities are worth their expense. Finally, marketing control may be difficult because it is very hard to develop exact performance standards for marketing personnel.

Methods of Evaluating Performance

There are specific methods for assessing and improving the effectiveness of a marketing strategy. A marketer should state in the marketing plan what a marketing strategy is supposed to accomplish. These statements should set forth performance standards, which usually are stated in terms of profits, sales, or costs. Actual performance must be measured in similar terms so that comparisons are possible. This section describes sales analysis and cost analysis, two general ways of evaluating the actual performance of marketing strategies. Wal-Mart, for example, has a reputation for conducting detailed sales and cost analysis, which contributes to its success. This strategy is discussed in Inside Marketing.

Wal-Mart's Strategy for Success

DISCOUNTERS LIKE Wal-Mart, K mart, and Target are seemingly immune to the current retailing debacle, boosting sales while other stores fail all around them. However, even the most profitable discount chains are noticing competition from specialized mass merchandisers like Toys "R" Us and Home Depot. Of the "Big Three" discounters, analysts agree that Wal-Mart is least likely to suffer. In 1990, the company toppled Sears from its long-held position as the nation's largest retailer; sales at Wal-Mart rose 26 percent to $32.6 billion, and on one particular day, 36 new outlets opened simultaneously.

The late Sam Walton, founder of Wal-Mart, initiated this spectacular growth by pursuing a strategy that has led some retailers to consider the company the "Scourge of Main Street." His earliest plan included building stores in isolated rural areas and small towns, offering the underserved residents low prices on everything from cosmetics and clothing to electronic equipment and lawn furniture, all the while absorbing sales from small businesses that were unable to compete on price or variety. Wal-Mart continues to sell its huge product assortments, in both small towns and big cities, for the lowest possible prices, which attracts more shoppers, which increases sales, which allows the company to lower prices even further. In a retail environment of inadequate customer service, Wal-Mart is an exception, stationing employees to greet entering shoppers and operating sufficient registers to prevent long check-out lines. Over the years, Wal-Mart has developed a loyal core of customers and a reputation for fast, friendly service at consistently low prices.

Offering products that consumers want is paramount at Wal-Mart. State-of-the-art satellite communications and "computer-to-computer" ordering ensure that customers are almost never disappointed when they look for an item on the shelves. Company executives employ the personalized Wal-Mart version of a marketing survey; they put in about two days every week visiting stores and talking to shoppers. In response to consumer input, Wal-Mart initiated its "Buy American" program, stocking and promoting U.S.–made products instead of imports whenever possible. For customers with environmental considerations, Wal-Mart recently began positioning signs throughout the store to identify "environmentally friendly" products and packages.

Of the top ten discounters operating in 1962, when Wal-Mart, K mart, and Target opened for business, not a single one remains today. Wal-Mart, however, barrels along like a locomotive, and stores in its path better watch out. Because of the phenomenal success of its 1,600 outlets throughout the South and Midwest, the firm is taking on big cities in the far West and the Northeast, opening 165 discount stores in California and others in New Jersey, New York, and Pennsylvania. By 1995, outlets will compete in 75 percent of K mart's territory, compared to only 35 percent today, and experts predict that Wal-Mart's sales will reach $125 billion by the turn of the century. Wal-Mart appears unstoppable with this strategy: Give customers products they want, prices they can afford, and the service they deserve.

Sources: Bill Saporito, "Is Wal-Mart Unstoppable?" *Fortune*, May 6, 1991, pp. 50–52, 54, 58–59; Janice Castro, "Mr. Sam Stuns Goliath," *Time*, Feb. 25, 1991, pp. 62–63; Jason Zweig, "Expand It Again, Sam," *Forbes*, July 9, 1990, p. 106; "Retailing in America: Pile 'Em High and Go Bust," *The Economist*, July 7, 1990, p. 70; and Christy Fisher and Patricia Strnad, "Wal-Mart Pulls Back on Hypermart Plans," *Advertising Age*, Feb. 19, 1990, p. 49.

Sales Analysis

Sales analysis uses sales figures to evaluate a firm's current performance. It is probably the most common method of evaluation because sales data partially reflect the target market's reactions to a marketing mix and often are readily available, at least in aggregate form.

Marketers use current sales data to monitor the impact of current marketing efforts. For example, Godiva attempts to measure the sales of its chocolates during selected holiday seasons. However, that information alone is not enough. To provide useful analyses, current sales data must be compared with forecasted sales, industry sales, specific competitors' sales, or the costs incurred to achieve the sales volume. For example, knowing that a variety store attained a $600,000 sales volume this year does not tell management whether its marketing strategy has been successful. However, if managers know that expected sales were $550,000, then they are in a better position to determine the effectiveness of the firm's marketing efforts. In addition, if they know that the marketing costs needed to achieve the $600,000 volume were 12 percent less than budgeted, they are in an even better position to analyze their marketing strategy precisely.

Types of Sales Measurements Although sales may be measured in several ways, the basic unit of measurement is the sales transaction. A sales transaction results in a customer order for a specified quantity of an organization's product sold under specified terms by a particular salesperson or sales group on a certain date. Many organizations record these bits of information about their transactions. With such a record, a company can analyze sales in terms of dollar volume or market share.

Firms frequently use dollar volume sales analysis because the dollar is a common denominator of sales, costs, and profits. However, price increases and decreases affect total sales figures. For example, if a company increased its prices by 10 percent this year and its sales volume is 10 percent greater than last year, it has not experienced any increase in unit sales. A marketing manager who uses dollar volume analysis should factor out the effects of price changes.

A firm's market share is the firm's sales of a product stated as a percentage of industry sales of that product. For example, Coca-Cola at one time sold 40 percent of all the cola sold annually in the United States and thus had a market share of 40 percent. Market-share analysis lets a company compare its marketing strategy with competitors' strategies. The primary reason for using market-share analysis is to estimate whether sales changes have resulted from the firm's marketing strategy or from uncontrollable environmental forces. When a company's sales volume declines but its share of the market stays the same, the marketer can assume that industry sales declined (because of some uncontrollable factors) and that this decline was reflected in the firm's sales. However, if a company experiences a decline in both sales and market share, it should consider the possibility that its marketing strategy is not effective.

Even though market-share analysis can be helpful in evaluating the performance of a marketing strategy, the user must interpret results cautiously. When attributing a sales decline to uncontrollable factors, a marketer must keep in mind that such factors do not affect all firms in the industry equally. Not all firms in an industry have the same objectives, and some change objectives from one year to the next. Changes in the objectives of one company can affect the market shares of one or all companies in that industry. For example, if a competitor significantly increases promotional efforts or drastically reduces prices to increase market share, then a company could lose market share despite a well-designed marketing strategy. Within an industry, the entrance of new firms or the demise of established ones also affects a specific firm's market share, and market-share analysts should attempt to account for these effects. KFC, for example, probably reevaluated its marketing strategies when McDonald's introduced its own fried chicken product.

Bases for Sales Analysis Whether it is based on sales volume or market share, sales analysis can be performed on aggregate sales figures or on disaggregated data. Aggregate sales analysis provides an overview of current sales. Although helpful, aggregate sales analysis is often insufficient because it does not bring to light sales variations within the aggregate. It is not uncommon for a marketer to find that a large proportion of aggregate sales comes from a small number of products, geographic areas, or customers. (This is sometimes called the "iceberg principle" because only a small part of an iceberg is visible above the water.) To find such disparities, total sales figures usually are broken down by geographic unit, salesperson, product, customer type, or a combination of these categories.

In sales analysis by geographic unit, sales data can be classified by city, county, district, state, country, or any other geographic designation for which a marketer collects sales information. Actual sales in a geographic unit can be compared with sales in a similar geographic unit, with last year's sales, or with an estimated market potential for the area. For example, if a firm finds that 18 percent of its sales are coming from an area that represents only 8 percent of the potential sales for the product, then it can be assumed that the marketing strategy is successful in that geographic unit.

Because of the cost associated with hiring and maintaining a sales force, businesses commonly analyze sales by salesperson to determine the contribution each salesperson makes. Performance standards for each salesperson are often set in terms of sales quotas for a given time period. Evaluation of actual performance is accomplished by comparing a salesperson's current sales to a preestablished quota or some other standard, such as the previous period's sales. If actual sales meet or exceed the standard and the sales representative has not incurred costs above those budgeted, that person's efforts are acceptable.

Sales analysis is often performed according to product group or specific product item. Marketers break down their aggregate sales figures by product to determine the proportion that each contributed to total sales. Columbia Pictures, for example, might break down its total sales figures by box-office figures for each film produced. A firm usually sets a sales volume objective—and sometimes a market share objective—for each product item or product group, and sales analysis by product is the only way to measure such objectives. A marketer can compare the breakdown of current sales by product with those of previous years. In addition, within industries for which sales data by product are available, a firm's sales by product type can be compared with industry averages. To gain an accurate picture of where sales of specific products are occurring, marketers sometimes combine sales analysis by product with sales analysis by geographic area or salesperson.

Analyses based on customers are usually broken down by types of customers. Customers can be classified by the way they use a firm's products, their distribution level (producer, wholesaler, retailer), their size, the size of orders, or other characteristics. Sales analysis by customer type lets a firm ascertain whether its marketing resources are allocated in a way that achieves the greatest productivity. For example, sales analysis by type of customer may reveal that 60 percent of the sales force is serving a group that makes only 15 percent of total sales.

A considerable amount of information is needed for sales analyses, especially if disaggregated analyses are desired. The marketer must develop an operational system for collecting sales information; obviously, the effectiveness of the system for collecting sales information largely determines a company's ability to develop useful sales analyses.

Marketing Cost Analysis

Although sales analysis is critical for evaluating the effectiveness of a marketing strategy, it gives only part of the picture. A marketing strategy that successfully generates sales may also be extremely costly. To get a complete picture, a firm must know the marketing costs associated with using a given strategy to achieve a certain sales level. **Marketing cost analysis** breaks down and classifies costs to determine which are associated with specific marketing activities. By comparing costs of previous marketing activities with results generated, a marketer can better allocate the firm's marketing resources in the future. Marketing cost analysis lets a company evaluate the effectiveness of an ongoing or recent marketing strategy by comparing sales achieved and costs incurred. By pinpointing exactly where a company is experiencing high costs, this form of analysis can help isolate profitable or unprofitable customer segments, products, or geographic areas.

In some organizations, personnel in other functional areas—such as production or accounting—see marketers as primarily concerned with generating sales, regardless of the costs incurred. By conducting cost analyses, marketers can undercut this criticism and put themselves in a better position to demonstrate how marketing activities contribute to generating profits. Even though hiring a spokesperson such as Nolan Ryan (see Figure 21.6) is costly, sales goals cannot be reached without large expenditures for promotion in the athletic shoe industry. Cost analysis should show whether promotion costs are effective in increasing sales.

Determining Marketing Costs The task of determining marketing costs is often complex and difficult. Simply ascertaining the costs associated with marketing a product is rarely adequate. Marketers must usually determine the marketing costs of serving specific geographic areas, market segments, or even specific customers.

A first step in determining the costs is to examine accounting records. Most accounting systems classify costs into **natural accounts**—such as rent, salaries, office supplies, and utilities—which are based on how the money was actually spent. Unfortunately, many natural accounts do not help explain what marketing functions were performed through the expenditure of those funds. It does little good, for example, to know that $80,000 is spent for rent each year. The

Figure 21.6

Marketing Costs Generate Sales

Hiring celebrities to promote products can be costly, but effective, especially in the competitive athletic shoe industry.

Source: Courtesy Nike, Inc.

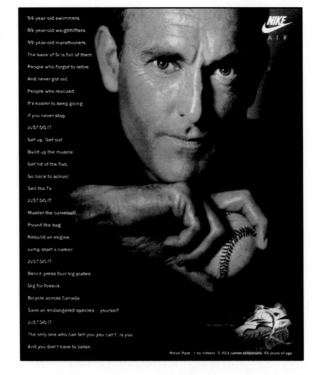

analyst has no way of knowing whether the money is spent for the rental of production, storage, or sales facilities. Therefore, marketing cost analysis usually requires that some of the costs in natural accounts be reclassified into **marketing function accounts**, which indicate the function performed through the expenditure of funds. Common marketing function accounts are transportation, storage, order processing, selling, advertising, sales promotion, marketing research, and customer credit.

Natural accounts can be reclassified into marketing function accounts as shown in the simplified example in Table 21.1. Note that a few natural accounts, such as advertising, can be reclassified easily into functional accounts because they do not have to be split across several accounts. For most of the natural accounts, however, marketers must develop criteria for assigning them to the various functional accounts. For example, the number of square feet of floor space used was the criterion for dividing the rental costs in Table 21.1 into functional accounts. In some instances, a specific marketing cost is incurred to perform several functions. A packaging cost, for example, could be considered a production function, a distribution function, a promotional function, or all three. The marketing cost analyst must reclassify such costs across multiple functions.

Three broad categories are used in marketing cost analysis: direct costs, traceable common costs, and nontraceable common costs. **Direct costs** are directly attributable to the performance of marketing functions. For example, sales force salaries might be allocated to the cost of selling a specific product item, selling in a specific geographic area, or selling to a particular customer. **Traceable common costs** can be allocated indirectly, using one or several

Table 21.1 Reclassification of Natural Accounts into Functional Accounts

Profit and Loss Statement		Functional Accounts					
		Advertising	Personal Selling	Transportation	Storage	Marketing Research	Non-Marketing
Sales	$250,000						
Cost of goods sold	45,000						
Gross profit	205,000						
Expenses (natural accounts)							
Rent	$ 14,000		$ 7,000		$ 6,000		$ 1,000
Salaries	72,000	$12,000	32,000	$7,000		$1,000	20,000
Supplies	4,000	1,500	1,000			1,000	500
Advertising	16,000	16,000					
Freight	4,000			2,000			2,000
Taxes	2,000				200		1,800
Insurance	1,000				600		400
Interest	3,000						3,000
Bad debts	6,000						6,000
Total	$ 122,000	$29,500	$40,000	$9,000	$ 6,800	$2,000	$34,700
Net profit	$ 83,000						

criteria, to the functions that they support. For example, if the firm spends $80,000 annually to rent space for production, storage, and selling, the rental costs of storage could be determined on the basis of cost per square foot used for storage. **Nontraceable common costs** cannot be assigned according to any logical criteria and thus are assignable only on an arbitrary basis. Interest, taxes, and the salaries of top management are nontraceable common costs.

The manner of dealing with these three categories of costs depends on whether the analyst uses a full-cost or a direct-cost approach. When a **full-cost approach** is used, cost analysis includes direct costs, traceable common costs, and nontraceable common costs. Proponents of this approach claim that if an accurate profit picture is desired, all costs must be included in the analysis. However, opponents point out that full costing does not yield actual costs because nontraceable common costs are determined by arbitrary criteria. With different criteria, the full-costing approach yields different results. A cost-conscious operating unit can be discouraged if numerous costs are assigned to it arbitrarily. To eliminate such problems, the **direct-cost approach**, which includes direct costs and traceable common costs but not nontraceable common costs, is used. Opponents say that this approach is not accurate because it omits one cost category.

Methods of Marketing Cost Analysis Marketers can use several methods to analyze costs. The methods vary in their precision. This section examines three cost analysis methods—analysis of natural accounts; analysis of functional accounts; and cost analysis by product, geographic area, or customer.

Marketers sometimes can determine marketing costs by performing an analysis of natural accounts. The precision of this method depends on how detailed the firm's accounts are. For example, if accounting records contain separate accounts for production wages, sales-force wages, and executive salaries, the analysis can be more precise than if all wages and salaries are lumped into a single account. An analysis of natural accounts is more meaningful, and thus more useful, when current cost data can be compared with those of previous periods or with average cost figures for the entire industry. Cost analysis of natural accounts frequently treats costs as percentages of sales. The periodic use of cost-to-sales ratios lets a marketer ascertain cost fluctuations quickly.

As indicated earlier, the analysis of natural accounts may not shed much light on the cost of marketing activities. In such cases, natural accounts must be reclassified into marketing function accounts for analysis. Whether certain natural accounts are reclassified into functional accounts and what criteria are used to reclassify them will depend to some degree on whether the analyst is using direct costing or full costing. After natural accounts have been reclassified into functional accounts, the cost of each function is determined by summing the costs in each functional account. Once the costs of these marketing functions have been determined, the analyst is ready to compare the resulting figures with budgeted costs, sales analysis data, cost data from earlier operating periods, or perhaps average industry cost figures, if these are available.

Although marketers ordinarily get a more detailed picture of marketing costs by analyzing functional accounts than by analyzing natural accounts, some firms need an even more precise cost analysis. The need is especially great if the firms sell several types of products, sell in multiple geographic areas, or sell to a wide variety of customers. Activities vary in marketing different products in

| Functional Accounts | | Product Groups | | |
		A	B	C
Advertising	$29,500	$14,000	$ 8,000	$ 7,500
Personal selling	40,000	18,000	10,000	12,000
Transportation	9,000	5,000	2,000	2,000
Storage	6,800	1,800	2,000	3,000
Marketing research	2,000		1,000	1,000
Total	$87,300	$38,800	$23,000	$25,500

Table 21.2 Functional Accounts Divided into Product-Group Costs

specific geographic locations to certain customer groups. Therefore the costs of these activities also vary. By analyzing the functional costs of specific product groups, geographic areas, or customer groups, a marketer can find out which of these marketing entities are the most cost effective to serve. In Table 21.2, the functional costs derived in Table 21.1 are allocated to specific product categories.

A similar type of analysis could be performed for geographic areas or for specific customer groups. The criteria used to allocate the functional accounts must be developed so as to yield results that are as accurate as possible. Use of faulty criteria is likely to yield inaccurate cost estimates that in turn lead to less effective control of marketing strategies. Marketers determine the marketing costs for various product categories, geographic areas, or customer groups and then compare them to sales. This analysis lets them evaluate the effectiveness of the firm's marketing strategy or strategies.

The Marketing Audit

A **marketing audit** is a systematic examination of the marketing group's objectives, strategies, organization, and performance. Its primary purpose is to identify weaknesses in ongoing marketing operations and plan the necessary improvements to correct these weaknesses.

Like an accounting or financial audit, a marketing audit should be conducted regularly instead of just when performance control mechanisms show that the system is out of control. The marketing audit is not a control process to be used only during a crisis, although a business in trouble may use it to isolate problems and generate solutions.

A marketing audit may be specific and focus on one or a few marketing activities, or it may be comprehensive and encompass all of a company's marketing activities. Table 21.3 lists many possible dimensions of a marketing audit.

Part I. The Marketing Environment Audit

Macroenvironment

A. Economic-demographic
1. What does the company expect in the way of inflation, material shortages, unemployment, and credit availability in the short run, intermediate run, and long run?
2. What effect will forecasted trends in the size, age distribution, and regional distribution of population have on the business?

B. Technological
1. What major changes are occurring in product technology? In process technology?
2. What are the major generic substitutes that might replace this product?

C. Political-legal
1. What laws are being proposed that may affect marketing strategy and tactics?
2. What federal, state, and local agency actions should be watched? What is happening with pollution control, equal employment opportunity, product safety, advertising, price control, etc., that is relevant to marketing planning?

D. Cultural
1. What attitude is the public taking toward business and the types of products produced by the company?
2. What changes in consumer lifestyles and values have a bearing on the company's target markets and marketing methods?

E. Ecological
1. Will the cost and availability of natural resources directly affect the company?
2. Are there public concerns about the company's role in pollution and conservation? If so, what is the company's reaction?

Task Environment

A. Markets
1. What is happening to market size, growth, geographical distribution, and profits?
2. What are the major market segments and their expected rates of growth? Which are high-opportunity and low-opportunity segments?

B. Customers
1. How do current customers and prospects rate the company and its competitors on reputation, product quality, service, sales force, and price?
2. How do different classes of customers make their buying decisions?
3. What evolving needs and satisfactions are the buyers in this market seeking?

C. Competitors
1. Who are the major competitors? What are the objectives and strategy of each major competitor? What are their strengths and weaknesses? What are the sizes and trends in market shares?
2. What trends can be foreseen in future competition and substitutes for this product?

D. Distribution and dealers
1. What are the main trade channels bringing products to customers?
2. What are the efficiency levels and growth potentials of the different trade channels?

E. Suppliers
1. What is the outlook for the availability of key resources used in production?
2. What trends are occurring among suppliers in their patterns of selling?

F. Facilitators and marketing firms
1. What is the outlook for the cost and availability of transportation services?
2. What is the outlook for the cost and availability of warehousing facilities?
3. What is the outlook for the cost and availability of financial resources?
4. How effectively is the advertising agency performing? What trends are occurring in advertising agency services?

G. Publics
1. Where are the opportunity areas or problems for the company?
2. How effectively is the company dealing with publics?

Part II. Marketing Strategy Audit

A. Business mission
1. Is the business mission clearly focused with marketing terms and is it attainable?

Table 21.3 **Dimensions of a Marketing Audit**

B. Marketing objectives and goals

1. Are the corporate objectives clearly stated? Do they lead logically to the marketing objectives?
2. Are the marketing objectives stated clearly enough to guide marketing planning and subsequent performance measurement?
3. Are the marketing objectives appropriate, given the company's competitive position, resources, and opportunities? Is the appropriate strategic objective to build, hold, harvest, or terminate this business?

C. Strategy

1. What is the core marketing strategy for achieving the objectives? Is it sound?
2. Are the resources budgeted to accomplish the marketing objectives inadequate, adequate, or excessive?
3. Are the marketing resources allocated optimally to prime market segments, territories, and products?
4. Are the marketing resources allocated optimally to the major elements of the marketing mix, i.e., product quality, service, sales force, advertising, promotion, and distribution?

Part III. Marketing Organization Audit

A. Formal structure

1. Is there a high-level marketing officer with adequate authority and responsibility over those company activities that affect customer satisfaction?
2. Are the marketing responsibilities optimally structured along functional, product, end user, and territorial lines?

B. Functional efficiency

1. Are there good communication and working relations between marketing and sales?
2. Is the product-management system working effectively? Are the product managers able to plan profits or only sales volume?
3. Are there any groups in marketing that need more training, motivation, supervision, or evaluation?

C. Interface efficiency

1. Are there any problems between marketing and manufacturing, R&D, purchasing, finance, accounting, and legal that need attention?

Part IV. Marketing Systems Audit

A. Marketing information system

1. Is the marketing intelligence system producing accurate, sufficient, and timely information about developments in the marketplace?
2. Is marketing research being adequately used by company decision makers?

B. Marketing planning system

1. Is the marketing planning system well conceived and effective?
2. Is sales forecasting and market-potential measurement soundly carried out?
3. Are sales quotas set on a proper basis?

C. Marketing control system

1. Are the control procedures (monthly, quarterly, etc.) adequate to ensure that the annual-plan objectives are being achieved?
2. Is provision made to analyze periodically the profitability of different products, markets, territories, and channels of distribution?
3. Is provision made to examine and validate periodically various marketing costs?

D. New-product development system

1. Is the company well organized to gather, generate, and screen new product ideas?
2. Does the company do adequate concept research and business analysis before investing heavily in a new idea?
3. Does the company carry out adequate product and market testing before launching a new product?

Part V. Marketing Productivity Audit

A. Profitability analysis

1. What is the profitability of the company's different products, served markets, territories, and channels of distribution?
2. Should the company enter, expand, contract, or withdraw from any business segments, and what would be the short- and long-run profit consequences?

B. Cost-effective analysis

1. Do any marketing activities seem to have excessive costs? Are these costs valid? Can cost-reducing steps be taken?

Table 21.3 Dimensions of a Marketing Audit (continued)

Part VI. Marketing Function Audits

A. Products

1. What are the product line objectives? Are these objectives sound? Is the current product line meeting these objectives?
2. Are there particular products that should be phased out?
3. Are there new products that are worth adding?
4. Are any products able to benefit from quality, feature, or style improvements?

B. Price

1. What are the pricing objectives, policies, strategies, and procedures? Are prices set on sound cost, demand, and competitive criteria?
2. Do the customers see the company's prices as being in or out of line with the perceived value of its products?
3. Does the company use price promotions effectively?

C. Distribution

1. What are the distribution objectives and strategies?
2. Is there adequate market coverage and service?
3. How effective are the following channel members: distributors, manufacturers' reps, brokers, agents, etc.?
4. Should the company consider changing its distribution channels?

D. Advertising, sales promotion, and publicity

1. What are the organization's advertising objectives? Are they sound?

2. Is the right amount being spent on advertising? How is the budget determined?
3. Are the ad themes and copy effective? What do customers and the public think about the advertising?
4. Are the advertising media well chosen?
5. Is the internal advertising staff adequate?
6. Is the sales promotion budget adequate? Is there effective and sufficient use of sales promotion tools, such as samples, coupons, displays, and sales contests?
7. Is the publicity budget adequate? Is the public relations staff competent and creative?

E. Sales force

1. What are the organization's sales-force objectives?
2. Is the sales force large enough to accomplish the company's objectives?
3. Is the sales force organized along the proper principle(s) of specialization (territory, market, product)? Are there enough (or too many) sales managers to guide the field sales reps?
4. Does the sales compensation level and structure provide adequate incentive and reward?
5. Does the sales force show high morale, ability, and effort?
6. Are the procedures adequate for setting quotas and evaluating performance?
7. How does the company's sales force compare to the sales forces of competitors?

Source: Philip Kotler, *Marketing Management: Analysis, Planning, and Control,* 7th ed. © 1991, pp. 726–728. Adapted by permission of Prentice-Hall, Inc., Englewood Cliffs, N.J.

Table 21.3 **Dimensions of a Marketing Audit (continued)**

An audit might deal with only a few of these areas, or it might include them all. Its scope depends on the costs involved, the target markets served, the structure of the marketing mix, and environmental conditions. The results of the audit can be used to reallocate marketing efforts and to reexamine marketing opportunities.

The marketing audit should aid evaluation by doing the following:

1. Describing current activities and results related to sales, costs, prices, profits, and other performance feedback
2. Gathering information about customers, competition, and environmental developments that may affect the marketing strategy

3. Exploring opportunities and alternatives for improving the marketing strategy
4. Providing an overall database to be used in evaluating the attainment of organizational goals and marketing objectives

Marketing audits can be performed internally or externally. An internal auditor may be a top-level marketing executive, a companywide auditing committee, or a manager from another office or of another function. Although it is more expensive, an audit by outside consultants is usually more effective because external auditors have more objectivity, more time for the audit, and greater experience.

There is no single set of procedures for all marketing audits. However, firms should adhere to several general guidelines. Audits are often based on a series of questionnaires that are administered to the firm's personnel. These questionnaires should be developed carefully to ensure that the audit focuses on the right issues. Auditors should develop and follow a step-by-step plan to guarantee that the audit is systematic. When interviewing company personnel, the auditors should strive to talk with a diverse group of people from many parts of the company.

The marketing audit lets an organization change tactics or alter day-to-day activities as problems arise. For example, marketing auditors often wonder whether a change in budgeted sales activity is caused by general market conditions or is due to a change in the firm's market share.

Although the concept of auditing implies an official examination of marketing activities, many organizations audit their marketing activities informally. Any attempt to verify operating results and to compare them with standards can be considered an auditing activity. Many smaller firms probably would not use the word *audit,* but they do perform auditing activities.

Several problems may arise in an audit of marketing activities. Marketing audits can be expensive in time and money. Selecting the auditors may be difficult because objective, qualified personnel may not be available. Marketing audits can also be extremely disruptive because employees sometimes fear comprehensive evaluations, especially by outsiders.

Summary

The organization of marketing activities involves the development of an internal structure for the marketing unit. The internal structure is the key to directing marketing activities. A centralized organization is one in which the top-level managers delegate very little authority to lower levels of the firm. In a decentralized organization, decision-making authority is delegated as far down the chain of command as possible. In a marketing-oriented organization, the focus is on finding out what buyers want and providing it in a way that lets the organization achieve its objectives. The marketing unit can be organized by (1) functions, (2) products, (3) regions, or (4) types of customers. An organization may use only one approach or a combination.

Implementation is an important part of the marketing management process. Proper implementation of a marketing plan depends on internal marketing to employees, the motivation of personnel who perform marketing activities, effective communication within the marketing organization, the coordination of marketing activities, and a focus on quality. Internal marketing refers to the managerial actions necessary to make all members of the marketing organization understand and accept their respective roles in implementing the marketing strategy. To attract, motivate, and retain qualified internal customers (employees), firms employ internal marketing by designing internal products (jobs) that satisfy employees' wants and needs. Marketing managers must also motivate marketing personnel. A company's communication system must allow the marketing manager to communicate with high-level management, with managers of other functional areas in the firm, and with personnel involved in marketing activities both inside and outside the organization. Marketing managers must coordinate the activities of marketing personnel and integrate these activities with those in other areas of the company and with the marketing efforts of personnel in external organizations. Total quality management is the coordination of efforts directed at improving customer satisfaction, increasing employee participation and empowerment, forming and strengthening supplier partnerships, and facilitating an organizational culture of continuous quality improvement.

The marketing control process consists of establishing performance standards, evaluating actual performance by comparing it with established standards, and reducing the difference between desired and actual performance. Performance standards, which are established in the planning process, are expected levels of performance with which actual performance can be compared. In evaluating actual performance, marketing managers must know what marketers within the firm are doing and must have information about the activities of external organizations that provide the firm with marketing assistance. Then actual performance is compared with performance standards. Marketers must determine whether a discrepancy exists and, if so, whether it requires corrective action, such as changing the performance standards or improving actual performance.

To maintain effective marketing control, an organization needs to develop a comprehensive control process that evaluates its marketing operations at a given time. The control of marketing activities is not a simple task. Problems encountered include environmental changes, time lags between marketing activities and their effects, and difficulty in determining the costs of marketing activities. In addition to these, it may be hard to develop performance standards.

Control of marketing strategy can be achieved through sales and cost analyses. For the purpose of analysis, sales are usually measured in terms of either dollar volume or market share. For a sales analysis to be effective, it must compare current sales performance with forecasted company sales, industry sales, specific competitors' sales, or the costs incurred to generate the current sales volume. A sales analysis can be performed on the firm's total sales, or the total sales can be disaggregated and analyzed by product, geographic area, or customer group.

Marketing cost analysis involves an examination of accounting records and, frequently, a reclassification of natural accounts into marketing function accounts. Such an analysis is often difficult because there may be no logical, clear-cut way to allocate natural accounts into functional accounts. The analyst may choose either direct costing or full costing. Cost analysis can focus on (1) an aggregate cost analysis of natural accounts or functional accounts or (2) an analysis of functional accounts for products, geographic areas, or customer groups.

To control marketing strategies, it is sometimes necessary to audit marketing activities. A marketing audit is a systematic examination of the marketing group's objectives, strategies, organization, and performance. A marketing audit attempts to identify what a marketing unit is doing, to evaluate the effectiveness of these activities, and to recommend future marketing activities.

Important Terms

Centralized organization
Decentralized organization
Marketing-oriented organization
Internal marketing
Total quality management
Marketing control process
Performance standard
Sales analysis
Marketing cost analysis
Natural accounts
Marketing function accounts
Direct costs
Traceable common costs
Nontraceable common costs

Full-cost approach
Direct-cost approach
Marketing audit

Discussion and Review Questions

1. What determines the place of marketing within an organization? Which type of organization is best suited to the marketing concept? Why?
2. What factors can be used to organize the internal aspects of a marketing unit? Discuss the benefits of each type of organization.
3. Why might an organization use multiple bases for organizing its marketing unit?
4. What is internal marketing? Why is it important in implementing marketing strategies?
5. Why is motivation of marketing personnel important in implementing marketing plans?
6. How does communication help in implementing marketing plans?
7. What are the major steps of the marketing control process?
8. List and discuss the five requirements for an effective control process.
9. Discuss the major problems in controlling marketing activities.
10. What is a sales analysis? What makes it an effective control tool?
11. Identify and describe three cost analysis methods. Compare and contrast direct costing and full costing.
12. How is the marketing audit used to control marketing program performance?

21.1   IBM Struggles to Maintain Leadership in the
       Computer Industry

International Business Machines, or "Big Blue," has been a leader in the computer industry since the 1960s. Several of its products, including the System/370 mainframe computers and the IBM PC line of personal computers, set the standards for many computer makers. Despite IBM's reputation for providing high-quality computers and strong service to its customers, there are those who have lost faith in the company. In a 1990 survey of more than 100 of IBM's major customers, common complaints included a lack of applications software, poor integration of IBM's different computer product lines, and systems that are difficult to use. Customer dissatisfaction has been translated into declining sales, profits, and market share.

Recognizing that IBM's performance is not up to par, Chairman John Akers is directing an ongoing reorganization to make the company more responsive to customers' needs and more competitive in a stagnating computer market. The reorganization effort is intended to boost sales, speed up new-product development, remove excessive corporate layers, and improve products and customer service. IBM has combined its personal computer and typewriter divisions because customers of those products have similar needs. It has also merged its mainframe division with the less profitable midsize-computer division. To help reduce bureaucracy that slows down new-product development and dissatisfies customers, the organization has been somewhat decentralized, giving decision-making responsibilities to six major product and marketing divisions. Initially, IBM asked 15,000 employees, mostly in management, to retire early and allowed another 25,000 positions to remain vacant. The latest employee reductions will leave the company's total work force well below its peak of 407,000—management alone will shrink 20 percent. By retraining and moving thousands of employees to new positions within the company, IBM has expanded the number of salespeople and support staff and is encouraging them to form long-term relationships with major customers. Although these efforts have improved the company's performance, IBM is still experiencing slow growth, in part because of increasing competition in its mainframe and personal computer markets.

Analysts believe that IBM's problems stem from having too many employees, high overhead, and too great a reliance on its cash cow, mainframe computers. Mainframe computer sales make up the largest percentage of the company's $65 billion annual sales. The multimillion-dollar mainframes link the company to its largest, most profitable customers and also heavily influence computer and software purchases. But as the IBM-dominated mainframe-computer market matures, growth is slow and competition is fierce. Amdahl Corp. and Hitachi Data Systems, marketers of IBM-compatible machines, and Fujitsu, Ltd. of Japan have been stealing market share with computers that are more powerful and less expensive than IBM's System/370 workhorse. In response to the increasing competition, not only from other mainframes, but from powerful minicomputers and personal computers that are able to tackle some jobs only mainframes could once handle, IBM introduced the powerful Enterprise System/9000. The ES/9000 is the company's first new mainframe since 1985. Intended to make IBM computes more useful to Fortune 500 companies, this new model uses fiber-optic data lines to carry information at twice the speed of its predecessor. Despite a price tag ranging from $70,480 to $22.8 million and the slow growth of mainframe revenues in the industry as a whole, IBM is hopeful that its new mainframe will put an end to flat sales and slow growth in this market segment.

IBM also faces problems in other segments of the computer market. For example, sales of the midrange AS/400 slipped about 40 percent in one year. As is the case with mainframes, slow sales of midrange computers can be attributed to increasingly powerful personal computers and workstations with the ability to handle more complex applications once requiring the power of a minicomputer or mainframe. IBM executives project a turnaround, however, expecting worldwide demand for midrange computers to grow about 19 percent in the next few years. In the workstation segment, IBM commands a mere 7 percent of a market that is growing 40 percent annually. That statistic may change with the company's introduction of a new generation of workstations, the RISC System/6000. This family of products, including POWERstation 730 with advanced graphic capability, will be competitively priced. Although the Japanese-dominated laptop-computer market is growing 40 percent annually, IBM still has no product to offer.

Everything is not all bad for IBM, however. It continues to lease System/370 and AS/400 equipment at rates that competitors find hard to match. (Leasing, however, accounts for only 4 percent of IBM's revenues). Analysts also praise the company's recent investments in software companies and use of faster chips in its PCs. In the personal computer market, IBM is recovering from a slow period with the help of new products such as the PS/2 systems that run on OS/2 software. Unit sales of this desktop system are up about 25 percent and demand continues to be strong.

To correct IBM's current poor performance—its expenses are up almost as much as its sales—the company is taking several steps. To increase sales, IBM discounted prices on many products by up to 40 percent. After the debut of its new mainframe, the company reduced the price of older 3090 models by 50 percent. Although many industry experts warn that IBM may confuse its customers by broadening its product line, this is just what the company did. Knowing that in the computer industry, equipment can become obsolete in a matter of a few years, IBM continues to develop products and technology critical to its survival. With the mainframe ES/9000 as its flagship, IBM is introducing the System/390, a 400-product package possessing a broad array of technology with the ability to network between IBM and non-IBM systems. IBM has also developed a super computer chip with four times the memory of today's most advanced chips. About the size of a thumbnail, it will store more than 2,000 pages of text on a sliver of silicon 200 times thinner than a sheet of paper. Hoping to capture an increased share in the industrial arena, IBM developed software packages for the plastics industry and designed them to run on workstation-class computers. IBM is cultivating a long-term approach by entering the education sector more aggressively, an arena it previously left to Apple and Radio Shack. Discounting means low profits from these sales, but company executives have come to realize that schools are a reliable and growing market, and that the children getting familiar with IBMs in the classroom today are the adults who will buy computers tomorrow.

Chairman John Akers vows that IBM will show "modest growth" in revenues over the next few years, but despite this forecast, analysts continue to predict gloom for Big Blue. They point out that IBM has repeatedly anticipated turnarounds that have yet to materialize. Hoopla surrounding its introduction of the new System/390 did not prevent IBM shares from falling 12.5 percent on the New York Stock Exchange. Critics continue to blame Akers for IBM's dismal performance in the last few years, particularly for manufacturing problems, product delays, and managerial decisions that have blemished IBM's reputation and its earnings. To reach Aker's goal of operating margins of 18 percent, IBM continues to cut costs even further and eliminate more jobs.

In addition to restructuring and drastic cost-cutting measures, IBM managers continue to monitor the marketing environment as well as the company's performance. Further changes in corporate and marketing strategies may be necessary to make IBM more profitable. Analysts agree that in the future, IBM's direction must be set by the needs of its customers as much as by the advance of information-processing technology. IBM executives are convinced the company can return to fast growth and maintain market leadership by proving to customers that it is market-driven. The down side is, they expect it will take ten years to see results.[16]

Questions for Discussion

1. In what ways can IBM benefit from the reorganizational steps that management has taken?
2. Why is the proper implementation of new-product introductions so important at IBM?
3. What types of control is IBM using to improve its performance?

21.2 Sears Searches for a Winning Marketing Strategy

For most of the 20th century, from main streets in small towns to shopping malls in big cities, Sears was the number-one retailer in the United States. Enjoying that position no longer, the company now trails as number three behind Wal-Mart and K mart. In one year, net income tumbled dramatically from $646.9 million to $257.4 million. Reducing pretax expenses still left Sears with higher operating costs than its major competitors. Despite an enormous increase in advertising during one recent holiday season, the organization suffered its worst Christmas sales in 15 years. Struggling to survive the 1990s (or join an expanding list of defunct retailers), Sears cut 33,000 jobs, froze 20,000 managers' salaries, and once again revamped its marketing strategy for all 863 stores.

For most of its history, Sears has chosen to compete on the basis of quality rather than price. Strategy included putting the Sears brand name on a variety of products, advertising that brand, and charging a higher price in exchange for quality. Over the years, the company developed a large loyal consumer base that associated the Sears brand name with value. However, when competitors like K mart and Wal-Mart came along offering well-known brands at discount prices, something previously unavailable to consumers, the competitive arena changed from quality to price, leaving Sears unprepared to do battle. The company could not vie with efficient discounters offering most merchandise at cheaper prices nor with upscale boutiques and department stores offering trendier goods in brighter surroundings. In addition, the company's traditional backbone, its reputation for reliability and excellent customer service, deteriorated.

Recognizing that radical changes would be required if Sears were to remain a viable retailer, the organization sought a new marketing strategy. Experts outside of Sears bombarded company executives with suggestions: Sell the catalog, get out of the general-merchandise business, split the departments into separate stores, give the women's clothing department an entirely new name. In the end, Sears tried and failed with what looks to outsiders like a random series of different strategies rather than a cohesive plan.

To lure brand-name bargain hunters, Sears initiated its "everyday low prices" strategy. Consumers were led to believe that the store offered the lowest prices every day without special sales. In reality, customers couldn't always find the promised bargains because many of Sears's prices were higher than those of its competitors. Of one thousand Sears shoppers responding to a consumer opinion poll, 37 percent believed Sears's prices were higher than other retailers and 63 percent rated the prices as about the same. To make matters worse, federal regulators investigated Sears for deceptive advertising, alleging that the company did not actually lower prices on most items as its advertisements claimed. Results of this investigation are not yet available. Other failing strategies included marketing McKids clothing and toys in free-standing specialty stores (these all closed), promoting Sears as the "Store of the Future" and the "Financial Supermarket" (these strategies were discarded), and upgrading women's fashions (Sears failed to overcome its poor image in this area).

CEO Edward Brennan is the architect of Sears's most recent marketing strategy, which includes a variety of physical and promotional changes. One facet of the new plan includes moving away from the "everything-for-everybody" approach, trimming the product mix, and positioning Sears as a powerful specialty merchant by installing more "Sears Brand Central" departments that offer non-Sears brand merchandise. "Power formats," separated boutiquelike sections that resemble trendy specialty shops, will flaunt track lighting, jazzy music, and videos of dancing models. The company is also experimenting with offering some merchandise, such as paint, hardware, and furniture, in free-standing formats. If the success of the Home Life furniture store in Madison, Wisconsin, which doubled Sears's Madison furniture market share in eight months, persists, consumers will probably see plenty of other individual Sears stores popping up.

Moving away from the "everyday low prices" strategy, Sears is bombarding consumers with advertising, sales, and special promotions. Included among these are a Presidents' Day Sale, a Carnival of Bargains sale, and the Sears Charge Bonus Club, which rewards shoppers who charge merchandise on their Sears credit card. Much of the new advertising focuses on product reliability and consumer trust, two traditional Sears strengths that were sacrificed to emphasize price. To shore up consumers' faith in Sears, "everyday low prices" will become "everyday fair prices." Point-of-sale signs stress trust and reliability, as will television and print advertisements. Shoppers can now go to conveniently placed kiosks to telephone Sears representatives for details concerning everything from availability of appliance replacement parts to delivery time for out-of-stock items.

Despite strong recognition, considerable customer loyalty, and the fact that 40 percent of U.S. households own Sears credit cards, company management cannot seem to overcome confusion over what the Sears name stands for. Because the Sears image hinges on Die Hard batteries and power drills, how can the company effectively market high-fashion women's cocktail dresses? What kind of store does Sears want to be? Insisting that Sears management has lost touch with its customers and its mission, critics insist that no plan for revitalizing the company is possible unless the management can communicate a clear vision. If the organization cannot do so and market that vision successfully to consumers, Sears will never again be the king of U.S. retailing.[17]

Questions for Discussion

1. Why did Sears's "everyday low prices" strategy fail?
2. On what dimensions or bases is Sears most likely to be able to compete successfully in today's highly competitive retail environment?
3. Evaluate Edward Brennan's most recent strategy.

Chapter Notes

1. Based on information from PepsiCo, Inc., 1991 Annual Report; Patricia Sellers, "Pepsi Keeps On Going After No. 1," *Fortune*, Mar. 11, 1991, pp. 62–64, 70; Laura Bird, "Pepsi's New Order: Snack Food, Global Growth and Profit," *Adweek's Marketing Week*, Dec. 17, 1990, pp. 4–5; Amy Dunkin, "PepsiCo: Why a Top Consumer Marketer Moved Up in Rank," *Business Week*, Apr. 13, 1990, pp. 26–30; John Oldland, "Plotting Strategy over a Pepsi," *Marketing*, Apr. 9, 1990, p. 10; Frederick H. Lowe, "New 'Rapping' for Pepsi Can," *Chicago Sun Times*, Apr. 5, 1990; and PepsiCo, Inc., *Products and Service*.
2. Larry Reibstein, "IBM's Plan to Decentralize May Set a Trend—But Imitation Has a Price," *Wall Street Journal*, Feb. 19, 1988, p. 17.
3. Rohit Despande and Frederick E. Webster, Jr., "Organizational Culture and Marketing: Defining the Research Agenda," *Journal of Marketing*, January 1989, pp. 3–15.
4. Michael D. Hutt and Thomas W. Speth, "The Marketing Strategy Center: Diagnosing the Industrial Marketer's Interdisciplinary Role," *Journal of Marketing*, Fall 1984, pp. 16–53.
5. John C. Narver and Stanley F. Slater, "Creating a Market-Oriented Business," *The Channel of Communications*, Summer 1989, pp. 5–8.
6. Dave Ulrich, "Strategic Human Resources Planning: Why and How?" *Human Resources Planning*, 10, no. 1, 1987, pp. 25–57.
7. Steven Lysonski, "A Boundary Theory Investigation of the Product Manager's Role," *Journal of Marketing*, Winter 1985, pp. 26–40.
8. Jennifer Lawrence, "Frito Reorganizes," *Advertising Age*, June 26, 1989, p. 4.
9. James H. Donnelly, Jr., Leonard L. Berry, and Thomas O. Thompson, *Marketing Financial Services* (Homewood, Ill.: Dow Jones-Irwin, 1985), pp. 229–245.
10. Sybil F. Stershic, "Internal Marketing Campaign Reinforces Service Goals," *Marketing News*, July 31, 1989, p. 11.

11. David C. Jones, "Motivation the Catalyst in Profit Formula," *National Underwriter,* July 13, 1987, pp. 10, 13.

12. The example is adapted from Edward B. Deakin and Michael W. Maher, *Cost Accounting,* 3rd ed. (Homewood, Ill.: Irwin, 1991), pp. 838–839.

13. Fred Steingraber, "Total Quality Management: A New Look at a Basic Issue," *Vital Speeches of the Day,* May 1990, pp. 415–416.

14. Bernard J. Jaworski, "Toward a Theory of Marketing Control: Environmental Context, Control Types, and Consequences," *Journal of Marketing,* July 1988, pp. 23–39.

15. Theo Haimann, William G. Scott, and Patrick E. Connor, *Management,* 5th ed. (Boston: Houghton Mifflin, 1985), pp. 478–492.

16. Robert L. Scheier, "IBM Redraws its Big Blueprint," *PC Week,* Dec. 2, 1991, pp. 1, 6; Carol J. Loomis, "Can John Akers Save IBM?" *Fortune,* July 15, 1991, pp. 40–56; Jim McNair, "IBM Rolls Out Next Generation," *Miami Herald,* Sept. 6, 1990; "Computer Makers Find Schools a Reliable Market," *Kansas City (MO) Business Journal,* Aug. 13, 1990; Louise Kehoe, "The New Big Blue," *Electronics,* July 1990, pp. 27–28; Mark Schlack, "IBM Makes Push into Plastics Software," *Plastics World,* July 1990, pp. 18–19; Sharon Machlis, "'Big Blue' Makes Push for Engineering Market," *Design News,* Mar. 26, 1990, p. 186; Harris Collingwood, "IBM May Be Crowding Its Own Turf," *Business Week,* Feb. 19, 1990, p. 42; Frank Ruiz, "IBM Blazes Trail with New 16-Megabit Computer Chip," *Tampa FL) Tribune,* Feb 14, 1990; Bob Freund, "IBM-Rochester Wins Award," *Rochester (MI) Post-Bulletin,* Jan. 19, 1990; Jeff Moad and Susan Kerr, "How Customers Help the New IBM," *Datamation,* Jan. 1, 1990, pp. 20–24; Craig Mellow, "A Delayered Big Blue," *Business Month,* January 1990, p. 13; John W. Verity, "A Slimmer IBM May Still Be Overweight," *Business Week,* Dec. 18, 1989, pp. 107–108; Paul B. Carroll, "Big Blues: Hurt by a Pricing War, IBM Plans a Writeoff and Cut of 10,000 Jobs," *Wall Street Journal,* Dec. 6, 1989, pp. A1, A8; John Hillikirk, "As IBM Falters, Shareholders and Critics Take Aim at Akers," *USA Today,* Dec. 6, 1989, p. 10B; and John W. Verity, "What's Ailing IBM? More Than This Year's Earnings," *Business Week,* Oct. 16, 1989, pp. 75–86.

17. Patricia A. Langan, "Sears' Need: More Speed," *Fortune,* July 15, 1991, pp. 88–90; Ellen Neuborne, "CEO Pitching New Vision for Retailer," *USA Today,* Apr. 10, 1991, p. 9B; Janice Castro, "Mr. Sam Stuns Goliath," *Time,* Feb. 25, 1991, pp. 62–63; Jon Berry, "Can Brennan Save the Big Store?" *Adweek's Marketing Week,* Feb. 18, 1991, pp. 4–5; Eric N. Berg, "Sears Says It Will Cut 21,000 Jobs," *New York Times,* Jan. 4, 1991, p. D1; "Sears Announces Sales Promotion," *New York Times,* Sept. 14, 1990, p. D4; Annetta Miller and Patricia King, "Retailing Perestroika: Troubled Sears Looks for a New Mix—Again," *Newsweek,* Sept. 3, 1990, p. 52; Kevin Kelly and Laura Zinn, "Can Ed Brennan Salvage the Sears He Designed?" *Business Week,* Aug. 27, 1990, p. 34; Kate Fitzgerald, "Sears Slipping from No. 1," *Advertising Age,* Aug. 6, 1990, pp. 1, 36; Henry H. Beam, "Strategic Discontinuities: When Being Good May Not Be Enough," *Business Horizons,* July–August, 1990, pp. 10–14; Steve Weiner, "It's Not Over Until It's Over," *Forbes,* May 28, 1990, pp. 58, 60, 64; Kate Fitzgerald, "Sears' Cudmore Takes 'Trust' Tack," *Advertising Age,* Jan. 28, 1990, pp. 3, 60; Amy Dunkin, "Slugging It Out for Survival," *Business Week,* Jan. 8, 1990, pp. 32–33; and Kate Fitzgerald, "Sears' Plan on the Ropes," *Advertising Age,* Jan. 8, 1990, pp. 1, 42.

USA Today: The Nation's Newspaper*

USA Today, billed as "the nation's newspaper," debuted in 1982 as America's first national general-interest daily newspaper. The paper was the brainchild of Allen H. Neuharth, Chairman of Gannett Co., Inc., a diversified news and information company that publishes newspapers, operates broadcasting stations and outdoor advertising businesses, and is involved in research, marketing, commercial printing, a newswire service, and news programming. Gannett is currently the largest U.S. newspaper group, with 82 daily newspapers, including USA Today, USA Weekend, and a number of non-daily publications.

Pre-launch Strategy

On February 29, 1980, Allen Neuharth met with "Project NN" task force members for the first time to discuss his vision for producing and marketing a unique wide-focus daily newspaper that would ultimately be distributed nationwide. National newspaper circulation had previously been technologically infeasible, but by 1980 satellite technology solved the problem of limited geographical distribution. Neuharth was ready to take advantage of two seemingly disparate trends in the reading public—an increasingly short attention span among a generation nurtured on television rather than print, coupled with a growing hunger for more information. Neuharth believed that readers face a time crunch in a world where so much information is available, but there is so little time to absorb it. USA Today's primary mission would be to provide more news about more subjects in less time. Task force members were enthusiastic about the concept. Research suggested that USA Today target primarily achievement-oriented men in professional and managerial positions who are heavy newspaper readers and frequent travelers.

In 1981 and early 1982, a team of news, advertising, and production personnel from the staffs of Gannett's 83 daily newspapers developed, edited, published, and tested several different prototypes. Gannett sent three different 40-page prototype versions of USA Today to almost 5,000 professional people. Along with each prototype, they sent readers a response card that asked what

*This case was developed and written by Geoffrey P. Lantos and Cheryl Anne Molchan, Stonehill College.

they liked best and least about the proposed paper, whether or not they would buy it, as well as whether they would give it overall approval. The content of each prototype was basically the same. What differed were the layout and graphics presentations. For example, one prototype included a section called "Agenda" that included comics and a calendar of meetings to be held by various organizations that day. According to marketplace feedback, readers liked the prototypes. The Gannett Board of Directors unanimously approved the paper's launch, and so on April 20, 1982, Gannett announced that in a few months, the first copies of USA Today would be available in the Washington/Baltimore area.

Product Launch

On September 15, 1982, 155,000 copies of the newspaper's first edition hit the newsstands. On page one, founder Neuharth wrote a short summary of USA Today's mission statement. He wanted to make USA Today enlightening and enjoyable to the public, informative to national leaders, and attractive to advertisers. The first issue featured a cover story on Batman, abridged the assassination of the Lebanese president-elect to a news brief, and included an article on celebrities talking about their weight problems. The issue sold out.

A little over a month following its debut, USA Today's circulation hit 362,879, double the original year-end projections, and by the end of January 1983, just three and a half months after launch, circulation reached 531,438. As early as April 1983, the newspaper's circulation topped the one million mark.

Gannett did not plan a grand nationwide debut for USA Today. In order to carefully monitor results and modify the paper and its marketing as needed, the paper implemented a regional rollout distribution strategy. Produced at facilities in Arlington, VA, USA Today was then transmitted via satellite to printing plants across the country. The newspaper's marketers divided the country into fifteen geographical market segments, and by the end of the first quarter of 1983 USA Today was available within a 200-mile radius of these fifteen major markets, making it accessible to 42 percent of U.S. households. On Monday through Friday mornings, readers in such cities as Chicago,

Houston, New York, Los Angeles, and Denver could pick up a copy of *USA Today*. Significantly, these markets contained 23 million of the 35 million adults who read two or more newspapers daily. Gannett's focus group research indicated that many readers were bringing the paper into their homes, rather than reading it on their commute or at work. Consequently, Gannett launched a home delivery subscription service in 1984. Home delivery caused problems at first, because the in-house computer technology could not handle subscription mailing lists efficiently, and the postal service was not always delivering the paper on its publication day. Nevertheless, subscriptions grew, and by 1991 nearly half of distribution was via home and office delivery.

Newspaper as Better Mousetrap

Clearly, the paper filled a gap in the market, satisfying several unmet needs and wants. At 25 cents per copy, the paper was competitively priced. *USA Today*'s success came not from low prices, but from listening to its readers and giving them what they want. *USA Today* communicated with readers on a personal level very quickly (many of the short, fact-filled stories are under 250 words), clearly, and directly, in an upbeat, positive, exciting way. The color is riveting, and so are the space-defying number of stories, factoids, larger-than-usual pictures, bar graphs, and charts, all squeezed onto each page without seeming too crowded. Instead of confusion, readers get neatness and order. Very few stories are continued on another page. The paper's dependably consistent organization enables readers to go directly to any one of *USA Today*'s four sections. It takes an average of only 25 minutes for a reader to peruse the paper.

President Tom Curly recently told readers that *USA Today* strives to be a balanced newspaper, reporting positive stories along with negative ones and reflecting America's diversity. The editorial page always presents opposing views. *USA Today*'s own editorial position on most major social, economic, and political issues can be described as middle-of-the-road, a position its staff believes is in tune with the general public. The newspaper's intent is to allow readers to have the information and opinions they need to form their own views.

By the summer of 1984, the size of the newspaper had expanded to 48 pages and the price had gone up 10 cents to 35 cents. Circulation was also growing, reaching 1,276,334 daily for the period ending March 31, 1985. This figure includes "blue chip" circulation, sales in bulk at reduced rates to airlines and hotels, which in turn provide *USA Today* free as a service to their clientele. By August 1985, the newspaper's cover price was up to 50 cents.

Growing Pains

During the mid-1980s, the media dubbed *USA Today* "McPaper"—the fast food of the newspaper business. Critics denounced what they called its junk-food journalism. In spite of the criticism, circulation surpassed 1.4 million by Oct. 1985, and by November of that year the paper expanded to 56 pages in length. The newspaper had become the second largest in the country with a circulation topped only by the *Wall Street Journal*. Although *USA Today* competes more directly with news weeklies and business newspapers than with local papers, many papers have adopted some of *USA Today*'s style. Publishers began adding color and beefing up circulation campaigns to compete with "The Nation's Newspaper."

By 1986, *USA Today* had become global, transmitting international editions via satellite to over 50 countries including Britain, Switzerland, and Singapore. *USA Today* competed with the *European Wall Street Journal* and the *Financial Times*, targeting American tourists, business travelers, and U.S. military personnel looking for news from home. The strategy proved successful. In July 1986, Simmons Market Research Bureau reported that *USA Today* had almost five million readers per day, the most of any U.S. daily newspaper.

Product Improvements

To stay ahead of the competition, which was increasingly borrowing its format, *USA Today* had to innovate. Beginning in the mid-1980s, Gannet began incorporating less traditional value-added features to keep readers interested. The paper added 800 and 900 "hot-line" numbers that readers could call for expert information on financial planning, college admissions, minority business development, taxes, and other subjects. In 1989, over three million readers called those numbers. Almost one and a half million called for up-to-the-minute information on sports, weather, stocks, and even lottery numbers, and tens of thousands responded to reader-opinion polls and write-in surveys on political and current event issues. In 1990 alone, over 22,000 wrote, phoned, or faxed letters to the editor. In 1991 the editorial page was redesigned to provide more room for guest columnists to encourage debate. The change was popular; the volume of letters increased by over 500%. Gannett initiated a high-school "Academic All-Star" program that it later expanded to include colleges and universities. By rolling the presses over four hours earlier than the *Wall Street Journal* and almost three hours later than the *New York Times*, *USA Today* offered more up-to-date coverage.

Promotional Strategies

On the promotional front, *USA Today* also became an innovator. Prior to 1986, the paper limited its promotions mostly to outdoor advertising and television. In 1986 and 1987 Neuharth undertook a BusCapade promotion tour, traveling to all 50 states and talking with all kinds of people, including the governors of each state. Neuharth succeeded in raising public awareness of his paper, and in 1987, *USA Today* broke into the black for the first time, recording profits of $1,093,756 for the month of May. Encouraged, Neuharth forged ahead with a "JetCapade" promotion. For seven months, Neuharth and a small news team traveled to 30 countries, stimulating global demand for the paper. During a visit to the troops of Operation Desert Storm in the Persian Gulf, General Norman Schwarzkopf expressed a need for news from home. *USA Today* arranged for delivery of 18,000 copies per day. By 1991, the separately published *USA Today* international edition was available in more than 90 countries in Western Europe, the Middle East, North Africa, and Asia, selling 55,000 copies a day.

The paper continued to drum up demand among advertisers by adding marketing enhancements. Getting Madison Avenue advertisers presented a challenge to *USA Today*, because those agencies weren't convinced that it would pay to advertise in the paper. Gannett's first strategy for enlisting advertisers was called the Partnership Plan, providing six months of free space with six months of paid advertising. In 1987, *USA Today* began to accept regional advertising on a controlled basis, confining it to a small number of categories such as regional travel, retail, tourism, and economic development. By 1989, the paper opened up regional advertising to all categories. Color advertisements could arrive as late as 6:00 p.m. the day before publication, giving local advertisers increased flexibility. In 1991 Gannett added a VIP program that allows advertisers to earn bonus pages for renewing or increasing their schedules. *USA Today*'s advertising revenues continue to climb, ranking them among the top ten of all consumer publications.

Almost a decade after *USA Today*'s launch, Gannett finds itself in the enviable position of owning one of America's most successful new newspapers. It remains the most widely read newspaper in the country, with daily readership of over 6.5 million. In an era when nearly all major national media are suffering declines in readership or viewing audience, *USA Today* continues to grow. Rising distribution costs and promotions, however, are currently making the newspaper slightly unprofitable, including recent yearly losses of $18 million. To reverse this trend, *USA Today* is creating several spinoffs, including its first special interest publication, *USA Today Baseball Weekly*. During its first month of operation, circulation reached 250,000. Venturing into new media, *USA Today* recently joined with Cable News Network to produce a football TV program and in 1992 launched *USA Today SkyRadio* to provide live radio on commercial flights. Some analysts insist that whatever the paper tries, huge distribution costs will keep the paper's profits marginal for the foreseeable future. For now, however, *USA Today* remains well-positioned as the United States' hometown paper and the print media's answer to television.

Questions for Discussion

1. What opportunities in the marketing environment did Gannett seize in launching *USA Today*? How did they learn about these opportunities? How did they respond to the opportunities identified?
2. Who is *USA Today*'s competition? What are the implications for their marketing strategy?
3. What competitive growth strategies did Gannett use in introducing *USA Today* and in growing the paper over time? Were these strategies appropriate?
4. Which performance standards did Gannett measure in assessing *USA Today*'s success? According to these measures, is the paper a success?

Sources: Thomas Curley, "Looking Ahead to the Opportunity," *USA Today*, Jan. 2, 1992, p. 12A; Dean Foust, "Patching the Cracks in the House That Al Built," *Business Week*, Dec. 16, 1991, pp. 86–87; "*USA Today* Readership Up," *USA Today*, Jul. 18, 1991, p. 2B; *USA Today Fact Sheet*, June 1991; *USA Today Timeline*, May 1991, P. 1; Tom Curley, "First, Fast, and Fair," *USA Today*, Jan. 7, 1991, p. 5A; "The Nation's Newspaper: A Case Study," prepared by Randy Grow, Pam Oliver, John Rutland, Terry Schadeberg, Memphis State University, 1991; Gannett Co. Inc., 1990 Annual Report, pp. 30, 50; Tom Curley, "1 Million New Readers Added in 1989," *USA Today*, Jan. 8, 1990, p. 13A; Gannett Co. Inc., 1989 Annual Report, p. 62; "*USA Today*'s Tomorrow," *The Economist*, Nov. 25, 1989, p. 80; William Gloede, "Here to Stay," *Advertising Age*, Aug. 24, 1987, p. 1; Steven Colford, "Profits Bolsters *USA Today*," *Advertising Age*, Jun. 22, 1987, p. 91; "BusCapade USA," *Editor and Publisher*, Mar. 21, 1987, p. 20; Peter Prichard, *The Making of McPaper* (Kansas City: McMeel & Parker, 1987); Edwin Diamond, "*USA Today* Today," *New York Magazine*, Oct. 20, 1986, p. 16; Steve Govoni, "Expensive Freebies," *Financial World*, Jan. 22, 1986, p. 12; "*USA Today* Tries to Take on the World," *Business Week*, Aug. 13, 1984, p. 78; Richard Gordon, "*USA Today* Sets Its Big Push for Advertising in 1984," *Advertising Age*, Dec. 29, 1983, p. 12; Kevin Higgins, "*USA Today* Nears Million Reader Mark," *Marketing News*, Apr. 15, 1983, p. 1, 5; "Sports & Weather Top Reader Items in *USA Today*," *Editor and Publisher*, Feb. 26, 1983, p. 8; "*USA Today* Unnerves Rivals Coast to Coast," *Business Week*, Feb. 7, 1983, p. 71; "*USA Today* Steps Up Market Rollout Plans," *Advertising Age*, Oct. 18, 1982, p. 3; "What Tomorrow Holds for *USA Today*," *Madison Avenue*, Sept. 1982, p. 118; B. G. Yovovich, "Tomorrow Arrives for today," *Advertising Age*, Jul. 19, 1982, p. 8; and "Ad Industry Skeptical on National Daily," *Advertising Age*, Dec. 21, 1981, p. 1.

McDonald's Social Responsibility

The McDonald's Corporation is the largest food service organization in the world. McDonald's competes on the basis of price and value by offering quality food products with speed and convenience in reliable, clean restaurants. In the United States, about 2 percent of all restaurants are McDonald's, but they account for 7 percent of all restaurant sales. McDonald's is one of the most advertised brands in the world, and the company spends a billion dollars a year on marketing.

Customer satisfaction is the cornerstone of McDonald's marketing strategy. The company wants to make every customer contact an enjoyable experience by serving quality food at affordable prices and providing fast, accurate, friendly service. Most people reading this case have had the McDonald's experience many times.

The philosophy of Ray Kroc, McDonald's founder, was that McDonald's and its franchisees should put something back into the communities in which they do business. In addition, McDonald's believes that being a good corporate citizen means treating people with fairness and integrity and sharing success in the communities where they operate. This philosophy is implemented in many different ways throughout the McDonald's corporation.

Education

Quality education for America's youth is a national priority, and McDonald's is committed to making a contribution. Many young people who work in McDonald's stores are taught the importance of responsibility, self-discipline, and good work habits. McDonald's works with parents, educators, and students, and believes in supporting education through various programs that encourage and recognize scholastic achievement. The "Black History Makers of Tomorrow" essay contest honors high school juniors who demonstrate exceptional leadership, character, and scholarship, along with the potential to become future history makers. McDonald's also offers college scholarships through the "Hispanic/American Commitment to Education Resources." In addition, McDonald's provides programs to encourage students to stay in school.

Equal Opportunity and Affirmative Action

McDonald's is concerned about equal opportunity and affirmative action. The company attempts to attract minorities, women, disabled, and older people and develop their potential without regard to race, sex, religion, ethnicity, educational or cultural background. McJobs is an employment program established to assist mentally and physically challenged individuals to develop their skills and confidence to succeed. The McMasters program attempts to recruit, train, and retain some of McDonald's most valued employees— people aged 55 and over. McDonald's franchisees represent the largest group of minority entrepreneurs in the United States.

Environment

As a responsible corporate citizen, McDonald's is committed to protecting the environment. The company has many ongoing efforts to manage solid waste, conserve and protect natural resources, and promote sound environmental practices. Although many studies indicated that foam packaging is environmentally sound, McDonald's phased out this packaging in 1990 because of customer feedback. There are programs within the McDonald's organization to reduce the weight and volume of packaging, to recycle, to implement reusable materials whenever feasible, and to purchase a minimum of $100 million a year of recycled materials for use in the construction, equipping, and operations of restaurants. In addition, McDonald's refuses to purchase beef from companies that destroy tropical rain forests to create cattle grazing lands. This policy is strictly enforced and closely monitored.

Ronald McDonald Children's Charities

Part of the philosophy of giving something back to the communities is dedicated to helping children achieve their fullest potential. Since its founding in 1984 in memory of Ray Kroc, Ronald McDonald Children's Charities (RMCC) has funded nearly 1,000 grants totaling $35 million to help support programs in the areas of health care and medical research, specially designed rehabilitation facilities, and special youth education programs.

The Ronald McDonald House program is the cornerstone of RMCC providing a "home away from home" for families of seriously ill children being treated at nearby hospitals. The first Ronald McDonald House was developed 17 years ago in Philadelphia when the NFL's Philadelphia Eagles, a children's hospital, and owner/operators of McDonald's restaurants wanted to create a place where parents of sick children could be with others who understood their situation and could provide emotional support.

Within a year after the Philadelphia Ronald McDonald House opened, the Philadelphia Eagles' general manager went to Chicago to help Children's Memorial Hospital and several area residents establish a second Ronald McDonald House. McDonald's owner/operators and their customers provided the fundraising effort. This time the promotion was developed in cooperation with the Chicago Bears NFL team, and the second Ronald McDonald House opened in 1977.

In 1991, the 150th Ronald McDonald House was opened. All totaled, more than 2,200 bedrooms are available for families serving some 4,000 family members each night. The largest house (50 rooms) is in Indianapolis; the smallest (4 rooms) is in Boise, Idaho. Each house is located close to a major medical facility.

Each Ronald McDonald House is run by a local nonprofit organization comprised of members of the medical community, McDonald's owner/operators, businesses and civic organizations, and parent volunteers. More than 12,000 volunteers provide the backbone of the program, helping with all aspects of House operations including fundraising, renovation, program development, and services to families. Families staying at Ronald McDonald Houses are asked to make a donation ranging from $5 to $15 per day. If that is not possible, their stay is free.

McDonald's Serves Communities

McDonald's attempts to contribute to all aspects of community life by supporting education, pursuing equal opportunity and affirmative action in employment practices, operating Ronald McDonald Children's Charities, and promoting sound environmental practices. All of these activities combined demonstrate a commitment to putting something back into the communities that spend 7 percent of their out-of-home food dollars in McDonald's restaurants. Few companies can compete with the high level of commitment McDonald's has made to communities.

Questions for Discussion

1. Why do you believe that McDonald's has selected Ronald McDonald Children's Charities as one of its more visible attempts to implement social responsibility?
2. Why are environmental, educational, and equal opportunity/affirmative action issues so important to McDonald's long-term success?
3. Currently 65 percent of all future owner/operators in training are minorities and women. What impact will this have on McDonald's operations in the future?

Sources: McDonald's 1990 Annual Report; *Ronald McDonald House Fact Sheet*, Ronald McDonald Children's Charities, Kroc Drive, Oakbrook, IL; *Ronald McDonald House Backgrounder*, Ronald McDonald Children's Charities, Kroc Drive, Oakbrook, IL; *Ronald McDonald House World*, a newsletter published for the Ronald McDonald House family, Winter 1991; and "Ronald McDonald's Children's Charities" videotape.

PREVIEW:

MICROMARKET COMPUTER APPLICATION VI

Morning Foods Corporation:
Interpreting Net Present Value

A net present value (NPV) analysis is conducted for each of three proposed new breakfast cereals. Using Lotus 1-2-3, NPV calculations are made by entering figures for company growth, sales, contribution to margin, costs, discount rate, and initial investment.

The case questions require an interpretation of NPV and evaluation of the cereals in different investment environments. A memo to a marketing executive must include a recommendation for investment.

VII *Selected Applications*

The remaining chapters in this book discuss and highlight strategic applications in business-to-business, services, and international marketing. We emphasize the features and issues that are unique to each of these selected areas of marketing. We also focus on aspects that impact formulating and implementing marketing strategies. Chapter 22 analyzes the development of business-to-business marketing strategies and discusses the decisions and activities that characterize business-to-business marketing. Chapter 23 explores selected aspects of services and nonbusiness marketing strategies. Chapter 24 focuses on international marketing and on the development and implementation of marketing strategies for foreign markets.

22 *Business-to-Business Marketing*

OBJECTIVES

- To understand some unique characteristics of business-to-business marketing

- To learn how to select and analyze business-to-business target markets

- To find out how business-to-business marketing mix components differ from the components in consumer product marketing mixes

At last, Simplesse is here. (And only here.)

You've heard the news about Simplesse. The all natural ingredient that takes the place of fat while doing something never before possible. It puts back the taste.

Now you can try Simplesse. Only in new Simple Pleasures.® It's everything you love about ice cream, but without the fat.

Simplesse is completely natural. Made with nothing artificial, nothing complicated. So products like ice cream, and soon salad dressing and mayonnaise, can taste just as rich, creamy and delicious as you've always loved them.

And since Simplesse® all natural fat substitute has no fat, there's no cholesterol. And a lot fewer calories.

Try Simplesse. Only in new Simple Pleasures. Any questions? Call 1-800-321-7254.

All Natural
Simplesse
Fat Substitute

Enjoy it now. Only in new Simple Pleasures.

NutraSweet Company's brand of sugar substitute has become a household name, but its exclusive patent and worldwide monopoly expires in 1992. Pressure is on the organization to produce an equally popular and profitable product. Nutra-Sweet believes it can present an encore performance with its fat substitute, Simplesse, a blend of proteins from milk and egg whites. Simplesse's recent approval by the Food and Drug Administration as the first low-calorie fat substitute opens the door to a potential $500 million market.

To separate its brand of fat substitute from its brand of sugar substitute, NutraSweet markets Simplesse through a newly formed subsidiary, Simplesse Company, and employs a marketing strategy aimed at establishing Simplesse as a "branded ingredient." The firm is working to assure that customers will look for Simplesse on product labels, not "microparticulated protein." NutraSweet's strategy for establishing brand identity includes persuading its customers to display the Simplesse logo—a spoon dipping into a dish—on their packaging, and introducing its own frozen dessert, Simple Pleasures.

Consumers can find Simplesse in two flavors of frozen treats at the nationwide Baskin-Robbins ice-cream chain, in Fat Freedom Eskimo Pie Sandwiches, and soon, in low-fat cheese spreads. Recent FDA approval for Simplesse's use in all foods means that consumers will soon find the product in many other places as well.

Although Simplesse benefits from being the first fat substitute on the market, its success is far from assured. Longer-than-expected FDA approval time hurt because the product is now entering a market where everything from cereal to potato chips is advertised as being low in fat and cholesterol. When its patent runs out in 2005, Simplesse will come up against packaged-food giant Procter & Gamble, Frito-Lay, Unilever, and A.E. Staley Manufacturing all of which are working on fat substitutes. NutraSweet's long-awaited second act depends on establishing brand identity before the curtain rises on the competition.[1]

Photo: The NutraSweet Company.

THE SIMPLESSE COMPANY IS a business-to-business marketer that will be facing strong competition. To prosper in the fat substitute market, Simplesse must develop effective business-to-business marketing strategies. Some of the problems that business-to-business marketers experience resemble those of consumer product marketers. Although business-to-business marketers rely on basic marketing concepts and decisions, they sometimes apply those concepts and decisions differently than consumer product marketers because of the nature of business-to-business markets and products.

This chapter focuses on dimensions unique to developing marketing strategies for business-to-business products. Initially, we take a brief look at the general nature of business-to-business marketing. Next, we examine the selection and analysis of business-to-business target markets by considering who potential customers are, where they are located, and estimating their purchase potential. We then discuss the distinctive features of business-to-business marketing mixes.

The Nature of Business-to-Business Marketing

Business-to-business (or **industrial**) **marketing** is a set of activities directed toward facilitating and expediting exchanges involving business-to-business products and markets. As mentioned in Chapter 8, a business-to-business product differs from a consumer product in that it is purchased to be used for resale, to be used directly or indirectly to produce other products, or to be used in the operations of an organization. As Chapter 4 explains, an organizational or business-to-business market consists of individuals or groups who purchase a specific kind of product for one of three purposes: resale, direct use in producing other products, or use in general daily operations. Business-to-business markets consist of numerous types of customers, including commercial producers, resellers, governments, and institutions.

Business-to-business products fall into seven categories:

1. *Raw materials* actually become a part of a physical product. They are the basic materials delivered from mines, farms, forests, oceans, and recycled solid wastes.
2. *Major equipment* includes large tools and machines used for production (see Figure 22.1).
3. Although it does not become a part of the product, *accessory equipment* consists of standardized items used in production and office activities.
4. *Component parts* become part of the physical product and are either finished items ready for assembly or products that need little processing before assembly.
5. *Process materials* are used directly in production but, unlike component parts, are not readily identifiable.
6. *Consumable supplies* facilitate a firm's production and operations but do not become an actual part of the finished product.
7. *Business-to-business services* are the intangible products (see Figure 22.2) that organizations use in their operations. (The Global Perspective presents examples of firms that provide business-to-business services.)

Figure 22.1

Major Equipment

Unisys provides major computer equipment to business-to-business customers in banking, government, telecommunications, and distribution.

Source: Unisys Corporation.

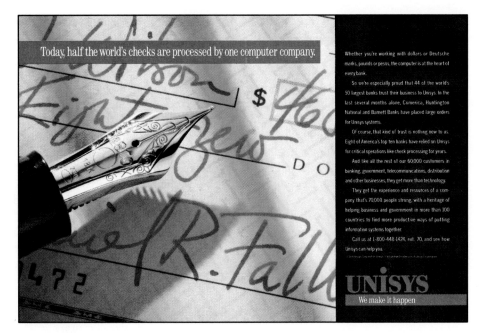

In addition to product differences, business-to-business marketing is considered unique for the following reasons: (1) the buyer's decision-making process, (2) characteristics of the product market, and (3) the nature of environmental influences.[2] These differences influence the development and implementation of business-to-business marketing strategies.

Selection and Analysis of Business-to-Business Target Markets

Marketing research is becoming increasingly important in business-to-business marketing, especially in selecting and analyzing target markets. Most of the marketing research techniques that we discuss in Chapter 7 can also be applied to business-to-business marketing. In this section we focus on important and unique approaches to selecting and analyzing business-to-business target markets.[3]

Business-to-business marketers have easy access to a considerable amount of information about potential customers, for much of this information appears in government and industry publications. However, comparable data about ultimate consumers are not available. Even though business-to-business marketers may use different procedures to isolate and analyze target markets, most follow a similar pattern: (1) determining who potential customers are and how many there are, (2) locating where potential customers are, and (3) estimating their purchase potential.

Determining Who Potential Customers Are and How Many There Are

Much information about business-to-business customers is based on the **Standard Industrial Classification (SIC) system**, which the federal government developed to classify selected economic characteristics of industrial, commercial, financial, and service organizations. Table 22.1 shows how the SIC system can be used to categorize products. Various types of business activities are separated into lettered divisions, and each division is divided into numbered two-digit major groups. For example, major group 22 includes all firms that manufacture textile mill products. Each major group is divided into three-digit-coded subgroups, and each subgroup is separated into detailed industry categories that are coded with four-digit numbers. The most recent *SIC Manual* lists 83 major groups, 596 subgroups, and 1005 detailed industry categories.[4] To categorize manufacturers in more detail, the *Census of Manufacturers* further subdivides manufacturers (Division D) into five- and seven-digit-coded groups. The fifth digit denotes the product category, and the sixth and seventh digits designate the specific product.

Much data are available for each SIC category through various government publications, such as *Census of Business, Census of Manufacturers,* and *County Business Patterns.* Table 22.2 shows types of information that can be obtained through government sources. Some data are available by state, county, and metropolitan area. Market data also appear in such nongovernment sources as Dun & Bradstreet's *Market Identifiers, Sales & Marketing Management's Survey of Industrial Purchasing Power,* and other trade publications.

Figure 22.2

Business-to-Business Service

Commercial insurance is an example of a business-to-business service.

Source: Courtesy of Cigna Corporation.

Fighting Oil Fires in Kuwait

NEAR THE END of the Persian Gulf War, retreating Iraqi troops set fire to over 650 Kuwaiti oil wells. Every day, more than five million barrels of crude oil valued at $87 million went up in a thick black blanket of smoke vast enough to stretch from New York City to Key West, Florida. Plumes of flame shot as high as 400 feet in the air, spewing deadly gas and turning the nearby vicinity into a 650-degree-centigrade inferno. Oil flowed into the desert out of some damaged pipelines at 800 miles per hour, and sand around the wells was hot enough to melt glass.

Facing a catastrophe the world has never encountered before, Kuwaiti officials hired Boots and Coots, Wild Well Control, and the celebrated Red Adair Company, all Texas-based oilfire fighting firms, and Canadian firm Safety Boss to come and put out the fires. Kuwait chose the services of these companies based primarily on their reputations for putting out oil fires from Alaska to Zaire, reputations enhanced by their images as gritty, tobacco-chewing "hellfighters." They speak their own language (novice firefighters are called "worms"), wear distinctive clothing, and drive showy cars. Red Adair personnel all wear fire-engine red coveralls and drive identical red Cadillacs. The acknowledged masters in their field, experts estimate that the firms charge about $1,000 per worker per day to battle the fires.

For the first few months, Kuwait was not a satisfied customer. Complaining that the North American firms weren't extinguishing the fires fast enough, some Kuwaiti officials expressed regret that there was no bonus clause in contracts to reward those firms that finished the job early. Hoping to speed things up and reduce losses to about $12.5 billion, Kuwait's oil minister negotiated with other firefighting companies and government groups from Britain, China, France, Germany, and Iran.

The American firms blamed worse-than-usual working conditions and bureaucratic red tape for the holdup. Kuwaiti government officials were slow to sign supply contracts. Firefighters had to wait until the oil fields could be cleared of unexploded mines and other war refuse. Then they had to wait until pipelines could be laid to bring enough water 40 miles uphill from the Persian Gulf. Housing for 11,000 workers had to be constructed. Equipment was slow to arrive. One Saudi Arabian border official searched an entire 52-truck convoy of oil equipment, and the Saudi government allowed only six trucks per day into Kuwait.

Once the slow and arduous task of getting people and equipment into place was over, work went surprisingly quickly. In addition to the four original companies, 27 other teams helped to put out fires, cap wells, and render support services, bringing the total to 10,000 workers from over 30 countries. On November 6, 1991, workers from Safety Boss extinguished the last burning oil well in Kuwait. When assessing the damage at the end of the war, experts predicted that it would take two years to put out the fires, costing over $4 billion to do it, and that Kuwait would lose about $43 billion worth of oil in the process. Instead, firefighters made Kuwait a very satisfied customer by finishing the job in eight months at a cost of $2.2 billion and holding the country's oil revenue losses to $12 billion.

Sources: David Coll, "Bringing Back the Sun," *Oilweek*, Dec. 16, 1991, p. 12; Matthew L. Wald, "Amid Ceremony and Ingenuity, Kuwait's Oil-Well Fires Are Declared Out," *New York Times*, Nov. 7, 1991, p. 3; D'Arcy Jenish, "A Desert Inferno," *Maclean's*, July 8, 1991, pp. 55–56; Joe Treen and Lorenzo Benet, "Fields of Fire," *People*, Apr. 29, 1991, pp. 42–44; "Kuwait: Firms Sought," *Los Angeles Times*, Apr. 14, 1991, pp. A1, A6–A7; Bob Drogin, "Hotshots in Kuwait's Fiery Hell," *Los Angeles Times*, Apr. 3, 1991; Charles Leerhsen, et al., "Hellfighters to the Rescue," *Newsweek*, Mar. 25, 1991, pp. 29–30; and William Dowell and Michael Riley, "Blazing Oil," *Time*, Mar. 18, 1991, p. 37.

Level	SIC Code	Description
Division	D	Manufacturing
Major group	22	Textile mill products
Industry subgroup	225	Knitting mills
Detailed industry	2251	Women's full-length and knee-length hosiery
Product category	22513	Women's finished seamless hosiery
Product item	2251311	Misses' finished knee-length socks

Sources: *1987 Standard Industrial Classification Manual,* U.S. Office of Management and Budget; and *Census of Manufacturers 1987,* U.S. Bureau of the Census.

The SIC system is a ready-made tool that allows business-to-business marketers to divide firms into market segments based mainly on the types of products manufactured or handled. Although the SIC system is a vehicle for segmentation, it must be used in conjunction with other types of data to enable a specific marketer to determine exactly which customers it can reach and how many of them.

Input-output analysis works well in conjunction with the SIC system. This type of analysis is based on the assumption that the output or sales of one industry are the input or purchases of other industries. **Input-output data** tell what types of industries purchase the products of a particular industry. A major source of national input-output data is the *Survey of Current Business,* published by the Office of Business Economics, U.S. Department of Commerce. It presents input-output data for eighty-three industries in matrix form.

After learning which industries purchase the major portion of an industry's output, the next step is to find the SIC numbers for those industries. Because firms are grouped differently in the input-output tables and the SIC system, ascertaining SIC numbers can be difficult. However, the Office of Business Economics does provide some limited conversion tables with the input-output data. These tables can assist business-to-business marketers in assigning SIC numbers to the industry categories used in the input-output analysis. For example, the motor vehicle and equipment industry, an industry that buys significant quantities of paint and related products, can be converted into SIC categories 3711 and 3715.

Having determined the SIC numbers of the industries that buy the firm's output, a business-to-business marketer is in a position to ascertain the number of firms that are potential buyers nationally, by state, and by county. Government publications such as the *Census of Business,* the *Census of Manufacturers,* and *County Business Patterns* report the number of establishments within SIC classifications, along with other types of data, such as those shown in Table 22.2. For manufacturing industries, *Sales & Marketing Management's Survey of Industrial Purchasing Power* contains state and county SIC information about the number and size of plants and shipment sizes. Unlike most government sources, this survey is updated annually.

Table 22.2

Types of Govern-ment Information Available About Business-to-Business Markets (based on SIC categories)

Value of industry shipments
Number of establishments
Number of employees
Exports as a percentage of shipments
Imports as a percentage of apparent consumption
Compound annual average rate of growth
Major producing areas

Locating Business-to-Business Customers

At this point, a business-to-business marketer knows what types of industries purchase the kinds of products his or her firm produces, as well as the number of establishments in those industries and certain other information. However, that marketer still has to find out the names and addresses of potential customers. To identify sales leads, Maxon, in Figure 22.3, uses a reply ad to encourage potential customers to send for more information about its valves.

One approach to identifying and locating potential customers is to use state or commercial industrial directories, such as *Standard & Poor's Register* and Dun & Bradstreet's *Middle Market Directory* or *Million Dollar Directory*. These

Figure 22.3

Locating Business-to-Business Customers

Maxon locates potential customers for its valves by advertising product benefits and applications and by providing information request forms.

Source: Maxon Corporation.

sources contain such information about a firm as its name, SIC number, address, phone number, and annual sales. By referring to one or more of these sources, a marketer can isolate business-to-business customers that have SIC numbers, determine their locations, and thus develop lists of potential customers by city, county, and state.

A second approach, more expedient but also more expensive, is to use a commercial data company. Dun & Bradstreet, for example, can provide a list of firms that fall into a particular four-digit SIC group. For each company on the list, Dun & Bradstreet gives the name, location, sales volume, number of employees, type of products handled, names of chief executives, and other information.

Either approach can effectively identify and locate a group of potential customers. However, a business-to-business marketer probably cannot pursue all firms on the list. Because some companies have a greater purchase potential than others, the marketer must determine which segment or segments to pursue.

In business-to-business marketing, situation-specific variables may be more relevant in segmenting markets than are general customer characteristics. Business-to-business customers concentrate on benefits sought; therefore, understanding end use of the product is more important than the psychology of decisions or socioeconomic characteristics. Segmenting by benefits rather than customer characteristics can provide insight into the structure of the market and opportunities for new customers.[5]

Estimating Purchase Potential

To estimate the purchase potential of business-to-business customers or groups of customers, a marketer must find a relationship between the size of potential customers' purchases and a variable available in SIC data, such as the number of employees. For example, a paint manufacturer might attempt to determine the average number of gallons purchased by a specific type of potential customer relative to the number of persons employed. If the marketer has no previous experience in this market segment, it will probably be necessary to survey a random sample of potential customers to establish a relationship between purchase sizes and numbers of persons employed. Once this relationship has been established, it can be applied to potential customer segments to estimate their purchases. After deriving these estimates, the marketer selects the customers to be included in the target market.

Despite their usefulness in isolating and analyzing target markets, SIC data pose several problems for users. First, a few industries do not have specific SIC designations. Second, because a transfer of products from one establishment to another is counted as a part of total shipments, double counting may occur when products are shipped between two establishments within the same firm. Third, because the Census Bureau is prohibited from publishing data that would identify a specific business organization, some data—such as value of total shipments—may be understated. Finally, because SIC data are provided by government agencies, there is usually a significant lag between the time the data are collected and when that information becomes available.

Characteristics of Business-to-Business Marketing Mixes

After selecting and analyzing a target market, a business-to-business marketer must create a marketing mix that will satisfy the customers in that target market. In many respects, the general concepts and methods involved in developing a business-to-business marketing mix are similar to those used in consumer product marketing. Here we focus on the features of business-to-business marketing mixes that differ from the marketing mixes for consumer products by examining each of the four components: product, distribution, promotion, and price.

Product

After selecting a target market, the business-to-business marketer has to decide how to compete. Production-oriented managers fail to understand the need to develop a distinct appeal for their product to give it a competitive advantage. Positioning the product (discussed in Chapter 8) is necessary to successfully serve a market, whether consumer or business-to-business.[6]

Compared with consumer marketing mixes, the product ingredients of business-to-business marketing mixes often include a greater emphasis on services, both before and after the sale. Services, including on-time delivery, quality control, custom design, and a nationwide parts distribution system, may be important components of the product.

Before making a sale, business-to-business marketers provide potential customers with technical advice regarding product specifications, installation, and application. Many business-to-business marketers depend heavily on long-term customer relationships that perpetuate sizable repeat purchases. Therefore business-to-business marketers also make a considerable effort to provide services after the sale. John Deere, long the leading manufacturer of heavy farming equipment, is striving to maintain its long-term relationships with American farmers through innovation and service. Because business-to-business customers must have products available when needed, on-time delivery is another service included in the product component of many business-to-business marketing mixes. A marketer unable to provide on-time delivery cannot expect the marketing mix to satisfy business customers. Availability of parts must also be included in the product mixes of many business-to-business marketers because a lack of parts can result in costly production delays. The business-to-business marketer that includes availability of parts within the product component has a competitive advantage over a marketer that fails to offer this service. Furthermore, customers whose average purchases are large often desire credit; thus some business-to-business marketers include credit services in their product mixes.

When planning and developing a business-to-business product mix, a business-to-business marketer of component parts and semifinished products must realize that a customer may decide to make the items instead of buying them. In some cases, then, business-to-business marketers compete not only with each other, but with their own potential customers as well.

Frequently, business-to-business products must conform to standard technical specifications that customers want. Thus business-to-business marketers often concentrate on functional product features rather than on marketing considerations. This fact has important implications for business-to-business salespeople. Rather than concentrate just on selling activities, they must assume the role of consultants, seeking to solve their customers' problems and influencing the writing of specifications.[7]

Because business-to-business products are rarely sold through self-service, the major consideration in package design is protection. There is less emphasis on the package as a promotional device.

Research on business-to-business customer complaints indicates that business-to-business buyers usually complain when they encounter problems with product quality or delivery time. On the other hand, consumers' complaints pertain to other problems, such as customer service and pricing. This type of buyer feedback allows business-to-business marketers to gauge marketing performance. It is important that business-to-business marketers respond to valid complaints because the success of most business products depends on repeat purchases. Because buyer complaints serve a useful purpose, many business-to-business firms facilitate this feedback by providing customer service departments.[8]

If a business-to-business marketer is in a mature market, growth can come from attracting market share from another business-to-business marketer, or a firm can look at new applications or uses for its products.

Distribution

The distribution ingredient in business-to-business marketing mixes differs from that of consumer products with respect to the types of channels used; the kinds of intermediaries available; and the transportation, storage, and inventory policies. Nonetheless, the primary objective of the physical distribution of business products is to ensure that the right products are available when and where needed.

As discussed in Chapter 11, distribution channels tend to be shorter for business-to-business products than for consumer products (refer back to Figure 11.3, which shows four commonly used business-to-business distribution channels). Although **direct-distribution channels**, in which products are sold directly from producers to users, are not used frequently in the distribution of consumer products, they are the most widely used for business-to-business products. More than half of all business products are sold through direct channels. Business-to-business buyers like to communicate directly with producers, especially when expensive or technically complex products are involved. For this reason, business buyers prefer to purchase expensive and highly complex mainframe computers directly from IBM, Cray, and other mainframe producers. In these circumstances, a business-to-business customer wants the technical assistance and personal assurances that only a producer can provide.

A second business-to-business distribution channel involves an industrial distributor to facilitate exchanges between the producer and customer (Channel F in Figure 11.3). An **industrial distributor** is an independent business organization that takes title to products and carries inventories. Thus industrial distributors are merchant wholesalers; they assume possession and ownership of goods, as well as the risks associated with ownership. Industrial distributors usually sell standardized items, such as maintenance supplies, production tools, and small operating equipment. Some industrial distributors carry a wide variety of product lines; others specialize in one or a small number of lines. Industrial distributors can be most effectively used when a product has broad market appeal, is easily stocked and serviced, is sold in small quantities, and is needed rapidly to avoid high losses (as is a part for an assembly line machine).[9]

Industrial distributors offer sellers several advantages. They can perform the needed selling activities in local markets at relatively low cost to a manufacturer. They can reduce a producer's financial burden by providing their customers with credit services. And because industrial distributors usually maintain close relationships with their customers, they are aware of local needs and can pass on market information to producers. By holding adequate inventories in their local markets, industrial distributors reduce the producers' capital requirements.

There are, though, several disadvantages to using industrial distributors. Industrial distributors may be difficult to control because they are independent firms. Because they often stock competing brands, an industrial seller cannot depend on them to sell a specific brand aggressively. Furthermore, industrial distributors maintain inventories, for which they incur numerous expenses; consequently, they are less likely to handle bulky items or items that are slow sellers relative to profit margin, need specialized facilities, or require extraordinary selling efforts. In some cases, industrial distributors lack the technical knowledge necessary to sell and service certain business-to-business products.

In the third business-to-business distribution channel (Channel G in Figure 11.4), a manufacturers' agent is employed. As described in Chapter 11, a manufacturers' agent or representative is an independent business person who sells complementary products of several producers in assigned territories and is compensated through commissions. Unlike an industrial distributor, a manufacturers' agent does not acquire title to the products and usually does not take possession. Acting as a salesperson on behalf of the producers, a manufacturers' agent has no latitude, or very little, in negotiating prices or sales terms.

Using manufacturers' agents can benefit a business-to-business marketer. These agents usually possess considerable technical and market information and have an established set of customers. For a business-to-business seller with highly seasonal demand, a manufacturers' agent can be an asset because the seller does not have to support a year-round sales force. That manufacturers' agents are paid on a commission basis also may be an economical alternative for a firm that has highly limited resources and cannot afford a full-time sales force.

Certainly, the use of manufacturers' agents is not problem-free. Even though straight commissions may be cheaper, the seller may have little control over manufacturers' agents. Because of the compensation method, manufacturers' agents generally want to concentrate on their larger accounts. They are often reluctant to spend adequate time following up sales, to put forth special selling efforts, or to provide sellers with market information when such activities reduce the amount of productive selling time. Because they rarely maintain inventories, manufacturers' agents have a limited ability to quickly provide customers with parts or repair services.

The fourth business-to-business distribution channel (Channel H in Figure 11.3) has both a manufacturers' agent and an industrial distributor between the producer and the business customer. This channel may be appropriate when the business-to-business marketer wishes to cover a large geographic area but maintains no sales force because of highly seasonal demand or because the firm cannot afford a sales force. This type of channel can also be useful for a business-to-business marketer that wants to enter a new geographic market without expanding the firm's existing sales force.

So far, our discussion has implied that all channels are equally available and that an industrial producer can select the most desirable option. However, in a number of cases, only one or perhaps two channels are available for the distribution of certain types of products. An important issue in channel selection is the manner in which particular products are normally purchased. If customers ordinarily buy certain types of products directly from producers, it is unlikely that channels with intermediaries will be effective. Other dimensions that should be considered are the product's cost and physical characteristics, the costs of using various channels, the amount of technical assistance customers need, and the size of product and parts inventory needed in local markets.

Physical distribution decisions regarding transportation, storage, and inventory control are especially important for business-to-business marketers. Some raw materials and other business-to-business products may require special handling; for example, toxic chemicals used in the manufacture of some products must be shipped, stored, and disposed of properly to ensure that they do not harm people or the environment. In addition, the continuity of most business-to-business buyer-seller relationships depends on the seller's having the right products available when and where the customer needs them. This requirement is so important that business-to-business marketers must sometimes make a considerable investment in order-processing systems, materials-handling equipment, warehousing facilities, and inventory control systems.

Many business-to-business purchasers are moving away from traditional marketing exchange relationships, in which the buyer buys primarily on price from multiple suppliers, to more tightly knit, relational exchanges, which are long-lasting agreements between manufacturers and suppliers that are less price-driven.[10] Just-in-time inventory management systems are providing the rationale underlying these new types of relationships. To reduce inventory costs and to eliminate waste, buyers purchase new stock just before it is needed in the manufacturing process. For this system to be effective, they must share a great deal of information with their suppliers since these relationships are collaborative.

Promotion

The combination of promotional efforts used in business-to-business marketing mixes generally differs greatly from those for consumer products, especially convenience goods. The differences are evident in the emphasis on various promotion mix ingredients and the activities performed in connection with each promotion mix ingredient.

For several reasons, most business-to-business marketers rely on personal selling to a much greater extent than do consumer product marketers (except, perhaps, marketers of consumer durables). Because a business-to-business seller often has fewer customers, personal contact with each customer is more feasible. Some business products have technical features that are too numerous or too complex to explain through nonpersonal forms of promotion. Moreover, business purchases are frequently high in dollar value and must be suited to the job and available where and when needed; thus business-to-business buyers want reinforcement and personal assurances from business-to-business sales personnel. Because business-to-business marketers depend on repeat purchases, sales personnel must follow up sales to make certain that customers know how to use the purchased items effectively, as well as to ensure that the products work properly. Inside Marketing discusses some of the problems that women involved in business-to-business selling face.

Salespeople need to perform the role of educators, showing buyers clearly how the product fits their needs. When purchase of a product is critical to the future profitability of the business-to-business buyer, buying decision makers gather extensive amounts of information about all alternative products. To deal with such buyers successfully, the seller must have an extremely well-trained sales force that is knowledgeable not only about its own company's products, but also about competitors' offerings. Besides, if sales representatives offer thorough and reliable information, they can reduce the business-to-business buyer's uncertainty, as well as differentiate their firm's product from the competition. Finally, the gathering of information lengthens the decision-making process. Thus it is important for salespeople to be patient; not to pressure their clients as they make important, new, and complex decisions; and to continue providing information to their prospects throughout the entire process.[11]

As Table 22.3 illustrates, the average cost of a business-to-business sales call varies from industry to industry. Selling costs are comprised of salaries, commissions, bonuses, and travel and entertainment expenses. The average cost of a business-to-business call is $259.[12] Keep in mind, though, that some business-to-business sales are very large and sometimes take years to complete —for example, sales of new Boeing aircraft to airline companies.

Because of the escalating costs of advertising and personal selling, telemarketing, the creative use of the telephone to enhance the salesperson's function, is on the upswing. Some of the activities in telemarketing include toll-free 800

Table 22.3

The Average Cost of a Business-to-Business Sales Call in Selected Industries

Industry	Average Cost of a Personal Sales Call
Electronics and Computer Manufacturing	$279.35
Non-Manufacturing/Services	267.79
Food Service	262.39
Building and Construction	242.99
Manufacturing	238.60
Industry Average	259.00

Source: *Cahners Advertising Research Report No. 542.2C* (Newton, MA: Cahners Publishing Co., 1990).

Breaking the Gender Barrier: Women in Business-to-Business Sales

AMERICANS AS A WHOLE are no longer surprised to encounter women bus drivers, physicians, attorneys, or construction workers; women are increasingly making inroads into traditionally male-dominated fields. But over the next decade, women will comprise almost two-thirds of new workers in the U.S. labor force. Many of these women will opt for careers that still cause some raised eyebrows—careers, for example, in business-to-business sales. Women entering this field make up a small minority, but that is changing. The Bureau of Labor Statistics reveals that from 1970 to 1989, the number of women employed in nonretail professional selling jobs rose from 6.6 percent to 20.7 percent of the total U.S. sales force. Those currently paving the way for women who will follow maintain that, although there is an up side to being a female in business-to-business sales, for the most part they face challenges their male counterparts rarely confront.

The consensus among saleswomen, their sales managers, and their customers is that it is often easier for a woman to get an appointment with a customer than it is for a man. Reasons commonly given for women's somewhat preferential treatment reflect a prevailing sexist attitude—the buyer is curious about the woman's looks or he is unwilling to hurt her feelings by refusing her an appointment. But some male customers honestly prefer dealing with a woman, saying they are less on guard with women salespeople, have more confidence that women follow through on promises, and believe that women listen and try to help more than men do. Some sales managers believe that women are more successful because they tend to do more research, know more about their accounts, strive harder to perform than many salesmen, and often express more personal concern for customers.

Among the disadvantages to being a woman in business-to-business sales, the one most often voiced is that whereas a man's competence is never challenged on the basis of his sex alone, a woman's is. When women sell cosmetics, clothing, or jewelry, customers are unlikely to say, "How can a woman know anything about this business?" Biased as it is, when she is selling fuel oil, heavy-duty cable, or rubber for tire manufacturing, the question comes up persis-

tently. A dubious male customer often demands that a saleswoman prove herself in some way before he will consider a sale; she may be intensely quizzed or required to go out on a dock, down into a quarry, or up on a catwalk. Sometimes buyers refuse to meet with a woman altogether. One woman in international sales of landfill and mine equipment reports that one of her clients admitted that if he had known before their first meeting that she was a woman, that meeting would never have taken place.

Other problems faced by women in business-to-business sales include isolation from other women (about 90 percent of buyers and purchasing agents are men); amount of travel (mothers with small children are especially burdened); and doubt over the kind of image to project (women worry about appearing too feminine, too meek, or even too aggressive).

Researchers interested in the role of women in business-to-business sales are studying male-female differences in job satisfaction, performance, motivation, and stress. Results so far suggest that female salespeople experience higher levels of job dissatisfaction and more turnover. However, when interviewed about their jobs, several women in the field expressed confidence and enthusiasm. One woman sales manager quipped that some of her customers still insist on talking to "the boss," but she is slowly convincing them that she is the boss. Most saleswomen believe that product knowledge and intense involvement can break down the gender barrier and lead to a fulfilling career.

Sources: Bill Kelley, "Selling in a Man's World," *Sales & Marketing Management,* January 1991, pp. 29–32, 34–35; Janice Castro, "Get Set: Here They Come!" *Time,* Fall 1990, pp. 50–52; "Women in Sales," *Agency Sales Magazine,* July 1990, pp. 17–28; Patrick L. Schul, Steven Remington, and Robert L. Berl, "Assessing Gender Differences in Relationships Between Supervisory Behaviors and Job-Related Outcomes in the Industrial Sales Force," *Journal of Personal Selling & Sales Management,* Summer 1990, pp. 1–16; and Bobbi Linkemer, "Women in Sales: What Do They Really Want?" *Sales & Marketing Management,* January 1989, pp. 61–65.

phone lines and data-terminal-assisted personal-sales workstations that take orders, check stock and order status, and provide shipping and billing information.

Although not all business-to-business salespeople perform the same sales activities, they can generally be grouped into the following categories, as described in Chapter 17: technical, missionary, and trade or inside order takers. An inside order taker could effectively use telemarketing. Regardless of how sales personnel are classified, business-to-business selling activities differ from consumer sales efforts. Because business-to-business sellers are frequently asked for technical advice about product specifications and uses, they often need technical backgrounds and are more likely to have them than consumer sales personnel. Compared with typical buyer-seller relationships in consumer product sales, the interdependence that develops between business-to-business buyers and sellers is likely to be stronger; sellers count on buyers to purchase their particular products, and buyers rely on sellers to provide information, products, and related services when and where needed. Although business-to-business salespeople do market their products aggressively, they almost never use hard-sell tactics because of their role as technical consultants and the interdependence between buyers and sellers.

Advertising is emphasized less in business-to-business sales than in consumer transactions. Some of the reasons given earlier for the importance of personal selling in business-to-business promotion mixes explain why. However, advertising often supplements personal selling efforts. Because the cost of a business-to-business sales call is high and continues to rise, advertisements that allow sales personnel to perform more efficiently and effectively are worthwhile for business-to-business marketers. Advertising can make business-to-business customers aware of new products and brands; inform buyers about general product features, representatives, and organizations; and isolate promising prospects by providing inquiry forms or the addresses and phone numbers of company representatives. To ensure that appropriate information is sent to a respondent, it is crucial that the inquiry be specific as to the type of information desired, the name of the company and respondent, the company's SIC number, and the size of the organization.

Because the demand for most business-to-business products is derived demand, marketers can sometimes stimulate demand for their products by stimulating consumer demand. Thus a business-to-business marketer occasionally sponsors an advertisement promoting the products sold by the marketer's customers. In Figure 22.4, Intel encourages its customers' customers to buy computers with Intel microprocessors.

When selecting advertising media, business-to-business marketers primarily choose such print media as trade publications and direct mail; they seldom use broadcast media. Trade publications and direct mail reach precise groups of business customers and avoid wasted circulation. In addition, they are best suited for advertising messages that present numerous details and complex product information (which are frequently the types of messages that business-to-business advertisers wish to get across).

Compared with consumer product advertisements, business-to-business advertisements are usually less persuasive and more likely to contain a large amount of copy and numerous details. In contrast, marketers that advertise to reach ultimate consumers sometimes avoid extensive advertising copy because consumers are reluctant to read it. Business-to-business advertisers, however, believe that

business-to-business purchasers with any interest in their products will search for information and read long messages.

Sales promotion activities, too, can play a significant role in business-to-business promotion mixes. They encompass such efforts as catalogs, trade shows, and trade sales promotion methods that include merchandise allowances, buy-back allowances, displays, sales contests, and other methods discussed in Chapter 17. Business-to-business marketers go to great lengths and considerable expense to provide catalogs that describe their products to customers. Customers refer to various sellers' catalogs to determine specifications, terms of sale, delivery times, and other information about products. Catalogs thus help buyers decide which suppliers to contact.

Trade shows can be effective vehicles for making many customer contacts in a short time. One study found that firms allocate 25 percent of their annual promotion budgets to trade shows to communicate with their current and potential customers, promote their corporate image, introduce new products, meet key account executives, develop mailing lists, identify sales prospects, and find out what their competitors are doing. Although trade shows take second place to personal selling, they rank above print advertising in influencing business-to-business purchases, particularly at the need recognition and vendor evaluation stages of the business-to-business buying process.[13]

Many firms that participate in trade shows lack specific objectives for what they hope to accomplish by such participation. Firms with the most successful trade show programs have written objectives for the tasks they wish to achieve, and they carefully select the type of show in which to take part so that the attendees match the firm's target market.[14]

How business-to-business marketers use publicity in their promotion mixes may not be much different from the way that marketers of consumer products use it.

Price

Compared with consumer product marketers, business-to-business marketers face many more price constraints from legal and economic forces. As indicated in Chapter 2, the Robinson-Patman Act significantly influences producers' and wholesalers' pricing practices by regulating price differentials and the use of discounts. When the federal government invokes price controls, ordinarily the effect is to regulate business-to-business marketers' prices directly and to a greater extent than consumer product prices are regulated. With respect to economic forces, an individual business-to-business firm's demand is often highly elastic, requiring the firm to approximate competitors' prices. This condition often results in nonprice competition and a considerable amount of price stability.

Today's route to sustainable competitive advantage lies in offering customers something that the competition does not offer—something that helps them increase their productivity and profitability. Firms achieve high market share not by offering low prices, but by offering their customers superior value and product quality.[15] Customers are willing to pay higher prices for quality products.[16] Companies such as Caterpillar Tractor Co., Hewlett-Packard Co., and 3M have shown that a value-based strategy can win a commanding lead over competition. Such firms emphasize the highest-quality products at slightly higher prices.

Although there are a variety of ways for determining prices of business-to-business products, the three most common are administered pricing, bid pricing, and negotiated pricing. With **administered pricing**, the seller determines the price (or series of prices) for a product, and the customer pays that specified price. Marketers who use this approach may employ a one-price policy in which all buyers pay the same price, or they may set a series of prices that are determined by one or more discounts. In some cases, list prices are posted on a price sheet or in a catalog. The list price is a beginning point from which trade, quantity, and cash discounts are deducted. Thus the actual (net) price a business-to-business customer pays is the list price less the discount(s). When a list price is used, a business-to-business marketer sometimes specifies the price in terms of list price times a multiplier. For example, the price of an item might be quoted as "list price × .78," which means the seller is discounting the item so that the buyer can purchase the product at 78 percent of the list price. Simply changing the multiplier lets the seller revise prices without having to issue new catalogs or price sheets.

With **bid pricing**, prices are determined through sealed or open bids. When a buyer uses sealed bids, select sellers are notified that they are to submit their bids by a certain date. Normally, the lowest bidder is awarded the contract, providing the buyer believes the firm is able to supply the specified products when and where needed. In an open-bidding approach, several but not all sellers are asked to submit bids. In contrast to sealed bidding, the amounts of the bids are made public. Finally, a business-to-business purchaser sometimes uses negotiated bids. Under this arrangement, the customer seeks bids from a number of sellers and screens the bids. Then the customer negotiates the price and terms of sale with the most favorable bidders, until a final transaction is consummated or until negotiations are terminated with all sellers.

Sometimes a buyer will be seeking either component parts to be used in production for several years or custom-built equipment to be purchased currently and through future contracts. In such instances, a business-to-business seller may submit an initial, less profitable bid to win "follow-on" (subsequent) contracts. The seller that wins the initial contract is often substantially favored in the competition for follow-on contracts. In such a bidding situation, a business-to-business marketer must determine how low the initial bid should be, the probability of winning a follow-on contract, and the combination of bid prices on both the initial and the follow-on contract that will yield an acceptable profit.[17]

For certain types of business-to-business markets, a seller's pricing component may have to allow for **negotiated pricing**. That is, even when there are stated list prices and discount structures, negotiations may determine the actual price a business-to-business customer pays. Negotiated pricing can benefit seller and buyer because price negotiations frequently lead to discussions of product specifications, applications, and perhaps product substitutions. Such negotiations may give the seller an opportunity to provide the customer with technical assistance and perhaps sell a product that better fits the customer's requirements; the final product choice might also be more profitable for the seller. The buyer benefits by gaining more information about the array of products and terms of sale available and may acquire a more suitable product at a lower price.

Some business-to-business marketers sell in markets in which only one of these general pricing approaches prevails. Such marketers can simplify the price components of their marketing mixes. However, a number of business-to-business marketers sell to a wide variety of business-to-business customers and must maintain considerable flexibility in pricing.

Summary

Business-to-business marketing is a set of activities directed at facilitating and expediting exchanges involving business-to-business products and customers in business-to-business markets.

Business-to-business marketers have a considerable amount of information available to them for use in planning their marketing strategies. Much of this information is based on the Standard Industrial Classification (SIC) system, which categorizes businesses into major industry groups, industry subgroups, and detailed industry categories. The SIC system provides business-to-business marketers with information needed to identify market segments. It can best be used for this purpose in conjunction with other information, such as input-output data. After identifying target industries, the marketer can locate potential customers by using state or commercial industrial directories or by employing a commercial data company. The marketer then must estimate the potential purchases of business-to-business customers by finding a relationship between a potential customer's purchases and a variable available in published sources.

Like marketers of consumer products, a business-to-business marketer must develop a marketing mix that satisfies the needs of customers in the business-to-business target market. The product component frequently emphasizes services because they are often of primary interest to business-to-business customers. The marketer must also consider that the customer may elect to make the product rather than buy it. Business-to-business products must meet certain standard specifications that business-to-business users want.

The distribution of business-to-business products differs from that of consumer products in the types of channels used; the kinds of intermediaries available; and transportation, storage, and inventory policies. A direct-distribution channel is common in business-to-business marketing. Also used are channels containing manufacturers' agents, indusrial distributors, or both agents and distributors. Channels are chosen on the basis of availability, the typical mode of purchase for a product, and several other variables.

Personal selling is a primary ingredient of the promotional component in business-to-business marketing mixes. Sales personnel often act as technical advisers both before and after a sale. Advertising sometimes is used to supplement personal selling efforts. Business-to-business marketers generally use print advertisements containing more information but less persuasive content than consumer advertisements. Other promotional activities include catalogs and trade shows.

The price component for business-to-business marketing mixes is influenced by legal and economic forces to a greater extent than it is for consumer marketing mixes. Pricing may be affected by competitors' prices, as well as by the type of customer who buys the product.

Important Terms

Business-to-business (industrial) marketing

Standard Industrial Classification (SIC) system

Input-output data

Direct-distribution channels

Industrial distributor

Administered pricing

Bid pricing

Negotiated pricing

Discussion and Review Questions

1. How do business-to-business products differ from consumer products?
2. What function does the SIC system help business-to-business marketers perform?
3. List some sources that a business-to-business marketer can use to determine the names and addresses of potential customers.
4. How do business-to-business marketing mixes differ from those of consumer products?
5. What are the major advantages and disadvantages of using industrial distributors?
6. Why do business-to-business marketers rely on personal selling more than consumer products marketers?
7. Why would a business-to-business marketer spend resources on advertising aimed at stimulating consumer demand?
8. Compare three methods for determining the price of business-to-business products.

The Mack Truck Company builds and services trucks for worldwide businesses ranging from logging to construction companies. Mack's traditional strengths have been its understanding of industrial customers' needs, its ability to positively influence purchase decisions, and its reputation for quality, service, and innovative design, engineering, and manufacturing. In America, the phrase "Built Like a Mack Truck" has become synonymous with "big, solid, and dependable." However, a declining truck market, union difficulties, and inconsistent product quality have brought Mack Truck to the brink of bankruptcy. The company's market share of the heavy-duty truck segment is only 12.4 percent, the lowest in a decade, and its finances have tumbled from a $31.8 million profit in 1988 to losses of $285 million in 1990 and $46.8 million in the third quarter of 1991. In *Fortune* magazine's Ninth Annual Corporate Reputations Survey, Mack Truck ranked number 300 out of 306 companies rated in categories such as quality of products and services, financial soundness, and long-term investment value.

Hoping to improve its profits and reputation, Mack is reducing costs to improve price competitiveness by reducing inventory, closing plants, laying off employees—particularly from its corporate staff—and converting from fully integrated manufacturing to using outside suppliers. Determining that it is more expensive to make its own power trains, diesel engines, transmissions, and rear axle carriers, Mack will begin incorporating components manufactured by companies like Caterpillar and Rockwell. By cutting the costs of materials, company executives believe they can reduce the cost of Mack's vehicles by about $3,000 per truck.

Mack's target markets have always been independent truckers, who typically select large, powerful, and well-equipped trucks, and fleet customers who have specific customized needs. For Mack, this means that many different variations of trucks are made for specific customers. One of Mack's largest, most visible fleet customers is United Parcel Service, which has been a client for about 30 years. However, in the long-haul, over-the-road segment, which accounts for 70 percent of the sales in this market, Mack has done poorly. To compete more vigorously for this segment, the company introduced a new line of over-the-road trucks, its CH600 series. Production problems forced Mack to construct the new line with old-model engines, resulting in customer disappointment and weak sales. However, now that the new engine is available, orders for CH600 trucks are up, and company representatives assert that soon all vehicles in this series will contain new-model externally manufactured engines.

Despite its attempts to reduce costs and its advantageous partnership with Renault (which owns 44.6 percent of the company), Mack continues to be beset by one problem after another. Hoping to escape paying union wages, Mack constructed an $80 million high-technology, nonunion plant in Winnsboro, South Carolina. However, the United Auto Workers Union and about 400 employees transferring from union plants in the North embroiled Mack in an extended legal battle resulting in bad feelings and bad relations. In the end, the union won the right for representation and its associated higher wages. Problems with a computer network established to keep track of inventory and facilitate distribution resulted in 1,200 partially assembled trucks parked in a field waiting for parts. Workers at the South Carolina plant were forced to empty a huge warehouse just to determine what parts they had and what parts they needed. Product quality continues to be erratic; one Detroit-area Mack dealer recently reported receiving trucks with paint runs and badly constructed interiors.

Mack's prospects currently look bleak, but the company is focusing on the future with commitments to improving product quality, maintaining environmentally responsible standards, and developing a product council consisting of key distributors and corporate engineering staff who will seek profitable niches for the company. Development of Mack's new E9 14-liter V-8 engine, already installed in Renault's top-of-the-line European truck, is calculated to provide growth for the firm. Mack's new CEO is hoping the company will own a 20 percent market share within the next five years, but the real key to Mack's success, insist industry analysts, is the recovery of the U.S. heavy-truck market. Right now, those prospects seem to be bleak, with sales projected to be well below the break-even point for the foreseeable future.[18]

Questions for Discussion

1. What are Mack Truck's target markets?
2. How are Mack Truck's financial problems influencing its marketing strategies?
3. Which environmental forces are having the most impact on Mack Truck's marketing strategies?

22.2 Compaq Computer Targets Business Customers

In businesses, banks, doctors' offices, department stores, and homes, computers make work and life easier in general. But no single class of computer is a perfect fit for every job, and computer companies continually develop and market a variety of models to fill a variety of niches. Compaq Computer, the world's fourth-largest manufacturer of desktop personal computers, primarily produces high-quality high-priced versions for businesses and professional organizations that require fast, rugged, and reliable machines and are willing to pay premium prices to get them. Compaq targets Fortune 500–type companies, including in its impressive list of clientele such organizations as ALCOA, the Louvre Museum in Paris, Dole Foods of Thailand, Lego Toys, and the *Chicago Tribune*.

In 1982, Rod Canion, Bill Murto, and Jim Harris left their executive positions with Texas Instruments, formed their own company, and introduced the Compaq Portable Computer. Just four years later, Compaq made *Fortune* magazine's list of the top 500 companies in the world, faster than any other business in the history of the list. By the end of 1987, sales topped the $1 billion mark. In 1989, boasting a net income of $333 million and about $2.9 billion in sales, Compaq became the second-largest supplier of business PCs in Europe, surpassing Apple. Although IBM still maintains better brand recognition, consumers now view Compaq as having joined its chief competitor at the top of the PC ladder.

Because the computer industry is typified by rapid technological innovation, systems become outmoded almost as soon as they become widely available. To keep in step with the market, computer companies must introduce products with enough frequency to stimulate demand for the "newest and best." To come up with the most innovative and advanced technology, Compaq's strategy has been to invest heavily in research and development. These expenses result in significantly higher prices; companies that do not spend as much in those areas can afford to sell their products at lower prices. As a result, Compaq leaves about 60 percent of the desktop market to its competitors, focusing on customers who can afford and are willing to pay Compaq's high prices. Compaq positions its products as extremely reliable, high-performance, no-nonsense machines perfect for heavy use in large firms, government, and engineering and other sciences. Compaq is almost exclusively a business-oriented company, and the majority of its customers are not individuals choosing computers for their personal use, but purchasing agents, information systems managers, and other corporate professionals choosing systems for the businesses they represent.

To target its fundamental market segment, Compaq produces businesslike and serious advertisements devoid of the show-business glamor prevalent in Apple and IBM campaigns. (Both of these spend more on advertising than Compaq.) The company's slogan, "It Simply Works Better," speaks directly to the utilitarian demands of its market. Compaq's advertisements appear in computer and business magazines because the people who read those particular publications are many of the same people who are most inclined to buy Compaq computers. Additionally, the company's high prices create an aura of prestige and in effect function as a subtle means of targeting Compaq's market. Businesses demand reputable and reliable computers and might view Compaq's premium prices as assurance of getting what they pay for.

Compaq's distribution system has, for the most part, attracted many business customers. Because local dealerships like BusinessLand and ComputerLand provide installation, warranty service, and postwarranty repairs, businesses believe they will get the prompt and personal assistance critical to limiting costly "down time." Obviously, mail-order computer companies cannot deliver that type of on-the-spot service. However, some customers complain that they are not always able to talk personally to someone at Compaq when technical problems arise. Recently, two other problems with the company's methods have surfaced. First, many of its dealers lack the technical expertise and experience to sell Compaq's new and highly sophisticated systems like the SystemPro line. Second, when dealerships choose, for a variety of reasons, to favor another brand over Compaq, the company loses sales. This problem became painfully apparent in Compaq's recent split with one of its dealerships, BusinessLand. When IBM offered that firm volume discounts, its salespeople all over the country began pushing IBMs more heavily than Compaqs. After Compaq dropped BusinessLand, which had accounted for about 7 percent of its sales, the organization reported the first earnings drop in its seven-year history. In addition, Compaq had relied on BusinessLand's nationwide coverage to effectively sell its networking SystemPro computers. After a one-year separation, Compaq reconciled with BusinessLand, but only after agreeing to match IBM's 44 percent product discounts.

Until recently, Compaq had been able to successfully attract the high end of the computer market by maintaining premium prices, low-key advertising, and a dealership distribution strategy. Although Compaq netted $92 million in the first three months of 1990, up 11 percent from the previous three months, and its stock went up almost 57 percent, slowing domestic sales and intense competition from lower-priced catalog companies are forcing the company to reevaluate its methods and initiate some changes. Compaq recently discounted prices up to 40 percent on several of its most advanced PCs. Calling it "creative pricing," one company executive said that his organization is responding to the growing view that its products are becoming too high-priced, especially for smaller companies that were previously loyal Compaq customers. Responding to the reality that few retailers are equipped to sell machines as complicated as the new $29,999 SystemPro 486, Compaq recently signed agreements with several computer consulting firms to sell the SystemPro line and opened up fifteen demonstration centers to help sell the network systems. Expanding its marketing techniques beyond simple and straightforward advertising, Compaq will introduce a joint worldwide promotion with Microsoft to introduce the Microsoft BallPoint Mouse, the first mouse pointing device designed specifically for use with laptop PCs. Compaq will offer free BallPoints to buyers of any of its laptop or notebook computers. Advertisements for the promotion will appear in the *Wall Street Journal, Forbes, Business Week, Fortune,* and *USA Today.*[19]

Questions for Discussion

1. Compare Compaq's new marketing strategy with its previous one.
2. Will the new strategy that Compaq is using to remain competitive diminish its premium image and thus adversely affect its efforts to market its products in the premium business segment of the personal computer market?
3. What types of problems result from Compaq's heavy reliance on retailers to reach the business segment?

Chapter Notes

1. Based on information from Robert Steyer, "Analysts Trim Hopes on Fake Fat," *St. Louis Post Dispatch,* Aug. 1, 1991; Robert Steyer, "Simplesse OK'd for All Foods," *St. Louis Post Dispatch,* Aug. 14, 1991; "Fake Fat of the Land," *Time,* June 24, 1991, p. 41; Robert McMath, "Footloose and Sugar-Free," *Adweek's Marketing Week,* June 3, 1991, p. 41; "Baskin-Robbins," *New York Times,* Apr. 17, 1991, p. D3; Julie Liesse, "Fat-Free: Fad or Food of the Future?" *Advertising Age,* Sept. 10, 1990, p. 6; Judith Crown, "NutraSweet Slips Up with Fat Substitute," *Advertising Age,* Aug. 20, 1990, p. 40; Anthony Ramirez, "Fake Fat: Another Sweet Deal?" *New York Times,* May 28, 1990, pp. 27–28; Jim Ostroff, "FDA OKs Use of Simplesse, Low-Calorie Fat Substitute," *Supermarket News,* Feb. 26, 1990, pp. 6, 42; Molly O'Neill, "First Low-Calorie Substitute for Fats Is Approved by U.S.," *New York Times,* Feb. 23, 1990; and Eben Shapiro, "Monsanto Shares Up Sharply on Hopes for Fat Substitute," *New York Times,* Feb. 23, 1990.
2. Edward F. Fern and James R. Brown, "The Industrial/Consumer Marketing Dichotomy: A Case of Insufficient Justification," *Journal of Marketing,* Spring 1984, pp. 168–177.

3. Some of the ideas in this section are from Robert W. Haas, *Industrial Marketing Management: Text and Cases* (Boston: PWS-Kent, 1989), pp. 35–61.

4. *1987 Standard Industrial Classification Manual* (U.S. Office of Management and Budget, Washington, D.C.).

5. Peter Doyle and John Saunders, "Market Segmentation and Positioning in Specialized Industrial Markets," *Journal of Marketing,* Spring 1985, p. 25.

6. Ibid., p. 25.

7. Erin Anderson and Anne T. Coughlan, "International Market Entry and Expansion via Independent or Integrated Channels of Distribution," *Journal of Marketing,* January 1987, pp. 71–82.

8. Hiram C. Barksdale, Jr., Terry E. Powell, and Ernestine Hargrove, "Complaint Voicing by Industrial Buyers," *Industrial Marketing Management,* May 1984, pp. 93–99.

9. James D. Hlavacek and Tommy J. McCuistion, "Industrial Distributors: When, Who, and How?" *Harvard Business Review,* March–April 1983, p. 97.

10. Gary L. Frazier, Robert E. Spekman, and Charles R. O'Neal, "Just-in-Time Exchange Relationships in Industrial Markets," *Journal of Marketing,* October 1988, pp. 52–67.

11. Daniel H. McQuiston, "Novelty, Complexity, and Importance as Causal Determinants of Industrial Buyer Behavior," *Journal of Marketing,* April 1989, pp. 66–79.

12. "What Is the Average Cost of a Personal Sales Call?" *Cahners Advertising Research Report, No. 542-1G* (Newton, MA: Cahners Publishing Co., 1990).

13. Roger A. Kerin and William L. Cron, "Assessing Trade Show Functions and Performance: An Exploratory Study," *Journal of Marketing,* July 1987, pp. 87–94.

14. Ibid.

15. John C. Narver and Stanley F. Slater, "Creating a Market-Oriented Business," *The Channel of Communications,* Summer 1989, pp. 5–8.

16. Robert Jacobson and David A. Aaker, "The Strategic Role of Product Quality," *Journal of Marketing,* October 1987, pp. 31–44.

17. Douglas G. Brooks, "Bidding for the Sake of Follow-On Contracts," *Journal of Marketing,* January 1978, p. 35.

18. Jim Henry, "Boss Says Mack Will Stay, Someday Engines May Be Imported," *Automotive News,* Nov. 25, 1991, p. 16; Joseph Bohn, "Freightliner to Cut Staff, Shut Field Office," *Automotive News,* April 22, 1991, p. 6; Jack Semple, "Mack a Heavy Load for Renault," *Automotive News,* Mar. 25, 1991, p. 19; Jun Ah Pak, "America's Most Admired Corporations," *Fortune,* Feb. 11, 1991, pp. 52–60; Daniel F. Cuff, "A Renault Executive Is Taking Over Mack," *New York Times,* Oct. 18, 1990; Joseph Weber, "These Days Mack Trucks Isn't Built Like a Mack Truck," *Business Week*, July 30, 1990, pp. 40–41; Richard Johnson, "Volvo, Renault Seek Truck Savings," *Automotive News,* June 4, 1990, pp. 1, 6; Joseph Bohn, "Mack: Lean, Hungry, and Mean," *Automotive News,* Apr. 23, 1990, p. 8i, 10i–11i; Joseph Bohn, "Mack Opens Up CH Models to Outside Vendors," *Automotive News,* Mar. 12, 1990, p. 16; Neal Templin, "Troubled Mack Trucks Finds Its Problems Are Mostly Homegrown," *Wall Street Journal,* Feb. 27, 1990, p. 1; Joseph Bohn, "Mack Tries to Reverse Morale, Profit Slide," *Automotive News,* Feb. 26, 1990, p. 14; Julie Candler, "Mack Trucks' Turnaround," *Nation's Business,* Nov. 1988, pp. 60–61; Robert Wrubel, "Putting the Hammer Down," *Financial World,* Oct. 20, 1987, pp. 25–29; Christopher S. Eklund, "The UAW Takes on Mack—and Its Own Members," *Business Week,* Mar. 23, 1987, p. 116H; and Greg Myers, "Bidding Wars," *Business and Economic Review,* Jan–March 1987, pp. 8–14.

19. "Compaq, Microsoft Team for Joint Promotion," *Adweek,* Mar. 11, 1991, p. 61; Mark Ivey, Barbara Buell, Jonathan B. Levine, and Neil Gross, "What's in a Clone: Price, Technology, Service . . . ," *Business Week,* Nov. 19, 1990, p. 137; Thomas C. Hayes, "Compaq Cuts Prices on Some Computers," *New York Times,* Sept. 12, 1990; Kevin Burke, Brett Graham, Dale Miller, Steve Rikli, and Chris Tiesman, *Compaq Computer Corporation Desktop Personal Computers: Marketing Plan,* Working Paper, Texas A&M University, Fall 1990; Todd Mason, "Compaq to Unveil 3 Personal Computers, Posing Big Sales Challenge for Dealers," *Wall Street Journal,* July 23, 1990, p. B2; Jim Bartimo and Deidre A. Depke, "Compaq's Muscular Mini Isn't Knocking Them Out," *Business Week,* July 2, 1990, pp. 34–35; Gregory Seay, "Overseas Sales Boost Compaq to New Heights," *Houston Post,* Apr. 27, 1990; Deidre A. Depke, "Bloody, Bowed, Back Together," *Business Week,* Mar. 19, 1990, pp. 42–43; and Carla Lazzareschi, "Compaq and Businessland Heal Their Yearlong Rift," *Los Angeles Times,* Mar. 8, 1990, p. D6.

23 *Services Marketing*

O B J E C T I V E S

- To understand the nature and characteristics of services

- To examine how services are classified

- To understand the development of marketing strategies for services

- To explore the nature of nonbusiness marketing

- To understand the development of marketing strategies in nonbusiness organizations

During the 1980s, the number of college-age students dropped by 10 percent and is expected to drop another 25 percent by the mid-1990s. This dwindling student pool has ended the days of bulging classrooms, forcing colleges to face lean times. Continuing to raise the price of tuition to compensate for a smaller student population is no longer a practical solution. Prospective students are increasingly reluctant to assume the burden of exorbitant tuition, whose average price tag has tripled since 1976. To stem declining enrollment, more institutions of higher learning are marketing themselves to the public.

Colleges and universities pinpoint markets that will be most receptive to their messages. Segmenting tools such as geodemographics use computer software to establish a geographic and demographic profile of enrolled and prospective students. These tools can tell an institution what its current students are like and where to find more of them.

Involving a university's own marketing faculty in researching and planning student recruitment is often a cost-effective way to help the admissions office. Universities find that including the marketing department not only makes judicious use of an existing pool of expertise and experience, but also provides faculty with an opportunity to put theories into practice.

Some individuals warn that marketing will tarnish the image of higher education. Nevertheless, many colleges and universities are raising enrollment by using promotion to communicate their messages. Using telemarketing, Rider College in New Jersey employs students to call college prospects and talk up Rider's merits. Cuyahoga Community College credits its full-blown marketing campaign—including research surveys, focus groups, animated television spots, radio jingles, and newspaper advertising—for the school's first enrollment increase in six years.

For many colleges and universities, using marketing techniques to enhance esteem and increase name recognition is no longer a luxury but an essential. Across the United States, admissions counselors are under the same pressure traditionally placed on coaches—either win or get fired.[1]

Photo: Terry Wild Studio.

E DUCATIONAL INSTITUTIONS are service providers and clearly are organizations that develop marketing strategies and engage in marketing activities. This chapter presents concepts that apply specifically to the marketing of services. Services marketing involves marketing in not-for-profit organizations such as educational institutions, churches, charities, and governments, as well as for-profit areas such as financial, personal, and professional services.

The chapter first focuses on the growing importance of service industries in our economy. Second, it addresses the unique characteristics of services and the problems they present to marketers. Third, it presents various classification schemes that can help service marketers develop marketing strategies. In addition, we discuss a variety of marketing mix considerations. Finally, we define nonbusiness marketing and examine the development of nonbusiness marketing strategies and the control of nonbusiness marketing activities.

The Nature and Characteristics of Services

As we mention in Chapter 8, all products—goods, services, or ideas—possess a certain amount of intangibility. A service is an intangible product involving a deed, a performance, or an effort that cannot be physically possessed.[2] We should note that few products can be classified as a pure good or a pure service. Consider, for example, an automobile. When consumers purchase a car, they take ownership of a physical item that provides transportation, but the warranty associated with the purchase is a service. When consumers rent a car, they purchase a transportation service that is provided through temporary use of an automobile. Most products, such as automobiles and automobile rentals, contain both tangible and intangible components. One component, however, will dominate, and it is this dominant component that leads to the classification of goods, services, and ideas.

Figure 23.1 illustrates the tangibility concept by placing a variety of products on a continuum of tangibility and intangibility. Tangible-dominant products are typically classified as goods, and intangible-dominant products are typically considered services. Thus, as defined in Chapter 8, services are intangible-dominant products that are the result of the application of human and mechanical efforts to people or objects.

Growth and Importance of Services

The increasing importance of services in the U.S. economy has led many people to call the United States the world's first service economy. The service industries—encompassing trade, communications, transportation, food and lodging, financial and medical services, education, government, and technical services—account for about 60 percent of the national income and three-fourths of the nonfarm jobs in the United States. In generating 44 million new jobs in the past thirty years, these industries have absorbed most of the influx of women and minorities into the work force and fueled every recent economic recovery.[3]

One major catalyst of the growth in consumer services has been long-term economic growth in the United States, which has led to increased interest in

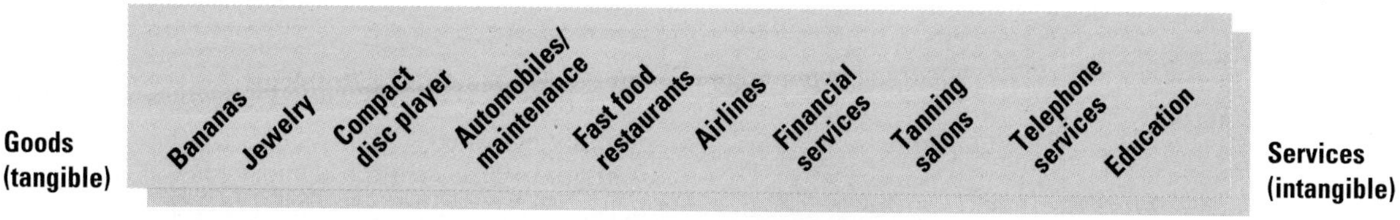

| Goods (tangible) | Bananas | Jewelry | Compact disc player | Automobiles/ maintenance | Fast food restaurants | Airlines | Financial services | Tanning salons | Telephone services | Education | Services (intangible) |

Figure 23.1 **A Continuum of Product Tangibility and Intangibility**

financial services, travel, entertainment, and personal care. Lifestyle changes have similarly encouraged expansion of the service sector. In the past forty years, the number of women in the work force has more than doubled. With approximately 70 percent of the women between the ages of 18 and 34 now working, the need for child care, domestic services, and other time-saving services has increased. Consumers want to avoid such tasks as meal preparation, house cleaning, home maintenance, and tax preparation; consequently franchise operations, such as Subway Sandwiches, Merry Maid, Chemlawn, and H&R Block, have experienced rapid growth. Furthermore, Americans have become more fitness- and recreation-oriented, and so the demand for fitness and recreational facilities has escalated. In terms of demographics, the U.S. population is growing older, and this change has promoted tremendous expansion of health-care services. Finally, the number and complexity of goods needing servicing have spurred demand for repair services.

Large retailers, such as Sears, are successfully incorporating additional services into their retail stores. Providing additional services at one location is an excellent way to satisfy and keep customers who need and want more and more services. Sears operates its traditional department stores but in addition offers optical services, financial services, automotive services, and others. If customers enter a store for one service, they will be more likely to eventually shop at the store again or try another service that the retailer provides.[4]

Not only have consumer services grown in our economy; business services have prospered as well. Business or industrial services include repairs and maintenance, consulting, installation, equipment leasing, marketing research, advertising, temporary office personnel, and janitorial services. Expenditures for business and industrial services have risen even faster than expenditures for consumer services. This growth has been attributed to the increasingly complex, specialized, and competitive business environment.

Characteristics of Services

The problems of service marketing are not the same as those of goods marketing. To understand these unique problems, it is first necessary to understand the distinguishing characteristics of services. Services have four basic characteristics: (1) intangibility, (2) inseparability of production and consumption, (3) perishability, and (4) heterogeneity.[5] Table 23.1 summarizes these characteristics and the marketing problems they entail.

Intangibility stems from the fact that services are performances. They cannot be seen, touched, tasted, or smelled, nor can they be possessed. Services have a

Table 23.1

Service Characteristics and Marketing Problems

Unique Service Features	Resulting Marketing Problems
Intangibility	Cannot be stored
	Cannot be protected through patents
	Cannot be readily displayed or communicated
	Prices are difficult to set
Inseparability	Consumer is involved in production
	Other consumers are involved in production
	Centralized mass production is difficult
Perishability	Services cannot be inventoried
Heterogeneity	Standardization and quality are difficult to control

Source: Valarie A. Zeithaml, A. Parasuraman, Leonard L. Berry, "Problems and Strategies in Services Marketing," *Journal of Marketing*, Spring 1985, pp. 33–46. Used by permission of the American Marketing Association.

few tangible attributes, called **search qualities**, that can be viewed prior to purchase. When consumers cannot view a product in advance and examine its properties, they may not understand exactly what is being offered. Even when consumers do gain sufficient knowledge about service offerings, they may not be able to evaluate the possible alternatives. On the other hand, services are rich in experience and credence qualities. **Experience qualities** are those qualities that can be assessed only after purchase and consumption (satisfaction, courtesy, and the like). **Credence qualities** are those qualities that cannot be assessed even after purchase and consumption.[6] An appendix operation is an example of a service high in credence qualities. How many consumers are knowledgeable enough to assess the quality of an appendectomy, even after it has been performed? In summary, it is difficult to go into a store, examine a service, purchase it, and take it home with you.

Related to intangibility is **inseparability** of production and consumption. Services are normally produced at the same time they are consumed. A medical examination is an example of simultaneous production and consumption. In fact, the doctor cannot possibly perform the service without the patient's presence, and the consumer is actually involved in the production process. With other services, such as air travel, many consumers are simultaneously involved in production. Because of high consumer involvement in most services, standardization and control are difficult to maintain.

Because production and consumption are simultaneous, services are also characterized by **perishability**. In other words, unused capacity in one time period cannot be stockpiled or inventoried for future time periods. Consider the airlines' seating-capacity dilemma. Each carrier maintains a sophisticated reservations system to juggle ticket prices and ensure maximum revenues for every flight. On a single day, airlines make thousands of fare changes in an attempt to maximize seat usage. This attempt to maximize revenues on most flights has led to overbooking, which means that airlines may sell tickets for more seats than are available to compensate for "no-shows"—people who have made reservations but who may not actually take that particular flight. The airlines' dilemma illustrates how service perishability presents problems very different from the supply-and-demand problems encountered in the marketing of goods.[7] Unoccupied seats on an airline flight cannot be stored for use on another flight that is booked to capacity.

Finally, because most services are labor-intensive, they are susceptible to **heterogeneity**. People typically perform services, and people do not always perform consistently. There may be variation from one service to another within the same organization or variation in the service that a single individual provides from day to day and from customer to customer. Thus standardization and quality are extremely difficult to control. But this fact may also lead to customizing services to meet consumers' specific needs. Because of these factors, service marketers often face a dilemma: how does one provide efficient, standardized service at some acceptable level of quality while simultaneously treating each customer as a unique person? Giving "good service" is a major concern of all service organizations, and it is often translated into more personalized service.[8]

Classification of Services

Services are a very diverse group of products, and an organization may provide more than one kind. Examples of services include car rentals, repairs, health care, barber shops, health spas, tanning salons, amusement parks, day care, domestic services, legal counsel, banking, insurance, air travel, education, business consulting, dry cleaning, and accounting. Nevertheless, services can be meaningfully analyzed by using a five-category classification scheme: (1) type of market, (2) degree of labor-intensiveness, (3) degree of customer contact, (4) skill of service provider, and (5) goal of the service provider. Table 23.2 summarizes this scheme.

Services can be viewed in terms of the market or type of customer they serve—consumer or business. The implications of this distinction are very similar to those for all products and therefore are not discussed here.

A second way to classify services is by degree of labor-intensiveness. Many services, such as repairs, education, and hair care, rely heavily on human labor. Other services, such as telecommunications, health spas, and public transportation, are more equipment-intensive. Satellite television services, discussed in the Global Perspective, are an example of equipment-intensive services.

Labor-intensive (people-based) services are more susceptible to heterogeneity than are most equipment-based services. Marketers of people-based services must recognize that service providers are often viewed as the service itself. Therefore, strategies relating to selecting, training, motivating, and controlling employees are very important. Figure 23.2 shows examples of labor-based and equipment-based services.

The third way services can be classified is by customer contact. High-contact services include health care, hotels, real estate agencies, and restaurants; low-contact services include repairs, movie theaters, dry cleaning, and spectator sports.[9] Note that high-contact services generally involve actions that are directed toward individuals. Because these services are directed at people, the consumer must be present during production. Although it is sometimes possible

Table 23.2

Classification of Services

Category	Examples
Type of Market	
Consumer	Repairs, child care, legal counsel
Business	Consulting, janitorial services, installation
Degree of Labor-Intensiveness	
Labor-based	Repairs, education, haircuts
Equipment-based	Telecommunications, health spas, public transportation
Degree of Customer Contact	
High contact	Health care, hotels, air travel
Low contact	Repairs, dry cleaning, postal service
Skill of the Service Provider	
Professional	Legal counsel, health care, accounting services
Nonprofessional	Domestic services, dry cleaning, public transportation
Goal of the Service Provider	
Profit	Financial services, insurance, health care
Nonprofit	Health care, education, government

for the service provider to go to the consumer, high-contact services typically require that the consumer go to the production facility. Thus the physical appearance of the facility may be a major component of the consumer's overall evaluation of the service. Because the consumer must be present during production of a high-contact service, the process of production may be just as important as its final outcome.

Low-contact service, in contrast, commonly involves actions directed at things. Consequently, the consumer is usually not required to be present during service delivery. The consumer's presence, however, may be required to initiate or terminate the service. A dry cleaner, for example, must provide and maintain dry cleaning equipment and a facility to house the equipment. Although they must be present to initiate the provision of the service, consumers need not be present during the cleaning process. The appearance of the production facilities and the interpersonal skills of actual service providers are thus not as critical in low-contact services as they are in high-contact services.[10]

Skill of the service provider is a fourth way to classify services. Professional services tend to be more complex and more highly regulated than nonprofessional services. In the case of legal counsel, for example, consumers often do not know what the actual service will involve or how much it will cost until the service is completed because the final product is very situation-specific. Additionally, attorneys are regulated both by law and by professional associations.

Finally, services can be classified according to the goal of the service provider—profit or nonprofit. Later in this chapter we examine nonbusiness marketing. Most nonbusiness organizations provide services rather than goods.

Developing Marketing Strategies for Services

Before we discuss the development of a marketing mix for service firms, we need to reiterate a major point: the marketing concept is equally applicable to goods, services, and ideas. The marketing of services, like the marketing of goods, requires the identification of a viable target market segment, the development of a service concept that addresses the consumer's needs within that segment, the creation and implementation of an operating strategy that will adequately support the service concept, and the design of a service delivery system that will support the chosen operating strategy.[11]

Table 23.3 illustrates the approaches that marketers of services can take to achieve consumer satisfaction. A basic requirement of any marketing strategy, however, is a development phase, which includes defining target markets and finalizing a marketing mix. The following seven precepts need to be considered when developing a service marketing strategy:

1. Make sure that marketing occurs at all levels, from the marketing department to the point where the service is provided.
2. Allow flexibility in providing the service—when there is direct interaction with the customers, customize the service to their wants and needs.
3. Hire and maintain high-quality personnel and market your organization or service to them; often it is the people in a service organization who differentiate one organization from another.
4. Consider marketing to existing customers to increase their use of the service or create loyalty to the service provider.

Figure 23.2   **Labor-Intensive versus Equipment-Intensive Services**   Health care services, such as Mountain Chiropractic, tend to be people-based whereas transportation services, such as Federal Express, are equipment-based.   Sources: Mountain Chiropractic; courtesy of Federal Express.

5. Quickly resolve any problems in providing the service, to avoid damaging your firm's reputation for quality.
6. Think high technology to provide improved services at a lower cost. Continually evaluate how to customize the service to each consumer's unique needs.
7. Brand your service to distinguish it from that of the competition. For example, instead of simply seeking a moving truck, a customer would seek a rental from U-Haul because of U-Haul's name recognition.[12]

In the following sections we discuss the marketing mix requirements for finalizing a services marketing strategy.

Product

Goods can be defined in terms of their physical attributes, but services cannot because they are intangible. As we point out earlier in the chapter, it is often difficult for consumers to understand service offerings and to evaluate possible service alternatives. To overcome this problem, five hospitals in the Tampa Bay area used the cartoon character Snuffy Smith in a promotional campaign to help senior citizens understand the complicated paperwork associated with obtaining free or low-cost medical services. The sixty-second commercials covered such

Table 23.3   **Examples of Approaches to Consumer Satisfaction for Marketers of Services**

Service Industry	Outcome Sought by Buyer	Technical Possibilities	Strategic Possibilities
Higher education	Educational attainment	Help professors to be effective teachers; offer tutoring	Admit better prepared students (or, for a fee, give them better preparation before entry)
Hospitals	Health	Instruct patients in how to manage their current problems and prevent others	Market preventive medicine services (weight loss, stress reduction, etc.)
Banks	Prosperity	Offer money management courses; provide management assistance to small businesses	Market financial expertise, probably by industry specialization
Plumbing repairs	Free-flowing pipes	Provide consumers with instructions and supplies to prevent further clogs	Diversify (e.g., point-of-use water-purification systems)

Source: Adapted from Betsy D. Gelb, "How Marketers of Intangibles Can Raise the Odds for Consumer Satisfaction," *Journal of Services Marketing,* Summer 1987, p. 15.

STAR Delivers the First Pan-Asian Satellite Television Service

COMBINE A THRIVING Asian economy with limited and poor-quality terrestrial television broadcasting in countries such as Kuwait, Japan, and New Zealand, and the result is the world's fastest-growing market for commercial satellite television. Although many companies have joined the battle for access into the homes of 2.7 billion potential viewers, as of 1991, STAR TV was the first pan-Asian service, currently sending its signal to satellite dishes in 38 countries throughout the region.

Honk Kong billionaire Li Kashing launched STAR, which stands for Satellite TV Asian Region, initially targeting major markets, such as Hong Kong, Taiwan, South Korea, Thailand, and India. He started with four channels: an Asian version of MTV, a sports channel, an entertainment channel, and one offering Chinese-language programming. Hourly news reports from the BBC will soon be incorporated into a 24-hour news channel that will go head-to-head with chief rival CNN. What makes STAR stand out is that its programming is free to anyone with a satellite dish; there is no signal scrambling or subscription fee. Advertisers like Mobil Oil, Mitsubishi, Nike, and Swatch International, who pay about $2 million each for a package of spots, make STAR possible. Despite the "free-to-air" nature of the broadcasts, only those owning a satellite dish or having cable or microwave hookups can see the programs. Although that makes STAR available primarily to the affluent, one-half million households already receive the signal, and analysts expect that number to rise to over four million in the next few years.

Thanks to technological advances that allow multichannel sound tracks, STAR is overcoming communication problems by broadcasting programs in many languages. Trying to get an advertising message to audiences with disparate cultural values and customs isn't as simple. For example, advertisers contend with variation in packaging and product names, making regional marketing complicated. What is posing STAR's biggest potential threat, however, is interference from some governments hoping to prevent the company from introducing their people to foreign programs and ideas. The government of Malaysia recently banned private satellite dishes to protect its large Muslim population from what it terms "undesirable values." In India, a government committee argues that satellite television exposes people to "foreign perceptions and alien values."

Neither STAR nor its many competitors seem daunted by the problems they face. CNN, seen by about 150,000 private subscribers in Japan, Taiwan, and Hong Kong, and ESPN are both broadcast on the Indonesian-operated Palaba B2 satellite. HBO and TV New Zealand are negotiating to join them, and Japan's state-controlled NHK and Hong Kong–based Business News Network are looking for regional satellite programming as well. Flaunting conventional wisdom that warns against offering satellite television with no subscription fee, STAR is succeeding by serving a market hungry for variety and quality in television programming. On its first day of service, 500,000 households tuned in.

Sources: "Asia's Hot New STAR," *Time,* Oct. 28, 1991, p. 92; Andrew Geddes, "Asian Satellite TV Blasts Off," *Advertising Age,* Oct. 28, 1991, p. S-14; Rhonda Palmer, "SAT Problems for CNN in Asia," *International,* July 15, 1991, pp. 31, 87; and Michael Westlake, "Reach for the Stars," *Far Eastern Economic Review,* May 30, 1991, pp. 60–61.

topics as how to fill out insurance forms and how to get quicker check-in at the hospital. The campaign was highly successful and resulted in thousands of calls to the toll-free number provided in the advertisement.[13]

There may also be tangibles (such as facilities, employees, or communications) associated with a service. These tangible elements help form a part of the product and are often the only aspects of a service that can be viewed prior to purchase. Consequently, marketers must pay close attention to associated tangibles and make sure that they are consistent with the selected image of the service product.[14] For example, because consumers perceive bus terminals as plagued by crime and therefore hesitate to use bus services for long-distance travel, Greyhound Lines, Inc. spent $30 million to update its terminals and open new ones. The company also installed a computer system to reduce the time consumers spend waiting for tickets.[15] Improving the physical appearance of Greyhound terminals and reducing the time required to provide some services are tangible cues that consumers can use to judge Greyhound's services.

The service product is often equated with the service provider; for example, the teller or the beautician becomes the service a bank or a beauty parlor provides. Because consumers tend to view services in terms of the service personnel and because personnel are inconsistent in their behavior, it is imperative that marketers effectively select, train, motivate, and control contact people. Service marketers are selling long-term relationships as well as performance.

After testing many variables, the Strategic Planning Institute (SPI) developed an extensive database on the impact of various business strategies on profits. The institute found that "relative perceived product quality" is the single most important factor in determining long-term profitability. In fact, because there are generally no objective measures to evaluate the quality of professional services (medical examination, legal services, and so forth), the customer is actually purchasing confidence in the service provider.[16] The strength or weakness of the service provided often affects consumers' perceptions of product quality. Of the companies in the SPI database, businesses that rate low on service lose market share at the rate of 2 percent a year and average a 1 percent return on sales. Companies that score high on service gain market share at the rate of 6 percent a year, average a 12 percent return on sales, and charge a significantly higher price.[17] These data indicate that firms having service-dominant products must score high on service quality.

Because services are performances rather than tangible goods, the concept of service quality is difficult to grasp. However, price, quality, and value are important considerations of consumer choice and buying behavior for both goods and services.[18] It should be noted that it is not objective quality that matters, but the consumer's subjective perceptions. Instead of quality meaning conformance to a set of specifications—which frequently determine levels of product quality—service quality is defined by customers.[19] Moreover, quality is frequently determined in a comparison context. In the case of services, quality is determined by contrasting what the consumer expected a service to be with her or his actual service experience.[20]

Service providers and service consumers may have quite different views of what constitutes service quality. Consumers frequently enter service exchanges with a set of predetermined expectations. Whether a consumer's actual experiences exceed, match, or fall below these expectations will have a great effect on future relationships between the consumer and the service provider. To improve service quality, a service provider must adjust its own behavior to be consistent with consumers' expectations or perceptions.

Research indicates that there are five elements that affect customers' perceptions of service quality. The first, and most important, is reliability, which is the ability to perform the service dependably and correctly. A second important element is the appearance of the tangibles, such as facilities, equpment, and

Figure 23.3

Complexity/Variability Grid for Medical Services

Source: Adapted from G. Lynn Shostack, 1985 American Marketing Association Faculty Consortium on Services Marketing, Texas A&M University, July 7–11. Reprinted by permission of the American Marketing Association.

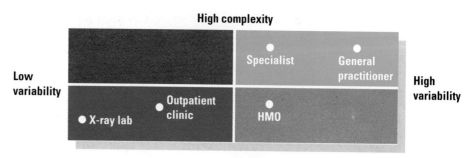

personnel. Third, responsiveness, which is the speed and willingness to provide service, influences perceptions of service quality. Assurance, employees' ability to convey trust and confidence, is the fourth dimension. Employee empathy, shown by caring, individualized attention to customers, is the fifth element found to affect customers' perceptions of service quality.[21]

Other product concepts discussed in Chapters 8, 9, and 10 are also relevant here. Management must make decisions regarding the product mix, positioning, branding, and new-product development of services. It can make better decisions if it analyzes the organization's service products as to complexity and variability. Complexity is determined by the number of steps required to perform the service. Variability reflects the amount of diversity allowed in each step of service provision. In a highly variable service, every step in performing the service may be unique, whereas in cases of low variability, every performance of the service is standardized.[22] For example, services provided by physicians are both complex and variable. Patient treatment may involve many steps, and the doctor has considerable discretion in shaping the treatment for each individual patient.

An examination of the complete service delivery process, including the number of steps and the number of decisions, enables marketers to plot their service products on a complexity/variability grid, such as the one in Figure 23.3. The position of a service on the grid has implications for its positioning in the market. Furthermore, any alterations in the service delivery process that shift the position of the service on the complexity/variability grid have an impact on the positioning of the service in the marketplace. Table 23.4 details the effects of such changes. When structuring the service delivery system, marketers should explicitly consider the firm's marketing goals and target market.

Promotion

As intangible-dominant products, services are not easily promoted. The intangible is difficult to depict in advertising, whether the medium is print, television, or radio. Service advertising should thus emphasize tangible cues that will help consumers understand and evaluate the service. For example, as illustrated in Figure 23.4, airlines frequently depict aircraft in their advertising. The cues may be the physical facilities in which the service is performed or some relevant tangible object that symbolizes the service itself.[23] For example, restaurants may stress their physical facilities—clean, elegant, casual, and so on—to provide cues

as to the quality or nature of the service. Insurance firms, such as Allstate Insurance Co. and Travelers Co., use objects as symbols to help consumers understand their services. Outstretched hands ("You're in good hands with Allstate") symbolize security, and the "Travelers Umbrella" suggests the protection Travelers' insurance plans provide. Service providers may also focus on the characteristics they believe customers want from their services in advertising. AT&T emphasizes the reliability of its long-distance telephone services, while its competitor Sprint focuses on the quality of its sound.[24]

To be successful, firms must not only maximize the difference between the value of the service to the customer and the cost of providing it; they must also design the service with employees in mind. Contact personnel are critical to the perception of quality service. They must be provided with sufficient tools and knowledge to furnish the type of service that the customer desires. Because service industries are information-driven, they can substitute knowledgeable, highly trained personnel for the capital assets used in more product-oriented businesses.[25]

Personal selling is potentially powerful in services because this form of promotion lets consumers and salespeople interact. When consumers enter into a service transaction, they must, as a general rule, interact with service firm employees. Customer contact personnel can be trained to use this opportunity to reduce customer uncertainty, give reassurance, reduce dissonance, and promote the reputation of the organization.[26] Once again, this emphasizes the importance of properly managing contact personnel.

Although consumer service firms have the opportunity to interact with actual customers and those potential customers who contact them, they have little opportunity to go out into the field and solicit business from all potential consumers. The very large number of potential customers and the high cost per sales call rule out such efforts. On the other hand, marketers of business-to-business services, like the marketers of business-to-business goods, are dealing with a much more limited target market and may find personal selling the most effective way of reaching customers.

Sales promotions, such as contests, are feasible for service firms, but other types of promotions are more difficult to implement. How do you display a service? How do you give a free sample without giving away the whole service? A complimentary visit to a health club or a free skiing lesson could possibly be considered a free sample to entice a consumer into purchasing a membership or taking lessons. Some banks have sponsored contests with prizes such as mortgages that the winner does not have to repay or credit cards for which the winner does not have to pay the balance for a year. The role of publicity and the implementation of a publicity campaign do not differ significantly in the goods and service sectors.

Consumers tend to value word-of-mouth communications more than company-sponsored communications. This preference is probably true for all products but especially for services because they are experiential in nature. For this reason, service firms should attempt to stimulate word-of-mouth communications.[27] They can do so by encouraging consumers to tell their friends about satisfactory performance. Many firms, for instance, prominently display signs urging customers to tell their friends if they like the service and to tell the firm if they do not. Some service providers, such as hair stylists, give their regular customers discounts or free services for encouraging friends to come in for a haircut. Word of mouth can be simulated through communications messages that feature a testimonial—for example, television advertisements showing consumers who vouch for the benefits of a service a particular firm offers.

One final note should be made in regard to service promotion. The promotional activities of most professional service providers, such as doctors, lawyers, and CPAs, are severely limited. Until recently, many professionals were prohibited by law or trade associations from advertising. Although these restrictions have now been lifted, there are still many obstacles to be overcome. Not used to

Table 23.4

Effects of Shifting Positions on the Complexity/Variability Grid

Downshifting Complexity/Variability	Upshifting Complexity/Variability
Standardizes the service	Increases costs
Requires strict operating controls	Indicates higher-margin/lower-volume strategy
Generally widens potential market	Personalizes the service
Lowers costs	Generally narrows potential market
Indicates lower-margin/higher-volume strategy	Makes quality more difficult to control
Can alienate existing markets	

Source: Adapted from G. Lynn Shostack, 1985 American Marketing Association Faculty Consortium on Services Marketing, Texas A&M University, July 7–11, 1985.

seeing professionals advertise, consumers may reject advertisements for those who do. Furthermore, professionals are not familiar with advertising and consequently do not always develop advertisements appropriate for their services. Increasingly, lawyers are being forced to consider advertising because many potential clients do not know that they need legal services, there is an oversupply of lawyers, and there are more franchised law firms in shopping centers, causing a distinct change in the competition. Consumers want more information about legal services, and lawyers have a very poor public image.[28] On the other hand, physicians are more skeptical of the impact of advertising on their image and business. Many physicians are attempting to expand their customer base by promoting extended office hours, making house calls, consulting by telephone, and opening more offices.[29] Despite the trend toward professional services advertising, the professions themselves exert pressure on their members not to advertise or promote because such activities are still viewed as highly unprofessional.

Price

Price plays both an economic and a psychological role in the service sector, just as it does with physical goods. However, the psychological role of price in respect to services is magnified somewhat because consumers must rely on price as the sole indicator of service quality when other quality indicators are absent. In its economic role, price determines revenue and influences profits.

Services may also be bundled together and then sold for a single price. Service bundling is a practical strategy because in many types of services there is a high ratio of fixed to variable costs and high cost sharing among service offerings. Moreover, the demand for certain services is often interdependent. For example, BankAmerica Corp. offers a package of banking services—checking and savings accounts and credit lines that become active when customers overdraw their other accounts—called Alpha, which the bank promotes as one-stop shopping for its customers. Linking these services together helped BankAmerica reverse a decline in its deposits.[30] Price bundling may help service marketers cross-sell to their current customers, or acquire new customers. The policy of price leaders also may be used by discounting the price of one service product when the customer purchases another service at full price.[31]

As noted in Table 23.1, service intangibility may complicate the setting of prices. When pricing physical goods, management can look to the cost of production (direct and indirect materials, direct and indirect labor, and overhead) as an indicator of price. It is often difficult, however, to determine the cost of service provision and thus identify a minimum price.

Many services, especially professional services, are situation-specific. Thus neither the service firm nor the consumer knows the extent of the service prior to production and consumption. Once again, because cost is not known beforehand, price is difficult to set. Despite the difficulties in determining cost, many service firms use cost-plus pricing. Others set prices according to the competition or market demand.

Pricing of services can also help smooth fluctuations in demand. Given the perishability of service products, this is an important function. A higher price may be used to deter or offset demand during peak periods, and a lower price may be used to stimulate demand during slack periods. For example, Domino's Pizza, the second-largest pizza chain in the United States, may offer two pizzas for the price of one to minimize sales declines during slow sales months.[32] Airlines rely heavily on price to help smooth their demand, as do many other operations, such as bars and entertainment clubs, movie theaters, resorts, and hotels.

Distribution

Almost by definition, service industries are limited to direct channels of distribution. Many services are produced and consumed simultaneously; in high-contact services in particular, service providers and consumers cannot be separated. In low-contact services, however, service providers may be separated from customers by intermediaries. Dry cleaners, for example, generally maintain strategically located retail stores as drop-off centers, and these stores may be independent or corporate-owned. Consumers go to the retail store to initiate and terminate service, but the actual service may be performed at a different location. The separation is possible because the service is directed toward the consumer's physical possessions, and the consumer is not required to be present during delivery.

Other service industries are developing unique ways to distribute their services. To make it more convenient for consumers to obtain their services airlines, car rental companies, and hotels have long been using intermediaries: travel agencies. In financial services marketing, the two most important strategic concerns are the application of technology and the use of electronic product delivery channels—such as automatic teller machines (ATMs) and electronic funds transfer systems—to provide customers with financial services in a more widespread and convenient manner.[33] Consumers no longer must go to their bank for routine transactions; they can now receive service from the closest ATM. Bank credit cards have enabled banks to extend their credit services to consumers over widely dispersed geographic areas through a nationwide network of intermediaries, namely, the retail merchants who assist consumers in applying for and using the cards.

Strategic Considerations

In developing marketing strategies, the marketer must first understand what benefits the customer wants, how the marketer is perceived relative to the competition, and what services consumers buy.[34] In other words, the marketer must develop the right service for the right people at the right price and at the right place. The marketer must remember to communicate with consumers so that they are aware of the need-satisfying services available to them. In Figure 23.5, American Airlines communicates with its customers about its services.

One of the unique challenges service marketers face is matching supply and demand. We have seen that price can be used to help smooth demand for a service. There are other ways, too, that marketers can alter the marketing mix to deal with the problem of fluctuating demand. Through price incentives, advertising, and other promotional efforts, marketers can remind consumers of busy

times and encourage them to come for service during slack periods. Additionally, the product itself can be altered to cope with fluctuating demand. Restaurants, for example, may change their menus, vary their lighting and decor, open or close the bar, and add or delete entertainment. A ski resort may install an alpine slide to attract customers during the summer. Finally, distribution can be modified to reflect changes in demand. Theaters have traditionally offered matinees during the weekend, when demand is greater, and some libraries have mobile units that travel to different locations during slack periods.[35]

Before understanding such strategies, service marketers must first grasp the pattern and determinants of demand. Does the level of demand follow a cycle? What are the causes of this cycle? Are the changes random?[36] The need to answer such questions is best illustrated through an example. An attempt to use price decreases to shift demand for public transportation to off-peak periods would most likely fail because of the cause of the cyclical demand for public transportation: employment hours. Employees have little control over working hours and are therefore unable to take advantage of pricing incentives.

Nonbusiness Marketing

Remember that earlier we broadly defined marketing as a set of individual and organizational activities aimed at facilitating and expediting satisfying exchanges in a dynamic environment through the creation, distribution, promotion, and pricing of goods, services, and ideas. Most of the previously discussed concepts and approaches to managing marketing activities also apply to nonbusiness situations. Of special relevance is the material offered in the first half of this chapter because many nonbusiness organizations provide services.

Nonbusiness marketing includes marketing activities conducted by individuals and organizations to achieve some goal other than ordinary business goals of profit, market share, or return on investment. Nonbusiness marketing can be divided into two categories: nonprofit-organization marketing and social marketing. Nonprofit-organization marketing is the application of marketing concepts and techniques to organizations such as hospitals and colleges. Social marketing is the development of programs designed to influence the acceptability of social ideas, such as contributing to a foundation for AIDS research or getting people to recycle more newspapers, plastics, and aluminum.[37] In Figure 23.6, the Ontario Head Injury Association encourages motorcyclists to wear helmets.

As discussed in Chapter 1, an exchange situation exists when individuals, groups, or organizations possess something that they are willing to give up in an exchange. In nonbusiness marketing, the objects of the exchange may not be specified in financial terms. Usually, such exchanges are facilitated through **negotiation** (mutual discussion or communication of terms and methods) and **persuasion** (convincing and prevailing upon by argument). Often negotiation and persuasion are conducted without reference to or awareness of the role that marketing plays in transactions. We are concerned with nonbusiness performance of marketing activities, whether the exchange is consummated or not.

In the rest of this chapter, we first examine the concept of nonbusiness marketing to determine how it differs from marketing activities in business organizations. Next we explore the overall objectives of nonbusiness organizations, their marketing objectives, and the development of their marketing strategies. We close the discussion by illustrating how controlling marketing activities can promote marketing awareness in a nonbusiness organization.

Figure 23.6

Social Marketing

In this example of a social marketing activity, the Ontario Head Injury Association uses this advertisement to encourage motorcyclists to wear helmets.

Source: Art Director, Wade Koniakowsky; Writer, Bob Kevsletter; Photographer, Chris Wimpey; Creative Directors, John Vitro and John Robertson.

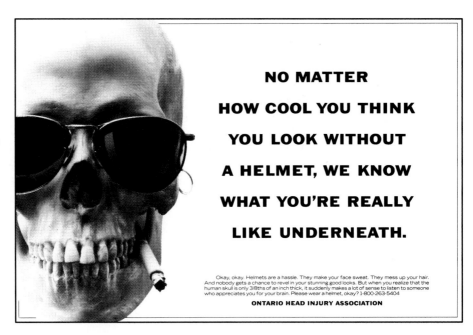

NO MATTER HOW COOL YOU THINK YOU LOOK WITHOUT A HELMET, WE KNOW WHAT YOU'RE REALLY LIKE UNDERNEATH.

Okay, okay. Helmets are a hassle. They make your face sweat. They mess up your hair. And nobody gets a chance to revel in your stunning good looks. But when you realize that the human skull is only 3/8ths of an inch thick, it suddenly makes a lot of sense to listen to someone who appreciates you for your brain. Please wear a helmet, okay? 1-800-263-5404

ONTARIO HEAD INJURY ASSOCIATION

Why Is Nonbusiness Marketing Different?

Many nonbusiness organizations strive for effective marketing activities. Charitable organizations and supporters of social causes are major nonbusiness marketers in this country. Political parties, unions, religious sects, and fraternal organizations also perform marketing activities, yet they are not considered businesses. Whereas the chief beneficiary of a business enterprise is whoever owns or holds stock in it, in theory the only beneficiaries of a nonbusiness organization are its clients, its members, or the public at large.

Nonbusinesses have a greater opportunity for creativity than most business organizations, but trustees or board members of nonbusinesses are likely to have trouble judging performance when services can be provided only by trained professionals. It is harder for administrators to evaluate the performance of doctors, professors, or social workers than it is for sales managers to evaluate the performance of salespersons in a for-profit organization.

Another way in which nonbusiness marketing differs from for-profit marketing is that nonbusiness is sometimes quite controversial. Nonbusiness organizations such as Greenpeace, the National Rifle Association, and the National Organization for Women spend lavishly on lobbying efforts to persuade Congress, the White House, and even the courts to support their interests, in part because acceptance of their aims by all of society is not always guaranteed. However, marketing as a field of study does not attempt to state what an organization's goals should be or to debate the issue of nonbusiness versus business goals. Marketing only attempts to provide a body of knowledge and concepts to help further an organization's goals. Individuals must decide whether they approve or disapprove of a particular organization's goal orientation. Most marketers would agree that profit and consumer satisfaction are appropriate goals for business enterprises, but there probably would be considerable disagreement about the goals of a controversial nonbusiness organization.

Nonbusiness Marketing Objectives

The basic aim of nonbusiness organizations is to obtain a desired response from a target market. The response could be a change in values, a financial contribution, the donation of services, or some other type of exchange. Nonbusiness marketing objectives are shaped by the nature of the exchange and the goals of the organization. For example, the Easter Seal telethon has raised more than $200 million since its inception in 1972; the telethon is the charity's largest annual fund-raising event. Telethons have three specific marketing objectives: (1) to raise funds to support programs, (2) to plead a case in behalf of disabled people, and (3) to inform the public about the organization's programs and services. Tactically, telethons have received support by presenting quality programs and services; generating extensive grassroots support; portraying disabled people in a positive and dignified way; developing national, regional, and local support; and providing quality entertainment.[38] Figure 23.7 illustrates how the exchanges and the purpose of the organization can influence marketing objectives. (These objectives are used as examples and may or may not apply to specific organizations.)

Figure 23.7

Examples of Marketing Objectives for Different Types of Exchanges

Source: Philip Kotler, *Marketing for Nonprofit Organizations,* 2nd ed., © 1982, p. 38. Adapted by permission of Prentice-Hall, Inc., Englewood Cliffs, N.J.

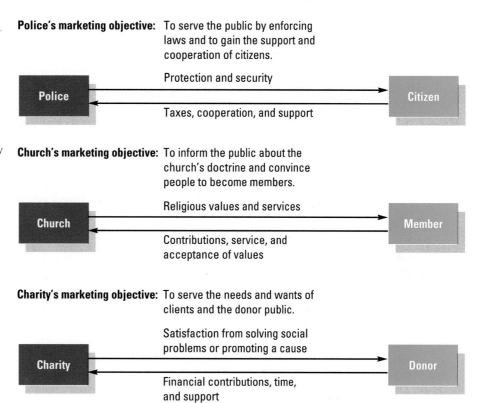

Police's marketing objective: To serve the public by enforcing laws and to gain the support and cooperation of citizens.

Police → Protection and security → Citizen
Police ← Taxes, cooperation, and support ← Citizen

Church's marketing objective: To inform the public about the church's doctrine and convince people to become members.

Church → Religious values and services → Member
Church ← Contributions, service, and acceptance of values ← Member

Charity's marketing objective: To serve the needs and wants of clients and the donor public.

Charity → Satisfaction from solving social problems or promoting a cause → Donor
Charity ← Financial contributions, time, and support ← Donor

Nonbusiness marketing objectives should state the rationale for an organization's existence. An organization that defines its marketing objective as providing a product can be left without a purpose if the product becomes obsolete. However, serving and adapting to the perceived needs and wants of a target public, or market, enhances an organization's chance to survive and achieve its goals.

Developing Nonbusiness Marketing Strategies

Nonbusiness organizations must also develop marketing strategies by defining and analyzing a target market and creating and maintaining a marketing mix that appeals to that market.

Target Markets   We must revise the concept of target markets slightly to apply it to nonbusiness organizations. Whereas a business is supposed to have target groups that are potential purchasers of its product, a nonbusiness organization may attempt to serve many diverse groups. For our purposes, a **target public** is broadly defined as a collective of individuals who have an interest in or concern about an organization, a product, or a social cause. The terms *target market* and *target public* are difficult to distinguish for many nonbusiness organizations. The target public of the Partnership for a Drug Free America is parents, adults, and concerned teenagers. However, the target market for the organization's advertisements is potential and current drug users. When an organization is concerned about changing values or obtaining a response from the public, it views the public as a market.[39]

In nonbusiness organizations, direct consumers of the product are called **client publics** and indirect consumers are called **general publics**.[40] For example, the client public for a university is its student body, and its general public includes parents, alumni, and trustees. The client public usually receives most of the attention when an organization develops a marketing strategy. The techniques and approaches to segmenting and defining target markets discussed in Chapter 4 apply also to nonbusiness target markets.

Developing a Marketing Mix   A marketing mix strategy limits alternatives and directs marketing activities toward achieving organizational goals. The strategy should outline or develop a blueprint for making decisions about product, distribution, promotion, and price. These decision variables should be blended to serve the target market.

In tackling the product variable, nonbusiness organizations deal more often with ideas and services than with goods. Problems may evolve when an organization fails to define what is being provided. What product does the Peace Corps provide? Its services include vocational training, health services, nutritional assistance, and community development. It also markets the ideas of international cooperation and the implementation of U.S. foreign policy. The Peace Corps' product is more difficult to define than the average business product. As indicated in the first part of this chapter, services are intangible and therefore need special marketing efforts. The marketing of ideas and concepts is likewise more abstract than the marketing of tangibles, and it requires much effort to present benefits.

Because most nonbusiness products are ideas and services, distribution decisions relate to how these ideas and services will be made available to clients. If the product is an idea, selecting the right media (the promotional strategy) to communicate the idea will facilitate distribution. The availability of services is closely related to product decisions. By nature, services consist of assistance, convenience, and availability. Availability is part of the total service. For example, making a product such as health services available calls for knowledge of such retailing concepts as site location analysis.

Developing a channel of distribution to coordinate and facilitate the flow of nonbusiness products to clients is a necessary task, but in a nonbusiness setting the traditional concept of the marketing channel may need to be reviewed. The independent wholesalers available to a business enterprise do not exist in most nonbusiness situations. Instead, a very short channel—nonbusiness organization to client—is prevalent because production and consumption of ideas and services are often simultaneous.

Making promotional decisions may be the first sign that nonbusiness organizations are performing marketing activities. Nonbusiness organizations use advertising and publicity to communicate with clients and the public. Direct mail remains the primary means of fund raising for social services such as those provided by the Red Cross and Special Olympics. In addition to direct mail, the Special Olympics uses telephone solicitation and television advertising.[41] Personal selling is also used by many nonbusiness organizations, although it may be called something else. Churches and charities rely on personal selling when they send volunteers to recruit new members or request donations. The U.S. Army uses personal selling when its recruiting officers attempt to convince men and women to enlist. Special events to obtain funds, communicate ideas, or provide services are sales promotion activities. Contests, entertainment, and prizes offered to attract donations resemble the sales promotion activities of business enterprises. Amnesty International, for example, has held worldwide concert tours, featuring artists such as Sting and Phil Collins, to raise funds and increase public awareness of political prisoners around the world.

The number of advertising agencies that are donating their time for public service announcements (PSAs) is increasing, and the quality of print PSAs is improving notably. Nonprofit groups are becoming increasingly interested in the impact of advertising on their organizations. Inside Marketing describes how the Partnership for a Drug Free America has been highly successful in using donated media time to disseminate its messages.

Although product and promotion techniques might require only slight modification when applied to nonbusiness organizations, pricing is generally quite different and the decision making more complex. The different pricing concepts that the nonbusiness organization faces include pricing in user and donor markets. There are two types of monetary pricing: *fixed* and *variable*. Admission fees to a zoo represent a fixed approach to pricing, whereas zoo fund-raising activities that lead to a donation represent a variable pricing structure.[42]

The broadest definition of price (valuation) must be used to develop nonbusiness marketing strategies. Financial price, an exact dollar value, may or may not be charged for a nonbusiness product. Economists recognize the giving up of alternatives as a cost. **Opportunity cost** is the value of the benefit that is given up by selecting one alternative rather than another. This traditional economic view of price means that if a nonbusiness organization can convince someone to donate time to a cause or to change his or her behavior, then the alternatives given up are a cost to (or a price paid by) the individual. Volunteers who answer phones for a university counseling service or suicide hotline, for example, give up the time they could have spent studying or doing other things, and the income they might have earned from working at a business organization.

For other nonbusiness organizations, financial price is an important part of the marketing mix. Nonbusiness organizations today are raising money by increasing the prices of their services or starting to charge for services if they have not done so before. They are using marketing research to determine what kinds of products people will pay for. Pricing strategies of nonbusiness organizations often stress public and client welfare over equalization of costs and revenues. If additional funds are needed to cover costs, then donations, contributions, or grants may be solicited.

Controlling Nonbusiness Marketing Activities

Control is designed to identify what activities have occurred in conformity with the marketing strategy and to take corrective action where any deviations are found. The purpose of control is not only to point out errors and mistakes, but to revise organizational goals and marketing objectives as necessary. One way to

Figure 23.8

Measuring Advertising Effectiveness

The Alaska Visitors Association can measure the success of this advertisement by monitoring the number of information requests received.

Source: The Alaska Visitors Association.

measure the effectiveness of the advertisement in Figure 23.8 is to monitor the number of requests for information.

Because of federal and state spending cuts, the need to encourage public support or donations is increasingly important. Many potential contributors decide which charities to support based on the amount of money actually used in charitable programs. Charities are more aggressively examining their own performance and effectiveness. For example, the Salvation Army contributes to the needy 86 cents out of every dollar it receives; its employees are basically volunteers who work for almost nothing. Charities are making internal changes to increase their effectiveness, and many are hiring professional managers to help with strategic planning in developing short-term and long-range goals.

To control nonbusiness marketing activities, managers must make a proper inventory of activities performed and prepare to adjust or correct deviations from standards. Knowing where and how to look for deviations and knowing what types of deviations to expect are especially important in nonbusiness situations. Because nonbusiness marketing activities may not be perceived as marketing, managers must clearly define what activity is being examined and how it should function.

It may be difficult to control nonbusiness marketing activities because it is often hard to determine whether goals are being achieved. A mental health center that wants to inform community members of its services may not be able to find out whether it is communicating with persons who need assistance. Surveying to discover the percentage of the population that is aware of a mental health program can show whether the awareness objective has been achieved, but it fails to indicate what percentage of the persons with mental health problems has been assisted. The detection and correction of deviations from standards is certainly a major purpose of control, but standards must support

Partnership for a Drug Free America

IN A RECENT SURVEY of American teenagers, 92 percent of those questioned said they had seen a commercial in which an egg is cracked into a hot frying pan and, as the egg fries and turns brown, a voice-over warns, "This is your brain on drugs." What is unusual about this commercial and many other powerful television and radio spots and print advertisements like it, is that the cost of development, production, and air time is donated as a public service. They are all part of an intensive antidrug campaign organized by the Partnership for a Drug Free America, a coalition of advertisers, media representatives, and drug experts. The campaign, acknowledged by many as the biggest pro bono advertising crusade since the World War II War Bond campaign, strives to get and keep American youngsters off drugs by deglamorizing the use of marijuana, cocaine, and crack.

The Partnership, created in 1986, is the concept of advertiser Phillip Joanou. At that time, cocaine enjoyed widespread use among young, upper-middle-class professionals, and the Partnership's first goal was to target those trendsetters and convince them that drug use is stupid, not glamorous. Soliciting free advertising time from the media and persuading some of the most creative people in advertising to work on the project were the first two orders of business. A 25-person creative committee evaluated over 270 submissions from volunteers, looking for high-quality hard-hitting messages. Those they finally accepted portrayed, in dramatic and sometimes gruesome fashion, images of death, dependency, mental and physical deterioration, and wasted lives. In one television spot, a narrator, already dead from a cocaine overdose, sings a lullaby to his daughter from his coffin; one print advertisement shows a young woman with a white gun, symbolizing cocaine, up her nose.

Since the first commercials aired, the Partnership has used over $800 million of donated media time and space, which translates into about $1 million worth of antidrug advertising going out to the public daily in the forms of 32 television commercials, 25 radio spots, and 80 newspaper and magazine advertisements. Functioning as a nonprofit organization

dependent on donated time and services, the Partnership for a Drug Free America now ranks second in advertising expenditure only to McDonald's and spends five times as much as Coca-Cola.

From recent survey evidence, it appears that the campaign is influencing negative attitudes toward drug use. Eighty-three percent of adults questioned said they "don't like hanging around drug users," up from 73 percent the year the Partnership's advertisements debuted. Partnership chairman James Burke contends that the group's efforts are working so well because they coincide with the beginning of a trend away from drug use among those in the target market.

The Partnership views as its two ongoing goals convincing the media of the continued importance of its involvement in developing effective advertising, and creating fresh advertising messages. Immediate plans include targeting hard-core drug users (a group largely ignored until now), increasing street-level promotional efforts, such as posters on street corners, and placing more advertisements in nontraditional media, such as movie theaters and videocassettes. Members of the Partnership are encouraged by recent contributions. Yellow Pages publishers pledged more than $41 million in advertising space for antidrug messages, and in a particularly poignant move, an independent video distributor agreed to place antidrug messages on the company's films, beginning with *Wired*, the biography of comedian John Belushi, who died of a drug overdose.

Sources: Joshua Levine, "Don't Fry Your Brain," *Forbes*, Feb. 4, 1991, pp. 116–117; Clifford R. Medney, "For Social Cause Advertising Try 'Disenfranchise Marketing,' " *Advertising Age*, June 4, 1990, p. 24; Steven W. Colford, "Anti-Drug Victory," *Advertising Age*, Apr. 30, 1990, p. 22; Steven W. Colford, "Anti-Drug Boost," *Advertising Age*, Nov. 24, 1989, p. 2; Debra Gersh, "Ads Help in Fight Against Drugs," *Editor & Publisher*, July 30, 1988, p. 24; Barbara Lippert, "Celebrities Speak Out Against Drugs," *Adweek's Marketing Week*, Aug. 31, 1987, p. 21; and Stewart Alter, "Ad, Media Group Starts Hard-Hitting War on Drugs," *Advertising Age*, Mar. 9, 1987, pp. 2, 96.

the organization's overall goals. Managers can refine goals by examining the results that are being achieved and analyzing the ramifications of those results.

Techniques for controlling overall marketing performance must be compatible with the nature of an organization's operations. Obviously, it is necessary to control the marketing budget in most nonbusiness organizations, but budgetary control is not tied to profit-and-loss standards; responsible management of funds is the objective. Central control responsibility can facilitate orderly, efficient administration and planning. For example, Illinois Wesleyan University evaluates graduating students' progress to control and improve the quality of the educational product. The audit phase relies on questionnaires sent to students and their employers after graduation. The employer completes a questionnaire to indicate the student's progress; the student completes a questionnaire to indicate what additional concepts or skills were needed to perform duties. In addition, a number of faculty members interview certain employers and students to obtain information for control purposes. Results of the audit are used to develop corrective action if university standards have not been met. Corrective action might include an evaluation of the deficiency and a revision of the curriculum.

Summary

Services are intangible-dominant products that cannot be physically possessed—the result of applying human or mechanical efforts to people or objects. They are a growing part of the U.S. economy. Services have four distinguishing characteristics: intangibility, inseparability of production and consumption, perishability, and heterogeneity. Because services include a diverse group of industries, classification schemes are used to help marketers analyze their products and develop the most appropriate marketing mix. Services can be viewed as to type of market, degree of labor-intensiveness, degree of customer contact, skill of the service provider, and goal of the service provider.

When developing a marketing mix for services, several aspects deserve special consideration. Regarding product, service offerings are often difficult for consumers to understand and evaluate. The tangibles associated with a service may be the only visible aspect of the service, and marketers must manage these scarce tangibles with care. Because services are often viewed in terms of the providers, service firms must carefully select, train, motivate, and control employees. Service marketers are selling long-term relationships as well as performance.

Promoting services is problematic because of their intangibility. Advertising should stress the tangibles associated with the service or use some relevant tangible object. Customer contact personnel should be considered an important secondary audience for advertising. Personal selling is very powerful in service firms because customers must interact with personnel; some forms of sales promotion, however, such as displays and free samples, are difficult to implement. The final component of the promotion mix, publicity, is vital to many service firms. Because customers value word-of-mouth communications, messages should attempt to stimulate or simulate word of mouth. Many professional service providers, however, are severely restricted in their use of promotional activities.

Price plays three major roles in service firms. It plays a psychological role by indicating quality and an economic role by determining revenues. Price is also a way to help smooth fluctuations in demand.

Service distribution channels are typically direct because of simultaneous production and consumption. However, innovative approaches such as drop-off centers, intermediaries, and electronic distribution are being developed.

Fluctuating demand is a major problem for most service firms. Marketing strategies (product, price, promotion, and distribution), as well as nonmarketing strategies (primarily internal, employee-based actions), can be used to deal with the problem. Before attempting to undertake any such strategies, however, service marketers must understand the patterns and determinants of demand.

Nonbusiness marketing includes marketing activities conducted by individuals and organizations to achieve goals other than normal business goals. Nonbusiness marketing uses most concepts and approaches applied to business situations.

The chief beneficiary of a business enterprise is whoever owns or holds stock in the business, but the beneficiary of a nonbusiness enterprise should be its clients, its members, or its public at large. The goals of a nonbusiness organization reflect its unique philosophy or mission. Some nonbusiness organizations have very controversial goals, but many organizations exist to further generally accepted social causes.

The marketing objective of nonbusiness organizations is to obtain a desired response from a target market. Developing a nonbusiness marketing strategy consists of defining and analyzing a target market and creating and maintaining a marketing mix. In nonbusiness marketing, the product is usually an idea or service. Distribution is not involved as much with the movement of goods as with the communication of ideas and the delivery of services, which results in a very short marketing channel. Promotion is very important in nonbusiness marketing; personal selling, sales promotion, advertising, and publicity are all used to communicate ideas and inform people about services. Price is more difficult to define in nonbusiness marketing because of opportunity costs and the difficulty of quantifying the values exchanged.

It is important to control nonbusiness marketing strategies. Control is designed to identify what activities have occurred in conformity with marketing strategy and to take corrective actions where deviations are found. The standards against which performance is measured must support the nonbusiness organization's overall goals.

Important Terms

Intangibility
Search qualities
Experience qualities
Credence qualities
Inseparability
Perishability
Heterogeneity

Nonbusiness marketing
Negotiation
Persuasion
Target public
Client publics
General publics
Opportunity cost

Discussion and Review Questions

1. Identify and discuss the distinguishing characteristics of services. What problems do these characteristics present to marketers?
2. What is the significance of "tangibles" in service industries?
3. Analyze a house-cleaning service in terms of the five classification schemes, and discuss the implications for marketing mix development.

4. How do search, experience, and credence qualities affect the way consumers view and evaluate services?

5. Discuss the role of promotion in services marketing.

6. Analyze the demand for dry cleaning, and discuss ways to cope with fluctuating demand.

7. Compare and contrast the controversial aspects of nonbusiness versus business marketing.

8. Relate the concepts of product, distribution, promotion, and price to a marketing strategy aimed at preventing drug abuse.

9. What are the differences among clients, publics, and consumers? What is the difference between a target public and a target market?

10. What is the function of control in a nonbusiness marketing strategy?

11. Discuss the development of a marketing strategy for a university. What marketing decisions should be made in developing this strategy?

Cases

23.1 Holiday Corporation Looks to "Promus" of Brighter Future

In 1989, the Holiday Corporation announced the sale of its entire Holiday Inn hotel chain to Bass PLC of London, a British brewing and hospitality company. This $2.25 billion sale followed a 1987 deal in which Holiday sold its international Holiday Inns to Bass.

The sale to Bass included all the Holiday Inns worldwide, Crowne Plaza Hotels, Holiday Inn University at Olive Branch, Mississippi, the Holidex reservation system, the Priority Club frequent-guest program, the Holiday Inn headquarters building in Memphis, Tennessee, and several other companies around the world. One condition of this sale was that Holiday drop its association with the ownership and management of the Holiday Inn hotel chain. The Holiday Corporation therefore assumed a new name, The Promus Companies. However, the new company retained the senior management team of the Holiday Corporation.

The sale made Bass the largest hotel company in the world in number of rooms (a title formerly held by Holiday), and second only to Best Western in the number of hotels. After the sale, Promus was left with four remaining businesses—Embassy Suites, Inc., Hampton Inns, Inc., Homewood Suites Equity Development Corp., and Harrah's hotels and casinos. After the sale, Promus became the world's thirteenth-largest hotel company in number of rooms and fourteenth in number of hotels.

Promus' five-year strategic plan includes a very aggressive expansion program for its 94 Embassy Suites, 240 Hampton Inns, and 10 Homewood Suites. Hampton Inns alone will grow by 50 units a year through 1993. However, now that the excessive real estate holdings have been sold along with Holiday Inn, the strategy specifically excludes the ownership of real estate assets. In this way, Promus can focus on being a developer, manager, and franchiser of hotels without the complications of owning the real estate.

Each of Promus's retained businesses operates in a separate and distinct market. Originally intended to compete in the limited-service, upper-economy segment against hotels such as La Quinta, Days Inn, and Comfort Inn, Hampton Inns is now positioned head-on against Holiday Inn and Marriott's Courtyard chain. With its "100% Satisfaction Guarantee" policy of a free room for any dissatisfied customer, Hampton hopes to differentiate itself from the competition. In a recent *Consumer Reports* survey, these hotels bested every economy and moderately priced chain for cleanliness of rooms and quality of staff. Promus will count on high-quality service to stimulate strong customer demand and increase occupancy rates in a slow-growth segment.

Embassy Suites, consisting almost entirely of two-room units, is positioned in the lower upscale segment against Crowne Plaza (now owned by Bass PLC), Hilton, Sheraton, and Ramada. Homewood Suites, a recent addition to the Promus family, is targeted at the extended-stay traveler who lodges for at least five nights. Homewood's only significant competition is Marriott's Residence Inns.

Although a great deal of Promus's business is in the hotel sector, a large part of its future lies in the gaming industry. Harrah's, the world's premier casino/hotel firm, is the only such company with properties in each of the five major U.S. gaming markets—Atlantic City, New Jersey, and Las Vegas, Reno, Lake Tahoe, and Laughlin, Nevada. Harrah's competitors include Caesar's Palace, Circus Circus, and the MGM Grand. Developments are underway that should help Harrah's achieve above-average growth for the next five years. Each of the five Harrah's hotels and casinos has plans to expand the number of rooms, the size of the casinos, and the number of restaurants. Despite these plans for expansion, industry experts believe that Promus wants to sell Harrah's in Reno and Lake Tahoe (possibly to Asian buyers for $550 million), but continue to manage the properties for a fee. Such a sale would help reduce Promus's current $1 billion debt. Basing his confidence in the company on the enthusiasm of its new CEO Michael Rose, one prominent investment advisor predicts that over the next few years, each segment of Promus will show strong growth.[43]

Questions for Discussion

1. What marketing problems did Holiday Corporation have before the sale of Holiday Inns to Bass PLC of London?
2. What marketing segmentation issues exist in positioning Embassy Suites, Hampton Inns, Homewood Suites, and Harrah's hotels and casinos?
3. Discuss the merits of being the number-one hotel in the world in number of rooms (Bass) versus the thirteenth-largest hotel company in number of rooms (Promus). How might this relative size difference affect service quality?

23.2   Kinder-Care: More Than Just Kids' Stuff

In 1965, 25 percent of the women working in the United States had children under six years old. To care for them, parents usually called on a family member or someone else they knew. By 1985, however, 56 percent of working women had to find supervision for children under age six, and analysts predict that by 1995, two out of three preschoolers will have mothers in the work force. Meeting these growing needs has transformed an infant day care business with a baby-sitter image into a giant industry.

With 1,250 centers in 40 states and Canada, Kinder-Care is the nation's oldest and largest child care company. In 1969, Kinder-Care's founders gave their firm a head start in the child care industry by anticipating early on the needs of an increasing number of two-career families. In neighborhood centers, children aged six weeks to 12 years get basic care and intellectual, physical, and social development for about $75 a week. All of Kinder-Care's age-specific programs, from Look at Me for toddlers to Klubmates, an after-school program for school-age children, are the company's registered trademarks. Although educators often question the quality of a uniform national curriculum that teaches the letter *B* to every three-year-old in every Kinder-Care center on the first Monday in February, about 130,000 children a day attend.

The company is organized into divisions by region and district, with a director and assistant director for each individual center. All managers participate in periodic training, and all personnel go through an internal certification procedure. Executives at corporate headquarters in Montgomery, Alabama, direct marketing for Kinder-Cares all over the country, budgeting about $5 million a year for advertising alone. Positioning itself as the quality child care leader, the company's theme is "Child Care Parents Trust." Local radio, television, and newspaper advertisements emphasize age-appropriate learning and dedication to providing a safe environment and well-trained caregivers. The firm also gets its message out through direct mailings that entice parents to enroll their children with offers of free trial visits and introductory discounts. To further strengthen its already powerful brand identity, Kinder-Care enters into promotions with well-known products like Cheerios, Jif peanut butter, Crest toothpaste, and Pampers disposable diapers.

Despite intense marketing efforts and increasing demand for child care, Kinder-Care recently recorded losses of $85.5 million and defaulted on some of its long-term debt. Company executives blame rising costs and higher insurance expenses for some of their difficulties. They also point to industrywide problems, including too many firms targeting the same group, competition from public school programs, and a worsening economy. Industry analysts, however, fault parent company Kinder-Care, Inc., for overexpanding into unrelated businesses, such as savings and loans and a chain of shoe stores. Not only did this expansion lead to debt, say the experts, but it distracted the company from doing what it does best, providing quality child care.

Kinder-Care's executives believe that the industry still has tremendous potential for growth and are taking action to get their firm back on track. To concentrate on day care, Kinder-Care Learning Centers separated from its parent company, quickly closed down 43 nonprofitable centers, and spent about $20 million renovating over 400 others. By providing higher wages, better benefits, and incentive plans to reward center managers and by strengthening its training programs, Kinder-Care hopes to upgrade the quality of its personnel. An improved computerized network and centralized maintenance frees caregivers from paperwork and other chores that take precious time away from the children. Efforts to enhance quality are already showing results. In three years, Kinder-Care improved its retention record from 28.6 weeks per child to 43 weeks.

Recognizing that a growing number of businesses want to offer child care as an employee benefit, Kinder-Care created a separate corporate division, Kinder-Care at Work. Working with companies in two ways, this unit operates on-site centers or enters into discount agreements so that employees get lower-than-usual rates when they bring children to a center located away from the workplace. Among others, Kinder-Care manages on-site day care for Walt Disney World, Citicorp, and LEGO Systems. Discounting partners number about 160, including corporate giants like J.C. Penney, AT&T, and Federal Express.

In Charlotte, North Carolina; Baton Rouge, Louisiana; and Minneapolis, Minnesota, Kinder-Care is test-marketing a broader concept of service. Results from consumer focus groups told company executives that many parents would be willing to pay for more help from their day care centers if they could get it. With the advertising theme "Helping America's Busiest Families" and an $8 million budget to support it, the new service provides evening child care, diapers, and baby food, and even takes clothes to the dry cleaners for harried parents. To offer such convenience, the company links up with national marketers like Procter & Gamble and Beech-Nut, who provide Pampers and Special Harvest organic baby food at supermarket prices.

Kinder-Care's continuing struggle to maintain the number-one slot should warn newcomers that operating quality day care services at a profit is no simple task. Informed parents are quick to leave centers with inadequate care and poor management, and the federal government recently tightened child care regulations. Because parents are demanding dependability and safety, many local governments are organizing their own offices to address these issues. Complying with strict requirements is proving too costly for small companies or home care services, allotting more market share to Kinder-Care and its hungry competitors like Discovery Learning Centers and La Petite Academy. Whether or not Kinder-Care can hold on to its position as market leader depends not only on how well it serves customers' needs, but on how well it can market those services to potential day care customers.[44]

Questions for Discussion

1. Using the dimensions in Table 23.2, how would day care services be classified or characterized?
2. How is Kinder-Care changing its target markets to be more successful?
3. What types of marketing mix changes is Kinder-Care making to remain competitive?

Chapter Notes

1. Based on information from Bob Sevier and Catherine Drew, "Precision Prospecting," *Case Currents,* April 1991, pp. 40, 42–44; Elaine Underwood, "Marketing the Halls of Ivy," *Adweek's Marketing Week,* Mar. 18, 1991, p. 26; Sandra Golden, "Sweat the Small Stuff and You'll Come Out Ahead," *AACJC Journal,* February– March 1991, pp. 36–41; Susan Tifft, "Hard Times on the Old Quad," *Time,* Oct. 29, 1990, p. 92; and Archer W. Huneycutt, Patsy B. Lewis, and Elizabeth A. Wibker, "Marketing the University: A Role for Marketing Faculty," *College and University,* Fall 1990, pp. 29–34.
2. Leonard L. Berry and A. Parasuraman, *Marketing Services: Competing Through Quality* (New York: The Free Press, 1991), p. 5.
3. James L. Heskett, "Lessons in the Service Sector," *Harvard Business Review,* March– April 1987, p. 118.
4. David Pottruck, "Building Company Loyalty and Retention Through Direct Marketing," *Journal of Services Marketing,* Fall 1987, p. 56.
5. Valerie A. Zeithaml, A. Parasuraman, and Leonard L. Berry, "Problems and Strategies in Services Marketing," *Journal of Marketing,* Spring 1985, pp. 33–46.

6. Valerie A. Zeithaml, "How Consumer Evaluation Processes Differ Between Goods and Services," in *Marketing of Services,* ed. James H. Donnelly and William R. George (Chicago: American Marketing Association, 1981), pp. 186–190.

7. Leonard L. Berry, Valarie A. Zeithaml, and A. Parasuraman, "Responding to Demand Fluctuations: Key Challenge for Service Businesses," in *AMA Educators Proceedings,* ed. Russell Belk et al. (Chicago: American Marketing Association, 1984), pp. 231–234.

8. Carol F. Surprenant and Michael R. Solomon, "Predictability and Personalization in the Service Encounter," *Journal of Marketing,* April 1987, p. 86.

9. Christopher H. Lovelock, "Classifying Services to Gain Strategic Marketing Insights," *Journal of Marketing,* Summer 1983, p. 15.

10. Christopher H. Lovelock, *Services Marketing,* 2nd ed. (Englewood Cliffs, N.J.: Prentice-Hall, 1991), pp. 55–56.

11. Heskett, pp. 118–126.

12. Leonard L. Berry, "Big Ideas in Services Marketing," *Journal of Services Marketing,* Fall 1987, pp. 5–9.

13. "Seniors Learn About Healthcare from Cartoon Character," *Services Marketing Newsletter,* Winter 1987, p. 2.

14. G. Lynn Shostack, "Breaking Free from Product Marketing," *Journal of Marketing,* April 1977, pp. 73–80.

15. Kevin Kelly, "Greyhound Is Bringing Travelers Down to Earth Again," *Business Week,* June 19, 1989, pp. 52–53.

16. Sak Onkvisit and John J. Shaw, "Service Marketing: Image, Branding, and Competition," *Business Horizons,* January–February 1989, p. 16.

17. Tom Peters, "More Expensive, But Worth It," *U.S. News & World Report,* Feb. 3, 1986, p. 54.

18. Valarie A. Zeithaml, "Consumer Perceptions of Price, Quality, and Value: A Means-End Model and Synthesis of Evidence," *Journal of Marketing,* July 1988, pp. 2–22.

19. Leonard L. Berry, "8 Keys to Top Service at Financial Institutions," *American Banker,* August 1987.

20. A. Parasuraman, Valarie A. Zeithaml, and Leonard L. Berry, "SERVQUAL: A Multiple-Item Scale for Measuring Consumer Perceptions of Service Quality," *Journal of Retailing,* Spring 1988, pp. 12–40.

21. Berry and Parasuraman, p. 16.

22. G. Lynn Shostack, "Service Positioning Through Structural Change," *Journal of Marketing,* January 1987, pp. 34–43.

23. Berry and Parasuraman, pp. 98–101.

24. Mark Lewyn, "AT&T, MCI, Sprint Battle for Business," *USA Today,* July 18, 1989, pp. 1B, 2B.

25. Heskett, pp. 118–125.

26. William R. George and J. Patrick Kelly, "The Promotion and Selling of Services," *Business,* July–September 1983, pp. 14–20.

27. Ibid.

28. Doris C. Van Doren and Louise W. Smith, "Marketing in the Restructured Professional Services Field," *Journal of Services Marketing,* Summer 1987, pp. 69–70.

29. Joyce Jensen and Steve Larson, "Nation's Physicians Adding Healthcare Services, Marketing Their Practices to Attract New Patients," *Modern Healthcare,* July 16, 1987, pp. 49–50.

30. Charles McCoy, "Combat Banking: A Slashing Pursuit of Retail Trade Brings BankAmerica Back," *Wall Street Journal,* Oct. 2, 1989, pp. A1, A4.

31. Joseph P. Guiltinan, "The Price Bundling of Services: A Normative Framework," *Journal of Marketing,* April 1987, p. 74.

32. Raymond Serafin, "Domino's Pizza Takes 'Fresh' Angle," *Advertising Age*, Feb. 29, 1988, p. 34.

33. Nigel A. L. Brooks, "Strategic Issues for Financial Services Marketing," *Journal of Services Marketing*, Summer 1987, p. 65.

34. Yoram Wind, "Financial Services: Increasing Your Marketing Productivity and Profitability," *Journal of Services Marketing*, Fall 1987, p. 8.

35. Lovelock, *Services Marketing*, pp. 279–289.

36. Ibid.

37. J. Whyte, "Organization, Person and Idea Marketing as Exchange," *Quarterly Review of Marketing* (U.K.), January 1985, pp. 25–30.

38. John Garrison, "Telethons—The Positive Story," *Fund Raising Management*, November 1987, pp. 48–52.

39. Philip Kotler, *Marketing for Nonprofit Organizations*, 2nd ed. (Englewood Cliffs, N.J.: Prentice-Hall, 1982), p. 37.

40. Ibid.

41. Eileen Norris, "Direct Marketing: Charities Step Up Solicitations," *Advertising Age*, July 27, 1987, pp. S4, S6.

42. Leyland F. Pitt and Russell Abratt, "Pricing in Non-Profit Organizations—A Framework and Conceptual Overview," *Quarterly Review of Marketing* (U.K.), Spring–Summer 1987, pp. 13–15.

43. Christopher W. L. Hart, "Hampton Inns Guests Satisfied with Satisfaction Guarantee," *Marketing News*, Feb. 4, 1991, p. 7; "Where to Stay?" *Consumer Reports*, September 1990, pp. 576–582; Brian Bremner, "America's Innkeepers Brace for the 90s," *Business Week*, Aug. 13, 1990, pp. 106–107; Gene G. Marcial, "Hotel Rooms with a Rosy View," *Business Week*, Mar. 12, 1990, p. 110; Susan A. Thorp, "Promus Faces Office Squeeze," *(Memphis) Commercial Appeal*, Jan. 31, 1990, pp. B4, B8; Mark Maremont and Chuck Hawkins, "No Time for Tea at Holiday Inns," *Business Week*, Jan. 8, 1990, pp. 38–39; Laura Koss, "Holiday Inns Sold to Bass," *Business Travel News*, Sept. 5, 1989, p. 4; Tom Graves, "Leisure and Hospitality Sizable Part of U.S. Economy," *Industry Surveys*, Mar. 10, 1988, pp. L34–L35; and Holiday Corporation, 1988 Annual Report.

44. Roger Neugebauer, "Status Report #2 on Employer Child Care," *Child Care Information Exchange*, July–August 1991, pp. 5–9; David Kiley, "Kinder-Care Broadens Its Service Line," *Adweek's Marketing Week*, July 29, 1991, p. 7; Deborah L. Cohen, "Kinder-Care Negotiating to Restructure Large Debt," *Education Week*, Jan. 30, 1991, p. 10; Jason Zweig, "Caring for Kinder-Care," *Forbes*, Aug. 20, 1990, p. 108; Cathy Trost, "Marketing-Minded Child-Care Centers Become More Than 9-to-5 Baby Sitters," *Wall Street Journal*, June 18, 1990, p. B1; Jennifer Caspar, "Entrepreneurs Find Day Care Isn't Child's Play," *Washington Post*, June 11, 1990, p. B6; Graham Button, "The Grass Is No Greener," *Forbes*, Apr. 30, 1990, pp. 46, 48; Stephen D. Solomon, "Head of the Class," *Inc.*, March 1990, pp. 76–77, 78, 80, 82–83; and Kinder-Care Learning Centers, 1990 Annual Report.

24 *International Marketing*

OBJECTIVES

- To define the nature of international marketing

- To understand the importance of international marketing intelligence

- To recognize the impact of environmental forces on international marketing efforts

- To become aware of regional trade alliances and markets

- To examine the potential of marketing mix standardization among nations

- To describe adaptation of the international marketing mix when standardization is impossible

- To look at ways of becoming involved in international marketing activities

PARKER
SCHREIBKULTUR IN HÖCHSTER VOLLENDUNG.

In the mid-1980s Parker Pen Company, at the time a Wisconsin firm, sold products in 154 countries, and its marketing executives were eager to design and implement a global strategy. Then-president James Peterson believed that global marketing would be crucial to the survival of the company. Profits were down, and most of the profits were generated by Manpower Temporary Services, a subsidiary. Peterson and his marketing team began production of cheap pens that could compete in the under-$3 market, and they standardized everything associated with Parker products. Worldwide advertising was handled by one agency using a single theme—"Make your mark with a Parker." In addition, advertising spotlighted Parker's new, inexpensive products instead of the quality pens that were the company's trademark.

Difficulties were encountered almost immediately. The manufacturing facilities which produced the new product line repeatedly shut down and the number of defective products soared. In addition, the standardized advertising strategy was so general that it appealed to no one in particular. Profits plummeted, Peterson resigned, and in 1986 Parker Pen was purchased by a group of British investors.

Now based in Newhaven, England, Parker Pen Ltd. is again a profitable company, with a new marketing strategy. Parker's inexpensive pens receive less emphasis, and plans to produce disposable pens have been shelved. Except for the company's Duofold Centennial $312 eighteen-carat gold-nib fountain pen, targeted to a tiny market segment, global advertising has been dropped. The company has worked hard to restore its reputation for quality and reliability. Perceived value, rather than volume, is the focus. Parker pens now hold the number-two position in the very competitive Japanese high-end pen market with a 17 percent market share and are again seen worldwide as high-quality writing instruments.[1]

Photo courtesy of Parker.

I NTERNATIONAL MARKETING is marketing activities that are performed to compete beyond the domestic market. The worldwide marketing operations of the Parker Pen Company provide a good example of how management of international marketing activities requires a grasp of the environmental complexities of foreign countries. In many cases, serving a foreign target market requires more than minor adjustments of marketing strategies.

This chapter looks closely at the unique features of international marketing and at the marketing mix adjustments businesses make when they cross national boundaries. We begin by examining American firms' levels of commitment to and degree of involvement in international marketing. We then consider the importance of international marketing intelligence when a firm is moving beyond its domestic market. Next we focus on the need to understand various environmental forces in international markets and discuss several regional trade alliances and markets. We also analyze marketing mix standardization and adaptation. At the close of the chapter, we describe a number of ways of getting involved in international marketing.

Involvement in International Marketing

Before international marketing could achieve its current level of importance, enterprises with the necessary resources had to develop an interest in expanding their businesses beyond national boundaries. Once interested, marketers engage in international marketing activities at several levels of involvement. Regardless of the level of involvement, however, they must choose either to customize their marketing strategies for different regions of the world or to standardize their marketing strategies for the entire world.

Multinational Involvement

The level of involvement in international marketing covers a wide spectrum, as shown in Figure 24.1. Casual or accidental exporting is the lowest level of commitment. For example, the products of a small medical supplies manufacturer might occasionally be purchased by hospitals or clinics in nearby countries; its products might also be purchased by other countries through an export agent. Active exporting concentrates on selling activities to gain foreign market acceptance of existing products. Full-scale international marketing involvement means that top management recognizes the importance of developing international marketing strategies to achieve the firm's goals. Globalization of markets requires total commitment to international marketing; it embodies the view that the world is a single market.

Globalization Versus Customization of Marketing Strategies

Only full-scale international marketing involvement and globalization of markets represent a full integration of international marketing into strategic market planning. Traditional full-scale international marketing involvement is based on products customized according to cultural, regional, and national differences. In

Casual or accidental exporting | Active exporting | Full-scale international marketing involvement | Globalization of markets

Occasional, unsolicited foreign orders are received. There is no real commitment to international marketing.

This is an attempt to create sales without significant changes in the firm's products and overall operations. An active effort to find foreign markets for existing products is most typical.

Markets across national boundaries are a consideration in the marketing strategy. International marketing activities are seen as a part of overall planning.

Companies try to operate as if the world were one large market, ignoring regional and national differences.

National or domestic orientation ← → Global orientation

Figure 24.1 **Levels of Involvement in International Marketing**   Source: Adapted figure from *International Marketing*, 4th ed., by Vern Terpstra. Copyright © 1987 by The Dryden Press, reproduced by permission of the publisher.

full-scale international marketing, marketing strategies are developed to serve specific target markets. From a practical standpoint, this means that to standardize the marketing mix, the strategy needs to group countries by social, cultural, technological, political, and economic similarities.

In contrast, **globalization** involves developing marketing strategies as though the entire world (or regions of it) were a single entity; a globalized firm markets standardized products in the same way everywhere.[2] For many years, organizations have attempted to globalize the marketing mix as much as possible by employing standardized products, promotion campaigns, prices, and distribution channels for all markets. The economic and competitive payoffs for globalized marketing strategies are certainly great. Brand name, product characteristics, packaging, and labeling are among the easiest marketing mix variables to standardize; media allocation, retail outlets, and price may be more difficult. In the end, the degree of similarity between the various environmental and market conditions determines the feasibility of globalization.

Some companies have moved from customizing or standardizing products for a particular region of the world to offering globally standardized products that are advanced, functional, reliable, and low-priced.[3] Nike, for example, provides a standardized product worldwide. As we stated earlier, a firm committed to globalization develops marketing strategies as if the entire world (or major regions of it) were a single entity. Examples of globalized products are electrical equipment, western American clothing, movies, soft drinks, rock music, cosmetics, and toothpaste. Sony televisions, Levi jeans, and American cigarette brands seem to make year-to-year gains in the world market. Even McDonald's, Pizza Hut, and Burger King restaurants seem to be widely accepted in markets throughout the world. Attempts are now being made to globalize industrial products, such as computers, robots, and carbon filters, and professional engineering products, such as earth-moving equipment and communications equipment. But the question remains whether promotion, pricing, and distribution of these products can also be standardized.

Debate about the feasibility of globalized marketing strategies has continued since the birth of the idea in the 1960s. Surprisingly, questions about standardized advertising policies are the leading concern. However, it should be remembered that there are degrees of both customization and globalization. Neither strategy is implemented in its pure form.[4] The debate will doubtless continue about which products, if any, can be fully globalized. Some firms, such as Black & Decker and Coca-Cola, have adopted globalized marketing strategies. Research seems to indicate that the key to operating successfully internationally lies in being global while acting according to local differences.[5] Consumer products, such as candy and beer, do best when accommodating local differences. The Global Perspective on page 784 describes how Kraft adjusts the marketing of its packaged cheese slices for different countries.

International Marketing Intelligence

Despite the debate over globalization of markets, most American firms perceive international markets as differing in some ways from domestic markets. Analyses of international markets and possible marketing efforts can be based on many dimensions. Table 24.1 lists the types of information that international marketers need.

Gathering secondary data (see Table 24.2) should be the first step in analyzing a foreign market. Sources of information include U.S. government publications, financial service firms, international organizations such as the United Nations, foreign governments, and international trade organizations. American firms seeking to market their products in Mexico, for example, can obtain information about Mexican markets and regulations from the U.S. Department of Commerce, the Mexican Chamber of Commerce and Industry, and numerous other organizations. Depending on the source, however, secondary data can be misleading. The reliability, validity, and comparability of data from some countries are often problematic.

To overcome these shortcomings, marketers may need primary data to understand consumers' buying behavior in the particular country under investigation. Marketers may have to adjust techniques of collecting primary data for foreign markets. Attitudes toward privacy, unwillingness to be interviewed, language differences, and low literacy rates can provide serious research obstacles. In a bicultural country such as Canada, a national questionnaire that uses identical questions is impossible because of the cultural and language differences. In many areas of Africa, where the literacy rate is low, self-administered questionnaires would never work.

Primary research should uncover significant cultural characteristics before a product is launched so that the marketing strategy is appropriate for the target market. It may be necessary to investigate basic patterns of social behavior, values, and attitudes to plan a final marketing strategy. Overall, the cost of obtaining such information may be higher than the cost of domestic research; the reasons include the large number of foreign markets to be investigated, the distance between the marketer and the foreign market, unfamiliar cultural and marketing practices, language differences, and the scarcity or unreliability of published statistics.[6]

Preliminary Screening	Analysis of Industry Market Potential	Analysis of Company Sales Potential
Demographic/Physical Environment Population size, growth, density Urban and rural distribution Climate and weather variations Shipping distance Product-significant demographics Physical distribution and communication network Natural resources **Political Environment** System of government Political stability and continuity Ideological orientation Government involvement in business Government involvement in communications Attitudes toward foreign business (trade restrictions, tariffs, nontariff barriers, bilateral trade agreements) National economic and developmental priorities **Economic Environment** Overall level of development Economic growth: GNP, industrial sector Role of foreign trade in the economy Currency, inflation rate, availability, controls, stability of exchange rate Balance of payments Per capita income and distribution Disposable income and expenditure patterns **Social/Cultural Environment** Literacy rate, educational level Existence of middle class Similarities and differences in relation to home market Language and other cultural considerations	**Market Access** Limitations on trade: tariff levels, quotas Documentation and import regulations Local standards, practices, and other nontariff barriers Patents and trademarks Preferential treaties Legal considerations: investment, taxation, repatriation, employment, code of laws **Product Potential** Customer needs and desires Local production, imports, consumption Exposure to and acceptance of product Availability of linking products Industry-specific key indicators of demand Attitudes toward products of foreign origin Competitive offerings Availability of intermediaries Regional and local transportation facilities Availability of manpower Conditions for local manufacture	**Sales Volume Forecasting** Size and concentration of customer segments Projected consumption statistics Competitive pressures Expectations of local distributors/agents **Landed Cost** Costing method for exports Domestic distribution costs International freight insurance Cost of product modification **Cost of Internal Distribution** Tariffs and duties Value-added tax Local packaging and assembly Margins/commission allowed for the trade Local distribution and inventory costs Promotional expenditures **Other Determinants of Profitability** Going price levels Competitive strengths and weaknesses Credit practices Current and projected exchange rates

Source: Adapted from S. Tamer Cavusgil, "Guidelines for Export Market Research," *Business Horizons,* November–December 1985, pp. 30–31. Used by permission.

Table 24.1 **Information Needed for International Marketing Analyses**

Kraft General Foods Adjusts to Global Markets

KRAFT GENERAL FOODS are marketed in over one hundred countries around the world, and about 25 percent of the firm's sales and earnings come from outside the United States. It is therefore extremely important for Kraft to be able to adapt its products and marketing strategies to international markets. Although today's packaged food industry is increasingly global, what a Korean family may choose to eat is probably different from what an American family would choose to eat. Similarly, product characteristics that appeal to various cultures are likely to be different. Kraft's successful worldwide promotion of its packaged cheese slices is a good example of how the concept of adaptive marketing can be applied.

Kraft discovered several years ago that many consumers were not aware that Kraft's packaged cheese slices were dairy products—that is, made from milk—whereas some of the competitors' cheese slices were not. Advertisements emphasizing that Kraft cheese was made from "five ounces of milk" proved very successful in the American market, and it was therefore decided to use this same "dairy" emphasis in foreign markets where the product had proved successful. However, because of differences in these overseas markets, the promotion of Kraft slices had to be altered. The result was specific advertising campaigns for each nation, tailored for unique differences, yet retaining the same basic theme. For example, in Canada a different formula was used in the slices—one with seven ounces of milk instead of five—and there were no direct competitors, so the advertisements made no direct comparisons with other products. In Australia a more dramatic visual presentation was made to illustrate how much milk is contained in each slice, using an implied health message directed at mothers. Finally, in England and Spain the differing number of slices contained in each package meant that the amount of milk shown to be included in Kraft slices had to be altered as well as being converted to metric volume measures such as pints and liters.

Kraft's adaptive strategy of marketing the company's cheese slices is an excellent example of how a firm often must find a blend between standardized and customized marketing. The company was able to retain the same basic message for all markets, but made changes in the message so that it was relevant to each different foreign market.

Source: James M. Kilts, "Company Study: Adaptive Marketing," *Journal of Consumer Marketing*, Summer 1990, pp. 39–45.

After analyzing secondary and primary data, marketers should plan a marketing strategy. After market entry, review and control will result in decisions to withdraw from the foreign market, to continue to expand operations, or to consider additional foreign markets.

Environmental Forces in International Markets

A detailed analysis of the environment is essential before a company enters a foreign market. If a marketing strategy is to be effective across national borders, the complexities of all the environments involved must be understood. In this section we see how differences in the cultural, social, economic, political and legal, and technological forces of the marketing environment in other countries affect marketing activities.

Type of Information	U.S. Department of Commerce Sources	Other Sources
Foreign market information	Business America Foreign economic trends Overseas business reports International economic indicators	Business International Dun & Bradstreet International Chase World Information Corp. Stanford Research Institute International Trade Reporter Accounting firms Foreign trade organizations
Export market research	Country market sectoral surveys Global market surveys International market research	Market research firms Advertising agencies Publishing companies Trade associations Library of Congress section tracking
International statistics	Export statistics profile Customer service statistics	Predicasts U.S. foreign trade reports Foreign brokerage houses United Nations International Monetary Fund OECD, EC, GATT
Overseas representatives	Customized export mailing list World traders data reports Agent/distributor service	Banks International Chambers of Commerce Consulting firms Direct telephone contact
Sales leads	Trade opportunities program Strategic and industrial product sales group Major export projects program Export information reference room	Banks International Chambers of Commerce Consulting firms State development agencies
Reference data on foreign markets	World traders data reports	Banks International Chambers of Commerce Consulting firms State development agencies Corporate information databases

Source: S. Tamer Cavusgil, "Guidelines for Export Market Research," *Business Horizons,* November–December 1985, p. 32; and Leonard M. Fuld, "How to Gather Foreign Intelligence Without Leaving Home," *Market News,* Jan. 4, 1988, pp. 24, 47. Data used by permission.

Table 24.2   **Sources of Secondary Information for International Marketing**

Cultural Forces

In Chapter 4 we define culture as the concepts, values, and tangible items, such as tools, buildings, and foods, that make up a particular society. Culture is passed on from one generation to another; in a way, it is the blueprint for acceptable behavior in a given society. This notion of culture, or national character, involves the idea that people of a given nation have distinctive patterns of behavior and distinctive personality characteristics.[7] When products are introduced into one nation from another, acceptance is far more likely if there are similarities between the two cultures.

The connotations associated with body motions, greetings, colors, numbers, shapes, sizes, and symbols vary considerably across cultures (Table 24.3 gives a few examples). For multinational marketers, these cultural differences have implications that pertain to product development, personal selling, advertising, packaging, and pricing. For example, the illustration of feet is regarded as despicable in Thailand. An international marketer also must know a country's customs regarding male-female social interaction. In Italy it is unacceptable for a salesman to call on someone's wife if the husband is not home. In Thailand certain Listerine television commercials that portrayed boy-girl romantic relationships were unacceptable. In Figure 24.2, Listerine is promoted in Spanish.

Product adoption and use are also influenced by consumers' perceptions of other countries. When consumers are generally unfamiliar with products from another country, their perceptions of the country itself affect their attitude toward and adoption of the product. If a country has a reputation for producing quality products, and therefore has a positive image in consumer's minds,

Figure 24.2

Adapting to Global Differences

A unique approach to promoting Listerine in Spanish.

Source: Courtesy of Warner-Lambert Company.

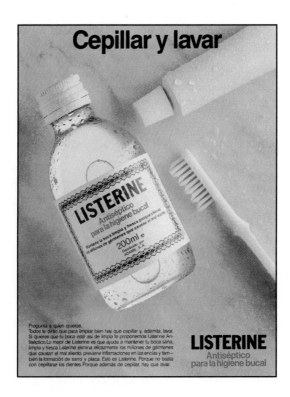

Country/ Region	Body Motions	Greetings	Colors	Numbers	Shapes, Sizes, Symbols
Japan	Pointing to one's own chest with a forefinger indicates one wants a bath. A forefinger to the nose indicates "me."	Bowing is the traditional form of greeting.	Positive colors are in muted shades. Combinations of black, dark gray, and white have negative overtones.	Positive numbers are 1, 3, 5, 8. Negative numbers are 4, 9.	Pine, bamboo, or plum patterns are positive. Cultural shapes such as Buddha-shaped jars should be avoided.
India	Kissing is considered offensive and not seen on television, in movies, or in public places.	The palms of the hands touch and the head is nodded for greeting. It is considered rude to touch or shake hands with a woman.	Positive colors are bold colors, such as green, red, yellow, or orange. Black and white are negative if they appear in the context of weddings.	To create brand awareness, numbers are often used as a brand name.	Animals such as parrots, elephants, tigers, or cheetahs are often used as brand names or on packaging. Sexually explicit symbols are avoided.
Europe	Raising only the index finger signifies a person wants two items. When counting on one's fingers, "one" is often indicated by thumb, "two" by thumb and forefinger.	It is acceptable to send flowers in thanks for a dinner invitation, but not roses (for sweethearts) or chrysanthemums (for funerals).	Generally, white and blue are considered positive. Black often has negative overtones.	The numbers 3 or 7 are usually positive. 13 is a negative number.	Circles are symbols of perfection. Hearts are considered favorably at Christmas time.
Latin America	General arm gestures are used for emphasis.	The traditional greeting is a hearty embrace and a friendly slap on the back.	Popular colors are generally bright or bold yellow, red, blue, or green.	Generally, 7 is a positive number. Negative numbers are 13, 14.	Religious symbols should be respected. Avoid national symbols, such as flag colors.
Middle East	The raised eyebrow facial expression indicates "yes."	The word *no* must be mentioned three times before it is accepted.	Positive colors are brown, black, dark blues, and reds. Pink, violets, and yellows are not favored.	Positive numbers are 3, 5, 7, 9; 13, 15 are negative.	Round or square shapes are acceptable. Symbols of six-pointed star, raised thumb, or Koranic sayings are avoided.

Source: James C. Simmons, "A Matter of Interpretation," *American Way*, April 1983, pp. 106–111; and "Adapting Export Packaging to Cultural Differences," *Business America*, Dec. 3, 1979, pp. 3–7.

Table 24.3 **Sampling of Cultural Variations**

marketers from that country will want to make the country of origin well known. For example, in Hungary a positive general image of Japan carries over to a favorable evaluation of Japanese products.[8] Conversely, marketers may want to dissociate themselves from a particular country. Because American cars have not been viewed by the world as being quality products, Chrysler, for example, may want to advertise in Japan that Colt is "not another American compact."[9]

Culture may also affect marketing negotiations and decision-making behavior on the part of marketers, industrial buyers, and other executives. Research has shown that when marketers use a problem-solving approach—that is, gain information about a particular client's needs and tailor products or services to meet those needs—it leads to increased customer satisfaction in marketing negotiations in France, Germany, the United Kingdom, and the United States. However, the attractiveness of the salesperson and his or her similarity to the customer increase the levels of satisfaction only for Americans. Furthermore, marketing negotiations proceed differently in the various cultures, and the role and status of the seller are more important in both the United Kingdom and France.[10] Cultural differences in the emphasis placed on personal relationships, status, decision-making styles, and approaches to bidding have all been shown to complicate business dealings between Americans and Japanese.[11] In the Far East a gift may be considered a necessary introduction before negotiation, but in the United States or Canada a gift may be considered a bribe.

Social Forces

Marketing activities are primarily social in purpose; therefore they are influenced by the institutions of family, religion, education, health, and recreation. For example, in Greece, where sunbathing is a commonplace form of recreation, U.S. products such as Johnson & Johnson Baby Sunblock have a large target market. In every nation, these social institutions can be identified. By finding major deviations in institutions among countries, marketers can gain insights into the adaptation of a marketing strategy. Although football is a popular sport in the United States and a major opportunity for many television advertisers, soccer is the most popular television sport in Europe. The role of children in the family and a society's overall view of children also influence marketing activities. For example, the use of cute, cereal-loving children in advertising for Kellogg's is illegal in France. In the Netherlands, children are banned from confectionery advertisements, and candy makers are required to place a little toothbrush symbol at the end of each confectionery spot.[12]

Economic Forces

Economic differences dictate many of the adjustments that must be made in marketing abroad. The most prominent adjustments are caused by differences in standards of living, availability of credit, discretionary buying power, income distribution, national resources, and conditions that affect transportation.

In terms of the value of all products produced by a nation, the United States has the largest gross national product in the world, $4,881 billion. **Gross national product (GNP)** is an overall measure of a nation's economic standing in terms of the value of all products produced by that nation for a given period of time. However, it does not take into account the concept of GNP in relation to population (GNP per capita). The United States has a GNP per capita of $19,840. The aggregate GNP of a very small country may be low. Austria's, for instance, is $124 billion, but the GNP per capita, a measure of the standard of living, is $16,330. China has a high GNP ($546 billion) but a GNP per capita of only $501.[13] This figure means that the average Chinese citizen has less discretionary income than do citizens in countries with higher GNPs per capita. Knowledge about per capita income, aggregate GNP, credit, and the distribution of income provides general insights into market potential.

Opportunities for international marketers are not limited to countries with the highest incomes. Some nations are progressing at a much faster rate than they were a few years ago, and these countries—especially in Latin America, Africa, Eastern Europe, and the Middle East—have great market potential. However, marketers must understand the political and legal environment before they can convert buying power into actual demand for specific products.

Political and Legal Forces

A country's political system, national laws, regulatory bodies, national pressure groups, and courts all have great impact on international marketing. A government's policies toward public and private enterprise, consumers, and foreign firms influence marketing across national boundaries. Some countries have established import barriers. Many nontariff barriers, such as quotas and minimum price levels set on imports, port-of-entry taxes, and stringent health and safety requirements, still make it difficult for American companies to export their products.[14] Just a few years ago, companies exporting electronic equipment to Japan had to wait for the Japanese government to inspect each item. A government's attitude toward cooperation with importers has a direct impact on the economic feasibility of exporting to that country.

Differences in political and government ethical standards are illustrated by what the Mexicans call *la mordida*, "the bite." The use of payoffs and bribes is deeply entrenched in many governments. Because U.S. trade and corporate policy, as well as U.S. law, prohibits direct involvement in payoffs and bribes, American companies may have a hard time competing with foreign firms that engage in this practice. Some U.S. businesses that refuse to make payoffs are forced to hire local consultants, public relations firms, or advertising agencies—which results in indirect payoffs. The ultimate decision about whether to give small tips or gifts where they are customary must be based on a company's code of ethics. However, it is illegal for U.S. firms to attempt to make large payments or bribes to influence policy decisions of foreign governments under the Foreign Corrupt Practices Act of 1977. The act also subjects all publicly held U.S. corporations to demanding internal control and record-keeping requirements related to their overseas operations.

Technological Forces

Much of the marketing technology used in North America and other industrialized regions of the world may be ill-suited for developing countries. For example, advertising on television or through direct-mail campaigns may be difficult in countries that lack up-to-date broadcast and postal services. Nonetheless, many countries—particularly China, South Korea, Mexico, and Poland—want to engage in international trade, often through partnerships with American and Japanese firms, so that they can gain valuable industrial and agricultural technology. But the export of technology that has strategic importance to the United States may require the approval of the U.S. Department of Defense.

Regional Trade Alliances and Markets

Although some firms are beginning to view the world as one huge marketplace, various regional trade alliances and specific markets may create difficulties or opportunities for companies engaging in international marketing. This section examines several regional trade alliances and changing markets, including the Free Trade Agreement between the United States and Canada, the proposed free trade agreement between the United States and Mexico, the *maquiladora* industries of Mexico, the 1992 unification of Europe, the Pacific Rim markets, and changing conditions in Eastern Europe, and the former Soviet Republics.

The U.S.–Canada Free Trade Agreement

In 1989 the United States and Canada signed the Free Trade Agreement (FTA), which essentially merged the American and Canadian markets and formed the largest free-trade zone in the world. The agreement calls for the elimination of most tariffs and other trade restrictions over a ten-year period so that goods and

Figure 24.3

Canada and United States Trade

Canadian Pacific Limited, a leading transportation, waste services, energy, forest products, real estate, tourism, telecommunications and manufacturing firm in Canada, should benefit from the Free Trade Agreement.

Source: Canadian Pacific Limited.

services can flow more easily each way across the U.S.–Canadian border. Trade between the United States and Canada already totals more than $175 billion annually. The FTA is making trade and investment across the border efficient, profitable, and secure.

Although passage of the trade pact was controversial and required lengthy negotiations, most experts believe that it will enable firms in both countries to compete more successfully against Asian and European rivals. When all the provisions are in effect in the year 2000, the treaty will enlarge Canada's markets ten times, and the United States will have unrestricted access to a market the size of California. Canadians are expected to ship more minerals, livestock, and forest products to the United States; American investments in Canada and sales of paper goods are likely to increase. In the first two years after the signing of the Free Trade Agreement, the volume of trade between the United States and Canada increased 8 percent.[15] Canadian Pacific Limited (Figure 24.3) should benefit from the Free Trade Agreement. The tariff reductions mandated by the FTA will especially benefit smaller American and Canadian firms because it will allow them to create more efficient economies of scale for the unified market and to earn higher profit margins.[16]

Free Trade Between the United States and Mexico and the *Maquiladora* Industries

Trade between the United States and Mexico has been flourishing in recent years. In 1990, a free trade agreement between Mexico and the United States similar to the Canadian FTA was proposed. A free trade area stretching from Canada to Mexico could mean faster growth, more jobs, better working conditions, and a cleaner environment for all three countries.[17] The trade agreement with Mexico could bring together 360 million consumers and $6 trillion in total annual output, possibly the largest market in the world. The potential free trade pact with Mexico has been made possible by reforms that have opened up the country to investment from outsiders and reduced the maximum tariff from 100 percent in 1982 to a maximum of 20 percent in 1992.[18] Between 1986 and 1991, Mexican exports to the United States rose 72 percent, and U.S. exports to Mexico doubled. In 1991 Mexicans spent 15 cents of every dollar they earned on U.S. goods and services.[19] Since Mexican production workers average a little over $2 per hour, free trade may result in the short-term loss of some U.S. manufacturing jobs, but free trade could also create higher-skilled, better-paying jobs in the United States as a result of growth in exports.

The Border Industrialization Plan of 1965 established the *maquiladora* system between the United States and Mexico. Under this system, U.S. firms establish labor-intensive assembly plants, called *maquilas,* in Mexico. A U.S. firm may lease a Mexican-owned *maquila,* subcontract production through a *maquila,* or assume part ownership of a *maquila.* The U.S. company supplies the *maquila* with components for assembly, processing, or repair, and the Mexican plant returns the finished products to the United States for further processing or shipment to customers. The company pays a U.S. tariff only on the value added to the product in Mexico. Although the original plan established a relationship between Mexico and U.S. companies, some Japanese, Korean, and European companies are also using *maquiladora* plants.[20]

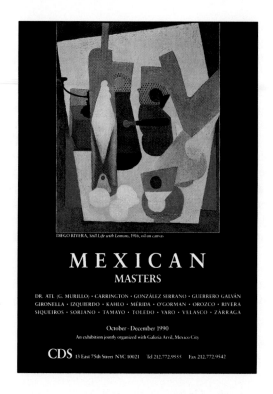

The system has many benefits for U.S. firms and for the Mexican economy. Mexico has one of the lowest labor-cost rates in the world. Furthermore, in recent years, the value of the peso has fallen dramatically relative to the value of the American dollar, making investment in Mexican plants more profitable. Finally, because of Mexico's proximity to the United States, it is less expensive to transport goods and components to and from Mexico than to and from other nations. Mexico derives benefits from the *maquiladora* system because the arrangement increases economic development by facilitating foreign exchange and providing employment. The Mexican economy is not as stable as Canada's and faces some serious issues in the near future. However, Mexico has shown a commitment to playing an active role in North American economic activity through trade agreements with both the United States and Canada, a political climate that encourages investment, and internal political and economic reforms designed to stabilize the economy.[21] Figure 24.4 is an advertisement for an exhibit of Mexican artwork in New York City.

Europe 1992

The unification of Europe in 1992 is an attempt to permit free trade between the twelve member nations of the European Community (EC). Although Germany, France, Italy, the United Kingdom, Spain, the Netherlands, Belgium, Denmark, Greece, Portugal, Ireland, and Luxembourg currently exist as separate markets, on January 1, 1993 they tried to merge into the largest single market in the world, with more than 320 million consumers. Currently, there are disputes and debates over the agreement between the member nations. If the unification succeeds, it will allow marketers to develop one standardized product for all twelve nations instead of customizing products to satisfy the regulations and restrictions of each country.[22]

Although the twelve nations of the EC are trying to function as one large market and consumers in the EC may become more homogeneous in their needs and wants, marketers must be aware that cultural and social differences between the twelve member nations may require modifications in the marketing mix for consumers in each nation. The European Community can be segmented into six markets on the basis of cultural, geographic, demographic, and economic variables: (1) the United Kingdom and Ireland; (2) central and northern France, southern Belgium, central Germany, and Luxembourg; (3) Spain and Portugal; (4) southern Germany, northern Italy, and southeastern France; (5) Greece and southern Italy; (6) Denmark, northern Germany, the Netherlands, and northern Belgium.[23] Differences in taste and preferences between these markets are significant for international marketers. For example, the British prefer front-loading washing machines, whereas the French prefer top-loading machines. Consumers in Spain eat far more poultry products than Germans do.[24] Preference differences may exist even within the same country, depending on the geographic region. Thus international marketing intelligence efforts are likely to remain very important in determining European consumers' needs and developing marketing mixes that satisfy those needs.

Pacific Rim Nations

Companies of the Pacific Rim nations—Japan, China, South Korea, Taiwan, Singapore, Hong Kong, the Philippines, Malaysia, Indonesia, Australia, and Indochina—have become increasingly competitive and sophisticated in their marketing efforts in the last three decades. The Japanese in particular have made tremendous inroads into world consumer markets for automobiles, motorcycles, watches, cameras, and audio and video equipment. Figure 24.5 illustrates the Japanese trade surplus with the United States and other countries. Products from Sony, Sanyo, Toyota, Mitsubishi, Canon, Suzuki, and others are sold all over the world and have set standards of quality by which other products are often judged. Managers from other nations study and imitate Japan's highly efficient management and manufacturing techniques. However, Japan's marketing muscle has not escaped criticism. The United States and Europe rely on Japan's informal trade restraints on its exports of cars, textiles, steel, and audio and video consumer products. The United States has also been critical of Japan's reluctance to accept imports from other nations.

South Korea has become very successful in world markets with familiar brand names such as Samsung, Daewoo, and Hyundai. But even before those companies became household words, their products achieved strong success under American company labels such as GE, GTE, RCA, and J.C. Penney. Korean companies are now taking market share away from Japanese companies in the world markets for videocassette recorders, color televisions, and computers, despite the fact that the Korean market for these products is limited. In Canada, the Hyundai Excel overtook Japan's Honda in just eighteen months.[25] With Europe and Japan blocking entry to some of their markets, Korean firms have decided to go head-to-head with Japanese and American manufacturers for a piece of the U.S. market. It has been speculated that Korea may be the next Asian "powerhouse" economy, particularly in light of the recent movement toward the reunification of North and South Korea, with South Korea contributing technological expertise and North Korea an abundance of cheap labor.[26]

Because of its drive toward modernization, the People's Republic of China was thought to have great market potential and opportunities for joint-venture projects. However, limited consumer demand and political instability dimmed those prospects. In particular, a 1989 student prodemocracy uprising in Beijing reversed several years of business progress in China. Given the political instability, many foreign companies reduced their presence in China or left altogether; other firms became more cautious in their relations with China.[27]

Less visible Pacific Rim regions, such as Singapore, Taiwan, and Hong Kong, are major manufacturing and financial centers. Singapore also has large world markets for pharmaceutical and rubber goods. Hong Kong, however, faces an uncertain future after it moves from British control to control by the People's Republic of China in 1997. Taiwan may have the most promising future of all the Pacific Rim nations. It has a strong local economy and has lowered many import barriers, thus increasing imports. Taiwan is beginning to privatize state-run banks and is also opening its markets to foreign firms. Some analysts believe that it may replace Hong Kong as a regional financial power center when Hong Kong reverts to Chinese control.[28] Firms from Thailand and Malaysia are also blossoming, carving out niches in the world markets for a variety of products, from toys to automobile parts.[29] In the case of virtually all Asian countries, the end of the Cold War has caused these nations to increasingly move toward forming trade links.[30]

Changing Relations with Eastern Europe and the Former Soviet Union

The countries that composed the former Soviet Union and other Eastern European nations (Poland, Hungary, East Germany, Yugoslavia, Czechoslovakia, Rumania, and Bulgaria) are experiencing great political and economic changes. The Communist party's centrally planned economies have been replaced by democratic institutions in most of these countries. In fact, changes in the Eastern European countries have been the fastest-breaking developments in international marketing. These countries are very different in terms of technology, infrastructure, foreign investment laws, and speed of change.[31] As a result, they are becoming increasingly market-oriented.

There have been widespread measures to improve the economic environment of what was the Soviet Union. These measures are aimed primarily at making the new nations more responsive to the forces of supply and demand. Other economic reform plans include replacing the system of state-owned enterprises and farms with independent businesses leased or owned by workers, shareholders, cooperatives, and joint ventures; overhauling the system of centrally determined prices; and setting free-market prices for many products. In the short-run these measures promise to cause economic difficulties, such as food shortages and unemployment. However, given sufficient time, the former Soviet Union could represent unique marketing opportunities.[32]

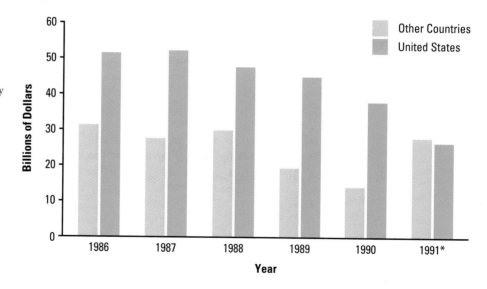

Figure 24.5

Japanese Trade Surplus, 1985–1991 (in billions of dollars)

Source: Japanese Ministry of Trade, 1991.

*1991 figure represents first three quarters

The reformers of the Russian, Polish, and Hungarian economies want to reduce trade restrictions on imports and offer incentives to encourage exports to and investment in their countries.[33] For example, General Motors agreed to a $150 million joint venture in Hungary in 1990. In addition, GM reached an agreement to build 150,000 Opels a year in an East German government-owned factory.[34] The cost to Germany promises to be great; already the expense of the reunification of East and West Germany has brought economic growth to a standstill. However, once the reunification is complete, the new Germany could easily emerge as an even more influential economic power than it was in years past.[35] Because of these economic and political reforms, productivity in Eastern Europe and Russia is expected to increase as workers are given more incentives and control, raising the possibility that Eastern Europe will become an economic powerhouse rivaling the United States and Japan. There is also speculation that some of the Eastern European nations will ultimately join the European Community, allowing freer trade across all European borders.[36]

Because of the changing economic conditions in Eastern Europe and the former Soviet Union, there are many marketing opportunities in these countries for American, Western European, and Asian firms. Some American firms, including Monsanto, Combustion Engineering, McDonald's, and Pizza Hut, are marketing products in Russia, either through joint ventures with Russian firms or through direct ownership.[37] Siemens, Federal Express, Procter & Gamble, and Occidental Petroleum are also among the many companies considering doing business in Eastern Europe. The countries of Eastern Europe are building new hotels and improving telephone, airline, and ground transportation services to facilitate international trade, as well as for the benefit of their citizens.[38] However, because of the swift and uncontrolled nature of the changes taking place in Eastern Europe and the former Soviet Union, firms considering marketing their products in these countries must carefully monitor events and proceed cautiously.

Strategic Adaptation of Marketing Mixes

Once a U.S. firm determines foreign market potentials and understands the foreign environment, it develops and adapts its marketing mix. Creating and maintaining the marketing mix is the final step in developing the international marketing strategy. Only if foreign marketing opportunities justify the risk will a company go to the expense of adapting the marketing mix. Of course, in some situations new products are developed for a specific country. In these cases, there is no existing marketing mix and no extra expense to consider in serving the foreign target market. The Global Perspective on page 797 illustrates that even small businesses may need to develop international marketing strategies to succeed.

Product and Promotion

As Figure 24.6 shows, there are five possible strategies for adapting product and promotion across national boundaries: (1) keep product and promotion the same worldwide, (2) adapt promotion only, (3) adapt product only, (4) adapt both product and promotion, and (5) invent new products.[39]

Keep Product and Promotion the Same Worldwide   This strategy attempts to use in the foreign country the product and promotion developed for the U.S. market, an approach that seems desirable wherever possible because it eliminates the expenses of marketing research and product redevelopment. PepsiCo and Coca-Cola use this approach in marketing their soft drinks. Although both translate promotional messages into the language of a particular country, they market the same product and promotional messages around the world. Despite certain inherent risks that stem from cultural differences in interpretation, exporting advertising copy does provide the efficiency of international standardization, or globalization. Global advertising embraces the same concept as global marketing, discussed earlier in this chapter. An advertiser can save hundreds of thousands of dollars by running the same advertisement worldwide.

Figure 24.6

International Product and Promotion Strategies

Source: Adapted from Warren J. Keegan, *Global Marketing Management*, 4th ed., Englewood Cliffs, N.J.: Prentice-Hall, 1989, pp. 378–382. Used by permission.

Global Marketing Makes the Difference for Auditronics

AUDITRONICS, A SMALL COMPANY with about sixty employees, was started in 1966 in the garages of its founders. Currently operating in a 15,000-square-foot manufacturing facility, the company designs and manufactures control panels for recording studios and television and radio stations. Originally, Auditronics custom-made recording consoles for recording studios, but after switching from totally custom manufacturing to larger production, they were able to cut costs and expand their market more rapidly.

What makes Auditronics different is that its consoles are designed and manufactured for specific radio and television station applications. For example, one of Auditronics' new products, the 1900Mix-Minus System, allows television news correspondents to simultaneously hear and communicate with their director and other correspondents in different locations. The television console also incorporates features found in recording studio consoles, thus helping television stations sound better. Auditronics' unique, specialized consoles employ cutting-edge technology that is potentially useful in every country that has television and radio stations and recording studios.

On the other hand, the specialized nature of Auditronics' products requires the volume of international markets for the company to maintain design and production efficiency.

While domestic sales have been good, it is the ability of this small company to capture international sales that has made the difference. In 1991 the firm had an order backlog of three months partially because of increased international sales. It shipped five television control consoles to Kuwait after the 1991 war in the Persian Gulf, and at the same time it was fulfilling orders with local radio stations and was shipping nine radio consoles to Hong Kong. By expanding its marketing to radio and television stations worldwide, Auditronics has been able to emerge as a successful small, privately owned business.

Sources: Mark Borowsky, "International Sales Set Auditronics Off to Good Start," *Memphis Business Journal*, Nov. 18–22, 1991, p. 32; and Mark Borowsky, "Auditronics Expanding Global Business with Console for TV Stations," *Memphis Business Journal*, Nov. 13–17, 1989, pp. 6–7.

Adapt Promotion Only This strategy leaves the product basically unchanged but modifies its promotion. In Figure 24.7 Kitchen Aid's mixers are unchanged, but the promotion is altered for various international markets. This approach may be necessary because of language, legal, or cultural differences associated with the advertising copy. When Polaroid introduced its SX-70 camera in Europe, for example, it used the same television commercials and print advertisements featuring "well-known" celebrities that it used in the United States. However, because the celebrities were not well known in Europe, the commercials were not effective, and sales of the SX-70 were low initially. Only when Polaroid adapted its promotion to appeal to regional needs and tastes did the SX-70 begin to achieve success.[40] Promotional adaptation is a low-cost modification compared with the costs of redeveloping engineering and production and physically changing products.

Generally, the strategy of adapting only promotion infuses advertising with the culture of people who will be exposed to it. Often promotion combines thinking globally and acting locally. At company headquarters, a basic global marketing strategy is developed, but promotion is modified to fit each market's needs.

Figure 24.7

Adapt Promotion Only

KitchenAid modifies its promotion, but not its product, for the French-Canadian market.

Source: ® Registered trademark of KitchenAid. Advertisement reprinted with permission.

Adapt Product Only The basic assumption in modifying a product without changing its promotion is that the product will serve the same function under different conditions of use. Soap and detergent manufacturers have adapted their products to local water conditions and washing equipment without changing their promotions. Household appliances also have been altered to use different types of electricity. Manufacturers must also sometimes alter brand names for international markets. It is not always possible to directly translate a brand name and still retain relative simplicity and positive connotations, yet these are vital considerations if the product is to be successful.[41]

A product may have to be adjusted for legal reasons. Japan, for example, has some of the most stringent automobile emission requirements in the world. American automobiles that fail emission standards cannot be marketed in Japan. Sometimes products must be adjusted to overcome social and cultural obstacles. For example, Jell-O introduced a powdered gelatin mix that failed in England because the English were used to buying gelatin in jelled form. Resistance to a product is frequently based on attitudes and ignorance about the nature of new technology. It is often easier to change the product than to overcome technological biases.

Adapt Both Product and Promotion When a product serves a new function or is used differently in a foreign market, then both the product and its promotion need to be altered. For example, when Procter & Gamble marketed its Cheer laundry detergent in Japan, it promoted the product as being effective in all temperatures, just as it does in the United States. Most Japanese, however, wash clothes in cold water and therefore do not care about all-temperature washing. Moreover, the Japanese often add a lot of fabric softener to the wash, and Cheer did not produce many suds under those conditions. Procter & Gamble thus reformulated Cheer so that it would not be affected by the addition of fabric softeners and changed the promotion to emphasize "superior" cleaning in cold water. Cheer then became one of Procter & Gamble's most successful products in Japan.[42] Adaptation of both product and promotion is the most expensive strategy discussed thus far, but it should be considered if the foreign market appears large enough.

Invent New Products   This strategy is selected when existing products cannot meet the needs of a foreign market. General Motors developed an all-purpose, jeeplike motor vehicle that can be assembled in underdeveloped nations by mechanics with no special training. The vehicle is designed to operate under varied conditions; it has standardized parts and is inexpensive. Colgate-Palmolive Co. developed an inexpensive, all-plastic, hand-powered washing machine that has the tumbling action of a modern automatic machine. The product, marketed in underdeveloped countries, was invented for households that have no electricity. Strategies that involve the invention of products are often the most costly, but the payoff can be great.

Distribution and Pricing

Decisions about the distribution system and pricing policies are important in developing an international marketing mix. Figure 24.8 illustrates different approaches to these decisions.

Distribution   A firm can sell its product to an intermediary that is willing to buy from existing market channels in the United States, or it can develop new international marketing channels. Obviously, a service company needs to develop its own distribution systems to market its products. However, many products, such as toothpaste, are distributed through intermediaries and brokers. The firm must consider distribution both between countries and within the foreign country.

Figure 24.8

Strategies for International Distribution and Pricing

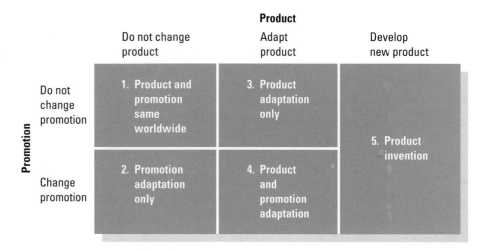

Product

	Do not change product	Adapt product	Develop new product
Do not change promotion	1. Product and promotion same worldwide	3. Product adaptation only	5. Product invention
Change promotion	2. Promotion adaptation only	4. Product and promotion adaptation	

(Promotion)

In determining distribution alternatives, the existence of retailers and wholesalers that can perform marketing functions between and within nations is one major factor. If a foreign country has a segmented retail structure consisting primarily of one-person shops or street vendors, it may be difficult to develop new marketing channels for such products as packaged goods and prepared foods. Quite often in developing countries, certain channels of distribution are characterized by ethnodomination. *Ethnodomination* occurs when an ethnic group occupies a majority position within a marketing channel. Indians, for example, own approximately 90 percent of the cotton gins in Uganda; the Hausa tribe in Nigeria dominates the trade in kola nuts, cattle, and housing; and Chinese merchants dominate the rice economy in Thailand. Marketers must be sensitive to ethnodomination and recognize that the ethnic groups operate in subcultures unique in social and economic organization.[43]

If the product being sold across national boundaries requires service and information, then control of the distribution process is desirable. Caterpillar, for example, sells more than half its construction and earth-moving equipment in foreign countries. Because it must provide services and replacement parts, Caterpillar has established its own dealers in foreign markets. Regional sales offices and technical experts are also available to support local dealers. A manufacturer of paintbrushes, on the other hand, would be more concerned about agents, wholesalers, or other manufacturers that would facilitate the product's exposure in a foreign market. Control over the distribution process would not be so important for that product because services and replacement parts are not needed. Distribution problems can arise, however, when an exporting firm sells, knowingly or unknowingly, to an unauthorized agent that competes with the exporter's official agent.[44]

Research suggests that international firms use independently owned marketing channels when they market in countries perceived to be highly dissimilar to their home markets. However, when they market complex products, they develop vertically integrated marketing channels to gain control of distribution. To manage the distribution process from manufacture to customer contact requires an expert sales force that must be trained to specifically sell the firm's products. Moreover, when products are unique or highly differentiated from those of current competitors, international firms also tend to design and establish vertically integrated channels.[45]

It is crucial to realize that a nation's political instability can jeopardize the distribution of goods. For example, when the United States invaded Panama in late 1989, the Panama Canal was closed for several days, delaying shipments of goods through the canal. Similarly, during the political unrest in China, military activity and fighting made it difficult to move goods into and out of certain areas. Thus we want to stress again the importance of monitoring the environment when engaging in international marketing. Companies that market products in unstable nations may need to develop alternate plans to allow for sudden unrest or hostility and ensure that the distribution of their products is not jeopardized.

Pricing The domestic and foreign prices of products are usually different. For example, the prices charged for Walt Disney videos in Spain may differ from U.S. prices for Walt Disney videos. The increased costs of transportation, supplies, taxes, tariffs, and other expenses necessary to adjust a firm's operations to international marketing can raise prices. A key decision is whether the basic pricing policy will change (as discussed in Chapter 17). If it is a firm's policy not to allocate fixed costs to foreign sales, then lower foreign prices could result.

American pharmaceutical manufacturers have been accused of selling their products in foreign markets at low prices (without allocating research and development costs) while charging American customers high prices that include all research and development expenses. The sale of U.S. products in foreign markets—or vice versa—at lower prices (when all costs have not been allocated or when surplus products are sold) is called **dumping**. Dumping is illegal in many countries if it damages domestic firms and workers.

A cost-plus approach to international pricing is probably the most common method used because of the compounding number of costs necessary to move products from the United States to a foreign country. Of course, as our discussion of pricing policies in Chapter 17 points out, understanding consumer demand and the competitive environment is a necessary step in selecting a price.

The price charged in other countries is also a function of foreign currency exchange rates. Fluctuations in the international monetary market can change the prices charged across national boundaries on a daily basis. There has been a trend toward greater fluctuation (or float) in world money markets. For example, a sudden variation in the exchange rate, which occurs when a nation devalues its currency, can have wide-ranging effects on consumer prices.

Developing Organizational Structures for International Marketing

The level of commitment to international marketing is a major variable in deciding what kind of involvement is appropriate. A firm's options range from occasional exporting to expanding overall operations (production and marketing) into other countries. In this section we examine exporting, licensing, joint ventures, trading companies, direct ownership, and other approaches to international involvement.

Exporting

Exporting is the lowest level of commitment to international marketing and the most flexible approach. A firm may find an exporting intermediary that can perform most marketing functions associated with selling to other countries. This approach entails minimum effort and cost. Modifications in packaging, labeling, style, or color may be the major expenses in adapting a product. There is limited risk in using export agents and merchants because there is no direct investment in the foreign country.

Export agents bring together buyers and sellers from different countries; they collect a commission for arranging sales. Export houses and export merchants purchase products from different companies and then sell them to foreign countries. They are specialists at understanding customers' needs in foreign countries.

Foreign buyers from companies and governments provide a direct method of exporting and eliminate the need for an intermediary. Foreign buyers encourage international exchange by contacting domestic firms about their needs and the opportunities available in exporting. Domestic firms that want to export with a minimum of effort and investment seek out foreign importers and buyers.

Licensing

When potential markets are found across national boundaries—and when production, technical assistance, or marketing know-how is required—**licensing** is an alternative to direct investment. The licensee (the owner of the foreign operation) pays commissions or royalties on sales or supplies used in manufacturing. An initial down payment or fee may be charged when the licensing agreement is signed. Exchanges of management techniques or technical assistance are primary reasons for licensing agreements. Yoplait yogurt is a French yogurt that is licensed for production in the United States; the Yoplait brand tries to maintain a French image.

Licensing is an attractive alternative to direct investment when the political stability of a foreign country is in doubt or when resources are unavailable for direct investment. Licensing is especially advantageous for small manufacturers wanting to launch a well-known brand internationally. For example, all Spalding sporting products are licensed worldwide. The Questor Corporation owns the Spalding name but produces no goods itself. Pierre Cardin has issued five hundred licenses and Yves St. Laurent two hundred to make their products.[46] Lowenbrau has used licensing agreements, including one with Miller in the United States, to increase sales worldwide without committing capital to build breweries.

Joint Ventures

In international marketing, a **joint venture** is a partnership between a domestic firm and a foreign firm or government. Joint ventures are especially popular in industries that call for large investments, such as natural resources extraction or automobile manufacturing. Control of the joint venture can be split equally, or one party may control decision making. Joint ventures are often a political necessity because of nationalism and governmental restrictions on foreign ownership. They also provide legitimacy in the eyes of the host country's citizens. Local partners have firsthand knowledge of the economic and sociopolitical environment, access to distribution networks, or privileged access to local resources (raw material, labor management, contacts, and so on). Moreover, entrepreneurs in many less-developed countries actively seek associations with a foreign partner as a ready means of implementing their own corporate strategy.[47]

Joint ventures are assuming greater global importance because of cost advantages and the number of inexperienced firms entering foreign markets. They may be the result of a trade-off between a firm's desire for completely unambiguous control of an enterprise and its quest for additional resources. They may occur when internal development or acquisition is not feasible or unavailable or when the risks and constraints leave no other alternative. As project sizes increase in the face of global competition and firms attempt to spread the huge costs of technological innovation, there is increased impetus to form joint ventures.[48] Several European truck makers are considering mergers and joint ventures with other European firms to consolidate their power after the unification of Europe in 1992 and the deregulation of the European trucking industry in 1993. Volvo and Renault have developed a partnership, and Britain's Leyland and the Netherlands' DAF have already joined forces.[49]

Increasingly, once a joint venture succeeds, nationalism spurs a trend toward expropriating or purchasing foreign shares of the enterprise. On the other hand, a joint venture may be the only available means for entering a foreign market. For example, American construction firms bidding for business in Saudi Arabia have found that joint ventures with Arab construction companies gain local support among the handful of people who make the contracting decisions.

Strategic alliances, the newest form of international business structure, are partnerships formed to create competitive advantage on a worldwide basis. They are very similar to joint ventures. The number of strategic alliances is growing at an estimated rate of about 20 percent per year.[50] In fact, in some industries, such as automobiles and computers, strategic alliances are becoming the predominant means of competing. International competition is so fierce and the costs of competing on a global basis so high that few firms have the individual resources to go it alone. Thus individual firms that lack all the internal resources essential for international success may seek to collaborate with other companies.[51]

The partners forming international strategic alliances often retain their distinct identities, and each brings a distinctive competence to the union. However, the firms share common long-term goals. As might be imagined, this "marriage" of two firms from different cultures is not without problems. Interestingly, research has shown that the firm experiencing the highest levels of conflict and lowest levels of satisfaction is often the company from the host country.[52] What distinguishes international strategic alliances from other business structures is that member firms in the alliance may have been traditional rivals competing for market share in the same product class.[53] An example of such an alliance is the New United Motor Manufacturing, Inc. (NUMMI), formed by Toyota and General Motors to make Chevrolet Novas and Toyota Tercels. This alliance united the quality engineering of Japanese cars with the marketing expertise and market access of General Motors.

Trading Companies

A **trading company** provides a link between buyers and sellers in different countries. A trading company, as its name implies, is not involved in manufacturing or owning assets related to manufacturing. It buys in one country at the lowest price consistent with quality and sells to buyers in another country. An important function of trading companies is taking title to products and undertaking all the activities necessary to move the products from the domestic country to a foreign country. For example, large grain-trading companies operating out of home offices in both the United States and overseas control a major portion of the world's trade in basic food commodities. These trading companies sell agricultural commodities that are homogeneous and can be stored and moved rapidly in response to market conditions.

Trading companies reduce risk for companies interested in getting involved in international marketing. A trading company will assist producers with information about products that meet quality and price expectations in domestic or international markets. Additional services a trading company may provide include consulting, marketing research, advertising, insurance, product research and design, legal assistance, warehousing, and foreign exchange.

In 1982 the Export Trading Company Act was passed to facilitate the efficient operation of trading companies in the United States. Besides allowing banks to invest in trading companies, the Export Trading Act created a new certification procedure that enables companies to apply for limited protection from antitrust laws when conducting export operations. The program has been less successful than the government had hoped. The best-known U.S. trading company is Sears World Trade, which specializes in consumer goods, light industrial items, and processed foods. A trading company acts like a wholesaler, taking on much of the responsibility of finding markets while facilitating all marketing aspects of a transaction.

Direct Ownership

Once a company makes a long-term commitment to marketing in a foreign nation that has a promising political and economic environment, **direct ownership** of a foreign subsidiary or division is a possibility. Although most discussions of foreign investment concern only manufacturing equipment or personnel, the expenses of developing a separate foreign distribution system can be tremendous. The opening of retail stores in Europe, Canada, or Mexico can require a large financial investment in facilities, research, and management.

Figure 24.9

Multinational Enterprise

Ford promotes its minivan in Germany as well as many other countries.

Source: Courtesy of Ford Motor Company.

1990 Rank	Company	Foreign Revenue (millions)	Total Revenue (millions)	Foreign Revenue as Percent of Total
1	Exxon	$79,015	$105,519	74.9%
2	IBM	41,886	69,018	60.7
3	General Motors	37,738	124,705	30.3
4	Ford Motor	35,879	97,650	36.7
5	Mobil	32,515	58,770	55.3
6	Citicorp	21,072	38,385	54.9
7	Texaco	17,520	40,899	42.8
8	E.I. du Pont de Nemours	17,413	40,047	43.5
9	ITT	11,628	25,734	45.2
10	Philip Morris	10,468	44,323	23.6
11	Dow Chemical	10,279	19,773	52.0
12	Procter & Gamble	9,618	24,081	39.9
13	Chevron	8,592	38,607	22.3
14	General Electric	8,272	58,414	14.2
15	Eastman Kodak	8,245	18,908	43.6
16	Amoco	8,227	29,201	28.2
17	Xerox	8,105	19,188	42.2
18	United Technologies	7,840	21,783	36.0
19	Hewlett-Packard	7,208	13,233	54.5
20	Digital Equipment	7,119	12,943	55.0

Source: Excerpted by permission of *Forbes* magazine, July 22, 1991. © Forbes Inc. 1991.

The term **multinational enterprise** refers to firms that have operations or subsidiaries located in many countries. Often the parent firm is based in one country and cultivates production, management, and marketing activities in other countries. The firm's subsidiaries may be quite autonomous to be able to respond to the needs of individual international markets. Firms such as General Motors, Citicorp, ITT, and Ford (see Figure 24.9) are multinational companies with worldwide operations. Table 24.4 lists the twenty largest U.S. multinationals. The contribution of foreign profit as a percentage of total profit shows how important international involvement can be. Many of these firms could not operate at an acceptable profit without their foreign subsidiaries.

A wholly owned foreign subsidiary may be allowed to operate independently of the parent company so that its management can have more freedom to adjust to the local environment. Cooperative arrangements are developed to assist in marketing efforts, production, and management. A wholly owned foreign subsidiary may export products to the home nation. Some American automobile manufacturers, for example, import cars built by their foreign subsidiaries. A foreign subsidiary offers important tax, tariff, and other operating advantages. One of the greatest advantages is the cross-cultural approach. A subsidiary usually operates under foreign management, so that it can develop a local identity. The greatest danger in such an arrangement comes from political uncertainty: a firm may lose its foreign investment.

Summary   Marketing activities performed across national boundaries are usually significantly different from domestic marketing activities. International marketers
must have a profound awareness of the foreign environment. The marketing
strategy ordinarily is adjusted to meet the needs and desires of foreign markets.

The level of involvement in international marketing can range from casual
exporting to globalization of markets. Although most firms adjust their marketing mixes for differences in target markets, some firms are able to standardize
their marketing efforts worldwide. Traditional full-scale international marketing
involvement is based on products customized according to cultural, regional,
and national differences. Globalization, however, involves developing marketing
strategies as if the entire world (or regions of it) were a single entity; a globalized firm markets standardized products in the same way everywhere.

Marketers must rely on international marketing intelligence to understand the
complexities of the international marketing environment before they can formulate a marketing mix. They therefore collect and analyze secondary and primary
data about international markets.

Environmental aspects of special importance include cultural, social, economic, political, and legal forces. Cultural aspects of the environment that are
most important to international marketers include customs, concepts, values,
attitudes, morals, and knowledge. Marketing activities are primarily social in
purpose; therefore they are influenced by the institutions of family, religion,
education, health, and recreation. The most prominent economic forces that
affect international marketing are those that can be measured by income and
resources. Credit, buying power, and income distribution are aggregate measures of market potential. Political and legal forces include the political system,
national laws, regulatory bodies, national pressure groups, and courts. Foreign
policies of all nations involved in trade determine how marketing can be conducted. The level of technology helps define economic development within a
nation and indicates the existence of methods to facilitate marketing.

Various regional trade alliances and specific markets are creating difficulties
and opportunities for firms, including the Free Trade Agreement between the
United States and Canada, the proposed free trade agreement between the
United States and Mexico, the *maquiladora* industries of Mexico, the unifica-
tion of Europe in 1992, the Pacific Rim markets, and changing conditions in
Eastern Europe and the former Soviet Union.

After a country's environment has been analyzed, marketers must develop a
marketing mix and decide whether to adapt product or promotion. There are
five possible strategies for adapting product and promotion across national
boundaries: (1) keep product and promotion the same worldwide, (2) adapt
promotion only, (3) adapt product only, (4) adapt both product and promotion,
and (5) invent new products. Foreign distribution channels are nearly always
different from domestic ones. The allocation of costs, transportation considerations, or the costs of doing business in foreign nations will affect pricing.

There are several ways of getting involved in international marketing. Exporting is the easiest and most flexible method. Licensing is an alternative to direct
investment; it may be necessitated by political and economic conditions. Joint
ventures and strategic alliances are often appropriate when outside resources are
needed, when there are governmental restrictions on foreign ownership, or
when changes in global markets encourage competitive consolidation. Trading
companies are experts at buying products in the domestic market and selling to

foreign markets, thereby taking most of the risk in international involvement. Direct ownership of foreign divisions or subsidiaries is the strongest commitment to international marketing and involves the greatest risk. When a company has operations or subsidiaries located in many countries, it is termed a multinational enterprise.

Important Terms

International marketing
Globalization
Gross national product (GNP)
Dumping
Licensing

Joint venture
Strategic alliances
Trading company
Direct ownership
Multinational enterprise

Discussion and Review Questions

1. How does international marketing differ from domestic marketing?
2. What must marketers consider before deciding whether to become involved in international marketing?
3. Why are the largest industrial corporations in the United States so committed to international marketing?
4. Why was so much of this chapter devoted to an analysis of the international marketing environment?
5. A manufacturer recently exported peanut butter with a green label to a nation in the Far East. The product failed because it was associated with jungle sickness. How could this mistake have been avoided?
6. Relate the concept of reference groups (Chapter 4) to international marketing.
7. How do religious systems influence marketing activities in foreign countries?
8. Which is more important to international marketers, a country's aggregate GNP or its GNP per capita? Why?
9. If you were asked to provide a small tip (or bribe) to have a document approved in a foreign nation where this practice was customary, what would you do?
10. In marketing dog food to Latin America, what aspects of the marketing mix need to be altered?
11. What should marketers consider as they decide whether to license or to enter into a joint venture in a foreign nation?
12. Discuss the impact of strategic alliances on marketing strategies.

Cases

24.1 Porsche AG

Founded in 1930 by Dr. Ferdinand Porsche, the company known today as Porsche AG began as a research and development firm. The original company accepted contracts from individuals and firms to design new automobiles, airplanes, and ships. The company built prototypes of each design and thoroughly tested them. If the firm that commissioned the work approved the design, the product was then produced by one of the large manufacturing companies in Germany. After World War II, the Porsche family experienced a period of hardship, disappointment, and personal tragedy but in 1948 Porsche's son, Dr. Ferry

Porsche, began a company to manufacture family-designed sports cars. Despite depressed economic conditions, the company persevered and prospered. By 1973, Porsche AG had built and sold some 200,000 Porsche automobiles, gaining world recognition for its cars and their promise of "driving in its purest form."

Porsche today is organized into three divisions located in three suburbs of Stuttgart: the factory, in Zuffenhausen; testing, engineering, and design, in Weissach; and marketing, in Ludwigsburg. The Porsche Research and Development Center has produced the 959 race car, an aircraft engine, the TAG motor, and designs for ambulances, mobile surgery units, gliders, fire engines, and forklift trucks. The company holds more than two thousand patents, and innovations developed by Porsche are in several manufacturers' car models.

The popularity of Porsche cars stems from their reputation for outstanding performance. Not only are the cars produced in a painstaking fashion, but Porsche AG also takes maintenance and repair very seriously. Porsche mechanics receive five days of classroom instruction each year at the Porsche marketing center in Ludwigsburg, more training than any other car company provides. Until 1984, U.S. Porsche mechanics also flew to Germany for training, but now they receive instruction at Porsche training centers at home. In its advertising, the company encourages customers to rely only on Porsche experts for repair and maintenance of their cars to avoid having unsatisfactory experiences with unqualified mechanics. This action further differentiates Porsche automobiles from the competition.

However, despite Porsche's reputation for excellence, the company has fallen on hard times. It was forced to raise prices on cars sold in the United States because of changes in the dollar-market exchange rate, and a recently implemented tax on luxury cars priced in excess of $30,000 has also damaged sales. Because of the price increases, the tax, a weakening U.S. dollar, and competitors such as the Chevrolet Corvette and the Japanese Acura NSX, Porsche sales in the United States dropped from over 30,000 cars in 1986 to about 9,000 in 1989. Sales in 1991 were down to 4,400 cars. Porsche expected to sell 5,000 cars in the United States in 1992. This decrease in sales is particularly serious for the firm as roughly 60 percent of all Porsches are sold in the United States. Overdependence on the shrinking U.S. market has caused Porsche AG to implement an austerity program, including laying off 22 percent of its U.S. employees, lowering production output, reducing costs, revamping all three model lines, lowering prices, and pulling out of the lower end of the luxury car market. The company is also trying to enter new markets, including Spain and Japan, to boost sales and increase profits. An additional move was the 1992 launch of the Porsche Credit Corporation, which makes financing easier for Porsche buyers. The financing subsidiary can accommodate the large sums, long terms and unusual lease or financing arrangements required for cars priced as high as $100,000.

Porsche is successful in markets in which the social climate favors people who want to demonstrate their success and the economic climate is conducive to the entrepreneur. Porsche management believes that its customers have high personal goals and a drive to achieve, do not like to compromise, and give their best efforts every time. Although not averse to risk, they prepare thoroughly for new ventures. Porsche customers are goers and doers, but not showoffs. To succeed, Porsche AG must exhibit some of its customers' traits. Customers must be able to identify with the firm, to see in the company the same characteristics they see in themselves. Unless Porsche can successfully convey, through the company's marketing efforts and in a difficult economic environment, what sets their cars apart from the competition, harder times are ahead.[54]

Questions for Discussion

1. Evaluate international marketing opportunities for Porsche AG. What are the company's strengths and weaknesses?
2. What obstacles must Porsche overcome to be successful selling Porsche automobiles in the United States?
3. What is the role of diversification in the Porsche AG corporate strategy?

24.2 Granada Corporation: "The Global Cattle Clone"

Texas-based Granada Corporation helps ranchers around the world improve the quality of their cattle through semen collection, artificial insemination, and embryo transfers, in which cattle embryos from superior animals are implanted in surrogate cows. Granada is also one of a growing number of firms conducting research in embryo cloning—the multiple replication of a fertilized embryo to produce genetically identical offspring—and gene-transfer technologies.

Much of the company's marketing effort focuses on educating ranchers about embryo transfer technology and its benefits. In 1990 Granada and magazine publisher Holstein-Friesian World Inc. (HFW) joined forces in an industry awareness program called "A Clone, Just for You." The program's primary objective was to emphasize the safe, timely, and cost-effective characteristics associated with utilizing commercial cloning in dairy herd management. Initial advertising included news releases, displays at conventions, and sales promotions, such as contests giving away free products and dollars-off coupons toward the purchase of embryo technology.

This type of marketing expertise has enabled Granada to bypass overseas sales agents and go directly to ranchers in its international marketing activities. Sometimes the ranchers approach Granada first. Because of this direct customer contact, the company makes sure its employees have, in addition to their technical expertise, well-developed interpersonal skills that are effective across a multitude of cultures.

Most of the foreign customers who are interested in the high-technology service offered by Granada can afford it and can arrange to pay in American dollars. Many ranchers arrange payment through letters of credit at an American bank. Thus Granada is somewhat insulated against fluctuating exchange rates and the economic woes of other nations.

The company does have to worry about customs regulations regarding the transfer of technology and the sale of services across international boundaries, however. In addition, some foreign governments have tried to obtain the technology for themselves. The issues associated with the transfer of science and technology across national boundaries and the international protection of proprietary products and processes promise to be at the forefront of international trade negotiations in the future.

With the apparent end of the Cold War and the political restructuring of Europe, bioscience technology will become an important element of foreign policy, just as military strength was a few short years ago. As with all companies engaged in international trade, Granada must be very careful to obey all laws and regulations and yet ensure that it receives all payment that it deserves for its services without unnecessarily "giving away" its unique products and ideas. All of this can be especially difficult when dealing across national boundaries.[55]

Questions for Discussion

1. What are the international environmental concerns in Granada's marketing?
2. What is the potential for marketing mix standardization at Granada?
3. What are alternative ways Granada can gain new international markets?

Chapter Notes

1. Based on information from Geoffrey E. Duin, "Parker Pen: An Old Japan Hand," *Tokyo Business Today,* July 1989, pp. 50–51; and Mike Stevens, "Premiums and Incentives: Designs on Your Desk," *Marketing,* Apr. 14, 1988, pp. 45, 47.
2. Theodore Levitt, "The Globalization of Markets," *Harvard Business Review,* May–June 1983, p. 92.
3. Ibid.
4. Subhash C. Jain, "Standardization of International Marketing Strategy: Some Research Hypotheses," *Journal of Marketing,* January 1989, pp. 70–79.
5. James Wills, A. Coskun Samli, and Laurence Jacobs, "Developing Global Products and Marketing Strategies: A Construct and a Research Agenda," *Journal of the Academy of Marketing Science,* Winter 1991, pp. 1–10.
6. Vern Terpstra, "Critical Mass and International Marketing Strategy," *Journal of the Academy of Marketing Science,* Summer 1983, pp. 269–282.
7. Terry Clark, "International Marketing and National Character: A Review and Proposal for an Integrative Theory," *Journal of Marketing,* October 1990, pp. 66–79.
8. Nicolas Papadopoulos, Louise A. Heslop, and Jozsef Beracs, "National Stereotypes and Product Evaluations in a Socialist Country," *International Marketing Review, 7,* no. 1, 1990, pp. 32–47.
9. C. Min Han, "Country Image: Halo or Summary Construct?" *Journal of Marketing Research,* May 1989, pp. 222–229.
10. Nigel G. G. Campbell, John L. Graham, Alain Jolibert, and Hans Gunther Meissner, "Marketing Negotiations in France, Germany, the United Kingdom, and the United States," *Journal of Marketing,* April 1988, pp. 49–62.
11. Brian Mark Hawrysh and Judith Lynne Zaichkowsky, "Cultural Approaches to Negotiations: Understanding the Japanese," *International Marketing Review, 7,* no. 2, 1990, pp. 28–42.
12. Laurel Wentz, "Local Laws Keep International Marketers Hopping," *Advertising Age,* July 11, 1985, p. 20.
13. *Statistical Abstract of the United States,* 1991, p. 841.
14. Earl Naumann and Douglas J. Lincoln, "Non-Tariff Barriers and Entry Strategy Alternatives: Strategic Marketing Implications," *Journal of Small Business Management,* April 1991, pp. 60–70.
15. Ann Reilly Dowd, "Viva Free Trade for Mexico," *Fortune,* June 17, 1991, p. 97.
16. Albert G. Holzinger, "A New Era in Trade," *Nation's Business,* September 1989, pp. 67–69.
17. Dowd, p. 97.
18. Ibid.
19. Ibid.

20. Thomas V. Greer, "The Maquiladora Program: Nature and Current Status," *Developments in Marketing Science,* vol. 12, Academy of Marketing Science Proceedings, 1989, pp. 108–111.

21. Stephen B. Shepard, "President Salinas: 'My People Are in a Hurry,'" *Business Week,* Aug. 12, 1991, pp. 34–36.

22. John Hillkirk, "It Could Be Trade Boom or Bust," *USA Today,* Jan. 12, 1989, p. 4B.

23. Sandra Vandermerwe and Marc-André L'Huillier, "Euro-Consumers in 1992," *Business Horizons,* January–February 1989, pp. 34–40.

24. Eric G. Friberg, "1992: Moves Europeans Are Making," *Harvard Business Review,* May–June 1989, p. 89.

25. Leslie Helm, with Laxmi Nakarmi, Jang Jung Soo, William J. Holstein, and Edith Terry, "The Koreans Are Coming," *Business Week,* Dec. 25, 1985, pp. 46–52.

26. Robert Neff and Laxmi Nakarmi, "Asia's Next Powerhouse: An All-but-Unified Korea?" *Business Week,* Oct. 14, 1991, p. 63.

27. Dori Jones Yang and Dinah Lee, with William J. Holstein and Maria Shao, "China: The Great Backward Leap," *Business Week,* June 19, 1989, pp. 28–32.

28. Dori Jones Yang, with Dirk Bennett and Bill Javerski, "The Other China Is Starting to Soar," *Business Week,* Nov. 6, 1989, pp. 60–62.

29. Louis Kraar, "Asia's Rising Export Powers," *Fortune,* Special Pacific Rim 1989 issue, pp. 43–50.

30. Dinah Lee, "Asia: The Next Era of Growth," *Business Week,* Nov. 11, 1991, pp. 56–59.

31. "East Bloc Business," *USA Today,* Mar. 19, 1990, p. 6B.

32. Rose Brady and Peter Galuszka, "Winter Is Coming, and the Soviet Cupboard Is Bare," *Business Week,* Nov. 4, 1991, p. 52.

33. Peter Gumbel, "Soviet Reformers Urge Bold Push to Liberalize Faltering Economy," *Wall Street Journal,* Oct. 27, 1989, p. A9.

34. "VW, GM Plan East German Ventures," *Chicago Tribune,* Mar. 13, 1990, Sec. 3, p. 1.

35. John Templeman, "Europe's Powerhouse Starts to Clank and Grind," *Business Week,* Oct. 28, 1991, pp. 50–51.

36. John Templeman, Thane Peterson, Gail E. Schares, and Jonathan Kapstein, "The Shape of Europe to Come," *Business Week,* Nov. 27, 1989, pp. 60–64.

37. Richard L. Kirkland, "Russia: Where Gorbanomics Is Leading," *Fortune,* Sept. 28, 1987, pp. 82–84; and Misha G. Knight, "The Russian Bear Turns Bullish on Trade," *Business Marketing,* April 1987, pp. 83–84.

38. Kevin Maney, "Eager East's Welcome Mat Is a Bit Shabby," *USA Today,* Oct. 23, 1989, pp. 1B, 2B; and Peter Gumbel, "Corporate America Flocking to Moscow," *Wall Street Journal,* Oct. 24, 1989, p. A18.

39. Warren J. Keegan, *Global Marketing Management,* 4th ed. (Englewood Cliffs, N.J.: Prentice-Hall, 1989), pp. 378–382.

40. Kamran Kashani, "Beware the Pitfalls of Global Marketing," *Harvard Business Review,* September–October 1989, pp. 93–94.

41. Allan K. Chan, "Localization in International Branding: A Preliminary Investigation on Chinese Names of Foreign Brands in Hong Kong," *International Journal of Advertising,* 9, no. 1, 1990, pp. 81–91.

42. Alecia Swasy, "After Early Stumbles, P&G Is Making Inroads Overseas," *Wall Street Journal,* Feb. 6, 1989, p. B1.

43. Douglass G. Norvell and Robert Morey, "Ethnodomination in the Channels of Distribution of Third World Nations," *Journal of the Academy of Marketing Science,* Summer 1983, pp. 204–235.

44. Aspy P. Palia and Charles F. Keown, "Combating Parallel Importing: Views of U.S. Exporters to the Asia-Pacific Region," *International Marketing Review,* 8, no. 1, 1991, pp. 47–56.

45. Erin Anderson and Anne T. Coughlan, "International Market Entry and Expansion via Independent or Integrated Channels of Distribution," *Journal of Marketing,* January 1987, pp. 71–82.

46. John A. Quelch, "How to Build a Product Licensing Program," *Harvard Business Review,* May–June 1985, pp. 186–187.

47. Andrew Kupfer, "How to Be a Global Manager," *Fortune,* Mar. 14, 1988, pp. 52–58.

48. Kathryn Rudie Harrigan, "Joint Ventures and Competitive Advantage," *Strategic Management Journal,* May 1988, pp. 141–158.

49. A. Dunlap Smith, "Europe's Truckmakers Face Survival of the Biggest," *Business Week,* Nov. 6, 1989, p. 68.

50. "More Companies Prefer Liaisons to Marriage," *Wall Street Journal,* Apr. 12, 1988, p. 35.

51. Thomas Gross and John Neuman, "Strategic Alliances Vital in Global Marketing," *Marketing News,* June 1989, pp. 1–2.

52. Ghazi M. Habib and John J. Burnett, "An Assessment of Channel Behavior in an Alternative Structural Arrangement: The International Joint Venture," *International Marketing Review,* 6, no. 3, 1989, pp. 7–21.

53. Margaret H. Cunningham, "Marketing's New Frontier: International Strategic Alliances," working paper, Queens University (Ontario), 1992.

54. James R. Henley, "Porsche Puts on Brakes," *USA Today,* Jan. 29, 1992, p. 2B; Karen Miller and Terrence Roth, "Porsche, a Favorite in Times of Plenty, Struggles to Survive in a More Frugal Era," *Wall Street Journal,* Jan. 27, 1992, pp. B1–B2; Thos. L. Bryant, "Miscellaneous Ramblings," *Road and Track,* December 1991, p. 53; Jim Henry, "Luxury Car Tax May Speed Sales," *Advertising Age,* Dec. 10, 1990, p. 17; "Japan's Supercars: The Next Samurai," *Economist,* Jan. 4, 1990, pp. 69–72; Joshua Levine, "What Price Perfection?" *Forbes,* Oct. 30, 1989, pp. 228–229; and Garel Rhys, "Smaller Car Firms: Will They Survive?" *Long Range Planning,* October 1989, pp. 22–29.

55. Stanley E. Bird and Diedra A. Johnson, "Diary: Promotion Highlights New Cloning Technology," *AgriMarketing,* March 1991, p. 26; Kenneth H. Keller, "Science and Technology," *Foreign Affairs,* Fall 1990, pp. 123–138; Kerry K. Litzenberg and Vernon E. Schneider, "A Profile of Tomorrow's Agribusiness Leaders: The U.S. Perspective," *Agribusiness,* May 1989, pp. 249–258; and Marj Charlier, "New Breed of Ranchers Is Cloning Cows," *Wall Street Journal,* Feb. 22, 1989, p. B4.

Federal Express Expands Services Internationally

Frederick W. Smith founded Federal Express Corp. in 1973 with part of an $8 million inheritance. At the time, the U.S. Postal Service and United Parcel Service (UPS) were the only means for delivering letters and packages, and they often took several days or more to get packages to their destinations. While a student at Yale in 1965, Smith wrote a paper proposing an independent overnight-delivery service. Although he received a C on the paper, he did not lose sight of his vision. Smith recognized that in today's high-tech world, time is money, and he believed that many businesses would be willing to pay more to get letters, documents, and packages delivered overnight. He was right.

Federal Express began shipping packages overnight from Memphis, Tennessee, on April 17, 1973. On that first night of operations, the company handled six packages, one of which was a birthday present sent by F. W. Smith himself. Today Federal Express handles about 1.5 million packages and documents per day—more than half of all the overnight package and document transactions with the United States—with total revenues of more than $7.69 billion for 1991. According to the company, Federal Express does not just transport packages anywhere in the United States and to much of the rest of the world; it moves *information* for both consumers and industrial customers.

Federal Express has tens of thousands of drop boxes in the United States, and 1,650 service centers and airport facilities around the world. It owns a fleet of over 350 airplanes and 29,000 trucks and vans for handling delivery. The company even has its own weather forecasting service, ensuring that most of its flights arrive within fifteen minutes of schedule. Most packages are sorted at the Memphis superhub (in the middle of the night), but other packages and documents are trucked directly to their destination whenever convenient. For international deliveries to the United Kingdom, Germany, Spain, and one hundred other countries, Federal Express uses a combination of direct services and independent contractors.

Promotion, Pricing, and Competition

As with other services, promotion of Federal Express' delivery service is difficult because of its intangible nature. Federal Express promotes its service, convenience, efficiency, price, and customer service. Its ongoing campaign, "When it absolutely, positively, has to be there overnight," appealed to businesspeople and was one of the most successful slogans in the service industry. Today, that slogan has been replaced with "Absolutely, positively, the best in the business," to further promote the company's record of efficiency and on-time delivery.

When Federal Express began opening service centers all over the United States, it promoted each one with a huge grand opening celebration, complete with direct mail invitations, radio remotes, and door prizes. It reinforced this promotion with excellent customer relations. In a 1985 campaign to highlight the company's international service, Federal Express used point-of-sale materials and gave a World Atlas to each new customer making an international shipment. The international campaign boosted international volume in the service centers 46 percent.

Because Federal Express depends on its employees to promote its service, the company hires the best people it can and offers them the best training and compensation possible. As a result, Federal Express employees are loyal and have very high levels of service and efficiency. In fact, most employees are so loyal they often claim to have "purple blood" that matches the company's official color.

Federal Express charges $15 for delivery of its Overnight Letter packages before 10:30 the next morning. Prices vary for larger packages and international shipments. Customers can save $3 by dropping packages off at a Federal Express office instead of having a courier pick it up. They can save more money by using the company's new Standard Overnight Service, which offers next-day afternoon delivery at a cost of $11.25 ($8.25 if dropped off) for letter packages. Although the U.S. Postal Service currently charges $8.75 for its Express Mail delivery service and the United Parcel Service charges $8.50 for its overnight letter delivery, Federal Express believes it offers customers more service and efficiency for its price.

Despite offering a vital service and having motivated employees and successful promotions, Federal Express faces a maturing market for its services. Figure 1 indicates relative market shares for companies in the

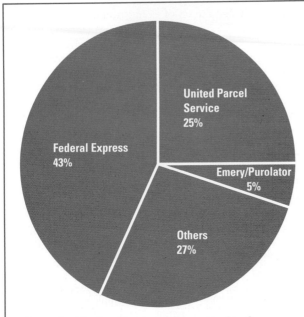

Figure 1 **Market Shares of Domestic Air-Cargo Shipments**

domestic air-cargo industry. The company that created the overnight delivery service now faces intense competition from the U.S. Postal Service, United Parcel Service, and electronic mail (facsimile machines and computer links). Many companies that once sent important documents overnight via Federal Express now fax those documents or send them via computer modem. Federal Express's own experiment in electronic mail service, ZapMail, was abandoned after only three years because it was never profitable. Some experts believe that Federal Express could lose as much as 30 percent of its letter business to electronic mail.

Expanding International Operations

Dropping ZapMail allowed Federal Express to focus on expanding its overseas operations, the most rapidly growing area of the overnight market. Because of the globalization of the economy, businesses need to be able to communicate quickly with employees around the world, with partners in other nations, and with other businesses. Thus Federal Express began international operations in 1975 with shipments to and from the United States' biggest trading partner, Canada. In 1984, Federal Express bought Gelco International, enabling it to start operations in Europe and the Far East. Federal Express was also named the official air express carrier for the 1988 Olympic Games in Seoul, a designation that the company used in promotions. More recent changes in the international arena, like

the establishment of the European Economic Community and the dismantling of closed economies, have allowed Federal Express to gain entry into vast new markets. By 1991, the company had taken advantage of many of these changes and was offering international service to over one hundred countries.

Federal Express's most important strategic move into international markets to date was its 1988 purchase of Tiger International Inc., the owner of the Flying Tiger Line air freight service, for $880 million. The purchase gave Federal Express valuable routes, airport facilities, and expertise in European and Asian markets which it had been struggling to enter. Such valuable assets would have taken Federal Express years to develop on its own. The purchase also gave Federal valuable landing slots in Sydney, Singapore, Bangkok, Hong Kong, Seoul, Paris, Brussels, and Tokyo.

The purchase of Tiger has created some problems for Federal Express. The purchase left the company with a debt of $2.1 billion. It also thrust the company into the heavy-freight distribution market, which is more cyclical and capital intensive than small-package distribution. In addition, many of Tiger's key customers, including UPS and a large number of freight forwarders, are Federal Express competitors. The new Federal Express may lose valuable business from freight forwarders because they will be shut out of the market when Federal Express begins shipping heavy freight door-to-door. Finally, Federal Express inherited 6,500 union employees from Tiger, which it had to weave into its own nonunion work force. Chairman, president, and CEO Fred Smith conceded that merging the two companies would be a challenge, but believed the effort will make Federal Express a powerful global delivery service.

Recent Developments

Although Federal Express' domestic sales and income continue to rise, recent losses in international operations have had a dramatic impact on earnings in the past two years. In 1991, Federal Express lost $391.4 million on international operations, while earnings fell to a low of 11 cents per share. Company officials point to several reasons for the losses. First, the company is still recovering from its buyout of Flying Tiger, a move which increased Federal's fixed costs of international operations. Second, the company has experienced poor sales performance due to very stiff competition. In international air shipments Federal Express holds a 12 percent market share, well behind industry leader DHL which owns a commanding 50 percent of the market. Figure 2 indicates the relative market shares of compet-

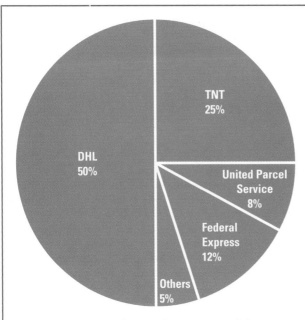

Figure 2 **Market Shares of International Air-Cargo Shipments**

itors in the international air-cargo industry. Finally, Federal Express has had difficulty in building a global infrastructure to support its operations. Negotiating for landing rights, dealing with foreign customs regulations, and establishing information networks have proved to be very costly to the company. Combined, these problems make Federal Express' international service much less reliable than its domestic service.

The Future

With the problems that Federal Express faces in its international operations, many wonder whether the decision to expand globally was a wise one. Others argue that the move was only premature; that is, the international market is not large enough as of yet to support Federal Express' full-scale involvement. Only time will tell whether the move to expand internationally was the best course of action.

In the meantime, Federal Express is counting on the current trend in just-in-time inventory to help boost its revenues. With its sophisticated computer tracking system and overnight delivery, Federal Express actually

manages the inventories of some customers at its Memphis, Oakland, and Newark hubs. IBM, for example, employs Federal Express to warehouse parts for its workstations, enabling it to cut its delivery costs and close 120 parts depots.

In an effort to retain its leading market share, Federal Express has entered UPS's traditional turf: loading-dock deliveries. The company has expanded its two-day ground delivery service of heavy packages and plans to add still more trucks and vans. If necessary, Smith says the company will cut its prices to compete with UPS, Airborne Express, DHL, and other air express companies. Federal Express also plans to shift its emphasis from letters to packages, which generate higher profits.

Federal Express continues to try to improve its services through more sophisticated computers and customer relations and further overseas expansion. The company has been highly successful because it recognized a need and filled it. There is no doubt Fred Smith's C paper has become an indispensable part of the business world.

Questions for Discussion

1. Was Federal Express' decision to expand into global markets a good one? Why or why not?
2. How could recent world events (i.e., German reunification, the break-up of the Soviet Union) affect the international overnight package-delivery market? How might these changes affect Federal Express' international operations?
3. What challenges does Federal Express face in maintaining its leading share of the domestic overnight delivery market?

Sources: Roland Klose, "FedEx Struggles for Profit Overseas," *The Commercial Appeal* (Memphis), Sept. 22, 1991, p. B1; Federal Express Corp. 1991 Annual Report; *Moody's CD Report on Federal Express Corp.*, Moody's Investors' Service, Inc., 1991, pp. 8–10; Glenn Ruffenach, "Federal Express Earnings Plunge 79% But Firm, Some Others See Turnaround," *Wall Street Journal*, Mar. 20, 1990, p. A3; Clemens P. Work, "The Flying-Package Trade Takes Off," *U.S. News and World Report*, Oct. 2, 1989, pp. 47, 50; and Dean Foust, with Jonathan Kapstein, Pia Farrell, Peter Finch, and Chris Power, "Mr. Smith Goes Global," *Business Week*, Feb. 13, 1989, pp. 66–72.

Martin Marietta's Commitment to Ethics

Headlines revealing unethical or illegal business practices seem almost commonplace. Not only is this type of conduct taking a financial toll—experts estimate that U.S. firms lose about $300 billion a year as result—but a toll in public confidence as well. In a recent *Time* magazine survey, about 75 percent of those interviewed said they believe that American business is contributing to a national decline in morals. Many organizations are becoming aware that it is not enough to have a nominal code of ethics written down somewhere if that code is not supported by a solid program of education and implementation. To regain the public's trust and ensure that making a profit doesn't take precedence over "doing the right thing," many U.S. companies are instituting rigorous ethics programs that go beyond mere words on paper.

For those companies relying predominately on government contracts, conducting business in a manner above reproach can be a matter of survival. The U.S. Congress, the Inspector General's Office, the Departments of Defense, Energy, and Transportation, NASA, and numerous federal and state agencies regularly investigate government contractors to ensure that they are adhering to federal regulations. When an inquiry leads to an indictment, the government suspends the contractor's eligibility to bid on or be awarded any government contract for a designated period of time, and the resulting bad press may permanently damage the organization's reputation. For Americans already skeptical about rockets that explode prematurely on the launch pad and $300 toilet seats, official sanctions confirm public suspicions. Martin Marietta Corporation, the sixth largest defense contractor in the United States, boasts an exemplary ethics program that helps the organization maintain profitability and preserve its reputation by guiding employees toward ethical job decisions.

Company Background

Founded in 1917 by Glen L. Martin, Martin Company manufactured America's first bombers as well as other military and commercial aircraft. Its "Clipper," flown by Pan American, made air service across the Pacific a practical reality. After World War II, the firm decreased aircraft production, turning instead to missile, electronics, and nuclear systems manufacturing. Work on the Titan, an intercontinental ballistic missile, eventually evolved into a space launch vehicle. By the time Martin joined with American-Marietta Company, a construction material and chemical products supplier, the firm had produced its last airplane. Even in the midst of today's defense downsizing, Martin Marietta employs about 68,000 workers at 360 plants in the United States and Canada and recently recorded net earnings of $327.6 million.

Company Operations

In 1989, Martin Marietta earned 79 percent of its revenue from defense contracts. Some of its weapons-related products include a night vision system, infra-red search and track devices, anti-tank missiles, and Patriot air defense missiles, made famous during the Persian Gulf War. However, operating five separate divisions, including the Astronautics Group, the Electronics, Information, and Missiles Group, the Materials Group, Energy Systems, and Air Traffic Systems, keeps Martin Marietta from being totally dependent on the Pentagon for its business.

According to company executives, Martin Marietta has acquired $5 billion in non-defense business in the last few years. Examples include contracts with the Social Security Administration, Department of Agriculture, and the Treasury Department; a $600-million agreement to make high-speed mail sorters for the United States Postal Service; a contract to design a U.S. air traffic control system for the 21st century; and a $525 million deal with the Department of Housing and Urban Development (HUD) to update and operate its information systems. The HUD project alone includes setting up an entirely new data system, establishing nationwide communications that link headquarters with eighty-one field offices nationwide, and replacing HUD's networking equipment with 50,000 new personal computers.

According to many industry experts, Martin Marietta continues to thrive because of innovative technologies, strong finances, diverse capabilities, and good management. It is important, however, to include the company's commitment to ethical business practices in the catalog of factors leading to its success.

Ethics Program

Initiated in 1985, Martin Marietta's corporate ethics program consists of a published *Code of Ethical Standards and Conduct* and a Corporate Ethics Office to handle formal complaints and investigations. Educational materials are also a vital component of the program. These include *Guidelines,* a companion publication to the code (to help with dilemmas that have no clear cut "right" and "wrong" answers) and an ethics videotape (defining ethics and providing decision-making direction).

When a company employee has a question involving ethical behavior on the job, (a conflict of interest or record keeping, for example), the formal code specifically outlines a course of action. If talking to a supervisor or a personnel representative doesn't resolve the situation, employees can call their local Ethics Representative whose number is always prominently displayed. Employees can also call the Ethics Office at corporate headquarters with phone lines available 24 hours a day, seven days a week. All calls are confidential, and those who wish may remain anonymous. Once the office receives a complaint, it conducts an internal investigation, reporting its findings to the person initiating that investigation. If the inquiry reveals ethical misconduct, potential sanctions include termination or resignation, suspension without pay, removal from job without termination, a written reprimand, or an oral reprimand and counseling.

Over the last several years, Martin Marietta has won over half of the contracts for which it competed, twice the industry average. Recently, the organization bid for the contract to manufacture several key components of the space-based missile defense system popularly known as SDI (or Star Wars). If Martin Marietta acquires the contract, some of the ongoing political controversy surrounding SDI might spill over onto Martin Marietta. Even so, experts acknowledge that in large part because of its reputation for a commitment to ethical standards, Martin Marietta will remain what it is today, one of the most respected companies worldwide in the defense industry.

Questions for Discussion

1. What types of ethical issues are likely to arise in an organization that relies heavily on government contracts?
2. Why is an effective ethics program especially important for a government contractor like Martin Marietta?
3. What are the most important components of Martin Marietta's ethics program?

Sources: Steven Pearlstein, "Contractors' New Watchword: Efficiency," *Washington Post,* Dec. 11, 1991, pp. A1, A18; Steven Pearlstein, "Martin Marietta: Offense is Best Defense," *Washington Post,* Dec. 11, 1991; "Martin Marietta Corp." *Washington Post,* April 8, 1991; "Martin Marietta Plans to Restructure Units, Eliminating 400 Jobs," *Wall Street Journal,* Jan. 8, 1991; Martin Marietta Corp., 1990 Report; Gary H. Anthes, "HUD Set to Outsource IS," *Computerworld,* Dec. 3, 1990, pp. 1, 119; Richard Pastore, "Peace Has A Price for Defense Firms' IS," *Computerworld,* June, 25, 1990, pp. 1, 118; and "Martin Marietta Corp," *Washington Post,* April 9, 1990; and "Good People Finish First," Martin Marietta Corp. videotape.

PREVIEW:

MICROMARKET COMPUTER APPLICATION VII

Grocery Products Corp.: Analyzing the Contribution of Functional Accounts.

This exercise assigns the expenses from functional accounts to specific product groups to determine the profit or loss generated by each product group. In particular, the appropriate percentages of promotional and general expenses are charged to detergents, foods, and drinks through entry of accounting data into a Lotus 1-2-3 worksheet. Sensitivity analysis is conducted by varying promotion and sales force allocations, gross sales, and taxes. The closing memo summarizes findings and makes recommendations for resource allocations.

Careers in Marketing

Some General Issues

As we note in Chapter 1, between one-fourth and one-third of the civilian work force in the United States is employed in marketing-related jobs. Although there obviously are a multitude of diverse career opportunities in the field, the number of positions in each area varies. For example, millions of workers are employed in many facets of sales, but relatively few people work in public relations and marketing research.

Many nonbusiness organizations now recognize that they do, in fact, perform marketing activities. For that reason, marketing positions are increasing in government agencies, hospitals, charitable and religious groups, educational institutions, and similar organizations.

Even though financial reward is not the sole criterion for selecting a career, it is only practical to consider how much you might earn in a marketing job. Table A.1 illustrates the top ten salary positions for middle managers in marketing. Note that all these careers relate directly to marketing. A national sales manager may earn $60,000 to $100,000 or an even higher salary. Brand managers make $35,000 to $60,000. A media manager could earn $30,000 to $55,000. Generally, entry-level marketing personnel earn more than their counterparts in economics and liberal arts but not as much as people who enter accounting, chemistry, or engineering positions. Average starting salaries for marketing graduates are approaching $25,000. Marketers who advance to higher-level positions often earn high salaries, and a significant proportion of corporate executives held marketing jobs before attaining top-level positions.

Many business recruiters know that students are unrealistic about desired salaries, responsibilities and perks that they demand. Michigan State University researchers questioned campus interviewers about the class of 1992. Only one-third of the recruiters indicated that 1992 job candidates had realistic expectations. One of the major problems seems to be that job candidates are more interested in "what's in it for me?" instead of "what can I do for the company?" In a fiercely competitive job market where the supply of candidates may exceed the demand for new hires, such an attitude can be fatal.[1] Competing effectively in today's market requires the student to be innovative and persistent by examining career opportunities in emerging areas, some of which are discussed in this Appendix.

In the 1990s, it has become more difficult to find a good job in marketing. Many of the largest companies are reorganizing, restructuring, or merging in ways that often result in fewer marketing jobs. Intense competition in the global arena has lead to many businesses cutting back on hiring in general. For example, the 1995 salaried and hourly workers at General Motors will be about half

Position	Salary Range
National sales manager	$60,000–$100,000
Corporate strategic market planner	55,000– 75,000
International sales	50,000– 75,000
Advertising account supervisor	40,000– 70,000
Distribution manager	40,000– 60,000
Sales promotion manager	40,000– 55,000
Product/brand manager	35,000– 60,000
Purchasing manager	35,000– 55,000
Media manager	30,000– 55,000
Retail manager	25,000– 45,000

the size of GM's 1985 workforce. Thus, you will be entering a highly competitive job market, and you will need to know what characteristics recruiters look for and how to present your skills and achievements effectively.

Another important issue is whether you can enjoy the work associated with a particular career. Because you will spend almost 40 percent of your waking hours on the job, you should not allow such factors as economic conditions or status to override your personal goals as you select a lifelong career. Too often, people do not weigh these factors realistically. You should give considerable thought to your choice of a career, and you should adopt a well-planned, systematic approach to finding a position that meets your personal and career objectives.

After determining your objectives, you should identify the organizations that are likely to offer desirable opportunities. Learn as much as possible about these organizations before setting up employment interviews; job recruiters are impressed with applicants who have done their homework.

When making initial contact with potential employers by mail, enclose a brief, clearly written letter of introduction. After an initial interview, you should send a brief letter of thanks to the interviewer. The job of getting the right job is important, and you owe it to yourself to take this process seriously.

The Résumé

The résumé is one of the keys to being considered for a good job. Because it states your qualifications, experiences, education, and career goals, the résumé is a chance for a potential employer to assess your compatibility with the job requirements. For the employer's and individual's benefit, the résumé should be accurate and current.

To be effective, the résumé can be targeted toward a specific position, as Figure A.1 shows. This document is only one example of an acceptable résumé. The job target section is specific and leads directly to the applicant's qualifica-

LORRAINE MILLER
2212 WEST WILLOW
(416) 862-9169

EDUCATION: B.A. Arizona State University, 1993, Marketing, achieved a 3.4 on a 4.0 scale throughout college.

POSITION DESIRED: PRODUCT MANAGER WITH AN INTERNATIONAL FIRM PROVIDING FUTURE CAREER DEVELOPMENT AT THE EXECUTIVE LEVEL.

QUALIFICATIONS:

* communicates well with individuals to achieve a common goal

* handles tasks efficiently and in a timely manner

* knowledge of advertising sales, management, marketing research, packaging, pricing, distribution, and warehousing

* coordinates many activities at one time

* receives and carries out assigned tasks or directives

* writes complete status or research reports

EXPERIENCES:

* Assistant Editor of college paper

* Treasurer of the American Marketing Association (student chapter)

* Internship with 3-Cs Advertising, Berkeley, CA

* Student Assistantship with Dr. Steve Green, Professor of Marketing, Arizona State University

* Solo cross-Canada canoe trek, summer 1992

WORK RECORD:

1993 – Present	Blythe and Co., Inc.	
	* Junior Advertising Account Executive	
1992 – Present	Assistantship with Dr. Steve Green	
	* Research Assistant	
1990 – 1991	The Men	
	* Retail sales and consumer relations	
1988 – 1990	Farmer	
	* Helped operate relative's blueberry farm in Michigan for three summers.	

tions for the job. Capabilities show what the applicant can do and that the person has an understanding of the job's requirements. Skills and strengths should be highlighted as to how they relate to the specific job. The achievement section indicates success at accomplishing tasks or goals within the job market and at school. The work experience section includes an unusual listing that might pique the interest of an interviewer: helped operate relative's blueberry farm in Michigan for three summers. That is something that could help launch an interview discussion. It tends to incite rather than satisfy curiosity, thus inviting further inquiry. The solo cross-Canada canoe trek elicited many highly favorable comments from interviewers. The listing is exceedingly brief, but interviewers never failed to bring it up.[2]

Common suggestions for improving résumés include deleting useless information, improving organization, using professional printing and typing, listing duties (not accomplishments), maintaining grammatical perfection, and avoiding an overly elaborate or fancy format.[3] The biggest problems in résumés are distortions and lies; 36 percent of the personnel experts surveyed thought that this was a major problem.[4] People lie most often about previous salaries and tasks performed in former jobs.

Types of Marketing Careers

In considering marketing as a career, the first step is to evaluate broad categories of career opportunities in the areas of marketing research, sales, public relations, industrial buying, distribution management, product management, advertising, retail management, and direct marketing. Keep in mind that the categories described here are not all-inclusive and that each encompasses hundreds of marketing jobs.

Marketing Research

Clearly, marketing research and information systems are vital aspects of marketing decision making. Marketing researchers survey Americans to determine their habits, preferences, and aspirations. The information about buyers and environmental forces that research and information systems provide improves a marketer's ability to understand the dynamics of the marketplace and make effective decisions.

Marketing researchers gather and analyze data relating to specific problems. Marketing research firms are usually employed by a client organization, which could be a provider of goods or services, a nonbusiness organization, the government, a research consulting firm, or an advertising agency. The activities performed include concept testing, product testing, package testing, advertising testing, test-market research, and new-product research.

A researcher may be involved in one or several stages of research, depending on the size of the project, the organization of the research unit, and the researcher's experience. Marketing research trainees in large organizations usually perform a considerable amount of clerical work, such as compiling secondary data from a firm's accounting and sales records and periodicals, government publications, syndicated data services, and unpublished sources. A junior analyst may edit and code questionnaires or tabulate survey results. Trainees also may participate in primary data gathering by learning to conduct mail and telephone surveys, conducting personal interviews, and using observational methods of primary data collection. As a marketing researcher gains experience, the researcher may become involved in defining problems and developing hypotheses; designing research procedures; and analyzing, interpreting, and reporting findings. Exceptional personnel may assume responsibility for entire research projects.

Although most employers consider a bachelor's degree sufficient qualification for a marketing research trainee, many specialized positions require a graduate degree in business administration, statistics, or other related fields. Today, trainees are more likely to have a marketing or statistics degree than a liberal arts degree, courses in statistics, data processing, psychology, sociology, communications, economics, and English composition are valuable preparations for a career in marketing research.

The U.S. Bureau of Labor Statistics indicates that marketing research provides abundant employment opportunity, especially for applicants with graduate training in marketing research, statistics, economics, and the social sciences. Generally, the value of information gathered by marketing information and research systems will become more important as competition increases, thus expanding the opportunities for prospective marketing research personnel.

The three major career paths in marketing research are with independent marketing research agencies/data suppliers, advertising agency marketing research departments, and marketing research departments in businesses. In a company in which marketing research plays a key role, the researcher is often a member of the marketing strategy team. Surveying or interviewing consumers is the heart of the marketing research firm's activities. A statistician selects the sample to be surveyed, analysts design the questionnaire and synthesize the gathered data into a final report, data processors tabulate the data, and the research director controls and coordinates all these activities so that each project is computed to the client's satisfaction (i.e., consumer and industrial product manufacturers).[5] In marketing research agencies, a researcher deals with many clients, products, and problems. Advertising agencies use research as an ingredient in developing and refining campaigns for existing or potentially new clients.[6]

Salaries in marketing research depend on the type, size, and location of the firm as well as the nature of the positions. Generally, starting salaries are somewhat higher and promotions somewhat slower than in other occupations requiring similar training. Typical starting salaries are $21,000 to $25,000 per year. Salaries range from $18,000 for a junior analyst to $35,000 or more for a senior analyst, and research directors often earn salaries of more than $60,000. In addition, the role of marketing in overall corporate planning is becoming more important as companies seek marketing information for strategic planning purposes. Marketing research directors are reporting to higher levels of management than ever before, and the number of corporate vice presidents who receive marketing research as regular input in decision making has doubled in recent years.

Sales

Millions of people earn a living through personal selling. Chapter 17 defines personal selling as a process of informing customers and persuading them to purchase products through personal communication in an exchange situation. Although this definition describes the general nature of many sales positions, individual selling jobs vary enormously with respect to the type of businesses and products involved, the educational background and skills required, and the specific activities sales personnel perform. Because the work is so varied, sales occupations offer numerous career opportunities for people with a wide range of qualifications, interests, and goals. A sales career offers the greatest potential compensation. Sales careers opportunities discussed in this section are both business-to-business sales types. The following two sections describe what is involved in wholesale and manufacturer sales.

Wholesale Sales Wholesalers perform activities to expedite transactions in which purchases are intended for resale or to be used to make other products. Wholesalers thus provide services to both retailers and producers. They can help match producers' products to retailers' needs and can provide accumulation and allocation services that save producers time, money, and resources. Some activities associated with wholesaling include planning and negotiating transactions; assisting customers with sales, advertising, sales promotion, and publicity; handling transportation and storage activities; providing customers with inventory control and data processing assistance; establishing prices; and giving customers technical, management, and merchandising assistance.

The background wholesale personnel need depends on the nature of the product handled. A drug wholesaler, for example, needs extensive technical training and product knowledge and may have a degree in chemistry, biology, or pharmacology. A wholesaler of standard office supplies, on the other hand, may find it more important to be familiar with various brands, suppliers, and prices than to have technical knowledge about the products. A new wholesale representative may begin a career as a sales trainee or hold a nonselling job that provides experience with inventory, prices, discounts, and the firm's customers. A college graduate usually enters the sales force directly out of school. Competent salespersons also transfer from manufacturer and retail sales positions.

The number of wholesale sales positions is expected to grow about as fast as the average for all occupations. Earnings for wholesale personnel vary widely because commissions often make up a large proportion of their incomes.

Manufacturer Sales Manufacturer sales personnel sell a firm's products to wholesalers, retailers, and industrial buyers; they thus perform many of the same activities wholesale salespersons handle. As is the case with wholesaling, the educational requirements for manufacturer sales depend largely on the type and complexity of the products and markets. Manufacturers of nontechnical products usually hire college graduates who have a liberal arts or business degree and give them training and information about the firm's products, prices, and customers. Manufacturers of highly technical products generally prefer applicants who have degrees in fields associated with the particular industry and market involved.

More and more sophisticated marketing skills are being utilized in industrial sales. Industrial marketing originally followed the commodity approach to complete a sale, whereby the right product is in the right place at the right time and for the right price. Today industrial sales use the same marketing concepts and strategies as do marketers selling to consumers.

Employment opportunities in manufacturer sales are expected to experience average growth. Manufacturer sales personnel are well compensated and earn above-average salaries. Most are paid a combination of salaries and commissions, and the highest salaries are paid by manufacturers of electrical equipment, food products, and rubber goods. Commissions vary according to the salesperson's efforts, abilities, and sales territory and the type of products sold.

Industrial Buying

Industrial buyers, or purchasing agents, are responsible for maintaining an adequate supply of the goods and services that an organization needs for operations. In general, industrial buyers purchase all items needed for direct use in producing other products and for use in the day-to-day operations. Industrial buyers in large firms often specialize in purchasing a single, specific class of products, for example, all petroleum-based lubricants. In smaller organizations, buyers may be responsible for purchasing many different categories of items, including such goods as raw materials, component parts, office supplies, and operating services.

An industrial buyer's main job is selecting suppliers who offer the best quality, service, and price. When the products to be purchased are standardized, buyers may compare suppliers by examining catalogs and trade journals, making purchases by description. Buyers who purchase highly homogeneous products often meet with salespeople to examine samples and observe demonstrations. Sometimes, buyers must inspect the actual product before purchasing; in other cases, they invite suppliers to bid on large orders. Buyers who purchase specialized equipment often deal directly with manufacturers to obtain specially designed items made to specifications. After choosing a supplier and placing an order, an industrial buyer usually must trace the shipment to ensure on-time delivery. Finally, the buyer sometimes is responsible for receiving and inspecting an order and authorizing payment to the shipper.

Training requirements for a career in industrial buying relate to the needs of the firm and the types of products purchased. A manufacturer of heavy machinery may prefer an applicant who has a background in engineering; a service company, on the other hand, may recruit liberal arts majors. Although it is not generally required, a college degree is becoming increasingly important for buyers who wish to advance to management positions. Entry-level positions are in the $20,000 to $25,000 range.

Employment prospects for industrial buyers are expected to increase faster than average through the 1990s. Opportunities will be excellent for individuals with a master's degree in business administration or a bachelor's degree in engineering, science, or business administration. In addition, companies that manufacture heavy equipment, computer equipment, and communications equipment will need buyers with technical backgrounds.

Public Relations

Public relations encompasses a broad set of communication activities designed to create and maintain favorable relations between the organization and its publics—customers, employees, stockholders, government officials, and society in general. Public relations specialists help clients create the image, issue, or message they wish to present and communicate it to the appropriate audience. According to the Public Relations Society of America, 120,000 persons work in public relations in the United States. Half the billings found in the 4,000 public relations agencies and firms come from Chicago and New York. The highest starting salaries can also be found there. Communication is basic to all public relations programs. To communicate effectively, public relations practitioners first must gather data about the firm's client publics to assess their needs, identify problems, formulate recommendations, implement new plans, and evaluate current activities.

Public relations personnel disseminate large amounts of information to the organization's client publics. Written communication is the most versatile tool of public relations, and good writing ability is essential. Public relations practitioners must be adept at writing for a variety of media and audiences. It is not unusual for a person in public relations to prepare reports, news releases, speeches, broadcast scripts, technical manuals, employee publications, shareholder reports, and other communications aimed at both organizational personnel and external groups. In addition, a public relations practitioner needs a thorough knowledge of the production techniques used in preparing various communications.

Public relations personnel also establish distribution channels for the organization's publicity. They must have a thorough understanding of the various media, their areas of specialization, the characteristics of their target audiences, and their policies regarding publicity. Anyone who hopes to succeed in public relations must develop close working relationships with numerous media personnel to enlist their interest in disseminating an organization's communications.

A college education combined with writing or media-related experience is the best preparation for a career in public relations. Most beginners have a college degree in journalism, communications, or public relations, but some employers prefer a business background. Courses in journalism, business administration, marketing, creative writing, psychology, sociology, political science, economics, advertising, English, and public speaking are recommended. Some employers require applicants to present a portfolio of published articles, television or radio programs, slide presentations, and other work samples. Other agencies are requiring written tests that include activities such as writing sample press releases. Manufacturing firms, public utilities, transportation and insurance companies, and trade and professional associations are the largest employers of public relations personnel. In addition, sizable numbers of public relations personnel work for health-related organizations, government agencies, educational institutions, museums, and religious and service groups.

Although some larger companies provide extensive formal training for new personnel, most new public relations employees learn on the job. Beginners usually perform routine tasks such as maintaining files about company activities and searching secondary data sources for information that can be used in publicity materials. More experienced employees write press releases, speeches, and articles and help plan public relations campaigns.

Employment opportunities in public relations are expected to increase faster than the average for all occupations through the 1990s. One caveat is in order, however: Competition for beginning jobs is keen. The prospects are best for applicants who have solid academic preparation and some media experience. Abilities that differentiate candidates such as a basic understanding of computers are becoming increasingly important.

Distribution Management

A distribution (or traffic) manager arranges for the transportation of goods within firms and through marketing channels. Transportation is an essential distribution activity that permits a firm to create time and place utility for its products. It is the distribution manager's job to analyze various transportation modes and select the combination that minimizes cost and transit time while providing acceptable levels of reliability, capability, accessibility, and security.

To accomplish this task, a distribution manager performs many activities. First, the individual must choose one or a combination of transportation modes from the five major modes available: railways, motor vehicles, inland waterways, pipelines, and airways. Then the distribution manager must select the specific routes the goods will travel and the particular carriers to be used, weighing such factors as freight classifications and regulations, freight charges, time schedules, shipment sizes, and loss and damage ratios. In addition, this person may be responsible for preparing shipping documents, tracing shipments, handling loss and damage claims, keeping records of freight rates, and monitoring changes in government regulations and transportation technology.

Distribution management employs relatively few people and is expected to grow about as fast as the average for all occupations in the near future. Manufacturing firms are the largest employers of distribution managers, although some traffic managers work for wholesalers, retail stores, and consulting firms. Salaries of experienced distribution managers vary but generally are much higher than the average for all nonsupervisory personnel.

Entry-level positions for distribution management are in the $20,000 to $25,000 per year salary range. Starting jobs are diverse, varying from inventory control, traffic scheduling, operations management, or distribution management. Inventory management is an area of great opportunity because many U.S. firms see inventory costs as high relative to foreign competition, especially that from the Japanese.

Most employers prefer graduates of technical programs or seek people who have completed courses in transportation, logistics, distribution management, economics, statistics, computer science, management, marketing, and commercial law. A successful distribution manager must be adept at handling technical data and be able to interpret and communicate highly technical information.

Product Management

The product manager occupies a staff position and is responsible for the success or failure of a product line. Product managers coordinate most of the marketing activities required to market a product; however, because they hold a staff position, they have relatively little actual authority over marketing personnel. Even so, they take on a large amount of responsibility and typically are paid quite well relative to other marketing employees. Being a product manager can be rewarding both financially and psychologically, but it can also be frustrating because of the disparity between responsibility and authority.

A product manager should have a general knowledge of advertising, transportation modes, inventory control, selling and sales management, sales promotion, marketing research, packaging, pricing, and warehousing. The individual must be knowledgeable enough to communicate effectively with personnel in these functional areas and to make suggestions and help assess alternatives when major decisions are being made.

Product managers usually need college training in an area of business administration. A master's degree is helpful, although a person usually does not become a product manager directly out of school. Frequently, several years of selling and sales management are prerequisites for a product management position, which often is a major step in the career path of top-level marketing executives. The average salary for an experienced product manager is $35,000 to $60,000.

Advertising

Advertising pervades our daily lives. Business and nonbusiness organizations use advertising in many ways and for many reasons. Advertising clearly needs individuals with diverse skills to fill a variety of jobs. Creative imagination, artistic talent, and expertise in expression and persuasion are important for copywriters, artists, and account executives. Sales and managerial ability are vital to the success of advertising managers, media buyers, and production managers. Research directors must have a solid understanding of research techniques and human behavior.

Advertising professionals disagree on the most beneficial educational background for a career in advertising. Most employers prefer college graduates. Some employers seek individuals with degrees in advertising, journalism, or business; others prefer graduates with broad liberal arts backgrounds. Still other employers rank relevant work experience above educational background.

"Advertisers look for generalists," says Kate Preston, a staff executive of the American Association of Advertising Agencies, "thus there are just as many economics or general liberal arts majors as M.B.A.s." Common entry-level positions in an advertising agency are found in the traffic department, account service (account coordinator), or in the media department (media assistant). Starting salaries in these positions are often quite low but to gain experience in the advertising industry, employees must work their way up in the system. The entry-level salaries of media assistants and account coordinators are often $15,000 or less.[7]

A variety of organizations employ advertising personnel. Although advertising agencies are perhaps the most visible and glamorous of employers, many manufacturing firms, retail stores, banks, utility companies, and professional and trade associations maintain advertising departments. Advertising jobs also can be found with television and radio stations, newspapers, and magazines. Other businesses that employ advertising personnel include printers, art studios, letter shops, and package-design firms. Specific advertising jobs include advertising manager, account executive, research director, copywriter, media specialist, and production manager.

Employment opportunities for advertising personnel are expected to decrease in the early nineties as agency acquisitions and mergers continue. General economic conditions, however, strongly influence the size of advertising budgets and, hence, employment opportunities.

Retail Management

More than 20 million people in the United States work in the retail industry.[8] Although a career in retailing may begin in sales, there is more to retailing than simply selling. Many retail personnel occupy management positions. Besides managing the sales force, they focus on selecting and ordering merchandise, promotional activities, inventory control, customer credit operations, accounting, personnel, and store security.

How retail stores are organized varies. In many large department stores, retail management personnel rarely get involved with actually selling to customers; these duties are performed by retail salespeople. However, other types of retail organizations may require management personnel to perform selling activities from time to time.

Large retail stores offer a variety of management positions besides those at the very top, including assistant buyers, buyers, department managers, section managers, store managers, division managers, regional managers, and vice president of merchandising. The following list describes the general duties of four of these positions; the precise nature of these duties varies from one retail organization to another.

A section manager coordinates inventory and promotions and interacts with buyers, salespeople, and ultimate consumers. The manager performs merchandising, labor relations, and managerial activities and can rarely expect to get away with as little as a forty-hour work week.

The buyer's task is more focused. In this fast-paced occupation, there is much travel and pressure and the need to be open-minded with respect to new and potentially successful items.

The regional manager coordinates the activities of several stores within a given area. Sales, promotions, and procedures in general are monitored and supported.

The vice president of merchandising has a broad scope of managerial responsibility and reports to the president at the top of the organization.

Traditionally, retail managers began their careers as salesclerks. Today, many large retailers hire college-educated people, put them through management training programs, and then place them directly into management positions. They frequently hire people with backgrounds in liberal arts or business administration. Sales and retailing are the greatest employment opportunities for marketing students.

Retail management positions can be exciting and challenging. Competent, ambitious individuals often assume a great deal of responsibility very quickly and advance rapidly. However, compensation programs for entry-level positions (management trainees) have historically been below average. This situation is changing rapidly with major specialty, department, and discount stores offering entry salaries in the $20,000 to $25,000 range. In addition, a retail manager's job is physically demanding and sometimes entails long working hours. Nonetheless, positions in retail management often provide numerous opportunities to excel and advance.

Direct Marketing

One of the most dynamic areas in marketing is direct marketing, in which the seller uses one or more direct media (telephone, mail, print, or television) to solicit a response. For example, Shell Oil uses its credit card billings (direct mail) to sell a variety of consumer products.

The telephone is a major vehicle for selling many consumer products. Telemarketing is direct selling to customers using a variety of technological improvements in telephone services. According to the American Telemarketing Association (Glenview, Illinois), $73 billion of the industry's sales come from business-to-business marketing, not from selling to consumers at home. In addition, the telemarketing industry has been growing an average of 30 percent per year.

The use of direct mail catalogs appeals to market segments such as working women or people who find going to retail stores difficult or inconvenient. Newspapers and magazines offer great opportunity, especially in special market segments. *Golf Digest*, for example, is obviously a good medium for selling golfing equipment. Cable television provides many new opportunities for selling directly to consumers. Home shopping channels, for example, have been very successful. Interactive cable will offer a new method to expand direct marketing by developing timely exchange opportunities for consumers.

The most important asset in direct marketing is experience. Employers often look to other industries to locate experienced professionals. This preference means that if you can get an entry-level position in direct marketing, you will have a real advantage in developing a career.

Jobs in direct marketing include buyers, such as department store buyers, who select goods for catalog, telephone, or direct mail sales. Catalog managers develop marketing strategies for each new catalog that goes into the mail. Research/mail-list management involves developing lists of products that will sell in direct marketing and lists of names that will respond to a direct mail effort. Order fulfillment managers direct the shipment of products once they are sold. Direct marketing's effectiveness is enhanced by periodic analysis of advertising and communications at all phases of contact with the consumer. Direct marketing involves all aspects of the marketing decision. It is becoming a more professional career area that provides great opportunity.

Notes

1. *Wall Street Journal's Managing Your Career,* Spring 1992, p. 3.
2. Donald Asher, "Use Your Resume to Show Versatility," *Wall Street Journal's Managing Your Career,* Spring 1992, pp. 20, 23.
3. T. Jackson, "Writing the Targeted Resume," *Business Week's Guide to Careers,* Spring 1983, pp. 26–27.
4. Burke Marketing Research for Robert Hall Inc. Reported in *USA Today,* Oct. 2, 1987, p. B-1.
5. Judith George, "Market Researcher," *Business Week Careers,* October 1987, p. 10.
6. "What It's Like to Work in Marketing Research Depends on Where You Work—Supplier, Ad Agency, Manufacturer," *Collegiate Edition Marketing News,* December 1985, pp. 1, 3.
7. Vincent Daddiego, "Making It In Advertising," *Business Week Careers,* February 1988, p. 42.
8. Eleanor May, *Future Trends in Retailing* (Cambridge, Mass.: Marketing Science Institute, 1987), p. 1.

Financial Analysis in Marketing

Our discussion in this book focused more on fundamental concepts and decisions in marketing than on financial details. However, marketers must understand the basic components of selected financial analyses if they are to explain and defend their decisions. In fact, they must be familiar with certain financial analyses if they are to reach good decisions in the first place. We therefore examine three areas of financial analyses: cost-profit aspects of the income statement, selected performance ratios, and price calculations.[1] To control and evaluate marketing activities, marketers must understand the income statement and what it says about the operations of their organization. They also need to be acquainted with performance ratios, which compare current operating results with past results and with results in the industry at large. In the last part of the appendix, we discuss price calculations as the basis of price adjustments. Marketers are likely to use all these areas of financial analysis at various times to support their decisions and to make necessary adjustments in their operations.

The Income Statement

The income, or operating, statement presents the financial results of an organization's operations over a period of time. The statement summarizes revenues earned and expenses incurred by a profit center, whether it is a department, brand, product line, division, or entire firm. The income statement presents the firm's net profit or net loss for a month, quarter, or year.

Table B.1 is a simplified income statement for a retail store. The owners of the store, Rose Costa and Nick Schultz, see that net sales of $250,000 are decreased by the cost of goods sold and by other business expenses to yield a net income of $83,000. Of course, these figures are only highlights of the complete income statement, which appears in Table B.2.

The income statement can be used in several ways to improve the management of a business. First, it enables an owner or manager to compare actual results with budgets for various parts of the statement. For example, Rose and Nick see that the total amount of merchandise sold (gross sales) is $260,000. Customers returned merchandise or received allowances (price reductions) totaling $10,000. Suppose the budgeted amount was only $9,000. By checking the ticket for sales returns and allowances, the owners can determine why these events occurred and whether the $10,000 figure could be lowered by adjusting the marketing mix.

---

1. We gratefully acknowledge the assistance of Jim L. Grimm, Professor of Marketing, Illinois State University, in writing this appendix.

Stoneham Auto Supplies
Income Statement for the Year Ended December 31, 1992

Net Sales	$250,000
Cost of Goods Sold	45,000
Gross Margin	$205,000
Expenses	122,000
Net Income	$ 83,000

After subtracting returns and allowances from gross sales, Rose and Nick can determine net sales from the statement. They are pleased with this figure because it is higher than their sales target of $240,000. Net sales is the amount the firm has available to pay its expenses.

A major expense for most companies that sell goods (as opposed to services) is the cost of goods sold. For Stoneham Auto Supplies, it amounts to 18 percent of net sales. Other expenses are treated in various ways by different companies. In our example, they are broken down into standard categories of selling expenses, administrative expenses, and general expenses.

The income statement shows that the cost of goods Stoneham Auto Supplies sold during fiscal year 1992 was $45,000. This figure was derived in the following way. First, the statement shows that merchandise in the amount of $51,000 was purchased during the year. In paying the invoices associated with these inventory additions, purchase (cash) discounts of $4,000 were earned, resulting in net purchases of $47,000. Special requests for selected merchandise throughout the year resulted in $2,000 of freight charges, which increased the net cost of delivered purchases to $49,000. Adding this amount to the beginning inventory of $48,000, the cost of goods available for sale during 1992 was $97,000. However, the records indicate that the value of inventory at the end of the year was $52,000. Because this amount was not sold, the cost of goods that were sold during the year was $45,000.

Rose and Nick observe that the total value of their inventory increased by 8.3 percent during the year:

$$\frac{\$52,000 - \$48,000}{\$48,000} = \frac{\$4,000}{\$48,000} = \frac{1}{12} = .0825 \text{ or } 8.3\%$$

Further analysis is needed to determine whether this increase is desirable or undesirable. (Note that the income statement provides no details concerning the composition of the inventory held on December 31; other records supply this information.) If Nick and Rose determine that inventory on December 31 is excessive, they can implement appropriate marketing action.

Gross margin is the difference between net sales and cost of goods sold. Gross margin reflects the markup on products and is the amount available to pay all other expenses and provide a return to the owners. Stoneham Auto Supplies had a gross margin of $205,000:

Stoneham Auto Supplies
Income Statement for the Year Ended December 31, 1992

Gross Sales			$260,000
Less: Sales returns and allowances			10,000
Net Sales			$250,000
Cost of Goods Sold			
Inventory, January 1, 1992 (at cost)		$48,000	
Purchases	$51,000		
Less: Purchase discounts	4,000		
Net purchases	$47,000		
Plus: Freight-in	2,000		
Net cost of delivered purchases		$49,000	
Cost of goods available for sale		$97,000	
Less: Inventory, December 31, 1992 (at cost)		52,000	
Cost of goods sold			$ 45,000
Gross Margin			$205,000
Expenses			
Selling expenses			
Sales salaries and commissions	$32,000		
Advertising	16,000		
Sales promotions	3,000		
Delivery	2,000		
Total selling expenses		$53,000	
Administrative expenses			
Administrative salaries	$20,000		
Office salaries	20,000		
Office supplies	2,000		
Miscellaneous	1,000		
Total administrative expenses		$43,000	
General expenses			
Rent	$14,000		
Utilities	7,000		
Bad debts	1,000		
Miscellaneous (local taxes, insurance, interest, depreciation)	4,000		
Total general expenses		$26,000	
Total expenses			$122,000
Net Income			$ 83,000

Net Sales	$250,000
Cost of Goods Sold	– 45,000
Gross Margin	$205,000

Stoneham's expenses (other than cost of goods sold) during 1992 totaled $122,000. Observe that $53,000, or slightly more than 43 percent of the total, constituted direct selling expenses:

$$\frac{\$53,000 \text{ selling expenses}}{\$122,000 \text{ total expenses}} = .434 \text{ or } 43\%$$

The business employs three salespersons (one full-time) and pays competitive wages for the area. All selling expenses are similar to dollar amounts for fiscal year 1991, but Nick and Rose wonder whether more advertising is necessary because inventory increased by more than 8 percent during the year.

The administrative and general expenses are also essential for operating the business. A comparison of these expenses with trade statistics for similar businesses indicate that the figures are in line with industry amounts.

Net income, or net profit, is the amount of gross margin remaining after deducting expenses. Stoneham Auto Supplies earned a net profit of $83,000 for the fiscal year ending December 31, 1992. Note that net income on this statement is figured before payment of state and federal income taxes.

Income statements for intermediaries and for businesses that provide services follow the same general format as that shown for Stoneham Auto Supplies in Table B.2. The income statement for a manufacturer, however, is somewhat different in that the "purchases" portion is replaced by "cost of goods manufactured." Table B.3 shows the entire Cost of Goods Sold section for a manufacturer, including cost of goods manufactured. In other respects, income statements for retailers and manufacturers are similar.

Selected Performance Ratios

Rose and Nick's assessment of how well their business did during fiscal year 1990 can be improved through selective use of analytical ratios. These ratios enable a manager to compare the results for the current year with data from previous years and industry statistics. Unfortunately, comparisons of the current income statement with income statements and industry statistics from other years are not very meaningful because factors such as inflation are not accounted for when comparing dollar amounts. More meaningful comparisons can be made by converting these figures to a percentage of net sales, as this section shows.

The first analytical ratios we discuss, the operating ratios, are based on the net sales figure from the income statement.

Operating Ratios

Operating ratios express items on the income, or operating, statement as percentages of net sales. The first step is to convert the income statement into percentages of net sales, as illustrated in Table B.4.

Stoneham Auto Supplies
Income Statement for the Year Ended December 31, 1992

Cost of Goods Sold			
Finished goods inventory January 1, 1992			$ 50,000
Cost of goods manufactured			
Work-in-process inventory, January 1, 1992		$ 20,000	
Raw materials inventory, January 1, 1992	$ 40,000		
Net cost of delivered purchases	240,000		
Cost of goods available for use	$280,000		
Less: Raw materials inventory December 31, 1992	42,000		
Cost of goods placed in production		$238,000	
Direct labor		32,200	
Manufacturing overhead			
Indirect labor	$ 12,000		
Supervisory salaries	10,000		
Operating supplies	6,000		
Depreciation	12,000		
Utilities	10,000		
Total manufacturing overhead		$ 50,000	
Total manufacturing costs		$320,000	
Total work-in-process		$340,000	
Less: Work-in-process inventory, December 31, 1992		22,000	
Cost of goods manufactured			$318,000
			$368,000
Cost of goods available for sale			
Less: Finished goods inventory, December 31, 1992			48,000
Cost of Goods Sold			**$320,000**

After making this conversion, the manager looks at several key operating ratios: two profitability ratios (the gross margin ratio and the net income ratio) and the operating expense ratio.

For Stoneham Auto Supplies, these ratios are determined as follows (see Tables B.2 and B.4 for supporting data):

$$\text{Gross margin ratio} = \frac{\text{gross margin}}{\text{net sales}} = \frac{\$205,000}{\$250,000} = 82\%$$

$$\text{Net income ratio} = \frac{\text{net income}}{\text{net sales}} = \frac{\$83,000}{\$250,000} = 33.2\%$$

$$\text{Operating expense ratio} = \frac{\text{total expense}}{\text{net sales}} = \frac{\$122,000}{\$250,000} = 48.8\%$$

The gross margin ratio indicates the percentage of each sales dollar available to cover operating expenses and achieve profit objectives. The net income ratio indicates the percentage of each sales dollar that is classified as earnings (profit) before payment of income taxes. The operating expense ratio indicates the percentage of each dollar needed to cover operating expenses.

If Nick and Rose feel that the operating expense ratio is higher than historical data and industry standards, they can analyze each operating expense ratio in Table B.4 to determine which expenses are too high and can then take corrective action.

After reviewing several key operating ratios, in fact, managers will probably want to analyze all the items on the income statement. For instance, by doing so, Nick and Rose can determine whether the 8 percent increase in inventory was necessary.

Inventory Turnover

The inventory turnover rate, or stockturn rate, is an analytical ratio that can be used to answer the question, "Is the inventory level appropriate for this business?" The inventory turnover rate indicates the number of times that an inventory is sold (turns over) during one year. To be useful, this figure is then compared with historical turnover rates and industry rates.

The inventory turnover rate can be computed on cost as follows:

$$\text{Inventory turnover} = \frac{\text{cost of goods sold}}{\text{average inventory at cost}}$$

Rose and Nick would calculate the turnover rate from Table B.2 as follows:

$$\frac{\text{Cost of goods sold}}{\text{Average inventory at cost}} = \frac{\$45,000}{\$50,000} = 0.9 \text{ time}$$

They find that inventory turnover is less than once per year (0.9 time). Industry averages for competitive firms are 2.8 times. This figure convinces Rose and Nick that their investment in inventory is too large and that they need to reduce their inventory.

Return on Investment

Return on investment (ROI) is a ratio that indicates management's efficiency in generating sales and profits from the total amount invested in the firm. For

Table B.4

Income Statement Components as Percentages of Net Sales

Stoneham Auto Supplies
Income Statement as a percentage of net sales for the year ended
December 31, 1992

		Percentage of net sales
Gross Sales		103.8%
Less: Sales returns and allowances		3.8
Net Sales		100.0%
Cost of Goods Sold		
Inventory, January 1, 1992 (at cost)		19.2%
Purchases	20.4%	
Less: Purchase discounts	1.6	
Net purchases	18.8%	
Plus: Freight-in	.8	
Net cost of delivered purchases		19.6
Cost of goods available for sale		38.8%
Less: Inventory, December 31, 1992 (at cost)		20.8
Cost of goods sold		18.0
Gross Margin		82.0%
Expenses		
Selling expenses		
Sales salaries and commissions	12.8%	
Advertising	6.4	
Sales promotions	1.2	
Delivery	0.8	
Total selling expenses		21.2%
Administrative expenses		
Administrative salaries	8.0%	
Office salaries	8.0	
Office supplies	0.8	
Miscellaneous	0.4	
Total administrative expenses		17.2%
General expenses		
Rent	5.6%	
Utilities	2.8	
Bad debts	0.4	
Miscellaneous	1.6	
Total general expenses		10.4%
Total expenses		48.8
Net Income		33.2%

example, for Stoneham Auto Supplies the ROI is 41.5 percent, which compares well with competing businesses.

We use figures from two different financial statements to arrive at ROI. The income statement, already discussed, gives us net income. The balance sheet, which states the firm's assets and liabilities at a given point in time, provides the figure for total assets (or investment) in the firm.

The basic formula for ROI is

$$ROI = \frac{net\ income}{total\ investment}$$

For Stoneham Auto Supplies, net income for fiscal year 1992 is $83,000 (see Table B.2). If total investment (taken from the balance sheet for December 31, 1992) is $200,000, then

$$ROI = \frac{\$83,000}{\$200,000} = 0.415\ or\ 41.5\%$$

The ROI formula can be expanded to isolate the impact of capital turnover and the operating income ratio separately. Capital turnover is a measure of net sales per dollar of investment; the ratio is figured by dividing net sales by total investment. For Stoneham Auto Supplies,

$$Capital\ turnover = \frac{net\ sales}{total\ investment} = \frac{\$250,000}{\$200,000} = 1.25$$

ROI is equal to capital turnover times the net income ratio. The expanded formula for Stoneham Auto Supplies is

$$ROI = \frac{net\ sales}{total\ investment} \times \frac{net\ income}{net\ sales}$$

$$= \frac{\$250,000}{\$200,000} \times \frac{\$83,000}{\$250,000}$$

$$= (1.25)\ (33.2\%) = 41.5\%$$

Price Calculations

An important step in setting prices is selecting a pricing method, as indicated in Chapter 19. The systematic use of markups, markdowns, and various conversion formulas helps in calculating the selling price and evaluating the effects of various prices. The following sections will provide more detailed information about price calculations.

Markups

As indicated in the text, markup is the difference between the selling price and the cost of the item. That is, selling price equals cost plus markup. The markup must cover cost and contribute to profit; thus markup is similar to gross margin on the income statement.

Markup can be calculated on either cost or selling price as follows:

$$\text{Markup as percentage of cost} = \frac{\text{amount added to cost}}{\text{cost}} = \frac{\text{dollar markup}}{\text{cost}}$$

$$\text{Markup as percentage of selling price} = \frac{\text{amount added to cost}}{\text{selling price}} = \frac{\text{dollar markup}}{\text{selling price}}$$

Retailers tend to calculate the markup percentage on selling price.

Examples of Markup

To review the use of these markup formulas, assume that an item costs $10 and the markup is $5.

$$\text{Selling price} = \text{cost} + \text{markup}$$

$$\$15 = \$10 + \$5$$

Thus

$$\text{Markup percentage on cost} = \frac{\$5}{\$10} = 50\%$$

$$\text{Markup percentage on selling price} = \frac{\$5}{\$15} = 33\tfrac{1}{3}\%$$

It is necessary to know the base (cost or selling price) to use markup pricing effectively. Markup percentage on cost will always exceed markup percentage on price, given the same dollar markup, so long as selling price exceeds cost.

On occasion, we may need to convert markup on cost to markup on selling price, or vice versa. The conversion formulas are

$$\text{Markup percentage on selling price} = \frac{\text{markup percentage on cost}}{100\% + \text{markup percentage on cost}}$$

$$\text{Markup percentage on cost} = \frac{\text{markup percentage on selling price}}{100\% - \text{markup percentage on selling price}}$$

For example, if the markup percentage on cost is $33\tfrac{1}{3}$ percent, then the markup percentage on selling price is

$$\frac{33\tfrac{1}{3}\%}{100\% + 33\tfrac{1}{3}\%} = \frac{33\tfrac{1}{3}\%}{133\tfrac{1}{3}\%} = 25\%$$

If the markup percentage on selling price is 40 percent, then the corresponding percentage on cost would be as follows:

$$\frac{40\%}{100\% - 40\%} = \frac{40\%}{60\%} = 66\tfrac{2}{3}\%$$

Finally, we can show how to determine selling price if we know the cost of the item and the markup percentage on selling price. Assume that an item costs $36 and the usual markup percentage on selling price is 40 percent. Remember that selling price equals markup plus cost. Thus if

$$100\% = 40\% \text{ of selling price} + \text{cost}$$

then

$$60\% \text{ of selling price} = \text{cost}$$

In our example, cost equals $36. Then

$$0.6X = \$36$$

$$X = \frac{\$36}{0.6}$$

$$\text{Selling price} = \$60$$

Alternatively, the markup percentage could be converted to a cost basis as follows:

$$\frac{40\%}{100\% - 40\%} = 66\tfrac{2}{3}\%$$

Then the computed selling price would be as follows:

$$\text{Selling price} = 66\tfrac{2}{3}\%(\text{cost}) + \text{cost}$$

$$= 66\tfrac{2}{3}\%(\$36) + \$36$$

$$= \$24 + \$36 = \$60$$

By remembering the basic formula—selling price equals cost plus markup—you will find these calculations straightforward.

Markdowns

Markdowns are price reductions a retailer makes on merchandise. Markdowns may be useful on items that are damaged, priced too high, or selected for a special sales event. The income statement does not express markdowns directly because the change in price is made before the sale takes place. Therefore separate records of markdowns would be needed to evaluate the performance of various buyers and departments.

The markdown ratio (percentage) is calculated as follows:

$$\text{Markdown percentage} = \frac{\text{dollar markdowns}}{\text{net sales in dollars}}$$

In analyzing their inventory, Nick and Rose discover three special automobile jacks that have gone unsold for several months. They decide to reduce the price of each item from $25 to $20. Subsequently, these items are sold. The markdown percentage for these three items is

$$\text{Markdown percentage} = \frac{3\,(\$5)}{3\,(\$20)} = \frac{\$15}{\$60} = 25\%$$

Net sales, however, include all units of this product sold during the period, not just those marked down. If ten of these items have already been sold at $25 each, in addition to the three items sold at $20, then the overall markdown percentage would be

$$\text{Markdown percentage} = \frac{3\,(\$5)}{10\,(\$25) + 3\,(\$20)}$$

$$= \frac{\$15}{\$250 + \$60} = \frac{\$15}{\$310} = 4.8\%$$

Sales allowances also are a reduction in price. Thus the markdown percentages should also include any sales allowances. It would be computed as follows:

$$\text{Markdown percentage} = \frac{\text{dollar markdowns} + \text{dollar allowances}}{\text{net sales in dollars}}$$

Discussion and Review Questions

1. How does a manufacturer's income statement differ from a retailer's income statement?

2. Use the following information to answer questions a through c:

   Company TEA
   Fiscal year ended June 30, 1993

Net Sales	$500,000
Cost of Goods Sold	300,000
Net Income	50,000
Average Inventory at Cost	100,000
Total Assets (total investment)	200,000

   a. What is the inventory turnover rate for TEA Company? From what sources will the marketing manager determine the significance of the inventory turnover rate?

   b. What is the capital turnover ratio for fiscal year 1993? What is the net income ratio? What is the return on investment (ROI)?

   c. How many dollars of sales did each dollar of investment produce for TEA Company in fiscal year 1993?

3. Product A has a markup percentage on cost of 40 percent. What is the markup percentage on selling price?

4. Product B has a markup percentage on selling price of 30 percent. What is the markup percentage on cost?

5. Product C has a cost of $60 and a usual markup percentage of 25 percent on selling price. What price should be placed on this item?

6. Apex Appliance Company sells twenty units of product Q for $100 each and ten units for $80 each. What is the markdown percentage for product Q?

PREVIEW:
MICROMARKET COMPUTER APPLICATION
FOR APPENDIX B

Locke Stores: Analyzing Financial Ratios for Marketing Decisions

This exercise provides input for a decision regarding the purchase of one of three existing retail outlets. Gross margin, net income ratio, operating expense ratio, inventory turnover, return on investment, and capital turnover are calculated using Lotus 1-2-3 to allow a meaningful comparison between the three retail outlets. A second set of ratios is calculated when new information is discovered. The outcome of the financial ratio analysis must be tempered by environmental factors in the final memo.

Accessory equipment Equipment used in production or office activities; does not become a part of the final physical product.

Accommodation strategy Used when a business assumes responsibility for its actions in reaction to outside pressures.

Accumulation A process through which an inventory of homogeneous products that have similar production or demand requirements is developed.

Administered pricing A process in which the seller sets a price for a product, and the customer pays that specified price.

Advertising A paid form of nonpersonal communication about an organization and/or its products that is transmitted to a target audience through a mass medium.

Advertising appropriation The total amount of money that a marketer allocates for advertising for a specific time period.

Advertising campaign The creation and execution of a series of advertisements to communicate with a particular target audience.

Advertising platform The basic issues or selling points that an advertiser wishes to include in the advertising campaign.

Advertising target The group of people at whom advertisements are aimed.

Aesthetic modification Modification directed at changing the sensory appeal of a product by altering its taste, texture, sound, smell, or visual characteristics.

Agent A marketing intermediary who receives a commission or fee for expediting exchanges; represents either buyers or sellers on a permanent basis.

Aided recall test A posttest method of evaluating the effectiveness of advertising in which subjects are asked to identify advertisements they have seen recently; they are shown a list of products, brands, company names, or trademarks to jog their memory.

Allocation The breaking down of large homogeneous inventories into smaller lots.

Allowance Concession in price to achieve a desired goal; for example, industrial equipment manufacturers give trade-in allowances on used industrial equipment to enable customers to purchase new equipment.

Approach The manner in which a salesperson contacts a potential customer.

Arbitrary approach A method for determining the advertising appropriation in which a high-level executive in the firm states how much can be spent on advertising for a certain time period.

Area sampling A variation of stratified sampling, with the geographic areas serving as the segments, or primary units, used in random sampling.

Artwork The illustration in an advertisement and the layout of the components of an advertisement.

Assorting Combining products into collections, or assortments, that buyers want to have available at one place.

Assortment A combination of similar or complementary products put together to provide benefits to a specific market.

Atmospherics The conscious designing of a store's space to create emotional effects that enhance the probability that consumers will buy.

Attitude The knowledge and positive or negative feelings about an object.

Attitude scale A measurement instrument that usually consists of a series of adjectives, phrases, or sentences about an object; subjects are asked to indicate the intensity of their feelings toward the object by reacting to the statements in a certain way. It can be used to measure consumer attitudes.

Automatic vending Nonstore, nonpersonal retailing; includes coin-operated, self-service machines.

Average cost Total costs divided by the quantity produced.

Average fixed cost The fixed cost per unit produced; it is calculated by dividing the fixed costs by the number of units produced.

Average revenue Total revenue divided by the quantity produced.

Average total cost The sum of the average fixed cost and the average variable cost.

Average variable cost The variable cost per unit produced; it is calculated by dividing the variable cost by the number of units produced.

Barter The trading of products.

Base-point pricing A geographic pricing policy that includes the price at the factory, plus freight charges from the base point nearest the buyer.

Benefit segmentation The division of a market according to the various benefits that customers want from the product.

Better Business Bureau A local, nongovernmental regulatory group supported by local businesses that aids in settling problems between specific business firms and consumers.

Bid pricing A determination of prices through sealed bids or open bids.

Bonded storage A storage service provided by many public warehouses, whereby the goods are not released until U.S. customs duties, federal or state taxes, or other fees are paid.

Brand A name, term, symbol, design, or combination of these that identifies a seller's products and differentiates them from competitors' products.

Brand-extension branding A type of branding in which a firm uses one of its existing brand names as part of a brand for an improved or new product that is usually in the same product category as the existing brand.

Brand manager A type of product manager responsible for a single brand.

Brand mark The element of a brand, such as a symbol or design, that cannot be spoken.

Brand name The part of a brand that can be spoken —including letters, words, and numbers.

Breakdown approach A general approach for measuring company sales potential based on a general economic forecast—or other aggregate data—and the market sales potential derived from it; company sales potential is based on the general economic forecast and the estimated market sales potential.

Breakeven point The point at which the costs of producing a product equal the revenue made from selling the product.

Broker A functional middleman who performs fewer functions than other intermediaries; the primary function is to bring buyers and sellers together for a fee.

Buildup approach A general approach to measuring company sales potential in which the analyst initially estimates how much the average purchaser of a product will buy in a specified time period and then multiplies that amount by the number of potential buyers; estimates are generally calculated by individual geographic areas.

Business analysis An analysis providing a tentative sketch of a product's compatibility in the marketplace, including its probable profitability.

Business-to-business buying behavior *See* Organizational buying behavior.

Business-to-business market A market consisting of individuals, groups, or organizations that purchase specific kinds of products for resale, for direct use in producing other products, or for use in day-to-day operations; also called organizational market.

Business-to-business marketing A set of activities directed toward facilitating and expediting exchanges involving business-to-business markets and business-to-business products.

Business-to-business product A product purchased to be used directly or indirectly to produce other products or to be used in the operations of an organization.

Business-to-business service An intangible product that an organization uses in its operations, such as a financial product or a legal service.

Buy-back allowance A certain sum of money given to a purchaser for each unit bought after an initial deal is over.

Buying allowance A temporary price reduction to resellers for purchasing specified quantities of a product.

Buying behavior The decision processes and acts of people involved in buying and using products.

Buying center The group of people within an organization who are involved in making organizational purchase decisions; these people take part in the purchase decision process as users, influencers, buyers, deciders, and gatekeepers.

Buying power Resources such as money, goods, and services that can be traded in an exchange situation.

Buying power index A weighted index consisting of population, effective buying income, and retail sales data. The higher the index number, the greater the buying power.

Captioned photograph A photograph with a brief description that explains the picture's content.

Cash-and-carry wholesaler A limited service wholesaler that sells to customers who will pay cash and furnish transportation or pay extra to have products delivered.

Cash discount A price reduction to the buyer for prompt payment or cash payment.

Catalog retailing A type of mail-order retailing in which selling may be handled by telephone or in-store visits and products are delivered by mail or picked up by the customers.

Catalog showrooms A form of warehouse showroom in which consumers shop from a mailed catalog and buy at a warehouse where all products are stored out of buyers' reach. Products are provided in the manufacturer's carton.

Causal study Research planned to prove or disprove that x causes y or that x does not cause y.

Centralized organization An organization in which the top-level managers delegate very little authority to lower levels of the organization.

Cents-off offer A sales promotion device for established products whereby buyers receive a certain amount off the regular price shown on the label or package.

Channel capacity The limit on the volume of information that a communication channel can handle effectively.

Channel conflict Friction between marketing channel members, often resulting from role deviance or malfunction; absence of an expected mode of conduct that contributes to the channel as a system.

Channel cooperation A helping relationship among channel members that enhances the welfare and survival of all necessary channel members.

Channel of distribution *See* marketing channel.

Channel leadership The guidance that a channel member with one or more sources of power gives to other channel members to help achieve channel objectives.

Channel power The ability of one channel member to influence another channel member's goal achievement.

Clayton Act Passed in 1914, this act prohibits specific practices, such as price discrimination, exclusive dealer arrangements, and stock acquisitions, whose effect may substantially lessen competition and tend to create a monopoly.

Client public The direct consumers of the product of a nonbusiness organization; for example, the client public of a university is its student body.

Closing The element in the selling process in which the salesperson asks the prospect to buy the product.

Code of ethics Formalized statement of what a company expects of its employees with regard to ethical behavior.

Coding process The process by which a meaning is placed into a series of signs that represent ideas; also called encoding.

Cognitive dissonance Dissatisfaction that may occur shortly after the purchase of a product, when the buyer questions whether he or she should have purchased the product at all or would have been better off purchasing another brand that was evaluated very favorably.

Combination compensation plan A plan by which salespeople are paid a fixed salary and a commission based on sales volume.

Commercialization A phase of new-product development in which plans for full-scale manufacturing and marketing must be refined and settled and budgets for the product must be prepared.

Commission merchant An agent often used in agricultural marketing who usually exercises physical control over products, negotiates sales, and is given broad powers regarding prices and terms of sale.

Communication A sharing of meaning through the transmission of information.

Community shopping center Shopping center that includes one or two department stores and some specialty stores, as well as convenience stores; serves several neighborhoods and draws consumers who are not able to find desired products in neighborhood shopping centers.

Company sales forecast The amount of a product that a firm actually expects to sell during a specific period at a specified level of company marketing activities.

Comparative advertising Advertising that compares two or more identified brands in the same general product class; the comparison is made in terms of one or more specific product characteristics.

Competition Generally viewed by a business as those firms that market products similar to, or substitutable for, its products in the same target market.

Competition-matching approach A method of ascertaining the advertising appropriation in which an advertiser tries to match a major competitor's appropriations in terms of absolute dollars or in terms of using the same percentage of sales for advertising.

Competition-oriented pricing A pricing method in which an organization considers costs and revenue secondary to competitors' prices.

Competitive advertising Advertising that points out a brand's uses, features, and advantages that benefit consumers but may not be available in competing brands.

Competitive structure The model used to describe the number of firms that control the supply of a product and how it affects the strength of competition; factors include number of competitors, ease of entry into the market, the nature of the product, and knowledge of the market.

Component part A finished item ready for assembly or a product that needs little processing before assembly and that becomes a part of the physical product.

Comprehensive spending patterns The percentages of family income allotted to annual expenditures for general classes of goods and services.

Concentration strategy A market segmentation strategy in which an organization directs its marketing efforts toward a single market segment through one marketing mix.

Concept testing The stage in the product development process in which initial buying intentions and attitudes regarding a product are determined by presenting a written or oral description of the product to a sample of potential buyers and obtaining their responses.

Conflict of interest Results from marketers' taking advantage of situations for their own selfish interests rather than for the long-run interest of the business.

Consumable supplies Items that facilitate an organization's production and operations, but do not become part of the finished product.

Consumer buying behavior The buying behavior of ultimate consumers—people who purchase products for personal or household use and not for business purposes.

Consumer buying decision process The five-stage decision process consumers use in making purchases.

Consumer contest A sales promotion device for established products based on the analytical or creative skill of contestants.

Consumer Goods Pricing Act Federal legislation that prohibits the use of price maintenance agreements among producers and resellers involved in interstate commerce.

Consumer jury A panel used to pretest advertisements; it consists of a number of persons who are actual or potential buyers of the product to be advertised.

Consumer market Purchasers and/or individuals in their households who intend to consume or benefit from the purchased products and who do not buy products for the main purpose of making a profit.

Consumer movement A social movement through which people attempt to defend and exercise their rights as buyers.

Consumer movement forces The major forces in the consumer movement are consumer organizations, consumer laws, consumer education, and independent consumer advocates. The three major areas stressed are product safety, disclosure of information, and protection of the environment.

Consumer product Product purchased for ultimate satisfaction of personal and family needs.

Consumer Product Safety Commission A federal agency created to protect consumers by setting product standards, testing products, investigating product complaints, banning products, and monitoring injuries through the National Electronic Surveillance System.

Consumer protection legislation Laws enacted to protect consumers' safety, to enhance the amount of information available, and to warn of deceptive marketing techniques.

Consumer sales promotion technique A sales promotion method that encourages or stimulates customers to patronize a specific retail store or to try and/or purchase a particular product.

Consumer spending patterns Information indicating the relative proportions of annual family expenditures or the actual amount of money that is spent on certain types of goods or services.

Consumer sweepstakes A sales promotion device for established products in which entrants submit their names for inclusion in a drawing for prizes.

Containerization The practice of consolidating many items into one container that is sealed at the point of origin and opened at the destination.

Convenience products Relatively inexpensive, frequently purchased items for which buyers want to exert only minimal effort.

Cooperative advertising An arrangement in which a manufacturer agrees to pay a certain amount of a retailer's media costs for advertising the manufacturer's products.

Copy The verbal portion of advertisements; includes headlines, subheadlines, body copy, and signature.

Corporate strategy The strategy that determines the means for utilizing resources in the areas of production, finance, research and development, personnel, and marketing to reach the organization's goals.

Correlation methods Methods used to develop sales forecasts as the forecasters attempt to find a relationship between past sales and one or more variables, such as population, per capita income, or gross national product.

Cost comparison indicator Allows an advertiser to compare the costs of several vehicles within a specific medium relative to the number of persons reached by each vehicle.

Cost-oriented pricing A pricing policy in which a firm determines price by adding a dollar amount or percentage to the cost of a product.

Cost-plus pricing A form of cost-oriented pricing in which first the seller's costs are determined and then a specified dollar amount or percentage of the cost is added to the seller's cost to set the price.

Count and recount A sales promotion method based on the payment of a specific amount of money for each product unit moved from a reseller's warehouse in a given period of time.

Coupon A new-product sales promotion technique used to stimulate trial of a new or improved product, to increase sales volume quickly, to attract repeat purchasers, or to introduce new package sizes or features.

Credence qualities Qualities of services that cannot be assessed even after purchase and consumption; for example, few consumers are knowledgeable enough to assess the quality of an appendix operation, even after it has been performed.

Culture Everything in our surroundings that is made by human beings, consisting of tangible items as well as intangible concepts and values.

Cumulative discount Quantity discount that is aggregated over a stated period of time.

Customary pricing A type of psychological pricing in which certain goods are priced primarily on the basis of tradition.

Customer forecasting survey The technique of asking customers what types and quantities of products they intend to buy during a specific period so as to predict the sales level for that period.

Customer orientation An approach to marketing in which a marketer tries to provide a marketing mix that satisfies the needs of buyers in the target market.

Cycle analysis A method of predicting sales by analyzing sales figures for a period of three to five years to ascertain whether sales fluctuate in a consistent, periodic manner.

Dealer brand *See* Private distributor brand

Dealer listing An advertisement that promotes a product and identifies the names of participating retailers that sell the product.

Dealer loader A gift, often part of a display, that is given to a retailer for the purchase of a specified quantity of merchandise.

Decentralized organization An organization in which decision-making authority is delegated as far down the chain of command as possible.

Decline stage The stage in a product's life cycle in which sales fall rapidly and profits decrease.

Decoding process The stage in the communication process in which signs are converted into concepts and ideas.

Defense strategy Used when a business tries to minimize or avoid additional obligations linked to a problem or problems.

Defensive advertising Advertising used to offset or lessen the effects of a competitor's promotional program.

Demand curve A line showing the relationship between price and quantity demanded.

Demand-oriented pricing A pricing policy based on the level of demand for the product—resulting in a higher price when demand for the product is strong and a lower price when demand is weak.

Demand schedule The relationship, usually inverse, between price and quantity demanded; classically, a line sloping downward to the right, showing that as price falls, quantity demanded will increase.

Demographic factors Personal characteristics such as age, sex, race, nationality, income, family, life cycle stage, and occupation; also called socioeconomic factors.

Demonstration A sales promotion method manufacturers use temporarily to encourage trial use and purchase of the product or to show how the product works.

Department store A type of retail store having a wide product mix; organized into separate departments to facilitate marketing efforts and internal management.

Dependent variable A variable contingent on, or restricted to, one or a set of values assumed by the independent variable.

Depression A stage of the business cycle during which unemployment is extremely high, wages are very low, total disposable income is at a minimum, and consumers lack confidence in the economy.

Depth of product mix The average number of different products offered to buyers in a firm's product line.

Depth interview Personal interview with an open, informal atmosphere; this interview may take several hours. It is used to study motives.

Derived demand A characteristic of industrial demand that arises because industrial demand derives from the consumer demand.

Descriptive study A type of study undertaken when marketers see that knowledge of the characteristics of certain phenomena is needed to solve a problem; may require statistical analysis and predictive tools.

Direct cost approach An approach to determining marketing costs in which cost analysis includes direct costs and traceable common costs but does not include nontraceable common costs.

Direct costs Costs directly attributable to the performance of marketing functions.

Direct distribution channels Distribution channels in which products are sold directly from producer to ultimate users.

Direct marketing The use of nonpersonal media to introduce products by mail or telephone.

Direct ownership A long-run commitment to marketing in a foreign nation in which a subsidiary or division is owned by a foreign country through purchase.

Discount store A self-service, general merchandise store positioned as having low prices.

Discretionary income Disposable income that is available for spending and saving after an individual has purchased the basic necessities of food, clothing, and shelter.

Disposable income After-tax income.

Distribution The activities that make products available to customers when and where they want to purchase them.

Distribution center A large, centralized warehouse that receives goods from factories and suppliers, regroups the goods into orders, and ships the orders to customers quickly, with the focus on active movement of goods rather than passive storage.

Distribution variable The marketing mix variable in which marketing management attempts to make products available in the quantities desired, with adequate service, to a target market and to keep the total inventory, transportation, communication, storage, and materials handling costs as low as possible.

Diversified growth A type of growth that occurs in three forms, depending on the technology of the new products and the nature of the new markets the firm enters; the three forms are horizontal, concentric, and conglomerate.

Drop shipper A limited service wholesaler that takes title to products and negotiates sales but never physically handles products.

Dual distribution A channel practice whereby a producer distributes the same product through two or more different channels.

Dumping The sale of products in foreign markets at lower prices than those charged in the domestic market (when all costs are not allocated or when surplus products are sold).

Early adopters Individuals who choose new products carefully and are viewed by persons in the early majority, late majority, and laggard categories as being "the people to check with."

Early majority Individuals who adopt a new product just prior to the average person; they are deliberate and cautious in trying new products.

Economic forces Forces that determine the strength of a firm's competitive atmosphere and affect the impact of marketing activities because they determine the size and strength of demand for products.

Economic institutions An environmental force in international markets made up of producers, wholesalers, retailers, buyers, and other organizations that produce, distribute, and purchase products.

Economic order quantity (EOQ) The order size that minimizes the total cost of ordering and carrying inventory.

Effective buying income Similar to disposable income; it includes salaries, wages, dividends, interest, profits, and rents, less federal, state, and local taxes.

Electronic data interchange (EDI) Process that lets a company integrate order processing, production planning, inventory, accounting, and transportation planning into a total information system.

Encoding *See* Coding process.

Environmental monitoring The process of seeking information about events and relationships in a company's environment to assist marketers in identifying opportunities and in planning.

Environmental scanning The collecting of information about the forces in the marketing environment.

Equalized workload method A method of determining sales-force size in which the number of customers multiplied by the number of sales calls per year required to serve these customers effectively is divided by the average number of calls each salesperson makes annually.

Ethical issues Identifiable problems, situations, or opportunities requiring an individual or organization to choose from among several actions that must be evaluated as right or wrong, ethical or unethical.

Ethical pricing A form of professional pricing in which the demand for the product is inelastic and the seller is a professional who has a responsibility not to overcharge the client.

Exchange Participation by two or more individuals, groups, or organizations, with each party possessing something of value that the other party desires. Each must be willing to give up its "something of value" to get "something of value" held by the other, and all parties must be willing to communicate with each other.

Exclusive dealing A situation in which a manufacturer forbids an intermediary to carry products of competing manufacturers.

Exclusive distribution A type of market coverage in which only one outlet is used in a geographic area.

Executive judgment A sales forecasting method based on the intuition of one or more executives.

Experience curve pricing A pricing approach in which a company fixes a low price that high-cost competitors cannot match and thus expands its market share; this approach is possible when a firm gains cumulative production experience and is able to reduce its manufacturing costs to a predictable rate through improved methods, materials, skills, and machinery.

Experience qualities Qualities of services that can be assessed only after purchase and consumption (taste, satisfaction, courtesy, and the like).

Experimentation Research in which the factors that are related to or may affect the variables under investigation are maintained as constants so that the effects of the experimental variables may be measured.

Expert forecasting survey Preparation of the sales forecast by experts, such as economists, management consultants, advertising executives, college professors, or other persons outside the firm.

Exploratory studies A type of research conducted when more information is needed about a problem and the tentative hypothesis needs to be made more specific; it permits marketers to conduct ministudies with a very restricted database.

Extensive decision making The considerable time and effort a buyer spends seeking alternative products, searching for information about them, and then evaluating them to determine which one will be most satisfying.

External search The process of seeking information from sources other than one's memory.

Facilitating agency An organization that performs activities helpful in performing channel functions but does not buy, sell, or transfer title to the product; it can be a transportation company, an insurance company, an advertising agency, a marketing research agency, or a financial institution.

Family packaging A policy in an organization that all packages are to be similar or are to include one major element of the design.

Feature article A form of publicity that is up to three thousand words long and is usually prepared for a specific publication.

Federal Trade Commission A governmental group, consisting of five commissions, established to prevent the free enterprise system from being stifled or fettered by monopoly or anticompetitive practices; it provides direct protection to consumers from unfair or deceptive trade practices.

Federal Trade Commission Act (1914) Established the Federal Trade Commission and currently regulates the greatest number of marketing practices.

Feedback The receiver's response to a decoded message.

Field public warehouse A warehouse established by a public warehouse at the owner's inventory location; the warehouser becomes the custodian of the products and issues a receipt that can be used as collateral for a loan.

Fixed cost The cost that does not vary with changes in the number of units produced or sold.

F.O.B. (free-on-board) destination Part of a price quotation, used to indicate who must pay shipping charges. F.O.B. destination price means that the producer absorbs the costs of shipping the merchandise to the customer.

F.O.B. (free-on-board) factory Part of a price quotation; used to indicate who must pay shipping charges. F.O.B. factory price indicates the price of the merchandise at the factory, before it is loaded onto the carrier vehicle; the buyer must pay for shipping.

Food broker An intermediary that sells food and other grocery products to retailer-owned and merchant wholesalers, grocery chains, industrial buyers, and food processors. Both buyers and sellers use food brokers to cope with fluctuating market conditions.

Franchising An arrangement in which a supplier (franchisor) grants a dealer (franchisee) the right to sell products in exchange for some type of consideration.

Free merchandise A sales promotion method aimed at retailers whereby free merchandise is offered to resellers that purchase a stated quantity of product.

Free samples A new-product sales promotion technique that marketers use to stimulate trial of a product, to increase sales volume in early stages of the product's life cycle, or to obtain desirable distribution.

Freight absorption pricing Pricing for a particular customer or geographical area whereby the seller absorbs all or part of the actual freight costs.

Freight forwarders Businesses that consolidate shipments from several organizations into efficient lot sizes, which increases transit time and sometimes lowers shipping costs.

Full-cost approach An approach to determining marketing costs in which cost analysis includes direct costs, traceable common costs, and nontraceable common costs.

Full-service wholesaler A marketing intermediary that provides most services that can be performed by wholesalers.

Functional discount *See* trade discount.

Functional middleman A marketing intermediary that does not take title to products but usually receives a fee for expediting exchanges.

Functional modification A change that affects a product's versatility, effectiveness, convenience, or safety, usually requiring the redesigning of one or more parts of the product.

Functional wholesaler A marketing intermediary that expedites exchanges among producers and resellers and is compensated by fees or commissions.

General merchandise wholesaler Full-service merchant wholesaler that carries a very wide product mix.

General public The indirect consumers of the product of a nonbusiness organization; for instance, the general public of a university includes alumni, trustees, parents of students, and other groups.

Generic brand A brand that indicates only the product category (such as *aluminum foil*), not the company name and other identifying terms.

Geographic pricing A form of pricing that involves reductions for transportation costs or other costs associated with the physical distance between the buyer and the seller.

Globalization of markets The development of marketing strategies as if the entire world (or regions of it) were a single entity; products are marketed the same way everywhere.

Good A tangible item.

Government markets Markets made up of federal, state, county, and local governments, spending billions of dollars annually for goods and services to support their internal operations and to provide such products as defense, energy, and education.

Green marketing Refers to the specific development, pricing, promotion, and distribution of products that do not harm the environment.

Gross National Product (GNP) An overall measure of a nation's economic standing in terms of the value of all products produced by that nation for a given period of time.

Group interview A method of uncovering people's motives relating to some issue, such as product usage, with an interviewer generating discussion on one or several topics among the six to twelve people in the group.

Growth stage The product life cycle stage in which sales rise rapidly; profits reach a peak and then start to decline.

Heterogeneity A condition resulting from the fact that people typically perform services; there maybe variation from one service provider to another or variation in the service provided by a single individual from day to day and from customer to customer.

Heterogeneous market A market made up of individuals with diverse product needs for products in a specific product class.

Horizontal channel integration The combining of institutions at the same level of operation under one management.

Hypothesis A guess or assumption about a certain problem or set of circumstances; reasonable supposition that may be right or wrong.

Idea A concept, image, or issue.

Idea generation The search by businesses and other organizations for product ideas that help them achieve their objectives.

Idea Screening A stage in the product development process in which the ideas that do not match organiza-tional objectives are rejected and those with the greatest potential are selected for further development.

Illustrations Photographs, drawings, graphs, charts, and tables, used to encourage an audience to read or watch an advertisement.

Implicit bargaining A method of employee motivation that recognizes the various needs of different employees and is based on the theory that there is no one best way to motivate individuals.

Impulse buying An unplanned buying behavior that involves a powerful, persistent urge to buy something immediately.

Income The amount of money received through wages, rents, investments, pensions, and subsidy payments for a given period.

Incremental productivity method A plan by which a marketer should continue to increase the sales force as long as the additional sales increases are greater than the additional selling costs that arise from employing more salespeople.

Independent variable A variable free from the influence of, or not dependent on, other variables.

Individual branding A branding policy in which each product is named differently.

Industrial distributor An independent business organization that takes title to industrial products and carries inventories.

Inelastic demand A type of demand in which a price increase or decrease will not significantly affect the quantity demanded.

Inflation A condition in which price levels increase faster than incomes, causing a decline in buying power.

Information inputs The sensations we receive through our sense organs.

In-home retailing A type of nonstore retailing that involves personal selling in consumers' homes.

Innovators The first consumers to adopt a new product; they enjoy trying new products and tend to be venturesome, rash, and daring.

Input-output data A type of information, sometimes used in conjunction with the SIC system, that is based on the assumption that the output or sales of one industry are the input or purchases of other industries.

Inseparability A condition in which the consumer frequently is directly involved in the production process because services normally are produced at the same time that they are consumed.

Institutional advertising A form of advertising promoting organizational images, ideas, and political issues.

Institutional market A market that consists of organizations seeking to achieve goals other than such normal business goals as profit, market share, or return on investment.

Intangibility A characteristic of services: because services are performances, they cannot be seen, touched, tasted, or smelled, nor can they be possessed.

Integrated growth The type of growth that a firm can have within its industry; three possible growth directions include forward, backward, and horizontal.

Intense growth The type of growth that can occur when current products and current markets have the potential for increasing sales.

Intensive distribution A form of market coverage in which all available outlets are used for distributing a product.

Intermodal transportation Combining and coordinating two or more modes of transportation.

Internal marketing Managerial actions aimed at making members of the marketing organization understand and accept their respective roles in implementing a marketing strategy.

Internal search An aspect of an information search where buyers first search their memory for information about products that might solve their problem.

International marketing Marketing activities performed across national boundaries.

Introduction stage The stage in a product's life cycle beginning at a product's first appearance in the marketplace, when sales are zero and profits are negative.

Job enrichment A method of employee motivation that gives employees a sense of autonomy and control over their work, with employees being encouraged to set their own goals.

Joint demand A characteristic of industrial demand that occurs when two or more items are used in combination to produce a product.

Joint venture A partnership between a domestic firm and foreign firms and/or governments.

Just-in-time (JIT) Calls for companies to maintain low inventory levels and purchase products and materials in small quantities, just at the time they are needed for production.

Kinesic communication Commonly known as body language, this type of interpersonal communication occurs in face-to-face selling situations when the salesperson and customers move their heads, eyes, arms, hands, legs, and torsos.

Labeling An important dimension of packaging for promotional, informational, and legal reasons; regulated by numerous federal and state laws.

Laggards The last consumers to adopt a new product; they are oriented toward the past and suspicious of new products.

Late majority People who are quite skeptical of new products; they eventually adopt new products because of economic necessity or social pressure.

Layout The physical arrangement of the illustration, headline, subheadline, body copy, and signature of an advertisement.

Learning A change in an individual's behavior that arises from prior behavior in similar situations.

Legal forces Forces that arise from the legislation and interpretation of laws; these laws, enacted by government units, restrain and control marketing decisions and activities.

Level of involvement The intensity of interest that one has for a particular product in a particular buying decision.

Licensing (international) An arrangement in international marketing in which the licensee pays commissions or royalties on sales or supplies used in manufacturing.

Limited decision making The type of consumer decision making used for products that are purchased occasionally and when a buyer needs to acquire information about an unfamiliar brand in a familiar product category.

Limited-line wholesaler Full-service merchant wholesaler that carries only a few product lines.

Limited service wholesaler A marketing intermediary that provides only some marketing services and specializes in a few functions.

Line family branding A branding policy in which an organization uses family branding only for products within a line, not for all its products.

Long-range plan A plan that covers more than five years.

Mail-order retailing A type of nonpersonal, nonstore retailing that uses direct mail advertising and catalogs and is typified by selling by description. The buyer usually does not see the actual product until it is delivered.

Mail-order wholesaler An organization that sells through direct mail by sending catalogs to retail, industrial, and institutional customers.

Mail surveys Questionnaires sent to respondents, who are encouraged to complete and return them.

Major equipment A category of industrial products that includes large tools and machines used for production purposes.

Manufacturer brand A brand initiated by a producer; makes it possible for a producer to be identified with its product at the point of purchase.

Manufacturers' agent An independent business person who sells complementary products of several producers in assigned territories and is compensated through commissions.

Marginal cost The cost associated with producing one more unit of a product.

Marginal revenue (MR) The change in total revenue that occurs after an additional unit of a product is sold.

Market An aggregate of people who, as individuals or as organizations, have needs for products in a product class and who have the ability, willingness, and authority to purchase such products.

Market attractiveness–business position model A two-dimensional matrix designed to serve as a diagnostic tool to highlight SBUs that have an opportunity to grow or that should be divested.

Market density The number of potential customers within a unit of land area, such as a square mile.

Marketing manager The individual responsible for managing the marketing activities that serve a particular group or class of customers.

Marketing Individual and organizational activities that facilitate and expedite satisfying exchange relationships in a dynamic environment through the creation, distribution, promotion, and pricing of goods, services, and ideas.

Marketing audit A systematic examination of the objectives, strategies, organization, and performance of a firm's marketing unit.

Marketing audit report A written summary produced after the marketing audit has been conducted; it includes recommendations that will increase marketing productivity and develops a recommendation as to the business' general direction.

Marketing channel A group of interrelated intermediaries who direct products to customers; also called channel of distribution.

Marketing concept A managerial philosophy that an organization should try to satisfy customers' needs through a coordinated set of activities that at the same time allows the organization to achieve its goals.

Marketing control process A process that consists of establishing performance standards, evaluating actual performance by comparing it with established standards, and reducing the differences between desired and actual performance.

Marketing cost analysis A method for helping to control marketing strategies whereby various costs are broken down and classified to determine which costs are associated with specific marketing activities.

Marketing databank A file of data collected through both the marketing information system and marketing research projects.

Marketing environment The environment that surrounds both the buyer and the marketing mix; it consists of political, legal, regulatory, societal, consumer movement, economic, and technological forces. Environmental variables affect a marketer's ability to facilitate and expedite exchanges.

Marketing ethics Moral evaluation of decisions based on accepted principles of behavior that result in an action being judged right or wrong.

Marketing experimentation A set of rules and procedures under which the task of data gathering is organized to expedite analysis and interpretation.

Marketing function account Classification of costs that indicates which function was performed through the expenditure of funds.

Marketing information system (MIS) A system that establishes a framework for the day-to-day managing and structuring of information gathered regularly from sources both inside and outside an organization.

Marketing intelligence All the data gathered as a basis for marketing decisions.

Marketing intermediary A member of a marketing channel, usually a merchant or an agent, acting to direct products to buyers.

Marketing management A process of planning, organizing, implementing, and controlling marketing activities to facilitate and expedite exchanges effectively and efficiently.

Marketing mix Consists of four major variables: product, price, distribution, and promotion.

Marketing objective A statement of what is to be accomplished through marketing activities.

Marketing-oriented organization An organization that attempts to determine what target market members want and then tries to produce it.

Marketing plan The written document or blueprint for implementing and controlling an organization's marketing activities related to a particular marketing strategy.

Marketing planning A systematic process that involves assessing marketing opportunities and resources, determining market objectives, and developing a plan for implementation and control.

Marketing planning cycle Obtaining and utilizing feedback at each stage of marketing planning in order to control and coordinate those stages.

Marketing program A set of marketing strategies that are implemented and used at the same time.

Marketing research The part of marketing intelligence that involves specific inquiries into problems and marketing activities to discover new information so as to guide marketing decisions.

Marketing strategy A plan for selecting and analyzing a target market and creating and maintaining a marketing mix.

Market manager A person responsible for the marketing activities that are necessary to serve a particular group or class of customers.

Market opportunity An opportunity that arises when the right combination of circumstances occurs at the right time to allow an organization to take action toward generating sales from a target market.

Market orientation The organizationwide generation of market intelligence pertaining to current and future customer needs, dissemination of the intelligence across departments, and organizationwide responsiveness to it.

Market planning cycle The five-step cycle that involves developing or revising marketing objectives relative to performance, assessing marketing opportunities and resources, formulating marketing strategy, developing the plan for implementation and control, and implementing the marketing plan.

Market potential The total amount of a product that customers will purchase within a specified period at a specific level of industrywide marketing activity.

Market requirement Related to customers' needs or desired benefits, the market requirement is satisfied by components of the marketing mix that provide benefits to buyers.

Market segment A group of individuals, groups, or organizations sharing one or more similar characteristics that make them have relatively similar product needs.

Market segmentation The process of dividing a total market into groups of people with relatively similar product needs, for the purpose of designing a marketing mix (or mixes) that more precisely matches the needs of individuals in a selected segment (or segments).

Market share A firm's sales in relation to total industry sales, expressed as a decimal or percentage.

Market test A stage of new-product development that involves making a product available to buyers in one or more test areas and measuring purchases and consumer responses to promotion, price, and distribution efforts.

Markup A percentage of the cost or price of a product added to the cost.

Markup pricing A pricing method where the price is derived by adding a predetermined percentage of the cost to the cost of the product.

Mass merchandiser A retail operation that tends to offer fewer customer services than department stores and to focus its attention on lower prices, high turnover, and large sales volume; the category includes supermarkets and discount houses.

Materials handling Physical handling of products.

Maturity stage A stage in the product life cycle in which the sales curve peaks and starts to decline as profits continue to decline.

Mechanical observation devices Cameras, recorders, counting machines, and equipment to record movement, behavior, or physiological changes in individuals.

Media plan A plan that sets forth the exact media vehicles to be used for advertisements and the dates and times that the advertisements are to appear.

Medium of transmission That which carries the coded message from the source to the receiver or audience; examples include ink on paper and vibrations of air waves produced by vocal cords.

Medium-range plans Plans that usually encompass two to five years.

Megacarrier A freight transportation company that provides many methods of shipment, such as rail, truck, and air service.

Merchandise allowance A sales promotion method aimed at retailers; it consists of a manufacturer's agreement to pay resellers certain amounts of money for providing special promotional efforts, such as setting up and maintaining a display.

Merchant A marketing intermediary who takes title to merchandise and resells it for a profit.

Merchant wholesaler A marketing intermediary who takes title to products, assumes risk, and is generally involved in buying and reselling products.

Missionary salesperson A support salesperson, usually employed by a manufacturer, who assists the producer's customers in selling to their own customers.

Modified rebuy purchase A type of industrial purchase in which a new-task purchase is changed the second or third time, or the requirements associated with a straight-rebuy purchase are modified.

Money refund A new-product sales promotion technique in which the producer mails a consumer a specific amount of money when proof of purchase is established.

Monopolistic competition A market structure in which a firm has many potential competitors; to compete, the firm tries to develop a differential marketing strategy to establish its own market share.

Monopoly A market structure existing when a firm produces a product that has no close substitutes and/or when a single seller may erect barriers to potential competitors.

Moral philosophies Principles or rules that individuals use to determine the right way to behave.

Motive An internal energizing force that directs a person's behavior toward his or her goals.

MRO items An alternative term for supplies: supplies can be divided into Maintenance, Repair, and Operating (or overhaul) items.

Multinational enterprise A firm that has operations or subsidiaries in several countries.

Multisegment strategy A market segmentation strategy in which an organization directs its marketing efforts at two or more segments by developing a marketing mix for each selected segment.

Multivariable segmentation Market division achieved by using more than one characteristic to divide the total market; this approach provides more information about the individuals in each segment than does single-variable segmentation.

National Advertising Review Board A self-regulatory unit created by the Council of Better Business Bureaus and three advertising trade organizations; it screens national advertisements to check for honesty and processes complaints about deceptive advertisements.

Natural account Classification of costs based on what the money is actually spent for; typically a part of a regular accounting system.

Negotiated pricing A determination of price through bargaining even when there are stated list prices and discount structures.

Negotiation Mutual discussion or communication of the terms and methods of an exchange.

Neighborhood shopping center A shopping center that usually consists of several small convenience and specialty stores and serves consumers who live less than ten minutes' driving time from the center.

New product Any product that a given firm has not marketed previously.

New-product development A process consisting of six phases: idea generation, screening, business analysis, product development, test-marketing, and commercialization.

News release A form of publicity that is usually a single page of typewritten copy containing fewer than three hundred words.

New-task purchase A type of industrial purchase in which an organization is making an initial purchase of an item to be used to perform a new job or to solve a new problem.

Noise A condition in the communication process existing when the decoded message is different from what was coded.

Nonbusiness marketing Marketing activities conducted by individuals and organizations to achieve some goal other than ordinary business goals such as profit, market share, or return on investment.

Noncumulative discount A one-time price reduction based on the number of units purchased, the size of the order, or the product combination purchased.

Nonprice competition A policy in which a seller elects not to focus on price and instead emphasizes distinctive product features, service, product quality, promotion, packaging, or other factors to distinguish its product from competing brands.

Nonprofit organization marketing The application of marketing concepts and techniques to such nonprofit groups as hospitals and colleges.

Nonstore retailing A type of retailing where consumers purchase products without visiting a store.

Nontraceable common costs Costs that cannot be assigned to any specific function according to any logical criteria and thus are assignable only on an arbitrary basis.

Objective-and-task approach An approach to determining the advertising appropriation: marketers first determine the objectives that a campaign is to achieve, and then ascertain the tasks required to accomplish those objectives; the costs of all tasks are added to ascertain the total appropriation.

Observation method A research method where researchers record the overt behavior of subjects, noting physical conditions and events. Direct contact with subjects is avoided; instead, their actions are examined and noted systematically.

Odd-even pricing A type of psychological pricing that assumes that more of a product will be sold at $99.99 than at $100.00, indicating that an odd price is more appealing than an even price to customers.

Off-price retailer A store that buys manufacturers' seconds, overruns, returns, and off-season merchandise for resale to consumers at deep discounts.

Oligopoly A competitive structure existing when a few sellers control the supply of a large proportion of a product; each seller must consider the actions of other sellers to changes in marketing activities.

Open bids Prices submitted by several, but not all, sellers; the amounts of these bids are not made public.

Opportunity cost The value of the benefit that is given up by selecting one alternative rather than another.

Order getter A type of salesperson who increases the firm's sales by selling to new customers and by increasing sales to present customers.

Order processing The receipt and transmission of sales order information in the physical distribution process.

Order taker A type of salesperson who primarily seeks repeat sales.

Organizational buying behavior The purchase behavior of producers, government units, institutions, and resellers; also called industrial buying behavior.

Organizational market Individuals or groups who purchase a specific kind of product for one of three purposes: resale, direct use in producing other products, or use in general daily operations; also called industrial market.

Overall family branding A policy of branding all of a firm's products with the same name or at least a part of the name.

Patronage motives Motives that influence where a person purchases products on a regular basis.

Penetration price A lower price designed to penetrate the market and thus quickly produce a larger unit sales volume.

Percent-of-sales approach A method for establishing the advertising appropriation whereby marketers simply multiply a firm's past sales, forecasted sales, or a combination of the two by a standard percentage based on both what the firm traditionally has spent on advertising and what the industry averages.

Perception The process by which an individual selects, organizes, and interprets information inputs to create a meaningful picture of the world.

Perfect competition Ideal competitive structure that would entail a large number of sellers, none of which could significantly influence price or supply.

Performance standard An expected level of performance against which actual performance can be compared.

Perishability A condition where, because of simultaneous production and consumption, unused capacity to produce services in one time period cannot be stockpiled or inventoried for future time periods.

Personal interview survey A face-to-face interview that allows more in-depth interviewing, probing, follow-up questions, or psychological tests.

Personality An internal structure in which experience and behavior are related in an orderly way.

Personal selling A process of informing customers and persuading them to purchase products through personal communication in an exchange situation.

Personal factors Factors influencing the consumer buying decision process that are unique to particular individuals.

Persuasion The activity of convincing or prevailing upon an individual or organization to bring about an exchange.

Physical distribution An integrated set of activities that deal with managing the movement of products within firms and through marketing channels.

PIMS (Profit Impact on Marketing Strategy) A Strategic Planning Institute (SPI) research program which provides reports on the products of SPI member firms; these reports assist the member firms in analyzing marketing performance and formulating marketing strategies.

Pioneer advertising A type of advertising that informs persons about what a product is, what it does, how it can be used, and where it can be purchased.

Point-of-purchase materials A sales promotion method that uses such items as outside signs, window displays, and display racks to attract attention, to inform customers, and to encourage retailers to carry particular products.

Political and legal institutions Public agencies, laws, courts, legislatures, and government bureaus.

Political forces Forces that strongly influence the economic and political stability of our country not only through decisions that affect domestic matters but through their authority to negotiate trade agreements and to determine foreign policy.

Population All elements, units, or individuals that are of interest to researchers for a specific study.

Posttest An evaluation of advertising effectiveness after the campaign.

Premiums Items that are offered free or at a minimum cost as a bonus for purchasing.

Press conference A meeting used to announce major news events.

Prestige pricing Setting prices at a high level to facilitate a prestige or quality image.

Pretest Evaluation of an advertisement before it is actually used.

Price The value placed on what is exchanged.

Price competition A policy whereby a marketer emphasizes price as an issue and matches or beats the prices of competitors also emphasizing low prices.

Price differentiation A demand-oriented pricing method whereby a firm uses more than one price in the marketing of a specific product; differentiation of prices can be based on several dimensions, such as type of customers, type of distribution used, or the time of the purchase.

Price discrimination A policy of charging some buyers lower prices than other buyers, which gives those paying less a competitive advantage,

Price elasticity of demand A measure of the sensitivity of demand to changes in price.

Price leaders Products sold at less than cost to increase sales of regular merchandise.

Price lining A form of psychological pricing in which an organization sets a limited number of prices for selected lines of products.

Price skimming A pricing policy whereby an organization charges the highest possible price that buyers who most desire the product will pay.

Price variable A critical marketing mix variable in which marketing management is concerned with establishing a value for what is exchanged.

Pricing method A mechanical procedure for setting prices on a regular basis.

Pricing objectives Overall goals that describe the role of price in an organization's long-range plans.

Pricing policy A guiding philosophy or course of action designed to influence and determine pricing decisions.

Primary data Information observed and recorded or collected directly from subjects.

Private brand *See* private distributor brand.

Private distributor brand A brand that is initiated and owned by a reseller; also called private brand.

Private warehouse A storage facility operated by an organization for the purpose of distributing its own products.

Proactive strategy Used when a business assumes responsibility for its actions and responds to accusations made against it without outside pressure or the threat of government intervention.

Problem definition The first step in the research process toward finding a solution or launching a research study; the researcher thinks about the best ways to discover the nature and boundaries of a problem or opportunity.

Process materials Materials used directly in the production of other products; unlike component parts, they are not readily identifiable.

Procompetitive legislation Laws enacted to preserve competition.

Producer market A market consisting of individuals and business organizations that purchase products for the purpose of making a profit by using them to produce other products or by using them in their operations.

Product Everything (both favorable and unfavorable) that one receives in an exchange; it is a complexity of tangible and intangible attributes, including func-

tional, social, and psychological utilities or benefits. A product may be a good, a service, or an idea.

Product adoption process The five-stage process of buyer acceptance of a product: awareness, interest, evaluation, trial, and adoption.

Product advertising Advertising that promotes goods and services.

Product assortment A collection of a variety of different products.

Product deletion The elimination of some products that no longer satisfy target market customers or contribute to achievement of an organization's overall goals.

Product development A stage in creating new products that moves the product from concept to test phase and also involves the development of the other elements of the marketing mix (promotion, distribution, and price).

Product differentiation The use of promotional efforts to differentiate a company's products from its competitors' products, with the hope of establishing the superiority and preferability of its products relative to competing brands.

Product elimination The process of deleting a product from the product mix when it no longer satisfies a sufficient number of customers.

Production orientation The viewpoint that increasing the efficiency of production is the primary means of increasing an organization's profits.

Production-oriented organization A firm that concentrates on either improving production efficiency or producing high-quality, technically improved products; it has little regard for customers' desires.

Product item A specific version of a product that can be designated as a unique offering among an organization's products.

Product life cycle The course of product development, consisting of several stages: introduction, growth, maturity, and decline. As a product moves through these stages, the strategies relating to competition, pricing, promotion, distribution, and market information must be evaluated and possibly changed.

Product line A group of closely related products that are considered a unit because of marketing, technical, or end-use considerations.

Product manager A person who holds a staff position in a multiproduct company and is responsible for a product, a product line, or several distinct products that are considered an interrelated group.

Product mix The composite of products that an organization makes available to consumers.

Product mix depth *See* depth (of product mix).

Product mix width *See* width (of product mix).

Product modification The changing of one or more of a product's characteristics.

Product-portfolio analysis A strategic planning approach based on the philosophy that a product's market growth rate and its relative market share are important considerations in determining its marketing strategy.

Product-portfolio approach An approach to managing the product mix that attempts to create specific marketing strategies to achieve a balanced mix of products that will produce maximum long-run profits.

Product positioning The decisions and activities that are directed toward trying to create and maintain the firm's intended product concept in customers' minds.

Product-specific spending patterns The dollar amounts families spend for specific products within a general product class.

Product variable That aspect of the marketing mix dealing with researching consumers' product wants and planning the product to achieve the desired product characteristics.

Professional pricing Pricing used by persons who have great skill or experience in a particular field or activity, indicating that a price should not relate directly to the time and involvement in a specific case; rather, a standard fee is charged regardless of the problems involved in performing the job.

Professional services Complex and frequently regulated services that usually require the provider to be highly skilled; for example, accounting or legal services.

Projective technique A test in which subjects are asked to perform specific tasks for particular purposes while in fact they are being evaluated for other purposes; assumes that subjects will unconsciously "project" their motives as they perform the tasks.

Promotion The communication with individuals, groups, or organizations to directly or indirectly facilitate exchanges by influencing audience members to accept an organization's products.

Promotion mix The specific combination of promotional methods that an organization uses for a particular product.

Promotion variable A major marketing mix component used to facilitate exchanges by informing an individual or one or more groups of people about an organization and its products.

Prospecting Developing a list of potential customers for personal selling purposes.

Prosperity A stage of the business cycle characterized by a combination of low unemployment and relatively high aggregate income, which causes buying power to be high (assuming a low inflation rate).

Proxemic communication A subtle form of interpersonal communication used in face-to-face interactions when either party varies the physical distance that separates them.

Psychological factors Factors that operate within individuals to partially determine their general behavior and thus influence their behavior as buyers.

Psychological pricing A pricing method designed to encourage purchases that are based on emotional reactions rather than rational responses.

Publicity Nonpersonal communication in news story form, regarding an organization and/or its products, that is transmitted through a mass medium at no charge.

Public relations A broad set of communication activities used to create and maintain favorable relations between the organization and its publics, such as customers, employees, stockholders, government officials, and society in general.

Public warehouses Business organizations that provide rented storage facilities and related physical distribution facilities.

Pull policy Promotion of a product directly to consumers with the intention of developing strong consumer demand.

Purchasing power A buyer's income, credit, and wealth available for purchasing products.

Push money An incentive program designed to push a line of goods by providing salespeople with additional compensation.

Push policy The promotion of a product only to the next institution down the marketing channel.

Quality modification A change that relates to a product's dependability and durability and is generally executed by alterations in the materials or production process used.

Quality of life The enjoyment of daily living, enhanced by leisure time, clean air and water, an unlittered earth, conservation of wildlife and natural resources, and security from radiation and poisonous substances.

Quantity discounts Deductions from list price that reflect the economies of purchasing in large quantities.

Quota sampling Nonprobability sampling in which the final choice of respondents is left to the interviewers.

Rack jobbers Intermediaries (also called service merchandisers) similar to truck wholesalers but providing the extra service of cleaning and filling a display rack.

Random factor analysis A method of predicting sales whereby an attempt is made to attribute erratic sales variations to random, nonrecurrent events, such as a regional power failure or a natural disaster.

Random sampling A type of sampling in which all the units in a population have an equal chance of appearing in the sample; probability sampling.

Raw materials Basic materials that become part of a physical product; obtained from mines, farms, forests, oceans, and recycled solid wastes.

Reaction strategy Adopted when a business allows a condition or potential problem to go unresolved until the public learns about it.

Real-estate brokers Brokers who, for a fee or commission, bring buyers and sellers together to exchange real estate.

Receiver The individual, group, or organization that decodes a coded message.

Recession A stage in the business cycle during which unemployment rises and total buying power declines, stifling both consumers' and businesspeople's propensity to spend.

Reciprocity A practice unique to business-to-business sales in which two organizations agree to buy from each other.

Recognition test A posttest method of evaluating the effectiveness of advertising; individual respondents are shown the actual advertisement and asked whether they recognize it.

Recovery A stage of the business cycle during which the economy moves from recession toward prosperity.

Recruiting A process by which the sales manager develops a list of applicants for sales positions.

Reference group A group with which an individual identifies so much that he or she takes on many of the values, attitudes, or behaviors of group members.

Regional issues Versions of a magazine that differ across geographic regions and in which a publisher can vary the advertisements and editorial content.

Regional shopping center A type of shopping center that usually has the largest department stores, the widest product mix, and the deepest product lines of all shopping centers in an area; usually there are at least 150,000 customers in the target area.

Regulatory forces Forces arising from regulatory units at all levels of government; these units create and enforce numerous regulations that affect marketing decisions.

Reinforcement advertising An advertisement attempting to assure current users that they have made

the right choice and telling them how to get the most satisfaction from the product.

Reliability A condition existing when a sample is representative of the population; it also exists when repeated use of an instrument produces almost identical results.

Reminder advertising Advertising used to remind consumers that an established brand is still around and that it has certain uses, characteristics, and benefits.

Reorder point The inventory level that signals that more inventory should be ordered.

Reseller market A market consisting of intermediaries, such as wholesalers and retailers, that buy finished goods and resell them for the purpose of making a profit.

Retailer An intermediary that purchases products for the purpose of reselling them to ultimate consumers.

Retailer coupon A sales promotion method used by retailers when price is a primary motivation for consumers' purchasing behavior; usually takes the form of a "cents-off" coupon that is distributed through advertisements and is redeemable only at a specific store.

Retailing Activities required for exchanges in which ultimate consumers are the buyers.

Retail positioning Involves identifying an unserved or underserved market niche, or segment, and serving the segment through a strategy that distinguishes the retailer from others in the minds of persons in that segment.

Robinson-Patman Act A law directly influencing pricing and promotions policies; the law prohibits price differentials and promotional allowances that are discriminatory.

Role A set of actions and activities that a person in a particular position is supposed to perform, based on the expectations of both the individual and the persons around the individual.

Routine response behavior The type of decision making used by a consumer when buying frequently purchased, low-cost items that require very little search and decision effort.

Safety stock The inventory needed to prevent a stockout (running out of a product).

Sales analysis A process for controlling marketing strategies whereby sales figures are used to evaluate performance.

Sales branches Similar to merchant wholesalers in their operations; may offer credit, delivery, give promotional assistance, and furnish other services.

Sales contest A sales promotion method used to motivate distributors, retailers, and sales personnel through the recognition of outstanding achievements.

Sales-force forecasting survey Estimation by members of a firm's sales force of the anticipated sales in their territories for a specified period.

Sales forecast The amount of a product that a company expects to sell during a specific period at a specified level of marketing activities.

Sales office Provides service normally associated with agents; owned and controlled by the producer.

Sales orientation A focus on increasing an organization's sales as the major way to increase profits.

Sales-oriented organization An organization acting on its belief that personal selling and advertising are the primary tools used to generate profits and that most products—regardless of consumers' needs—can be sold if the right quantity and quality of personal selling and advertising are used.

Sales potential The maximum percentage of market potential that an individual firm within an industry can expect to obtain for a specific product.

Sales promotion An activity and/or material that acts as a direct inducement to resellers, salespersons, or consumers; it offers added value or incentive to buy or sell the product.

Sample A limited number of units that are believed to be representative of the total population under study for marketing research purposes.

Sampling Selecting representative units from a total population.

Scientific decision making An approach that involves systematically seeking facts and then applying decision-making methods other than trial and error or generalization from experience.

Scrambled merchandising The addition of unrelated products and product lines to an existing product mix, particularly fast-moving items that can be sold in large volume.

Sealed bids Prices submitted to a buyer, to be opened and made public at a specified time.

Search qualities Tangible attributes of services that can be viewed prior to purchase.

Seasonal analysis A method of predicting sales whereby an analyst studies daily, weekly, or monthly sales figures to evaluate the degree to which seasonal factors, such as climate and holiday activities, influence a firm's sales.

Seasonal discounts A price reduction that sellers give to buyers who purchase goods or services out of season; these discounts allow the seller to maintain steadier production during the year.

Secondary data Information compiled inside or outside the organization for some purpose other than the current investigations.

Segmentation variable A dimension or characteristic of individuals, groups, or organizations that is used to divide a total market into segments.

Selective distortion The changing or twisting of currently received information that occurs when a person receives information inconsistent with his or her feelings or beliefs.

Selective distribution A form of market coverage in which only some available outlets in an area are chosen to distribute a product.

Selective exposure Selection of some inputs to be exposed to our awareness while many others are ignored because of the inability to be conscious of all inputs at one time.

Selective retention The phenomenon of remembering information inputs that support personal feelings and beliefs and forgetting inputs that do not.

Self-concept One's own perception of oneself.

Selling agents Intermediaries who market all of a specified product line or the entire output of a manufacturer; they have control over the manufacturer's marketing effort and may be used in place of a marketing department.

Service An intangible that results from applying human and mechanical efforts to people or objects.

Service heterogeneity *See* heterogeneity.

Service inseparability *See* inseparability.

Service intangibility *See* intangibility.

Service perishability *See* perishability.

Sherman Antitrust Act Legislation passed in 1890 to prevent businesses from restraining trade and monopolizing markets.

Shopping product An item for which buyers are willing to put forth considerable effort in planning and making the purchase.

Short-range plans Plans that cover a period of one year or less.

Single-variable segmentation The simplest form of segmentation, achieved by using only one characteristic to divide—or segment—the market.

Situational factors The set of circumstances or conditions that exist when a consumer is making a purchase decision.

Social class An open aggregate of people with similar social ranking.

Social factors The forces that other people exert on one's buying behavior.

Social institutions An environmental force in international markets, including the family, education, religion, health, and recreational systems.

Social marketing Marketing that involves the development of programs designed to influence the acceptability of social ideas or causes.

Social responsibility An approach to marketing decisions that takes into account how these decisions may affect society as a whole and various groups and individuals within society.

Societal forces Forces that pressure marketers to provide high living standards and enjoyable lifestyles through socially responsible decisions and activities; the structure and dynamics of individuals and groups and the issues of concern to them.

Socioeconomic factors *See* demographic factors.

Sole sourcing Situation when a buyer chooses only one supplier.

Sorting activities The way channel members divide roles and separate tasks, including the roles of sorting out, accumulating, allocating, and assorting products.

Sorting out The first step in developing an assortment; involves breaking down conglomerates of heterogeneous supplies into relatively homogeneous groups.

Source A person, group, or organization that has a meaning that it intends and attempts to share with a receiver or an audience.

Special-event pricing Advertised sales or price cutting to increase revenue or lower costs.

Specialty-line wholesaler A merchant wholesaler that carries a very limited variety of products designed to meet customers' specialized requirements.

Specialty product An item that possesses one or more unique characteristics that a significant group of buyers is willing to expend considerable purchasing efforts to obtain.

Specialty retail A type of store that carries a narrow product mix with deep product lines.

Standard Industrial Classification (SIC) System A system developed by the federal government for classifying industrial organizations, based on what the firm primarily produces; also classifies selected economic characteristics of commercial, financial, and service organizations; uses code numbers to classify firms in different industries.

Statistical interpretation An analysis that focuses on what is typical or what deviates from the average; indicates how widely respondents vary and how they are distributed in relation to the variable being measured.

Stockout A condition that exists when a firm runs out of a product.

Store brand *See* distributor brand.

Storyboard A blueprint used by technical personnel to produce a television commercial; combines the copy with the visual material to show the sequence of major scenes in the commercial.

Straight commission compensation plan A plan according to which a salesperson's compensation is determined solely by the amount of his or her sales for a given time period.

Straight-rebuy purchase A type of industrial purchase in which a buyer purchases the same products routinely under approximately the same terms of sale.

Straight salary compensation plan A plan according to which salespeople are paid a specified amount per time period.

Strategic alliances Partnerships formed to create competitive advantage on a worldwide basis.

Strategic business unit (SBU) A division, product line, or other profit center within a parent company that sells a distinct set of products and/or services to an identifiable group of customers and competes against a well-defined set of competitors.

Strategic marketing planning A process through which an organization can develop marketing strategies that, when properly implemented and controlled, will contribute to achieving the organization's overall goals.

Strategic market plan A comprehensive plan that takes into account not only marketing but all other functional areas of a business unit that must be coordinated, such as production, finance, and personnel, as well as concern about the environment.

Strategy The key decision or plan of action required to reach an objective or set of objectives.

Stratified sampling A type of sampling in which units in a population are divided into groups according to a common characteristic or attribute; then a probability sample is conducted within each group.

Subculture A division of a culture based on geographic regions or human characteristics, such as age or ethnic background.

Superficial discounting A deceptive markdown sometimes called "was-is pricing" (the firm never intended to sell at the higher price); this is fictitious comparative pricing.

Supermarket A large, self-service store that carries broad and complete lines of food products, and perhaps some nonfood products.

Superstore A giant store that carries all food and nonfood products found in supermarkets, as well as most products purchased on a routine basis; sales are much greater than at discount stores or supermarkets.

Supplies *See* consumable supplies.

Support personnel Members of the sales staff who facilitate the selling function but usually are not involved only with making sales.

Survey methods Interviews conducted by mail, telephone, or in person to obtain factual information from or about those being interviewed, or to find out their opinions and values.

Symbolic pricing A type of psychological pricing in which prices are set at an artificially high level to provide prestige or a quality image.

Syndicated data services External sources of information that a marketer uses to study a marketing problem. Examples include American Research Bureau (ARB), Selling Areas Marketing, Inc. (SAMI), the A.C. Nielsen Company Retail Index, the Market Research Corporation of America (MRCA); they collect general information that is sold to subscribing clients.

Tactile communication Interpersonal communication through touching.

Target market A group of people for whom a firm creates and maintains a marketing mix.

Target public A group of people who have an interest in or a concern about an organization, a product, or a social cause.

Technical salesperson A support salesperson who directs efforts toward the organization's current customers by providing technical assistance in system design, product application, product characteristics, or installation.

Technological forces Forces that influence marketing decisions and activities because they affect people's lifestyles and standards of living, influence their desire for products and their reaction to marketing mixes, and have a direct impact on maintaining a marketing mix by influencing all its variables.

Technology The knowledge of how to accomplish tasks and goals.

Technology assessment A procedure by means of which managers try to foresee the effects of new products and processes on the firm's operation, on other business organizations, and on society in general.

Telemarketing A form of personal selling where highly trained account executives do everything over the telephone that face-to-face salespeople do.

Telephone retailing A type of nonstore retailing based on a cold canvass of the telephone directory or a screening of prospective clients before calling.

Telephone surveys The soliciting of respondents' answers to a questionnaire over the telephone, with the answers being written down by the interviewer.

Test marketing A limited introduction of a product in areas chosen to represent the intended market to determine probable buyers' reactions to various parts of a marketing mix.

Time series analysis A technique in which the forecaster, using the firm's historical sales data, tries to discover patterns in the firm's sales volume over time.

Total costs The sum of fixed costs and variable costs.

Total market approach An approach in which an organization designs a single marketing mix and directs it at an entire market for a specific product category; also called undifferentiated approach.

Total revenue The price times quantity.

Traceable common costs Costs that can be allocated indirectly, using one or several criteria, to the functions that they support.

Trade (or functional) discount A reduction off the list price a producer gives to an intermediary for performing certain functions.

Trademark A legal designation indicating that the owner has exclusive use of a brand or part of a brand and that others are prohibited by law from using it.

Trade mart A relatively permanent facility that firms can rent to exhibit products year-round.

Trade name The legal name of an organization, rather than the name of a specific product.

Trade salesperson A type of salesperson not strictly classified as support personnel because he or she performs the order-taking function as well.

Trade sales promotion method A category of sales promotion techniques that stimulate wholesalers and retailers to carry a producer's products and to market these products aggressively.

Trade show A show whose purpose is to let manufacturers or wholesalers exhibit products to potential buyers; therefore assists in the selling and buying functions; commonly held annually at a specified location.

Trading company A company that provides a link between buyers and sellers in different countries; it takes title to products and provides all the activities necessary to move the product from the domestic country to a market in a foreign country.

Trading stamps A sales promotion method used by retailers to attract consumers to specific stores and to increase sales of specific items by giving extra stamps to purchasers of those items.

Traditional specialty retailer A store that carries a narrow product mix with deep product lines.

Transfer pricing The type of pricing used when one unit in a company sells a product to another unit; the price is determined by one of the following methods: actual full cost, standard full cost, cost plus investment, or market-based cost.

Transit time The total time that a carrier has possession of the goods.

Transportation Moving a product from where it is made to where it is purchased and used, and thus adding time and place utility to the product.

Transportation modes Railways, motor vehicles, waterways, pipelines, and airways used to move goods from one location to another.

Trend analysis An analysis that focuses on aggregate sales data, such as company's annual sales figures, over a period of many years to determine whether annual sales are generally rising, falling, or staying about the same.

Truck wholesaler A wholesaler that provides transportation and delivery of products directly to customers for inspection and selection.

Tying contract An agreement in which a supplier agrees to sell certain products to a dealer if the dealer consents to buy other products the supplier sells.

Unaided recall test A posttest method of evaluating the effectiveness of advertising; subjects are asked to identify advertisements that they have seen or heard recently but are not shown any clues to stimulate their memories.

Undifferentiated approach An approach in which an organization designs a single marketing mix and directs it at an entire market for a specific product category; same as total market approach.

Unfair trade practices acts State laws, enacted in more than half the states, that prohibit wholesalers and retailers from selling products below their costs or below their costs plus a certain percentage of markup.

Uniform geographic pricing A type of pricing, sometimes called "postage-stamp price," that results in fixed average transportation; used to avoid the problems involved in charging different prices to each customer.

Unit loading Grouping one or more boxes on a pallet or skid.

Universal Product Code A series of thick and thin lines that can be read by an electronic scaner to identify the product and provide inventory and pricing information.

Unsought products Products purchased because of a sudden need that must be solved (e.g., emergency automobile repairs) or when aggressive selling is used to obtain a sale that otherwise would not take place (e.g., encyclopedias).

Validity A condition that exists when an instrument does measure what it is supposed to measure.

Variable cost A cost that varies directly with changes in the number of units produced or sold.

Vending *See* automatic vending.

Venture team An organizational unit established to create entirely new products that may be aimed at new markets.

Vertical channel integration The combining of two or more stages of a marketing channel under one management.

Vertical marketing system A marketing channel in which channel activities are coordinated or managed by a single channel member to achieve efficient, low-cost distribution aimed at satisfying target market customers.

Warehouse showroom A type of retail store with high volume and low overhead; lower costs are effected by shifting some marketing functions to consumers, who must transport, finance, and perhaps even store merchandise.

Warehouse/wholesale club A large-scale, members-only establishment that combines features of cash-and-carry wholesaling with discount retailing.

Warehousing Designing and operating facilities for storing and moving goods.

Warranty Document that specifies what the producer will do if the product malfunctions.

Wealth The accumulation of past income, natural resources, and financial resources.

Wheeler-Lea Act Makes unfair and deceptive acts or practices unlawful, regardless of whether they injure competition.

Wheel of retailing A hypothesis that holds that new types of retailers usually enter the market as low-status, low-margin, low-price operators but eventually evolve into high-cost, high-price merchants.

Wholesaler An intermediary that buys from a producer or another intermediary and sells to another reseller; performs such marketing activities as transportation, storage, and information gathering necessary to expedite exchanges.

Wholesaling All marketing transactions in which purchases are intended for resale or are used in making other products.

Width of product mix The number of product lines a company offers.

Willingness to spend A disposition toward expected satisfaction from a product; influenced by the ability to buy, as well as numerous psychological and social forces.

Zone prices Regional prices that vary for major geographic zones, as the transportation costs differ.

Webster, Cynthia, 241n
Webster, Frederick E., Jr., 204n, 711n
Weight Watchers, 172
Weinberger, Marc G., 538n
Weinstein, Steve, 395n
Welles, Chris, 103n
Wells, Ken, 675n
Wendy's, 585, 605
Wentz, Laurel, 810n
Werner, Ray O., 69n
Westbrook, Robert A., 175n
West Coast, 165
Westerman, Mary, 141n
Western Drug Distributors Drug Emporiums, 324
Westinghouse Electric Corp., 383
Wetterau, 392
Wheeler-Lea Act (1936), 38 (table), 39, 81, 595
When Harry Met Sally, 661
White, Joseph B., 31n, 501n
White, Randy, 173
White House, 764
Whittle, Chris, 137
Whittle Communications, 137
Wholesome Meat Act (1967), 91
Whyte, J., 777n

Wibker, Elizabeth A., 775n
Wickes Furniture, 407
Wide Glide motorcycle, 297
Wieffering, Eric J., 103n
Wilcox, James B., 605n
Wilcox, Robert D., 573n
Wild Well Control, 725
Wilke, John R., 102n
Williams-Sonoma, 412
Willow Creek Community Church, 6
Wills, James, 810n
Wilson, Les, 27, 28
Wind, Yoram, 204n, 676n, 777n
Winn-Dixie Stores, Inc., 403, 405, 416
Winnebago Industries, 311
Winters, Patricia, 607n
Wired, 769
Wolff, Cindy, 31n
Wong, Betty, 103n
Wood, Donald F., 466n
Woodruff, David, 676n
Woodward & Lothrop, 409
WordPerfect Corporation, 218
WorkGroup Technologies, Inc., 433
World Book Encyclopedia, 410
World Bowl, 281
World League of American Football, 281

Wotruba, Thomas A., 572n
Wrangler, 17, 419
Wright, Sylvia H., 204n
Wrigley's gum, 339, 624 (illus.)
WRTV (Waiting Room Television), 138

Xerox Corporation, 21, 22, 213, 278, 432, 805 (table)

Yang, Dori Jones, 811n
Yates, Deborah, 204n
Yawn, David, 465n
Yellow Freight, 451, 452 (table)
Yellow Pages, 769
Youngblood, Stuart, 102n
Yugoslavia, 802
Yves St. Laurent, 830

Zaichkowsky, Judith Lynne, 810n
Zazarine, Paul, 30n
Zeithaml, Valerie A., 605n, 776n
Zellner, Wendy, 241n, 501n
Zeltzer Seltzer, 392
Zenith Electronics Corporation, 249
Zeren, Linda, 325n
Zinn, Laura, 433n, 434n
Zinszer, Paul H., 367n